Communications
in Computer and Information Science   1864

Rationale

The CCIS series is devoted to the publication of proceedings of computer science conferences. Its aim is to efficiently disseminate original research results in informatics in printed and electronic form. While the focus is on publication of peer-reviewed full papers presenting mature work, inclusion of reviewed short papers reporting on work in progress is welcome, too. Besides globally relevant meetings with internationally representative program committees guaranteeing a strict peer-reviewing and paper selection process, conferences run by societies or of high regional or national relevance are also considered for publication.

Topics

The topical scope of CCIS spans the entire spectrum of informatics ranging from foundational topics in the theory of computing to information and communications science and technology and a broad variety of interdisciplinary application fields.

Information for Volume Editors and Authors

Publication in CCIS is free of charge. No royalties are paid, however, we offer registered conference participants temporary free access to the online version of the conference proceedings on SpringerLink (http://link.springer.com) by means of an http referrer from the conference website and/or a number of complimentary printed copies, as specified in the official acceptance email of the event.

CCIS proceedings can be published in time for distribution at conferences or as post-proceedings, and delivered in the form of printed books and/or electronically as USBs and/or e-content licenses for accessing proceedings at SpringerLink. Furthermore, CCIS proceedings are included in the CCIS electronic book series hosted in the SpringerLink digital library at http://link.springer.com/bookseries/7899. Conferences publishing in CCIS are allowed to use Online Conference Service (OCS) for managing the whole proceedings lifecycle (from submission and reviewing to preparing for publication) free of charge.

Publication process

The language of publication is exclusively English. Authors publishing in CCIS have to sign the Springer CCIS copyright transfer form, however, they are free to use their material published in CCIS for substantially changed, more elaborate subsequent publications elsewhere. For the preparation of the camera-ready papers/files, authors have to strictly adhere to the Springer CCIS Authors' Instructions and are strongly encouraged to use the CCIS LaTeX style files or templates.

Abstracting/Indexing

CCIS is abstracted/indexed in DBLP, Google Scholar, EI-Compendex, Mathematical Reviews, SCImago, Scopus. CCIS volumes are also submitted for the inclusion in ISI Proceedings.

How to start

To start the evaluation of your proposal for inclusion in the CCIS series, please send an e-mail to ccis@springer.com.

Ngoc Thanh Nguyen · János Botzheim ·
László Gulyás · Manuel Nunez · Jan Treur ·
Gottfried Vossen · Adrianna Kozierkiewicz
Editors

Advances in Computational Collective Intelligence

15th International Conference, ICCCI 2023
Budapest, Hungary, September 27–29, 2023
Proceedings

 Springer

Editors
Ngoc Thanh Nguyen 🆔
Wrocław University of Science
and Technology
Wrocław, Poland

Faculty of Information Technology
Nguyen Tat Thanh University
Ho Chi Minh, Vietnam

László Gulyás 🆔
Eötvös Loránd University
Budapest, Hungary

Jan Treur 🆔
Vrije Universiteit Amsterdam
Amsterdam, The Netherlands

Adrianna Kozierkiewicz 🆔
Wrocław University of Science
and Technology
Wrocław, Poland

János Botzheim 🆔
Eötvös Loránd University
Budapest, Hungary

Manuel Nunez 🆔
Universidad Complutense de Madrid
Madrid, Spain

Gottfried Vossen 🆔
University of Münster
Münster, Germany

ISSN 1865-0929   ISSN 1865-0937 (electronic)
Communications in Computer and Information Science
ISBN 978-3-031-41773-3   ISBN 978-3-031-41774-0 (eBook)
https://doi.org/10.1007/978-3-031-41774-0

This Springer imprint is published by the registered company Springer Nature Switzerland AG
The registered company address is: Gewerbestrasse 11, 6330 Cham, Switzerland

Paper in this product is recyclable.

Preface

This volume contains the second part of the proceedings of the 15th International Conference on Computational Collective Intelligence (ICCCI 2023), held in Budapest, Hungary between 27–29 September 2023. The conference was organized in a hybrid mode which allowed for both on-site and online paper presentations. The conference was hosted by the Eötvös Loránd University (ELTE), Hungary and jointly organized by Wrocław University of Science and Technology, Poland in cooperation with IEEE SMC Technical Committee on Computational Collective Intelligence, European Research Center for Information Systems (ERCIS), International University-VNU-HCM (Vietnam) and John von Neumann Computer Society (NJSZT).

Following the successes of the 1st ICCCI (2009), held in Wrocław - Poland, the 2nd ICCCI (2010) in Kaohsiung - Taiwan, the 3rd ICCCI (2011) in Gdynia - Poland, the 4th ICCCI (2012) in Ho Chi Minh City - Vietnam, the 5th ICCCI (2013) in Craiova - Romania, the 6th ICCCI (2014) in Seoul - South Korea, the 7th ICCCI (2015) in Madrid - Spain, the 8th ICCCI (2016) in Halkidiki - Greece, the 9th ICCCI (2017) in Nicosia - Cyprus, the 10th ICCCI (2018) in Bristol - UK, the 11th ICCCI (2019) in Hendaye - France, the 12th ICCCI (2020) in Da Nang - Vietnam, the 13th ICCCI (2021) in Rhodes - Greece, and the 14th ICCCI (2022) in Hammamet - Tunisia, this conference continued to provide an internationally respected forum for scientific research in computer-based methods of collective intelligence and their applications.

Computational collective intelligence (CCI) is most often understood as a subfield of artificial intelligence (AI) dealing with soft computing methods that facilitate group decisions or processing knowledge among autonomous units acting in distributed environments. Methodological, theoretical, and practical aspects of CCI are considered as the form of intelligence that emerges from the collaboration and competition of many individuals (artificial and/or natural). The application of multiple computational intelligence technologies such as fuzzy systems, evolutionary computation, neural systems, consensus theory, etc. can support human and other collective intelligence, and create new forms of CCI in natural and/or artificial systems. Three subfields of the application of computational intelligence technologies to support various forms of collective intelligence are of special interest but are not exclusive: the Semantic Web (as an advanced tool for increasing collective intelligence), social network analysis (as a field targeted at the emergence of new forms of CCI), and multi-agent systems (as a computational and modeling paradigm especially tailored to capture the nature of CCI emergence in populations of autonomous individuals).

The ICCCI 2023 conference featured a number of keynote talks and oral presentations, closely aligned to the theme of the conference. The conference attracted a substantial number of researchers and practitioners from all over the world, who submitted their papers for the main track and 9 special sessions.

The main track, covering the methodology and applications of CCI, included: collective decision-making, data fusion, deep learning techniques, natural language processing, data mining and machine learning, social networks and intelligent systems, optimization, computer vision, knowledge engineering and application, as well as Internet of Things: technologies and applications. The special sessions, covering some specific topics of particular interest, included: cooperative strategies for decision making and optimization, artificial intelligence, speech communication, IOT applications, natural language processing, deep learning, intelligent systems, machine learning, collective intelligence in medical applications and computer vision.

We received 218 papers submitted by authors coming from 41 countries around the world. Each paper was reviewed by at least three members of the international Program Committee (PC) of either the main track or one of the special sessions; reviews were single blind. Finally, we selected 63 papers for oral presentation and publication in one volume of the Lecture Notes in Artificial Intelligence series and 59 papers for oral presentation and publication in one volume of the Communications in Computer and Information Science series.

We would like to express our thanks to the keynote speakers: Loo Chu Kiong from Universiti Malaya (Malaysia), A.E. Eiben from Vrije Universiteit Amsterdam (The Netherlands), Aleksander Byrski from AGH University of Science and Technology (Poland), and Diego Paez-Granados from ETH Zürich (Switzerland).

Many people contributed toward the success of the conference. First, we would like to recognize the work of the PC co-chairs and special sessions organizers for taking good care of the organization of the reviewing process, an essential stage in ensuring the high quality of the accepted papers. The workshop and special session chairs deserve a special mention for the evaluation of the proposals and the organization and coordination of the work of 9 special sessions. In addition, we would like to thank the PC members, of the main track and of the special sessions, for performing their reviewing work with diligence. We thank the Local Organizing Committee chairs, Publicity chairs, Web chair, and Technical Support chairs for their fantastic work before and during the conference. Finally, we cordially thank all the authors, presenters, and delegates for their valuable contribution to this successful event. The conference would not have been possible without their support.

Our special thanks are also due to Springer for publishing the proceedings and to all the other sponsors for their kind support.

It is our pleasure to announce that the ICCCI conference series continues to have a close cooperation with the Springer journal Transactions on Computational Collective Intelligence, and the IEEE SMC Technical Committee on Transactions on Computational Collective Intelligence.

Finally, we hope that ICCCI 2023 contributed significantly to the academic excellence of the field and will lead to the even greater success of ICCCI events in the future.

September 2023

Ngoc Thanh Nguyen
János Botzheim
László Gulyás
Manuel Núñez
Jan Treur
Gottfried Vossen
Adrianna Kozierkiewicz

Organization

Organizing Committee

Honorary Chairs

László Borhy — Rector of Eötvös Loránd University, Hungary
Arkadiusz Wójs — Rector of Wrocław University of Science and Technology, Poland

General Chairs

Ngoc Thanh Nguyen — Wrocław University of Science and Technology, Poland
János Botzheim — Eötvös Loránd University, Hungary

Program Chairs

László Gulyás — Eötvös Loránd University, Hungary
Manuel Núñez — Universidad Complutense de Madrid, Spain
Jan Treur — Vrije Universiteit Amsterdam, The Netherlands
Gottfried Vossen — University of Münster, Germany

Steering Committee

Ngoc Thanh Nguyen — Wrocław University of Science and Technology, Poland
Piotr Jędrzejowicz — Gdynia Maritime University, Poland
Shyi-Ming Chen — National Taiwan University of Science and Technology, Taiwan
Kiem Hoang — VNU-HCM University of Information Technology, Vietnam
Dosam Hwang — Yeungnam University, South Korea
Lakhmi C. Jain — University of South Australia, Australia
Geun-Sik Jo — Inha University, South Korea
Janusz Kacprzyk — Polish Academy of Sciences, Poland
Ryszard Kowalczyk — Swinburne University of Technology, Australia
Yannis Manolopoulos — Open University of Cyprus, Cyprus

Toyoaki Nishida	Kyoto University, Japan
Manuel Núñez	Universidad Complutense de Madrid, Spain
Klaus Söilen	Halmstad University, Sweden
Khoa Tien Tran	VNU-HCM International University, Vietnam

Organizing Chairs

Udo Bub	Eötvös Loránd University, Hungary
Marcin Pietranik	Wrocław University of Science and Technology, Poland

Special Session Chairs

Adrianna Kozierkiewicz	Wrocław University of Science and Technology, Poland
Paweł Sitek	Kielce University of Technology, Poland
András Lőrincz	Eötvös Loránd University, Hungary
Ellák Somfai	Eötvös Loránd University, Hungary

Doctoral Track Chair

Marek Krótkiewicz	Wrocław University of Science and Technology, Poland

Publicity Chairs

Attila Kiss	Eötvös Loránd University, Hungary
Marcin Jodłowiec	Wrocław University of Science and Technology, Poland
Rafal Palak	Wrocław University of Science and Technology, Poland

Webmaster

Marek Kopel	Wrocław University of Science and Technology, Poland

Local Organizing Committee

Kaan Karaköse	Eötvös Loránd University, Hungary
Márk Domonkos	Eötvös Loránd University, Hungary
Natabara Gyöngyössy	Eötvös Loránd University, Hungary
Patient Zihisire Muke	Wrocław University of Science and Technology, Poland
Thanh-Ngo Nguyen	Wrocław University of Science and Technology, Poland
Jose Fabio Ribeiro Bezerra	Wrocław University of Science and Technology, Poland

Keynote Speakers

Loo Chu Kiong	Universiti Malaya, Malaysia
Agoston E. Eiben	Vrije Universiteit Amsterdam, The Netherlands
Aleksander Byrski	AGH University of Science and Technology, Poland
Diego Paez-Granados	ETH Zürich, Switzerland

Special Session Organizers

AISC 2023: Special Session on AI and Speech Communication

Ualsher Tukeyev	al-Farabi Kazakh National University, Kazakhstan
Orken Mamyrbayev	Institute of Information and Computational Technologies, Kazakhstan

EIIOT 2023: Special Session on Edge Intelligence for IOT Applications

Suresh Sankaranarayanan	King Faisal University, KSA
Pascal Lorenz	University of Haute Alsace, France

CCINLP 2023: Special Session on Computational Collective Intelligence and Natural Language Processing

Ismail Biskri	University of Québec at Trois-Rivières, Canada
Nadia Ghazzali	University of Québec at Trois-Rivières, Canada

DISADA 2023: Special Session on Deep Learning and Intelligent Systems for Arabic Document Analysis

Mounir Zrigui	University of Monastir, Tunisia
Sadek Mansouri	University of Monastir, Tunisia
Nafaa Haffar	University of Monastir, Tunisia
Dhaou Berchech	DB Consulting, France

CSDMO 2023: Special Session on Cooperative Strategies for Decision Making and Optimization

Piotr Jędrzejowicz	Gdynia Maritime University, Poland
Dariusz Barbucha	Gdynia Maritime University, Poland
Ireneusz Czarnowski	Gdynia Maritime University, Poland

MLRWD 2023: Special Session on Machine Learning in Real-World Data

Jan Kozak	University of Economics in Katowice, Poland
Artur Kozłowski	Łukasiewicz Research Network, Poland
Przemysław Juszczuk	Polish Academy of Sciences, Poland
Barbara Probierz	University of Economics in Katowice, Poland
Tomasz Jach	University of Economics in Katowice, Poland

AIIMTH 2023: Special Session on AI and Internet of Medical Things in Healthcare

Octavian Postolache	ISCTE-University Institute of Lisbon, Portugal
Madina Mansurova	al-Farabi Kazakh National University, Kazakhstan

DICV 2023: Special Session on Recent Advances of Deep Learning and Internet of Things in Computer Vision-Related Applications

Wadii Boulila	Prince Sultan University, KSA
Jawad Ahmad	Edinburgh Napier University, UK
Maha Driss	Prince Sultan University, KSA
Anis Koubaa	Prince Sultan University, KSA
Mark Elliot	University of Manchester, UK

Innov-Healthcare 2023: Special Session on Innovative use of Machine Learning and Deep Learning for HealthCare Empowerment

Yassine Ben Ayed — University of Sfax, Tunisia
Wael Ouarda — Ministry of Higher Education and Scientific Research, Tunisia

Senior Program Committee

Plamen Angelov — Lancaster University, UK
Costin Badica — University of Craiova, Romania
Nick Bassiliades — Aristotle University of Thessaloniki, Greece
Maria Bielikova — Slovak University of Technology in Bratislava, Slovakia
Abdelhamid Bouchachia — Bournemouth University, UK
David Camacho — Universidad Autónoma de Madrid, Spain
Richard Chbeir — University of Pau and Pays de l'Adour, France
Shyi-Ming Chen — National Taiwan University of Science and Technology, Taiwan
Paul Davidsson — Malmo University, Sweden
Mohamed Gaber — Birmingham City University, UK
Daniela Godoy — ISISTAN Research Institute, Argentina
Manuel Grana — University of the Basque Country, Spain
William Grosky — University of Michigan, USA
Francisco Herrera — University of Granada, Spain
Tzung-Pei Hong — National University of Kaohsiung, Taiwan
Dosam Hwang — Yeungnam University, South Korea
Lazaros Iliadis — Democritus University of Thrace, Greece
Mirjana Ivanovic — University of Novi Sad, Serbia
Piotr Jedrzejowicz — Gdynia Maritime University, Poland
Geun-Sik Jo — Inha University, South Korea
Kang-Hyun Jo — University of Ulsan, South Korea
Janusz Kacprzyk — Systems Research Institute, Polish Academy of Sciences, Poland
Ryszard Kowalczyk — Swinburne University of Technology, Australia
Ondrej Krejcar — University of Hradec Kralove, Czech Republic
Hoai An Le Thi — University of Lorraine, France
Edwin Lughofer — Johannes Kepler University Linz, Austria
Yannis Manolopoulos — Aristotle University of Thessaloniki, Greece
Grzegorz J. Nalepa — AGH University of Science and Technology, Poland

Toyoaki Nishida	Kyoto University, Japan
Manuel Núñez	Universidad Complutense de Madrid, Spain
George A. Papadopoulos	University of Cyprus, Cyprus
Radu-Emil Precup	Politehnica University of Timisoara, Romania
Leszek Rutkowski	Częstochowa University of Technology, Poland
Tomasz M. Rutkowski	University of Tokyo, Japan
Ali Selamat	Universiti Teknologi Malaysia, Malaysia
Edward Szczerbicki	University of Newcastle, Australia
Ryszard Tadeusiewicz	AGH University of Science and Technology, Poland
Muhammad Atif Tahir	National University of Computer and Emerging Sciences, Pakistan
Jan Treur	Vrije Universiteit Amsterdam, The Netherlands
Serestina Viriri	University of KwaZulu-Natal, South Africa
Bay Vo	Ho Chi Minh City University of Technology, Vietnam
Gottfried Vossen	University of Münster, Germany
Lipo Wang	Nanyang Technological University, Singapore
Michał Woźniak	Wrocław University of Science and Technology, Poland
Farouk Yalaoui	University of Technology of Troyes, France
Slawomir Zadrozny	Systems Research Institute, Polish Academy of Sciences, Poland

Program Committee

Muhammad Abulaish	South Asian University, India
Sharat Akhoury	University of Cape Town, South Africa
Stuart Allen	Cardiff University, UK
Ana Almeida	GECAD-ISEP-IPP, Portugal
Bashar Al-Shboul	University of Jordan, Jordan
Adel Alti	University of Setif, Algeria
Taha Arbaoui	University of Technology of Troyes, France
Thierry Badard	Laval University, Canada
Amelia Badica	University of Craiova, Romania
Hassan Badir	École Nationale des Sciences Appliquées de Tanger, Morocco
Dariusz Barbucha	Gdynia Maritime University, Poland
Paulo Batista	Universidade de Evora, Portugal
Khalid Benali	University of Lorraine, France
Morad Benyoucef	University of Ottawa, Canada

Szymon Bobek	Jagiellonian University, Poland
Grzegorz Bocewicz	Koszalin University of Technology, Poland
Urszula Boryczka	University of Silesia, Poland
János Botzheim	Eötvös Loránd University, Hungary
Peter Brida	University of Zilina, Slovakia
Ivana Bridova	University of Zilina, Slovakia
Krisztian Buza	Budapest University of Technology and Economics, Hungary
Aleksander Byrski	AGH University of Science and Technology, Poland
Alberto Cano	Virginia Commonwealth University, USA
Frantisek Capkovic	Institute of Informatics, Slovak Academy of Sciences, Slovakia
Roberto Casadei	Università di Bologna, Italy
Raja Chiky	Institut Supérieur d'Electronique de Paris, France
Amine Chohra	Paris-East Créteil University (UPEC), France
Kazimierz Choros	Wrocław University of Science and Technology, Poland
Robert Cierniak	Częstochowa University of Technology, Poland
Mihaela Colhon	University of Craiova, Romania
Antonio Corral	University of Almeria, Spain
Rafal Cupek	Silesian University of Technology, Poland
Ireneusz Czarnowski	Gdynia Maritime University, Poland
Camelia Delcea	Bucharest University of Economic Studies, Romania
Konstantinos Demertzis	Democritus University of Thrace, Greece
Shridhar Devamane	Global Academy of Technology, India
Muthusamy Dharmalingam	Bharathiar University, India
Tien V. Do	Budapest University of Technology and Economics, Hungary
Márk Domonkos	Eötvös Loránd University, Hungary
Abdellatif El Afia	ENSIAS-Mohammed V University in Rabat, Morocco
Nadia Essoussi	University of Tunis, Tunisia
Rim Faiz	University of Carthage, Tunisia
Marcin Fojcik	Western Norway University of Applied Sciences, Norway
Anna Formica	IASI-CNR, Italy
Bogdan Franczyk	University of Leipzig, Germany
Dariusz Frejlichowski	West Pomeranian University of Technology in Szczecin, Poland
Mauro Gaspari	University of Bologna, Italy
K. M. George	Oklahoma State University, USA

Janusz Getta	University of Wollongong, Australia
Chirine Ghedira	Jean Moulin Lyon 3 University, France
Daniela Gifu	Romanian Academy - Iasi Branch, Romania
Arkadiusz Gola	Lublin University of Technology, Poland
László Gulyás	Eötvös Loránd University, Hungary
Natabara Gyöngyössy	Eötvös Loránd University, Hungary
Petr Hajek	University of Pardubice, Czech Republic
Kenji Hatano	Doshisha University, Japan
Marcin Hernes	Wrocław University of Economics, Poland
Huu Hanh Hoang	Hue University, Vietnam
Jeongky Hong	Yeungnam University, South Korea
Frédéric Hubert	Laval University, Canada
Zbigniew Huzar	Wrocław University of Science and Technology, Poland
Agnieszka Indyka-Piasecka	Wrocław University of Science and Technology, Poland
Dan Istrate	Université de Technologie de Compiegne, France
Fethi Jarray	Gabes University, Tunisia
Joanna Jedrzejowicz	University of Gdansk, Poland
Gordan Jezic	University of Zagreb, Croatia
Ireneusz Jóźwiak	Wrocław University of Science and Technology, Poland
Przemysław Juszczuk	University of Economics in Katowice, Poland
Arkadiusz Kawa	Poznań School of Logistics, Poland
Zaheer Khan	University of the West of England, UK
Attila Kiss	Eötvös Loránd University, Hungary
Marek Kopel	Wrocław University of Science and Technology, Poland
Petia Koprinkova-Hristova	Bulgarian Academy of Sciences, Bulgaria
Szilárd Kovács	Eötvös Loránd University, Hungary
Ivan Koychev	University of Sofia "St. Kliment Ohridski", Bulgaria
Jan Kozak	University of Economics in Katowice, Poland
Dalia Kriksciuniene	Vilnius University, Lithuania
Stelios Krinidis	Centre for Research and Technology Hellas (CERTH), Greece
Dariusz Krol	Wrocław University of Science and Technology, Poland
Marek Krotkiewicz	Wrocław University of Science and Technology, Poland
Jan Kubicek	VSB -Technical University of Ostrava, Czech Republic

Elzbieta Kukla	Wrocław University of Science and Technology, Poland
Marek Kulbacki	Polish-Japanese Academy of Information Technology, Poland
Piotr Kulczycki	Polish Academy of Science, Systems Research Institute, Poland
Kazuhiro Kuwabara	Ritsumeikan University, Japan
Halina Kwasnicka	Wrocław University of Science and Technology, Poland
Mark Last	Ben-Gurion University of the Negev, Israel
Nguyen-Thinh Le	Humboldt-Universität zu Berlin, Germany
Philippe Lemoisson	French Agricultural Research Centre for International Development (CIRAD), France
Florin Leon	"Gheorghe Asachi" Technical University of Iasi, Romania
Mikołaj Leszczuk	AGH University of Science and Technology, Poland
Doina Logofatu	Frankfurt University of Applied Sciences, Germany
Aphilak Lonklang	Eötvös Loránd University, Hungary
Juraj Machaj	University of Zilina, Slovakia
George Magoulas	Birkbeck, University of London, UK
Bernadetta Maleszka	Wrocław University of Science and Technology, Poland
Marcin Maleszka	Wrocław University of Science and Technology, Poland
Adam Meissner	Poznań University of Technology, Poland
Manuel Méndez	Universidad Complutense de Madrid, Spain
Jacek Mercik	WSB University in Wrocław, Poland
Radosław Michalski	Wrocław University of Science and Technology, Poland
Peter Mikulecky	University of Hradec Kralove, Czech Republic
Miroslava Mikusova	University of Zilina, Slovakia
Jean-Luc Minel	Université Paris Ouest Nanterre La Défense, France
Javier Montero	Universidad Complutense de Madrid, Spain
Anna Motylska-Kuźma	WSB University in Wrocław, Poland
Manuel Munier	University of Pau and Pays de l'Adour, France
Phivos Mylonas	Ionian University, Greece
Laurent Nana	University of Brest, France
Anand Nayyar	Duy Tan University, Vietnam
Filippo Neri	University of Napoli Federico II, Italy
Linh Anh Nguyen	University of Warsaw, Poland

Loan T. T. Nguyen	VNU-HCM International University, Vietnam
Sinh Van Nguyen	VNU-HCM International University, Vietnam
Adam Niewiadomski	Lodz University of Technology, Poland
Adel Noureddine	University of Pau and Pays de l'Adour, France
Alberto Núñez	Universidad Complutense de Madrid, Spain
Mieczysław Owoc	Wrocław University of Economics, Poland
Marcin Paprzycki	Systems Research Institute, Polish Academy of Sciences, Poland
Isidoros Perikos	University of Patras, Greece
Elias Pimenidis	University of the West of England, UK
Nikolaos Polatidis	University of Brighton, UK
Hiram Ponce Espinosa	Universidad Panamericana, Brazil
Piotr Porwik	University of Silesia, Poland
Paulo Quaresma	Universidade de Evora, Portugal
David Ramsey	Wrocław University of Science and Technology, Poland
Mohammad Rashedur Rahman	North South University, Bangladesh
Ewa Ratajczak-Ropel	Gdynia Maritime University, Poland
Virgilijus Sakalauskas	Vilnius University, Lithuania
Ilias Sakellariou	University of Macedonia, Greece
Khouloud Salameh	University of Pau and Pays de l'Adour, France
Imad Saleh	Université Paris 8, France
Sana Sellami	Aix-Marseille University, France
Yeong-Seok Seo	Yeungnam University, South Korea
Andrzej Sieminski	Wrocław University of Science and Technology, Poland
Dragan Simic	University of Novi Sad, Serbia
Paweł Sitek	Kielce University of Technology, Poland
Vladimir Sobeslav	University of Hradec Kralove, Czech Republic
Stanimir Stoyanov	University of Plovdiv "Paisii Hilendarski", Bulgaria
Grażyna Suchacka	University of Opole, Poland
Libuse Svobodova	University of Hradec Kralove, Czech Republic
Martin Tabakov	Wrocław University of Science and Technology, Poland
Yasufumi Takama	Tokyo Metropolitan University, Japan
Trong Hieu Tran	VNU University of Engineering and Technology, Vietnam
Maria Trocan	Institut Superieur d'Electronique de Paris, France
Krzysztof Trojanowski	Cardinal Stefan Wyszyński University in Warsaw, Poland
Ualsher Tukeyev	Al-Farabi Kazakh National University, Kazakhstan

Olgierd Unold	Wrocław University of Science and Technology, Poland
Serestina Viriri	University of KwaZulu-Natal, South Africa
Thi Luu Phuong Vo	VNU-HCM International University, Vietnam
Roger M. Whitaker	Cardiff University, UK
Izabela Wierzbowska	Gdynia Maritime University, Poland
Adam Wojciechowski	Lodz University of Technology, Poland
Krystian Wojtkiewicz	Wrocław University of Science and Technology, Poland
Drago Zagar	University of Osijek, Croatia
Danuta Zakrzewska	Lodz University of Technology, Poland
Constantin-Bala Zamfirescu	"Lucian Blaga" University of Sibiu, Romania
Katerina Zdravkova	University of Ss. Cyril and Methodius, Macedonia
Haoxi Zhang	Chengdu University of Information Technology, China
Jianlei Zhang	Nankai University, China
Adam Ziebinski	Silesian University of Technology, Poland

Contents

Natural Language Processing

Data Minning and Machine Learning

Social Networks and Speek Communication

Cybersecurity and Internet of Things

Cooperative Strategies for Decision Making and Optimization

Digital Content Understanding and Application for Industry 4.0

Computational Intelligence in Medical Applications

Collective Intelligence and Collective Decision-Making

Assessing the Effects of Expanded Input Elicitation and Machine Learning-Based Priming on Crowd Stock Prediction

Harika Bhogaraju[1], Arushi Jain[2], Jyotika Jaiswal[2],
and Adolfo R. Escobedo[3]($\boxtimes$) ⓘ

[1] Arizona State University, Tempe, AZ 85281, USA
[2] Vellore Institute of Technology, Chennai, India
[3] North Carolina State University, Raleigh, NC 27606, USA
arescobedo@ncsu.edu

Abstract. The stock market is affected by a seemingly infinite number of factors, making it highly uncertain yet impactful. A large determinant of stock performance is public sentiment, which can often be volatile. To integrate human inputs in a more structured and effective manner, this study explores a combination of the wisdom of crowds concept and machine learning (ML) for stock price prediction. A crowdsourcing study is developed to test three ways to elicit stock predictions from the crowd. The study also assesses the impact of priming participants with estimates provided by an Long Short Term Model (LSTM) model herein developed for this context.

Keywords: Wisdom of Crowds · Machine Learning · Priming · Stock Prediction

1 Introduction

Human beings have always had an inherent interest in predicting the unpredictable. The journey may have started with fortune tellers, oracles, and prophets, using sun signs, planetary positions, and star alignments to predict the future. But today, artificial intelligence takes their place using statistics, big data analytics, and at the heart of it all, machine learning (ML). ML has permeated every modern industry to provide predictive insights. A non-comprehensive list is as follows. In healthcare, ML models have been used to predict COVID-19 surges, death numbers, and recovery rates during the pandemic [17]. In manufacturing, they have been applied to improve the efficiency of smart factories [19]. In surveillance, Karpathy et al. [12] evaluate the performance of Convolutional Neural Networks(CNNs) on broadly 487 categories of videos, totaling 1 million YouTube videos to further surveillance automation. In the mental health space, Fathi et al. [7] train an ANFIS model on a large dataset with seven input features to detect social anxiety disorder in healthcare.

© The Author(s), under exclusive license to Springer Nature Switzerland AG 2023
N. T. Nguyen et al. (Eds.): ICCCI 2023, CCIS 1864, pp. 3–16, 2023.
https://doi.org/10.1007/978-3-031-41774-0_1

There are seemingly more applications of ML emerging for forecasting highly uncertain yet impactful events. One representative use case is the stock market, whose irregular nature puzzles day traders, investors, and scientists alike. While stock trading is often thought of as a 'zero-sum game', there are tangible factors that play a role in measuring the performance of a stock. For instance, historical prices and other financial data about a company are often good indicators of the potential of a stock to be profitable for an investor. With the advances in ML, processing large quantities of financial data has become a routine task. Using neural networks, millions of data points can be processed to produce a prediction of the stock price of a company. For example, Shen and Shafiq [23] compare different ML models to determine which model has more accurate predictions; a comprehensive Long Short Term Memory (LSTM) network achieves the highest accuracy.

LSTMs have certainly brought us a step closer to unraveling the stock market, but what makes stock trading so mercurial is public sentiment due to its very subjective and inconsistent nature. Moreover, the stock market is a victim of second-order effects; trading activity leads to chain reactions of consequent trading activity. This makes public sentiment difficult to track, and yet it remains an essential determinant in stock performance. Many have tried to find concrete ways to measure public sentiment. For example, Das et al. [4] use tweets, social media comments, news headlines, and other news sources to predict stock prices during the COVID-19 pandemic. The paper concludes that using public sentiment from social media and news in combination with stock data improves stock prediction accuracy. However, social media users are often easily influenced by others' opinions resulting in biased and polarized public sentiment that does not accurately represent personal views [20]. Similarly, Checkley et al [3] find that bloggers can add uncertainty to the market rather than bring clarity. The study concludes that using sentiment collected from blogs improves forecasts of volatility and trading volume but not of price direction.

The *wisdom of crowds* can be a promising approach to obtaining a more stable estimate of public sentiment since it gathers people's inputs in a more structured and controlled setting. This concept builds on the notion that "the sum is greater than the sum of the parts", to derive aggregate judgments that are often more accurate and reliable than those of any individual, including subject matter experts [25]. To achieve these effects, each crowd member's opinion must be elicited independently from others. In addition, this private information must be obtained from a diverse set of individuals. The wisdom of crowds has many commonplace applications including in the healthcare industry, where it is used for diagnosis, nutrition, surveillance, and public health [27]. It is also utilized in more narrow applications such as recommendation systems [22]. In a context closely related to this work, prediction markets rely on the wisdom of crowds to derive accurate estimates by engaging large participant pools in simple prediction tasks like binary classification (up-down movement of stocks) and simple price estimations. However, more complex forms of input elicitation that may require higher cognitive power from the participant pool but potentially enhance the wisdom of crowd effects have received little attention.

To explore this potential, this paper develops a wisdom of crowds approach that combines different input elicitation techniques and machine learning-based priming to augment stock performance prediction. The approach is deployed via a custom user interface on a crowdsourcing platform (Amazon MTurk) in order to engage a diverse pool of participants who can draw on their own independent knowledge to provide the requested estimates.

2   Literature Review

2.1   Machine Learning in Finance

It is important to understand specific financial indicators that have been integral to analyzing stocks. An elementary analysis of a stock can be performed by analyzing five key variables: Opening price, high of the day, low of the day, volume, and adjusted closing price [21]. The indicators are primarily used in making short-term predictions. On the other hand, long-term predictions tend to use 52-week high, price-earnings ratio (P/E ratio), and moving averages (MAs). Performance metrics such as these use varying ratios of revenue, profits, debt, and assets to quantify the health of a company.

While these indicators are good at summarizing the current health of a stock, ML can be a great source for looking into the future. Many different neural networks including LSTMs, MDWDNNs (Multi-Dimensional Wide Neural Networks), and MDRNNs (Multi-Dimensional Recurrent Neural Networks) have been developed to predict time-stamped data such as temperature fluctuations and annual retail sales. For example, Khodabakhsh et al. [14] use crude oil and byproduct flow rates to predict a petrochemical plant's crude oil purchase amount. Although various neural network models can be employed to predict stock prices [1,18], LSTMs are simple, easily accessible, and more popular than their more complex counterparts. Therefore, we adopt LSTMs in the present study to shift attention to the crowd rather than on model performance, since the latter has been the primary focus of the majority of other works in this space. In the featured context, LSTMs have been used to read historical stock prices and predict future stock price values [16]. Nevertheless, LSTMs have evolved to utilize more than historical data alone [10,15].

2.2   Public Sentiment and Stock Performance

In addition to financial factors, public sentiment can be used as a feature to support ML model predictions. For example, Siah and Myers [24] measured public sentiment through Google Trends and Bloomberg Businessweek. "Positive" and "Negative" words were first categorized and then data was mined to obtain a public sentiment score. The study found that Google Trends were unhelpful in improving model accuracy. Such findings highlight the volatility of social media and news as sources of public sentiment and the need to gather data in a more structured manner.

2.3 Wisdom of Crowds

The wisdom of crowds can be applied to obtain a more stable form of public sentiment. This concept can be leveraged by eliciting and aggregating the judgments or predictions from multiple participants to reduce errors and thereby better approximate the ground truth. Traditional wisdom of crowds techniques can be applied to gauge the potential value of a stock by eliciting price estimates (numerical input) or up/down estimates (binary choice) [6]. However, the former can lead to marked under/overestimation due to cognitive biases [9], while the latter may fail to capture nuanced information. In fact, a recommended practice in prediction markets is to normalize the market price and to interpret the elicited crowd inputs as the probability that the market believes in the stock [2]. The latter observation motivates experimenting with a wider variety of input elicitation techniques for this context. This is further supported by recent studies showing that richer crowd information can be extracted on human computation tasks by eliciting and combining multiple modalities of estimates [13, 28].

2.4 ML and Crowdsourcing

ML and crowdsourcing have complementary strengths, meaning that they can work better together than alone. This has been shown across various applications. For example, Yasmin et al. [29] use crowdsourcing inputs as features within several standard ML algorithms for image classification; they show that these hybrid algorithms perform better than a state-of-the-art fully automated classification algorithm, when the training sets are small to medium in size. In addition, Demartini et al. [5] combine inputs from machine learning algorithms, crowdsourcing workers, and experts to combat the spread of online misinformation. Similar approaches can be extrapolated to many different use cases including the stock market. Indeed, Hill and Ready-Campbell [8] use over 2 million users' stock picks on the investment platform CAPS to train an ML model that ranks stocks and builds stock portfolios. These works provide a glimpse of the potential advantages of combining ML and the wisdom of crowds. Following in these footsteps, this paper employs a combination of an ML model and crowdsourcing inputs to predict the performance of stocks.

3 Experiment Design

Three experiments were deployed on Amazon MTurk, a crowdsourcing platform, on a total of 308 participants. Each experiment was deployed on the first weekend of the months of September 2022 (Experiment A), October 2022 (Experiment B), and November 2022 (Experiment C). Weekends were chosen so as to avoid frequent and momentary fluctuations in the current stock price. Experiments A and B use a common set of 22 stocks, and Experiment C uses 10 stocks selected from the larger set of the two other experiments.

The user interface asked participants to provide estimates on several stocks through a combination of different input elicitation techniques and representations of ML predictions (i.e., priming), the latter of which were obtained from the outputs of an LSTM model. Depending on the complexity of the question, a time limit of either 90 s or 120 s was imposed. It is important to remark that Experiments A and B were conducted at a time when the Dow Jones Index (DJI) was trending downward, while Experiment C was conducted at a time when the DJI was trending upward, as is shown in Fig. 1.

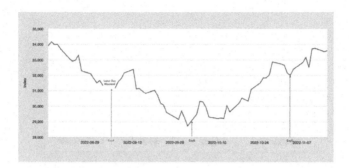

Fig. 1. The Dow Jones Index from Aug 15, 2022 to Nov 15, 2022.

3.1   The ML Model

An LSTM model is trained on the historical stock prices of a select set of stocks to obtain short-term (1 month) and long-term predictions (3 months and 1 year). It is optimized using the Adam optimization algorithm [26]. This univariate model uses the closing price of a stock recorded over the past 3 years from Aug 31, 2019 to Aug 31, 2022, to train and the last 60 days to make a prediction for Day 61; the sliding window is altered to incorporate a new prediction for Day 62. For Experiment A, this process is repeated until a prediction for Sep 30, 2022 and a prediction for Nov 30, 2022 are acquired. For Experiment B, a similar process is repeated using data from Sep 30, 2019 to Sep 30, 2022 to retrieve a prediction for Oct 31, 2022 and for December 31, 2022. For Experiment C, a similar process is repeated using data from Oct 31, 2019 to Oct 31, 2022 to retrieve a prediction for Nov 30, 2022 and for January 31, 2023. Due to time constraints, the accuracy of the three-month predictions could not be verified.

3.2   Input Elicitation Techniques

Each study consists of a total of 10 questions that deploy a selection of three types of input elicitation techniques: percentage growth via a slider, price movement via a graph, and investment allocation via a pie chart. The percentage growth questions measure the projected percentage growth of a stock on a scale of −25%

to +25%; −25% corresponds to the leftmost point on the scale (in the darkest red), and +25% corresponds to the rightmost point on the scale (in the darkest green). The slider increments by 5% for each change in color/shade allowing users to choose a percentage of growth within the given range. Each related question asks users to provide predictions over different time windows. Based on the data obtained in Experiments A and B, the granularity of the slider was reduced for Experiment C. For questions that use ML-based priming, a note with the percentage growth predicted by the LSTM model for the stock is provided above the slider. Figure 2 shows the user interface for this type of input elicitation.

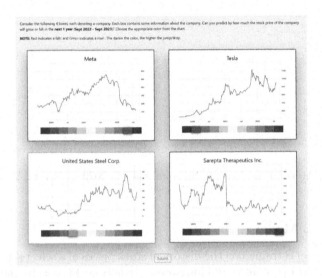

Fig. 2. Interface Example of a Percentage Growth Question.

The price movement questions use an interactive graph to display projected stock prices and elicit the participant's estimate. The historical stock price for the past year is provided to the user, who is then asked to move from a fixed data point indicating the stock price for the upcoming month to the user's estimated price. For questions that use ML-based priming, the upcoming month's price is set to the predicted value; for questions that do not, the upcoming month's price is set to the same value as the current month. Figure 3 shows the user interface for this type of input elicitation.

Each investment allocation question asks users to allocate a budget of virtual funds across a basket of stocks. The total amount of virtual money available to the user is $100,000. A user can invest the full amount in any single company or distribute it among multiple companies. An interactive pie chart is used to illustrate the fund proportions allocated by the user. Users move the slider of each stock to specify the amount of virtual money they would like to allocate to it. The users are presented with the current stock price of all the companies in the basket but, for the question involving ML-based priming, a projected

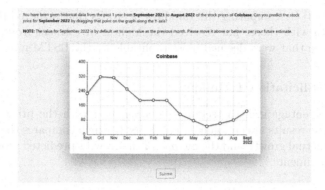

Fig. 3. Interface Example of a Price Movement Question.

percentage growth for each of the stocks in the basket is also shown. Figure 4 shows the user interface for this type of input elicitation.

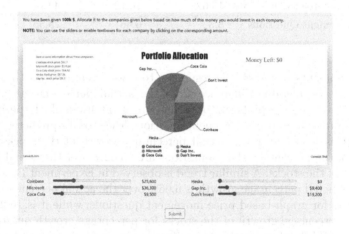

Fig. 4. Interface Example of an Investment Allocation Question.

4 Analysis

This section assesses the performance of the tested input elicitation techniques based on the resulting differences between the actual growth and the median of the crowd's predicted growth for the individual stocks. In addition, it analyzes the effect of priming on participant performance in three ways: (1) by measuring the correlation between the predictions by ML vs predictions by the crowd and between the actual price vs the crowd's predictions; (2) by comparing the differences between the actual growth and the median of the crowd's predicted growth; and (3) by comparing the rankings of stocks that achieved the highest actual growth with those that received the highest investment from the crowd and with those that were deemed most profitable by the LSTM model.

4.1 Input Elicitation Techniques

First, the percentage growth technique is compared with the price movement technique. The results are summarized in Table 1, which compares the difference between the actual growth and the median of the crowd's predicted growth across all three experiments.

Table 1. Comparison of the accuracy achieved via percentage growth questions vs via price movement questions.

	Crowd's Predicted Growth - Actual Growth (%)		
Question Type	Experiment A	Experiment B	Experiment C
Percentage Growth Questions	15.62	16.12	4.91
Price Movement Questions	5.3	6.66	75.55

In Experiments A and B, the responses to the percentage-growth questions had a more considerable difference from the actual percentage growth than the responses to the graph-based price movement questions. In Experiment A, across all graph-based price movement questions, the crowd's predicted percentage growth is 5.30% over the actual percentage growth of the stocks; on the other hand, the percentage slider questions are 15.62% over the actual percentage growth of the stocks. A similar trend is observed in Experiment B, where the crowd's predicted percentage growth is 6.66% over the actual percentage growth of the stocks for graph-based price movement questions, while it is 16.26% over the actual percentage growth of the stocks for percentage growth questions.

One plausible explanation for this difference in performance can be that 5% increments in the slider of the percentage-growth questions are not sufficiently granular, leading to large differences between the crowd's responses. To explore this issue, the increments for Experiment C were altered to reduce the increment gap. The modified slider contains the values −20%, −10%, −5%, −2%, −1%, 0%, 1%, 2%, 5%, 10%, 20%.

After modifying the slider scale, participant performance improved considerably. In Experiment C, the crowd's predicted percentage growth is 4.91% over the actual percentage growth of the stocks. On the other hand, the price movement questions performed much worse in this experiment than in the previous two. Specifically, the crowd's predicted percentage growth is 75.55% over the actual percentage growth of the stocks. However, an interesting observation can be made here. Participants overestimated a few stocks (META, TSLA, AAL, and X) by nearly 3 times their actual price. A reason for this could be that at the time of this study, these stocks were very popular, as measured by high Google Trends scores (>60) causing people to be overly optimistic about their performance. In addition, unlike Experiments A and B, the market was trending upward at the time Experiment C was deployed, which can explain why the participants overestimated the prices on popular stocks. Indeed, when META, TSLA, AAL, and X are removed, the price movement questions outperformed the percentage growth questions, with a difference of only 0.12% between the actual growth and the crowd's predicted growth.

In summary, with a more granular calibration of the slider, the percentage movement questions yield closer estimations than the price movement questions but, after removing outliers, the price movement questions elicit more accurate predictions. These results motivate the need to further research these two techniques before a more definitive statement on their comparative performance can be made. Due to the nature of the input elicitation techniques, only the percentage growth and price movement questions can be directly compared to each other. Next, the investment allocation questions reveal some interesting findings. This information can be found in Table 2, which shows the performance of investment allocation questions across all three studies.

Table 2. Rankings of stocks based on their actual profitability vs based on the proportion of funds allocated to them by the crowd.

Rankings of Stocks					
Experiment A		Experiment B		Experiment C	
Actual	Crowd	Actual	Crowd	Actual	Crowd
COIN	KO	GPS	KO	META	X
MSFT	GPS	KO	COIN	X	META
KO	COIN	COIN	GPS	KO	AAPL
GPS	HSKA	MSFT	MSFT	AAPL	KO
HSKA	MSFT	HSKA	HSKA	VISA	VISA

In Column 1, stocks are ordered from most to least profitable in Experiment A. In Column 2, the stocks are ordered based on the proportion of funds invested by participants in each stock from highest to lowest. This is repeated for all the experiments across the rest of the columns. Based on the data in the table, it appears that the crowd tended to invest most of their funds in the most profitable stocks. In Experiment A, KO and COIN were heavily invested stocks; they are also the among the most profitable companies among the set of stocks given to users. In Experiment B, most participants invested the largest proportion of money in KO, which has the second-highest actual growth. Lastly in Study C, most people invested the most on X and the second-most on META. The actual growth of META and X were the first and second highest, respectively, among the bucket of stocks for this question.

4.2   Priming

The correlations between the crowd's predicted price, ML's predicted price, and the actual price of a stock were measured using Pearson's correlation coefficient. This measure calculates the linear correlation between two vectors, with -1 representing a total negative linear relationship, $+1$ representing a total positive linear relationship, and 0 representing no linear correlation.

Table 3 contains the correlation coefficients between ML's predicted prices, the crowd's predicted prices, and the actual price. For questions with priming, the correlation between the crowd's predictions and ML along with the correlation between the crowd's predictions and actual price are represented. For questions without priming, only the correlation between the crowd's prediction and the actual price is shown. The experimental results show that the crowd's predictions were influenced by ML. Indeed, the table shows that there is a strong positive linear correlation between ML's predicted prices and the median of the crowd's predicted prices. In addition, for questions with ML-based priming, there was a higher correlation between the median prices predicted by participants and those predicted by ML.

Table 3. Correlation between the predictions by ML vs predictions by the crowd and between the actual price vs the crowd's predictions, with and without priming.

| | Pearson's Correlation | | | | | |
| | Experiment A | | Experiment B | | Experiment C | |
Question Type	ML & Crowd	Actual & Crowd	ML & Crowd	Actual & Crowd	ML & Crowd	Actual & Crowd
Priming	0.9244	0.8628	0.9091	0.8918	0.925	0.9485
No priming	-	0.7381	-	0.8216	-	0.6982

Next, the effect of priming on each input elicitation technique is analyzed. However, due to previously discussed differences in the nature of the input elicitation techniques (e.g., mismatches in data types) and the time frame of certain questions, certain direct comparisons could not be made.

First, the effect of priming on the percentage growth questions is observed. The data pertaining to this can be found in Table 4, which contains the difference between the actual growth of a stock and the crowd's predicted growth across all three experiments.

Experiments A and B did not feature questions with priming within the 1-month time period and, thus, could not be used. However, the data from Experiment C suggests that priming did not help participants to make more accurate predictions for the percentage growth questions. In particular, the absolute value of the difference between the actual growth and the median of the crowd's predicted growth is higher for questions where an ML suggestion was provided. However, there is an interesting observation to be made here. Priming appears

Table 4. Assessment of the effects of priming on percentage growth questions.

Question Type	Crowd's Predicted Growth - Actual Growth (%)		
	Experiment A	Experiment B	Experiment C
Priming	-	-	4.91
No priming	−15.62	16.26	−2.67

to have made the crowd's predictions more optimistic, specifically, the difference between the actual growth and the crowd's predicted growth is 4.91% with priming, while it is −2.67% without priming. That said, the difference between the two numbers is not large enough to close the debate on priming.

When it comes to the price movement questions, ML-based priming boosted participant performance (up to 3 times better). This information can be found in Table 5 which contains the difference between actual growth and the median of the crowd's predicted growth across all three experiments.

Table 5. Assessment of the effects of priming on price movement questions.

Question Type	Crowd's Predicted Growth - Actual Growth (%)		
	Experiment A	Experiment B	Experiment C
Priming	17.93	3.75	31.96
No priming	18.41	12.45	114.33

Based on the data in the table, priming seems to help participants make more accurate predictions. One explanation for this could be that participants were able to refine their estimations against the ML prediction. Just as the percentage growth questions give participants a set of values to choose from, the predicted ML price serves as a suggestion for the price movement question. Lastly, when looking at the investment allocation questions, priming seems to have influenced the crowd's investment decision-making processes. This information can be found in Table 6, which contains the data from the investment allocation questions that are primed across all three experiments.

The first three table columns apply to Experiment A: Column 1 orders the stocks from most to least profitable, column 2 from highest to lowest proportion of funds allocated by the crowd, and column 3 from most to least profitable as predicted by the ML model. This is repeated for Experiments B and C in the remaining table columns. In Experiments A and C, most people invest in stocks that are deemed most profitable by the ML model (BAC and PYPL in Exp A and NFLX and TSLA in Exp C). In Experiment B, there is an equal split between people who invested the largest proportion of their money in the least profitable and the most profitable stocks (XOM, PYPL). This could speak to participants' risk-taking appetite. Low-risk investors tend to invest in stocks

Table 6. Rankings of stocks based on actual profitability, proportion of funds allocated by the crowd, and ML's profitability projections.

Rankings of Stocks								
Experiment A			Experiment B			Experiment C		
Actual	Crowd	ML	Actual	Crowd	ML	Actual	Crowd	ML
PFE	GOOG	XOM	XOM	GOOG	GOOG	GPS	AAL	SRPT
PYPL	BAC	BAC	BAC	(PYPL, XOM)	PFE	SRPT	NFLX	NFLX
XOM	PYPL	PYPL	PFE	(BAC, PFE)	XOM	NFLX	TSLA	TSLA
BAC	PFE	GOOG	GOOG		BAC	AAL	GPS	AAL
GOOG	XOM	PFE	PYPL		PYPL	TSLA	SRPT	GPS

that are already profitable with expectations of slow growth, whereas high-risk investors tend to invest in stocks that are currently not profitable with the hopes of rapid growth in a short span of time.

5 Conclusion

The relationship between the wisdom of crowds and ML is complex but certainly worth exploring in the pursuit of building more effective hybrid AI systems. The stock market is one case for hybrid AI systems to improve forecasts. In order to utilize crowdsourcing, it is important to determine which input elicitation techniques tend to yield higher-quality estimates. In the case of this study, while the percentage growth questions perform better with a more granular calibration of the slider, the price movement questions often yield more accurate results on certain types of stocks. Further testing of these techniques is needed on a more consistent selection of stocks to advance this research. Investment allocation (via a pie chart) is also an interesting approach to analyzing the crowd's investment tendencies. Most people invested in companies that had the highest actual growth. A wider variety of stocks with more context on the previous performance of the stocks is a promising direction of further study.

In addition to the right crowdsourcing technique, at the heart of hybrid AI systems is establishing a symbiotic relationship between people and ML models. Based on participant data from this study, there was a strong correlation between the crowd's predictions and those made by the ML model. In fact, there is a stronger correlation between the crowd's predictions and the actual stock price when the crowd is exposed to suggestions from ML than when they are not.

While ML was not helpful in improving participant performance for percentage growth questions, there is a considerable improvement in participant performance for price movement questions. This could have broader implications on other ML crowdsourcing tasks. For questions that can be ambiguous or rather open-ended, ML might be a great source of support and direction for participants. This could be tested further with more types of activities across different contexts beyond the stock market. In addition, participants were aligned with ML's projected growth of stocks for investment allocation questions in all three studies. To reach a more definitive conclusion, additional studies with a larger participant pool need to be conducted. Based on the participant data, 101 out of 308 participants claim to engage in stock trading on a monthly basis, 73 participants traded on a weekly basis, and 55 never traded. Using these different expertise levels, more nuanced aggregation techniques can be employed to better engage the crowd in the prediction process. Another important area to explore is the different prediction windows presented to users. Considering the accessibility and speed at which information disseminates, prediction windows within hours or minutes might be more relevant and could lead to more accurate predictions [11]. Lastly, ML model performance can be tested by experimenting with different types of models and input features.

Acknowledgements. The authors thank all participants in this study, which received institutional IRB approval prior to deployment. The lead PI of the project (the fourth author) and one of the students (the first author) also gratefully acknowledge support from the National Science Foundation under Award Number 1850355.

References

1. Machine learning approaches in stock price prediction: A systematic review. https://iopscience.iop.org/article/10.1088/1742-6596/2161/1/012065
2. Bassamboo, A., Cui, R., Moreno, A.: Wisdom of crowds in operations: Forecasting using prediction markets (2015). Available at SSRN 2679663
3. Checkley, M.S., Higón, D.A., Alles, H.: The hasty wisdom of the mob: How market sentiment predicts stock market behavior. Expert Syst. Appl. **77**, 256-263 (2017). https://www.sciencedirect.com/science/article/abs/pii/S0957417417300398
4. Das, N., Sadhukhan, B., Chatterjee, T., Chakrabarti, S.: Effect of public sentiment on stock market movement prediction during the COVID-19 outbreak. Soc. Netw. Anal. Min. **12**(1), 92 (2022)
5. Demartini, G., Mizzaro, S., Spina, D.: Human-in-the-loop artificial intelligence for fighting online misinformation: Challenges and opportunities. IEEE Data Eng. Bull. **43**(3), 65–74 (2020)
6. Endress, T., et al.: deliberated intuition in stock price forecasting. Econ. Sociol. **11**(3), 11–27 (2018)
7. Fathi, S., Ahmadi, M., Birashk, B., Dehnad, A.: Development and use of a clinical decision support system for the diagnosis of social anxiety disorder. Comput. Methods Programs Biomed. **190**, 105354 (2020)
8. Hill, S., Ready-Campbell, N.: Expert stock picker: the wisdom of (experts in) crowds. Int. J. Electron. Commer. **15**(3), 73–102 (2011)
9. Honda, H., Kagawa, R., Shirasuna, M.: On the round number bias and wisdom of crowds in different response formats for numerical estimation. Sci. Rep. **12**(1), 1–18 (2022)
10. Huang, Y., Capretz, L.F., Ho, D.: Machine learning for stock prediction based on fundamental analysis. In: 2021 IEEE Symposium Series on Computational Intelligence (SSCI), pp. 01–10. IEEE (2021)
11. Martins, C.J.L., et al.: Information diffusion, trading speed and their potential impact on price efficiency-Literature review. Borsa Istanbul Rev. **22**(1), 122-132 (2021). https://www.sciencedirect.com/science/article/pii/S2214845021000193

12. Karpathy, A., Toderici, G., Shetty, S., Leung, T., Sukthankar, R., Fei-Fei, L.: Large-scale video classification with convolutional neural networks. In: Proceedings of the IEEE conference on Computer Vision and Pattern Recognition, pp. 1725–1732 (2014)
13. Kemmer, R., Yoo, Y., Escobedo, A., Maciejewski, R.: Enhancing collective estimates by aggregating cardinal and ordinal inputs. https://ojs.aaai.org/index.php/HCOMP/article/view/7465
14. Khodabakhsh, A., Ari, I., Bakır, M., Alagoz, S.M.: Forecasting multivariate time-series data using LSTM and mini-batches. In: Bohlouli, M., Sadeghi Bigham, B., Narimani, Z., Vasighi, M., Ansari, E. (eds.) CiDaS 2019. LNDECT, vol. 45, pp. 121–129. Springer, Cham (2020). https://doi.org/10.1007/978-3-030-37309-2_10
15. links open overlay panelAdil Moghar a, A., a, b, has never been easy to invest in a set of assets, A.: Stock market prediction using lstm recurrent neural network (2020). https://www.sciencedirect.com/science/article/pii/S1877050920304865
16. Mohanty, S., Vijay, A., Gopakumar, N.: Stockbot: Using lstms to predict stock prices. arXiv preprint arXiv:2207.06605 (2022)
17. Mojjada, R.K., Yadav, A., Prabhu, A., Natarajan, Y.: Machine learning models for COVID-19 future forecasting. Materials Today: Proceedings (2020)
18. Wang, Q., Xu, W., Zheng, H.: Combining the wisdom of crowds and technical analysis for financial market prediction using deep random subspace ensembles. Neurocomputing, **299**, 51-61 (2018). https://www.sciencedirect.com/science/article/abs/pii/S0925231218303540
19. Rai, R., Tiwari, M.K., Ivanov, D., Dolgui, A.: Machine learning in manufacturing and industry 4.0 applications. Int. J. Prod. Res. **59**, 4773–4778 (2021)
20. Remias, R.: President Trump's Tweets and their Effect on the Stock Market: The Relationship Between Social Media, Politics, and Emotional Economic Decision-Making. Ph.D. thesis, Wittenberg University (2021)
21. Seethalakshmi, R.: Analysis of stock market predictor variables using linear regression. Int. J. Pure and Appl. Math. **119**(15), 369–378 (2018)
22. Shang, S., Hui, P., Kulkarni, S.R., Cuff, P.W.: Wisdom of the crowd: incorporating social influence in recommendation models. In: 2011 IEEE 17th International Conference on Parallel and Distributed Systems, pp. 835–840. IEEE (2011)
23. Shen, J., Shafiq, M.O.: Short-term stock market price trend prediction using a comprehensive deep learning system. J. big Data **7**(1), 1–33 (2020)
24. Siah, K.W., Myers, P.: Stock market prediction through technical and public sentiment analysis (2016)
25. Surowiecki, J.: The wisdom of crowds. Anchor (2005)
26. Team, K.: Keras documentation: Adam. https://keras.io/api/optimizers/adam/#::text=Adam
27. Wazny, K.: Applications of crowdsourcing in health: an overview. J. Global Health **8**(1), 010502 (2018)
28. Yasmin, R., Grassel, J.T., Hassan, M.M., Fuentes, O., Escobedo, A.R.: Enhancing image classification capabilities of crowdsourcing-based methods through expanded input elicitation. https://ojs.aaai.org/index.php/HCOMP/article/view/18949
29. Yasmin, R., Hassan, M.M., Grassel, J.T., Bhogaraju, H., Escobedo, A.R., Fuentes, O.: Improving crowdsourcing-based image classification through expanded input elicitation and machine learning. Front. Artif. Intell. **5**, 848056 (2022)

RaReSi: An Approach Combining Ratings and Reviews to Measure User Similarity in Neighbor-Based Recommender Systems

Ho Thi Hoang Vy[1,2] , Do Thi Thanh Ha[1,2] , Tiet Gia Hong[1,2] ,
Thi My Hang Vu[1,2] , Cuong Pham-Nguyen[1,2] , and Le Nguyen Hoai Nam[1,2(✉)]

[1] Faculty of Information Technology, University of Science, Ho Chi Minh City, Vietnam
{hthvy,dttha,tghong,vtmhang,pncuong,lnhnam}@fit.hcmus.edu.vn
[2] Vietnam National University, Ho Chi Minh City, Vietnam

Abstract. Neighbor-based recommender systems are highly valued for their interpretability. These systems focus on determining the similarity between users to find neighbor sets. In this paper, we combine observed ratings and reviews from users to calculate their similarity, named RaReSi. This combination is reflected not only in the calculation of user similarity but also in the transformation of the user representation space. Thus, our method effectively addresses the issue of sparse data, a typical challenge in the field of recommender systems. Experimental results on datasets Baby, Tools-Home Improvement, and Beauty show that our proposed method yields better RMSE results than rating-only, review-only, and other combined methods.

Keywords: User similarity · Rating prediction · Recommender systems

1 Introduction

Recommender systems help people avoid information overload [1, 2]. They find the items that best match the preferences of the users. Besides the accuracy of the recommended item set, the interpretability of the recommendation process is also of great interest. Neighbor-based recommender systems are always interpretive [3, 4]. They recommend an item to a user only if it is highly appreciated by his/her neighbors [5].

In this manner, the neighbor set is a determining factor for the accuracy of neighbor-based recommender systems. The notion of a user's neighbors mentions users who are similar to him/her. Thus, neighbor-based recommender systems focus on defining a measure of similarity between users [3, 4].

In reality, a user's characteristics are conveyed through ratings and reviews observed by him/her [6]. Ratings are a concise numerical representation of the users' satisfaction with the items while reviews are text expressions of the users' experience with the items [7]. These two types of data complement each other to clarify user preferences, leading to improved accuracy in recommendations [6, 8]. However, in neighbor-based recommender systems, the similarity between users is primarily defined by their ratings.

N. T. Nguyen et al. (Eds.): ICCCI 2023, CCIS 1864, pp. 17–29, 2023.
https://doi.org/10.1007/978-3-031-41774-0_2

As a result, we aim to propose a method for calculating the similarity between users that combines both their observed ratings and reviews. Specifically, the contribution of this paper is as follows:

- At present, similarity measures are encountering challenges regarding the sparse representation of users [9, 10]. As a result, we first integrate the reviews and ratings obtained from users to discover a fully-specified and low-dimensional space for their representation.
- In the space identified above, we propose a method to determine the similarity between users.

The structure of this paper is as follows: Section 1 presents the context and research contributions. Section 2 reviews related works. In Sect. 3, we establish the objectives of the study. Section 4 details the proposed method steps. The experimental results and methodology are reported in Sect. 5. Lastly, Sect. 5 summarizes our conclusions and outlines future works. Table 1 lists the symbols in this paper.

Table 1. The symbols used in this paper.

Symbol	Description
$r_{u,i} = *$	The unknown rating of user u for item i
$r_{u,i} \neq *$	The observed rating of user u for item i
$t_{u,i} \neq *$	The observed review of user u for item i
$r'_{u,i}$	The rating extracted from thcorsponding review
$\hat{r}_{u,i}$	The predicted rating of user u for item i
$sim_{u,v}$	The similarity between two users u and v
$corr_{u,f}$	The correlation between user u and influencer f
μ_u	The average rating of users u
c_u	The consistency of user u
e_u	The experience of user u
$\overrightarrow{q_u}$	The Bert embedding vector of user u
$\mathbb{P}_{u,i}$	The neighbor set of u concerning item i
$\mathbb{I}_u$	The item set rated by user u
$|\mathbb{I}_u|$	The number of elements in the $\mathbb{I}_u$

2 Related Works

2.1 Problem Definition

For an active user u, recommender systems need to predict his/her unknown ratings ($r_{u,i} = *$). This process is based on models trained from previously observed ratings ($r_{u,i} \neq *$) and observed reviews ($t_{u,i} \neq *$). As depicted in Fig. 1, the ratings of the active user u_1 for items i_2, i_3, and i_5 are calculated. Items with the highest predicted ratings ($\hat{r}_{u,i}$) will be ultimately selected to make recommendations to the active user u_1.

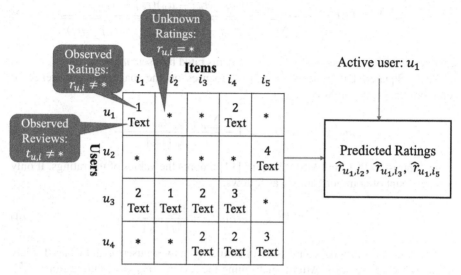

Fig. 1. An example of predicting ratings in a recommender system.

2.2 Neighbor-Based Recommender Systems

Nowadays, recommender systems are more concerned with explaining their results. This is essential in earning the trust of users. One of the best-explained recommender systems is those based on neighbors [1, 3]. These systems recommend an item i to user u based on the fact that the neighbor set of u has tried and enjoyed item i. Thus, the user u's rating for item i will be predicted as follows [3, 11]:

- Step 1: Identify users similar to user u who have rated item i, referred to as the neighbor set of u concerning item i:$\mathbb{P}_{u,i}$
- Step 2: Compute the average of the ratings of the neighbors $v \in \mathbb{P}_{u,i}$ for item i to estimate user u's rating for item i, denoted by $\hat{r}_{u,i}$, as flows:

$$\hat{r}_{u,i} = \mu_u + \frac{\sum_{v \in \mathbb{P}_{u,i}} sim_{u,v} \cdot (r_{v,i} - \mu_v)}{\sum_{v \in \mathbb{P}_{u,i}} |sim_{u,v}|} \tag{1}$$

where μ_u and μ_v respectively represent the average ratings given by users u and v; $sim_{u,v}$ is the similarity between two users u and v.

2.3 User Similarity Measure

The neighborhood set of a user will be determined based on the similarity between him/her and each other user. Following are some of the typical methods for calculating user similarity.

Pearson Correlation Coefficient (PCC) [12] is the cosine between two vectors containing the common ratings of two corresponding users, as follows:

$$sim_{u,v}^{PCC} = PCC_{u,v} = \frac{\sum_{i \in \mathbb{I}_u \cap \mathbb{I}_v} (r_{u,i} - \mu_u)(r_{v,i} - \mu_v)}{\sqrt{\sum_{i \in \mathbb{I}_u \cap \mathbb{I}_v} (r_{u,i} - \mu_u)^2} \sqrt{\sum_{i \in \mathbb{I}_u \cap \mathbb{I}_v} (r_{v,i} - \mu_v)^2}} \quad (2)$$

where $\mathbb{I}_u$ and $\mathbb{I}_v$ are respectively the sets of items rated by users u and v;

Mean Squared Difference (MSD) [13] focuses on the magnitude difference of common ratings, as follows:

$$sim_{u,v}^{MSD} = MSD_{u,v} = 1 - \frac{\sum_{i \in \mathbb{I}_u \cap \mathbb{I}_v} |r_{u,i} - r_{v,i}|}{|\mathbb{I}_u \cap \mathbb{I}_v|} \quad (3)$$

In contrast to PCC and MSD, Jaccard [14] ignores the values of the ratings. It only uses the count of common ratings, as follows:

$$sim_{u,v}^{Jaccard} = Jaccard_{u,v} = \frac{|\mathbb{I}_u \cap \mathbb{I}_v|}{|\mathbb{I}_u \cup \mathbb{I}_v|} \quad (4)$$

The study [15] proposes a measure of similarity between users u and v based solely on their observed reviews. After transforming the reviews $(t_{u,i} \neq *)$ into vectors $(\overrightarrow{x_{u,i}})$, it calculates the average distance between the vectors representing the reviews for the common items, as follows:

$$sim_{u,v}^{review-based} = \frac{\sum_{i \in \mathbb{I}_u \cap \mathbb{I}_v} ||\overrightarrow{x_{u,i}} - \overrightarrow{x_{v,i}}||}{|\mathbb{I}_u \cap \mathbb{I}_v|} \quad (5)$$

In [16], the authors propose a formula for calculating user similarity by combining both reviews and ratings. Specifically, it is the average of the rating-based similarity ($sim_{u,v}^{PCC}$ as Eq. (2)) and the review-based similarity ($sim_{u,v}^{review-based}$, as follows:

$$sim_{u,v}^{combination} = \frac{1}{2} sim_{u,v}^{review-based} + \frac{1}{2} sim_{u,v}^{PCC} \quad (6)$$

3   Motivation

The inherent nature of recommender systems is sparse data. In reality, after experiencing items, users rarely reveal their ratings and reviews. For example, the sparsity of some datasets can reach up to 99%. Therefore, we aim to combine the **Ratings** and **Reviews** observed by users to calculate their **Similarity**, taking into account this issue. Therefore, our proposed method is named **RaReSi.**

A solution to this issue is to change the representation of the users from a high-dimensional and sparse space of items to a lower-dimensional and fully specified one [9, 10]. This new space is often referred to as the latent space, which is formed by linear or non-linear combinations of the original space. However, this process is computationally expensive. Therefore, inspired by the study [3], we choose the influencers in the user set to serve as the new space for user representation. The key difference of our proposed method lies in determining influences and their correlation with other users based on both the observed review and rating. This process will be presented in Subsects. 4.1, 4.2.

Next, we re-represent the users through influencers and then compute their similarities. Its details will be shown in Sect. 4.3.

4   Our Proposed Method, RaReSi

4.1   Determining Influencers

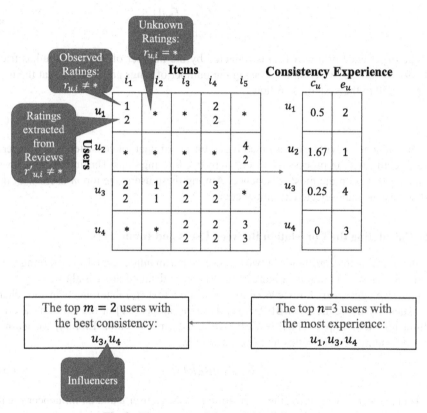

Fig. 2. The process of determining influencers.

Figure 2 shows our process of selecting users as influencers. Specifically, an influencer in the recommender systems must meet two criteria: consistency [17] and experience [18, 19]. According to the observation in [20], there exist some ratings that are inconsistent with the corresponding reviews. For example, some users might rate an item poorly even though they wrote positive reviews about it. Therefore, an influencer must be a user who provides the most consistent preferences. To measure the consistency of users, we use the method proposed by [20], denoted by function g, to convert reviews $(t_{u,i} \neq *)$ to ratings $(r'_{u,i})$, as follows:

$$r'_{u,i} = g(t_{u,i}) \tag{7}$$

Concretely, this method obtains ratings by comparing each word in the review with a sentiment dictionary. It is efficient, cost-effective, and has proven to be highly accurate in recommender systems. Now, a user's consistency (c_u) can be evaluated by comparing the ratings he/she has given $(r_{u,i} \neq *)$ with the ratings extracted from his/her reviews $(r'_{u,i})$, as follows:

$$c_u = \frac{\sum_{i \in \mathbb{I}_u} \left| r_{u,i} - r'_{u,i} \right|}{|\mathbb{I}_u|} \tag{8}$$

The experience of a user (e_u) is reflected by the number of items he/she has tried [18, 19]. Therefore, we compute it using the number of rangs and reviews that the user has provided to the system, as follows:

$$e_u = |\mathbb{I}_u| \tag{9}$$

The influencers will be determined based on a combinati of consistency and experience. Specifically, this process is carried out by two filtering steps. The first filter retrieves the top n users with the most experience. Among these users, the top m users with the best consistency are selected as influencers.

4.2 Calculating the Correlation Between Users and Influencers

We aim to define the correlation between a user u and an influencer f by combining their observed reviews and ratings. Figure 3 illustrates the detailed process above.

First, we aggregate all reviews of a user u into a text (t_u) that reflects his/her characteristics. By using the DistilBERT deep learning model [21] of the istilbert-base-nli stsb-mean-tokens implemented in Sentence-transformers Python Library, we learn a Bert embedding vector for this text $(\overrightarrow{q_u})$, as follows:

$$\overrightarrow{q_u} = DistilBERT(t_u) \tag{10}$$

Then, in terms of reviews, the correlation between a user u and an influencer f will be the cosine between their embedding vectors $(cosine_{\overrightarrow{q_u}, \overrightarrow{q_f}})$. In terms of ratings, the correlation between u and f can be calculated by the cosine between the two vectors that hold their ratings for common items $(PCC_{u,f}$ as Eq. (2)). As influencers are selected based on their extensive experiences, the existence of common items rated by u and f is fully possible. The final correlation between u and f $(corr_{u,f})$ is calculated by taking the average of their correlations in terms of reviews and ratings, as follows:

$$corr_{u,f} = \tfrac{1}{2} cosine_{\overrightarrow{q_u}, \overrightarrow{q_f}} + \tfrac{1}{2} PCC_{u,f} \tag{11}$$

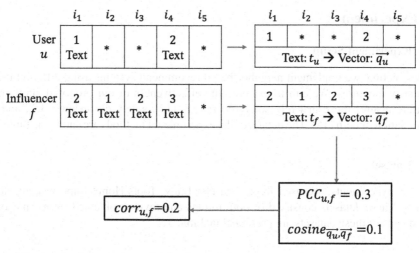

Fig. 3. The process of calculating the correlation between a user and an influencer.

4.3 Computing the User Similarity in the Space of Influencers

Each user will be represented by a vector where each entry contains the correlation between him/her and an influencer. This vector is completely-specified, low-dimensional, and especially reflects the user's characteristics in both reviews and ratings. The similarity between two users u and v is computed by the cosine between their vectors in the space of influencers. The detailed implementation of this formula is as follows:

$$sim_{u,v}^{RaReSi} = \frac{\sum_{f \in \mathbb{F}} corr_{u,f} \cdot corr_{v,f}}{\sqrt{\sum_{f \in \mathbb{F}} corr_{u,f}^2} \cdot \sqrt{\sum_{f \in \mathbb{F}} corr_{v,f}^2}} \tag{12}$$

where $\mathbb{F}$ is the influence set identified in Sect. 4.1.

Table 2. The description of experimental methods.

User similarity measures for identifying neighbor sets	The average of the ratings given by the neighbors	Abbreviation
Rating-based Similarity: $sim_{u,v}^{PCC}$[12] as Eq. (2)	Eq. (1)	RaSi
Review-based Similarity: $sim_{u,v}^{Review-based}$ [15] as Eq. (5)	Eq. (1)	ReSi
Combined Similarity: $sim_{u,v}^{Combination}$[16] as Eq. (6)	Eq. (1)	ComSi
Our proposed **Similarity:** $sim_{u,v}^{RaReSi}$ as Eq. (12)	Eq. (1)	RaReSi

5   Experiment

5.1   Experiment Setup

In this section, we implement neighbor-based recommend systems using different user similarity measures. We aim to examine the effectiveness of our proposed similarity measure against those that rely solely on ratings [12], solely on reviews [15], and a combination of both [16]. The details of the experimental methods are shown in Table 2.

5.2   Dataset

For our experiments, we used three datasets: Baby, Tools-Home Improvement, and Beauty. These datasets consisted of both ratings and reviews obtained from Amazon. The details of these datasets are presented in Table 3.

Table 3. The description of experimental datasets.

	# users	# items	# ratings and reviews
Baby	19,445	7,050	160,792
Tools-Home Improvement	19,856	10,217	134,476
Beauty	22,365	12,101	198,502

We randomly split each dataset into 65% for training and 35% for testing. This procedure was carried out three times to produce three different training-test pairs. The average outcome of these three training-test pairs was then employed to assess the effectiveness of the experimental methods.

5.3   Measure

To ensure user satisfaction with the recommendations, recommender systems should first suggest items that the user likes. Additionally, the most favored items should be placed at the top of the recommendation list. Both of these objectives can only be accomplished if the predicted ratings ($\hat{r}_{u,i}$) match the actual ratings ($\tilde{r}_{u,i}$) in the test set ($\mathbb{T}$). This is assessed by the RMSE measure as follows:

$$RMSE = \sqrt{\frac{\sum_{(u,i)\in\mathbb{T}}\left(\hat{r}_{u,i} - \tilde{r}_{u,i}\right)^2}{|\mathbb{T}|}} \tag{13}$$

5.4   Experimental Result

First, we investigate the RMSE results for each size of the neighbors set when the number of selected influencers is fixed at 40. As shown in Figs. 4, 5 and 6, when the number of selected neighbors is low, the two similarities that combine both reviews and ratings, i.e. ComSi and RaReSi, deliver significantly better RMSE results than the similarities that use one of them, i.e. RaSi and ReSi. That is because this scenario requires high accuracy in the similarity between users. As the number of selected neighbors increases, the superiority of ComSi and RaReSi compared to RaSi and ReSi decreases because the neighbor sets begin to become noisy. This reinforces the idea that the combination of ratings and reviews accurately captures the similarities between users in neighbor-based recommender systems. A comparison of the two combined methods reveals that our proposed method, i.e. RaReSi, has an RMSE result of 1.4111 across all three datasets, while the recently proposed combined method, i.e. ComSi, has an RMSE result of 1.4307 across all three datasets.

Next, we select users with high sparsity on all three experimental datasets. Specifically, users with the minimum number of observed ratings and reviews, that is, less than 10, are selected to compute the RMSE instead of the RMSE of the whole system. As shown in Fig. 7, the RMSE results on the sparse users of RaReSi across all three experimental datasets are significantly better than those of ComSi. Specifically, when the number of neighbors is selected as 20 and 25, the RMSE result of RaReSi decreases by 5,77% and 4,43% compared to those of ComSi. The reason is that RaReSi is designed to account for sparse data by transforming the user representation space, while ComSi solely focuses on the user similarity calculation process.

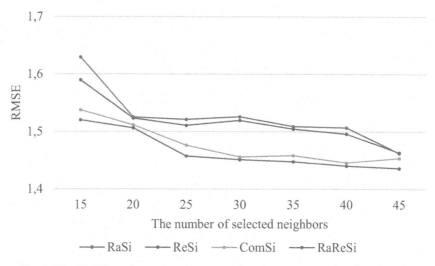

Fig. 4. The RMSE results produced by the experimental methods in the Baby dataset

The number of selected influencers is a crucial parameter that determines the effectiveness of our proposed method, i.e. RaReSi. Figure 8 shows the RMSE results on each experimental dataset when the number of influencers increases from 30 to 60 and the number of selected neighbors is fixed at 25. It can be seen that as the number of influencers increases, the accuracy of rating predictions by RaReSi gradually increases because users

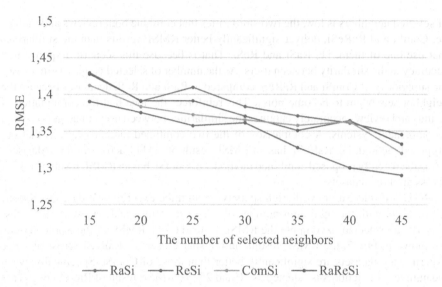

Fig. 5. The RMSE results produced by the experimental methods in the Tools-Home Improvement dataset

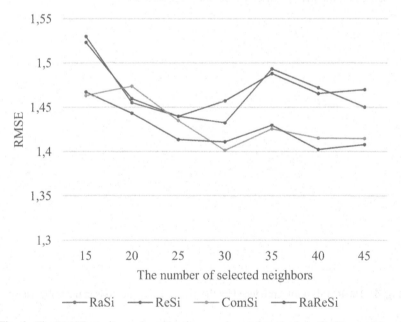

Fig. 6. The RMSE results produced by the experimental methods in the Beauty dataset

are represented more comprehensively. However, when deploying neighbor-based recommender systems, the offline phase requires calculating the similarity of each pair of

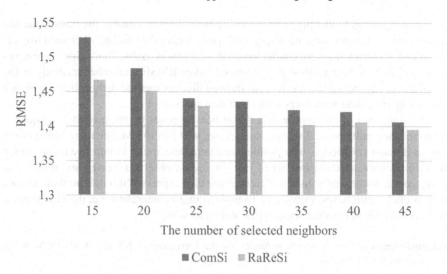

Fig. 7. The RMSE result across all three experimental datasets for sparse users with less than 5 observed ratings and reviews.

users. Therefore, if the number of influencers is chosen to be too large, the computational cost for the offline phase will increase significantly.

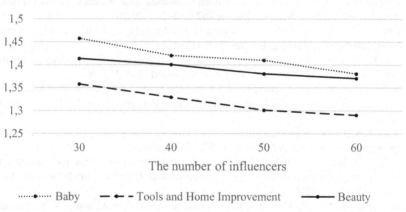

Fig. 8. The RMSE results on each experimental dataset when the number of influencers increases from 30 to 60.

6 Conclusion and Future Work

This paper presents a combination of observed reviews and ratings to improve the accuracy of similarity calculations, namely RaReSi, in neighbor-based recommender systems. Our proposed method addresses the issue of data sparsity by utilizing the observed reviews and ratings to identify influencers. These influencers enable the transformation of user representations into a fully specified space, where the similarity between users is calculated. Experiments were conducted on three datasets: Baby, Tools-Home Improvement, and Beauty. Our method demonstrated better RMSE than other methods in the experiments. Moreover, the results also showed that our method demonstrated a higher superiority in dealing with users with large data sparsity.

The limitation of our approach is that it heavily relies on the quantity and quality of the selected influencers. In future studies, we will aim to leverage more information such as domain knowledge, user profiles, and item description to improve the accuracy of the influencer selection instead of just relying on observed ratings and reviews as in this paper. Additionally, user preferences are also expressed through implicit actions such as clicks, purchases, views, etc. To make it more comprehensive, the next version of RaReSi needs to consider these types of data as well.

Acknowledgments. This research is funded by the University of Science, VNU-HCM under grant number CNTT 2022-04.

References

1. Valcarce, D., Landin, A., Parapar, J., Barreiro, Á.: Collaborative filtering embeddings for memory-based recommender systems. Eng. Appl. Artif. Intell. **85**, 347–356 (2019)
2. Khan, Z.Y., Niu, Z., Yousif, A.: Joint deep recommendation model exploiting reviews and metadata information. Neurocomputing **402**, 256–265 (2020)
3. Lima, G.R., Mello, C.E., Lyra, A., Zimbrao, G.: Applying landmarks to enhance memory-based collaborative filtering. Inf. Sci. **513**, 412–428 (2020)
4. Cai, W., Pan, W., Liu, J., Chen, Z., Ming, Z.: k-Reciprocal nearest neighbors algorithm for one-class collaborative filtering. Neurocomputing **381**, 207–216 (2020)
5. Valcarce, D., Parapar, J., Barreiro, Á.: Language models for collaborative filtering neighborhoods. In: European Conference on Information Retrieval, pp. 614–625. Springer, Cham (2016)
6. Nam, L.N.H.: Incorporating textual reviews in the learning of latent factors for recommender systems. Electron. Commer. Res. Appl. **52**, 101133 (2022)
7. Chehal, D., Gupta, P., Gulati, P.: Implementation and comparison of topic modeling techniques based on user reviews in e-commerce recommendations. J. Ambient. Intell. Humaniz. Comput. **12**(5), 5055–5070 (2021)
8. Hernández-Rubio, M., Cantador, I., Bellogín, A.: A comparative analysis of recommender systems based on item aspect opinions extracted from user reviews. User Model. User-Adap. Inter. **29**(2), 381–441 (2019)
9. Hoang, B.N.M., Vy, H.T.H., Hong, T.G., Hang, V.T.M., Nhung, H.L.T.K.: Using bert embedding to improve memory-based collaborative filtering recommender systems. In: 2021 RIVF International Conference on Computing and Communication Technologies (RIVF), pp. 1–6. IEEE (2021)
10. Aggarwal, C.C.: Recommender Systems, vol. 1. Springer International Publishing, Cham (2016)
11. Gazdar, A., Hidri, L.: A new similarity measure for collaborative filtering based recommender systems. Knowl.-Based Syst. **188**, 105058 (2020)

12. Su, X., Khoshgoftaar, T.M.: A survey of collaborative filtering techniques. Adv. Artif. Intell. **2009**, 1–19 (2009)
13. Herlocker, J.L., Konstan, J.A., Borchers, A., Riedl, J.: An algorithmic framework for performing collaborative filtering. In: ACM SIGIR Forum, vol. 51, No. 2, pp. 227–234. ACM, New York, NY, USA (2017)
14. Koutrika, G., Bercovitz, B., Garcia-Molina, H.F.: Expressing and combining flexible recommendations. In: Proceedings of the 35th SIGMOD International Conference on Management of Data (SIGMOD'09), Providence, RI, USA, vol. 29
15. Musto, C., de Gemmis, M., Semeraro, G., Lops, P.: A multi-criteria recommender system exploiting aspect-based sentiment analysis of users' reviews. In: Proceedings of the eleventh ACM conference on recommender systems, pp. 321–325 (2017)
16. Ghasemi, N., Momtazi, S.: Neural text similarity of user reviews for improving collaborative filtering recommender systems. Electron. Commer. Res. Appl. **45**, 101019 (2021)
17. Nam, L.N.H.: Towards comprehensive profile aggregation methods for group recommendation based on the latent factor model. Expert Syst. Appl. **185**, 115585 (2022)
18. Wang, W., Zhang, G., Lu, J.: Member contribution-based group recommender system. Decis. Support Syst. **87**, 80–93 (2016)
19. Ortega, F., Hernando, A., Bobadilla, J., Kang, J.H.: Recommending items to group of users using matrix factorization based collaborative filtering. Inf. Sci. **345**, 313–324 (2016)
20. Shen, R.P., Zhang, H.R., Yu, H., Min, F.: Sentiment based matrix factorization with reliability for recommendation. Expert Syst. Appl. **135**, 249–258 (2019)
21. Sanh, V., Debut, L., Chaumond, J., Wolf, T.: DistilBERT, a distilled version of BERT: smaller, faster, cheaper and lighter. arXiv preprint arXiv:1910.01108 (2019)

Personalized Quiz-Based Perfume Recommender System Using Social Data

Elena-Ruxandra Luțan[✉][iD] and Costin Bădică[✉][iD]

Department of Computers and Information Technology,
University of Craiova, 200585 Craiova, Romania
elena.ruxandra.lutan@gmail.com, costin.badica@edu.ucv.ro

Abstract. In this paper we propose a method for obtaining perfume recommendations by considering lifestyle and contextual aspects. The method was validated using a dataset collected from *Fragrantica* – an online encyclopedia of perfumes. The dataset was obtained using a custom scraper to collect perfume information from *Fragrantica* website. We used a quiz GUI in order to collect user preferences and expectations perfume-wise, and to generate the personalized top-most recommendation using our dataset. Lastly we propose two performance measures and discuss our algorithm performances.

Keywords: Recommender System · Web Scrapping

1 Introduction

Finding the loved perfume is a very difficult task, as the perfume reflects a person's individuality, style and personality [9]. Aspects like mood or lifestyle are important, because the perfume should suit our daily activities and make us feel comfortable [19].

Recommending a perfume is hard. On one hand, most websites selling perfumes and colognes advise the users to choose fragrances based on their notes [14]. On the other hand, specialized perfumers advise to not make a notes-based choice of perfumes, as a certain note can be obtained from a variety of compounds, and it might smell completely different based on the compound that is actually used.

In this paper, we propose a method for obtaining perfume recommendations starting from user lifestyle, and considering daily and contextual aspects when providing recommendations, such as season when the user would like to wear the perfume or time of day, for example if the user plans to wear the perfume during the day (office, regular daily activities) or during the night (events, parties).

We created a perfume dataset with data collected from *Fragrantica* website [8], which is an online encyclopedia of perfumes, containing 76.693 perfumes and 1.372.745 fragrance reviews (values available on *Fragrantica* website on 21.12.2022). Based on this dataset, we created a system which collects the preferences of the user and checks the perfume dataset for the most suitable perfumes. Then, running the recommendation algorithm, it displays the top-most recommendation for the user.

The perfume recommendation algorithm we propose uses the concept of *Fragrance Family* instead of *Fragrance Notes* or *Fragrance Accords*. *Fragrance Family* refers to a narrowed classification of perfumes into distinctive olfactory groups. *Fragrance Notes*

N. T. Nguyen et al. (Eds.): ICCCI 2023, CCIS 1864, pp. 30–43, 2023.
https://doi.org/10.1007/978-3-031-41774-0_3

are individual scents which can be sensed when smelling a fragrance, while *Fragrance Accords* are a combination of *Fragrance Notes* [11]. Based on literature, fragrance notes are not sufficient to describe a perfume or to find similarities between perfumes ([11, 20]). Therefore, we did not rely our recommender system solely on perfumes notes.

The paper is structured as follows. Section 2 covers related works. Section 3 describes the main system functionalities for gathering the perfume data and providing fragrance recommendations. In Sect. 4, we provide the dataset overview and then we discuss the experimental results. The last section presents the conclusions.

2 Related Works

According to [13], four main fragrance families can be identified: fresh, floral, oriental and woody, which can be further split into multiple subcategories.

Joel Lee [11] considers that the notes list used to describe a perfume shows only the prominent ones, which actually generates an incomplete list of individual scents, as there are more aspects to the overall scent of a fragrance than what is described using the notes. In the same direction, the author proposes to never use the *Fragrance Notes* when comparing perfumes, as one note may come from different compounds and therefore it can produce a slightly different scent. On the other hand, accords are obtained by balancing and harmonizing a set of components in order to create a unique scent. [15] describes the accords as the skeleton of a perfume.

Michael Edwards, a perfume expert, studied the fragrance families and developed a *Fragrance Wheel*, which has multiple versions. In 1983, he identified 11 blended subcategories for the 4 families: floral family (floral, soft floral, floral oriental), oriental family (soft oriental, oriental, wordy oriental), woody family (mossy words, dry woods) and fresh (citrus, green, water). In 2008 version [5], 2 new subcategories were added, "woods" for woody family and "fruity" for the fresh family. The latest version, from 2010 [6], contains an additional subclass called "Aromatic Fougère" for the woody family and refers the oriental family also as amber family. Using the fragrance wheel, one can categorize the scents based on their dominant accords.

[7] proposes a division of fragrances into 11 categories, based on the following notes: citrus, green leaves, aquatic, aromatic, leather, chypre, woody, oriental, gourmand, floral, fruity. Although we will not use this exact division, we were inspired by this proposal when choosing the accords applicable for each category.

[10] divides the perfumes into two categories: traditional perfumes and modern perfumes. The traditional perfumes are divided into 7 subcategories: single floral, floral bouquet, oriental or amber, wordy, leather, chypre, fougere, while the modern ones are: bright floral, green, "aquatic, oceanic or ozonic", citrus and gourmand.

Seven main olfactory families from 1984 were reviewed by the French Society of Perfumers: citrus, floral, ferns, chypre, woody, orientals or amber, leathers [3]. Along them there are different facets which can be assigned to a perfume, such as aldehydic facet (for metallic and orange notes), marine facet, gourmand facet or powdery facet.

[21] identifies 8 major fragrance families: 4 feminine ones (Chypre, Citrus, Floral and Oriental) and 4 masculine ones (Aromatic, Citrus, Oriental, Woody). Each of the major fragrance families is then split into multiple subclasses and described based on the dominant accords.

In [23], Michael Zarzo proposes an approach to visualize the spectrum of fragrances as a two-dimensional plot, depending on olfactory classes. The fragrances are mapped into a series of categories, derived from the 14 categories proposed by M. Edwards.

[12] proposes the emotion classification of fragrances based on their main accords. We will not use the concept of emotion classification in this research, but it is a very interesting path to follow as future work.

On [22] we found a dataset which best matched our expectation, containing details about perfumes from *Fragrantica* website. It contains the main data available on the website for each perfume, like name, gender type, rating, accords, description and notes. Although the dataset was consistent, it misses some statistics which we consider valuable inputs for our system, such as suitable season or part of the day when wearing the perfume will bring the best user experience.

In [17], Kalina Zeligowska Serej creates a model for making predictions based on perfumes statistics available on *Fragrantica* website. For experiments and observations, she uses a dataset from *Kaggle*, which unfortunately is no more available. The article provides interesting insights about the nature of *Fragrantica* statistics.

3   System Design

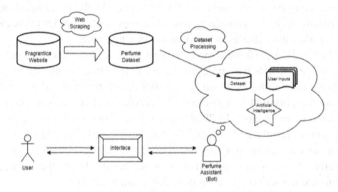

Fig. 1. System Design.

The proposed system contains multiple sub-systems working together for a common aim: to interact with the user using natural language, to understand his or her scent preferences and to recommend an appropriate fragrance the user might enjoy. Therefore, the workflow can be divided as follows (see Fig. 1):

1. Dataset gathering.
2. Interaction with the chatbot in natural language or using a quiz GUI (the NLP part of the chat bot from the block diagram in Fig. 1 is not described in this paper).
3. Dataset manipulation for recommending the user a perfume based on his/her query.

3.1   Dataset Gathering

The experimental dataset was collected from *Fragrantica* website [8], using our own customized web scraper. It uses *Beautiful Soup* and *Selenium* Python libraries for Web crawling and HTML download and parsing. On the website, the perfumes are displayed as lists of 30 elements. There is no page division of the list of displayed perfumes, and to see more results, there is a button at the bottom of the page for loading more results.

The website offers the possibility to sort perfumes by a variety of fields. Some of the fields on which filters can be set, such as release year or country are not visible on the perfume details web page.

Algorithm 1. *Fragrantica* Scraping Algorithm

1: **for** each year-category URL **do**
2:     Navigate to the category on *Fragrantica* website
3:     Load the first $n = 150$ perfumes
4:     **for** each perfume available on the page **do**
5:         Identify the Perfume URL
6:         Store the Perfume URL in the *perfume_url.txt* file
7:     **end for**
8: **end for**
9: **for** each URL in the *perfume_url.txt* file **do**
10:     Navigate to the URL
11:     Collect the defined Perfume Entity fields
12:     Store the perfume details in the Perfumes Dataset
13: **end for**

The scraper works in two steps (Algorithm 1). At first it goes to the URL given as input. The URL refers to a category of perfumes on the website, obtained by setting filters on the perfume year criteria. A category refers to a decade between 1920–2022. After the filter is set, the perfumes are sorted by their popularity.

Since there is no perfume pagination on *Fragrantica* website, in order to make visible the entire list of perfumes to be collected, the scraper must repeatedly press the button available on the lower part of the screen to load more content on the page. We decided to collect the topmost $n = 150$ perfumes from each year-category. This means that the button for loading more content must be checked and pressed 4 times. Afterwards, the URLs of the available perfumes are retrieved and stored inside a text file.

The second step of the scraper refers to sequentially explore through the list of perfume URLs available in the text file, to navigate to each perfume details web page, to collect the actual perfume data and to store it inside the perfumes dataset.

Although the task to collect the data seems pretty easy, it proved to be rather difficult. The first issue is that the HTML code of the page is poorly structured, making difficult to identify the fields. The second difficulty comes from the website protections, which are very strict. Although we used random big times between accessing each web page, the website still restricted our access based on the browser signature or IP address.

The dataset is represented in tabular format and it is stored in a CSV file. On *Fragrantica* website, each bottle of perfume is described by several parameters, captured as separate columns. Table 1 shows the perfume parameters that we extracted.

Table 1. Perfume Entity Description.

Field Name	Field Description
URL	The URL which uniquely identifies the perfume
Name	The name of the perfume
Brand	The brand of the perfume
Accords	List of tuples (perfume accord, associated weight)
Rating value	Float number representing the rating of the perfume
Rating count	Natural number representing the number of ratings for the perfume
Wanted statistics	List of tuples (value, weight) which shows in percentage how many users have, had or want the perfume
Sentiment statistics	List of tuples (value, wight) which shows in percentage how many users love, like, dislike, hate or have a neural sentiment for the perfume
Season	List of tuples (value, weight) which shows in percentage how many users voted the perfume suitable for each season (winter, spring, summer, fall)
Time of day	List of tuples (value, weight) which shows in percentage how many users voted the perfume suitable for day-time or night-time
Description	The description of the perfume
Perfumer	List of strings referring to the expert or experts who created the perfume
Top Notes	List of strings referring to the top notes of the perfume
Middle Notes	List of strings referring to the middle notes of the perfume
Base Notes	List of strings referring to the base notes of the perfume
Longevity	List of tuples (value, weight) showing how many users voted the respective perfume longevity category available on the website (very week, weak, moderate, long lasting, eternal)
Silage	List of tuples (value, weight) showing how many users voted the respective perfume silage category (intimate, moderate, strong, enormous)
Gender	List of tuples (value, weight) showing how many users voted the respective perfume gender category (female, more female, unisex, more male, male)
Price Value	List of tuples (value, weight) showing how many users voted the respective perfume price value category (way overpriced, overpriced, ok, good value, great value)

3.2 Perfume Recommendation

In order to simplify the process of retrieving the user fragrance preferences, we use a short 5 questions quiz. After the user fills in and submits the quiz answers, the system retrieves the best matching item from the perfume dataset.

Depending on the initial answer, we have one of the following use cases: no matching perfume is found, a single perfume is found or multiple perfumes are found. If no perfume is found, the system apologizes to the user and offers the possibility to reconsider the quiz selection. If only one perfume matches the selection, it is directly recommended to the user. Lastly, if multiple perfume matches are found, the user is asked to provide his/her preferred fragrance families. After grabbing the user answer, the system recommends the most highly rated perfume matching the selection (see Algorithm 2).

Our algorithm uses the concept of *Fragrance Families*, which are extracted from the *Perfume Description* available on *Fragrantica* website. We created a customized mapping of the *Fragrance Families* in order to improve the categorization of perfumes and to ensure that users lacking advanced perfume industry knowledge can distinguish between the different fragrance families. More details about the rationale and definition of this procedure are given in Sect. 4.2.

Algorithm 2. Perfume Recommendation Algorithm

1: Get the user inputs for the quiz
2: **for** each question in the quiz **do**
3:     **if** at least one check is detected **then**
4:         Filter the perfumes dataset based on the selected checkboxes
5:     **else**
6:         Skip the filtering on current question
7:     **end if**
8: **end for**
9: **if** filtered dataset contains no item **then**
10:     Apologize to the user that no recommendation can be done for selected answers
11: **else if** dataset contains exactly one item **then**
12:     Recommend the perfume to the user
13: **else**
14:     Select all Fragrance families from the filtered dataset
15:     Display to the user the Fragrance families and ask for the preferred one(s)
16:     **if** no Fragrance family is selected **then**
17:         Skip the filtering
18:     **else**
19:         Filter by selected Fragrance family/families
20:     **end if**
21:     Select the most highly rated perfume
22:     Recommend the perfume to the user
23: **end if**

---

4 Experiments and Discussions

4.1 Dataset Overview

Our dataset consists in 855 perfumes spanning years 1920–2022 and their parameters extracted from *Fragrantica* website using our customized web scraper.

Considering the perfume brands, the dataset contains perfumes from 242 brands and one perfume which is not assigned any brand. From these, 180 brands occur between 1 and 3 times, 45 brands feature between 4 and 9 perfumes and 18 brands have 10 or more perfumes available in our dataset (Fig. 2).

Figure 3a shows the season distribution of the perfumes. A perfume might be suitable for multiple seasons. For example, according to [2], warm, oriental notes can be worn for both fall and winter. In the same direction, citrus notes are suitable for spring and summer ([2,16]). For each perfume of our dataset, weights (defined as percents) are available for each of the four seasons. We considered that a perfume is suitable for a certain season if its weight is at least 75%. Note that the total sum of the weights of a perfume is not 100%, as it refers to a scaled rating given per season, rather than a direct seasonal classification of a perfume. For example, perfume "Versace Pour Homme" by Versace (Index 460) is 100% suitable for summer, 77.4401% suitable for spring, 25.5161% for fall and only 10.5367% for winter. Therefore, Fig. 3a must be interpreted as 437 perfumes out of 855 are considered suitable for fall, 345 perfumes out of 855 are considered suitable for spring and so on, with the mention that a certain perfume can belong to multiple seasons.

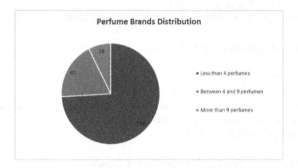

Fig. 2. Perfume Brands Distribution.

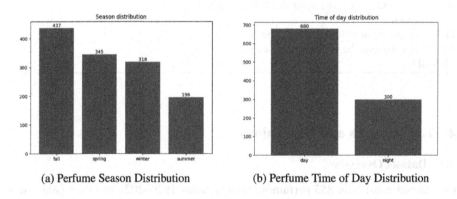

(a) Perfume Season Distribution

(b) Perfume Time of Day Distribution

Fig. 3. Perfume Statistics.

Similarly, we have a time of the day perfume classification (Fig. 3b), showing when a perfume can be suitable for both daytime and night time. For example, "Mahora" by

Guerlain (Index 372) is 76.455% suitable for day time use and 100% for night time use. For a perfume to be classified in day or night category, the weight of the category must be at least 75%.

The rest of perfume statistics collected from *Fragrantica* (Longevity, Silage, Gender and Price Value) are defined as counters of votes. We are not using the Price Value statistic, as we considered it will most likely shadow our results. The classification as way overpriced, overpriced, good value or great value is too subjective with regard to the users' financial statements and the money they are willing to invest in perfumery. Longevity, Silage and Gender preferences are aspects we gather from the user using the quiz. For Gender detection, there would be two possibilities: the first refers to the brand classification of the perfume and the second refers to using the Gender statistics. [22] used the first approach for the gender classification. We chose to use the second method, as it is grounded in the user opinions, while the other is provided by the perfume brand. We considered that a perfume is suitable for a certain gender, if the Gender has at least 50% votes. For example, "Vega Guerlain" by Guerlain is tagged in the Perfume Name as "for women", but if we check the gender statistics, 50% of the persons who voted considered that the fragrance is "unisex", i.e. it would be suitable for men too.

4.2   Fragrance Family Mapping Procedure

The *Fragrance Family* classification on *Fragrantica* is included in the beginning of the *Perfume Description* and it uses the following text pattern: "[Perfume Name] by [Perfume Brand] is a [Fragrance family/families] fragrance for [men/women/men and women]". So we can easily extract the *Fragrance Family(ies)* that are written in the *Perfume Description* using regular expressions. Following the extraction process, we obtained 33 unique families, or more precisely 33 unique sub-classes, because most of them are combinations of major fragrance families defined in the literature. Figure 4 shows the *Fragrance Families* distribution, as extracted from *Fragrantica* website.

The first motivating aspect of the usefulness of a fragrance family mapping to a simplified description is the complexity of fragrance family descriptions. In order to directly understand some of the sub-classes, a considerable amount of fragrance knowledge is required. Therefore we created our own simplified fragrance families system, by combining and reducing the literature classification presented in Sect. 2, in order to use only terms which can be comprehended by most non-expert users.

Another motivating aspect of the utility of a fragrance family mapping procedure is the fact that the same family might be represented under different names, depending on the way the words are placed in the *Perfume Description* text.

For example, in Fig. 4, we can see that there are two classes "Floral Woody Musk" and "Woody Floral Musk". Using our mapping, the fragrances will be assigned the new class "Floral Woody Oriental", because "Musk" is a sweet note specific for "Oriental" perfumes [18]. Also, in the Description "Citric" and "Citrus" define similar notes, so we decided to merge them into term "Citric".

There are also some derived fragrance families which we mapped into the source fragrances. For example, most of us may understand how "Leather" or "Gourmand" could smell, but for a person not familiarized with the fragrance notes terminology, "Chypre" or "Fougere" will probably mean nothing.

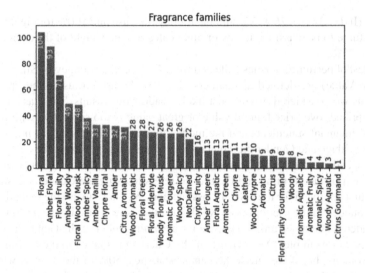

Fig. 4. Perfume*Fragrance Families* Distribution.

Following the description "A'classic' chypre scent typically starts with a fresh hit of citrus notes, followed by florals and an earthy, woody base to round it off. It playfully contrasts light and airy with deep and musky, to dramatic effect." from [4], we mapped "Chypre" to "Citric Floral Woody".

On the other hand, the description "The Fougere is a diverse group that focuses on the blend of a citrus top note, frequently bergamot, an aromatic heart of lavender, and a touch of rose which can also be replaced by the more herbal rosiness of geranium, balanced with deeper notes of oakmoss, vetiver and coumarin (a warm hay like note found in tonka beans)" from [1] suggested to classify the "Fougere" family as "Citric", "Floral", "Green", "Oriental".

Finally, our system includes the following *Fragrance Families*: *Floral*, *Citric*, *Acquatic*, *Fruity*, *Green*, *Oriental (Sweet)*, *Woody*, *Aromatic (Spices)* and *Not defined*. The "Not Defined" family refers to the case when the *Fragrance Family* was not found inside the *Perfume Description* field, and therefore could not be extracted and mapped.

We emphasize that although our new classification might not map the terms by entirely preserving their original semantics, our aim was to use more user-friendly terms which are more likely to be understood by any user of our application.

After mapping the new fragrance families using our mapping table defined in file *fragrance_family_mapping.txt*, the resulted fragrance families distribution is shown in Fig. 5. Note that each perfume can belong to one or multiple fragrance families.

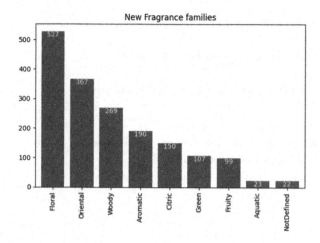

Fig. 5. *Fragrance Families* Distribution after applying the Mapping Procedure.

4.3   Experimental Results

Our initial plan was to use natural language processing to detect the user fragrance preferences. However we realized that most users would not directly give too much information of their preferences, because they are simply not able to say what they actually like or would like in a perfume. We concluded that the assistant bot might better ask a set of questions, to direct the user towards describing his/her fragrance preferences. But we realized that most likely this would bore the user, since no one actually likes to be asked too many questions. Therefore, we concluded that best solution would be to give the user a short quiz. The quiz has 5 questions and all of them refer to general aspects the user would expect from a perfume: gender, season, time of day, longevity and silage. The quiz GUI (Fig. 6) was created using *Tkinter* Pyhon Library.

After the user submits the answers, the system checks the perfume database for best matching items. In case on one question no answer is selected, the system will skip the question. Also, the user can select multiple answers for the same questions.

For example, let us assume that the user is looking for a women perfume, for day time winter wear, which means the user has selected the corresponding quiz checkboxes. Considering moreover that the user has preferences only for long-lasting or very long-lasting perfumes with a strong or very strong silage, the perfume assistant will set the corresponding filters from the perfume dataset and it will conclude that only one perfume matches the user expectations. This result is most often expected, because although winter perfumes are stronger and more long-lasting than perfumes for the rest of the seasons', during the day time, lighter perfumes are used.

On the other hand, if the user would not have any preference for longevity or silage, and he/she will be only looking for day time winter women perfumes, 115 perfumes from the dataset would match the selection. In this case, in the quiz window, the user will be asked to fill the preferred fragrance family or families from the available ones.

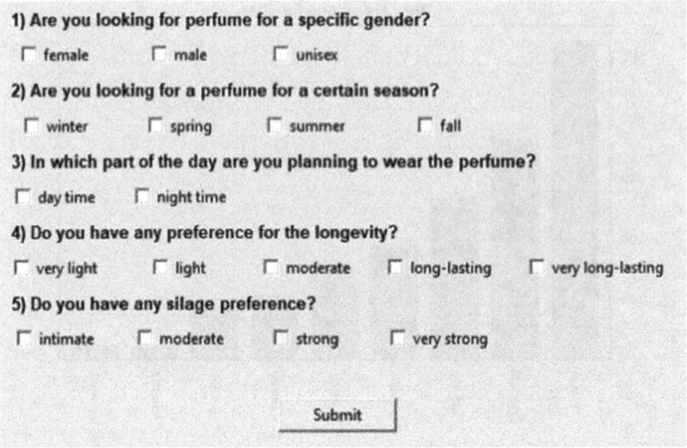

Fig. 6. Quiz used to get user preferences in order to provide perfume recommendations.

The perfume assistant will make an additional processing of the 115 identified perfumes regarding the fragrance families that are available for them.

Let us consider that the user is interested only on aromatic, spicy fragrances. In this case, the recommended perfumes list will contain 4 entries (Table 2). Based on our algorithm, the perfume with the highest *Rating Value* is considered the best match, so the user will be recommended "Shalimar Eau de Cologne by Guerlain" (Table 2).

Table 2. Sample Recommended Perfumes Set.

Index	Perfume Name	Rating Value
330	Tendre Madelein by Les Senteurs Gourmandes	4.3
346	Kenzo Jungle le Tigre by Kenzo	4.19
705	Shalimar Eau de Cologne by Guerlain	4.44
730	Maja by Myrurgia	4.05

The algorithm evaluation was performed by analyzing the sentiment statistics of the recommended perfume, in order to decide if the recommendation is useful or not.

The perfume dataset "Sentiment Statistics" column was collected from *Fragrantica*. It shows users ratings regarding loving, liking, hating or disliking that particular perfume. We divide the sentiments into two categories: positive (love, like) and negative (hate, dislike) and use them to validate our algorithm. In order to be considered correct, our algorithm provided recommendation must satisfy (we set *threshold* = 50%):

$$positive\ sentiment - negative\ sentiment > threshold$$

We defined two performance measures for our recommendation algorithm. For their evaluation we tested the system by submitting a population of quiz instances representing a population of users seeking a recommendation. The measures use the parameters:

- *Total number of recommendations* that represents the number of quiz instances for which users actually received recommendations.
- *Total number of relevant recommendations* that represents the number of quiz instances for which users received relevant recommendations according to our criterion based on sentiment statistics.
- *Total number of quiz instances* that represents the total number of quiz instances submitted by users in our experiment.

Our proposed performance measures are as follows:

- *Effectiveness* shows the proportion of quiz instances for which users have received recommendations.

$$Effectiveness = \frac{Total\ number\ of\ recommendations}{Total\ number\ of\ quiz\ instances}$$

- *Relevance* shows what proportion of quiz instances for which users received recommendations identified as relevant.

$$Relevance = \frac{Total\ number\ of\ relevant\ recommendations}{Total\ number\ of\ quiz\ instances}$$

Table 3. Evaluation of recommendation per algorithm branch.

Recomm. Algorithm Branch	*Effectiveness*			*Relevance*		
	Correct	Total	Score	Correct	Total	Score
No Recomm	192	1000	0.192	-	-	-
Exactly 1 Recomm	26	1000	0.026	19	1000	0.019
Recomm. Using Fragrance Family	782	1000	0.782	730	1000	0.73

Table 3 shows the results of the evaluation. We used a set of 1000 randomly generated quiz inputs by sampling quiz fields from uniform probability distributions, to simulate 1000 users filling the quiz, seeking their suitable perfume. 192 quiz answers did not receive any recommendation, i.e. no perfume in our perfume dataset matched the expected perfume performances selected in the quiz. For 26 quiz answers only one perfume in the dataset matched the selection. Majority of recommendations, 782, were issued considering the additional user input regarding the *Fragrance Family*.

We obtained an *Effectiveness* of 78.2% for providing recommendation using *Fragrance Family*, i.e. a good score in our opinion. Our algorithm has a lower *Effectiveness* score for cases when exactly one perfume from dataset matches the user selection (2.6%). There are also few cases when no recommendation can be provided to the user (19.2%). We appreciate that the situation of not being able to provide any recommendation can be improved by expanding the dataset.

For *Relevance*, we obtained a score of 1.9% for the cases when exactly one perfume from dataset matcheds the user selection and 73% for providing recommendation using *Fragrance Family*. The *Relevance* metrics cannot be computed for the cases when no recommendation was provided to the user, since it relies on evaluating the relevance of the recommendation actually made.

5   Conclusions

In this paper we presented a method for providing perfume recommendations considering user lifestyle and daily activities. In order to receive recommendations, the user fills a quiz about perfume preferences and expectations, such that the system can understand his or her tastes. We consider the quiz approach to be most beneficial method to get the information from both user and application design point of view. On one hand, the user will be kept happy as the quiz is pretty short and he/she can easily fill in the questions using checkboxes. Another solution would be to directly ask these questions, but we the user avoided asking too many individual questions, as this might make the user bored or angry. On the other hand, from application point of view, all user inputs are simultaneously available such that the recommendation can be easily provided.

Another important aspect is that in designing the quiz we assumed that the user is not expert in perfumes, so we did not ask him/her to provide expert knowledge for making the recommendations. Instead, we assumed that the user might not be familiarized with perfume industry and so we decided to inquire him/her about more meaningful aspects like the season or time of the day when he or she would like to wear the perfume, together with the details about the expected longevity and silage of the perfume. Afterwards we use social data available in the dataset to find the best matching perfume.

Lastly, we performed the evaluation of the recommendation algorithm by proposing two performance measures: *Effectiveness* and *Relevance*, which show the proportion of quiz instances for which recommendations were received, respectively the proportion of quiz instances for which the recommendation was identified as relevant.

References

1. Angela Flanders Perfumery: What is a Fougere Perfume? (2021). https://angelaflanders-perfumer.com/blogs/news/what-is-a-fougere-scent. Accessed 23 Dec 2022
2. Choosing a seasonal perfume. https://www.bonparfumeur.com/pages/how-to-choose-a-seasonal-perfume. Accessed 23 Dec 2022
3. La Carrément Belle équipe: The 7 olfactory families. https://www.carrementbelle.com/blog/en/2020/09/16/the-7-olfactory-families/. Accessed 23 Dec 2022
4. Chow, E.: What is a chypre? (2022). https://www.theperfumeshop.com/blog/expertise/what-is-chypre-in-perfume/. Accessed 23 Dec 2022
5. Edwards, M.: Fragrances of the world. Michael Edwards & Co. (2008)
6. Edwards, M.: Fragrances of the world. Michael Edwards & Co. (2011)

7. The classification of fragrance notes. A detailed explanation of the classification of fragrance notes. https://flavoursogood.com/new/The-classification-of-fragrance-notes.html. Accessed 23 Dec 2022
8. Fragrantica website. https://www.fragrantica.com/. Accessed 23 Dec 2022
9. Global Perfume Market (2022 to 2027) - Industry Trends, Share, Size, Growth, Opportunity and Forecasts (2022). https://www.globenewswire.com/en/news-release/2022/05/03/2434555/28124/en/Global-Perfume-Market-2022-to-2027-Industry-Trends-Share-Size-Growth-Opportunity-and-Forecasts.html. Accessed 23 Dec 2022
10. Perfume Types - Perfume Classification and Notes. http://www.historyofperfume.net/perfume-facts/perfume-classification-and-fragrance-notes/. Accessed 23 Dec 2022
11. Lee, J.: What Are Notes and Accords? How to Make Sense of Fragrances (2019). https://modernratio.com/fragrance-notes-and-accords/. Accessed 23 Dec 2022
12. McBride, G.: How are fragrances notes classified? (2015). https://www.quora.com/How-are-fragrance-notes-classified/answer/George-McBride-2ch=10&oid=13571646&share=2831f2e9&target_type=answer. Accessed 23 Dec 2022
13. A guide to fragrance strengths & types. https://www.perfumedirect.com/pages/a-guide-to-perfume-strengths-and-types. Accessed 23 Dec 2022
14. How to choose the right perfume?. https://www.scentrique.com/post/how-to-choose-the-right-perfume. Accessed 23 Dec 2022
15. The accord. https://www.sylvaine-delacourte.com/en/guide/the-accord. Accessed 23 Dec 2022
16. Choose a perfume according to the season. https://www.sylvaine-delacourte.com/en/guide/choose-a-perfume-according-to-the-season. Accessed 23 Dec 2022
17. Serej, K.Z.: Capstone project: Perfumes Ratings (2020). https://medium.com/@kalina.zeligowska/capstone-project-perfumes-ratings-f8c9c449eae0. Accessed 11 Mar 2023
18. Serras, L.: Your fragrance wheel and scent families guide (2021). https://www.fragrancex.com/blog/fragrance-wheel/. Accessed 23 Dec 2022
19. Sinks, T.: How to choose the right perfume or cologne for you (2019). https://www.nytimes.com/2019/02/21/smarter-living/how-to-choose-perfume-cologne-fragrance.html. Accessed 23 Dec 2022
20. Stragier, K.: The (un)importance of notes. A story about music and perfume (2020). https://www.smellstories.be/en/blogs/blog/the-unimportance-of-notes-a-story-about-music-and/. Accessed 23 Dec 2022
21. Fragrance Families. https://www.theperfumedcourt.com/fragrance_families.aspx. Accessed 23 Dec 2022
22. Veras, C., Vadakan, D., Dean, J., Volosin, J., Lacerda, K., Moreno, O.M.: Scent Angels (2021). https://github.com/sir-omoreno/perfume_designer_app. Accessed 23 Dec 2022
23. Zarzo, M.: Multivariate analysis of olfactory profiles for 140 perfumes as a basis to derive a sensory wheel for the classification of feminine fragrances. Cosmetics **7**(1), 11 (2020). https://doi.org/10.3390/cosmetics7010011

LSTM-Based QoE Evaluation for Web Microservices' Reputation Scoring

Maha Driss[1,2]([✉]) [iD]

[1] Computer Science Department, CCIS, Prince Sultan University,
Riyadh, Saudi Arabia
mdriss@psu.edu.sa

[2] RIADI Laboratory, ENSI, University of Manouba, Manouba, Tunisia

Abstract. Sentiment analysis is the task of mining the authors' opinions about specific entities. It allows organizations to monitor different services in real time and act accordingly. Reputation is what is generally said or believed about people or things. Informally, reputation combines the measure of reliability derived from feedback, reviews, and ratings gathered from users, which reflect their quality of experience (QoE) and can either increase or harm the reputation of the provided services. In this study, we propose to perform sentiment analysis on web microservices reviews to exploit the provided information to assess and score the microservices' reputation. Our proposed approach uses the Long Short-Term Memory (LSTM) model to perform sentiment analysis and the Net Brand Reputation (NBR) algorithm to assess reputation scores for microservices. This approach is tested on a set of more than 10,000 reviews related to 15 Amazon Web microservices, and the experimental results have shown that our approach is more accurate than existing approaches, with an accuracy and precision of 93% obtained after applying an oversampling strategy and a resulting reputation score of the considered microservices community of 89%.

Keywords: Sentiment Analysis · Reputation · Web Microservices · Long Short-Term Memory Model · Net Brand Reputation

1 Introduction

In the current era, many customer reviews are available on different platforms and applications: e-commerce, Web services, games, social networks, etc. What interests us in this paper are the web microservices-based applications. A web microservice is a tiny, self-contained component of an online application that performs a specific function or task. The microservices architecture is a methodology for developing software systems consisting of loosely coupled, independently deployable services [13]. Customers post reviews online as feedback on microservices they have purchased, used, or experienced. These reviews are one of the most effective ways to motivate and encourage potential customers to

N. T. Nguyen et al. (Eds.): ICCCI 2023, CCIS 1864, pp. 44–56, 2023.
https://doi.org/10.1007/978-3-031-41774-0_4

use services. They reflect users' quality of experience (QoE), which can influence potential customers' perceptions. Positive reviews can enhance the microservice's reputation and encourage new users to try it out, while negative reviews can harm its reputation and discourage potential users. The main issue with these reviews is that they may be ambiguous and unclear, and this is due to various factors such as attitude, emotions, used vocabulary, and previous experiences of the customer. To solve this issue, sentiment analysis techniques [4] are employed to automatically transform these unstructured reviews into structured data that can be extremely valuable for commercial concerns like reputation management. Having positive reviews and a good reputation as a service can play an important role in its success. It helps attract customers' attention and interest and establish trust and confidence in the service. In this paper, we aim to perform sentiment analysis techniques on web microservices' reviews to exploit the provided information for services' reputation assessment and scoring. Our proposed approach is designed and implemented to mine microservices' reviews by categorizing them into different polarity labels and providing a score that is used to measure the microservices' community reputation. This approach applies a deep learning-based sentiment classification that performs the Long Short-Term Memory (LSTM) model [14] and employs the Net Brand Reputation (NBR) algorithm [3] to assess reputation scores for concerning microservices. This work makes a significant contribution by leveraging the outputs of the LSTM model to classify reviews as positive or negative. These results are then utilized to calculate the overall reputation score of the microservices' community provider through the application of the NBR algorithm. The proposed approach is tested on a set of 10,000 reviews related to 15 Amazon Web microservices. The experimental results have shown that our approach is more accurate than existing approaches, with an accuracy and a precision of 93% after applying oversampling strategy and a resulting reputation score of 89%. The remainder of this paper is structured as follows: Sect. 2 provides a brief background about Web microservices, sentiment analysis, and reputation assessment. Section 3 presents pertinent related works that implement sentiment classification and reputation assessment for Web microservices. Section 4 details the proposed approach. Section 5 illustrates the implementation of the proposed approach and discusses the experiments that are conducted to test and validate this approach. Section 6 presents the concluding remarks and future works.

2 Background

This section presents fundamental concepts related to Web microservices, sentiment analysis, and reputation management.

2.1 Web Microservices

A web microservice is a tiny, self-contained component of an online application that performs a specific function or task. The microservices architecture is a methodology for developing software systems consisting of loosely coupled, independently deployable services [5,11]. Each microservice is often responsible for a specific business function and connects with other services through common web protocols. Online microservices are frequently employed to develop sophisticated web systems that demand scalability, fault tolerance, and flexibility. By splitting a web application into smaller, more manageable services, developers may work on each component individually, making it easier to update, test, and deploy changes. The quality of service characteristics (e.g., response time, availability, scalability, security, usability, etc.), which are provided by these Web microservices, have become a primary concern for the users as well as the providers [6]. One way to improve these characteristics is to analyze the feedback generated by users' reviews. Mining users' feedback is crucial since it reflects the service's reputation and leads to its improvement. It generally gives an idea of whether users like the microservice, and if the users do not like it, it indicates what factors contributed to this negative feedback.

2.2 Web Microservices and Reputation Management

According to the Concise Oxford Dictionary [2], "Reputation is generally said or believed about a person's or thing's character or standing". Informally, reputation combines the measure of reliability derived from feedback, reviews, and ratings gathered from users in a certain society. The QoE and the reputation of web microservices are closely related. A positive quality of experience can lead to a strong reputation, while a negative quality of experience can harm the reputation of the microservice. When users have a positive experience while using a web microservice, they are more likely to recommend it to others and leave positive reviews or feedback. This can help to build the microservice's reputation and attract new users. On the other hand, if users have a negative experience while using a web microservice, they may leave negative reviews or feedback, which can harm the microservice's reputation. A reputation model [12] in the context of Web microservices is a method that enables decision-makers to distinguish good and satisfying services from bad and poor ones based on users' feedback and reviews. In this context, the importance of reputation is derived from the need to help users and service providers to distinguish the quality of the functionalities and performances among similar services based on these services' history of use and how they behaved in the past.

2.3 Sentiment Analysis

Sentiment Analysis (SA) is defined as analyzing authors' opinions, emotions, or attitudes about specific entities such as products, services, events, and individuals [10]. These entities are most likely to be covered by users' reviews. Sentiment analysis is a process that aims to classify sentiments, and that consists of three different steps [10]: 1) sentiment identification, 2) feature selection, and 3) sentiment classification. The input of this process is a dataset of users' reviews; the output is a set of sentiment polarities (i.e., positive/negative/neutral or positive/negative). There are three main classification levels for SA [15]: document-level, sentence-level, and aspect-level SA. In this paper, we tackle the second class of SA since considered users' opinions will be grouped into a single document that will be analyzed at the sentence level to determine users' orientations.

3   Related Works

Many statistical, fuzzy-logic, and data mining-based approaches for computing web service reputation have been proposed in the literature. These are the most recent and relevant related works.

In [9], the authors presented a collaborative Service Level Agreement (SLA) and Reputation-based Trust Management (RTM) solution for federated cloud environments. The SLA service explicitly set performance standards and evaluated the real performance of cloud applications installed. Based on the SLA, the collaborative solution's RTM service utilized many technical and user experience parameters to calculate the cloud providers' dependability and customers' trust. The collaborative approach was demonstrated and proven in a genuine federated setting. The study, presented in [8], uses a trust prediction and confusion matrix to rank web services based on throughput and response time. For a benchmark web services dataset, AdaBoostM1 and J48 classifiers were utilized as binary classifiers. The confusion matrix was used to compute trust scores. Correct prediction of trustworthy and untrusted web services has enhanced the overall selection process in a pool of comparable web services. Kappa statistics values were used to evaluate the suggested method and compare the performance of AdaBoostM1 and J48 classifiers. [7] discussed web service selection utilizing a well-known machine learning technique, REPTree, to forecast trustworthy and untrusted services correctly. Using web services datasets, the performance of REPTree is compared to that of five machine learning models. The authors tested web services datasets using a ten k-fold cross-validation approach. They utilized performance measures, like sensitivity and specificity measures, to assess the effectiveness of the REPTree classifier. The evaluation results of the suggested web services selection technique showed a link between the final selection and the recommended web service trust score. The authors in [1] presented a reputation-based trust assessment technique using online user evaluations to combine the NBR measure with a deep learning-based sentiment analysis model called CBiL-STM. The suggested deep learning model combined the layers of Convolutional Neural Networks (CNN) and Bidirectional Long Short-Term Memory (BiLSTM). The CNN layers coped with the high dimensionality of text inputs, and the BiL-STM layer investigated the context of the derived features in both forward and backward directions.

The existing works using a reputation-based selection of web services have several limitations, including:

- Limited scope: Reputation-based selection approaches typically rely on feedback from a small subset of users, which may not be representative of the broader user community. This can result in biased or incomplete reputation scores.

- Difficulty in interpretability: Deep learning-based solutions are often complex and difficult to interpret, making it difficult to understand how they arrive at their reputation scores. This can limit the transparency of the reputation assessment process.
- Computational requirements: Hybrid deep learning models used for reputation assessment can be computationally intensive and require significant resources to train and evaluate. This can make them less suitable for use in resource-constrained environments, such as on mobile devices or in low-bandwidth networks.
- Limited generalization performance: Imbalanced datasets with few instances of negative feedback may result in biased reputation scores, as the model may be more likely to assign positive scores to services even if they are not of high quality.
- Difficulty in feature extraction: Imbalanced datasets may make it difficult for the deep learning model to extract meaningful features that accurately represent the characteristics of the service. This can result in poor model performance and inaccurate reputation scores.

4   Proposed Approach

Our proposed approach for computing Web services' reputation focuses on using deep learning models. This choice is justified by the fact that these models have proven their efficiency in sentiment analysis in several applications (i.e., social media monitoring, brand monitoring, market analysis, etc.), as demonstrated in the study presented in [15]. Our approach consists of four phases: 1) the data preprocessing phase, 2) the embedding generation phase, 3) the sentiment analysis phase, and 4) the reputation assessment phase. Figure 1 presents our approach with its different phases.

4.1   Data Collecting Phase

This phase encloses four consecutive tasks, which are:

1. Removing the invalid reviews: the reviews' dataset is examined to filter out invalid reviews. A review is considered invalid if: 1) it is empty, 2) it contains mainly tagged usernames, and 3) it provides mainly commercial URLs.
2. Word tokenizing and stemming: for each review, tokenization and stemming tasks are performed. Tokenization aims to divide a text into small units called tokens, which refer in our context to words composing the whole review. Stemming aims to reduce a word to its word stem. For example, the stem word of "understanding" is "understand", which is obtained by removing the affix from "understanding".

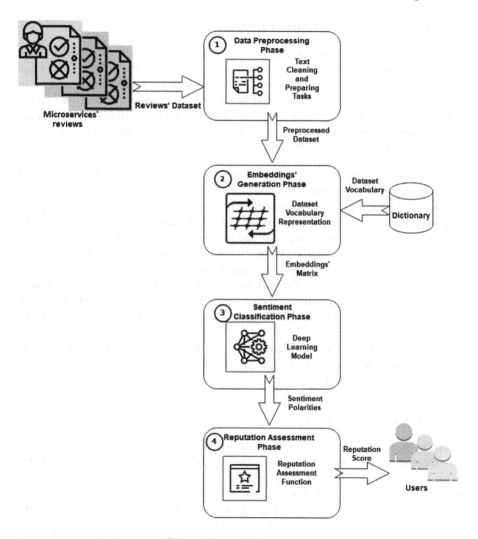

Fig. 1. Proposed approach.

3. Stop words, special characters, and punctuation marks removing: stop words such as "a", "of", and "in" are words that need to be filtered out since they do not contribute much to the overall meaning of the review. Also, special characters (i.e., "@", "%", "/", etc.) and punctuation marks are eliminated to increase the accuracy of the sentiment classification phase.

4. Part-of-speech (POS) tagging: This task aims to convert each review into a set of tuples where each tuple has a form (word, tag). The tag signifies whether the word is a noun, adjective, verb, etc. After applying POS tagging, only nouns, and adjectives are kept since they both play a key role in the distinction of the sentiment polarity of the review.

4.2 Embeddings' Generation Phase

A word embedding is a learned representation for text where words that have the same meaning have a similar representation. Word embeddings are a class of techniques where individual words are represented as real-valued vectors in a predefined vector space. Each word is mapped to one vector, and the vector values are learned in a way that resembles a neural network. Hence the technique is often lumped into the field of deep learning. To represent the preprocessed data, we proceed with the following successive steps:

1. Create a word-to-index dictionary: each word will be assigned to a key, and the unique matching index is used as the value for the key.
2. Padding: Padding is the process of setting a fixed length to sentences. Every sentence has a different length so we will set the maximum size of each list of sentences to 50 as an example. If the list's size is greater than 50, it will be trimmed to 50. And for the lists with a length of less than 50, we will add 0 at the end until it reaches the maximum length.
3. Create a feature matrix: We will load the GloVe word embeddings, which is an algorithm for obtaining vector representations for words. And build a dictionary that will include words as keys and their corresponding embedding list as values.
4. Create embedding matrix: The matrix will have columns where all columns contain the GloVe word embeddings for the words, and each row will match the corresponding index.

4.3 Classification Phase

We propose a deep learning-based sentiment analysis method to ensure review classification. This method relies on the LSTM model. LSTM is a Recurrent Neural Network (RNN) variant specifically designed to better handle long-term dependencies in sequential data. Compared to traditional RNNs, LSTM can selectively forget or remember previous inputs and outputs, allowing it to capture more complex patterns in sequential data. In the context of text classification for sentiment analysis, LSTM can bring several improvements over traditional RNNs:

- Better handling of long-term dependencies: Sentiment analysis often requires understanding the context and meaning of words and phrases over long sequences of text. LSTM can better capture these dependencies and make more accurate predictions compared to traditional RNNs.
- Improved memory: Since LSTM can selectively remember or forget previous inputs and outputs, it can retain useful information and discard irrelevant information more effectively. This makes it easier for LSTM to identify important features for sentiment analysis and make more accurate predictions.
- Reduced vanishing gradient problem: Traditional RNNs can suffer from the vanishing gradient problem, where the gradients become very small, and the model stops learning effectively. LSTM can alleviate this problem by using

gating mechanisms to control the flow of information and gradients through the network.

Figure 2 presents the architecture of the LSTM model used for microservices' reviews classification.

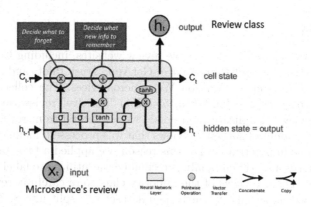

Fig. 2. LSTM Architecture for Microservices' Reviews Classification.

4.4 Reputation Assessment Phase

The objective of this phase is to use the NBR formula to assess the reputation of Web microservice providers. This will validate the proposed model's effectiveness used for reputation assessment. The NBR formula determines the net value of a brand's reputation based on published reviews, utilizing sentiment analysis to measure customer satisfaction. The NBR index emphasizes positive feedback from brand advocates more than negative feedback, and its output can range from -100 to 100, with higher values indicating a greater number of positive reviews. Equation 1 illustrates the NBR formula.

$$NBR = \frac{PositiveReviews - NegativeReviews}{PositiveReviews + NegativeReviews} * 100 \qquad (1)$$

5 Experiments

In this section, firstly, we will present the details of the implementation. Next, we will describe the dataset and the performance metrics. Finally, we will provide a detailed explanation of the results and make comparisons with existing deep-learning models used for text mining.

5.1 Implementation Environment

The experiments in this paper are carried out on a PC with the following configuration properties: an x64 CPU, an Intel Core i9-11900H (11th Gen), 32 GB RAM, and an NVIDIA GeForce RTX 3080 (8G) graphics card. All experiments were carried out on Google Colab14, with Python 3.7.1015 and Keras 2.4.3.

5.2 Dataset

The reviews are scraped from multiple review websites, including Capterra, g2, Gartner, TrustRadius, Software Advice, GetApp, Trust Pilot, and Spiceworks. The reviews are about 15 Amazon Web microservices. The collected dataset contains 10,676 reviews, including 10,155 (95%) "Positive" reviews and 521 (5%) "Negative" reviews. Duplicates and noises were removed from reviews. Due to the enormous amount of gathered reviews that was processed, manual labeling of this dataset was impracticable. For this reason, we applied a two-stage labeling approach. Firstly, a sentiment analysis technique was utilized to label the dataset automatically. Then, reviews of the minority class were carefully reviewed and re-labeled based on specific features. The dataset was split into 80% for model training and 20% for validation and testing.

5.3 Performance Metrics

The overall accuracy performance of the proposed approach is measured through the accuracy, precision, recall, and F1-score, which are expressed in the following: In order to assess the performance of the proposed approach, accuracy, precision, recall, and F1-score metrics were used. The statistical measures are represented mathematically in Eqs. 2–5, where: TP, TN, FP, and FN represent the number of True Positives, True Negatives, False Positives, and False Negatives, respectively.

Accuracy: it is used to evaluate the model's overall performance throughout all categories.

$$Accuracy = \frac{TP + TN}{TP + TN + FP + FN} \tag{2}$$

Precision: it is used to assess the model's accuracy in classifying a sample as positive or negative.

$$Precision = \frac{TP}{TP + FP} \tag{3}$$

Recall : it is employed to assess the model's ability to identify the positive samples.

$$Recall = \frac{TP}{TP + FN} \tag{4}$$

F1-score: it combines the accuracy and recall measurements to produce a value-added rating for performance verification.

$$F1 - score = \frac{2 * Precision * Recall}{Precision + Recall} \tag{5}$$

5.4   Results and Discussion

The main goal of the proposed approach is to classify microservice reviews properly. This was accomplished using RNN, GRU, CNN, and LSTM. Across 20 epochs, the five deep-learning architectures were trained. The Adam optimizer, the cross-entropy loss function, and the SoftMax activation function have been employed for the models' configuration.

Table 1. Weighted Average Measures of Accuracy, Precision, Recall, and F1-score for RNN, GRU, CNN, and LSTM Models Used for Microservices' Reviews Classification.

Deep Learning Model	Accuracy (%)	Precision (%)	Recall (%)	F1-score (%)
RNN	87	88	86	88
GRU	81	87	90	91
CNN	88	92	87	89
LSTM (Proposed Model)	91	92	90	92

As shown by the performance results in Table 1, our model outperforms all the other models for the weighted average by ensuring an overall accuracy of 91%, a precision and an F1-score of 92%, and a recall of 90%. The training time for each model is shown in Table 2. The results show that CNN takes the least training time, followed by LSTM. As compared to the training times of RNN and GRU models, the training time of our suggested classifier was acceptable. The considered dataset was a highly imbalanced dataset. It is challenging for any classifier to predict a class accurately based on a few hundred instances. Only 521 negative reviews are included in the whole dataset, with only 104 of them used for testing and validation. To address the imbalance problem, various resampling strategies were tested. These include oversampling, undersampling, SMOTE, and ADASYN strategies. Figure 3 shows the training and validation loss learning curves of CBiLSTM with different resampling techniques. All of the other techniques, with the exception of oversampling, appear to be unable to solve the typical underfitting problem during model training. Figure 4 shows the classification report obtained after applying oversampling by considering the

Table 2. Training Time for RNN, GRU, CNN, and LSTM Models Used for Microservices' Reviews Classification.

Deep Learning Model	Training Time (ms)
RNN	698.13
GRU	785.66
CNN	352.33
LSTM (Proposed Model)	398.41

same number of positive and negative reviews in the testing, which is 1000. The results confirmed the oversampling strategy's effectiveness since it provided considerable improvements in performance compared to testing results without a resampling strategy. Before oversampling, the model had an accuracy of 91% and a precision of 92%. However, after oversampling the data, the model's accuracy and precision increased to 93%.

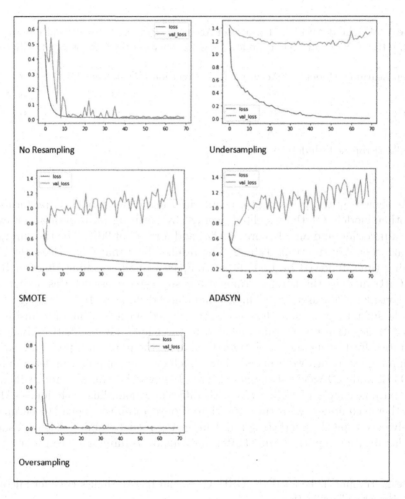

Fig. 3. Training Loss and Validation Loss Learning Curves of LSTM Plotted as a Function of the Epoch Number after Applying Different Resampling Strategies.

The analysis of the binary matrix revealed that the number of positive reviews was 2039, denoted by the TP value, while the number of negative reviews was 112, represented by the TN value. Substituting these values into Eq. 1, the NBR score for AWS microservices was computed as 89.58%. Moreover, the testing

	precision	recall	f1-score	support
0	0.90	0.99	0.94	67
1	0.98	0.85	0.91	47
accuracy			0.93	114
macro avg	0.94	0.92	0.93	114
weighted avg	0.93	0.93	0.93	114

Fig. 4. Classification report.

dataset comprised 2,031 positive reviews and 104 negative reviews, leading to an estimated reputation score of 90.25% for AWS microservices. Comparing the NBR score generated using LSTM-based techniques for reputation assessment with the score obtained from the original dataset revealed close similarity between the two values. These results imply that the LSTM-based approach can be a reliable and effective technique for assessing the reputation of microservices providers.

6 Conclusion and Future Work

This study develops a deep learning model to classify web microservice user-related reviews based on sentiments derived from collected users' reviews. The proposed deep learning model, LSTM, outperforms other existing models used in text classification for sentiment analysis, such as RNN, GRU, and CNN. The aim of this approach is to establish a reputation ranking for microservices providers by analyzing the QoE of their users. The QoE is gauged by classifying reviews as "positive" or "negative" and comprehensively evaluating users' opinions towards the service providers. Our upcoming work involves the integration of advanced natural language processing techniques to enhance the precision of sentiment analysis. This may entail the use of sophisticated deep learning models, like Transformers, that leverage attention mechanisms to more effectively comprehend the nuances of language and context in reviews. Additionally, we will investigate the impact of the suspicious user punishment mechanism on the reputation of service providers and we will propose viable solutions to address the challenges posed by unjust feedback ratings.

Acknowledgment. The author would like to thank Prince Sultan University for financially supporting the conference registration fees.

References

1. Al Saleh, R., Driss, M., Almomani, I.: CBiLSTM: a hybrid deep learning model for efficient reputation assessment of cloud services. IEEE Access **10**, 35321–35335 (2022)
2. Baldick, C.: The Concise Oxford Dictionary of Literary Terms. Oxford University Press, Oxford (1996)

3. Bilecki, L.F., Fiorese, A.: A trust reputation architecture for cloud computing environment. In: 2017 IEEE/ACS 14th International Conference on Computer Systems and Applications (AICCSA), pp. 614–621. IEEE (2017)
4. Birjali, M., Kasri, M., Beni-Hssane, A.: A comprehensive survey on sentiment analysis: approaches, challenges and trends. Knowl.-Based Syst. **226**, 107134 (2021)
5. Driss, M.: Ws-advising: a reusable and reconfigurable microservices-based platform for effective academic advising. J. Ambient Intell. Hum. Comput. **13**, 1–12 (2022)
6. Driss, M., Ben Atitallah, S., Albalawi, A., Boulila, W.: Req-WSComposer: a novel platform for requirements-driven composition of semantic web services. J. Ambient Intell. Hum. Comput. **13**, 1–17 (2022)
7. Hasnain, M., Ghani, I., Pasha, M.F., Jeong, S.R.: Machine learning methods for trust-based selection of web services. KSII Trans. Internet Inf. Syst. (TIIS) **16**(1), 38–59 (2022)
8. Hasnain, M., Pasha, M.F., Ghani, I., Imran, M., Alzahrani, M.Y., Budiarto, R.: Evaluating trust prediction and confusion matrix measures for web services ranking. IEEE Access **8**, 90847–90861 (2020)
9. Papadakis-Vlachopapadopoulos, K., González, R.S., Dimolitsas, I., Dechouniotis, D., Ferrer, A.J., Papavassiliou, S.: Collaborative SLA and reputation-based trust management in cloud federations. Future Gener. Comput. Syst. **100**, 498–512 (2019)
10. Saberi, B., Saad, S.: Sentiment analysis or opinion mining: a review. Int. J. Adv. Sci. Eng. Inf. Technol **7**(5), 1660–1666 (2017)
11. Surianarayanan, C., Ganapathy, G., Pethuru, R.: Essentials of Microservices Architecture: Paradigms, Applications, and Techniques. Taylor & Francis, Abingdon (2019)
12. Wahab, O.A., Bentahar, J., Otrok, H., Mourad, A.: A survey on trust and reputation models for web services: single, composite, and communities. Decis. Support Syst. **74**, 121–134 (2015)
13. Wolff, E.: Microservices: Flexible Software Architecture. Addison-Wesley Professional, Boston (2016)
14. Yu, Y., Si, X., Hu, C., Zhang, J.: A review of recurrent neural networks: LSTM cells and network architectures. Neural Comput. **31**(7), 1235–1270 (2019)
15. Yue, L., Chen, W., Li, X., Zuo, W., Yin, M.: A survey of sentiment analysis in social media. Knowl. Inf. Syst. **60**, 617–663 (2019)

Previous Opinions is All You Need—Legal Information Retrieval System

Maciej Osowski[1][ID], Katarzyna Lorenc[1][ID], Paweł Drozda[2][ID],
Rafał Scherer[3][✉][ID], Konrad Szałapak[4], Kajetan Komar-Komarowski[4],
Julian Szymański[5][ID], and Andrzej Sobecki[5][ID]

[1] Emplocity Ltd, Warsaw, Poland
[2] University of Warmia and Mazury, Olsztyn, Poland
pdrozda@matman.uwm.edu.pl
[3] Czestochowa University of Technology, Czestochowa, Poland
rafal.scherer@pcz.pl
[4] Lex Secure 24H Opieka Prawna, Sopot, Poland
{ks,kkk}@lexsecure.com
[5] Gdansk University of Technology, Faculty of Electronics,
Telecommunications and Informatics, Gdańsk, Poland
{julian.szymanski,andrzej.sobecki}@eti.pg.edu.pl,
http://emplocity.com/, https://lexsecure.pl/

Abstract. We present a system for retrieving the most relevant legal opinions to a given legal case or question. To this end, we checked several state-of-the-art neural language models. As a training and testing data, we use tens of thousands of legal cases as question-opinion pairs. Text data has been subjected to advanced pre-processing adapted to the specifics of the legal domain. We empirically chose the BERT-based HerBERT model to perform the best in the considered scenario.

Keywords: Transformer · BERT neural network · text retrieval · HerBERT · legal recommendation

1 Introduction

Over the past few years, the development of natural language processing (NLP) practical solutions has been very dynamic, and this advancement led to massive improvements in the quality of AI models. This work focuses on the niche domain of the law and legal technology applications. Legal opinions are time-consuming to prepare because they often require a thorough analysis of complex legal issues, as well as a review of a large amount of legal cases, statutes, and regulations. The process of researching and synthesizing this information can be time-consuming and labor-intensive. The use of artificial intelligence and machine learning in preparing legal opinion could help to streamline this process and make it more efficient. AI methods can relatively fast search vast amounts of data to find relevant information, and can also assist in organizing and analysing this information, even in generating legal output and answers. This can save time and

© The Author(s), under exclusive license to Springer Nature Switzerland AG 2023
N. T. Nguyen et al. (Eds.): ICCCI 2023, CCIS 1864, pp. 57–67, 2023.
https://doi.org/10.1007/978-3-031-41774-0_5

increase accuracy, allowing lawyers to focus on more high-level tasks such as applying the law to the facts of a case, or considering the potential implications of a legal decision. Additionally, AI can help to reduce the risk of human error, which is particularly important in the legal field where precision is key.

The goal of information retrieval is to find information that matches an information need from a set of resources that contain different types of data, such as text [1], images [9], sound or video. Information retrieval systems apply various methods to compare user queries with the resources and order them by their relevance. Some examples of information retrieval systems are web search engines, library catalogues and recommender systems.

We explore a specific application of Transformer networks, i.e. we present an AI-powered text information retrieval which offers attorneys a new way to deliver legal opinions. Namely, the system automatically proposes several past cases similar to the considered one by analysing its content. We compare three machine learning models for this task and select the best one. With our document automation and machine learning method, one can read past documents, data mine existing information, and use retrievals to produce legal opinions in a fraction of the time needed in the case of traditional methods. The presented retrieval system is aimed especially towards facilitating and accelerating the work of lawyers. The task of this transformer-based model is to match one or more legal opinions from the database to a new query from the client. This allows the person providing legal advice to automate part of their work. Moreover, it can suggest cases that could be overlooked by a human due to fatigue or distraction.

The rest of the paper is organized as follows. The Transformer model is described shortly in Sect. 2. In Sect. 3 we describe other NLP-related works and models used by them. Our method for legal information retrieval, the collected data and the experiments are described in Sects. 4 and 5. Section 6 concludes the paper.

2 Transformer Model

Transformer neural networks have recently gained a lot of attention in the field of artificial intelligence and machine learning. These networks are particularly useful for a variety of natural language processing tasks, such as machine translation, language modelling, and text classification.

The Transformer architecture was introduced by Vaswani et al. in 2017 [27], and has since become a widely used model in natural language processing. It is based on the concept of self-attention, which allows the model to weight different input tokens differently based on their relevance to a given task. This allows the model to effectively capture long-range dependencies in the input data, which is crucial for many natural language tasks. The attention mechanism [2,12] mimics cognitive attention in neural networks to help to focus on important parts of a sequence. Self-attention mechanism allows the model to weight different input tokens differently based on their relevance to a given task. The model is able to effectively capture long-range dependencies in the input data, which is crucial for many natural language tasks.

Another key advantage of the Transformer architecture is that it allows for efficient parallelization during training and inference. This is because the self-attention mechanisms allow the model to process the input data in parallel, rather than sequentially like many previous models. This makes it possible to train and deploy Transformer models more quickly and efficiently. Transformer models are highly adaptable and can be fine-tuned for a wide range of tasks and languages with relatively little data. This makes them particularly useful for scenarios where there is limited annotated training data available. The combination of self-attention mechanisms, efficient parallelization, and adaptability makes Transformer models a powerful tool for natural language processing tasks.

The transformer model (Fig. 1) accepts whole sequences as the input. Firstly, the byte pair encoding tokenizer breaks down the input text into tokens, after which each token is transformed into a vector through word embedding. Afterwards, the positional details of the token are incorporated into the word embedding.

In each encoder layer, its primary task is to create encodings that contain relevant information regarding the relationships between different parts of the inputs. These encodings are then forwarded to the subsequent encoder layer as inputs. On the other hand, each decoder layer functions in the opposite manner. It takes all the encodings and applies the contextual information they contain to produce a sequence of output. This is achieved through the employment of the attention mechanism in every encoder and decoder layer.

Once a sentence is fed into a transformer model, attention weights are computed for each token in parallel. These attention weights enable the attention unit to produce embeddings for each token in its contextual surroundings. These embeddings contain details about the token as well as a weighted mix of other significant tokens, each weighted by their respective attention weight. The attention is calculated using the softmax function

$$Attention(Q, K, V) = softmax\left(\frac{QK^T}{\sqrt{d_k}}\right)V \tag{1}$$

where Q, K, V are matrices of query, key and value vectors, respectively. One set of query, key and value weights is an attention head. Many such attention head can be used to discover various relations in data.

3   Related Work

As training Transformers is computationally demanding, there emerged many pre-trained models, such as GPT [19], RoBERTa [13] or BERT [6].

The transformer-based BERT (Bidirectional Encoder Representations from Transformers) model has been developed by Google for natural language processing tasks such as language translation, language modelling, and question answering. BERT is a pre-trained model that can be fine-tuned for specific tasks by adding task-specific layers on top of the pre-trained model. BERT is a specific model developed using the transformer architecture for natural language

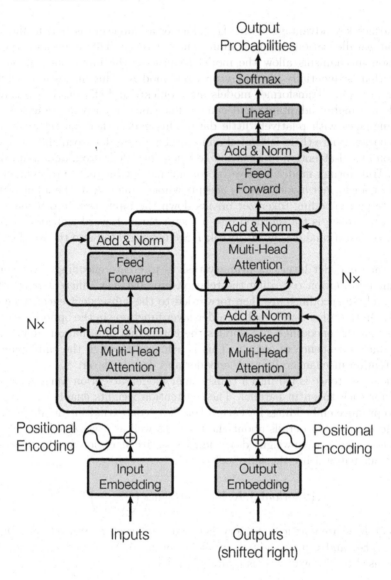

Fig. 1. Architecture of the Transformer model [27].

processing tasks, while the transformer is a general architecture that can be used to develop a variety of models for different tasks.

One key contribution of the BERT model is its ability to process input text in a bidirectional manner, meaning that it takes into account both the left and right context of each word in the input. This allows BERT to better capture the context and meaning of words in the input and improve performance on tasks that require understanding of the entire input, such as natural language inference and question answering. The BERT model was trained on a large corpus of text data and can be fine-tuned for specific tasks by adding task-specific layers on top of the pre-trained model. The authors demonstrated the effectiveness of the BERT model on several benchmark datasets, achieving state-of-the-art results on several tasks. The BERT model has since become widely adopted in the natural language processing community and has been used to achieve state-of-the-art results on many tasks.

In [14] the authors published the Chinese Legal Case Retrieval Dataset (LeCaRD) with 107 query cases and over 43,000 candidate cases. They implemented several popular retrieval models, such as BM25 [20], LMIR [17], TF-IDF [21] as traditional bag-of-words IR models, and BERT [22]. The last method achieved the best results. Biagoli et al. [3] computed text statistics, namely an unsupervised min frequency threshold over the number of times a term has been found in the entire training set, aiming at eliminating terms with poor statistics and a supervised threshold over the information gain of terms, which measures how much a term discriminates between documents belonging to different classes. Then, the Support Vector Machines were used to classify provisions.

Shao et al. [23] conducted a user study involving 45 participants majoring in law to collect users' rich interactions and relevance assessments. With the collected data, they scrutinized the characteristics of the search process in legal case retrieval practice. In [22] they applied the BERT architecture at the paragraph level to the retrieval of similar cases from the COLIEE 2019 dataset [18]. Vu Tran et al. [25] used the same the COLIEE 2019 dataset. Their work consisted in two main elements. The first was a machine learning model to extract catchphrases for new documents with the knowledge from previously seen documents and the expert drafted catchphrases. They were used as important phrases for a particular document. The second is a subsystem for document summarization into continuous vector space which is used to rank documents.

In [15] similar legal cases are retrieved by semantic language processing and checked on cases from the Canadian Supreme Court. Jain et al. [10] proposed a DCESumm method for sentence scoring as supervised sentence-level summary relevance prediction joined with unsupervised clustering-based document-level score enhancement. They used the BillSum and Forum of Information Retrieval Evaluation (FIRE) legal document summarization datasets, and obtained very high scores.

Legal text summarization was studied in [26]. The documents were compared by TF-IDF and Rouge-L scores, and summarization was performed by glowworm swarm optimization (GSO) with bidirectional gated recurrent neural network model.

Several studies have demonstrated the effectiveness of Transformer networks for machine translation. For example, Vaswani et al. (2017) [27] showed that a Transformer model outperformed previous state-of-the-art machine translation models on the WMT 2014 English-to-German and English-to-French translation tasks. Similarly, Chen et al. (2018) [4] found that a Transformer-based model achieved superior results on the WMT 2014 English-to-Chinese translation task. In [5] transformer is used to deobfuscate PowerShell scripts.

In addition to machine translation, Transformer networks have also been applied to language modelling tasks. For instance, Radford et al. (2018) [19] used a Transformer-based model to set a new state-of-the-art on the Penn Treebank language modelling benchmark. Similarly, Devlin et al. (2019) [6] used a Transformer model to achieve state-of-the-art results on the Google Billion Words language modelling benchmark.

Transformer networks have also been used for text classification tasks, with promising results. For example, Kim (2014) [11] used a Convolutional Neural Network (CNN) and a Transformer model for text classification, and found that the Transformer model outperformed the CNN on several benchmarks. Similarly, Zhang et al. (2019) [29] used a Transformer model for text classification and found that it outperformed other state-of-the-art models on several benchmarks.

Multi-QA Transformer is a type of transformer architecture designed for the task of multi-hop question answering, which requires the model to reason over multiple pieces of evidence to answer a given question. This architecture was introduced in [24] and has been further developed in subsequent work.

The Multi-QA Transformer consists of multiple modules, each of which is responsible for processing a different type of input. These modules include a document encoder, a question encoder, and an answer decoder. The document encoder processes the input documents to create a set of document embeddings, while the question encoder creates a question embedding. The answer decoder then takes these embeddings and generates an answer.

One key aspect of the Multi-QA Transformer is its ability to incorporate information from multiple sources. In addition to processing the input documents and questions, the model can also incorporate external knowledge sources, such as knowledge graphs or ontologies, to enhance its reasoning capabilities.

The effectiveness of the Multi-QA Transformer has been demonstrated on a variety of benchmark datasets, including the HotpotQA dataset (Yang et al. 2018) and the TriviaQA dataset (Joshi et al. 2017). These results show that the Multi-QA Transformer can achieve state-of-the-art performance on multi-hop question answering tasks.

LaBSE (Language-agnostic BERT Sentence Embedding) is a pre-trained transformer-based architecture developed for cross-lingual natural language processing (NLP) tasks. It was introduced by Fang et al. in 2020 [7] and has been shown to outperform existing cross-lingual sentence embedding models on several benchmark datasets.

LaBSE is based on the BERT architecture and is pre-trained on large amounts of monolingual and parallel data. During pre-training, LaBSE learns a joint representation space for sentences from multiple languages. This enables it to map semantically similar sentences in different languages to similar points in the embedding space. To achieve this, LaBSE employs a parallel data mining technique that allows it to mine parallel sentences from monolingual corpora. The mined parallel sentences are then used to train the model in a supervised fashion using a cross-lingual contrastive loss function. This loss function encourages the model to map semantically similar sentences in different languages to nearby points in the embedding space, while keeping distant points separated.

LaBSE has been shown to outperform existing cross-lingual sentence embedding models on several benchmark datasets, including the Cross-lingual Sentiment Analysis (CLSA) and BUCC corpora (Fang et al., 2020). It has also been used as a building block in several downstream cross-lingual NLP tasks, such as cross-lingual information retrieval (CLIR) (Wu et al. 2021) and cross-lingual text classification (CLTC) (Li et al. 2021).

4 Data

The corpus we had at our disposal contained about 10,000 legal cases. It was crucial that each record contained a legal question and answer in the text. Two main elements in preprocessing can be distinguished. Specifically, the first is to remove redundant texts from legal opinions such as encouraging contact with the low firm, e.g. "More information con be found on our Facebook page". The second important component is handling non-informative questions like "What possibilities does the client have?" We developed an algorithm for identifying unspecified questions and then concatenated the extracted context to such queries (Fig. 2).

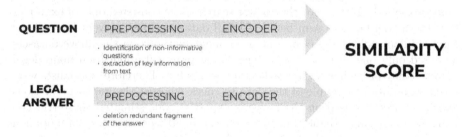

Fig. 2. General workflow of the method.

5 Experiments

The research began with testing three models: LaBSE [8]. Herbert [16] and a model specific to the QA problem—multi-QA (six-layer version of MiniLM [28] fine-tuned on 215M QA pairs) in a zero-shot learning configuration. Surprisingly high results were achieved by the LaBSE model in this way (see Table 1). The probability of finding on appropriate legal opinion is more than 40% cases when the model has not seen the data before. However, after model fine-tuning, we noticed that Herbert gains the highest score and finds the best semantic relations in legal texts.

Moreover, we conducted numerous analyses, among others, by adding negative examples during training or by attempting to match the question with tokenized sentences from a legal opinion. Nevertheless, classic training performed best, i.e. comparing the similarity between the full text of the question and the answer. In the next section, only the Herbert model will be considered due to its high performance.

Table 1. Comparison of three language models for a various number N of top predictions.

TopN	Zero-shot			Fine-tuned		
	LaBSE	Herbert	multi-qa	LaBSE	Herbert	multi-qa
1	0.413	0.011	0.217	0.459	0.604	0.423
2	0.520	0.013	0.295	0.488	0.730	0.518
3	0.564	0.015	0.323	0.643	0.792	0.596
5	0.644	0.020	0.384	0.710	0.844	0.665
7	0.703	0.028	0.426	0.763	0.865	0.714
10	0.737	0.032	0.451	0.811	0.888	0.752

The final results are shown in Fig. 3. To experimentally test our method, we used two sets: I) Test data—the answer search space consisted only of examples that the model hod not seen before, 2) Full data—seeking answers from all the legal opinions collected so far. The assessment methods on the above datasets accepted only one correct answer, whereas in practical application many legal opinions may prove helpful in reaching a new verdict. Therefore, specialists were given an additional sample of the data to check whether the model predictions would be useful. Based on the lawyer's expertise, we estimated the retriever's realistic performance (light blue on the chart). In 80% of cases, a helpful opinion already appears among the first two model predictions.

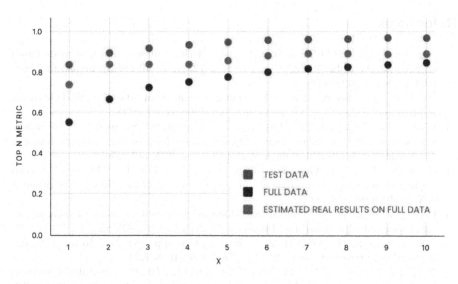

Fig. 3. Retrieval accuracy results for various numbers of top N predicted results of the Herbert model, which was the best-performing model of all the considered ones. The accuracy metric is the F1 score estimated by expert lawyers.

6   Conclusions

The usefulness of various intelligent algorithms has been appreciated in many aspects of our lives, and AI in our workplaces is becoming increasingly ubiquitous. This study shows that using sophisticated state-of-the-art transformer-based neural models, it is possible to create a tool that will invaluably support and optimize the work of lawyers. Namely, based on tens of thousands of legal cases, we created an NLP retrieval system for matching the best legal opinion for a query question. We analysed some models and the Herbert model turned out to achieve the best accuracy. In creating this system, we were guided by its usability and this condition has been met, as the model achieves high results even when seeking answers among all opinions.

Acknowledgments. The work was supported by founds of the project "A semi-autonomous system for generating legal advice and opinions based on automatic query analysis using the transformer-type deep neural network architecture with multitasking learning", POIR.01.01.01-00-1965/20.

The project financed under the program of the Polish Minister of Science and Higher Education under the name "Regional Initiative of Excellence" in the years 2019–2023 project number 020/RID/2018/19 the amount of financing PLN 12,000,000.

References

1. Aghdam, M.H.: Automatic extractive and generic document summarization based on NMF. J. Artif. Intell. Soft Comput. Res. **12**(1), 37–49 (2023). https://doi.org/10.2478/jaiscr-2023-0003
2. Bahdanau, D., Cho, K., Bengio, Y.: Neural machine translation by jointly learning to align and translate. arXiv preprint arXiv:1409.0473 (2014)
3. Biagioli, C., Francesconi, E., Passerini, A., Montemagni, S., Soria, C.: Automatic semantics extraction in law documents. In: Proceedings of the 10th International Conference on Artificial Intelligence and Law, pp. 133–140 (2005)
4. Chen, Y., Feng, Y., Gao, D., Li, J., Xiong, D., Liu, L.: The best of both worlds: Combining recent advances in neural machine translation. arXiv preprint arXiv:1804.09847 (2018)
5. Dedek, M., Scherer, R.: Transformer-based original content recovery from obfuscated powershell scripts. In: Tanveer, M., Agarwal, S., Ozawa, S., Ekbal, A., Jatowt, A. (eds.) ICONIP 2022. CCIS, vol. 1794, pp. 284–295. Springer, Singapore (2022). https://doi.org/10.1007/978-981-99-1648-1_24
6. Devlin, J., Chang, M.W., Lee, K., Toutanova, K.: BERT: pre-training of deep bidirectional transformers for language understanding. In: Proceedings of the 2019 Conference of the North American Chapter of the Association for Computational Linguistics: Human Language Technologies, Volume 1 (Long and Short Papers), pp. 4171–4186. Association for Computational Linguistics, Minneapolis, Minnesota (2019). https://doi.org/10.18653/v1/N19-1423, https://aclanthology.org/N19-1423
7. Feng, F., Yang, Y., Cer, D., Arivazhagan, N., Wang, W.: Language-agnostic BERT sentence embedding. In: Proceedings of the 60th Annual Meeting of the Association for Computational Linguistics (Volume 1: Long Papers), pp. 878–891 (2022)
8. Feng, F., Yang, Y., Cer, D., Arivazhagan, N., Wang, W.: Language-agnostic BERT sentence embedding. In: Proceedings of the 60th Annual Meeting of the Association for Computational Linguistics (Volume 1: Long Papers), pp. 878–891. Association for Computational Linguistics, Dublin, Ireland (2022). https://doi.org/10.18653/v1/2022.acl-long.62, https://aclanthology.org/2022.acl-long.62
9. Grycuk, R., Scherer, R., Marchlewska, A., Napoli, C.: Semantic hashing for fast solar magnetogram retrieval. J. Artif. Intell. Soft Comput. Res. **12**(4), 299–306 (2022). https://doi.org/10.2478/jaiscr-2022-0020
10. Jain, D., Borah, M.D., Biswas, A.: A sentence is known by the company it keeps: improving legal document summarization using deep clustering. Artif. Intell. Law, 1–36 (2023)
11. Kim, Y.: Convolutional neural networks for sentence classification. arXiv preprint arXiv:1408.5882 (2014)
12. Kim, Y., Denton, C., Hoang, L., Rush, A.M.: Structured attention networks. In: International Conference on Learning Representations (2017)
13. Liu, Y., et al.: Roberta: a robustly optimized BERT pretraining approach. arXiv preprint arXiv:1907.11692 (2019)
14. Ma, Y., et al.: LeCaRD: a legal case retrieval dataset for Chinese law system. In: Proceedings of the 44th International ACM SIGIR Conference on Research and Development in Information Retrieval, pp. 2342–2348 (2021)
15. Maxwell, K.T., Oberlander, J., Lavrenko, V.: Evaluation of semantic events for legal case retrieval. In: Proceedings of the WSDM 2009 Workshop on Exploiting Semantic Annotations in Information Retrieval, pp. 39–41 (2009)

16. Mroczkowski, R., Rybak, P., Wróblewska, A., Gawlik, I.: HerBERT: efficiently pretrained transformer-based language model for Polish. In: Proceedings of the 8th Workshop on Balto-Slavic Natural Language Processing, pp. 1–10. Association for Computational Linguistics, Kiyv, Ukraine (2021). https://aclanthology.org/2021.bsnlp-1.1

17. Ponte, J.M., Croft, W.B.: A language modeling approach to information retrieval. ACM SIGIR Forum **51**(2), 202–208 (2017)

18. Rabelo, J., Kim, M.-Y., Goebel, R., Yoshioka, M., Kano, Y., Satoh, K.: A summary of the COLIEE 2019 competition. In: Sakamoto, M., Okazaki, N., Mineshima, K., Satoh, K. (eds.) JSAI-isAI 2019. LNCS (LNAI), vol. 12331, pp. 34–49. Springer, Cham (2020). https://doi.org/10.1007/978-3-030-58790-1_3

19. Radford, A., Narasimhan, K., Salimans, T., Sutskever, I., et al.: Improving language understanding by generative pre-training (2018)

20. Robertson, S.E., Walker, S., Jones, S., Hancock-Beaulieu, M.M., Gatford, M., et al.: Okapi at trec-3. Nist Special Publication Sp 109, 109 (1995)

21. Salton, G., Buckley, C.: Term-weighting approaches in automatic text retrieval. Inf. Process. Manage. **24**(5), 513–523 (1988)

22. Shao, Y., et al.: BERT-PLI: modeling paragraph-level interactions for legal case retrieval. In: IJCAI, pp. 3501–3507 (2020)

23. Shao, Y., Wu, Y., Liu, Y., Mao, J., Zhang, M., Ma, S.: Investigating user behavior in legal case retrieval. In: Proceedings of the 44th International ACM SIGIR Conference on Research and Development in Information Retrieval, pp. 962–972 (2021)

24. Talmor, A., Berant, J.: MultiQA: an empirical investigation of generalization and transfer in reading comprehension. In: Proceedings of the 57th Annual Meeting of the Association for Computational Linguistics, pp. 4911–4921 (2019)

25. Tran, V., Le Nguyen, M., Tojo, S., Satoh, K.: Encoded summarization: summarizing documents into continuous vector space for legal case retrieval. Artif. Intell. Law **28**, 441–467 (2020)

26. Vaissnave, V., Deepalakshmi, P.: Modeling of automated glowworm swarm optimization based deep learning model for legal text summarization. Multimedia Tools Appl. **82**, 1–20 (2022)

27. Vaswani, A., et al.: Attention is all you need. In: Advances in Neural Information Processing Systems, pp. 5998–6008 (2017)

28. Wang, W., Wei, F., Dong, L., Bao, H., Yang, N., Zhou, M.: Minilm: deep self-attention distillation for task-agnostic compression of pre-trained transformers. In: Larochelle, H., Ranzato, M., Hadsell, R., Balcan, M., Lin, H. (eds.) Advances in Neural Information Processing Systems, vol. 33, pp. 5776–5788. Curran Associates, Inc. (2020). https://proceedings.neurips.cc/paper/2020/file/3f5ee243547dee91fbd053c1c4a845aa-Paper.pdf

29. Zhang, Y., Chen, Y., Feng, Y., Gao, D., Liu, L.: HiBERT: hierarchical attention networks for document classification. arXiv preprint arXiv:1909.09610 (2019)

An Agent-Based Network Model
for Interpersonal Emotion Regulation
in a Human-Bot Interaction

Filippos Dimopoulos[1], Edgar Eler[1,2][✉] ⓘ, Marieke Timmers[1], Jan Treur[1] ⓘ,
and Sander L. Koole[2] ⓘ

[1] Vrije Universiteit Amsterdam, Social AI Group, Department of Computer Science,
Amsterdam, The Netherlands
f.dimopoulos@student.vu.nl, {e.eler,j.treur}@vu.nl
[2] Vrije Universiteit Amsterdam, Department of Clinical Psychology, Amsterdam,
The Netherlands
s.l.koole@vu.nl

Abstract. This study analyses the effects of emotional coregulation in the interaction between a distressed human and a bot. Through the coregulation premises, an emotion contagion process impacts the emotional system, which initially increases the distress level of the bot due to the influence of the human's emotions. Configuring the bot with optimal emotion regulation decreases its distress levels as it can self-regulate its emotions, which affects the human's emotions, regulating them by the emotion contagion process. The results show how this coregulation process occurs.

1 Introduction

Emotions have traditionally been viewed as a barrier to effective decision-making. However, there is a positive and a negative aspect to this. In case of the second, a negative state can hinder our decision-making process, introducing a negative bias in making the "correct" decisions. In order to perform a favourable action, humans need to regulate their emotions. This can happen by using various tactics. Consider the following loop: shown in Fig. 1 first a *situation*, second a thought process (*attention*), thirdly an *appraisal* of the situation and lastly a *response* to this process. The feedback loop would connect the response to the situation. For example, an individual is participating in an interview, they feel the interviewer is distant and interpret it as displeasure with the interviewee, which results in fear. The regulation happens when comparing the situation in-hand and the ideal one. This discrepancy drives the interviewee to make a different choice, eg. instead of showing the fear, to try and show excitement and change the emotional status of the interviewer.

In a social environment, the decision-making processes of individuals affect each other. This process is based on social contagion. The particular kind of social contagion addressed in this paper and in the example above, is emotion contagion. By expressing their opinions, for example, individuals affect other individuals' emotions, which triggers the loop mentioned before.

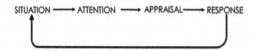

Fig. 1. Sequential Model of emotion generation [1]

In this paper, we present a social agent model that supports interpersonal emotion regulation, based on the emotion contagion process. Following this section, the necessary theoretical background is provided. The third chapter describes the computational model used. The fourth section presents the results of the simulations for different settings. The fifth and sixth sections include the conclusion of our research and a discussion around future work and ambitions based on this project.

2 Background

Emotion theorists have put forward different definitions of what emotion is. According to the American Psychological Association (APA), emotion is defined as "a complex reaction pattern, involving experiential, behavioural and physiological elements" [5]. In the Dictionary of Cognitive Psychology [6], although not formally defined, it is described as a mental state. Subsequently, according to the James-Lange theory (William James, Carl Lange, 1880s), emotional stimuli first induce peripheral physiological variations, which occur without consciousness of affect. These bodily responses are further interpreted by the brain to produce the feeling state of an emotion [7].

Over the last decades, emotional regulation has become a more and more interesting research topic for diverse fields, such as psychology and neuroscience, where a point of interest is the mechanism that governs the emotions biology-wise, and, more recently, artificial intelligence, where a recreation of the emotion regulation that takes place by an interaction between prefrontal cortex and amygdala is addressed computationally [8, 9]. Most of this literature focuses on individual emotion regulation, but recently the interest in interpersonal emotion regulation has grown as well.

In the remainder of this section, the agent modeling approach by (self-modeling) temporal-causal networks used is briefly introduced [2–4]. In this approach *nodes* Y in a network have activation values $Y(t)$ that are dynamic over time t; therefore, they serve as state variables and will usually be called *states*. To specify these dynamics, the states are considered to affect each other by the connections within the network. Following [2], a basic *network structure* is characterised by:

- **connectivity characteristics**
  Connections from a state X to a state Y and their *weights* $\omega_{X,Y}$
- **aggregation characteristics**
  For any node Y, some *combination function* $c_Y(..)$ defines aggregation that is applied to the *single impacts* $\omega_{X_i,Y} X_i(t)$ on Y from its incoming connections from states $X_1, \ldots, X_k$
- **timing characteristics**
  Each state Y has a *speed factor* η_Y defining how fast it changes upon given impact

Here, the states X_i and $Y(t)$ have activation levels $X_i(t)$ and $Y(t)$ that vary (often within the [0, 1] interval) over time, described by real numbers. The dynamics of such networks are described by the following difference (or differential) equations that incorporate in a canonical manner the network characteristics $\omega_{X,Y}$, $\mathbf{c}_Y(..)$, η_Y:

$$Y(t + \Delta t) = Y(t) + \eta_Y[\mathbf{c}_Y(\omega_{X_1,Y}X_1(t), \ldots, \omega_{X_k,Y}X_k(t)) - Y(t)]\,\Delta t \qquad (1)$$

for any state Y and where $X_1, \ldots, X_k$ are the states from which Y gets its incoming connections. The Eq. (1) are useful for simulation purposes and also for analysis of properties of the emerging behaviour of such network models. The overall combination function $\mathbf{c}_Y(..)$ for state Y is taken as the weighted average of some of the available basic combination functions $\mathbf{c}_j(..)$ by specified weights $\gamma_{j,Y}$, and parameters $\pi_{1,j,Y}$, $\pi_{2,j,Y}$ of $\mathbf{c}_j(..)$, for Y:

$$\mathbf{c}_Y(V_1, \ldots, V_k) = \frac{\gamma_{1,Y}\mathbf{c}_1(V_1, \ldots, V_k) + \ldots + \gamma_{m,Y}\mathbf{c}_m(V_1, \ldots, V_k)}{\gamma_{1,Y} + \ldots + \gamma_{m,Y}} \qquad (2)$$

Such Eqs. (1), (2) are hidden in the dedicated software environment that can be used for simulation and analysis; see [3, 4], Ch 9. This software environment is freely downloadable from URL https://www.researchgate.net/project/Network-Oriented-Mod eling-Software

For the combination functions used here, see Table 1.

Table 1. Combination functions from the library used here

Name	Notation	Formula	Parameters
Euclidean	$\mathbf{eucl}_{n,\lambda}(V_1, \ldots, V_k)$	$\sqrt[n]{\dfrac{V_1^n + \cdots + V_k^n}{\lambda}}$	Order n Scaling factor λ
Advanced logistic	$\mathbf{alogistic}_{\sigma,\tau}(V_1, \ldots, V_k)$	$\left[\dfrac{1}{1+e^{-\sigma(V_1+\cdots+V_k-\tau)}} - \dfrac{1}{1+e^{\sigma\tau}}\right](1 + e^{-\sigma\tau})$	Steepness $\sigma > 0$ Threshold τ

3   The Introduced Social Agent Model

The social multi-agent model introduced in this paper was designed by considering the mechanisms involved in the internal emotion regulation processes of two agents a and b, a human and a bot, and the dynamics of their interaction for emotion contagion. The cyclic mechanisms for individual emotion regulation are based on the conceptual causal model from [2], Ch 3. The conceptual representation of the social agent model is illustrated in Fig. 2, in which the circles represent the mental states, the arrows represent the connections, and the shaded areas in the background represent the individuals.

The individual emotion regulation process is modelled in the same way for both agents a and b. For each agent:

- the stimulus from the world/environment is represented by the *ws* states
- the *ps* state represents the preparation for the emotional response
- the *es* state represents the expressed emotion.
- the *fs* state represents the felt emotion
- the *cs* state represents the internal emotion regulation control

The connections that involve the emotion regulation control states *cs* are displayed as dotted arrows to illustrate the emotion control processes of monitoring the stimulus (incoming connections) and suppressing the emotional response *ps* and felt emotion *fs* (outgoing connections).

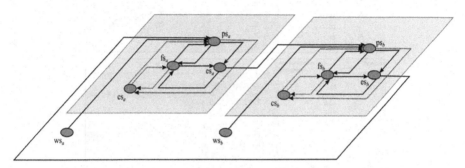

Fig. 2. Social (multi-)agent model for the human-bot interaction

The interpersonal emotion regulation process conceptualized in Fig. 2 has the premise that the expressed emotion *es* of both individuals will be the interface by which the emotions of one individual will impact the emotions of the other individual and vice-versa. Skipping for the sake of simplicity the process of sensing and representing incoming stimuli, there are direct connections from the *es* state of one agent to the emotional response preparation state *ps* of the other. This preparation state is used as the primary state that receives the external stimuli (from *ws* and *ps*), the suppression effect from the emotion regulation control state *cs* and the impact of the emotion feeling state *fs*. The latter feeling state receives impacts from the emotion preparation state *ps*, the expressed emotion state es, and from the regulation control state *cs* that suppresses it. The expressed emotion state *es* receives impact from the emotion preparation and feeling states *ps* and *fs*. As the expressed emotion and the emotion felt mutually affect each other, which also impacts the emotion preparation state in a bi-directional manner [2], some loops were included in the model to simulate the cyclic form in which those states affect each other.

The base idea of this scenario is a distressed human (agent *a*) with a poorly functioning individual emotion regulation system that gets in contact with a bot (agent *b*), and due to the interaction with the bot, the human's emotion is regulated. The tables in Fig. 3 are the role matrices of the designed social (multi-)agent model. They show the values of the network characteristics (serving as the model parameters) defined for the main simulation. In this scenario, the human had its ability to regulate emotions individually reduced due to its distress situation, so the table *mcwv* illustrated in Fig. 3, shows that the two incoming connections for the emotion regulation control state of the human (cs_a) have weight 0.1 while the bot has its internal emotion regulation fully operational, with the two incoming connections to the bot's emotion regulation control state (cs_b) have the maximum weight 1.0.

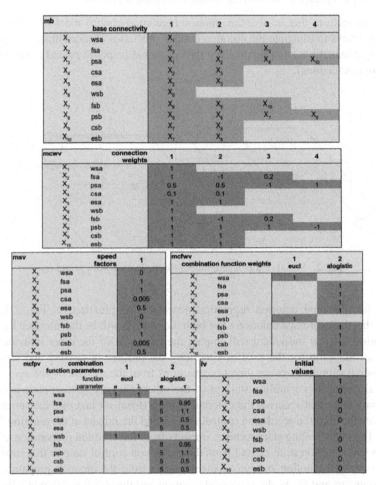

Fig. 3. Network characteristics representing the multi-agent model

4 Simulation Results

The expected outcome of the interaction between the distressed human and the bot is an initial increase in the bot's distress levels due to the emotional contagion from the high level of distress of the human. Once the well-functioning internal emotion regulation control of the bot gets activated, its distress level drops significantly. Due to that, by emotion contagion also the human's emotion gets regulated. This will support the idea of interpersonal emotion regulation through coregulation, as described by [10]. Figure 4 illustrates the expected results, with the curves representing the feeling states fs_a of the human (agent a) and fs_b of the bot (agent b).

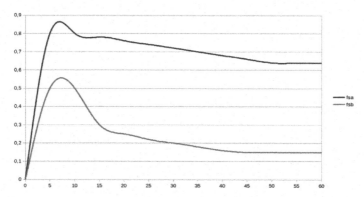

Fig. 4. Expected results for the main simulation

Simulation 1 - Main Scenario

For the main scenario, the simulation was performed following all values illustrated in Fig. 3. The human is considered to have a high distress level, while having very poor individual emotion control, and the bot with a perfectly operational individual emotion control. The results for Simulation 1 are displayed in Fig. 5. The results start with a steep and rapidly increasing activation level in all non-control states. After this, once the control state cs_b of the bot gets activated, the feeling state fs_b of the bot immediately starts to decrease, which by emotion contagion also impacts the human feeling state fs_a. A tipping point occurs at time point 441.5, significantly dropping all states' values.

Simulation 2 - Human with Better Emotion Regulation Control

In Simulation 2, we increased the emotion regulation control of the human by increasing the weight of the two incoming connections of cs_a from 0.1 to 0.5, which resulted in a similar outcome to Simulation 1, but with the emotion being regulated almost four times faster, which is noticeable by the tipping point moving from the timepoint 441 to around 120. Figure 6 illustrates those results.

Simulation 3 - Bot with Poorer Emotion Regulation Control

A third simulation was performed for further validation of the model, but now decreasing the emotion regulation control of the bot. In this simulation, the effects of the changes in an individual's emotions have less impact on the other's emotions, which makes this a more realistic scenario when compared to the expected results. Figure 7 illustrates this simulation.

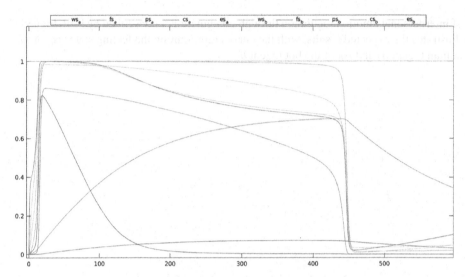

Fig. 5. Main simulation result

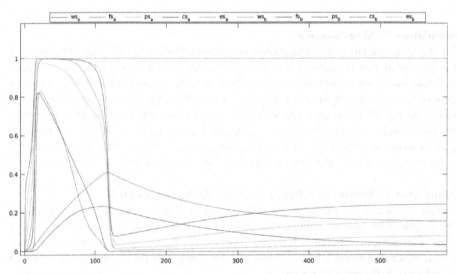

Fig. 6. Simulation results with the human configured with an increased emotion control

5   Verification of the Model by Mathematical Analysis

To verify the results obtained from the simulations, analysis of stationary points can be done. For any state Y, a time point in which it is stationary can be selected, a time t where approximately $dY(t)/dt = 0$, or approximately $Y(t + \Delta t) = Y(t)$. Given (1) from Sect. 2, this is equivalent to approximately

$$\mathbf{c}_Y(\omega_{X_1,Y}X_1(t), \ldots, \omega_{X_k,Y}X_k(t)) - Y(t) = 0$$

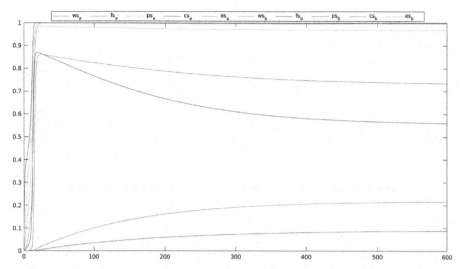

Fig. 7. Simulation results with the bot configured with a poorer emotion regulation control

For this t, from the simulation values and network characteristics (using the values and weights of the connected states in the combination function), the aggregated impact $\mathbf{c}_Y(\omega_{X_1,Y}X_1(t), \ldots, \omega_{X_k,Y}X_k(t))$. Then by comparing that to the value $Y(t)$ from the simulation, the deviation can be found:

$$\text{Deviation} = \mathbf{c}_Y(\omega_{X_1,Y}X_1(t), \ldots, \omega_{X_k,Y}X_k(t)) - Y(t)$$

Tables 2, 3 and 4 display the absolute values of these deviations.

Table 2. Verification of the agent model for Simulation 1

	ws_a	fs_a	ps_a	cs_a	es_a	ws_b	fs_b	ps_b	cs_b	es_b
Maxima										
time point	27	27	27	27	27	27	27	27	27	27
state value	1	0.860604	0.983853	0.000632922	0.996291	1	0.782143	0.999657	0.0939761	0.998228
aggimpact	1	0.86558205331	0.999599612034	0.001684590169	0.999219780921	1	0.775906251462	0.999999072862	0.998712672848	0.998712672848
deviation	0	0.00497805331	0.015746612034	0.001051668169	0.000928780921	0	0.006236748538	0.000342072862	0.904736572848	0.000484672848
Minima										
time point	1168	1168	1168	1168	1168	1168	1168	1168	1168	1168
state value	1	0.000590792	0.093897	0.00512246	0.0437967	1	0.00082221	0.25034	0.160733	0.159971
aggimpact	1	0.000590920134	0.085907780713	0.00003927452	0.000564674225	1	0.000822337324	0.370455615714	0.00321993606	0.00321993606
deviation	0	0.000000128134	0.007989219287	0.00508318548	0.043232025775	0	0.000000127324	0.120115615714	0.15751306394	0.15675106394

In Table 2, most of the results performed by the simulation match the results obtained from the verification formula, except for the state cs_b, which is highly decreasing its value in the timepoint 27, so it is not stationary. This is also applicable to the results obtained in Table 3.

Simulation 3 results in the best matching among all simulations, as described in Table 4. The deviation values are more consistent because, in timepoints selected from Simulation 3, the states are more stationary than in the other simulations.

Table 3. Results of the verification of the agent model for Simulation 2

	ws_a	fs_a	ps_a	cs_a	es_a	ws_b	fs_b	ps_b	cs_b	es_b
Maxima										
time point	22	22	22	22	22	22	22	22	22	22
state value	1	0.827915	0.979885	0.0332754	0.990933	1	0.811244	0.999712	0.0710132	0.996856
aggimpact	1	0.826032257842	0.999401092419	0.4085351643	0.998954171125	1	0.805955223948	0.999999351634	0.998980219085	0.998980219085
deviation	0	0.001882742158	0.019516092419	0.3752597643	0.008021171125	0	0.005288776052	0.000287351634	0.927967019085	0.002124219085
Minima										
time point	596	598	598	598	598	596	598	598	596	598
state value	1	0.000272811	0.0802717	0.0329552	0.0362027	1	0.000782667	0.245267	0.158441	0.155139
aggimpact	1	0.000230428065	0.067304828865	0.000190105539	0.000452357302	1	0.000783319838	0.297179171286	0.003071373016	0.003071373016
deviation	0	0.000042382935	0.012966871135	0.032765094461	0.035750342698	0	0.000000652838	0.051912171286	0.155369626984	0.152067626984

Table 4. Results of the verification of the agent model for Simulation 3

	ws_a	fs_a	ps_a	cs_a	es_a	ws_b	fs_b	ps_b	cs_b	es_b
Maxima										
time point	23	23	23	23	23	23	23	23	23	23
state value	1	0.861055	0.983893	0.00472622	0.996088	1	0.866407	0.999837	0.0170026	0.998299
aggimpact	1	0.861343555915	0.999587269006	0.001685446746	0.998222837234	1	0.865224124617	0.999999740222	0.009319172361	0.990344406597
deviation	0	0.000288555915	0.015694269006	0.003040773254	0.003134837234	0	0.001182875383	0.000162740222	0.007683427639	0.001045498597
Minima										
time point	596	598	598	598	598	596	598	598	598	598
state value	1	0.73439	0.966465	0.0887453	0.997337	1	0.559623	0.997971	0.216742	0.994869
aggimpact	1	0.644741941855	0.9998619114642	0.001447913094	0.97754296147	1	0.5597749555	0.9998789599	0.005517176954	0.992323213233
deviation	0	0.089848058145	0.032154114642	0.087297386906	0.00020596147	0	0.0000480445	0.0019079599	0.211224823046	0.002245786767

6 Validation by Parameter Tuning for the Expected Results

To validate the model, data was extracted from the expected results described in Sect. 4 and illustrated in Fig. 4. Six distinct time points of the *fs* and *cs* states of both individuals were selected to represent expected data to be compared with the results obtained by the model. Table 5 displays the values of the *fs* and *cs* states for the selected time points.

Table 5. Expected data for states at given time points

	10	20	50	100	300	500
fs_a	0.05	0.3	0.9	0.75	0.7	0.65
cs_a	0.00	0.01	0.02	0.05	0.08	0.09
fs_b	0.01	0.28	0.6	0.45	0.4	0.35
cs_b	0.02	0.06	0.16	0.3	0.4	0.5

To compare the expected results to the results obtained by the model, a computational iterative parameter tuning process was performed, running Simulation 1 and obtaining the deviations between the simulated data and the expected data from Table 5. The speed factor parameters η_{csa}, η_{esa}, η_{csb}, η_{esb} of the *cs* and *es* states of both individuals were selected to be tuned by Simulated Annealing [11] in order to reach simulation values close to the expected data. Those parameters started with a random value of 0.5 and could get any value between 0 and 1 over the iterations.

After tuned by this Simulated Annealing algorithm, the parameters obtained the value as follows: $\eta_{csa} = 0.9797$, $\eta_{esa} = 0.5357$, $\eta_{csb} = 0.0013$, $\eta_{esb} = 0.1469$. The lowest deviation found by the Simulated Annealing is Root Mean Square Error RMSE = 0.1298, illustrated in Fig. 8.

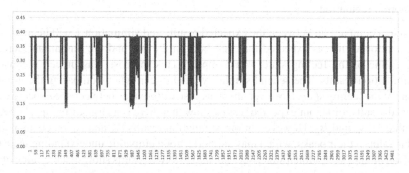

Fig. 8. RMSE errors over the Simulated Annealing process

Figure 9 illustrates the results of Simulation 1 when applied the tuned parameters, including the reference points (with *ref_* prefix) of the expected data from Table 5.

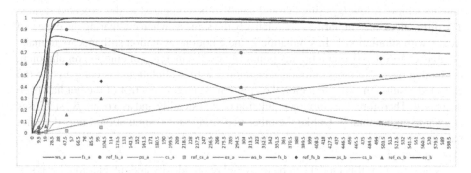

Fig. 9. Simulation 1 after applying tuned parameters

7   Discussion

In this section, first, the focus will be on the comparison between the expected results and the achieved results. This comparison allows for further elaboration on the next steps in making the model more realistic. Lastly, possibilities for further research will be discussed as this will bring more specific information about how to make the emotion-regulation model more realistic. The simulation results consisted of three different simulations:

1) Human with reduced individual emotion regulation and bot with perfect individual emotion regulation

2) Human with better individual emotion regulation and bot with perfect individual emotion regulation
3) Human with reduced individual emotion regulation and bot with reduced individual emotion regulation

First, a comparison between the expected results and simulation 1 will be made. As aforementioned, it was expected that first both in the bot and the human an increase of the value of the feeling state would appear. This increase was indeed notable in our simulation results. The second similarity can be seen when comparing the gradual decline of the feeling state. However, there are also differences between the expected and achieved results. First, our expected results show that there is a large difference between the value of fs_a and fs_b. However, in our simulation results fs_a and fs_b reach an almost similar value at their peaks, which may support a good empathic understanding from the bot of the human's emotional state. Second, the expected results show that the value of fs_b would have a steep decline, but would stabilise at a value above 0. The final results show a steep decline, but the value of fs_b rapidly stabilises at 0. Similarly, it was expected that fs_a would decrease its value and stabilise at a value above zero. Nonetheless, at a tipping point the value of fs_a rapidly declined all the way to 0. If simulation 2 is compared to simulation 1, the most notable difference is the speed with which the emotion is regulated. Due to increased emotion regulation control in the human, the bot needs less time to achieve a low fs_a. Simulation 2 can also be compared to the expected results. The differences and similarities are relatively the same as when comparing the expected results with simulation 1. In simulation 2, the emotion regulation still appears to make fs_a go back to value 0 after a tipping point. Hence, the increase of emotion regulation in the human results in rapid emotion regulation. Lastly, simulation 3 is compared to the expected results. In this simulation the emotion regulation control of the bot had been decreased. Therefore, the emotion regulation occurs steadily and as a result fs_a stabilises at a value higher than 0. Unlike the other two simulations, simulation 3 thus does not have a tipping point. Consequently, this simulation shows many similarities with the expected results.

A next step for this model can be to extend the model by adding additional ways of coregulation which can make it more realistic. Currently, the model represents emotional regulation by the bot based on social contagion. State es_b does not represent any specific action such as a hug or a pat on the shoulder, that would affect the fs_a in the human but just the expressed emotion. The consequence of adding such other actions as well could be that the fs_a in the human could be affected in different ways by the different actions. This may contribute to optimising the bots response in its attempt to regulate the human emotion fs_a. Furthermore, the model can be made adaptive so that by learning emotion regulation is improved over time. In this paper, it was assumed that internal emotion regulation in the human is very poor and internal emotion regulation in the bot is excellent. In short, this means that in the current model the human does not have the quality to regulate its own emotions well, while the bot has the power to both regulate its own emotions and those of the human. However, in reality the human most likely has more capacities to regulate its own emotions. In order to explore this, additional states in this model may be specified. In the current model, this was not done because for this first step this would have complicated the model too much.

References

1. McRae, K.: Emotion regulation. Emotion **20**(1), 1 (2020). https://doi.org/10.1037/emo000 0703
2. Treur, J.: Network-Oriented Modeling: Addressing Complexity of Cognitive, Affective and Social Interaction. Springer, Cham (2016)
3. Treur, J.: A modeling environment for reified temporal-causal networks: modeling plasticity and metaplasticity in cognitive agent models. In: Baldoni, M., Dastani, M., Liao, B., Sakurai, Y., Wenkstern, R.Z. (eds.) PRIMA 2019. LNCS (LNAI), vol. 11873, pp. 487–495. Springer, Cham (2019). https://doi.org/10.1007/978-3-030-33792-6_33
4. Treur, J.: Network-Oriented Modeling for Adaptive Networks: Designing Higher-Order Adaptive Biological, Mental and Social Network Models. Springer Nature (2020)
5. APA Dictionary of Psychology
6. Oatley, K. (2000). Emotion: Theories
7. Critchley, H.D.: Psychophysiology of neural, cognitive and affective integration: fMRI and autonomic indicants. Int. J. Psychophysiol. **73**(2), 88–94 (2009)
8. Gross, J.J.: Emotion regulation: current status and future prospects. Psychol. Inq. **26**(1), 1–26 (2015). https://doi.org/10.1080/1047840X.2014.940781
9. Phelps, E.A., Delgado, M.R., Nearing, K.I., LeDoux, J.E.: Extinction learning in humans: role of the Amygdala and vmPFC. Neuron **43**(6), 897–905 (2004). https://doi.org/10.1016/j.neuron.2004.08.042
10. Butler, E.A., Randall, A.K.: Emotional coregulation in close relationships. Emot. Rev. **5**(2), 202–210 (2013). https://doi.org/10.1177/1754073912451630
11. Kirkpatrick, S., Gelatt, C.D., Vecchi, M.P.: Optimization by simulated annealing. Science, New Series **220**, 671–680 (1983)

Deep Learning Techniques

Optimizing Deep Learning for Computer-Aided Diagnosis of Lung Diseases: An Automated Method Combining Evolutionary Algorithm and Transfer Learning

Hassen Louati[1]([✉]) [iD], Ali Louati[2] [iD], Elham Kariri[2] [iD], and Slim Bechikh[1] [iD]

[1] SMART Lab, University of Tunis, ISG, Tunis, Tunisia
hassen.louati@stud.acs.upb.ro, slim.bechikh@fsegn.rnu.tn
[2] Department of Information Systems, College of Computer Engineering
and Sciences, Prince Sattam bin Abdulaziz University, Al-Kharj 11942, Saudi Arabia
{a.louati,e.kariri}@psau.edu.sa

Abstract. Recent advancements in Computer Vision have opened up new opportunities for addressing complex healthcare challenges, particularly in the area of lung disease diagnosis. Chest X-rays, a commonly used radiological technique, hold great potential in this regard. To leverage this potential, researchers have proposed the use of deep learning methods for building computer-aided diagnostic systems. However, the design and compression of these systems remains a challenge, as it depends heavily on the expertise of the data scientists. To address this, we propose an automated method that utilizes an evolutionary algorithm (EA) to optimize the design and compression of a convolutional neural network (CNN) for X-Ray image classification. This method is capable of accurately classifying radiography images and detecting possible chest abnormalities and infections, including COVID-19. Additionally, the method incorporates transfer learning, where a pre-trained CNN model on a large dataset of chest X-ray images is fine-tuned for the specific task of detecting COVID-19. This approach can help to reduce the amount of labeled data required for the specific task and improve the overall performance of the model. Our method has been validated through a series of experiments against relevant state-of-the-art architectures.

Keywords: Computer-Aided Diagnosis · Deep Learning ·
Evolutionary algorithms · Transfer Learning

1 Introduction

Chest X-ray is one of the most often used radiological procedures for diagnosing a range of lung diseases. In modern hospitals, X-ray imaging studies are archived in various image archiving and communication systems [22,25]. However, the

N. T. Nguyen et al. (Eds.): ICCCI 2023, CCIS 1864, pp. 83–95, 2023.
https://doi.org/10.1007/978-3-031-41774-0_7

use of these databases, which contain vital image data, to aid deep learning models in the development of computer-assisted diagnostic systems has yet to be thoroughly investigated [23,24].

Several methods for detecting chest radiograph image views have been proposed in recent years, with deep convolutional neural networks (DCNNs) showing promise in various computer vision challenges [6,18]. AlexNet, VggNet, and ResNet, three of the most popular CNN architectures, have demonstrated excellent accuracy in image recognition and identification tasks. However, these designs were created manually, which has led researchers in the fields of machine learning and optimization to believe that better architectures can be discovered using automated methods [22,26].

This task is modeled as an optimization issue and solved with an appropriate search algorithm. The designs are then subjected to the training procedure, which determines the optimal settings for the network's weights, activation functions, and kernels. Prior research has demonstrated that the convolution topology within each block of a CNN corresponds to an optimization problem with a large search space [19]. Unfortunately, there are no clear guidelines for designing an architecture that is suitable for a particular task, which makes the design process subjective and heavily dependent on the knowledge of data scientists.

To address this, we propose an automated method called **CNN-XRAY-E-T**, which combines evolutionary algorithms and transfer learning to optimize the design and compression of CNNs for X-ray image classification and detecting possible chest abnormalities and infections, including COVID-19. The proposed method utilizes evolutionary algorithms to optimize the architecture of a CNN for the task of X-ray image classification. Evolutionary algorithms are powerful optimization techniques that are capable of exploring the large search space of possible CNN architectures thand identifying the optimal one for a given task. The method also incorporates transfer learning, which is a technique that allows a model that has been trained on one task to be reused and fine-tuned for another related task [11]. In this context, transfer learning can be used to pre-train the CNN model on a large dataset of chest X-ray images and then fine-tune the model on the specific task of detecting COVID-19. This can help to reduce the amount of labeled data required for the specific task and improve the overall performance of the model [15]. The proposed method aims to compress the CNN model, which is a crucial technique for minimizing and reducing the size of a deep learning model by eliminating redundant and ineffective components. Nevertheless, compressing deep models without significant loss of precision is an impressive challenge [11]. Recent research has centered on the development of evolutionary algorithms that reduce the computational complexity of CNNs while maintaining their performance. The proposed CNN-XRAY-E-T method has been validated through a series of experiments against relevant state-of-the-art architectures. The outcomes of these experiments indicate that the method is capable of achieving high accuracy in classifying radiography images and detecting potential chest abnormalities and infections, including COVID-19, while simultaneously reducing the number of parameters and computational complexity of the model [3].

The proposed method, CNN-XRAY-E-T, presents a viable option for optimizing the design and compression of CNNs for X-ray image classification and detecting potential chest abnormalities and infections, including COVID-19. By combining evolutionary algorithms and transfer learning, the method is able to explore the huge search space of different CNN designs, choose the ideal one for a particular task, and reduce the number of parameters and computing complexity of the model. This strategy can enhance the diagnostic procedure for lung disorders, such as COVID-19, and make it more accessible to hospitals with low resources.

The following is a summary of this work's key contributions:

- Proposing an automated method, CNN-Xray-D-C, for optimizing the design and compression of CNNs for X-ray image classification and detecting possible chest abnormalities and infections, including COVID-19.
- Incorporating evolutionary algorithms and transfer learning to improve the performance of the CNN model and reduce the amount of labeled data required for the specific task.
- Justifying the suggested technique against relevant state-of-the-art architectures, demonstrating great accuracy in categorizing radiography images and identifying possible chest anomalies and infections, including COVID-19.
- Reducing the number of parameters and computational complexity of the model, making it more accessible to hospitals with limited resources.

2   Related Work

In recent years, the use of CNNs for the classification of X-ray images has gained a lot of attention in the field of medical diagnosis. This approach has proven to be very effective in identifying thoracic diseases by analyzing chest X-rays. Researchers have proposed various methods to improve the accuracy of this technique. For instance, Wang et al. developed a semi-supervised framework for multi-label classification of X-ray images [1], Islam et al. created advanced network architectures for improved classification [2],Rajpurkar et al. discovered that a standard DenseNet architecture was more accurate at detecting pneumonia than radiologists [3]. Yao et al. proposed a method for maximizing performance by optimizing label dependencies [4]. Irvin et al. created CheXNet, a deep learning network that makes optimization more tractable by employing dense connections and batch normalization [5]. Prabira et al. used pretrained CNN models to extract deep features, which were then fed into an SVM classifier. These studies demonstrate the diagnostic potential of CNNs in the field of thoracic disease and the need for additional research in this area.

In recent years, the use of evolutionary optimization for the design of CNNs has gained significant attention in the field of machine learning. This approach has been shown to be successful in various tasks due to its global search capabilities, which allow it to avoid local optima while finding a near-globally optimal solution [7]. Researchers have proposed different methods to optimize the structure and parameters of CNNs using evolutionary algorithms. Several studies have investigated the optimization of CNNs using evolutionary algorithms. Shinaozaki et al. utilized a genetic algorithm to optimize a DNN's structure and parameters [7]. CMA-ES, a continuous optimizer, converted discrete structural variables to real values through an indirect encoding [8]. Xie et al. improved recognition accuracy by representing the network topology as a binary string [8]. However, the high computing cost of this approach limited its use to small-scale data sets. Sun et al. proposed an evolutionary method for optimizing CNNs for image classification applications, including the development of a novel weight initialization method, an encoding scheme for variable-length chromosomes, a slack binary tournament selection technique, and an efficient fitness assessment technique [9]. Lu et al. modeled the architectural search problem as a multi-objective optimization problem, balancing classification error rate and computational complexity, as quantified by FLOPS, using the NSGA-II algorithm [10].

Channel pruning is a technique that aims to reduce the number of channels in the input supplied to the intermediate layers of a CNN model [11]. By decreasing the number of channels, it is possible to reduce computation and storage needs without compromising the model's accuracy. There have been several channel pruning techniques proposed in recent years, including training-based methods that add regularization terms to weights during the training stage [11,12]. Some studies have also focused on pruning pre-trained models with different criteria [13], without considering the pre-training procedure. Despite these efforts, there is still room for improvement when it comes to reducing model redundancy. Furthermore, most research has focused on accelerating networks during the inference stage, with little attention paid to off-line pruning efficiency [11–13]. Recent techniques have also focused on inference-based channel pruning, which define selection criteria to identify and remove unnecessary channels [12,14]. Li et al. proposed removing filters with lower weights, which are assumed to yield weaker activations [13]. However, this criterion may remove some important filters, especially in thin layers. Hu et al. Thinet advocated using a greedy strategy to eliminate filters based on statistical data acquired from the next layer [11]. However, a greedy strategy may not be the optimal answer for combinatorial optimization problems, particularly if the solution space is expansive. In addition, its off-line pruning technique is time-consuming since each iteration traverses the whole training set.

Transfer learning (TL) is a technique that allows for the transfer of knowledge from one task to another, similar task in order to improve performance [15]. It is based on the idea that people can accomplish similar tasks by applying previous knowledge. According to Pan and Yang, TL is defined as using knowledge from a source domain and task to improve learning of a target prediction function in a target domain and task. Formally, a domain is made up of a feature space X and a marginal probability distribution $P(X)$, where $X = x_1, ..., x_n \epsilon X$. Given a certain domain represented by $Do = X, P(X)$, a task is represented by $T = Y, f(.)$ where Y represents a label space and $f(.)$ represents an objective prediction function. The goal of transfer learning is to "increase learning of the target prediction function $f_T(.)$ in D_T by leveraging knowledge in the source domain D_S and the learning task T_S. In the context of CNNs, TL can be applied by transferring knowledge at the parameter level [16]. For example, in medical image classification, a CNN model that has been trained on a natural image classification task (source task) can be used to improve performance on a medical image classification task (target task) when labels are available in both domains [5]. CNNs have been used successfully in various medical applications, such as the detection of brain tumors from MRI images, the recognition of breast cancer, and the classification of illnesses from X-ray images [17].

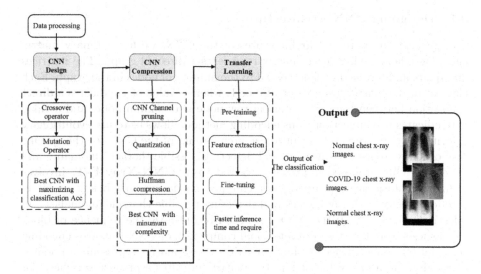

Fig. 1. The Operational Mechanism of **CNN-Xray-E-T** on X-Ray Images.

3   Proposed System

The following question motivates our strategy:

- What is the optimal way to design and compress a CNN architecture for X-ray image classification using evolutionary optimization and transfer learning?
- How can transfer learning be applied to improve the performance of CNNs for X-ray image classification in detecting COVID-19 and other chest abnormalities?

To answer this research question, we propose the **CNN-Xray-E-T** method, which utilizes evolutionary optimization and transfer learning to create a robust CNN architecture for analyzing X-ray images for anomaly detection and infectious disease monitoring, particularly for the detection of COVID-19 and other thoracic pathologies. The method first maximizes accuracy by identifying the best graph topology sequence for X-ray image classification, and then it minimizes the computational complexity of CNNs by optimizing the number of hyperparameters chosen for the convolution layer using methods of a CNN architecture compression process. Additionally, by incorporating transfer learning, the approach utilizes pre-trained CNN models on a large dataset of chest X-ray images to fine-tune for the specific task of detecting COVID-19, which helps to reduce the amount of labeled data required and improve the overall performance of the model. As shown in Fig. 1, our proposed approach **CNN-Xray-E-T**, combines evolutionary optimization, compression and transfer learning techniques to design an efficient CNN architecture for X-ray image classification. The details of this approach will be discussed in the following sections.

3.1   Designing CNN Architecture

To represent the potential architectures of the CNN, we use a binary matrix encoding scheme, where each matrix represents a directed graph. The matrices are square and have a dimension equal to the number of nodes in the graph. Each element in the matrix has a value of 0 or 1, where a value of 1 indicates a direct connection between the corresponding row node and column node, and a value of 0 indicates no connection. This encoding method allows us to use evolutionary algorithms to explore and optimize the architecture of the CNN for the specific task of X-ray image classification and detecting possible thoracic anomalies and infections. Our proposed approach, referred to as **CNN-Xray-E-T**, involves utilizing evolutionary optimization techniques to design an efficient architecture for classifying X-ray images and detecting possible thoracic anomalies and infections, such as COVID-19. Our solution to optimize the sequence of block topologies and reduce the computational complexity of CNNs involves encoding the solution as a sequence of binary matrices. Each matrix represents a possible directed graph and a value of 1 in the matrix indicates a predecessor-successor relationship between the row node and column node, while a value of 0 means they are not connected. To ensure that the solution follows certain constraints, the active convolution nodes must have at least one preceding node, either from a previous layer or as an input node. Additionally, each active convolution node must have predecessors in its preceding layers. The first convolution node must only have a single predecessor, serving as the input node, and the output node of the last convolution node must have a single successor node.

Our approach utilizes a two-point crossover operator to generate variation in all parts of the solution. This operator takes in two parent solutions, which are represented as sets of binary strings. It then selects two cutting points on each parent and swaps the bits between them to create two new offspring solutions. However, sometimes the crossover operator may generate solutions that do not meet the feasibility constraints outlined previously. To address this, we use a local adjustment process to repair any infeasible solutions created by the crossover. Similarly, the mutation operator is applied by converting the solution into a binary string before using a one-point mutation method.

3.2   Compressing CNN and Transfer Learning

Our proposed technique employs genetic algorithms to determine the optimal channels to prune in each layer of the CNN. This is a challenging task, as the number of channels available in each layer can vary, and determining which channels to keep and which to discard can greatly impact the overall performance of the model. The genetic algorithm works as follows:

- Only a limited number of chromosomes, C, are considered for each layer with a size of LLC, meaning only a subset of the total 2^C possibilities are used.
- Each chromosome, M_i, is encoded as a binary sequence of length C. The probability of a 1 or 0 being present is determined by a Bernoulli distribution with a mean of p, where p represents the desired fraction of channels to be pruned.
- For instance, if there are 3 channels, the possible initializations are $1, 1, 0$, $0, 1, 1$, and $1, 0, 1$, with a p value of 0.666. This would result in pruning the first kernel channel while preserving the other two.

To introduce genetic variation into our population, we utilize the two-point crossover operator. This allows for changes across all chromosomes at once. The parent solutions are represented as sets of binary strings and two offspring solutions are created by exchanging the bits between two cutting points. This method is selected to maintain as much of the chromosome's local structure and solution feasibility as possible.

The mutation operator converts the solution into a binary string, then applies one-point mutation. Regarding the Fitness Function:

- The goal of the current technique is to minimize the error by identifying the optimal pruned chromosome (Wp) through the use of a layer-wise error difference. This is achieved by finding the solution that decreases the term E(Yp) using an equation.

$$E(Y) = \frac{1}{N} \sum_{i=1}^{N} \|Y - Y_i\| \tag{1}$$

- However, through the application of the Taylor expansion of the equation and using approximations as described in "Optimal Brain Damage (OBD)," the goal function is simplified to a more manageable form.

$$\delta E = \frac{1}{2} \delta W^T H \delta W \tag{2}$$

To decrease the storage size of the weights file even further, we use quantization, a method that converts 32-bit floating point values into 5-bit integer levels. This process distributes the values linearly between the minimum and maximum weights (Wmin and Wmax), as it has been found to produce more accurate results compared to density-based quantization. This is crucial as low probability weights with high values can have a significant impact and may be underestimated if quantized to a lesser value, resulting in a compressed sparse row of quantized weights. Another compression technique, Huffman compression, can also be applied to further reduce the size of the weights file, but requires additional hardware, such as a Huffman decompressor and a converter for the compressed sparse row to weights matrix.

After performing the weight pruning and quantization techniques, the next step is to utilize transfer learning. This involves using the pre-trained, compressed model as a starting point for a new task, such as classifying X-ray images for a specific disease. The convolutional layers of the pre-trained model can be used as a feature extractor, where the weights of these layers are kept fixed and only the fully connected layers are retrained using the new dataset. This allows the model to utilize the generic features learned from the pre-training task, while fine-tuning them for the specific task at hand. Additionally, transfer learning can also be applied at the feature level, where the output of the pre-trained model's convolutional layers can be used as input for a new classifier, without retraining the entire model. This approach can also be useful when the amount of labeled data for the new task is limited.

4   Experiments Study

4.1   Configuration and Setup

The Chest X-Ray14 dataset is comprised of 112,120 frontal-view radiographs and X-Ray images of 30,805 distinct patients. The images were obtained through the use of natural language processing techniques on radiological reports stored in hospital image archiving and communication systems. The data can be found at the following link: https://www.kaggle.com/paultimothymooney/chest-xray-pneumonia. In addition to this dataset, X-Ray images of COVID-19 patients were obtained from Dr. Joseph Cohen's open-source GitHub repository: https://github.com/ieee80 23/covid-chestxray-dataset. To evaluate the algorithms being compared, the parameters were determined through trial and error, and the TensorFlow framework was implemented in Python 3.5 and analyzed using eight Nvidia 2080Ti GPU cards. The accuracy of the models was established through the use of the holdout validation technique, which involves randomly selecting 80% of the data for training and 20% for testing. The settings used in the experiments include a batch size of 128, 50 or 350 epochs, a learning rate of 0.1, momentum of 0.9, and weight decay of 0.0001 for gradient descent. The search strategy includes 40 generations, a population size of 60, a crossover probability of 0.9, and a mutation probability of 0.1. These settings were used to optimize the CNN architectures generated from the test data.

Table 1. Obtained results for AUROC and number of parameters on ChestX-Ray14 dataset.

Method	Search Method	AUROC Test(%)	#Params
Yao et al. [4]	manual	79.8	–
Wang et al. [1]	manual	73.8	–
CheXNet [5]	manual	84.4	7.0M
Google AutoML [2]	RL	79.7	–
LEAF [20]	EA	84.3	–
NSGANet-X [21]	EA	84.6	2.2M
CNN-XRAY [22]	EA	87.12	5.1M
CNN-Xray-D-C [18]	EA	86.98	1.1M
CNN-Xray-E-T	EA	89.8	1.0M

4.2   Results and Discussion

Table 1 appears to be a comparison of different methods for X-Ray image classification using different search methods (manual, RL, or EA) and the obtained results in terms of AUROC (Area Under the Receiver Operating Characteristic Curve) and the number of parameters (#Params). The study, **CNN-Xray-E-T** is considered the most impactful in the three main categories of techniques for designing CNNs. Table 1 showcases the comparison of the various CNN design methods when applied to X-Ray images. As we can see, the manual approaches, such as Yao et al. and Wang et al., have an AUROC range between 79.8% and 87.12%, and the number of parameters range from 2.2M to 7.0M. On the other hand, the performance of Google AutoML is lower, with an AUROC of only 79.7%. When looking at the evolutionary approaches, we see that the AUROC values are higher, with LEAF achieving 84.3%, NSGANet-X achieving 84.6%, and CNN-XRAY achieving 87.12%. However, the most impressive result is from **CNN-Xray-E-T**, which uses an evolutionary algorithm combined with transfer learning. This approach is capable of automatically designing a CNN architecture that produces high AUROC values of 89.8% while using fewer parameters, only 1.0M.

The significance of **CNN-Xray-E-T** is reinforced by Fig. 2, which highlights its ability to detect multiple diseases including COVID-19 with a high level of accuracy and using fewer parameters. This is demonstrated through a comparison of its disease curve and AUROC with other methods. Overall, **CNN-Xray-E-T** demonstrates its superiority over other methods in terms of both accuracy and efficiency. Table 1 showcases the results of various CNN designs applied to X-Ray images. The AUROC of manually designed CNNs ranges from 79.8 to 87.12%, with parameters ranging from 2.2M to 7.0M. Google AutoML, a non-manual method, produced the lowest AUROC of 79.7%. The evolutionary methods showed superior performance, with AUROC values of 84.3% for LEAF, 84.6% for NSGANet-X, and 87.12% for CNN-XRAY. Among these,

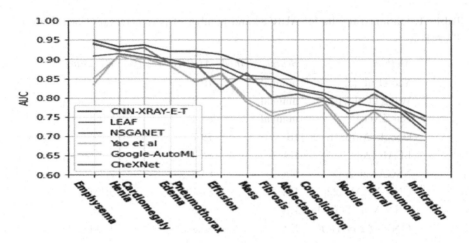

Fig. 2. Comparison of Class-Wise Mean Test AUROC in ChestX-Ray14 Using **CNN-Xray-E-T** Multi-Label Classification Performance with Peer Works.

CNN-Xray-E-T performed best with an AUROC of 89.8% and the least number of parameters at 1.0M. These results suggest that automatically designing CNNs with evolutionary methods can produce high AUROC values and be more efficient in terms of the number of parameters used.

Manual CNN design is challenging due to the vast number of possible architectures, requiring high expertise and time investment. To overcome these difficulties, RL-based and evolutionary methods have been developed to automate the design process. Evolutionary methods have proven to be more effective than RL-based methods, which can get stuck in local optima, because they have global search capabilities and allow for the acceptance of less-performing individuals through mating selection. Optimizing the network architecture plays a critical role in improving classification accuracy as it governs the interactions between nodes in the neural network

Furthermore, incorporating transfer learning into the design of **CNN-Xray-E-T** has greatly improved its performance compared to the other approaches. Transfer learning allows the utilization of pre-trained models as a starting point, reducing the time and computational resources required for training the network. Additionally, it provides the network with prior knowledge and understanding of image features, which can greatly improve the accuracy of the final model. This highlights the importance of transfer learning in the design of deep learning models and the positive impact it can have on the performance and efficiency of the model. The results from Table 1 demonstrate the effectiveness of **CNN-Xray-E-T**, which has achieved the highest AUROC values while having a relatively low number of parameters compared to other methods (Table 2).

The **CNN-Xray-D-C** method shows promising results in reducing the complexity of CNN designs while preserving a high level of accuracy. The design and compression process of **CNN-Xray-D-C** takes into account only the accuracy

Table 2. Obtained accuracy values on Chest X-Ray images.

Detection Method	Test Acc (%)	Sensitivity	Specificity
Deep features-based SVM	95.4	97.29	93.47
ResNet101	89.26	91.23	87.29
Inceptionv3	91.08	91.11	91.05
GoogleNet	91.44	89.82	93.05
VGG16	92.76	97.47	88.05
VGG19	92.91	95.11	90.70
XceptionNet	93.92	94.76	93.05
Inceptionresnetv2	93.32	94.76	93.05
AlexNet	93.32	93.41	93.23
DenseNet201	93.88	94.35	93.41
CNN-Xray-D-C	97.82	98.82	96.28

and computational complexity of the DCNN, thus making it possible to obtain high-quality results even without additional regularization. This makes **CNN-Xray-D-C** a standout, as it's the only system that combines the design and compression of CNN architecture for detecting COVID-19 using Evolutionary Algorithms. However, **CNN-Xray-E-T** takes this a step further by incorporating transfer learning, which has the potential to enhance the overall performance of the CNN. Transfer learning involves using pre-trained models on large datasets as a starting point for training on a smaller, similar task. This allows the CNN to leverage the knowledge gained from previous tasks, making the training process faster and more effective. The combination of design, compression, and transfer learning in **CNN-Xray-E-T** makes it a more superior method compared to **CNN-Xray-D-C** in detecting COVID-19 infections.

5   Conclusion

The design of a suitable DCNN architecture is crucial for obtaining high accuracy in the classification of thoracic diseases, including COVID-19. To address this issue, several recent works have proposed Evolutionary Algorithm-based innovative ways for decreasing the computational complexity of DCNNs (EAs). Although channel pruning has been commonly employed to simplify DCNNs, it may produce an extremely high-dimensional space, which may compromise the model's performance. We present a new method for developing DCNN architectures in an effort to overcome this difficulty. Our method for diagnosing COVID-19 and other thoracic disorders is based on an evolutionary algorithm that strives for the best possible sequence of block topologies. Furthermore, we incorporate channel pruning, quantization, and other compression techniques to reduce the complexity of the resulting architecture while maintaining high accuracy. The proposed approach demonstrates promising results in detecting thoracic diseases, and outperforms other state-of-the-art methods in terms of accuracy and computational efficiency.

To further enhance the performance of our proposed approach, we suggest several future directions for research. First, incorporating additional knowledge such as domain-specific information, prior medical knowledge, and other related information can further improve the accuracy of the model. Additionally, exploring other advanced techniques such as neural architecture search and reinforcement learning can provide further improvement in the design of the DCNN architecture. Finally, evaluating our approach on other large-scale medical imaging datasets and other thoracic diseases can provide more comprehensive insights into the performance of our approach and its potential applications in the medical field.

Funding. Deputyship for Research & Innovation, Ministry of Education in Saudi Arabia. Project No. (IF2/PSAU/2022/01/21577).

References

1. Wang, X., Peng, Y., Lu, L., Lu, Z., Bagheri, M., Summers, R.M.: ChestX-ray8: hospital-scale chest x-ray database and benchmarks on weakly-supervised classification and localization of common thorax diseases. In IEEE Conference on Computer Vision and Pattern Recognition, pp. 3462–3471 (2017)
2. Islam, M.T., Aowal, M.A., Minhaz, A.T., Ashraf, K.: Abnormality detection and localization in chest X-rays using deep convolutional neural networks. CoRR, abs/1705.09850 (2017)
3. Rajpurkar, P., et al.: Deep learning for chest radiograph diagnosis: a retrospective comparison of the CheXNeXt algorithm to practicing radiologists. PLoS Med. **15**(11), 1–17 (2018)
4. Yao, L., Poblenz, E., Dagunts, D., Covington, B., Bernard, D., Lyman, K.: Learning to diagnose from scratch by exploiting dependencies among labels. CoRR, abs/1710.1050 (2017)
5. Irvin, J., et al.: Chexpert: a large chest radiograph dataset with uncertainty labels and expert comparison. In: Thirty-Third AAAI Conference on Artificial Intelligence, pp. 590–597 (2019)
6. Louati, H., Bechikh, S., Louati, A., et al.: Joint design and compression of convolutional neural networks as a Bi-level optimization problem. Neural Comput. Appl. (2022). https://doi.org/10.1007/s00521-022-07331-0
7. Shinozaki, T., Watanabe, S.: Structure discovery of deep neural network based on evolutionary algorithms. In: 2015 IEEE International Conference on Acoustics, Speech and Signal Processing, pp. 4979–4983 (2015)
8. Xie, S., Girshick, R., Dollar, P., Tu, Z., He, K.: Aggregated residual transformations for deep neural networks. In: IEEE Conference on Computer Vision and Pattern Recognition, pp. 1492–1500 (2017)
9. Sun, Y., Xue, B., Zhang, M., Yen, G.G.: Completely automated CNN architecture design based on blocks. IEEE Trans. Neural Netw. Learn. Syst. **33**(2), 1242–1254 (2019)
10. Lu, Z., et al.: Nsga-net: neural architecture search using multi-objective genetic algorithm. In: Genetic and Evolutionary Computation Conference, pp. 419–427 (2019)

11. Luo, J., Wu, J., Lin, W.: Thinet: a filter level pruning method for deep neural network compression, arXiv preprint arXiv: 1707.06342 (2017)
12. He, Y., Zhang, X., Sun, J.: Channel pruning for accelerating very deep neural networks. In: International Conference on Computer Vision (ICCV), vol. 2, p. 6 (2017)
13. Liu, Z., Li, J., Shen, Z., Huang, G., Yan, S., Zhang, C.: Learning efficient convolutional networks through network slimming. In: International Conference on Computer Vision (ICCV), pp. 2755–2763 (2017)
14. Hu, H., Peng, R., Tai, Y., Tang, C.: Network trimming: A datadriven neuron pruning approach towards efficient deep architectures, arXiv preprint arXiv: 1607.03250 (2016)
15. Pan, S.J., Yang, Q.: A survey on transfer learning. IEEE Trans. Knowl. Data Eng. **22**, 1345–59 (2010)
16. Yao, L., Poblenz, E., Dagunts, D., Covington, B., Bernard, D., Lyman, K.: Learning to diagnose from scratch by exploiting dependencies among labels. CoRR, vol. abs/1710.1050 (2017)
17. Sethy, P.K., Behera, S.K.: Detection of coronavirus disease (covid-19) based on deep features. Int. J. Math. Eng. Manage. Sci. **5**(4), 643–651 (2020)
18. Louati, H., Louati, A., Bechikh, S., Ben Said, L.: Design and compression study for convolutional neural networks based on evolutionary optimization for thoracic x-ray image classification. In: ICCCI 2022 (2022). https://doi.org/10.1007/978-3-031-16014-1_23
19. Louati, H., Bechikh, S., Louati, A., Aldaej, A., Said, L.B.: Evolutionary optimization of convolutional neural network architecture design for thoracic x-ray image classification. In: Fujita, H., Selamat, A., Lin, J.C.-W., Ali, M. (eds.) IEA/AIE 2021. LNCS (LNAI), vol. 12798, pp. 121–132. Springer, Cham (2021). https://doi.org/10.1007/978-3-030-79457-6_11
20. Liang, J., Meyerson, E., Hodjat, B., Fink, D., Mutch, K., Miikkulainen, R.: Evolutionary neural automl for deep learning (2019). https://doi.org/10.1145/3321707.3321721
21. Lu, Z., et al.: Multi-criterion evolutionary design of deep convolutional neural networks. ArXiv: abs/1912.01369 (2019)
22. Louati, H., Bechikh, S., Louati, A., Aldaej, A., Said, L.B.: Evolutionary optimization for CNN compression using thoracic x-ray image classification. In: Fujita, H., Fournier-Viger, P., Ali, M., Wang, Y. (eds.) IEA/AIE 2022. LNCS, vol. 13343, pp. 112–123. Springer, Cham (2022). https://doi.org/10.1007/978-3-031-08530-7_10
23. Louati, H., Louati, A., Bechikh, S., et al.: Topology optimization search of deep convolution neural networks for CT and X-ray image classification. BMC Med. Imaging **22**, 120 (2022). https://doi.org/10.1186/s12880-022-00847-w
24. Louati, H., Bechikh, S., Louati, A., Hung, C.C., Ben Said, L.: Deep convolutional neural network architecture design as a bi-level optimization problem. Neurocomputing **439**, 44–62 (2021). https://doi.org/10.1016/j.neucom.2021.01.094
25. Louati, H., Bechikh, S., Louati, A., Aldaej, A., Said, L.B.: Evolutionary optimization of convolutional neural network architecture design for thoracic x-ray image classification. In: Fujita, H., Selamat, A., Lin, J.C.W., Ali, M. (eds.) IEA/AIE 2021. LNCS, vol. 12798, pp. 121–132. Springer, Cham (2021). https://doi.org/10.1007/978-3-030-79457-6_11
26. Louati, H., Louati, A., Bechikh, S., et al.: Embedding channel pruning within the CNN architecture design using a bi-level evolutionary approach. J. Supercomput. (2023). https://doi.org/10.1007/s11227-023-05273-5

Deep Bidirectional LSTM Network Learning-Based Sentiment Analysis for Tunisian Dialectical Facebook Content During the Spread of the Coronavirus Pandemic

Samawel Jaballi[1,2,3]([✉]), Manar Joundy Hazar[1,2,4], Salah Zrigui[5], Henri Nicolas[3], and Mounir Zrigui[1,2]

[1] Department of Computer Science, Faculty of Sciences of Monastir, University of Monastir, Monastir, Tunisia
samawel.jaballi@u-bordeaux.fr
[2] Research Laboratory in Algebra Numbers Theory and Intelligent Systems, Monastir, Tunisia
[3] LaBRI, University of Bordeaux, Talence, France
[4] Computer Center, University of Al -Qadisiyah, Qadisiyah, Iraq
[5] Laboratory LIG, CS 40700, 38058 Cedex Grenoble, France

Abstract. Sentiment analysis (SA) is a multidisciplinary field that aims to predict sentiment tone or attitude expressed in a text, SA using social media data has become a popular topic especially during critical events such as natural disasters, social movements and recently the spread of the Coronavirus Pandemic. Sentiments can be expressed explicitly or implicitly in text and identifying these expressions can be challenging. SA in Tunisian dialect is particularly difficult due to the complexity of the language, its morphological richness and the lack of contextual information. Recently, deep learning (DL) models have been widely adopted in the field of SA, especially in the context of Arabic SA. These models, such as Bi-directional LSTM networks (Bi-LSTM) and LSTM networks, have shown to achieve high accuracy levels in sentiment classification tasks for Arabic and dialectical text. Despite the successes of DL models in Arabic SA, there are still areas for improvement in terms of contextual information and implicit mining expressed in different real-world cases. In this paper, the authors introduce a deep Bi-LSTM network to ameliorate Tunisian SA during the spread of the Coronavirus Pandemic. The experimental results on Tunisian benchmark SA dataset demonstrate that our model achieves significant improvements over the state-of-art DL models and the baseline traditional machine learning (ML) methods. We believe that this contribution will benefit anyone working on Tunisian pandemic management or doing comparative work between Tunisian and other jurisdictions, which can provide valuable insights into how the public is responding to the crisis and help guide pandemic management decisions.

Keywords: COVID-19 · Social Media · Sentiment Analysis · Tunisian Dialect · Deep Learning · Bi-LSTM · Text Processing · Pandemic governance · Public Health

© The Author(s), under exclusive license to Springer Nature Switzerland AG 2023
N. T. Nguyen et al. (Eds.): ICCCI 2023, CCIS 1864, pp. 96–109, 2023.
https://doi.org/10.1007/978-3-031-41774-0_8

1 Introduction

Arabic is the official language of 27 countries and spoken by over 400 million people. The language has two commonly used varieties: Modern Standard Arabic (MSA) and Dialectal Arabic (DA). MSA is used in formal written and oral communication, while DA is used in informal exchanges [1]. DA is divided into two main groups: Middle Eastern (Mashriq) and North African (Maghrebi) dialects. Mashriq dialects include Egyptian, Levantine, and Gulf dialects, while Maghrebi dialects include Algerian, Tunisian, and Moroccan dialects [2].

DA is prevalent on social media and microblogging channels, but it poses challenges for thematic classification and SA [6]. These challenges include a lack of resources for these dialects, as some dialects are better researched than others. Additionally, Arabic is a morphologically rich and complex language with complex morphosyntactic conventions, irregular forms, and numerous dialectal variants with no spelling norms. This makes it difficult to learn robust general models about Arabic text without proper processing. Furthermore, there are fewer resources available for Arabic sentiment analysis, such as sentiment dictionaries and annotated corpora, compared to French or English. These challenges have led to a significant interest in Arabic sentiment analysis [3].

SA is the process of identifying and extracting specific sentiments from text using Natural Language Processing (NLP), computational linguistics, and data mining techniques. It can be applied at different levels of analysis, such as document level, sentence level, aspect level, and word level. In addition, SA in Arabic dialectical text is an important and timely topic, as Arabic is one of the most widely spoken languages in the world and is the official or native language of many countries [4].

Tunisian dialect is a subset of the Arabic dialects spoken in the Maghreb region. The goal of this work is to develop an efficient SA tool for Tunisian textual productions on Facebook networks during the spread of Coronavirus Pandemic. Despite recent progress in the study of this dialect, there is still important work to be done. However, the development of these tools faces several challenges, including a limited number and availability of resources and a lack of standard linguistic rules for this dialect [5]. This makes the task of sentiment classification more complicated as there is no agreement on semantic analysis conventions [3].

In our approach, we have proposed a deep Bi-LSTM sentiment classification model to improve the state-of-the-art performance of Tunisian dialectical SA. Our contribution can be summarized as follows:

1. We examine the benefits of our pre-processing method such as tokenization, punctuation removal, light stemming and Latin character removal.
2. Our work has used the bidirectional Deep LSTM with the ability to extract contextual information from the feature sequences of Tunisian dialectical sentences.
3. Our Bi-LSTM model significantly outperforms other DL models and the baseline traditional ML algorithms in terms of accuracy and F1-measure on Tunisian benchmark SA dataset.

The rest of this paper is organized as follows. We will first provide an overview of some related recent work on approaches and methods of Arabic and Tunisian dialectical

SA. Then, in Sect. 3, we will detail our Tunisian dialectical SA system using the deep Bi-LSTM learning model. Section 4 provides the experimental study, the results obtained and the discussion. Finally, Sect. 5 gives the conclusion of this paper and highlights future works.

2   Related Work

SA aims to classify subjective texts into two or more categories. The most obvious are negative and positive. We refer to this problem as Binary Sentiment Analysis. Some works contain a third category for neutral text. We refer to this problem as Ternary Sentiment Analysis. A final option is to consider sentiment based on a rank score or rating system, such as the 5-star rating system. This is known as Multi-Way Sentiment Analysis [6]. Thus, ML, lexicon-based, hybrid and DL approaches are among the existing research on Arabic and Tunisian dialectical SA approaches.

2.1   Machine Learning Approach

ML is the most applied approach in SA, where algorithms are trained on labeled data to predict the sentiment of a given text. Shoukry et al. [7] performed SA of tweets written in Egyptian dialects and MSA. They have collected 1,000 tweets, consisting of 500 positive and 500 negative tweets, and they have used standard n-gram features. Then, they have experimented with two classifiers, Support Vector Machines (SVM) and Naive Bayes (NB), to classify the sentiment of the tweets.

In [8], authors have created a SA method for both informal Arabic and MSA to assess the sentiment in social media. They used the K-Nearest Neighbors (KNN) algorithm as a classifier to classify 1,080 Arabic reviews from social media and news websites. In [9], authors have used two ML algorithms, SVM and NB to perform SA on Arabic reviews and comments from the Yahoo Maktoob website. Abdul-Mageed et al. [10] have created a supervised system for Arabic social media named SAMAR. The system was built using an SVM classifier.

In [11], authors have presented the Tunisian SA Corpus (TSAC[1]), which focuses on the Tunisian dialect. They have collected 17,000 user comments from the official Facebook accounts of Tunisian radio and television stations. To test the performance of their collected corpus, they have employed three ML algorithms, Multilayer Perceptron, Multinomial Naive Bayes and SVM.

Salamah et al. [12] have collected 340,000 tweets in the Kuwaiti dialect. To measure the performance of the suggested corpus, they have used three ML algorithms, Random Forests (RF), SVM J48, and Decision Trees (DT).

2.2   Lexicon-Based Approach

The lexicon-based approach also known as knowledge-based approach is another commonly used method for Arabic sentiment analysis, especially when there is limited

---

[1] https://github.com/fbougares/TSAC.

labeled data available. It involves using pre-existing sentiment dictionaries containing words and their associated sentiment scores to identify and classify the sentiment of a given text. The sentiment dictionaries used in this approach are created manually by annotating words with sentiment polarity (positive, negative, neutral) or assigning them a sentiment orientation score (score between 0 and 5). The overall sentiment of a text is then computed by aggregating the sentiment scores of the individual words in the text [13]. This method can be fast and effective, but its accuracy may be limited by the quality and completeness of the sentiment dictionary used.

In [14], authors have presented a system consisting of two parts. The first part is a free online game that aims to build a lexicon of positive and negative words, while the second part is a SA system that classifies reviews based on their sentiment, using the lexicon created in the first part. This approach leverages the knowledge of users who participate in the online game to build the sentiment dictionary, which can be used for SA in the second part of the system. Al-Ayyoub et al. [15] have created a lexicon of 120,000-word Arabic linguistic terms by collecting a large number of articles from the Arabic news website. This lexicon includes Arabic linguistic features, which can be used in SA to classify the sentiment of text written in Arabic, as it provides a comprehensive list of words and their sentiment scores.

In [16], authors have proposed to investigate the impact of pre-processing techniques on SA of Tunisian dialect. They have compared the performance of two SA models, a lexicon-based model and a supervised ML-based model (SVM and NB). The results showed that including pre-processing methods such as emoji handling, negation tagging, and stemming improved the performance of the SA of Tunisian dialect.

In [17], authors have proposed a subjectivity SA system for Egyptian tweets and have developed a new Arabic lexicon by combining two existing standard Arabic lexicons (ArabSenti and MPQA) with two Egyptian Arabic lexicons. The new lexicon consisted of 900 tweets (300 positive, 300 negative, and 300 neutral) and the results showed that their lexicon-based model outperformed with an accuracy of 87%. This study highlights the importance of considering dialect-specific lexicons in SA and the potential improvement it can bring to the performance of SA models.

2.3 Hybrid Approach

The hybrid approach merges the strengths of both ML and lexicon-based approaches. Briefly, it leverages the high accuracy of ML and the stability of the lexicon-based approach to improve overall performance. Authors in [18] have proposed a hybrid SA method that combined lexicon-based and ML approaches. They used the SentiStrength English lexicon for translation and applied Maximum Entropy (ME) and KNN for classification. In [19], authors have developed a semantic model called ATSA (Arabic Twitter Sentiment Analysis) that uses supervised ML algorithms (NB, SVM and semantic analysis) and a vocabulary built from freely available dictionaries like Arabic WordNet. The performance of the model improved compared to the basic bag-of-words representation with an increase of 5.78% for the NB classifier and 4.48% for the SVM classifier.

Soliman et al. [20] have tested and evaluated different configurations to develop an Arabic SA tool. They have conducted three experiments. The first experiment used the SVM-based approach, the second experiment used only the lexicon-based approach with

SSWIL lexicon, and the third experiment combined both the SSWIL lexicon and the SVM-based approach. In [21], authors have tackled the SA of dialectical Arabic words and MSA by using the SVM and NB classifiers. To handle dialectical words, they have employed a dialect vocabulary that maps dialectical words to their corresponding MSA words.

2.4 Deep Learning Approach

DL models are based on neural network architectures to model high-level abstractions in data and to automatically extract features and perform complex tasks such as SA [22]. These models often outperform traditional ML methods in terms of accuracy and can handle noisy and unstructured data, making them well suited for SA tasks. Only a few studies have explored DL models in Arabic dialect text and Tunisian dialect.

Masmoudi et al. [23] have created a corpus of 43K comments in Tunisian dialect from Tunisian supermarkets' Facebook pages and have tested its performance using CNN, LSTM, and Bi-LSTM models. The best results were achieved by LSTM and Bi-LSTM, with an F-Measure of 87%. In [24], Jerbi et al. have proposed a DL approach for SA of code-switched Tunisian Dialect. They have evaluated the performance of four variants of RNNs: LSTM, Bi-LSTM, deep LSTM, and deep Bi-LSTM. The results, based on the TSAC corpus [11], showed that a deep LSTM model achieved the highest accuracy of 90% compared to other DL models.

Authors in [25] have introduced the TUNIZI[2] corpus as a SA dataset for Tunisian Arabizi[3]. The corpus consists of 17K comments collected from YouTube, written using Latin characters and numerals. The dataset is balanced with 47% positive and 53% negative comments and has been preprocessed for analytical studies and NLP tasks. In [26], Bsir et al. have explored the Bi-LSTM learning model for Arabic SA with the ability of extracting the semantic information to predict the sentiment of Arabic text. Experiments showed that their proposed model achieves significant improvements in the Accuracy and F1-measure results over the existing models and it can handle both forward and backward dependencies from feature sequences.

3   Proposed Methodology

Basically, our approach consists of three major phases: Firstly, the data exploration phase, where we explore an online corpus of Tunisian Facebook comments during the spread of Coronavirus Pandemic. During this phase, we thoroughly analyze the data to gain insights and understanding of the content. Secondly, the data pre-processing phase, where we apply various techniques to preprocess the collected data and make it suitable for further analysis. This involves tasks such as cleaning the text, removing irrelevant information, handling dialectical words, and performing other necessary transformations. Finally, the model training phase where we train and test our deep Bi-LSTM model and evaluate it as compared to several ML classifiers (e.g., SVM, DT, NB, etc.) and DL models (e.g., LSTM, CNN, etc.)

---

[2] Arabizi: Arabizi refers to Arabic written using the Roman script.

[3] https://github.com/chaymafourati/TUNIZI-Sentiment-Analysis-Tunisian-Arabizi-Dataset.

3.1 Data Exploration

The CTSA[4] dataset (Corona Tunisian Sentiment Analysis) constitute a good representative sample of the Tunisian Facebook comments and posts during the COVID-19
pandemic. The dataset covers the prevalent topics discussed on Facebook during the
critical period from 28th June to 27th August 2021, when the Pandemic started to spread
in Tunisia. We have analyzed the textual content of Tunisian Facebook posts; in particular, we have identified the most-frequent words, hashtags, posts and comments posted
in this period and tracking their frequency over time, as the virus started to disperse in
many Tunisian governorates. Figure 1 shows the time series (over days) of the top 10
most frequent words.

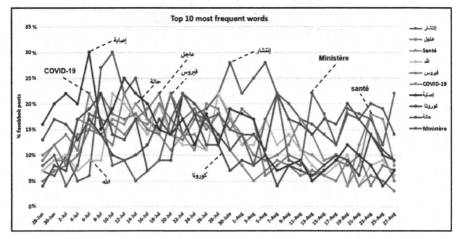

Fig. 1. Time series of the frequency (in percentage of Facebook posts) of top 10 most frequent
word for the period of 28th June to 27th August 2021.

The 10 most-frequent words shown in Fig. 1 appear to belong to two distinct categories: those related to COVID-19 (such as "santé", "COVID-19") and those related to
prayers and supplications (such as " الله", "God"). The frequency of the word " الله" rose
early on when news about the virus started to spread, as it may reflect discussions about
whether the pandemic is a punishment from God. The frequency of the word declines
over time but rises again as the virus starts to spread more widely in Tunisia. Thus,
we have collected more than 40,000 posts and comments from Facebook. We obtained
9,396 Tunisian French code-mixed posts after cleaning the corpus. Table 1. shows the
distribution of Emotion tags in the code-mixed corpus. We used hashtags related to the
Covid-19 pandemic, recent sanitary trends and words which depict emotions in Tunisian
dialect like (" فرحان", "far7an" for happy, etc.).

Afterwards, we have utilized language identification for each word to have a better
understanding of the corpus, using the tool[5] from the study [27]. We have shown the

---

[4] https://www.kaggle.com/naim99/tsnaimmhedhbiv2.

[5] https://github.com/irshadbhat/litcm.

distribution of words present in the corpus between Tunisian Dialect (Arabic and Arabizi) and Latin languages in Table 2., which provides insight into the code-mixing nature of the data.

Table 1. Distribution of Emotion tags in the code-mixed corpus.

Emotion	Related emojis	Sentences
Happy	😄	725
Sad	😢	1457
Angry	😠	1118
Disgust	🤢	349
Fear	😨	937
Surprise	😮	83
Total	-- --	4669

Table 2. Distribution of total and unique words in the code-mixed corpus.

Language	Word Count	Unique Words
Tunisian Dialect	17631	8517
Latin	11309	6031
Total	28940	14548

3.2 Data Pre-processing

The collected corpus must be preprocessed for use. Figure 2 depicts the data pre-processing pipeline.

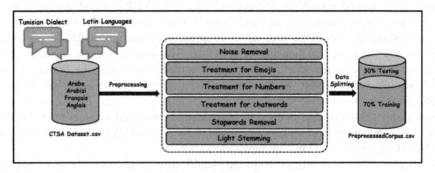

Fig. 2. The pipeline of the data pre-processing phase.

Noise Removal

As the corpus's comments are web scrapped, chances are they contain some URLs, HTML tags, and links. Since these tags are useless, it is better to remove them for effective classification results. Thus, Noise removal involves eliminating special characters, mentions, hashtags, and multiple whitespaces.

Treatment for Emojis & Numbers

Tunisian Facebook users frequently use emoji and emoticons instead of words to express emotions. To preserve this information, a small emoji-to-word converter has been developed. As for our treatment of numbers, two steps are taken: The first step is to remove numbers that are not part of words, as numbers do not carry sentimental information in SA. The second step is to replace numbers concatenated with letters with substitute letters (e.g., 5 to kh and 7 to h, as seen in the case of Arabizi words.)

Treatment for Chat Words and Stopwords.

The treatment for chat words involves removing character redundancy while preserving meaning (e.g., " خطيررررر " to " خطير ", "Urgenceeeee" to "Urgence"). Also, common chat words will be converted back to their original forms (e.g., "Slm" to "Salem"). We have used the Unigram model to identify the frequent chat words. Recall that in our contribution, we are interested in the SA of Tunisian French code-mixed posts and since publicly available stopwords extraction tools work only with monolingual corpora such as the example of NLTK[6] library, that's why we have developed a multilingual stopwords extractor. To do this, we have utilized two N-gram models (Unigrams and Bigrams) for stopwords extraction and then manually reviewed the results to eliminate words that do not carry significant meaning. As an illustration, some examples of stopwords in our research are ("cette", " بعد ", "eni", " أنت ", "inty", " عن ", etc.)

Light Stemming

The light stemming approach involves removing a small set of suffixes and/or prefixes to find the root of a word. Our contribution uses the ISRI stemmer from the Information Science Research Institute (ISRI). It operates similarly to the Khoja stemmer, but without utilizing a root dictionary. If a word cannot be rooted, the ISRI stemmer normalizes it by removing specific end patterns and determinants instead of leaving it unchanged. It also recognizes a set of diacritical marks and affix classes, as demonstrated by the example ("إنتشار - نشر " , "ستمرض - مرض ").

3.3 Model Training

After performing the processing of the Facebook posts, a vocabulary size was defined to convert the words into vectors. The sentiment labels (positive, negative and neutral) were encoded as well, and padding step was done to bring all the vectors to a specific length. The Bi-LSTM network architecture included the following layers: the Embedding layer to convert incoming words into vectors, the Bi-LSTM layer for processing the word vectors, the Dropout layers to avoid overfitting, the Conv1D layer to summarize the

---

[6] https://www.nltk.org.

vector along one dimension, the Global MaxPooling1D layer to find the maximum value in each feature map and finally the last layer as a fully connected layer with a Softmax activation function and three neurons for the output predicted label (positive, negative and neutral) producing a one-hot encoded result. Thus, Bi-LSTM combines the two LSTM hidden layers to the output layer, improving the learning of long-term dependencies and better model performance. Previous studies [22] have demonstrated that bidirectional networks are more effective than standard networks in various areas, including SA. The structure of a Bi-LSTM layer, made up of a forward and backward LSTM, is depicted in Fig. 3. As the forward LSTM layer output sequence $\overrightarrow{h}$, is obtained in a common way as the unidirectional one, the backward LSTM layer output sequence $\overleftarrow{h}$, is measured using the reversed inputs from time $t-1$ to $t-n$. Then, these output sequences fed to σ function to combine them into an output vector y_t[19]. Similar to the LSTM layer, the final output of a Bi-LSTM layer can be represented by a vector, $Y_t = [y_{t-n}, \ldots, y_{t-1}]$, in which the last element, y_{t-1}, is the estimated analysis label for the next iteration [28].

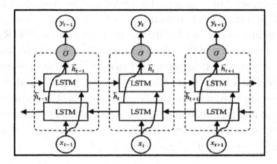

Fig. 3. The workflow of Bidirectional LSTM layer

4 Experiments and Results

4.1 Baseline and Evaluation Metrics

We have randomly divided our collected dataset into two corpora, 70% of the dataset for training and 30% for testing. The number of training iterations (epochs) is fixed at 10 for all experiments. To prevent overfitting, Dropout regularization is applied with a dropout rate of 40%. The goal of the experiments is to find the optimal parameters for the model. Notice that only the parameters that yield the best results are reported. To evaluate the performance of our proposed SA system, we have conducted experiments using various classification algorithms. The first set of experiments is designed to measure the performance of traditional ML methods such as NB, SVM, RF and Logistic Regression (LR) classifiers. These classifiers are applied to different combinations of preprocessed data. For feature extraction, we have used three embedding models: Bag Of Words (BOW), Term Frequency-Inverse Document Frequency (TF-IDF), and GloVe (Global Vectors for

Word Representation). Furthermore, to evaluate the performance of our system as well as the other classifiers, we have used the most widely popular measures retrieval namely, Accuracy, Precision and Recall Their corresponding formulas are recalled respectively in 1, 2 and 3, where tp, tn, fp and fp represent True Positive[7], True Negative[8], False Positive[9] and False Negative[10] respectively.

$$Accuracy = \frac{tp + tn}{tp + tn + fp + fn} \tag{1}$$

$$Recall = \frac{tp}{tp + fp} \tag{2}$$

$$F_1 measure = 2 * \frac{Precision * Recall}{Precision + Recall} \tag{3}$$

4.2 Experimental Results

In the experiment, DL models were performed using Keras[11] library, while ML models were performed using Scikit-Learn[12] library. Table 3. displays the results of the ML classifiers after applying the pre-processing method. Table 4. presents the results of the second set of experiments, which were done using different configurations of DL models during the training phase.

4.3 Discussion

Our study aims to present a new method for Tunisian Dialectical SA to surpass the limitations of feed-forward models by considering multilingual contextual features and Tunisian French code-mixed information in both directions (forward and backward) of the Tunisian Dialectical written comments. From the results showed in Sect. 4.2, we can highlight that our proposed method yielded the highest sentiment prediction accuracy results. According to Tables 4. and 5., deep Bi-LSTM and Bi-LSTM outperformed other DL models (CNN and LSTM) on the benchmark CTSA dataset. This is due to the fact that Bi-LSTM networks can better capture context in the text by combining both forward and backward hidden layers. This allows it to access both preceding and succeeding contextual features, resulting in richer semantic information and the ability to make full use of contextual information than the Unidirectional LSTM networks. Additionally, according to Table 3., in which we have performed five ML algorithms applied with three embeddings models (BOW, TF-IDF, GloVe), we can clearly see that DL algorithms typically have better accuracy than traditional ML methods and as noted in [29], the SVM becomes inefficient and costly when dealing with large training data as it is not capable of

---

[7] The number of correctly classified positive comments.

[8] The number of correctly classified negative comments.

[9] The number of incorrectly classified positive comments.

[10] The number of incorrectly classified negative comments.

[11] https://keras.io.

[12] https://scikit-learn.org.

Table 3. Experimental results obtained with machine learning classifiers on CTSA Corpus

Label prediction after pre-processing						
Classifier + Embedding	Metrics	SVM	RF	LR	NB	DT
Classifier + BOW	**Recall** **F1- Measure** **Accuracy**	65.3264.53 **71,14**	69.16 65.78 70,09	72.1769.6774,91	73.82 72.23 74,57	71.6570.42 **71,78**
Classifier + TF-IDF	**Recall** **F1- Measure** **Accuracy**	65.7462.58 69,94	70.0969.60 71,49	72.24 71.89 **75,12**	71,13 72.12 **75,84**	68.8664.97 69,29
Classifier + GloVe	**Recall** **F1- Measure** **Accuracy**	68.8965.47 70,32	71.9669.64 **72,82**	69.83 70.79 74,43	72.19 71.51 73,43	70.69 68.21 71,03

Table 4. Experimental results obtained with Deep Learning models on CTSA Corpus

Model Configuration	Recall	F1 score	Accuracy
CNN (fully connected layer size = 100)	72.81	72.52	74.09
LSTM (dropout rate = 0.4)	69.54	70.89	72.89
RNTN	70.49	72.29	74.97
RNN	72.82	73.82	75.12
CNN + LSTM	75.42	76.08	77.62
Combined LSTM	75.12	74.17	76.79
Bi-LSTM	**76.32**	**77.58**	**78.10**

Table 5. Comparison of accuracy results of different DL models after applying light stemming

Classifier + Embedding	Metrics	Deep Bi-LSTM	LSTM	CNN
Without Stemming	**Recall** **F1- Measure** **Accuracy**	75.79 74.24 **77.89**	69.05 75.78 75.92	74.17 75.42 74,40
Arabic Light Stemming (ISRI Stemmer)	**Recall** **F1- Measure** **Accuracy**	79.25 77.93 **79,80**	77.57 78.15 77,49	78.21 77.04 78,61

handling such big size data. Moreover, when the training data is unbalanced and noisy, it can negatively impact the SVM performance due to its high computational cost and low generalization error [30]. For the RF algorithm, the complexity increases as the number of trees in the forest and the number of training samples increase, because more trees and more training samples increases the model's complexity, leading to longer processing times and higher computational resource requirements. Furthermore, our model was improved by adding morphological features, including stems, to overcome the problem of limited vocabulary, ambiguity issue and the lexical sparsity.

According to results in Table 5., experiments clearly indicate that using light stemming leads to an average improvement of 2.56% across the three tested DL models. According to similar studies [31, 32, 33], including morphological features, such as stems, improved performance quality on data containing a mixture of Dialectal Arabic and MSA. This approach offers several benefits, including improvement in sentiment prediction accuracy through the implementation of various Arabic pre-processing techniques like punctuation removal, digits, tokenization, Latin characters removal, light stemming and the ability to consider the code-mixed contextual information by considering both forward and backward dependencies.

5 Conclusion and Perspectives

We tackled in this paper, the SA problem for Tunisian textual productions on Facebook during the spread of the Coronavirus pandemic. To address this challenge, we have proposed an efficient deep Bi-LSTM learning model to extract multilingual and code-mixed contextual features, improving in richer semantic information to overall quality of the sentiment prediction. Experiments on Tunisian benchmark dataset (TSAC) showed the effectiveness of the deep Bi-LSTM model, outperforming state-of-the-art algorithms in terms of accuracy and F1-measure. We believe that our model will contribute to future exploration in the field of SA and text mining especially during critical events.

Our future works will focus on comparing the effect of different recent contextualized word embeddings models such as BERT, ELMO, ULMFiT, XLNet and GPT-3 on their previously presented DL model for Arabic dialectical SA. Additionally, we plan to study the media press and news articles related to COVID-19 in order to identify bias and track the spread of misinformation and fake news.

Acknowledgment. The authors would like to express their deep gratitude towards the members of the Research Laboratory in Algebra, Numbers theory and Intelligent Systems (RLANTIS) for their unwavering support and contribution in the realization of this paper.

References

1. Guellil, I., Saâdane, H., Azouaou, F., Gueni, B., Nouvel, D.: Arabic natural language processing: an overview. J. King Saud Univ.-Comp. Inf. Sci. **33**(5), 497–507 (2021)
2. Merhben, L., Zouaghi, A., Zrigui, M.: Lexical disambiguation of Arabic language: an experimental study. Polibits (46), 49–54 (2012)

3. Sghaier, M.A., Zrigui, M.: Sentiment analysis for Arabic e-commerce websites. In: 2016 International Conference on Engineering & MIS (ICEMIS), pp. 1–7. IEEE (2016)

4. Mahmoud, A., Zrigui, M.: Deep neural network models for paraphrased text classification in the Arabic language. In: Métais, E., Meziane, F., Vadera, S., Sugumaran, V., Saraee, M. (eds.) Natural Language Processing and Information Systems. LNCS, vol. 11608, pp. 3–16. Springer, Cham (2019). https://doi.org/10.1007/978-3-030-23281-8_1

5. Merhbene, L., Zouaghi, A., & Zrigui, M.: A semi-supervised method for Arabic word sense disambiguation using a weighted directed graph. In: Proceedings of the Sixth International Joint Conference on Natural Language Processing, pp. 1027–1031, Oct (2013)

6. Batita, M.A., Zrigui, M.: Derivational relations in Arabic wordnet. In: Proceedings of the 9th Global WordNet Conference, pp. 136–144, Jan (2018)

7. Shoukry, A., Rafea, A.: Sentence-level Arabic sentiment analysis. In: 2012 International Conference on Collaboration Technologies and Systems (CTS), pp. 546–550. IEEE (2012)

8. Maraoui, M., Zrigui, M., Antoniadis, G.: Use of NLP tools in CALL system for Arabic. Int. J. Comp. Process. Lang. **24**(02), 153–165 (2012)

9. Abdulla, N.A., Al-Ayyoub, M., Al-Kabi, M.N.: An extended analytical study of Arabic sentiments. Int. J. Big Data Intell. **1**(1–2), 103–113 (2014)

10. Abdul-Mageed, M., Diab, M., Kübler, S.: SAMAR: Subjectivity and sentiment analysis for Arabic social media. Comp. Speech Lang. **28**(1), 20–37 (2014)

11. Medhaffar, S., Bougares, F., Esteve, Y., Hadrich-Belguith, L.: Sentiment analysis of tunisian dialects: linguistic ressources and experiments. In: Proceedings of the third Arabic natural language processing workshop (WANLP), Valencia, Spain, pp. 55–61 (2017)

12. Salamah, J.B., Elkhlifi, A.: Microblogging opinion mining approach for Kuwaiti Dialect. In: Proceedings of the International Conference on Computing Technology and Information Management, pp. 388–396 (2014)

13. Ayadi, R., Maraoui, M., Zrigui, M.: Intertextual distance for Arabic texts classification. In: 2009 International Conference for Internet Technology and Secured Transactions, (ICITST), pp. 1–6 (2009)

14. Albraheem, L., Al-Khalifa, H. S.: Exploring the problems of sentiment analysis in informal Arabic. In: Proceedings of the 14th International Conference on Information Integration and Web-based Applications & Services (2012)

15. Al-Ayyoub, M., Essa, S.B., Alsmadi. I.: Lexicon-based sentiment analysis of Arabic tweets. Int. J. Social Netw. Mining **2**(2), 101–114 (2014)

16. Mulki, H., Haddad, H., Ali, C.B., Babaoğlu, I.: Tunisian dialect sentiment analysis: a natural language processing-based approach. Comput. y Sist. **22**(4), 1223–1232 (2018)

17. Stoyanov, V., Cardie, C., Wiebe, J.: Multi-perspective question answering using the opqa corpus. In: Proceedings of Human Language Technology Conference and Conference on Empirical Methods in Natural Language Processing, pp. 923–930, Oct (2005)

18. Brahimi, B., Touahria, M., Tari, A.: Improving Arabic sentiment classification using a combined approach. Comput. y Sist. **24**(4), 1403–1414 (2020)

19. Haffar, N., Hkiri, E., Zrigui, M.: TimeML annotation of events and temporal expressions in Arabic texts. In: Computational Collective Intelligence: 11th International Conference, ICCCI 2019, Hendaye, France, September 4–6, 2019, Proceedings, Part I 11, pp. 207–218. Springer International Publishing, Cham (2019)

20. Soliman, T.H., Elmasry, M.A., Hedar, A., Doss, M.M.: Sentiment analysis of Arabic slang comments on facebook. Int. J. Comp. Technol. **12**(5), 3470–3478 (2014)

21. Zrigui, S., Ayadi, R., Zouaghi, A., Zrigui, S.: ISAO: an intelligent system of opinions analysis. Res. Comput. Sci., **110**, 21–30 (2016)

22. Jaballi, S., Zrigui, S., Sghaier, M.A., Berchech, D., Zrigui, M.: Sentiment analysis of Tunisian users on social networks: overcoming the challenge of multilingual comments in the

Tunisian dialect. In: Computational Collective Intelligence: 14th International Conference, ICCCI 2022, Hammamet, Tunisia, 28–30 Sept 2022, Proceedings, pp. 176–192. : Springer International Publishing, Cham (2022)

23. Masmoudi, A., Hamdi, J., Belguith, L.: Deep learning for sentiment analysis of Tunisian dialect. Comp. y Sist. **25**(1), 129–148 (2021)

24. Jerbi, M.A., Achour, H., Souissi, E.: Sentiment analysis of code-switched Tunisian dialect: exploring RNN-based techniques. In: Smaïli, K. (ed.) ICALP 2019. CCIS, vol. 1108, pp. 122–131. Springer, Cham (2019). https://doi.org/10.1007/978-3-030-32959-4_9

25. Fourati, C., Messaoudi, A., Haddad, H.: TUNIZI: a Tunisian Arabizi sentiment analysis Dataset. arXiv preprint arXiv:2004.14303 (2020)

26. Haffar, N., Hkiri, E., Zrigui, M.: Using bidirectional LSTM and shortest dependency path for classifying Arabic temporal relations. KES **2020**, 370–379 (2020)

27. Bhat, I.A, Mujadia, V., Tammewar, A.: IIIT-H system submission for FIRE2014 shared task on transliterated search. In: Proceedings of the Forum for Information Retrieval Evaluation on – FIRE '14, New York, New York, USA, pp. 48–53 (2015)

28. Sghaier, M.A., Zrigui, M.: Rule-based machine translation from Tunisian dialect to modern standard Arabic. Proc. Comp. Sci. **176**, 310–319 (2020)

29. Abd Allah, M.A.H., Haffar, N., Zrigui, M.: Contribution to the methods of indexing Arabic textual documents to improve the performance of IRS. In: 2022 International Conference on Innovations in Intelligent Systems and Applications (INISTA), pp. 1–6. IEEE (2022)

30. Jabnoun, J., Haffar, N., Zrigui, A., Nsir, S., Nicolas, H., Trigui, A.: An image retrieval system using deep learning to extract high-level features. In: Advances in Computational Collective Intelligence: 14th International Conference, ICCCI 2022, Hammamet, Tunisia, September 28–30, 2022, Proceedings, pp. 167–179. Springer International Publishing, Cham (2022)

31. Slimi, A., Nicolas, H., Zrigui, M.: Hybrid time distributed CNN-transformer for speech emotion recognition. In: Proceedings of the 17th International Conference on Software Technologies ICSOFT, Lisbon, Portugal, pp. 11–13 (2022)

32. Bellagha, M.L., Zrigui, M.: Speaker Naming in Arabic TV programs. Int. Arab J. Inf. Technol. **19**(6), 843–853 (2022)

33. Trigui, A., Terbeh, N., Maraoui, M., Zrigui, M.: Statistical approach for spontaneous Arabic speech understanding based on stochastic speech recognition module. Res. Comput. Sci. **117**, 143–151 (2016)

Interpretation of Immunofluorescence Slides by Deep Learning Techniques: Anti-nuclear Antibodies Case Study

Oumar Khlelfa[1(✉)], Aymen Yahyaoui[1,2(✉)], Mouna Ben Azaiz[3], Anwer Ncibi[1], Ezzedine Gazouani[3], Adel Ammar[4], and Wadii Boulila[4,5(✉)]

[1] Military Academy of Fondouk Jedid, 8012 Nabeul, Tunisia
oumarkh1997@gmail.com
[2] Science and Technology for Defense Lab (STD), Ministry of National Defense, Tunis, Tunisia
aymen.yahyaoui@ept.rnu.tn
[3] Immunology Department, The Principal Military Hospital of Instruction of Tunis, Tunis, Tunisia
[4] Robotics and Internet-of-Things Laboratory, Prince Sultan University, Riyadh, Saudi Arabia
[5] RIADI Laboratory, National School of Computer Sciences, University of Manouba, Manouba, Tunisia
wboulila@psu.edu.sa

Abstract. Nowadays, diseases are increasing in numbers and severity by the hour. Immunity diseases, affecting 8% of the world population in 2017 according to the World Health Organization (WHO), is a field in medicine worth attention due to the high rate of disease occurrence classified under this category. This work presents an up-to-date review of state-of-the-art immune diseases healthcare solutions. We focus on tackling the issue with modern solutions such as Deep Learning to detect anomalies in the early stages hence providing health practitioners with efficient tools. We rely on advanced deep learning techniques such as Convolutional Neural Networks (CNN) to fulfill our objective of providing an efficient tool while providing a proficient analysis of this solution. The proposed solution was tested and evaluated by the immunology department in the Principal Military Hospital of Instruction of Tunis, which considered it a very helpful tool.

Keywords: CNN · e-health · immune systems · immunofluorescence slides · antinuclear antibodies · artificial intelligence · deep learning

1 Introduction

In the current era, the significant spread of chronic diseases is much higher than ever before, especially those related to immune problems [1]. On this note, the fact that the rate of affection by immune diseases is increasing extensively

© The Author(s), under exclusive license to Springer Nature Switzerland AG 2023
N. T. Nguyen et al. (Eds.): ICCCI 2023, CCIS 1864, pp. 110–122, 2023.
https://doi.org/10.1007/978-3-031-41774-0_9

underlines the need to provide a solution for the doctors to help save time and provide them with precision while treating the immunofluorescence slides. In fact, the analysis of immunofluorescence [2] results based solely on the knowledge of a single doctor is a method that lacks precision, and also could be a significant source of potential misdiagnosis due to the massive amount of details present in the Indirect immunofluorescence (IIF) images [3]. This creates dangerous risks for immunologists working under enormous responsibility and likewise for the patient, who is the most significant beneficiary. Therefore, the presented solution is very effective in this matter, as it helps to save time, leading to faster results; thus, more patients can be treated by a single expert doctor. On the other hand, the certainty factor also plays a major part in this study, as the error rate is very minimal thanks to this model, which made it possible to reach a 94.48% accuracy for diagnosing positive and negative IIF images. This will lead to another level of performance that will help newly graduated doctors to go through their medical career with more confidence based on the automated results.   This work is carried out in collaboration with the immunology department of the Principal Military Hospital of Instruction of Tunis. The objective is to offer a tool in the form of a computer application, where the greatest benefits are to effectively assist the doctors of the immunology department in diagnosing autoimmune diseases through the analysis of IIF images. This should make interpreting IIF images much easier in terms of time and level of certainty.

The main contributions of this work are as follows:

- It presents an overview of the different state-of-the-art techniques, methods, and tools related to AI and the interpretation of immunofluorescence sides.
- It treats the multiple cases of immunofluorescence slides using a combination of a DL model and a NASNet model leading to accurate results.
- It presents the interactive tool developed for the specific needs of the medical staff at the military hospital of Tunis immunology department. This tool was developed, deployed, and tested on many patients. The medical staff confirmed it as an interesting and useful tool for IIF interpretation.

The science of immunology was revealed in the late 18th century, and from that moment on, it can be admitted that it gained its rightful recognition as a branch of knowledge.

Autoimmune diseases, one of the most common issues in immunology, is a disease that results from a dysfunction of the immune system leading it to attack the normal constituents of the body: Normally, the immune system preserves the cells of the body. Whereas during autoimmune disease, it identifies them as foreign agents and attacks them. Statistics have shown that 5 to 8% of the world's population is affected by this type of disease [5].

Immunofluorescence technique: It is a method that consists of detecting and locating, by fluorescence emission, a protein of interest produced by an Antigen, with the help of a specific antibody related to the agent in question. Thus, it makes it possible to determine the presence or absence of a protein and its localization in the cell or tissue analyzed. In immunofluorescence, two types of labeling can be carried out as shown in Fig. 1:

- Direct immunofluorescence [4] where the fluorescent protein, called fluorochrome, is not coupled to a secondary antibody but to the primary antibody.
- Indirect immunofluorescence [2] where a primary antibody binds to the antigen. Then, a secondary antibody with a strong affinity for the primary antibody is added.

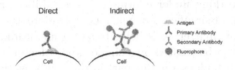

Fig. 1. Direct vs Indirect Immunofluorescence [16].

2   Related Work

Indirect immunofluorescence (IIF) is considered the reference test for the detection of autoimmune diseases. As a well-established and challenging issue in the field of medical image analysis, HEp-2 image classification has become one of the growing centers of interest in the last decade. For this reason, three international IIF image classification competitions were held in 2012, 2014, and 2016. These competitions were very significant in this progress by facilitating the collection of a large amount of data. As a classical image classification problem, traditional machine learning techniques have been greatly applied to HEp2 image classification.

2.1   Machine Learning-Based Solutions

In this context, several research works have been considered using various methods such as gradient features with intensity order pooling by [6] who were capable of reaching 74.39% cell level accuracy and 85.71% image level accuracy on the ICPR dataset. Also, multiple linear projection descriptors were considered by [7], who adopt the feature learning method to learn the appropriate descriptor from the image data itself. They were able to reach 66.6% classification accuracy. Machine Learning (ML) can learn from the data, while non-learning-based techniques depend on rules that depend critically on domain knowledge. However, traditional machine learning techniques rely on predefining feature representations, which is a crucial step and necessitates complicated engineering [8].

2.2   Deep Learning Based Solutions

Several deep learning-based approaches proposed in the literature have shown great progress in healthcare for disease diagnosis [9–15]. Deep learning was considered in two subfields of HEp2 image classification (HEp2IC) that have attracted the attention of researchers: the classification of individual HEp-2 cells and the classification of HEp-2 specimens.

Cell-Level HEp-2 Image Classification (CL-HEP2IC) Methods: there are two methods for Deep Neural Networks (DNN) to be used; DNN as a feature extractor and DNN as a classifier. As shown in Fig. 2, the amount of research based on the last method is more important than the other. In fact, more than 30 publications adopt this method on three of the most popular datasets (ICPR 2012, I3A, and SNPHEp-2). In contrast, less than ten publications are adopting the method of using the DNN as a feature extractor.

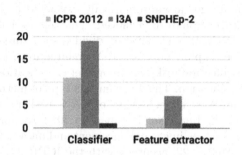

Fig. 2. Number of publications based on the use of DNNs [17].

1) CL-HEp2IC methods that use DNN as feature extractor:
Extraction is frequently used in HE2IC approaches based on handcrafted features. It allows extracting features from the input image to carry out the classification performed generally with support vector machines or k-nearest neighbors. There are two kinds of feature extraction: feature extraction from a pre-trained DNN model and feature extraction from a fine-tuned DNN model: First, in [18], authors used a pre-trained CNN model but with an intensity-aware classification schema with two steps accompanied by an approach to pull out the features that can differentiate between the classes which allowed them to reach 77.1% average class accuracy. One year later, authors in [19] proposed a much simpler idea of replacing the SIFT with the CNN features, enabling them to achieve a 98% classification accuracy. Second, feature extraction from a fine-tuned DNN model consists of improving a pre-trained model. One of the methods in this context involves a modern pooling strategy to overcome and remove the fixed-size constraint of the CNNs known by resizing the input images. They used a CaffeNet model to extract features and then a K-spatial pooling to support the HEp2 cell images with arbitrary sizes. This method allowed them to reach an accuracy of 98.41% [17]. Unlike all previous works, authors of [21] used the convolutional auto-encoder (CAE) as a feature extractor. In fact, it is not only CAE, but they train two different CAEs, one for normal images with RGB colors and another one for the gradient images, which are images that have been subject to a directional change in intensity or color. The first is used to learn the geometric properties of HEp-2 cells, while the second is used to learn the local intensity changes in HEp-2 cells. They were able to reach 98.27% accuracy with the SNPHEp-2 [21] dataset and 98.89 with the I3A dataset [21].

2) CL-HEp2IC methods that use DNN as a classifier:
The following methods combine the feature extraction step and the classification step as one part. In fact, in this kind of method, the features of the input images are automatically extracted and relying on these features, the classification phase is achieved.

The cell-level HEp2 image classification that uses DNN as a classifier is divided into three groups. The following methods combine the feature extraction step and the classification step as one part. In fact, in this kind of method, the features of the input images are automatically extracted and relying on these features, the classification phase is achieved. The cell-level HEp2 image classification that uses DNN as a classifier is divided into three groups. Generic DNN-based approaches exploit popular DNN architectures, primarily designed for general image classification tasks like ImageNet classification, to perform cell-level HEp2 image classification. The focus on this type of method began in 2015 with [22] who used an AlexNet, a variant of CNN used in the competition of image classification of the ImageNet Database in 2012, reinforced by some pre-processing techniques such as image enhancement and data augmentation. They were able to achieve 80.3% [22] accuracy with the ICPR 2012 dataset. A later study conducted by [23] concerning other generic CNN models, specially ImageNet, GoogleNet, and LetNet-5, shows that even without any pre-processing methods used in the procedure, GoogleNet exceeds the performance of the two remaining methods and gets as far as 95.53% accuracy. In [23], the authors focused on three other generic CNNs, which are VGG-16, ResNet-50, and InceptionV3. Their work confirms that this last generic CNN, named InceptionV3 is more efficient in the HEp2 image classification than the other models considered in their research without any pre-processing procedures with a 98.28% accuracy [24]. As mentioned earlier, the generic CNN is strengthened with techniques such as image enhancing and DA, another idea brought by [25] who suggested to use of the generative adversarial network (GAN), which generates images with a different composition than the initial images different from rotating or reversing, and train generic CNN like the GoogleNet model with those images provided. It reaches 98.6% accuracy [25]. Despite its high accuracy, this method shows its weaknesses while facing a large intra-class variation of data. Second, Generic DNN-based methods with partial changes in layers or training schemes consist of making smaller changes in the generic model. Two major studies were shown in this context: The first one is proposed by [26], who added two additional convolutional layers with a 1×1 filter before the LeNet5 CNN architecture. It aims to boost the number of feature channels to facilitate the task of the classification layers to attain a 79.13% [26] accuracy, which outperforms the accuracy of the basic LeNet-5 by a significant amount. The second method by the same group of researchers two years later in 2018: they chose to concentrate on the ResNet model and merge the first layers' predictions into the final classification layers using a bridging mechanism to go far as 97.14% accuracy on the ICPR 2012 dataset and 98.42% [27] accuracy on the I3A dataset. Despite the high accuracy achieved in this study, it is accompanied by an increasing number of network parameters.

Specimen-Level HEp-2 Image Classification (SL-HEP2IC) Methods:
The specimen-level methods deal with the images of the HEP2 as an entire block and classify the whole image. These methods were decomposed into two main types: single-cell processing-based SL-HEP2IC methods and multi-cell processing-based methods.

1) Single-cell processing-based SL-HEP2IC methods:
Single-cell processing methods consist of feeding this kind of model with a specimen image as input. It will be split into singular cell images using ground truth labeling at the cell level, such as bounding box annotations or segmentation masks. Then a majority voting strategy is employed to obtain the specimen-level result by accumulating the cell results. It is considered the extension of the Cell-level HEp2 image classification. According to the utilization of DNNs, we can split this part of the related work concerning the HEp2 image classification into two main parts:

- Feature extraction-based methods: Those methods are much the same as those previously discussed. They are divided into two parts: feature extraction from each cell of the specimen and then passed into a classifier to obtain the cell class. In this context, the authors [26] proposed a modification to the LeNet-5 model by adding a 1×1 convolutional block. Then, after the cell classes are identified, a majority voting strategy (MVS) is applied by choosing the most dominant cell label as the specimen label. This strategy leads them to reach 95.83% accuracy [26]. Confusion can be present while applying the majority voting strategy. That is why another approach is used to overcome such a critical issue: representing the population histogram (PH).
- Pure DNN-based methods: The pure DNN means that the DNN is used as a direct classifier in this kind of method. They are similar to the methods discussed previously. One of the studies concerning this type of method is the [26] study, which used modified LeNet-5 for the classification issue for each cell image obtained from specimen images and reached a 79.13% accuracy [26].

The drawbacks of the single-cell processing based on specimen level are:

- The requirement of single cell classification to obtain the specimen classification.
- When numerous cells are presented in a specimen image, the single cell processing based on specimen level faces many problems while first of all segmenting and also while classifying specimen-cells.

2) Multi-cell processing-based methods:
Multi-cell processing methods treat a whole specimen image at once. They are more efficient and can be divided into two types:

- Pixel-wise prediction-based methods: In this prediction, each pixel of the specimen image is contributed to a class label. Then, the results of these pixels are fed to a majority voting method to classify the whole specimen. The basis of this method is the fully convolutional network, a variant of the CNN that replaces the fully connected layers with convolutional ones.

Senior 2		Senior 1							
		Negative	Homog.	Fine S.	Coarse S.	Nucleol.	Centrom.	Dot	TOT
	Negative	117	6	10	5	3			141
	Homog.	5	110	15	3	1			134
	Fine S.	26	22	49	24	1			122
Senior 2	Coarse S.	23	4	20	67				114
	Nucleol.	1				38			39
	Centrom.						31		31
	Dot					1		7	8
	TOT	172	142	94	99	44	31	7	589

Fig. 3. Level of concordance between two seniors [20].

- Image-wise prediction-based methods: In this type of method, only one prediction is given to the whole specimen image. A recent method is introduced in this context which resizes the specimen image. Consequently, the local information disappears. That is why handcrafted features are used to make the model stronger, showing a good classification performance that outperforms some other methods.

3 Proposed Approach

In this section, the proposed approach is described, and we mention details about the dataset as well as model architectures.

3.1 Immunofluorescence Slides Interpretation

Medical decisions must be made carefully and with high precision. In this regard, the detection of the IIF image class is very crucial because of two factors:

- The need for a double reading of these images, which is not always possible in many cases.
- Even with the availability of two senior physicians, the difficulty of analyzing IIF images is always present due to the great detail in this type of image.

Fig. 3 visualizes the level of concordance between two seniors Immunologist readers. We note that they had, on average, 71% of concordance despite their expertise in the field.

3.2 Global Approach Process

As shown in Fig. 4, the user (who is either the doctor or the technician) must be able to:

- Identify whether the input image provided is positive or negative in the first instance.
- Provide prediction of the exact class of the IIF image if it is positive: The developed application, whose purpose is assisting Immunologists in diagnosing different cases, must be able to provide predictions with nearly perfect accuracy of the anomalies present in the patient's IIF images.

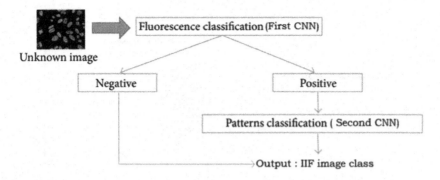

Fig. 4. Proposed approach.

3.3   Dataset

For Binary classification, the dataset is a mixture of an open-source dataset called AIDA HEp-2 and a set of IIF images taken from the department of immunology of the military hospital of Tunis. The AIDA HEp-2 dataset is a part of the complete AIDA database, resulting from international cooperation between Tunisia and Italy. In Table 1, the number of patients from whom the IIF images were taken is mentioned, as well as the positive and the negative patients. The total number of images acquired is equal to 2080, about 2 images from each patient.

Table 1. Dataset Description.

Number of patients	Positive fluorescence intensity	Negative fluorescence intensity
1000	470	530

For multi-class classification, a dataset containing 2668 IIF images distributed into 7 classes is used to train, validate and test the model. Figure 5 describes the representation of how these images are divided.

3.4   Model Architecture

Two models were proposed for the prediction of the IIF image class. The first one is dedicated to the binary classification of the image provided as input: an IIF image is either positive (presence of antibody) or negative (otherwise). The model consists of multiple layers, one enveloping the other so that the output of the first becomes the input of the second and so on, until the last layer, which is the output of the whole model. In this work, the first model is sequential, i.e., the output of each layer is the input of the next layer. It is composed of the layers put in the following arrangement:

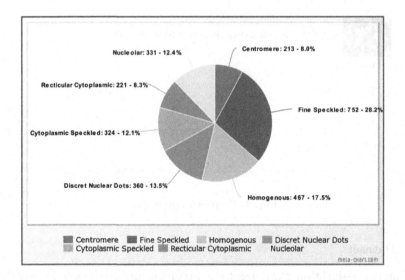

Fig. 5. Distribution of samples over classes.

- 6 sets of Convolutional followed by a Max Pooling layer.
- A Flatten layer (with the shape of 256).
- 3 Dense layers (with the respective shapes of 64, 128, and 1).

For the second model, the proposed pre-trained NASNet neural network provides accurate results. We enhanced the architecture by adding a dense layer to the model which led to better results.

4 Results

In this section, the obtained results through the training and testing phases are presented.

4.1 Training

For the binary classification, a model was trained using two classes: positive and negative. Figure 6 shows a screen capture of results during the training phase. Then, the performance was evaluated using a range of metrics. Next, the proposed approach was extended to the multiclass model, which was trained on a total of 7 different classes, as shown in Fig. 7, and again evaluates the model's performance using a range of metrics.

Binary Model. To investigate the performance of the proposed approach, we began by training a binary classification model with two classes: positive and negative. The positive class represented instances of the existence antibody in the cell, while the negative class represented instances that did not exhibit the phenomenon. A dataset of 2080 samples for training and testing the model and evaluating its performance was used.

```
Epoch 15/25
5/5 [==============================] - 34s 7s/step - loss: 0.3033 - accuracy: 0.8875 - val_loss: 0.5726 - val_accuracy: 0.7965
Epoch 16/25
5/5 [==============================] - 34s 7s/step - loss: 0.2032 - accuracy: 0.9250 - val_loss: 0.3926 - val_accuracy: 0.8372
Epoch 17/25
5/5 [==============================] - 36s 7s/step - loss: 0.4305 - accuracy: 0.8308 - val_loss: 0.3939 - val_accuracy: 0.8372
Epoch 18/25
5/5 [==============================] - 34s 7s/step - loss: 0.2482 - accuracy: 0.9000 - val_loss: 0.4150 - val_accuracy: 0.8256
Epoch 19/25
5/5 [==============================] - 38s 8s/step - loss: 0.2789 - accuracy: 0.8625 - val_loss: 0.4099 - val_accuracy: 0.8488
Epoch 20/25
5/5 [==============================] - 34s 7s/step - loss: 0.2279 - accuracy: 0.9125 - val_loss: 0.4900 - val_accuracy: 0.8023
Epoch 21/25
5/5 [==============================] - 35s 7s/step - loss: 0.1600 - accuracy: 0.9375 - val_loss: 0.4376 - val_accuracy: 0.8372
Epoch 22/25
5/5 [==============================] - 35s 7s/step - loss: 0.2127 - accuracy: 0.9000 - val_loss: 0.5030 - val_accuracy: 0.8547
Epoch 23/25
5/5 [==============================] - 30s 6s/step - loss: 0.3217 - accuracy: 0.8923 - val_loss: 0.6194 - val_accuracy: 0.7849
Epoch 24/25
5/5 [==============================] - 34s 7s/step - loss: 0.2517 - accuracy: 0.9125 - val_loss: 0.4399 - val_accuracy: 0.8372
Epoch 25/25
5/5 [==============================] - 34s 7s/step - loss: 0.2396 - accuracy: 0.8923 - val_loss: 0.4312 - val_accuracy: 0.8314
```

Fig. 6. Training the binary classification model.

Multi Class Classification. A Multi-class model was trained to distinguish the different interpretable classes. There are seven classes, as explained previously, and the model was trained using Google Colab Pro as its training exceeded the locally provided resources.

```
Epoch 1/10
25/25 [==============================] - 837s 34s/step - loss: 7.8566 - accuracy: 0.8550 - val_loss:6.2548 - val_accuracy: 0.5897
Epoch 2/10
25/25 [==============================] - 828s 34s/step - loss: 4.2056 - accuracy: 0.8625 - val_loss:6.2052 - val_accuracy: 0.6124
Epoch 3/10
25/25 [==============================] - 831s 34s/step - loss: 2.4525 - accuracy: 0.9200 - val_loss:4.3657 - val_accuracy: 0.6275
Epoch 4/10
25/25 [==============================] - 830s 34s/step - loss: 0.9253 - accuracy: 0.8450 - val_loss:4.0078 - val_accuracy: 0.5852
Epoch 5/10
25/25 [==============================] - 830s 34s/step - loss: 1.0039 - accuracy: 0.8325 - val_loss:3.2055 - val_accuracy: 0.6305
Epoch 6/10
25/25 [==============================] - 826s 34s/step - loss: 0.9023 - accuracy: 0.8503 - val_loss:1.9825 - val_accuracy: 0.6109
Epoch 7/10
25/25 [==============================] - 823s 34s/step - loss: 0.8947 - accuracy: 0.8604 - val_loss:1.2874 - val_accuracy: 0.6576
Epoch 8/10
25/25 [==============================] - 830s 34s/step - loss: 0.7528 - accuracy: 0.8925 - val_loss:0.9245 - val_accuracy: 0.6667
Epoch 9/10
25/25 [==============================] - 828s 34s/step - loss: 0.6780 - accuracy: 0.8575 - val_loss:0.8125 - val_accuracy: 0.5551
Epoch 10/10
25/25 [==============================] - 828s 34s/step - loss: 0.5127 - accuracy: 0.8925 - val_loss:0.6822 - val_accuracy: 0.6154
```

Fig. 7. Training the multi-class classification model.

4.2   Testing Results

The first model achieved an accuracy of 94.48% on a challenging classification task. The model was trained using a convolutional neural network architecture as explained in the previous section on a dataset of 2080 images. Then it was evaluated using a standard test set and obtained a precision-recall curve, which showed that the model's accuracy was consistent across a range of thresholds. The results of this study demonstrate the effectiveness of this approach and provide a foundation for future research.

The second model achieved an accuracy of 69.61% on the multiclass classification task. The second model was trained using a more complex neural network architecture with additional layers and a larger number of parameters. A similar dataset of 2668 images was used for training and testing the second model. The evaluation of the second model's performance showed that it had lower accuracy compared to the first model, which may be due to the lack of images or the increased complexity of the architecture.

5   Conclusion

In this work, an overview of the different state-of-the-art techniques, methods, and tools related to AI for the Interpretation of Immunofluorescence slides is depicted. Also, a solution that treats the multiple cases of immunofluorescence slide interpretation is presented using a combination of a DL model and a NAS-Net model leading to accurate results, especially in binary classification. In future works, a fusion between the two methods, cell level and specimen level, is a must-try approach to reach better results. In fact, with the use of the cell-level method, a population diagram representing the distribution of the cells within the sample can be produced. Then, with the use of the prediction based on the specimen-level method, a comparison of the two results will lead to a better verification of the decision-making process. Finally, we note that AI is a powerful tool in the Immunology field, however, human beings are exposed to a variety of diseases that target their immunity, therefore, new AI solutions evolving with theses diseases are required.

Acknowledgment. The authors would like to thank Prince Sultan University for financially supporting the conference attendance fees.

References

1. Bagatini, M.D., et al.: Immune system and chronic diseases 2018. J. Immunol. Res. (2018)
2. Van Hoovels, L., et al.: Variation in antinuclear antibody detection by automated indirect immunofluorescence analysis. Ann. Rheum. Dis. **78**(6), e48–e48 (2019)
3. Cascio, D., et al.: Deep CNN for IIF images classification in autoimmune diagnostics. Appl. Sci. **9**(8), 1618 (2019)
4. Jain, S., et al.: Role of direct immunofluorescence microscopy in spectrum of diffuse proliferative glomerulonephritis: a single-center study. J. Microsc. Ultrastruct. **9**(4), 177 (2021)
5. Boyer, O., Candon, S.: Autoimmune diseases: The breakdown of self-tolerance (2021). https://www.inserm.fr/information-en-sante/dossiers-information/maladies-auto-immunes

6. Shen, L., Lin, J.: HEp-2 image classification using intensity order pooling based features and bag of words. Pattern Recognit. **47**(7), 2419–2427 (2014)

7. Liu, L., Wang, L.: HEp-2 cell image classification with multiple linear descriptors. Pattern Recognit. **47**(7), 2400–2408 (2014)

8. Qawqzeh, Y., Bajahzar, A., Jemmali, M., Otoom, M., Thaljaoui, A.: Classification of diabetes using photoplethysmogram (PPG) waveform analysis: logistic regression modeling. BioMed Res. Int. 2020 (2020)

9. Driss, K., Boulila, W., Batool, A., Ahmad, J.: A novel approach for classifying diabetes' patients based on imputation and machine learning. In: 2020 International Conference On UK-China Emerging Technologies (UCET), pp. 1–4 (2020)

10. Al-Sarem, M., Alsaeedi, A., Saeed, F., Boulila, W., AmeerBakhsh, O.: A novel hybrid deep learning model for detecting COVID-19-related rumors on social media based on LSTM and concatenated parallel CNNs. Appl. Sci. **11**, 7940 (2021)

11. Al-Sarem, M., Saeed, F., Boulila, W., Emara, A.H., Al-Mohaimeed, M., Errais, M.: Feature selection and classification using CatBoost method for improving the performance of predicting Parkinson's disease. In: Saeed, F., Al-Hadhrami, T., Mohammed, F., Mohammed, E. (eds.) Advances on Smart and Soft Computing. AISC, vol. 1188, pp. 189–199. Springer, Singapore (2021). https://doi.org/10.1007/978-981-15-6048-4_17

12. Ben Atitallah, S., Driss, M., Boulila, W., Ben Ghezala, H.: Randomly initialized convolutional neural network for the recognition of COVID-19 using X-ray images. Int. J. Imaging Syst. Technol. **32**, 55–73 (2022)

13. Rasool, M., Ismail, N., Boulila, W., Ammar, A., Samma, H., Yafooz, W., Emara, A.: A hybrid deep learning model for brain tumour classification. Entropy **24**, 799 (2022)

14. Jemmali, M., Melhim, L., Alourani, A., Alam, M.: Equity distribution of quality evaluation reports to doctors in health care organizations. PeerJ Comput. Sci. **8**, e819 (2022)

15. Alam, M., Melhim, L., Ahmad, M., Jemmali, M.: Public attitude towards covid-19 vaccination: validation of covid-vaccination attitude scale (c-vas). J. Multidisc. Healthc., 941–954 (2022)

16. https://www.abcam.com/secondary-antibodies/direct-vs-indirect-immunofluorescence

17. Han, X.-H., Lei, J., Chen, Y.-W.: HEp-2 cell classification using k-support spatial pooling in deep CNNs. In: Carneiro, G., et al. (eds.) LABELS/DLMIA -2016. LNCS, vol. 10008, pp. 3–11. Springer, Cham (2016). https://doi.org/10.1007/978-3-319-46976-8_1

18. Phan, H.T.H., et al.: Transfer learning of a convolutional neural network for HEp-2 cell image classification. In: 2016 IEEE 13th International Symposium on Biomedical Imaging (ISBI), pp. 1208–1211. IEEE (2016)

19. Lu, M., et al.: Hep- 2 cell image classification method based on very deep convolutional networks with small datasets. In: Ninth International Conference on Digital Image Processing (ICDIP 2017), vol. 10420, p. 1042040. Inter- national Society for Optics and Photonics (2017)

20. Benammar Elgaaied, A., et al.: Computer-assisted classification patterns in autoimmune di- agnostics: the AIDA project. BioMed Res. Int. (2016)

21. Vununu, C., Lee, S.-H., Kwon, O.-J., Kwon, K.-R.: A dynamic learning method for the classification of the hep-2 cell images. Electronics **8**(8), 850 (2019)

22. Bayramoglu, N., et al.: Human epithelial type 2 cell classification with convolutional neural networks. In: 2015 IEEE 15th International Conference on Bioinformatics and Bioengineering (BIBE), pp. 1–6. IEEE (2015)

23. Rodrigues, L.F., et al.: HEp-2 cell image classification based on convolutional neural networks. In: 2017 Workshop of Computer Vision (WVC), pp. 13–18. IEEE (2017)
24. Rodrigues, L.F., et al.: Comparing convolutional neural networks and preprocessing techniques for hep-2 cell classification in immunofluorescence images. Comput. Biol. Med. **116**, 103542 (2020)
25. Majtner, T., Bajić, B., Lindblad, J., Sladoje, N., Blanes-Vidal, V., Nadimi, E.S.: On the effectiveness of generative adversarial networks as HEp-2 image augmentation tool. In: Felsberg, M., Forssén, P.-E., Sintorn, I.-M., Unger, J. (eds.) SCIA 2019. LNCS, vol. 11482, pp. 439–451. Springer, Cham (2019). https://doi.org/10.1007/978-3-030-20205-7_36
26. Li, H., et al.: Deep CNNs for hep-2 cells classification: A cross-specimen analysis. arXiv preprint arXiv:1604.05816 (2016)
27. Lei, H., et al.: A deeply supervised residual network for hep-2 cell classification via cross-modal transfer learning. Pattern Recognit. **79**, 290–302 (2018)

An Improved Approach for Parkinson's Disease Classification Based on Convolutional Neural Network

Jihen Fourati[1(✉)], Mohamed Othmani[2], and Hela Ltifi[3,4]

[1] National Engineering School of Sfax, University of Sfax, 1173 Sfax, Tunisia
jihen.fourati@enis.u-sfax.tn
[2] Faculty of Sciences of Gafsa, University of Gafsa, 2100 Gafsa, Tunisia
m.othmani@qu.edu.sa
[3] Faculty of Sciences and Techniques of Sidi Bouzid, University of Kairouan, Kairouan, Tunisia
[4] Research Groups in Intelligent Machines Lab, 3038 Sfax, Tunisia
Hela.ltifi@ieee.org

Abstract. Parkinson's Disease remains one of the most critical progressive neurological disorders that affect both motor and cognitive function. Therefore, the investigation into some solutions for Parkinson's disease classification is warranted. Our focus lies specifically on DaTscan images, which play a crucial role in diagnosing neurodegenerative Parkinsonian syndrome. In this study, we propose an approach utilizing convolutional neural networks, incorporating data augmentation and image preprocessing techniques, to accurately classify DaTscan images of both healthy control subjects and those with Parkinson's disease. To leverage the power of transfer learning, we have evaluated our CNN model against well-established pre-trained models such as vgg16, resnet50, and inception v3. Experiments carried out on the PPMI dataset proved the effectiveness of our proposed model compared to state-of-the-art methods.

Keywords: Parkinson's disease · Convolutional neural network · Transfer learning · Classification

1 Introduction

Parkinson's disease (PD) is the second most common neurodegenerative disorder of the population in the age group greater than 65 years [1]. The characteristic symptoms are tremors at rest, bradykinesia, and rigidity. The cause of PD is the loss of dopaminergic neurons in the substantia nigra of the brain [1]. People with PD lose the nerve endings that produce dopamine, the major chemical which controls most of the involuntary functions of the body. Dopamine is a substance produced by neurons that act as neurotransmitters. When the neurons in the substantia nigra begin to damage or die, less dopamine is produced, which is the main cause of the onset of Parkinson's disease in an individual [2]. The reason

N. T. Nguyen et al. (Eds.): ICCCI 2023, CCIS 1864, pp. 123–135, 2023.
https://doi.org/10.1007/978-3-031-41774-0_10

behind the impairment of these neurons is still unknown. Parkinson's disease cannot be cured, but an early diagnosis can help the individual receive adequate treatment and avoid the critical situation [3]. Early detection of Parkinson's disease is difficult for a number of reasons. Mainly, neurologists and movement order specialists can diagnose this disease only after reviewing the patient's complete medical history and repeated scans which are both time-consuming and inconvenient for the patients as most of them are above the age of sixty. The domain awareness of physicians who analyze the patient's data and symptoms plays a key role in accurately diagnosing and classifying Parkinson's disease. As a result, classifying Parkinson's disease is a difficult task, as experts are stressed by the high workload [4].

This study suggests a deep learning model that accurately classifies any given DaTSCAN as having Parkinson's disease or not. The transfer learning pretrained: vgg16, resnet50, and inception v3 models, are used for the discrimination of healthy control and PD subjects. The proposed method improves classification accuracy without significantly rising computing costs, in contrast to many previous deep learning-based approaches that are computationally intensive. We used deep learning as the primary methodology due to its varied capabilities including feature extraction. We construct the main problem of this study as a classification problem to make it traceable. We demonstrate the effectiveness of our proposed model on the PPMI benchmark dataset. As a consequence, the proposed approach was able to reach 98.5% accuracy.

2   Literature Review

Many studies have used various methods including gait freezing, electromyography signals, Single-photon emission computed tomography images, magnetic resonance imaging images, and image sketches for Parkinson's diagnosis [21–30]. Researchers applied approaches based on machine learning for the diagnosis of PD falling primarily into discrimination between PD and healthy control, differential diagnosis, and early detection of PD [9]. There are numerous methods that have been reported in the literature which has focused on the early detection of Parkinson's disease. For example, Brahim et al. [5] performed their experiments for classifying PD using shape and surface-fitting-based features and a support vector machine classifier. They achieved a 92.6% accuracy, a 91.2% sensitivity, and a specificity of 93.1%. Furthermore, Rumman et al. [6] suggested convolutional neural networks detect patterns in DaTSCAN images associated with PD. An artificial neural network was designed with the sigmoid function as the activation function, and the model was trained using this architecture. They obtained an accuracy of 94%, a sensitivity of 100%, and a specificity of 88% as a result. Whereas, Ortiz et al. [7] trained two CNN architectures, LeNet and AlexNet, to classify DaTScan images with an average accuracy of 95.1% and AUC = 97%.

Moreover, Sivaranjini et al. [8] proposed pre-trained AlexNet for 2D MRI scan classification to improve PD diagnosis. The study reached 88.90% accuracy. Their proposed architecture exhibited true positive rate and true negative rate values of 89.30 and 88.40%, respectively. Indeed, Esmaeilzadeh et al. [9] used a deep learning framework for simultaneous classification and regression of Parkinson's disease diagnosis based on MR-Images and personal information. They achieved an accuracy of 81.2 and 84.1%, respectively, for the original and simplified model. Indeed, Pavan et al [10] proposed a DL-based model using LIME and VGG16 to distinguish PD from non-PD. They obtained 95.20% accuracy which is relatively less than our proposed technique. Quan et al. [11] utilize the inceptionV3 architecture in their experiment on predicting PD. In order to account for the small dataset size, they implemented a ten-fold cross-validation to evaluate the model's performance. They obtained a 98.4% accuracy, a sensitivity score of 98.8%, and a specificity score of 97.6%. Besides, Ankit et al [12] applied a fuzzy fusion logic-based ensemble approach to an ensemble of deep learning models to predict Parkinson's using DaTscan images. They accomplished 98.45% of accuracy. Furthermore, Prashant et al. [33] developed various classification models that can discriminate between scans of healthy normal, early PD, and SWEDD subjects. Their proposed model achieved an accuracy of 96.14%, a sensitivity score of 95.74%, and 77.35% specificity.

3   Methodology

This section highlights and details the proposed research methodology for Parkinson's disease classification. The proposed method is mainly represented in three steps. First, we conducted image preprocessing. Secondly, we performed data augmentation to balance the imbalanced dataset before we fed data to the proposed model. Then, we thoroughly elaborated on the proposed CNN-based approach and its architecture to classify the patients based on the dopamine level inside the brain from DaTscan images.

3.1   Data Preprocessing

Before dealing with the data, some signal manipulations were needed. First, we converted all DaTscan images from DICOM format into png format. Since the brains of men and women differ in size, we cropped the superfluous dark edges. As a result, the dimensions of the extracted images became irregular. To this end, we resized them to 224×224 resolution and scaled them between zero and one value.

3.2   Data Augmentation

To increase the dataset size, we employed data augmentation and pre-processing techniques. In practical terms, we have a limited amount of data. There are different types of data augmentation techniques that we have applied including vertical flip, shift augmentation, image rotation with the range between $-20°$ and $20°$, and changing brightness from the range of 0.9 to 1.5. The data are fed into the model through ImageDataGenerator class of the TensorFlow deep learning library. To execute the data augmentation process, input data are segregated into a directory named train, test, and validation.

3.3   Convolutional Neural Network Backbones

Transfer learning focuses on transferring knowledge from one domain to another [34]. It refers to machine learning techniques that consist of adopting features learned on source problems and leveraging them on a new but similar target problem. The key advantage of transfer learning is that it reduces the time taken to develop and train a model by reutilizing the weights of previously developed models [35]. For this study, the dataset is preprocessed to make it suitable for transfer learning tasks. Indeed, we used convolutional neural networks with transfer learning to early detect Parkinson's disease. The convolutional neural network architectures covered in this article were chosen not at random but rather based on their popularity and performance in different state-of-the-art disease classification models. The three CNNs (vgg16, inceptionv3, and restnet50) that serve as the baseline architectures for our suggested approach are briefly introduced in this section to keep the study self-contained [36]. Different pre-trained convolutional neural network variants are utilized, including vgg16, inceptionv3, and restnet50 to figure out the well-fitting model.

Vgg16 Network. The vgg16 network is an improved version of the AlexNet deep CNN model. It was one of the best-performing architectures in the ImageNet Large Scale Visual Recognition Challenge [14]. The vgg16 network consists of 16 hidden layers (13 convolutional layers and three fully connected layers) and has a small receptive field of 3×3. It contains five max-pooling layers of size 2×2. There are 3 fully connected layers after the last max-pooling layer. It uses the softmax classifer as the final layer. Every hidden layer is provided with the ReLU activation function [14].

Resnet50 Network. The resnet50 model introduces a 50-layer deep residual learning and has over 23 million trainable parameters. It consists of 5 stages each with a convolution and Identity block [15]. Each convolution block has 3 convolution layers and each identity block also has 3 convolution layers. The architecture involves two concepts for model optimization [15]. The layers possess the same number of filters for the same type of output feature maps. Moreover, when the output feature map's size is halved, the number of filters is doubled to preserve each layer's time complexity [15].

InceptionV3 Network. The inceptionV3 module is a widely used model for image classification tasks. It usually includes three different convolution sizes and maximum pooling [16]. For the network output of the previous layer, the channel is aggregated after the convolution operation, followed by non-linear fusion. Thus, network expression and adaptability at different scales can be improved, and overfitting can be prevented [16].

3.4   Convolutional Neural Network Model

The convolutional neural network is a very useful neural network inspired by the human nervous system and achieves high performance in a wide range of applications compared to traditional methods [17]. Typical CNN is a mathematical construct that is composed of multiple building blocks [18]: two computational layers (convolution layer, subsampling layer), and an ultimate classification through a fully connected layer as shown in Fig. 1. The convolutional layer computes the convolutional operation of the input data using kernel filters to extract high-level features. It contains a set of filters, the parameters of which are to be learned throughout the training. Each kernel is convolved with the input data to perform an activation feature map. The output volume of the convolutional layer is obtained by stacking the activation maps of all filters along the depth dimension [19]. The subsampling layer provides typical downsampling of the output size dimension by average pooling or max-pooling over the feature maps in the convolutional layer [18]. It is used to reduce both overfitting as well as a computational burden. The fully-connected layer performs a high-level logical operation by collecting the features from the pooling layer. It generates the CNN model output data [18]. Figure 1 shows the processing of CNN where M denotes the number of input features. C_i and S_i denote ith convolutional and subsampling layers, respectively. Let CK_i denote the kernel size in C_i layer; also, SP_i denotes the pooling size in S_i layer. Then, CM_i and SM_i denote the number of filter output in C_i layer and the number of output in S_i layer, respectively. FNN is a fully connected layer; the output of which is the output from the entire network [18]. Thus, CNN performs training on data by alternating between convolutional and subsampling layers to reflect the characteristics of sequence data.

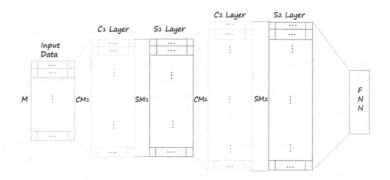

Fig. 1. Network structure of the CNN.

3.5 Convolutional Neural Network for Parkinson's Diseases Classification

The convolutional neural network is a category of models dedicated to extracting features from 2D inputs (e.g., images). A typical CNN is constructed by three types of layers: the convolutional layer, the max-pooling layer, and the fully connected layer. In this work, CNN has been used successfully as a Parkinson's disease classifier. The training strategy used in this study is based on PD and non-PD patches because of its rapid convergence time compared with whole image-based training. Our proposed model utilizes an iterative structure consisting of convolutional and max pooling layers repeated five times. This sequence is followed by a flattened layer, which transforms the multidimensional feature maps into a one-dimensional vector, and two fully connected layers. This architecture allows the model to learn hierarchical representations through multiple levels of feature extraction and abstraction. To delve deeper, the inputs go through a stack of a couple of convolutions and a max-pooling layer, followed by one flattened layer, one fully connected layer and dropout layer, and an output layer. The convolution layers (1, 2, 3, 4, 5) are convolved with their respective kernel number (16, 32, 64, 64, and 128). After each one of the convolution layers, the max-pooling layer, also known as a down-sampling layer, is applied to the feature maps. It was employed to minimize computational complexity and supervise overfitting. The stride for the previous layers is set at 3. The model exhibits nonlinearity by providing all layers with the rectified linear unit (ReLU) activation function. ReLU doesn't reach saturation, it prevents gradients from saturating in deep networks, and thus mitigates the incidence of vanishing gradients compared to sigmoid and hyperbolic tangent activation functions. The mathematical form of the ReLU function is as follows:

$$f(x) = max(0, x) \tag{1}$$

where x is the input to a neuron. 3×3 filters are employed in all the convolutional layers. The pool size of each max-pooling size is set to 2×2. To prevent the problem of overfitting, we inject dropout several times. Dropout [20] is a regularization model with low calculation cost and strong deep learning ability. In dropout, a hyper-parameter of neuron sampling probability (p) is chosen. While the default value is set as 0.5, it is not a norm, and thus, it must be constantly tested with different data and networks. The output of our model is a probability, firstly, we end our network with a single-unit layer with a sigmoid activation that classifies every data point into one of the two different categories, and binary cross-entropy is used as the loss function. Sigmoid permits each class to have higher probabilities. The predicted probabilities using the sigmoid function are given as follows [31],

$$Pr(Y_i = 0) = \frac{e^{-\beta.Xi}}{1 + e^{-\beta.Xi}} \tag{2}$$

$$Pr(Y_i = 0) = 1 - Pr(Y_i = 0) = \frac{1}{1 + e^{-\beta.Xi}} \tag{3}$$

The details of each layer parameter of the proposed Parkinson's disease classification CNN model are presented in Table 1. For the training parameters of the proposed network, we adopted 85% of samples for training and the remaining 15% for testing.

Table 1. The architecture of our classification model.

Layers No	Type	Rate	No. kernels/Units	Output shape
Layer 1	Conv2D		16, (3,3)	224 × 224 × 3
Layer 2	MaxPool2D		(2, 2)	127 × 127× 16
Layer 3	Conv2D		32, (3,3)	127 × 127× 32
Layer 4	MaxPool2D		(2, 2)	63 × 63 × 32
Layer 5	Conv2D		64, (3,3)	63 × 63 × 64
Layer 6	MaxPool2D		(2, 2)	31 × 31 × 64
Layer 7	Conv2D		64, (3,3)	16 × 16 × 64
Layer 8	MaxPool2D		(2, 2)	8 × 8 × 64
Layer 9	Conv2D		128, (3,3)	4 × 4 × 128
Layer 10	MaxPool2D		(2, 2)	2 × 2 × 128
Layer 11	Flatten			128
Layer 12	Dense		64	64
Layer 13	Dropout	0.2		64
Layer 14	Dense			2

Given that the main objective of this research study described in the paper is to distinguish between individuals with Parkinson's disease and healthy controls, i.e., a binary classification problem, the optimal choice entails configuring the model with the adaptive moment estimation (ADAM) optimizer. and the hinge loss function plus an L2 Regularization. ADAM algorithm ensures that the learning steps, during the training process, are scale-invariant relative to the parameter gradients [32]. Finally, we trained our network in 400 epochs with 128 batch sizes.

4   Experiments and Results

4.1   Dataset Description

The present experiments were conducted using a dataset containing DaTscan images for 1290 PD and healthy control (HC) subjects extracted from the Parkinson's Progression Markers Initiative (PPMI). DaTscan images have been extensively used for the automatic diagnosis of Parkinson's disease after pre-processing and reordering from PPMI images. The dataset consists of a total of 1290 images (1097 instances are related to PD patients and the rest are related to healthy individuals).

4.2   Experiment Setup and Result Analysis

Our model experiments were developed in Keras and trained using an Intel Pentium N3520 CPU on 64-bit Windows 10 OS. All methods were executed using Jupyter Notebooks (Python 3.9.10). For our study, the proposed approach was tested on the PPMI dataset. The Keras deep learning framework is used and includes a variety of pre-trained deep learning models along with their weights networks used for this work including vgg16, resnet50, and inceptionV3. Figure 2 shows the results of the accuracy and loss of our proposed model on the PPMI dataset during the training phase. The blue graph illustrates the training set and the orange graph illustrates the validation set. We reached a training binary accuracy = 0.9952, validation binary accuracy = 0.985, training loss = 0.1743, and validation loss = 0.0479.

To compare our experiments with previous works, we defined four metrics: accuracy, recall, precision, and F-measure. While accuracy is one of the measures used to test a network, it tends to be misleading. In such cases, other evaluation metrics should be considered in addition to accuracy. Recall, precision, and F-measure are excellent quantification measures for binary classifications. Accuracy was computed using the following expression:

$$Accuracy = \frac{TP + TN}{TP + FP + TN + FN} \tag{4}$$

where TP is true positive, TN is true negative, FP is false positive, and FN is false negative (Table 2).
Recall was computed as:

$$Recall = \frac{TP}{TP + FN} \tag{5}$$

Precision was computed as:

$$Precision = \frac{TP}{TP + FP} \tag{6}$$

F-measure was computed as:

$$F - measure = \frac{2 \times recall \times precision}{recall + precision} \tag{7}$$

In order to show the performance of the proposed method, we referred to several other pre-trained models with different structures (vgg16, restnet0, and inceptionV3). We reported evaluation results in Table 3. The performance evaluation was conducted by training and testing using the same data in each model. Table 4 illustrates the comparison between our proposed approach and other previous studies. The proposed approach which is based on the CNN achieved 98.5%, 100%, 96.9%, and,98.4% for accuracy, recall, precision, and F-measure, respectively. The vgg16 model attained 96.364% accuracy, 97.4% precision, 98.4% recall, and 97.54% F-measure, which are higher than inceptionV3 and resnet50 but low compared to CNN. The resnet50 model attained 89.094%

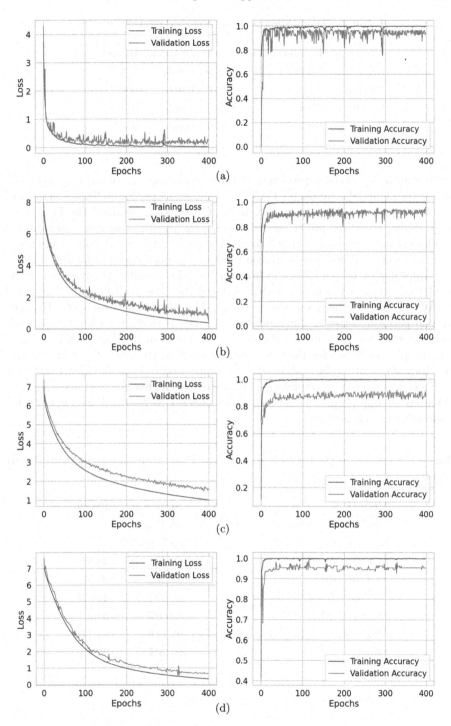

Fig. 2. Accuracy and Loss curves (training and validation) (a) Proposed CNN (b) Vgg16 (c) Resnet50 (d) InceptionV3.

Table 2. Classification performances in three CNN models.

	Proposed CNN	Vgg16	Resnet50	InceptionV3
Accuracy	0.985	0.9636	0.8909	0.9545
Precision	1	0.97	0.965	0.97
Recall	0.969	0.98	0.965	0.98
F-measure	0.954	0.975	0.965	0.975

testing accuracy, 96.54% precision, 96.54% recall, and 96.54% F-measure. The inceptionV3 model attained 95.454% accuracy, 97.4% precision, 98.4% recall, and 97.54% F-measure. We observed that the CNN model attained the best accuracy among the three pre-trained deep-learning models, and resnet50 attained the lowest accuracy as compared to other models. The receiver operating characteristic curve (ROC) has been also used as a performance parameter. ROC is a graphical plot by which the performance of the classifier is presented. ROC is plotted between the true-positive rate and the false-positive rate. The value of AUC is ranging between zero and one. The higher the values of AUC, the system perform better in differentiating between patients with healthy individuals. All the classifiers have performed well in terms of AUC as shown in Fig. 3. The results could be classified as favorable since to the best of our knowledge, it achieved one of the best accuracies in comparison to state-of-the-art methods of Parkinson's disease classification. It can be noted that the best accuracy was achieved by our proposed method, which attests to its excellent capacity for addressing the challenge.

Table 3. Proposed method classification accuracy rate with existing methods (PPMI dataset).

Method	Accuracy	Recall
CNN models + FRLF [12]	98.45%	–
LeNet and AlexNet [7]	95% ±0.30%	–
InceptionV3 [11]	98.40%	98.8%
VGG-16 [10]	95.20%	97.5%
Custom ANN [6]	94.00%	**100%**
PCA with SVM [5]	92.60%	91.2%
SVM with Striatal Binding Ratio [33]	96.14%	95.74%
Ours	**98.5%**	96.9%

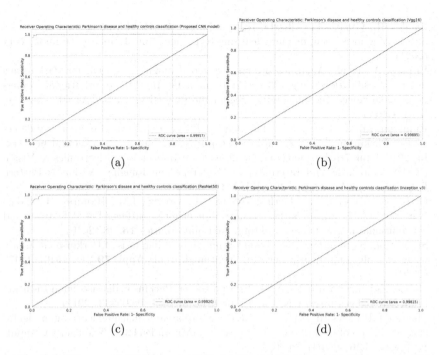

Fig. 3. ROC curve (a) Proposed CNN (b) Vgg16 (c) Resnet50 (d) InceptionV3.

5   Conclusion

This paper proposed a convolutional neural network approach, along with data augmentation and image preprocessing to classify the DaTscan images of healthy control and Parkinson's disease subjects. We have exploited the high-level feature extraction of the convolutional neural network model. The premise of our work is that it should be possible to characterize different subjects based on DaTscan images. As exhibited in experiments, the proposed approach outperforms state-of-the-art methods in terms of accuracy. In the future, we intend to expand the proposed model to be able to deal with multiclass Parkinson's disease classification.

References

1. Mhyre, T.R., Boyd, J.T., Hamill, R.W., Maguire-Zeiss, K.A.: Protein Aggregation and Fibrillogenesis in Cerebral and Systemic Amyloid Disease, vol. 65, p. 389 (2012)
2. National Institute of Neurological Disorders and Stroke (US) (1994). Parkinson's disease: Hope through research (No. 94–139). National Institute of Neurological Disorders and Stroke, National Institutes of Health
3. Emamzadeh, F.N., Surguchov, A.: Parkinson's disease: biomarkers, treatment, and risk factors. Front. Neurosci. **12**, 612 (2018). https://doi.org/10.3389/fnins.2018.00612

4. Lamba, R., Gulati, T., Alharbi, H.F., Jain, A.: A hybrid system for Parkinson's disease diagnosis using machine learning techniques. Int. J. Speech Technol., 1–11 (2021)
5. Brahim, A., et al.: A proposed computer-aided diagnosis system for Parkinson's disease classification using 123 I-FP-CIT imaging. In: 2017 International Conference on Advanced Technologies for Signal and Image Processing (ATSIP), pp. 1–6. IEEE (2017)
6. Rumman, M., Tasneem, A.N., Farzana, S., Pavel, M.I., Alam, M.A.: Early detection of Parkinson's disease using image processing and artificial neural network. In: 2018 Joint 7th International Conference on Informatics, Electronics & Vision (ICIEV) and 2018 2nd International Conference on Imaging, Vision & Pattern Recognition (icIVPR), pp. 256–261. IEEE (2018)
7. Ortiz, A., Munilla, J., Martínez-Ibañez, M., Górriz, J.M., Ramírez, J., Salas-Gonzalez, D.: Parkinson's disease detection using isosurfaces-based features and convolutional neural networks. Front. Neuroinformatics 13, 48 (2019)
8. Sivaranjini, S., Sujatha, C.M.: Deep learning based diagnosis of Parkinson's disease using convolutional neural network. Multimed. Tools Appl. 79(21), 15467–15479 (2020)
9. Esmaeilzadeh, S., Yang, Y., Adeli, E.: End-to-end Parkinson disease diagnosis using brain MR-images by 3d-CNN. arXiv preprint arXiv:1806.05233 (2018)
10. Magesh, P.R., Myloth, R.D., Tom, R.J.: An explainable machine learning model for early detection of Parkinson's disease using LIME on DaTSCAN imagery. Comput. Biol. Med. 126, 104041 (2020)
11. Quan, J., Xu, L., Xu, R., Tong, T., Su, J.: DaTscan SPECT Image Classification for Parkinson's Disease. arXiv preprint arXiv:1909.04142 (2019)
12. Kurmi, A., Biswas, S., Sen, S., Sinitca, A., Kaplun, D., Sarkar, R.: An ensemble of CNN models for Parkinson's disease detection using DaTscan images. Diagnostics 12(5), 1173 (2022)
13. Parkinson's Progression Markers Initiative. https://www.ppmi-info.org/. Accessed 2 Mar 2019
14. Ghosh, S., Bandyopadhyay, M.: Detection of coronavirus (COVID-19) using deep convolutional neural networks with transfer learning using chest x-ray images. In: Bandyopadhyay, M., Rout, M., Chandra Satapathy, S. (eds.) Machine Learning Approaches for Urban Computing. SCI, vol. 968, pp. 63–77. Springer, Singapore (2021). https://doi.org/10.1007/978-981-16-0935-0_4
15. Bhagyalaxmi, D., Babu, B.S.: Using deep neural networks for predicting diseased cotton plants and leafs. In: Raj, J.S., Kamel, K., Lafata, P. (eds.) Innovative Data Communication Technologies and Application. LNCS, vol. 96, pp. 385–399. Springer, Singapore (2022). https://doi.org/10.1007/978-981-16-7167-8_28
16. Gu, J., et al.: Recent advances in convolutional neural networks. Pattern Recognit. 77, 354–377 (2018)
17. Ko, B.C.: A brief review of facial emotion recognition based on visual information. Sensors 18(2), 401 (2018)
18. Pak, U., Kim, C., Ryu, U., Sok, K., Pak, S.: A hybrid model based on convolutional neural networks and long short-term memory for ozone concentration prediction. Air Qual. Atmos. Health 11(8), 883–895 (2018)
19. Mostafa, S., Wu, F.X.: Diagnosis of autism spectrum disorder with convolutional autoencoder and structural MRI images. In: Neural Engineering Techniques for Autism Spectrum Disorder, pp. 23–38. Academic Press (2021)

20. Srivastava, N., Hinton, G., Krizhevsky, A., Sutskever, I., Salakhutdinov, R.: Dropout: a simple way to prevent neural networks from overfitting. J. Mach. Learn. Res. **15**(1), 1929–1958 (2014)
21. Fourati, J., Othmani, M., Ltifi, H.: A hybrid model based on convolutional neural networks and long short-term memory for rest tremor classification. In: ICAART , no. 3, pp. 75–82 (2022)
22. Fourati, J., Othmani, M., Ltifi, H.: A hybrid model based on bidirectional long-short term memory and support vector machine for rest tremor classification. Signal Image Video Process. **16**(8), 2175–2182 (2022)
23. Othmani, M.: A vehicle detection and tracking method for traffic video based on faster R-CNN. Multimed. Tools Appl. **81**(20), 28347–28365 (2022)
24. Ben Salah, K., Othmani, M., Kherallah, M.: Long short-term memory based photo-plethysmography biometric authentication. In: Badica, C., Treur, J., Benslimane, D., Hnatkowska, B., Krotkiewicz, M. (eds.) ICCCI. LNCS, vol. 1653, pp. 554–563. Springer, Cham (2022). https://doi.org/10.1007/978-3-031-16210-7_45
25. Benjemmaa, A., Ltifi, H., Ayed, M.B.: Design of remote heart monitoring system for cardiac patients. In: Barolli, L., Takizawa, M., Xhafa, F., Enokido, T. (eds.) AINA 2019. AISC, vol. 926, pp. 963–976. Springer, Cham (2020). https://doi.org/10.1007/978-3-030-15032-7_81
26. Ltifi, H., Ayed, M.B., Kolski, C., Alimi, A.M.: HCI-enriched approach for DSS development: the UP/U approach. In: 2009 IEEE Symposium on Computers and Communications, pp. 895–900. IEEE (2009)
27. Ltifi, H., Ayed, M.B., Trabelsi, G., Alimi, A.M.: Using perspective wall to visualize medical data in the Intensive Care Unit. In: 2012 IEEE 12th International Conference on Data Mining Workshops, pp. 72–78. IEEE (2012)
28. Ellouzi, H., Ltifi, H., Ayed, M.B.: New multi-agent architecture of visual intelligent decision support systems application in the medical field. In: 2015 IEEE/ACS 12th International Conference of Computer Systems and Applications (AICCSA), pp. 1–8. IEEE (2015)
29. Salah, K.B., Othmani, M., Kherallah, M.: A novel approach for human skin detection using convolutional neural network. Vis. Comput. **38**(5), 1833–1843 (2021). https://doi.org/10.1007/s00371-021-02108-3
30. Ben Salah, K., Othmani, M., Kherallah, M.: Contactless heart rate estimation from facial video using skin detection and multi-resolution analysis (2021)
31. Basly, H., Ouarda, W., Sayadi, F.E., Ouni, B., Alimi, A.M.: DTR-HAR: deep temporal residual representation for human activity recognition. Vis. Comput., 1–21 (2021). https://doi.org/10.1007/s00371-021-02064-y
32. Livieris, I.E., Pintelas, E., Pintelas, P.: A CNN-LSTM model for gold price time-series forecasting. Neural Comput. Appl. **32**(23), 17351–17360 (2020)
33. Prashanth, R., Roy, S.D., Mandal, P.K., Ghosh, S.: High-accuracy classification of Parkinson's disease through shape analysis and surface fitting in 123I-Ioflupane SPECT imaging. IEEE J. Biomed. Health Inf. **21**(3), 794–802 (2016)
34. Ying, W., Zhang, Y., Huang, J., Yang, Q.: Transfer learning via learning to transfer. In: International Conference on Machine Learning, pp. 5085–5094. PMLR (2018)
35. Theckedath, D., Sedamkar, R.R.: Detecting affect states using VGG16, ResNet50 and SE-ResNet50 networks. SN Comput. Sci. **1**, 1–7 (2020)
36. Ukwuoma, C.C., Hossain, M.A., Jackson, J.K., Nneji, G.U., Monday, H.N., Qin, Z.: Multi classification of breast cancer lesions in histopathological images using DEEP_Pachi: multiple self-attention head. Diagnostics **12**(5), 1152 (2022)

A Convolutional Recurrent Neural Network Model for Classification of Parkinson's Disease from Resting State Multi-channel EEG Signals

Fatma Salah$^{(\boxtimes)}$ [iD], Dhouha Guesmi [iD], and Yassine Ben Ayed [iD]

Multimedia, InfoRmation Systems and Advanced Computing Laboratory: MIRACL,
University of Sfax, Sfax, Tunisia
bensalahfatma60@gmail.com

Abstract. Parkinson's disease (PD) is an evolutionary neurologic disorder which affects the functioning of the brain by the progressive loss of dopaminergic nerve cells. Parkinson's signs such as tremor, slowed movement and muscles rigidity are all common motor symptoms. In addition, other non-motor symptoms such as cognitive changes, dementia, and anxiety that are difficult to detect in early stages. Thus, early diagnosis of the disease is very important to take the preventive measures. Therefore, the analysis of EEG signals based on deep learning models have shown a great power in the diagnosis process. This work develops a deep learning approach based on Convolutional Recurrent Neural Network (CRNN) in order to discriminate between patients suffering from Parkinson's and Healthy Controls (HC) using Electro Encephalo Graphy (EEG) signals. The hybrid neural network algorithms CRNN consist of a mixture of recurrent neural network (RNN) and convolutional neural network (CNN). Parkinson's disease dataset was used in a resting state, which is consists of twenty PD and twenty normal subjects. The main objectives of CRNN use are that can extract automatically multiple characteristics from the input signals such as spatial and temporal features. For testing and evaluating our approach, the model was assessed using a non-overlapping 2-s EEG segments and a 10-fold cross-validation strategy. A significantly high accuracy of 96.16% was achieved with the developed model.

Keywords: Parkinson · Convolutional recurrent neural network · EEG · Preprocessing · Deep learning · Computer-Aided Diagnostic (CAD)

1 Introduction

Human brain presents a major challenge in the modern science since it still holds secrets for us, even though humanity has been very persistent to understand the brain. The human body is made up of trillions of cells. The human brain has about 86 billion neurons [1]. Many neurological disorders can cause brain dysfunction and affect the health of patients, such as PD.

PD is inevitably recognized to be one of the brain neurodegenerative disorders of the central nervous system that affects small areas of the brain. When functioning normally,

© The Author(s), under exclusive license to Springer Nature Switzerland AG 2023
N. T. Nguyen et al. (Eds.): ICCCI 2023, CCIS 1864, pp. 136–146, 2023.
https://doi.org/10.1007/978-3-031-41774-0_11

the nerve cells in an area of the brain called substantia nigra produce chemical known as dopamine. Dopamine serves as chemical messenger allowing communication between the substantia nigra and the basal ganglia. The lack of dopamine often impairs the patient's motor skills, speech, and other functions [2]. It is ranked as the second most common neurodegenerative disorder in the world after Alzheimer's Disease (AD). Based on information from the World Health Organization (WHO), PD affects more than 10 million people worldwide. Tunisia has up to 10,000 people with PD, and this number does not reflect the hundreds of undetected cases. The incidence of PD increases with age, which mostly affects the elderly population (age > 65 years old). But regardless of age, it affects not only the affected person, but also everyone around him, sooner or later, to varying degrees [3].

Diagnosing the disease is difficult because symptoms vary from person to person. There are a number of other diseases that have similar symptoms, and sometimes motor or non-motor symptoms are not observed, which means that a misdiagnosis can occur. Recently, CAD has become more popular and has been gradually being used in the detection of neurodegenerative diseases [4, 5] to improve the accuracy of clinical tests to identify PD and make it robust. There are also a variety of techniques in the field of neurology that are used individually or in combination to support clinical diagnosis.

The neuroimaging methods, such as Single Photon Emission Computed Tomography (SPECT) [6] MRI [7, 8], Positron Emission Tomography (PET) scans with radiologically marked tracers and Computed Tomography (CT) [9, 10] are commonly used to facilitate early diagnosis and detection for PD.

EEG is a non-invasive technique recording the brain neurons electrical activity, to pick up their function with excellent temporal resolution. For these reasons, the EEG is widely used in many areas of clinical work and research.

It has been used to study neurological diseases such as epilepsy, schizophrenia, and AD [11, 12]. According to previous studies, they are basically non-linear and non-stationary, and their statistical properties change over time, therefore, we can overcome these difficulties by applying Deep Learning (DL) techniques.

In the current study, we designed a DL model to extract the hidden information and changes in the resting-state EEG signals from individuals with PD and HC to help the diagnostic of PD. The rest of the paper describes the participants and the EEG dataset used in this study. Next, we explain the description of methodology includes preprocessing strategy, classification method and the design of the proposed model. Finally, we deal with the performance of the system and the interpretation of the results.

2 Materials and Methods

2.1 Study Participants

The Parkinson's disease resting state EEG data used in this paper was downloaded on OSF open platform https://osf.io/pehj9/.

EEG data were obtained from 20 patients (11 women and 9 men) diagnosed using the UK Brain Bank criteria and 20 age-matched healthy participants (12 women and 8 men) without neurological disease.

Table 1 includes demographical information, and clinical and neuropsychological measurements of patients and healthy controls. The severity of disease was measured using the Movement Disorder Society Unified Parkinson's Disease Rating Scale (MDS-UPDRS). Eight patients had an average score at PD onset. Seven patients had MDSUP-DRS 22–35, and the remaining five patients had MDS-UPDRS $\geq$ 35. Cognitive impairment was evaluated using Mini Mental-State Exam (MMSE). During the day of the study, EEG recordings was collected from 13 PD patients when they not taking their morning medication (at least 12 h break in medication). These patients were considered as those in OFF phase.

Table 1. Participants clinical and neuropsychological information.

	Control(n = 20)	PD(n = 20)
sex (male/female)	8/12	9/11
Age (mean ± SD)	68 (6.0)	70 (7.2)
Disease duration, years (mean ± SD)	n/a	6 (4.9)
Mini-mental state score (mean ± SD)	28 (2.0)	28 (1.8)
MDS-UPDRS, motor (mean ± SD)	5 (3.0)	29 (16.4)

2.2 EEG Signal Recordings

The EEG data was measured with 64 active electrodes at 500 Hz sampling rate, and 0.16–125 Hz filtering during recording using a NeurOne Tesla amplifier.

The EEG recordings lasted two minutes of eyes-open and two minutes of eyes-closed in resting state per participant (except, due to a technical failure, the first patient's eyesclosed data was lost). In addition, the participants and patients also took part in an experiment investigating speech deficits in PD [15].

2.3 Preprocessing Phase

The EEG data were preprocessed in MATLAB using custom scripts and EEGLAB toolbox. In the preprocessing pipeline [16], we implemented a series of crucial steps to enhance the quality and extract meaningful information from the raw data.

Initially, each electrode's mean was removed then 50 Hz line noise was removed and EEG was referenced to robust average reference. To eliminate artifacts caused by eye movements and blinks the two EOG channels were removed. A high-pass filter at 0.5 Hz was employed to suppress low-frequency drifts. To further enhance the quality of the EEG recordings, data were manually examined to identify and eliminate any noticeable artifacts, such as eye blinks, electrode pops, electrode drifts, and muscle activity. Then, the regions containing these artifacts were rejected. Finally, we chose to divide the data into non-overlapping 2-second segments (1000 samples), which leads to produce large number of EEG samples. Thus, each EEG signal is represented as a data matrix of size $64 \times 2 \times 500$ where 64 is the number of electrodes and 500 the sampling rate.

After the preprocessing step and before feeding the deep convolution network, the input data was normalized to the Z-score normalization using the Eq. (1):

$$z = \frac{x - \mu}{\sigma} \tag{1}$$

Where μ, σ denote zero mean and unit standard deviation, respectively.

2.4 CRNN Model

DL networks is consisting of algorithms inspired originally by the workings of the human brain neurons. In recent decades, DL models have been successfully applicated for early detection of the neurodegenerative diseases. The point of using CRNN model is that can extract a set of various features automatically from the EEG signals including

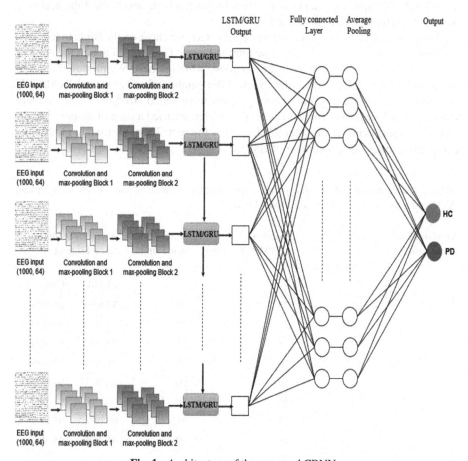

Fig. 1. Architecture of the proposed CRNN.

spatial and temporal information. Furthermore, the generated features can help to make performance better. In the CRNN network, we used the segmented signals as input for the convolutional layer. The signals dimensions are 1000×64, where 1000 is the number of points of signal in each sample and 64 is the number of EEG channels. At first, we started by using one convolutional layer, at each time we have added new layer the accuracy was on the rise. The accuracy started to decreases gradually when we combined the third convolutional layer. For this reason, we used only two convolutional layers, each of which are followed by a maximum pooling layer. After these layers, two fully connected layers time distributed are laid. We used the activation function Rectified Linear Unit (ReLU) for all layers. We also used the global average pooling after the fully connected layer. The final decision is made by using the softmax for the last layer to calculating the probability of the PD and HC classes. The proposed CRNN model was trained using Adam optimizer. For the classification problem, we applied categorical crossentropy loss function. The architecture is illustrated in the Fig. 1.

Firstly, we keep varied the number of layers and the regularization parameters that includes the number of filters and kernel sizes. We chose the number of hidden layers between the input layer and output layer by keep adding layers until the accuracy increased and the test error decreased.

As shown in Table 2, to obtain the best parameters, we chose on the begin to fixed the kernel on small size of 3 for the two convolution layers. Then, we increased the number of filters from 16 to 64 layer by layer to choose which is best. We proposed a set of values varied from 20 to 40 in order to select the number of units for the LSTM/GRU cells and dense layers. Two max pooling layers were added sized of 3 to learn more features. To helping our network to generalize better, we tried a suite of dropout values. From this experiment, we find that 0.5 dropout is the best. Then, we tried to modify the learning rate every certain number of epochs.

Table 2. Configuration information of the hyperparameter search of the CRNN model using LSTM and GRU units. *CL: Convolutional Layer.

Number of filters of the first C-L	Number of filters of the second CL	Number of LSTM/GRU units	Number of dense units	Accuracy using Kernel size of 3	
				LSTM	GRU
16	32	20	20	87.85%	85.20%
		25	25	87.76%	89.03%
		35	35	89.36%	92.51%
		40	40	81.93%	87.30%
32	64	20	20	96.00%	94.88%
		25	25	96.14%	94.34%
		35	35	96.07%	95.84%
		40	40	96.16%	95.38%

Upon tried a suite of dropout values, we find that the dropout of percentage 0.5 better than other percentages. Using two values of learning rate include 0,001 and 0,0001 the best diagnostic performance was achieved with the learning rate of 0.0001.

The Table 3 show the architecture with the best parameters of the CRNN model.

Table 3. Details of architecture and parameters of the CRNN model.

Layer	Kernel size	Number of filters	Output shape
Input	—	—	(1000,64)
1D convolution	3	32	(998,32)
Max-pooling	3	32	(332,32)
Dropout rate (0.5)	—	—	—
1D convolution	3	64	(330,64)
Max-pooling	3	64	(110,64)
Dropout rate (0.5)	—	—	—
LSTM	—	40	(110,40)
Time distributed	—	40	(110,40)
Global average pooling	—	40	(1,40)
Dense	—	40	(1,2)

As seen in the Table 3 using LSTM units the accuracy increased upon 96,16%. We can conclude that the proposed network work well with LSTM cells than GRU cells. After many experiments, we can notice that 32 maps in the first convolutional layer and 64 maps in the second convolutional layer is the best. Using small kernel sizes of 3 is much efficient. It appears that 40 units for the LSTM is the best. Dense layers with 40 units only perform slightly better and are not worth the additional computational cost.

2.5 Performance Evaluation

Without proper evaluation of the DL model using different scales, and depending only on the accuracy, it can lead to many problems and poor predictions. To improve the overall predictive power of the PD detection model we used different rating scales such as:

$$Accuracy = \frac{(TP + TN)}{(TN + TP + FN + FP)}. \tag{2}$$

$$Sensitivity-Recall = \frac{(TP)}{(FN + TP)}. \tag{3}$$

$$Specificity = \frac{(TN)}{(TN + FP)}. \tag{4}$$

$$Precision = \frac{(TP)}{(FP + TP)}. \tag{5}$$

$$F-measure = \frac{2 \times (Precision \times Recall)}{(Precision \times Recall)}. \tag{6}$$

2.6 Confusion Matrix

To improve the overall predictive power of the PD model, the confusion matrix has been also used. The confusion matrix counts the number of correct and incorrect predictions and shows the type of errors that are being made by the classifier. The matrix contains four key terms which are given as follows (Fig. 2):

		Predicted Class	
		Negative	Positive
True Class	Negative	True Negative (TN)	False Positive (FP)
	Positive	False Negative (FN)	True Positive (TP)

Fig. 2. Confusion matrix.

Where (TN) denotes True Negatives that represent the number of healthy participants who were correctly labeled.

False Positives (FP) is defined as the case where the number of healthy participants incorrectly classified as having PD.

The False Negatives (FN) is equal to the number of PD patients incorrectly classified as healthy participants and the True Positives (TP) is equal to the number of correctly classified Parkinson's patients.

3 Results and Discussion

The model was constructed in python using the powerful DL library keras with tensorflow and using google colab 12GB NVIDIA Tesla K80 GPU was provided. The batch size for the data was selected as 100.

To estimate the efficiency of our model, we used a k-fold Cross Validation (CV) strategy. We split our complete data into 10 uniform parts, fold 1, fold 2, fold 3 and so on, each part consisting of 143 segments. Then we built ten different models, each model being trained on nine out of ten parts and the rest being kept for testing. This procedure is repeated ten times so that all ten parties participate in both the training and testing phases. The final performance consists of average K-tests. The purpose of this method is to avoid overfitting the CRNN model during training. Therefore, the final accuracy and rating scales presented in this work are the average of all folds. The results per fold are summarized in the Table 4.

Table 4. Classification result of CRNN model per fold.

CV	Accuracy (%)	Specificity (%)	Sensitivity (%)	Precision (%)	F measure (%)
CV 1	97.90	100	98	97	98
CV 2	91.60	99	100	84	92
CV 3	95.80	100	90	100	95
CV 4	95.10	99	95	94	96
CV 5	99.30	91	98	100	99
CV 6	96.50	99	97	95	97
CV 7	88.11	100	100	79	88
CV 8	93.00	97	100	86	93
CV 9	97.20	99	100	94	97
CV10	89.51	95	100	81	90
Tenfold Average	96.16	97,9	97,8	91,0	94,5

We used metrics such as accuracy, specificity, sensitivity, precision, and F-measure to evaluate the obtained experimental results. The performance results in Table 4 showed that the proposed CRNN approach provided an ideal classification accuracy, specificity and sensitivity. According to Table 4, We can see all the accuracy of each test fold and the average of these tests that gives an accuracy of 96,16%.

An average classification accuracy of 96.16%, specificity of 97,9%, sensitivity of 97,8% were achieved with the proposed CRNN.

We found that the CRNN network with hybrid architecture composed of CNN and LSTM cells work better than with GRU cells.

According to Fig. 3, only 67 EEG epochs from the HC (Healthy Control) group were misclassified incorrectly as Parkinson's patient group, and 13 out of 630 epochs from the PD group were misclassified as healthy group.

Still, research in Parkinson's disease has made remarkable progress. There is very real hope that the precise effects of the genetics or environmental causes on brain function will be understood. In the recent years, several studies used different imaging data, such as MRI and handwritten images, as well as PET and CT imaging and Dopamine Transporter scan (DaTscan) imaging. However, studies were not limited to imaging data; they also used voices and signal data such as biomedical voice and biometric signal and

Predicted Class

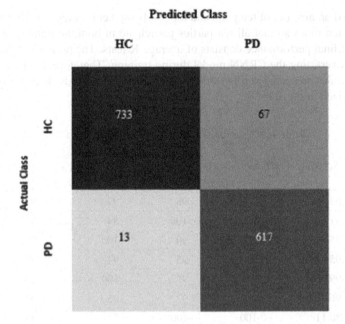

Fig. 3. Confusion matrix of the classification results obtained from the proposed CRNN model.

a few of the studies used EEG and ElectroMyoGram (EMG) signals. Oh et al. [13] proposed a CNN model for differentiating PD from healthy controls and they achieved a result of 88.25% accuracy, 84.71% sensitivity, and 91.77% specificity in a private dataset. Lee et al. [14] also designed a DL model, specifically a CNN combined with RNN with LSTM cells and promising performances were achieved with accuracy of 96.9%, precision of 100%, and recall of 93.4%. These remarkable researches give real hope for the future.

By comparing the different DL techniques, it is evident that the highest accuracy of PD classification was obtained using the CRNN algorithm. Unlike traditional ML techniques that typically require manual design and selection of features, DL techniques can automatically learn features from raw data. DL methods have the advantage of potentially capturing more complex and abstract features.

The CRNN model can extract hidden spatial and temporal features from the EEG signals. Even with a limited number of normal and PD subjects (20 HC and 20 PD), good performance was obtained with the CRNN model.

In the future, we will be able to use a large database with information on other brain disorders to validate the proposed model. Therefore, instead of detecting a single disease, the proposed model can detect other brain disorders such as sleep disorders and AD.

4   Conclusion

Entering the 21st century, our biggest challenge is that we still don't know much about the human brain. Therefore, early detection of neurological diseases is very beneficial as it assists the patient in taking preventive measures. Current work focuses on spontaneous diagnosis of PD from EEG signals using a DL model CRNN based on CNN and RNN with LSTM cells to distinguish HC from patients suffering from PD. Furthermore, our proposed CRNN model shows great potential for automatic PD detection with high accuracy of 96.16%, 97,9% specificity and 97,8% sensitivity. Our study may help to early detect of PD based on EEG brain activity.

References

1. Azevedo, F.A.C., et al.: Equal numbers of neuronal and nonneuronal cells make the human brain an isometrically scaled-up primate brain. J. Comp. Neurol. **513**(5), 532–541 (2009). https://doi.org/10.1002/cne.21974
2. Jankovic, J.: Parkinson's disease: clinical features and diagnosis. J. Neurol. Neurosurg. Psychiatr. **79**(4), 368–376 (2008)
3. Parkinson's Disease Foundation, https://www.parkinson.org/Understanding-Parkinsons/Statistics, last accessed 11 October 2022
4. Salvatore, C., et al.: Machine learning on brain MRI data for differential diagnosis of Parkinson's disease and Progressive Supranuclear Palsy. J. Neurosci. Methods **222**, 230–237 (2014). https://doi.org/10.1016/j.jneumeth.2013.11.016
5. Pizarro, R.A., et al.: Automated quality assessment of structural magnetic resonance brain images based on a supervised machine learning algorithm. Front. Neuroinform. **10**, 52 (2016). https://doi.org/10.3389/fninf.2016.00052
6. Antikainen, E., Cella, P., Tolonen, A., van Gils, M.: SPECT image features for early detection of Parkinson's disease using machine learning methods. In: Annual International Conference of the IEEE Engineering in Medicine and Biology Society 2021, pp. 2773–2777, Mexico (2021)
7. Zhang, X., et al.: Multi-view graph convolutional network and its applications on neuroimage analysis for Parkinson's disease. AMIA Symp. **5**(12), 1147–1156 (2018)
8. Gong, B., et al.: Neuroimagingbased diagnosis of Parkinson's disease with deep neural mapping large margin distribution machine. Neurocomputing **320**, 141–149 (2018)
9. Dai, Y., Tang, Z., Wang, Y., Xu, Z.: Data driven intelligent diagnostics for Parkinson's disease. IEEE Access **29**(7), 106941–106950 (2019)
10. Zhao, Y., et al.: A 3D deep residual convolutional neural network for differential diagnosis of Parkinsonian syndromes on 18F-FDG PET images. In: Annual International Conference of the IEEE Engineering in Medicine and Biology Society. IEEE Engineering in Medicine and Biology Society. Annual International Conference, vol. 2019, pp. 3531–3534 (2019)
11. Gandal, M.J., Edgar, J.C., Klook, K., Siegel, S.J.: Gamma synchrony: towards a translational biomarker for the treatment resistant symptoms of schizophrenia. Neuropharmacology **62**(3), 1504–1518 (2012)
12. Hampal, H., et al.: Biomarker for Alzheimer's disease: academic, industry and regulatory perspectives. Nat Rev Drug Discov **9**(7), 560–574 (2010)
13. Oh, S.L., et al.: A deep learning approach for Parkinson's disease diagnosis from EEG signals. Neural Comput. Appl. **32**, 10927–10933 (2020)

14. Lee, S., Hussein, R., McKeown, M.J.: A deep convolutional-recurrent neural network architecture for Parkinson's disease EEG classification. In: IEEE Global Conference on Signal and Information Processing (GlobalSIP), pp. 1–4. Ottawa, ON, Canada (2019)
15. Railo, H., Nokelainen, N., Savolainen, S., Kaasinen, V.: Deficits in monitoring self-produced speech in Parkinson's disease. Clin. Neurophysiol. **131**(9), 2140–2147 (2020). https://doi.org/10.1101/823674
16. Bigdely-Shamlo, N., Mullen, T., Kothe, C., Su, K.M., Robbins, K.A.: The PREP pipeline: standardized preprocessing for large-scale EEG analysis. Front. Neuroinform. **9**, 16 (2015). https://doi.org/10.3389/fninf.2015.00016

Recognition of Alzheimer's Disease Based on Transfer Learning Approach Using Brain MR Images with Regularization

Dhouha Guesmi[2]([✉]) [iD], Fatma Salah[1] [iD], and Yassine Ben Ayed[1] [iD]

[1] Multimedia, Information Systems and Advanced Computing Laboratory: MIRACL,
University of Sfax, Sfax, Tunisia
[2] Multimedia, Information Systems and Advanced Computing Laboratory: MIRACL,
University of Sfax, ELHARA, 4100 Medenine, Tunisia
dhouhaguesmi21@gmail.com

Abstract. Alzheimer's Disease (AD) is a progressive, permanent and irreversible neurological disorder of the brain that causes brain atrophy, death of brain cells, destruction of memory skills, and deterioration of thinking and social interactions. It has become a serious disease all over the world. Although there is no cure to reverse the progression of Alzheimer's disease, early detection of Alzheimer's disease would be very effective in the medical field and it could help for the treatment. This paper focuses on the early detection of stages of cognitive impairment and Alzheimer's disease using neuroimaging with transformative Learning (TL). Magnetic Resonance Imaging (MRI) images obtained from the Alzheimer's Disease Neuroimaging Database (OASIS) are categorized using a TL approach. Our proposed pre-trained networks such as InceptionV3-M and VGG16-M are modified applying batch normalization and regularization. The classification performance of these two networks is analyzed with the help of confusion matrix and its parameters. Simulation results have shown that the VGG16 model gives 97.06% accuracy. It also observed that the proposed system gives more accurate results than any previous studies performed previously on the OASIS dataset. These findings could help drive the development of computer-aided diagnosis.

Keywords: Alzheimer · Deep neural networks · MRI · OASIS · Preprocessing · Transfer learning

1 Introduction

The three most frequently caused neurologic diseases are Parkinson's Disease (PD), Alzheimer's Disease (AD), and SchiZophrenia (SZ) distinguished as disorders from regular healthy brain functioning [1]. Individuals affected with either of these three diseases trigger the family with enormous trouble along with health care services. Thus, it is very difficult to identify these brain diseases at their early stage [1, 2]. AD is a very significant public health problem and a chronic neuronal disorder that relentless procession affects human retentivity, analytical capabilities, and memory, as it actually affects a very large number of individuals, often the elderly. According to epidemiological data, AD (confusion of a few years with old age) now affects about 26 million people

N. T. Nguyen et al. (Eds.): ICCCI 2023, CCIS 1864, pp. 147–160, 2023.
https://doi.org/10.1007/978-3-031-41774-0_12

around the world, including 50,000 in Tunisia [3]. AD is caused by excess tau-hyper phosphorylation and Aβ (Amyloid-β) production [4]. The hippocampus part is affected first due to this disease as it is inextricably linked with analysis and memory; thus, the common and earliest symptom is memory loss [5]. To date, the main cause of this disease is obscure, and it's considered hereditary. Thus, detecting disease in the early stages impedes development [6, 7]. Various image techniques like Magnetic Resonance Imaging (MRI), Positron Emission Tomography (PET), and Computed Tomography (CT) are used for detecting AD. However, it's challenging for practitioners to manually examine and extract significant features from enormous and complicated data. Since MRI scans contain different interoperator and intra-operator variability concerns; analyzing MRI scans manually becomes a time-consuming, difficult task and subject to errors [8].

MRI is widely used to analyze, detect and classify AD. Standard machine learning algorithms require domain experts for feature extraction and it observed that user-specified feature approaches are confined to certain limitations and produce diminished outcomes. The performance of the system can be enhanced by using approaches proficient in automatic feature learning (i.e., deep learning) based on inputs and problems specified. Since deep learning stipulates instinctive feature extraction, the performance of the system can be enhanced with accurate outcomes. Among all DL approaches CNN based its variant mostly use via DNN, RNN, and so on. MRI scans are used to segment the brain's abnormal tissues to detect and classify AD [9].

Deep learning techniques are applied classification of different stages of AD using MRI [10], three various preprocessing techniques were applied i.e., skull-striping, cerebellum removal, and spatial normalization, and autoencoder was applied for feature extraction. Whereas, for classification, SVM is applied and obtained with around 95% accuracy. Research by Saikumar et al. [11], 3D CNN algorithm and autoencoder were proposed for classifying AD stages using MRI scans. Developed a model based on multimodal deep learning techniques for detecting stages of AD in the early stage [12, 13]. Denoising autoencoder was applied for feature extraction classification using CNN. The proposed model identifies three different affected regions of the brain i.e., amygdala region, hippocampus region, and rey auditory verbal learning test (RAVLT) using ADNI datasets.

Ioffe and Szegedy [14] implemented CNN variant algorithm for the detection and classification of AD using the OASIS dataset. Various AD detection machine learning algorithms were compared such as SVM along with automated extracted features and SVM with manually extracted features, and AdaBoost. Higami et al. [15] developing a multi-modal DL network to predict AD using MRI data, CSF biomarkers, longitudinal cognitive measures, and cross-sectional neuroimaging modalities. The system also predicted the risk of developing AD. In developed a model using deep residual learning integrated with transfer learning algorithms for classifying six different stages of AD Alzheimer's disease. Ebrahimighahnavieh et al. [16] proposed a method for classification of AD using CNN variant i.e., LeNet architecture, and obtained around 96.86% accuracy and it also assists to predict the different stages of AD for a mixed range of ages. In 2021, Authors in [17] used the SqueezeNet, ResNet18, AlexNet, Vgg11, DenseNet, and InceptionV3 pre-trained models and they achieved nearly 99.38% accuracy by SqueezeNet model for training and testing. In 2019, Authors in [18] worked on an efficient technique of utilizing transfer learning to classify the images by fine-tuning a pre-trained convolutional network, AlexNet.

However, we find some limitations in the current research work which we have to mention as follows: (1) There are some models that have achieved higher accuracy, but their performance has not been proven adequately, and this is certainly against the previously trained models [20], (2) Some achieved lower accuracy than others [19], (3) Other research focuses only on the performance of pre-trained models for detecting Alzheimer's disease, but they have not suggested any other modifications [21]. Therefore, in this paper, we propose a model to overcome the above limitations. We used two pretrained models with two architectures, namely InceptionV3 and VGG16 using the regularization and batch normalization. The major contributions of the study are as follows:

- We investigated two models of different architectures. The pretrained models and their number of convolutional layers are listed in Table 1.
- The study compares the performance of different pretrained models such as InceptionV3 and VGG16 by applying a transfer learning method based on the regularization and batch normalization.
- We achieved the optimal results with the VGG16 model in terms of classifying AD and NOAD, which is higher than any other previous studies that have been done before.

Table 1. Pretrained models and their number of convolutional layers.

Classification Model	No. of Convolutional Layers
InceptionV3-S	48
VGG16-S	16

2 Materials and Methods

In this study, we aimed to predict Alzheimer's disease based on brain MRI images showing the presence or absence of Alzheimer's disease.

2.1 Data Selection

In our research work, we used OASIS open-access dataset [22]. These datasets investigate during preparation by Daniel S. Marcus from Neuroimaging Informatics Analysis Center (NIAC) at Washington University School of medicine. We have 382 images obtained from the OASIS database; "Includes 218 subjects aged 18 to 59 years and 198 subjects aged 60 to 96 years". Each group includes an approximately equal number of male and female subjects, ranging from no dementia to moderate level.

The image preprocessing is the major part to extract efficient and accurate results for those algorithms. There are different sizes of images in the dataset. The different sizes of images can influence the architecture towards low accuracy. Image resizing reduces the time of neural network model training. The OASIS [22] dataset image size is 256 * 256 (Fig. 1).

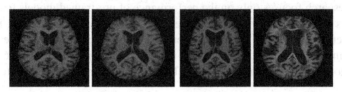

Fig. 1. Examples of OASIS MRI image data. (1) Patient with no dementia; (2) patient with very mild AD; (3) patient with mild AD; (4) patient with moderate AD.

2.2 Image Preprocessing

For the proposed model, the training, validation and testing on medical images go through the preprocessing steps. MRI images during the process of their forming endure deterioration, such as low variation due to bad brightness produced by the visual devices. To overcome this issue for the improvement of MRI scans, image enhancement approaches were applied for the upgrade of the distribution of pixels over an extensive range of intensities, linear contrast stretching was applied on the images.

During the image acquisition process, some undesirable information was added to the image due to nonlinear light intensity conceded as noise. Specifically, non-linear light intensity affects the overall performance-accuracy of the image processing [23]. The dynamic range of light intensity was increased by using contrast stretching because the output images after this process were the ones having improved contrast and appropriate light distribution. Images in the OASIS repository to get better performance on the latter stages were enhanced using the linear contrast stretching.

MRI images were obtained from the public OASIS repository and have been improved using the extraction of the green channel, the log transformation for the linear contrast stretching, the global thresholding, the closure or the morphological opening and the overlay mask on the green channel. We segmented images were resized to 224 * 224 as per model requirements (Fig. 2).

2.3 Data Augmentation

In neuroimaging, a large number of scans related to AD patient's availability are a major issue because few hundreds of image samples are available. It is a common thing for a deep learning model to provide more effective results on more data. In medical research, the classification of cancer and AD are problematic due to lack of availability of data. The small imbalanced dataset is quite difficult to train and creates overfitting problems during training of the model, which affects the model efficiency. Obviously, overfitting

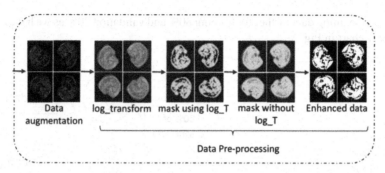

Fig. 2. Image enhancement.

is a main risk. To overcome this issue, we need more data to enhance the effective accuracy in our proposed model. We used the augmentation technique to create 10 more images on each available MRI image. We can see that now the process of applying the geometric transformation to each image of the dataset has become a widely used approach and also helps to increase the proportion of training data. It can be increased by rotating, translating and reflecting the existing images, using the socalled label preserving transformations [36].

Table 2. Data augmentation.

Rotation Range	10 selected angles Θ; in the interval $0 \leq \Theta \leq 360$
Zoom range	0.5, 1.5
Shear range	0.15 Degree
Height shift range	0.1 Degree
Width shift range	0.1 Degree
Channel shift range	150.0

In Table 2, data augmentation is described for the parameters used for augmentation, where in our case, each image is randomly rotated by 10 selected angles Θ; in the interval $0 \leq \Theta \leq 360$, width and height shift range 0.1 degrees, and shear range 0.15 degree.

2.4 Characterization of Data

After pre-processing, we labeled our data for binary classification and fixed our sample size. Since we are doing the binary classification, we labeled the records in the dataset with a Clinical Dementia Ratio (CDR) 0 or 1. Note that CDR 0 indicates healthy Alzheimer's disease (i.e., NOAD), and CDR 1 indicates severe Alzheimer's (i.e., AD). For classification purposes, we considered 200 Alzheimer's patients and 100 No-Demented patients (Table 3). Each patient has ten images. During the experiment, we divide each class of data into three steps. In the first step, we split data 20% for testing and retain remaining data further for training 80% and validation 20% as we have shown in the flow chart in Fig. 3.

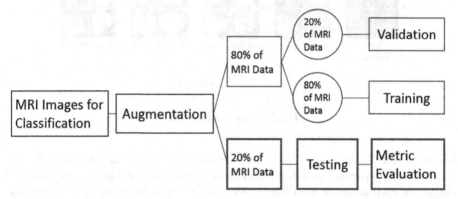

Fig. 3. Framework of the proposed method on MRI data of each classification task (NOAD, AD). Augmentation is applied to all data samples, i.e., 80% for training, and 20% testing. NOAD = No Alzheimer's disease, and AD = Alzheimer's disease.

Table 3. Summary of the global clinical dementia rating (CDR).

Clinical Dementia Rate (RATE)	No. of Samples
CDR-0 (No Dementia)	100
CDR-1 (Moderate AD)	200

2.5 Classification Model Training

InceptionV3-Standard
Inception-v3 is a convolutional neural network that is 48 layers deep. We can load a pre-trained version of the network trained on more than a million images from the ImageNet databas. The pretrained network can classify images into 1000 object categories, such as keyboard, mouse, pencil, and many animals. As a result, the network has learned rich feature representations for a wide range of images. The network has an image input size of 299-by-299.

VGG16-Standard
VGG16-S is a convolutional neural network model proposed by K. Simonyan and A. Zisserman from the University of Oxford in the paper "Very Deep Convolutional Networks for Large-Scale Image Recognition". The model achieves 92.7% top-5 test accuracy in ImageNet, which is a dataset of over 14 million images belonging to 1000 classes. It was one of the famous model submitted to ILSVRC-2014. It makes the improvement over

AlexNet by replacing large kernel-sized filters (11 and 5 in the first and second convolutional layer, respectively) with multiple 3 × 3 kernel-sized filters one after another. VGG16-S was trained for weeks and was using NVIDIA Titan Black GPU's.

Proposed Modified Models

In this study, we selected two different classification models. These two DNN models, InceptionV3-S and VGG16-S, were selected to achieve our primary aim of identifying Alzheimer's disease. It is noted that after loading each pre-trained model, we added our classifiers, which are based on fully connected layers, and the dropout layers had a 50% dropout rate with each model. This classifier adds a stack of fully connected layers that is fed by the features extracted from the convolutional base. The final layer was a softmax layer, which was stacked at the end, followed by the FC layer output to determine whether the image should be classified as NOAD or AD. We applied transfer learning to the models for Alzheimer's disease identification. For image classification problems, the standard approach is to use a stack of fully-connected layers followed by a softmax activated layer. The softmax layer outputs the probability distribution over each possible class label and then we just need to classify the image according to the most probable class.

The main reason we chose those architectures is because they have already produced higher precision results and more efficient and excellent performance in computer-aided diagnostic problems. The InceptionV3-S model consists of 315 layers in total. In the InceptionV3-M model, Relu is used as the activation function, batch normalization for normalization, and max pooling and average pooling are used together for pooling. We modify the last two fully connected layers and final classification layers as per our problem. These two fully connected layers are 1000 and 512 with binary classification. For the VGG16-M model, we modify the last two fully connected layers and final classification layers as per our problem. We applied transport marking to freeze the convolutional layers. Since in many applications while performing the transfer learning process, they only focus on a fully connected layer trained on the training data and convolutional layers are kept constant. In the proposed model, we used different hyperparameters as presented in Table 4.

While training the models, we want to get the best possible result according to the chosen metric. At the same time, we want to keep a similar result on the new data. But the cruel truth is that we can't get 100% accuracy. Even if we did, the result is still not without errors. There are simply too few test situations to find them. Batch normalization allows us to not only work as a regularizer but also reduce training time by increasing a learning rate. The problem is that during a training process the distribution on each layer is changed. So we need to reduce the learning rate that slows our gradient descent optimization. But, if we will apply a normalization for each training mini-batch, then we can increase the learning rate and find a minimum faster. To address overfitting, we can at the first time apply weight regularization to the both of models. This will add a cost to the loss function of the network for large weights (or parameter values). As a result, we get a simpler model that will be forced to learn only the relevant patterns in the train data. There are L1 regularization and L2 regularization. L2 regularization will add a cost with regards to the squared value of the parameters. We have tried with L2 regularization. This results in smaller weights.

Table 4. Hyper-parameters for the proposed method, used during training and testing, ReLU (Rectified Linear Unit).

HYPERPARAMETERS	
Activation Function	ReLU
Base Learning Rate	1e5
Epochs	20
Batch Size	32
Optimizer	Adam
Loss Function	Binary Cross Entropy

While training the models, we want to get the best possible result according to the chosen metric. At the same time, we want to keep a similar result on the new data. But the cruel truth is that we can't get 100% accuracy. Even if we did, the result is still not without errors. There are simply too few test situations to find them.

Batch normalization allows us to not only work as a regularizer but also reduce training time by increasing a learning rate. The problem is that during a training process the distribution on each layer is changed. So we need to reduce the learning rate that slows our gradient descent optimization. But, if we will apply a normalization for each training mini-batch, then we can increase the learning rate and find a minimum faster.

To address overfitting, we can at the first time apply weight regularization to the four models. This will add a cost to the loss function of the network for large weights (or parameter values). As a result, we get a simpler model that will be forced to learn only the relevant patterns in the train data. There are L1 regularization and L2 regularization. L2 regularization will add a cost with regards to the squared value of the parameters. We have tried with L2 regularization. This results in smaller weights (Fig. 4).

2.6 Model Evaluation

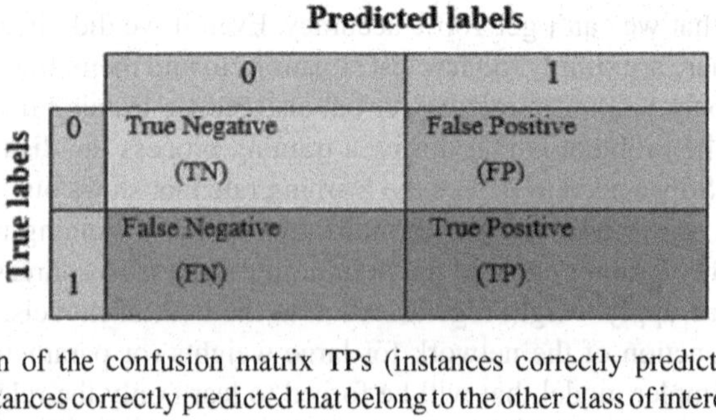

Predicted labels

		0	1
True labels	0	True Negative (TN)	False Positive (FP)
	1	False Negative (FN)	True Positive (TP)

Fig. 4. Illustration of the confusion matrix TPs (instances correctly predicted to the class of interest), TNs (instances correctly predicted that belong to the other class of interest), FPs (instances assigned to the class of interest but do not belong to it), and FNs (instances assigned to the class of interest but belong to the complementary class).

Figure 5 shows the schematic of the entire workflow of the classification process. The entire dataset was first divided into training, validation and test datasets. These datasets then underwent preprocessing. After model testing and hyper parameter tuning to obtain the optimal results on the validation dataset, the model was deployed to the test dataset for binary classification. The model performance was then evaluated in terms of prediction accuracy.

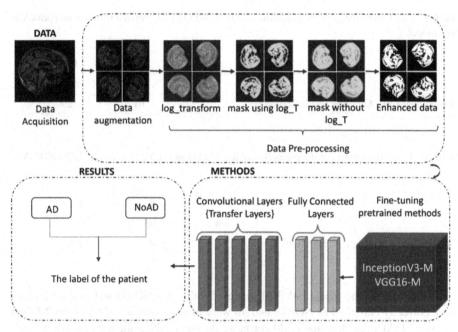

Fig. 5. Schematic of the classification process.

3   Results and Discussion

We implemented the proposed model using Tensorflow [24], Keras [25] and Python on a Windows X86–64 machine with Intel(R) Pentium(R) 3825U, 4 GB RAM and 1.90 GHz. We extracted the feature from the 3820 data samples after preprocessing. The classification was performed on training, validation, and test datasets. We split data 20% for testing and retain remaining data further for training 80% and validation 20%, more detail is shown in Fig. 3. We used full test data and validated the model, so the final epoch result of the validation accuracy could be said, as validation accuracy.

To be careful not to the overfitting, we used early stopping and applied the SGD training with a minibatch size of 64, a learning rate of 0.01, a weight decay of 0.06 and a momentum factor of 0.9 with Nesterov optimization. We first performed a classification study using two pretrained deep learning models on the datasets to select the model that most accurately predicts the presence or absence of the disease from the patients. These images were fed into the classification model to record the performance of the model. After a model was sufficiently trained, the test cases were predicted. A set of images from a patient was given as input, and the output was obtained as an array. It included the prediction of the model; the output predicted by the model was labeled as either 0 or 1 for NOAD and AD, respectively. All the test cases were predicted in the same manner; the results are listed in Tables 5 and 6.

Table 5. Confusion matrix of the prediction of the NOAD and AD derived from the InceptionV3-M's model.

		0	**1**
	0	52	48
InceptionV3-M (Applying regularization)	**1**	61	129

Table 6. Confusion matrix of the prediction of the NOAD and AD derived from the VGG16-M's model.

		0	**1**
	0	95	5
VGG16-M (Applying regularization)	**1**	4	196

In the case of the InceptionV3-M model, for the 100 NOAD test cases, 52 cases were correctly classified as NOAD, and 48 were misclassified as AD. For the 200 test cases of NOAD, the InceptionV3-M correctly classified 129 of the test cases as AD and misclassified 61 test cases as NOAD. Similarly, in the case of the VGG16-M model, for the 100 No dementia test cases, 95 cases were correctly classified as No dementia (TN), and 5 cases were misclassified as AD (FP). Likewise, for the 200 AD test cases, 196 were correctly classified as AD (TP), and 4 were misclassified as No dementia (FN).

Table 7. Performance evaluation of the two deep neural network (DNN) models.

Models	Accuracy on testing data	
	InceptionV3-M	VGG16-M
Baseline model	67.65%	99.90%
Batch normalization	57.35%	94.85%
Regularization	**60.29%**	**97.06%**

Tables 5 and 6 show the performance obtained for each of the pre-trained CNN models during training and validation for binary classification. Our results revealed that VGG16-M outperformed the other model in identifying AD with accuracies of the InceptionV3-M and VGG16-M models were 60.29% and 97.06%, respectively. Transfer learning helps develop robust models. However, without preprocessing, batch normalization and regularization, we obtained poor results in the identification of the disease, where the VGG16-M model exhibited the highest accuracy with a prediction accuracy of 97.06%. This could be explained because the first convolution layer of the classifier extracts deep image features that the final classification layer uses to classify the input image.

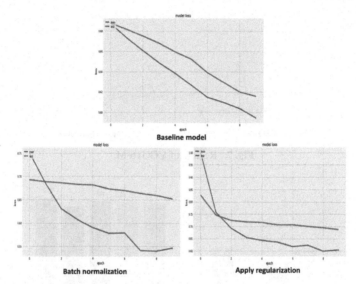

Fig. 6. Results of InceptionV3-M.

A comparative analysis of these two models with the test dataset suggested that the VGG16-M model was the best in identifying the presence or absence of AD. All these results obtained from the binary classification corroborates the results reported by [26] where the results of the pre-trained deep learning models show the effectiveness of pre-trained models in AD classification. The graphical representation of training loss vs validation loss and training accuracy vs validation accuracy of all the models is displayed from Figs. 6 and 7.

As shown in Table 7, the L2 regularization and Batch normalization help to improve the training of deep neural networks. Until this sight, the regularization models seems to be the best model for generalization. We manage to increase the accuracy on the validation data substantially. Hence, transfer learning as feature extraction using VGG16-M is an effective technique to classify MR images into Dementia, and No Dementia. The InceptionV3-M achieved 60.29% and VGG16-M achieved 97.06%. This proves that VGG16-M is by far the best deep learning method to predict the binary classification of Alzheimer's disease.

From Fig. 8, the performance comparison of per-class classification results of the pre-trained models has demonstrated outstanding performance for accurately positively

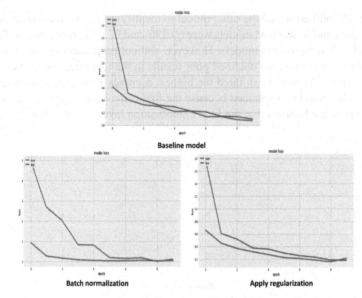

Fig. 7. Results of VGG16-M.

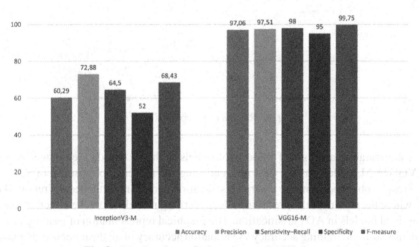

Fig. 8. Results of transfer learning on OASIS dataset.

classifying dementia in the case of InceptionV3-M and VGG16-M with 60.29% and 97.06% respectively. The poor performance of the pre-trained models for positively classifying mild dementia could be due to the close brain changes between dementia and mild dementia as the two classes are both associated with reduced cortical thickness and surface area in the brain regions [27].

We can conclude from Tables 5 and 6 that VGG16-M is a strong pre-trained model for MR image classification. VGG16-M produced the best training and validation accuracy among the other model.

4   Conclusion

We can consider that the early detection of Alzheimer's disease remains a challenge, and because of the flexibility of the classification of deep learning and its ability to generate optimal results, it has aroused the interest of researchers. With pre-trained models on large imageNet labeled datasets, reliable training models are available for detailed feature representation. Therefore, comparative analysis and evaluation of two different pre-trained CNN architectures are presented in this study. We utilized transfer learning with a feature extraction approach using two CNN models which include VGG16-M, and InceptionV3-M for accurate classification of MR images. Though it has been tested only on AD dataset, we believe it can be used successfully for other classification problems of medical domain.

For future studies, with Transfert Learning (TL) at the layer level, we plan to use the VGG architecture family with pre-trained weights. We also plan to try other neural networks as a base model to build the classifier. Additionally, we can also improve the overall performance by thinning, i.e. training the pre-trained convolutional layers of the base model, provided that enough data is used and we plan to exploit the results obtained from our analysis to design new discriminative features for recognizing other task in the medical imaging field.

References

1. Francolini, G., et al.: Artificial intelligence in radiotherapy: state of the art and future directions. Med. Oncol. **37**(6), 1–9 (2020)
2. Kwak, K., Niethammer, M., Giovanello, K.S., Styner, M., Dayan, E.: Differential role for hippocampal subfields in Alzheimer's disease progression revealed with deep learning. Cereb. Cortex **32**(3), 467–478 (2022)
3. Mathers, C.D., et al.: Global Burden of Disease 2000: Version 2 methods and results, In the Journal of Global Programme on Evidence for Health Policy Discussion, vol. 50. World Health Organization (2002)
4. Venugopalan, J., Tong, L., Hassanzadeh, H.R., Wang, M.D.: Multimodal deep learning models for early detection of Alzheimer's disease stage. Sci. Rep. **11**(1), 1–13 (2021)
5. Fang, X., Liu, Z., Xu, M.: Ensemble of deep convolutional neural networks based multi-modality images for Alzheimer's disease diagnosis. IET Image Proc. **14**(2), 318–326 (2020)
6. Lee, R., Choi, H., Park, K.-Y., Kim, J.-M., Seok, J.W.: Prediction of post-stroke cognitive impairment using brain FDG PET: deep learning-based approach. Eur. J. Nucl. Med. Mol. Imaging **49**(4), 1254–1262 (2022)
7. Tyrrell, D.A.J., Parry, R.P., Crow, T.J., Johnstone, E., Ferrier, I.N.: Possible virus in schizophrenia and some neurological disorders. The Lancet **313**(8121), 839–841 (1979)
8. Clarke, L.P., et al.: MRI segmentation: methods and applications. Magn. Reson. Imaging **13**(3), 343–368 (1995)
9. Sharma, S., Mandal, P.K.: A comprehensive report on machine learning-based early detection of Alzheimer's disease using multi-modal neuroimaging data. ACM Comput. Surv. **55**(2), 1–44 (2023)
10. Basheera, S., Sai Ram, M.S.: Convolution neural network–based Alzheimer's disease classification using hybrid enhanced independent component analysis based segmented gray matter of T2 weighted magnetic resonance imaging with clinical valuation. Alzheimer's & Dementia: Translational Research & Clinical Interventions **5**(1), 974–986 (2019)

11. Saikumar, K., Rajesh, V., Babu, B.S.: Heart disease detection based on feature fusion technique with augmented classification using deep learning technology. Traitement du Signal **39**(1), 31–42 (2022)

12. Zeitzer, J.M., et al.: Phenotyping apathy in individuals with Alzheimer disease using functional principal component analysis. Am. J. Geriatr. Psychiatry **21**(4), 391–397 (2013)

13. Lindberg, O., et al.: Hippocampal shape analysis in Alzheimer's disease and frontotemporal lobar degeneration subtypes. Journal of Alzheimer's Disease **30**(2), 355–365 (2012)

14. Ioffe, S., Szegedy, C.: Batch normalization: accelerating deep network training by reducing internal covariate shift. Proceedings of the 32nd International Conference on Machine Learning, vol. 37, pp. 448–456 (2015)

15. Higami, Y., Yamakawa, M., Shigenobu, K., Kamide, K., Makimoto, K.: High frequency of getting out of bed in patients with Alzheimer's disease monitored by non-wearable actigraphy. Geriatrics & Gerontology International **19**(2), 130–134 (Feb. 2019)

16. Ebrahimighahnavieh, M.A., Luo, S., Chiong, R.: Deep learning to detect Alzheimer's disease from neuroimaging: a systematic literature review. Comput. Methods Programs Biomed. **187**, 1–48 (2020)

17. Odusami, M., et al.: Comparable Study of Pre-trained Model on Alzheimer Disease Classification. In: Gervasi, O., et al. (ed.) Computational Science and Its Applications – ICCSA 2021. In the ICCSA 2021, Lecture Notes in Computer Science, vol. 12953 (2021)

18. Maqsood, M., et al.: Transfer Learning Assisted Classification and Detection of Alzheimer's Disease Stages Using 3D MRI Scans. The Journal of Sensors **19**, 2645 (2019)

19. Islam, J., Zhang, Y.: A novel deep learning based multi-class classification method for alzheimer's disease detection using brain MRI data. In: the Proc. International Conference on Brain Informatics, pp. 213–222 (2017)

20. Wang, S., et al.: Classification of alzheimer's disease based on eight-layer convolutional neural network with leaky rectified linear unit and max pooling. The Journal of Med Syst **42**(85) (2018)

21. Khagi, B., et al.: CNN Models Performance Analysis on MRI images of OASIS dataset for distinction between Healthy (i.e. Non Demented) and Alzheimer's patient (i.e. Demented). In: the 2019 International Conference on Electronics Information and Communication (ICEIC), pp. 1–4 (2019)

22. Khagi, B., et al.: Models Performance Analysis on MRI images of OASIS dataset for distinction between Healthy and Alzheimer's patient. In: the 2019 International Conference on Electronics, Information, and Communication (ICEIC), pp. 1–4 (2019)

23. Tsafas, V., et al.: Application of a deep-learning technique to non-linear images from human tissue biopsies for shedding new light on breast cancer diagnosis. IEEE J. Biomed. Health Inform. **26**(3), 1188–1195 (2022)

24. Abadi, M., et al.: TensorFlow: Large-scale machine learning on heterogeneous systems (2015)

25. Lee, H., Song, J.: Introduction to convolutional neural network using Keras; an understanding from a statistician, Communications for Statistical Applications and Methods, vol. 26, no. 6. Communications for Statistical Applications and Methods, pp. 591–610 (30-Nov 2019)

26. Xia, Z., et al.: A novel end-to-end hybrid network for Alzheimer's disease detection using 3D CNN and 3D CLSTM. In: the IEEE 17th International Symposium on Biomedical Imaging (ISBI), pp. 1–4. IEEE (2020)

27. Yang, H., et al.: Study of brain morphology change in Alzheimer's disease and amnestic mild cognitive impairment compared with normal controls. In: the General Psychiatry, vol. 32 (2019)

Detection and Analyzing Satellite Images by Using Conventional Neural Network

Atheer Joudah[1]([✉]), Souheyl Mallat[2], and Mounir Zrigui[1]

[1] Department of Computer Science, Faculty of Sciences of Monastir, University of Monastir, Monastir, Tunisia
atheermubs@gmail.com
[2] Research Laboratory in Algebra, Numbers Theory and Intelligent System, Ottawa, Canada

Abstract. Maintenance and recordkeeping require agricultural field data. These agricultural fields may have text, schematic drawings, logos, barcodes, and serial numbers. Rectangular metal or synthetic farming fields. This study classifies satellite images of the region using CNN and deep learning. Manufacturers change field dimensions. Satellite image localization aids pest control, scene analysis, and field tracking. Context—the flow of information between a satellite picture and a Convolutional Neural Network—is as important as satellite image data for interpretation. CNN classifiers identify satellite fields. Quadrilaterals localize satellite images better than rectangles. A convolutional neural network processes the noise-reduced regions (CNN). CNN's preprocessing sorts of comparable qualities by size and arranges them into text lines. CNN's tech is industry wide. If the CNN scored at least one text region low, the user is invited to take a new image of that portion of the field, which is compared to the original image and text processing is repeated. Operation ends after a certain number of attempts or when all regions score sufficiently. Following 300 rounds of training and testing, the CNN has 98.17% accuracy and outputs the type of field detected, a list of regions containing extracted text, and its reliability. 70%, 20%, and 10% of the data trained, tested, and verified the suggested system. A dataset with several classes showed the feature vector's utility. Python deep learning was used for the study. Our architecture has three distinct but equally critical functional head networks, therefore training simultaneously may cause instability. If the model fails to converge, the head design may be hidden. We gradually incorporated each functional head throughout design to ensure the single-head design concept was strong.

Keywords: Satellite imagery · Deep learning · Agriculture fields · CNN · Image analysis · Segmentation · Detection

1 Introduction

Modern society relies on electricity. Hence, power pylons, circuit breakers, and other electrical infrastructure like transformers are worldwide. As seen in [1], consistent electricity requires preventative infrastructure maintenance. Agricultural field data is essential for maintenance and documentation. These agricultural fields may contain text,

N. T. Nguyen et al. (Eds.): ICCCI 2023, CCIS 1864, pp. 161–174, 2023.
https://doi.org/10.1007/978-3-031-41774-0_13

schematic drawings, logos, barcodes, and serial numbers. Metal or synthetic agricultural fields are rectangular. Manufacturers vary field dimensions, design, typography, and construction. The first sample field is rusty aluminum with a hard-to-read barcode. The fields are slightly larger than the previous field, made of synthetic material, smooth and shiny, and include schematic designs, according to [3]. Maintenance personnel formerly input field data manually. As indicated in [4], this transcription may be degraded or even become dark if typos or important information are deleted. Most farming is intricate, so this takes time. Harvest samples are visible on the fields. As they've never been opened, they're perfect. A handheld device holds a weathered metal farmland. The illustrations below show the challenges of automatic content extraction and manual transcription (described in [5]). Weather exposure deteriorates agricultural land over time. Old agricultural fields may have flaking paint, making the lettering unintelligible. Shadows, reflections, lighting changes, and partial occlusions make outdoor shooting difficult. In [6], the field exhibits a specular reflection along its upper edge (Fig. 1).

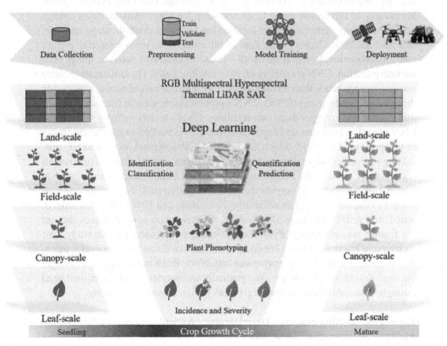

Fig. 1. The applications of deep learning and satellite image based agricultural field recognition in real-times [6].

Converting text images to machine-readable text allows access to field semantic data. OCR is this method (CNN). CNN software is widely available, and many methods have been devised for this task [7]. Most systems are designed to manage digital paper documents. Given this, the four shown agricultural regions show another issue: incompatible fonts with text processing fonts [8]. One-part embossed font has lower contrast and thinner strokes than painted or printed type. Hence, CNN solutions will yield poor outcomes.

This paper presents a novel method for recognizing, categorizing, and retrieving agricultural field text. Rectangular fields connected to electricity-generating equipment with human-readable text. Diagrams and barcodes are processable. Steps in our process: The field in the supplied image is clipped, deformed, and inverted. Machine learning classifies the qualities. Each category has job titles and descriptions from [9]. Preprocessing removes dust, text fragments, and neighboring frames that create noise and clutter. CNN engines process filtered areas. The user is asked to take a new picture of a field section if its recognition score falls below a threshold.

1.1 Motivation

Information technology helps us understand numerous interrelated fields. We study object detection in scanned photos, text extraction from satellite images, and form categorization since no other methods are perfect for our purpose. We want to create an algorithm that recognizes fields and converts the data into human-readable language. The new image is compared to the original, which may have had a bigger field, and the CNN is run again. This multi-view approach reliably extracts text even with occlusions or reflections. The methodoutputs the detected text, its position on the field, its confidence, and the field type [10]. This practical task involves creating a deep learning application prototype that lets users take photos for content extraction.

Field classification efficiency and combination are evaluated. We also show the CNN's applicability to three more fields and the effect of training it for the field's typefaces. Finally, illumination affects field classification and text extraction. Here are few catastrophic failures (Fig. 2).

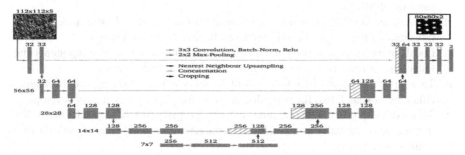

Fig. 2. Convolutional Neural Network Schema [10].

1.2 Problem Statement

Satellite photo content extraction and field detection and categorization are similar. Rectangular satellite photos show text. So, a Convolutional Neural Network (CNN) must be run on each agricultural zone in a picture to retrieve their data. We locate and track satellite photos for traffic control [11]. Maximally Stable Extremal Regions identify the satellite in the supplied image (MSER). MSER + labels satellite images with dark borders surrounding light zones, while MSER- labels agricultural land using the same method. This study shows three satellite pictures and MSER output. Satellite imaging confirms MSER + regions with many MSER- zones. Black areas should also have fairly uniform dimensions and straight lines through their centers. The light region surrounding the dark sections must have the same average height [12]. Using field photos to train the deep convolutional neural network may improve segmentation. Writing or logos might help estimate the playing field's limits. Classifiers sometimes mix classes. Three visually diverse photos in the first group are hard to categorize. Reflections make the second one visually diverse. The preparatory method should improve correlation acknowledgment performance under certain conditions. Their findings showed that primitive visual system neurons were built to partition fields via shape, variety, and differential release. All field segmentation organizations may use the new data. Flagging organizations usually comply with data better than feedforward ones. The research used a convolutional neural network (CNN) with a one-vs-one technique to recognize characters using the different types of agriculture, each represented by an MSER-region. Tracking the satellite image through multiple frames improves categorization accuracy by providing multiple field perspectives. The best character results across all frames determine the satellite image detection result.

1.3 Research Contributions

The research contributions of this dissertation are given by:

   i. The objective of this study is to present a novel method for automatically recognizing and classifying satellite imagery in photographs of the real world. Nevertheless, research defines Category-Specific Extremal Areas using extreme regions, a superset of MSER.
  ii. The suggested CNN method based on deep learning counts all extreme regions by thresholding the image at each gray level, beginning with level one.
 iii. Local binary patterns are used to construct descriptors, and related components that reflect the extreme regions are eliminated for each intensity level.
  iv. There appear to be just three ways in which the current extreme zones could change: either they expand, two formerly distinct ones merge, or a new region develops.
   v. This work exploits the incremental updating property of CNN by selecting CNN that are also gradually computable for character recognition, hence minimizing runtime complexity.
  vi. The research suggests employing the normalized central algebraic moments, compactness, Euler number, entropy of the cumulative histogram, number of convexities, and convex hull area. To determine the Euler number of an object, one must first determine the total number of holes in the object (although the last two descriptors are not incrementally computable).
 vii. CNN descriptors based on deep learning employ a classifier to identify whether the region of interest is present at each intensity level of the input image. This necessitates the inclusion of rotating or sloping agricultural fields in training samples to assure detection.

viii. It should be noted that this algorithm detects fields in actual photos. Therefore, a distinct grouping and filtering procedure is required to simply collect satellite images.

The CNN detection process and an example of a discovery. In addition to the image itself, it is possible to discern the agricultural fields of the country portrayed on the sticker placed over the satellite image. In addition, this method is not limited to the field alone; it may also be used to locate other objects.

In first section talked about introduction, problem statement and aim of study and second session talked about literature review, and third section talked about proposed of method and in forth section talked about experiments and evaluation and fifth section talked about conclusion and reference.

2 Literature Review

Satellite photo content extraction and field detection and categorization are similar. Satellite images are rectangular and human readable. So, a Convolutional Neural Network (CNN) must be run on each agricultural zone in a picture to retrieve their data. Researchers propose using satellite pictures for traffic control by recognizing and tracking items [13]. Maximally Stable Extremal Regions identify the satellite in the supplied image (MSER). MSER + labels satellite images with dark borders surrounding light zones, while MSER- labels agricultural land using the same method. Three satellite photographs show MSER production. Satellite imaging confirms MSER + regions with many MSER- zones. According to [14], the black squares must have similar diameters and straight lines across their centers. The adjacent light zone must almost match the adjacent dark zone's average height. The authors use SVM using the one-vs-one method and feed it the MSER-regions from [15]. Tracking the satellite image through multiple frames improves categorization accuracy by providing multiple field perspectives. The satellite image field detection result is a vote-based grouping of the best images from all frames (Fig. 3).

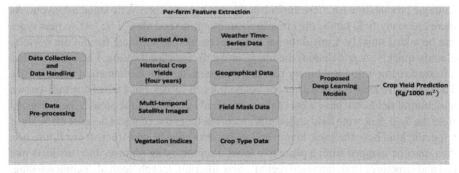

Fig. 3. Crop yield detection using automated feature extraction and deep learning-based models [15].

[16] researchers use a similar method to recognize field in photos. Extremal Regions—a superset of MSER—define Category-Specific Extremal Regions (CSER). The suggested technique thresholds the image at each gray level, starting at level one, to count extremal points [17]. Each intensity level generates descriptors and deletes related components indicating extreme regions. According to research, the present severe zones can only expand, merge, or form a third zone (detailed in [18]). Selecting progressively computable descriptors reduces runtime complexity. In addition to the descriptors described in [19], they suggest utilizing normalized central algebraic moments, compactness, the Euler number (the number of holes in the objects divided by the number of objects), the cumulative histogram entropy, the number of convexities, and the area of the convex hull. Using field photos to train the deep convolutional neural network may improve segmentation. Field locations can help estimate field borders more accurately. Classifiers sometimes mix classes. Three visually diverse photos in the first group are hard to categorize. Reflections make the second one visually diverse. The preparatory method should improve correlation acknowledgment performance under certain conditions. Their findings showed that primitive visual system neurons were built to partition fields via shape, variety, and differential release. All field segmentation organizations may use the new data. Flagging organizations usually comply with data better than feed-forward ones. The classifier uses these attributes at each intensity level to determine if the area is interesting. For the [20] method to work, training samples must comprise tilted or rotating farms. This approach finds fields in real-world photos. Hence, [21] requires a unique grouping and filtering mechanism to obtain just satellite photos. CSER detection and output example the satellite image's sticker shows the country's agricultural areas. This method can also be used to find other things outside the field [22–24].

3 Proposed Method

In this section I will work on dataset rated to satellite image data for interpretation and apply this dataset on CNN algorithm and will see flowchart of CNN algorithm as show in Fig. 4 shows the technique's schematic. Identify, remove, and deform the field. The image shows only the upright field, which can be used to identify it. Each producer builds a unique product line for these agricultural lands because there is no standard layout. As there are many field kinds, the classifier's training method should be fast so new types can be added quickly. Convolutional neural networks, appropriate for mobile devices, classify quickly. A grid divides the image into cells for classification. Each grid cell has a feature vector with local binary pattern histograms and the median color value (LBP). The field's size ratio is added after concatenating cell values. For each of our well-known agricultural fields, we have a list of the names and locations of the areas to be harvested from the field. Knowing field region placements helps extract content because all fields of a specific kind have the same layout and no borders must be constructed. For future use, data must be mapped from a place to a label. Preprocessing removes field artifacts like dirt and structures from retrieved regions. Size filtering, morphological opening/closing, and character grouping are preprocessing. The Tesseract Convolutional Neural Network (CNN) engine one repeats CNN operations on preprocessed field areas. The results are saved once the maximum number of retries, or all regions have scored enough. The result includes the detected field type, identified field, confidence, and field position. To simplify processing, a field should be extracted precisely after confirming its existence and position. The previous boundary is unsuitable due to thresholding and morphological opening errors. The provided rectangle's rotation is a rough approximation based on the extracted related components, making its precision questionable.

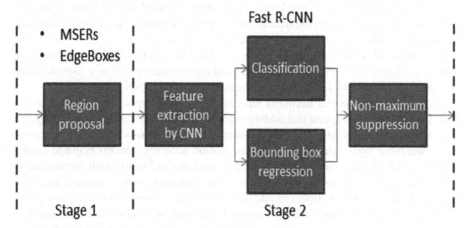

Fig. 4. The employment of CNN and MSER based proposed system for satellite field image classification.

As shown in Fig. 4, a CCN consists of multiple hierarchical levels, including feature map layers, classification layers, and totally linked layers. CNN receives an image as input, analyzes it, and assigns one of multiple class labels to classify an image into a preset set of categories. In a deep CNN, the input image traverses several layers, including a feature extraction with customized filters (kernels), a pooling layer, a fully connected layer, and a classification layer or bounding regression. In the first layer of a conventional CNN, convolution employs filters to build output feature maps. The filters in convolutional layers can be used to detect edges, blur them, or sharpen them. The feature maps generated by the convolution layers are forwarded to the sample layers to reduce the size of following levels. If the input image is quite huge, they assist in minimizing the parameter size. The size has been decreased without sacrificing any of the essential information, and any unnecessary ones have been omitted. When available, the vectorized feature maps are given to the completed layers. The photos are then categorized using the activation and classification functions. CNN's categorization procedure is enhanced with the use of backpropagation.

3.1 Proposed in CNN Algorithm

Each layer of the convolutional neural networks that have been constructed uses a different proportion of the total training data. Bagging, a method for selecting elements at random and with restitution, is used to generate the subgroups' elements. Hence, a sample may appear multiple times. We randomly select a subset of the features from the feature vector and use it to divide the data for each node when training the layers. In our example, the number of features used for divides is half the square root of the total number of features. After computing all feasible splits, the one with the greatest information gain for the label histogram and the least entropy loss is chosen. In our situation, learning is complete when CNN-Layers are formed or when the expected classification error is less than 1%. During training, the error is estimated by detecting instances that the bagging method missed. The layers of this convolutional neural network are not trimmed. Each tree classifies the data according to its own rules, and a simple majority determines the final label, There is a simple formula to do so:

Dimension of image = (n, n) Dimension of filter = (f,f) Dimension of output will be ((n-f + 1), (n-f + 1)) You should have a good understanding of how a convolutional layer works at this point. Let us move to the next part of the CNN architecture.

As convolutional neural networks have so many advantages, they are commonly used. In response, we suggest that adding extra layers does not result in overfitting. To conclude, it is secure to utilize a huge number as doing so boosts precision. Nevertheless, when more layers are added, the classification accuracy benefits begin to erode. Additionally, both the training and classification periods rise linearly with the number of layers. The capability to evaluate several trees simultaneously reduces training and classification times. A primary aspect should be the efficiency of the categorizing operation. In supervised deep learning, common methods like support vector machines, boosted layers, convolutional neural networks, and others are contrasted. A dataset with binary classification problems is used for testing. While no individual performed best across all tasks, the research concludes that there is no universally superior algorithm. Based on the outcomes of their research, bagged layers, convolutional neural networks, and calibrated boosted layers offer the maximum performance. Often, CNN algorithms are utilized for the purpose of sign recognition. Their test set comprises of about 5000 photos in 43 distinct categories. To round out the top three deep learning algorithms, the results show that convolutional neural networks perform admirably. We analyze the efficacy of convolutional neural networks. Using the most stable extremes, the approach locates satellite photos. By looking for many smaller locations within the bigger region, the satellite photos can be located. CNN develops most of these algorithms to identify field in photographs captured in the real world. While the congestion in our field photographs is not nearly as severe as that in natural images, advanced techniques such as SWT are unnecessary. Instead, we apply the same MSER and grouping-based technique employed for text extraction from agricultural areas to recognize satellite images. We have access to both the recovered up-right field image and a list of the section names, positions, and content types. Because the field is not always extracted correctly, the highlighted areas need to be changed to match the field's content (Fig. 5).

4   Experiments and Evaluation

The opened image is removed pixel-by-pixel. Character width is minimal compared to structural element; therefore, they stay intact. The first example region graph shows this. Several lines remain unleveled. The identical method would remove most of the field when removing vertical lines. To avoid this, borders are first identified and only those

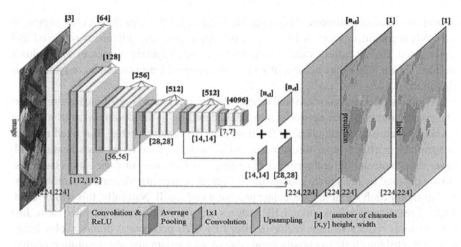

Fig. 5. A CNN architecture for processing the satellite images of fields.

regions are screened. Peaks appear in the first 20% of the left and right sides. A column's peak is 70% black pixels. Assuming the field is generally centered, the distance of the first detected peak on either side to the image border should be similar. The opening result is subtracted pixel-by-pixel again. Since deleted lines are rarely exactly horizontal or vertical, some debris remains. Second-region filtering result. Extracting and filtering related components removes noise. A connected component is eliminated if its bounding box meets the image borders, its width and height are less than three pixels, or its area is less than (Fig. 6).

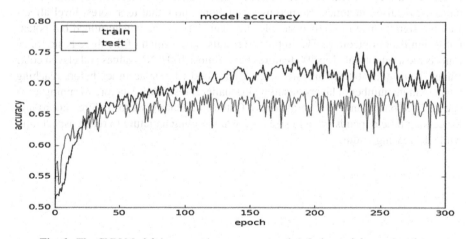

Fig. 6. The CNN Model Accuracy (accuracy vs epochs) during training and testing.

We organize and collect field data in this article. CNN locates the field using contours after creating a mask. A convolutional neural network classifies the extracted field using local binary patterns, median color values, and size ratio. Field and type extracted pieces start at the same coordinates. After preprocessing, a CNN helps detect each region. If the CNN recognition score is low, a user-provided issue area picture is retrieved and reprocessed. Field studies evaluate recommendations. Lighting successes and failures are also shown. Classifier vectors often contain pairs of features. Each combination is classified.

A domain-specific convolutional neural network receives a N-attribute feature vector. The convolutional neural network splits data according to the optimal partition during training, when each node takes m features from the feature vector. The fixed number of attributes m affects layer-forest tree classification. Improve forest classification with lower layer correlation and stronger classifiers. m increases linkages and classifiers. Divide the total by the square root of the number of active variables and use three example values for each variable to calculate precision and recall. Naturally, this will be used. These three elements look alike. LBP features are more influential than size ratio. Just LBP features reduce feature vector accuracy by 0.26 percentage points. Color information contributes little to classifications due to scarce data and low-resolution photos. Fuzzy, twisted fields approximate median blurring. The report describes classification results for the full feature vector and LBP features alone for a range of median blur kernel widths. Avoid leave-one-out cross-validation. Instead, the full dataset trains the classifier. Classification's feature vector comes from image blurring. Both feature vectors can identify all photos (Fig. 7 and Table 1).

After training, convolutional neural networks rank feature vector component vectors effectively. Four variables are assessed for relevance in the reference convolutional neural network user guide. The forest reclassifies data based on feature randomness after sampling. We provide the number of people that voted for the proper class in each tree using the original and updated sample sizes. Averaging variance or precision across all levels determines the feature's relevance. Problems arise when well-intentioned procedures yield false outcomes. Numerous simulations show that user forest level affects variable significance more than sample size. This lets us see undetermined but potentially significant outcomes. The imprecise results show which of the three basic forest traits is most important. Top 100 features have almost 100 CNN values and eleven color values. Pairing attributes hurts size ratio. CNNs boost forest accuracy before reaching the maximum number of layers, resulting in smaller forests. All-data forest training averages 3.21 s (based on five separate runs). Gather the feature vector before classifying. Processing time depends on field size ratio when scaling a picture to retain aspect ratio while decreasing width.

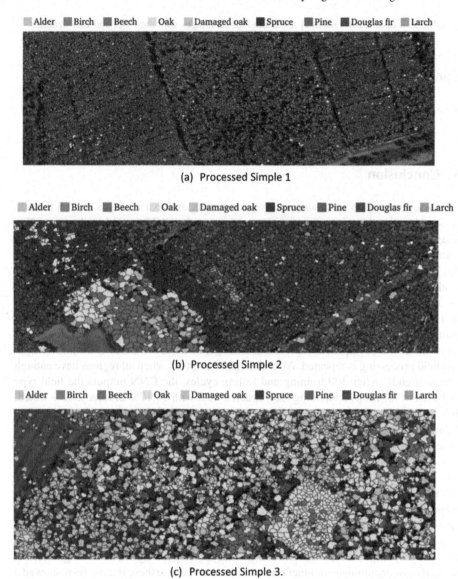

Alder Birch Beech Oak Damaged oak Spruce Pine Douglas fir Larch

(a) Processed Simple 1

Alder Birch Beech Oak Damaged oak Spruce Pine Douglas fir Larch

(b) Processed Simple 2

Alder Birch Beech Oak Damaged oak Spruce Pine Douglas fir Larch

(c) Processed Simple 3.

Fig. 7. Classification results for processed sample images using CNN.

Table 1. Classification results for median blurred images with the CNN and LBP features.

Kernel Size	9×9	19×19	29×29	39×39
LBP	124 (99.2%)	104 (83.2%)	60 (48.0%)	35 (28.0%)
	1 (0.8%)	21 (16.8%)	65 (52.0%)	90 (72.0%)
CNN Feature Vector	125 (100.0%)	114 (91.2%)	73 (58.4%)	45 (36.0%)
	0 (0.0%)	11 (8.8%)	52 (41.6%)	80 (64.0%)

5 Conclusion

This study uses deep learning to detect, categorize, and extract fields from a dataset. A deep learning-based convolutional neural network (CNN) would evaluate satellite image components to produce agricultural fields or areas of interest (ROI). Machine learning detects, segments, and tags the satellite image in the input image. CNN classifies images using LBP histograms, feature size ratios, and color. It got species-specific field arrangement and segment coordinates. It compares field fields to defined fields to fix field extraction errors. Preprocessing minimizes noise before introducing recent data into a convolutional neural network (CNN). CNN preprocesses by similarity, size, and plane of focus. CNN-based. If the CNN gives at least one field region a low confidence score, the user is prompted to capture a new image, which is compared to the prior image, and field processing is repeated. After enough attempts or when all regions have enough points, it ends. After 300 training and testing cycles, the CNN outputs the field type and a list of locations containing the extracted field with 98.17% accuracy. 10% tested, 10% validated, and 20% trained the suggested system. The feature vector was tested on a dataset with unique classes from a subset of field types. New vs. old. Local binary pattern histograms, color characteristics, and field size ratios most affected categorization. The composite feature vector correctly categorized specular reflections, shadows, and insufficient illumination-induced fuzzy or miscolored pictures. We demonstrated that training the CNN with test field typography lowers recognition errors. Field region preprocessing removes short hyphens, commas, and dots that mix with field borders, causing most remaining issues. Filters consider previously used fields. Constant field region preprocessing removes chipped or discolored characters. Indistinguishable field and backdrop improve field localization accuracy. Overpainting the field's edges, letting dirt and moss accumulate, or other circumstances may cause these issues: Tests showed a three-field CNN with font detection training performed effectively. The prototype lacks a manual focus dial and struggles to photograph highly reflective fields. Most fields aren't connected to gadgets since their surfaces deteriorate quickly after environmental contact. It collects field data quickly.

References

1. Rizvi, S., Patti, D., Björklund, T., Cabodi, G., Francini, G.: Deep classifiers-based satellite image detection, localization and recognition on GPU-powered mobile platform. Future Internet **9**, 66 (2017)

2. Rafique, M.A., Pedrycz, W., Jeon, M.: Field satellite images detection using region-based convolutional neural networks. Soft Comput. **22**, 6429–6440 (2018)
3. Salau, A.O., Yesufu, T.K., Ogundare, B.S.: Field field number localization using a modified GrabCut algorithm. J. King Saud Univ. Comput. Inf, Sci (2019)
4. Kakani, B.V., Gandhi, D., Jani, S.: Improved CNN based automatic field number field recognition using features trained neural network. In: Proceedings of the 2017 8th International Conference on Computing, Communication and Networking Technologies (ICCCNT), Delhi, India (3–5 July 2017)
5. Arafat, M.Y., Khairuddin, A.S.M., Paramesran, R.A.: Vehicular satellite image recognition framework for skewed images. KSII Trans. Internet Inf. Syst., 12 (2018)
6. Available Online: https://melabglobal.com/blogs/news/why-use-field-field-recognition-par king-system
7. Ansari, N.N., Singh, A.K., Student, M.T.: Field number field recognition using temfield matching. Int. J. Comput. Trends Technol. **35**, 175–178 (2016)
8. Samma, H., Lim, C.P., Saleh, J.M., Suandi, S.A.: A memetic-based fuzzy support vector machine model and its application to satellite image recognition. Memetic Comput. **8**, 235–251 (2016)
9. Tabrizi, S.S., Cavus, N.: A hybrid KNN-SVM model for iranian satellite image recognition. Procedia Comput. Sci. **102**, 588–594 (2016)
10. Available Online: https://medium.datadriveninvestor.com/convolutional-neural-networks-explained-7fafea4de9c9
11. Abbood, Z.A., Yasen, B.T., Ahmed, M.R., Duru, A.D.: Speaker identification model based on deep neural networks. Iraqi J. Comp. Sci. Math. **3**(1), 108–114 (2022)
12. Shaker, A.S., Ahmed, S.R.: Information retrieval for cancer cell detection based on advanced machine learning techniques. Al-Mustansiriyah J. Sci. **33**(3), 20–26 (2022)
13. Yaseen, B.T., Kurnaz, S., Ahmed, S.R.: Detecting and Classifying Drug Interaction using Data mining Techniques. In : 2022 International Symposium on Multidisciplinary Studies and Innovative Technologies (ISMSIT), pp. 952–956. IEEE (2022, October)
14. Abdulateef, O.G., Abdullah, A.I., Ahmed, S.R., Mahdi, M.S.: Vehicle license plate detection using deep learning. In: 2022 International Symposium on Multidisciplinary Studies and Innovative Technologies (ISMSIT), pp. 288–292. IEEE (2022, October)
15. Ahmed, S.R., Sonuç, E., Ahmed, M.R., Duru, A.D.: Analysis survey on deepfake detection and recognition with convolutional neural networks. In: 2022 International Congress on Human-Computer Interaction, Optimization and Robotic Applications (HORA), pp. 1–7. IEEE (2022, June)
16. Ahmed, S.R.A., Sonuç, E.: Deepfake detection using rationale-augmented convolutional neural network. Applied Nanoscience 1–9 (2021)
17. Ahmed, M.R., Ahmed, S.R., Duru, A.D., Uçan, O.N., Bayat, O.: An expert system to predict eye disorder using deep convolutional neural network. Academic Platform-Journal of Engineering and Science **9**(1), 47–52 (2021)
18. Sivaraman, S., Trivedi, M.M.: A general active learning framework for on-road field recognition and tracking. IEEE Transactions on Intelligent Transportation Systems (2010)
19. Silva, S., Jung, C.: Real-time Brazilian satellite image detection and recognition using deep convolutional neural networks. In: 14th IAPR International Conference on Document Analysis and Recognition (ICDAR) (2017)
20. Matas, J., Zimmermann, K.: Unconstrained licence field and field localization and recognition 225–230 (2015). https://doi.org/10.1109/ITSC.2005.1520111
21. Girshick, R.: Fast R-CNN. In: IEEE International Conference on Computer Vision (ICCV) (2015)

22. Amari, R., Zrigui, S., Nicolas, H., Zrigui, M.: Deep Convolutional Neural Network for Speech Recognition. In : International Conference on Computational Collective Intelligence (ICCCI) (2022, September)

23. Slimi, A., Hafar, N., Zrigui, M., Nicolas, H.: Multiple models fusion for multi-label classification in speech emotion recognition systems. Procedia Computer Science **207**, 2875–2882 (2022)

24. Mounir, A.J., Mallat, S., Zrigui, M.: Analyzing satellite images by apply deep learning instance segmentation of agricultural fields. Periodicals of Engineering and Natural Sciences **9**(4), 1056–1069 (2021)

25. Mansouri, S., Charhad, M., Zrigui, M.: A new approach for automatic Arabic-text detection and localisation in video frames. Int. J. Adva. Intelli. Paradi. **22**(1–2), 72–83 (2022)

26. Bassem, B., Zrigui, M.: Gender identification: a comparative study of deep learning architectures. In: Intelligent Systems Design and Applications: 18th International Conference on Intelligent Systems Design and Applications (ISDA 2018) held in Vellore, India, December 6–8, 2018, Volume 2, pp. 792–800. Springer International Publishing (2020)

27. Farhani, N., Terbeh, N., Zrigui, M.: Object recognition approach based on generalized hough transform and color distribution serving in generating arabic sentences. Int. J. Comp. Info. Eng. **13**(6), 339–344 (2019)

28. Farhani, N., Terbeh, N., Zrigui, M.: Image to text conversion: state of the art and extended work. In: 2017 IEEE/ACS 14th International Conference on Computer Systems and Applications (AICCSA), pp. 937–943. IEEE (2017, October)

29. Rabbouch, H., Saâdaoui, F., Ibrahim, H., Zrigui, M.: Multiresolutional Hybrid NLM-Wiener Filters for X-Ray Image Denoising. In : 2022 8th International Conference on Control, Decision and Information Technologies (CoDIT), Vol. 1, pp. 343–348. IEEE (2022, May)

Classifying Chicken-Made Food Images Using Enhanced MobilNetV2

Abdulaziz Anorboev[1]($\boxtimes$) , Javokhir Musaev[1] , Sarvinoz Anorboeva[1] ,
Jeongkyu Hong[4] , Ngoc Thanh Nguyen[2,3] , Yeong-Seok Seo[1] ,
and Dosam Hwang[1]

[1] Yeungnam University, Daegu, Republic of Korea
abdulaziz.anorboev@gmail.com
[2] Wroclaw University of Science and Technology, 50-370 Wroclaw, Poland
Ngoc-Thanh.Nguyen@pwr.edu.pl
[3] Nguyen Tat Thanh University, Ho Chi Minh 70000, Vietnam
[4] University of Seoul, Seoul, Republic of Korea
jhong0301@uos.ac.kr

Abstract. We focused on the development of a classification model for
Chicken food images using convolutional neural networks (CNNs) for
diet management apps. While previous studies have proposed methods
for classifying food images in specific countries, little research has been
done on Chicken food image classification. To address this gap, we collected images from various platforms and search engines and evaluated
the proposed model's performance using a Chicken food image dataset.
The results showed that transfer learning can be used to achieve successful classification, but the model's performance varied depending on
the type of food being classified. Thus, further research is necessary to
improve the accuracy of the model for specific food types. This study
has implications for the training process of the classification model and
the public Chicken food image dataset, which can be useful for future
studies aiming to enhance the model's performance.

Keywords: Image Classification · Transfer Learning · Deep Learning

1 Introduction

The app assists users in monitoring their daily dietary intake, including calories,
nutrient types, and other pertinent information pertinent to their health objectives, via analysis of food images. Food image classification algorithms adopt
machine learning techniques to recognize different types of food based on their
visual characteristics. These algorithms can identify specific foods or ingredients, as well as estimate portion sizes, which helps users accurately track their
daily calorie intake and nutrient consumption. Furthermore, food image classification [1] can be leveraged to customize dietary recommendations tailored
to the user's health objectives and preferences. For example, the app may recommend specific meals or recipes based on the user's dietary restrictions [2],

N. T. Nguyen et al. (Eds.): ICCCI 2023, CCIS 1864, pp. 175–188, 2023.
https://doi.org/10.1007/978-3-031-41774-0_14

such as vegan or gluten-free diets, or their weight loss goals. Foods can have similar visual appearances, particularly when prepared or presented in different ways [3]. A piece of grilled chicken may appear similar to a piece of grilled tofu or tempeh, making it difficult for a food image classification algorithm to differentiate between them. Similarly, different types of pasta dishes may appear similar, thereby making it challenging to accurately identify the type of pasta being used in a particular dish.

To address these challenges, food image classification algorithms often use advanced machine learning techniques that can analyze multiple features of food images, such as texture, color, shape, and other visual characteristics. These algorithms may also consider contextual information, such as ingredients used in a particular dish and cultural and regional variations in food preparation. Food image classification algorithms can be trained on large datasets of food images to improve their accuracy and discriminatory ability. By continuously learning and adapting to new data [4], these algorithms can become more accurate over time, increasing their suitability for food image classification. Using machine learning algorithms [5] to automatically identify and classify different types of food, these applications can offer various benefits such as improved speed, service efficiency, accuracy in tracking dietary intake, and personalized dietary recommendations.

Despite these potential benefits, automatic food classification has not yet been fully integrated into numerous real-world applications. This is because the technology is still relatively new and requires further research and development to improve its accuracy and effectiveness. Another challenge is that automatic food classification often requires large amounts of high-quality data to train machine learning algorithms. This data can be challenging and costly to gather, particularly when considering diverse and varied dishes that are prepared and served differently. Moreover, there are potential concerns about privacy and security, particularly in the context of personal health management. Users may be hesitant to share information regarding their dietary intake and habits, and there may be concerns regarding the security of sensitive health data. Veggie Vision [6] was one of the first attempts at food classification, specifically for identifying food items during supermarket checkouts. The system uses a combination of visual features, including color (hue, saturation, and intensity), shape, and density, to analyze and classify images of food items. Veggie Vision uses a nearest-neighbor algorithm to classify food items, which involves comparing the visual features of an unknown item to the features of known items in a database. The system then assigns the unknown item to the class of the most similar known item.

This system was designed to facilitate automated checkout in supermarkets by identifying items without manual scanning. This could potentially accelerate checkout times and reduce item identification errors. Although Veggie Vision was a pioneering effort in food classification, the system had limitations in terms of accuracy and scalability. It can only recognize a limited number of food items and is prone to errors when items are presented in different orientations or lighting conditions. The pre-trained model used in [7] used a convolutional neural network (CNN) that was trained on a large dataset of general images, rather than specifically on food images. The researchers fine-tuned this pre-trained model by training it on a small dataset of food images, which enabled it to recognize different types of food items. The Food-5K database consists of 5,000 images of 250 food items, and the Food-11 database consists of 16643 images with 11 food categories. Both databases were used to evaluate the performance of the pre-trained model, along with a dataset of nonfood images. The results indicated that the pre-trained model could accurately classify food and non-food images with accuracies of over 90% and 85% on the Food-5K and Food-11 databases, respectively. The model also outperformed other state-of-the-art food image classification methods in terms of accuracy and speed.

Food image classification has not specifically focused on chicken food image classification. However, some studies [8–14] have classified specific types of chicken dishes or poultry products, such as fried chicken, chicken nuggets, and grilled chicken. Nevertheless, the development of a food image classification model that can classify over 23 types of chicken food remains a significant contribution to the field, as it expands the scope of food items that can be recognized and classified automatically. Additionally, examining the characteristics of the chicken food image dataset can provide insights into the challenges and opportunities of food image classification in this domain. Understanding the differences between food categories is important for accurate classification because foods within the same category can have subtle differences in appearance that affect their visual features. By examining the characteristics of the chicken food image dataset, such as color, texture, and shape, researchers can identify key features that can be used to distinguish between different types of chicken dishes. Pre-trained deep neural networks, such as DenseNet121 [15], ResNet50 [16], and MobileNetV2 [17], were used for food classification through transfer learning. Pre-trained models, having been trained on extensive datasets of general images, can be fine-tuned to specific tasks, such as food image classification, thereby conserving time and resources compared to training a model from scratch. In addition to fine-tuning the pre-trained models, another approach considered is feature extraction. This involves using pre-trained models as feature extractors, where the output of certain layers in the network is used as input features for a conventional classification method, such as AlexNet [18]. This approach can prove advantageous when training data is scarce or when experimenting with varying classification techniques.

The research has contributed to the intended users of the model, which is capable of automatically categorizing visually similar chicken food images, in the following ways:

First, the study offers a classification algorithm that can correctly categorize pictures of visually comparable chicken food classes. This contribution is important since it can be challenging to distinguish between food items that appear identical on the surface, and the automated categorization model can be a helpful resource for the target audience.

Secondly, the study also offers a pre-processed dataset that can be used to train models for categorizing images of chicken food. The intended consumers, who might not have the knowledge or resources to pre-process the data on their own, can gain time from this.

Lastly, the study also evaluates how well different pre-trained CNNs perform when used to train a model to categorize photos of chicken meal. Based on accuracy and learning time, this comparison can help the intended users choose the best pre-trained CNN for their particular use case.

2   Methodology

The study collected images from a Chicken food image dataset. This dataset was used to train the classification model. To prepare the image data for model training, the study performed image pre-processing and augmentation. Image pre-processing involves techniques such as resizing, normalization, and filtering to improve the quality of the images. Augmentation involves creating new training examples by applying transformations such as rotation, flipping, and cropping to the existing images. The classification model was trained using the pre-processed and augmented image data. The model was trained to classify chicken food images into different categories.

2.1   Dataset

We developed a novel database with 23 distinct categories of chicken-based food items. This database is designed for health-related applications that enable auto-mated food identification and daily nutrient calculation. The database comprises of 10,360 images, with each category containing at least 400 sample images. The images were collected from diverse sources, including Google, Bing, Naver, and Kaggle image search engines. Although the resolution of the images varied, we have provided detailed category-specific information in Table 1.

2.2   CNN

In this research, we used a CNN, a commonly used method for image classification, to extract features from the images. Specifically, we employed four pre-trained models, AlexNet, ResNet50, DenseNet121, and MobileNetV2, which were previously trained with ImageNet data, to classify our dataset. To accomplish this, we connected the pre-trained feature extraction network with a classification model network that incorporates fully connected layers activated with ReLu and employs Softmax for the output layers. In this study, we used transfer learning techniques to train our model using pre-trained weights obtained from a dataset. This process involves fine-tuning the hyperparameters to optimize accuracy and minimize loss. Each input image underwent feature extraction, which was performed in the convolution and pooling layers. The final layer has a fully connected layer that classifies the features extracted in the previous step. We evaluated the classification results using a loss function and measured the accuracy and loss at each epoch for both the training and validation data. Once the training process was completed, the performance of the model was tested using a separate test dataset.

Table 1. Dataset Information.

Chicken-Food Types	Abbreviated Version	Train Samples	Test Samples
Buffalo Wings	BW	396	50
Butter Chicken	BC	400	50
Chicken 65	C65	400	50
Chicken Biriyani	CB	400	50
Chicken Fried Steak	CFS	400	50
Chicken Nuggets	CN	400	50
Chicken Parmigiana	CP	400	50
Chicken Tajine	CTaj	400	50
Chicken Tikka	CTik	400	50
Chicken and Waffles	CnW	400	50
Chicken with Chestnuts	CwC	400	50
Chili Chicken	CC	400	50
Chinese Chicken Salad	CCS	400	
Creamy Chicken Marsala	CCM	400	50
Creamy Lemon Parmesan Chicken Piccata	CLPCP	400	50
Garlic Soya Chicken	GSC	400	50
General Tso's Chicken	GTC	400	50
Italian Braised Chicken	IBC	400	50
Italian Chicken Meal Prep Bowls	ICMPB	398	50
Italian Skillet Chicken with Tomatoes And Mushrooms	ISCwTnM	410	56
Italian Style Chicken Mozzarella Skillet	ISCMS	400	50
Nashville Hot Chicken	NHC	400	50
Tandoori Chicken	TC	400	50

3 Experimental Setup and Results

3.1 Training Setup

We implemented the proposed model using Python version 3.9.13 and the TensorFlow library. We initialized the model weights using a Gaussian distribution and did not incorporate any bias parameters. During training, we used a GPU with 24 GB of memory, specifically, a GeForce RTX 3090 Ti with CUDA 11.6. A mini-batch size of 32 was used for training. The model was trained for 50 epochs using the Adam optimizer and a sparse categorical loss function with a default learning rate of 0.001. These technical specifications and training details are essential for accurately reproducing and comprehending the results of the proposed model.

3.2   Evaluation Metrics

A method was proposed that mainly focuses on the accuracy of the model. In previous studies, different metrics were used, such as the F1 score, recall, and ROC. For this research, two metrics were mainly focused on that meaningfully explained the method's achievements for different datasets. To present comparable results, precision, recall and f1 scores were used. All the datasets used were balanced, and wasn't evaluated the effects of different class weights on the final results. The accuracy was defined as the ratio of the number of true predictions to the total number of cases used to evaluate the model.

$$Accuracy = \frac{TP + TN}{TP + TN + FP + FN}. \tag{1}$$

$$Precision = \frac{TP}{TP + FP}. \tag{2}$$

$$Recall = \frac{TP}{TP + FN}. \tag{3}$$

$$F1\ score = \frac{2 \times Precision \times Recall}{Precision + Recall}. \tag{4}$$

TP corresponds to the true predicted positive results, TN corresponds to the true predicted negative results, FP corresponds to the false predicted positive results, and FN corresponds to the false predicted negative results.

$$UTP(X,Y) = X - X \cap Y \tag{5}$$

The second evaluation metric was the unique true prediction UTP Eq. 5, which identifies the percentage of unique predictions for each model with respect to another. $UTP(X,Y)$ finds unique true predictions for model X with respect to model Y. X represents the prediction scope of model X, and Y represents the prediction scope of model Y. These metrics explain why the proposed model achieved better results than the main model, in which only the main dataset was trained. The indices of the true predicted images differed among the models, even though they had the same accuracy. This allowed the ensemble to achieve better results.

3.3   Results and Discussions

A set of images was used to test each model's performance, and similarities and differences between the models were found. With an average top-1 recall of 0.9 for all models based on transfer learning, the accuracy of each model and food category was reported. As depicted in Figs. 1 through 4 for AlexNet, ResNet50,

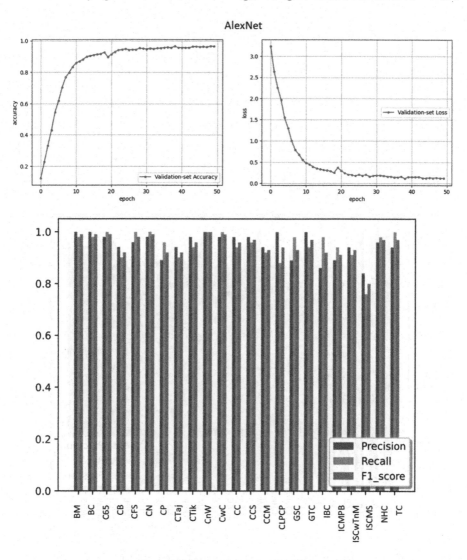

Fig. 1. Experimental results using AlexNet.

DenseNet121, and the Proposed model in Fig. 2, respectively, the paper provides the findings of trials on a validation dataset using accuracy-based metrics.

ResNet50 in Fig. 2 exhibited the lowest accuracy-related scores when compared to the other models, while having a continuous improvement in accuracy and loss during training. In contrast, DenseNet121 in Fig. 3 obtained the second-best ratings, while the other models had comparable results in loss, accuracy, precision, recall, and F1. When compared to other models, the proposed technique performed better, earning almost 2% higher scores when assessed using AS and F1.

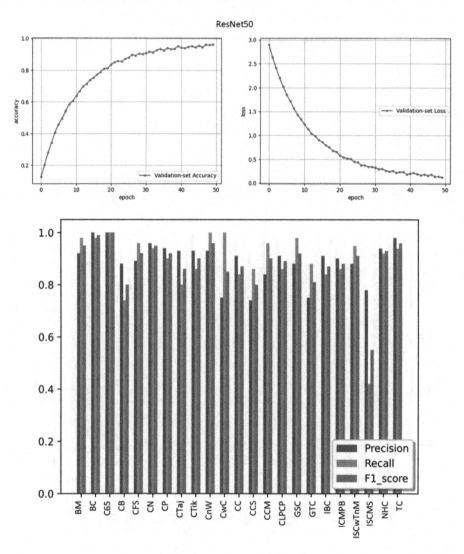

Fig. 2. Experimental results using ResNet50.

It also received the top scores in AS and F1 in the dataset. The results indicate that the proposed model has a lot of potential to be a successful model. Among the pre-trained models, proposed exhibited the best performance. It was observed that various models that utilized different feature extraction networks attained a similar result. The evaluation outcomes indicated notable variations in recall and precision across each food category. The recall of the 23 main categories, comprising the remaining food types, was depicted in Fig. 3, while Fig. 4 presented the precision and recall of each food type, accompanied by representative images.

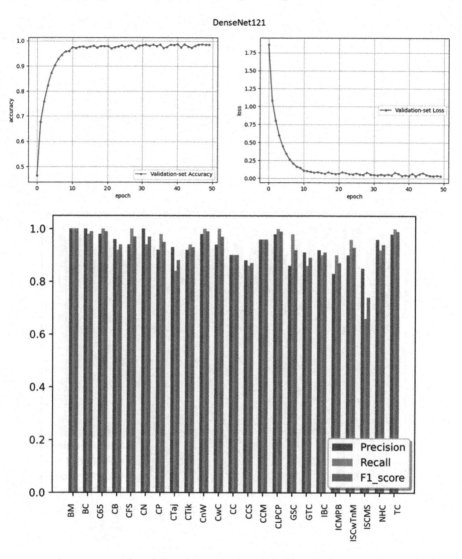

Fig. 3. Experimental results using DenseNet121.

To evaluate the generalization ability of the baseline and proposed methods in terms of accuracy, precision, recall, and F1 on unseen data during inference, we conducted tests on the test set of the considered datasets. Table 2 displays the findings from the experiment. With a few exceptions, the AlexNet approach achieved the highest F1 score of 1.0 on several BM, BC, CLPCP, and some classes of the dataset. Based on the data in the table, the suggested system displayed greater performance when compared to the baseline methods. The improvement

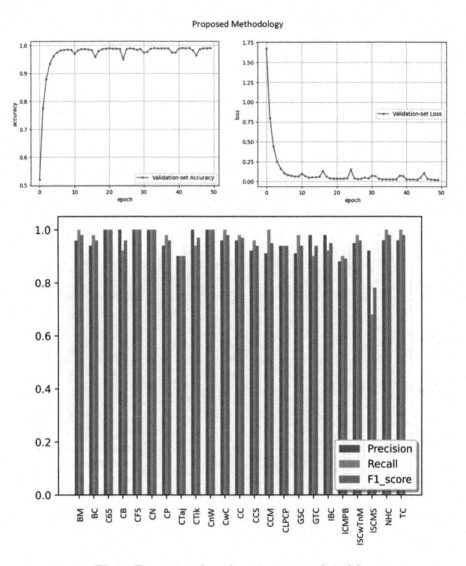

Fig. 4. Experimental results using proposed models.

above the suggested strategy, however, was only 0.01%. It is remarkable that the suggested technique showed the best accuracy-to-efficiency ratio early on, particularly in the fourth epoch, and that it consistently performed well.

Table 2. Classification recall, precision and f1-score of Chicken-Made food categories.

Dataset Classes	AlexNet			ResNet50			DenseNet121			Proposed Methodology		
	precision	recall	f1-score	precision	recall	f1-score	precision	recall	f1-score	precision	recall	f1-score
BM	1.00	1.00	1.00	0.92	0.98	0.95	1.00	0.98	0.99	0.96	1.00	0.98
BC	1.00	0.98	0.99	1.00	0.98	0.99	1.00	0.98	0.99	0.94	0.98	0.96
C65	0.98	1.00	0.99	1.00	1.00	1.00	0.98	1.00	0.99	1.00	1.00	1.00
CB	0.96	0.92	0.94	0.88	0.74	0.80	0.94	0.90	0.92	1.00	0.92	0.96
CFS	0.94	1.00	0.97	0.89	0.96	0.92	0.96	1.00	0.98	1.00	1.00	1.00
CN	1.00	0.94	0.97	0.96	0.94	0.95	0.98	1.00	0.99	1.00	1.00	1.00
CP	0.92	0.98	0.95	0.94	0.90	0.92	0.89	0.96	0.92	0.94	0.98	0.96
CTaj	0.93	0.84	0.88	0.93	0.80	0.86	0.94	0.90	0.92	0.90	0.90	0.90
CTik	0.92	0.94	0.93	0.93	0.86	0.90	0.98	0.94	0.96	1.00	0.94	0.97
CnW	0.98	1.00	0.99	0.93	1.00	0.96	1.00	1.00	1.00	1.00	1.00	1.00
CwC	0.94	1.00	0.97	0.75	1.00	0.85	0.98	1.00	0.99	0.96	1.00	0.98
CC	0.90	0.90	0.90	0.91	0.84	0.87	0.98	0.94	0.96	0.96	0.98	0.97
CCS	0.88	0.86	0.87	0.74	0.86	0.80	0.98	0.96	0.97	0.92	0.96	0.94
CCM	0.96	0.96	0.96	0.84	0.96	0.90	0.94	0.92	0.93	0.91	1.00	0.95
CLPCP	0.98	1.00	0.99	0.91	0.86	0.89	1.00	0.88	0.94	0.94	0.94	0.94
GSC	0.86	0.98	0.92	0.88	0.98	0.92	0.89	0.98	0.93	0.91	0.98	0.94
GTC	0.91	0.86	0.89	0.75	0.88	0.81	1.00	0.94	0.97	0.98	0.90	0.94
IBC	0.92	0.90	0.91	0.91	0.84	0.87	0.86	0.98	0.92	0.98	0.92	0.95
ICMPB	0.83	0.90	0.87	0.90	0.86	0.88	0.89	0.94	0.91	0.88	0.90	0.89
ISCwTnM	0.90	0.96	0.93	0.88	0.95	0.91	0.94	0.91	0.93	0.95	0.98	0.96
ISCMS	0.85	0.66	0.74	0.78	0.42	0.55	0.84	0.76	0.80	0.92	0.68	0.78
NHC	0.96	0.92	0.94	0.94	0.92	0.93	0.96	0.98	0.97	0.96	1.00	0.98
TC	0.98	1.00	0.99	0.98	0.94	0.96	0.94	1.00	0.97	0.96	1.00	0.98
accuracy			0.94			0.89			0.95			0.96
macro avg	0.94	0.93	0.93	0.89	0.89	0.89	0.95	0.95	0.95	0.96	0.95	0.95
weighted avg	0.94	0.94	0.93	0.89	0.89	0.89	0.95	0.95	0.95	0.96	0.96	0.95

3.4   Confusion Matrices

The Fig. 5 evaluated a classification models' performance on 23 classes of chicken-based food images. The model achieved high accuracy in classifying most of the images, despite their high similarity. However, some images were misclassified, and the baseline models and proposed model had different levels of error in misclassification. The confusion matrix showed instances of misclassification, such as DenseNet121 misclassifying 4 instances of Italian Style Chicken with Mozzarella Skillet out of 50 as Chicken Parmigiana. Evaluation results from AlexNet indicated that 5 incorrect predictions of Italian Style Chicken with Mozzarella Skillet belonged to a different category, Chili Chicken. ResNet50 had 6 classes with high confusion, as demonstrated in Fig. 5. The proposed model had the lowest error in misclassification, suggesting opportunities for further improvement in accurately classifying similar food types.

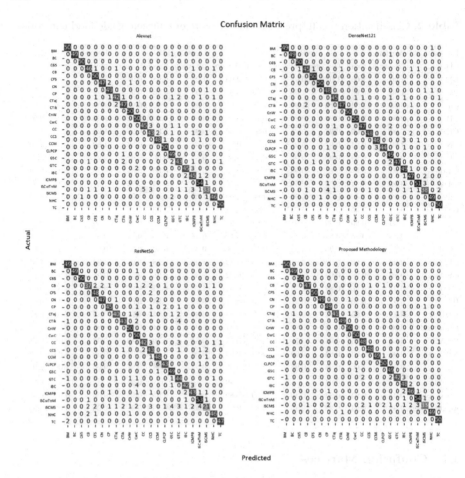

Fig. 5. Classification result of Chicken-Made food images using model based on Confusion Matrix.

4   Conclusion

The research findings indicated that regardless of the feature extraction networks employed, the models' categorization accuracy remained constant across all food categories. However, because to the complex combination of foods in an image and the significant similarity across particular image classes, low classification accuracy was seen in some food image classes. When identifying food photos comprising a mixture of different food categories or items with similar forms and colors, the classification model's performance was found to be subpar.

The study had several limitations because it was not possible to solve the poor classification performances for particular food classes, despite the fact that a model for categorizing chicken meal photos was constructed. Therefore, it is essential to increase the classification accuracy for these food groups in order to improve the model's overall performance.

Future studies should focus on improving the performance of the categorization model and assessing the viability of the suggested models in order to progress the field's study. Correcting the classification accuracy for particular food classes is one method for raising the performance of the classification model. Additionally, research on usability with prospective users should be done to determine how useful the classification models are. The length of time it takes for the models to receive input data and produce output results, for instance, can be measured during a usability research.

For the future work we plan also to use data from social media for improving the effectiveness of our method. Analyzing the reactions of users in social networks can bring valuable information in evaluating the images [19]. Integration methods can be here useful for making consistent decision regarding the social media data [20, 21].

References

1. McAllister, P., Zheng, H., Bond, R., Moorhead, A.: Towards personalised training of machine learning algorithms for food image classification using a smartphone camera. In: García, C.R., Caballero-Gil, P., Burmester, M., Quesada-Arencibia, A. (eds.) UCAmI 2016. LNCS, vol. 10069, pp. 178–190. Springer, Cham (2016). https://doi.org/10.1007/978-3-319-48746-5_18
2. Waltner, G., et al.: Personalized dietary self-management using mobile vision-based assistance. In: Battiato, S., Farinella, G.M., Leo, M., Gallo, G. (eds.) ICIAP 2017. LNCS, vol. 10590, pp. 385–393. Springer, Cham (2017). https://doi.org/10.1007/978-3-319-70742-6_36
3. Chun, M., Jeong, H., Lee, H., Yoo, T., Jung, H.: Development of Korean food image classification model using public food image dataset and deep learning methods. IEEE Access 10, 128732–128741 (2022). https://doi.org/10.1109/ACCESS.2022.3227796
4. Musaev, J., Anorboev, A., Nguyen, N.T., Hwang, D.: KeepNMax: keep N maximum of epoch-channel ensemble method for deep learning models. IEEE Access 11, 9339–9350 (2023)
5. Musaev, J., Nguyen, N.T., Hwang, D.: EMaxPPE: epoch's maximum prediction probability ensemble method for deep learning classification models. In: Wojtkiewicz, K., Treur, J., Pimenidis, E., Maleszka, M. (eds.) ICCCI 2021. LNCS, vol. 1463, pp. 293–303. Springer, Cham (2021). https://doi.org/10.1007/978-3-030-88113-9_23
6. Haas, R.B.J.C.N., Taubin, R.M.G.: Veggievision: a produce recognition system. IBM TJ Watson Research Center, PO Box, vol. 704 (2012)
7. Singla, A., Yuan, L., Ebrahimi, T.: Food/non-food image classification and food categorization using pre-trained Googlenet model. In: Proceedings of the 2nd International Workshop on Multimedia Assisted Dietary Management, pp. 3–11. ACM (2016)
8. Islam, K.T., Wijewickrema, S., Pervez, M., O'Leary, S.: An exploration of deep transfer learning for food image classification. In: Digital Image Computing: Techniques and Applications (DICTA), Canberra, ACT, Australia 2018, pp. 1–5 (2018). https://doi.org/10.1109/DICTA.2018.8615812

9. Beijbom, O., Joshi, N., Morris, D., Saponas, S., Khullar, S.: Menu-Match: restaurant-specific food logging from images. In: 2015 IEEE Winter Conference on Applications of Computer Vision, Waikoloa, HI, USA, 2015, pp. 844–851 (2015). https://doi.org/10.1109/WACV.2015.117

10. Barbon, S., Costa Barbon, A.P.A.D., Mantovani, R.G., Barbin, D.F.: Machine learning applied to near-infrared spectra for chicken meat classification. J. Spectrosc. 2018, 12 (2018). Article ID 8949741. https://doi.org/10.1155/2018/8949741

11. Geronimo, B.C., et al.: Computer vision system and near-infrared spectroscopy for identification and classification of chicken with wooden breast, and physicochemical and technological characterization. Infrared Phys. Technol. 96, 303–310 (2019)

12. Mirzaee-Ghaleh, E., Taheri-Garavand, A., Ayari, F., et al.: Identification of fresh-chilled and frozen-thawed chicken meat and estimation of their shelf life using an e-nose machine coupled fuzzy KNN. Food Anal. Methods 13, 678–689 (2020). https://doi.org/10.1007/s12161-019-01682-6

13. Perez, I.M.N., Badaró, A.T., Barbon, S., Barbon, A.P.A., Pollonio, M.A.R., Barbin, D.F.: Classification of chicken parts using a portable near-infrared (NIR) spectrophotometer and machine learning. Appl. Spectrosc. 72, 1774–1780 (2018)

14. Xiong, Y., et al.: Non-destructive detection of chicken freshness based on electronic nose technology and transfer learning. Agriculture 13(2), 496 (2023). https://doi.org/10.3390/agriculture13020496

15. Huang, G., et al.: Densely connected convolutional networks. In: 2017 IEEE Conference on Computer Vision and Pattern Recognition (CVPR) (2017).https://doi.org/10.1109/cvpr.2017.243

16. He, K., Zhang, X., Ren, S., Sun, J.: Deep residual learning for image recognition. In: 2016 IEEE Conference on Computer Vision and Pattern Recognition (CVPR), pp. 770–778 (2015)

17. Sandler, M., Howard, A., Zhu, M., Zhmoginov, A., Chen, L.C.: MobileNetV2: inverted residuals and linear bottlenecks. In: 2018 IEEE/CVF Conference on Computer Vision and Pattern Recognition, pp. 4510–4520 (2018)

18. Krizhevsky, A., Sutskever, I., Hinton, G.E.: ImageNet classification with deep convolutional neural networks. Commun. ACM 60(6), 84–90 (2017)

19. Tran, V.C., Hwang, D., Nguyen, N.T.: Hashtag recommendation approach based on content and user characteristics. Cybern. Syst. 49(5–6), 368–383 (2018). https://doi.org/10.1080/01969722.2017.1418724

20. Sliwko, L., Nguyen, N.T.: Using multi-agent systems and consensus methods for information retrieval in internet. Int. J. Intell. Inf. Database Systems 1(2), 181–198 (2007). https://doi.org/10.1504/IJIIDS.2007.014949

21. Nguyen N.T: Metody wyboru consensusu i ich zastosowanie w rozwiązywaniu konfliktów w systemach rozproszonych. Oficyna Wydawnicza Politechniki Wrocławskiej (2002)

Natural Language Processing

Initial Approach to Pharmaceutical Opinion Search in Polish Language

Grzegorz Dziczkowski[1,2] and Grzegorz Madyda[2(✉)]

[1] University of Economics in Katowice, Bogucicka 3a, 40-228 Katowice, Poland
grzegorz.dziczkowski@ue.katowice.pl
[2] Institute of Innovative Technologies, EMAG, Leopolda 31, 40-189 Katowice, Poland
grzegorz.madyda@emag.lukasiewicz.gov.pl

Abstract. In recent years, the Internet has tended to speed up the publication of opinions on almost every topic. The volume of published texts results in a huge amount of data that the average Internet user is not able to analyze. At the same time, it can be observed that a very important topic that is becoming increasingly popular on the web is drugs and pharmaceuticals. Taking these two facts into account, we can assume that the customer of websites providing and reviewing medical and pharmaceutical services and products is also becoming a victim of information overload. In this situation, artificial intelligence solutions become helpful. Thanks to modern solutions, an appropriate algorithm is able to perform Opinion Mining, that is, analyze a significant amount of texts, posts and opinions and then aggregate their content into a form suitable for the average person. The following article shows how novel methods of Machine Learning are able to perform analysis of texts in polish language related to the medical and pharmaceutical industries, and then extract key information on a given topic.

Keywords: Machine Learning · Sentiment Analysis · Opinion Mining · Medical · Pharmaceutical

1 Project Objective

The aim of the project is to create a completely innovative system based on the latest scientific achievements. Presented project aims to achieve the following results:

- automatically search online resources (online forums, blogs, archives) to retrieve reviews containing opinions of other users,
- automatically assign a rating to the emotions contained in users' texts (ratings: very positive, positive, neutral, negative, very negative).

Mentioned innovative system will be dedicated to individual customers. It will be designed to provide the customer with an aggregate analysis of medical and pharmaceutical products of interest. With help of the algorithm it will be possible

N. T. Nguyen et al. (Eds.): ICCCI 2023, CCIS 1864, pp. 191–202, 2023.
https://doi.org/10.1007/978-3-031-41774-0_15

to perform an analysis of other users' opinions on the topic specified by the client. An example of functionality of the algorithm: The user is interested in a new medicine, hospital or medical and pharmaceutical product. After retrieving given phrase, analysis can be performed with help of the algorithm, and then the result of analysis is presented.

The analysis is based on automatically found opinions of other web users, which can potentially be found in forums, newsgroups, thematic blogs, thematic online newspapers or thematic digital archives. Communication with the customer will be realized through a minimalist and intuitive panel on a dedicated platform, where a search field for phrases of interest will be specified. After parametrization of input, an analysis (linguistic and statistical) will be carried out to determine the opinion intensity rating (from very negative to very positive). After this stage, the system is ready to present results of analysis. The results will be presented in graphical form, detailing the sources of the documents found, the date they were created, the opinions contained, and statistical graphs of the ratings generated.

In order to implement described system, an IT analysis (linguistic and statistical) of the learning base, consisting of sample documents, is necessary. Natural language is difficult to analyze and varies depending on the industry being described. For this reason, industry being analyzed must be precisely selected and specified so that algorithms are as precise as possible. Choice of the medical and pharmaceutical industry is dictated by the great interest of this industry in investments related to innovative IT solutions. In addition, there is a large base of available online forums, discussion groups, thematic blogs, online pharmacies and online publications related to selected industry.

This article presents the results of opinions' intensity analysis of Internet users evaluating doctors. We present only preliminary results to show the desirability of further research in the project. Actual opinions written in Polish are analyzed. The opinions were taken from publicly available websites on which Internet users evaluate doctors.

2   Motivation and Current State of Knowledge

Nowadays, the Internet has become an indispensable tool for exchanging information, offering unlimited access to ever-growing resources. With the development of technology, the Internet and its resources have grown in size to a great extent over the years. Today, access to information is easier than ever. Information can be received from many sources through the Internet. In Poland, the percentage of households with Internet access has increased from 75.7% in 2017 to 89.6% in 2020. If only households with children are considered, as many as 99.1% have access to the Internet [1]. Access to the Internet means not only easier access to information, but also to material goods. The development of online sales (e-commerce) has increased significantly in recent years.

In April 2017 - 46% of people surveyed in Poland bought something online in the last month, in June 2020 the percentage was 67% this is an increase of up to 21% [2]. In 2021, total sales of pharmaceutical and para-pharmaceutical products in Poland amounted to PLN 56 million. According to estimates, retail sales will grow by PLN 11 billion between 2022 and 2027, and online sales will account for 10% of the market share [3].

The Internet provides an opportunity to consult experiences with other users in almost all areas of life, e.g.: Internet users read reviews of a product or service before buying it. Consumers have always been guided by other people's opinions when shopping. Nowadays, opinions about a product can be easily found in online stores, online forums, social media, etc. People who buy online, often suggest the opinions of other Internet users. Their positive or negative opinion can be crucial when deciding to buy or choose a particular product or brand. Portals that allow people to comment on movies or TV series are also popular, it is worth using them, for example: before buying a movie ticket to avoid regretting the money spent.

However, with the development of Internet accessibility and increasingly widespread e-commerce services, a new problem is emerging: information overload. This is a sociological effect of increasing globalization, offering access to a huge number of products that a person is unable to analyze and evaluate personally. Therefore, the basic problem on the Internet is not the existence of information itself but searching for it, making the extraction of data from the entries of internauts require adequate tools. Buying on the Internet without verifying reviews may end up with the delivery of a product or service that does not meet the consumer's expectations. Considering:

- the ever-growing number of Internet users,
- the growing number of people using e-commerce services,
- the fact that about 30% of Internet users make entries on the Internet [2],

it should be concluded that on the Internet, the number of emerging product rating entries will steadily increase.

Given facts shows it may be difficult for the average user to decide: "which product should I choose?", and this problem will be escalated as the number of added reviews increases. To help users come the latest scientific advances in the field that allow automatic analysis of emotions expressed by the author of the text, i.e. natural language processing techniques for sentiment analysis. However, in order for data analysis to produce notable results it must be carried out on a large amount of data, fast enough and automatically. Artificial intelligence (AI) and machine learning (ML) solutions are ideal for this purpose. Tools that particularly support the process of data mining (DM) contained in Internet users' entries are natural language processing (NLP). Through the use of appropriate tools, a computer program is able to analyze a huge number of consumer entries, on the basis of which data can be presented on a specific topic concerning product opinions. Statistical analyses can then be carried out based on the data obtained from the program [4,5]. Analysis of the market, trends and opinions of Internet users is the main purpose of the presented article; due to the existing need for automatic opinion analysis solutions to provide invaluable data, as well as due to the huge niche in the global market for the above products, related to the lack of adequate knowledge and algorithms. Main purpose of paper is show possibility of automated analysis performed with help of ML solutions. It is initial work which (in future) will be expanded into form of a bigger project. Project that will allow users to acquire opinion summary of certain medical or pharmaceutical product/service based on analysis of online resources. The scientific fields of the project are sentiment analysis (SA) and opinion mining (OM), which aim to analyze the intensity of emotions and polarity of opinions written in natural languages. Two basic approaches implementing opinion analysis can be distinguished: a linguistic approach using linguistic resources such as dictionaries, grammars, lexical-grammar tables, and a statistical approach using machine learning models such as Bayes networks, rule-based methods, decision trees, SVMs or Markov models, for example. Sentiment analysis has been an area of research since the early 2000s. The interest in AI solutions can be evidenced by the increase in the number of scientific papers published on the subject and the constant search for new solutions in this field. The combination of sentiment analysis methods and high amount of data is opinion mining, a field that provides information on the opinions of people making posts on, for example, online forums, e-commerce, social media [17,18].

Despite the rapid development of the fields of sentiment analysis and opinion mining, resulting in the increasing proficiency of the emotion intensity analysis techniques used, commercial projects are applied in very narrow subject areas and for a specific natural language. The reason for this is the complexity of natural language. There is a different way to express an opinion about movies, for example, and a different way to express an opinion about cars, for example. In addition, natural language is not restructured and, for example, the detection of sarcasm is a serious challenge for the machine. A solution that seems to be promising is a combination of linguistic and statistical approaches.

It would be to use the most accurate linguistic analysis possible before implementing machine learning models.

2.1   Existing Technological Solutions

For English, there are tools for narrow opinion analysis, such as Sentiment140, Twiends, Twittratr, SocialMention, TipTop, TweetFeel, Americaspeaks, CEECN, PEP-Net. In addition, English has the largest number of linguistics dictionaries, such as SentiWordNet, Bing Liu lexicon, MPQA, LIWC, among others. The richness of linguistic resources for English and its versatility have resulted in the existence of many European projects, for example FP7 Cockpit, FP7 E-policy, FP7 Limousine, FP7 Acronym, FP7 Trend Miner. Unfortunately, opinion analysis in Polish is not as heavily researched as in English, due to the different grammatical structure of the two languages. The mentioned tools, linguistic resources and supervised machine learning models cannot be directly implemented for Polish. Due to the complex structure of the Polish language, data preprocessing requires an appropriate data resource. The resources are specific to both the Polish language and the categories of texts to be analyzed (medical, pharmaceutical). Nevertheless, there are associations and organizations dealing with NLP in Polish, i.e.:

- CLIP - Computational Linguistics in Poland [7],
- Language Technology Group of Wroclaw University of Technology [8],
- Laboratory of Linguistic Engineering - Information Processing Center - State Research Institute [9].

In the publicly available resources of the listed organizations tools, data and dictionaries relating to the Polish language can be found. The publicly available corpus of the Polish language is the "Narodowy Korpus Jezyka Polskiego" - NKJP [10]. On the basis of the NKJP Corpus, the TaKIPI Polish language tagger [11] was created, which establishes for words in the text their morpho-syntactic description, and then determines the correct interpretation of individual words depending on the context of their occurrence. Linguistic resources available for the Polish language include, for example, "Słowosieć" [12], a project that creates a lexical knowledge base by semi-automatically constructing lexical resources by recognizing semantic relations based on morpho-syntactic and semantic data in text corpora. This project is equivalent to the project for the English language "WordNet". An example of a project in the fields of sentiment analysis and opinion mining is the Po IG - Next project [13], which provides a system that analyzes the content of available electronic documents, performs clustering and is capable of finding documents of interest to the user. Another project for the Polish language is the Clarin-pl project [14]. The project provides tools for syntactic and morphological analysis in a pan-European scientific infrastructure enabling researchers to work comfortably with very large collections of texts.

Bridging the gap between research in Polish and other languages is also being addressed by the NCN Core project [15], which aims to develop techniques, tools and resources that accomplish the task of automatically identifying references in Polish. The basic task of the system is to extract the right information from the source documents by searching for those documents and those parts of them that are relevant to the formulated problem. Given the application domain of the proposed work, which is the medical and pharmaceutical industry, it seems important to highlight the fact that there is a corpus of medical expressions in Polish, which can be found in the resources of the UFAL Medical Corpus [16].

2.2 Literature Review

Analyzing the scientific literature, it can be concluded that the creation of a solution for the medical and pharmaceutical market based on sentiment analysis of the opinions of Internet users written in Polish is important, timely and needed [6]. Literature reviews on sentiment analysis present various aspects of research [4,5,17,18]. It can be noted that the data sets used in the research most often come from online sources, where a patient shares his or her opinion about a service or product in the form of a comment or forum post [20–23,25]. The most frequently commented aspect is:

- medicine,
- medical service,
- doctor,
- vaccine,

According to the authors [19], the basic machine learning methods used in sentiment analysis research on health and well-being are:

- Support Vector Machine (SVM),
- Naive Bayes classifier (NB),
- Decision Trees,
- maximum entropy principle,
- logistic regression,

ML models need a resource of data on which to "learn" the relationships between data. The prepared texts are preprocessed into a form that will be suitable for the classifier model. ML methods require text preprocessing before the learning process. Texts must be cleared of irrelevant information, e.g.: web links. The analyzed text is divided into individual words (tokenization). Then irrelevant tokens (stop-word) are removed from the text. The remaining tokens are reduced to their basic grammatical form (stemming or lemmatization). Also used is the assignment to tokens of the part of speech (Part of speech) they represent. After the appropriate operations - tokens are processed to the appropriate numerical representation. The data is transferred to the ML model. The model then analyzes the data and creates patterns to classify opinions accordingly.

Then, based on the learned patterns, they recognize and classify completely new information. The source of information for ML models can be a web portal, an e-commerce site, social media, thematic forums [20].

The authors of the paper [21] present a study made on the basis of online opinions of patients about hospital services in the United Kingdom. The data is used by ML models to classify the statements. The results obtained from the classification are compared with a sample data with a known category. Basic and well-studied ML algorithms such as Naive Bayes classifier, Decision Trees, Support Vector Method are able to match an opinion to a given category with high efficiency. ML methods are able to evaluate texts from different perspectives, for example: how satisfied the patient was with the service on a five-point scale or which of the three preset categories the opinion is about.

Deep-learning methods, or neural networks, are also being tested in research [22], where the authors tested various neural network architectures trained on data sets derived from Internet user reviews. The opinions of Internet users contained in the website "drugs.com" were used as a data source. In addition to entering opinions in free text, Internet users also rated drugs on a 10-point scale. Various architectures were trained to classify drug opinions. It turned out that both ML methods and neural networks were able to achieve an efficiency of more than 80%. A correlation was also presented showing that ML models have higher efficiency on larger learning sets. In the case of neural networks, the same small size of the training set yielded better results compared to ML models.

The researchers [23] also proposed using multi-level methods, where they compared the effectiveness of an SVM, two types of neural network and a classifier formed from a combination of a neural network and SVM.

The data set for the study consisted of opinions of Internet users from the website "www.askapatient.com." The opinions were about two types of drug. After performing the classification, the authors concluded that multistage methods have higher efficiency than single-stage methods.

The experiments presented in the paper [24] showed that with the help of machine learning methods, a lot of relevant information about drugs can be collected from customer reviews. Data downloaded from websites were used in this analysis. The opinions were divided according to the category of the drug (contraception, depression, pain, anxiety, diabetes). During the experiment, several model variants were prepared to verify whether a model learned on a certain data set could cope with classifying data on a different type of drug or data from a completely different source. In the analyzed texts it was decided to evaluate:

- overall product evaluation,
- whether there were side effects,
- whether the patient's condition improved while taking the drug,

Models, learned and verified on data from the same category of drug achieved more than 90% success rate. Models learned on data from one drug category but verified on data from another drug category achieved lower values due to the presence of specific expressions. However, combinations of closely related categories (e.g.: depression and anxiety) showed increased effectiveness.

Models learned on a data set from one source (Drugs.com) but verified on data from another source (Druglib.com) also achieved over 70% effectiveness.

Satvik Garg presented in [25] a solution that recommends a drug for a given problem based on the opinions of other patients.

Patient reviews from the Drugs.com website were used as a data set. The author shows the data flow from the data cleaning stage to the recommendation stage. Various types of classifiers were trained on the processed data. Then to create a recommendation system, the author averaged the opinions from four different models (Perceptron, LinearSVC, LGBM, RandomForest). When queried for a given problem, the system makes several drug suggestions along with an accuracy rating.

A. Sobkowicz in his work [26] showed the dictionary needed to classify opinions, for the construction of which he used commonly available tools - python programming language, Tweepy and Scrapy libraries. Morphological analysis was performed using the Morfologik tool. The author performed sentiment analysis using the three main tools of NEAT neural network, NB classifier and SVM method. The results presented gave good results for the NEAT method (80% accuracy) and SVM (77% accuracy).

The authors of the paper [27] showed that there is a low number of publications and tools in Polish compared to the leading languages (English, Chinese).

One of the important elements is benchmarking (reference/comparison method). The authors presented the KLEJ tool - which is able to comparatively evaluate NLP tools in Polish in different categories. They then present a model based on the HerBERT architecture and its results obtained after training based on the "National Corpus of the Polish Language" and the "Free Reading" corpus. The average of the scores received in the nine tests was 80.5% effectiveness.

3   System Architecture

From a scientific point of view, an interesting problem is how to classify criticism according to the intensity of the author's emotions. The proposed opinion mining solution consists of three different classifiers that assign a rating to a user's reviews. Presented work use web resources that are characterized by fact that in addition to the opinion itself written in natural language, it contains also fine grained opinion. For the purposes of presented research work, the ratings were unified into 5 classes expressing intensity of the opinion and they are as follows: very negative, negative, neutral, positive and very positive. For purposes of the research, 100 opinions were collected from each of the classes presented. In order to assign a rating to opinions, three classifiers were used: statistical classifier, group character classifier, linguistic classifier. Simplified schematic of solution is presented on Fig. 1. Detailed description of classifiers is placed on next page.

- **statistical classifier:** the use of two classifiers - a classifier that filters objective/subjective sentences and a classifier that assigns a rating to criticism. Various data mining models will be tested in this classifier: Naive Bayes, SVM, DT. The intermediate steps of the classifier are as follows: text preprocessing, lemmatization, vectorization, computation of the complete index, preparation of the learning set for each classifier, reduction of the index allocated to each classifier, addition of synonyms, and text classification;
- **group character classifier:** it is based on statistical analysis of linguistic data to determine the behavior of groups - opinions that have the same emotion intensity rating. Examples of features are characteristic words, sentence length, opinion size, negation detection, characteristic expressions or punctuation or special characters. For a new review, the distances between the features of the new review and the features of the groups are calculated;
- **linguistic classifier:** use of local grammars - representation of linguistic phenomena by recursive transitions, and electronic dictionaries. Creation of five grammars corresponding to each assigned grade. Each grammar has multiple grammar rules - local grammars. Local grammars are produced manually by analyzing the corpus;

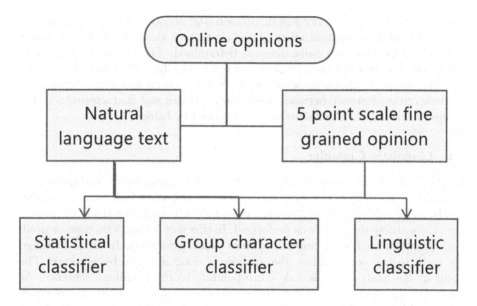

Fig. 1. Simplified schematic of proposed solution.

4   Experimental Results

4.1   Statistical Classifier

This section presents a general approach used in the data mining and opinion mining. Statistical linguistic classifier is based on machine learning with supervision: decision trees, Naive Bayes classifier, SVM method. The aim is to give a rating that expresses the opinion of an internet user. Only subjective sentences are analysed. Two classifications are performed for each sentence. Firstly, it is checked whether the sentence is subjective, and if so, it is classified to assign one of five scores. The final rating is calculated as average of the ratings received. The best results were obtained with Bayes classifier. In the research, this classifier was first used to determine subjective and objective sentences and then to assign a score to the ratings. In general, the process prepares learning data basis for two classifiers: a classifier that filter subjective/objective and classifier that assign a score. The results are summarised in Table 1.

4.2   Group Character Classifier

The general approach in group character classifier is based on the verification whether the reviews with the same fine grained rating have common characteristics. Firstly, all the critics are regrouped according to their score. This creates 5 different groups of critics. Group character classifier is based on statistical analysis of linguistic data to determine the common characteristic of groups - opinions that have the same emotion intensity rating. Examples of features are:

characteristic words, sentence length, opinion size, negation detection, character-istic expressions or punctuation or special characters. Based on that - behaviour of reviews that have the same score is determined. The results shows strong differences between the characteristics of defined groups. Creation of the com-mon characteristic allows to determine to which group a new critic belongs to. For new critics, distance between their characteristics and characteristics of the groups is calculated. The results are summarised in Table 1.

4.3   Linguistic Classifier

All the critics are regrouped according to the fine grained user rating (mark). A grammar is created for each group. The grammar is based on a learning database. In order to create grammar rules for each mark, the study of reviews from the learning database was performed. In this way 5 grammars were created. Each grammar contains a number of rules - local grammars. In order to assign the mark to the new opinion, the analysis is done sentence by sentence. The result of the analysis is the rule corresponding to the examined sentence. At the end of this operation, selected sentences of new opinions with corresponding rules are obtained. To obtain the prediction of user rating, the average mark corresponding to the main grammars is calculated. The construction of the local grammars was done manually by analysis of the reviewed sentences with the same mark associated. The results are summarised in Table 1.

Table 1. Experimental results - F-score.

	Statistical classifier	group character classifier	linguistic classifier
Very positive	72.4%	69.1%	74.5%
Positive	70.2%	64.8%	74.6%
Neutral	64.5%	47.6%	67.6%
Negative	52.4%	45.7%	55.2%
Very negative	70.4%	69.4%	82.6%
F-score all classes	66.0%	59.3%	70.9%

5   Contribution and Future Works

Presented system automatically assigns a rating that expresses the intensity of the emotions contained in the reviews. The reviews are written in Polish and refer to doctors' reviews. The data was collected from publicly available portals. The aim of the work was to automate assignment of a rating that reflects the user's emotions using knowledge from the field of opinion mining.

The focus of this research is on automatic acquisition of information in the corpus, and more specifically on linguistic sentiment analysis. The aim was to prepare the data and create complex local grammars. The results obtained were compared with a general statistical method using classification.

The article succeeded in presentation of a linguistic approach to automatic classification. The adaptation of linguistic resources, such as the creation of complex local grammars and the adaptation of dictionaries, was an important part of work.

The paper presents preliminary results of the project. It focuses only on reviews in which doctors are described. The goal for future work is to create a much more general analysis of the entire medical market. Moreover, the market includes more product types, i.e. medicines and medical services. In order to carry out a more detailed study, it is necessary to deepen the linguistic analysis and to continue to develop the linguistic resources.

It is certainly demonstrated that in-depth linguistic analysis for a closed subject area such as the pharmaceutical market produces correct results and can compete with a purely statistical approach based on machine learning.

The work presented in this article is a prelude to work on a larger project that aims to create a system for automated research into pharmaceutical market trends. Future work will be based on the extension of NLP analysis and the adaptation of linguistic resources in Polish. The next step will also be to automate the creation of grammars in order to improve the linguistic processes in the project.

References

1. Społeczenstwo informacyjne w Polsce w 2020 r. https://stat.gov.pl. Accessed Oct 2022
2. Komunikat CBOS. https://www.cbos.pl/SPISKOM.POL/2020/K08520.PDF. Accessed Oct 2022
3. Statistical data. www.pmrmarketexperts.com. Accessed Oct 2022
4. Mejova, Y.: Sentiment analysis: an overview. University of Iowa, Computer Science Department (2009)
5. Ahmad, M., et al.: Machine learning techniques for sentiment analysis: a review. Int. J. Multidiscip. Sci. Eng. 8(3), 27 (2017)
6. "Polityka dla rozwoju sztucznej inteligencji w Polsce od roku 2020" appendix to the resolution no. 196 Council of Ministers of December 28, 2020. (item 23)
7. Computational Linguistics in Poland. http://clip.ipipan.waw.pl/. Accessed Oct 2022
8. On-line resources. http://nlp.pwr.wroc.pl/. Accessed Oct 2022
9. On-line resources. https://opi.org.pl/. Accessed Oct 2022
10. On-line resources. http://korpus.pl/. Accessed Oct 2022
11. On-line resources. http://nlp.pwr.wroc.pl/narzedzia-i-zasoby/takipi. Accessed Oct 2022
12. On-line resources. http://nlp.pwr.wroc.pl/projekty/slowosiec2. Accessed Oct 2022
13. On-line resources. http://nekst.ipipan.waw.pl/index.php. Accessed Oct 2022
14. On-line resources. http://www.clarin-pl.eu/. Accessed Oct 2022
15. On-line resources. http://glass.ipipan.waw.pl/wiki/core. Accessed Oct 2022
16. On-line resources. https://ufal.mff.cuni.cz/. Accessed Oct 2022

17. Casas-Valadez, M.A., et al.: Research trends in sentiment analysis and opinion mining from knowledge management approach: a science mapping from 2007 to 2020. In: 2020 International Conference on Innovation and Intelligence for Informatics, Computing and Technologies (3ICT). IEEE (2020)
18. Birjali, M., Kasri, M., Beni-Hssane, A.: A comprehensive survey on sentiment analysis: approaches, challenges and trends. Knowl.-Based Syst. **226**, 107134 (2021)
19. Zunic, A., Corcoran, P., Spasic, I.: Sentiment analysis in health and well-being: systematic review. JMIR Med. Inform. **8**(1), e16023 (2020)
20. Tavoschi, L., et al.: Twitter as a sentinel tool to monitor public opinion on vaccination: an opinion mining analysis from September 2016 to August 2017 in Italy. Hum. Vaccines Immunotherapeutics **16**(5), 1062–1069 (2020)
21. Greaves, F., et al.: Use of sentiment analysis for capturing patient experience from free-text comments posted online. J. Med. Internet Res. **15**(11), e2721 (2013)
22. Colón-Ruiz, C., Segura-Bedmar, I.: Comparing deep learning architectures for sentiment analysis on drug reviews. J. Biomed. Inform. **110**, 103539 (2020)
23. Padmavathy, P., Mohideen, S.P.: An efficient two-pass classifier system for patient opinion mining to analyze drugs satisfaction. Biomed. Sig. Process. Control **57**, 101755 (2020)
24. Gräßer, F., et al.: Aspect-based sentiment analysis of drug reviews applying cross-domain and cross-data learning. In: Proceedings of the 2018 International Conference on Digital Health (2018)
25. Garg, S.: Drug recommendation system based on sentiment analysis of drug reviews using machine learning. In: 2021 11th International Conference on Cloud Computing, Data Science and Engineering (Confluence). IEEE (2021)
26. Sobkowicz, A.: Automatic sentiment analysis in Polish language. In: Ryżko, D., Gawrysiak, P., Kryszkiewicz, M., Rybiński, H. (eds.) Machine Intelligence and Big Data in Industry. SBD, vol. 19, pp. 3–10. Springer, Cham (2016). https://doi.org/10.1007/978-3-319-30315-4_1
27. Rybak, P., et al.: KLEJ: comprehensive benchmark for Polish language understanding. arXiv preprint arXiv:2005.00630 (2020)

WSDTN a Novel Dataset for Arabic Word Sense Disambiguation

Rakia Saidi[1]([⊠]) [ID], Fethi Jarray[3] [ID], Asma Akacha[2], and Wissem Aribi[2]

[1] LIMTIC Laboratory, UTM University, Tunis, Tunisia
saidi.rakya@gmail.com, rakya.saidi@fst.utm.tn
[2] ESLI Laboratory, Faculty of Letters Arts and Humanities of Manouba, UMA University, Tunis, Tunisia
[3] Higher Institute of Computer Science of Medenine, Gabes University, Medenine, Tunisia

Abstract. Word sense disambiguation (WSD) task aims to find the exact sense of an ambiguous word in a particular context. It is crucial for many applications, including machine translation, information retrieval, and semantic textual similarity. Arabic WSD faces significant challenges, primarily due to the scarcity of resources, which hinders the development of robust deep learning models. Additionally, the semantic sparsity of context further complicates the task, as Arabic words often exhibit multiple meanings. In this paper, we propose WSDTN, a manually annotated corpus, designed to fill this gap and to enable the automatic disambiguation of Arabic words. It consists of 27530 sentences collected from different resources and spanning different domains, each with a target word and its appropriate sense. We present the novel corpus itself, its creation procedure for reproducibility and a transformer based model to disambiguate new words and evaluate the performance of the corpus. The experimental results show that the baseline approach achieves an accuracy of around 90%. The corpus is publically available upon request and is open for extension.

Keywords: Word sense disambiguation · Arabic Text · Natural language processing · BERT · Fusion strategy

1 Introduction

Given a polysemic target word and a fixed inventory of word senses, word sense disambiguation (WSD) aims to determine the right sense of the ambiguous target. Since many words in natural language are ambiguous, their meanings might vary depending on the context in which they are used. It is a crucial step for many NLP applications, such as sentiment analysis, machine translation and information retrieval.

The main challenge in Arabic WSD is the lack of annotated large resources. All the publically available corpora as Arabic WordNet (AWN) [24],

© The Author(s), under exclusive license to Springer Nature Switzerland AG 2023
N. T. Nguyen et al. (Eds.): ICCCI 2023, CCIS 1864, pp. 203–212, 2023.
https://doi.org/10.1007/978-3-031-41774-0_16

OntoNotes [25], the Arabic version of Semcor [15] and the Arabic gloss datasets [8,18] suffer from some issues. For example, the AWN [24] dataset uses only English annotations, OntoNotes is a small test corpus and, Semcor [15] is a translated version of the original English Semcor. In addition, the context-gloss dataset [8] is relatively small and contains a lot of duplication, with many missing contextual fields, without distinction between nominal word and verbal one, without clear steps of WSD, the user of dataset thinks the word is the original base, but he finds that it is a derived one, the defined word is not extracted from the example or utterance, and in arabglossbert there is no mention of the source or the reference of the disambiguated word by its SIT. The dataset created in [18] is neither very reliable nor accessible. In this paper, our aim is to address these issues by creating a new Arabic WSD, named WSDTN. We validate the data set through a FusionBert based model evaluated by the test set accuracy.

The rest of the manuscript is structured as follows: The state-of-the-art is presented in Sect. 2. Section 3 presents our Arabic benchmark. Section 4 describes our strategies for Arabic WSD. Section 5 discusses the numerical results. We summarize our contributions and discuss some potential future extensions in the conclusion section.

2   State of the Art

The Arabic WSD (AWSD) is cast as a supervised learning problem that predicts the sense (tag) for a given target work. The early approaches are based on traditional machine learning [2–5]. Recent approaches are based on context-free embedding, such as word2vec for word representation and BILSTM and GRU for layers classification [6,7,17,21]. Their main drawback is the static embedding of targets independently of the context. This issue is addressed by the most recent approaches which are based on transformer based language model such as BERT and its Arabic version [8,16,18,20]. They offer the possibility of simultaneously encoding the target word and its context, which is an important factor in predicting the correct sense of a word. Globally, they construct context-gloss pairs and cast WSD as a binary classification problem that outputs 1 if the gloss corresponds to the sense of the target word. For example, et-Razzaz et al. [8], Saidi et al. [16], Al-hajj and Jarrar [18] and Saidi et al. [20] obtained 76%, 96.33%, 84% and 88.88% in terms of accuracy, respectively. Even if Bert-based approaches have achieved a great step toward solving many NLP tasks, their effects on handling Arabic WSD remain far from the expected results. This is mainly due to the lack of large size annotated Arabic WSD datasets.

The contribution of this paper is two-fold. First, we manually create a novel Arabic WSD dataset (WSDTN) and automatically augment it by a data augmentation techniques Second, we design a BERT-based model (FusionBert) for Arabic WSD.

3   Dataset Creation

The Arabic nominal and verbal units are extracted from The Doha Historical Dictionary of Arabic (DHDA) [26]. Unlike other digital Arabic dictionaries [27], DHDA is an etymological one, made by Arabic scientists and experts. Accordingly, the significations of our AVU are quantified by their first, second and third contextual appearances in Arabic Language, in DHDA. The first signification is the central, like [قِطَار](Qita:r) ("caravan of camels"); the others are connotational or metaphorical senses in particular uses that are lexicalized; by the lexicalization, these senses run to be lexical significations, and we get a polysemous verbal unit, like [قِطَار ١](Qita:r 1) ("caravan of camels"), [قِطَار ن](Qita:r n) ("train"). This process is internal because of its semantical aspect, where Time is the most important semantic quantifier that guides WSD.

3.1   Creation Procedure

We follow many steps to build our WSDTN (see Algorithm 1). First, we select the target word from the DHDA dictionary, second choose the target POS, third find the polysemous lexical units, forth pick-up their SIT from their utterances, fifth delete proclitics, sixth remove diacritics from three columns, lexical entry, gloss and examples, because of the inability of our WSDTN to treat its, seventh made examples for the lexical entries that haven't utterances.

Algorithm 1: Dataset WSDTN creation procedure

Output: Select the source of corpus

1 **for** *each selected word* **do**
2 | - Choose the POS Tagging
3 | - Find the polysemous lexical units
4 | - Pick-up their SIT from their utterance
5 | - Delete proclitics
6 | - Associate a gloss for the word
7 | **for** *each gloss* **do**
8 | | - Associate a context example for the word
9 | | - Remove diacritics
10 | - Remove diacritics
11 **for** *each context example* **do**
12 | - Remove diacritics

We prepare our dataset of polysemous Arabic nominal and verbal units, as polysemy the major cause of Word Signification Ambiguity (WSA), with their significations ordered etymologically, mentioned in their first utterances; every signification has its own context; every context has more than two examples. The WSDTN architecture is presented in Fig. 1.

We care about some WSD cases in DHDA which give a dialectal use of its standard pronunciation, as [ذكر] (akar) (dialectal) from [ذكر] (dakar) (standard),

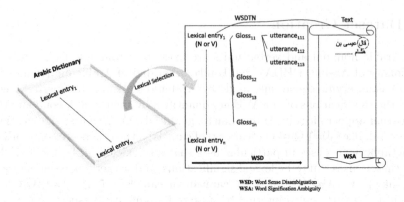

Fig. 1. WSDTN architecture.

refer to gloss by another, as the lexical entry [جلد] (alada) in [قطعه] and its synonym [قطع] (qataa).

We enriched our dataset with many types of ambiguity, such as:

- Duplication sign: the meaning of word [نَصَرَ] (made him victorious) is different from the meaning of word [نَصَّرَ] (made him Christian)

- Hamza form: the meaning of word [أَقْبَلَ] (came) is different from the meaning of word [اقْبَلْ] (Accept).

- Diacritization Marks: the meaning of word [عَلَمّ] (Flag) is different from the meaning of word [عِلْمّ] (Science).

- Root difference: the meaning of word [أسِف] (Get close to the ground) which root is [س ف ف] is different from the meaning of word [أسِف] (being Sorry) which root is [ء س ف].

- POS Tag: the meaning of the word [ذهب] (gold) which POS Tag is [اسم] is different from the meaning of word [ذهب] (go) which POS Tag is [فعل]

- Contextual multiplicity: the meaning of the word [عين] (Eye) is different from the meaning of word [عين] (spy), determined by context.

- Times change: in the past, the meaning of the word [قطار] (caravan of camels) is different from the meaning of word [قطار] (train) at this age.

The component of our WSDTN corpus are shown in Fig. 2.

WSDTN provides other useful information such as word Diacritization, stem, root and affixes that can used for other tasks such as proclitics and enclitics detection and stemming. Figure 3 shows our benchmark statistics.

Fig. 2. WSDTN component.

Fig. 3. WSDTN statistics.

3.2 Backtranslation for Arabic WSD Data Augmentation

Data augmentation (DA) consists of artificially generating new samples from the training data set by applying various techniques. It is mainly used to improve the performance of deep neural networks for small training data sets, as in the case of low-resource languages.

In this paper, we adopt the backtranslation technique (see Algorithm 2). It translates an Arabic sentence into English and then back translates it into Arabic. It is a well-known sense-preserving approach and suitable for text classification [1] and WSD task. From each original sentence (context-example), we generate three backtranslated sentences. For example, from the original sentence (S), we generate three new sentences ($g1, g2, g3$):

(S) أبقى الباب مفتوحا أمام المزيد من العروض

(g1) أبقت الباب مفتوحًا على المزيد من العروض

(g2) أبقت الباب مفتوحًا أمام المزيد من العروض

(g3) أبقى الباب مفتوحًا على المزيد من العروض

Algorithm 2: Data augmentation for Arabic WSD by backtranslation
Input   : Select a target word
1 **for** *each context-example with a target word* **do**
2   - Translate context-example to english
3   - Re-Translate context-example three times into arabic

4   A BERT Based Fusion Approach for Arabic WSD

Bidirectional Encoder Representations from Transformers (BERT) [14] is a transformer-based language model, specifically the encoder part of the transformer. In this paper, we take advantage of five different available pre-trained Arabic BERT models that are currently available: AraBERT [9], Arabic-BERT [11], ArBERT [28], MarBERT [22] and CAMeL-BERT [23] and the multilingual mBERT [12], which supports texts in Arabic. The features of each model are shown in Table 1.

Table 1. Characteristics of pretrained Arabic BERT models.

Model	Ara-BERT	Arabic-BERT	CAMeL-BERT	Mar-BERT	Ar-BERT	mBERT
Parameters	135M	110M	108M	163M	163M	110M
Normalization	yes	no	yes	yes	no	yes
Textual Data	27 GB	95 GB	167 GB	61 GB	61 GB	61 GB
Tokenization	wordpieces	wordpieces	wordpieces	wordpieces	wordpieces	character

We follow an intermediate fusion strategy to integrate the embedding of the target word and its context. In general, it consists of the following four blocks: Word Embedding, Interaction Layer, Aggregation Layer, and Prediction Layer. Our FusionBert is presented in Fig. 4.

1. **Word Embedding:** it consists of encoding each word using the BERT pre-training language model. Thus, each input word is represented as a 768-dimensional vector.
2. **Interaction Layer:** represents the attention mechanism, where the sharing of information between the context-example and the target word is measured by the attention mechanism.
3. **Aggregation Layer:** First, we apply a simple maximum-pooling of target words in the sentence to obtain the encoding of the sentence. Second, we concatenate the word and sentence embeddings to get the target word and sentence embedding.
4. **Prediction Layer:** We fed the sentence and the target word embedding into a fully connected network. The entire model is end-to-end trained with softmax as the activation function and sparse categorical cross entropy as the loss function.

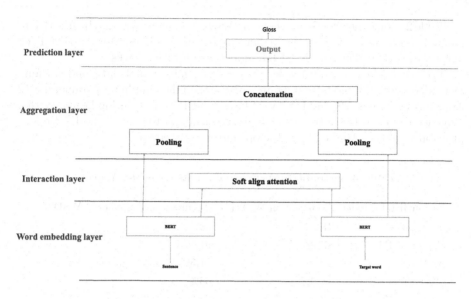

Fig. 4. FusionBert architecture for Arabic WSD.

5   Experimental Results

To do a credible comparison with the existing Glossbert benchmark [8,18], we choose firstly to use the Arabic available BERT model without data augmentation, and secondly we implement our WSD network (FusionBert) and apply it on the augmented WSDTN corpora. For all experiments, we divided our dataset to two parts: 80% for training and 20% for test.

Table 2 displays the simple BERT results. We used the same hyperparameters values as in [18] (With a warm up step count of 1412, a batch size of 16 and the first learning rate is 2e−5.). However, we trained the model for 20 epochs as in [8].

Table 2. Simple BERT results for Arabic WSD, NF stands for not found.

Model	Accuracy on [8] data	Accuracy on [18] data	Accuracy on our benchmark
AraBERT-V2	67%	84%	**88.3%**
Camel BERT	NF	82%	86.5%
ArBERT	50%	NF	64.2%
MarBERT	NF	NF	60.9%
Arabic BERT	NF	NF	58%
mBERT	NF	NF	53.7%

Table 2 shows the effectiveness of our WSDTN benchmark, maybe it is due to manual creation of data and the higher number of examples. Our AraBERT-V2 outperforms the other Arabic BERT model for all benchmarks.

Table 3 displays the FusionBert results on the original data and its augmented version. All models are trained using the following hyperparameters: 12 Transformer blocks, 768 hidden layer blocks, and 12 self-attention heads. With a sequence length of 128, a batch size of 64, a learning rate of $2e-5$, and a dropout probability of 0.2, Adam [19] as the optimizer and 100 epochs.

Table 3. FusionBert experimental results for Arabic WSD.

FusionBERT Model	Accuracy on WSDTN	Accuracy on augmented WSDTN
AraBERT-V2	91.2%	93%
Camel BERT	87.6%	91.5%
ArBERT	67%	71.5%
MarBERT	63.7%	66%
Arabic BERT	63%	65.3 %
mBERT	55 %	58.6 %

Table 3 proved the idea that as we increase the training data the results will get better in a system using a deep learning model, the accuracy on the augmented WSDTN outperform the accuracy on the original WSDTN for all FusionBERT models.

Our FusionBERT system outperforms the simple BERT models, maybe it's due to the attention mechanism represented in the interaction layer.

6   Conclusion

This manuscript presented a new benchmark for Arabic WSD. We validate it using the BERT-based intermediate fusion strategy. The results demonstrate that our new benchmark outperforms the available gloss datasets by 88.3% in terms of accuracy using the WSDTN data and 93% on the FusionBert with the augmented data. As a future extension, we aim to augment our data by using a deep learning generative model such us GPT.

References

1. Ma, J., Li, L.: Data augmentation for Chinese text classification using back-translation. In: Journal of Physics: Conference Series, vol. 1651, no. 1, p. 012039. IOP Publishing (2020)
2. Elmougy, S., Taher, H., Noaman, H.: Naïve Bayes classifier for Arabic word sense disambiguation. In: Proceeding of the 6th International Conference on Informatics and Systems, pp. 16–21 (2008)

3. El-Gedawy, M.N.: Using fuzzifiers to solve word sense ambiguation in Arabic language. Int. J. Comput. Appl. **79**(2) (2013)
4. Alkhatlan, A., Kalita, J., Alhaddad, A.: Word sense disambiguation for Arabic exploiting Arabic wordnet and word embedding. Procedia Comput. Sci. **142**, 50–60 (2018)
5. Hadni, M., Ouatik, S.E.A., Lachkar, A.: Word sense disambiguation for Arabic text categorization. Int. Arab J. Inf. Technol. **13**(1A), 215–222 (2016)
6. Merhbene, L., Zouaghi, A., Zrigui, M.: An experimental study for some supervised lexical disambiguation methods of Arabic language. In: Fourth International Conference on Information and Communication Technology and Accessibility (ICTA), pp. 1–6. IEEE (2013)
7. Laatar, R., Aloulou, C., Belghuith, L.H.: Word2vec for Arabic word sense disambiguation. In: Silberztein, M., Atigui, F., Kornyshova, E., Métais, E., Meziane, F. (eds.) NLDB 2018. LNCS, vol. 10859, pp. 308–311. Springer, Cham (2018). https://doi.org/10.1007/978-3-319-91947-8_32
8. El-Razzaz, M., Fakhr, M.W., Maghraby, F.A.: Arabic gloss WSD using BERT. Appl. Sci. **11**(6), 2567 (2021)
9. Antoun, W., Baly, F., Hajj, H.: AraBERT: transformer-based model for Arabic language understanding. arXiv preprint arXiv:2003.00104 (2020)
10. Abdul-Mageed, M., Elmadany, A., Nagoudi, E.M.B.: ARBERT & MARBERT: deep bidirectional transformers for Arabic. arXiv preprint arXiv:2101.01785 (2020)
11. Safaya, A., Abdullatif, M., Yuret, D.: KUISAIL at SemEval-2020 Task 12: BERT-CNN for offensive speech identification in social media. In: Proceedings of the Fourteenth Workshop on Semantic Evaluation, pp. 2054–2059 (2020)
12. Libovický, J., Rosa, R., Fraser, A.: How language-neutral is multilingual BERT? arXiv preprint arXiv:1911.03310 (2019)
13. Vaswani, A., et al.: Attention is all you need. arXiv preprint arXiv:1706.03762 (2017)
14. Devlin, J., Chang, M.W., Lee, K., Toutanova, K.: BERT: pre-training of deep bidirectional transformers for language understanding. arXiv preprint arXiv:1810.04805 (2018)
15. Vial, L., Lecouteux, B., Schwab, D.: UFSAC: unification of sense annotated corpora and tools. In: Language Resources and Evaluation Conference (LREC) (2018)
16. Saidi, R., Jarray, F.: Combining BERT representation and POS tagger for Arabic word sense disambiguation. In: Abraham, A., Gandhi, N., Hanne, T., Hong, T.-P., Nogueira Rios, T., Ding, W. (eds.) ISDA 2021. LNNS, vol. 418, pp. 676–685. Springer, Cham (2022). https://doi.org/10.1007/978-3-030-96308-8_63
17. El-Gamml, M.M., Fakhr, M.W., Rashwan, M.A., Al-Said, A.B.: A comparative study for Arabic word sense disambiguation using document preprocessing and machine learning techniques. In: Arabic Language Technology International Conference, Bibliotheca Alexandrina, CBA, vol. 11 (2011)
18. Al-Hajj, M., Jarrar, M.: ArabGlossBERT: fine-tuning BERT on context-gloss pairs for WSD. arXiv preprint arXiv:2205.09685 (2022)
19. Kingma, D.P., Ba, J.: Adam: a method for stochastic optimization. arXiv preprint arXiv:1412.6980 (2014)
20. Saidi, R., Jarray, F., Kang, J., Schwab, D.: GPT-2 contextual data augmentation for word sense disambiguation. In: Pacific Asia Conference on Language, Information and Computation (2022)
21. Saidi, R., Jarray, F., Alsuhaibani, M.: Comparative analysis of recurrent neural network architectures for Arabic word sense disambiguation. In: Proceedings of

the 18th International Conference on Web Information Systems and Technologies, WEBIST 2022, 25–27 October 2022 (2022)
22. MarBERRT model. https://huggingface.co/UBC-NLP/MARBERT. Accessed 10 Nov 2022
23. Camel Bert. https://huggingface.co/CAMeL-Lab/bert-base-arabic-camelbert-ca. Accessed 10 Nov 2022
24. Arabic WordNet. http://globalwordnet.org/resources/arabic-wordnet/awn-browser/. Accessed 20 Mar 2021
25. Ontonotes. https://goo.gl/peHdKQ. Accessed 10 Feb 2023
26. Doha dictionnaries. https://www.dohadictionary.org/. Accessed 14 Dec 2022
27. Arabic Digital dictionnaries. https://www.almaany.com/. Accessed 18 Jan 2023
28. ArBERT. https://huggingface.co/UBC-NLP/ARBERT. Accessed 10 Nov 2022

CNN-BiLSTM Model for Arabic Dialect Identification

Malek Hedhli[✉][iD] and Ferihane Kboubi[iD]

National School of Computer Science, ENSI's RIADI Laboratory, Manouba, Tunisia
{malek.hedhli,ferihane.kboubi}@ensi-uma.tn

Abstract. Dialectal Arabic is a term that covers Arabic dialects, resulting from linguistic interference between the Arabic language and local or neighboring languages. The automatic identification of dialects is a task that allows to recognize automatically the dialect used to write a text. This task is very important for several other NLP tasks, where a priory knowledge of the dialect of an input text can be useful for the rest of the process, such as sentiment analysis, machine translation and hate speech detection. The general objective of this paper is to propose a new approach for the identification of Arabic dialects in textual content. The first obstacle to the development of this task is the lack of resources and especially of balanced dataset. To address this issue and achieve our goal we started by building a balanced dataset by merging together and filtering 7 datasets. Then we proposed a new approach for Arabic dialect identification based on the combination of CNN with BiLSTM. To evaluate our model, we conducted a comparative study of several machine learning and deep learning models using a bunch of features. We considered these models as baseline and compared their results against the ones obtained by our model. The evaluation of our approach showed about 2% improvement in accuracy, compared to the best baseline models.

Keywords: Natural Language Processing · Arabic Dialect Identification · Text Classification · Embedding Models · AraVec · CNN · BiLSTM

1 Introduction

Dialect identification can be considered as a special case of linguistic recognition, that involves differentiating between members of the same language family using language identification techniques. Dialects, in contrast to languages, often share similar phonetics and a written system. Therefore, it is essential to emphasize the distinctive linguistic features, such as words, characters, and phonemes, that characterize each dialect. The study of dialectical Arabic has gained considerable importance, particularly due to the increasing prevalence of informal online communication and the appearance of Arabic dialects in written form through the trans-formative impact of social media over the past decade. The identification of Arabic dialects is considered to be the first pre-processing component

N. T. Nguyen et al. (Eds.): ICCCI 2023, CCIS 1864, pp. 213–225, 2023.
https://doi.org/10.1007/978-3-031-41774-0_17

for any natural language processing problem. This task is useful for automatic translation, sentiment analysis and hate speech detection [1]. In [2] the authors identified several challenges regarding Arabic dialect identification. These challenges concern the limited number of resources, homographs recognition, use of Arabizi and the variations caused by dialectical phoneme sounds and pronunciation of Arabic letters. In this article, we focused on identifying the Arabic dialect from textual content. We addressed the lack of resources by building a balanced dataset by merging and filtering seven datasets. We experienced many models of Machine Learning and Deep Learning for this task. Then we proposed a new approach based on the combination of CNN and BiLSTM.

In Sect. 2, we present related works about the Arabic dialects identification. In Sect. 3, we introduce our proposed approach by presenting the architecture of the model, and we describe the preprocessing, embedding and classification layers of our model. In Sect. 4, we describe the data sources corresponding to the dataset used in our work, we also present the baseline models and the parameters used for each model. Finally, in Sect. 5, we present the results of our approach as well as the results of the baseline models. Then we present a detailed discussion in order to interpret and analyse these results.

2   Related Work

In the last decade, there are several works that have focused on the task of Arabic dialects identification. In this section we present a review of the most interesting works. A. Ali et al. 2015 [3] combined the characteristics of the generative and discriminating classifiers with the Multi-Class Support Vector Machine (SVM). They considered Egyptian, Gulf, Levantine, Maghreb and MSA. In [4], R. Tachicart et al. 2017, introduced a distinction between Moroccan dialect and MSA using two different methods: (1) a rule-based method relying on stop word frequency and (2) a statically-based method using several machine learning classifiers. In [5], M. El-Haj et al. 2018, proposed an approach using language bivalency and written code-switching. They considered four Arabic dialect regions: Egypt, North Africa, Gulf and Levant in addition to MSA. In addition to the word and n-gram features they integrated also additional grammatical and stylistic features and defined a subtractive bivalency profiling approach to address issues of bivalent words. In [6] S. Shon et al. 2018, used acoustic features and language embeddings with text-based linguistic features. They used Siamese neural network to extract language embeddings. They addressed three dialects: Egypt, Maghreb and the Levant.

More recently, Arabic Dialect Identification gained much more attention as several works have been proposed such as the shared-task NADI series (2020 and 2021). Abdul-Mageed et al. 2020 [7] and Abdul-Mageed et al. 2021 [8] provided a common evaluation framework and a benchmark dataset for researchers to evaluate and compare the performance of their dialect identification systems. The mission involved 21 Arab countries and 100 towns in total in those countries.

The main differences between the two versions concern the number of the proposed tasks. Indeed Abdul-Mageed et al. 2021 [8] included four subtasks:

country-level MSA identification, country-level dialect identification, province-level MSA identification, and province-level sub-dialect identification.

Y. Aseri et al. 2022 [9], used Logistic Regression, Multinominal Naïve Bayes and Support Vector Machine (SVM) for the identification of Saudi and MSA dialects, this configuration was built using two levels of language models: unigram and bi-gram, as feature sets for system training. S. M. Alzanin et al 2022 [10], presented short text classification of tweets on social media in Arabic, they presented the integration of words using Word2vec and (TF-IDF) with Support Vector Machine (SVM), Gaussian Naïve Bayes (GNB) and Random Forest (RF). In Table 1, we present a comparison of some existing work according to several criteria. Indeed, we present for each work the features types and the classification algorithms as well as the performance accuracy (Acc) measures and the F1-score for the best tested model (bold).

Table 1. Related work comparison

Ref	Features	Algorithm	Best perf	Level
[11]	1, 2, 3 word grams, 1 to 5 character grams	multi-class Bayesian, SVM, **RF**	83.3% (Acc)	Binary
[12]	1 to 6 character grams, Word unigrams	**SVM**, ensembles	68% (Acc), 51% (F1)	Region
[13]	Word n-grams, Character n-grams	**MNB**	90% (Acc), 69% (F1)	Region
[14]	Embeddings models, 1, 2, 3 word grams, TF-IDF	LR, **MNB**, SVM, CNN, LSTM, CLSTM, **BiLSTM**, BiGRU	87.81% (Acc)	City
[15]	Subtask 1: WC	Subtask 1: ML, **Ensemble methods**	city: 67% country: 75% region: 85% (F1)	City, Country, Region
[15]	Subtask 2: Embeddings	Subtask 2: **Neural**	71.70% (F1)	Country
[16]	surface features, static embeddings, AraBERT, mBERT	SVM, Transformer model, **AraBERT**, mBERT	60.6% (F1)	Country
[17]	N-grams character	**RB meta-classifiers**	74% (Acc)	Country
[18]	1 to 5 N-grams	language model scoring	85.7% (Acc)	Binary
[19]	TF-IDF, one-hot enc, embedding layer	LR, CNN, CNN + GRU	92% (Acc), 57.6% (F1)	Region

3 Proposed Approach

Our objective is to identify the dialect in a textual content written in Arabic characters. To solve this problem, we propose to follow a methodology based on three phases: (1) Preprocessing phase, (2) Embedding phase, and (3) Classification phase. Our main contribution concerns the text modeling and classification phases. Indeed, we propose a new classification architecture based on the combination of CNN-BiLSTM models with AraVec as features. The architecture of our model is illustrated in Fig. 1. In the remaining of this section, we present the pipeline of our proposed approach. Then, we describe the steps one by one.

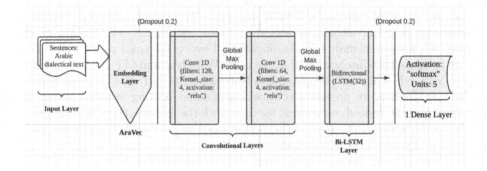

Fig. 1. The proposed Arabic dialect identification approach

Preprocessing Phase: Preprocessing plays a vital role in text mining due to the inherent complexities of unstructured and linguistically diverse natural language text documents. We applied some data cleaning and preprocessing techniques to prepare the data for the next layer, these techniques are dedicated to Arabic texts and include: removal of Arabic Stop Words, removal of hashtags, removal of punctuation, removal of diacritics, removal of repeating characters, normalizing the text, stemming, replacing @username with empty string, removal of Links and encoding dialects. To facilitate the way of learning, we have encoded the labels of each dialect in numbers from 0 to n − 1, where n is the number of the considered dialects.

Embedding Phase: The sentences in our data are actually series of (ordered) words. In order to run machine learning and deep learning algorithms, we need to convert text files into digital feature vectors. In the literature there are several classical modeling techniques like Bag Of Words (BOW), Term Frequency (TF), Term Frequency - Inverse Document Frequency (TF-IDF), and N-gram, which are classic features. There are also more recent techniques like Continuous Bag Of Words (CBOW), Word2Vec, Glove, FastText, AraBert or AraVec. In our work, we choose to experiment with a number of recent techniques, namely: AraVec [20], Glove[1] and Transformer [21]. AraVec provides six different word embedding models, where each text domain (Tweets, WWW and Wikipedia) has two different models; one built using CBOW techniques and the other using the Skip-Gram technique. In our work we choose the Twt-CBOW. The Twt-CBOW model was trained on a dataset containing 66.9 millions of documents, 1090 millions of tokens with the minimum word frequency count value set to 500 and a window size of 3.

---

[1] https://github.com/tarekeldeeb/GloVe-Arabic.

Classification Phase: Our classification layer is based on the combination of Convolutional Neural Network (CNN) and Bidirectional Long Short Term Memory (BiLSTM). The convolutional neural network is a deep learning classification model which uses a mathematical operation called convolution instead of the overall matrix multiplication in at least one of their layers. CNN are generally used in computer vision, but have recently been applied to various NLP tasks and the results were promising. Bidirectional recurrent neural networks simply join two independent RNNs. This structure allows networks to have upstream and downstream information about the sequence at each time step. Using bi-directional means executing entries in two ways, the model is an inverse execution for the analysis of each word, using the two hidden states combined, we are able at any time to preserve the information not just the previous word, but also to the coming word. In our proposed classification model we used 2 convolutional layers with AraVec embedding matrix as input, then we used a Bidirectional layer with 32 filters, finally we used a dense layer with Softmax activation function. In the following we give a description of the hyperparameters used for our model: Optimizer: Adam provided by TensorFlow, Loss function: sparse_categorical _crossentropy, Number of epochs: 5, Batch size: 32, Validation_split: 0.2, Embedding size: 100, Convolutional layer 1D (filters: 128, Kernel_size: 4, activation: "relu"), Convolutional layer 1D (filters: 64, Kernel_size: 4, activation: "relu"), Dropout: 0.2, Bidirectional Layer (LSTM(32)), 1 Dense layer: Activation function: Softmax.

4 Experimental Setup

In this section we present two principal parts, the first subsection considers the description of the process of constructing the dataset used for the experiments. This process is based on the filtering and merging of seven existing datasets. In the second sub-section, we present the models we have chosen as a basis for comparing the performances of our approach. In our work we considered two sets of models: the first set includes machine learning models while the second set contains deep learning models.

4.1 Dataset

This contribution, aims to address the issue of unbalanced resources in the automatic processing of Arabic dialects. In order to mitigate the impact of this challenge, we undertook the task of collecting seven annotated corpora, despite their inherent imbalance. Through a meticulous process of filtering and merging, we successfully curated a balanced dataset comprising five dialects, which served as the foundation for our experimentation. This effort in creating a balanced dataset highlights the significance of our work in addressing the lack of balanced resources in Arabic dialect processing. In order to construct our dataset, we collected 116,650 sentences with their respective labels: Tunisian (TUN), Maghreb (MGH), Egyptian (EGY), Levantine (LEV), Gulf (GLF) and Iraqi (IRQ), the data source and the distribution of dialects are presented in the Table 2.

Table 2. Datasets used

Corpus	Dialects	Source	Size	Used Data
TUNIZI [22]	TUN	Y	3,000 S	1,000 S
TSAC [23]	TUN	F	17,064 S	10,000 S
T-HSAB [24]	TUN	F and Y	6,024 S	5,000 S
DART [25]	EGY MGH LEV GLF IRQ	T	25,000 S	25,000 S
SHAMI [26]	LEV	F and Y	117,805 S	43,250 S
PADIC [27]	LEV MGH	W	31,234 S	31,000 S
AOC [28]	EGY MGH LEV GLF IRQ	SM	1.400 S	1,400 S

*Y: Youtube *F: Facebook *T: Twitter *W: Web sites *SM: Social media *S: Sentence

Then, we have followed three filtering procedures, the first focused on the MGH dialect, which was present in the DART, PADIC, and AOC corpora. MGH composes three dialects: Tunisian, Algerian, and Moroccan. In order to treat the Tunisian dialect as a distinct class, we began by eliminating sentences annotated as Tunisian from these corpora. Consequently, after applying this filtering process, the MGH dialect exclusively comprised the Algerian and Moroccan dialects. The other two filtering procedures we performed are to balance the number of sentences in each dialect. In fact we noticed that the data is very unbalanced, which can impact the learning performance and potentially lead to overfitting for certain dialects while underfitting for others. To mitigate these challenges associated with unbalanced data, it is essential to employ specific balancing techniques. Due to the significantly low number of Iraqi sentences, we decided to exclude the IRQ dialect from our analysis. When comparing the sentence counts across dialects, we found that there were only 216 Iraqi sentences, whereas the subsequent dialect, Egyptian, had 4,830 sentences.

Among the remaining dialects, Egyptian has the lowest number of sentences. To ensure a balanced distribution of sentences across the dialects, the number of sentences in the other dialects is reduced accordingly using random under sampling. By doing so, each dialect has a comparable number of sentences for a more equitable representation in the dataset. The final composition of our dataset includes five dialects represented in a balanced way as follow: 4834 TUN, 4834 MGH, 4832 GLF, 4832 LEV and 4830 EGY. The dataset has 2 columns "Sentence" and "Dialect", Table 3 gives some details about the composition of the dataset in terms of the number of sentences and words, the vocabulary size and the maximum length of sentences, for each dialect and for the whole dataset. We have made our dataset available to the scientific community in an open-access manner.[2]

---

[2] https://github.com/malek-hedhli/Arabic-Dialects-Dataset.

Table 3. Data description

Dialect	Sentences	Total Words	Vocab Size	Max Sent Len
LEV	4 832	65 324	20 982	228
MGH	4 834	25 697	7 412	41
GLf	4 832	55 937	23 238	403
EGY	4 830	92 701	31 359	1131
TUN	4 834	56 134	22 694	382
Total	24 162	295 793	105 685	1 131

4.2 Baseline Models

To evaluate our model, we compared its performance against a set of reference algorithms. We chose to deal with two subsets: (1) classical machine learning algorithms (non-neural) and (2) deep learning algorithms. To ensure optimal hyperparameter selection for our experiment, we used the grid search method. For each algorithm we determined its precision, recall, accuracy and f1-score. In the following we give a description of the parameters used with each algorithm.

Machine Learning Algorithms. During our first set of experimentation, we tested and evaluated several non neural algorithms: Logistic Regression (LR), Decision Tree Classifier (DT), Multinomial Naive Bayes Classifier (MNB), Support Vector Machines (SVM) (with C = 1, gamma = scale, kernel = linear), Random Forests (RF) (with Estimators-number = 350, Max-depth = 60), and Xtreme Gradient Boost (XGB) (with Learning-Rate = 0.2, use LabelEncoder = False). With this first subset we used a Tfidf vectors as features. In addition, we evaluated the performance of the One-vs-Rest (OvR) and One-vs-One (OvO) techniques in combination with binary classifiers such as logistic regression (LR) and support vector machines (SVM) for handling the multi-class classification aspect of our case. These techniques allowed us to extend the capabilities of LR and SVM to effectively classify instances across multiple classes.

Deep Learning Algorithms. In the second set of experimentation, we tested and evaluated several deep learning algorithms: Convolutional Neural Networks (CNN), Recurrent Neural Networks (RNN), Long Short-Term Memory (LSTM), Bidirectional Long ShortTerm Memory (BiLSTM), CNN-LSTM and CNN-BiLSTM which is our proposed model. As regarding to the second subset we used Aravec with EMBEDDING_DIM = 300, Glove with EMBEDDING_DIM = 256 and Transformer as features.

For the deep learning models, we used the following hyperparameters:

Loss function: sparse_categorical_crossentropy, activation function: Softmax, optimizer: Adam provided by TensorFlow, number of epochs: 5, batch size: 32, validation_split: 0.2, embedding size: 50, 1 convolutional layer 1D (filters: 32, Kernel_size: 4), and 1 dense layer: (None, 5). For the models that have the RNN, LSTM and Bi-LSTM layers, we use dropout: 0.2, LSTM layer (32) and LSTM (64) for models that have Bidirectional layer.

5   Results and Discussion

In this section we start by presenting the results of our proposed approach, then we present those obtained by machine learning and deep learning algorithms, and finally we present a discussion and a comparison of all the obtained results. To evaluate our model, we conducted multiple experiments. Specifically, we trained our model three times, each using a different set of feature vectors: AraVec, Glove, and Transformer. These vectors were formed by training models on our Arabic text corpora, enabling them to capture semantic relationships, co-occurrence statistics, or contextual information of words through distinct approaches. Each time we measured the performance of the model. Table 4 showcases the obtained values. With AraVec we obtained the highest results 88% of accuracy, 89% of precision, 88% of recall and 88% of F1-score, with Transformer we got lower results 80% accuracy, 81% precision, 80% recall and 80% F1-score. Glove gave the lowest results 78% of accuracy, 79% of precision, 78% of recall and 78% of F1-score. Since AraVec gave the best values we chose to keep it for the remaining tests.

Table 4. Performance of our CNN-BiLSTM model

CNN-BiLSTM	Transformer	Glove	AraVec
Accuracy	80%	78%	**88%**
Precision	81%	79%	**89%**
Recall	80%	78%	**88%**
F1-Score	80%	78%	**88%**

To better study and understand the performance of our model we calculated the precision, recall and F1-score values for each dialect of the dataset. The results presented in the following Table 5, show the measures obtained with each dialect. We find that the best precision value 93%, is obtained with the Tunisian dialect. The worst value is about 86% and is obtained with Maghreb dialect. For the recall values, we obtained the best result with the Levantine dialect 96%, and the worst with the Maghreb dialect 80%. Finally when we evaluate the F1-score, we find the best result obtained with the Levantine and Tunisian dialect 91% and the worst with the Maghreb dialect 83%.

In the remaining of this section we present a set of experimentation to evaluate several machine learning and deep learning baseline models for Arabic dialect identification task and compare their results with our AraVec CNN-BiLSTM model. The performance values obtained by the machine learning models are presented in Table 6. While observing the accuracy of each machine learning model, we find that the **Multinomial Naive Bayes** model is the most efficient with an accuracy rate of **86%**, 87% of precision, **87%** of recall, and **87%** of F1-score. **Support Vector Machine** and **Logistic Regression** gave slightly lower results with an accuracy of **85%**, **86%** of precision, **86%** of recall, and **86%** of

Table 5. Performance of our AraVec CNN-BiLSTM model

Dialect	Precision	Recall	F1-Score
EGY	88%	88%	88%
MGH	86%	80%	83%
GLF	91%	89%	90%
LEV	87%	**96%**	**91%**
TUN	**93%**	89%	**91%**
Weighted AVG	89%	88%	88%

F1-score. The worst result is obtained by **Decision Tree** with an accuracy of **64%**, **65%** of precision, **64%** of recall, and **64%** of F1-score. Compared to the best machine learning model, our model's performance is better by 2% accuracy, 2% precision, 1% recall and 1% F1-score. In Fig. 2, we have presented an evaluation curve of the accuracy, precision, recall and F1-score for the different Machine Learning models and our proposed model.

Table 6. Machine Learning performance results

Models	Accuracy	Precision	Recall	F1-Score
Logistic Regression	85%	86%	86%	86%
Decision Tree	64%	65%	64%	64%
Multinomial Naive Bayes	**86%**	**87%**	**87%**	**87%**
Support Vector Machine	85%	86%	86%	86%
Random Forest	76%	78%	76%	77%
XGBoost	68%	73%	69%	71%
AraVec CNN-BiLSTM*	**88%**	**89%**	**88%**	**88%**
Improv%[1]	2%	2%	1%	1%

*: Proposed model, [1]: improvement over the best model

The performance of the deep learning models values are presented in the Table 7. The best values are in bold, the second best values are underlined and italicized. With Transformer, the CNN model gave the best performances among the baseline models with 81% of accuracy, 82% of precision, 81% of recall and 81% of F1-score. RNN gave the poorest value with an accuracy equal to 58%, 59% of precision, 58% of recall and 58% of F1-score. Compared to our approach, CNN with transformer had lower performance of around 7% in accuracy, precision, recall and F1-score.

The second modeling was tried with Glove. Again CNN gave the best performance compared to the baseline models with an accuracy of 71%, 72% of precision, 72% of recall and 72% of F1-score with the CNN model. The poorest

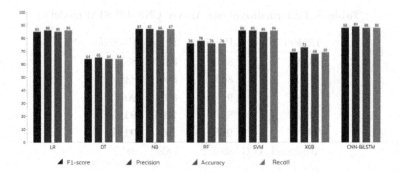

Fig. 2. Performance scores for machine learning models

Table 7. Deep Learning performances results

Models	Accuracy	Precision	Recall	F1-Score
CNN	+T 81%	+T 82%	+T 81%	+T 81%
	+G 71%	+G 72%	+G 72%	+G 72%
	+A 70%	+A 71%	+A 71%	+A 71%
LSTM	+T 68%	+T 69%	+T 68%	+T 68%
	+G 65%	+G 66%	+G 65%	+G 65%
	+A 68%	+A 69%	+A 68%	+A 68%
BiLSTM	+T 62%	+T 63%	+T 62%	+T 62%
	+G 70%	+G 71%	+G 70%	+G 70%
	+A 86%	*+A 87%*	*+A 86%*	*+A 86%*
RNN	+T 58%	+T 59%	+T 58%	+T 58%
	+G 54%	+G 56%	+G 55%	+G 55%
	+A 55%	+A 57%	+A 54%	+A 55%
CNN-LSTM	+T 68%	+T 69%	+T 68%	+T 68%
	+G 62%	+G 64%	+G 62%	+G 63%
	+A 67%	+A 69%	+A 67%	+A 68%
AraVec CNN-BiLSTM*	**88%**	**89%**	**88%**	**88%**
Improv%	2%	2%	2%	2%

T: Transformer G: Glove A: AraVec *: Proposed model

performance values are obtained with RNN model which gave 54% of accuracy, 56% of precision, 55% of recall and 55% of F1-score. Once again our approach had a better performance compared to the best performing baseline model with Glove embedding. The improvement is around 17% in accuracy and precision, and around 16% in recall and F1-score.

The final evaluation was with AraVec using the Twt-CBOW technique. This time the best performances compared to the base models are obtained by BIL-STM with 86% of accuracy, 87% of precision, 86% of recall and 86% of F1-score, with Bi-LSTM model. The minimum value is obtained by RNN model and is equal to 55% of accuracy, 57% of precision, 54% of recall and 55% of F1-score. Compared to the best deep learning model, our model's performance is better by 2% in accuracy, 2% in precision, 2% in recall and 2% in f1-score. In Fig. 3, we have presented an evaluation curve of the accuracy, precision, recall and F1-score for the different Deep Learning models and our proposed model.

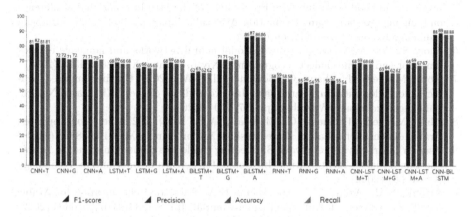

Fig. 3. Performance scores for deep learning models

6 Conclusion

Our work focuses in particular on the identification of Arabic dialects which poses a great challenge due to the lack of resources and the variety of these dialects for the 22 countries that officially speak Arabic (420 million speakers).

In this paper we propose a new Arabic Dialect Identification approach based on the combination of CNN and BiLSTM models and using AraVec embedding. We constructed a balanced dataset containing 5 dialects by filtering and merging seven existing unbalanced datasets. We evaluated our approach and compared its results against two sets of baseline models. Experiments have shown that the performances of our approach exceed those of the best baseline model. In the field of natural language processing, research is still under way, with a number of researchers focusing on Arabic dialects. In the future we can concentrate on more dialects and we can deepen our work towards a classification by city for each country.

References

1. Badri, N., Kboubi, F., Habacha Chaibi, A.: Towards automatic detection of inappropriate content in multi-dialectic Arabic text. In: Bădică, C., Treur, J., Benslimane, D., Hnatkowska, B., Krótkiewicz, M. (eds.) ICCCI 2022. CCIS, vol. 1653, pp. 84–100. Springer, Cham (2022). https://doi.org/10.1007/978-3-031-16210-7_7
2. Mousa, A.: Deep identification of Arabic dialects. Thèse de doctorat, Informatics Institute (2021)

3. Ali, A., Dehak, N., Cardinal, P.: Automatic dialect detection in Arabic broadcast speech. arXiv preprint arXiv:1509.06928 (2015)
4. Tachicart, R., Bouzoubaa, K., Aouragh, S.L., Jaafa, H.: Automatic identification of Moroccan colloquial Arabic. In: Lachkar, A., Bouzoubaa, K., Mazroui, A., Hamdani, A., Lekhouaja, A. (eds.) ICALP 2017. CCIS, vol. 782, pp. 201–214. Springer, Cham (2018). https://doi.org/10.1007/978-3-319-73500-9_15
5. El-Haj, M., Rayson, P., Aboelezz, M.: Arabic dialect identification in the context of bivalency and code-switching. In: Proceedings of the 11th International Conference on Language Resources and Evaluation, Miyazaki, Japan, pp. 3622–3627. European Language Resources Association (2018)
6. Shon, S., Ali, A., Glass, J.: Convolutional neural networks and language embeddings for end-to-end dialect recognition. arXiv preprint arXiv:1803.04567 (2018)
7. Abdul-Mageed, M., Zhang, C., Bouamor, H.: NADI 2020: the first nuanced Arabic dialect identification shared task. In: Proceedings of the Fifth Arabic Natural Language Processing Workshop, pp. 97–110 (2020)
8. Abdul-Mageed, M., Zhang, C., Elmadany, A.R.: NADI 2021: the second nuanced Arabic dialect identification shared task. arXiv preprint arXiv:2103.08466 (2021)
9. Aseri, Y., Alreemy, K., Alelyani, S.: Meeting challenges of modern standard Arabic and Saudi dialect identification. In: Computer Science & Information Technology (CS & IT) (2022)
10. Alzanin, S.M., Azmi, A.M., Aboalsamh, H.A.: Short text classification for Arabic social media tweets. J. King Saud Univ.-Comput. Inf. Sci. **34**(9), 6595–6604 (2022)
11. Darwish, K., Sajjad, H., Mubarak, H.: Verifiably effective Arabic dialect identification. In: Proceedings of the 2014 Conference on Empirical Methods in Natural Language Processing (EMNLP), pp. 1465–1468 (2014)
12. Malmasi, S., Zampieri, M.: Arabic dialect identification in speech transcripts. In: Proceedings of the Third Workshop on NLP for Similar Languages, Varieties and Dialects (VarDial3), pp. 106–113 (2016)
13. Salameh, M., Bouamor, H., Habash, N.: Fine-grained Arabic dialect identification. In: 27th International Conference on Computational Linguistics, COLING 2018, pp. 1332–1344. Association for Computational Linguistics (ACL) (2018)
14. Elaraby, M., Abdul-Mageed, M.: Deep models for Arabic dialect identification on benchmarked data. In: Proceedings of the Fifth Workshop on NLP for Similar Languages, Varieties and Dialects (VarDial 2018) (2018)
15. Bouamor, H., Hassan, S., Habash, N.: The MADAR shared task on Arabic fine-grained dialect identification. In: Proceedings of the Fourth Arabic Natural Language Processing Workshop (2019)
16. Abdelali, A., Mubarak, H., Samih, Y.: QADI: Arabic dialect identification in the wild. In: Proceedings of the Sixth Arabic Natural Language Processing Workshop, pp. 1–10 (2021)
17. Malmasi, S., Refaee, E., Dras, M.: Arabic dialect identification using a parallel multidialectal corpus. In: Hasida, K., Purwarianti, A. (eds.) Computational Linguistics. CCIS, vol. 593, pp. 35–53. Springer, Singapore (2016). https://doi.org/10.1007/978-981-10-0515-2_3
18. Zaidan, O.F., Callison-Burch, C.: Arabic dialect identification. Comput. Linguist. **40**(1), 171–202 (2014)
19. Ali, M.: Character level convolutional neural network for Arabic dialect identification. In: VarDial@ COLING 2018, pp. 122–127 (2018)
20. Soliman, A.B., Eisa, K., El-Beltagy, S.R.: AraVec: a set of Arabic word embedding models for use in Arabic NLP. In: Proceedings of the 3rd International Conference on Arabic Computational Linguistics (ACLing 2017), Dubai, UAE (2017)

21. Gillioz, A., et al.: Overview of the transformer-based models for NLP tasks. In: 2020 15th Conference on Computer Science and Information Systems (FedCSIS). IEEE (2020)
22. Fourati, C., Messaoudi, A., Haddad, H.: TUNIZI: a Tunisian Arabizi sentiment analysis dataset. arXiv preprint arXiv:2004.14303 (2020)
23. Mdhaffar, S., Bougares, F., Esteve, Y.: Sentiment analysis of Tunisian dialects: linguistic ressources and experiments. In: Third Arabic Natural Language Processing Workshop (WANLP), pp. 55–61 (2017)
24. Haddad, H., Mulki, H., Oueslati, A.: T-HSAB: a Tunisian hate speech and abusive dataset. In: Smaïli, K. (ed.) ICALP 2019. CCIS, vol. 1108, pp. 251–263. Springer, Cham (2019). https://doi.org/10.1007/978-3-030-32959-4_18
25. Alsarsour, I., Mohamed, E., Suwaileh, R.: DART: a large dataset of dialectal Arabic tweets. In: Proceedings of the Eleventh International Conference on Language Resources and Evaluation (LREC 2018) (2018)
26. Kwaik, K.A., Saad, M., Chatzikyriakidis, S.: Shami: a corpus of Levantine Arabic dialects. In: Proceedings of the Eleventh International Conference on Language Resources and Evaluation (LREC 2018) (2018)
27. Meftouh, K., Harrat, S., Jamoussi, S.: Machine translation experiments on PADIC: a parallel Arabic dialect corpus. In: Proceedings of the 29th Pacific Asia Conference on Language, Information and Computation (2015)
28. Zaidan, O., Callison-Burch, C.: The Arabic online commentary dataset: an annotated dataset of informal Arabic with high dialectal content. In: Proceedings of the 49th Annual Meeting of the Association for Computational Linguistics: Human Language Technologies, pp. 37–41 (2011)

Active Learning with AraGPT2 for Arabic Named Entity Recognition

Hassen Mahdhaoui, Abdelkarim Mars$^{(\boxtimes)}$, and Mounir Zrigui

Research Laboratory in Algebra, Numbers Theory and Intelligent Systems,
University of Monastir, Monastir, Tunisia
hassenmahdhaoui@gmail.com, Abdelkarim.mars@gmail.com,
Mounir.Zrigui@fsm.rnu.tn

Abstract. Arabic Named Entity Recognition (ANER) is a crucial task in natural language processing that aims to identify and classify named entities in text into predefined categories such as person, location, and organization. In this study, we propose an active learning approach for Arabic Named Entity Recognition (ANER) using the pre-trained language model AraGPT2. Our approach utilizes the model's uncertainty in making predictions to select the most informative examples for annotation, reducing the need for a large annotated dataset. We evaluated our approach on three datasets: AQMAR, NEWS, and TWEETS. The results demonstrate that our active learning approach outperforms state-of-the-art models and tools such as MADAMIRA, FARASA, and Deep Co-learning methods on AQMAR and NEWS datasets. Additionally, our approach demonstrates robustness on TWEETS dataset, which primarily contains text written in the Egyptian dialect and often includes mistakes or misspellings. Our findings suggest that the active learning approach can significantly improve the performance of ANER models, particularly when dealing with noisy or dialectal text.

Keywords: Natural Language Processing · Arabic Named Entity Recognition (ANER) · Large Language Models · AraGPT2 · active learning

1 Introduction

Natural Language Processing (NLP) is a field of artificial intelligence that focuses on the interaction between computers and human language. It involves developing algorithms and models that enable machines to understand, interpret, and generate human language in a meaningful way. NLP has gained significant attention and popularity due to its wide range of applications and its ability to extract insights and value from large volumes of text data. NLP models excel in a wide range of tasks across different fields, including sentiment analysis [3,5,18], speech recognition [13,19,25,26], text classification [8,23], named entity recognition [11,28,31,32], etc. In this paper, we focus on the task of Arabic Named

© The Author(s), under exclusive license to Springer Nature Switzerland AG 2023
N. T. Nguyen et al. (Eds.): ICCCI 2023, CCIS 1864, pp. 226–236, 2023.
https://doi.org/10.1007/978-3-031-41774-0_18

Entity Recognition (ANER), a fundamental task in natural language processing that aims to identify and classify named entities such as persons, organizations, locations, etc. in text written in the Arabic language. However, ANER in Arabic is a challenging task due to the complexity and variability of the Arabic language, such as the presence of diacritics, complex morphological features, and the rich use of synonyms and idiomatic expressions.

Traditionally, ANER models were based on rule-based and dictionary-based approaches, which require a significant amount of human effort to create and maintain the rules and dictionaries. However, these approaches are prone to errors and are not robust to variations in writing styles and dialects. With the recent advancements in deep learning techniques, many ANER models have been proposed that are based on neural networks. These models have shown to be more robust and accurate than traditional methods.

Recently, pre-trained language models such as BERT, GPT-2, and RoBERTa have been fine-tuned to perform various NLP tasks, including ANER. These models have been pre-trained on large amounts of text data and have been fine-tuned on specific tasks with small amounts of labeled data, which reduces the need for large annotated datasets. The fine-tuning process allows these models to adapt to new tasks and domains quickly and effectively.

Another approach that has been gaining popularity in recent years is active learning. Active learning is a semi-supervised learning approach that aims to reduce the need for large annotated datasets by selecting the most informative examples for annotation. The model's uncertainty in making predictions is used to select examples that are likely to improve its performance. This study presents an active learning approach for ANER using the AraGPT2 model, which is a pre-trained language model that has been fine-tuned to perform ANER. The results showed that our active learning approach achieved superior performance compared to other models and tools, including the MADAMIRA, FARASA, and Deep Co-learning methods, on the AQMAR and NEWS datasets. The approach also demonstrated robustness on the TWEETS dataset, which primarily contains text written in the Egyptian dialect and often includes mistakes or misspellings. Furthermore, the results of the comparison with the LLM model showed that our active learning approach outperforms LLM in terms of F-measure.

This paper aims to investigate various techniques for Arabic Named Entity Recognition (ANER) based on rules, machine learning, and deep learning. We will begin by reviewing the existing related work in this field. Then, we will outline our methodology, including the dataset used and the preprocessing steps applied. Our proposed approach will be presented, incorporating the concepts of Aragpt and active learning. The evaluation of our model will be conducted on three datasets, demonstrating its superiority over other methods. Finally, we will conclude by summarizing our findings and discussing the implications of our research.

2   Related Work

2.1   Traditional and Machine Learning Methods

Before machine learning approaches, rule-based methods have also been employed for Arabic named entity recognition (ANER). Rule-based ANER systems rely on predefined patterns or linguistic rules to identify entities. These rules can be based on specific word patterns, syntactic structures, or other language-specific characteristics.

Rule-based ANER systems typically involve the manual creation or extraction of rules from linguistic resources or domain knowledge. These rules are then applied to the text to identify and classify named entities. In 2015, Emna Hkiri et al. [33] developed a bilingual Arabic-English lexicon of named entities (NE) to enhance the performance of Arabic rule-based systems. Their approach involved pre-editing DBpedia linked data entities, applying an automatic model for detecting, extracting, and translating Arabic-English named entities. They achieved an accuracy of 82.59%.

In [1], an ANER system based on Hidden Markov Model (HMM) was proposed, which used stemming to address inflection and ambiguity in the language. In [2], an ML system using Decision Trees was proposed, which was able to extract various types of named entities with an F-measure of 81.35%. The authors of [12] used the Conditional Random Field (CRF) method to improve their system's performance and reported high accuracy with recall of 72.77%, precision of 86.90% and F-measure of 79.21%. In [4], a combination of two ML systems, pattern recognition using CRF and bootstrapping, was used to handle Arabic NER and various features such as POS tagging, BPC, gazetteers, and morphological features were used. In [20], a neural network architecture was developed for ANER, which compared the performance of Decision Trees and Neural Networks. The results showed that the neural network approach achieved 92% precision, while the DT had 87% precision. Nafaa Haffar et al. [21] proposed the TimeML Annotation of Events and Temporal Expressions in Arabic Texts, where they utilized their annotated corpus to carry out the annotation process. In [6], the authors built multiple classifiers using SVM combined with the CRF approach and used ACE datasets for evaluation. The results showed that each NE type was sensitive to different features and thus, each feature had a different role in recognizing the NE with different degrees. In [7], the authors investigated the impact of word representations on ANER systems and presented different approaches for integrating word representations with NER. They also provided a comparison of commonly used neural word embedding algorithms and concluded that the performance was improved when combining different approaches together [25].

2.2   Recent Deep Learning Methods

In recent research on Arabic named entity recognition (ANER), there has been a notable trend towards adopting deep learning methods. These approaches leverage the power of neural networks to improve the accuracy and effectiveness of NER models specifically designed for Arabic text.

The authors of [22] introduced a novel method for detecting and classifying Arabic Named Entities (ANER) using deep co-learning, a semi-supervised learning algorithm. They first developed a Wikipedia article classifier using LSTM-DNN to obtain a semi-labeled dataset for ANER. The evaluation was carried out on three different ANER datasets and the results were compared with various state-of-the-art and off-the-shelf ANER methods. It was found that their method produced significant results that outperformed the compared approaches applied to the different three datasets. Similarly, the authors of [9] proposed a neural network model with a multi-attention layer for extracting ANEs. They claimed that their approach improved performance, particularly for unseen word labeling, with an F1 score of 91% on the ANERCorpus dataset, surpassing existing methods by a significant margin. In 2021, Norah Alsaaran and Maha Alrabiah [10] proposed a BERT-BGRU Approach. They demonstrate that the proposed model outperformed state-of-the-art ANER models achieving 92.28% and 90.68% F-measure values on the ANERCorp dataset and the merged ANERCorp and AQMAR dataset, respectively. Chadi Helwe et al. [27] proposed a semi-supervised learning approach to train a BERT-based NER model using labeled and semi-labeled datasets. They achieve 65.5% and 78.6. F-measure values on AQMAR and NEWS datasets respectively.

Our improved approach combines semi-supervised learning with active learning to train the AraGPT2 model. By leveraging both labeled and unlabeled data, we achieve higher accuracy and performance. This enhancement is demonstrated by significant improvements in the F-measure values on the AQMAR and NEWS datasets.

3   Methodology

3.1   Datasets

In this study, the datasets utilized for training, validation, and testing were similar to those utilized by Helwe and Elbassuoni [10]. We employed six different datasets with one set for training, one for validation, three for testing and one semi-annotated set for training our semi-supervised model. The training dataset, ANERCorp dataset (ANE, 2007), which consists of 114,926 labeled tokens, was used to train the teacher model and fine-tune the student model. The validation dataset, NewsFANE Gold corpus with 71,067 labeled sentences, was used to fine-tune the model's hyperparameters. Our approach was then evaluated on three Arabic NER benchmarks, starting with AQMAR dataset, an annotated corpus for Arabic NER task which contains 2,456 sentences from 28 articles from Arabic Wikipedia from four different domains. The second dataset used for evaluation is the NEWS dataset, which is also an annotated corpus for Arabic NER task which consists of 292 sentences retrieved from the RSS feed of the Arabic (Egypt) version of news.google.com from October 6, 2012. The last dataset used for evaluation in this study is the TWEETS dataset, which was created by Darwish in 2013. This dataset includes 982 tweets that were randomly selected from tweets posted between November 23, 2011 and November 27, 2011, and retrieved from Twitter API using the query "lang: ar" (language = Arabic). Additionally, this study used a semi-labeled dataset that was generated by annotating entities in randomly selected Wikipedia articles using an LSTM neural network model. The dataset includes a total of 1,617,184 labeled and unlabeled tokens, with each line containing a set of tokens and their corresponding labels if they exist. The annotation process was conducted using the summary of each entity's Wikipedia article, and the LSTM model was trained to classify the entities into one of four classes: person, location, organization, or other (Fig. 1).

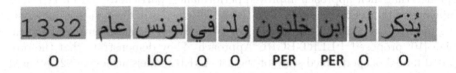

Fig. 1. Instance of Labeled Dataset.

3.2 Pre-processing

To prepare the Arabic dataset for Named Entity Recognition (NER), we performed preprocessing steps to unify the tagging scheme used in the dataset. We also removed the "object" and "miscellaneous" classes from the dataset to focus solely on the Named Entity classes (person, location, organization, etc.). Additionally, to address the complex morphological and syntactic features of the Arabic language [26], we applied several text normalization techniques such as diacritics removal, tokenization, and stemming. These preprocessing steps aimed to simplify the text and improve the performance of the NER model [31].

3.3 Proposed Approach

Large Language Model (GPT). A Large Language Model (GPT) is a type of artificial intelligence model that is trained to generate natural language text. GPT stands for "Generative Pre-training Transformer," which refers to the process used to train the model. The model is trained on a large dataset of text, such as books or articles, and uses this training data to generate new text that is similar in style and content. GPT models have been used for a wide range of tasks, including language translation, text summarization, and question answering. They are also used for more creative tasks such as writing fiction.

AraGPT2 Model. The AraGPT2 model is based on the transformer architecture, which is a type of neural network that has been shown to be particularly effective for natural language processing tasks. The transformer architecture uses self-attention mechanisms to allow the model to weigh the importance of different parts of the input when making predictions.

AraGPT uses a variant of the transformer architecture called the GPT, which is a deep neural network with 12 layers and a hidden size of 768. It is pre-trained on a large corpus of Arabic text data, which includes a wide variety of text styles and formats, such as news articles, books, and social media posts. Once the model is pre-trained, it can be fine-tuned for various NLP tasks by training it on a smaller dataset with task-specific labels. This allows the model to learn the specific characteristics of the task and generate more accurate predictions.

Aragpt has consistently demonstrated superior performance compared to other techniques in various NLP tasks like speech recognition sentiment analysis and arabic named entity recognition. By integrating Aragpt into our models, we effectively harness its advanced language understanding capabilities, further enhancing the quality and accuracy of our results.

AraGPT2 has shown to be a powerful tool for Arabic language tasks, but it's important to note that it's always good to evaluate the performance of the model on specific data and tasks to ensure that it's able to achieve the desired accuracy. Additionally, as with any model, the quality of the data used for pre-training and fine-tuning is also crucial for the performance of the model.

Active Learning. The process of labeling data for named entity recognition (NER) often requires manual annotation by human experts, which is costly when scaling. Active learning [17] aims to address this challenge by strategically selecting annotated examples, leading to better performance with fewer annotations. In this setup, the active learning algorithm works in multiple rounds. At the beginning of each round, the algorithm selects sentences to annotate within a given budget. Once the annotations are in place, the model parameters are updated by training on the extended dataset, and the process proceeds to the next round. This approach assumes that the cost of annotating a sentence is proportional to the number of words in the sentence, and that each selected sentence requires full annotation, regardless of or considering partial annotations. Active learning has been shown to be an effective approach for various NLP tasks like speech recognition [15], sentiment analysis [16] and ANER [29], etc.

Active Learning Model for Arabic NER. Our method utilizes two datasets, one that is small but fully labeled and another that is large but partially labeled. We first train a AraGPT2 teacher model using the fully labeled dataset. Next, we use the trained model to predict labels for the unlabeled parts of the partially labeled dataset and save them. Then, we calculate the average confidence score for the predicted labels of each predicted instance and check if it surpasses a set threshold. If so, we select those instances and save them in order to select the most accurate data from the teacher model's annotation. After that, We then train another AraGPT2 model, called the student model, with the same architecture as the teacher model, using the instances that have a confidence score that surpasses a predefined threshold. Finally, we fine-tune the student model using the fully labeled dataset (Fig. 2).

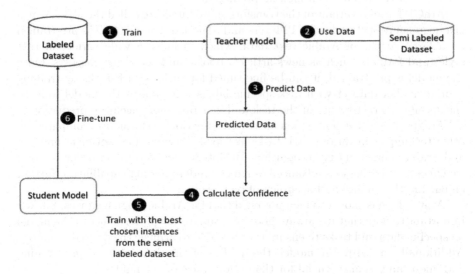

Fig. 2. Proposed Active Learning Approach.

4 Evaluation

In this section, we investigate the performance of our semi-supervised approach for the task of Arabic Named Entity Recognition. In our approach, the fully supervised AraGPT2 model was trained over 40 epochs with batch size of 32, dropout of 0.2 and early stopping technique, ADAM optimization algorithm was used during the training process. In order to train our active learning model, we selected instances from the semi-labeled dataset that were predicted by the fully supervised model with a confidence score greater than 0.95 as the threshold.

In order to evaluate the performance of our semi-supervised approach for Arabic Named Entity Recognition, we utilized the commonly used F-measure metric. This metric is widely used in the field of NER for Arabic text, as seen in previous studies such as FARASA [24] and MADAMIRA [14]. All experiments were conducted on a Windows 10 machine equipped with 12 GB of RAM, an Intel Core I7 CPU, and an NVIDIA GeForce GTX 1060 6 GB GPU.

5 Results

5.1 AQMAR Dataset

In evaluating our active learning model, we first tested it on the AQMAR dataset. The results, as shown in Table 1, indicate that traditional machine learning techniques such as MADAMIRA and FARASA, which rely on feature engineering, performed less favorably compared to deep learning approaches. The Deep Co-learning approach, which utilizes a semi-supervised learning method utilizing semi-labeled data during training, achieved a slightly higher F-measure than the Fully Supervised AraGPT2-based model. However, our active learning approach utilizing AraGPT2 achieved the highest F-measure of 67.2.

Table 1. Comparing the Performance of Arabic NER Tools and Various Models on the AQMAR Dataset using the F-measure Metric.

Model	LOC	ORG	PER	Avg
MADAMIRA	39.4	15.1	22.3	29.2
FARASA	60.1	30.6	52.5	52.9
Deep Co-learning	67.0	38.2	65.1	61.8
AraGPT2 Fully Supervised	64.5	32.3	70.9	63.4
AraGPT2 Semi-Supervised	70.4	35.7	76.2	67.2

5.2 NEWS Dataset

In the NEWS dataset, as demonstrated in Table 2, the performance of various techniques and tools closely mirrors the results obtained from the AQMAR dataset. Notably, the MADAMIRA and FARASA methods exhibit lower scores in comparison to the deep learning techniques. The Deep Co-learning approach demonstrates superior performance with an F-measure of 81.3, surpassing even the fully supervised AraGPT2 model. Our active learning approach outperforms all other methods and tools.

Table 2. Comparing the Performance of Arabic NER Tools and Various Models on the NEWS Dataset using the F-measure Metric.

Model	LOC	ORG	PER	Avg
MADAMIRA	39.4	15.1	22.3	29.2
FARASA	73.1	42.1	69.5	63.9
Deep Co-learning	81.6	52.7	82.4	74.1
AraGPT2 Fully Supervised	74.9	55.3	86.6	75.7
AraGPT2 Semi-Supervised	82.4	62.4	90.2	81.3

5.3   TWEETS Dataset

The final dataset evaluated in this study is the TWEETS dataset. As shown in Table 3, the MADAMIRA and FARASA tools yielded poor results in comparison to the deep learning approaches, with an F-measure of 24.6 and 39.9 respectively. Notably, only in this dataset, the Deep Co-learning approach achieved the highest score, outperforming both the fully supervised and semi-supervised AraGPT2 models with an F-measure of 59.2.

Table 3. Comparing the Performance of Arabic NER Tools and Various Models on the TWEETS Dataset using the F-measure Metric.

Model	LOC	ORG	PER	Avg
MADAMIRA	40.3	8.9	18.4	24.6
FARASA	47.5	24.7	39.8	39.9
Deep Co-learning	65.3	39.7	61.3	59.2
AraGPT2 Fully Supervised	58.1	30.9	61.5	56.9
AraGPT2 Semi-Supervised	63.7	43.5	60.4	58.9

6   Conclusion

Our research presents compelling evidence for the effectiveness of an active learning approach in Arabic Named Entity Recognition (ANER) using the AraGPT2 model. Our experimental results demonstrate significant improvements in performance compared to several state-of-the-art models and tools, including, FARASA, MADAMIRA and Deep Co-learning methods, on AQMAR and NEWS datasets. The success of our active learning approach highlights its potential to enhance ANER models, especially in scenarios where labeled data is scarce or expensive to obtain. Active learning allows the model to intelligently select the most informative samples for annotation, thereby optimizing the use of available resources.

Our research opens avenues for further exploration and investigation. Future studies can delve into the application of active learning in different languages and tasks, aiming to replicate and extend the positive outcomes observed in Arabic ANER. Additionally, exploring the combination of active learning with other techniques, such as transfer learning or data augmentation, may yield even more significant improvements in ANER performance.

References

1. Dahan, F., Touir, A., Mathkour, H.: First order hidden Markov model for automatic Arabic name entity recognition. Int. J. Comput. Appl. **123**(7), 37–40 (2015)
2. Al-Shoukry, S.A.H., Omar, N.: Arabic named entity recognition for crime documents using classifiers combination. Int. Rev. Comput. Softw. **10**(6), 628 (2015)
3. Abdellaoui, H., Zrigui, M.: Using tweets and emojis to build TEAD: an Arabic dataset for sentiment analysis. Computación y Sistemas **22**(3), 777–786 (2018)
4. AbdelRahman, S., Elarnaoty, M., Magdy, M., Fahmy, A.: Integrated machine learning techniques for Arabic named entity recognition. Int. J. Comput. Sci. Issues **7**, 27–36 (2010)
5. Laroussi, O., Mallat, S., Nicolas, H., Zrigui, M.: An opinion analysis method based on disambiguation to improve a recommendation system. In: Bădică, C., Treur, J., Benslimane, D., Hnatkowska, B., Krótkiewicz, M. (eds.) ICCCI 2022. CCIS, vol. 1653, pp. 42–56. Springer, Cham (2022). https://doi.org/10.1007/978-3-031-16210-7_4
6. Benajiba, Y., Diab, M., Rosso, P.: Arabic named entity recognition: an SVM-based approach. In: Proceedings of 2008 Arab International Conference on Information Technology (ACIT), pp. 16–18. Association of Arab Universities, Amman (2008)
7. Bazi, I.E., Laachfoubi, N.: Arabic named entity recognition using word representations. arXiv preprint arXiv:1804.05630 (2018)
8. Mahmoud, A., Zrigui, M.: Deep neural network models for paraphrased text classification in the Arabic language. In: Métais, E., Meziane, F., Vadera, S., Sugumaran, V., Saraee, M. (eds.) NLDB 2019. LNCS, vol. 11608, pp. 3–16. Springer, Cham (2019). https://doi.org/10.1007/978-3-030-23281-8_1
9. Ali, M.N.A., Tan, G., Hussain, A.: Boosting Arabic named-entity recognition with multi-attention layer. IEEE Access **7**, 46575–46582 (2019)
10. Alsaaran, N., Alrabiah, M.: Arabic named entity recognition: a BERT-BGRU approach. Comput. Mater. Continua **68**, 471–485 (2021)
11. Hkiri, E., et al.: Constructing a lexicon of Arabic-English named entity using SMT and semantic linked data. Int. Arab J. Inf. Technol. (IAJIT) **14**(6) (2017)
12. Benajiba, Y., Rosso, P.: Arabic named entity recognition using conditional random fields. In: Proceedings of the Workshop HLT NLP Arabic World LREC, vol. 8, pp. 143–153 (2008)
13. Zouaghi, A., Zrigui, M., Antoniadis, G.: Automatic understanding of the spontaneous Arabic speech. Traitement Automatique des Langues **49**(1), 141–166 (2008)
14. Pasha, A., et al.: MADAMIRA: a fast, comprehensive tool for morphological analysis and disambiguation of Arabic. In: LREC 2014, pp. 1094–1101 (2014)
15. Hakkani-Tür, D., Riccardi, G., Gorin, A.: Active learning for automatic speech recognition. In: 2002 IEEE International Conference on Acoustics, Speech, and Signal Processing, vol. 4. IEEE (2002)
16. Asli, S.A.A., et al.: Optimizing annotation effort using active learning strategies: a sentiment analysis case study in persian. In: Proceedings of the 12th Language Resources and Evaluation Conference (2020)
17. Ren, P., et al.: A survey of deep active learning. ACM Comput. Surv. (CSUR) **54**(9), 1–40 (2021)
18. Jaballi, S., Zrigui, S., Sghaier, M.A., Berchech, D., Zrigui, M.: Sentiment analysis of Tunisian users on social networks: overcoming the challenge of multilingual comments in the Tunisian dialect. In: Nguyen, N.T., Manolopoulos, Y., Chbeir, R., Kozierkiewicz, A., Trawiński, B. (eds.) ICCCI 2022. LNAI, vol. 13501, pp. 176–192. Springer, Cham (2022). https://doi.org/10.1007/978-3-031-16014-1_15

19. Amari, R., Noubigh, Z., Zrigui, S., Berchech, D., Nicolas, H., Zrigui, M.: Deep convolutional neural network for Arabic speech recognition. In: Nguyen, N.T., Manolopoulos, Y., Chbeir, R., Kozierkiewicz, A., Trawiński, B. (eds.) ICCCI 2022. LNAI, vol. 13501, pp. 120–134. Springer, Cham (2022). https://doi.org/10.1007/978-3-031-16014-1_11

20. Mohammed, N.F., Omar, N.: Arabic named entity recognition using artificial neural network. J. Comput. Sci. **8**(8), 1285–1293 (2012)

21. Haffar, N., Hkiri, E., Zrigui, M.: TimeML annotation of events and temporal expressions in Arabic texts. In: Nguyen, N.T., Chbeir, R., Exposito, E., Aniorté, P., Trawiński, B. (eds.) ICCCI 2019. LNCS (LNAI), vol. 11683, pp. 207–218. Springer, Cham (2019). https://doi.org/10.1007/978-3-030-28377-3_17

22. Helwe, C., Elbassuoni, S.: Arabic named entity recognition via deep co-learning. Artif. Intell. Rev. **52**(1), 197–215 (2019). https://doi.org/10.1007/s10462-019-09688-6

23. Mahmoud, A., Zrigui, M.: Semantic similarity analysis for corpus development and paraphrase detection in Arabic. Int. Arab J. Inf. Technol. **18**(1), 1–7 (2021)

24. Abdelali, A., Darwish, K., Durrani, N., Mubarak, H.: Farasa: a fast and furious segmenter for Arabic. In: Proceedings of the 2016 Conference of the North American Chapter of the Association for Computational Linguistics: Demonstrations, San Diego, California, pp. 11–16. Association for Computational Linguistics (2016)

25. Amari, R., et al.: Deep convolutional neural network for speech recognition. In: International Conference on Computational Collective Intelligence (ICCCI) (2022)

26. Dabbabi, K., Mars, A.: Spoken utterance classification task of Arabic numerals and selected isolated words. Arab. J. Sci. Eng. **47**, 10731–10750 (2022). https://doi.org/10.1007/s13369-022-06649-0

27. Helwe, C., et al.: A semi-supervised BERT approach for Arabic named entity recognition. In: Proceedings of the Fifth Arabic Natural Language Processing Workshop (2020)

28. Li, J., et al.: A survey on deep learning for named entity recognition. IEEE Trans. Knowl. Data Eng. **34**(1), 50–70 (2020)

29. Alsaaran, N., Alrabiah, M.: Arabic named entity recognition: a BERT-BGRU approach. Comput. Mater. Continua **68**, 471–485 (2021)

30. Nayel, H.A., Medhat, W., Rashad, M.: BENHA@ IDAT: improving irony detection in Arabic tweets using ensemble approach. In: FIRE (Working Notes) (2019)

31. Hkiri, E., Mallat, S., Zrigui, M.: Integrating bilingual named entities lexicon with conditional random fields model for Arabic named entities recognition. In: 2017 14th IAPR International Conference on Document Analysis and Recognition (ICDAR), vol. 1. IEEE (2017)

32. Haffar, N., Ayadi, R., Hkiri, E., Zrigui, M.: Temporal ordering of events via deep neural networks. In: Lladós, J., Lopresti, D., Uchida, S. (eds.) ICDAR 2021. LNCS, vol. 12822, pp. 762–777. Springer, Cham (2021). https://doi.org/10.1007/978-3-030-86331-9_49

33. Hkiri, E., Mallat, S., Zrigui, M.: Improving coverage of rule based NER systems. In: 2015 5th International Conference on Information & Communication Technology and Accessibility (ICTA). IEEE (2015)

FreMPhone: A French Mobile Phone Corpus for Aspect-Based Sentiment Analysis

Sarsabene Hammi[✉], Souha Mezghani Hammami, and Lamia Hadrich Belguith

ANLP Research Group, MIRACL Lab, FSEGS, University of Sfax, Sfax, Tunisia
souha.hammami@ihecs.usf.tn, lamia.belguith@fsegs.usf.tn

Abstract. Aspect-Based Sentiment Analysis (ABSA) task is one of the Natural Language Processing (NLP) research fields that has seen considerable scientific advancements over the last few years. This task aims to detect, in a given text, the sentiment of users towards the different aspects of a product or service. Despite the big number of annotated corpora that have been produced to perform the ABSA task in the English language, resources are still stingy, for other languages. Due to the lack of French corpora created for the ABSA task, we present in this paper the French corpus for the mobile phone domain "FreMPhone". The constructed corpus consists of 5217 mobile phone reviews collected from the Amazon.fr website. Each review in the corpus was annotated with its appropriate aspect terms and sentiment polarity, using an annotation guideline. The FreMPhone contains 19257 aspect terms divided into 13259 positives, 5084 negatives, and 914 neutrals. Moreover, we proposed a new architecture "CBCF" that combines the deep learning models (LSTM and CNN) and the machine learning model CRF and we evaluated it on the FreMPhone corpus. The experiments were performed on the subtasks of the ABSA: Aspect Extraction (AE) and Sentiment Classification (SC). These experiments showed the good performance of the CBCF architecture which overrode the LSTM, CNN, and CRF models and achieved an F-measure value equal to 95.96% for the Aspect Extraction (AE) task and 96.35% for the Sentiment Classification (SC) task.

Keywords: Aspect-based Sentiment Analysis · Aspect Extraction · CBCF · FreMPhone · Sentiment Analysis

1 Introduction

In recent years, online platforms and commercial websites have witnessed a significant increase in the mass of exchanged information. This huge amount of information made the major trading houses scramble to obtain this information and exploit it to achieve their commercial and political interests. In fact, comprehending what customers think about services, products, political personalities, etc., can significantly influence the changing of the course of events for the better, including the enhancement of commercial products or changing of political strategies, etc. With the growing desire to analyze this electronic content, researchers [1] put forward, for the first time in 2004, a new scientific task that

N. T. Nguyen et al. (Eds.): ICCCI 2023, CCIS 1864, pp. 237–249, 2023.
https://doi.org/10.1007/978-3-031-41774-0_19

they called sentiment analysis (SA). This task aims to detect from the online available content the sentiment of customers about someone or something [1]. However, the sentiment analysis task may not be enough in some cases, especially with the increase of requirements of companies. In fact, some companies tend to know not only the opinions of customers about their industrialized products but also about the different aspects of these products. From here, came the Aspect-Based Sentiment Analysis (ABSA) task which provides more fine-grained sentiment analysis. This task enables companies to improve the different aspects that customers did not like in a product and thus ameliorate the satisfaction rate. Taking the following review "*I fell in love with this **camera***", the ABSA task aims to identify the positive sentiment expressed for the aspect term "**camera**" of the entity "**phone**".

Early studies have divided the ABSA task into two sub-tasks: The Aspect Extraction (AE) task and the Sentiment Classification (SC) task. The AE task aims to extract the aspect terms in which customers express their opinion about them ("**quality**", "**screen**", "**facial recognition**", etc.), while the SC tends to assign sentiment polarity ("**positive**", "**negative**" or "**neutral**") to the aspects extracted in the AE task.

Since the accomplishment of any ABSA task needs the use of a well-annotated corpus, we found many corpora that have been constructed for this purpose in the English language. Among these corpora, we mention the Amazon Customer Reviews corpus [1], TripAdvisor corpus [2], Epinions corpus [3], SemEval-2014 ABSA corpus [4], etc. However, the number of publicly available French corpora for the ABSA task is still scarce. For this reason, we propose in this study the first available Mobile Phone corpus "FreMPhone" for the ABSA task. FreMPhone corpus serves as a complementary resource to existing French resources and it is composed of 19257 aspect terms. In addition, we introduce a new neural network architecture CBCF to evaluate the reliability of the FreMPhone corpus. This architecture combines the CNN, Bi-LSTM, and CRF models. It uses first the Bi-LSTM and CNN models to select the pertinent features for classification and then employs the CRF model to detect the appropriate label for each word. This architecture surpasses the LSTM, CNN, and CRF models and achieves encouraging results for both AE and SC tasks.

The rest of the paper is organized as follows. Section 2 presents the ABSA-related corpora constructed for the French language. Section 3 describes the process of data collection, the annotation manner, and the characteristics of the created corpus. Section 4 details the CBCF architecture proposed to solve the AE task and SC task on the FreMPhone corpus. Section 5 illustrates the obtained experimental results. Section 6 provides the conclusion and some perspectives.

2 Related Works

Despite the abundance of ABSA-annotated corpora for the English language, there is a scarcity of corpora for the French language. After a survey study effectuated on the existing French corpora for the ABSA task, we concluded that only a little number of them are available. In this section, we present only the available French corpora for the ABSA task. These corpora are CANÉPHORE [5], the SemEval-2016 restaurant corpus [6], and the SemEval-2016 museum corpus [6]. The CANÉPHORE [5] corpus was created in 2015 and it contains 5372 tweets that discuss the "Miss France" event elaborated in 2012. This corpus was annotated using the annotation tool Brat[1]. For each tweet, the annotators identify the entities (subjects, aspects, or markers) and their sentiment polarities which can be positive or negative. As a result of this annotation, a set of 292 aspects was extracted. The SemEval-2016 restaurant corpus [6] was built within the fifth task of the SemEval international workshop. It was collected from the Yelp[2] website and consists of 457 restaurant reviews (2365 sentences) that reflect the attitudes of consumers concerning the restaurant domain. The annotation of this corpus was released in two steps. For the first time, the whole corpus was annotated by a French native speaker linguistic. After that, the annotation was verified by the organizers of this task. For each review, the annotator identifies the entities and their attributes and then assigns to them a sentiment polarity. The annotation in this work was effectuated based on 6 categories of entities (*restaurant, food, drinks, ambiance, service, location*), 5 categories of attributes (*general, prices, quality, style_options, miscellaneous*), and 3 sentiment classes (*positive, negative, neutral*). As a result of this annotation, a set of 3484 tuples was produced. Within the same task, [6] built the second French corpus for the museum domain. This corpus consists of 162 (655 sentences) French museum reviews crawled from the Yelp website for the ABSA task. This corpus was annotated based on 6 entities (*museum, collections, facilities, service, tour_guiding, location*) and 8 attributes (*general, prices, comfort, activities, architecture, interest, setup, miscellaneous*). Each entity-attribute pair was annotated into positive, negative, or neutral. At the end of the annotation, a set of 891 tuples was obtained.

These presented corpora are freely available online. Table 1 contains the different details of the three presented French corpora.

Table 1. Overview of ABSA available corpora.

Corpus	Size	Entity-Attribute	Number of Aspects	Source
CANÉPHORE	5372 tweets	-	292	Twitter
SemEval-2016 restaurant	2365 sentences	30	3841	Yelp
SemEval-2016 museums	655 sentences	48	891	Yelp

3 Corpus and Annotation

This section presents the created corpus "FreMPhone" (source, structure, statics, etc.) and details the different steps followed in its annotation. In the following paragraphs, we mean by aspect terms both aspects and entities.

---

[1] http://brat.nlplab.org/

[2] https://www.yelp.com/

3.1 Corpus Presentation

The FreMPhone corpus was collected from the Amazon[3] website. For this research, Amazon was selected as the data source owing to its substantial volume of available comments. Amazon is one of the big American e-commerce companies that was founded in 1994. It sells several kinds of products (books, dvds, mobile phones, etc.) around the world and it gives its customers, by writing reviews on its website, the opportunity to express their opinions about the products that they purchased. This makes Amazon one of the largest websites that contain the biggest database of customer reviews. In this work, we have only been interested in the mobile phone domain. A corpus of 5651 mobile phone reviews was collected for this purpose from May 2022 until August 2022. To make our corpus more appropriate for the development of the ABSA method, we deleted the reviews that contain senseless sentences and that consisted only of one word. Also, we removed the reviews that are written in a language other than French. The final number of reviews obtained is 5217. These reviews encompass over six brands represented in Table 2.

Table 2. Number of reviews in the corpus by type of brand.

Brand	Samsung	iPhone	Nokia	Huawei	Oppo	Other brands
Number of reviews	2152	1445	589	456	328	274

To collect the FreMPhone corpus, we used the data extraction tool "Instant data scarper"[4] which is based on AI (artificial intelligence) to predict which data is most relevant on the HTML page.).

3.2 Corpus Annotation

To well annotate our French mobile phone corpus, we studied some of the most referenced annotation guidelines for ABSA corpora such as, [2, 4], and [6]. After that, a subset of 1000 reviews was chosen randomly from the corpus and was annotated by two annotators separately. As a result, a set of 42 aspect terms were found in these reviews. Then, we prepared an annotation guideline, based on the studied guidelines. This guideline contains a brief definition of the ABSA task and rules for the aspect's polarity classification.

To ensure a better process of annotation, we have divided the corpus into five sets, with each set containing approximately 1000 reviews. Every set was subjected to annotation by a minimum of two annotators, and each one of them worked individually on the same copy of the file. After the annotation of each set, the three annotators discuss the disagreement, divergences, and inconsistencies found in the annotation and fix the

---

[3] https://fr.wikipedia.org/wiki/amazon
[4] https://chrome.google.com/webstore/detail/instant-datascraper/ofaokhiedipichpaobibbnahnkd oiiah

misinterpretations. The final decision is taken by the first author. It is important to mention that in certain cases the first author might require to affect a series of improvements and adjustments in the guideline to enhance the process of annotation.

The process of annotation continued for more than 3 months. The annotators labeled approximately 50 reviews each day where each review contain a number of sentences ranging between 1 (at least) and 30 (at most). For each review text in the corpus, the annotators are required to identify the aspect terms and then assign to them a sentiment polarity. This sentiment polarity can be positive (+1), negative (-1), or neutral (0).

3.3 Annotation Scheme

As discussed above, the annotation process takes place in two steps. In the first step, the annotators are charged to identify the different aspect terms in a specific corpus. For this purpose, we have used the IOB [7] tagging scheme. Each identified aspect term is labeled as being at the beginning (B) or inside (I). The other words (non-aspects) in the corpus are labeled as outside (O). The following example represents the annotation manner of a review using the IOB format.

The	iPhone	is	just	perfect	but	I'm	disappointed	by	the	storage	capacity
O	B	O	O	O	O	O	O	O	O	B	I

As it is shown by the example above, when the aspect is composed of only one term, the tag "B" is given to the aspect term ("**iPhone**"). If the aspect term is composed of more than one term, the annotation scheme gives the first term of the compound aspect the tag "B" ("**storage**") and gives the other words composing the compound aspect term the tag "I" ("**capacity**").

After the identification of aspect terms, we will give each term of them a sentiment polarity. At this level, the label "POS" (if the customer expresses a positive sentiment toward the aspect), "NEG" (if the customer expresses a negative sentiment toward the aspect), or "NEUT" (if the customer mentions the aspect term in the review without expressing any sentiment) is assigned for each aspect term. The following example represents the annotation manner of a review using the POS, NEG, NEUT, and O labels.

The	iPhone	is	just	perfect	but	I'm	disappointed	by	the	storage	capacity
O	B	O	O	O	O	O	O	O	O	B	I
O	POS	O	O	O	O	O	O	O	O	NEG	NEG

3.4 Corpus Statistics

In this section, we provide the results of the statistical study performed on the collected corpus. The FreMPhone corpus contains a total number of words equal to 71461 distributed among 10758 sentences. Statistical information demonstrated in Fig. 1 proves the big variability in the number of words in reviews which ranges between 2 words and 322 words in each review. As it is clearly demonstrated in Fig. 1, the majority of reviews (38%) are composed of less than 50 words. 29% of reviews contained a number of words ranging between 50 and 100 words. The rest of the reviews are distributed as follows, 19% are composed of a number of words that varies between 100 and 200 words, 9% contain a number of words ranging between 200 and 300 words and only 5% are composed of more than 300 words.

After the annotation of our corpus with IOB schema and sentiment labels (POS, NEG, NEUT), we obtained 19257 aspect terms. Figure 2 shows the distribution of these aspect terms according to the number of sentiment classes. 13259 aspect terms are classified as positive, 5084 aspect terms are classified as negative and 914 aspect terms are classified as neutral.

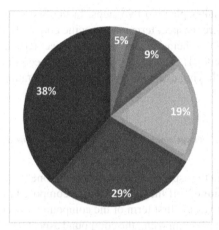 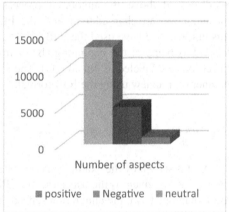

Fig. 1. Distribution of reviews according to the number of words.

Fig. 2. Distribution of aspect terms according to the sentiment classes.

In addition, we present in Fig. 3 the 10 most used aspect terms in the corpus. As is shown, the most three discussed aspect terms in the corpus are "telephone/*telephone*" (appeared 2146 times in the corpus), "produit/*product*" (appeared 1025 times in the corpus), and "prix/*price*" (appeared 979 times in the corpus).

4   CBCF: A New Architecture for AE and SC

As discussed above, the ABSA task is divided into two subtasks: Aspect Extraction (AE), and Aspect Sentiment Classification (ASC). To solve these subtasks, we propose a new neural network-based architecture "CBCF" which is a combination of Bi-LSTM, CNN, and CRF models. As shown in Fig. 4, the proposed CBCF architecture consists of four main components: the embedding layer, the CNN model, the Bi-LSTM model, and the CRF model. In the embedding layer, the Word2Vec [8] model is used to create word embedding vectors. This model was trained on 20 000 mobile phone reviews collected from Amazon Website. After that, a CNN [9] model is employed to select features useful for the classification. This model is applied due to its capacity to detect proficient local features. However, this model still enables to capture of distant information related to the target word. For that, we applied the Bi-LSTM model, which is capable of learning long-term dependencies. This model takes as input the features extracted by the CNN model and produces new features as output, incorporating contextual information of the target word. Subsequently, the generated features are incorporated into the CRF [11] model in order to detect the label of a given word. This model takes into account the dependencies between labels, where it exploits the neighboring labels to identify the current label of a target word.

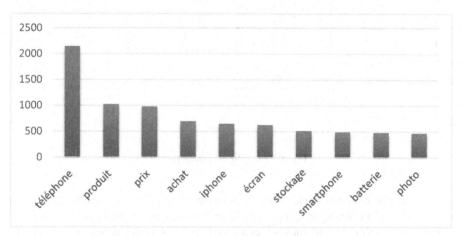

Fig. 3. The top 10 most used aspect terms in the corpus.

Embedding Layer. The objective of this step is to transform the words contained in the corpus into numerical vectors which are comprehensible by the deep learning algorithms. In fact, many methods are used to achieve this purpose in ABSA-related studies such as the One-hot encoding method, the Term Frequency-Inverse Document Frequency (TF-IDF), etc. However, the main issue with such methods is related to their inability to capture contextual information which is important information in the ABSA task. For that, we employed in this study the word embeddings method. This method represents the words that appear in a similar context with word vectors relatively close.

Many models have been developed to create embeddings of words (such as Glove, ELMO, etc.). In this study, we employed the Word2Vec model. Similar to any model that is characterized by neural networks-based architecture, the Word2Vec model needs to be trained on a huge mass of information to give reliable word vectors that take into consideration contextual information. In fact, there are numerous publicly available word embedding models that have been trained on a big number of data collected from several sources (e.g. Twitter, Wikipedia, etc.). However, these models are inefficient in our task since they have been trained on multi-domain corpora and not on a mobile phone corpus. For that, we used 20 000 mobile phone Amazon reviews to train the Word2Vec model for both AE and SC tasks. Each word in the corpus is represented as a 350-dimensional vector.

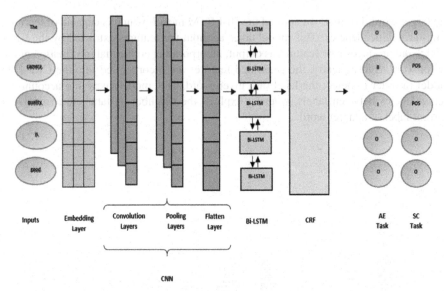

Fig. 4. The CBCF architecture.

Convolution Neural Network. The Convolution Neural Network (CNN) model is a multi-layers deep learning model presented for the first time by [9] to perform the task of forms recognition. In this study, we employed the CNN model in order to extract efficient local features. This model is composed of convolution layer (s), pooling layer(s), and flatten layer. In the first step, by receiving word embedding vectors from the embedding layer, it employs convolution operations to generate feature maps. This operation multiplies (or convolves) the matrix representation "M" by another convolution matrix (or filter) to produce a feature map. After that, the CNN model uses a pooling layer in order to decrease the number of parameters. Finally, the CNN model utilizes a flatten layer to convert the high-dimensional vectors, into one-dimensional vectors.

In this step, we used two convolution layers with 200 feature maps, the activation function ReLU, two pooling layers, each with a pool size equal to 200, and a flatten layer.

Long Short-Term Memory. The Long Short-Term Memory (LSTM) [10] is an artificial neural network model created to treat sequential data. It is an RNN model with a supplementary cell of memory. This model has been designed to solve the problems of vanishing gradients and long-term dependencies learning faced by traditional RNNs. For that, the main advantage of using LSTM lies in its ability to maintain long-term memory and control the flow of information within the network. The LSTM model follows the mechanism of forward propagation and treats the input sequence in one direction from left to right. It considers only the information coming from the previous units to detect the new outputs. In this study, we used a bidirectional LSTM (Bi-LSTM) model which is an enhanced version of the LSTM model. This model predicts the label of a word based on the information coming from the previous units (forward propagation) and the next units (backward propagation).

The Bi-LSTM model is composed of a series of Bi-LSTM neurons, each of which contains a memory cell, and three gates: an input gate, an output gate, and a forget gate. The input gate determines which information must be conveyed to the memory. The output gate chooses the value of the next node. The forget gate decides which information should be deleted.

At instant t, the Bi-LSTM model takes as input the one-dimensional vectors outputted by the flatten layer and produces new vectors of words that take into consideration the long-term dependencies between the words and the local information. These newly produced vectors are incorporated into the CRF model.

In this step, we used a Bi-LSTM model composed of 300 neurons.

Conditional Random Field. The Conditional Random Field (CRF) [11] is a statistical model that is often used for sequence labeling tasks, such as named entity recognition, sentiment analysis, etc. The CRF model assigns a label to each word of a sequence based on a set of parameters, known as transition parameters, to model the probability of a label transition from one word to the other. The CRF model has been used in multiple ABSA-related studies ([12, 13]) and it has achieved good classification results.

At instant t, the outputs of the Bi-LSTM model are passed to the CRF model in order to classify a given word. This model utilizes the interdependence or contextual connection between neighboring tags to predict the final output labels.

5 Experiments and Results

In this section, two experiments were conducted. The first experiment was realized to evaluate the performance of the proposed CBCF architecture for the Aspect Extraction (AE) task and Sentiment Classification (SC) task, as well as the reliability of the FreM-Phone corpus. However, in the second experiment, the performance of the Word2Vec model was assessed in comparison to the FastText model. This experiment aims to detect which model is more suitable to construct word embeddings for AE and SC tasks.

To achieve the experiments, we divided the constructed FreMPhone corpus into 80% for the training phase and 20% for the test phase. The performance of the models was evaluated using three metrics which are Precision (P), Recall (R), and F1-score (F1).

5.1 Experiment 1: Evaluation of the CBCF Architecture

As presented in Table 3, the best classification performances were achieved by the proposed CBCF architecture with an F-measure value equal to 95.97% where it surpassed the LSTM model (91.07%) by approximately 4%, the CNN model (67.14%) by approximately 28%, and the CRF model (72.95%) by approximately 23%.

Table 4 summarized the results obtained by the CBCF architecture and the other deep-learning models for the Sentiment Classification (SC) task on the FreMPhone. As shown in Table 4, we obtained promising results in the SC task where the best F-measure value was obtained after the use of the proposed CBCF (96.35%). This architecture overrode the LSTM model (with approximately 6%), the CNN model (with approximately 7%), and the CRF model (with approximately 40%) for the FreMPhone corpus.

The obtained F-measure (Table 3 and Table 4), using the CBCF architecture significantly surpassed the CNN, Bi-LSTM, and CRF models. So, the combination of CNN, Bi-LSTM, and CRF models gives better results than using each one of them separately and enhances obviously the AE and SC tasks. In addition, the obtained results prove the reliability of our created FreMPhone corpus.

Table 3. Results of the FreMPhone evaluation in the AE task using the CBCF architecture and other models.

Corpus	Model	Aspect Extraction Task		
		Precision	Recall	F-measure
FreMPhone	**LSTM**	87.76%	94.65%	91.07%
	CNN	76.11%	60.14%	67.19%
	CRF	81.90%	65.76%	72.95%
	CBCF	97.95%	94.08%	95.97%

Table 4. Results of the FreMPhone evaluation in the SC task using the CBCF architecture and other models.

Corpus	Model	Sentiment Classification Task		
		Precision	Recall	F-measure
FreMPhone	**LSTM**	91.62%	88.78%	90.17%
	CNN	83.81%	95.93%	89.46%
	CRF	61.14%	51.29%	55.78%
	CBCF	93.10%	99.83%	96.35%

5.2 Experiment 2: Comparison of the Word2Vec Model with the FastText Model for AE and SC Tasks

In this experiment, we compared the accuracy of the Word2Vec used model with the Fast-Text [14] model with the aim of determining which model is more suitable for building word embeddings for the AE task and SC task. FastText [14] is a model that utilizes the skip-gram model to generate word embeddings. Each word is transformed into a group of n-grams, and each n-gram is assigned a vector representation. The embedding of a word is obtained by summing up the vectors of all its character n-grams. This method allows FastText to handle out-of-vocabulary words and morphological variations by breaking them down into sub-words and utilizing the information from the sub-words to generate a vector representation for the word. Figure 5 highlights the F-measure results achieved by the CBCF model when employing the Word2Vec and FastText models in the AE task and SC task on the FreMPone corpus. As it is clear in Fig. 5, the FastText model achieved much better results than the Word2Vec model for the AE task. This result aligns with the nature of the task as it aids in better learning the context information of the aspects within the review. Also, unlike the Word2Vec model, FastText has the capability to create representations for words that did not appear in the training data which can improve mainly the process of aspects detection. However, we remarked that the Word2Vec model achieved better results than the FastText model in the SA task. These findings can be explained for many reasons. Firstly, the Word2Vec model captures the semantic and syntactic relationships between words, which can be beneficial for the detection of opinion words describing the aspect terms, and thus the SC task. Also, Word2Vec's embeddings are based on the co-occurrence statistics of words in the training data, which can better detect the sentiment of a word based on the words that appear in the same context.

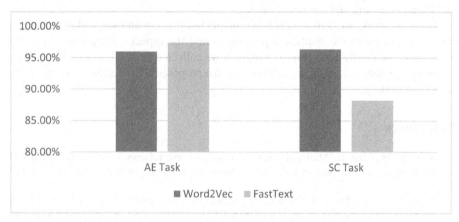

Fig. 5. Illustration of FreMPhone corpus F-measure results using Word2Vec and FastText representation models.

6 Conclusion

In this paper, we presented the French mobile phone corpus FreMPhone constructed for the ABSA task. This corpus was collected from the Amazon website and contains 5217 mobile phone reviews. In this study, we described the process followed in the collection and the annotation of the corpus. Also, we provided a statistical study of the corpus including the number of aspects found, and their distribution according to the positive, negative, and neutral classes. In addition, we proposed a new architecture "CBCF" to evaluate the FreMPhone corpus constructed. This architecture combines the strength of the deep learning models, namely CNN and Bi-LSTM, with the machine learning model CRF. This architecture surpassed the deep learning models and achieved very encouraging results reach to 95.97% for the AE task and 96.35% for the SC task. The obtained results validate the effectiveness and high performance of our proposed architecture in accurately extracting aspect terms and their associated sentiment. Furthermore, they demonstrate that combining deep learning models with machine learning models yields superior results compared to using each model separately. Deep learning models excel at capturing complex patterns and relationships in textual data, while machine learning models provide a structured framework for labeling and sequence tagging tasks. Moreover, we compared the performance of the word embedding models namely, Word2Vec and FastText. Findings show that the FastText constructs more pertinent embedding vectors for the AE task, while the Word2Vec model ensures a better SA. These outcomes prove that the choice of a suitable word embedding model can have a significant impact on the performance of aspect-based sentiment analysis tasks.

Overall, this research contributes valuable insights into the field of ABSA, providing a comprehensive corpus, an effective architecture, and a comparative analysis of word embedding models. These findings pave the way for future advancements in aspect-based sentiment analysis and hold significant potential for various applications in natural language processing and sentiment mining.

In future work, we will enhance the annotation process and we will annotate the corpus according to the implicit aspect terms and the aspect's categories. Also, we will extend the FreMPhone corpus, with reviews collected from other domains such as restaurants, hotels, etc. Also, we will improve the proposed CBCF architecture by using BERT embedding.

References

1. Minqing, H., Bing, L.: Mining and summarizing customer reviews. In: 10th ACM SIGKDD International Conference on Knowledge Discovery and Data Mining ACM, pp. 168–177 (2004)
2. Wang, H., Lu, Y., Zhai, C.: Latent aspect rating analysis on review text data: A rating regression approach. In: Proceedings of the 16th ACM SIGKDD International Conference on Knowledge Discovery and Data Mining (KDD 2010), pp. 783–792. Washington, US (2010)
3. Samaneh, M., Martin, E.: Opinion Digger: An unsupervised opinion miner from unstructured product reviews. In: 19th ACM International Conference on Information and Knowledge Management (CIKM 2010), pp. 1825–1828 (2010)
4. Pontiki, M., et al.: Semeval-2014 task 4: Aspect based sentiment analysis. In: ProWorkshop on Semantic Evaluation. Association for Computational Linguistics, pp. 20–31
5. Lark, J., Morin, E., Saldarriaga, S.: CANÉPHORE: un corpus français pour la fouille d'opinion ciblée. In : 22e conférence sur le Traitement Automatique des Langues Naturelles (2015)
6. Pontiki, M., et al.: Semeval-2016 task 5: Aspect based sentiment analysis. In: ProWorkshop on Semantic Evaluation Association for Computational Linguistics, pp.19–30 (2016)
7. Ramshaw, L., Marcus, M.: Text chunking using transformation-based learning. Natural language processing using very large corpora, pp 157–176 (1999)
8. Mikolov, T., Chen, K., Corrado, G., Dean, J.: Efficient estimation of word representations in vector space. arXiv preprint arXiv:1301.3781 (2013)
9. Fukushima, K., Sei, M.: Neocognitron: A self-organizing neural network model for a mechanism of visual pattern recognition. In: Competition and cooperation in neural nets, pp. 267–285. Springer, Berlin, Heidelberg (1982)
10. Graves, A.: Long short-term memory. Supervised sequence labeling with recurrent neural networks, pp. 37–45 (2012)
11. Lafferty, J., McCallum, A., Pereira, F.: Conditional random fields: Probabilistic models for segmenting and labeling sequence data (2001)

12. Heinrich, T., Marchi, F.: Teamufpr at absapt 2022: Aspect extraction with crf and bert. In: Proceedings of the Iberian Languages Evaluation Fórum (IberLEF 2022), co-located with the 38th Conference of the Spanish Society for Natural Language Processing, Online. CEUR (2022)
13. Lei, S., Xu, H., Liu, B.: Lifelong learning crf for supervised aspect extraction. arXiv preprint arXiv:1705.00251 (2017)
14. Joulin, A., Grave, E., Bojanowski, P., Mikolov, T.: Bag of tricks for efficient text classification. arXiv preprint arXiv:1607.01759 (2016)

OTSummarizer an Optimal Transport Based Approach for Extractive Text Summarization

Imen Tanfouri[1] and Fethi Jarray[1,2]

[1] LIMTIC Laboratory, UTM University, Tunis, Tunisia
fjarray@gmail.com
[2] Higher Institute of Computer Science of Medenine, Medenine, Tunisia

Abstract. Automatic text summarization (ATS) consists of automatically generating a coherent and concise summary of the original document. It is a fundamental task in Natural Language Processing (NLP) with various applications, including news aggregation and social media analysis. The most recent approaches are based on transformer architecture, such as BERT and its different descendants. However, these promising approaches face input length limitations, such as 512 tokens for the BERT-base model. To alleviate these issues, we propose an Optimal Transport (OT) based approach for ATS called OTSummarizer. It represents a sentence by a distribution over words and then applies an OT solver to get similarities between the original document and a candidate summary. We design a Beam Search (BS) strategy to efficiently explore the summary search space and get the optimal summary. We develop theoretical results to justify the use of OT in ATS. Empirically, we evaluate the model on the CNN Daily Mail and PubMed datasets, ensuring a ROUGE score of 41.66%. The experimental results show that the OTSummarizer performs better than previous extractive summarization state-of-the-art approaches in terms of ROUGE-1, ROUGE-2 and ROUGE-L scores.

Keywords: Automatic text summarization · Natural language processing · Optimal transport · Deep learning

1 Introduction

Automatic text summarization (ATS) is a fundamental task in natural language processing (NLP) that aims to generate a shorter version of the original text while preserving its coherence and meaning. It gained a lot of interest in the last years due to its large applications in various domains such as social media summarization, customer feedback summarization, and medical summarization. Additionally, ATS reduces reading time, accelerates the process of information retrieval, and is less biased than human summarizers.

Automatic text summarization techniques are continually evolving, with recent advancements in deep learning and neural networks leading to more accurate and sophisticated summarization models. Despite these advancements, text

© The Author(s), under exclusive license to Springer Nature Switzerland AG 2023
N. T. Nguyen et al. (Eds.): ICCCI 2023, CCIS 1864, pp. 250–261, 2023.
https://doi.org/10.1007/978-3-031-41774-0_20

summarization remains a challenging task, and further research is needed to improve its accuracy and effectiveness.

ATS can be categorized into abstractive [18,19,21] and extractive [14,20] methods, depending on the creative way (see Fig. 1). The former generates a shorter text by distilling the relevant information from the original document. The latter aims to extract the salient sentences while respecting a length constraint and avoiding redundancy.

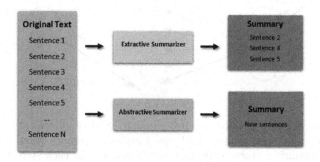

Fig. 1. Extractive summarization extracts a subset of sentences from the original document. Abstractive text summarization generates a short and concise summary of the source document.

Each summarization category has its advantages and disadvantages. Even if abstractive approaches gain in flexibility of generating the summary, they suffer from high computation due to the generation process and hallucination where a model may generate factually invalid statements [11]. In contrast, extractive approaches are less time-consuming and more efficient, and more structured, especially in formal writing such as the legal domain. However, they are prone to redundancy where similar sentences are extracted. In this paper, we are concerned with extractive summarization, and we aim to fix its issues by proposing an Optimal Transport (OT) scoring method that combines local and global contexts. Figure 2 provides an overview of the proposed method applied on a toy source document. The contribution of this manuscript can be summarized as follows:

1. Propose OTsummarizer a hybrid approach of BEAM Search, BERT embedding and Optimal transport for single document extractive summary.
2. Use optimal transport as a loss function for training, and theoretically show its suitability for the summarization task.
3. Validate OTsummarizer on the CNN/Daily Mail and PubMed datasets and achieve state-of-the-art performance.

The remainder of this paper is organized as follows. Section 2 reviews the relevant work on ATS. Section 3 presents our proposed method for ATS. Section 4 describes the experiments and results. Section 5 concludes this paper and discusses some future extensions.

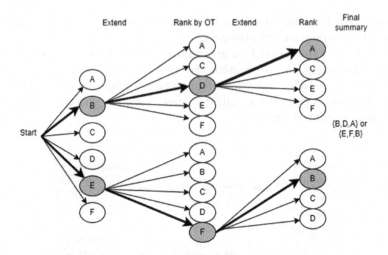

Fig. 2. OTSummarizer applied on toy example. Source document is the set of (A,B,C,D,E,F) sentences, Beam Search size equals 2, summary length equals 3 sentences. OTSummarizer starts with an empty summary. In each step, the algorithm extends the current summary by the sentences that are not yet included, then compute the optimal transport between the candidate summary and the source document and finally keep the two (beam width = 2) best summaries. For example, in the second steps, the best summaries are (B,D) and (E,F).

2   Related Work

Extractive summarization methods can be classified into two approaches, namely, machine learning and combinatorial optimization according to the stages of using datasets. The former uses the datasets in both levels of sentence representation and selection, whereas the latter uses datasets for representation and implements an optimization strategy for selection.

The most recent machine learning approaches are based on the transformer framework and its descendants. Nada et al. [1] proposed a BERT-based clustering approach by using BERT as word embedding. Finally, sentences near the centroid are chosen for summarization. The main limitation of this approach is that sentences are encoded separately with fixed-size embeddings. This issue was leveraged by Yang Liu [2] who proposed BERTSUM that inputs the entire sequence of texts and outputs the embedding of each sentence. BERTSUM handles multiple sentences by inserting a [CLS] token before each sentence, contrary to the original BERT model, which is limited to two sentences [3,4]. LEAD [5] presents a neural model for single document summarization based on joint extraction and syntactic compression. They extract the sentences from the document and then evaluate possible constituent-based compression units to produce the final compression summary. Zhong et al. [6] proposed MatchSUM as the first summary-level method for extractive text summarization. They cast the summarization task as a semantic text matching task instead of the commonly used sequence-labeling model. They implemented a Siamese-based neural network to evaluate the semantic similarity between the original document and a candidate summary. Tanfouri and Jarray [12,13] proposed GASUM model by combining Bidirectional Encoder Representations from Transformers (BERT) and a Genetic Algorithm (GA).

Combinatorial optimization approaches rely on sentence embedding and ranking scenarios to extract the top relevant sentences. Bouscarrat et al. [7] proposed a clustering-based approach by selecting the sentences with the closest embeddings to the document embedding and learning a transformation of the document embedding to maximize the similarity between the generated and golden summaries. Zheng and Lapata [8] proposed an unsupervised system using pre-trained language models to compute sentence similarities to construct a sentence graph and select important sentences based on their centrality. Srivastava, Ridam, et al. [9] proposed a combination of clustering with topic modeling to reduce topic bias. They used Latent Dirichlet Allocation (LDA) for topic modeling and employed K-Medoids clustering for summary generation. The approach was evaluated on three datasets-Wikihow, CNN/DailyMail, and the DUC2002 corpus. Tang et al. [10] formulated the extractive summarization task as an optimal transport problem from the original document distribution to the semantic distribution of the candidate summary, namely OTExtSUM. They applied a beam search strategy to find the lowest-cost transportation summary. OTExtSUM have achieved state-of-the-art among combinatorial based approach for extractive summarization

Generally, deep learning approaches are more accurate and more time-consuming than combinatorial optimization approaches because they train huge models with billions of parameters. However, combinatorial approaches can be generalized to others because they depend on the language only on the step of sentence encoding. For this purpose, we propose a novel extractive summarization approach that takes advantage of the progress in language modeling and the promising optimal transport metric to quantify similarities between candidate and original summaries.

3 Proposed Methodology

We start with a reminder of the optimal transport problem, TF-IDF vectorization, BERT embedding, and Beam Search because they are the cornerstone of our model.

3.1 Optimal Transport

The optimal transport (OT) problem consists in minimizing the cost or distance of transporting a given amount of mass between two probability distributions or measures, subject to mass conservation constraints (see Fig. 3). In machine learning, OT is used as distribution's similarity measurement metric.

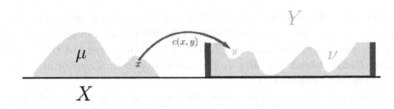

Fig. 3. Optimal transport problem. Transform the initial distribution X into a final distribution Y using a minimal cost. OTSummarizer adopts the Euclidean distance between the BERT words embeddings of every pair of tokens x in the candidate summary and x in the original document.

Formally, let X (e.g. a candidate summary) be an m-dimensional distribution, i.e. a positive vector of size m (e.g. m is the number of different tokens) whose elements add up to 1. Similarly, let Y (e.g. the source document) be an n-dimensional distribution. Let $c(x_i, y_j)$ be the cost of transporting a unit of mass from position $x_i \in X$ (e.g., i-th word) to $y_j \in Y$. A transportation plan is a $m \times n$ matrix π such that π_{ij} represents the amount of mass transported from x_i to y_j. We observe that the transportation plan can be equivalently defined as a joint distribution with marginal distributions equal to the original distributions. Mathematically, OT can be formulated as the following optimization problem (1).

$$W(X,Y) = \min_{\pi} \quad \langle \pi, C \rangle = \sum_{i=1}^{m}\sum_{j=1}^{n} C_{ij}\pi_{ij}$$

$$\text{s.t.} \qquad \sum_{j=1}^{n} \pi_{ij} = X_i, \ \forall\, i \tag{1}$$

$$\sum_{i=1}^{m} \pi_{ij} = Y_j, \ \forall\, j$$

$$\pi_{ij} \geq 0 \quad i = 1,\ldots m; j = 1\ldots, n$$

In Eq. (1), the objective function is the total transport cost. The decisions variables are the transport plans π. The first constraint ensures that a feasible transport plan pushes forward the distribution X into Y while the second constraint guarantees the conservation of the transportation flow, i.e., it does not lose or gain mass while transport. The last constraint is known as the non-negativity constraint and ensures that all plans are non-negative. OT is intrinsically a linear program, but it can be efficiently solved by a more advanced solver, such as Entropic regularization OT solver [15] to obtain a more stable solution. $W(X,Y)$ is also known as Wasserstein distance between the distributions X and Y.

3.2   TFIDF Vectorization

TF-IDF (Term Frequency-Inverse Document Frequency) is a popular technique used in information retrieval and natural language processing to transform textual data into numerical features that can be used in machine learning models. The basic idea behind TF-IDF vectorization is to weigh each word in a document by its importance, which is a function of how frequently it appears in the document and how rare it is in the entire corpus of documents. Formally, given a document preprocessed by tokenization and stop word removal. The term frequency TF_{ij} is defined as the number of times a word i appears in a sentence, j normalized by the total number of words in the sentence. For a given document, the inverse document frequency IDF_i refers to the log of the total number of sentences in the document divided by the number of sentences containing the word i. $TFIDF(i,j)$ is defined as the product of the term frequency $TFij$ and the inverse document frequency IDF_i. Therefore, a sentence s_i is represented by a normalized vector of TFIDF values of its terms, where each value is divided by the total sum of the values. Normalization is necessary to ensure that all sentences are represented by a distribution vector of length equal to the vocabulary size. The distribution of a document is equal to the average of its sentence distribution.

In the subsequent, we denote by $TFIDF_S$ and $TFIDF_D$ the TFIDF representation of the candidate summary and the original document, respectively.

3.3   BERT Language Model

BERT (Bidirectional Encoder Representations from Transformers) [16] is a pre-trained NLP model based on the transformer architecture, which is a type of deep neural network designed to process sequential data, such as text. The transformer is composed of an encoder-decoder architecture.

Unlike conventional NLP models that treat text in a unidirectional way, BERT is a bidirectional model that takes into account the entire context of a word or phrase by looking at both the words that come before and after it in a sentence. Hence, it can better understand the meaning and context of words and sentences and therefore produce more accurate results.

BERT is pre-trained on a massive amount of text data, using a process called masked language modeling, in which certain words are randomly replaced with a [MASK] token, and the model must predict the original word based on the context. BERT is also trained on a task called next sentence prediction, in which the model is given two sentences and must predict whether they are sequential or not. It has achieved state-of-the-art performance on a wide range of NLP tasks and is widely used in industry and academia. There are many BERT versions trained in various languages with different sizes of transformer block fineness.

3.4   Beam Search

Beam Search (BS) is a heuristic search algorithm used to explore the space of possible solutions and find the best possible solution. In Beam Search, a set of candidate solutions, known as the "beam", is maintained at each step of the search process. The beam is initialized with a single candidate solution, which is usually the empty sequence or a special symbol that represents the start of the sequence. At each step, the beam is expanded by generating a set of possible next steps for each candidate solution in the beam. The candidate solutions are then ranked according to a scoring function and the top candidates are then selected to form the new beam for the next step. This process is repeated until a stopping criterion is met, such as reaching a maximum length. The final candidate solution is typically the one with the highest score in the final beam.

The size of the beam (B) determines the compromise between computation efficiency and solution quality. A larger beam size allows for more exploration and a higher-quality solution, but it is a time-consuming and memory-intensive process. However, a smaller beam size is faster but may get stuck in a local optimum. In particular, Beam Search is equivalent to hill climbing when $B = 1$ and equivalent to breadth-first search for a very large beam size.

3.5 OTSummarizer

Figure 2 shows the architecture of the proposed system applied to a toy source document with five sentences. Globally, the OTSummarizer consists of exploring the summary space using the beam search strategy to find the closest summary to the original document. The full description is given by Algorithm 15. The procedure $ExtendCandidates(\mathbb{S})$ extends a generated summary $\mathbb{S}$ by sentences that are not yet selected. The main block BeamSearch (K = length of desired summary, B = beam width, D = source document) starts with an empty summary, then iteratively extend the current summaries and retain the best B summaries.

Each generated summary is scored (line 13), by solving an OT problem between the candidate summary and the original document. Figure 4 illustrates the scoring of candidates summaries. It involves four steps. First, we apply a word embedding technique (line 12). In this paper, we adopt a TFIDF vectorization strategy. Second, define a transportation cost between every pair of tokens $x_i \in S$ and $x_j \in D$. In this paper, we adopt the Euclidean distance between two embeddings of the tokens. However, we check different word embeddings such as BERT and its descendants. Third, we call an OT solver to solve the model (1) and compute the distance between the summary, S, and the original document D (line 13). Finally, we implement BS as an exploration strategy to find the summary having the minimum distance from the original document (loop in line 10).

Let's develop some theoretical results concerning optimal transport-based extractive summarizers.

Lemma 1 (Combination of input distributions). *Let X_1 and X_2 be two initial distributions, Y be the final distribution and $Z = \alpha X_1 + (1 - \alpha)X_2$ then*

i) $W(Z,Y) \leq \alpha W(X_1,Y) + (1 - \alpha)W(Y)$
ii) The combination of input distributions is better than the worst distribution.

Algorithm 1. OTSummarizer an extractive text summarizer. ExtendSummary($\mathbb{S}$), for every candidate summary, generates all possible extensions by a sentence that is not yet included. Beam Search iteratively extends a summaries population and takes the best B summaries. The algorithm returns the best summary found so far.

Input: D: the original, B the number of sentences and K: the beam width.
Output: S^* the extractive summary.

1: Compute the cost matrix between word pairs, C
2: Compute the document's TFIDF encoding $TFIDF_D$;
3: **function** EXTENDSUMMARY($\mathbb{S}$) // generate all possible extensions
4:     $Extend = \emptyset$
5:     **for** $S, s; S \in \mathbb{S}, s \in D, s \notin S$ **do**
6:         $Extend = Extend \cup (S \oplus s)$ // extend S by sentence s
7:     **return** $Extend$
8: **function** BEAMSEARCH(K, B, D) // main function
9:     $\mathbb{S} = \emptyset, k = 0$
10:     **for** k =1 to K **do** // iteratively append a new sentence
11:         $\mathbb{S}$=ExtendCandidates($\mathbb{S}$)
12:         Compute TF-IDF encoding TF_S of $S \in \mathbb{S}$;
13:         Compute $W(TFIDF_D, TFIDF_S)$ // summary scoring
14:         $\mathbb{S}$= the best B summaries with the lowest $W(TFIDF_D, TFIDF_S)$
15:     **return** $S^* = \underset{S \in \mathbb{S}}{argmin} W(TFIDF_D, TFIDF_S)$

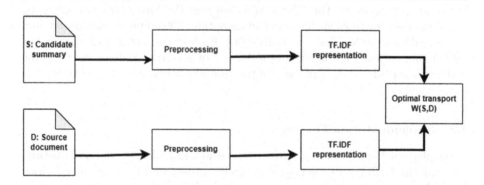

Fig. 4. Computation of distance between a candidate summary and the source document. Firstly, both summary and source are preprocessed, then their Tf.IDFs representations are computed. Finally, the optimal transport cost between the representations is computed.

Proof. i) Let π_1 be the optimal transport plan from X_1 to Y, π_2 be the optimal transport plan from X_2 to Y and $\pi = \alpha\pi_1 + (1-\alpha)\pi_2$. Firstly, we note that π is a feasible solution to $OP(Z, Y)$ because it satisfies both constraints of (1). Moreover, $\langle \pi, C \rangle = \langle \alpha\pi_1 + (1-\alpha)\pi_2, C \rangle = \alpha \langle \pi_1, C \rangle + (1-\alpha) \langle \pi_2, C \rangle = \alpha W(X_1, Y) + (1-\alpha)W(X_2, Y)$. The last equality is due to the fact that π_1 and π_2 are optimal transport plans. Finally, since OT is a minimization problem and π is a feasible solution, we deduce that $W(Z,Y) \leq \langle \pi, C \rangle = \alpha W(X_1, Y) + (1-\alpha)W(X_2, Y)$

ii) From i), we conclude $W(Z,Y) \leq \max(W(X_1, Y), (W(X_2, Y))$. ∎

The following theorem justifies the use of OT in extractive summarization, where a candidate summary can be seen as a fusion of many summaries.

Theorem 1 (Combination of summaries). *The combination of summaries is better than the worst summary.*

Proof. Le $S1$ and $S2$ be two candidate summaries with sizes $n1$ and $n1$, respectively. They are concatenated into a summary S that has a distribution $Z = \alpha X_1 + (1-\alpha)X_2$ where X_1 and X_2 are the distribution of $S1$ and $S2$, respectively, and $\alpha = \frac{n1}{n1+n2}$. According to the previous lemma, the cost of S is less than the maximum cost of $S1$ and $S2$. ∎

4   Experiments and Results

In this section, we describe the datasets used for text summarization and provide an overview of OTSummariser's implementation strategy.

4.1   Summarization Dataset

We run experiments on the CNN/DailyMail and PubMed extractive datasets. The former is a large English dataset of more than 300,000 news articles written by journalists at CNN and the Daily Mail. Each document is paired with 3–4 golden summaries. PubMed [17] is a dataset of scientific articles in which the abstract is considered the summary of the ground truth and the rest of the article the original document.

4.2   Implementation Details

We implement Beam Search strategy with beam width of 10. In our architecture, we used the BERT base case model which consists of 12 transformer blocks, 768 hidden blocks and 12 self-attention heads. We solve the optimal transport problem (OT) with an entropic regularization OT solver [15]. Figure 5 illustrates an example of extractive summary on CNN dataset where the selected sentences are highlighted.

The machine-generated summaries are often evaluated using the well-known ROUGE (for Recall-Oriented Understudy for Gisting Evaluation) metric. It is a set of metrics, including ROUGE-1, ROUGE-2 and ROUGE-L, that relies on precision and recall by counting the number of overlapping n-grams between the golden summary and the machine summary. A higher ROUGE score indicates that the machine summary has captured the silent content of the reference summary. ROUGE-1 calculates the recall of unigrams in the generated summary with respect to the unigrams in the reference summary. ROUGE-2 calculates the recall of bigrams in the generated summary with regard to the bigrams in the golden summary. ROUGE-L measures the recall of longest common subsequence (LCS) in the candidate summary with respect to the LCSs in the golden summary.

Table 1 compares the performance of OTSummarizer and state-of-the-art approaches such as LEAD and OTEXSum over CNN/DailyMail and PubMed datasets. The experimental result shows that the OTSummarizer outperforms by a large margin OTExtSum according to ROUGE-1 (R-1), ROUGE-2 (R-2) and ROUGE-L (R-L) metrics. OTSummarizer achives a 41.66%. ROUGE-1 evaluation score on CNN dataset and 43.06%. ROUGE-1 score on PubMEd dataset. It was shown that OTExtSUm claims achieves state-of-the-art results in combinatorial based approaches for extractive summarization [10]. Besides, it also outperforms LEAD method, which is a machine learning based approach. Moreover, OTSummarizer is faster and more intelligent in the search for the optimal summary. This outperformance is due to the use of BERT as a word enconcoding, TFIDF as a vectorization scheme, Optimal Transport as a candidate summary scoring function, and Beam search as an exploration strategy that efficiently explores the summary search space to find near-optimal summaries. Indeed, the search space is exponential in the number of sentences in the source document, and the exploration strategy should be chosen carefully to avoid discarding some areas or searching exhaustively for the best summary.

Table 1. Comparison of the numerical results of OTSummarizer, LEAD and OTEXSum on CNN/Daily Mail and PubMEd data sets using ROUGE-1 (R-1), ROUGE-2 (R-2) and ROUGE-L (R-L) metrics.

Dataset	CNN/DailyMail			PubMed		
Model	R-1	R-2	R-L	R-1	R-2	R-L
LEAD	40.43	17.62	**36.67**	34.00	8.60	27.10
OTExtSum	34.5	12.8	27.8	39.80	13.60	32.30
OTSummarizer	**41.66**	**19.82**	33.58	**43.06**	**20.33**	**35.41**

Input Text: CNN/Daily Mail dataset

Ronda Rousey recorded the fastest-ever finish in a UFC title fight as she submitted Cat Zingano after just 14 seconds in Los Angeles. Rousey was expected to face the toughest examination of her reign as bantamweight champion against the unbeaten Zingano. But having avoided a flying knee in the opening seconds, Rousey took her opponent down and set to work trying to execute her trademark armbar. Scroll down to watch Rousey beat Zingano in 14 seconds. Ronda Rousey manoeuvres herself into position to submit Cat Zingano after 14 seconds of their fight. Rousey attempts to lock in her trademark arm bar finish as she defended her bantamweight title. Rousey consoles Zingano after her stunning victory inside 14 seconds at the Staples Center in Los Angeles. Rousey grapples with Zingano before celebrating in the Octagon after her record-breaking victory. Ronda Rousey bt Cat Zingano via sub. Holly Holm bt Raquel Pennington via KO. Jake Ellenberger bt Josh Koscheck via sub. Alan Jouban bt Richard Walsh via KO. Tony Ferguson bt Gleison Tibau via sub. Roan Carneiro bt Mark Munoz via sub. Roman Salazar bt Norifumi Yamamoto N/C. Tim Means bt Dhiego Lima via TKO. Derrick Lewis bt Ruan Potts via TKO. Valmir Lazaro bt James Krause via SD. Masio Fullen bt Alexander Torres via SD. Rousey had landed on her head but the champion gracefully flipped Zingano on to up and manoeuvred swiftly into position to wrench Zingano's arm grotesquely. Rousey forced the challenger to tap out. 'We were expecting that she might come out and do something flying at me right away,' Rousey said. 'That's not usually how you land an armbar at that angle, but it works. It was a lot like judo transitions, where you scramble the second you hit the ground. 'I made that up on the fly, to be honest.' But it was kind of funny: We were going toward the ground, and I kind of reverted back to judo mode and was thinking. 'Don't touch your back. It's a point.' 'That's where the acrobatic thing came from, was thinking about not touching your back in judo.' It was hard to work out who was more stunned, Zingano or the sell-out 17,000-crowd at the Staples Center. 'She's really good ... but that wouldn't happen again,' the beaten challenger said. 'It was a knee and then a throw and then a scramble, and then she was wrapped around my arm. I got caught. I was ready to do a million different things. I planned on getting in a fist fight tonight.' Zingano looks in pain as Rousey moves herself into position to execute the armbar finish. Rousey celebrates as Zingano is attended to by the referee following her early defeat in Los Angeles. Dublin featherweight Conor McGregor (left) and light-heavyweight champion Jon Jones were in attendance. Former UFC heavyweight champion Brock Lesnar was Octagon side as Rousey eased to victory. For the first time in the promotion's history, two women's fights headlined a pay-per-view event as boxer Holly Holm made her debut with a split-decision victory over Raquel Pennington in the co-main event. Middleweight champion Chris Weidman originally was scheduled to fight Vitor Belfort but had to withdraw injured. Zingano had earned her title shot two years ago with an upset victory over Miesha Tate, but was forced to wait after suffering a serious knee injury before she was hit by her estranged husband's suicide last year. Holm, meanwhile, ended an 11-year pro boxing career to concentrate on MMA two years ago but looked far from the complete package against Pennington. Both fighters landed big shots during a stand-up fight, and while Holm finished with a bloody nose, she left Pennington with a swollen left eye. UFC Octagon girls Vanessa Hanson, Brittney Palmer, Arianny Celeste and Chrissy Blair pose for pictures. Vanessa and Brittney introduce the first round of the respective fights during UFC 184 in Los Angeles. Holly Holm (right) made a winning debut with a split-decision victory over Raquel Pennington. Holm moved from a boxing career to mixed martial arts and remains unbeaten. Pennington lands a left hand on Holm as she battled hard only to lose by split decision. Actresses Mandy Moore (left) and Minka Kelly pose for a photograph during the UFC 184 event. Vin Diesel was also at the Staples Center (left) as UFC president Dana White poses with Mark Wahlberg.

Output: Generated Summary

Rousey was expected to face the toughest examination of her reign as bantamweight champion against the unbeaten Zingano. But having avoided a flying knee in the opening seconds, Rousey took her opponent down and set to work trying to execute her trademark armbar. Rousey had landed on her head but the champion gracefully flipped Zingano on to her back, got up and manoeuvred swiftly into position to wrench Zingano's arm grotesquely. It was a lot like judo transitions, where you scramble the second you hit the ground. 'I made that up on the fly, to be honest. Rousey has won all 11 of her mixed martial arts fights and all but one inside the first round. Actresses Mandy Moore (left) and Minka Kelly pose for a photograph during the UFC 184 event. Vin Diesel was also at the Staples Center (left) as UFC president Dana White poses with Mark Wahlberg. Zingano had earned her title shot two years ago with an upset victory over Miesha Tate, but was forced to wait after suffering a serious knee injury before she was hit by her estranged husband's suicide last year.

OTSummarizer

Fig. 5. Example of running OTSummarizer system over a source document from CNN/DailyMail dataset. The extracted sentences are highlighted in the original document.

5   Conclusion

In this paper, we propose an optimal transport-based approach (OTsummarizer) for extractive summarization. We prove that optimal transport based on BERT embedding can be effectively used for machine summaries scoring, and Beam Search can be used as a space exploration strategy to find the best summary. OTsummarizer outperforms the state-of-the-art of combinatorial-based extractive approaches on the famous CNN Daily Mail dataset and the PubMed datasets. For future works, we are going to improve the performance of our approach by adopting sentence transformers as the embedding model instead of TF.IDF. Another future research direction will be to automatically determines the size of the generated summary.

References

1. Abu Nada, A.M., Alajrami, E., Al-Saqqa, A.A., Abu-Naser, S.S.: Arabic text summarization using arabert model using extractive text summarization approach (2020)
2. Liu, Y., Lapata, M.: Text summarization with pretrained encoders. arXiv preprint arXiv:1908.08345 (2019)

3. Nallapati, R., et al.: Abstractive text summarization using sequence-to-sequence RNNs and beyond. arXiv preprint arXiv:1602.06023 (2016)
4. Hermann, K.M., et al.: Teaching machines to read and comprehend. Adv. Neural Inf. Process. Syst. **28** (2015)
5. Xu, J., Durrett, G.: Neural extractive text summarization with syntactic compression. arXiv preprint arXiv:1902.00863 (2019)
6. Zhong, M., et al.: Extractive summarization as text matching. arXiv preprint arXiv:2004.08795 (2020)
7. Bouscarrat, L., Antoine, B., Thomas, P., Cécile, P.: STRASS: a light and effective method for extractive summarization based on sentence embeddings. arXiv preprint arXiv:1907.07323 (2019)
8. Zheng, H., Lapata, M.: Sentence centrality revisited for unsupervised summarization. arXiv preprint arXiv:1906.03508 (2019)
9. Srivastava, R., et al.: A topic modeled unsupervised approach to single document extractive text summarization. Knowl.-Based Syst. **246**, 108636 (2022)
10. Tang, P., Hu, K., Yan, R., Zhang, L., Gao, J., Wang, Z.: OTExtSum: extractive text summarisation with optimal transport. arXiv preprint arXiv:2204.10086 (2022)
11. Maynez, J., Narayan, S., Bohnet, B., McDonald, R.: On faithfulness and factuality in abstractive summarization. arXiv preprint arXiv:2005.00661 (2020)
12. Tanfouri, I., Jarray, F.: GaSUM: a genetic algorithm wrapped BERT for text summarization. In: International Conference on Agents and Artificial Intelligence (2023)
13. Tanfouri, T.G., Jarray, F.: An automatic Arabic text summarization system based on genetic algorithms. Procedia Comput. Sci. **189**, 195–202 (2021)
14. Tanfouri, I., Jarray, F.: Genetic Algorithm and Latent Semantic Analysis based Documents Summarization Technique (2022)
15. Cuturi, M.: Sinkhorn distances: lightspeed computation of optimal transport. Adv. Neural Inf. Process. Syst. **26** (2013)
16. Devlin, J., Chang, M.W., Lee, K., Toutanova, K.: Bert: pre-training of deep bidirectional transformers for language understanding. arXiv preprint arXiv:1810.04805 (2018)
17. Cohan, A., et al.: A discourse-aware attention model for abstractive summarization of long documents. arXiv preprint arXiv:1804.05685 (2018)
18. Paulus, R., Xiong, C., Socher, R. : A deep reinforced model for abstractive summarization. arXiv preprint arXiv:1705.04304 (2017)
19. Bai, Y., Gao, Y., Huang, H.: Cross-lingual abstractive summarization with limited parallel resources. arXiv preprint arXiv:2105.13648 (2021)
20. Liu, Y.: Fine-tune BERT for extractive summarization. arXiv preprint arXiv:1903.10318 (2019)
21. Nallapati, R., Zhou, B., Gulcehre, C., Xiang, B.: Abstractive text summarization using sequence-to-sequence RNNs and beyond. arXiv preprint arXiv:1602.06023 (2016)

Towards a Hybrid Document Indexing Approach for Arabic Documentary Retrieval System

Rasha Falah kadhem[1,2,3]([✉]), Souheyl Mallat[1,2], Emna Hkiri[2,3,4], Atheer Joudah[1,2], Abdullah M. Albarrak[5], and Mounir Zrigui[1,2]

[1] Department of Computer Science, Faculty of Sciences of Monastir, University of Monastir, Monastir, Tunisia
rashakadhum@yahoo.com
[2] Research Laboratory in Algebra, Numbers Theory and Intelligent Systems, Monastir, Tunisia
[3] Department of Computer Science, University of Al Qadisiyah, Al Diwaniyah, Iraq
[4] Higher Institute of Computer Science and Management of Kairouan, Kairouan, Tunisia
[5] Imam Mohammad Ibn Saud Islamic University, Riyadh, Saudi Arabia

Abstract. We present in this paper, a semantic indexing approach based on the meanings of words, or concepts, in the representation of documents. These concepts are identified by the word sense disambiguation, using in jointly the Arabic Wordnet linguistic resource. Subsequently, to calculate the score and to evaluate the semantic proximity between the concepts, we based on the measures of similarities between the different meanings of the terms (candidate concepts). In addition, we propose an association rule-based model for extracting concepts belonging to the contextual domain that are hidden and implicitly defined. The evaluation of the proposed method shows the advantage of the contextual relations in the quality of the semantic indexing We obtained a high precision by validating 80.2% of rules and detecting other semantic and contextual relations between concepts. Intended to be generic because it can be used both in an documentary retrieval system.

Keywords: Semantic Indexing · Disambiguation · Arabic Wordnet · Association Rules Model · Contextual Relations · NLP · Information Retrieval System

1 Introduction

1.1 A Subsection Sample

Nowdays, the digitization of documents and the development of Internet technologies are generating an incessant increase in the mass of documents available; Faced with this mass of documents, the future reader feels disoriented and needs tools to help him filter documents to access relevant documents. For this purpose, the Information Retrieval Systems (IRSs) provide the user with a list of documents responding to his need for information formulated in the form of a request. In order to achieve this, one of the main tasks of an information retrieval system (IRS) is indexing. The indexing of documents is primarily intended to sort the documents in order of relevance [1]. It aims

N. T. Nguyen et al. (Eds.): ICCCI 2023, CCIS 1864, pp. 262–271, 2023.
https://doi.org/10.1007/978-3-031-41774-0_21

to extract the keywords that best represent a document and to construct simplified representations describing the informational content of documents and queries in order to facilitate research. Most of the work in this area has been devoted mainly to Western languages, including English. On the other hand, the Arabic language [18, 22, 23, 26, 31], being a morphological rich and strongly inflectional language, has had few studies at the level of extraction of descriptors. This is due to the major problem of the complexity of its automatic process. In traditional IRSs, documents and queries are represented (indexed) by keywords, they can be automatically extracted from their texts. In such systems, the matching (or matching) document-query is lexicon based on the presence or absence of the words of the query in the document [2]. Or, the words of the language are inherently ambiguous. The same word used in the document can define different meanings (case polysemy and homonymy), and several lexically different words used in the document can reflect the same meaning (case of synonymy).Thus, documents yet irrelevant are found, while semantically relevant documents are not found [11].To address this shortcoming, in this paper, we propose a novel approach to indexing and weighting documents.Our proposed approach for the indexing of Arabic textual documents is essentially composed of two phases, the first of which consists of improving the semantic indexing method by making it possible to find the correct meanings of the ambiguous words [19] by disambiguating the meanings of the words [3, 21]. For this step, we performed a comparative study between three similarity measures to be able to identify the correct meaning of the target word to be disambiguated based on the Arabic wordnet (AWN) language resource.

The second phase is used to improve this indexing process by identifying an association rule-based model to discover the non-taxonomic relationships that are implicitly defined between the concepts (see example in Table 4) leading to a more expressive representation of the documents.

In the third step, we are interested in exploiting our indexing method's contribution to improving the Arabic documentary research system.

The paper is organized as follows: Sect. 2 presents the existing problems, namely the disparity of terms and ambiguity faced in the indexing process. In Sect. 3, details our indexing approach; we will describe Lesk's extended disambiguation algorithm and the contextual relation detection algorithm we implement to produce the indexing process and integrate it into the SR documentary.In Sect. 4, we present an experimental comparison and discussion of the results provided by the evaluation of the contribution.

2 Related Works

In this section, we present a literature review of the different methods of indexing documents:

Mallak [4] indexes documents and queries by clusters of concepts that are most representative of their semantic content. To do this, he uses the same mapping technique proposed by Baziz [5] for detecting the key terms of a document. Each identified key term can be attached in the WordNet ontology to one or more concepts (so-called term-concepts). To find the best concept that describes the meaning of a term in its context of appearance [12], Mallak proposes a new method of disambiguation based on the notion of centrality [4, 6].

Dinh's work [7, 8] presents a semantic indexing approach based on the concepts of the MeSH thesaurus. This approach begins with extracting concepts from a document or query, projecting its textual content onto a pre-established list of all the concepts belonging to the MeSh thesaurus.

Zaki's work [9] introduces the notion of semantic neighborhood [24]. They propose a hybrid system for contextual and semantic indexing of Arabic documents, bringing an improvement to classical models based on n-grams and the Okapi model. They calculate the similarity between the words using a hybridization of N-grams, Okapi and a kernel function. In order to have a robust descriptor index, they used a semantic graph to model the semantic connections between the terms, relying on an auxiliary dictionary to increase the connectivity of the graph.

For better knowledge, our basic idea is to exploit the advantages of different approaches. In short, we note that the combination of these methods, thus introducing hybrid methods, to perfect the result of indexing. However, our method is interested in indexing based on the meanings of words, or concepts, in the representation of documents.

3   Description of the Approch

We propose a hybrid approach that combines the semantic approach and the statistical approach: A semantic approach: focuses mainly on the representation of documents by the meanings of the words they contain rather than by the words themselves, based on the semantic disambiguation of words.

A statistical approach: is concerned with the representative terms of a document extracted, it is about assigning them a weight that determines their respective importance in the latter.

Weighting can characterize not only the presence or absence of the term in the documents, but also their relative importance in describing the content of the document.

Indeed, the representation that we propose for the document, is a representation similar to that of the semantic network with the difference that the arcs are quantified by a real value denoting the semantic proximity between the concepts. This semantic proximity value is calculated using semantic similarity measures and taking into account other contextual relationships. With this in mind, we will use the association rules model [13, 20] in the indexing step, which is mainly aimed at discovering non-taxonomic relationships (contextual relations) between index terms (keywords or concepts) of a collection of documents. These are latent relationships, embedded in the texts, carried by the semantic context of the co-occurrence of the terms in the document. The goal of our approach, therefore, is to improve the representation of indexed entities and to overcome the problems of classical word-based indexing and to better represent the semantic content of documents.

3.1   Preprocessing

This is the first step to perform in our indexing method.

Segmentation. The segmentation phase therefore consists of identifying the boundaries of words, ie autonomous lexical units that we seek to label at the level of the main parts of speech (verb, noun, adjective, adverb, determinant, etc.). Segmentation also aims at detaching morphemic units that have no free form, such as clitics, and that appear attached to other words [27, 30] (for example, the determinant for the noun and conjugation preposition for the verb). These units are difficult to identify in Arabic because they are graphically ambiguous (by their similarity to other constituent parts of words) [10, 15].

Standardization. Standardization is subject to a standard [21]. A standard is a reference document. Obviously, if everyone establishes and follows their own standard, standardization is useless. This is why standardization is only relevant if it is applied by a large community.

Suppression of "Empty Words". The empty words represent the words very frequently used in the current language, they represent the words used for the construction of a sentence. They are so common that it's useless to index them or use them in a search. For this reason we eliminate these words before the lemmatisation phase. The elimination of these words returns the most important words. As an example we can mention the words ('في ' ,' كل ' ,' لم ' ,' لن ' ,' له ' ,' من ' ,' هو ' ...)..

Example :   " انطلقت الأشغال في اليوم السادس من هذا الشهر"
⇩
" انطلقت الأشغال اليوم السادس الشهر "

3.2 Extraction of Candidate Concepts and Semantic Disambiguation

The purpose of this step is to extract all the concepts from the significant terms of the semantic [25, 28] content of the documents, by projection on the AWN semantic network. If this projection generates for a given term several corresponding concepts, then this term will be disambiguated [16]. The descriptive terms of the document (or a query) are the meaningful words extracted from the textual content of the document. They can take many forms (eg simple words, terms, phrases, thesaurus entries, etc.) and are more or less difficult to extract.

Arabic WordNet is used, first of all, to retrieve the different possible meanings of the terms used in order to choose for each term a unique meaning that corresponds to it in the text. Subsequently, to calculate the score and to evaluate the semantic proximity [17, 29] between the concepts (to which the terms of the documents are attached), we based ourselves on the measures of similarities between the different meanings of the terms (candidate concepts).

We performed a comparison between the three methods of similarity measures. it turns out that the measure of Leacok and Chodorow has the advantage of being simple to calculate in addition to the performances it presents, while remaining as expressive as the others, it is for this reason that we adopted this measure as a foundation in our work. Table 1 gives an example of index selection for some concepts identified in the document:

Table 1. Example of selecting concepts from Arabic Wordnet

Words	Examples of synsets	Index
عصر	{بعد الزوال ، أيام ، أصيل ، عهد ،عصر ، يوم}	{عهد}
سحر	{إستهوى، فتن، أغوى ، تيّم، سحر،}	{فتن}
عين	{،رقيب جاسوس سري، عميل ، ينبوع ، عين}	{ينبوع}

3.3 Weighting of Index Terms

The objective of this step is to assign weights to the identified concepts (synsets) which express their importance in the document. Several weighting functions of terms have been proposed. We are interested in classical TF * IDF (term frequency - inverse document frequency). The table below represents the weighting result (Table 2).

Table 2. Weighted Concepts.

Concepts	Weight
مصر	0.4
الاسكندرية	0.1
بحار	0.6
محيط	0.6
جزيرة	0.21
شاطئ	0.11
القاهرة	0.12
جمهورية مصر	0.3
حرب	0.55
قتال	0.5
صراع	0.53
ضحايا	0.13
عصابات	0.20
سفن	0.12
ميناء	0.11

3.4 Improvement of Indexing Process: Extraction of Contextual Relations Between Concepts

The Arabic WordNet only integrates the semantic proximity relations between the concept nodes. In addition, we note the absence of useful contextual relationships between relevant concepts, hence the need to identify these relationships. This phase is the most delicate phase in our work since the terms related to the context of a word are implicitly represented in the documents and for this reason they are difficult to extract [14] contrary to the semantic variations of a term that are provided by the external resource Arabic Wordnet. In this step we used the association rules model which represents a knowledge extraction model.

We use the apriori algorithm to extract the relations, which reflect a semantic proximity between the nodes (concepts). This algorithm consists of two steps: The first step extracts all frequent itemsets from the document. The second is the generation of association rules between frequent itemsets discovered in the first step. We detail the operation of each of these steps in the following:

Generation of Frequent Itemsets. This step comprises the following three phases:

- Construction of the E1 set of 1-itemsets which corresponds to the most frequent concepts in the document, which have a weight P1-itemsets higher than given threshold (sup1min $= 0.3$);
- From the set E1 of the frequent 1-itemsets computed in the previous step, we generate all the 2-itemsets candidates, in order to build E2, which have a weight P2-items $=$ sup (1-itemset1, 1-itemset2) greater than sup1min. With P2-items $=$ min (P1-itemsets (1-itemset1), P1-itemsets (1-itemset2));
- The stop condition of the algorithm is when there are no new candidate itemsets to generate, in order to return the set E $=$ E1 $\cup$ E2 of all itemsets frequent in the document;

Generation of Semantic Association Rules. After the construction of the set E corresponding to all the important itemsets in the document. The semantic association rules are generated [51].

A semantic association rule between X and Y, we denote X $\rightarrow$ sem Y, is defined as follows:

$$X \rightarrow \text{sem } Y \; \exists Xi \in \text{Dom}(X), \exists Yj \in \text{Dom}(Y)/Xi \rightarrow Yj \tag{3.6}$$

Such that Xi $\rightarrow$ Yj is an association between the terms (1-itemsets) Xi and Yj.

The intuitive meaning of the rule X $\rightarrow$ sem Y is that, if a document is around ie by the semantic relation (is-a) of the concept X, it also tends to be around the concept Y. This interpretation s' also applies to the rule X i $\rightarrow$ Y j. Thus, the rule R: X i $\rightarrow$ Y j expresses the probability that the semantics of the content of the document relate to Y j knowing that it is about Xi. With respect to this semantics, the confidence associated with the rule R is based on the degree of importance of Y j in the document d.

However, some problems can occur when discovering rules such as redundancy and cycles. The redundant rules generally derive from the property of transitivity: X $\rightarrow$ sem Y, Y $\rightarrow$ sem Z and X $\rightarrow$ sem Z. To eliminate the redundancies, we propose to construct the minimal coverage of the set of extracted rules (ie that is, the minimal subset of non-transitive rules, and the existence of cycles is usually due to the simultaneous discovery of association rules X $\rightarrow$ sem Y and Y $\rightarrow$ sem X or association rules such that X $\rightarrow$ sem Y, Y $\rightarrow$ sem Z and Z $\rightarrow$ sem X. To solve this problem, we eliminate the weakest rule (with the weakest support) from the rules that led to the cycle. Support, we randomly eliminate a rule from the cycle.

Example. Returning to the previous example (Sect. 2.4), whose objective is to extract the contextual relations by the application of the Apriori algorithm: The terms are the most frequent 1-itemsets in the document, which are used to build the set of 2-itemset (set of two terms). We then calculate the weight of each 2-itemsets: P2-itemsets ({ضحايا, حرب}) = Som (0.55, 0.21) = 0.76... Etc. We only retain rules that have a confidence threshold ≥ minConf. These association rules are used to construct the semantic rules that form the basis for identifying the relationship between the document concept nodes. The Table 9 below shows the generation of validated assciation rules (Table 3).

Table 3. Example of extraction of non-taxonomic relationships.

Itemset	Rule	Confidence	Support	Rule validity
{ضحايا ، حرب }	R1: حرب ◄ ضحايا	0.75	1	Valid
{حرب ،عصابات}	R2 حرب ◄ عصابات	0.66	1	Valid
{ جزيرة ، بحار }	R3 : بحار ◄ جزيرة	0.83	1	Valid

It can be seen that the validation of rules presented in the table leads to a marked change in the concept of representative documents. This change due to the variation of the weights of each concept. Finally, the selected (validated) rules allow the identification of semantic and contextual relationships between document node concepts. The following table represents the final result of the index concepts by indicating the weight of each concept.

Table 4. Conceptual indexes.

Concept-node	Domaine (concept)	Weight
حرب	{عصابات ، صراع ، قتال، ضحايا،}	0.86
بحار	{ميناء، شاطئ ، جزيرة ، سفن، بحار ، محيط}	0.93
مصر	{جمهورية مصر ، الاسكندرية ، القاهرة ،}	0.82

4   Experimentation and Result Evaluation

4.1   Corpus

As part of our work, we have collected various Arabic texts from the web. Our corpus contains a set of documents that touches on three domains (environment, war, history) and can be named expansion corpus. We built our corpus so that it is compatible with the contexts of use of some ambiguous Arabic words that we will test.

4.2   Experiment and Results

We have generated a set of rules (328 rules) of which 68% are selected validated rules whereas 32% are selected not validated. This leads to improving our indexing approach.We describe in the following a comparative table that illustrates the contribution of our indexing method compared to the classical method and the preliminary semantic method, then we discuss the results obtained (Table 5).

Table 5. Variation of assessment measures by type of indexation.

Type of Indexing	Precision	Recall
Classic indexing	40.5%	25.3%
Preliminary semantic indexation	60.4%	57.5%
Improved semantic indexing	80.2%	66.9%

This can be explained by the generation of association rules with a configuration of conf-min and sup-min metrics is set, respectively. A sharp improvement in results presented in precision (20%) is obtained by validating 68% of rules and by the fusion of the two approaches: classical and semantic.

This means that the latter methodconsiders the frequency of appearance of the term and all its semantic relations. However, classical indexing only considers the separated terms' frequency. This will allow us to estimate the importance of the term in the document not only by its frequency of appearance but also by the importance of semantic and contextual relations (detection of other contextual relations between concepts by the model of rules of association) with the rest of the terms in the document.

In the end, we base our evaluation on the three experiments (Ex1, Ex2 and Ex3) in the comparison of information retrieval system performance on a list of 50 query according to three indexing approaches respectively (classic indexing, preliminary semantic indexing, or indexing) (Table 6).

Table 6. Precisions at five levels of recall for each retrieval type

Recall	Precision		
	Ex1	Ex2	Ex3
0	0.68	0.82	1
0.2	0.56	0.7	0.83
0.4	0.39	0.65	0.76
0.6	0.36	0.54	0.68
0.8	0.32	0.42	0.59
1	0.16	0.22	0.44

5 Conclusion

In this paper, we have presented a novel approach to automatic concept-based document indexing. we started our method by applying a set of treatments on the documents of our expansion corpus using the tools of NLP. We used the external Arabic Wordnet resource as an identity source to identify the correct meaning of each word displayed in a document. To choose the one-way meaning of these words, we calculated the measure of similarity between the different proposed meanings. The set of terms are then weighted by the TF * IDF scheme. As soon as we obtained the terms of the index, we moved to the phase of discovering the implicit contextual relations between the concepts, at the phase that was the most important and the most difficult in our work. In this phase, we proposed a model of association rules dealing with the relationships between the terms of the document, namely the concepts. We apply, therefore, the Apriori algorithm. This is first to identify all common elements, corresponding to individual concepts. A frequent concept is, in our context, a concept whose weight is greater than or equal to a fixed minimum threshold. Secondly, association rules are discovered between n-elements frequent sets (concepts). We finished our work by experimenting with our indexing approach to show its impact on the performance of the document retrieval system in terms of precision and recall respectively 80.2% and 66.9%.

References

1. Merhbene, L., Zouaghi, A., Zrigui, M.: Combination of information retrieval methods with LESK algorithm for Arabic word sense disambiguation. Artificial Intelligence Review, December (2012)
2. Mallat, S., Zouaghi, A., Hkiri, E., Zrigui, M.: Method of lexical enrichment in information retrieval system in arabic. Int. J. Info. Retrie. Res. octobre 2013. China (2013)
3. Mallat, S., Ben Mohamed, M.A., Hkiri, E., Zouaghi, A., Zrigui, M.: Semantic and contextual knowledge representation for lexical disambiguation: case of arabic-french query translation. J. Comp. Info. Technol. (2014)
4. Ihab, M.: New factors for the exploitation of the semantics of a text in Information Research, Thesis Phd, Toulouse University (2011)
5. Mustapha, B., Mohamed, B., Aussenac-Gilles, N.: A Conceptual Indexing Approach based on Document Content Representation, IRIT, Toulouse III University Campus, Toulouse (2005)
6. Boughanem, M., Mallak, I., Prade, H.: A new factor computing the relevance of a document to a query, IEE World Congress on Computational Intelligence (WCCI 2010), Barcelona (2010)
7. Duy, D., Tamine, L.: Towards a Semantic Indexing Model Adapted to Patient Medical Records, Francophone Conference on Information Retrieval and Applications, CORIA (2010)
8. Duy, D.: Access to biomedical information: towards an approach of indexing and research of conceptual information based on the fusion of termino-ontological resources, Thesis Phd. Toulouse University (2012)
9. Zaki, T., Mammass, D., Ennaji, A., Nicolas, S.: A kernel hybridization NGram-Okapi for indexing and classification of Arabic papers. J. Info. Comp. Sci. England (2014)
10. Lamia, B., Leila, B., Ghassan, M.: Segmentation of Arabic texts based on the contextual analysis of punctuation marks and certain particles. Tunisia (2005)
11. Mallat, S., Hkiri, E., Maraoui, M., Zrigui, M.: Proposal of statistica l method of semantic indexing for multilingual documents. FUZZ-IEEE **2016**, 2417–2424 (2016)

12. Mallat, S., Hkiri, E., Maraoui, M., Zrigui, M.: Semantic network formalism for knowledge representation: towards consideration of contextual information. Int. J. Semantic Web Inf. Syst. **11**(4), 64–85 (2015)
13. Mallat, S., Hkiri, E., Maraoui, M., Zrigui, M.: Lexical network enrichment using association rules model. CICLing **1**(2015), 59–72 (2015)
14. Hkiri, E., Mallat, S., Maraoui, M., Zrigui, M.: Automating event recognition for SMT systems. ICCCI **1**, 494–502 (2015)
15. Mohamed, M.A.B., Mallat, S., Nahdi, M.A., Zrigui, M.: Exploring the potential of schemes in building NLP tools for arabic language. Int. Arab J. Inf. Technol. **12**(6), 566–573 (2015)
16. Laroussi, S.M., Nicolas, H., Zrigui, M.: An opinion analysis method based on disambiguation to improve a recommendation system. ICCCI (CCIS Volume) 42–56 (2022)
17. Hkiri, E., Mallat, S., Zrigui, M., Mars, M.: Constructing a lexicon of arabic-english named entity using SMT and semantic linked data. Int. Arab J. Inf. Technol. **14**(6), 820–825 (2017)
18. Zrigui, M.: Contribution au traitement automatique de l'Arabe. HDR en informatique. Stendhal University, Grenoble 3 (2008)
19. Merhbene, L., Zouaghi, A., Zrigui, M.: ambiguous arabic words disambiguation: the results. Proceedings of the Student Research Workshop, pp. 45–52 (2010)
20. Hkiri, E, Mallat, S, Zrigui, M.: Semantic and contextual enrichment of Arabic query leveraging NLP resources and association rules model. 33rd International Business Information Management IBIMA. Granada, Spain (2020)
21. Merhbene, L, Zouaghi, A, Zrigui, M.: A semi-supervised method for Arabic word sense disambiguation using a weighted directed graph. Proceedings of the Sixth International Joint Conference on Natural Language (2009)
22. Maraoui, M., Antoniadis, G., Zrigui, M.: CALL System for Arabic Based on Natural Language Processing Tools. IICAI, 2249–2258 (2009)
23. Ayadi, R., Maraoui, M., Zrigui, M.: Intertextual distance for Arabic texts classification. In: 2009 International Conference for Internet Technology and Secured (2009)
24. Zouaghi, A., Zrigui, M., Antoniadis, G., Merhbene, L.: Contribution to semantic analysis of Arabic language. Advances in Artificial Intelligence **2012**, 11 (2011)
25. Charhad, M., Zrigui, M., Quénot, G.: Une approche conceptuelle pour la modélisation et la structuration sémantique des documents vidéos SETIT-3rd International Conference: Sciences of Electronic, Technologies (2017)
26. Haffar, N., Hkiri, E., Zrigui, M.: Enrichment of Arabic TimeML corpus. Computational Collective Intelligence: 12th International Conference, ICCCI (2020)
27. Maraoui, M., Antoniadis, G., Zrigui., M.: Un système de génération automatique de dictionnaires étiquetés de l'arabe. CITALA 2007, pp. 18–19 (2007)
28. Zouaghi, A., Zrigui, M., Ahmed, M,B.: Un étiqueteur sémantique des énoncés en langue arabe.Actes de la 12ème conférence sur le Traitement Automatique des Langues (2010)
29. Abdellaoui, H., Mohamed, M.A.B., Bacha, K., Zrigui, M.: Ontology based description of an accessible learning object. Fourth International Conference on Information and Communication Technology (2011)
30. Maraoui, M., Zrigui, M., Antoniadis, G.: Use of NLP tools in CALL system for Arabic. Int. J. Comp. Proce. Lang. **24**(02), 153–165 (2012)
31. Ayadi, R., Maraoui, M., Zrigui, M.: SCAT: a system of classification for Arabic texts International Journal of Internet Technology and Secured Transactions (2011)

Sh-DistilBERT: New Transfer Learning Model for Arabic Sentiment Analysis and Aspect Category Detection

Hasna Chouikhi[1]([⊠]) and Fethi Jarray[2]

[1] LIMTIC Laboratory, UTM University, Tunis, Tunisia
hasna.chouikhi@fst.utm.tn
[2] Higher Institute of Computer Science of Medenine, Medenine, Tunisia

Abstract. Arabic sentiment analysis is the process of computationally identifying and categorizing opinions expressed in a piece of text, particularly to assess whether the writer's attitude toward a given topic, product, etc. is positive, negative, or neutral. In sentiment analysis, aspect category detection (ACD) attempts to identify the aspect categories mentioned in a sentence. Our study investigates the effects of transfer learning across several Arabic NLP tasks. We proposed a new shared DistilBERT model, which is a fine-tuned version of the basic DistilBERT. Our results demonstrate the outperforming of the proposed approach for the two tasks presented in the study, with a small variation. We also showed the limited effects of transfer learning on the performance of the proposed approach, particularly for highly dialectic comments.

Keywords: Arabic Text · Arabic BERT-based models · DistilBERT model · Arabic Sentiment Analysis · Aspect Category Detection · Transfer learning

1 Introduction

Sentiment analysis (SA) is the process of using a machine to analyze subjective information such as opinions, sentiments, evaluations, and attitudes contained in texts. It is currently being researched in the field of natural language processing, as well as in data mining, text mining, and web mining.

Furthermore, as it becomes more prevalent in management and society as a whole, sentiment analysis is expanding its prospect beyond computer science to include social science and management science as well.

The importance of sentiment analysis is highlighted further by the growth of social media platforms such as reviews and Twitter. It is now used in research in fields such as finance and pharmaceuticals. Because of the Internet, people are increasingly expressing their ideas and finding information through social media or comments. According to this trend, sentiment analysis is being investigated on a regular basis, and research in more interdisciplinary areas is very likely.

N. T. Nguyen et al. (Eds.): ICCCI 2023, CCIS 1864, pp. 272–283, 2023.
https://doi.org/10.1007/978-3-031-41774-0_22

SA may be treated on three different levels: document, sentence, and aspect. The first two levels determine the overall sentiment polarity of the text or sentence, which is not always useful. Users can express diverse opinions on distinct aspects or entities inside the same text or review, making the aspect level, also known as aspect-based sentiment analysis (ABSA), more appropriate and practical for real-world circumstances.

The ABSA task was divided into four subtasks for SemEval 2014 Task 4 [6]. Firstly, Aspect Term Extraction (ATE), in which the goal is to extract features or aspects of services, items, or themes presented in a phrase or sentence. For example, "This phone's camera is pretty strong." In this phrase, the reviewer evaluated the phone's camera. Aspect Term Extraction (ATE) problems, such as Named Entity Recognition (NER), are seen as sequence tagging issues. Secondly, Aspect Polarity Detection (APD) is the process of identifying the semantic orientation, whether positive, negative, neutral, or conflict, for each aspect that is evaluated inside a sentence, such as "The voice on this phone is fantastic". This review is a favorable and positive assessment of the product, the camera. Thirdly, Aspect Category Detection (ACD), also known as a prepared list of aspect categories, is applied in the ATE job of identifying the aspect category being researched in a given statement, such as "The pizza was really good." The aspect category is food. It is the hypernym for the pizza aspect term. Finally, Aspect Category Polarity (ACP) aims to determine the polarity of the sentiment of the investigated aspect categories in a given phrase. "The dishes were amazing, but the music was dreadful," for example, is the purpose of the "Aspect Category Polarity" assignment. In this review, the author had a favorable, positive opinion of the food category but an unfavorable, negative opinion of the ambiance category.

There has recently been a surge in interest in applying Transfer Learning (TL) approaches for NLP applications [1]. The process of adapting a pre-trained model on a certain task to a new task, often by fine-tuning the model on a new dataset, is referred to as TL. One advantage of TL is that it can greatly minimize the quantity of labeled data and computing resources required to train a model for a new task, particularly when the new task is linked to the original one. The proposed model will be based on previously trained language models that have proved state-of-the-art performance on a variety of NLP tasks [2–4].

In particular, we apply TL approaches based on several well-performed pre-trained language models in this study to perform SA and ACD tasks. In addition, We present a Shared DistilBERT-based model (Sh-DistilBERT) for jointly learning different tasks simultaneously.

The rest of this paper is structured as follows. Section 2 summarizes past research on Arabic Sentiment Analysis and Aspect Category Detection. The suggested model is explained in Sect. 3. Section 4 describes the experimental setup as well as the assessment results. Section 5 summarizes the paper and suggests future research topics.

2   Related Work

Most of the relevant work in sentiment analysis may be divided into three categories: machine learning, deep learning, and hybrid.

Abdul-Mageed et al. [16] introduced a manually annotated corpus for Modern Standard Arabic (MSA) as well as a new polarity lexicon for subjectivity and sentiment analysis (SSA). They used a two-stage classification technique, the first for subjectivity classification and the second for sentiment classification. Language-independent data were combined with MSA-morphological features to train a binary SVM classifier.

The authors of [17] expanded on the work in [16] and presented SAMAR, a sentence-level SSA system for Arabic social media texts such as synchronous chat, Twitter, web discussion forums, and Wikipedia talk pages. In a two-stage SVM classifier, they employed automatically predicted morphological features, standard features, dialectal Arabic features, and gene-specific features.

Heikal et al. [12] used a CNN and LSTM model to evaluate sentiment in a corpus of 10,000 Arabic tweets [13]. The corpus' polarity was classified into four groups: positive, negative, biased, and objective. Nevertheless, the research was restricted to just three categories (positive, negative, and biased), reducing the real size of the corpus to 3315 tweets. Both models have an accuracy of roughly 64%.

The authors in [14] created a corpus of 2026 Arabic tweets that cover three health-related topics. The corpus was manually identified and annotated into positive and negative polarity. They evaluated CNN's performance to those of other machine learning approaches such as SVM, NB, and logistic regression. They also used the N-grams methodology (unigrams and bigrams) to extract features. The findings showed that SVM beat CNN with an accuracy of 91.37%.

On the basis of an Arabic tweet, Alayba et al. [15] suggested a recurrent convolutional neural network (RCNN). They employed three separate small corpora of tweets with sizes of 1732, 1975, and 2479, respectively, covering health services, political subjects, and general topics. Each corpus was divided into two categories: positive and negative. They used several levels of sentiment analysis for each corpus in their work: char level, Ch5gram level, and word level. Nevertheless, in their suggested method, they did not work directly on Arabic, but instead translated all tweets into English and divided each word into independent letters to maximize the number of features. Using word-level sentiment analysis on the health services corpus, their proposed approach attained the highest accuracy of 94 %.

The authors of [19] proposed a hybrid approach that integrated both the machine learning approach using SVM and the semantic orientation approach. The authors of [18] merged lexical features extracted from an Arabic sentiment lexicon and a machine learning-based sentiment analysis model. These findings were applied to Egyptian, Saudi, Levantine, and MSA Arabic social media datasets.

Despite extensive efforts in applying deep learning to English sentiment analysis, limited progress has been made in the context of Arabic data. For Arabic text sentiment classification, In [20] RAE was used. Baly et al. [21] applied an RNTN to predict the sentiment of Arabic tweets. They created a sentiment tree bank [22] for their model to use. They reported on the performance of two cutting-edge algorithms for opinion mining in the English language when compared to Arabic data. They proved that deep learning produced state-of-the-art results for Arabic sentiment analysis.

Bidirectional Encoder Representations from Transformers (BERT) is a language representation model developed by Jacob Devlin and his Google colleagues [23]. It has become a frequent baseline in natural language processing research since its inception [24]. Unlike existing language representation algorithms that only record the context in one way, BERT was developed to anticipate words based on both the left and right context [25]. BERT was also designed as an unsupervised model that can be trained using the vast amount of plain text corpus accessible on the web in most languages. This combination of traits enables BERT to perform a variety of natural language processing tasks, including sentiment classification [26].

Several BERT models were pre-trained to handle Arabic. Devlin and his team, for example, created a multilingual model that supports over 100 languages, including Arabic. Antoun et al. [27] created an Arabic model known as **AraBERT**. The model was trained on around 24 gigabytes of text. ArabicBERT [28] employed the standard BERT setup, which included 512 tokens as the maximum sequence length, 12 attention heads, 768 hidden dimensions, and 12 transformer blocks.

CAMeLBERT-MSA [29] is a collection of pre-trained BERT models on Arabic texts of various sizes and variants (Modern Standard Arabic (MSA), Dialectal Arabic (DA), Classic Arabic (CA), and a combination of the three). MARBERT [30] is a massive pre-trained masked language model that focuses on Dialectal Arabic (DA) and MSA.

Chouikhi et al. [31] proposed a BERT-based approach to sentiment analysis in Arabic (ASA-medium BERT [32]). Their study demonstrated that Arabic Sentiment Analysis (ASA) has become one of the research areas that have drawn the attention of many researchers.

Saidi and Jarray [39] propose a two-stage method for Arabic WSI. In the first stage, they used a Transformer-based encoder such as BERT or DistilBERT to convert the input sentence into context representations. In the second step, they used KMeans and Agglomerative Hierarchical Clustering to cluster the embedded corpus acquired in the previous stage (HAC). For the Arabic WSI summarization challenge, they evaluated their suggested technique. Their experiment results indicate that the proposed model outperforms the Open Source Arabic Corpus (OSAC) [40] and the SemEval Arabic corpus (2017).

The scientific community devotes less attention to Arabic Aspect-Based Sentiment Analysis compared to the English language. In the meanwhile, the ACD task has received less attention than other ABSA tasks, such as aspect term extraction and aspect sentiment polarity classification.

Al-Smadi et al. [5] was the first work in AABSA. They submitted the first annotated AABSA corpus using SemEval 2014 task 4 annotation rules [6]. They also provided baseline values for each ABSA task, including ACD, which scored 15.2% on the F1 score.

Al-Dabet and Tedmori [7] suggested another attempt to improve on prior achievements. They approached the ACD challenge as a multi-label classification problem with a binary relevance (BR) classification method. The suggested model integrated CNN and IndyLSTM [8], and it was divided into a series of independent binary classifiers to train each aspect category separately. The F-1 score for the experimental results was 58.1%.

Obaidat and Mohawesh [9] used a lexicon-based approach to build on the prior findings. For each category, fourteen lexicons were created using seed words and Pointwise Mutual Information (PMI). The suggested technique searched each lexicon for the words in a given review, combined their weights, and then allocated the review to the aspect category with the highest sum value. The improvement over the baseline result, however, was not impressive (23.4% vs. 15.18%).

Tamchyna and Veselovská [10] proposed their model, which was also submitted in slot 1 in numerous languages, including Arabic, to the same competition. They used a Long short-term memory (LSTM) as an encoded layer to capture long-term dependencies in the data and reduce the need for feature engineering and linguistic tools, and a logistic regression classifier to output label probabilities, to implement a binary classifier for each category (E#A pair). For the ACD task, the model received an F1-score of 47.3%.

To accomplish the ACD task on an Arabic reference dataset, Bensoltane and Zaki [11] proposed a BiGRU-based model. Moreover, we investigated the impact of employing various word embeddings, such as word-level, character-level, domain-specific, and contextualized word embeddings. The experimental findings demonstrate that BERT-BiGRU gets the highest F1-score (65.5%) among the assessed models and beats the baseline and related work on the same dataset substantially. Furthermore, despite being trained on a small dataset, domain-specific embeddings have yielded beneficial results.

In this paper, we propose a Shared DistilBERT-based model [33] which will be fine-tuned for the two tasks sentiment analysis and aspect category detection. A comparison study is applied between the proposed model and two Arabic BERT-based models (ASA-medium BERT [32] and AraBERT base model [27]).

3   Proposed Method

We start with a reminder of the DistilBERT architecture and an explanation of the new fine-tuned DistilBERT model (Shared DistilBERT) and the Arabic BERT-based model compared with in this study.

3.1 DistilBERT and Shared DistilBERT (Sh-DistilBERT) Model

Smaller, faster, cheaper, lighter: The DistilBERT Model was proposed in the blog post Presenting DistilBERT, a distilled form of BERT, and the paper DistilBERT: smaller, quicker, cheaper, and lighter. DistilBERT is a compact, quick, inexpensive, and light Transformer model that has been educated by distilling BERT base. It has 40% fewer parameters than bert-base-uncased, runs 60% faster, and maintains more than 95% of BERT's performance on the GLUE language understanding benchmark.

Among DistilBERT characteristics that are different from BERT based model, we can mention that since DistilBERT lacks token type ids, you do not need to specify which token belongs to which segment. Simply use the tokenizer.sep token to split your parts (or [SEP]). Also, DistilBERT does not support selecting input positions (position ids input). This might be added if necessary.

DistilBERT has the same general architecture as BERT, with the exception of the elimination of the token-type embeddings and pooler, as well as a 2x reduction in the number of layers.

The optimal practices for training the BERT model are integrated into DistilBERT. DistilBERT is distilled in large batches using gradient accumulation, dynamic masking, and no next sentence prediction (NSP) objective.

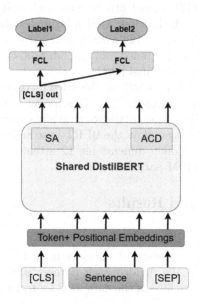

Fig. 1. Shared DistilBERT-based architecture.

For the shared DistilBERT layers (Fig. 1), we adopt "Distilbert-base-uncased," which has 12 layers. We preserve the first eight layers of the model

Table 1. Hyperparameters Setting.

Parameters	Values/Selection
Epochs	50
Learning rate (Lr)	5e-5
Optimizer	Adam
Max seq length	256
Batch size	32
Weight decay	1e-3

and fine-tune just the last four layers for fine-tuning the model using the transfer learning technique. We also use learning rate decay and weight decay to further improve our fine-tuning effect. Table 1 presents the hyperparameters used for fine-tuning of Sh-BistilBERT model.

3.2   Arabic BERT Models

In this study, we used as a term of comparison with the proposed model Sh-DistilBERT two Arabic BERT-based models (ASA-Medium-BERT [31] and AraBERT [27])

ASA-Medium-BERT model [31] is used with only 8 encoders (Medium case [28]). The output of the last four hidden layers is concatenated to get a size representation vector $512 \times 4 \times 128$ with 16 batch size. The pooling operation's output is concatenated and flattened too, and later on, crossed a dense layer and a Softmax function to get the final label.

AraBERT model [27] is based on the BERT concept, which is a stacked Bidirectional Transformer Encoder [23]. This model is widely regarded as the foundation for the majority of cutting-edge results from different NLP tasks across several languages. It employs the BERT-base architecture, which includes 12 encoder blocks, 768 hidden dimensions, 12 attention heads, 512 maximum sequence lengths, and 110M parameters in total.

4   Experiments and Results

4.1   Datasets

In this paper, we used a variety of datasets according to the tasks that are appointed to each task. We divided each dataset into two subsets using the conventional method, with 80% of the data used for training and 20% for testing.

Sentiment Analysis Task: For this task, we used five datasets:

– **ASTD**: The Arabic Sentiment Twitter Dataset [13] has around 10 K arabic tweets from different dialects. Tweets were annotated as positive, negative, neutral, and mixed.

- **HARD**: The Hotel Arabic Reviews Dataset [36] contains 93,700 reviews. Each one has two parts: positive comments and negative comments. It covers 1858 hotels contributed by 30889 users (68% positive, 13% negative, and 19% neutral).
- **LABR**: The Large-scale Arabic Book Reviews [37] contains over 63,000 book reviews in arabic.
- **AJGT**: The Arabic Jordanian General Tweets [38] contains 1,800 tweets annotated as positive and negative.
- **Large scale Arabic Sentiment Analysis (LargeASA)** [32]. We aggregate HARD, LABRR, and AJGT datasets into a large corpus for ASA. This dataset is publicly available upon request.

Aspect Category Detection Task: We performed experiments in this study using two available datasets: the HAAD and ABSA Arabic Hotels datasets.

- **HAAD dataset** [5] is considered as the most readily accessible dataset. There are 1513 Arabic book reviews. There are 2838 aspect words in HAAD, and 17 categories.
- **ABSA Arabic Hotels Dataset** was introduced in SemEval-2016 on the side of ABSA's multilingual task, including tasks in 8 dialects and 7 areas [6,34,35]. There are 19,226 preparation tuples and, 4802 testing tuples in the dataset. The dataset includes many reviews, and each review contains multiple sentences. Each sentence includes three parts: the aspect category, the extracted opinion term, and the aspect polarity. The dataset contains 35 categories.

4.2 Evaluation Method

In order to determine the effectiveness of the proposed model, the accuracy metric was adopted, which was defined as follows:

$$Accuracy = \frac{correct predictions number}{overall samples number} \tag{1}$$

Accuracy measures the number of correct samples to all samples, higher accuracy indicates better performance.

4.3 Results and Discussion

Below are presented in detail the results found for this study for different tasks. For the SA task (Table 2), Sh-DistilBERT gives the best result with HARD, ASTD, and LargeASA datasets. ASA-medium BERT gives the best result with the rest of the datasets. This drop in results from Sh-DistilBERT especially with the LABR dataset is explicative by the nature of this dataset because it is a dialect one. For the ACD task, our proposed model gives the best result with the ABSA Arabic Hotels dataset. For the HAAD dataset, ASA-medium BERT

Table 2. Comparison between Shared DistilBERT-based model and Arabic BERT models for Arabic Sentiment Analysis task.

Datasets	Sh-DistilBERT	ASA-medium BERT	AraBERT
HARD	**96.44**	95	96.2
ASTD	**94.10**	91	92.6
AGJT	96.03	**96.11**	93.8
LABR	85.07	**87**	86.7
LargeASA	**91.21**	90	85

Table 3. Comparison between Shared DistilBERT-based model and Arabic BERT models for Arabic Aspect Category Detection task.

Datasets	Sh-DistilBERT	ASA-medium BERT	AraBERT
ABSA Arabic Hotels	**96.54**	96.09	95.41
HAAD	97.15	**97.55**	96.45

outperforms all the models. As the categories in ABSA Arabic Hotels are in the English language, it is more suitable for the proposed model to give good results. However, the categories in HAAD dataset are in the Arabic language, that is why the Arabic BERT-based model gives results better than the Sh-DistilBERT model.

5   Conclusion

In this paper, we've shown how transfer learning, the newest natural language processing revolution, can outperform all prior models. We demonstrated that, with adequate fine-tuning, transformer models such as DistilBERT may play an important role in sentiment analysis and aspect category detection. As the Arabic language has a specificity, especially for the dialect form, the proposed model needs to set other parameters. In our future work, we will try to find these parameters and apply this model to other Arabic NLP tasks.

References

1. Mozafari, M., Farahbakhsh, R., Crespi, N.: A BERT-based transfer learning approach for hate speech detection in online social media. In: Cherifi, H., Gaito, S., Mendes, J.F., Moro, E., Rocha, L.M. (eds.) COMPLEX NETWORKS 2019. SCI, vol. 881, pp. 928–940. Springer, Cham (2020). https://doi.org/10.1007/978-3-030-36687-2_77
2. Bensoltane, R., Zaki, T.: Towards Arabic aspect-based sentiment analysis: a transfer learning-based approach. Soc. Netw. Anal. Min. **12**, 1–16 (2022)
3. Chouikhi, H., Alsuhaibani, M.: Deep transformer language models for Arabic text summarization: a comparison study. Appl. Sci. **12**(23), 11944 (2022)

4. Chouikhi, H., Alsuhaibani, M., Jarray, F.: BERT-based joint model for aspect term extraction and aspect polarity detection in Arabic text. Electronics **12**(3), 515 (2023)
5. Al-Smadi, M., Qawasmeh, O., Talafha, B., Quwaider, M.: Human annotated Arabic dataset of book reviews for aspect based sentiment analysis. In: 2015 3rd International Conference on Future Internet of Things and Cloud, pp. 726–730. IEEE, August 2015
6. Pontiki, M., et al.: Semeval-2016 task 5: aspect based sentiment analysis. In: ProWorkshop on Semantic Evaluation (SemEval-2016), pp. 19–30. Association for Computational Linguistics (2016)
7. Al-Dabet, S., Tedmori, S., Mohammad, A.S.: Enhancing Arabic aspect-based sentiment analysis using deep learning models. Comput. Speech Lang. **69**, 101224 (2021)
8. Gonnet, P., Deselaers, T.: Indylstms: independently recurrent LSTMs. In: ICASSP 2020–2020 IEEE International Conference on Acoustics, Speech and Signal Processing (ICASSP), pp. 3352–3356. IEEE, May 2020
9. Obaidat, I., Mohawesh, R., Al-Ayyoub, M., Mohammad, A.S., Jararweh, Y. Enhancing the determination of aspect categories and their polarities in Arabic reviews using lexicon-based approaches. In: 2015 IEEE Jordan Conference on Applied Electrical Engineering and Computing Technologies (AEECT), pp. 1–6. IEEE, November 2015
10. Tamchyna, A., Veselovská, K.: Ufal at semeval-2016 task 5: recurrent neural networks for sentence classification. In: Proceedings of the 10th International Workshop on Semantic Evaluation (SEMEVAL-2016), pp. 367–371, June 2016
11. Bensoltane, R., Zaki, T.: Comparing word embedding models for Arabic aspect category detection using a deep learning-based approach. In: E3S Web of Conferences, vol. 297, p. 01072. EDP Sciences (2021)
12. Heikal, M., Torki, M., El-Makky, N.: Sentiment analysis of Arabic tweets using deep learning. Procedia Comput. Sci. **142**, 114–122 (2018)
13. Nabil, M., Aly, M., Atiya, A.: Astd: Arabic sentiment tweets dataset. In: Proceedings of the 2015 Conference on Empirical Methods in Natural Language Processing, pp. 2515–2519, September 2015
14. Alayba, A.M., Palade, V., England, M., Iqbal, R.: Arabic language sentiment analysis on health services. In: 2017 1st International Workshop on Arabic Script Analysis and Recognition (ASAR), pp. 114–118. IEEE, April 2017
15. Alayba, A.M., Palade, V., England, M., Iqbal, R.: A combined CNN and LSTM model for Arabic sentiment analysis. In: Holzinger, A., Kieseberg, P., Tjoa, A.M., Weippl, E. (eds.) CD-MAKE 2018. LNCS, vol. 11015, pp. 179–191. Springer, Cham (2018). https://doi.org/10.1007/978-3-319-99740-7_12
16. Abdul-Mageed, M., Diab, M., Korayem, M.: Subjectivity and sentiment analysis of modern standard Arabic. In: Proceedings of the 49th Annual Meeting of the Association for Computational Linguistics: Human Language Technologies, pp. 587–591, June 2011
17. Abdul-Mageed, M., Diab, M., Kübler, S.: SAMAR: subjectivity and sentiment analysis for Arabic social media. Comput. Speech Lang. **28**, 20–37 (2014)
18. El-Beltagy, S.R., Khalil, T., Halaby, A., Hammad, M.: Combining lexical features and a supervised learning approach for Arabic sentiment analysis. In: Gelbukh, A. (ed.) CICLing 2016. LNCS, vol. 9624, pp. 307–319. Springer, Cham (2018). https://doi.org/10.1007/978-3-319-75487-1_24

19. Shoukry, A., Rafea, A.: A hybrid approach for sentiment classification of Egyptian dialect tweets. In: 2015 First International Conference on Arabic Computational Linguistics (ACLing), pp. 78–85. IEEE, April 2015

20. Al Sallab, A., Hajj, H., Badaro, G., Baly, R., El-Hajj, W., Shaban, K.: Deep learning models for sentiment analysis in Arabic. In: Proceedings of the Second Workshop on Arabic Natural Language Processing, pp. 9–17, July 2015

21. Baly, R., et al.: A characterization study of Arabic twitter data with a benchmarking for state-of-the-art opinion mining models. In: Proceedings of the third Arabic Natural Language Processing Workshop, pp. 110–118, April 2017

22. Baly, R., Hajj, H., Habash, N., Shaban, K.B., El-Hajj, W.: A sentiment treebank and morphologically enriched recursive deep models for effective sentiment analysis in Arabic. ACM Trans. Asian Low-Resour. Lang. Inf. Process. (TALLIP) **16**(4), 1–21 (2017)

23. Devlin, J., Chang, M.W., Lee, K., Toutanova, K.: Bert: pre-training of deep bidirectional transformers for language understanding. arXiv preprint arXiv:1810.04805 (2018)

24. Rogers, A., Kovaleva, O., Rumshisky, A.: A primer in BERTology: what we know about how BERT works. Trans. Assoc. Comput. Linguist. **8**, 842–866 (2021)

25. Zaib, M., Sheng, Q.Z., Emma Zhang, W.: A short survey of pre-trained language models for conversational AI-a new age in NLP. In: Proceedings of the Australasian Computer Science Week Multiconference, pp. 1–4, February 2020

26. Alshalan, R., Al-Khalifa, H.: A deep learning approach for automatic hate speech detection in the Saudi twitter sphere. Appl. Sci. **10**(23), 8614 (2020)

27. Antoun, W., Baly, F., Hajj, H.: Arabert: transformer-based model for Arabic language understanding. arXiv preprint arXiv:2003.00104 (2020)

28. Safaya, A., Abdullatif, M., Yuret, D.: Kuisail at semeval-2020 task 12: bert-cnn for offensive speech identification in social media. In: Proceedings of the Fourteenth Workshop on Semantic Evaluation, pp. 2054–2059, December 2020

29. Inoue, G., Alhafni, B., Baimukan, N., Bouamor, H., Habash, N.: The interplay of variant, size, and task type in Arabic pre-trained language models. arXiv preprint arXiv:2103.06678 (2021)

30. Abdul-Mageed, M., Elmadany, A., Nagoudi, E.M.B.: ARBERT & MARBERT: deep bidirectional transformers for Arabic. arXiv preprint arXiv:2101.01785 (2020)

31. Chouikhi, H., Chniter, H., Jarray, F.: Arabic sentiment analysis using BERT model. In: Wojtkiewicz, K., Treur, J., Pimenidis, E., Maleszka, M. (eds.) ICCCI 2021. CCIS, vol. 1463, pp. 621–632. Springer, Cham (2021). https://doi.org/10.1007/978-3-030-88113-9_50

32. Chouikhi, H., Chniter, H., Jarray, F.: Stacking BERT based models for Arabic sentiment analysis. In: Proceedings of the 13th International Joint Conference on Knowledge Discovery, Knowledge Engineering and Knowledge Management - Volume 2: KEOD, pp. 144–150 (2021). https://doi.org/10.5220/0010648400003064, ISBN 978-989-758-533-3, ISSN 2184-3228

33. Sanh, V., Debut, L., Chaumond, J., Wolf, T.: DistilBERT, a distilled version of BERT: smaller, faster, cheaper and lighter. arXiv preprint arXiv:1910.01108. (2019)

34. Mohammad, A.S., Qwasmeh, O., Talafha, B., Al-Ayyoub, M., Jararweh, Y., Benkhelifa, E.: An enhanced framework for aspect-based sentiment analysis of hotels' reviews: Arabic reviews case study. In: 2016 11th International Conference for Internet Technology and Secured Transactions (ICITST), pp. 98–103. IEEE, December 2016

35. Al-Smadi, M., Talafha, B., Al-Ayyoub, M., Jararweh, Y.: Using long short-term memory deep neural networks for aspect-based sentiment analysis of Arabic reviews. Int. J. Mach. Learn. Cybern. **10**, 2163–2175 (2019)

36. Elnagar, A., Khalifa, Y.S., Einea, A.: Hotel Arabic-reviews dataset construction for sentiment analysis applications. In: Shaalan, K., Hassanien, A.E., Tolba, F. (eds.) Intelligent Natural Language Processing: Trends and Applications. SCI, vol. 740, pp. 35–52. Springer, Cham (2018). https://doi.org/10.1007/978-3-319-67056-0_3

37. Aly, M., Atiya, A.: LABR: A Large Scale Arabic Book Reviews Dataset. Meetings of the Association for Computational Linguistics (ACL) At: Sofia, Bulgaria (2013)

38. Alomari, K.M., ElSherif, H.M., Shaalan, K.: Arabic tweets sentimental analysis using machine learning. In: Benferhat, S., Tabia, K., Ali, M. (eds.) IEA/AIE 2017. LNCS (LNAI), vol. 10350, pp. 602–610. Springer, Cham (2017). https://doi.org/10.1007/978-3-319-60042-0_66

39. Saidi, R., Jarray, F.: Sentence transformers and DistilBERT for Arabic word sense induction. In: Proceedings of the 15th International Conference on Agents and Artificial Intelligence, vol. 3, pp 1020–1027 (2023). ISBN 978-989-758-623-1. ISSN 2184-433X

40. Saad, M.K., Ashour, W.: Osac: open source Arabic corpora. In: 6th ArchEng International Symposiums, EEECS, vol. 10, November 2010

Data Minning and Machine Learning

A Hybrid Method of K-Nearest Neighbors with Decision Tree for Water Quality Classification in Aquaculture

Mahdi Hamzaoui$^{(\boxtimes)}$ ⓘ, Mohamed Ould-Elhassen Aoueileyine ⓘ, and Ridha Bouallegue ⓘ

Innov'COM Lab - SUPCOM - University of Carthage, Carthage, Tunisia
`mahdi.hamzaoui@supcom.tn`

Abstract. Water is a main factor in aquaculture, its quality plays an important role in fish farming management. The non-linearity, dynamics and non-stability of its parameters make it a very complex system to manage. The classical methods used to judge if the water quality is valid for fish farming or not are not very effective. To have good results, the involvement of technology is necessary. The use of artificial intelligence and a machine learning techniques is a good solution in this context. A DTKNN+ model is proposed in this paper. It is a new hybrid approach that combines decision tree with k-nearest neighbors(KNN). Many machine learning techniques were used in this new approach. The results showed the DTKNN+ effectiveness compared to a simple KNN. Its accuracy score is worth 99.28% and its mean absolute error value did not exceed 0.0071. The error rate is also decreased from 1674 misclassifications on 103544 with KNN to 743 on 103544 with DTKNN+.

Keywords: Aquaculture · Water quality · Machine learning · Decision tree · K-Nearest neighbors

1 Introduction

Aquaculture, a method for cultivating aquatic animals, is crucial for the human food security. Fishing has been important in resolving the food crisis, guaranteeing food safety, enhancing people's quality of life, and increasing exports. According to the FAO, since 1961, global consumption of these products (excluding algae) has increased at an average annual rate of 3.0%, which is nearly twice as fast as the annual growth in the world's population. Consumption is now at 20.2 kg per person, more than twice the level observed in the 1960s. Production of aquatic animals was 30% greater in 2020 than it was on average during the 2000s and was more than 60% higher than it was on average during the 1990s. Despite the effects of the COVID-19 pandemic, more than 157 million tons (89%)

Supported by SUPTECH UNIVERSITY.

of aquatic animal production in 2020 was intended for direct human consumption. In aquaculture, water is a very important element. Its quality plays a vital role in fish farming. Good water quality helps the farmer having a maximum fish growth, guarantee a high quality product and minimize the diseases and deaths rate. All these factors increase fish production and consequently influence national and international economic growth.

Water contains many parameters that can judge its quality. In aquaculture there are intervals of standard values [1]; if a value of a parameter exceeds the limits, the water quality will be influenced. The main parameters of aquaculture water are dissolved oxygen(DO), ammonia(NH3, NH4+), nitrite(NO2-), nitrate, turbidity, pH and temperature [2]. Many factors can interact in water quality such as biology, physics and human activities; they make it a very complex, nonlinear and dynamic system. Water quality classification is very important for intensive aquaculture. It can help provide early change warnings of water quality and reduce the aquaculture loss. Older methods of water quality classification are not very effective because of the complex composition of water. An outdated classification models does not help to have better results. Therefore, the use of new technologies by introducing artificial intelligence and machine learning can be an effective solution.

This section reviews relevant works on water quality classification and prediction that uses machine learning. The main methods for predicting water quality parameters include the time-series method, the Markov method, the support vector regression machine method, and the grey system theory method [3–5]. However, there are also downsides to these frequently used methodologies, such as the weak generalization issue, low processing efficiency, and poor, uncertain forecasting accuracy. As a result, these conventional methods can rarely satisfy the expanding demands of precision aquaculture. In recent years, various models based on ANN and DL have been suggested for forecasting water quality indicators in the aquaculture context [6,7]. To create a water quality forecasting model for aquaculture, some of these models used a BP neural network technique with various activation functions, including tansig, logsig, and purelin. Tingting Li & Al. used BPNN, RBFNN, SVM, and LSSVM methods in aquaculture to predict the values of water parameters DO, pH, ammonium-nitrogen (NH3 - N), nitrate nitrogen (NO3 -N), and nitrite-nitrogen (NO2 -N) [8]. They found that the prediction results of SVM are the best with high stability. Probabilistic neural network (PNN) was the subject of a study on drinking water classifications by Donya Dezfooli & al. [9], which showed that PNN performs better than K-nearest neighbors and support vector machine . Neha Radhakrishnan & al. compared several classification methods to conclude that decision tree is the best classification method [10]. Smail Dilmi & al. implemented a new approach based on deep learning and feature extraction techniques to monitor and classify water quality [11]. DL-LSTM-based forecasting models for water quality metrics have also been the subject of numerous other notable studies [12]. Zhuhua Hu & Al. developed a model prediction technique using the LSTM deep learning network [13]. The water quality data is first repaired and corrected using linear interpolation, smoothing and moving average filtering techniques. Next, the correlation coefficient is used to determine the order of the correlations between pH, water temperature, and other factors. Finally, employing the preprocessed data and their correlation, an LSTM-based water quality prediction model is built. By using a decomposition method on the original signal, multi-scale forecast techniques have been demonstrated to get more characteristics for the predicted signals than single-scale features [14]. Each segment of the original signal can be broken down and its distinctive intrinsic characteristics revealed. Many other works have proposed hybrid models to predict water quality. Elias Eze & Al. proposed a hybrid model based on EEMD, DL and LSTM, EEMD is responsible for the decomposition of the water parameters. EEMD and DL are used to predict the values of these parameters [15]. Shuangyin Liu & Al. proposed a hybrid approach to predict DO and water temperature values in a crab rearing environment, this method is based on the two algorithms RGA and SVR, it searches for the optimal SVR parameters using real-valued genetic algorithms, and then adopts the optimal parameters to build the SVR models [16].

In this paper, we describe a study that uses machine learning techniques to water quality classification. To provide a comprehensive overview, studies conducted earlier on the same subject and their results, is discussed at the end of the "Introduction" section. In addition, the "Background" section provides theoretical definitions of the different methods used in this work. The "Methodology" section describes the data acquisition phase and outlines the data preprocessing methods used in the study. This section compares different algorithms for water quality classification and introduces the new approach DTKNN+. The ensuing section, "Results and Discussion", reports the study's findings and evaluates the performance of DTKNN+ compared to previous approaches. The results of other research similar to this study will also be presented in this section. Finally, the paper concludes in the "Conclusion" section, which presents a forward-looking vision and insight into future works.

2   Background

This section provides background on the field of artificial intelligence and machine learning. General terms used throughout this paper are also defined.

2.1   Min-Max Normalization

Min-Max normalization is the process of converting data that has been measured in engineering units to a value between 0 and 1. Where by setting the highest (max) value to 1 and the lowest (min) value to 0. This makes it simple to compare numbers that were obtained using various scales or measurement units [17]. The definition of the normalized value is:

$$MM(X_{i,j}) = \frac{X_{i,j} - X_{min}}{X_{max} - X_{min}} \tag{1}$$

2.2   Machine Learning Classification Models

Decision Tree. Decision trees perform best with classification algorithms whose model relies on a set of input parameters to predict an output value. Among the advantages of the tree is the speed of execution, the efficiency with large data sets and the ability to evolve and assimilate rules [18]. Indeed, the decision tree is an algorithm based on the principle of iterations which divides the individuals in n groups (n = 2 in the case of binary trees), at each iteration, and this to explain the target result. The first split gives sub-sets of the first node of the tree. Then, this fragmentation continues until the splitting process is finished.

Multilayer Perceptron. Generally, the training of ANN (artificial neural network) models is often done with a BPNN (backpropagation neural network). The MLP is an advanced representation of ANNs. The MLP is a class of FFNN (Feed Forward neural network) that builds its network of nodes based on supervised learning of BP. It is a simple model based on a high number of layers. Nevertherless, its optimization is a bit difficult [19]. Retropercolation learning algorithms are often used to measure the propagation error in each node of the network [20].

Support Vector Machines (SVM). SVM algorithms have been very successful due to the quality of the experimental results obtained. The approach of SVM algorithms is to find a hyperplane in an N-dimensional medium that separates data points. To separate two categories of data points, there are several possible hyperplanes. The goal is to find a plane with maximum margin that can classify future data with more confidence. Data points falling on either side of the hyperplane can be assigned to different classes. Also, the dimension of the hyperplane depends on the number of entities. It is a hyperplane in the form of a line if the number of input entities is two. If the number of input entities is equal to three, then the hyperplane becomes a two-dimensional plane [18].

Naïve Bayes. Naïve Bayes Classifier is a classification method based on Bayes' theorem. When comparing classification methods, Naïve Bayes Classifier is known to be better than some other classification methods. This can be explained by its strong independence assumption and a very strong (naive) assumption in front of conditions or situations. It can also be judged that the realization of the model is quite simple and easy. The model can be implemented for large datasets [21].

The formula used in the Naïve Bayes method is the following:

$$P(C|X) = \frac{P(C)P(X|C)}{P(X)} \tag{2}$$

X: attributes, C:class, $(C|X)$: probability of even C given X has occured, (X—C): probability of even X given C has occurred

Logistic Regression. The LR model assigns to each predictor a coefficient to see its independent contribution to the variation of the dependent variable.

$$\ln\left[\frac{P(Y)}{1 - P(Y)}\right] = \beta_0 + \beta_1 X_1 + \beta_2 X_2 + ... + \beta_k X_k \tag{3}$$

$$\frac{P(Y)}{1 - P(Y)} = e^{\beta_0 + \beta_1 X_1 + \beta_2 X_2 + ... + \beta_k X_k} \tag{4}$$

$$P(Y) = e^{\beta_0 + \beta_1 X_1 + \beta_2 X_2 + ... + \beta_k X_k} - P(Y)e^{\beta_0 + \beta_1 X_1 + \beta_2 X_2 + ... + \beta_k X_k} \tag{5}$$

$$P(Y) = \frac{e^{\beta_0 + \beta_1 X_1 + \beta_2 X_2 + ... + \beta_k X_k}}{1 + e^{\beta_0 + \beta_1 X_1 + \beta_2 X_2 + ... + \beta_k X_k}} \tag{6}$$

The model for the predicted probabilities is represented as a natural. In Eq. (6), the logistic regression model creates a direct link between the probability of Y and the predictor variables. The objective is to predict the k+1 unknown parameters β in Eq. (6). This is done by estimating maximum likelihood and is done with the goal of finding the set of parameters for which the probability of the data is greatest. The regression coefficients show the degree of association between each independent variable and the outcome. LR then calculates the probability of success over the probability of failure and finally displays the results as a rib ratio [22].

K-Nearest Neighbors. KNN is a non-parametric method that looks for the optimal k-Nearest Neighbors and predicts the traffic flow at the next time. The size of k will influence the accuracy of the prediction. It can be set between 5 and 30 in first experiments. Finally, the results will show whether the value of k is reasonable or not [23].

2.3   Metric Evaluation Models

Mean Absolute Error (MAE)). MAE is the basic evaluation metric; it is used to compare the advantages and disadvantages of different algorithms [13].

$$MAE = \frac{1}{N}\sum_{i=1}^{N}|Y_i - \overline{Y_i}| \tag{7}$$

Root Mean Squared Error (RMSE). RMSE refers to the average error, which is more sensitive to extreme values. If there is an extreme value at the time of learning, the RMSE will be affected by the increase in error. The change in the evaluation index can be used as a benchmark for the robustness test of the model [13].

$$RMSE = \sqrt{\frac{1}{N}\sum_{i=1}^{N}\left(|Y_i - \overline{Y_i}|\right)^2} \tag{8}$$

Evaluation of Accuracy (ACC). ACC is calculated as the total number of right predictions divided by the overall dataset population [16].

$$ACC = \frac{TP + TN}{P + N} = 1 - ERR \qquad (9)$$

Confusion Matrix. A confusion matrix is a two-dimensional array of size N × N used to evaluate a classification model; N is the number of resultant (target) classes. The matrix makes a comparison between the actual target values and the values predicted by the learning model. The confusion matrix is a summary table that displays the correct and incorrect number of predictions.

2.4 Feature Importance in Decision Tree

The Feature Importance values represent the degree of influence of a parameter on the class. In other words, it is the expected probability of knowing the value of the class $Y = y_i$ if the value of the attribute X is known. The Feature Importance I_x of a characteristic X is the expected probability of Y given X. $I_x = E\left[Pr(Y = y_i|X)\right] \forall i$ While relying on this definition, it is assumed that I_x can provide a useful result for choosing the best features in the decision tree construction [17].

3 Methodology

3.1 Data Source

Data Acquisition. As system performance depends on accurate data, collecting data for experiments is a crucial activity. Twelve fishponds were used to create the dataset. The data are gathered at Nsukka Nigeria between June,18th and July,24th 2021 using six sensors (temperature, turbidity, dissolved oxygen, pH, ammonia, nitrate) controlled by an ESP 32 microcontroller. Data collection is done every 5 s. This project is developed by HiPIC Research Group, Department of Computer Science, University of Nigeria Nsukka, Nigeria.

Data Preprocessing. The dataset contains more than 345,000 records. Data losses have been reported and this is due to the large number of records on the one hand and the state of the data sensors on the other hand which could be influenced by the climate (especially the wireless sensors). Data preprocessing mechanisms have been used to fill in the empty fields. It is also very important to normalize the data to improve the performance of the algorithms.

3.2 Water Parameters Values in Aquaculture

Numerous characteristics in water can be used to determine its quality; in aquaculture, these parameters have defined value ranges, and if a parameter's value exceeds these ranges, the water's quality may be impacted [1]. The following Table 1 shows the suitable ranges of water parameters in aquaculture:

Table 1. Table of water parameter suitable ranges in aquaculture.

Parameters	Ranges	Units
PH	7–8.5	–
Temperature	27–30	c
Dissolved Oxygen	4–9	g/ml
Nitrate	<350	g/ml

3.3   Comparison Between the Different Algorithms

In order to define a good classification model for water quality in aquaculture, a comparison between several algorithms must be made. In this study, the five classification algorithms, Naïve Bayes, SVM, Logistic Regression, Multilayer perceptron and KNN, were tested on the same dataset which is cleaned and pre-processed in advance. The most successful algorithm is the one with the lowest false classification. The evaluation models used to measure the performance of the algorithms are MAE, RMSE, ACC and confusion matrix.

3.4   DTKNN+ Approach

DTKNN+ is a hybrid approach that combines two models, decision tree and KNN to make a classification of water quality in aquaculture. DTKNN+ starts with the raw data acquisition of water parameters. After preliminary dataset pre-processing, it is passed to the decision tree algorithm for training. The latter has the ability to return the degree of importance of each feature in the model by invoking the Feature importance function. A specific python module is developed in this work allowing to keep only the most important features in the training phase. Only the most important features will be passed to KNN for training (see Fig. 1). This new DTKNN+ approach optimises its performance by choosing the best number of neighbors to be passed to KNN as hyperparameter. It also uses the GridSearchCv technique for the training phase validation. The comparison between a simple KNN and DTKNN+ showed that the latter performs better in the water quality classification process.

4   Results and Discussion

4.1   Water Quality Parameters Correlation

The results shows that Nitrate has a strong negative correlation with pH, a moderate positive correlation with temperature and almost no correlation with DO. PH has a weak correlation with temperature and DO, the correlation between DO and temperature is also weak. We deduce the strong negative correlation between pH and Nitrate. The increase of the pH value implies the decrease of the Nitrate value and vice versa(see Fig. 2).

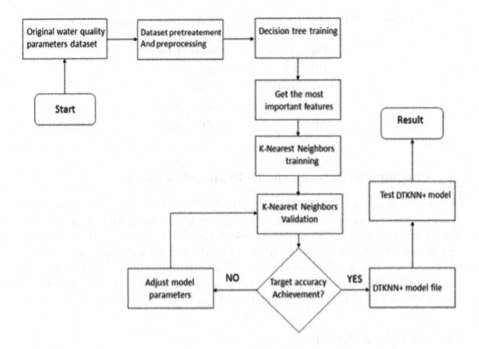

Fig. 1. DTKNN+ flowchart.

4.2 Evaluation of Different Algorithms

The evaluation of the confusion matrix, the evaluation metrics models and the test scores of the algorithms showed that the Naïve Bayes performance is low; the values of MAE/ RMSE and ACC found are 0.1848/0.4299 and 81.51% respectively. The SVM, Logistic Regression and MLP algorithms had MAE/ RMSE and ACC values between 0.0831 and 0.0775/ between 0.2882 and 0.2785 and between 91.68% and 92.24% respectively. The result with KNN is more accurate than the other models, the obtained values of MAE/ RMSE and ACC are respectively 0.0643/0.2535 and 93.56%. The following Table 2 shows the evaluation of the different models compared.

The results obtained clearly show that KNN is the best performer among the five models compared since it had the highest score and the lowest error rates compared to the remaining models. KNN made fewer misclassifications, 6659 on 103544 samples, while Naïve Bayes made 15948 misclassifications on 103544 samples (see Fig. 3). The results obtained with KNN gave that it is the most qualified model to be a third of our new hybrid approach DTKNN+, which is implemented by combining the two models KNN and Decision Tree.

Table 2. Evaluation table of the different models.

Model	MAE	RMSE	ACC %
Naïve Bayes	0.1848	0.4299	81.51
SVM	0.0831	0.2882	91.68
Logistic Regression Bayes	0.0820	0.2864	91.79
Multilayer Perceptron	0.0775	0.2785	92.24
K-Nearest Neighbors	0.0643	0.2535	93.56

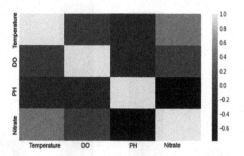

Fig. 2. Water parameters correlations.

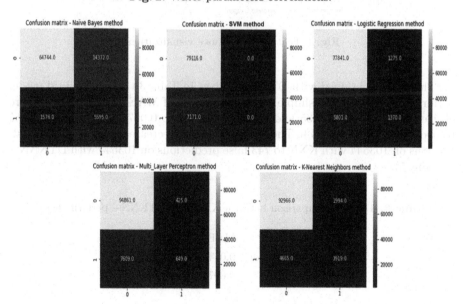

Fig. 3. Confusion matrix models evaluation.

4.3   DTKNN+ Approach Performances

Features Most Important. After training, the decision tree algorithm gave the degree of each features importance. The results showed that pH and Dissolved Oxygen are the main parameters of high importance to judge the water quality and whether it is valid for fish farming or not. The parameters nitrate and temperature are of less importance (see Fig. 4).

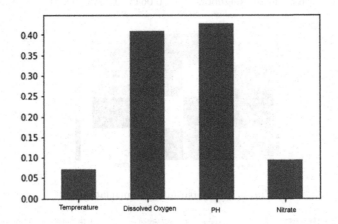

Fig. 4. Feature importance visualization.

The results obtained with DTKNN+ gives in Table 3 that this hybrid model performs better than the simple KNN. The values of MAE/RMSE and ACC are evolved from 0.0643/0.2535 and 93.56% of KNN to 0.0071/0.0847 and 99.28% respectively with DTKNN+. The error rate is also decreased from 1674 misclassifications on 103544 with KNN to 743 false predictions on 103544 with DTKNN+ (see Fig. 5).

Table 3. Table of comparison between KNN and DTKNN+ performances.

Model	MAE	RMSE	ACC %
K-Nearest Neighbors	0.0643	0.2535	93.56
DTKNN+	0.0071	0.0847	99.28

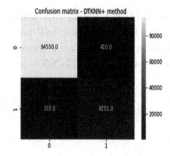

Fig. 5. Confusion matrix DTKNN+ evaluation.

4.4 Further Discussion

To evaluate the performance of the new hybrid DTKNN+ approach, the results of this study are compared with several other similar studies. An analysis was performed to evaluate the methods used, the characteristics of the data, the performance indicators and the results obtained. Based on these comparisons, the advantages and limitations of these water quality classification methods are elaborated. Richa Babbar & Al. compared between several algorithms for water quality classification in a river. They proved that Decision Tree is the best technique with an accuracy rate that reaches 100%. Ten water quality parameters were present in the dataset to train the models [24]. Fereshteh Modaresi & Al. made a comparison between SVM, KNN and Probabilistic Neural Networks. They showed that SVM is the best algorithm for water quality classification [25]. Nida Nasir & Al. found that CATBoost is the best algorithm for classifying drinking water quality [26]. All these works cannot be applied to the aquaculture domain. There are water quality parameters that cannot be useful in our context. Therefore, the data used in this work cannot be useful in the field of aquaculture. We can conclude that our DTKNN+ approach is developed specifically to monitor water quality and to see if it is really comfortable for the life of marine species or not.

5 Conclusion

Following several problems in water quality, this study is started by comparing classification algorithms such as Naïve Bayes, Logistic Regression, K-Nearest Neighbors, Multilayer Perceptron, to judge that KNN is the best. Based on this last method, a new hybrid approach DTKNN+ that combines it with decision tree is proposed. After the acquisition of the dataset, preprocessing and pretreatment operations have been applied. Then the decision tree model is trained on this dataset to determine the most important features. These were passed to KNN for training, validation and testing. Several machine-learning techniques were applied on this new DTKNN+ approach for optimization. An evaluation showed that the accuracy score evolved with DTKNN+ to reach a rate of 99.28%.

All the experiments done with DTKNN+ in this work have shown that this new approach is very efficient. In the future, an IoT solution will be implemented to capture in real time data related to water parameters from a pond in the Tunisian context, train these data with DTKNN+ and visualize the result from a mobile or web application.

Acknowledgements. This work was supported by SUPTECH University.

References

1. Kassem, T., Shahrour, I., El Khattabi, J., Raslan, A.: Smart and sustainable aquaculture farms. Sustainability **13**(19), 10685 (2021)
2. Abdullah, A.H., et al.: Development of aquaculture water quality real-time monitoring using multi-sensory system and internet of things. J. Phys. Conf. Ser. **2107**(1), 012011. IOP Publishing (2021)
3. Rozario, A.P., Devarajan, N.: Monitoring the quality of water in shrimp ponds and forecasting of dissolved oxygen using Fuzzy C means clustering based radial basis function neural networks. J. Ambient. Intell. Humaniz. Comput. **12**(5), 4855–62 (2021)
4. Liu, S., Xu, L., Jiang, Y., Li, D., Chen, Y., Li, Z.: A hybrid WA-CPSO-LSSVR model for dis-solved oxygen content prediction in crab culture. Eng. Appl. Artif. Intell. **29**, 114–24 (2014)
5. Li, Z., Jiang, Y., Yue, J., Zhang, L., Li, D.: An improved gray model for aquaculture water quality prediction. Intell. Autom. Soft Comput. **18**(5), 557–67 (2012)
6. Xiao, Z., Peng, L., Chen, Y., Liu, H., Wang, J., Nie, Y.: The dissolved oxygen prediction method based on neural network. Complexity **9**, 2017 (2017)
7. Liu, J., et al.: Accurate prediction scheme of water quality in smart mariculture with deep Bi-S-SRU learning network. IEEE Access **8**, 24784–98 (2020)
8. Li, T., Lu, J., Wu, J., Zhang, Z., Chen, L.: Predicting aquaculture water quality using machine learning approaches. Water **14**(18), 2836 (2022)
9. Dezfooli, D., Hosseini-Moghari, S.M., Ebrahimi, K., Araghinejad, S.: Classification of water quality status based on minimum quality parameters: application of machine learning techniques. Model. Earth Syst. Environ. **4**, 311–24 (2018)
10. Radhakrishnan, N., Pillai, A.S.: Comparison of water quality classification models using machine learning. In: 2020 5th International Conference on Communication and Electronics Systems (ICCES), pp. 1183–1188. IEEE, 10 June 2020
11. Dilmi, S., Ladjal, M.: A novel approach for water quality classification based on the integration of deep learning and feature extraction techniques. Chemom. Intell. Lab. Syst. **214**, 104329 (2021)
12. Li, Z., Peng, F., Niu, B., Li, G., Wu, J., Miao, Z.: Water quality prediction model combining sparse auto-encoder and LSTM network. IFAC-PapersOnLine **51**(17), 831–6 (2018)
13. Hu, Z., et al.: A water quality prediction method based on the deep LSTM network considering correlation in smart mariculture. Sensors **19**(6), 1420 (2019)
14. Li, C., Li, Z., Wu, J., Zhu, L., Yue, J.: A hybrid model for dissolved oxygen prediction in aquaculture based on multi-scale features. Inf. Process. Agric. **5**(1), 11–20 (2018)
15. Eze, E., Halse, S., Ajmal, T.: Developing a novel water quality prediction model for a South African aquaculture farm. Water **13**(13), 1782 (2021)

16. Liu, S., Tai, H., Ding, Q., Li, D., Xu, L., Wei, Y.: A hybrid approach of support vector regression with genetic algorithm optimization for aquaculture water quality prediction. Math. Comput. Model. **58**(3–4), 458–65 (2013)

17. Al Iqbal, M.R., Rahman, S., Nabil, S.I., Chowdhury, I.U.: Knowledge based decision tree construction with feature importance domain knowledge. In: 2012 7th International Conference on Electrical and Computer Engineering, pp. 659–662. IEEE, 20 December 2012

18. Jalal, D., Ezzedine, T.: Decision tree and support vector machine for anomaly detection in water distribution networks. In: 2020 International Wireless Communications and Mobile Compu-ting (IWCMC), pp. 1320–1323. IEEE, 15 June 2020

19. Senthil Kumar, A.R., Sudheer, K.P., Jain, S.K., Agarwal, P.K.: Rainfall-runoff modelling using artificial neural networks: comparison of network types. Hydrol. Process. Int. J. **19**(6), 1277–91 (2005)

20. Mosavi, A., Ozturk, P., Chau, K.W.: Flood prediction using machine learning models: literature review. Water **10**(11), 1536 (2018)

21. Salmi, N., Rustam, Z.: Naïve Bayes classifier models for predicting the colon cancer. In: IOP Conference Series: Materials Science and Engineering, vol. 546, no. 5, p. 052068. IOP Publishing, 1 June 2019

22. Boateng, E.Y., Abaye, D.A.: A review of the logistic regression model with emphasis on medical research. J. Data Anal. Inf. Process. **7**(4), 190–207 (2019)

23. Zhang, L., Liu, Q., Yang, W., Wei, N., Dong, D.: An improved k-nearest neighbor model for short-term traffic flow prediction. Procedia. Soc. Behav. Sci. **96**, 653–62 (2013)

24. Babbar, R., Babbar, S.: Predicting river water quality index using data mining techniques. Environ. Earth Sci. **76**, 1–5 (2017)

25. Modaresi, F., Araghinejad, S.: A comparative assessment of support vector machines, probabilistic neural networks, and K-nearest neighbor algorithms for water quality classification. Water Resour. Manag. **28**, 4095–111 (2014)

26. Nasir, N., et al.: Water quality classification using machine learning algorithms. J. Water Process Eng. **48**, 102920 (2022)

Evaluating Web Crawlers with Machine Learning Algorithms for Accurate Location Extraction from Job Offers

Paweł Drozda[1,2]([envelope]) [ORCID], Bartosz A. Nowak[1,2]([envelope]) [ORCID], Arkadiusz Talun[2]([envelope]),
and Leszek Bukowski[2]([envelope])

[1] Faculty Mathematics and Computer Science, University of Warmia and Mazury,
Olsztyn, Poland
{pdrozda,bnowak}@matman.uwm.edu.pl
[2] Emplocity S.A., Warsaw, Poland
{arkadiusz.talun,leszek.bukowski}@emplocity.pl

Abstract. This article focuses on systems designed to extract the location of a job listing from a job advertisement on web pages. It presents the use of classifiers to improve the reliability of automata used to collect this information. Three different algorithms - SVM, Random Forest and XGBoost - were used for this purpose. Accuracy, precision, recall and F1 score were used to evaluate the performance of each algorithm. While XGBoost performed best with an accuracy and F1 score of nearly 94%, all three algorithms showed very similar results. This suggests that each of the three algorithms can be effectively used to improve the accuracy of indexing robots in identifying jobs in job listings.

Keywords: Web Crawling · Web Content Extraction · XGBoost · Random Forests · SVM

1 Introduction

Recently, in many cases, finding suitable employees for vacancies has become a huge problem on the labor market. Especially in industries where experienced professionals with precisely defined competences are sought, a lot of time and financial resources are needed to find and hire the suitable candidate. Most medium and large companies have recruitment departments employing many specialists whose main task is to find and try to hire suitable candidates. Usually, the recruitment process is manual, where a lot of effort is directed to find and encourage the right people to interview and, if the candidate meets the job requirements, to present him a job offer. Another popular channel for recruiting people to work is the paid referral system. Both in the case of regular recruitment and the referral system, the costs of recruiting a new person to work are enormous, often exceeding six months of earnings.

On the other hand, a jobseeker encounters the barrier of many websites collecting job offers, both domestic and from around the world, where it is very

N. T. Nguyen et al. (Eds.): ICCCI 2023, CCIS 1864, pp. 300–312, 2023.
https://doi.org/10.1007/978-3-031-41774-0_24

often difficult to find job offers that match their skills. Often, even in the case of finding the perfect offer, it turns out later that the offer is no longer available. In many cases, this causes frustration of the jobseeker and reluctance to visit more websites.

This results in the need to improve the process of finding appropriate employees for the proposed positions. The Emplobot project is mainly aimed at automating the entire recruitment process and minimizing the effort needed to connect ideal candidates for job offers. The first works under the project [15] defined the proper preparation of the architecture of the entire recruitment bot system, while the second part of the project [14] allowed for the development of solutions allowing for crawling websites with job offers and finding job advertisements with high accuracy among all available subpages.

The next step in the project will concern the automatic indication of the exact location of the workplace for each job advertisement found on the most important job portals. The proposed research in this work is novel and, to the best of the authors' knowledge, no other paper deals with the problem of specifying the workplace in the advertisements. Of course, there are other ways to achieve similar results, for example by implementing crawlers that allow you to find interesting information on specific portals. However, they are mainly based on the structure of HTML elements on web portals, which makes them highly sensitive to changes in the HTML structure on portals. In addition, each of the job advertisement portals has a completely different structure and to obtain location information for each site, so there is a need to write a separate crawler, which is both very time-consuming and hard to maintain. The proposed research solves this problem, because having job offers, the proposed solutions work in a universal manner, independent of the website from which the ads come from.

The research concerned mainly the Polish market, as the system is offered on the Polish market. However, due to the high complexity of the Polish language and the emerging problems with inflection and word endings in Polish during the research, it should be assumed that the prepared solutions should be successfully applied to other, less complex languages (eg English). Automatic indication of the location in each advertisement from among several hundred thousand will allow the candidate to quickly select interesting advertisements. These studies will also be used in the next stages of the project, where the Emplobot system will collect information about candidates and will generate CVs from the collected data, and then will match appropriate job offers to the candidate database.

The proposed algorithms in the experimental phase were designed to evaluate correctness of the leading location found by the crawler for each advertisement. As part of solving the problem, classification algorithms were implemented and tested, the evaluation of which was based on the most commonly used measures of algorithm quality: accuracy, precision and recall. In particular, the XGBoost, SVM and Random Forests algorithms were used with different parameter setups and the various feature sets for advertise text representation. From the experiments turned out that the all methods achieved similar values of aforementioned measures, where all parameters reached between 93% and 94%. Moreover, the experimentation phase included the feature importance evaluation. From considered set of features included in the training dataset, it turned out that the **count** and **tag** features were of the greatest importance in almost all experiment settings.

The rest of the paper is structured as follows. The next section presents the related works. The Sect. 3 shows the main contribution of this paper, which is evaluated in Sect. 4. Conclusions and possible future directions are shown in the last section.

2   Related Work

With the significant growth of the World Wide Web there is a need to create some kind of algorithms responsible to classify content of web pages [1,2], although most of the search engines focus on finding collections of key-words and evaluation of a page [3]. There is an approach that uses typical machine learning algorithms for text classification [4]. A number of leading Machine Learning algorithms are also used to classify the content of a page after appropriate adaptation, pre/post processing and/or development, for example SVM [5], NN [6], XgBoost [7]. Learning algorithms are also used to classify page content after appropriate adaptation and/or enhancement.

They often don't take into consideration the structure of a web page and place of text clippings. Also other contents such as ads and parts of a page responsible for navigation on the site adds many unimportant and even garbage content. A good algorithm responsible for classification of web pages has to extract valuable content and description of the web page and then use it for the main task of classification.

Despite the fact that the problem of automatic matching of candidates to job offers was noticed many years ago, work is still underway to prepare solutions [8, 9], that will significantly reduce the workload of recruiters in the entire process of hiring new employees and increase the automation of this process [10]. Moreover, it should be noted that no major studies have addressed the problem considered in this area, i.e. automatic extraction of job's positions and job's locations from job's advertisements [11].

It is worth noting that the webscraping technique is being used more and more [12]. Mainly because more and more useful information is being put on web pages. Much of this posted data is given in a form that is very inconvenient to process by the computer system. However, there are many effective implementations of this type of solution in very different applications. An example is the attempt to determine the prices of a given product on the free market [13], which is especially interesting in the case of used or completely illegal products.

Suspiciously few works have been published on the use of this technique to predict the price of shares for the purpose of facilitating so-called short-term trading.

In the previous paper [14] Authors focused on the problem of detection if a single web page is a job offer and predicting location, position and aggregating information into database. This article continues the work and examines whether the system has correctly determined the location of a job offer.

3 Methodology

The chapter covers the entire process: from collecting information from the site to assessing whether the automated system correctly predicted the job location presented on the site.

The whole process can be described in a few steps:

1. extraction of site's general information,
2. check if website is a job offer,
3. further processing of data from the site,
4. find all possible site elements about job location,
5. predict location of job offer,
6. evaluate whether the location has been predicted correctly.

Although the solution was designed for processing job offers in the Polish language, it should be useful also for other languages, especially in the Indo-European family with some minor modifications.

The first task of the system is to check if the supplied page is a job offer. For that task WebCrawler extracts following features about the page:

- **page_l** = length of raw text in whole HTML page,
- **text_l** = length of extracted text, without HTML, CSS, etc.,
- **link_n** = number of HTML elements with tag "A",
- **container_n** = number of HTML elements with tag "DIV",
- **list_n** = number of HTML elements with tag "LI",
- **image_n** = number of HTML elements with tag "IMG",
- **input_n** = number of HTML elements with tag "INPUT",
- **form_n** = number of HTML elements with tag "FORM",
- **button_n** = number of HTML elements with tag "BUTTON",
- **head_l** = length of raw text responsible for site header,
- **text2page** = the result of dividing **text_l** by **page_l**,
- **containers2text** = the result of dividing **container_n** by **text_l**.

Although the collection of extracted features does not look to be very sophisticated, in most cases it is sufficient in order to correctly check if it is a job offer. Then the system uses XGBoost classifier [16] in order to check if the page seems to be a job offer. More details of this process is presented in the paper [14]. The next part of the algorithm is responsible for preprocessing of the web site. That process is done in a few sub-steps:

1. Extraction of raw text from html, removing JavaScript, CSS etc.
2. Conversion of words into its lower-case version.
3. Deletion of irrelevant elements such as: dots, commas or end of line.
4. Creating a simple list of consecutive words.

5. Creating a duplicate list of words and submitting it to the lemmatization [17, 18] process. This task is especially important in the Polish language, because of verb conjugation and case conjugation. For example, Polish nouns: "kot", "kota", "kotu", "kotem", "kocie" can be translated into English: "cat" or "cat's".

The next significant parts of the whole system are responsible for the assignment of location of the job in processed job offers, usually just a city's name.

The first of all the systems seeks in the processed list of words the ones that are also in the predefined dictionary of possible jobs location (mostly just city names). The next part is responsible for counting occurrences of all theses found words (in the most cases it just counts uses of all cities appearing in the website). After that the system gathers information about all cases of words associated with a job's location. Additionally, if the page constraints longer phase all other sub phases are ignored. For example if the site contains the phrase "new york" it ignores the sub-phase "york". Using that data the system once again uses Random Forest [19] in order to determine which location is the most probable true location mentioned at the website. All theses data is collected in the table with following columns:

- **count** - number of occurrences of this phrase (usually just a city name) on the website,
- **tag** - name of HTML tag of the element with the phrase,
- **child** - name of HTML tag of the first HTML child (if exists), or "x" otherwise,
- **parent** - name of HTML tag of element's HTML parent (if exists), or "x" otherwise,
- **xpath** - length of full path to the current HTML element (XPath),
- **raw_text** - length of text in current HTML element,
- **elements** - number of child HTML elements for current element,
- **city_name** - current phrase, the most probable name of the job's location.

The next stage of the work was to evaluate which sites were correctly classified. This was primarily done in order to improve the confidence of the data obtained.

Semi-automated samples were prepared to create the machine learning system. For this purpose, a sizable database of pages was collected, each of which was additionally manually labeled with information about the main location of the work presented on the page. Each page was then processed according to the method outlined earlier, including predicting which job location was the main one. The task of the next system was to test whether the predicted location was correct.

The algorithms worked on the same data as in the previously described table. All columns except city_name were used as input attributes, while an additional column with binary values was given as an output attribute, which determined whether the true location was identified correctly. The Authors tested many different Machine Learning systems for this purpose.

The first two algorithms tested were RandomForest [19] and XGBoost [16]. These two algorithm use a ensemble of decision trees [20,21]. The first one uses a technique called Bagging [22] and the second called Boosting [23].

The RandomForest algorithm builds a set of decision trees, each of which is created independently of the rest. Each individual tree is created on a data set that is not complete, but much larger than a tiny slice of the data. As a result, each individual tree should perform at least at an acceptable (and usually correct) level. However, since each tree is created on not the entire data set, therefore the resulting tree will naturally generalize knowledge much more strongly than a single large tree working on the entire data. The disadvantage of the reduced efficiency of a single component tree is neutralized by the fact that the final decision is made by a set of trees. As a result, a set of decision trees (formed on a varying, limited set of data) usually produces better results than a single large decision tree formed on whole data.

The XGBoost algorithm works in a slightly different way. Decision trees are built sequentially. At first, it is assumed what the default answer is, and based on this the errors between the current (default) answer and the correct one are calculated. Based on these errors, a decision tree is created, enforcing that the created tree should not be too complex. After the tree is created, it is checked how it performs and if it returns at least an acceptable level it is added to the set of trees. In the next step, the error between the desired values and the resulted values of the whole ensemble is calculated. In this way, new errors are taken into account when creating the next tree. In this way, the algorithm creates an ensemble of decision trees. It is believed that the XGBoost algorithm usually performs slightly better than RandomForest, but this is not certain and depends on the used parameters of both algorithms.

Another algorithm is SVM (Support Vector Machine) [24]. It works in a completely different way. The main task of the algorithm is selecting those samples (later called support vectors) that lie closest to the boundary separating samples belonging to different classes. This is not easy, because usually the resulting boundary is not a straight line or (hyper) space. Support vectors are also chosen so that the resulting margin between samples from different classes is as large as possible. In addition, it is allowed that some samples may not be correctly separated by the resulting boundary. After all, sometimes it is worth that some of the reference samples are not correctly classified, but the separating boundary is much simpler and usually generalizes knowledge better.

4 Experiments

The experimental phase consisted of two complementary paths. In the first, the features included in the input vector for the classification algorithms were analyzed for the importance. The second part of the research work was directed to the training process and testing of the three classification methods in terms of effectiveness and training time.

4.1 Feature Importance

The first part of the evaluation phase in this study was to identify the features that were most significant in terms of affecting the quality of the classification among all the features considered in the evaluation process. It should be noted that some of these features, nominally represented as qualitative, were encoded using One Hot Encoder. The evaluation of the validity of the features was carried out with the XGBoost and Random Forest algorithms using different sets of input parameters. For the XGBoost algorithm, the effect of max_depth was studied, as well as for Random Forest.

The average parameter importance scores for the learning process for all sets of hyperparameters are presented in Tables 1 and 2 for XGBoost and Random Forest.

Table 1. Feature Importance Scores for XGBoost.

No	Feature	Importance	No	Feature	Importance
1	child_ul	0.153	7	tag_label	0.049
2	tag_h3	0.118	8	child_div	0.038
3	count	0.105	9	parent_h3	0.035
4	tag_div	0.087	10	xpath	0.034
5	tag_p	0.072	11	tag_strong	0.021
6	tag_a	0.071	12	child_x	0.020

Table 2. Feature Importance Score for Random Forest.

No	Feature	Importance	No	Feature	Importance
1	count	0.404	7	elements	0.042
2	raw_text	0.123	8	xpath	0.036
3	tag_a	0.115	9	child_x	0.032
4	tag_div	0.076	10	parent_x	0.010
5	child_ul	0.056	11	tag_h3	0.009
6	tag_p	0.046	12	child_div	0.009

In addition, the Fig. 1 presents graphs of the most significant features for the models that for XGBoost and Random Forest achieved the best classification results.

It should be noted the most significant feature was **count** containing information about the number of occurrences of the word or group of words on the

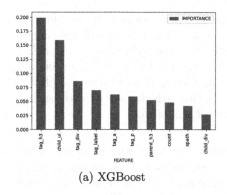

(a) XGBoost

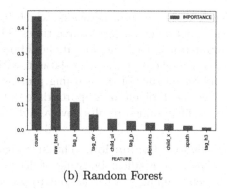

(b) Random Forest

Fig. 1. Feature Importance.

website. This feature should be considered important due to the fact that frequent occurrences of a particular geographic place may indicate the correct location for the job ad. Moreover, the high importance for **raw_text** is observed as well. Other characteristics identified as important were those created with One Hot Encoding method. Among them, the features that described the HTML tag of the element in which the ad appears gained particularly high importance in the context of classification. The **a, div, p, h3** tags were most often considered relevant. It is also noteworthy that the child and parent tags also appeared in the high relevance features (namely, **ul, h3, x**).

On the other hand, in the case of the second algorithm evaluated in terms of feature importance, a similar trend can be observed, which would indicate a good selection of features. However, slight differences can be noted. In particular, the higher relevance of features on **child, tags** compared to Random Forest algorithm should be pointed out, and the lower importance for the feature **count**. In conclusion, it should be noted that in the main the relevant features in the learning process should be the following: **count, tag, child, parent, xpath, raw_text**.

4.2 Classification Results

The main objective of the second stage of the research was to prepare models that effectively assess the correctness of automatic job identification on job ads that were collected within the prepared crawlers. This allows an effective way for job candidates to quickly find geographically interesting ads, but also to implement this solution in the Emplobot tool, which allows automatic matching of candidates and job offers taking into account the location of vacancies.

As part of the training, three classification algorithms from the field of Machine Learning were considered, which have shown high performance in a number of classification problems. The choice of these solutions was also dictated by a much faster training process than in the case of more advanced solutions,

such as deep neural networks, which in the first tests showed similar effectiveness, but much longer training times. The following subsections will describe the
evaluation of each method. It should be noted that the training of all algorithms
was carried out on the same dataset, with the same hardware parameter settings,
and for all runs of the learning process a 5-fold cross-validation was applied to
avoid the problem of inappropriate data selection, which allows us to conclude
that the obtained results have a high degree of reliability.

XGBoost Evaluation. The first algorithm considered was XGBoost, which
is based on gradient boosting of decision trees. As part of the study, hyperparameter tuning was carried out to prepare the most effective model. The training was carried out for the parameters: max_depth, min_child_weight, but the
obtained results show a very little impact of min_child_weight on effectiveness of
the XGBoost, which being the reason it has been omitted. The summary of the
results is shown in Table 3.

Table 3. XGBoost Results.

max_depth	Accuracy	Precision	Recall	F1	Training Time
4	92.27%	92.32%	92.27%	92.26%	3 s
6	92.94%	92.95%	92.94%	92.94%	4 s
8	93.30%	93.31%	93.30%	93.30%	5 s
10	93.48%	93.48%	93.48%	93.48%	7 s
12	93.59%	93.59%	93.59%	93.59%	8 s
16	93.69%	93.69%	93.69%	93.69%	8 s
20	**93.72%**	**93.72%**	**93.72%**	**93.72%**	10 s

From the table, it can be seen that the effectiveness of the algorithm varied
in the range of 92.27%–93.72% depending on the choice of max_depth. The
results illustrate the increasing trend of the effectiveness of the algorithm as
the max_depth increases. As can be seen, the best results were achieved for the
value of 20, where the final parameter values were: accuracy = 93.72% and F1
= 93.72%. Figure 2a shows the confusion matrix for the model that proved to
be the most effective.

It can be seen that nearly 160k cases were correctly classified, while the wrong
prediction concerned over 10k cases.

Random Forest Evaluation. The second method that was chosen to evaluate
the problem of evaluating the effectiveness of job ad crawlers for correct location
identification is Random Forest. The evaluation was conducted for max_depth,
n_estimators and criterion, but the last two did not affect the effectiveness of
the classification. The results for the evaluation of the parameter max_depth are
shown in Table 4.

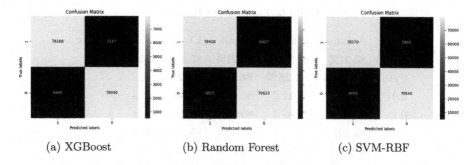

| (a) XGBoost | (b) Random Forest | (c) SVM-RBF |

Fig. 2. Confusion Matrices for XGBoost, Random Forst with max_depth = 20 and SVM with RBF Kernel with C = 10, gamma = 1.

Table 4. Random Forest Results.

max_depth	Accuracy	Precision	Recall	F1	Training Time
4	83.01%	83.26%	83.01%	82.97%	4 s
8	89.42%	89.53%	89.42%	89.41%	6 s
12	91.86%	91.96%	91.86%	91.86%	7 s
16	93.00%	93.05%	93.00%	93.00%	8 s
20	**93.58%**	**93.59%**	**93.58%**	**93.58%**	9 s

As can be observed, the parameter max_depth significantly increases the effectiveness of the algorithm as the value increases. The best results were achieved for the value 20, for which the confusion matrix in the Fig. 2b was presented.

The results also illustrate nearly identical training time as for XGBoost, as well as the values of parameters for the best model. On the other hand, the Random Forest is much more sensitive to changing max_depth values.

SVM Evaluation. The last of the algorithms considered in this paper is the Support Vector Machine algorithm (SVM). As a part of the experiments, a learning process was prepared for the two most commonly used kernels: linear and RBF along with changes in the most relevant parameters, i.e. for the linear kernel C = 0.0001, 0.001, 0.01, 0.1, 1, 10, 100, and for the RBF kernel the C = C = 0.01, 0.1, 1, 10, 100 and gamma = 0.01, 0.1, 1, 10, 100 parameters. The results for both cases are shown in the Tables 5 and 6. For clarity of results for the RBF kernel, only the best results for each choice of parameter C are listed.

It should be noted foremost the much longer SVM training for the RBF kernel compared to all the other methods considered. Among all the learning runs, it should be noted that the best results were achieved for kernel RBF, C = 1 and gamma = 1, where the individual parameters reached accuracy = 93.63 and F1 = 93.63. For this case, the confusion matrix in the Fig. 2c was also

Table 5. Linear SVM Results.

C	Accuracy	Precision	Recall	F1	Training Time
0.0001	85.21%	85.85%	85.21%	85.21%	25 s
0.001	**86.21%**	**86.26%**	**86.21%**	**86.20%**	32 s
0.01	86.01%	86.12%	86.01%	86.00%	33 s
0.1	85.70%	85.87%	85.69%	85.68%	32 s
1	85.40%	85.66%	85.40%	85.36%	30 s
10	82.97%	84.16%	82.97%	82.82%	29 s
100	80.85%	81.82%	80.85%	80.78%	29 s

Table 6. SVM Results with RBF Kernel.

C	gamma	Accuracy	Precision	Recall	F1	Training Time
0.01	0.1	82.32%	84.25%	82.32%	82.07%	417 s
0.1	1	88.55%	89.76%	88.55%	88.46%	344 s
1	10	93.55%	93.58%	93.55%	93.55%	703 s
10	1	**93.63%**	**93.64%**	**93.63%**	**93.63%**	576 s
100	1	93.11%	93.15%	93.10%	93.11%	533 s

presented, from which it can be seen that correctly the prediction ran for almost 160k test cases, similarly to other solutions.

Discussion. Considering all the solutions presented, it should be noted that the best results were achieved for the XGBoost algorithm, where also the learning time was the best. In addition, similar results were also achieved for Random Forest and SVM with RBF kernel along with worse training time for SVM. This allows us to conclude that for the problem posed, the best solution is a model based on XGBoost or Random Forest.

The authors noted that for Random Forest and XGBoost the best results are achieved for high values of max_depth, and for RBF-SVM for high values of C. This is probably due to the low level of "noise", or accurate preprocessing. The case of Linear-SVM is different. Here the best results were obtained for low C, in addition, the results obtained by this classifier were clearly lower than for RBF-SVM. This suggests that this classifier is just too simple for this task.

5   Conclusions

This paper evaluates the correctness of the location of the job extracted from a job advertisement by universal crawlers provided by Emplocity. In particular, based on the HTML document returned during the crawling process, the input vector parameters for the machine learning algorithms: SVM, Random

Forest and XGBoost have been defined. The relevance of the features was measured and models were trained to evaluate the correctness of the returned job location by Crawlers. Experimental results showed that the proposed approach achieved a high level of accuracy of nearly 94% for all tested methods, proving the correctness of the proposed approach. The next step of the project will be the implementation of the final version of the Emplobot system for automatic mapping of candidate profiles with available job postings.

Acknowledgements. This work is part of the Emplobot project No POIR.01.01.01-00-1135/17 "Development of autonomous artificial intelligence using the learning of deep neural networks with strengthening, automating recruitment processes" funded by the National Centre for Research and Development.

References

1. Zhang, J., Niu, Y., Nie, H.: Web document classification based on fuzzy k-NN algorithm. In: 2009 International Conference on Computational Intelligence and Security, 2009, pp. 193–196 (2009). https://doi.org/10.1109/CIS.2009.28
2. Dilip Patel, A., Pandya, V.N.: Web page classification based on context to the content extraction of articles. In: 2017 2nd International Conference for Convergence in Technology (I2CT), 2017, pp. 539–541 (2017). https://doi.org/10.1109/I2CT.2017.8226188
3. Weir, G. R. S., Dos Santos, E., Cartwright, B., Frank, R.: Positing the problem: enhancing classification of extremist web content through textual analysis. In: 2016 IEEE International Conference on Cybercrime and Computer Forensic (ICCCF), 2016, pp. 1–3 (2016). https://doi.org/10.1109/ICCCF.2016.7740431
4. Shen, D.: Text categorization. In: Liu, L., Ozsu, M.T. (eds.) Encyclopedia of Database Systems. Springer, Boston (2009). https://doi.org/10.1007/978-0-387-39940-9_414
5. Joachims, T.: Text classification. In: Learning to Classify Text Using Support Vector Machines. The Springer International Series in Engineering and Computer Science, vol. 668. Springer, Boston (2002). https://doi.org/10.1007/978-1-4615-0907-3_2
6. Singh, A.K., Goyal, N.: Detection of malicious webpages using deep learning. In: 2021 IEEE International Conference on Big Data (Big Data), 2021, pp. 3370–3379 (2021). https://doi.org/10.1109/BigData52589.2021.9671622
7. Atari, M., Al-Mousa, A.: A machine-learning based approach for detecting phishing URLs. In: 2022 International Conference on Intelligent Data Science Technologies and Applications (IDSTA), 2022, pp. 82–88 (2022). https://doi.org/10.1109/IDSTA55301.2022.9923050
8. Liao, G.D., You, M.Z., Wang, G.C.: Experimental economic research for matching job positions. In: 2015 International Conference on Behavioral, Economic and Socio-cultural Computing (BESC), 2015, pp. 96–101 (2015). https://doi.org/10.1109/BESC.2015.7365965
9. Elizabeth, M.G., Rivera, M.F.M., Alfonso, C.G.E.: Grouping mixed documents: Mexico job offers case study. In: Mata-Rivera, M.F., Zagal-Flores, R., Arellano Verdejo, J., Lazcano Hernandez, H.E. (eds.) GIS LATAM 2020. CCIS, vol. 1276, pp. 151–159. Springer, Cham (2020). https://doi.org/10.1007/978-3-030-59872-3_11

10. Di Meglio, E., Grassia, M., Misuraca, M.: The ideal candidate. Analysis of professional competences through text mining of job offers. In: Fabbris, L. (eds.) Effectiveness of University Education in Italy. Physica-Verlag HD, Heidelberg (2007). https://doi.org/10.1007/978-3-7908-1751-5_19

11. Pektor, O., Walek, B., Martinik, I.: A data mining approach for finding similar job positions to upgrade a job position in a system for evaluating competencies. In: 2020 21th International Carpathian Control Conference (ICCC), 2020, pp. 1–5 (2020). https://doi.org/10.1109/ICCC49264.2020.9257298

12. Liu, B., Menczer, F.: Web crawling. In: Web Data Mining. Data-Centric Systems and Applications. Springer, Berlin, Heidelberg (2011). https://doi.org/10.1007/978-3-642-19460-3_8

13. Khder, M.: Web scraping or web crawling: state of art, techniques, approaches and application. Int. J. Adv. Soft Comput. Appl. **13**(3), 145–168 (2021). https://doi.org/10.15849/IJASCA.211128.11

14. Talun, A., Drozda, P., Bukowski, L., Scherer, R.: FastText and XGBoost content-based classification for employment web scraping. In: Rutkowski, L., Scherer, R., Korytkowski, M., Pedrycz, W., Tadeusiewicz, R., Zurada, J.M. (eds.) ICAISC 2020. LNCS (LNAI), vol. 12416, pp. 435–444. Springer, Cham (2020). https://doi.org/10.1007/978-3-030-61534-5_39

15. Drozda, P., Talun, A., Bukowski, L.: Emplobot-design of the system. In: Proceedings of the 28th International Workshop on Concurrency, Specification and Programming (2019)

16. Chen, T., Guestrin, C.E: XGBoost: a scalable tree boosting system. In: KDD '16: Proceedings of the 22nd ACM SIGKDD International Conference on Knowledge Discovery and Data Mining, pp. 785–794, August 2016. https://doi.org/10.1145/2939672.2939785

17. Małyszko, J., Abramowicz, W., Filipowska, A., Wagner, T.: Lemmatization of multi-word entity names for polish language using rules automatically generated based on the corpus analysis. In: Vetulani, Z., Mariani, J., Kubis, M. (eds.) LTC 2015. LNCS (LNAI), vol. 10930, pp. 74–84. Springer, Cham (2018). https://doi.org/10.1007/978-3-319-93782-3_6

18. Gallay, L., Šimko, M.: Utilizing vector models for automatic text lemmatization. In: Freivalds, R.M., Engels, G., Catania, B. (eds.) SOFSEM 2016. LNCS, vol. 9587, pp. 532–543. Springer, Heidelberg (2016). https://doi.org/10.1007/978-3-662-49192-8_43

19. Ho, T.K.: Random decision forests. In: Proceedings of 3rd International Conference on Document Analysis and Recognition, 1995, vol. 1, pp. 278–282 (1995). https://doi.org/10.1109/ICDAR.1995.598994

20. Quinlan, J.R.: Induction of decision trees. Mach. Learn. **1**, 81–106 (1986). https://doi.org/10.1007/BF00116251

21. Costa, V., Pedreira, C.: Recent advances in decision trees: an updated survey. Artif. Intell. Rev. (2022). https://doi.org/10.1007/s10462-022-10275-5

22. Breiman, L.: Bagging predictors. Mach. Learn. **24**, 123–140 (1996). https://doi.org/10.1007/BF00058655

23. Breiman, L.: Arcing classifiers. Ann. Stat. **26**(3), 801–824 (1998). pp. 801–823. https://www.jstor.org/stable/120055

24. Cortes, C., Vapnik, V.: Support-vector networks. Mach. Learn. **20**, 273–297 (1995). https://doi.org/10.1007/BF00994018

A Design Science Research Approach Towards Knowledge Discovery and Predictive Maintenance of MEMS Inertial Sensors Using Machine Learning

Itilekha Podder[(✉)] [ID] and Udo Bub [ID]

Faculty of Informatics, Institute of Academia-Industry Innovation, Eötvös Loránd University, Egyetem tér 1-3, Budapest 1053, Hungary
`itilekha19@inf.elte.hu` `udobub@inf.elte.hu`

Abstract. Knowledge discovery is the process of extracting relevant and practical information from a collection of structured or unstructured data. In numerous applications, such as marketing, fraud detection, telecommunication, and manufacturing, it is an unavoidable step. The complexity of the discovery process has risen along with the volume of data during the past few decades. In this situation, artificial intelligence (AI)-based solutions have emerged as the most advantageous. However, there is a lack of a rigorous strategy in the knowledge extraction and reuse processes. A qualitative research paradigm known as Design Science Research (DSR), provides systematic recommendations for the generalization and transferability of newly produced knowledge utilizing artifacts. In this research, we present an artifact for the early prediction of impacted micro-electromechanical systems (MEMS)-based inertial sensors. MEMS-based inertial sensor manufacturing is complex and time-consuming. Moreover, there is a persistent need for more precise products, streamlined production stages, and quicker solutions. One way of achieving this is through optimized manufacturing processes using AI-based solutions. However, many difficulties are encountered, including problems with data collection, data analysis, computational power availability, platform compatibility, etc. Thorough and systemic guidelines can ensure the avoidance of all these issues. The proposed artifact is created using a DSR approach utilizing various machine learning algorithms for predictive maintenance of MEMS-based inertial sensors along with providing optimal feature selection methods. A thorough demonstration of the artifact designing and evaluation process is provided using a real use case. The manufacturing process has been improved by further investigation of the results to help with knowledge discovery and re-usability.

Keywords: Predictive maintenance · Machine learning · Classification · Micro electromechanical systems · Design science research · Knowledge discovery

N. T. Nguyen et al. (Eds.): ICCCI 2023, CCIS 1864, pp. 313–325, 2023.
https://doi.org/10.1007/978-3-031-41774-0_25

1   Introduction

Micro-electromechanical systems (MEMS)-based inertial sensor manufacturing is a complicated domain due to its multidisciplinary nature incorporating fields, such as material science, chemical engineering, mechanical engineering, electrical engineering, IC fabrication, packaging, etc. Due to its versatile applications in several industries, including communication, automotive, medicine, military, and consumer electronics, there is a constant demand for improved products. Thus, there is an ongoing need to optimize the production process with better and smarter solutions. An enormous database is created from the real-time data that was recorded throughout those process control phases. It is quite difficult and laborious to analyze the vast quantity of data in real-time with a high sample rate during manufacturing in order to eventually discover and anticipate faults. By far, human eye inspection cannot correlate the data with failure or success in the industrial process.

The development of artificial intelligence (AI) based solution, opens up new opportunities for investigating huge data sets and discovering complicated hidden patterns from complex and unstructured data, that may be used for early failure prediction and root cause investigation. Industry 4.0 now heavily relies on the field of AI, which encompasses everything from process to product innovation. Yet, the majority of AI applications are still created as tools. This is currently changing as the industry becomes more aware of its potential and uses AI more as an intelligent agent in the creation of sophisticated automation systems. Knowledge discovery is one of the key strengths of AI. It may assist humans-in-the-loop in discovering phenomena and linkages that would otherwise go undiscovered. Since this field is still developing, the process of knowledge discovery may occasionally be quite difficult and intimidating. A universal approach would be beneficial in many study areas given how quickly and differently AI is being used across diverse sectors.

Design Science Research (DSR) can play a fundamental role by helping to find structured ways of obtaining generalized knowledge. DSR is a qualitative research paradigm where researchers look into user insight to formulate a systematic design solution, by creating innovative artifacts in the form of constructs, models, methods, and instantiations [6]. DSR offers a variety of approaches, from problem identification to method development to assessment and conclusion, to addressing problems that may emerge in many design elements. The information acquired can also be useful for developing a framework that can be further generalized for knowledge discovery and re-usability through the set of procedures and guidelines. Due to the high dimensionality and non-linearity of the data, it becomes a complicated and cumbersome task which is why an effective AI application technique is required. In addition, the knowledge and information developed via the use of AI are not always effectively shared and/or reused. For this reason, we suggest using the DSR technique to provide descriptive or prescriptive information that might aid other researchers.

The rest of the paper is structured as follows. A brief introduction to DSR and the proposed artifact design using the cyclic evaluation process is described in

Sect. 2. Section 3 provides the problem description and discussion of the related work done in the field of predictive maintenance using DSR and AI. Section 4 discusses in depth the AI methods used for predictive maintenance for MEMS inertial sensor manufacturing. Finally, Sect. 5 draws a conclusion along with direction for future work.

2   Research Methodology

The Design Science Research (DSR) methodology served as the foundation for the research technique used in this study. The two primary DSR actions are "build" and "evaluate". The "build" activity seeks to create an implementable artifact that solves a specific problem, whereas the "evaluate" activity concentrates on producing descriptive data, such as observations, hypotheses, and theories.

Conceptualization, utilization, and sharing of the newly acquired knowledge all depend heavily on DSR. It places a greater focus on the creation of knowledge that may be used to accomplish predetermined goals, such as IT artifacts and practice-related advice. Three fundamental rules for artifact assessment are put forward to guarantee the significance and reliability of the prescriptive knowledge produced during the "build" process.

The following are the guidelines [5,7,16]:

- Distinguishing between Interior and Exterior Modes: The researcher must describe the emergent artifact in a form that enables reasoning about its purpose, inner structure, intended environment, practical usage processes, and testable hypotheses for external evaluation.
- Documenting Artifacts as Design Theories: To facilitate the interior mode of DSR, it is critical to record artifacts as design theories. The elements of design theory put forward by Gregor et al. [7] can be used to accomplish this documentation procedure. The accuracy and usefulness of the prescriptive knowledge are improved by documenting objects as design ideas.
- Ex-ante and ex-post assessments: Before creating or implementing a DSR artifact, an ex-ante evaluation is performed to confirm design choices and guarantee relevance. Ex-post evaluation is carried out following implementation to analyze the effectiveness and impact of the artifact. Together, they offer continual evaluations and suggestions for enhancing the artifact while it is being developed.

A cyclic evaluation process model for DSR artifacts has been proposed to establish evaluation procedures and related standards as depicted in Fig. 1. The model offers a structured method for assessing artifacts as they proceed through the DSR process. To create true claims about the artifact, relevant prescriptive knowledge must be obtained.

The appropriateness, relevance, validity, design correctness, construction quality, and usability of the artifact should all be taken into account during

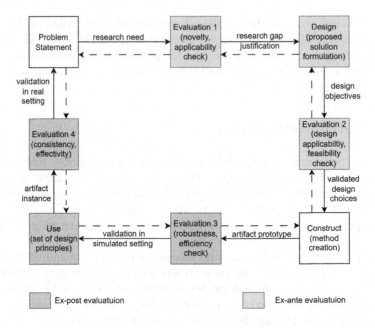

Fig. 1. Cyclic evaluation of the proposed process model.

evaluation. Early on in the DSR process, evaluations should start by determining the viability of incremental design changes.

There are four phases to the assessment process used for this research work as mentioned below:

- Evaluation of the Problem: This stage ensures sure that a pertinent DSR problem is identified and articulated. Surveys, expert interviews, and literature reviews can be used as supplementary evidence to show the planned DSR project's uniqueness, value in practice, and addition to knowledge.
- Evaluation of the Design Activity: The design activity's output is assessed to determine how well the artifact's design solves the specified issue. Since the artifact has not yet been utilized in a real-world situation or instantiated, this evaluation is being done in a controlled environment.
- Evaluation of Artifact Functionality: The goal of this stage is to assess how well the artifact interacts with other organizational components. It enables reflection on the artifact's design and offers insights into its usefulness. Ex-post assessments are carried out after the artifact has been built, whereas ex-ante evaluations are carried out before construction. If necessary, this stage makes it easier to iteratively enhance the design.
- Real-World Usability Assessment: The artifact's usability and efficacy in real-world contexts are evaluated in this last assessment phase while taking the organizational context into account. This evaluation uses the integration of artifact instances inside the organizational context as inputs.

A process model is presented in Sect. 4 to guide the evaluation design for predictive maintenance in MEMS-based inertial sensor manufacturing. Both ex-ante (Problem Statement, Evaluation 1, Design, and Evaluation 2) and ex-post (Evaluation 3, Use, and Evaluation 4) assessments are included in the approach. These assessments validate the artifact's functionality and usability as well as the accuracy of the design choices.

3   Problem Statement

MEMS-based inertial measurement unit (IMU) unit comprises a multi-axis gyroscope and an accelerometer that is utilized for positioning and navigation when combined with a global positioning system(GPS). Compared to conventional systems, a MEMS IMU system is preferable because of its precision, compact design, and cheaper price. MEMS-based IMUs are more prone to deterministic and random errors, such as measurement, quantization noise, alignment, bias, etc. than fiber or laser-based IMUs. Such uncorrected inaccuracies build up over time and have a negative effect on the sensitivity and accuracy of the inertial sensors. Sampaio et al. [14], Ciner et al. [2], and Gupta et al. [8] have shown that using AI-based solutions have significant advantages for predictive maintenance in MEMS-based inertial manufacturing.

Temperature dependency is a major problem in MEMS inertial sensors as it can affect the accuracy of the inertial sensors; Over a large temperature range, the sensors must meet specific offset requirements, such as drift, absolute failure, etc., that result from vibration, temperature, age (or mechanical stress), and humidity. The scope of this research is limited to the correction of the offset effects generated from excessive drift over temperature. These effects are only detectable after production test operations have been completed which may lead to yield loss.

The nonlinear behavior of a monitoring signal (P) caused by high-frequency components over temperature (T) is described here as the drift effect. It is calculated as the difference between the maximum and minimum value of the internal monitoring parameter over temperature, i.e., $maxP(T) - minP(T)$. Figure 2

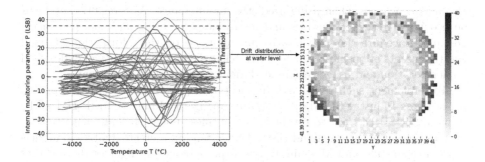

Fig. 2. Temperature drift distribution at wafer level.

shows the drift effect on a single wafer. When the drift value exceeds a prede-fined threshold, such as a 35 LSB difference between the minimum and maximum value of the parameter P, the sensor behavior is impacted. High drift values are marked with darker colors. Generally, this effect is too small to be noticed, mak-ing it impossible to quantify directly. Thus, analyzing the measurement data and process parameters can indicate the root cause behind it. Based on the drift threshold value, the sensors used for this analysis are categorized into two classes, i.e., (i) impacted (label 0) and (ii) good (label 1). One thing that has to be kept in mind is that the two classes are highly imbalanced, where label 0 is only 0.5% of the entire dataset. The data contains 1.5 million senor points, 212 characteristics, and 2 target classes.

3.1   Related Work

To address the temperature drift in MEMS gyroscopes, Yang et al. [22] devel-oped a solution combining a genetic algorithm (GA) with the widely used and well-known ML model support vector machine (SVM). Wang et al. [18] used GA with back propagation neural network (BPNN) to target a similar issue which proved to be much faster than the traditional polynomial fitting. Fontanella et al. [4], Shiau et al. [15], Xing et al. [21], and Xia et al. [20], Podder et al. [12] have shown that using artificial neural network based solutions for thermal cali-bration of MEMS inertial sensors have improved performance. Although all the aforementioned authors have achieved astounding results, authors faced issues, such as limited computational resources, unsatisfactory amount of training data availability, imbalanced and noisy data, or the data collection procedure was cumbersome.

By highlighting difficulties encountered in the field for its implementation and applications, Dalzochio et al. [3] also contribute to the field of predictive maintenance. Authors [10] use a random forest approach to showcase a machine-learning architecture for predictive maintenance. This system was tested on a real-world example, and the results indicate good accuracy. None of the afore-mentioned research projects take the DSR method into account while creating, installing, and transferring artifacts in predictive maintenance. While Tiddens et al. [17] assert that current research is creating new ways, organizations must also make decisions when using predictive maintenance. As a result, they focus on providing fresh perspectives and instructions for using and choosing meth-ods and procedures for preventative maintenance on the information at hand and the intents of businesses. The study acknowledges the scarcity of end-to-end implementation and usage recommendations for predictive maintenance.

To implement such solutions, the most widely used data mining approach is the Cross Industry Standard Procedure for Data Mining (CRSIP-DM). The steps of CRISP-DM are to establish the business issue (Business Understand-ing), examine the data at hand (Data Understanding), create analytical models (Data Preparation and Modeling), assess the outcomes in light of the business requirement (Evaluation), and implement the model (Deployment) [19]. The entire process is intended to be iterative, repeating as often as required to maintain up-to-date and efficient models. The project phases of CRISP-DM, however, exclude certain essential elements of the data science project life cycle. Moreover, the task-focused approach of CRISP-DM ignores how a team should prioritize tasks as well as interact and communicate generally [13]. To summarize, this method (i) lacks synergy between the business problem and analytics team, (ii) has no guidance for implementation and maintenance of the AI solution, and (iii) does not provide for theorizing, re-utilization, and transfer of newly obtained knowledge.

Moreover, [9]argues that data mining standards methods, such as CRISP-DM, do not offer a broad perspective that can help both the development of the model and its implementation in an information system. Thus, to create a supervised machine learning process model, which includes model initiation, error estimation, and deployment, the article uses DSR. This paper focuses mainly on predictive maintenance and uses DSR by taking into account the twin goals of creating artifacts by addressing problems and, concurrently, generalizing design and action theories.

4   Experiment and Result

The proposed method follows methodical and multiple evaluation-based strategies which are called an artifact in terms of a process model. Not only does the process model provide a thorough set of guidelines, but also a necessary set of design principles that can be translated to another manufacturing-based problem context as knowledge transfer. This provides the novelty of this research work.

Figure 3 describes the proposed process model (DSR artifact) to predict affected MEMS inertial sensors effectively and systematically, through root cause analysis using AI and DSR. It demonstrates the assessment procedure used to produce and assess the finished artifact in the ongoing research which is an extension of the work presented at [1]. The fundamental "build-evaluate" steps of DSR are used in the assessment process, although there are several modifications.

The process begins with the Problem Statement, where the "pain area" for the study is examined to create the research question(s) as explained in Sect. 3. Offset effects, such as excessive drift over temperature, can dramatically affect the sensor performance and are only detectable after production testing operations. Finding the true cause of this drift aberration and identifying the damaged components as early as feasible is thus necessary. A variety of techniques were used for this, including literature reviews, expert interviews, domain expertise, etc. as discussed in the Subsect. 3.1.

The next part of this DSR evaluation procedure is called "Evaluation 1". This step determines the importance of the issue, which in this case is to optimize the procedure by identifying the causes of the excessive temperature drift. Moreover, this results in more accurate sensors, which raises the yield percentage. A collection of design criteria specified to address the chosen problem can be seen as the "Design" phase and it is described in Table 1.

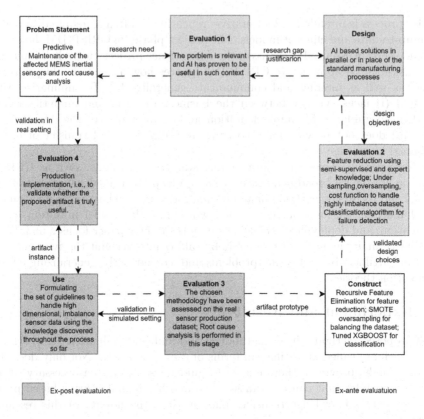

Fig. 3. Process model evaluation design for predictive maintenance in MEMS-based inertial sensor manufacturing.

After careful research and initial analysis, methods mentioned in Table 1 have been chosen as the desirable choices among the plethora of options keeping the problem statement in mind. The "Evaluation 2" phase is an experimental phase where many techniques and algorithms as mentioned before, have been employed and evaluated to get the best response.

For the experimental analysis, a real dataset containing 212 variables and over 1.5 million data points was used that contains information related to yaw rate sensors, inertial sensors, acceleration sensors, process measurements, temperature measurements, infrastructure measurements, etc. The focus was given to understanding the parameters that contribute to the high drift effect in temperature-sensitive sensors. Based on the temperature drift value, classification analysis was performed to distinguish between affected and unaffected sensors.

With the abundance of AI technologies available, this step took a long time, i.e. selecting the correct set of trial algorithms and methods that are consistent with the problem description was exhaustive. During the initial data preparation

Table 1. Overall Design Description.

Criterion	Methods Used
Data Preprocessing	Missing Value treatment, Outlier Detection and Removal, Data Scaling
Feature Selection	Correlation Analysis, Principal Component Analysis (PCA), Recursive Feature Elimination (RFE), Tree-based Feature Importance, Subject Matter Expert (SME) Knowledge
Sampling	Synthetic Minority Oversampling Technique (SMOTE), Resampling, NearMiss
Algorithms	XGBoost Classification Algorithms, Decision Trees, Random Forest (RF), Gaussian Naive Bayes (GNB), Support Vector Machines (SVM)
Evaluation Metrics	Accuracy, Precision, Recall, Receiver Operating Characteristic (ROC) Curve, Area Under the ROC Curve (AUC)

phase, data consistency was checked to remove outliers, missing values, data type mismatches, etc. using statistical methods. Uni-variate and bi-variate methods were used to understand the behavior of every input variable or feature and their dependencies on the target variable. The Z-score method, which is a measure of how far away each data point is from the mean in terms of standard deviation, was employed for the detection of outliers. The Z-score

To address the unbalanced nature of the data used for the current research, various approaches, including SMOTE oversampling, undersampling, and cost function, were used. The model prediction is generally influenced by the variables or features used during the training phase. An unnecessary amount of variables can lead to the model overfitting or inaccurate model prediction. Thus, the high dimensionality of the data was reduced using a variety of feature reduction approaches, including principal component analysis (PCA), Subject Matter Expert (SME), correlation analysis, recursive feature elimination (RFE), and tree-based feature significance from supervised techniques. Finally, 45 features were selected for model evaluation to maintain around 95% variance in the next phase.

Evaluation 1, Design, and Evaluation 2 are part of the "Ex-ante Evaluations". These are used to confirm the design decisions taken to produce an artifact for the problem statement. To discover the best solution set for early failure prediction of the impacted sensors in this instance, many rounds of experimentation were conducted on various combinations of algorithms. The last phase in this procedure is the "Construct," which is the complete solution set. The most effective method for choosing features was RFE [11]. The technique to balance the two classes in the data set was SMOTE oversampling for the minority class. The XGBoost classification algorithm was selected as the final predictive model. The number of gradient-boosted trees used was 2000 and the learning rate was set to 0.01 for better generalization. Logarithmic loss aka 'Log Loss' was used as the evaluation parameter which is a probabilistic measure that penalizes false classification.

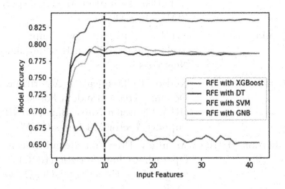

Fig. 4. Feature reduction process using Recursive Feature Elimination (RFE) to find the optimal feature space for classifying the affected MEMS-based inertial sensors.

The chosen classification model XGBoost, outperformed alternative tree-based approaches, naive Bayes, and support vector machines in terms of accuracy in the analysis as shown in Fig. 4.

Figure 5 displays the outcome of applying the XGBoost model on MEMS inertial sensor manufacturing data. After analyzing the model result and using the domain knowledge, a few observations were made. There could be some missing features or variables which could describe the behavior of the affected sensors and were not included in the data set. There could also be the presence of noise, imparted by the used input features. To reduce the noise of the neighboring data points, a 3 X 3 convolution window was used to average the neighborhood values for every input parameter. The averaged values were used again as a new feature to train the model.

Using the built-in "Feature Importance" for the XGBoost model, the most important input parameters influencing the model prediction were identified. It can be seen from Fig. 5, that the drift value is higher around the edges which indicates that the vacuum variation in the MEMS sensor is creating a large technological distribution of the affected sensors. The topmost parameter obtained from the feature importance of the XGBoost model confirmed the same. The modeling results also showed a strong correlation to one of the coupling coefficients in the sensing element which was the second parameter of the feature

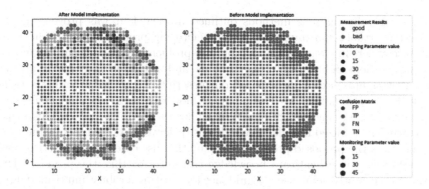

Fig. 5. Model prediction analysis to find the root cause behind the factors causing temperature-induced high drift.

importance. By visualizing the model results, the physical causes behind the measured effect on the sensors became more understandable. This newly produced information provided a new physical working mechanism for the monitoring parameter, which was not known before the analysis.

It became evident what physical factors were responsible for the detected effect on the sensors after completing a thorough examination of the sensors associated with false negatives (FN) and false positives (FP) near the wafer's borders. Using the whole data set, the XGBoost model was able to predict 96% of the good sensors (marked green in Fig. 5) and 88% of the impacted sensors (marked red). The final set of recommendations is created in the phase "Use," after employing the significant information obtained through research analysis and expert consultation. In the last phase, "Evaluation 4," artifact instances are verified using a real production implementation. The suggested artifact prototype is now being utilized in manufacturing to classify wafers based on drift behavior.

5   Conclusion and Future Work

The research paper discusses a novel artifact for MEMS inertial sensor predictive maintenance analysis incorporating AI solutions with the DSR technique. The resilience and potential of the XGBoost classification algorithm for early failure identification were demonstrated. The prediction was performed on individual sensors irrespective of the complete wafer. This implies that the model can predict the affected parts at the sensor level. By counting the number of affected sensors on a single wafer, the model can predict the chances of the wafer being good or affected. Under the current process, the impacted sensors can only be found once the finished product has been produced. But using the proposed solution in production, the impacted sensors can be detected earlier. Detecting and filtering these sensors from the component data before the final product is important to save production costs.

Through the rigorous methods outlined in Sect. 4, it was proven that the suggested artifact can improve the manufacturing process. A clear framework aids researchers in choosing the appropriate problem domain, designing and validating solutions in line with research needs, and ultimately creating an artifact. The artifact presented here is based on prescriptive knowledge and it satisfied three design principles: two DSR inquiry modes, process documentation, and continuous assessment, which qualify it to have a truth-like value. This helped in creating generalized knowledge which is transferable. As a part of future work, validation of the proposed process model in other use cases in other settings will be performed to authenticate knowledge transfer. For this, the proposed DSR artifact is currently being used as guidance for creating a robust multi-modal sensor fusion algorithm for blood pressure estimation in spinal cord injury patients. As the future domain of application and problem context is dissimilar to that presented in this paper, this will validate the re-usability, generalization, and transferability of the artifact. Further discussion is out of the scope of this paper.

Acknowledgements. The research was co-funded by the project Strengthening the EIT Digital Knowledge Innovation Community in Hungary (2021-1.2.1-EIT-KIC-2021-00006), implemented with the support provided by the Ministry of Innovation and Technology of Hungary from the National Research, Development and Innovation Fund, financed under the 2021-1.2.1-EIT-KIC funding scheme.

References

1. (cs)2; the 13th conference of phd students in computer science, June 2022. https://www.inf.u-szeged.hu/cscs/
2. Çınar, Z.M., Abdussalam Nuhu, A., Zeeshan, Q., Korhan, O., Asmael, M., Safaei, B.: Machine learning in predictive maintenance towards sustainable smart manufacturing in industry 4.0. Sustainability **12**(19), 8211 (2020)
3. Dalzochio, J., et al.: Machine learning and reasoning for predictive maintenance in industry 4.0: current status and challenges. Comput. Ind. **123**, 103298 (2020)
4. Fontanella, R., Accardo, D., Moriello, R.S.L., Angrisani, L., De Simone, D.: Mems gyros temperature calibration through artificial neural networks. Sens. Actuators A **279**, 553–565 (2018)
5. Gregor, S.: Building theory in the sciences of the artificial. In: Proceedings of the 4th International Conference on Design Science Research in Information Systems and Technology, pp. 1–10 (2009)
6. Gregor, S., Hevner, A.R.: Positioning and presenting design science research for maximum impact. MIS Q. **37**, 337–355 (2013)
7. Gregor, S., Jones, D., et al.: The anatomy of a design theory. Assoc. Inf. Syst. (2007)
8. Gupta, S., Mittal, M., Padha, A.: Predictive analytics of sensor data based on supervised machine learning algorithms. In: 2017 International Conference on Next Generation Computing and Information Systems (ICNGCIS), pp. 171–176. IEEE (2017)
9. Hirt, R., Koehl, N.J., Satzger, G.: An end-to-end process model for supervised machine learning classification: from problem to deployment in information systems. In: Designing the Digital Transformation: DESRIST 2017 Research in

Progress Proceedings of the 12th International Conference on Design Science Research in Information Systems and Technology. Karlsruhe, Germany, 30 May–1 June, pp. 55–63. Karlsruher Institut für Technologie (KIT) (2017)

10. Paolanti, M., Romeo, L., Felicetti, A., Mancini, A., Frontoni, E., Loncarski, J.: Machine learning approach for predictive maintenance in industry 4.0. In: 2018 14th IEEE/ASME International Conference on Mechatronic and Embedded Systems and Applications (MESA), pp. 1–6. IEEE (2018)

11. Podder, I., Fischl, T., Bub, U.: Smart feature selection for fault detection in the mems sensor production process using machine learning methods. In: 2nd International Conference on Industry 4.0 and Artificial Intelligence (ICIAI 2021), pp. 21–25. Atlantis Press (2022)

12. Podder, I., Fischl, T., Bub, U.: Artificial intelligence applications for mems-based sensors and manufacturing process optimization. Telecom **4**(1), 165–197 (2023). https://doi.org/10.3390/telecom4010011, https://www.mdpi.com/2673-4001/4/1/11

13. Saltz, J.S.: CRISP-DM for data science: strengths, weaknesses and potential next steps. In: 2021 IEEE International Conference on Big Data (Big Data), pp. 2337–2344 (2021). https://doi.org/10.1109/BigData52589.2021.9671634

14. Scalabrini Sampaio, G., Vallim Filho, A.R.D.A., Santos da Silva, L., Augusto da Silva, L.: Prediction of motor failure time using an artificial neural network. Sensors **19**(19), 4342 (2019)

15. Shiau, J.K., Ma, D.M., Huang, C.X., Chang, M.Y.: Mems gyroscope null drift and compensation based on neural network. Adv. Mater. Res. **255**, 2077–2081. Trans Tech Publ (2011)

16. Sonnenberg, C., vom Brocke, J.: Evaluation patterns for design science research artefacts. In: Helfert, M., Donnellan, B. (eds.) EDSS 2011. CCIS, vol. 286, pp. 71–83. Springer, Heidelberg (2012). https://doi.org/10.1007/978-3-642-33681-2_7

17. Tiddens, W., Braaksma, J., Tinga, T.: Exploring predictive maintenance applications in industry. J. Qual. Maint. Eng. **28**(1), 68–85 (2022)

18. Wang, S., Zhu, W., Shen, Y., Ren, J., Gu, H., Wei, X.: Temperature compensation for mems resonant accelerometer based on genetic algorithm optimized backpropagation neural network. Sens. Actuators A **316**, 112393 (2020)

19. Wirth, R., Hipp, J.: CRISP-DM: towards a standard process model for data mining. In: Proceedings of the 4th International Conference on the Practical Applications of Knowledge Discovery and Data Mining, vol. 1, pp. 29–39. Manchester (2000)

20. Xia, D., Chen, S., Wang, S., Li, H.: Temperature effects and compensation-control methods. Sensors **9**(10), 8349–8376 (2009)

21. Xing, H., Hou, B., Lin, Z., Guo, M.: Modeling and compensation of random drift of mems gyroscopes based on least squares support vector machine optimized by chaotic particle swarm optimization. Sensors **17**(10), 2335 (2017)

22. Yang, Y., Liu, Y., Liu, Y., Zhao, X.: Temperature compensation of mems gyroscope based on support vector machine optimized by GA. In: 2019 IEEE Symposium Series on Computational Intelligence (SSCI), pp. 2989–2994. IEEE (2019)

Efficient Pruning Strategy for Mining High Utility Quantitative Itemsets

Loan T. T. Nguyen[1,2] ⓘ, Anh N. H. Pham[1,2], Trinh D. D. Nguyen[3] ⓘ,
Adrianna Kozierkiewicz[4] ⓘ, Bay Vo[5] ⓘ, and N. T. Tung[5(✉)] ⓘ

[1] School of Computer Science and Engineering, International University, Ho Chi Minh City,
Vietnam
nttloan@hcmiu.edu.vn, ITITIU18007@student.hcmiu.edu.vn
[2] Vietnam National University, Ho Chi Minh City, Vietnam
[3] Faculty of Information Technology, Industrial University of Ho Chi Minh City, Ho Chi Minh
City, Vietnam
20126291.trinh@student.iuh.edu.vn
[4] Faculty of Computer Science and Management, Wroclaw University of Science and
Technology, Wrocław, Poland
Adrianna.kozierkiewicz@pwr.edu.pl
[5] Faculty of Information Technology, HUTECH University, Ho Chi Minh City, Vietnam
{vd.bay,nt.tung}@hutech.edu.vn

Abstract. High Utility Quantitative Itemset Mining (HUQIM), which is an extension of the original High Utility Itemset Mining (HUIM), has become an important research area that answers the ever-growing need for useful information from
the copious pool of data in reality. Due to the nature of the HUQIM problem,
its search space is huge and could heavily affect the execution time. Thus, the
recently proposed FHUQI-Miner has overcome these limits with novel pruning
strategies to narrow the space and outperform previously introduced algorithms.
However, there are certain shortcomings that the algorithm still faces. One of
the limitations is that the proposed strategies would not operate as efficiently on
dense datasets as they would on sparse datasets, resulting from the similarity in
structure of the transactions and thus increasing the number of join operations in
progress. To address this limitation, this work introduces an enhanced version of
the FHUQI-Miner algorithm with an improved TQCS structure to reduce mining
time and the number of joins performed.

Keywords: High Utility Quantitative · Itemset Mining · High Utility Itemset
Mining · Data mining

1 Introduction

In recent years, one of the most studied areas in the field of Data Mining is High Utility
Itemset Mining (HUIM) [1]. The task reveals patterns with high importance associated
with a utility function. For example, the discovered information can be used in market analysis to study customer behaviors [1] or the time user stays on webpages when

© The Author(s), under exclusive license to Springer Nature Switzerland AG 2023
N. T. Nguyen et al. (Eds.): ICCCI 2023, CCIS 1864, pp. 326–338, 2023.
https://doi.org/10.1007/978-3-031-41774-0_26

applied in click-stream analysis [2, 3], etc. This mining task has variations to fit several application targets, such as high utility sequential itemsets, high utility periodic itemsets, etc. HUIM aims to discover a complete set of patterns that have their utility value satisfies a user-specified threshold (μ). Unlike FIM, which only considers the appearance of items in transactions, HUIM extends the inputs further. Each item now has its quantity per transaction instead of a binary occurrence. In addition, they can carry another value known as unit utility, representing their level of importance, such as profit, cost, time, etc. [1]. HUIM is extensively studied and has many applications, resulting in a series of algorithms introduced in recent years [4]. However, the outcomes of HUIM do not contain information about quantities of the discovered patterns. Thus, an extension to HUIM to address this critical drawback was introduced. The task is known as High Utility Quantitative Itemset Mining (HUQIM); its outputs are now containing information about item quantities that yield the utility, besides knowing they are high utility [5, 6]. For instance, a discovered high utility itemset containing the following items {*cheese, coffee, champagne*} could help retailers co-promote them to boost sales. However, the discovered pattern does not provide about the quantities often purchased. HUQIM addresses this limitation to return patterns containing quantities that yield high profit besides the items, such as {*cheese:2, coffee:5, champagne:8*}. Furthermore, quantity ranges are also revealed by HUQIM. For example, an itemset such as {*ham:4–8, lettuce:2–5*} suggests that the combinations of items with their purchased quantity range yield high profit. Useful information like this could help retailers adjust their marketing policies to fit user needs better. Thus, HUQIM is considered more useful than the traditional HUIM task. However, considering more information makes HUQIM more complex and more challenging than HUIM. An item with different quantities is considered a different quantitative item (*Q-item* for short). The same is applied to the set of quantitative items (*Q-itemset*). This expands the search space of the problem further than HUIM. A quantitative item/itemset is called a high utility quantitative item/itemset if its utility is greater or equal to the μ threshold, which is specified by the users.

This work addresses the limitations of the previously proposed algorithm, the FHUQI-Miner [6], to improve the mining performance in terms of execution time, and memory usage and reduce the number of joins taken.

The remainder of this paper is organized as follows. A literature review of recent work related to HUIM and HUQIM is presented in the next section. Section 3 describes the backgrounds of the HUQIM task. Section 4 introduces our proposed techniques to improve mining performance. Evaluations are carried out and discussed in Sect. 5. Conclusions are drawn in Sect. 6, as well as future research opportunities are also discussed.

2 Related Works

Frequent Itemset Mining (FIM) is fundamental to the world of data mining, whose goal is to determine all sets of items that occurred at least a certain number of times in a transaction database [7]. In a transaction database, items are either appear or absent in each transaction, and thus they are all considered equally in FIM. Many approaches were introduced to reveal the set of frequent items [6, 7]. These approaches utilize the frequency measure's anti-monotonic property to improve the mining performance. Over time, the need for more important knowledge is raised besides the ones obtained from the discovered frequent patterns. Among the factors, the most focused is on the profit gained from the mined patterns. This is where HUIM took the focus of research interests [8].

HUIM extends FIM to address its limitations [8], removing the binary occurrence barrier. Each item appearing in the transaction now has a quantity linked. Besides, its level of importance (profit, weight, etc.) is also considered. For example, each pound of cherry is priced at $2, thus selling 3 lb yield $6 in profit. HUIM is targeting to reveal all combinations of items that provide profit no less than a user-specified threshold, known as minimum utility. Unlike FIM, the numeric function used in HUIM is neither anti-monotonic nor monotonic, as the frequency measure does. Thus, HUIM is considered more challenging than FIM. Several HUIM algorithms were introduced. The early algorithms followed the two-phase model. As its name implies, the two-phase methods reveal high utility itemsets (HUIs) in two phases. Some notable methods are Two-Phase [9], IHUP [10], TWU-Mining [11], etc. These algorithms rely on an upper bound known as Transaction Weighted Utilization (TWU), which satisfies the downward-closure property [9], to reduce the search space. Generating candidates is time and memory consuming. Thus, the one-phase method stepped in to resolve the limitations. Generated candidates are eliminated as soon as they are considered unpromising, saving further computation time and memory needed to check and store them. Several notable algorithms can be named, such as HUI-Miner [12], EFIM [13], iMEFIM [14], etc.

However, all these mentioned algorithms only discovered the high utility patterns to the user, no information, such as quantities, is returned. To address this drawback, the task of HUQIM is proposed to discover HUQIs. However, until recently, only a few approaches were proposed, as the task is more complex than HUIM. Some important algorithms are HUQA [15], HUQI-Miner [5] and FHUQI-Miner [6]. The most recent approach is the FHUQI-Miner. It comes with several optimizations, such as TQCS, and RQCPS, to overcome the limitations of previous approaches.

3 Preliminaries

This section introduces the foundation principles expected when mining HUQIs. As the study of HUQIM has been previously inspired by the abundance of knowledge from its predecessor HUIM, well-known definitions will not be presented here to keep the paper concise.

Let D be the input quantitative transaction database containing m transactions and is denoted as $D = \{T_1, T_2, \ldots, T_m\}$, $I = \{i_1, i_2, \ldots, i_n\}$ be a set of n distinctive items in the database D. A transaction $T_q \in D$, $T_q \subseteq I (1 \leq q \leq m)$ have a unique *transaction identifier*, denoted as T_{ID}. Each item $i \in I$ appears in transaction T_q has an associated positive number $q(i, T_q)$, referred to as the *internal utility* or its quantity in each transaction T_q. Another value called *external utility*, denoted by $p(i)$, will be used to keep track of the unit profit that each item i possesses. Table 1 introduces an exemplary transaction database D containing five transactions. Each transaction contains a set of items and their respective internal utilities. Considering transaction T_1, four items are currently being purchased, namely item a, c, h and i, with the respective quantities of 2, 7, 4, and 9. Moreover, Table 2 expresses the external utility values (profit) of the items $i \in I$. By reference, item a will always have a value of 20 profit units, and item c will always be worth 70 profit units. These external utility values are uniform across all transactions within the database D.

Table 1. An example of a Quantitative Transaction Database

TID	Items	Internal utilities
T_1	a, c, h, i	2, 7, 4, 9
T_2	a, c	3, 8
T_3	a, b, c, g, h	2, 1, 7, 7, 4
T_4	b, c, g, h	2, 9, 8, 5
T_5	a, d, e, f	2, 5, 1, 1

Table 2. The corresponding profit for each item in Table 1

Item	a	b	c	d	e	f	g	h	i
Profit	20	10	70	54	11	100	75	47	96

An *exact Q-item* x is a paired value in the form of (i, q) where $i \in I$ is the identifier for item x and q is its respective quantity. Furthermore, each transaction $T_q \in D$ can be viewed as a list of exact Q-items [6]. A *range Q-item* x considers the quantity of an item not as an exact value but rather a range of values. Therefore, a range Q-item will feature both a lower bound as well as a larger upper bound value, denoted as a tuple (i, l, u), where $i \in I$ is the identifier for that item x, l is the lower bound and u refers to the upper bound. The internal size of a *Q-item*, also known as the *Q-interval* can be calculated as following $Q - interval = (u - l + 1)$. A range *Q-item* among the mentioned would be able to represent all the different exact *Q-items* as an entirety [6]. It is important to remember that *range Q-items* do not inherently exist within a database, but rather a concept formed for the purpose of mining quantitative items. In other words, an item from a transaction can only have exactly one definite value, which is the exact *Q-item* mentioned above. Another characteristic that is often overlooked at this point is that exact *Q-items* of the form (i, q) can also be represented using the notion for *range Q-items* (i, l, u), where $q = l = u$.

Definition 1: Quantitative Itemset [6]

A set of *Q-items* that are collected together under a group will be referred to as a quantitative itemset X. A k-*Q-itemset* means a *Q-itemset* that consists of k distinctive *Q-items*, $X = [x_1, x_2, \ldots, x_k]$. If there is at least one *range Q-item* among the items in the set, the itemset would be referred to as a *range Q-itemset*. Otherwise, if and only if all of the Q-*items* in the set are *exact Q-items*, then it would be called an *exact Q-itemset*.

Definition 2: Inclusion of Q-item [6]

With an exact Q-item $X = (i, q)$ and a range Q-item $y = (j, l, u)$, y includes x or x is included in y if $i = j$ and $l \leq q \leq u$. Similarly, with two range Q-items $x = (i, l, u)$ and $y = (j, l\prime, u\prime)$, y *includes x or x is included in y* if $i = j$, $l \geq l\prime$ and $u \leq u\prime$.

Definition 3: Occurrence of a Q-item, Q-itemset [6]

For any exact Q-item $x = (i, q)$, it will be considered to occur in a particular transaction T_d, if $x \in T_d$. A range Q-item $x = (i, l, u)$ occurred in T_d if at least one of the exact Q-items in x is covered by that range occurs in the transaction. A Q-itemset $X = [x_1, x_2, \ldots, x_k]$ occurs in a transaction T_d if $\forall x \in X$, x occurs in T_d.

Definition 4: Occurrence Set and Support Count of a Q-itemset [6]

The occurrence-set of a Q-itemset X, $OCC(X)$, is the set of transactions where X appears. Given a Q-itemset X, the support count of X, $SC(X)$, is defined as the number of transactions containing X, $SC(X) = |OCC(X)|$.

Definition 5: Utility of a Q-item, Q-itemset [6]

- The utility of an exact Q-item $x = (i, q)$ in transaction T_d, denote $u(x, T_q)$ is determined as $u(x, T_q) = q(i, T_q) \times p(i)$.
- The utility of a range Q-item $x = (i, l, u)$ in transaction T_q is defined as the sum of all utility of the Q-items included in x: $u(x, T_q) = \sum_{j=l}^{u} u((i, j), T_q)$.
- Considering a Q-itemset $X = [x_1, x_2, \ldots, x_k]$, the utility of a Q-itemset X in transaction T_q, denoted as $u(X, T_q)$, is defined as the sum of utilities of Q-items of X in T_q: $u(X, T_q) = \sum_{i=1}^{k} u(x_i, T_q)$.
- The utility of the Q-itemset X in database D, denoted as $u(X)$, is determined as the sum of utilities of X in all transactions containing X, $u(X) = \sum_{T_q \in OCC(X)} u(X, T_q)$.

Definition 6: Transaction and Database Utility [6]

- The utility of a transaction $T_q = \{x_1, x_2, \ldots, x_k\}$, $T_q \in D$, denoted as $TU(T_q)$, is defined as the sum of utilities of all Q-items contained in T_q: $TU(T_q) = \sum_{i=1}^{k} u(x_i, T_q)$.
- The total utility of a database D, denoted as $\sigma(D)$, is determined as the sum of utilities of all transactions in D: $\sigma(D) = \sum_{i=1 \wedge T_i \in D}^{m} TU(T_i)$.

Definition 7: High Utility Quantitative Itemset (HUQI) [6]

Let D be a quantitative transaction database, a user-specified minimum utility threshold and μ, a Q-itemset X. X is called a high utility quantitative itemset if and only if its utility is no less than μ.

As the task of HUIQM is inherited from HUIM, the utility measure does not satisfy the downward-closure property. Thus, a proper utility-based upper bound is required to adapt the efficient pruning strategies from HUIM. The Transaction Weighted Utilization (TWU) upper bound is used to reduce the search space [9]. The base definition of TWU and the extended TWU definitions to be applied in HUIQM were described in detail in [6]. In addition, our work extends the original FHUQI-Miner algorithm. Thus all the *combining strategies* (Combine All, Combine Min, Combine Max), and *Q-itemset utility list* used in FHQUI-Miner are also employed [6]. The related definitions are also given discussed in [6]. Thus, to keep the paper compact, they will not be presented in this section. The core contribution of our work is to improve the effectiveness of the FHUQI-Miner algorithm; the related definitions are presented as follows.

Definition 8: Promising Q-itemsets [6]
Let X be a Q-itemset, a minimum utility threshold μ, and a quantitative related coefficient qrc ($qrc > 0$). X is considered a promising Q-itemset if $TWU(X) \geq \frac{\mu}{qrc}$. Otherwise, X is an unpromising Q-itemset.

Property 1: (Pruning Using TWU).
Let X be a Q-itemset, if X is an unpromising Q-itemset then X and all of its extensions are low utility itemsets and can be safely pruned from the search space [6].

Definition 9: TQCS Structure [6]
The TCQS structure is comprised of tuples in the form of $\langle a, b, c \rangle$, whereas a and b are the two Q-items that co-occurred in the database D; c are the TWU of the 2-Q-itemset constructed from a, b, $c = TWU(\{ab\})$. The concept of TQCS is mainly based on the EUCS structure proposed in the work of the FHM algorithm [6]. Differing from EUCS, the TQCS only keeps track of all the 2-Q-itemsets that really co-occur in the database D.

Property 2: (Exact Q-items Pruning – EQCPS). Given two Q-items x, y, a quantitative related coefficient qrc ($qrc > 0$), if there does not exist a tuple $\langle a, b, c \rangle$ such that $x = a, y = b$ and $c > \frac{\mu}{qrc}$, then the Q-itemset $\{xy\}$ is not a high utility Q-itemset as well as all of its extensions [6].

Property 3: (Range Q-items Pruning – RQCPS). Let $x = (i, l, u)$ be a range Q-item, and y be an exact Q-item, consider $x_i = (i, q)$ to be an exact Q-item within the range of (l, u) and is extracted from x. Then, if $\sum_{i=l}^{u} c_i < \frac{\mu}{qrc}$, the Q-itemset $\{xy\}$ and all of its extensions are not high utility Q-itemset [6].

4   Proposed Approach

Our goal is to enhance the effectiveness of the FHUQI-Miner algorithm based on a thorough analysis of the TQCS structure [5]. This strategy is named the Improved TQCS Strategy. As presented in the previous section, the underestimated property points toward the fact that both exact Q-items and range Q-items could be represented in a similar fashion via the format (i, l, u), where i is the identifier of that item in a given transactional database, l and u sequentially acting as the lower and upper bounds to the range of quantities that item will exist across the transactions of that database. Re-using the example transactional database given in Table 1, any randomly picked exact Q-item in those transactions could be represented as a range Q-item. $(i, 9)$ and $(f, 1)$ are by exact nature Q-items, but they can also be viewed as range Q-items under the form of $(i, 9, 9)$ and $(f, 1, 1)$, as their lower and upper bounds are basically the same, and the Q-interval of the "range" is simply 0.

Algorithm 1. iFHUQI-Miner

Input: D — quantitative transaction database; μ — minimum utility threshold; CM — combining method; qrc — quantitative related coefficient

Output: Complete set of HUQIs.

1: Scans D to calculate the TWU of each item.
2: Creates set of promising Q-items P^*: $\forall x \in P^*: TWU(X) \geq \frac{\mu}{qrc}$
3: Scans D to sort transactions in the decreasing order of utility $<$;
    create the utility list of promising items $UL(P^*)$; build the TQCS.
4: **FOREACH** $x \in P^*$ **DO**
5:      **IF** $UL(x).SumEutil \geq \mu$ **THEN**
6:          $H = H \cup x$; Output x
7:      **ENDIF**
8:      **ELSE**
9:          **IF** $UL(X).SumEutil + UL(X).SumRutil \geq \mu$ **THEN**
10:             $E = E \cup x$
11:         **ENDIF**
12:         **IF** $\frac{\mu}{qrc} \leq UL(X).SumEutil \leq \mu$ **THEN**
13:             $C = C \cup x$
14:         **ENDIF**
15:     **ENDELSE**
16: **ENDFOR**
17: Discover high utility range Q-itemset (HR) using CM and C
18: $QI \leftarrow sort(H \cup E \cup HR)$ using the $<$ order
19: **Improved_DFS_Mining**$(\emptyset, QI, UL(QI), P^*, qrc, CM, \mu)$

This change in the notation of any Q-item can easily make a difference through implementation, enabling the possibility of uniting the strategies that Nouioua et al. [5] initially and distinctively proposed. It is the default for every Q-item to contain both lower and upper bounds, and that exact Q-items to keep the same quantities for these variables. The detail of our proposal, the iFHUQI-Miner algorithm, is presented in Algorithm 1. The algorithm's pseudo-code is no different from the original FHUQI-Miner. It is shown here for the reader easier to catch up on the changes presented in Algorithm 2, which is the search space exploration phase.

Please note that in Algorithm 1, the set H contains all the HUQIs, the set C contains all the candidates Q-itemsets that can be combined to form high utility range Q-itemsets, the set E contains all Q-itemsets that should be explored further to discover possible HUQIs from the extensions, and the set HR contains all the high utility range Q-itemsets obtained by combining Q-items in C. The last line of Algorithm 1 invokes the recursive DFS-based function to scan the search space, the `Improved_DFS_Mining` function. This is where the *Improved TQCS Strategy* will be applied with respect to the previous assimilation of exact Q-items notation to range Q-items notation.

Comparing the original `Recursive_Mining_Search` in [6] versus the *Improved TQCS Strategy* presented here, the prominent distinction surfaces right at the extension traversal step when it scans through the set of promising Q-items. For the original FHUQI-Miner algorithm, it will explore all possible combination of Q-itemsets of the form $[Pxy]$, and prune away any combinations that are low-utility using the two pruning strategies. This approach, described from *line 9 to line 15* in the pseudo-code of the `Recursive_Mining_Search` [6], implies the different treatment between exact Q-items and range Q-items.

The strategy used in FHUQI-Miner can be summarized as follows.

– When both x and y are exact Q-items, the original FHUQI-Miner algorithm will compose the TQCS structure $\langle x, y, c \rangle$ and evaluate the TWU of between x and y. If the TWU does not satisfy the $\frac{\mu}{qrc}$ threshold, the next extension will be checked. This is the Exact Q-items Co-occurrence Pruning Strategy.
– When x is a range Q-item, the algorithm considers each exact Q-item x_i of $[Px]$ across all transactions and sums up all c values gathered under $\langle x_i, y, c \rangle$. If the sum is less than $\frac{\mu}{qrc}$, then the Q-itemset and its extensions will be dropped immediately. This is the Range Q-items Cooccurrence Pruning Strategy.

On the contrary, the proposed iFHUQI-Miner algorithm follows the principle of similar notation and shortens the validation stage to only *line 4* to *line 9*. In other words, this will treat range Q-items and exact Q-items in the same manner and unanimously apply the notation (i, l, u) to all items regardless of which side of the spectrum the current item falls under. In other words, the exact Q-items are now considered as a subset of the range Q-items, and this is done in line 4 of Algorithm 2. For example, using the transactional database D given in Table 1, any exact Q-item in D can be represented as a range Q-item. Such as $(a, 2)$ or $(e, 1)$ are exact Q-items by nature. But these exact Q-items can be represented as range Q-items of $(a, 2, 2)$ and $(e, 1, 1)$ with their ranges equal to zero.

Algorithm 2. Improved_DFS_Mining

Input: P — prefix Q-itemset, QI — Q-itemset list, $UL(QI)$ — utility list of Q-itemsets, P^* - promising Q-itemsets, qrc — quantitative related co-efficient, CM — combining method, μ — predefined minimum utility threshold

Output: the set of HUQIs with respect to prefix P.

1: **FOREACH** $[Px]$ such that $x \in QI$ **DO**
2:      $QI_s \leftarrow \emptyset$; $P_s^* \leftarrow \emptyset$
3:      **FOREACH** $[Py]$ such that $y \in QI$ **AND** $x \prec y$ **DO**
4:          **FOREACH** exact Q-item $x_i \in [Px]$ **DO**
5:              $c \leftarrow \sum_{i=l}^{u} TQCS(x_i, y)$
6:              **IF** $c == null$ **OR** $c \leq \dfrac{\mu}{qrc}$ **THEN**
7:                  next $[Py]$
8:              **ENDIF**
9:          **ENDFOR**
10:         $Z \leftarrow [Pxy]$; $UL(Z) \leftarrow$ Construct(x, y, P)
11:         **IF** $UL(Z) \neq null$ **AND** $TWU(Z) \geq \dfrac{\mu}{qrc}$ **THEN**
12:             $P_s^* \leftarrow P_s^* \cup Z$
13:             **IF** $UL(Z).SumEutil \geq \mu$ **THEN**
14:                 $H_s \leftarrow H_s \cup Z$; Output Z
15:             **ENDIF**
16:         **ELSE**
17:             **IF** $UL(Z).SumEutil + UL(Z).SumRutil \geq \mu$ **THEN**
18:                 $E_s \leftarrow E_s \cup Z$
19:             **ENDIF**
20:             **IF** $\dfrac{\mu}{qrc} \leq UL(Z).SumEutil \leq \mu$ **THEN**
21:                 $C_s \leftarrow C_s \cup Z$
22:             **ENDIF**
23:         **ENDELSE**
24:         **ENDIF**
25:     **ENDFOR**
26:     Discover high utility range Q-item (HR_s) using CM and C_s
27:     $QI_s \leftarrow sort(H_s \cup E_s \cup HR_s)$ using $\prec$ order
28:     **Improved_DFS_Mining**$(Px, QI_s, UL(QI_s), P_s^*, qrc, CM, \mu)$
29: **ENDFOR**

With this approach, the proposed algorithm will still be able to maintain the resources delegated to validate both exact Q-item and range Q-item as before and make the real implementation more manageable. In the case of exact Q-items because both boundaries will be referring to the same quantity, every item will still have only one tuple $\langle x, y, c \rangle$ created for it and validated with the same principles. As for the case of range Q-items, the procedure of retrieving the exact component Q-items within the range and validating their $\langle x_i, y, c \rangle$ tuples will also stay untouched. With this approach, the implementation of the first proposed algorithm will be improved compared to the original algorithm as it reduces the number of conditions required to validate before the mining process is performed any further. Therefore, although the idea might appear very basic, it can still surprisingly lead the iFHUQI-Miner algorithm to better overall performance.

Adopting the *Improved TQCS Strategy* into the FHUQI-Miner does not reduce the theoretical complexity, especially in the worst case. The pruning phase is now a straight-forward process with both exact Q-items and range Q-items considered using the same mechanism. However, the *Improved TQCS Strategy* does reduce the number of branch-ing and joins that need to be carried out while pruning. Thus, the complexity of the iFHUQI-Miner remains the same as FHUQI-Miner [6]. The improvement in terms of execution time and join counts can be observed in the experimental evaluation section of this work.

5   Evaluation Studies

To assert the proposed algorithm's performance, a series of experiments on different datasets were conducted. All the datasets are acquired directly from the SPFM library [16]. These four datasets were selected as they are used in several HUIM kinds of literature to evaluate the mining performance. Besides, since the FHUQI-Miner miner algorithm was evaluated using these datasets, it would provide fair comparisons on how the iFHUQI-Miner improved the mining performance. The information regarding all the datasets is summarized in Table 3. All the experiments were carried out on a computer with a fifth generation, 64-bit Intel® Core® i5-5257U processor, running macOS® Monterey has 8.0GB of RAM. Both algorithms are implemented in Java. Thus, Java API is used to measure the execution time as well as memory usage of the evaluated algorithms.

Table 3. Datasets characteristics

Dataset	$|D|$	$|I|$	$Trans_{AVG}$	Density	Type
BMS1	59,061	497	2.42	0.51%	Sparse
BMS2	77,512	3,340	4.62	0.14%	Sparse
Retail	88,162	16,470	10.30	0.06%	Sparse
Connect	67,557	129	43	33.33%	Dense

In all experiments, the performance of the proposed iFHUQI-Miner (with Improved TQCS Strategy) was directly compared with the original FHUQI-Miner across the three combining methods. A varying set of minimum utility thresholds μ is also selected and applied to all the runs for all methods. The obtained results of runtime, memory usage and number of joins can be viewed in Fig. 1, Fig. 2, and Fig. 3, respectively.

It can be seen in all the evaluated results throughout all combination methods, the iFHUQI-Miner has a better performance compared to the original algorithm. On the sparse datasets such as Retail (Fig. 1a), BMS1 (Fig. 1c), BMS2 (Fig. 1d), the mining time of iFHUQI-Miner reduced by up to 37% those of FHUQI-Miner, thanks to the Improved TCQS Strategy. In addition, this strategy also helps cut down the number of

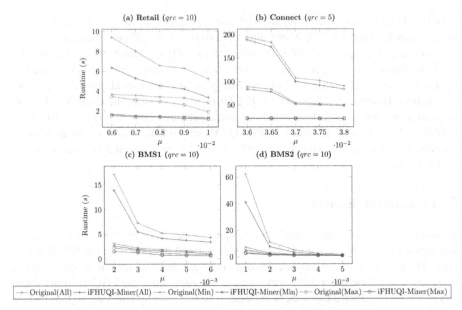

Fig. 1. Runtime comparisons of FHUQI-Miner and iFHUQI-Miner

joins operations needed (Fig. 3a, Fig. 3c and Fig. 3d) and thus lowers the memory usage (Fig. 2a, Fig. 2c and Fig. 2d). For the dense dataset Connect, the improved performance is also observed on all combination methods; however, it is not as high as in the sparse datasets. The execution time improvements are only up to 10% faster (Fig. 1b). As the Improve TQCS Strategy can only reduce a small number of join operations needed (Fig. 3b). This is also reflected in the memory usage of the Connect dataset (Fig. 2b).

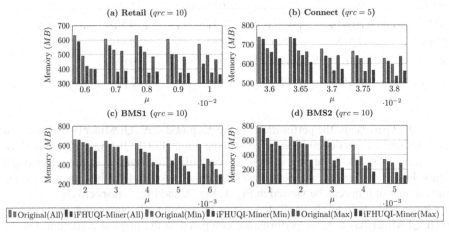

Fig. 2. Memory usage comparisons of FHUQI-Miner and iFHUQI-Miner

Generally, the iFHUQI-Miner algorithm has the fastest execution time among all of the experiments that were involved in this research. By overlooking the difference between exact Q-items and range Q-items as well as other restraints that were implemented in the original algorithm, with careful attention to a basic concept and an efficient execution of it in the real implementation of the algorithm, the first proposed algorithm was still able to apply the same evaluation method with TWU to all Q-items and eliminate low-utility Q-items beforehand, therefore also reducing the number of cases when the mining process is performed. All of the HUQIs generated by all algorithms were eventually compared with each other. This algorithm was eventually guaranteed to generate the same high utility itemsets but also eliminate a considerable amount of necessary join operations, as seen in the performance of the original algorithm.

6 Conclusion and Future Works

With respect to the works of Nouioua et al. on the FHUQI-Miner algorithm as the foundation, this work has presented an enhanced version of the algorithm, namely iFHUQI-Miner, equipped with the *Improved TCQS Strategy*, and has performed the necessary experiments to measure their performance against the original version. Results have shown that the iFHUQI-Miner, by considering exact Q-items and range Q-items as the same, is more efficient than the original FHUQI-Miner in pruning unpromising Q-items during the mining process, and thus reduces both the execution time and the number of join operations required for it to achieve the same output.

Besides the contribution of this work to enhance the mining performance of the quantitative high utility itemset, there are still is still for further improvements, such as: studying for a better upper bound could result in tighter search space and better execution time; adding new optimization to speed up the utility list construction and the combining methods; applying parallel computing methods onto the algorithm to make the algorithm scales better with the system it operates on.

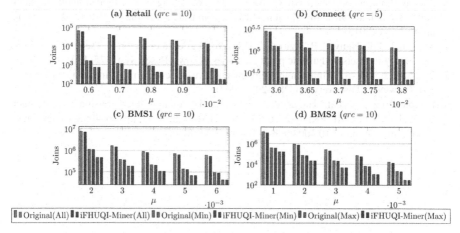

Fig. 3. Join counts comparisons of FHUQI-Miner and iFHUQI-Miner

References

1. Yao, H., Hamilton, H.J.: Mining itemset utilities from transaction databases. Data Knowl. Eng. **59**(3), 603–626 (2006)
2. Zhang, C., Han, M., Sun, R., Du, S., Shen, M.: A survey of key technologies for high utility patterns mining. IEEE Access **8**, 55798–55814 (2020)
3. Fournier-Viger, P., Chun-Wei Lin, J., Truong-Chi, T., Nkambou, R.: A survey of high utility itemset mining. In: Fournier-Viger, P., Lin, J.C.-W., Nkambou, R., Vo, B., Tseng, V.S. (eds.) High-Utility Pattern Mining. SBD, vol. 51, pp. 1–45. Springer, Cham (2019). https://doi.org/10.1007/978-3-030-04921-8_1
4. Gan, W., Lin, J.C.-W., Fournier-Viger, P., Chao, H.-C., Tseng, V.S., Yu, P.S.: A survey of utility-oriented pattern mining. IEEE Trans. Knowl. Data Eng. **33**(4), 1306–1327 (2021)
5. Li, C.-H., Wu, C.-W., Huang, J., Tseng, V.S.: An efficient algorithm for mining high utility quantitative itemsets. In: 2019 International Conference on Data Mining Workshops (ICDMW), pp. 1005–1012 (2019)
6. Nouioua, M., Fournier-Viger, P., Wu, C.-W., Lin, J.C.-W., Gan, W.: FHUQI-miner: fast high utility quantitative itemset mining. Appl. Intell. (2021)
7. Agrawal, R., Srikant, R.: Fast algorithms for mining association rules in large databases. In: 20th International Conference on Very Large Data Bases (VLDB 1994), pp. 487–499 (1994)
8. Yao, H., Hamilton, H.J., Butz, G.J.: A foundational approach to mining itemset utilities from databases. In: SIAM International Conference on Data Mining, vol. 4, pp. 482–486 (2004)
9. Liu, Y., Liao, W.K., Choudhary, A.: A two-phase algorithm for fast discovery of high utility itemsets. In: 9th Pacific-Asia Conference on Advances in Knowledge Discovery and Data Mining, vol. 3518, pp. 689–695 (2005)
10. Ahmed, C.F., Tanbeer, S.K., Jeong, B.S., Lee, Y.K.: Efficient tree structures for high utility pattern mining in incremental databases. IEEE Trans. Knowl. Data Eng. **21**(12), 1708–1721 (2009)
11. Le, B., Nguyen, H., Cao, T.A., Vo, B.: A novel algorithm for mining high utility itemsets. In: First Asian Conference on Intelligent Information and Database Systems, pp. 13–17 (2009)
12. Liu, M., Qu, J.: Mining high utility itemsets without candidate generation. In: ACM International Conference on Information and Knowledge Management, CIKM, pp. 55–64 (2012)
13. Zida, S., Fournier-Viger, P., Wu, C.-W., Lin, J.C.-W., Tseng, V.S.: Efficient mining of high-utility sequential rules. In: Machine Learning and Data Mining in Pattern Recognition, pp. 157–171 (2015)
14. Nguyen, L.T.T., Nguyen, P., Nguyen, T.D.D., Vo, B., Fournier-Viger, P., Tseng, V.S.: Mining high-utility itemsets in dynamic profit databases. Knowl.-Based Syst. **175**, 130–144 (2019)
15. Yen, S.-J., Lee, Y.-S.: Mining high utility quantitative association rules. In: Data Warehousing and Knowledge Discovery, pp. 283–292 (2007)
16. Fournier-Viger, P., et al.: The SPMF open-source data mining library version 2. In: Berendt, B., et al. (eds.) ECML PKDD 2016. LNCS (LNAI), vol. 9853, pp. 36–40. Springer, Cham (2016). https://doi.org/10.1007/978-3-319-46131-1_8

AAPL Forecasting Using Contemporary Time Series Models

Krzysztof Ziółkowski[✉] [iD]

WSB Merito University Gdańsk, Aleja Grunwaldzka 238A, 80-266 Gdansk, Poland
kziolkowski@wsb.gda.pl

Abstract. Predicting the value of stock prices is separate from external investment exposure to the stock market. The aim of the article is to evaluate selected time series forecasting models in forecasting stock data – exactly Apple Inc. (AAPL) stock price. There are not many articles in the literature on the possibility of using ML models in forecasting stock prices. It is important to ask the question whether ML models give better results than traditional models. To answer this question, in this article following regression models ARIMA, Logistic Regression were analyzed but also were used VEC, LSTM, XGBoost, Prophet.

Keywords: LSTM · ARIMA · Prophet

1 Introduction

This article presents the possibilities of using classical and non-classical methods of forecasting time series with daily frequency. A time series is one of the types of statistical series that can be defined as a series of observations of a certain phenomenon in successive time units (years, quarters, months, days, etc.). Time series analysis is based on the main assumption that successive the values of the considered feature (variable) represent successive measurements made in the same unit of time (at regular intervals) [13].

The ARIMA model is one of the most effective forecasting methods for time series. The equivalent of the ARIMA model is the SARIMA model, which takes seasonal factors into account. The next model that was analyzed was the logistic regression model, which is one of the simplest and most used algorithms for two-class classification. Logistic regression can also be used in time series forecasting. Logistic regression is a variant of regular Linear Regression used when the dependent variable takes two values (usually the occurrence and absence of something). The logistic regression model predicts the probability of a phenomenon as a function of independent variables. Another analyzed model was the Prophet model created by Meta, which combines a complicated mathematical apparatus with uncertainty modeling capabilities [9]. The Extreme Gradient Boosting (XGBoost) algorithm, derived from classical decision trees and random forests, was developed in 2014, popularized in 2016, whose usefulness in forecasting stock prices will be analyzed. The last model will be a neural network. Neural networks provide an opportunity building models representing complex relationships between input and output data for phenomena whose structure, laws of operation or causal relationships have not been fully understood sufficient to build effective mathematical models [11].

N. T. Nguyen et al. (Eds.): ICCCI 2023, CCIS 1864, pp. 339–350, 2023.
https://doi.org/10.1007/978-3-031-41774-0_27

2   Theoretical Framework

2.1   Autoregressive Approach in Timeseries Forecasting

Recall that we understand a time series as a set of equivalents in the time of observation of the studied phenomenon in a given time. In the presented calculations, which will constitute a time series as single implementations of the stochastic process, by which we mean a sequence of individual random arguments presented.

Having a single series, trying to create dynamic relationships that may occur between specialized observations of the phenomenon under study.

The abovementioned process is referred to as the autoregressive process of the 1st order AR(1). It means that the current value of the series is equal to the previous one times the parameter plus the disturbance. The processes of this kind appear when we analyze the autocorrelation of the random disturbance in the classic model of the linear regression. This is the autoregressive process of the p order: AR(p).

The notation AR(p) indicates an autoregressive model of order p. The AR(p) model is defined as:

$$y_t = C + \phi_1 y_{t-1} + \phi_2 y_{t-2} + \cdots + \phi_p y_{t-p} +_t,$$

where ϵ_t denotes white noise.

The autoregressive processes and the moving average can be combined into one process: autoregressive with the moving average referred to as the ARMA (p,q) [7, 8, 24]. The identification of the ARMA (p,q) processes [2] is possible with the use of the function of autocorrelation and partial autocorrelation. While observing a single series, we can only determine its average, variance and covariance between evenly distributed observations. So far, we have assumed that the analyzed series are stationary. A process can be considered as stationary if its average and variance are constant and the covariance depends exclusively on the lag which appears between two time periods, and it does not depend on the particular time period, starting from which this covariance is calculated [4, 10, 17, 19, 23].

Economic processes are often of non-stationary character. It is most frequently the non-stationarity in relation to the average, and only sometimes in relation to the variance. The non-stationarity in relation to the average can be observed not only on the series chart, on which some increasing or decreasing trends can be noticed, but it can be also traced in the function of autocorrelation. This function does not disappear even for several dozens of lags but its values decrease very slowly. The non-stationarity in relation to the average clears away differencing of the series, whereas the non-stationarity in relation to the variance considerably eliminates logarithming of the series. We shall concentrate mainly on the non-stationarity in relation to the average [6].

If yt is the ARMA (p,q) process, which comes from the yt process by its single differencing, then yt is referred to as an integrated process of the 1st order: I(1) which is described as: ARIMA(p,1,q), coming from an English abbreviation of Autoregressive Integrated Moving Average [1]. We can state that the yt process has the unit root [15].

2.2 Artificial Neural Networks

Artificial neural networks (ANN) are also used in forecasting time series (also stocks). ANN is a computational tool imitating the operation of the human brain in a simplified way.

The basic unit of a neural network is the neuron. A neuron is a simple computing element that processes signals and communicates and interacts with other such objects. Each signal is multiplied by its corresponding weight, which are subject to the learning process.

In prediction, the task of the network is to determine future answers based on a string of values from the past. Having information about values of the variable x in the moments preceding the predictions $x(t-1)$, $x(t-2)$, ..., $x(t-n)$, the network decides what will be estimated value $x(t)$ of the examined string at the current time t.

In contrast to the classic models whose construction is based on an algorithm that implements a specific method of solving a given problem, a network neural does not require prior definition of the processing method it does not require a programming process that uses a priori knowledge. This process is replaced by network training, during which knowledge is "acquired" on the basis of presented learning data [16].

Neural networks can be classified into different types. The simplest neural network is the single threshold perceptron, developed by McCulloch and Pitts [14]. The above model was significantly developed by Frank Rosenblatt. ANNs are divided into single-layer, double-layer and multi-layer networks (MMLs). Single-step networks can only solve a narrow class of problems. Two-layer and multi-layer networks can solve a much wider class. MMLs are comprised of an input layer, a hidden layer or layers, and an output layer.

This paper checks a recursive neural network to forecast the stock price. Recursive neural networks are a neural structure designed for sequential data. It is often used in time series forecasting. The most well-known types of recursive network include the Long Short-Term Memory Neural Network (LSTM) and the Gated Recurrent Unit (GRU). In the analyzed example, the LSTM network was used.

2.3 Logistic Regression

Logistic Regression is a variant of regular Linear Regression used when the dependent variable takes two values. The logistic regression model predicts the probability of a phenomenon as a function of independent variables. The advantage of logistic regression is that the interpretation of the results is very similar to methods used in classical regression [12].

In its general form, the linear multivariate regression model is presented as using the following equation [18]:

$$Y_t = b_0 X_0 t + b_1 X_{1t} + \ldots + b_m X_m + \epsilon_t,$$

where: Y – explained variable (regressive), X_0, X_1,..., X_m – explanatory variables (regression), $b_0, b_1,\ldots, b_m$ – structural parameters of the model, e – random component, t = 1..,T – observation number, j = 0, 1,..., m – explanatory variable number.

In the logit model it is assumed that we are dealing with the hidden variable y*, which is not directly observed. However, we observe:

$$y_i = \begin{cases} 1, \ dla \ y^* > 0 \\ 0, \ dla \ y^* \leq 0 \end{cases}$$

The hidden variable y* represents the propensity of the ith object to take the value $y_i = 1$.

The probability that the independent variable i y will be zero or 1, is therefore a function of explanatory variables and parameters:

$$P_i = F\left(x_i^T b\right) = \frac{1}{1 + \exp\left(-x_i^T b\right)} = \frac{\exp\left(x_i^T b\right)}{1 + \exp\left(x_i^T b\right)},$$

where: F – distribution function of the logistic distribution.

2.4 Support Vector Machines

The Support Vector Machines (SVM) method is based on the concept of decision space, which is divided by building boundaries separating objects of different class affiliation. The SVM method proposed by Vapnik is a kind of generalization of the idea of classification by means of discriminant hyperplanes. This method of supervised learning, particularly effective in classification and approximation problems, consists in maximizing the margin of separation, e.g. between two given classes. This method is widely used in many learning problems, for example, the problem of classification, density function estimation, determining the regression function or forecasting the values of time series [5]. The basic idea behind SVM is to transfer the training set to a larger dimension space; for this purpose, a mapping function is used [20].

Support Vector Classification (SVC) solves the following primal problem [21]:

$$\min_{\omega, b, \varsigma} \frac{1}{2} \omega^T \omega + C \sum_{i=1}^{n} \varsigma_i$$

subject to $y_i\left(\omega^T \phi(x_i) + b\right) \geq 1 - \varsigma_i, \varsigma_i \geq 0, i = 1, \ldots, n$.

trying to maximize the margin by minimizing while incurring a penalty when a sample is misclassified or within the margin boundary [21].

2.5 XGBoost

XGBoost is a collective tree-based machine learning algorithm using a gradient boosting framework. XGBoost provides a parallel tree boosting. The XGBoost algorithm was the result of a research project organized at the University of Washington and was presented by Carlos Guestrin and Tianqi Chen at the SIGKDD conference in 2016. In the taxonomy of machine learning methods, this algorithm is in the group of supervised learning procedures (it divides the set into test and training) [25].

XGBoost objective is a function of functions, which "cannot be optimized using traditional optimization methods in Euclidean space" [3].

XGBoost allows you to use a wide range of applications to solve user-defined problems of prediction, ranking, classification and regression.

2.6 Prophet

Prophet is an open source model created by Meta which allows you to create predictive models approximately semi-automatic where non-linear trends are fit with yearly, weekly, and daily seasonality, including holiday effects. Prophet can be used in forecasting time series data which have any of the following characteristics [22]:

- daily, quarterly, yearly observations,
- multiple seasonality's: day of week and time of year,
- important holidays that occur at irregular intervals,
- historical trend changes.

Prophet uses the decomposition of the time series into three main components: trend, seasonality, and holidays. The pattern is as follows:

$$Y(t) = g(t) + s(t) + h(t) + \epsilon_t,$$

where $g(t)$ represents the trend, $s(t)$ – seasonality, and $h(t)$ represents the effect of holidays.

The estimation of the parameters of the fitted model is carried out using principles of Bayesian statistics (finding the posterior maximum (MAP) method). Modern forecasting methods include the Prophet system that connects complex mathematical apparatus with uncertainty modeling capabilities. Advantages forecasting using Prophet is the speed of model determination and ease of forecasting [9].

3 Comparison Models Output

For stock market investors, the following quotation parameters of a given company/share are important. Investors are primarily interested in data: opening price, highest price in a given time interval, the lowest and closing price (O-open, H-High, L-Low, C-Close-OHLC). The main interval is the daily interval, but it should be emphasized that within the day there is so-called intraday trading that determines the opening price and closing price as well as the maximum and minimum price. In the analyzed case, the daily quotation of Apple Inc. (AAPL) from January 1, 2010 to January 20, 2023 was used (Fig. 1).

	Date	Open	High	Low	Close	Adj Close	Volume
0	2010-01-04	7.622500	7.660714	7.585000	7.643214	6.515212	493729600
1	2010-01-05	7.664286	7.699643	7.616071	7.656429	6.526476	601904800
2	2010-01-06	7.656429	7.686786	7.526786	7.534643	6.422666	552160000
3	2010-01-07	7.562500	7.571429	7.466071	7.520714	6.410789	477131200
4	2010-01-08	7.510714	7.571429	7.466429	7.570714	6.453412	447610800

Fig. 1. Apple stock price – OHLC and Volume.

From the above dataset we could observe that some data might be missing but it need to be underlined that there is no trade during holidays, weekend during this time the exchange is closet, just OTC trade might happen which is not considered during this analysis. Since 1st Jan was on Friday 2010, so that 1st traiding day took place on 4th Jan 2010 (Fig. 2).

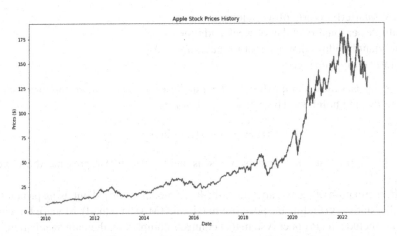

Fig. 2. Close price for Apple stock for analyzed period.

During the analyzed period there was an upward trend which we could observe on the chart above, of course, when analyzing this period, one cannot forget about the economic shocks that caused temporary drops in share prices, I mean the COVID-19 pandemic and the Russian-Ukrainian war.

In the analyzed case, the closing price was considered, but not the adjusted closing price. The difference between both prices is that the adjusted closing price amends a stock's closing price to reflect that stock's value after accounting for any corporate actions.

The first model considered for time series forecasting (close price) was classical ARIMA. According to the data it looks like time series variance is not constant throughout the time. The series were stabilized using logarithm. Afterwards as mentioned above the data was split for train and test data set [0.8/0.2].

The ACF plot shows the correlations with the lags are high and positive with very slow decay. While the PACF plot shows the partial autocorrelations have a single spike at lag 1. We could conclude that our time series is not stationary. According to ADF test p-value fails to reject null hypothesis. As result classical differentiating was used to have series more stationary. Afterwards was used Auto-fit the Arima to find the best p I q according to AIC (Akaike Information Criterion). According to the output the best order is (1,1,0) (Figs. 3 and 4).

For evaluation purposes were following metrics taken account MAE (Mean Absolute Error – 0.210), MAPE (Mean Absolute Percentage Error -: 0.042), and RMSE (Root Mean Squared Error – 0.234).

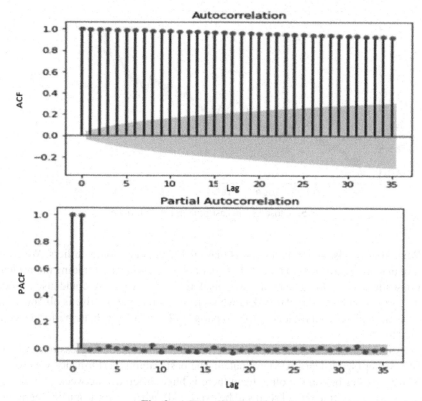

Fig. 3. ACF and PAC analysis.

SARIMAX Results

Dep. Variable:	y	No. Observations:	2628
Model:	SARIMAX(1, 1, 0)	Log Likelihood	6912.131
Date:	Tue, 31 Jan 2023	AIC	-13818.261
Time:	16:02:49	BIC	-13800.641
Sample:	0	HQIC	-13811.880
	- 2628		

Covariance Type: opg

	coef	std err	z	P>|z|	[0.025	0.975]
intercept	0.0010	0.000	2.753	0.006	0.000	0.002
ar.L1	-0.0489	0.012	-4.007	0.000	-0.073	-0.025
sigma2	0.0003	4.45e-06	68.164	0.000	0.000	0.000

Ljung-Box (L1) (Q):	0.00	Jarque-Bera (JB):	4631.82
Prob(Q):	0.98	Prob(JB):	0.00
Heteroskedasticity (H):	1.12	Skew:	-0.39
Prob(H) (two-sided):	0.09	Kurtosis:	9.46

Warnings:
[1] Covariance matrix calculated using the outer product of gradients (complex-step).

Fig. 4. ARIMA model output.

Above metrics show that ARIMA can be used for stock forecasting. Moreover, SARIMAX packed could accommodate seasonality and exogenous variables, which could improve time series forecast accuracy (Fig. 5).

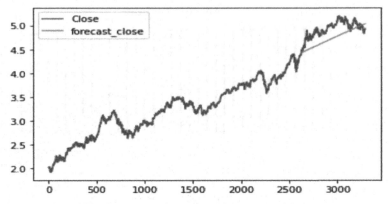

Fig. 5. Close vs forecast price for AAPL ticker.

We could see also from the boxplots that OHLC data has some outliers. We could observe that prices are higher at the end of quarters which typical for trading many clearing houses/traders try to close their positions during this period. We could also observe strong correlation between OHLC data which from trading perspective is obvious. The data was normalized and divided into two parts 80/20 ratio to evaluate performance of the model.

For validation of AAPL Inc stock price prediction was Logistic Regression, SVC and XGBClassifier (scikit-learn API) evaluated. The best training performance we observe for XGBClassifier but on the other hand there is huge difference between training and validation accuracy (the model seems to be overfitted), whereas for Logistic Regression and SVC model we do not observe such difference, but overall performance is lower (Fig. 6).

```
LogisticRegression() :
Training Accuracy :   0.5154577328117032
Validation Accuracy :   0.5197585994282619

SVC(kernel='poly', probability=True) :
Training Accuracy :   0.4793054652230746
Validation Accuracy :   0.48683694250854803

XGBClassifier() :
Training Accuracy :   0.7285119092860114
Validation Accuracy :   0.5232432129444518
```

Fig. 6. Models' accuracy output.

Above tested models give not good performance. It could be determined that there is too much data and among the period volatility is high. Apart from that mentioned shocks also affect the model. War effect is reflected at the stock price but also external factors which indirectly influence the market, e.g. economic slowdown.

The last two models which were tested was LSTM and Prophet. LSTM is a particular case of a recurrent neural network (RNN). For our case was used the LSTM model from Keras, which is an open source software library that provides a Python interface for artificial neural networks. Prior modeling the data was scaled by MinMaxScaler. It was chosen the most popular optimization algorithm, the Adam Optimization Algorithm, which is an extension to stochastic gradient descent. The loss function was selected from mean Squared Error class (Fig. 7).

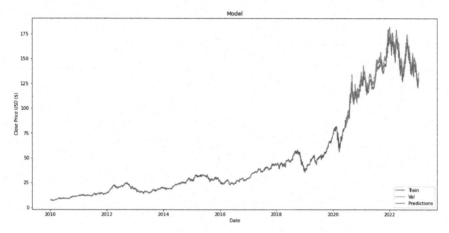

Fig. 7. LSTM model, trained, validated, predicted data.

For evaluation purposes were following metrics taken account MAE (Mean Absolute Error -5.835), MAPE (Mean Absolute Percentage Error – 0.041), and RMSE (Root Mean Squared Error – 6.497).

Above metrics show that LSTM can be used for stocks prediction. Moreover, this example was a simple RNN more advanced models could give better performance.

The last model explored in this article is Prophet. These advanced functions can be separated into three categories: visualization, performance diagnosis, and hyperparameter tuning. Moreover, Prophet algorithm implements a forecasting procedure taking into account nonlinear trends with multiple seasonal periods (yearly, monthly, weekly, and daily). Prophet comes with many methods that allow us to quickly visualize a model's predictions or its different components. The below graph displays the components of our model. Here our model uses a trend component and two different seasonal components—one with a weekly period and the other with a yearly period (Fig. 8).

The yellow curve denotes actual price whereas black curve denotes price prediction. We could conclude that prediction for close price is quite close actual value (Fig. 9).

The chart below show prediction for the next 365 days, whereas table presents boundaries for our prediction. Last day predicted is 20th Jan 2024, and the price would be 198.79, and considering unexpected events, it evaluates the low and high as 184.94 and 211.64, respectively (Fig. 10, Table 1).

According to the metrics MSE (7.91), MAE (4.75) and MAPE (0.09) Prophet could be used for daily prediction where data have seasonality and is expected holidays effect. Undoubtedly, the recent economic situation has a negative impact on the stock market. High market uncertainty causes large fluctuations in stock prices, which makes prediction more and more difficult.

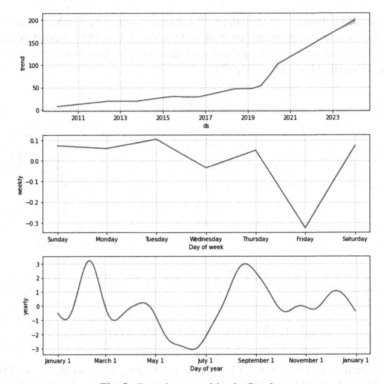

Fig. 8. Data decomposition by Prophet.

Fig. 9. Actual vs predicted price.

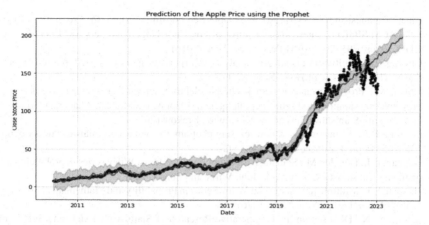

Fig. 10. Price prediction – next 365 days.

Table 1. Forecast boundaries last days of forecast.

Ds	yhat (ŷ)	yhat_lower	yhat_upper
16/01/2024	198.0492	184.74086	209.5346
17/01/2024	198.0784	184.64176	210.1324
18/01/2024	198.3503	185.22937	211.3295
19/01/2024	198.1771	184.62805	210.7985
20/01/2024	198.7973	184.97489	211.6469

4 Conclusion

Our forecast is obviously subject to error, but this is affected by geopolitical conditions such as war or the political situation in China, where Apple Inc. Factories are located. Certainly, the disadvantage of forecasting share prices is that they do not depend only on changes in time, but many economic and social as well as geopolitical factors affect the share prices in a specific time period. Nevertheless, it seems that the ARIMA, LSTM or Prophet algorithms are suitable for forecasting stock prices.

It should be emphasized that the author faced a difficult choice whether to present more forecasting methods for one company or less methods but for many companies. The author has chosen the first approach.

References

1. Asteriou, D., Hall, S.G.: Applied Econometrics, 2nd edn. Palgrave Macmillan, New York (2011)
2. Brockwell, P.J., Davis, R.A.: Time Series: Theory and Methods, 2nd edn. Springer, New York (2009)

3. Chen, T., Guestrin, C., XGBoost: A scalable tree boosting system. In: Proceedings of the 22nd ACM SIGKDD International Conference on Knowledge Discovery and Data Mining – KDD'16, pp. 785–794. ACM Press, New York (2016)

4. Cheung, C.P.: Multivariate time series analysis on airport transportation. Unpublished master's thesis, The University of Hong Kong ((1991)

5. Dutka, M.: Prognozowanie generacji energii elektrycznej z odnawialnych źródeł energii przy wykorzystaniu metod sztucznej inteligencji, rozprawa doktorska, Akademia Górniczo-Hutnicza im. Stanisława Staszica w Krakowie , Kraków (2020)

6. Górecki, B.: Podstawowy kurs nowoczesnej ekonometrii. www.uczelniawarszawska.pl/upl/1223105394.pd. Last accessed 21 Dec 2021

7. Hannan, E.J., Deistler, M.: Statistical theory of linear systems. Wiley series in probability and mathematical statistics. New York: John Wiley and Sons (1988)

8. Hannan, E.J.: Multiple time series. In: Wiley Series in Probability and Mathematical Statistics. John Wiley and Sons, New York (1970)

9. Kashpruk, N., Dissertation, P.: Comparative Research of Statistical Models and Soft Computing for Identification of Time Series and Forecasting. Opole University of Technology, Opole (2020)

10. Kawad, S., Prevedouros P.D.: Forecasting air travel arrivals: Model development and application at the Honolulu International Airport. Transportation Research Board, 1506 (1995)

11. Lula, P., Tadeusiewicz, R.: Wprowadzenie do sieci neuronowych. StatSoft, Kraków (2001)

12. Mach, Ł.: Zastosowanie regresji logistycznej do określenia prawdopodobieństwa sprzedaży zasobu mieszkaniowego. In: Knosal (ed.) Komputerowo Zintegrowane Zarządzanie 2 (2010)

13. Malska, W., Wachta, H.: Wykorzystanie modelu ARIMA do analizy szeregu czasowego, Zeszyty Naukowe Politechniki Rzeszowskiej 292, Elektrotechnika 34, RUTJEE, z. 34 (2015)

14. McCulloch, W.S., Pitts, W.: A logical calculus of the ideas immanent in nervous activity. Bull. Math. Biophys. **5**, 115–133d (1943)

15. Mills, T.C.: Time Series Techniques for Economists. Cambridge University Press, Cambridge (1990)

16. Morajda, J.: Wykorzystanie perceptronowych sieci neuronowych w zagadnieniu wyceny nieruchomości, Zeszyty Naukowe Małopolskiej Wyższej Szkoły Ekonomicznej w Tarnowie. Prace z zakresu informatyki i zarządzania (2005)

17. Payne, J.E., Taylor, J.P.: Modelling and forecasting airport passengers: a case study for an introductory forecasting course. Int. J. Inform. Operat. Manag. Educ. **2**(2), 167 (2007). https://doi.org/10.1504/IJIOME.2007.015282

18. Pełka, M.: Regresja logistyczna dla danych symbolicznych interwałowych, Econometrics. Ekonometria. Advances in Applied Data Analytics, Wydawnictwo Uniwersytetu Ekonomicznego we Wrocławiu (2015)

19. Prevedouros, P.D.: Origin-specific visitor demand forecasting at honolulu international airport. Transport. Res. Record: J. Transport. Res. Board **1600**(1), 18–27 (1997). https://doi.org/10.3141/1600-03

20. Radomska, S.: Prognozowanie indeksu WIG20 za pomocą sieci neuronowych NARX i metody SVM. Bank i Kredyt, Narodowy Bank Polski **52**(5), 457–472 (2021)

21. Scikit-learn: https://scikit-learn.org/stable/modules/svm.html#mathematical-formulation. Last accessed 21 Jan 2022

22. Taylor, S.J., Letham, B.: Forecasting at Scale. Am. Stat. **72**(1), 37–45 (2018)

23. Uddin, W., Mc Cullough, B.F., Crawford, M.M.: Methodology for forecasting air travel and airport expansion needs. Transp. Res. Board **1025**, 7–14 (1985)

24. Whittle, P.: Hypothesis Testing in Time Series Analysis. Almquist and Wicksell (1951)

25. Wójcik, F.: Prognozowanie dziennych obrotów przedsiębiorstwa za pomocą algorytmu XGBoost – Studium Przypadku, Studia Ekonomiczne. Zeszyty Naukowe Uniwersytetu Ekonomicznego w Katowicach 375 (2018)

Improving Gossip Learning via Limited Model Merging

Gábor Danner[1], István Hegedűs[1(✉)], and Márk Jelasity[1,2]

[1] University of Szeged, Szeged, Hungary
{danner,ihegedus,jelasity}@inf.u-szeged.hu
[2] ELKH SZTE Research Group on Artificial Intelligence, Szeged, Hungary

Abstract. Decentralized machine learning provides a unique opportunity to create data-driven applications without the need for large investments in centralized infrastructure. In our previous works, we introduced gossip learning for this purpose: models perform random walks in the network, and the nodes train the received models on the locally available data. We also proposed various improvements, like model sub-sampling, merging, and token-based flow control. Gossip learning is robust to failures, and does not require synchronization. Efficiency in terms of network bandwidth is also a major concern in the case of decentralized learning algorithms, especially when they are deployed in a network of IoT devices or smartphones. Here, we improve the model merging method to allow gossip learning to benefit more from token-based flow control. We experimentally evaluate our solution over several classification problems in simulations using an availability trace based on real-world smartphone measurements. Our results indicate that the improved variant significantly outperforms previously proposed solutions.

Keywords: Gossip learning · Decentralized machine learning · Model aggregation

1 Introduction

The widespread presence of smart devices provides the possibility for numerous applications that use machine learning. The traditional approach to machine learning is to collect the data at a central location for processing, but this can cause privacy concerns. This motivated a number of approaches to implement distributed machine learning algorithms. Perhaps the most notable approach is federated learning that is being used for mining data stored on smartphones without collecting it at a central location [12,15]. Although the nodes perform

This work was supported by the European Union project RRF-2.3.1-21-2022-00004 within the framework of the Artificial Intelligence National Laboratory and project TKP2021-NVA-09, implemented with the support provided by the Ministry of Innovation and Technology of Hungary from the National Research, Development and Innovation Fund, financed under the TKP2021-NVA funding scheme.

N. T. Nguyen et al. (Eds.): ICCCI 2023, CCIS 1864, pp. 351–363, 2023.
https://doi.org/10.1007/978-3-031-41774-0_28

the updates locally, there is still a need for a central server that aggregates and distributes the global model. Furthermore, the cost of such infrastructure can be prohibitive for startups or communities with limited resources.

To mitigate the problem of the requirement of a central infrastructure, a number of proposals have been made. Some of these utilize the blockchain infrastructure. Li et al. [14] proposed a blockchain-based, decentralized federated learning framework against malicious central servers or nodes. Ramanan and Nakayama [21] also proposed a blockchain-based federated learning framework that eliminates the role of a centralized aggregator. The selection of the device that updates a given chunk of the global model is based on the norm difference caused by the update. However, although the blockchain offers a number of benefits, blockchain-based distributed algorithms are not efficient.

Gossip learning [19] offers a more radical solution to the problem of central servers. Gossip learning is a fully distributed approach, not using any infrastructure (including blockchains) that avoids the collection of sensitive data, which remains on the devices instead. The devices communicate directly, sending their model to each other, and they train the received models on the locally available data. In addition to smartphones, this method has the potential to be employed on other platforms, such as smart metering or the Internet of Things. We presented a systematic comparison of federated learning and gossip learning in [11].

Gossip learning has been applied in a number of areas. For example, Guo et al. [10] proposed a gossip learning-aided user-centric online training framework to improve channel state information feedback performance and Belal et al. [3] proposed a decentralized recommender system based on gossip learning principles, which uses a personalized peer-sampling protocol and a model aggregation function that weights models by performance.

Giaretta and Girdzijauskas [9] assessed the applicability of gossip learning to real-world scenarios in general and introduced extensions that mitigate some of its limitations related to networks in which the node degree or the communication speed is correlated with the data distribution. Other improvements include the work of Onoszko et al. [18] that proposed a method for training personalized models in a decentralized setting with non-iid client data. Peers focus on communicating with neighbors that share similar data distributions, found based on training loss. Niwa et al. [17] extend Edge-Consensus Learning, an asynchronous decentralized DNN optimization algorithm, with the gradient modification of Stochastic Variance Reduction to improve performance on heterogeneous data.

There have also been a number of proposals to improve gossip learning specifically. Among these are model merging, model sub-sampling, and token-based flow control [8,11]. However, these do not always work well together. In this paper, we propose a novel method for merging that improves its synergy with token-based flow control, resulting in a significant speed-up even without subsampling. We evaluated our algorithm experimentally over several datasets and using a real-world smartphone availability trace (based on data collected by STUNner [4]).

The rest of the paper is structured as follows. In Sect. 2, we explain the concepts related to gossip learning. In Sect. 3, we describe our novel algorithm. In Sect. 4, we describe the experimental setup and discuss the simulation results. Finally, we conclude the paper in Sect. 5.

2 Background

Here, we introduce the necessary notations and concepts of gossip learning.

2.1 Supervised Classification

In the supervised learning problem, we aim to build a model based on a dataset $X = \{(x_1, y_1), \ldots, (x_n, y_n)\}$. Here, n is the size of the dataset (the number of samples). We assume that every sample x_i is a real valued feature vector of d elements ($x_i \in R^d$). In addition, for every example x_i, a class label y_i is also given that is an element of a discrete set K of possible class labels.

The learning task can be formulated as an optimization problem. The aim of the learning procedure is to find the parameters w of a given hypothesis function $h_w : R^d \rightarrow K$ that minimizes the objective function

$$J(w) = \frac{1}{n} \sum_{i=1}^{n} \ell(h_w(x_i), y_i) + \frac{\lambda}{2} \|w\|^2. \tag{1}$$

This objective function is the average of the losses ℓ computed on the training samples. To improve generalization, a regularization term is also often added, where λ is the regularization coefficient. A common solution for this optimization problem is the Gradient Descent (GD) method, where we iteratively update the parameters of the model, based on the partial derivative of the objective function.

$$w_{t+1} = w_t - \frac{\partial J(w)}{\partial w}(w_t) \tag{2}$$

Stochastic Gradient Descent (SGD) [6] approximates this update using the derivative of the loss of only one sample at a time. It iteratively selects a training example, sampled uniform randomly, and performs the parameter update of the model using the update rule

$$w_{t+1} = w_t - \eta_t \left(\frac{\partial \ell(h_w(x_i), y_i)}{\partial w}(w_t) + \lambda w_t \right), \tag{3}$$

where η_t is called the learning rate.

Logistic regression [5] is a linear model that specifies the hypothesis function as

$$h_{(w,b)}(x_i) = \frac{1}{1 + e^{(w^T x_i + b)}}, \tag{4}$$

where b is an additional model parameter, called bias, and $y_i \in \{0, 1\}$. The loss function is

$$\ell(h_{(w,b)}(x_i), y_i) = -y_i \ln h_{(w,b)}(x_i) - (1 - y_i) \ln(1 - h_{(w,b)}(x_i)). \tag{5}$$

Algorithm 1. Basic version of gossip learning

1: $(x, y) \leftarrow$ local sample
2: $(w, t) \leftarrow$ initialize()   ▷ local model
3: **loop**
4:      wait(Δ)
5:      $p \leftarrow$ selectPeer()   ▷ returns a random online neighbor
6:      send (w, t) to p
7: **end loop**
8:
9: **procedure** ONRECEIVEMODEL(w_r, t_r)
10:      $(w, t) \leftarrow (w_r, t_r)$
11:      $(w, t) \leftarrow$ update($(w, t), (x, y)$)   ▷ the model is trained and t is incremented
12: **end procedure**

2.2 Gossip Learning

In traditional machine learning, the model is trained on one machine or on a cluster of servers that stores the model and the dataset and performs the model updates. But in gossip learning [19], we have a network of computational units that are typically connected via the Internet. The dataset is distributed on these devices horizontally, that is, every node in this network holds only a few or maybe just one sample from the dataset. Models perform random walks (series of random steps) in this network, and when a node receives a model, it updates it by applying the SGD method using the local samples. More precisely, each node in the network first initializes a new model, and stores it locally. After that it periodically sends its local model to one of its neighbors in the network. When a node receives a model, it updates and stores this model locally.

The neighborhood management is provided by a peer sampling service. If this service can provide a node picked uniformly at random from the network, the model will be updated on training examples sampled uniformly at random.

An advantage of this decentralized approach is that, due to every node storing a model locally, they can predict the label of unseen examples without any communication cost.

The basic version of gossip learning can be seen in Algorithm 1. Every node holds only one data sample (x, y) and has a model (w, t) locally, where the model age t is the number of times the model has been updated. Δ denotes the gossip cycle length.

We call this communication pattern *proactive* because messages are sent based on a gossip cycle, independently of other events. In this proactive scheme, the number of the randomly walking models in the network approximately equals the number of online nodes. In the case of a linear model, the model size (the number of parameters) is the same as the size of an example, plus an extra bias term. In the case of more complex models, like neural networks, the model can be much larger.

Various techniques can be employed to improve the above algorithm, as listed below.

Token-based flow-control The communication pattern can be adjusted so that models perform "hot potato"-like random walks, that is, models do not wait for the clock at each node [8]. This technique is detailed in Sect. 2.3.

Model merging Instead of overriding the local model by the received one, the average of the model parameters is stored. One way to do this is to weight the models by their age [11].

Model partitioning This is a sub-sampling technique where there is a predefined partitioning of the model parameters; instead of sending the whole model to a neighbor, only a uniformly random partition is sent [11]. This reduces the communication cost of each message, meaning we can send messages more frequently. When such a partial model is received, it is merged with the corresponding parameters, leaving the rest unchanged (but the whole model is updated afterwards using the local samples). Each partition has its own age, which is used during weighted model merging.

Transfer learning We can use a large, pre-trained model (that was trained on a related, but different task) as a feature extractor [22]. This can result in a more useful and/or smaller feature set, the latter reducing communication costs. This can be the equivalent of training only the last layer of a deep neural network.

2.3   Token Gossip Learning

The proactive approach, that is, periodically sending the local model is suboptimal when the model transfer time is much shorter than the cycle length, that is, when the allowed average bandwidth utilization is much smaller than the maximum available bandwidth. This is because a lot of time is wasted between receiving a model and forwarding it to another node. The purely reactive approach, that is, forwarding a model immediately after receiving (and updating) it, is prone to extinction due to message loss. (Even reliable protocols like TCP can't guard against churn, the prolonged unavailability of a node.) The solution is the token account algorithm [8], a hybrid approach that enables a small number of models to travel (and learn) quickly in the network, and manages the number of such models implicitly, in an emergent way.

Similarly to the token bucket algorithm [20], a token is granted periodically at each node which can be later spent on outgoing network communication, and there is a cap on the number of tokens that can be accumulated. However, here, message sending is not completely reactive. Messages can also be sent proactively (spending a newly granted token immediately), to avoid starvation. Moreover, to preemptively mitigate the impact of message loss, multiple copies of a received model may be transmitted to various neighbors. If the number of tokens is approaching the capacity, it is an indication that there might be too few random walks in the network, therefore the algorithm becomes more inclined to send a proactive message (starting a new random walk) or multiple reactive messages (duplicating a random walk). The exact behavior is defined by functions PROACTIVE(a) and REACTIVE(a), where a is the number of tokens

---

Algorithm 2. Token gossip learning

1: $(x, y) \leftarrow$ local sample
2: $(w, t) \leftarrow$ initialize()   ▷ can include initial update
3: $a \leftarrow 0$ ▷ number of tokens
4: **loop**
5:     wait(Δ)
6:     **do with probability** proactive(a)   ▷ randomized branching
7:         $p \leftarrow$ selectPeer()
8:         send (w, t) to p
9:     **else**
10:        $a \leftarrow a + 1$ ▷ we did not spend the token so it accumulates
11:    **end do**
12: **end loop**
13:
14: **procedure** ONRECEIVEMODEL(w_r, t_r)
15:    $(w, t) \leftarrow$ merge($(w, t), (w_r, t_r)$)
16:    $(w, t) \leftarrow$ update($(w, t), (x, y)$)
17:    $x \leftarrow$ randRound(reactive(a)) ▷ randRound(x) rounds up with probability $\{x\}$
18:    $a \leftarrow a - x$ ▷ we spend x tokens
19:    **for** $i \leftarrow 1$ to x **do**
20:        $p \leftarrow$ selectPeer()
21:        send (w, t) to p ▷ queued for sequential sending
22:    **end for**
23: **end procedure**

---

in the node's account. PROACTIVE(a) returns the probability of sending a proactive message, and REACTIVE(a) returns the number of reactive messages to be sent. REACTIVE(a) is allowed to return a non-integer; we round it up with the probability equaling the fractional part, and round it down otherwise.

Here, we shall use the (slightly simplified) randomized strategy [8] that defines these functions as

$$
\text{PROACTIVE}(a) = \begin{cases} 0 & \text{if } a < A - 1 \\ \dfrac{a - A + 1}{C - A + 1} & \text{if } a \in [A - 1, C] \end{cases}
$$

and REACTIVE(a) = a/A. C is the capacity of the token account, and A influences the size of the token reserve the algorithm tries to maintain. The algorithm guarantees that a node will not send more than $\lceil t/\Delta \rceil + C$ messages within a period of time t. The pseudocode for the token account algorithm as applied to gossip learning is shown in Algorithm 2, also including model merging. This technique can result in a much faster growth of model age, since the (on average) $\Delta/2$ waiting period between the steps of the random walk is eliminated, leaving only the transfer time.

There is also a variant of this algorithm for use with partitioned model sampling [11]. It uses a separate token account for each partition, and reactive messages contain the same partition as the received one.

Algorithm 3. Limited merging

1: **procedure** MERGE($(w_a, t_a), (w_b, t_b)$)
2:     **if** $t_a > t_b + L$ **then**
3:         $w \leftarrow w_a$
4:     **else if** $t_b > t_a + L$ **then**
5:         $w \leftarrow w_b$
6:     **else**
7:         $w \leftarrow (t_a \cdot w_a + t_b \cdot w_b)/(t_a + t_b)$
8:     **end if**
9:     $t \leftarrow \max(t_a, t_b)$
10:     **return** (w, t)
11: **end procedure**

---

3 Limited Merging

Previous approaches to model merging used unweighted [19] or weighted [11] averaging, where the weights are the model ages. More precisely, for two models (w_a, t_a) and (w_b, t_b) the merged model is given by

$$\frac{t_a \cdot w_a + t_b \cdot w_b}{t_a + t_b}.$$

The age of the resulting model is $\max(t_a, t_b)$.

There are a number of situations, however, when one of the models has significantly more fresh updates. For example, one of the models might have collected many updates during a "hot potato" run due to the token account algorithm. Another possibility is that one of the models was not updated for some time due to its node having been offline. In such situations, it is a problem if unweighted merging is used, because this essentially halves the contribution of the freshly updated model. Weighted averaging does not solve this problem, because after a certain amount of time the age of both of the models will be so large that weighted averaging will effectively work as unweighted averaging due to the relative age difference becoming too small.

To deal with this problem, we propose limited merging. Here, when the age difference of the models to be merged is above a threshold L, we simply take the model with the higher number of updates and throw away the other one, instead of performing weighted averaging. The pseudocode is shown in Algorithm 3. In the case of partitioned models, this rule can be applied to the received partition and its counterpart based on their age.

4 Experiments

We performed the experimental evaluation using simulations[1] building upon PeerSim [16] to measure the gain in convergence speed resulting from our novel algorithm. In this section, we describe the datasets, system model, availability trace, and hyperparameters we used, then present our results.

---

[1] https://github.com/ormandi/Gossip-Learning-Framework/tree/privacy.

4.1 Datasets

We used three different classification datasets in our experiments: the Pendigits and HAR datasets, and a transformed version of the MNIST dataset. The Pendigits [2] and the MNIST [13] samples represent hand-written numbers from [0–9], forming 10 classes. The Pendigits dataset represents the numbers using 16 attributes, while MNIST contains images of 28 × 28 pixels. In a previous study [7], we performed transfer learning to extract new, high-quality features from the MNIST database using a CNN model that was trained over another dataset: Fashion-MNIST. The Fashion-MNIST [24] dataset has the same properties as MNIST, but it contains images of clothes and shoes instead of digits. We assume that the nodes have downloaded this pre-trained model and use it to transform the local samples. The feature set was compressed to 78 attributes using Gaussian Random Projection, to reduce the bandwidth consumption of gossip learning through the smaller models. In the HAR (Human Activity Recognition Using Smartphones) [1] dataset, the labels are walking, walking upstairs, walking downstairs, sitting, standing and lying, and the attributes are high level features extracted from smartphone sensor measurement series (acceleration, gyroscope and angular velocity). The features of all the datasets were standardized, that is, scaled and shifted to have a mean of 0 and a standard deviation of 1. Some important statistics of the datasets can be seen in Table 1.

Table 1. Data set properties. Note that the transformed version of MNIST, that we used in the experiments, has only 78 features.

	Pendigits	HAR	MNIST	F-MNIST
Training set size	7494	7352	60000	60000
Test set size	3498	2947	10000	10000
Number of features	16	561	784*	784
Number of classes	10	6	10	10
Class-label distribution	≈ uniform	≈ uniform	≈ uniform	≈ uniform

4.2 System Model

We consider a network of unsynchronized nodes. The size of the network is assumed to be identical to the training set size of the given database. Thus, each node has a unique training sample. Each node also has a random list of 20 nodes it can connect to, as this provides a favorable mixing time. (In practice, such a list can be obtained and maintained by a decentralized peer sampling service like Newscast [23]). In the churn scenario, we assume that the nodes may go offline at any time, and later may come back online (with their state intact). For a message to be successfully delivered we require that both the sender and the receiver remain online for the duration of the transfer. The allowed average bandwidth utilization was set so that a continuously online node can send 1000

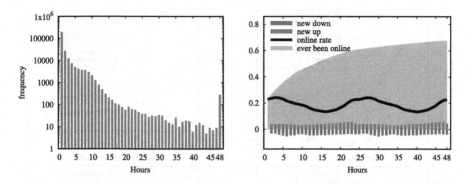

Fig. 1. Histogram of online session lengths (left) and device churn (right).

full models in 24 h. We assumed that nodes communicate during 1% of their online time, that is, the allowed average bandwidth utilization is much lower than the allowed maximum bandwidth utilization, enabling bursts. To model a platform where different learning tasks are solved one after the other, we simulated 48 h, but performed learning only during the second 24 h; this is to ensure a realistic distribution of token counts in the network at the beginning of the learning task.

4.3   Smartphone Trace

In our experiments involving churn, we used a smartphone availability trace collected from 1191 users by an application called STUNner [4], which monitors the NAT (network address translation) type, bandwidth, battery level, and charging status. The time series was split into 40,658 2-day segments (with a one-day overlap) based on the UTC time of day. By assigning one of these segments to each simulated node, it becomes possible to simulate a virtual 48-hour period. The segments are randomly sampled without replacement, but whenever the pool of segments runs out, the pool is reset. We define a device to be available after it has been on a charger as well as connected to the Internet (with a bandwidth of at least 1 Mbit/s) for at least one minute. This means we consider a user-friendly scenario in which battery power is not used at all.

Some important properties of this trace are shown in Fig. 1. On the right, the blue and red bars represent the ratio of the nodes that joined or left the network (at least once), respectively, in a given hour. Observe that usually only about 20% of the nodes are online. The average online session length is 81.37 min.

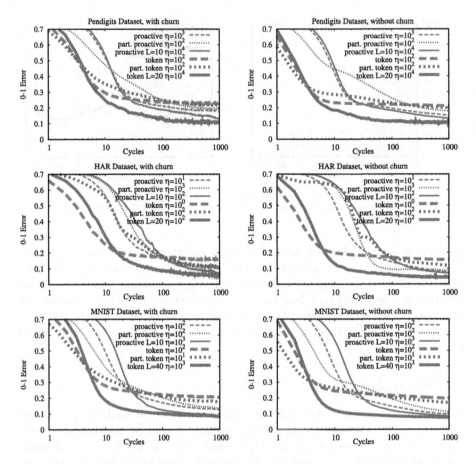

Fig. 2. Classification error of the various algorithm variants as a function of time, with trace-based churn (left) and without failures (right). "part." denotes partitioned.

4.4 Hyperparameters

Over a given dataset, we trained logistic regression models for each class separately, embedded in a one-vs-all meta-classifier. We set the cycle length Δ to one thousandth day (86.4 s). The algorithm variants using partitioned subsampling sent a random partition containing 10% of the model parameters at a time, and the gossip cycle time was proportionally shorter so that the overall bandwidth utilization is the same. For token gossip learning, we used the randomized strategy with parameters $A = 10$ and $C = 20$. We used a dynamic learning rate $\eta_t = \eta/t$, where t is the model age (not the elapsed wall-clock time). The regularization coefficient was set to $\lambda = 1/\eta$. In the case of the baseline algorithms, we chose η from the set of values $\{10^0, ..., 10^5\}$ so as to minimize the classification error at the end of the churn-based simulation.

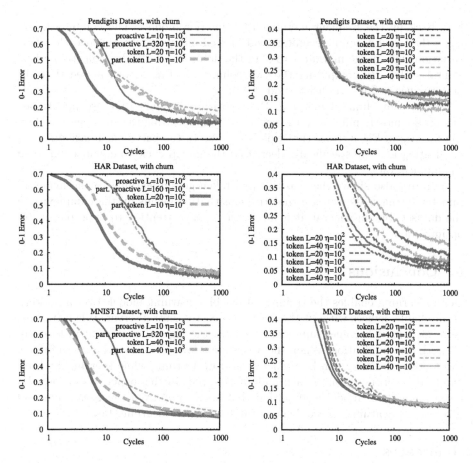

Fig. 3. Merge-limited gossip learning with and without partitioned subsampling (left) and the effect of different hyperparameter settings (right).

The hyperparameters of the novel variants (η and L) were also optimized using a simple grid search. For the error-free scenario, we used the same hyperparameters that were used in the churn scenario. We note here that if there is more than one sample in a node then the parameter L should be scaled proportionally because the age of the models will be scaled as well.

4.5 Results

Our results are shown in Fig. 2. The plots show the average ratio of misclassified test samples over the models of the online nodes. The horizontal axis is time (measured in cycles), which is also an upper bound on the total communication cost.

We can see that the token gossip learning method benefits greatly from the novel merging method, as the models performing hot potato walks are no longer held back by the frequent merging with inferior models. The combination of using the token account technique and limited merging outperformed the other variations by a large margin across all the datasets. (Note the logarithmic horizontal scale). By comparing the two columns in Fig. 2, we can see that the performance is fairly robust to node failures.

When using limited merging, the algorithm variants that use partitioned models are mostly inferior to the variants communicating the entire model. This can be seen in Fig. 3. Note that this is not due to the partitioned variants communicating less: we specifically decreased the gossip cycle to equalize expected communication.

Figure 3 also shows the sensitivity of token gossip learning to the hyperparameter settings. We can see that the sensitivity depends on the complexity of the dataset, but in general, it is advisable to pay attention to hyperparameter optimization.

5   Conclusions

Gossip learning enables the training of machine learning models over a network of unreliable devices without the need for a costly central server. When training large models, it becomes important to make the algorithm efficient in terms of network communication. When the nodes are allowed to communicate in bursts, token gossip learning can be used to speed up learning while keeping the total bandwidth consumption of each node unchanged. In this paper, we proposed a novel method for model aggregation that vastly improved the performance of token gossip learning, as we demonstrated on several learning tasks.

References

1. Anguita, D., Ghio, A., Oneto, L., Parra, X., Reyes-Ortiz, J.L.: A public domain dataset for human activity recognition using smartphones. In: Esann, vol. 3, p. 3 (2013)
2. Bache, K., Lichman, M.: UCI machine learning repository (2013)
3. Belal, Y., Bellet, A., Mokhtar, S.B., Nitu, V.: PEPPER: empowering user-centric recommender systems over gossip learning. Proc. ACM Interact. Mob. Wearable Ubiquit. Technol. **6**(3), 1–27 (2022)
4. Berta, Á., Bilicki, V., Jelasity, M.: Defining and understanding smartphone churn over the internet: a measurement study. In: Proceedings of the 14th IEEE International Conference on Peer-to-Peer Computing (P2P 2014). IEEE (2014). https://doi.org/10.1109/P2P.2014.6934317
5. Bishop, C.M., Nasrabadi, N.M.: Pattern Recognition and Machine Learning, vol. 4. Springer, Heidelberg (2006)
6. Bottou, L.: Stochastic gradient descent tricks. In: Montavon, G., Orr, G.B., Müller, K.-R. (eds.) Neural Networks: Tricks of the Trade. LNCS, vol. 7700, pp. 421–436. Springer, Heidelberg (2012). https://doi.org/10.1007/978-3-642-35289-8_25
7. Danner, G., Hegedűs, I., Jelasity, M.: Decentralized machine learning using compressed push-pull averaging. In: Proceedings of the 1st International Workshop on Distributed Infrastructure for Common Good, pp. 31–36 (2020)

8. Danner, G., Jelasity, M.: Token account algorithms: the best of the proactive and reactive worlds. In: Proceedings of The 38th International Conference on Distributed Computing Systems (ICDCS 2018), pp. 885–895. IEEE Computer Society (2018). https://doi.org/10.1109/ICDCS.2018.00090

9. Giaretta, L., Girdzijauskas, Š.: Gossip learning: off the beaten path. In: 2019 IEEE International Conference on Big Data (Big Data), pp. 1117–1124. IEEE (2019)

10. Guo, J., Zuo, Y., Wen, C.K., Jin, S.: User-centric online gossip training for autoencoder-based CSI feedback. IEEE J. Sel. Top. Signal Process. **16**(3), 559–572 (2022)

11. Hegedűs, I., Danner, G., Jelasity, M.: Decentralized learning works: an empirical comparison of gossip learning and federated learning. J. Parallel Distrib. Comput. **148**, 109–124 (2021)

12. Konečný, J., McMahan, H.B., Yu, F.X., Richtárik, P., Suresh, A.T., Bacon, D.: Federated learning: strategies for improving communication efficiency. arXiv preprint arXiv:1610.05492 (2016)

13. LeCun, Y., Bottou, L., Bengio, Y., Haffner, P.: Gradient-based learning applied to document recognition. Proc. IEEE **86**(11), 2278–2324 (1998). http://yann.lecun.com/exdb/publis/pdf/lecun-98.pdf

14. Li, Y., Chen, C., Liu, N., Huang, H., Zheng, Z., Yan, Q.: A blockchain-based decentralized federated learning framework with committee consensus. IEEE Netw. **35**(1), 234–241 (2020)

15. McMahan, B., Moore, E., Ramage, D., Hampson, S., y Arcas, B.A.: Communication-efficient learning of deep networks from decentralized data. In: Artificial Intelligence and Statistics, pp. 1273–1282. PMLR (2017)

16. Montresor, A., Jelasity, M.: PeerSim: a scalable P2P simulator. In: Proceedings of the 9th IEEE International Conference on Peer-to-Peer Computing (P2P 2009), pp. 99–100. IEEE, Seattle (2009). https://doi.org/10.1109/P2P.2009.5284506. Extended abstract

17. Niwa, K., Zhang, G., Kleijn, W.B., Harada, N., Sawada, H., Fujino, A.: Asynchronous decentralized optimization with implicit stochastic variance reduction. In: International Conference on Machine Learning, pp. 8195–8204. PMLR (2021)

18. Onoszko, N., Karlsson, G., Mogren, O., Zec, E.L.: Decentralized federated learning of deep neural networks on non-IID data. arXiv preprint arXiv:2107.08517 (2021)

19. Ormándi, R., Hegedűs, I., Jelasity, M.: Gossip learning with linear models on fully distributed data. Concurr. Comput.: Pract. Exp. **25**(4), 556–571 (2013)

20. Partridge, C.: Gigabit Networking. Addison-Wesley Professional (1994)

21. Ramanan, P., Nakayama, K.: BAFFLE: blockchain based aggregator free federated learning. In: 2020 IEEE International Conference on Blockchain (Blockchain), pp. 72–81. IEEE (2020)

22. Shin, H., et al.: Deep convolutional neural networks for computer-aided detection: CNN architectures, dataset characteristics and transfer learning. IEEE Trans. Med. Imaging **35**(5), 1285–1298 (2016)

23. Tölgyesi, N., Jelasity, M.: Adaptive peer sampling with newscast. In: Sips, H., Epema, D., Lin, H.-X. (eds.) Euro-Par 2009. LNCS, vol. 5704, pp. 523–534. Springer, Heidelberg (2009). https://doi.org/10.1007/978-3-642-03869-3_50

24. Xiao, H., Rasul, K., Vollgraf, R.: Fashion-MNIST: a novel image dataset for benchmarking machine learning algorithms. arXiv preprint arXiv:1708.07747 (2017)

Ensemble Machine Learning-Based Egg Parasitism Identification for Endangered Bird Conservation

Wiem Nhidi[1]([⊠]) [iD], Najib Ben Aoun[2,3] [iD], and Ridha Ejbali[1] [iD]

[1] RTIM: Research Team in Intelligent Machines, National Engineering School
of Gabes (ENIG), University of Gabes, 6029 Gabes, Tunisia
nhidiwiem@gmail.com, ridha_ejbali@ieee.org
[2] College of Computer Science and Information Technology, Al-Baha University,
Al Baha 65779-7738, Saudi Arabia
najib.benaoun@ieee.org
[3] REGIM-Lab: Research Groups in Intelligent Machines, National School
of Engineers of Sfax (ENIS), University of Sfax, 3038 Sfax, Tunisia

Abstract. The phenomenon of intraspecific nest parasitism is of a great
interest to biologists because it helps in the conservation of critically
endangered birds like the Slender-billed Gull. Indeed, upon detecting a
parasitic egg in the nest, the Slender-Billed Gull female abandon it. This
behavior results in loosing large number of future birds and leads to its
extension. So, a nest cleaning from parasitic eggs has been an urgent
need. Therefore, in this paper, we suggest a Slender-Billed parasitic egg
identification system from the egg visual information to clean the nest
and avoid the female leaving. Encouraged by the success of the machine
learning models in pattern recognition and classification, we have built a
system which extracts the most important egg visual features and classify
them using a set of machine learning models which have been aggregated
together to attain a high parasitic egg identification accuracy. In fact, a
set of egg visual features have been extracted from the eggshell using the
SpotEgg tool which have provided information about the egg coloration
and patterning such as the egg shape, size, color and spottiness. Our
model has been evaluated on a 31-nest dataset and has given an accuracy
of 88.3% which has outperformed other machine learning models.

Keywords: Ensemble Machine Learning · Stacked Model · SpotEgg ·
Voting classifier · Slender-Billed Gull · Parasitic Egg Identification

1 Introduction

Egg-laying parasitism is a behavior seen in a wide range of animal species including birds, amphibians and fish [7]. In birds, the parasite lays its eggs in the nest
of another bird (host), putting the task of raising its brood on the host such as
cuckoo finch, Anomali Spiza, tawny-flanked prinia [24]. Interspecific parasitism,

N. T. Nguyen et al. (Eds.): ICCCI 2023, CCIS 1864, pp. 364–375, 2023.
https://doi.org/10.1007/978-3-031-41774-0_29

in which the parasite lays eggs in the nest of a different species, and intraspecific parasitism, which affects members of the same species, are the two types of parasitism that can be distinguished. The Slender Billed Gull species is one of the birds that suffers from the intraspecific parasitism issue [9]. In fact, the Slender-billed gulls can lay up to three eggs in one nest [2]. While, we can observe four or five eggs in certain nests, indicating the presence of parasitic eggs. Generally, nests are spaced 45 cm apart, but in the center of colonies, nests can be as near as 15 cm away (see Fig. 1), which increase the risk of egg parasitism. Indeed, the big problem for the egg parasitism is that Slender Billed Gull female will leave the nest alone once it detects a parasitic egg. This will results in the loss of a large number of new birds. Furthermore, the slender-billed gull is one of the species protected by the African-Eurasian Migratory Waterbirds Agreement (AEWA) [9] which aims in protecting the endangered species. Therefore, decreasing egg parasitism for this species is essential to preserve it.

In this paper, we propose a method for identifying slender-billed gull parasitic eggs to help in maintaining the nest clean, avoiding the female leaving and preserving this specie. Our method extracts significant egg visual characteristics (egg color, spottiness, size, etc.) using the SpotEgg tool [13,14] and classify them using an ensemble machine learning model. Actually, five models have been trained on the egg dataset and a majority voting is conducted on the predictions of these models which helps in aggregating the models results and giving very promising egg parasitism identification.

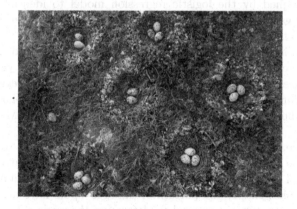

Fig. 1. Nest distribution of Slender-billed Gulls colony in Sfax city (Tunisia).

Our paper is organized as follows: in Sect. 2, we present the related work. While, we detail the proposed approach in Sect. 3. Afterwards, Sect. 4 provides the experimental results of our method variants as well as a comparative study with other machine learning models. Finally, the paper is concluded by giving the main findings and future work extensions.

2   Related Work

Most studies on parasitic egg identification [18,19,24,25,27] have focused on the ability of an automatic system to quantify the eggs. Indeed, many methods have been used to characterize the birds' eggs and to classify them in order to identify possible parasitism (see Table 1).

A technique for identifying parasite eggs has been proposed in [24]. It identifies the egg of the Anomali Spiza (host) from the egg of the Cuckoo finch (parasite) by using a fast Fourier transform followed by isotropic band-pass filters to extract egg features. This method computes a granularity spectrum for each egg region. Then, to enhance the egg characterization, the color difference between the parasite's eggs and the host as well as the pattern dispersion are extracted from each egg. Afterwards, a logistic regression model is used to classify these features. The method has been tested on a dataset collected in southern Zambia's Choma District.

Moreover, in [25], egg features such as the egg color difference and the pattern dispersion were extracted after granularity analysis (pattern filter size and pattern proportion energy calculated from the granularity spectrum which is obtained by applying fast Fourier transform and band-pass filtering on the egg region) to characterize the eggshell. Additionally, the shape and orientation of markings inside the eggshell are captured by the Scale Invariant feature transform (SIFT) high-level features extracted by the Nature Pattern Match (NPM) [26] generated by histogram equalization and median filtering. These features have been classified by the logistic regression model to identify the parasite cuckoo finch eggs (parasite) from tawny-flanked prinia eggs (host). The method has been evaluated on the same dataset in [24].

Afterwards, in [12], an egg classification method was proposed. The objective is to classify each egg into its corresponding clutches using its visual features. This method uses the SpotEgg tool [13] to extract 27 features of eggs such as egg shape, size, color and spottiness from calibrated images of Eurasian coot (Fulica atra) specie. These features are classified by the Support Vector Machine (SVM) algorithm.

Furthermore, in [27], sulk et al. have proposed a method to identify the parasitic cuckoo eggs from the Eurasian Reed Warbler and Great Reed Warbler based on visual features of eggs. In fact, a granularity spectrum analysis for measuring the size, shape, and pattern of the eggs' spots have been performed. In addition, spectrometry was used to determine the egg's color. The dataset has been collected from a fishpond location in South Moravia, Czech Republic. Then, using a combination of Hierarchical clustering and Random Forest, the extracted features have been classified to detect the egg parasitism.

In addition, to classify the egg of Slender Billed Gull species, a deep learning-based method has been proposed in [19]. This method trains a Convolution Neural Networks (CNN) model on a Slender Billed Gull dataset formed by 31 clutches and collected from Sfax region, Tunisia. Subsequently, in [18], Discrete Wavelet Transform (DWT) egg filtering operation has been conducted and given four sub-bands which are used to train a CNN model. As a result, the parasitic eggs have been identified using this CNN model and has giving encouraging results.

Table 1. Parasitic egg identification and egg classification techniques.

Study	Features	Classifier
[24]	Color, Pattern filter size, Pattern proportion energy, pattern dispersion,	Logistic regression
[25]	Pattern filter size, Pattern proportion energy	Logistic Regression
[12]	SpotEgg tool	SVM
[27]	Spotty coloring Egg-shaped size	Hierarchical clustering Random Forest
[18]	DWT+CNN	SVM Softmax
[19]	CNN	Softmax

As it can be seen from the summary in Table 1, different machine learning techniques has been used for parasitic egg identification. Indeed, machine learning models have proven their efficiency in many tasks including image segmentation and classification [3–6,16] which encourages us more to adopt a machine learning based method in our system. The promising results obtained demonstrate the effectiveness of these techniques in identifying parasitic eggs as well as saving new birds that were threatened due to their mother's departure. That is what motivated us to propose a parasitic egg recognition method based on an ensemble of machine learning model resulted from the aggregation of several models which are trained with accurate egg visual features.

3 The Proposed Method

To efficiently identify parasitic eggs of the Slender Billed Gull bird, we have build an ensemble machine learning based model trained using egg visual features. In fact, before extracting the visual features of the egg using the SpotEgg tool, a preprocessing step has been performed to improve the egg image quality and normalize all egg images size. Then, all the extracted features are concatenated together and introduced to an ensemble machine learning model. Two of the most successful ensemble machine learning strategies have been evaluated: model stacking strategy [15] and voting ensemble strategy [1]. As it can be seen in the experimental study section, the second strategy has given the best parasitic egg identification results. The pipeline of our proposed method is illustrated in Fig. 2 and the main phases will be described subsequently.

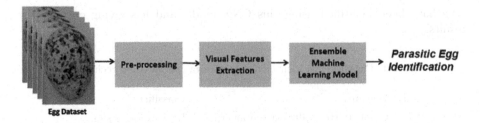

Fig. 2. Proposed method pipeline.

3.1   Egg Images Pre-processing

In order to extract accurate egg visual features, a preprocessing step has been conducted. Indeed, the egg images quality and illumination have been enhanced. In addition, since the egg RGB images in the dataset are of different sizes, all the egg images have been resized to $1024 \times 2048 \times 3$ (where 3 refers to the RGB channels).

3.2   Visual Features Extraction

Egg differentiation can not be achieved without precise egg characterization. That is why we have used the powerful SpotEgg tool [13] which extracts the egg coloration and patterning such as the egg shape, size, color and spottiness. SpotEgg tool has been developed by Gómez and Liñán-Cembrano [13] and it is implemented in MATLAB and an executable version is available. Indeed, SpotEgg conducts 3 steps to extract the egg visual features as shown in the Fig. 3. Firstly, image linearisation is performed to all the images in the dataset to obtain equivalent RGB average reflectance images which helps in normalizing all the images. Secondly, a region of Interest (ROI) definition step is executed. In this step the egg is detected from the image either by the SpotEgg tool itself (automatically) or manually where the ROI is drawn by the user. Thirdly, during the spot detection step, egg spots are identified from the detected egg. Then, egg spottiness and coloration features (length, width, fractal dimension of spottiness pattern, location of each spot, physical size, eccentricity of its shape, average reflectance in each of the camera's RGB colour channels, etc.) are extracted.

3.3   Ensemble Machine Learning Model

In order to model the egg visual features, two modeling strategies have been conducted and evaluated. The first strategy, is model stacking while the second one is voting ensemble strategy. Model staking [11,20] consists in training heterogeneous learners. Then, the resulted predictions of these learners are inputted to a meta-learner (e.g. neural network, logistic regression, etc.) which provides the final prediction result. However, voting ensemble [1] is manifested in training

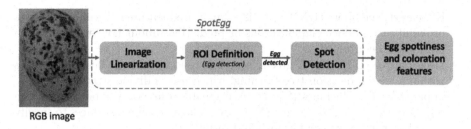

Fig. 3. SpotEgg visual feature extraction steps.

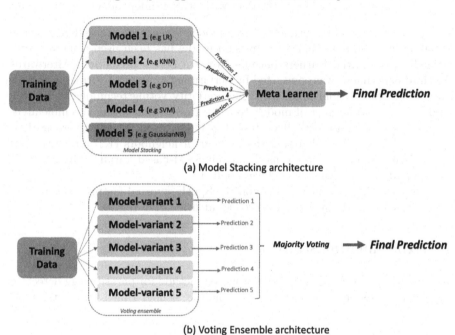

Fig. 4. Ensemble models architectures.

several learners and aggregating their predictions through a voting operation to get the final classification decision (see Fig. 4).

For our method, we have conducted three experiments. In the first experiment, five single models have been used to classify the egg visual features. These models are:

- Logistic Regression (LR) [17]: is a statistical technique for examining a dataset in which one or more independent variables affect an outcome. It is used to predict a categorical value by estimating the connection between a dependent variable and one or more independent variables.

- K-Nearest Neighbors (KNN) [21]: is a supervised learning classifier that uses proximity to produce classifications or predictions about how a specific data points will be grouped.
- DecisionTree (DT) [22]: A greedy search is used to find the best split points within a tree in decision tree learning, which uses a divide strategy.
- Support Vector Machines (SVM) [8]: it creates a line or a hyperplane which separates the data into classes. SVMs use multidimensional surfaces to specify the relationship between features and results.
- Gaussian Naive Bayes (GaussianNB) [23]: is a probabilistic classification method based on the Bayes theorem with strong independence assumptions.

Then, for the second experiment, these models have been stacked together as initial learners and the logistic regression model has been used a meta-learner trained on the initial learners outputs to get a better prediction. Afterwards, the third experiment was conducted by performing a majority voting among five learners to get the final prediction. The majority voting technique is typically used with an odd number of models to avoid ties. In this voting ensemble architecture, three variants have been tested: a KNN-based variant where we have applied 5 KNNs while changing the number of neighbors (K), an SVM-based variant with different kernels used and an SVM-based variant where 5 SVM models of different kernels have been applied.

Using a voting classifier trained on the SpotEgg visual features, our method has achieved very promising parasitic egg identification results.

4   Experimental Study

To evaluate the performance of the proposed method for parasitic egg detection, we performed extensive experiments on the the Slender Billed Gull dataset.

4.1   Dataset

In 2015, 31 Slender-billed Gull clutches from the Sfax salt flats in Tunisia [10] have been collected. In each nest, 2 to 4 eggs have been found. In total, the dataset contains 91 eggs photographed in very similar camera settings. However, the egg RGB images are of different sizes which may need a resizing step to normalize them based on their use. After genetic tests conducted by the biologists and involving egg-cracking, the parasitic eggs have been identified. Accordingly, the dataset has been labelled. In addition, the dataset is split into 70% for the training phase and 30% for the testing phase. Samples from the dataset are illustrated in Fig. 5.

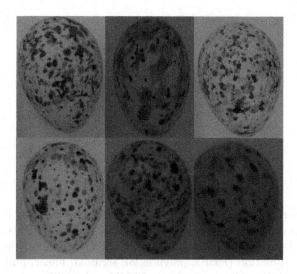

Fig. 5. Samples from Slender Billed Gull egg dataset.

4.2 Performance Evaluation Metric

To evaluate our method, we have adopted the classification accuracy metric which represents the percentage of the correctly classified test images (see Eq. 1) since it is the commonly used image classification metric.

$$Accuracy = \frac{\text{The number of test samples recognized correctly}}{\text{Total number of test samples}} \qquad (1)$$

4.3 Experimental Results

As previously discussed in the proposed method section, five models (LR, KNN, SVM, DecisionTree, GaussianNB) have been tested individually. Each algorithm will be evaluated using default model hyperparameters (KNN with K = 5 and SVM with 'rbf' kernel). As it can be seen from Table 2, the SVM (84.3%) and the KNN (84.9%) classifiers have achieved the highest accuracies, while the GuassianNB, the LR and the decision tree classifier have given accuracies of 76.1%, 74.7% and 69.6% respectively.

In order to enhance the efficiency of these models, we have conducted a model stacking operation as illustrated in Fig. 4. Indeed, these five models have been stacked together and the logistic regression classifier has been used a meta-learner. This stacked model has leads to an accuracy increase of 2% in comparison with the best individual classifier and gives an accuracy of 86.3%.

Moreover, encouraged by the success of the voting ensemble approach and the results reached by the single classifiers which has demonstrated that the SVM and the KNN are the best individual classifiers, three voting classifiers have been implemented. In the first voting classifier, five KNNs variants with

Table 2. The accuracy results for our different classifiers and model stacking.

Classifier	Accuracy
Logistic Regression (LR)	74.7%
K-Nearest Neighbors (KNN)	84.9%
Decision Tree (DT)	69.6%
Support Vector Machines (SVM)	84.3%
Gaussian Naive Bayes (GaussianNB)	76.1%
Model Stacking	**86.3%**

different number of neighbors (1, 3, 5, 7 and 9) have been used a initial learners. However, in the second voting classifier, the implemented model is a voting SVM with different kernels. We used multiple SVMs with different kernels such as the radial basis function (RBF), polynomial, sigmoid, linear, and precomputed kernels. By combining the predictions of SVMs with different kernels through voting, we obtained an ensemble model that can leverage the strengths of each individual SVM. The voting SVM model with different kernels demonstrated impressive accuracy, with results ranging from 70.4% for the precomputed kernel to 86.8% for the ensemble. Then, we explored the effectiveness of Support Vector Machines (SVMs) with different polynomial kernel degrees for our classification task.

Indeed, in the last voting classifier, five SVMs variants with different polynomial kernel degrees have been used a initial learners. Afterwards, for each voting classifier, a majority voting operation is conducted to identify the class with the highest majority of votes which will be considered as the final prediction. As a result, the first KNN-based voting classifier has given an accuracy of 85.4% which outperforms the individual KNNs results while the second SVM with different kernel has given an accuracy of 86.8%. Then th last model SVM-based voting classifier has given an accuracy of 88.3% which is better than using a single SVM as shown in Table 3. Consequently, the SVM-based voting classifier is adopted for our method since it gives the best Slender-Billed Gull's parasitic egg identification result.

Table 3. The accuracy results for the KNN and SVM based voting classifiers.

Classifier	Accuracy
KNN (k = 1)	83.3%
KNN (k = 3)	84.2%
KNN (k = 5)	84.9%
KNN (k = 7)	85%
KNN (k = 9)	83.9%
KNN-based voting classifier	**85.4%**
SVM (kernel = 'rbf')	84.3%
SVM (kernel = 'poly')	82.1%
SVM (kernel = 'sigmoid')	76%
SVM (kernel = 'linear')	79 %
SVM (kernel = 'precomputed')	70.4 %
SVM-based kernels voting classifier	**86.8%**
SVM (polynomial degree = 1)	79.8%
SVM (polynomial degree = 2)	81.9%
SVM (polynomial degree = 3)	82.1%
SVM (polynomial degree = 4)	75.3%
SVM (polynomial degree = 5)	74.6%
SVM-based voting classifier	**88.3%**

5   Conclusion

In this paper, we have proposed a method for identifying Slender-Billed Gull parasitic eggs based on the eggshell visual features which helps in saving this endangered species. In fact our method extracts visual features from prepro-cessed egg image using SpotEgg tool. Then these features are introduced to an SVM-based voting classifier to classify them and detect wither the query egg belongs to the host or to the parasite bird. The reached promising results prove the robustness and efficiency of our method. As for the future works, we plan to use more egg image features to better characterize the eggshell and evaluate our method on other egg datasets to upgrade it and confirm its effectiveness.

Acknowledgement. The authors would like to acknowledge the financial support of this work through grants from the General Direction of Scientific Research (DGRST), Tunisia, under the ARUB program.

References

1. Atallah, R., Al-Mousa, A.: Heart disease detection using machine learning major-ity voting ensemble method. In: 2nd International Conference on New Trends in Computing Sciences (ICTCS), pp. 1–6 (2019)

2. Barbosa, A., Leonild, L., Hanlon, T.: Changeable cuttlefish camouflage is influenced by horizontal and vertical aspects of the visual background. J. Comp. Physiol. **194**, 405–13 (2008)

3. Ben Aoun, N., Mejdoub, M., Ben Amar, C.: Bag of sub-graphs for video event recognition. In: 39th IEEE International Conference on Acoustics, Speech, and Signal Processing (ICASSP 2014), pp. 1566–1570 (2014). https://doi.org/10.1109/ICASSP.2014.6853857

4. Brahimi, S., Ben Aoun, N., Ben Amar, C.: Very deep recurrent convolutional neural network for object recognition. In: International Conference on Machine Vision (ICMV 2016), vol. 10341, p. 1034107 (2016). https://doi.org/10.1117/12.2268672

5. Brahimi, S., Ben Aoun, N., Ben Amar, C.: Improved very deep recurrent convolutional neural network for object recognition. In: IEEE International Conference on Systems, Man, and Cybernetics (SMC 2018), pp. 2497–2502 (2018). https://doi.org/10.1109/SMC.2018.00428

6. Brahimi, S., Ben Aoun, N., Ben Amar, C., Benoit, A., Lambert, P.: Multiscale fully convolutional densenet for semantic segmentation. J. WSCG **26**(2), 104–111 (2018)

7. Cassey, P., et al.: Avian eggshell pigments are not consistently correlated with colour measurements or egg constituents in two Turdus thrushes. J. Avian Biol. **43**, 503–12 (2012)

8. Chandra, M.A., Bedi, S.: Survey on SVM and their application in image classification. Int. J. Inf. Technol. **13**, 1–11 (2021)

9. Chokri, M.A., Sadoul, N., Medhioub, K., Bechet, A.: Analyse comparative de la richesse avifaunistique du salin de Sfax dans le contexte tunisien et méditerranéen. Rev. d'Ecol. Terre et Vie **63**(4), 351–369 (2008)

10. Chokri, M.A., Selmi, S.: Nesting phenology and breeding performance of the slender-billed gull Chroicocephalus genei in Sfax Salina, Tunisia. Ostrich **83**(1), 13–18 (2012)

11. Dietterich, T.G.: Ensemble methods in machine learning. In: Kittler, J., Roli, F. (eds.) MCS 2000. LNCS, vol. 1857, pp. 1–15. Springer, Heidelberg (2000). https://doi.org/10.1007/3-540-45014-9_1

12. Gomez, J., Gordoi, O.: EGG recognition: the importance of quantifying multiple repeatable features as visual identity signals. PLoS One **16**, 0248021 (2021)

13. Gómez, J., Liñán-Cembrano, G.: SpotEgg: an image-processing tool for automatised analysis of colouration and spottiness. J. Avian Biol. **48**(4), 502–512 (2016)

14. Liñán-Cembrano, G., Gómez, J.: SpotEgg: measuring coloration and patterning. J. Avian Biol. **48**(4), 502–512 (2017)

15. Malmasi, S., Dras, M.: Native language identification with classifier stacking and ensembles. Comput. Linguist. **44**(3), 403–446 (2018)

16. Mejdoub, M., Ben Aoun, N., Ben Amar, C.: Bag of frequent subgraphs approach for image classification. Intell. Data Anal. **19**(1), 75–88 (2015)

17. Ng, A., Jordan, M.: On discriminative vs. generative classifiers: a comparison of logistic regression and naive bayes. In: Advances in Neural Information Processing Systems, vol. 14 (2001)

18. Wiem, N., Ali, C.M., Ridha, E.: Wavelet feature with CNN for identifying parasitic egg from a Slender-Billed's nest. In: Abraham, A., Hanne, T., Castillo, O., Gandhi, N., Nogueira Rios, T., Hong, T.-P. (eds.) HIS 2020. AISC, vol. 1375, pp. 365–374. Springer, Cham (2021). https://doi.org/10.1007/978-3-030-73050-5_37

19. Nhidi, W., Ejbali, R., Dahmen, H.: An intelligent approach to identify parasitic eggs from a Slender-Billed's nest. In: Twelfth International Conference on Machine

Vision (ICMV 2019), vol. 11433, p. 1143309. International Society for Optics and Photonics (2020)

20. Pavlyshenko, B.: Using stacking approaches for machine learning models. In: 2018 IEEE Second International Conference on Data Stream Mining & Processing (DSMP), pp. 255–258. IEEE (2018)

21. Pribisova, A., Martinez, C.: Model decision tree. Technical report, Sandia National Lab. (SNL-NM), Albuquerque, NM, USA (2021)

22. Priyam, A., Abhijeeta, G., Rathee, A., Srivastava, S.: Comparative analysis of decision tree classification algorithms. Int. J. Curr. Eng. Technol. 3(2), 334–337 (2013)

23. Pushpakumar, R., Prabu, R., Priscilla, M., Renisha, P., Prabu, R.T., Muthuraman, U.: A novel approach to identify dynamic deficiency in cell using gaussian NB classifier. In: 2022 7th International Conference on Communication and Electronics Systems (ICCES), pp. 31–37. IEEE (2022)

24. Spottiswoode, C.N., Stevens, M.: Visual modeling shows that avian host parents use multiple visual cues in rejecting parasitic eggs. Proc. Natl. Acad. Sci. 107(19), 8672–8676 (2010)

25. Stoddard, M.C., Hogan, B.G., Stevens, M., Spottiswoode, C.N.: Higher-level pattern features provide additional information to birds when recognizing and rejecting parasitic eggs. Philos. Trans. R. Soc. B 374(1769), 20180197 (2019)

26. Stoddard, M.C., Kilner, R.M., Town, C.: Pattern recognition algorithm reveals how birds evolve individual egg pattern signatures. Nat. Commun. 5, 4117 (2014)

27. Šulc, M., et al.: Automatic identification of bird females using egg phenotype. Zool. J. Linn. Soc. 195(1), 33–44 (2022)

Social Networks and Speek Communication

A Comparative Analysis of Long Covid in the French Press and Twitter

Brigitte Juanals[1](✉) and Jean-Luc Minel[2]

[1] CentreNorbert Elias, Aix Marseille University- CNRS - EHESS, Marseille, France
brigitte.Juanals@univ-amu.fr
[2] MoDyCo, CNRS - University Paris Nanterre, Nanterre, France
jl.minel@orange.fr
https://cv.hal.science/brigitte-juanals

Abstract. This research focuses, in the media public sphere, on the modalities of construction and progressive visibility of persistent symptoms of certain forms of Covid-19, designated by the category "Long Covid". The aim is to analyze the process according to which this particular form of the disease appeared in the media in June 2020, was the subject of debates and contradictory - even conflicting - positions of the actors, until its institutional and public recognition in 2022. The article conducts a comparative analysis on the French national and regional press and on the digital social network Twitter.

Keywords: COVID-19 · Long Covid · Topic Modeling · Media · Sentiment Analysis

1 Introduction

We propose to interrogate the role played by the media and stakeholders involved in the production and circulation of information and knowledge about the Covid-19 epidemic in France from 2020 in the public sphere. We focused on persistent symptoms following an initial SARS-COV-2 infection, referred to as "Long Covid" (Covid Long in French) subject of debate in the media ecosystem. "Long Covid", also known as "post-COVID-19 syndrome" or "long-haul COVID" is called Post-acute Sequelae of COVID-19 (PASC) by medical scholars. It designs convalescent individuals in whom prolonged and often debilitating sequelae persist [1]. Many symptoms are associated with PASC. They include severe fatigue, frequent discomfort, nausea, headaches, and can lead to seriouspsychiatric disorders such as depression, anxiety and post-traumatic stress disorder [2,7]. The motivation to address this topic stems from the observation that these "post-Covid conditions", according to the World Health Organization (WHO) clinical definition, affect a significant number of people, i.e. "30% of people who had an SARS-CoV-2 infection more than three months before", which "would correspond to 2.06 million people over 18 years old affected in the French population at the beginning of April 2022" (Santé Publique France, 07/21/2022). However, these conditions, despite the number of people affected, appear to be less visible and are the subject of debate in the media ecosystem.

N. T. Nguyen et al. (Eds.): ICCCI 2023, CCIS 1864, pp. 379–392, 2023.
https://doi.org/10.1007/978-3-031-41774-0_30

1.1   The "Long Covid", a Public and Media Issue in Debate

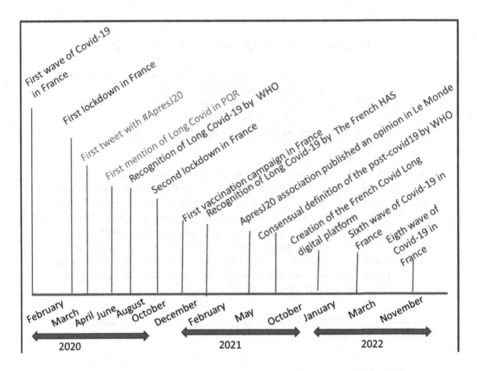

Fig. 1. Timeline of main events of the Covid-19 outbreak in France

The "Long Covid" category remains subject to debate and contention, particularly in the medical community. On the diagnostic dimension, many people in spring 2020 were not screened for Covid-19 because they had moderate symptoms and/or were not hospitalized. Therefore, the "Long Covid" labeling was often challenged by the healthcare professionals due to the lack of this initial diagnosis. Conversely, for the patients, the category "Long Covid" encompasses a set of symptoms that has gradually led to the recognition of a common experience: the lasting consequences of the disease in their bodies and their social lives, which encourage therapeutic wandering. In France, in May 2020, a collective was created to gather the acquired knowledge about long covid, disseminate information supports, contact journalists, deputies, physicians, politicians, provide support to patients and make their voices heard in the hope of being recognized and cured one day. On October 06, 2020, this collective created a non-profit organization called ApresJ20 (i.e. after 20 days) (https://www.apresj20.fr/) to have the long covid recognized as a disease. In particular, its communication campaign will be based on the hashtag #ApresJ20.

The recognition by the World Health Organization (WHO) in August 2020 (cf. Fig. 1) then by the French High Authority for Health (HAS) in February 2021, of persistent or prolonged Covid symptoms is a direct result of the advocacy carried out by patients and the healthcare professionals who accompany them. Numerous research projects are underway, both internationally and in France, that will refine the findings and improve our understanding of long Covid and its symptoms. In clinical practice and treatment, progress has been made in recent months. However, many uncertainties remain regarding the medium- and long-term experience of Covid, and its social consequences for patients. This justifies in our view the development of a social science perspective on the media visbility of these issues.

The outline of this paper is the following. First, in Sect. 2, we present the litterature review and then specify the contribution of the proposed methodology based on Latent Dirichlet Analysis (LDA) and Natural Language Processing (NLP) to tackle this field. In Sect. 3, we will present how articles of newspapers and tweets were collected. In Sect. 4, we will present the results of the comparative analysis. In Sect. 5, we put the focus on emotions in Tweets. Finally, we conclude in Sect. 6.

2 Literature Review and Methodology

2.1 Literature Review

There are many text mining works that rely on (LDA) to analyze texts or tweets related to COVID 19. Scapino et al. [7] studied how to extract meaningful insights in the Italian narration of COVID-19 pandemic. Specifically, they compared writings by health professionals with those of the lay public. At the beginning of the pandemic in 2020, Medford et al. [8] analyzed the polarity of emotions in tweets related to COVID19 based on a topic modeling approach. In the same way Valdez et al. [9] relied on LDA model to identify topics in a corpus of tweets related to COVID19. Important results of this study showed that the social network helped patients to cope with feelings of isolation but also contributed to disinformation [10].

Concerning the analysis of press articles, research work focused on whether the media delivered the latest COVID-19 information to the lay public [22,23]. Liu et al. [11] collected news articles about the coronavirus from major China press media between January and February 2020. They aimed to investigate the role of the media in this ongoing COVID-19 crisis in China. They concluded that the major themes identified by topic modeling in theses articles focused on the society rather than on individuals. In a large study covering 4 countries, [12] collected from January 1st, 2020 to December 1st, 2020 100,000 news headlines and articles related with COVID19 of eight major newspapers from four countries (United Kingdom, India, Japan, South Korea). They analyzed this data set relying on topic modeling and sentiment classification. They showed that there is a possible correlation between negative COVID-19 news and a countries' affectedness. In particular they pointed out that United Kingdom, the worst affected country at that time, had the highest negative headlines.

Our research is very similar to [13] who collected news articles and tweets related to COVID-19 written in Portuguese language from January to May 2020.

News were gathered from the Brazilian web site Universo Online which published the leading Brazilian daily newspaper, Folha de São Paulo. Tweets collected was filtered by 15 hashtags COVID-19-related topics but none of these hashtags concern the long covid.

2.2 An Instrumented Methodology

To identify topics and stakeholders' standpoints we carried out topic modeling and text mining analysis. Topic modeling, or Latent Dirichlet Analysis (LDA), is based on the construction of a probabilistic model [3]. LDA builds a generative probabilistic model that combines two Dirichlet distributions and two multinomial distributions [3]. The model, which is not computable, is estimated from different heuristics, the most common of which is the Gibbs algorithm. Topic modeling assigns to each text a topic, the one with the computed highest probability. One of the interests of topic modeling is that it is possible to study the variation of the importance of topics over time, as well as to compare the distribution of topics between different articles or different texts category.

Topic modeling algorithms are implemented in different languages (R, Python). We choose to use the R package topicmodels [4]. Using topic modeling call for to fix the number of topics as an input parameter. Several experiences argued for the choice of a smaller number of topics. In order to help the analyst in the choice of the number of topics, [5] proposed an approach that relies on the use of interactive visualization tools associated with the computation of two scores, salience and relevance. In their article, [5] present several experiments that allow to fix the value of the parameter that optimally weights the calculation of the salience and the relevance. We carried out this method [18]. We point out that press corpus was lemmatized and tagged with part of speech categories using TreeTagger Part-of-Speech [14]; only adjective, adverb, noun, verb categories were kept before processing topic modeling step. Taking into account the particularities of the writing of tweets, such as numerous abbreviations, non respect of the French syntax, tweets were not lemmatized.

To identify and categorize stakeholders, a classifier of named entities built with neural networks (https://v2.spacy.io/) was used. First, we kept the categorized entities "Person" (PER) and "Organization" (ORG) then we used a Python script developed by [6] to identify morphological variants of person names in order to enrich classifier results.

3 Corpora

3.1 Newspapers

We selected 5 titles from the French national daily press (PQN) and 39 titles from the regional daily press (PQR) whose annual circulation is greater than 30,000 copies. Articles were collected from the Europresse platform with the query "Covid%1long or covid%1persistant or affections%1post-covid". The %1 operator expresses a constraint of proximity between the words; these words must not be separated by more than one word in the sentence where they co-occur. After the collection step, a curation step removed articles in which the words of the search equation appear unrelated to the Covid Long. Finally, 988 articles, published between June 5, 2020 and December 31, 2022, were kept; 170 articles appeared in the national press and 818 in the regional press. The first articles mentioning the French term "covid persistant", appeared on June 5, 2020 in several PQR newspapers.

3.2 Tweets

The corpus of tweets was collected by exploiting the Academic Research Access API proposed by Twitter. This API allows collecting and filtering all tweets containing a combination of words and features during a time period. The first tweet that mentioned the long covid and proposed the hashtag "#ApresJ20" was sent on April 12, 2020 by the account @lapsyrevolte. The harvesting was limited to French tweets, by using the "lang" features, which contained hashtags "#ApresJ20" (After 20 days) or "#covidlong" sent between April 12, 2020 and December 30, 2022. The main figures are the following: 297,478 French tweets of which 92,494 original tweets and 204,984 retweets sent by 58,272 accounts, but only 11,245 accounts sent an original tweet.

4 Analysis

In order to examine the media visibility of this issue, Two research questions guided our comparative analysis. RQ1: How do the topics highlighted in the press and in the tweets differ? RQ2: What are the main categories of people and organizations mentioned in the press and in Twitter and how do they differ?

Figure 2 shows monthly evolution of the number of articles published in the press and the number of tweets. Concerning the flow of articles, there is a first strong increase in the number of articles in February 2021, followed by a relative stability until the end of the year 2021. A second strong progression is observed from January 2022 until March 2022. After this period an up and down flow of articles is observed with a last peak in October 2022. Peaks are more important for the PQR category but the general trend is similar in both categories. In 2021, peaks from February to May are related with the recognition by the HAS of the "Long Covid" (cf. Fig. 1).

Concerning the flow of tweets there is a first strong increase in the number of tweets and retweets in June 2020, followed by a slight decrease until January 2021 followed by second strong increase in February. The highest peak is observed in November 2021. The flow during the year 2022 is rather weak with a peak in October and November.

There are some differences between the two flows. The flow of tweets for the year 2020 is already important while it remains low for the press and especially

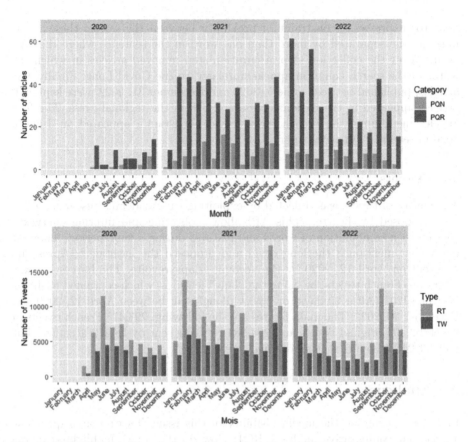

Fig. 2. Monthly evolution of the number of articles published by category and the number of tweets

for the national press. The flow of year 2022 is the most important for the press while it is the one of 2021 for the tweets.

To answer more precisely to our research questions, the topic modeling step allowed us, for all the topics found, to emphasize the number of texts indexed by a topic and the words with the highest probability in each topic. Relying on [5] we choose to set the number of topics at 8.

Table 1 shows the list of topics with the most significant words for each of them and the number of articles indexed by these topics. We note that the topics that deal with the daily life of patients and symptoms are the most important.

Figure 3 shows monthly evolution of these topics. The press devotes the greatest number of articles to the daily life topic (especially on the working issue) with a peak in march 2021. But from July 2021, the vaccination topic will give rise to a large number of articles with a peak in December 2021 which corresponds to the beginning of the vaccination campaign in France. It is also worth noting the peak of articles in May 2021 dedicated to the issue of symptoms (pain, fatigue,

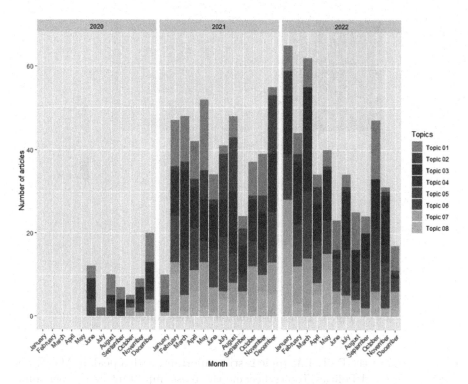

Fig. 3. Monthly evolution of topics in the press

Table 1. Topics for the press corpora

Number	Themes of Topic	Most probable words	Number of articles
01	Symptoms	symptômes, trouble, fatigue, douleur	181
02	Vaccination	vaccin, dose, risque, protèger	78
03	Research	étude, chercheur, publier, résultat	74
04	Daily Life	vivre, problème, retrouver, travail	208
05	Crisis	pouvoir, entreprise, travail, projet	119
06	Outbreak	vague, millions, masques, variants	108
07	Patient Care	patient, médecin, rééducation	122
08	Politics	loi, député, association	98

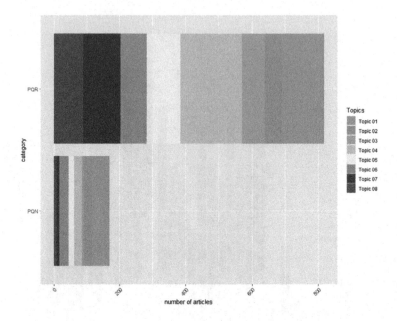

Fig. 4. Topics distribution by press category

etc.). In 2022, if the Daily Life topic is still important, with a peak in March, the Patient Care and Politics Topics became the most important at the beginning of the year.

Figure 4 shows topics distribution by press category. It can be observed that Daily Life (topic 4, 32%) and Patient Care (topic 7, 14%) topics are the most important in the PQR while it is the Symptoms topic (topic 1, 31%) for the PQN.

Applying a Topic Modeling algorithm does not produce relevant results on short texts like tweets [15]. Quan et al. [16] present a solution for sparse documents, finding that automatic text aggregation is able to produce more interpretable topics from short texts than the standard approach. Consequently, in a first step, we assembled tweets sent by a same account to form a text. In a second step we kept the texts with a length of more than 1000 words. This gave us a corpus of 125 texts, over the period April 2020 to December 2022. Adopting the same approach as for press texts to choose the most appropriate number of topic, we choose to set the number of topics at 5. Table 2 shows the list of topics with the most significant words for each of them and the number of texts indexed by these topics. The most important topic is "Testimonials" which gathers texts in which users relate their difficulties to live with the long covid.

As the texts on which the topic modeling is applied are aggregates of tweets sent at different dates, it is not possible to follow the temporal evolution of these tweets. We were therefore more interested in the most retweeted tweets and conversations. Concerning retweets, the most retweeted tweets are the following:

Table 2. Topics for the tweets corpora

Number	Themes of Topic	Most probable words	Number of texts
01	Patients	patients, nous, malades	15
02	Coming out	j'ai, nous, aujourd'hui, virus	12
03	Dispute	psychologisation, 1000 études, prouvé	7
04	Testimonials	douleurs, fatigue, mal de tête	67
05	Claim	prise en charge, parcours de soins	15

In the year 2020: *#apresJ20 RETURN ON THE 2nd INFECTIOLOGY RDV - COLD SHOWER. I thought a lot before writing this thread because I'm about to recount a very painful experience of MEDICAL MALTREATMENT and because I'm not going to be able to skip over the medical considerations (1538 retweets)*

In the year 2021: *#apresj20 #longcovid I don't usually do "threads", I don't even know if this is really a thread but I need to talk. I'm 28 and feel like I'm living in an 80 year old body that doesn't belong to me. I got sick during the Christmas vacations (1398 retweets)*

In the year 2022: *Disbarred for treating #CovidLong patients abandoned by fellow physicians. "I couldn't let people suffer in such a state!" His scientific arguments and long experience were not taken into account. Laissonslespre1 france soir (885 retweets)*

A conversation is a new feature proposed by Twitter in the new API. A conversation groups all the tweets that are sent by accounts that use the "Reply" feature. The conversation with the most participants are the following:

In 2020, the tweet that started the conversation with 26 participants was sent on 12/09/2020 with the following content: *"#J284 - Today, it's fatigue that dominates. Chest tightness returns tonight, not sure why. #LongCovid #apresJ20 @apresj20 Otherwise, I'm speaking tomorrow, Thursday 10/12 starting at 10:10am, live on RFI to talk about the disease".*

In 2021, the tweet that started the conversation with 64 participants was sent on 11/16/2021 with the following content: *"THE SHAME LIVE! (Thread) With an absence of empathy, humility, rigor, veracity and decency, #EricCaumes and #YvesCalvi just mocked 800,000 French #CovidLong live on @BFMTV. @apresj20 @FrAssosSante @LeMonde @franceinter @France @LEXPRESS..."*

In 2022, the tweet that started the conversation with 633 participants was sent on 11/29/2022 with the following content: *"This is how my legs are because of the covid, and these doctors who tell you it's stress ?mdrrrr, nobody gives explanations, all the analyses are good, if not @EmmanuelMacron @Sante_Gouv @FrcsBraun @apresj20 can give me some Ps I am vaccinated 3 times @Pfizer".*

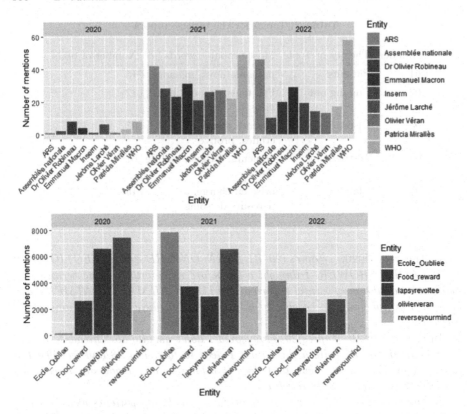

Fig. 5. Temporal evolution of mentioned people and organizations in the press and in tweets

We searched for persons or organizations mentioned in the press by using a classifier (see Sect. 2.2). Table 3 and Fig. 5 shows the main people and organization mentioned in the press over the three years. The press mentioned international (WHO) and national (ARS, INSERM) health institutions as well as one political organization (French National Assembly) and political people in charge of the executive power (President of the Republic, Minister of Health). The other two people strongly mentioned are physicians. Furthermore, analyzing all the persons mentioned showed a strong presence of medical personalities, 56 mentions of professors of medicine, 87 mentions of physicians, who were generally mentioned only once. It should be noted that the #ApresJ20 association (see Sect. 1.1), which represents the majority of patients, is mentioned only 5 times, 4 times in the PQN and 1 times in the PQR.

Concerning the corpus of tweets, we used software developed by [17] to compute several scores. Table 4 shows the most mentioned Twitter accounts in the tweet corpus over the three years among the 21,559 accounts mentioned. If the account of the Minister of Health is also the most mentioned, all the other accounts are those of long covid patients, two of whom are the founders of the association #ApresJ20, and one is the account of the Ecole_Oublie association. Concerning the passing score (that is to say accounts who tweet and retweet a lot) the three highest scores are those of two Covid Long patients and the Ecole_Oubliee association.

Table 3. Most mentioned people and organizations in the press

Names	Type	Occurence	Number of Sources	Comments
WHO	ORG	115	21	World Health Organization
ARS	ORG	88	22	Health Regional Agency
Emmanuel Macron	PER	64	20	President of Republic
Dr Olivier Robineau	PER	51	12	Physician
Dr Jérôme Larché	PER	46	6	Physician
Patricia Mirallès	PER	42	9	Member of National Assembly
INSERM	ORG	41	14	French Health Research Agency
Assemblée nationale	ORG	40	13	French National Assembly
Olivier Véran	PER	40	18	Minister of Health

Table 4. Most accounts mentioned in tweets

Account	Occurence	Comments
@olivierveran	16612	Minister of Health
@Ecole_Oubliee	12012	Parents for a Safe School against #Covid19
@lapsyrevoltee	11097	Co-founder of #ApresJ20
@reverseyourmind	9084	Patient Long Covid
@food_reward	8277	Co-founder of #ApresJ20

5   Focus on Emotions in Tweets

In line with [19], we carried out a sentiment analysis using R library package syuzhet [20]. This classifier scores each tweet with 2 sentiments (positive, negative) and 8 emotions (anger, fear, anticipation, trust, surprise, sadness, joy, and disgust) defined in the Canadian National Research Council's Word-Emotion Association Lexicon [21]. It must be pointed out that we did not carry out any change in proposed emotions, that explain the absence of neutral emotion. This is clearly a limitation of this work. Figure 6 shows the numbers of positive and negative sentiments and the distribution of each emotions. The negative sentiment is the most important and the two predominant emotions are sadness and

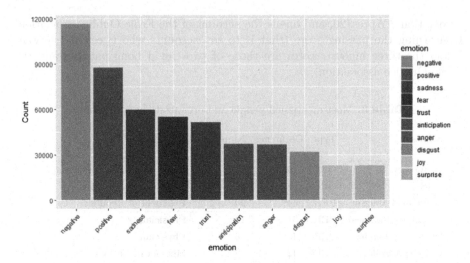

Fig. 6. Sentiments and emotions in tweets

fear. These results are in agreement with those obtained by the topic modeling. Indeed, the most important topic is the one called testimonial corresponding to tweets in which are evoked the headaches, pain and fatigue.

6   Conclusion

The result of our analysis show that the press put forward the topic of daily life and then that of the symptoms, whereas the tweets insist much more on the patients' testimonies and their emotions. These differences are corroborated by the highlighting in the press of personalities from the political and medical world, whereas the tweets mention patient groups or actors from the associative world who could not obtain the necessary visibility to have the long Covid recognized as a disease in the press and have come together using digital media.

Acknowledgments. This study was partially funded by the Institute of Public Health Sciences (ISSPAM - Aix-Marseille University), the Labex DRIIHM (ANR-11-LABX-0010, OHM Pima County) and iGLOBES (UMI 3157).

References

1. Mehandru, S., Merad, M.: Pathological sequelae of long-haul COVID. Nat. Immunol. **23**, 194–202 (2022)
2. Taquet, M., Luciano, S., Geddes, J.R., Harrison, P.J.: Bidirectional associations between COVID-19 and psychiatric disorder: retrospective cohort studies of 62,354 COVID-19 cases in the USA. Lancet Psychiatry **8**, 130–140 (2021)
3. Blei, D., Ng, A.Y., Jordan, M.J.: Latent Dirichlet allocation. Mach. Learn. Res. **3**, 993–1022 (2003)

4. Grün, B., Hornik, K.: Topicmodels: an R package for fitting topic models. J. Stat. Softw. **40**(13), 1–30 (2011)
5. Sievert, C., Shirley, K.E.: LDAvis: a method for visualizing and interpretring topics. In: Workshop on Interactive Language Learning, Visualisation, and Interfaces, pp. 63–70. ACL, USA (2014)
6. Brooks, C.F., Juanals, B., Minel, J.-L.: Trends in media coverage and information diffusion over time: the case of the American earth systems research centre biosphere 2. J. Creat. Commun. **17**(1), 88–107 (2022)
7. Scarpino, I., Zucco, C., Vallelunga, R., Luzza, F., Cannataro, M.: Investigating topic modeling techniques to extract meaningful insights in Italian long COVID narration. In: BioTech 2022, vol. 11, p. 41 (2022)
8. Medford, R.J., Saleh, S.N., Sumarsono, A., Perl, T.M., Lehmann, C.U.: An "Infodemic": leveraging high-volume twitter data to understand early public sentiment for the coronavirus disease 2019 outbreak. Open Forum Infect. Dis. **7** (2020)
9. Valdez, D., Ten Thij, M., Bathina, K., Rutter, L.A., Bollen, J.: Social media insights into US mental health during the COVID-19 pandemic: longitudinal analysis of twitter data. J. Med. Internet Res. **22**(12), e21418 (2020)
10. Rosenberg, H., Syed, S., Rezaie, S.: The Twitter pandemic: the critical role of Twitter in the dissemination of medical information and misinformation during the COVID-19 pandemic. CJEM **22**(4), 418–421 (2020)
11. Liu, Q., Zheng, Z., et al.: Health communication through news media during the early stage of the COVID-19 outbreak in China: digital topic modeling approach. J. Med. Internet Res. **22**(4), e19118 (2020)
12. Ghasiya, P., Okamura, K.: Investigating COVID-19 news across four nations: a topic modeling and sentiment analysis approach. IEEE Access **9**, 36645–36656 (2021)
13. de Melo, T., Figueiredo, C.M.: Comparing news articles and tweets about COVID-19 in Brazil: sentiment analysis and topic modeling approach. JMIR Public Health Surveill. **7** (2021)
14. Schmid, H.: Probabilistic part-of-speech tagging using decision trees. In: Proceedings of International Conference on New Methods in Language Processing, Manchester, UK, pp. 44–49 (1994)
15. Steinskog, A., et al.: Twitter topic modeling by tweet aggregation. NODALIDA (2017)
16. Quan, X., Kit, C., Ge, Y., Pan, S.: Short and sparse text topic modeling via self-aggregation. In: IJCAI 2015, pp. 2270–2276. AAAI Press (2015)
17. Juanals, B., Minel, J.-L.: Analysing cultural events on Twitter. In: Nguyen, N.T., Papadopoulos, G.A., Jędrzejowicz, P., Trawiński, B., Vossen, G. (eds.) ICCCI 2017. LNCS (LNAI), vol. 10449, pp. 376–385. Springer, Cham (2017). https://doi.org/10.1007/978-3-319-67077-5_36
18. Juanals, B., Minel, J.L.: Using topic modeling and nlp tools for analyzing long Covid coverage by French press and Twitter. In: 7th World Conference on Smart Trends in Systems, Security and Sustainability. LNNS. Springer, Heidelberg (2023)
19. Kwok, S.W.H., Vadde, S.K., Wang, G.: Tweet topics and sentiments relating to COVID-19 vaccination among Australian Twitter users: machine learning analysis. J. Med. Internet Res. **23**(5), e26953 (2021)
20. Jockers, M.L.: Syuzhet: extract sentiment and plot arcs from text. GitHub (2015). https://github.com/mjockers/syuzhet. Accessed 06 Dec 2022
21. Mohammad, S.M., Turney, P.D.: Crowdsourcing a word-emotion association lexicon. Comput. Intell. **29**(3), 436–465 (2013)

22. Bhattacharyya, A., Seth, A., Rai, S.: The effects of long COVID-19, its severity, and the need for immediate attention: analysis of clinical trials and Twitter data. Front. Big Data **5** (2022)
23. Bankston, J.F., Ma, L.: A study on people's mental health on Twitter during the COVID-19 pandemic. In: ICCDA (2022)

Semantic Analysis of Transit Related Tweets in London and Prague

Martin Zajac$^{(\boxtimes)}$ ⓘ, Jiri Horak ⓘ, and Pavel Kukuliac ⓘ

Department of Geoinformatics, Faculty of Mining and Geology, VSB-Technical University of Ostrava, 70800 Ostrava, Czech Republic
martin.zajac@vsb.cz

Abstract. The semantic analysis is an important tool for processing people's opinions, but processing data from social networking sites like Twitter is still challenging. Transit related tweets in London and Prague collected during the COVID-19 pandemic were analyzed using two corpus-based approaches – Bag-of-Words and Latent Dirichlet Allocation. Punctuality was the most frequent issue in both cities, followed by COVID-19 in London and Comfort in Prague. Analysis for the busiest London station enhanced the importance of the Breakdowns topic. Specific issues were found for some stations such as Victoria Station in London. The BoW method in our cases provides more robust results, namely for large heterogeneous samples, while LDA is well-suited for topic extraction using narrow well-specified samples focused on the explored theme.

Keywords: LDA · bag-of-words · Twitter · transit · semantic analysis

1 Introduction

Growing penetration, usage and impact of social networks in everyday life [12, 15] increases researchers' interests to understand the behaviour of these nets and their users. One of the frequent challenges is to analyse unstructured content to obtain essential information for various purposes. Public transport, especially in cities, represents a complex system with many agents and factors based on collaboration of transit providers and transit users. Both main actors are dependent on timely and accurate information about the transit system operation which may be instantly available on social networks. Typically, they are used for providing real-time status messaging and warnings, service information such as fares, restrictions, etc., interaction with customers (complaints, questions and answers), advertisement, recruitment and awareness creation [10, 11, 18].

One of the most promising platforms is Twitter, generating massive real-time data which are publicly available and easily accessible through Twitter's API [6].

The semantic analysis is a demanding task due to processing of natural language, identifying dominant or specific topics, and found text similarities. Among various methods, bag-of-words (BoW), Shallow Window-Based Methods (Word2vec, Bert) and Matrix Factorization Methods (e.g., LDA, LSA) are frequently applied. In this paper we

N. T. Nguyen et al. (Eds.): ICCCI 2023, CCIS 1864, pp. 393–405, 2023.
https://doi.org/10.1007/978-3-031-41774-0_31

will compare the performance of two of them – BoW and LDA, as the most popular methods – to evaluate topics discussed on official transit accounts of London and Prague.

The paper is organised as follows: after the introduction, the state-of-the-art about semantic analysis of natural languages is provided. Data collection and processing is explained in the 3rd chapter. Here, bag-of-words and LDA methods are applied and results are discussed. Small subchapters are dedicated to explaining relationships to metro lines and number of travellers. The following discussion is focused mainly on comparison with previous analysis of Madrid metro tweets and to discussed advantages and disadvantages of LDA and BoW from our perspective.

2   Semantic Analysis

The semantic analysis is an essential part of processing peoples' opinions. Hot topics of users' discussions can be discovered and with the appropriate preprocessing we can detect problems in fields of interest [4]. In our case, the semantic analysis enables understanding of topics discussed in tweets. Such analysis can be based on measuring of semantic similarity or semantic distance of the texts. Two main approaches of text similarity are text distance based or text representation based. The division is made by common characteristics of the particular methods. The distance methods algorithms describe the semantic proximity based on various approaches of distance measurements (length, distribution, semantic distance). Text representation methods see text as numerical features, and they differ in input structure of texts. Methods are string-based, corpus-based and graph structure methods. An advantage of the corpus-based methods that were utilized in this paper is their ability to work across languages as they do not consider actual meaning of the text, just the occurrence of words [20]. Also, machine learning techniques are currently used, for example, Almohammad and Georgakis [1] used the Random Forest model [24].

The Bag-of-Words model interprets the document as a combination of series of words without considering the order in which words appear in document. The main idea is a count vectorization. Text is represented by the count of the numbers of words that appear in a document. Word counts are then used in applications such as classification and topic modelling [17]. An advantage of this approach is mainly that the lexicons can be fully adapted to the investigated topic, such as topics about local government [22] or customer satisfaction in public transport [18] where they created eight relevant lexicons. The most represented topics were about customer satisfaction, along with service delivery, travel time and safety. On the other hand, using this method it is possible to discover only known topics which are established in advance (the supervised approach [21], and overlooks many latent topics. Such topics can be discovered using unsupervised topic modelling methods like LDA.

LDA belongs to text representation – corpus-based – matrix factorization methods [5]. Text representation methods consider texts as numerical features. Texts can be similar lexically and semantically [20]. Words are similar lexically if they have a similar character sequence, and semantically if they are used in the same context. Regarding corpus-based methods, they use information obtained from the corpus to calculate text similarity. From the matrix factorization methods point of view, they generate low-dimensional word representations to decompose large matrices that capture statistical information about the corpus. LDA is considered a generative probabilistic model based on a three-level hierarchical Bayesian model [6]. This method assumes that documents consists of words, each belonging to a topic, and a document partially relates to several subjects. Each document will contain several topics having overlapping topics in a document [4]. The optimal number of topics is determined by the coherence score, which highlights the overall coherence achieved in each topic [16]. The words in each document contribute to these topics. Each document has a discrete distribution on all topics, and each topic has a discrete distribution on all words [9]. The model is initialized by assigning each word in each document to a random topic. Then, we iterate through each word, cancel the assignment to its current topic, reduce the corpus scope of the topic count, and reassign the word to a new topic on the basis of local probability that the topic is assigned to the current document as well as global (corpus scope) probability that the word is assigned to the current topic [20]. This approach takes advantage of the ability to discover latent topics in a data sample. On the other hand, it is more computationally demanding. LDA can be utilized not only for modeling topics but also for filtering out irrelevant documents or tweets [7].

The semantic analysis of tweets faces issues with processing of a special language used in social networks such as abbreviations, slang, often excited emotions, misspellings and emoticons which often replace certain words. Therefore, special approaches are needed to either filter out or decode these special expressions for example, correction of misspellings using the Levenshetein distance algorithm [8].

3 Case Study: Evaluation of Activity About Transport Topics in London and Prague

To analyse transit topics, *rtweet* script was used to download the Twitter data from the accounts of the main transit integrators in London (@TfL) and Prague (@DPPoficialni). Data was collected during the COVID-19 pandemic between 26.3.2020 and 31.1.2021. The same original data collection (London: 545,295, Prague: 4,949) was used in [21]. First, collected data is preprocessed in a standard way using *dplyr* and *tidytext* R libraries. They remove hashtags, URLs, special characters, and convert letters to lowercase [7, 18]. We select tweets only from verified users and from users sending less than 20,000 tweets (to focus only on "human" users). Other restrictions are to select tweets only in the English language and posted from a mobile phone (twitter for iPhone, twitter for Android). Further, sentiment analysis is conducted by lexicon-based method (the BING lexicon contained in *tidytext* library). According to Osorio-Arjona et al. [14], only tweets with a negative sentiment score are used in following analyses to focus on mapping the main problems as they are mostly discussed in negative tweets.

Finally, we obtained 110,007 records for London and 991 for Prague. The low number in Prague is due to low usage of Twitter for discussions about public transport despite the increasing penetration of Twitter in the Czech population (0.75mil people in 2022 [23]).

Due to the high data volume of input data for LDA in London, data was randomly sampled to 40,000 tweets (maximum number that our computer can handle).

3.1 Bag-of Words Analysis

First, an exploratory data analysis of tweets was conducted to find out the most frequently used words. This frequency analysis enabled the identifcation of important topics such as issues in public transport, comfort at stations and transportation hubs, problems with overcrowding in public transport and COVID-19-related issues. The most discussed theme seems to be Punctuality due to the fact that delayed connections are the most common issue related to public transport. As a next step of processing, the list of tokens was prepared for each topic. Personal auditing of individual tweets assured good relationships between words and topics and enabled the exclusion of ambiguous tokens [21]. Each token was assigned to only one topic to simplify the processing and interpretation.

Distribution of topics in London and Prague is surprisingly similar (Fig. 1). In both cities, Punctuality (London 53%; Prague 45%) was the most discussed topic. The reason behind the high number of tweets about Punctuality is probably the general issue with delays in both cities. Non-punctual connections might have several causes. They may be caused by emergency situations or maintenance reasons. However, the data is from the Covid-19 period, so the reason might be a shortage of drivers because of illness and inability to keep every transit trip.

We expected that the most discussed topic would be Covid-19 as we collected data during the pandemic year. In Prague, the Punctuality topic was followed by Comfort (20%) and Breakdown (16%). Prague is constantly maintaining and repairing parts of its public transport infrastructure.

On the other hand, in London there were very little complaints about Breakdowns. Obviously, there are other much more important issues in negative tweets. The most problematic topics according to their shares are Punctuality and Covid-19.

Interestingly, overcrowding is the least presented topic in our sample for both cities. It seems during the pandemic overcrowding was not a hot topic and travelers adapted to the "usual" crowding and did not complain about it. E.g., the ridership in London dropped to 5% at the end of the march [19], therefore vehicles were probably not crowded. On the other hand, concerns about infection in the transit system may enforce the criticism of crowded transit but such complaints (crowded + infection) were classified as part of the Covid-19 topic. Also, for Prague, a significant decrease of ridership occurred, however not such a big drop as in London occured. A decrease of usual commuters accompanied the fact that tourism dropped close to zero due to travelling restrictions. The Breakdown topic was recorded mainly in Prague (16%). In London only 702 tweets complained about breakdowns (partly due to georeferencing issues), thus their share is almost 0%. However, this topic is significant in semantic analysis for stations described later.

A big difference between cities is recognized also in shares of tweets related to Covid-19 (London 21%, Prague 14%). It represents the second highest share of complaints in London but only the fourth one in Prague. It is assumed that far more restrictive precautions for Covid-19 were applied in the Czech Republic than in the UK. Also, the Czech population might be more prevention aware and have better accepted these precautions than in the UK which had more serious pandemic waves and larger groups of people disapproving protection measures [3].

The Comfort topic was expressed much more in Prague than in London. It is focused mainly on problems regarding homeless people, dirt, and overall conditions in stations in terms of temperature, smell and purity. The higher amount of complaints about comfort in Prague might be due to worse conditions in public transport compared to London. Smaller, non-frequented stations are liked by homeless and minorities who are worsening the comfort of travelers.

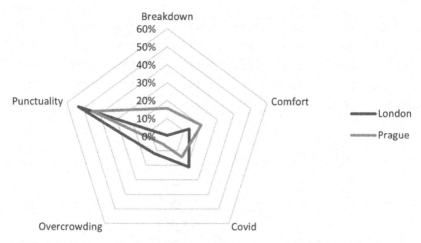

Fig. 1. Distribution of traffic topics for London, and Prague (Bag-of-Words approach)

To have a better picture of the situation in London, the semantic analysis was repeated for the busiest stations in the London transport system.

At Victoria station (Table 1), people discussed each problem evenly with the exception of a low share of overcrowding.

Specific features can be found for Stratford and Liverpool Street where complaints concerning breaks of services dominate among other topics. The breaks in service might be due to the situation surrounding Covid-19 together with traveling restrictions; fewer people traveled, so trains were not overcrowded. But, at peak hours where overcrowding is present most, problems such as not wearing masks and not obeying regulations bother people more.

People complain about Waterloo station mostly due to breakdowns and punctuality, which we believe depend on each other. We found that the situation at other stations is identical; travelers are most unsatisfied with breakdowns, punctuality, and COVID-19. Dissatisfaction with comfort and overcrowding is minimal. Conversely, up to 50% of tweets from Liverpool Street station contain complaints about breakdowns (Fig. 2).

The pattern of regular topics may be disrupted by some extraordinary events. At the London Victoria station we identified a topic about a tragical incident, where a covid infected person on purpose spat at a metro worker, who died afterwards of this virus [25].

Table 1. Shares of transit related tweet topics on main London stations

	Waterloo	Victoria	Stratford	Paddington	London Bridge	Liverpool Street	King's Cross St. Pancras
Breakdown	34%	23%	40%	42%	33%	52%	34%
Comfort	8%	24%	8%	3%	12%	4%	12%
Covid-19	17%	23%	22%	10%	21%	12%	14%
Overcrowding	4%	5%	5%	1%	3%	2%	4%
Punctuality	37%	25%	25%	44%	31%	30%	36%

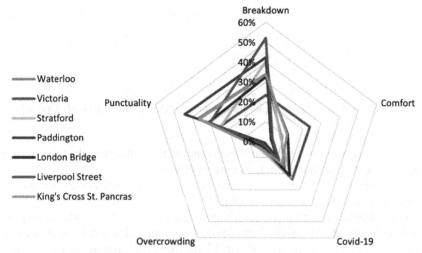

Fig. 2. Distribution of traffic topics in main London stations

Two additional topics were discovered in discussions of individual stations – transport cards (London Oyster) and new connections (e.g., new trains between Liverpool Street and Chesthunt).

Metro Lines

For London, we tried to find the reason of breakdown problems (often related to transport service) in modeled topics for Stratford and Liverpool Street stations. These stations are connected by the Central line (Fig. 3). We identified discussions about bad traffic situations and frequent need to reschedule the journey. On Central, District and Jubilee lines there was a strong topic about overcrowded morning connections and impossibility of keeping safe distance. For each line there was modelled at least one topic speaking about failure of connections, delays, as well as closure of some stations located on the tube line.

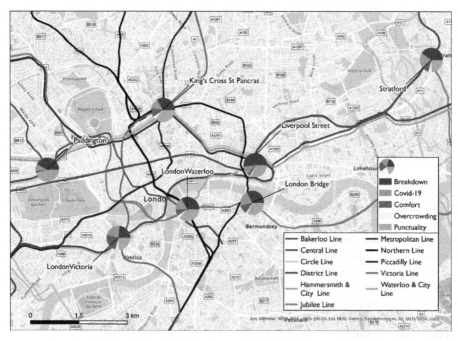

Fig. 3. Distribution of traffic complaints

3.2 LDA Results

As the whole processing was done in R, we decided to utilize R for this part as well. For computing the coherence score (estimation of topics contained in dataset), tools from *ldatuning* package and for modelling itself *topicmodel* package were used. For each topic, 20 relevant words were assigned. Finally, two researchers interpreted meanings of the topics independently. We were able to identify the following topics.

LDA for London (Table 2) identified a dominant topic about Covid-19 in particular problems with staff not obeying the precautions, staff not wearing facemasks and lack of hygiene at the stations. This topic was easy to recognize as the words were quite straightforward. A general problem in this sample was also regarding congestion and the bad morning traffic situation. There is also a topic with names of city officials and words like *blame, debt, failed lies*. We reckon that this discussion is mainly about blaming the mayor of London and city officials for the situation around public transport and unfulfilled promises.

The London transport system also has a problem with its customer service and website downtimes. To find the remaining topics that were established in the supervised part of the analysis we had to dig deeper and compute LDA on the level of busiest stations. Results can be found in the section below.

LDA for Prague confirmed that people discuss punctuality. The main punctuality concern is a bad continuity of tram and bus connections. When the connection is delayed for a few minutes, the subsequent connection will not wait. Breakdowns and maintenance were also detected but with more insight. Breakdowns were mostly caused by alternate

Table 2. Results of LDA analysis for London

Topic	Words
Covid-19	People, mask, wearing, staff, face, don't, wear, risk, virus
Congestion, morning traffic	Services, morning, work, people, trains, tube, rail, late
City officials	Khan, mayor, London, money, crime, blame, debt, bankrupt, failed, lies, money
Customer service	Issue, don't, card, wrong, response, account, evidence, data, back

tram transport due to maintenance of metro networks. Topic modelling showed more insight into the Covid-19 topic, where users were concerned about safety precautions and wearing of masks. Specifically, people complain they have to press the button to open the door which could be a hotspot for Covid-19 particles. Several discussions were also about ticket systems, SMS tickets, customer service and lack of night lines. People also tweeted about intervention of firefighters in the metro, unfortunately from the analysis results we were unable to identify the station.

Stations in London
Travelers in London stations complained mostly about punctuality in traffic. Pandemic circumstances were projected as the second most complained about issue which was COVID-19. People were complaining about violating the rules (wearing masks, distancing, sanitizing hands). This topic is also interrelated with other topics such as comfort and overcrowding as travelers were scared of infection and tweeted more on this behalf. The reason that these topics are weakly represented might be also that people stopped travelling heavily.

We were able to identify topics established in supervised topic modelling for each of the selected stations. At each station we found overlapping topics regarding Covid-19, Punctuality, Breakdowns. We also found new, unexpected topics such as bad air quality on London Victoria, issues with the London Oyster transport card, tickets and prices of the fare. We were also able to detect a general problem with noisy trains on Northern line stations.

Relationship to Travelers
When evaluating the representation of individual problems at stations, the dependence on the number of passengers per year handled by a particular station was also taken into account. The significant positive dependency was found for overcrowding (as expected) (Fig. 4 left), but also for the Comfort (Fig. 4 right), which indicates more comfort conditions in larger stations. Contrarily, a negative dependence was discovered between breakdown complaints and traveler counts (Fig. 5 left). The big stations might be better organised and maintained to better manage high volumes of travelers. But the regression line is almost horizontal which means a very small effect (Fig. 5). Almost no dependency can be seen for Punctuality (Fig. 5) as well as for COVID-19 (Fig. 6). The Pandemic

topic was frequently discussed focusing on mask wearing and fees for violation of related rules, for passengers as well as for staff.

The graphs also show some deviated points. In the Stratford station 5% of people complained about overcrowding with only 65 mil. Passengers (Fig. 4). The problem is that Stratford station has insufficient room on specific platforms and around entrances. This is a well-known issue and upgrades will take place across several phases starting in late 2022 [26]. In Fig. 4 (right) the most deviating station is Victoria with 24% of tweets about (dis)comfort. People complained about flocks of pigeons that produce mess and a bad smell. There is also a problem with a severe shortage of toilets [27].

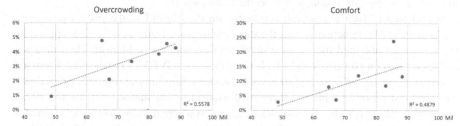

Fig. 4. Dependence of the share of selected topics on the number of passengers in London (overcrowding left, comfort right)

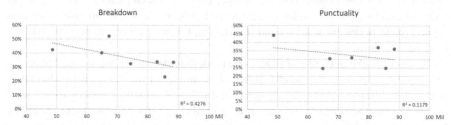

Fig. 5. Dependence of the share of selected topics on the number of passengers in London (breakdown left, punctuality right)

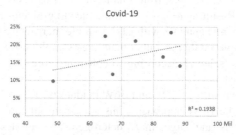

Fig. 6: Dependence of the share of COVID-19 complaints on the number of passengers in London

4 Discussion

Despite the fact that investigated tweets come from the pandemic period, COVID-19 is not the main topic in transit related tweets. Passengers discussed mainly Punctuality which remains the main issue for them. COVID-19 was the 2nd topic in London, but only the 4th one in Prague. The higher importance in London could be due to much higher transit loads than in Prague, and therefore difficulties keeping safe distances and not meeting maladaptive people without masks. A lower position of COVID-19 discussion was found in analysis for stations. In all investigated London stations, COVID-19 was the 3rd topic by share. E.g., Liu et al. [13] identified Pandemic prevention as the 4th topic in Chinese Weibo discussion, which seems to be similar.

Compared to similar research conducted on the Madrid metro system in the pre-covid period [14], Punctuality was the most commented issue as well, and, oppositely, Overcrowding obtained the smallest number of complaints in Madrid. Their data was collected between 16.9.2019 and 17.11.2019, thus no COVID-19 issues were discussed.

Also, the results of semantic analysis for stations show similar findings. Breakdowns was the most reported topic in all reported Madrid metro stations, similar to London where the only exception is London Victoria station where the Comfort topic dominates. This result can be accepted as we found out that there are outstanding problems with air quality and other issues that can be considered comfort issues. In Madrid, they discovered a pattern that punctuality is a bigger issue in the city center contrary to Breakdowns that is the more discussed problem on the city periphery. No such pattern is evident in our results in London, but our analysis was limited only to the seven top busiest stations and no typical periphery was covered. In Madrid, Overcrowding was recognized only on transfer stations.

We discovered that results of LDA topic modelling depend on the size and nature of the sample. Topics that were modelled from the sample for the whole of London (even after precise filtration) were vague. Individual word clusters representing topics were hard to interpret and there was a need to carefully consider how the topic should be classified. It was difficult to recognize preliminary established topics. In our opinion, the vagueness of topics derived by LDA for London transit (@Tfl) is caused by the complexity of various influences and themes discussed in such a large system. Much better results of LDA were obtained from smaller samples ($\pm$1500 tweets) selected only for transport stations. Resulting topics were more meaningful and easier to classify. It is recommended for semantic analysis with LDA to prefer narrow well-specified samples, best focused on the explored theme, rather than large samples covering various aspects. Also, topics should be selected according to coherent score to get best possible (not overlapping) word clusters.

When we compare results of LDA and BoW in identification of topics, better results were obtained using the BoW approach. This approach only follows the occurrence of words from lexicons and large, more heterogeneous samples do not deteriorate results. The example of such a heterogenous sample may be a study of user satisfaction with "London's Oyster" where Alshehri et al. [2] identified the following categories: system (system faults, problems with usage), Twitter communication (feedback, support, helpdesk), organization (technical support, competence of employees), and market coverage (ubiquity). We were able to identify topics used in BoW at a much higher rate.

To summarise, each method provides different advantages related to different kinds of data. The BoW approach is preferred for big datasets as it is computationally less demanding. It is also more robust so the results are not skewed by many weak themes in large heterogeneous samples. A disadvantage of this method is that a preliminary exploratory analysis is required to precisely setup the lexicons with words used for given topics. LDA is more useful on smaller datasets from narrower selections. In such cases, LDA is well-suited for topic extraction and detection of latent topics. LDA can be used for any language without changing settings or creating new lexicons.

5 Conclusion

Twitter enables the collection of a large volume of transit-related user messages. The semantic analysis of selected tweets after appropriate preprocessing improves our understanding of transit passengers' troubles. The transit provider may benefit from such periodically conducted analysis to better address the development of the transport system and their services.

Punctuality was the most important topic in London and Prague. In London the second most important topic was Covid-19 while in Prague it was Comfort. A slightly different importance of topics was found in semantic analysis of London stations, where Punctuality was followed by Breakdowns with quite similar values, and the Covid-19 topic was less discussed.

Two of the corpus-based methods were compared for public transport related tweets namely Bag-of-words and LDA. Based on our experiences, the BoW approach is recommended for big datasets especially in the case of heterogeneous data sets. Contrarily, LDA is more suitable for topic extraction from smaller and homogeneous data sets.

For future research, machine learning methods should be more employed. Also, the low penetration of Twitter in some countries such as Czechia requires analysis of topics also in other social networks. We plan to use a commercial service, SentiOne [28], which is able to follow keywords or hashtags in feeds on various SNS and compute simple analyses (sentiment, gender detection, impact of the tweet, wordclouds).

Acknowledgements. This research was funded by the grant SP2023/023 of the Faculty of Mining and Geology of the Technical University of Ostrava "Possibilities of using artificial intelligence in geodata science for the purpose of predicting real estate prices" and grant "Podpora vědy a výzkumu v Moravskoslezském kraji 2022" of the Faculty of Mining and Geology of the Technical University of Ostrava.

References

1. Almohammad, A., Georgakis, P.: Public twitter data and transport network status. In: 2020 10th International Conference on Information Science and Technology (ICIST). IEEE, Bath, London, and Plymouth, United Kingdom, pp. 169–174 (2020)
2. Alshehri, A., O'Keefe, R.: Analyzing social media to assess user satisfaction with transport for London's oyster. Int. J. Hum.-Comput. Interact. **35**, 1378–1387 (2019). https://doi.org/10.1080/10447318.2018.1526442

3. Anthony, A.: To mask or not to mask? Opinion split on London underground. The Observer (2021)
4. Azizi, F., Hajiabadi, H., Vahdat-Nejad, H., Khosravi, M.H.: Detecting and analyzing topics of massive COVID-19 related tweets for various countries. Comput. Electr. Eng. **106**, 108561 (2023). https://doi.org/10.1016/j.compeleceng.2022.108561
5. Blei, D.M., Ng, A.Y., Jordan, M.I.: Latent Dirichlet allocation. J. Mach. Learn. Res. **3**, 993–1022 (2003). Submitted 2/02; Published 1/03
6. Brzustewicz, P., Singh, A.: Sustainable consumption in consumer behavior in the time of COVID-19: topic modeling on twitter data using LDA. Energies **14**, 5787 (2021). https://doi.org/10.3390/en14185787
7. Dahal, B., Kumar, S.A.P., Li, Z.: Topic modeling and sentiment analysis of global climate change tweets. Soc. Netw. Anal. Min. **9**, 24 (2019). https://doi.org/10.1007/s13278-019-0568-8
8. Davis, C.A., Fonseca, F.T.: Assessing the certainty of locations produced by an address geocoding system. GeoInformatica **11**, 103–129 (2007). https://doi.org/10.1007/s10707-006-0015-7
9. Garcia-Martinez, A., Cascajo, R., Jara-Diaz, S.R., Chowdhury, S., Monzon, A.: Transfer penalties in multimodal public transport networks. Transp. Res. Part Policy Pract. **114**, 52–66 (2018). https://doi.org/10.1016/j.tra.2018.01.016
10. Georgiadis, G., Nikolaidou, A., Politis, I., Papaioannou, P.: How public transport could benefit from social media? evidence from european agencies. In: Nathanail, E.G., Adamos, G., Karakikes, I. (eds.) Advances in Mobility-as-a-Service Systems, pp. 645–653. Springer International Publishing, Cham (2021)
11. Howard, J.M.: Trains, Twitter and the social licence to operate: an analysis of Twitter use by train operating companies in the United Kingdom. Case Stud. Transp. Policy **8**, 812–821 (2020). https://doi.org/10.1016/j.cstp.2020.06.002
12. Huang, J.-W., Ma, H.-S., Chung, C.-C., Jian, Z.-J.: Unknown but interesting recommendation using social penetration. Soft. Comput. **23**, 7249–7262 (2019). https://doi.org/10.1007/s00500-018-3371-y
13. Liu, X., Ye, Q., Li, Y., Fan, J., Tao, Y.: Examining public concerns and attitudes toward unfair events involving elderly travelers during the COVID-19 pandemic using weibo data. Int. J. Environ. Res. Public. Health **18**, 1756 (2021). https://doi.org/10.3390/ijerph18041756
14. Osorio-Arjona, J., Horak, J., Svoboda, R., García-Ruíz, Y.: Social media semantic perceptions on Madrid Metro system: using Twitter data to link complaints to space. Sustain Cities Soc. **64**, 102530 (2021). https://doi.org/10.1016/j.scs.2020.102530
15. Paszto, V., Darena, F., Marek, L., Fuskova, D.: SGEM Spatial Analyses of Twitter Data – Case Studies, pp. 785–792 (2014)
16. Politis, I., Georgiadis, G., Kopsacheilis, A., Nikolaidou, A., Papaioannou, P.: Capturing twitter negativity pre- vs. mid-COVID-19 pandemic: an LDA application on london public transport system. Sustainability **13**(23), 13356 (2021). https://doi.org/10.3390/su132313356
17. Salton, G., Buckley, C.: Term-weighting approaches in automatic text retrieval. Inf. Process. Manag. **24**, 513–523 (1988). https://doi.org/10.1016/0306-4573(88)90021-0
18. Shalaby, A., Hosseini, M.: Linking social, semantic and sentiment analyses to support modeling transit customers' satisfaction: towards formal study of opinion dynamics. Sustain Cities Soc. **49**, 101578 (2019). https://doi.org/10.1016/j.scs.2019.101578
19. Vickerman, R.: Will Covid-19 put the public back in public transport? A UK perspective. Transp. Policy **103**, 95–102 (2021). https://doi.org/10.1016/j.tranpol.2021.01.005
20. Wang, J., Dong, Y.: Measurement of text similarity: a survey. Information **11**, 421 (2020). https://doi.org/10.3390/info11090421

21. Zajac, M., Horák, J., Osorio-Arjona, J., Kukuliač, P., Haworth, J.: Public transport tweets in London, Madrid and Prague in the COVID-19 period—temporal and spatial differences in activity topics. Sustainability **14**, 17055 (2022). https://doi.org/10.3390/su142417055

22. Zhang, S., Feick, R.: Understanding public opinions from geosocial media. ISPRS Int. J. Geo.-Inf. **5**, 74 (2016). https://doi.org/10.3390/ijgi5060074

23. Digital 2022: Czechia. In: DataReportal – Glob. Digit. Insights. https://datareportal.com/reports/digital-2022-czechia (2022). Accessed 22 Feb 2023

24. twitteR package – RDocumentation. https://www.rdocumentation.org/packages/twitteR/versions/1.1.9. Accessed 20 Nov 2022

25. Belly Mujinga's death: Searching for the truth – BBC News. https://www.bbc.com/news/uk-54435703. Accessed 27 Feb 2023

26. Stratford station secures funding for plans set to relieve overcrowding. In: Rail Technol. Mag. https://www.railtechnologymagazine.com/articles/stratford-station-secures-funding-plans-set-relieve-overcrowding. Accessed 27 Feb 2023

27. Sadly the worst underground service in history – London Victoria Station, London Traveller Reviews. In: Tripadvisor. http://www.tripadvisor.co.uk/ShowUserReviews-g186338-d8388711-r575092501-London_Victoria_Station-London_England.html. Accessed 27 Feb 2023

28. Conversational AI platform & social listening tool – SentiOne. https://sentione.com/. Accessed 27 Feb 2023

k-Shell Without Decomposition

Yayati Gupta[1]([✉])([iD]), Sanatan Sukhija[1]([iD]), and S. R. S. Iyengar[2]

[1] Mahindra University, Hyderabad, India
yytgpt@gmail.com
[2] Indian Institute of Technology Ropar, Rupnagar, India

Abstract. Identifying the influential nodes in a network is crucial for super-spreading information and trends. For a long time, such nodes are identified by decomposing the network to determine the k-core. The nodes in k-core are proven to be efficient spreaders. However, the algorithm requires the global information of the network. In this paper, we present a local variant (based on only neighborhood information) of the k-shell decomposition algorithm that can reliably estimate the shell number. The proposed iterative strategy identifies a small subgraph that is sufficient to accurately bind the maximum core number (shell number) of a node. The experimental results on diverse networks validate the efficacy of the proposed method.

Keywords: complex networks · k-shell decomposition · spreading power · influence maximization · social network analysis

1 Introduction

"You can have brilliant ideas, but if you can't get them across, your ideas won't get you anywhere" – Lee Iacocca [1]

Employing social networks for information diffusion plays an important role in the spreading of information, ideas, and trends. Further, not all nodes in a network have the same influence on others. Certain nodes have a greater power to spread ideas and trends. Identifying these influential nodes is critical for successful information dissemination. This is particularly important in today's world of social media, where viral content can reach millions of people in a matter of hours. According to Kevin Allocca, the trends manager at YouTube, seemingly mundane videos such as "Friday" and "Double Rainbow" gained popularity due to promotion by influential personalities [2]. For example, Jimmy Kimmel's tweet about the "Double Rainbow" video led to its instant popularity. Understanding the efficient spreaders is essential for comprehending the diffusion of trends. These influential spreaders determine the fate of an idea in a network, and if convinced, they can promote it to the entire world.

Many methods have been proposed in the literature to assess a node's spreading power, with one of the most commonly utilized being k-shell decomposition

© The Author(s), under exclusive license to Springer Nature Switzerland AG 2023
N. T. Nguyen et al. (Eds.): ICCCI 2023, CCIS 1864, pp. 406–418, 2023.
https://doi.org/10.1007/978-3-031-41774-0_32

[3]. K-shell decomposition works by recursively pruning nodes from a network [4]. This algorithm is simple, scalable, and time-efficient, but it requires the entire network to be available, which is often not feasible in today's world of big data. As networks with millions of nodes are loaded with trillions of edges, it is difficult to store them, and even if they are, it is often next to impossible to access them. Therefore, there is a need for smart local algorithms that can analyze the vicinity of a node and predict its influential power without requiring the entire network.

In this paper, we adopt a local perspective to analyze the k-shell decomposition algorithm. We show that the shell number of a node can be bounded above and below accurately using only its local information. These bounds can further be tightened by exploring the network to a few more levels. We then show that for every node i in a network, there exists a subgraph $S(V', E') \in G(V, E)$ such that i has the same shell number in S as in G. Finally we propose an approximation algorithm, which intelligently builds the above-mentioned subgraph S corresponding to a given node i. All the findings of this research have been validated using several real-world networks of varying nature and sizes.

2   Literature Review

Understanding the spreading of information in different social, biological, and economic networks is a problem of high significance [8]. It has been observed that the influence of nodes in a network varies in terms of their spreading power. Therefore, the identification of such influential nodes remains a major research problem that can help in superspreading or controlling the diffusion of information and diseases in various social, biological, and technical networks [9].

One of the widely accepted algorithms for determining such influential nodes is k-shell decomposition [3]. It has been used in diverse applications like finding central proteins in PPI (Protein-Protein Interaction) networks [10], identifying drug targets [11], understanding mutation rates [12], text visualization and summarization [13], real-time keyword extraction from conversations [15], corporate networks [16], banking networks [17], etc. The algorithm is computationally efficient, having a run time complexity of $O(|V| + |E|)$ where $|V|$ is the number of nodes and $|E|$ is the number of edges in the network, respectively.

Despite being time-efficient, k-shell decomposition turns infeasible for large-scale dynamic graphs. Various approaches have been taken to resolve this problem. One approach is to use parallel algorithms for core maintenance in dynamic graphs to speed up the process [18]. In the case of dynamically changing networks, Li et al. [19] show that the shell numbers of only a few nodes need to be updated on the insertion or deletion of an edge in the network. They devised an efficient algorithm to identify and recompute the shell numbers of such nodes in the graph. For very large-scale networks whose global information is not available, local methods to approximate shell numbers have been proposed.

Recent theoretical work has explored the limits of approximating the k-core or k-shell of a graph. In particular, it has been shown that for certain classes

of graphs, such as power-law graphs, there exists a constant factor approximation algorithm that can compute the k-core or k-shell in polynomial time [20].
However, for more general classes of graphs, such as random graphs, it has been
shown that any algorithm that computes a constant factor approximation to
the k-core or k-shell must take exponential time [22]. These results highlight the
importance of understanding the underlying structure of a graph when designing algorithms for approximating the k-core or k-shell. Many studies [23] also
consider community structure for more efficiently identifying the superspreaders.

Our paper takes a different approach from previous studies by providing
explicit bounds on the coreness of a graph and then attempting to tighten these
bounds. This allows for a more precise approximation of the k-core or k-shell, and
could potentially lead to more efficient algorithms for computing these structures
in large-scale graphs.

3   Finding Upper and Lower Bounds on Node Coreness

3.1   k-Shell Decomposition

K-shell decomposition [21] is a graph theoretical method for finding the shell
number δ_i of each node i in a network. The method works by iteratively removing
nodes with degree less than or equal to k, where k is the current shell number
being computed, until all remaining nodes have degree greater than k. The shell
number of each removed node is assigned to be k. The algorithm continues
until all nodes have been removed. The k-shell decomposition algorithm can be
formalized as follows:

1. Initialize $k = 1$.
2. Find all nodes with degree less than or equal to k, and remove them from the
   network.
3. Assign shell number k to each removed node.
4. Increment k and repeat from step 2 until all nodes have been removed.

Figure 1 depicts a schematic representation of the k-shell decomposition algorithm.

3.2   Proposed Approach

Our approach involves finding upper and lower bounds on the coreness of a node
and then iteratively refining these bounds. Table 1 provides a list of frequently
used notations in this project.

Lemma 1. $UB_i = d_i$

Proof. During the kth iteration of the algorithm, nodes with degrees $\leq k$ are
recursively removed. If a node has degree k and has not been removed in previous
iterations, it will be removed during the kth iteration. Therefore, a node i with
degree d_i can have a maximum coreness value of d_i since the node cannot remain
in the network beyond the d_i iteration.

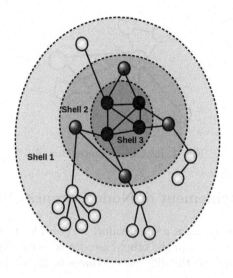

Fig. 1. k-shell Decomposition: An illustrative example

Table 1. Frequently used notations

Notation	Meaning
d_i	Degree of node i
c_i	Size of maximal clique containing i
δ_i	Coreness value of i
UB_i	Upper bound on δ_i
LB_i	Lower bound on δ_i

Lemma 2. $LB_i = c_i - 1$

Proof. If a node belongs to a clique of size k, it implies that the node has at least $k - 1$ neighbors whose degrees are also at least $k - 1$. Consequently, the node's degree is at least $k - 1$. The same holds true for all the neighbors of the node. Therefore, none of these k nodes can be removed before the $k - 1^{th}$ iteration. Consider Fig. 2, where node i does not belong to any clique of size greater than 4. In this case, node i cannot be removed before the third iteration, as all its clique-participating neighbors will remain intact until the third iteration. Since node i is tightly connected to these neighbors, it also cannot be removed. Hence, the coreness of node i is at least $c_i - 1$.

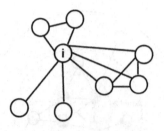

Fig. 2. Initialising Lower Bound

4   Iterative Refinement of Node Coreness Bounds

If $UB_i - LB_i \leq \Delta$ where Δ is a small value, we consider to have approximated the coreness for the node i. In the other case, we keep modifying the upper and lower bounds of node i till the difference reduces to the desired value.

Lemma 3. *Let S be the set of neighbours of i such that $\forall j \in S, UB_j \leq UB_i$. Also, let $MUB = max(UB_j)$ where $j \in S$. Then $UB_i = max(MUB, d_i - |S|)$*

Proof. Consider Fig. 3.

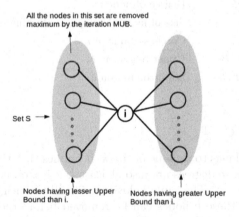

All the nodes in this set are removed maximum by the iteration MUB.

Set S →

Nodes having lesser Upper Bound than i.

Nodes having greater Upper Bound than i.

Fig. 3. Modifying Upper Bound

Consider a node i and its set of neighbors S such that $\forall j \in S$, $UB_j \leq UB_i$. Let $MUB = \max UB_j \mid j \in S$.

First, assume that $d_i - |S| \leq MUB$. Then, by the definition of MUB, all nodes in S are removed before or at the MUB iteration. Thus, node i will also be removed before or at the MUB iteration because it is connected to nodes in S and cannot survive without them. Therefore, $UB_i = \max MUB, d_i - |S|$ in this case.

Now, assume that $d_i - |S| > MUB$. Then, in the first MUB iterations, all nodes in S are removed, leaving $d_i - |S|$ remaining edges for node i. Since $d_i - |S| > MUB$, we know that there are still some nodes remaining in the network with degrees greater than MUB. Therefore, node i cannot be removed until all such nodes are removed. The last such node will be removed at the $d_i - |S|$ iteration, since node i has $d_i - |S|$ remaining edges and there are no nodes left with degrees greater than $d_i - |S|$. Thus, $UB_i = \max MUB, d_i - |S|$ in this case as well.

Therefore, we have shown that $UB_i = \max MUB, d_i - |S|$ holds in both cases, and the lemma is proven.

Lemma 4. *Let S be the set of neigbours of i such that $\forall j \in S, LB_j > UB_i$. Then $\delta_i = LB_i = UB_i$*

Proof. UB_i denotes the maximum time by which the node i can be removed. $\forall j \in S, LB_j > UB_i$ implies that none of its neighbour can be removed before UB_i. In that case, the node i will be removed exactly at the UB_ith step. Hence proved.

Lemma 5. *Let S be the set of neigbours of i. If $\forall j \in S, LB_j > LB_i$ and $\exists j \in S$ such that $d_i > LB_j$. Then $LB_i = min(LB_j)$ where $j \in S = MLBsay$*

Proof. According to the condition, none of the neighbours of i can be removed before the iteration MLB. Then at the least, i can be removed at the iteration MLB. Figure 4 describes it.

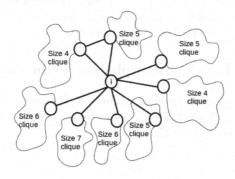

Fig. 4. Modifying Lower Bound

5   Proposed Algorithm

To determine the coreness of a node i, we first calculate its initial upper bound ($UB_i = d_i$) and lower bound ($LB_i = c_i$). If the difference between these bounds is large, we compute d_j and c_j for all neighbors $j \in N_i$ and update UB_i and

LB_i based on Lemmas 3, 4, and 5. If the difference still remains significant, we calculate d_k and c_k for $k \in N_i^2$, update the lower and upper bounds of all neighbors, and then update LB_i and UB_i again. If the difference does not reduce significantly, we continue the process for higher network levels.

Input   : A network graph $G = (V, E)$ and a node $i \in V$
Output: Coreness of node i

`// Initialization`
Compute initial UB_i and LB_i based on Lemmas 1 and 2; $\Delta \leftarrow$ a small
  value;

while $UB_i - LB_i > \Delta$ **do**
 foreach $j \in neighbor(i)$ **do**
  Compute d_j and c_j based on Lemmas 1 and 2; Update UB_j and
  LB_j based on Lemmas 3, 4, and 5;
 end
 Update UB_i and LB_i based on Lemmas 3, 4, and 5;
end

return Average of UB_i and LB_i;
Algorithm 1: Compute Coreness of a Node

The proposed algorithm explores the graph in a breadth-first search manner to minimize the difference between the upper and lower bounds of a given node i until it is less than or equal to a predefined value Δ. The convergence rate of the algorithm is influenced by the level of branching present in the network. As the branching factor increases, the algorithm converges slower. Figure 5 illustrates the most challenging scenario for the algorithm, although such graphs are infrequent in real-world networks. Therefore, a detailed investigation is necessary to estimate the level of branching in these networks.

6   Leveraging Local Subgraphs for Tight Bounds

This section aims to discuss a technique for obtaining accurate upper and lower bounds by leveraging k-shell decomposition on modified or smaller networks derived from the original network.

6.1   Lower Bound

Let $G'(V', E')$ be any subgraph containing node i. The coreness of node i in this subgraph can be determined using k-shell decomposition on G'. We denote the computed value as $\delta_{G'}(i)$.

Lemma 6. $\delta_i \geq \delta_{G'}(i)$

Proof. This lemma holds because the actual k-shell decomposition runs on the graph G, which has additional vertices and edges compared to G'. Adding more vertices and edges to G' can only increase the coreness of i, thereby proving the lemma.

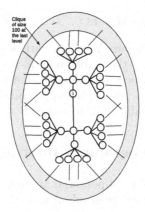

Fig. 5. Example of a graph with high branching factor, leading to slow convergence of the algorithm

Note: The choice of subgraph will depend on the research question, and the optimal subgraph type for obtaining the tightest lower bound needs to be further investigated.

6.2 Finding Tight Upper Bounds

To obtain an upper bound on the coreness of node i, we consider the Breadth-First Search (BFS) graph from node i up to a certain level l, denoted by $G_b(V_b, E_b)$ where V_b and E_b are subsets of V and E, respectively. To obtain a modified subgraph $G''(V'', E'')$ that yields the maximum possible value of δ_i when fed to the k-shell decomposition algorithm, we extend G_b in such a way that the last layer of the BFS traversal of this graph is part of a large clique, as shown in Fig. 6.

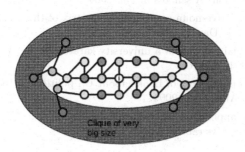

Fig. 6. Tight Upper Bound

It is important to note that not every subgraph can be used to obtain the tightest upper bound. The subgraph should be strictly formed using the BFS traversal on node i.

Lemma 7. *The coreness of node i in G″ is an upper bound on δ_i.*

Proof. Since the nodes in the last layer are part of a large clique, they cannot be easily removed. Therefore, the algorithm will first remove the nodes in the vicinity of node i, which reduces the upper bound to less than d_i. However, it still keeps it high enough to provide an upper bound, since the nodes in the outermost levels are not capable of decreasing δ_i.

7   Extracting the Subgraph of Interest

In this section, we present several potential approaches that may be utilized in the future to identify the exact subgraph of interest

7.1   The Top-Down Approach

The subgraph of interest, denoted by S, is initially set to the complete social network G, which includes the current node. To maintain the coreness of S at a specified value λ, we remove vertices from S iteratively that do not contribute to the coreness of the current node. However, it should be noted that this method may only provide a local minimum, as the order in which vertices are removed can influence the final result.

Table 2. Description and properties of popular social network datasets

Table 2. Datasets

Dataset	Description	# Nodes	# Edges
Dolphins	Social network of bottlenose dolphins in a community in New Zealand	62	159
Football	American college football games between Division IA schools in Fall 2000	115	613
Adjnoun	Adjective-noun co-occurrence matrix of the novel "David Copperfield"	112	425
Karate club	Social network of a university karate club in the 19701970ss	34	78
Polbooks	Co-purchasing of books about US politics on Amazon in 2004	105	441
Lesmiserables	Co-appearance of characters in the novel "Les Miserables" by Victor Hugo	77	254

To obtain a more accurate solution, we conducted experiments on various real-world networks [14] (shown in Table 2)for each node i in G. For each node $j \neq i$ in the network, we performed the following steps: First, a backup copy of the subgraph of interest S was created and denoted by H. Then, we removed the node j from S and computed the coreness of node i in S. If the coreness of node i in S was the same as its actual coreness in G, we kept the node j removed from S. Otherwise, we reverted S back to the backup copy H.

During this process, we recorded the fraction of the network explored, and computed the average and standard deviation of this fraction. The results of a single run are presented in Table 3, which displays the mean and standard deviation of the number of nodes and edges explored for each network. Specifically, $\mu_{|V|}$ and $\sigma_{|V|}$ represent the average and standard deviation of the number of nodes explored, while $\mu_{|E|}$ and $\sigma_{|E|}$ represent the average and standard deviation of the number of edges explored.

Table 3. Mean and Standard Deviation of nodes and edges explored

Network	$\mu_{|V|}$	$\sigma_{|V|}$	$\mu_{|E|}$	$\sigma_{|E|}$
Dolphins	0.172	0.113	0.137	0.110
Football	0.537	0.289	0.441	0.241
Adjnoun	0.157	0.081	0.139	0.094
Karate	0.151	0.0597	0.108	0.0637
Polbooks	0.115	0.0498	0.0799	0.0396
Lesmis	0.0894	0.062	0.0930	0.0982

The Football network has a high expected value of the fraction of nodes explored because it only contains two shells.

To account for the local maxima produced by the hill climbing approach, we repeated the algorithm 10 times and computed the mean and standard deviation of the results. We also calculated the mean and standard deviation of the mean and standard deviation values to show that the results are consistent across iterations. Table 4 displays the average and standard deviation of the mean values.

Table 4. Mean and Standard Deviation for the averages

Network	$\mu_{\mu_{|V|}}$	$\sigma_{\mu_{|V|}}$	$\mu_{\mu_{|E|}}$	$\sigma_{\mu_{|E|}}$
Dolphins	0.171	0.005	0.136	0.004
Football	0.521	0.016	0.427	0.005
Adjnoun	0.155	0.003	0.135	0.002
Karate	0.148	0.002	0.106	0.002
Polbooks	0.115	0.002	0.079	0.001
Lesmis	0.091	0.001	0.095	0.002

The table shows that the mean of the mean values $\mu_{|V|}$ and $\mu_{|E|}$ is very close to the value obtained from a single experiment. Additionally, the standard deviation is also very small. This indicates that the algorithm produces consistent results across multiple runs. To further analyze the consistency, one can determine the maximum error in the mean and standard deviation (Table 5).

Table 5. Mean and Standard Deviation for the standard deviations

Network	$\mu_{\sigma_{|V|}}$	$\sigma_{\sigma_{|V|}}$	$\mu_{\sigma_{|E|}}$	$\sigma_{\sigma_{|E|}}$
Dolphins	0.117	0.006	0.111	0.006
Football	0.285	0.007	0.238	0.006
Adjnoun	0.079	0.002	0.092	0.002
Karate	0.058	0.004	0.064	0.003
Polbooks	0.05	0.003	0.037	0.001
Lesmis	0.065	0.002	0.101	0.002

7.2   Bottom-Up Approach

In the bottom-up approach, we start with a subgraph S containing only one node, which is initially isolated and has coreness equal to zero in S. Then, we examine the neighbors of S and choose one that brings the coreness of the node closest to λ, and add it to S. We repeat this process by iteratively adding vertices until no more vertices can be added.

However, this approach has a drawback of discovering some unnecessary vertices. Unlike the previous approach, we cannot stop once we reach a plateau in our hill climbing approach. Instead, we stop when we can no longer move in any direction, i.e., all directions take us downhill. Although this approach may be faster than the previous one, it also has the disadvantage of potentially adding unnecessary vertices.

To address this issue, we can first find a local maxima using the bottom-up approach, and then remove the unnecessary vertices using the top-down approach described earlier. It is worth noting that the previous approach may encounter a scenario where deleting one vertex decreases coreness, while deleting another vertex increases it and again makes it equal to λ. Such cases require careful consideration.

8   Conclusion

We have presented accurate bounds on the k-shell number of a node in a network at different levels of resolution, which can help identify nodes with high spreading power in large and complex networks. Moreover, we have proposed a novel node removal strategy that allows for the efficient determination of a node's k-shell number based on a smaller subgraph, making it possible to analyze the influential power of nodes in even larger networks. Our work demonstrates the potential for local algorithms to be used in place of more computationally intensive global approaches, which have traditionally been used to identify influential nodes in a network. These findings could have important implications for fields such as social network analysis, disease propagation modeling, and information diffusion in complex systems. Overall, our paper provides new insights and tools for the analysis of complex networks, contributing to the ongoing effort to understand the mechanisms underlying the spread of information and ideas.

References

1. Iacocca, L.: Where Have All the Leaders Gone? Scribner (2007)
2. Allocca, K.: Why videos go viral. TED Talks (2011). https://www.ted.com/talks/kevin-alloca-why-videos-go-viral
3. Kitsak, M., et al.: Identification of influential spreaders in complex networks. Nat. Phys. **6**(11), 888–893 (2010)
4. Callaway, D.S., Newman, M.E.J., Strogatz, S.H., Watts, D.J.: Network robustness and fragility: percolation on random graphs. Phys. Rev. E **69**(2) (2004)
5. Leskovec, J., Lang, K., Dasgupta, A., Mahoney, M.: Microscopic evolution of social networks. In: Proceedings of the 14th ACM SIGKDD International Conference on Knowledge Discovery and Data Mining, pp. 462–470 (2008)
6. Sonkar, S.B., Kumar, V., Kumar, A.: Exact computation of k-core decomposition and its application in clustering. Phys. Rev. E **92**(1) (2015)
7. Gupta, M., Menon, D.S., Pandey, S.: Approximating k-shell decomposition in massive graphs. arXiv preprint arXiv:2107.08906 (2021)
8. Newman, M.E.: Networks: An Introduction. Oxford University Press, Oxford (2010)
9. De Domenico, M., et al.: Mathematical formulation of multilayer networks. Phys. Rev. X **3**(4), 041022 (2013)
10. Emerson, A.F., Williams, C.R., Hong, K., Xie, X.S.: K-shell decomposition predicts protein fold specificity. J. Mol. Biol. **427**(1), 192–196 (2015)
11. Huang, C.Y., Chen, C.Y., Chen, Y.A., Huang, C.C., Peng, Y.H.: Identification of druggable targets by protein microenvironments similarity search. PLoS ONE **11**(1), e0147084 (2016)
12. Zhang, Y., Chen, W., Gu, X., Chen, T.: Efficient algorithms for k-core decomposition in massive networks. IEEE Trans. Knowl. Data Eng. **30**(4), 725–738 (2018)
13. Tixier, A.J., Géry, M., Boyer, A.: GoWvis: interactive graph visualization for the web using the dependency graph of packages from the NPM registry. J. Open Sour. Softw. **1**(6), 102 (2016)
14. Leskovec, J., Krevl, A.: SNAP datasets: Stanford large network dataset collection (2014). http://snap.stanford.edu/data
15. Meladianos, P., Gidaris, S., Androutsopoulos, I.: Real-time keyword extraction from conversations. In: Proceedings of the 2017 ACM on Conference on Information and Knowledge Management, pp. 2259–2262 (2017)
16. Zhao, L., Wu, F., Ma, J.: Investigating corporate networks using the k-shell decomposition method. J. Bus. Res. **70**, 70–76 (2017)
17. Kim, K.J., Kwon, Y.E., Han, I.: Network analysis of interbank transactions in a small open economy. J. Bus. Res. **88**, 235–242 (2018)

18. Wang, W., Wei, Y., Gao, X., Cheng, X.: Parallel k-core decomposition on distributed memory systems. Futur. Gener. Comput. Syst. **74**, 233–243 (2017)
19. Li, R., Wang, X., Chen, E.: Efficient algorithms for k-core decomposition of large-scale dynamic graphs. In: Proceedings of the 22nd ACM International Conference on Conference on Information & Knowledge Management, pp. 899–904 (2013)
20. Cohen, R., Havlin, S.: Complex Networks: Structure, Robustness and Function. Cambridge University Press, Cambridge (2010)
21. Seidman, S.B.: Network structure and minimum degree. Soc. Netw. **5**(3), 269–287 (1983)
22. Bodlaender, H.L., Kloks, T.: On approximating the k-core of a graph. Theoret. Comput. Sci. **365**(1), 21–33 (2006)
23. Sun, P.G., Miao, Q., Staab, S.: Community-based k-shell decomposition for identifying influential spreaders. Pattern Recognit. **120**, 108130 (2021). ISSN 0031-3203

Difficulties Developing a Children's Speech Recognition System for Language with Limited Training Data

Dina Oralbekova[1,2](✉) [iD], Orken Mamyrbayev[1] [iD], Mohamed Othman[3] [iD],
Keylan Alimhan[4] [iD], NinaKhairova[5] [iD], and Aliya Zhunussova[6] [iD]

[1] Institute of Information and Computational Technologies, Almaty, Kazakhstan
d.oralbekova@aues.kz
[2] Almaty University of Power Engineering and Telecommunications, Almaty, Kazakhstan
[3] Universiti Putra Malaysia, Kuala Lumpur, Malaysia
[4] L.N. Gumilyov Eurasian National University, Nur-Sultan, Kazakhstan
[5] National Technical University "Kharkiv Polytechnic Institute", Kharkiv, Ukraine
[6] Narxoz University, Almaty, Kazakhstan

Abstract. Automatic speech recognition is a rapidly developing area in the field of machine learning and is a necessary tool for controlling various devices and automated systems. However, such recognition systems are more aimed at adults than at the younger generation. The peculiarity of the development of a child's voice leads to an increase in the error in the recognition of children's speech in applications developed based on adult speech data. In addition, many applications do not consider the peculiarities of children's speech and the data used when children communicate between other children and adults. Thus, there is currently a huge demand for systems that understand adult and child speech and can process them correctly. In addition, there is the problem of the lack of these languages, which are part of the agglutinative, i.e. Turkic languages, especially Kazakh language. The difficulty of assembling and developing a high-quality and large case is still an unsolved problem. This paper presents studies of children's speech recognition based on modified data from adults and their impact on the quality of recognition for Kazakh language. Two models were built, namely the Transformer model and the insert-based model. The results obtained are satisfactory, but still require improvement and expansion of the corpus of children's speech.

Keywords: Automatic Speech Recognition · Children's Speech · Low-Resource Languages · End-to-End Models

1 Introduction

Speech recognition is a necessary tool for human interaction with various devices, work-technical and automated systems. There is a traditional speech recognition system, which usually consists of separate elements that are trained independently of each other. For a long time, in the task of speech recognition, the model based on hidden Markov

© The Author(s), under exclusive license to Springer Nature Switzerland AG 2023
N. T. Nguyen et al. (Eds.): ICCCI 2023, CCIS 1864, pp. 419–429, 2023.
https://doi.org/10.1007/978-3-031-41774-0_33

models (HMM) was widely used and was the main technology [1]. HMM is mainly used for dynamic time warping at the frame level and a mixture of Gaussian probability density distributions (GMM) is used to represent signal distributions over a fixed small period, which usually corresponds to a pronunciation unit [2]. For a long time, the HMM-GMM model was the general framework for speech recognition. Recently, deep learning has brought significant improvements in many studies, and in the development of speech recognition. The active use of artificial neural networks on each element of the scenario of the classical speech recognition system increases the efficiency of its work, which is reflected in many research papers. With the development of deep learning technologies, deep neural networks (DNN) began to be used in speech recognition for acoustic modeling [3]. The role of the DNN is to calculate the posterior probability of the state of the HMM, which can be converted into probabilities, replacing the usual probability of observing the GMM [4]. Thus, the HMM-GMM model turns into HMM-DNN, which achieves better results, and becomes a popular automatic speech recognition model.

With the development of deep learning technologies and computing technology, it has become easier to design and build speech recognition models. End-to-end (E2E) models have completely replaced traditional models, and almost all modern speech recognition and generation systems use the capabilities of neural networks at each step of the system processing element. The basic principle of work is that modern end-to-end models are trained based on big data. From the above it is possible to detect the main problem, it concerns the recognition of languages with limited training data, such as Kazakh, Kyrgyz, Turkish, etc.

There are many speech recognition technologies, but many of them do not consider the difference between a child's voice and an adult. And what is the peculiarity of the child's voice? Due to the specificity of the vocal apparatus, such as vocal cords, low lung capacity, etc., a child's voice differs from an adult's voice. The vocal cords in men are usually longer and more massive than in women, the tone frequency of a man's voice is usually in the range from 80 Hz to 240 Hz, and that of a woman's - from 140 Hz to 500 Hz. The frequency of the fundamental tone of a child's voice ranges from 170 Hz to 600 Hz [5]. A child's voice is characterized by a "high" sound, a smaller range, and a characteristic softness. Only tone frequency can be considered when processing speech data. However, the child's body is growing all the time, and this affects the frequency response of the voice. This feature of voice development leads to an increase in errors in the recognition of children's speech in applications developed based on adult speech data. In addition, it must be considered that children have a huge variation in phonetic, grammatical and syntactic forms. Compared to adults, children build sentences in a peculiar way, change the pitch, pull some sounds.

Some apps only understand certain forms of phrases or sentences, so adults will deliberately adapt their speaking style when accessing voice assistants. Children, in turn, do not change their way of speaking, but express their own phrases, as they are used to talking with their relatives or friends. If this feature of the child's voice is not considered when developing educational interactive material that requires voice contact with the child, this will negatively affect the level of education and the mental and emotional state of children [6].

Various experiments and works related to the recognition of children's speech for languages with sufficiently large training data have been investigated and performed. For languages with limited speech data that are included in the group of agglutinative languages, such as Kazakh [7–10], Uighur [11], Kyrgyz [12], Uzbek [13, 14], Hindi [15], etc. speech recognition systems based on hybrid, end-to-end models and Transformer were developed. But for such low-resource languages, corpora of children's speech have not been created and developed, and models and methods for recognizing children's agglutinative speech have not been developed.

The structure of the research work is given in the following order: in Sect. 2, an analytical review of the scientific direction is carried out. Section 3 describes the principles of operation of the Connectionist temporal classification (CTC) and attention-based models, as well as the insertion model. Further in Sect. 4, our experimental data, corpus of speech, and equipment for the experiment are described, and the results obtained are analyzed. The conclusions are given in the final section.

2 Literature Review

Children's voice can be divided into three stages of its development: 7–9 years old – younger age, primary school children (grades 1–4); 10–13 years old – middle age, children in grades 5–8; 13–15 years old – adolescence (grades 8–9); 16–18 years old - senior age (grades 10–11, 1st year students), the formation of the voice of an adult [16]. When collecting data, these features must be taken into account and properly categorized.

Special algorithms for speech recognition were not developed for children. To address the issues of recognition of children's speech, it is necessary to consider their speech pronunciation, some indiscriminate use of words, combined with grammar that defies any rules. All this must be considered when building models and finding solutions to this problem is much more difficult [16].

Sensory AI [17] and Soapbox Labs [18] have been developing a public speech corpus and child speech recognition model for many years. Sensory has already created a special model that considers the linguistic features of children's speech, and as a result, the model showed a 33% improvement compared to other models trained on adult speech data.

In [19], an automatic speech recognition (ASR) system was developed for children in Punjabi, which has a low level of data resources. A mixture of speech data from adults and children was used as training data and tested on children's speech. Due to discrepancies in acoustic attributes such as speech rate, pitch, and frequency between adult and pediatric speech, vocal tract length normalization (VTLN) was applied. In order to avoid errors due to lack of data, data extension outside the subject area based on prosody modification was applied to increase the amount of training data. These approaches have significantly reduced the error rate in children's speech recognition.

In [20] proposed several improvements to address the lack of large corpora of children's speech and address the domain mismatch when decoding children's speech by systems developed on adult data. Two approaches have been proposed. 1) A data augmentation method based on a speech model with a source filter to avoid a gap in the subject area between the speech data of adults and children. This method makes it possible to use these adult speech corpora, changing them and making them look like children's speech. 2) They applied the transfer learning method on the Transformer model, pre-trained on adult data. Using this model for a speech recognition task using adult data, supplemented by the proposed original filter distortion strategy and a limited amount of children's speech in the subject area, significantly improved the previous state-of-the-art results for British-English children's speech PF-STAR with 4.86% WER on the official test set.

The authors of [21] combined several small corpora of children's speech from languages other than English. Multilingual learning and transfer learning were applied. The obtained results gave a positive effect of using transfer learning on top of a multilingual model for languages with a limited set of data and outperformed conventional training in a single language.

The work [22] explores numerous methods to improve the performance of both hybrid and end-to-end ASR models in children's speech recognition. Three approaches have been proposed for child speech recognition: 1) use of compact model parameterization: Time Delay Factorized Neural Networks (TDNN-F) have been used as more efficient on Acoustic Model (AM) data for DNN-HMM hybrid ASR models. 2) Adaptation of models trained on data outside the domain: Transfer learning was used to adapt an end-to-end ASR model trained on adult speech to children's speech recognition. 3) Creative use of available domain data: Various data augmentation techniques have been applied to enhance existing child speech data for training hybrid ASR models. Thus, the author has improved the performance of hybrid and end-to-end ASR models in children's speech recognition.

In [23] compared a standard cepstral feature-based ASR approach with a CNN-based end-to-end acoustic modeling approach that jointly learns the corresponding features and a phonemic classifier from raw speech for children's speech recognition. Studies of the PF-STAR enclosure have shown that CNN-based end-to-end acoustic modeling produces better systems than systems with standard features such as MFCC. The authors' research has also shown that supplementing child data with adult speech data can further improve the system. An analysis of trained CNNs showed that CNNs learn to model formant information that is invariant to acoustic differences in the speech of children and adults.

The authors of [24] presented a detailed empirical study of children's speech recognition using modern end-to-end architectures. It was found that an end-to-end speech recognition system trained on adult speech has disadvantages for children's speech recognition. The benefits of end-to-end ASR for adult speech do not fully transfer to children's speech. Error studies show that the end-to-end system has fewer substitutions and insertions and a large number of deletions for children's speech recognition compared to the hybrid DNN-HMM. End-to-end architectures trained on large amounts of adult speech data can improve children's speech performance. The addition of a large amount of adult speech has been found to be more beneficial when the acoustic mismatch between children and adults is large.

In [25], the linguistic and acoustic characteristics of children's speech are considered in the context of automatic speech recognition. Acoustic variability is considered to be a major barrier to creating high performance ASR applications for children. It was found that a simple speaker normalization algorithm combining frequency warping and spectrum shaping reduces acoustic variability and significantly increases the efficiency of recognition of speaking children. Acoustic modeling, depending on age, further reduces the number of errors in words by 10%. Piecewise linear and phonemically dependent frequency deformation algorithms are proposed to reduce the acoustic discrepancy between the acoustic spaces of children and adults.

3 Methodology

CTC and Attention. In this work, we applied a hybrid CTC + attention model (Fig. 1) for recognition of continuous speech in children [9] and a model based on insertions using the example of the Kazakh language [26].

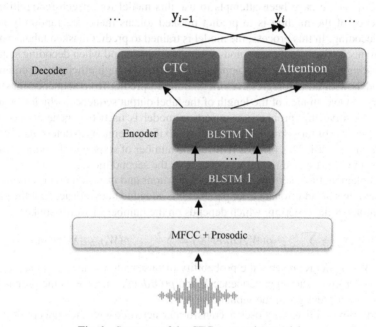

Fig. 1. Structure of the CTC + attention model

The CTC function was used to train the decoder, since the CTC algorithm uses monotonic alignment between speech and label sequences and quickly trains the network. And besides, the proposed model will be effective in speech recognition in noisy environments. In addition, CTC helps to speed up the process of estimating the desired alignment without the help of rough estimates of this process, which requires a lot of work and time. The model includes the attention model and CTC as follows:

$$L_{CTC/Att} = \tau L_{CTC}(x) + (1 - \tau)L_{Att}(x) \tag{1}$$

where τ – configurable parameter and satisfies the condition $- 0 \leq \tau \leq 1$.

Bidirectional LSTM networks with a pyramidal structure were used as an encoder, and the attention mechanism and CTC are the decoder, for sequential decoding of the network output.

Insertion-Based Model. E2E models work on a sequence-to-sequence (seq2seq) basis, autoregressively generating utterances from left to right, because speech is sequential. Speech-to-word or sentence decoding occurs on the basis of previous utterances, which does not take into account future utterances. And it has not been proven that this decoding method is the best in text-to-speech. We can, of course, predict the next word based on previous utterances, but this method will not work if some of the previous words were slurred or too quiet. In this case, future information can be used to determine what was said before. You need to understand that when decoding, you need to consider not only the previous context, but also the future one, which plays an important role in converting audio to text [27].

Machine translation technologies actively use the non-autoregressive transformer model [28]. There have been attempts to use this model for speech recognition [29]. The essence of the method is to predict masked tokens that were randomly masked during decoding. In this process, the model is trained to predict masked labels using the attention mechanism. And uses a non-autoregressive method when decoding sequences by evaluating hidden labels. This approach has achieved high efficiency in comparison with models with an autoregressive orientation. To predict from sequence masks, it is necessary to have an idea of the length of the label output sequence, which is a difficult process. To solve this problem, an insertion model is used that generates an output sequence in an arbitrary order without adding auxiliary elements to determine the length of output labels [30]. This process reduces the number of steps and decoding time.

Thus, the insert-based model was chosen as the second model.

To implement the insertion model, word positions and insertion order must be determined, and thus an additional Order parameter is added to take into account the possible permutations of the ordering, which depends on the number of words spoken eq. (2):

$$P(W|X) = \sum\nolimits_{Order} p(W, Order|X) = \sum\nolimits_{Order} p(W_{Order}|X) p(Order|X) \qquad (2)$$

where $p(W_{Order}|X)$ represents the probability of observing the target sequence W in a specific order given the input sequence X and $p(Order|X)$ represents the probability of a specific word order given the input sequence X.

Insertion-based decoding uses a Transformer network with the concept of position order (Fig. 2).

This model is trained in a completely end-to-end way, retaining all the benefits of decoding. This approach allows you to ignore the need to determine the length of the sequences in advance.

As shown in Eq. (2), word position prediction is performed by insertion into having words. Since the word position update does not change with respect to precomputed representations, the word position information can be reused in the next decoding step.

During sequence decoding, we model the conditional probability of a sequence of words by matching the distribution of words and their positions in the correct order.

4   Experiments and Results

This section contains descriptions of the case, preliminary model settings, experimental data, as well as the results obtained, and a comparative analysis of the data obtained.

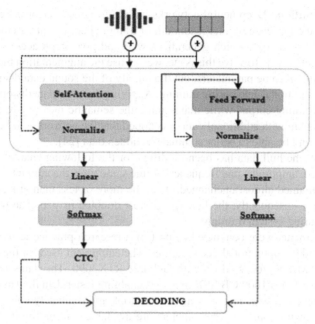

Fig. 2. Insertion-based model

Feature Extraction. Feature extraction is a process that extracts from a signal a small amount of data that is essential to solving a problem. The most popular feature extraction method is the Mel Frequency Cepstral Coefficients (MFCC) method.

The level of sound perceived by the human ear is related to the volume level and timbre, and therefore chalk is used as the unit for measuring the pitch of perceived sound. The human ear perceives the lower frequencies of sound much better, so these windows are concentrated closer to the low frequencies. Because of this, relying on MFCC functions alone is not enough to extract meaningful elements from audio data. We used the approach proposed in [19], the Prosodic function was used in conjunction with MFCC, and this set of functions helps to set the tone and pitch of speech. These changes in feature extraction work improve the quality and accuracy of speech recognition and the reliability of the system.

Data. To train the system, a ready-made corpus of the Kazakh language was used, containing about 50 h of adult speech, collected in the laboratory of "Computer Engineering of Intelligent Systems" of the Institute of High Temperatures of the Ministry of Education and Science of the Republic of Kazakhstan (https://iict.kz/). Data on children's speech amounted to 1.6 h (Fig. 3). To collect children's speech, 10 students from grades 4–6 were selected, text data was extracted from children's books, which children learn from. In order to somehow bring the speech of adults closer to children's, some acoustic characteristics have been changed: the height and frequency of speech data have been increased. The corpus consists of sound files, which are divided into training and test sets, accounting for 90% and 10% of the total respectively.

Data Augmentation. Deep neural networks with high model performance are highly dependent on the presence of a large amount of training data to learn a nonlinear function from input to output, which generalizes well and gives high accuracy of hidden object classification [8]. To solve this issue, we can use the augmentation method, which changes the data in some parameters, but the quality of the sound data does not change and is used as additional data during training. Applying different data distortion can lead to additional training corpus while maintaining the semantic meaning of the data. By training the system with additional data, it is hoped that the network will be sensitive to these changes and be able to better summarize hidden data [24].

As a result, the hull data has been modified for the following characteristics, such as tempo, speed, amplitude, and frequency. At the same time, the amount of data during the change remained almost unchanged, it can be more or less than at least 5% of the original value. Consequently, the hull was almost doubled in size. The modified data was applied during system training.

The experiments were conducted as part of a research practice at the Institute of Information and Computational Technologies. The equipment used for the experiments consisted of AMD Ryzen 9 GPUs with GeForce RTX3090. The datasets used in the study were stored on a 1000 GB SSD memory, enabling faster data flow during training and recognition processes. The training process took approximately one week to complete. The following main hyperparameters are available for configuring the training process: num_epochs, num_hidden, num_layers, batch_size, initial_learning_rate, and dropout_rate.

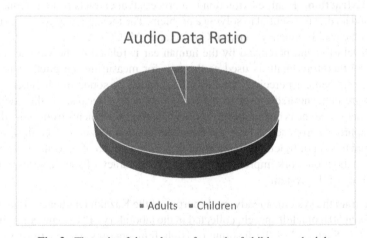

Fig. 3. The ratio of the volume of speech of children and adults

All audio materials are in.wav format. The PCM method was used to convert the data into digital form. Discrete frequency 44.1 kHz, bit depth 16 bits.

Conducting Experiments. For the experiments, the CTC models and attention were considered jointly and separately, the insertion model (Table 1). When extracting features, the MFCC function was supplemented. The metric used to evaluate the results was Word Error Rate (WER), which measures the percentage of incorrectly recognized words. However, the obtained results were not particularly impressive. This could be due to limited training data, suboptimal model architectures, or the need to explore alternative feature extraction approaches.

Table 1. Results of the work of the model based on the end-to-end approach for recognition of children's speech.

Model	WER, %	Data volume, h
CTC	46.3	101.6
Encoder-Attention-Decoder	44.7	101.6
CTC + attention	36.2	101.6
Insertion-based model	35.8	101.6

Based on the experiment's results, it can be noted that the Insertion-based model performed better compared to other models, achieving a WER of 35.8%. When testing the voice recognition system for children (regardless of gender), it performed similarly to adult voices in all considered models. This indicates that adult speech data can be included in the corpus, contributing to improving the quality of child speech recognition.

5 Conclusion

The paper considered methods for building integrated speech recognition systems, namely, the joint use of CTC and a coder-decoder based on the attention mechanism and an insert model for recognizing children's speech. The results of the experiments showed that the augmented MFCC function, together with the insertion model, showed satisfactory results as a CTC model with an attention mechanism. The results obtained can be improved by collecting and expanding the existing corpus of children's speech, and in the process of extracting features from audio, as well as building effective end-to-end models, it is necessary to pay more attention to the features of the language and children's speech.

The obtained results can be used in the automatic speech recognition system for the Kazakh language, for computer shorthand writing, for voice control of a computer, robotic and automated systems, which will allow not only adults, but also children with disabilities to simultaneously perform several functions not related to devices. Entering the car.

In the future, we plan to collect a corpus of children's speech, develop effective methods and models for the correct conversion of children's speech into text for the Kazakh language.

Acknowledgement. This research has been funded by the Committee of Science of the Ministry of Science and Higher Education of the Republic of Kazakhstan (Grant No. AP19174298).

References

1. Juang, B.H., Rabiner, L.R.: Hidden markov models for speech recognition. Technometrics **33**(3), 251 (1991). https://doi.org/10.2307/1268779
2. Brown, J.C., Smaragdis, P.: Hidden Markov and Gaussian mixture models for automatic call classification. J. Acoustical Soc. Am. **125**(6), EL221–EL224 (2009). https://doi.org/10.1121/1.3124659
3. Hinton, G., et al.: Deep neural networks for acoustic modeling in speech recognition. IEEE Signal Process. Magazine **29**(6), 82–97 (2012)
4. Ghaffarzadegan, S., Bořil, H., Hansen, J.H.L.: Deep neural network training for whispered speech recognition using small databases and generative model sampling. Int. J. Speech Technol. **20**(4), 1063–1075 (2017). https://doi.org/10.1007/s10772-017-9461-x
5. Children's Art School No. 4, Engels Homepage. https://engels-dshi4.ru/index.php?option=com_content&view=article&id=86:tormanova-o-v-detskij-golos-i-osobennosti-ego-razvitiya&catid=18&Itemid=131. Last accessed 16 Mar 2023
6. https://te-st.org/2021/06/02/voice-assistants-and-problems/
7. Mamyrbayev, O., Oralbekova, D., Alimhan, K., Othman, M., Turdalykyzy, T.: A study of transformer-based end-to-end speech recognition system for Kazakh language. Sci. Rep. **12**, 8337 (2022). https://doi.org/10.1038/s41598-022-12260-y
8. Mamyrbayev, O.Z., Oralbekova, D.O., Alimhan, K., Nuranbayeva, B.M.: Hybrid end-to-end model for Kazakh speech recognition. Int. J. Speech Technol. **26**(2), 261–270 (2022). https://doi.org/10.1007/s10772-022-09983-8
9. Oralbekova, D., Mamyrbayev, O., Othman, M., Alimhan, K., Zhumazhanov, B., Nuranbayeva, B.: Development of CRF and CTC based end-to-end kazakh speech recognition system. In: Nguyen, N.T., Tran, T.K., Tukayev, U., Hong, TP., Trawiński, B., Szczerbicki, E. (eds.) Intelligent Information and Database Systems. ACIIDS 2022. Lecture Notes in Computer Science(), vol. 13757. Springer, Cham (2022). https://doi.org/10.1007/978-3-031-21743-2_41
10. Mamyrbayev, O., Oralbekova, D., Kydyrbekova, A., Turdalykyzy, T., Bekarystankyzy, A.: End-to-end model based on RNN-T for Kazakh speech recognition. In: 2021 3rd International Conference on Computer Communication and the Internet (ICCCI), pp. 163–167 (2021). https://doi.org/10.1109/ICCCI51764.2021.9486811
11. Abulimiti, A., Schultz, T.: Automatic speech recognition for uyghur through multilingual acoustic modeling. In: Proceedings of the Twelfth Language Resources and Evaluation Conference, pp. 6444–6449. European Language Resources Association, Marseille, France (2020)
12. Du, W., Maimaitiyiming, Y., Nijat, M., Li, L., Hamdulla, A., Wang, D.: Automatic speech recognition for Uyghur, Kazakh, and Kyrgyz: an overview. Appl. Sci. **13**(1), 326 (2022). https://doi.org/10.3390/app13010326
13. Mukhamadiyev, A., Khujayarov, I., Djuraev, O., Cho, J.: Automatic speech recognition method based on deep learning approaches for Uzbek Language. Sensors **22**, 3683 (2022). https://doi.org/10.3390/s22103683
14. Ren, Z., Yolwas, N., Slamu, W., Cao, R., Wang, H.: Improving hybrid CTC/attention architecture for agglutinative language speech recognition. Sensors **22**, 7319 (2022). https://doi.org/10.3390/s22197319
15. Rathor, S., Jadon, R.S.: Speech recognition and system controlling using Hindi language. In: 2019 10th International Conference on Computing, Communication and Networking Technologies (ICCCNT), pp. 1–6. Kanpur, India (2019). https://doi.org/10.1109/ICCCNT45670.2019.8944641
16. TechInsider Homepage: https://www.techinsider.ru/technologies/1122303-raspoznavanie-rechi-v-medicine-zachem-nam-eto-nuzhno/. Last accessed 16 Mar 2023

17. Sensory Inc. Homepage: https://www.sensory.com/. Last accessed 16 Mar 2023
18. SoapBox Inc. Homepage. https://www.soapboxlabs.com/. Last accessed 16 Feb 2023
19. Kadyan, V., Shanawazuddin, S., Singh, A.: Developing children's speech recognition system for low resource Punjabi language. Appl. Acoustics **178**, 108002 (2021). https://doi.org/10.1016/j.apacoust.2021.108002
20. Jenthe, T., Kris, D.: Transfer Learning for Robust Low-Resource Children's Speech ASR with Transformers and Source-Filter Warping (2022). https://doi.org/10.48550/arXiv.2206.09396
21. Rong, T., Lei, W., Bin, M.: Transfer learning for children's speech recognition, pp. 36–39 (2017). https://doi.org/10.1109/IALP.2017.8300540
22. Dissertation thesis. https://jscholarship.library.jhu.edu/bitstream/handle/1774.2/62766/WU-THESIS-2020.pdf?sequence=1. Last accessed 2 Feb 2023
23. Dubagunta, S.P., Hande Kabil, S., Magimai.-Doss, M.: Improving children speech recognition through feature learning from raw speech signal. In: ICASSP 2019 – 2019 IEEE International Conference on Acoustics, Speech and Signal Processing (ICASSP), pp. 5736–5740. Brighton, UK (2019). https://doi.org/10.1109/ICASSP.2019.8682826
24. Shivakumar, P.G., Narayanan, S.: End-to-end neural systems for automatic children speech recognition: an empirical study. Comput. Speech Lang. **72**, 101289 (2022). https://doi.org/10.1016/j.csl.2021.101289
25. Potamianos, A., Narayanan, S., Lee, S.: Automatic speech recognition for children (1997). https://doi.org/10.21437/Eurospeech.1997-623
26. Ignatenko, G.S.: Classification of audio signals using neural networks. In: Ignatenko, G.S., Lamchanovsky, A.G. (eds.) Text: direct // Young scientist. - No. 48 (286), pp. 23–25 (2019). https://moluch.ru/archive/286/64455/
27. Mamyrbayev, O., Oralbekova, D., Othman, M., Turdalykyzy, T., Zhumazhanov, B., Mukhsina, K.: Investigation of insertion-based speech recognition method. Int. J. Signal Process. **7**, 32–35 (2022)
28. Gu, J., Bradbury, J., Xiong, C., Li, V.O., Socher R.: Non-autoregressive neural machine translation. arXiv preprint arXiv:1711.02281 (2017)
29. Chen, N., Watanabe, S., Villalba, J., Zelasko, P., Dehak, N.: Non-autoregressive transformer for speech recognition. IEEE Signal Process. Lett. **28**, 121–125 (2021)
30. Fujita, Y., Watanabe, S., Omachi, M., Chan, X.: Insertion-Based Modeling for End-to-End Automatic Speech Recognition. INTERSPEECH 2020 (2020). https://doi.org/10.48550/arXiv.2005.13211

Kazakh-Uzbek Speech Cascade Machine Translation on Complete Set of Endings

Tolganay Balabekova[ID], Bauyrzhan Kairatuly[ID], and Ualsher Tukeyev[(✉)] [ID]

Al-Farabi Kazakh National University, Almaty, Kazakhstan
ualsher.tukeyev@gmail.com

Abstract. Studies of speech-to-speech machine translation for Turkic languages are practically absent due to the difficulties of creating parallel speech corpora for training neural models. Therefore, the actual problem is creation of synthetic parallel corpora for investigation of speech machine translation of Turkic languages. In this work, a technology of formation of Turkic speech parallel corpora on the base of CSE (Complete Set of Endings) morphology model is proposed. For this technology of formation of Turkic speech parallel corpora is used the cascade scheme: speech-to-text, text-to-text and text-to-speech. A feature of this scheme is that it is used for the phase "text-to-text" a relational model of translation based on CSE morphology model. The scientific contribution of this work is the development of the technology of forming parallel speech corpora of the Kazakh-Uzbek language pairs, based on a cascade scheme for machine translation of speech on relational models. In the future, the formed synthetic parallel speech corpora will be used to train the neural machine translation of the speech of the Turkic languages.

Keywords: Automatic formation · speech · synthetic · parallel corpora · Kazakh-Uzbek

1 Introduction

Most Turkic languages are classified as languages with small electronic resources. The problem of computer processing of natural languages with small electronic resources is one of the most critical problems in the field of neural machine translation [1].

For Turkic languages, studies of machine translation speech-to-speech are practically absent due to the difficulties of creating parallel speech corpora for training neural models. The creation of machine translation of speech according to the cascade scheme (STT – TTT – TTS), where S is speech (speech), T is text (text), is also complex due to the absence of the TTT (Text-To-Text) phase for most Turkic languages. Therefore, in this paper, it is proposed to explore the approach of constructing machine translation of speech according to a cascade scheme for the formation of synthetic parallel speech corpora, which can be used to study neural machine speech-to-speech translation. The cascade scheme is proposed to be solved using relational models for the TTT phase based on the morphology model on the complete set of endings (CSE models) [2–9].

© The Author(s), under exclusive license to Springer Nature Switzerland AG 2023
N. T. Nguyen et al. (Eds.): ICCCI 2023, CCIS 1864, pp. 430–442, 2023.
https://doi.org/10.1007/978-3-031-41774-0_34

The scientific contribution of this work is to study the technology of forming parallel speech corpora of the Kazakh-Uzbek language pair with the development of a cascade scheme for machine translation of speech on relational models. In the future, this technology of obtaining synthetic parallel speech corpora will be used for other Turkic languages.

2 Related Works

In direct machine translation of speech S2ST (Speech to Speech Translation), intensive research is being carried out using neural network training technologies [10–20]. These studies include only Turkish from the Turkic languages.

Recently, the creation of direct models of machine speech translation into text under limited resources has been considered [21–24]. However, studies of natural models of speech-to-speech machine translation for low-resource languages have not yet been found.

The problem of parallel corpora for training machine translation of speech S2ST (Speech to Speech Translation) is currently being intensively studied [25–27]. Parallel corpora for S2ST (Speech to Speech Translation) are created specifically for this task and require special equipment for speech recording and significant financial costs.

This problem is especially relevant for the Turkic languages, since there are practically no parallel speech corpora for pairs of Turkic languages. However, monolingual speech corpora are already appearing for individual languages of the Turkic group: Kazakh, Uzbek [28, 29]. There are several domestic research of speech recognition for the Kazakh, Uzbek languages [28, 30–33].

However, research of neural machine translation of speech for Turkic languages is difficult now due to the lack of parallel speech corpora S2ST (Speech to Speech Translation) for training. The creation of machine translation of speech according to the cascade scheme (STT – TTT – TTS), where S is speech, T is text, is also difficult due to the absence of the TTT (Text-To-Text) phase for most Turkic languages.

Since the construction of the TTT (Text-To-Text) phase of machine translation of speech based on the CSE morphology model is feasible without constructing parallel corpora and is not resource-intensive compared to the cost of creating parallel corpora, it is possible to research the cascade scheme for constructing machine translation speeches of the Turkic languages. Moreover, in the presence of a single language corpus of speech of one of the Turkic languages, the cascade scheme for machine translation of the speech of the Turkic languages can be used for automatic machine translation into another Turkic language. By combining these two corpora of speech: the original and the translated corpora, and aligning them by sentences, can obtain a parallel corpus of speech for a pair of Turkic languages. The resulting parallel corpus of speech of a pair of Turkic languages can be used to train a neural model for machine translation of speech for improving of quality of speech machine translation.

Thus, in this article is proposed to build machine translation of S2ST (Speech to Speech Translation) according to a cascade scheme, where the TTT (Text-To-Text) phase is proposed to be solved for Kazakh-Uzbek using relational models of machine translation of texts based on a new model morphology according to the complete set of endings (CSE-models). Then this system of machine translation of speech S2ST (Speech to Speech Translation) according to the cascade scheme can be used to generate a synthetic parallel corpus of speech of the Kazakh-Uzbek languages. Next, the resulting parallel speech corpus will be used to train the neural model for improving of quality of speech translation.

3 Method

To develop the technology of the speech machine translation of Kazakh-Uzbek according to the cascade scheme for the formation of parallel corpora of Kazakh-Uzbek speech, the following tasks are set in the work:

- development and research of models and algorithms for a cascade scheme for speech machine translation of Kazakh-Uzbek on relational models using the CSE (Complete Set of Endings) morphology model;
- formation of parallel speech corpora using cascade technology of machine translation of Kazakh-Uzbek speech;

The task of developing and researching models and algorithms for a cascade scheme for speech machine translation of Kazakh-Uzbek on relational models will be solved by:

- development of a CSE-model of morphology for Kazakh and Uzbek languages;
- development of relational models, algorithms and programs for machine translation of Kazakh-Uzbek texts;
- selection of speech-to-text recognition tools (STT – Speech-To-Text) for Kazakh;
- selection tools of speech synthesis from text (TTS – Text-To-Speech) for Uzbek;
- development of text-to-text machine translation for Kazakh and Uzbek using relational models.

The task of forming parallel speech corpora using cascade technology of machine translation of Kazakh and Uzbek speech will be solved by:

- selection of the Kazakh language corpus;
- formation of a parallel corpus of speech of the Uzbek languages according to the Kazakh corpus of speech using the constructed cascade scheme of machine translation of speech.

3.1 Development of Linguistic Resources for Kazakh-Uzbek Text-to-Text Machine Translation

The steps for text-to-text machine translation of the Kazakh-Uzbek language pair based on the CSE model are as follows:

1. development of a complete set of endings for Kazakh and Uzbek languages using the CSE morphology model;
2. creation of a morphological analysis of the endings of Kazakh and Uzbek;
3. creation of a correspondence table of Kazakh-Uzbek endings on the base of morphological analysis description of endings;

4. creation of a correspondence table of stem words of the Kazakh-Uzbek languages pair;
5. creation of a correspondence table of stop words of the Kazakh-Uzbek languages pair;
6. creation of an algorithm for machine translation into the Kazakh-Uzbek language based on the CSE model;
7. creation of software based on created algorithms.

The steps listed above are described separately below.

Development the Complete Set of Endings of the Uzbek Language. Let's consider the scheme of derivation of combinations of possible placements of basic affix types on example of nominal words [2]. The set of affixes to the nominal words in the Uzbek language has four types: – plural affixes (denoted by K); – possessive affixes (denoted by T); – case affixes (denoted by C); – personal affixes (denoted by J). The stem will be denoted by S. The number of placements is determined by the formula (1):

$$A_{nk} = n!/(n - k)! \tag{1}$$

Let's look at all possible options for placing suffix types: one type, two types, and three types.

Total possible placement options of one type of endings – 4, two types – 6, three types – 4, four types – 1. Thus, the total number of possible placements of types of nominal words endings are 15. Inferring of complete set of endings of Kazakh is presented in [3]. The Table 1 shows the type and numbers of noun endings in the Uzbek language for one-type endings.

Table 1. Endings of one-type endings.

Suffix type	Suffixes	Number of endings
K	-lar	1
T	-im, m,-ing,-ng, -i, -si, -imiz, -miz, ingiz, -ngiz, – niki	11
C	-ning, -ga, -ka, -qa, -ni, -dan, -da	7
J	-man, -san, -miz, -siz, -dir, -dirlar	6

The placements of two types of endings are (KT, KC, KJ, TC, TJ, and CJ). Consider the endings number of KC placement as example.

Number of endings in KC placement: $K * C = 5$. The inferring of total number of endings of KC placement is given in Table 2.

Three and four affixes type placements of nouns considered in the same way. The number of endings for Uzbek nominal base words – 339.

Inferring of endings for Uzbek verb base words presents below on the example of definite past tense.

O'tgan zamon aniq fe'li (Uzbek name of definite past tense). The definite past tense of verb is formed by adding -di to the stem. An example of the formation of the verb in the definite past tense is shown in Table 3.

Table 2. The number of endings of the KC placement .

Example of stem	Plural	Case	Endings number
kitob(book)-	-lar	-ning, -ga, -ni, -da, -dan	**5**

Table 3. An example of the formation of the verb in the definite past tense.

Examples of stem	Endings	1 person	2 person	2 person (polite)	3 person	Number of endings
kel(come)- uxla(sleep)- yoz(write)-	**-di**	-m -k	-ng -ngiz	-ngiz -ngizlar	- -lar	4 3 4+3=**7**

In addition, in accordance with the tenses of the verbs, the forms of the negative and question were considered.

The number of Uzbek endings for verb words – 295.

The system of participle endings includes the following types: participle's base affixes (R) – 12 (-gan, -qan, -kan, -ayotgan, -yotgan, -adigan, – ydigan, -ar, -r, -mas, -ajak, -mish); case affixes (C); plural affixes (K); personal affixes (J); possessive affixes (T). Then, semantically acceptable affix type's placements are considered. For one type affixes semantically acceptable placements: RK, RT, RC, RJ. From two type affixes semantically acceptable placements: RKT, RTC, RCJ, RKC, RKJ. For three type affixes semantically acceptable placements: RKTC, RKCJ. From four type affixes semantically acceptable placements is zero.

Thus, the quantity of semantically acceptable placements of suffix types of participles is 11. Using the combinatorial procedure for deriving endings described above, below are data on their number for participles and voices.

The number of Uzbek participles endings – 1344. The number of voices endings – 252.

The number of endings for verb base words – 1916.

The total number of endings for Uzbek – 2255.

Creation of Correspondence Tables of Endings, Stems and Stop Words of Kazakh-Uzbek Pair. The creation of correspondence tables of endings, compiled according to the descriptions of the Kazakh and Uzbek morphological analysis is important parts of proposed technology of machine translation on CSE morphology model.

The correspondence table of endings of nominal stems for Kazakh and Uzbek words is presented in Table 4. Since the number of correspondences of endings is large, as an example, we have given a table of correspondences of the plural and possessive endings.

The constructed correspondence table of endings for Kazakh-Uzbek languages pair have 6042 rows, where the Uzbek language endings correspond to the Kazakh endings. The correspondence table of stems for Kazakh-Uzbek languages pair have 20285 words.

Table 4. The correspondence table of Kazakh-Uzbek endings (segment).

Kazakh-endings	Kazakh-morph description	Uzbek-morph description	Uzbek-endings
myn	\<NB\>*myn\<per\>\<sg\>\<p1\>	\<NB\>*man\<per\>\<sg\>\<p1\>	man
byn	\<NB\>*byn\<per\>\<sg\>\<p1\>	\<NB\>*man\<per\>\<sg\>\<p1\>	man
pyn	\<NB\>*pyn\<per\>\<sg\>\<p1\>	\<NB\>*man\<per\>\<sg\>\<p1\>	man
syŋ	\<NB\>*syŋ\<per\>\<sg\>\<p2\>	\<NB\>*san\<per\>\<sg\>\<p2\>	san
syz	\<NB\>*syz\<per\>\<sg\>\<p2\>\<frm\>	\<NB\>*siz\<per\>\<sg\>\<p2\>\<frm\>	siz
mın	\<NB\>*mın\<per\>\<sg\>\<p1\>	\<NB\>*man\<per\>\<sg\>\<p1\>	man
bın	\<NB\>*bın\<per\>\<sg\>\<p1\>	\<NB\>*man\<per\>\<sg\>\<p1\>	man
pın	\<NB\>*pın\<per\>\<sg\>\<p1\>	\<NB\>*man\<per\>\<sg\>\<p1\>	man
sıŋ	\<NB\>*sıŋ\<per\>\<sg\>\<p2\>	\<NB\>*san\<per\>\<sg\>\<p2\>	san
sız	\<NB\>*sız\<per\>\<sg\>\<p2\>\<frm\>	\<NB\>*siz\<per\>\<sg\>\<p2\>\<frm\>	siz
myz	\<NB\>*myz\<per\>\<pl\>\<p1\>	\<NB\>*miz\<per\>\<pl\>\<p1\>	miz
byz	\<NB\>*byz\<per\>\<pl\>\<p1\>	\<NB\>*miz\<per\>\<pl\>\<p1\>	miz
syŋdar	\<NB\>*syŋdar\<per\>\<pl\>\<p2\>	\<NB\>*siz\<per\>\<pl\>\<p2\>	siz
syzdar	\<NB\>*syzdar\<per\>\<pl\>\<p2\>\<frm\>	\<NB\>*sizlar\<per\>\<pl\>\<p2\>\<frm\>	sizlar
mız	\<NB\>*mız\<per\>\<pl\>\<p1\>	\<NB\>*miz\<per\>\<pl\>\<p1\>	miz
bız	\<NB\>*bız\<per\>\<pl\>\<p1\>	\<NB\>*miz\<per\>\<pl\>\<p1\>	miz
sıŋder	\<NB\>*sıŋder\<per\>\<pl\>\<p2\>	\<NB\>*siz\<per\>\<pl\>\<p2\>	siz
sızder	\<NB\>*sızder\<per\>\<pl\>\<p2\>\<frm\>	\<NB\>*sizlar\<per\>\<pl\>\<p2\>\<frm\>	sizlar

The correspondence table of stop words for Kazakh-Uzbek languages pair have 198 words.

For the TTT phase of the proposed cascade technology for machine translation of speech from Kazakh into Uzbek, a universal machine translation program based on the CSE morphology model was used [6, 34].

3.2 Selection of Speech-to-Text Recognition Tool (STT – Speech-To-Text) for the Kazakh Language

In the context of automatic speech recognition, several papers have shown that transformer-based models achieve advanced results on large data sets due to their ability to process long input sequences and take into account the context of the input data [35].

For speech-to-text recognition tools (STT – Speech-To-Text) for the Kazakh language is took a finely tuned model based on a pre-trained wav2vec2-large-xlsr-53 transformer-based model with Connectionist Temporal Classification (CTC) [36]. This model is based on the idea of non-self-guided learning, which means that it is trained on a large amount of unlabeled audio data, rather than labeled data (data with appropriate transcriptions).

The models facebook/wav2vec2-xls-r-300m and facebook/wav2vec2-large-xlsr-53 are both versions of the Wav2vec2 model, but they differ in the amount of data they were trained on and the size of the model.

The facebook/wav2vec2-large-xlsr-53 model was trained on 53,000 hours of audio data and has a model size of about 1.5 GB. This version of the model is considered to be a larger version of the Wav2vec2 models. It is worth noting that the larger the model and the more data it has been trained on, the better its performance is expected, but this also comes at the cost of a larger model and more computational resources required.

3.3 Selection Tool of Speech Synthesis from Text (TTS – Text-To-Speech) for Uzbek

We used TurkicTTS speech synthesis open-source tool [37]. The E2E-TTS models based on the Tacotron 2 [38] and Transformer [39] architectures were built using the ESPnet-TTS toolkit. The LJ Speech recipe was followed, and the latest ESPnet-TTS developments were used to configure the model building recipe. The input for each model is a sequence of characters consisting of 42 letters and 5 symbols, and the output is a sequence of 80-dimensional log Mel-filter bank features. WaveGAN was found to perform best for transforming these acoustic features into time-domain waveform samples and was used in the final E2E-TTS systems. No additional speech preprocessing was applied.

For the Tacotron 2 system, the encoder module was modeled as a single bi-directional LSTM layer with 512 units, while the decoder module was modeled as a stack of two unidirectional LSTM layers with 1,024 units. The parameters were optimized using the Adam algorithm with a dropout rate of 0.5.

The Transformer system was modeled using six encoder and six decoder blocks with the number of heads in the self-attention layer set to 8 with 512-dimension hidden states, and the feed-forward network dimensions set to 1,024. The model parameters were optimized using the Adam algorithm with a dropout rate of 0.1.

Further details on model specifications and training procedures are available in the authors' GitHub repository.

4   Experiments and Results

Initial data, results of the experiment on the proposed technology of speech cascade machine translation of Kazakh into Uzbek and their evaluation are presented in Table 5. The correspondence table of endings for Kazakh-Uzbek languages pair have 6042 rows. The correspondence table of stems for Kazakh-Uzbek languages pair have 20285 words. The correspondence table of stop words for Kazakh-Uzbek languages pair have 198 words.

Four metrics WER, BLEU, TER and chrF2 were used for evaluation using the sacrebleu tool [40]. The wrong recognized and wrong translated words are marked in bold. The words translated by synonyms are in bold and italics.

The first column of Table 5 contains sentences in Kazakh that must be voiced. The second column represents the result of the STT phase of speech recognition. The third column of the table presents the STT phase score for the specified metrics. The fourth column of the table presents the 'gold standard' of sentence translation into Uzbek. The fifth column of the table presents the result of the TTT phase, i.e. machine translation into Uzbek. The last column represents the TTT phase estimate. Google Translate was used to present the English translation of texts in Kazakh and Uzbek. The TTS phase, voicing the translated text into Uzbek, works without errors, but with some emphasis on the pronunciation of Kazakh.

Table 5. Initial data, results of the experiment on the proposed technology of speech cascade machine translation of Kazakh into Uzbek and their evaluation.

Qazaq (source text for speech)	audio recognition	Qazaq STT estimation	Uzbek (gold standard)	Uzbek machine translation	Uzbek machine translation estimation
Мен шай ішкенді жақсы көремін (I like to drink tea)	мен шай ішкенді жақсы көремін (I like to drink tea)	WER: 0.00 BLEU: 100.00 TER: 0.00 chrF2: 100.00	Men choy ichishni yaxshi ko'raman (I like to drink tea)	men choy *ichishkanni* yaxshi ko'raman (I like to drink tea)	WER: 9.09 BLEU: 30.21 TER: 20.00 chrF2: 88.12
Ол университетте француз тілін үйренуде (He is studying French at university)	ол университетте француз тілін үйренуде (he is studying French at university)	WER: 0.00 BLEU: 100.00 TER: 0.00 chrF2: 100.00	U universitetda fransuz tilini o'rganmoqda.(He is studying French at university)	u universitetda fransuz tilini *o'rganishda* (he is studying French at university)	WER: 9.52 BLEU: 39.76 TER: 20.00 chrF2: 84.39
Олар қазір кино тамашалауда (They are watching a movie now)	олар қазір кино тамашалау-да (They are watching a movie now)	WER: 0.00 BLEU: 100.00 TER: 0.00 chrF2: 100.00	Ular hozir kino tomosha qilishmoqda. (They are watching a movie now)	ular hozir kino tomosha qilishmoqda (They are watching a movie now)	WER: 0.00 BLEU: 100.00 TER: 0.00 chrF2: 100.00
Менің сүйікті түсім көк (My favorite color is blue)	менің **сүйікі** түсім көк (My favorite color is blue)	WER: 8.70 BLEU: 31.95 TER: 25.00 chrF2: 73.91	Mening sevimli rangim ko'k. (My favorite color is blue)	mening сүйікі rangim ko'k (My favorite color is blue)	WER: 23.08 BLEU: 35.36 TER: 25.00 chrF2: 58.10
Ол бос уақытында кітап оқуды жақсы көреді (He likes to read in his spare time)	ол бос уақытында кітап оқуды жақсы көреді (He likes to read in his spare time)	WER: 0.00 BLEU: 100.00 TER: 0.00 chrF2: 100.00	U bo'sh vaqtlarida kitob o'qishni yaxshi ko'radi. (He likes to read in his spare time)	u bo'sh vaqtlarida kitob *o'qishmoqda* yaxshi ko'radi (He likes to read in his spare time)	WER: 14.29 BLEU: 37.68 TER: 28.57 chrF2: 77.06

(*continued*)

Table 5. (*continued*)

Qazaq (source text for speech)	audio recognition	Qazaq STT estimation	Uzbek (gold standard)	Uzbek machine translation	Uzbek machine translation estimation
Ол орта мектепте мұғалім болып істейді (He works as a teacher in high school)	ол орта мектепте мұғалім болып істейді (He works as a teacher in high school)	WER: 0.00 BLEU: 100.00 TER: 0.00 chrF2: 100.00	U o'rta maktabda o'qituvchi bo'lib ishlaydi. (He works as a teacher in high school)	u o'rta maktabda o'qituvchi bo'lib ishlaydi (He works as a teacher in high school)	WER: 0.00 BLEU: 100.00 TER: 0.00 chrF2: 100.00
Біз өткен жылы парижге бардық (We went to Paris last year)	біз өткен жылы парижге бардық (We went to Paris last year)	WER: 0.00 BLEU: 100.00 TER: 0.00 chrF2: 100.00	Biz o'tkan yili Parijga borgan **edik**. (We went to Paris last year)	biz o'tgan yili parijga bordik (We went to Paris last year)	WER: 17.14 BLEU: 19.36 TER: 50.00 chrF2: 68.39
Олар келесі айда Африкаға саяхат қылуды жоспарлауда (They are planning a trip to Africa next month)	олар келесі айда африкаға саяхат қылуды жоспарлауда (They are planning a trip to Africa next month)	WER: 0.00 BLEU: 100.00 TER: 0.00 chrF2: 100.00	Ular kelasi oy Afrikaga sayohat qilishni rejalashtirmoqda. (They are planning a trip to Africa next month)	ular **keyingisi oyda** afrikaga sayohat qilishni **rejaishmoqda** (They are planning a trip to Africa next month)	WER: 21.05 BLEU: 26.27 TER: 42.86 chrF2: 67.29
Тыныш теңізге жылы алтын нұрын шашып, күн көкжиектен баяу батты (The sun slowly sank below the horizon, casting a warm golden light on the calm sea)	тыныш теңізге жылы алтын мұрын ша шып күн көпжеектен баяу батты (The sun slowly sank below the horizon, casting a warm golden light on the calm sea)	WER: 9.52 BLEU: 18.36 TER: 40.00 chrF2: 74.02	Sokin dengizga iliq oltin nurin sochip quyosh ufq ostida asta-sekin botdi. (The sun slowly sank below the horizon, casting a warm golden light on the calm sea)	sokin dengizga **yili** oltin **burun** ша шып kun көпжеек**dan** astasekin botdi (The sun slowly sank below the horizon, casting a warm golden light on the calm sea)	WER: 32.88 BLEU: 11.21 TER: 54.55 chrF2: 46.93

5 Discussion

An assessment was made of the influence of the phases of machine translation of speech on the result. The total number of words in the Kazakh text is 73. The total number of erroneous words in machine translation into Uzbek is 14. In the STT phase, the number of erroneous words is 6. In the TTT phase, the number of erroneous words is 8. In the TTS phase, the number of erroneous words is 0. The percentage of errors for the STT phase will be $6/73 = 8\%$, for the TTT phase it will be $8/73 = 10\%$. Influence (percentage) of speech translation phases on the overall quality: STT – $6/14 = 42\%$; TTT- $8/14 = 58\%$; TTS – $0/14 = 0\%$.

An analysis of STT phase errors shows that word errors occur due to errors in the recognition of individual phonemes in words. Analysis of TTT phase errors shows that out of 10 erroneous words, eight words are synonyms, so we can assume that there are only two real errors. That shows what in the speech translation there are some errors in the STT phase that not translated in the TTT phase and negative influence on the common result. Average scores for the text of the experiment: WER: 15.98; BLUE: 47.23; TER: 27.30; chrF2: 75.43.

In general, judging by the estimates, the quality of speech translation from Kazakh to Uzbek using the proposed technology seems good.

6 Conclusion

The paper considers the possibility of forming parallel speech corpora for low-resource languages of the Turkic group according to a cascade scheme, where the TTT phase uses the technology of relational models based on the CSE morphology model that does not require parallel corpora. The proposed technology is shown on the example of the Kazakh-Uzbek pair of languages. The results of experiments on machine translation of speech from Kazakh to Uzbek show a good level, which allows us to hope for the formation of synthetic parallel speech corpora for future training of neural models. At the same time, there are issues that need to be addressed to improve the quality of translation, namely, the issue of choosing the right stem when there are several translation options in the table of stems for the target language. Further work is related to increasing the number of stems, to solving the issue of choosing the most appropriate stem for translation, the generation of synthetic parallel speech corpora for the Kazakh-Uzbek pair and using them to train neural models of speech translation for these languages for improving of speech translation quality, as well using this technology for other low-resource languages of the Turkic group.

References

1. Koehn, P., Knowles, R.: Six challenges for neural machine translation. In: Proceedings of the First Workshop on Neural Machine Translation, pp. 28–39, Vancouver, Canada (2017)
2. Tukeyev, U.: Automaton models of the morphology analysis and the completeness of the endings of the Kazakh language. In: Proceedings of the international conference "Turkic languages processing" TURKLANG-2015 September 17–19, pp. 91–100. Kazan, Tatarstan, Russia (2015). (in Russian)
3. Tukeyev, U., Karibayeva, Ai.: Inferring the complete set of Kazakh endings as a language resource. In: Hernes, M., Wojtkiewicz, K., Szczerbicki, E. (eds.) Advances in Computational Collective Intelligence: 12th International Conference, ICCCI 2020, Da Nang, Vietnam, 30 Nov–3 Dec 2020, Proceedings, pp. 741–751. Springer International Publishing, Cham (2020). https://doi.org/10.1007/978-3-030-63119-2_60
4. Tukeyev, U., Sundetova, A., Abduali, B., Akhmadiyeva, Z., Zhanbussunov, N.: Inferring of the morphological chunk transfer rules on the base of complete set of Kazakh endings. In: Nguyen, N.-T., Manolopoulos, Y., Iliadis, L., Trawiński, B. (eds.) ICCCI 2016. LNCS (LNAI), vol. 9876, pp. 563–574. Springer, Cham (2016). https://doi.org/10.1007/978-3-319-45246-3_54
5. Tukeyev, U., Karibayeva, A., Zhumanov, Z.: Morphological segmentation method for Turkic language neural machine translation. Cogent Eng. 7(1), 1856500 (2020). https://doi.org/10.1080/23311916.2020.1856500

6. Tukeyev, U., Karibayeva, A., Turganbayeva, A., Amirova, D.: Universal programs for stemming, segmentation, morphological analysis of Turkic words. In: Thanh Nguyen, N., Iliadis, L., Maglogiannis, I., Trawiński, B. (eds.) Computational Collective Intelligence: 13th International Conference, ICCCI 2021, Rhodes, Greece, September 29 – October 1, 2021, Proceedings, pp. 643–654. Springer International Publishing, Cham (2021). https://doi.org/10.1007/978-3-030-88081-1_48

7. Matlatipov, S., Tukeyev, U., Aripov, M.: Towards the uzbek language endings as a language resource. In: Hernes, M., Wojtkiewicz, K., Szczerbicki, E. (eds.) Advances in Computational Collective Intelligence: 12th International Conference, ICCCI 2020, Da Nang, Vietnam, 30 Nov–3 Dec 2020, Proceedings, pp. 729–740. Springer International Publishing, Cham (2020). https://doi.org/10.1007/978-3-030-63119-2_59

8. Toleush, A., Israilova, N., Tukeyev, U.: Development of morphological segmentation for the kyrgyz language on complete set of endings. In: Nguyen, N.T., Chittayasothorn, S., Niyato, D., Trawiński, B. (eds.) Intelligent Information and Database Systems: 13th Asian Conference, ACIIDS 2021, Phuket, Thailand, 7–10 Apr 2021, Proceedings, pp. 327–339. Springer International Publishing, Cham (2021). https://doi.org/10.1007/978-3-030-73280-6_26

9. Qamet, A., Zhakypbayeva, K., Turganbayeva, A., Tukeyev, U.: Development Kazakh-Turkish machine translation on the base of complete set of endings model. In: Szczerbicki, E., Wojtkiewicz, K., Van Nguyen, S., Pietranik, M., Krótkiewicz, M. (eds.) Recent Challenges in Intelligent Information and Database Systems: 14th Asian Conference, ACIIDS 2022, Ho Chi Minh City, Vietnam, 28–30 Nov 2022, Proceedings, pp. 543–555. Springer Nature Singapore, Singapore (2022). https://doi.org/10.1007/978-981-19-8234-7_42

10. Lavie, A., et al.: JANUS-III: Speech-to-speech translation in multiple languages. In: Proceedings of the ICASSP 1997 (1997)

11. Wahlster, W. (ed.): Verbmobil: Foundations of Speech-to-Speech Translation. Springer, Berlin, Heidelberg (2000)

12. Nakamura, S., et al.: The ATR multilingual speech-to-speech translation system. IEEE Trans. Audio Speech Language Process. **14**(2), 365–376 (2006)

13. Guo, M., Haque, A., Verma, P.: End-to-end spoken language translation, arXiv preprint arXiv: 1904.10760 (2019)

14. Jia, Y., et al.: Direct speech-to-speech translation with a sequence-to-sequence model arXiv: 1904.06037v2 (2019)

15. Papi, S., Gaido, M., Negri, M., Turchi, M.: Speechformer: Reducing Information Loss in Direct Speech Translation arXiv:2109.04574v1 (2021)

16. Kano, T., Sakti, S., Nakamura, S.: Transformer-based direct speech-to-speech translation with transcoder. In: 2021 IEEE Spoken Language Technology Workshop (SLT), pp. 958–965. IEEE (2021)

17. Papi, S., Gaido, M., Karakanta, A., Cettolo, M., Negri, M., Turchi, M.: Direct Speech Translation for Automatic Subtitling. CoRR abs/2209.13192 (2022)

18. Bentivogli, L., et al.: Cascade versus Direct Speech Translation: Do the Differences Still Make a Difference? ACL/IJCNLP (1) 2021, pp. 2873–2887 (2021)

19. Niehues, J., Salesky, E., Turchi, M., Negri, M.: Tutorial Proposal: End-to-End Speech Translation. EACL (Tutorial Abstracts) 2021, pp. 10–13 (2021)

20. Wang, C., et al.: Simple and Effective Unsupervised Speech Translation. arXiv:2210.10191v1 [cs.CL] (2022)

21. Bansal, S., Kamper, H., Livescu, K., Lopez, A., Goldwater, S.: Low resource speech-to-text translation. Proc. Interspeech **2018**, 1298–1302 (2018)

22. Bansal, S., Kamper, H., Livescu, K., Lopez, A., Goldwater, S.: Pretraining on high-resource speech recognition improves low-resource speech-to-text translation. In: Proceedings of the 2019 Conference of the North American Chapter of the Association for Computational Linguistics: Human Language Technologies, vol. 1 (Long and Short Papers), pp. 58–68 (2019)

23. Cheng, Y.-F., Hung-Shin Lee, H.-S., Wang, H.-M.: AlloST: Low-Resource Speech Translation Without Source Transcription. In: Proceedings of the Interspeech 2021, pp. 2252–2256 (2021)
24. Chung, Y.-A., Weng, W.-H., Tong, S., James Glass, J.: Towards unsupervised speech-to-text translation. In: ICASSP 2019-2019 IEEE International Conference on Acoustics, Speech and Signal Processing (ICASSP), pp. 7170–7174. IEEE (2019)
25. Karakanta, A., Negri, M., Turchi, M.: MuST-Cinema: a Speech-to-Subtitles corpus. LREC 2020, pp. 3727–3734 (2020)
26. Jia, Y., Ramanovich, M.T., Wang, Q., Zen, H.: Cvss corpus and massively multilingual speech-to-speech translation. arXiv preprint arXiv:2201.03713 (2022)
27. Bentivogli, L., Mauro, C., Marco, G., Alina, K., Matteo, N., Marco, T.: Extending the MuST-C Corpus for a Comparative Evaluation of Speech Translation Technology. EAMT 2022, pp. 359–360 (2022)
28. Musaev, M., Mussakhojayeva, S., Khujayorov, I., Khassanov, Y., Ochilov, M., Varol, H.A.: USC: An Open-Source Uzbek Speech Corpus and Initial Speech Recognition Experiments. In: Karpov, A., Potapova, R. (eds.) SPECOM 2021. LNCS (LNAI), vol. 12997, pp. 437–447. Springer, Cham (2021). https://doi.org/10.1007/978-3-030-87802-3_40
29. Mussakhojayeva, S., Janaliyeva, A., Mirzakhmetov, A., Khassanov, Y., Varol, H.A.: KazakhTTS: an open-source kazakh text-to-speech synthesis dataset. In: Proceedings of the Interspeech 2021, pp. 2786–2790. https://doi.org/10.21437/Interspeech.2021-2124Open-Source Kazakh Text-to-Speech Synthesis Dataset. arXiv preprint arXiv:2104.08459 (2021)
30. Mamyrbayev, O., Alimhan, K., Zhumazhanov, B., Turdalykyzy, T., Gusmanova, F.: End-to-End Speech Recognition in Agglutinative Languages. In: Nguyen, N.T., Jearanaitanakij, K., Selamat, A., Trawiński, B., Chittayasothorn, S. (eds.) ACIIDS 2020. LNCS (LNAI), vol. 12034, pp. 391–401. Springer, Cham (2020). https://doi.org/10.1007/978-3-030-42058-1_33
31. Mamyrbayev, O., Alimhan, K., Oralbekova, D., Bekarystankyzy A., Zhumazhanov, B.: Identifying the influence of transfer learning methods in developing an end-to-end automatic speech recognition system with a low data level. Eastern-European J. Enterprise Technol. 1(9(115)), 84–92 (2022). https://doi.org/10.15587/1729-4061.2022.252801
32. Мамырбаев, О.Ж., Оралбекова, Д.О., Алимхан, К., Othman, M., Жумажанов, Б.: Применение гибридной интегральной модели для распознавания казахской речи. News of the National academy of sciences of the republic of Kazakhstan. 1(341), 58–68 (2022). https://doi.org/10.32014/2022.2518-1726.117
33. Khassanov, Y., Mussakhojayeva, S., Mirzakhmetov, A., Adiyev, A., Nurpeiissov, M., Varol, H.A.: A crowdsourced open-source Kazakh speech corpus and initial speech recognition baseline. In: Proceedings of the 16th Conference of the European Chapter of the Association for Computational Linguistics: Main Volume, pp. 697–706. Association for Computational Linguistics (2021). https://issai.nu.edu.kz/ru/%d0%b3%d0%bb%d0%b0%d0%b2%d0%bd%d0%b0%d1%8f/#research
34. NLP-KAZNU/Kazakh-Uzbek machine translation. https://github.com/NLP-KazNU/Kazakh-Uzbek-machine-translation-on-the-base-of-CSE-model. Access date: 1 Mar 2023
35. Wolf, T., et al.: HuggingFace's Transformers: State-of-the-art Natural Language Processing. arXiv (2020). https://doi.org/10.48550/arXiv.1910.03771
36. Baevski, A., Zhou H., Mohamed A., Auli, M.: wav2vec 2.0: A Framework for Self-Supervised Learning of Speech Representations. arXiv (2020). https://doi.org/10.48550/arXiv.2006.11477
37. Mussakhojayeva, S., Janaliyeva, A., Mirzakhmetov, A., Khassanov, Y., Varol, H.A.: KazakhTTS: An Open-Source Kazakh Text-to-Speech Synthesis Dataset. arXiv:2104.08459v3 [eess.AS] (2021)
38. Shen, J., et al.: Natural TTS synthesis by conditioning Wavenet on MEL spectrogram predictions. In: Proceedings of the IEEE International Conference on Acoustics, Speech and Signal Processing (ICASSP), pp. 4779–4783. IEEE (2018)

39. Li, N., Liu, S., Liu, Y., Zhao, S., Liu, M.: Neural speech synthesis with transformer network. Proc. AAAI Conf. Artif. Intell. **33**(01), 6706–6713 (2019). https://doi.org/10.1609/aaai.v33 i01.33016706
40. Sacrebleu: https://github.com/mjpost/sacrebleu. Access date 1 Mar 2023

Cybersecurity and Internet of Things

Human-Related Security Threats and Countermeasures of Electronic Banking and Identity Services - Polish Case Study

Wojciech Wodo[1(✉)] and Natalia Kuźma[2]

[1] Wroclaw University of Science and Technology, Wybrzeze Wyspianskiego 27,
50-370 Wroclaw, Poland
wojciech.wodo@pwr.edu.pl
[2] 360 Degrees ltd., Sienkiewicza 111/13, 50-346 Wroclaw, Poland
natalia@360degrees.pl

Abstract. The paper is a synthesis of findings on the financial sector's cybersecurity analysis and e-identity management from the perspective of human-related vulnerabilities. Extensive desk research was conducted to gain a complete picture of the coexisting digital services and their relationship. Based on that, we defined challenges and synthesized our observations, identifying the most severe security risks associated with digital banking and identity services. Our study points out that human errors are the weakest link in the security chain. COVID-19 has accelerated the development of the digital revolution, thus forcing users to use digital services with greater commitment. The acceleration of digital transformation has not been indifferent to hackers, who have quickly adapted to the changing environment. Thus, the risk of exposing inexperienced users to cyberattacks has increased. Human-led attacks, based on naivety, emotion, and lack of relevant knowledge, have posed the most significant threat. Adversaries skillfully maneuver between the offline and online worlds by using fake IDs and sending fake emails. Only proactive countermeasures can stop attacks. Using our expertise, we identified best practices and defined recommendations for the issues discussed, which is our most significant contribution to this study.

Keywords: banking · electronic banking · human factor · security · threats · cybersecurity · countermeasures

1 Introduction

Due to the digital revolution and the COVID-19 epidemic, new inexperienced people have begun using digital banking services, different mechanisms for identification or authorization, and trust services for electronic identity [8].

Many companies developed security policies and were able to assess the risks associated with cyberattacks in the workplace. However, the COVID-19 pandemic significantly accelerated the inevitable process of digital transformation

© The Author(s), under exclusive license to Springer Nature Switzerland AG 2023
N. T. Nguyen et al. (Eds.): ICCCI 2023, CCIS 1864, pp. 445–458, 2023.
https://doi.org/10.1007/978-3-031-41774-0_35

[2]. Employees who previously only worked from the office started working from their homes overnight. Most employers and employees focused on adapting processes to the new realities quickly and efficiently, thus creating new opportunities for cybercriminals. In April 2020, as many as 94% of all cyberattacks were phishing attacks (sent emails with attachments linked to "COVID-19", creation of new pages linked to the topic "Coronavirus"). From January to March 2020, more than 50,000 domains linked to COVID-19 were registered[1].

In this paper, we have focused on users, who are the weakest point of even the best-protected systems. Inexperienced users put their and their loved ones' data at risk of being leaked. A growing number of social engineering attacks like phishing and smishing rely on human weaknesses, making them highly effective.

Social engineering attacks target various social groups. Attackers aim both top managers and average employees, each time the effectiveness of attacks can be equally high because the level of intelligence or skills of a victim does not determine the success of an attack, but primary emotions like fear, happiness, and excitement. As a result, users often make irrational decisions like clicking a dangerous link or transferring money to a suspicious account. Attackers skillfully maneuver between online and offline worlds and exploit users' gullibility.

1.1 Motivation and Contribution

We considered the comprehensive ecosystem of digital services, including identity management, modern banking, and user awareness level, and analyzed them from a cybersecurity perspective. Extensive desk research was performed to get the whole image of the co-existing digital services and relationships among them. Based on various cited reports, legal acts, scientific and industrial papers, we defined challenges and synthesized our remarks by identifying the most severe security threats associated with digital banking and identity services.

Using our expert knowledge, we have identified *good practices* and defined *recommendations* to the particular discussed issues, which constitutes our most essential contribution to this paper.

Many issues associated with the scope of this paper are elaborated based on their current status in Poland as a case study. However, the outcomes impact is more powerful and applies mainly to the European countries, as they are very similar to Poland in many described regards, face the same challenges, and are subject to the same regulations and directives of the EU.

2 Human Factor as a Fundamental Security Threat

Fatigue, poor management, lack of tools and competencies to effectively verify identity documents and assess the compatibility of the person holding the document with the document itself, as well as the infiltration of the adversary into

---

[1] https://securityboulevard.com/2020/04/phishing-statistics-the-29-latest-phishing-stats-to-know-in-2020/.

the units performing identity confirmation, are proven to be some of the most severe security threats we face.

The digital world is evolving at an express pace. Unfortunately, even the best network security is not enough if an adversary shows up at the time of the initial identity verification. Officials who issue primary identity documents are a sensitive part of the process. It is on them to verify the accuracy and authenticity of the data provided and to confirm whether the person applying for an ID card or other document is the person standing in front of them.

Suppose a deliberately substituted official confirms a false identity and allows the issuance of primary documents on these data. In that case, such a document will be registered as a legitimate document in official databases. What follows at further stages will be a confirmation of a reliable identity, based on which the adversary will be able to carry out transactions, conclude contracts or produce other documents.

In many places, proof of identity is provided by primary documents such as an ID card or passport. There are companies that sell these documents as collectibles[2], which are confusingly similar to actual documents. An employee responsible for confirming the credibility of individuals states a critical security point of the system. If one confirms the identity based on a forged document will expose the system to severe danger. Fictitious identities are created based on forged documents[3]

Good Practice: In Poland, a register of public documents has been created[4], which is available from mid-2020 and allows verification of the authenticity of the presented data. It contains templates of currently valid documents and descriptions of security elements, both visible in visible light and ultraviolet light. The establishment of the register is an attempt to mitigate the risk related to incorrect confirmation of the authenticity of a forged document. It is a step in a good direction. However, without sufficient education in that field, it may turn out to be insufficient.

A serious risk is the lack of appropriate tools and competence to effectively verify identity documents and assess the conformity of the person holding the document with the document itself. Reasons for incorrect verification may be due to many reasons, such as the crowd of customers, poor attention to the employee, or fatigue. Employees are an essential part of the security chain, so it is worth emphasizing the importance of raising the competence of persons verifying identity documents and providing them with appropriate tools to reduce the possibility of error. Even a person who knows how to distinguish an authentic document from a fake one "by eye" may make a mistake due to fatigue.

---

[2] https://dokumencik.com.pl/.

[3] https://www.gov.pl/web/mswia/mozna-juz-korzystac-z-rejestru-dokumentow-publicznych.

[4] https://www.gov.pl/app/rdp/.

Good Practice: The EU Regulation no 2019/1157[5] is one of the ways to mitigate the risks of creating a false identity. Introducing ID cards with an electronic layer and biometric features allows linking the identity appearing on the documents to an existing natural person.

Recommendation: The recommended action is to spread knowledge about publicly available tools for verifying the authenticity of primary identity documents. Another action should be disseminating tools to allow verification of these documents, which will exclude human error. In particular, attention should be paid to the functionalities offered by the new electronic ID card - checking the correctness and integrity of data using a secure cryptographic protocol (including the possibility of comparing biometrics) and confirming the presence or personal signature. However, relevant institutions must be equipped with appropriate readers and trained staff to use these functions.

Businesses and banks are attractive targets for cybercriminals. In 2018, as many as 70% of the companies surveyed in the KPMG *Cyber Security Barometer* [7] reported at least one cyber incident. Interestingly, the human factor is the biggest challenge for companies (63%), the lack of adequate cyber security competence is a bigger problem than too little budget [7]. According to another report - *Cyber Security - Trends 2019*, employee mistakes or recklessness was the leading cause of company data leaks (48%) [16].

Employee training on cyber security and data protection is the most neglected component of many companies' cyber security policies [16]. Without the right level of education, regular training, and improving employee competency in this area, human error will always be the weakest link in the security chain [16].

Good Practice: Republic of Poland governmental website[6] provides instructions for a three-step verification of the authenticity of the mObywatel application. The verification was divided into three sections - visual, functional, and cryptographic. The detailed instruction and indication of crucial elements of the application are excellent help for the verifier.

There is an urgent need to prepare for man-made cyber threats. According to the *Cybersecurity: The Human Challenge* report [12], there is an increased awareness level among employers related to the human factor in the cybersecurity process. 48% of the respondents have implemented policies into their security procedures, considering threats resulting from user activity, and another 48% plan to implement them within a year.

Improving cybersecurity requires competent professionals, their knowledge and skills directly affect the protection of systems. According to the survey [12], 27% of managers said that finding and retaining qualified IT security experts is the biggest challenge for them, affecting the ability of companies to ensure the security of systems. At the same time, 54% addressed this criterion as one of the main challenges.

---

[5] https://eur-lex.europa.eu/legal-content/EN/TXT/PDF/?uri=CELEX: 32019R1157&from=EN.

[6] https://www.gov.pl/web/mobywatel/zabezpieczenia1.

Recommendation: We should define new competencies of a human of the future, or maybe already a human of the present (a human functioning in the space of two worlds: real and cyber). The set of these competencies will include, among others, navigating the digital world and using its services in an aware and safe way [10].

3   Inadequate or No User Education

The pace of implementation of new technologies is much faster than the development of methods to secure data online. It needs to be reflected in information and education campaigns to ensure the safe and informed use of digital services. The growing number of mobile banking users is accelerating the growth and effectiveness of cyber attacks. With the rise in popularity of digital banking come new challenges in the area of cyber security [10].

Users' level of knowledge and competence translates directly into how they act in the digital world. Therefore, it is fundamental to educate users about cybersecurity. According to the *CyberLabs* report [1], there are many areas for improvement in the way IT professionals are taught and in the knowledge, they are given. The basis of learning about cybersecurity is practical knowledge, a holistic approach to the topics discussed and continuous updating of the knowledge transferred by academics.

Cyber security subjects should appear in all universities (not only technical), thus raising the level of knowledge of all network users [1]. For many years, computer literacy has been an essential requirement for most jobs. Digital transformation concerns all areas (law, medicine, business, etc.), with the level of education of future users not changing adequately to their needs, especially in terms of potential risks and threats.

The study *Security of electronic and mobile banking systems in Poland. User Survey 2019* [15] shows that most people feel safe using mobile banking services. Most people have heard of cyber attacks and consider them dangerous, but their other responses indicate insufficient knowledge about cyber threats. Additionally, many recipients are unconcerned about potential attacks, claiming that the problem does not affect them. Users claim that their accounts are adequately secured or indicate that they do not have enough cash to be an attractive target for an attacker.

The low level of citizens' awareness regarding the possibility of using (secure) public digital solutions is evidenced, among other things, by the responses from the report [15]. Most of the respondents (64.5%) do not use the services of the ePUAP platform (Polish governmental e-services platform), and almost half of them (27.4% of the total) do not know what the platform is used for. The low use of public solutions is primarily insufficient education of citizens, which results in a lack of trust in this solution.

The demand for cybersecurity positions and competencies will increase in the near future [13]. In order to bridge the competency gap, employees should be familiarized with the company's security and data protection policies and trained in the basics of mitigating the risk of attacks [16].

Good Practice: Due to the current trends of digitalization and the transfer of digital banking services to the network, the number of attacks in this particularly attractive sector, is increasing. Therefore, the Polish Banks Association (ZBP) Qualification Standard was developed to respond to the need to improve the competence of financial services employees, an important element of which is strengthening the security of the financial system in Poland [9]. The qualification defines four key areas related to basic knowledge of data and identity protection, detecting cyber attacks, and responding skillfully when they occur. The ZBP standard focuses on employees in the financial services industry. However, it could be implemented in other industries as well. The scope covered by this qualification standard would also need to be monitored on an ongoing basis and updated periodically.

4   Digital Transformation, User Perceptions, Cultural Constraints, Naivety, and Social Engineering

Hacker attacks also affect individuals unaware of online threats and do not know how to secure their digital identities. As a result, they do not pay attention to their online security or think they are not at risk. Users lack awareness of how hacking attacks take place, and they do not realize that they are not targeted but automated based on phishing and installation of malware on victims' devices [15].

Attackers looking for ways to bypass security measures or obtain relevant information do not target only weak points of systems but also decide to attack users. Sociotechnique in cybersecurity means a set of psychological actions aimed at a group or individuals. In cybersecurity, the human factor is assumed to be the strongest and weakest element in the security chain. Numerous cybercriminals exploit the weakness of this element, and they design their attacks to take advantage of user mistakes. Such adversaries have been called social engineers, and the type of attacks they use - are social engineering attacks.

Phishing is one of the categorized attack methods, an attempt to fake a website or send a fake email resembling a message from a known or trusted service. The attacker uses people's unawareness of the threat to influence the victim by evoking extreme emotions (fear, curiosity etc.). Such an attack usually aims to persuade the victim to download a dangerous attachment, click on a link, or provide personal details.

Phishing is one of the biggest computer security threats for individual users, companies, and government entities. Phishing accounts for 77% of all social engineering attacks. The scale of danger resulting from phishing attacks is shown by the data concerning sending emails. It is estimated that worldwide, 294 billion emails are sent daily. Alarmingly, according to Social Engineer organization[7], as much as 90% of all sent emails are spam and malware.

A notification about the possibility of blocking an account, a letter from the bank about running out of funds in an account, or information about a

---

[7] https://www.social-engineer.org/resources/social-engineering-infographic/.

problem with a delivery from a courier company are all messages that many people receive. The success of phishing attacks is based on targeting these types of messages when users are less vigilant, which makes them forget about security rules and become careless.

In addition to the aforementioned sociotechnical reasons, the success of these attacks is often based on ignorance and low awareness of the threats of those who have access to sensitive data. In 2019, as many as 88% of organizations reported Spear Phishing attacks[8].

Good Practices: ZBP guide for digital banking users with basic security principles[9].

Recommendation: Practical educational campaigns with a psychological impact should be developed in response to this challenge. Such activities can be implemented through a tool to conduct simulated sociotechnical attacks based on phishing together with educational content. The basis of this solution should be to determine the level of awareness and competence of employees (users of digital banking services) in social engineering attacks. Based on the research outcomes, effective ways of informing about the conducted attacks and potential threats should be developed, combined with effective user education.

Most people have never experienced a hacking attack and therefore have no idea what emotions are involved. Lack of awareness about cyber security is partly due to a lack of understanding of the consequences of an attack and the associated emotions. Simulating a social engineering attack in a controlled environment is supposed to be a kind of shock associated with emotional stress, which will allow us to effectively assimilate the information, understand what the attack is and what emotions are experienced by the victim of a social engineering attack.

Even before the COVID-19 pandemic, many solutions were created to prepare citizens and institutions for digital transformation. For this purpose, trust services were created, operating under the European Parliament Regulation 910/2014 on eIDAS [4]. Some citizens used a trusted profile, and some institutions used electronic signatures. However, the current situation has accelerated the slow transformation triggering a kind of digital revolution. The COVID-19 pandemic highlights some shortcomings and errors. An example is the electronic document workflow, which was used inside one company but was not adapted to securely exchange documentation with other business entities [8].

Qualified electronic signatures are known to entrepreneurs, but their potential is not yet used. There are only 600 thousand qualified certificates registered in Poland, which, compared to issued credit cards (43 million units), is not a large number [8]. It is worth noting that over a period of 12 months (June 2019-June 2020), the number of issued certificates increased by one hundred thousand, that is, by as much as 17% [8]. Interest in digital tools has increased this year;

---

[8] https://securityboulevard.com/2020/04/phishing-statistics-the-29-latest-phishing-stats-to-know-in-2020/.

[9] https://zbp.pl/dla-klientow/bezpieczne-bankowanie/bankowosc-internetowa.

for example, usage of the mobile qualified electronic signature tool was as much as 600% higher than last year at the same time.

The year 2020 positively influenced the development of other related tools, i.e. signature platforms that secure the entire process of the electronic signature of documents. According to the Executive Vice President of Autenti [8], e-signature has become an essential tool for business. Only in March and April 2020, the interest in this solution quadrupled.

Businesses use qualified signatures mainly for administrative activities, with less than 50% planning to use them during the transformation process. From this, it follows that trust services are not (yet) a widely used solution. According to the *Trusted Economy* report [8], these services should be more easily integrated with companies' existing IT solutions, take into account the ergonomics of use and be cheap enough to dramatically increase the availability of their applications.

The limitation of using the mentioned solutions is the lack of reliable knowledge and verification of legal requirements by entrepreneurs [8]. Citizens of Poland, out of habit, assume that a paper signature will be required, even when it is not legally specified. On the other hand, this is not surprising since electronic document circulation does not inspire trust and is not a popular solution, especially in the public sector. This should indicate the potential of using trust services, thus encouraging citizens to get acquainted with their possibilities. Lack of trust or fear regarding electronic versions of documents is largely due to low levels of education in this regard.

Recommendation: The recommended action should be the development of publicly available and presented accessible form information campaigns on trusted services. There is an information gap in the Polish market regarding common knowledge of the tools mentioned above; consequently, few potential users decide to use them.

Good Practice: Another example of exciting solutions available on the Polish market is the eDO application, which facilitates the use of e-card[10]. The application allows eID-card holders to confirm their identity, enable signature or sign their own documents. Unfortunately, the application is not yet a popular solution; by June 2020, more than 3 million citizens had received their eIDs, of which more than 1 million had activated the new document, allowing them to use its electronic layer[11]. Currently, out of all e-card users, only more than 100,000 have downloaded eDo to their phone[12].

Recommendation: More e-signature platforms like Autenti[13] should be developed to secure the process of signing electronic documents and exchanging e-documents (EDI). The purpose of these platforms is to facilitate and secure the process of electronic document exchange. Their advantage is the generation of a digital trail documenting the whole process. An electronic time stamp or an

---

[10] https://www.edoapp.pl/.

[11] https://www.gov.pl/web/cyfryzacja/e-dowod-w-dloni-edo-app-w-telefonie.

[12] https://play.google.com/store/apps/details?id=pl.pwpw.edohub&hl=pl&gl=US.

[13] https://autenti.com/.

electronic seal authenticates the issued document and protects it against possible changes/attacks.

Good Practice: For the duration of the COVID-19 pandemic, the Ministry of Digitization launched a temporary Trusted Profile service that allows all interested parties to handle official matters online. Previously, a personal visit to a confirmation point was required to set up a Trusted Profile. Currently, the online Trusted Profile can be set up for a limited period of time, i.e. three months. One of the steps of setting up the trusted profile online is video verification, i.e. a conversation with an official. The pandemic period has increased the interest of Poles in the trusted profile. Only this year, almost 1,600,000 people have set up a trusted profile[14].

5   Legal and Regulatory Issues

During the FinTech industry development conference at the UKNF headquarters[15], a live survey on the barriers to growth in the financial market was conducted. The most significant barriers were considered to be "paper forms", "unclear and excessive regulations", "time of proceedings" and "changing guidelines". It is worth noting that paper forms were indicated as a greater barrier than, for example, lack of capital. The indicated barriers emphasize the need for efficient digitalization and, above all, the need to normalize the intricate legal aspects.

UKNF also published an updated list of barriers to fintech sector development. The document contains 194 items divided into 5 thematic subgroups, one related to identity and AML (Anti-Money Laundering issues. The key barrier was indicated as little work by regulators to bring SSI (Self Sovereign Identity) to the legal market.

SSI is a solution for creating a digital identity by assigning identifying characteristics to an entity. SSI is ultimately intended to be used to securely confirm an entity's identity when interacting with both private and public entities. Sovereign Identity could provide many benefits such as secure and fast identity authentication, confirmation of specific characteristics (e.g. age) or authorizations (e.g. driver's license), and transfer of data confirmed by third parties without their active participation in an ongoing process.

The potential for using SSI is very high, but this solution is in the early stages of development. The legal issues governing SSI as a means of digital identity or the need to provide standards/rules for the operation of sovereign identity remain to be resolved.

Recommendation: The recommended action is to start working on the implementation of the legal framework governing SSI. Another important aspect is to educate market participants/stakeholders about the possibilities of using SSI.

---

[14] https://www.gov.pl/web/cyfryzacja/tymczasowy-profil-zaufany--juz-jest.

[15] https://fintek.pl/nowa-lista-barier-w-rozwoju-fintechow-jest-ich-prawie-200-wszyscy-biora-sie-do-pracy/.

In Poland, there is a lack of unambiguous legal regulations concerning, among others, automatic video verification of the identity of a person applying for a qualified signature certificate. This is risky due to the possibility of the same service being provided by a foreign provider, which results in Polish companies not being competitive as trust service providers not only in European markets but even in their home country [8]. The increasing popularity of video verification in the commercial sector and trusted profile in the public administration in Poland indicates a huge demand for electronic identification services, which can be satisfied by commercial solutions [8].

Good Practice: (new national identity card with electronic layer) The solution that offsets the risks mentioned above is the electronic identity card, on which an electronic layer has been imposed. The new documents include an obligation to implement biometric features, in this case, a photo, and since August 2021, also fingerprints. Increased security will contribute to reducing the risk of document forgery. Linking electronic identity to a natural person (photo/fingerprints) allows to authenticate this document and to strongly confirm the identity with an e-document[16].

Good Practice: In 2019, the Office of the Financial Supervision Authority (KNF) presented a recommendation on customer identification and identity verification in banks and credit institutions using video verification [14]. The recommendation was based on inspections conducted in the financial sector, which revealed the difficulty of selecting appropriate security measures when conducting transactions without the customer's physical presence.

Properly conducted video verification eliminates the risk of erroneous verification of the customer and excludes the likelihood of third-party involvement. KNF's recommendation specifies how to carry out video verification, indicates control mechanisms, and defines precautionary measures that should be taken in order to mitigate the risk of incorrect verification of customer identity.

One of the legal and legislative risks may be adapting proposed solutions to changing laws. Changes in banking regulations have been extremely frequent in recent years. New rules, directives, and regulations are frequently introduced in the banking sector. There is a fear that, as in the case of the introduction of the EU PSD2 directive [5], common and popular solutions will cease to be acceptable. The aim of minimizing this risk is to create a solution that fully complies with the requirements of current regulations and to be able to modify the results to meet future changes in regulations. Constant monitoring and awareness of the regulations being introduced into the market are necessary to be able to respond effectively to the changes taking place.

According to the KPMG report [17]: "The PSD2 Directive represents a whole new playing field in banking and huge challenges in ensuring information security. The new business models will involve vectors of cyber-attacks and fraud that are difficult to predict at this point". Respondents employed by banks and

---

[16] https://www.gov.pl/web/cyfryzacja/e-dowod-20--nowy-wzor-dokumentu-wieksze-bezpieczenstwo.

cooperative banks confirmed that business process and cyber-security-related changes would be necessary for their institutions (41% and 63%, respectively).

The implementation of legislation such as PSD2 should be done in a way that ensures not only compliance with the rules but, above all, really increases the level of security by allowing the choice of security mechanisms higher than the minimum required by the legislation. For example, most institutions implement two-factor authentication (compliant with the PSD2 directive), using SMS codes as one-time passwords (OTP), which in the case of digital banking may not be sufficient. There are known and effective attacks on SMS codes - duplicating the SIM card and taking over the victim's number, and intercepting SMS messages [15]. Then it is possible to add a trusted beneficiary to authorize the subsequent transactions regardless of any OTP.

Recommendation: It is worth considering the introduction of more secure forms of authorization as an alternative to SMS codes, e.g. software tokens such as applications for phones or hardware tokens. The advantage of a hardware token is that it works independently of the phone or mobile application, so it does not exclude people who do not have a phone or smartphone. A hardware token ensures that no one but the token holder has the right to authorize the transaction. This solution prevents remote attacks such as malware or remote access to the phone.

In connection with the regulations above, biometrics begins to play an increasingly important role in banking systems - both active (face or fingerprint recognition) and passive analyzing the behavior of users (behavioral) and responding in case of anomalies [11]. Launching biometric channels as a second verification and authorization factor will significantly improve digital banking security.

EU regulation no 1093/2010 [3] establishes a European Banking Authority (EBA). Article 10 of this regulation deals with regulatory technical standards (binding because they are issued in the form of a regulation or a decision, i.e. by law).

EBA issues regulatory technical standards after public consultation. The way of selecting representatives for these consultations is crucial. Ensuring the participation of relevant industry experts is the foundation for creating properly prepared and thoughtful recommendations.

In 2021 European Union published the proposal of amendment to the eIDAS establishing a framework for a European Digital Identity [6]. This is a huge regulatory step towards harmonizing the European market of electronic identity and creating a common framework and standards for implementing modern solutions in the area of trusted services. In the exploratory memorandum of this proposal, we found that the evaluation eIDAS [primary regulation] revealed its limitation in addressing these new market demands. It is primarily due to its inherent limitations to the public sector, the limited possibilities, and the complexity for private online providers to connect to the system. Moreover, it is about the insufficient availability of notified eID solutions in all Member States and the lack of flexibility to support a variety of use cases.

In response, the new regulation would offer the European Digital Identity framework so that at least 80% of citizens can use a digital ID solution to access key public services by 2030.

European Digital Identity is the legal instrument which aims to provide for cross-border use:

- access to highly secure and trustworthy electronic identity solutions,
- that public and private services can rely on trusted and secure digital identity solutions,
- that natural and legal persons are empowered to use digital identity solutions,
- that these solutions are linked to a variety of attributes and allow for the targeted sharing of identity data limited to the needs of the specific service requested,
- acceptance of qualified trust services in the EU and equal conditions for their provision.

The security and control offered by the European Digital Identity framework should give citizens and residents full confidence that the European Digital Identity framework will offer everyone the means to control who has access to their digital twin and to which data exactly [6].

6 Conclusions

Many risks are associated with digital and mobile banking, electronic identity, and trust services. COVID-19 just accelerated digitization and exposed weaknesses in security systems. Attacks carried out on people in banking are particularly vulnerable.

We can observe evolution in a proper direction, like the register of public documents or the introduction of ID cards with an electronic layer and biometric features and issuing the proposal of amendment to the eIDAS regulation. On the other hand, there is still room for improvement, electronic ID should be more widespread, and biometric security features should be an integral part of security systems. Human issues like fatigue or mismanagement often make it easier for adversaries to infiltrate security systems.

Continuous education seems to be a neglected element when it is a fundamental component without which investment in better security will not make much sense. This should take place simultaneously on many levels: public information campaigns run by states or public trust institutions like banks, schools and universities, and workplaces. Internet users should know what dangers they are exposed to and what mistakes they make when using digital services.

Sociotechnical attacks are one of the most dangerous and the most efficient. Their success lies in exploiting people's gullibility and emotions. Therefore, improving user competence should be an integral part of the modern world. If we do not start to educate in the right way, cybercriminals will do it for us. The consequences of such "educational campaigns" will bring unpleasant effects such as leaking sensitive data or stealing money.

As the main focus for future work in this area, we would like to investigate the specifics of sociotechnical attacks and the most effective way of raising user awareness. We strongly believe that it will not be possible to raise the level of security of banking or electronic trust systems if, in parallel with improving the systems themselves, we do not raise the level of education of all digital services users.

References

1. Bridge Foundation: CyberLabs Raport 2020 (2020). https://98145a31-5189-415e-8474-41672cd6acb7.filesusr.com/ugd/2b3cfe_6421fe7dedef4dd186b1ca3398e37bc5.pdf
2. ESET: Cybersecurity Trends 2021: Staying secure in uncertain times (2021). https://www.welivesecurity.com/wp-content/uploads/2020/11/ESET_Cybersecurity_Trends_2021.pdf
3. European Parliament: Regulation (EU) no 1093/2010 of the European parliament and of the council of 24 November 2010 establishing a European banking authority and amending decision no 716/2009/EC and repealing commission decision 2009/78/EC. Official Journal of the European Union (2010). https://eur-lex.europa.eu/legal-content/EN/TXT/PDF/?uri=CELEX:32010R1093&from=EN
4. European Parliament: Regulation (EU) no 910/2014 of the European parliament and of the council of 23 July 2014 on electronic identification and trust services for electronic transactions in the internal market and repealing directive 1999/93/EC. Official Journal of the European Union (2014). https://eur-lex.europa.eu/legal-content/EN/TXT/PDF/?uri=CELEX:32014R0910&from=EN
5. European Parliament: Directive (EU) 2015/2366 of 25 November 2015 on payment services in the internal market. Official Journal of the European Union (2015). https://eur-lex.europa.eu/legal-content/EN/TXT/PDF/?uri=CELEX:32015L2366&from=EN
6. European Parliament: Proposal of the regulation of the European parliament and of the council of amending regulation (EU) no 910/2014 as regards establishing a framework for a European digital identity. Official Journal of the European Union (2021). https://eur-lex.europa.eu/legal-content/EN/TXT/?uri=CELEX%3A52021PC0281
7. KPMG: Barometer cyberbezpieczeństwa, w obronie przed cyberatakami (2019). https://assets.kpmg/content/dam/kpmg/pl/pdf/2019/04/pl-Raport-KPMG-Barometr-Cyberbezpieczenstwa-W-obronie-przed-cyberatakami.pdf
8. Obserwatorium.biz: TRUSTED ECONOMY in the new reality (2020). https://obserwatorium.biz/en/raport-trusted-economy.html
9. Polish Banks Association: Standard Kwalifikacyjny ZBP - Stosowanie zasad cyberbezpieczeństwa przez pracowników instytucji finansowych (2019). https://zbp.pl/getmedia/076a1ce8-2850-4415-8a45-0f13389e8f97/Standard-Kwalifikacyjny-Stosowanie-zasad-cyberbezpieczenstwa.pdf
10. Polish Banks Association: Cyberbezpieczny portfel (2020). https://www.zbp.pl/getmedia/156b5c44-bfcc-46cb-a5d1-bd0d141e9ed0/ZBP_CyberbezpiecznyPortfel2020
11. Puls Biznesu: Zloty Bankier 2020 (2020). https://www.bankier.pl/static/att/281000/7908761_zloty_bankier_2020_final.pdf

12. Sophos: Cybersecurity: the human challenge (2020). https://www.sophos.com/en-us/medialibrary/pdfs/whitepaper/sophos-cybersecurity-the-human-challenge-wp.pdf
13. SRK SF: Raport SBKL 2018 (2018). www.rada.wib.org.pl
14. UKNF: Stanowisko UKNF dotyczące identyfikacji klienta i weryfikacji jego tożsamości w bankach oraz oddziałach instytucji kredytowych w oparciu o metodę wideoweryfikacji (2019). https://www.knf.gov.pl/o_nas/komunikaty?articleId=66067&p_id=18
15. Wodo, W., Stygar, D.: Security of digital banking systems in Poland: user study 2019. In: Proceedings of the 6th International Conference on Information Systems Security and Privacy: ICISSP 2020, pp. 221–231. INSTICC, SciTePress (2020)
16. XOPERO: Cyberbezpieczeństwo: Trendy 2019 (2019). https://lp.xopero.com/raport-2019-trendy-cyberbezpieczenstwo
17. Zwiazek Bankow Polskich: PSD2 i Open Banking - Rewolucja czy ewolucja? (2019). https://assets.kpmg/content/dam/kpmg/pl/pdf/2019/03/pl-raport-kpmg0-zbp-psd2-i-open-banking-rewolucja-czy-ewolucja.pdf

Design and Development of IoT Based Medical Cleanroom

Bibars Amangeldy$^{(\boxtimes)}$, Nurdaulet Tasmurzayev , Madina Mansurova ,
Baglan Imanbek , and Talsyn Sarsembayeva

Al-Farabi Kazakh National University, Al-Farabi avenue, 71, Almaty, Kazakhstan
a.s.bibars@gmail.com

Abstract. In this study, we have developed and analyzed the implementation of an IoT system for a clean room, which encompasses an automated monitoring system utilizing IoT sensors. The performance of the proposed system was evaluated through experiments conducted at the Faculty of Information Technology, KazNU (Kazakhstan). Manual tests were performed to verify the accuracy of the sensor data, resulting in a data accuracy rate of approximately 99%. The findings indicate the reliability of the system, making it suitable for effectively connecting urban and suburban park communities. The article focuses on addressing the issue of regulating heat supply and air conditioning within enclosed spaces. We describe an automated system designed to monitor the dynamic characteristics of these sensors, comprising a software and hardware complex for configuring a test bench and analyzing sensor parameters related to dynamic temperature control and air conditioning. The primary objective of this system is to automate the control of air conditioning and maintain a desired temperature within a single room.

The system performs several functions, including control of the Google Coral USB Accelerator, configuration of the ADC, and determination of the amplitude-frequency and phase-frequency characteristics of temperature sensors, switches, leak sensors, and air conditioning units. These determinations are based on experimental studies conducted on a sensor dynamics monitoring stand and monitored using the SCADA Genesis64 program. The article presents the test bench schematic, the general algorithm of system operation, and screenshots of the program interface. The software for the automated temperature control and air conditioning system is developed using ModBus TCP, OPC UA, and SCADA programs as the foundation.

Keywords: SCADA Genesis 64 · intelligent system · air and conditioning system · microcontrollers

1 Introduction

When assessing air quality transitions between seasons, atmospheric dynamics and meteorological conditions play a crucial role. According to the World Health Organization, approximately 30% of newly constructed and industrial businesses experience significant indoor air quality (IAQ) issues [1]. It is essential to consider medical expenses and

© The Author(s), under exclusive license to Springer Nature Switzerland AG 2023
N. T. Nguyen et al. (Eds.): ICCCI 2023, CCIS 1864, pp. 459–469, 2023.
https://doi.org/10.1007/978-3-031-41774-0_36

production losses, as they represent substantial costs that can impact company performance [2]. Environmental pollution poses a serious challenge for industrial businesses, as it can lead to unhealthy working conditions. Maintaining a healthy and comfortable working environment requires effective management of IAQ within the company [3]. In the industrial sector, IAQ is measured based on solid particle count (PM10), temperature, and humidity, following Kazakhstani standards [4].

Air quality is a critical concern in clean rooms of semiconductor manufacturing plants. The clean room's entry and exit can influence particle count, humidity, and temperature. In industrialized nations like South Korea, around 80 to 90% of individuals spend their time indoors within buildings and businesses [5]. Prolonged exposure to air pollution has adverse effects on human health, causing irritation of the nose, eyes, and throat. This study focuses on how the "clean room" maintains optimal temperature and humidity levels. To address this issue, we have developed a monitoring system that adheres to Kazakhstan's established standards for clean rooms [6]. By implementing IoT technology, indoor pollutants can be effectively monitored. Maintaining air quality requires consideration of primary pollutants, such as PM10, as well as carbon monoxide, sulfur dioxide, carbon dioxide, formaldehyde, nitrogen dioxide, ozone, total suspended particles, and total volatile organic compounds [7]. Several studies have demonstrated a strong correlation between PM exposure and air quality [8, 9].

Hung et al. proposed the uSense monitoring system, which provides real-time displays of pollutant concentrations throughout the city using cost-effective materials [10]. The uSense system proves to be cost-effective and capable of generating substantial amounts of data. Furthermore, the system was subjected to on-site experiments [11]. PM2.5 measurements significantly influence the findings of this study. PM2.5 is commonly emitted from industrial exhaust gases, coal combustion exhaust gases, and vehicle emissions. Consequently, various researchers have focused on designing sensors to measure PM2.5 concentrations [12]. Elbayumi et al. proposed an IAQ system to identify potential sources impacting air quality [13]. Models for IAQ monitoring were presented in [14], revealing conditions of PM10 and PM2.5 in both indoor and outdoor air quality.

In clean rooms, additional tests can be conducted to assess the presence of ultrafine or microparticles, including tests for airflow, air pressure differentials, leakproofness of installed filter systems, visualization of air flow direction, humidity and temperature measurements, electrostatic tests, particle deposition tests, recovery tests, and containment leakproofness tests [15]. However, most manuscripts focused solely on monitoring IAQ systems and did not explore the potential of utilizing IoT technology and artificial intelligence for real-time monitoring of room conditions.

The primary objective of this study is to develop an IoT-based system for controlling and monitoring temperature and humidity in a medical powder production "clean room." The clean room is situated in the Internet of Things laboratory within the smart campus of KazNU. A more detailed description and prospects for the development of the smart laboratory on the KazNU campus were discussed in a previous article [16].

As mentioned in our previous research works [17] and [18], a crucial component of the Laboratory is a software package built upon the renowned Internet of Things platform, Genesis 64. This software package represents the "upper" level of the Smart

City system, enabling process visualization, management, analysis of indicators, and predictive modeling of processes.

Furthermore, there has been an increase in the occurrence of viral respiratory disease pandemics in the past two decades, including SARS-CoV-1 in 2003, MERS-CoV in 2012, and SARS-CoV-2 in 2019. This trend suggests the potential emergence of new viruses causing severe acute respiratory syndrome in the forthcoming decades. Consequently, it becomes imperative to develop a state-of-the-art heating, ventilation, and air conditioning (HVAC) system with remote control capabilities. The contributions of HVAC systems in mitigating and improving such situations have already been discussed in the research works [19] and [20].

Air conditioning entails an automated process of maintaining a conducive micro-climate within a room, encompassing factors such as air temperature, humidity, air circulation rate, and air purity. It is essential for ensuring normal human functionality and meeting safety requirements in polluted work environments. Typically, large-scale air conditioning systems are governed by complex automated control systems. An auto-mated air conditioning system regulates the indoor climate independently of atmospheric conditions. The primary devices employed are housed within a unit known as an air con-ditioner. Before delving into the categorization of air conditioning systems, it should be noted that there is currently no standardized classification for such systems. This is evident from the diverse range of basic schemes, technical parameters, and functional characteristics of various systems, tailored for specific room requirements. Achieving air conditioning involves the implementation of a comprehensive array of technical and technological means, collectively referred to as an air conditioning system. This system comprises installations such as air intake units, air cleaning and processing equipment, heat exchangers, filters, dehumidifiers or humidifiers, air circulation systems (including fans), automation systems, and remote control functionalities. Typically, these air con-ditioning components are integrated within one or two enclosures, wherein the terms "air conditioning system" and "air conditioning" are often used interchangeably.

2   The Realization of Intelligent System

The term "intelligent system" typically refers to a complex system that leverages advanced information and computational technologies, such as artificial intelligence, machine learning, and process automation. Intelligent systems are capable of collecting, analyzing, and interpreting data, making decisions, learning, and self-organizing in order to accomplish tasks and achieve specific goals.

Intelligent systems are commonly used to automate and optimize complex and resource-intensive processes in various domains, including industry, energy, transporta-tion, healthcare, and others. They can perform functions such as forecasting, optimiza-tion, monitoring, resource management, data analysis, and decision-making based on collected and processed information.

Intelligent systems help improve efficiency, enhance the quality of decision-making, reduce costs and risks, and automate routine tasks. They can adapt to changing conditions and learn from accumulated experience and data, enabling them to continuously improve their performance and outcomes.

The intelligent system for regulating and controlling the temperature and air conditioning of the room performs the following functions:

- monitoring the condition of the room in real time;
- ability to control the heat tap and air conditioner using microcontrollers: Siemens SIMATIC S7–1200, Siemens SIMATIC IoT 2040 and Raspberry PI 4
- economical power consumption due to monitoring.

Fig. 1. Supervisory control and data acquisition System UI

The test stand of the intelligent temperature and air conditioning control system in Fig. 1 includes:

1. A control and control cabinet with a freely programmable controller and I/O modules.
2. Sensors and actuators located on the stand.
3. VEGA Absolute wireless data acquisition system, based on LoRaWAN technology.
4. Video surveillance system.
5. Automated workplace (hereinafter referred to as APM) with the installed SCADA Genesis64 software.
6. The bench of an automated and control system with controller and I/O modules-designed to receive signals from primary devices (temperature sensors, switches, leak sensors, etc.), process these signals according to the built-in algorithms, output control actions according to the built-in algorithms to the actuators (LED strips, control and shut-off valve), as well as interact with external systems, for example, SCADA Genesis64 [21].
7. Sensors and actuators located on the stand are designed to form primary signals for further processing, receiving and executing control actions from the control system.

8. The VEGA Absolute wireless data acquisition system, based on LoRaWAN technology, is designed to collect data from primary sensors, transmit the received data through the base station to the server, and then transmit it to the Genesis64 SCADA.
9. The video surveillance system is designed to monitor the audience and transmit the video stream to the SCADA Genesis64.

After selecting the devices, our next step is to integrate them into the monitoring program that will track the building's condition. We have opted to use the ModBus TCP protocol within an Ethernet network, where the device address corresponds to its IP address. Typically, these devices are situated within the same subnet, with IP addresses differing only in the last digits (e.g., 192.168.1.20) when utilizing the commonly used subnet mask of 255.255.255.0. The interface employed is an Ethernet network, with the data transfer protocol being TCP/IP. Specifically, TCP port 502 is utilized for communication [22].

To achieve more accurate result in this system, for the rest software programme we chose these two programmes, which were used in our previous researches [23]:

1. OPC UA.
2. SCADA.

Furthermore, we have established a cloud platform for data collection, enabling us to receive information from the building and manage controllers and programs.

To address the issue of information interface adaptivity with the OPC server, explicit object typing can be implemented within the OPC UA server's address space. This involves comparing similar groups of technological parameters to a template (class). By doing so, we can ensure control over the completeness of the received information in the client application and automatically respond to any changes in volume on the server side. In the OPC UA client, it is possible to deviate from the currently accepted scheme, where the list of exchange signals with the OPC server is defined as a list of tag names. The provision of semantic information in the OPC UA server, along with links from the class description to its instances, allows for the establishment of a template for the list of objects. This eliminates the need for the client to manually enter a list of names of class instances that exist at the time of setting up the interface. Additionally, the OPC UA client can subscribe to receive notifications from the server regarding changes in the address space [24].

The communication between the controller and the I/O modules is established through the utilization of the Modbus RTU protocol. In this setup, the controller acts as the master. The configuration of the interaction parameters, as depicted in Fig. 2, is performed both on the I/O module using the M110 Configurator program and in the controller, specifically in the PLC configuration section under the resources tab.

On the other hand, the communication between the controller and the Genesis64 SCADA system is achieved using the Modbus TCP protocol. In this scenario, the controller operates as a slave. The interaction parameters, as illustrated in Fig. 3, are configured both in the Genesis64 SCADA system and in the controller, within the resources tab in the PLC configuration section.

Figure 4 presents a structural diagram illustrating the sensors integrated into the test bench. The hardware components of the system are located at the lower level of the

Fig. 2. Control box of the intelligent control system

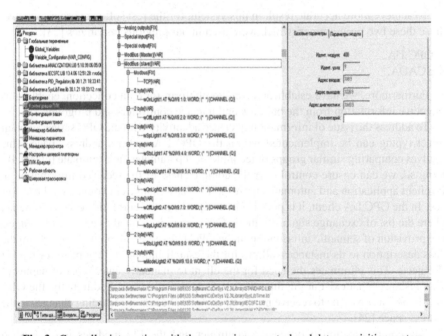

Fig. 3. Controller interaction with the supervisory control and data acquisition system

diagram and consist of pressure sensors, pumps, flow meters, and valves. We chose the Siemens PLC as the controller, which is situated at the intermediate level. The previously mentioned cloud and SCADA system are monitoring systems located at the top level of the architecture [25].

For data transmission, we utilized the Cloud through Telegram bot, Yandex Alice, and Yandex Maps. This allowed us to establish a connection with the test bench and retrieve real-time data from the sensors. Through integration between SCADA and other notification systems, we could receive alerts about changes in room parameters. These notifications could be sent in the form of SMS messages or emails, enabling prompt responses to any system changes.

Thus, our developed system not only facilitated monitoring and control of the test bench but also enabled integration and data exchange with other crucial systems and services, ensuring efficient management and oversight of processes within the room. This significantly enhanced the functionality and flexibility of our system, providing convenience and reliability in interacting with various user interfaces and notification systems.

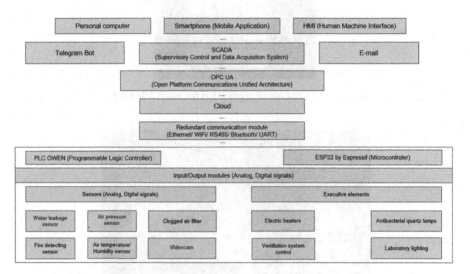

Fig. 4. Architecture of the intelligent control system

For our research, we have selected a laboratory within our department as the implementation site for this system, which will be utilized for our upcoming monitoring activities. The automated workstation, which serves as the teacher's workstation, is equipped with the Genesis 64 software. This software stands out as one of the most advanced and robust Internet of Things platforms globally. It is built upon the unified building management system from EXPO-2017 and has been employed in numerous international projects, including airports, administrative buildings, and government offices, among others. The software is developed by Iconics Corporation, a Microsoft gold partner, and possesses the technical capabilities for seamless integration with Microsoft Azure solutions, as depicted in Fig. 5 [26].

In the navigation menu, you can go to the screens:

1. Ventilation (window with 3D supply ventilation system);
2. Air conditioning (window with 3D VAV air conditioning);
3. Heat point (window with 2D mnemonic diagram of ITP);
4. Laboratory in Fig. 6 (transition to the graphic screen of the laboratory). The functionality of the other buttons is not used.

Fig. 5. Remote control application for smart laboratory

Fig. 6. Ventilation inlet for air quality control

To access the building layout and examine the internal infrastructure, one must click on the roof. Similarly, to observe the status of the equipment, specifically the air conditioner, it is necessary to select it on the plan. This action triggers the display of a pop-up window containing a 3D representation of the air conditioner. Furthermore, by clicking on the roof extension depicted in Fig. 7, a window showcasing the ventilation unit will open within the designated functional area.

The depicted layout in Fig. 8 illustrates a 3D design of an installation featuring a heating and cooling circuit, equipped with a single fan. The presented data within the layout is showcased in simulation mode. To control the installation, an enable/disable functionality can be accessed through the designated control button.

In this section of the project, the monitoring of the building's condition is facilitated. The "heat point" tab displays information pertaining to the heat point, specifically, three

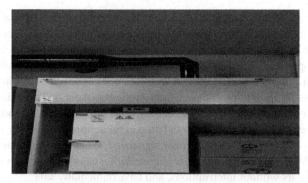

Fig. 7. The bactericidal module for air quality control

Fig. 8. The actuator for the microclimate control

hot water supply zones. The data presented within the layout is exhibited in simulation mode.

The intellectual aspect of this project involves integration with Yandex Alice, enabling both automated and manual control. In the former scenario, notifications are sent via a telegram bot, relaying information from sensors such as gas sensors, water level sensors, and motion sensors for security purposes. In the latter scenario, each laboratory is equipped with a temperature or humidity control mechanism to safeguard various types of equipment or medications. Even in the case of a chemical laboratory, the mobile application or the monitor shown in Fig. 5 will display the respective measurements. In the third scenario, control can be exercised through Alice, with the provision of Russian language support. Commands such as "Alice, turn on the air conditioning" or "turn off" can be given.

3   Conclusion

As a result of our research, an intelligent system has been developed to optimize the issue of heat supply and air conditioning consumption and waste within a room, utilizing a management and monitoring structure along with an intelligent system model [27].

The functionality of the system, supported by the intelligent automation, enables minimizing human intervention, enhancing system efficiency, local and remote management and control of all system states, analysis and examination of data over a specific time period, identification of deviations and failures in system elements and sections, as well as optimization of all operational processes.

The developed intelligent automation system effectively addresses the challenges associated with excessive heat usage and its associated costs. It operates as a centralized heat supply system, providing the necessary amount of heat and enabling year-round operation of air conditioning, independent of time of day or weather conditions.

By implementing monitoring and regulation of predefined parameters, the intelligent system ensures electricity is supplied only as needed, thereby minimizing unnecessary consumption. Moreover, the system is highly scalable, capable of continuous operation over multiple years without interruptions, and environmentally safe.

Acknowledgement. This work was funded by Committee of Science of Republic of Kazakhstan AP09260767 "Development of an intellectual information and analytical system for assessing the health status of students in Kazakhstan" (2021–2023).

References

1. Zheng, K., Zhao, S., Yang, Z., Xiong, X., Xiang, W.: Design and implementation of LPWA-based air quality monitoring system. IEEE Access **4**, 3238–3245 (2016). https://doi.org/10.1109/ACCESS.2016.2582153
2. Tong, S., Wang, T., Li, Y., Chen, B.: A combined backstepping and stochastic small-gain approach to robust adaptive fuzzy output feedback control. In: IEEE Trans. Fuzzy Syst. **21**(2), 314–327 (2013)
3. Daisey, J.M., Angell, W.J., Apte, M.G.: Indoor air quality, ventilation and health symptoms in schools: an analysis of existing information. Indoor Air **13**(1), 53–64 (2003)
4. Postolache, O.A., Dias Pereira, J.M., Silva Girao, P.M.B.: Smart sensors network for air quality monitoring applications. IEEE Trans. Instrum. Meas. **58**(9), 3253–3262 (2009)
5. Tran, T.V., Dang, N.T., Chung, W.Y.: Battery-free smart-sensor system for real-time indoor air quality monitoring. Sens. Actuators B Chem. **248**, 930–939 (2017)
6. On approval of sanitary rules "Sanitary and epidemiological requirements for objects in the field of circulation of medicines, medical devices and medical equipment". http://law.gov.kz/client/#!/doc/54528/rus/13.08.2010. Last accessed 22 Dec 2022
7. Ha, Q.P., Metia, S., Phung, M.D.: Sensing data fusion for enhanced indoor air quality monitoring. IEEE Sens. J. **20**(8), 4430–4441 (2020)
8. Pope, D.D., Ezzati, M.: Fine-particulate air pollution and life expectancy in the United States. New Eng. J. Med. **360**(4), 376–386 (2009)
9. Brienza, S., Galli, A., Anastasi, G., Bruschi, P.: A low-cost sensing system for cooperative air quality monitoring in urban areas. Sensors **15**, 12242–12259 (2015)
10. Hung, F.H.: An adaptive indoor air quality control scheme for minimizing volatile organic compounds density. IEEE Access **8**, 22357–22365 (2020)
11. Zheng, H., Xiong, K., Fan, P., Zhong, Z.: Data Analysis on Outdoor–Indoor Air Quality Variation: Buildings' Producing Dynamic Filter Effects. In: IEEE Systems Journal, vol. 13, no. 4, pp. 4386–4397, (2019)
12. Saad, S.M., Andrew, A.M., Shakaff, A.Y.M., Saad, A.R.M., Kamarudin, A.M.Y., Zakaria, A.: Classifying sources influencing indoor air quality (IAQ) using artificial neural network (ANN). Sensors **15**, 11665–11684 (2015)

13. Elbayoumi, M., Ramli, N.A., Md Yusof, N.F.F., Al Madhoun W.: Spatial and seasonal variation of particulate matter (PM10 and PM2.5) in Middle Eastern classrooms. Atmos. Environ. **80**, 389–397 (2013)
14. Wei, W., Ramalho, O., Malingre, L., Sivanantham, S., Little, J.C., Mandin, C.: Machine learning and statistical models for predicting indoor air quality. Indoor Air **29**(5), 704–726 (2019)
15. Zhao, L., Wu W., Li, S.: Design and implementation of an IoT-based indoor air quality detector with multiple communication interfaces. IEEE Internet of Things J. **6**(6), 9621–9632 (2019)
16. Mitova, M., Tomov, P., Kunicina, N., Patlins, A., Mansurova M., Namsrai, O.E.: Towards to sustainability of education: the mutual cooperation with partners in Smart city project. In: 2022 IEEE 7th International Energy Conference (ENERGYCON), pp. 1–6 (2022)
17. Tasmurzayev, N., Amangeldy, B., Baigarayeva, Z., Mansurova, M., Resnik, B., Amirkhanova, G.: Improvement of HVAC system using the intelligent control systemю In: 2022 IEEE 7th International Energy Conference (ENERGYCON), pp. 1–6 (2022)
18. Tasmurzayev, N.M., Amangeldy, B.S., Nurakhov, E.S., Mukhanbet, A.A., Yeltay, Z.: Implementation of an intelligent control system for heat distribution in rooms. In: 2021 IEEE International Conference on Smart Information Systems and Technologies (SIST), Nur-Sultan, Kazakhstan, pp. 1–5 (2021)
19. Sodiq, A., Moazzam, A.K., Mahmoud, N., Abdulkarem, A.: Addressing COVID-19 contagion through the HVAC systems by reviewing indoor airborne nature of infectious microbes: will an innovative air recirculation concept provide a practical solution? Environ. Res. **199**, 111329 (2021)
20. Junwei, D., Chuck W.Y., Shi-Jie C.: HVAC systems for environmental control to minimize the COVID-19 infection. Indoor Built Environ. **29**, 1195–1201 (2020)
21. Leonov A.V.: Internet of things: security problems. Omsk Scientific Bulletin, Russia (2015)
22. Varlamov, I.G.: New generation SCADA. Evolution of technologies-revolution of the building system. In: Automated Information and Control Systems in Power Engineering, Russia (2016)
23. Tasmurzayev, N., Amangeldy, B., Nurakhov, Y., Akhmed-Zaki, D., Baigarayeva, Z.: Intelligent thermal accumulator operation control system based on renewable energy sources. In: Proceedings of the 19th International Conference on Informatics in Control, Automation and Robotics – ICINCO, pp. 737–742 (2021)
24. Nolan, K.E., Guibene, W., Kelly, M.Y.: An evaluation of low power wide area network technologies for the internet of things. In: Proceeding of International Wireless, Germany (2016)
25. Soumaya, E.B., et al.: IoT-based smart airflow system for retrofitting commercial variable air volume HVAC systems. IFAC-PapersOnLine **55**, 444–449 (2022)
26. Pavlova, Z., Krasnov. A., Baltin, R.R.: Modern technologies for receiving and transmitting measurement information for the organization of sensor networks for monitoring oil and gas industry objects. Int. Res. J. 202–206 (2017)
27. Bartlett, G., Heidemann, J., Papadopoulos, C.: Understanding passive and active service discovery. In: Proceedings of the 7th ACM SIGCOMM conference on Internet measurement, ACM (2007)

Reliable Framework for Digital Forensics in Medical Internet of Things

Ines Rahmany[1]([envelope])[iD], Rihab Saidi[1][iD], Tarek Moulahi[2][iD], and Mutiq Almutiq[3][iD]

[1] Department of Computer Science, FST Sidi Bouzid, University of Kairouan, Sidi
Bouzid, Tunisia
`ines.rahmani@fstsbz.u-kairouan.tn`
[2] Department of Information Technology, College of Computer, Qassim University,
Buraydah 52571, Saudi Arabia
[3] Department of Management Information Systems and Production Management,
College of Business and Economics, Qassim University,
Buraydah 52571, Saudi Arabia

Abstract. Medical Internet of Things (MIoT) involves the use of connected devices and sensors. These devices can include wearable health monitors, smart medical devices, implantable sensors, and remote monitoring systems. These devices can collect a wide range of data, including vital signs, medication adherence, and activity levels, which can be used to diagnose and treat medical conditions remotely and make informed decisions based on real-time information. With the increasing use of medical Internet of Things (MIoT) devices, such as wearable health monitors and implantable medical devices, digital forensics has become a critical component of healthcare security. Digital forensics for medical IoT involves the use of specialized tools and techniques to investigate any suspected security breaches or incidents involving these devices. The main goal of this paper is to provide a reliable blockchain-based digital forensic framework in MIoT.

Keywords: Digital Forensics · Internet of Things · Cybercrime · Federated Learning · Medical Internet of Things · Blockchain · Healthcare

1 Introduction

Medical Internet of Things (MIoT) refers to the use of Internet of Things (IoT) technology in the field of healthcare. MIoT devices can include wearable health monitors, smart medical devices, implantable sensors, and remote monitoring systems. These devices can collect a wide range of data, including vital signs, medication adherence, and activity levels, which can be used to diagnose and treat medical conditions [6]. The use of MIoT devices has the potential to revolutionize healthcare by improving patient outcomes, reducing healthcare costs, and increasing access to care. However, it also raises concerns related to data privacy

© The Author(s), under exclusive license to Springer Nature Switzerland AG 2023
N. T. Nguyen et al. (Eds.): ICCCI 2023, CCIS 1864, pp. 470–480, 2023.
https://doi.org/10.1007/978-3-031-41774-0_37

and security, as these devices collect and transmit sensitive health information. Digital forensics for medical Internet of Things (IoT) refers to the process of investigating and analyzing medical devices connected to the internet for the purpose of collecting evidence in support of a legal case or for the purpose of improving the security and privacy of the devices [2, 7]. This type of forensics can involve the examination of devices such as wearable medical devices, smart pills, and telemedicine systems. The goal of digital forensics in the medical IoT context is to identify any data breaches, cyberattacks, or unauthorized access to medical devices, as well as to recover any lost or damaged data.

In order to perform digital forensics on medical IoT devices, investigators need to have a deep understanding of the devices and their underlying technology, as well as an understanding of the legal and regulatory framework surrounding medical data privacy and security. They may use a variety of tools and techniques, including data recovery, network analysis, and memory analysis, to uncover evidence of wrongdoing or to identify vulnerabilities in the devices.

It is important to note that digital forensics for medical IoT devices is a complex and rapidly evolving field, and it requires a specialized set of skills and knowledge to be performed effectively.

The core contribution of this paper is the development of a reliable framework for digital forensics in Medical Internet of Things. The main goals of this study are to:

- MIoT Threat modeling: using a structured process to identify and assess potential threats to a system or MIoT devices, networks, and data. It involves considering various scenarios and determining the likelihood and impact of each threat.
- Digital Forensics Framework: by establishing a reliable and systematic approach to collecting, analyzing, and presenting digital evidence based on Federated Learning protected by blockchain.

To rest of this paper is organized as follows: Sect. 2 presents a review of relevant literature, followed by Sect. 3, which proposes a digital forensic framework to develop a secure MIoT system. The proposed framework incorporates the digital forensics process of MIoT systems with three forensics levels. Finally, Sect. 5 presents conclusion and future work.

2   State of the Art of MIoT Forensics

The state of the art in Medical Internet of Things (MIoT) forensics methods involves the use of a combination of digital forensics techniques and a deep understanding of the medical devices and their underlying technology. The goal of these methods is to recover evidence of any wrongdoing or unauthorized access to medical devices, as well as to identify vulnerabilities in the devices that could be exploited by attackers.

Grispos et al. discussed in [3], the potential and the impact of digital forensics processes within the healthcare context.

Most of the currently used standard models adhere to the fundamental steps of a forensics investigation, including context setting, data collection, investigation, analysis, and reporting [5]. Other used forensic models include Digital Forensic Research Workshop (DFRW) which is based on seven phases (identification, preservation, collection, examination, analysis, presentation, and decision) [12]. Abstract Digital Forensic Model (ADFM) has three additional components (preparation, approach strategy, and return of evidence), which were lacking in DFRW [1]. In [4] the authors highlighted the needs of a Digital Forensic Investigation Process Model (DFIPM) for Internet of Medical Things devices so that to assure data privacy. Grispos et al. discussed in [3] the potential and the impact of digital forensics processes within the healthcare context.

Some of the current state of the art methods used in MIoT forensics include:

- Data recovery: This involves using specialized tools and techniques to recover data from damaged or corrupted medical devices. This can include the recovery of deleted or lost files, as well as the extraction of data from memory and storage devices [3,9].
- Network analysis: This involves analyzing network traffic from medical devices in order to identify any anomalies or signs of malicious activity. This can include the examination of network logs and packets, as well as the use of network forensic tools to identify and track malicious actors [7].
- Memory analysis: This involves analyzing the memory of medical devices in order to uncover any evidence of malware or unauthorized access. This can include the use of memory forensic tools to identify and extract malicious code, as well as the examination of memory dump files for signs of tampering or manipulation [11].
- Mobile device forensics: With the increasing use of mobile devices in the medical field, mobile device forensics has become an important aspect of MIoT forensics. This involves the recovery and analysis of data from smartphones and tablet devices used in medical settings [2].
- Cloud forensics: With the increasing use of cloud-based storage and processing in medical IoT, cloud forensics has become an important aspect of MIoT forensics. This involves the recovery and analysis of data stored in cloud-based systems, as well as the examination of cloud infrastructure for signs of malicious activity [10].

In the literature, MIoT forensics models have only gotten a modest level of attention [2,3,7,10,11]. The key topics covered in these papers include the necessity for digital forensics in MIoT, existing problems, and the various forensics phases. However, all the above mentioned papers do not present a reliable framework or a model for digital forensics in MIoT.

3   Proposed Framework for MIoT Forensics

We proposed a threat modeling framework for digital forensics in MIoT in order to identify security and privacy issues. Figure 1 depicts an intrusion detection system for the Medical Internet of Things (MIoT). We considered four basic components in the threat model: **medical devices**, including different types of wearable sensors or implantable devices of patients, **mobile devices** with e-health app, including mobiles phones and smart watches, a **fog layer** for processing and analyzing data and a **blockchain layer** for secure decision. Homomorphic cryptography is performed between the fog layer and the blockchain layer.

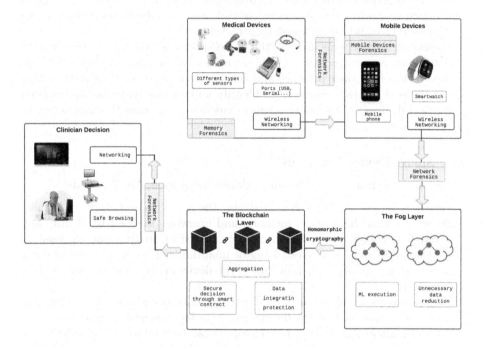

Fig. 1. A Threat Model for MIoT.

3.1 Memory Forensics

In the proposed framework, the memory forensics in MIoT include:

- Live memory analysis: This involves analyzing the memory of a running medical device in real-time in order to identify any anomalies or signs of malicious activity. This can include the use of live memory analysis tools to identify and track malicious actors, as well as the examination of memory for signs of suspicious activity.
- Memory dump analysis: This involves creating a copy of the memory of a medical device for the purpose of analysis. Memory dump analysis can be used to recover evidence of any wrongdoing or unauthorized access to medical devices, as well as to identify vulnerabilities in the devices that could be exploited by attackers.

- Volatile data analysis: This involves analyzing data stored in memory that is temporarily stored and can be lost when power to the device is lost. Volatile data analysis can be used to recover evidence of any wrongdoing or unauthorized access to medical devices, as well as to identify vulnerabilities in the devices that could be exploited by attackers.
- Memory artifact analysis: This involves analyzing the artifacts that are left behind in memory after a process or system event has occurred. Memory artifact analysis can be used to recover evidence of any wrongdoing or unauthorized access to medical devices, as well as to identify vulnerabilities in the devices that could be exploited by attackers.
- Rootkit detection: This involves the use of specialized tools and techniques to detect and remove rootkits, which are malicious software programs that are designed to hide their presence and activities on a system. Rootkit detection can be used in MIoT forensics to identify and remove malicious actors from medical devices, as well as to recover evidence of any unauthorized access to the devices.

3.2   Smart Device Forensics

In the proposed framework, the smart device forensics in MIoT include:

- Physical analysis: This involves analyzing the physical components of a smart device, such as the storage, memory, and firmware, in order to identify any anomalies or signs of malicious activity. Physical analysis can be used to recover evidence of any wrongdoing or unauthorized access to medical data, as well as to identify vulnerabilities in the devices that could be exploited by attackers.
- Logical analysis: This involves analyzing the data stored on a smart device in a logical format, such as the file system, in order to identify any anomalies or signs of malicious activity. Logical analysis can be used to recover evidence of any wrongdoing or unauthorized access to medical data, as well as to identify vulnerabilities in the devices that could be exploited by attackers.
- File system analysis: This involves analyzing the structure and contents of the file system on a mobile device in order to identify any anomalies or signs of malicious activity. File system analysis can be used to recover evidence of any wrongdoing or unauthorized access to medical data, as well as to identify vulnerabilities in the devices that could be exploited by attackers.
- Application analysis: This involves analyzing the applications installed on a smart device in order to identify any anomalies or signs of malicious activity. Application analysis can be used to recover evidence of any wrongdoing or unauthorized access to medical data, as well as to identify vulnerabilities in the devices that could be exploited by attackers.
- Cloud analysis: This involves analyzing data stored on cloud-based services associated with a smart device in order to identify any anomalies or signs of malicious activity. Cloud analysis can be used to recover evidence of any wrongdoing or unauthorized access to medical data, as well as to identify vulnerabilities in the devices that could be exploited by attackers.

3.3 The Fog Layer

The fog layer in Medical Internet of Things (MIoT) refers to the layer of computing resources that exist between the cloud and the edge devices in an IoT network. In MIoT forensics, the fog layer can play a critical role in the analysis and investigation of security incidents and data breaches, as it is responsible for processing, analyzing, and aggregating data from IoT devices before sending it to the cloud for storage and further analysis.

Unnecessary Data Reduction. In MIoT, large amounts of data are generated by medical devices and systems, such as wearable devices, remote monitoring systems, and electronic health records. This data can include sensitive and confidential information, such as patient health data, making it important to manage and process it in a secure and responsible manner. The use of unnecessary data reduction in MIoT can help to address some of the challenges associated with managing large and complex data sets, such as data storage and processing costs, data security and privacy, and data analysis and interpretation. By reducing the amount of data that needs to be stored and processed, unnecessary data reduction can help to minimize the risk of data breaches and unauthorized access, as well as improving the efficiency and speed of data analysis [8].

Machine Learning. In the fog layer in Medical Internet of Things (MIoT), machine learning (ML) can be used to enhance the capabilities and functionality of MIoT systems by providing real-time data analysis and decision-making capabilities.

ML algorithms can be deployed to process and analyze data generated by MIoT devices, such as wearable devices and remote monitoring systems, in real-time. This can enable real-time decision-making based on the data generated, without the need for data to be transmitted to a centralized data center for analysis. ML can be used in the fog layer of MIoT to ensure:

- Predictive maintenance: Using machine learning algorithms to analyze data from MIoT devices to predict when maintenance is needed, reducing the risk of equipment failure and increasing the efficiency of maintenance operations.
- Real-time diagnosis: Using machine learning algorithms to analyze data from wearable devices to detect symptoms of disease or other health conditions in real-time, allowing for early detection and intervention.
- Patient monitoring: Using machine learning algorithms to analyze data from remote monitoring systems to monitor patients in real-time, reducing the need for in-person visits and increasing patient safety and convenience.

3.4 The Blockchain Layer

Blockchain technology has the potential to play a significant role in the Medical Internet of Things (MIoT) by providing a secure, decentralized platform for storing and managing sensitive medical data. In MIoT, blockchain can help to address many of the privacy and security challenges associated with traditional centralized data storage solutions, including data breaches, unauthorized access, and data tampering.

One of the key benefits of blockchain in MIoT is its decentralized nature, which allows for the secure sharing of medical data between different stakeholders, such as patients, healthcare providers, and medical researchers, without the need for a centralized intermediary. This can help to improve the accuracy, completeness, and timeliness of medical data, which can in turn lead to better healthcare outcomes.

In addition to its security and privacy benefits, blockchain technology can also help to streamline and automate many of the processes involved in managing medical data in MIoT. For example, smart contracts can be used to automate the sharing and exchange of medical data between different stakeholders, based on predefined rules and conditions.

Overall, the integration of blockchain technology in MIoT has the potential to revolutionize the way medical data is stored, managed, and shared, while also helping to improve the overall quality and outcomes of healthcare. Blockchain technology has been increasingly used in the Medical Internet of Things (MIoT) for secure storage and management of sensitive medical data. In MIoT forensics, the blockchain layer can play a critical role in the analysis and investigation of security incidents and data breaches.

The blockchain layer in MIoT forensics typically involves the following steps:

- Data Collection: In this step, data is collected from the blockchain network, including blocks, transactions, and smart contracts.
- Data Analysis: In this step, the collected data is analyzed to identify any anomalies or signs of malicious activity, such as unauthorized access to medical data, data tampering, or network intrusion.
- Evidence Recovery: In this step, relevant evidence is recovered from the blockchain, including any data or artifacts that may be useful in reconstructing the events leading up to the security incident.
- Decision making: smart contracts can be used to automate processes and enforce policies, reducing the risk of human error and improving the overall efficiency and reliability of MIoT systems.
- Reporting: In this step, the results of the analysis are documented in a comprehensive report that outlines the findings, conclusions, and recommendations for remediation and future protection against similar security incidents.

3.5   Homomorphic Cryptography

Homomorphic cryptography is a form of encryption that allows computations to be performed on ciphertext data, without decrypting it first, and producing an encrypted result that can be decrypted to yield the same result as if the computations were performed on the plaintext data. This enables secure processing of sensitive information without revealing the data itself.

3.6   Network Forensics

Network forensics is the process of collecting, analyzing, and interpreting network data in order to investigate security incidents and support digital investigations. In the context of Medical Internet of Things (MIoT). In MIoT, network forensics is typically performed using a combination of network monitoring and analysis tools, such as network probes, intrusion detection systems, and log management solutions. These tools are used to collect and analyze network data, including traffic logs, system logs, and configuration files, in order to identify and understand the cause of a security incident.

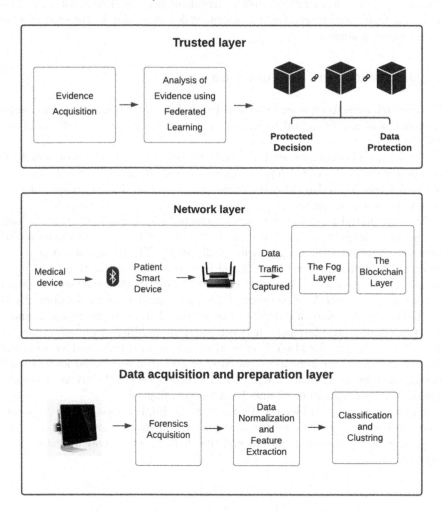

Fig. 2. Cyber threat detection system for MIoT.

Figure 2 illustrates a cyber threat detection system for MIoT. The proposed system for digital forensics in MIoT employs machine learning (ML) techniques at three levels of digital forensics: Data acquisition and preparation, network, and trusted level. The system acquires data from RAM memory, including information on running processes, logs, and events, which is then analyzed using various ML algorithms to detect intrusions. Network forensics involves analyzing data flow and extracting high-level features from network traffic. In the trusted level, an intrusion detection approach can be integrated into the cloud architecture to identify malicious activities. ML techniques, including supervised and unsupervised methods such as KNN, Naive Bayes, and ANN, as well as deep learning approaches such as CNN and deep belief networks, that can be used to evaluate evidence gathered from virtual disks, virtual memory, and network logs. This allows for faster and more accurate anomaly detection due to the cloud's high computing availability.

4   Discussion and Comparison

This research aims to raise awareness and stimulate discussions about the implementation and use of digital forensics tools, techniques, and standards in the medical field.

Table 1 presents comparison between the state of the art frameworks and our proposed framework. The comparison examines the type of the used data, the forensics level, the different architecture layers, the applied technique of each framework and whether the privacy and confidentiality are preserved.

Existing digital forensics frameworks and techniques tend to focus on hard drives and smartphones [5] medical implants [11], so there is a need to examine their effectiveness in the medical field. Additionally, The framework in paper [4] considers the following layers for digital forensics: data acquisition layer, data pre-processing layer, cloud layer, action layer. However, the framework in paper [5] considers Personal Area Network (PAN), Intermediate Area Network (IAN) and External Area Network (EAN). The proposed framework utilizes memory forensics, smart device forensics, network forensics on MIoT, and determines the most effective scheme for MIoT forensics by incorporating federated learning and blockchain. As for our knowledge, we are the first to use fedrated learning and blockchain in MIoT forensics framework. The other state of the art architectures employ ML LoS Algorithm [5] and Machine Learning [4].

Future work will consider the digital forensics implications from a corporate policy perspective, identifying the best way to integrate digital forensics processes into healthcare organizations and the challenges that may arise from this implementation.

Table 1. Frameworks comparison.

	Framework in [5]	Framework in [6]	Framework in [12]	Our Proposed Framework
Architecture layers	Data acquisition layer, data pre-processing layer, cloud layer and action layer	Personal Area Network (PAN), Intermediate Area Network (IAN) and External Area Network (EAN)	-	Data acquisition and preparation layer, network layer and trusted layer
Smart device	Personnel server (PS): WBAN, biomedical sensors, mobile networks...	Smartphones and tablets	Smartphones and medical implants	Mobile phone and smartwatch
Forensics level	-	-	IoT forensics investigation	Three forensics levels
Data	Scalar, images, radio ...	A file, an image, transaction history ...	IoT data can be available in any vendor-specific format	Scalar, images, radio ...
Techniques	Machine learning	LoS algorithm	A cryptographic Black-Berry 9900 PGP mobile phone method	Federated learning
Confidentiality	-	-	Symmetric-cryptography	Homomorphic encryption
Secure desicion	-	-	-	✓
Privecy-preservation	-	-	✓	✓

5 Conclusion and Future Work

The Medical Internet of Things (MIoT) is a rapidly growing technology that promises to revolutionize healthcare by enabling individualized e-health services that are accessible anytime and anywhere. However, security and privacy concerns arise with the increasing use of MIoT devices and the sharing of sensitive patient data. The challenge is to ensure the confidentiality and privacy of patients while also maintaining security. To succeed with MIoT, proper authentication and authorization measures must be put in place to prevent unauthorized access to linked equipment. Despite the security challenges, the adoption of MIoT in healthcare is expected to bring numerous benefits, including the digitization of healthcare and improved patient care. The use of connected devices in the healthcare system is still in its early stages of development, but the potential for disruption is significant and the future of healthcare looks promising with the integration of IoT. In the coming years, this novel framework, which enables the development of a forensically-conscious MIoT system, has the potential to make healthcare systems more reliable and trustworthy.

References

1. Bhatele, K.R., Jain, S., Kataria, A., Jain, P.: The fundamentals of digital forensics (2020)
2. Elhoseny, M., et al.: Security and privacy issues in medical internet of things: overview, countermeasures, challenges and future directions. Sustainability **13**(21), 11645 (2021)
3. Grispos, G., Bastola, K.: Cyber autopsies: the integration of digital forensics into medical contexts. In: 2020 IEEE 33rd International Symposium on Computer-Based Medical Systems (CBMS), pp. 510–513 (2020). https://doi.org/10.1109/CBMS49503.2020.00102
4. Jahankhani, H., Ibarra, J.: Digital forensic investigation for the internet of medical things (IoMT). Forensic Leg. Investig. Sci. **5** (2019)

5. Harbawi, M., Varol, A.: An improved digital evidence acquisition model for the internet of things forensic I: a theoretical framework. In: 2017 5th International Symposium on Digital Forensic and Security (ISDFS), pp. 1–6 (2017). https://doi.org/10.1109/ISDFS.2017.7916508

6. Lutta, P., Sedky, M., Hassan, M., Jayawickrama, U., Bakhtiari Bastaki, B.: The complexity of internet of things forensics: a state-of-the-art review. Forensic Sci. Int. Digit. Invest. **38**, 301210 (2021). https://doi.org/10.1016/j.fsidi.2021.301210. https://www.sciencedirect.com/science/article/pii/S2666281721001189

7. Perwej, Y., Akhtar, N., Kulshrestha, N., Mishra, P.: A methodical analysis of medical internet of things (MIoT) security and privacy in current and future trends. J. Emerg. Technol. Innov. Res. **9**(1), d346–d371 (2022)

8. Rahmany, I., Dhahri, N., Moulahi, T., Alabdulatif, A.: Optimized stacked auto-encoder for unnecessary data reduction in cloud of things. In: 2022 International Wireless Communications and Mobile Computing (IWCMC), pp. 110–115 (2022). https://doi.org/10.1109/IWCMC55113.2022.9825372

9. Rahmany, I., Mahfoudhi, S., Freihat, M., Moulahi, T.: Missing data recovery in the e-health context based on machine learning models. Adv. Artif. Intell. Mach. Learn. **2**(4), 516–532 (2022). https://doi.org/10.54364/aaiml.2022.1135

10. Ruan, K., Carthy, J., Kechadi, T., Crosbie, M.: Cloud forensics. In: Peterson, G., Shenoi, S. (eds.) DigitalForensics 2011. IAICT, vol. 361, pp. 35–46. Springer, Heidelberg (2011). https://doi.org/10.1007/978-3-642-24212-0_3

11. Shaaban, A., Abdelbaki, N.: Comparison study of digital forensics analysis techniques; findings versus resources. Procedia Comput. Sci. **141**, 545–551 (2018)

12. Yaqoob, I., Hashem, I.A.T., Ahmed, A., Kazmi, S.A., Hong, C.S.: Internet of things forensics: recent advances, taxonomy, requirements, and open challenges. Future Gener. Comput. Syst. **92**, 265–275 (2019). https://doi.org/10.1016/j.future.2018.09.058. https://www.sciencedirect.com/science/article/pii/S0167739X18315644

Federated Learning - Opportunities and Application Challenges

Mihailo Ilić$^{(\boxtimes)}$ and Mirjana Ivanović$^{(\boxtimes)}$

University of Novi Sad, Faculty of Sciences, Novi Sad, Serbia
{milic,mira}@dmi.uns.ac.rs
https://www.pmf.uns.ac.rs/en/

Abstract. In this paper our intention was to present a brief literature review focused on the latest research of the Federated Learning paradigm in order to identify current research trends, possible future directions of development, and challenges in this area. Federated learning as a new, powerful distributed intelligent paradigm can take on various forms in order to fit a diverse set of problems in a wide range of domains, economy, finance, medicine, agriculture and other industrial sectors. Based on presented research results, several key opportunities for future work can be identified and some emerging are connected to communication costs and performance of federated models trained by different algorithms.

Keywords: Federated Learning · Applications of Federated Learning · IoT and Federated Learning · Data Privacy Preserving

1 Introduction

Machine learning (ML) is nowadays a broad field with numerous research directions, opportunities, and limitless challenges. A wide range of ML techniques have been developed in modern research and one of the main challenges is the implementation of these techniques in areas where handling of sensitive data is of essential interest. As a characteristic example, we can mention the utilization of such techniques in the processing of very sensitive medical data. Privacy preservation and security of such data is essential and strictly guarded by numerous agreements and legal documents such as the General Data Protection Agreement (GDPR). Accordingly, new techniques have emerged which aim to protect the integrity of such sensitive data while also capitalizing on the knowledge hidden within this data. One of the ML approaches which nowadays is getting more and more popular and applicable in a wide range of domains, especially in highly distributed environments, is Federated Learning (FL). Known as decentralized machine learning, its main goal is to have each data center (edge node i.e. client) train local models on its local data. After this step, all of the trained models at different edge nodes are aggregated and combined somehow, either by collecting them at a central location (cloud i.e., server), or in a way that all of the edge nodes communicate their local models between them directly. In this paper we

© The Author(s), under exclusive license to Springer Nature Switzerland AG 2023
N. T. Nguyen et al. (Eds.): ICCCI 2023, CCIS 1864, pp. 481–492, 2023.
https://doi.org/10.1007/978-3-031-41774-0_38

give a brief overview of applications of FL in several important domains. Several insightful papers are grouped together according to the topics they cover. Also, we cover research on the utilization of FL in specific areas, different approaches and experimental evaluations of these techniques, and challenges which FL faces. We considered papers published after 2020. A simple methodological approach was applied based on the use of different keywords containing federated learning and searching within Google Scholar. The paper is organized as follows. In the second Section different approaches of FL implementation are presented. The third Section is devoted to the main challenges necessary to be solved when FL is employed in distributed environments. The fourth Section briefly presents several characteristic domains where FL approaches are natural solutions. Concluding remarks are given in the final section.

2   Different Approaches to Federated Learning

Federated learning is a form of decentralized learning where multiple clients work collaboratively with the main goal to train a global machine learning model without sharing their data. The reasons for such a style of processing data collected at the edge usually are oriented towards the reduction of the overhead cost of communication between edges and cloud or preservation of data privacy [13]. It is a powerful technique which attracts a lot of research and application interest in industry and academia. Application of FL depends on different circumstances, like high number of existing data centers, specific data distribution, great amount of data available at each center, orchestration method and so on. Depending on the mentioned characteristics, FL may take on many forms, with each form introducing different challenges like communication efficiency, security and protection against a variety of attacks, privacy protection, etc. From the first attempts mentioned in [19], the approach has significantly evolved and nowadays covers a broader scope of use cases. It exceeds the standard supervised edge learning orchestrated by a central server and moved away from supervised learning all together [5]. An interesting approach is the creation of personalized federated models [6,28,33] which are able to better support clients with different data distributions, developing new algorithms [2,10] and moving away from standard Federated Averaging [19].

The implementation of innovative FL algorithms may greatly benefit institutions where privacy preservation is crucial, like financial and medical sectors. Additionally, symbiosis with other modern approaches and technologies like digital twins may also push wider use of FL into fields such as agriculture, epidemiology and modeling the spread of diseases in urban areas.

Federated learning was first envisioned as a technique for coordinating edge devices in training ML models by a central server [19]. After that the approach has been quickly spread from the initial focus on edge and mobile devices and was broadened in order to encompass these new use cases. The terms "cross-silo" and "cross-device" federated learning were coined in [13] and cover two general settings. In the first case, focus is on applications with a relatively small number of reliable clients (like hospitals or banks). In the second case, focus is on initially envisioned applications, i.e. on the standard edge device setting. In this case applications can easily have hundreds of thousands or even millions of edge nodes.

Most research and implementations of FL imply having a central entity coordinating the learning process. However, there are some concerns regarding this approach. The minor concerns include favoritism when updating global models, which can have as a consequence that some edge nodes show better performance, while others show significantly worse ones. However, this issue can be alleviated by modifying the standard approach with techniques known as personalized federated learning [2,6,33]. More dangerous concerns regarding centralized FL include unsafe or even malicious central servers which may cause data leaks. This problematic situation in centralized coordination of FL has led to some research fully oriented on decentralized methods. Some of them rely on peer-to-peer communication [27], while others are oriented to contemporary approaches such as blockchain [17].

Depending on the orchestration method applied, we can distinguish:

- **Centralized FL** – The learning process is coordinated by a central server. The server takes care of orchestration and synchronization of the learning processes at each edge node. It is responsible for selecting a subset of edge nodes and having them iteratively or concurrently update the global model [13,31].
- **Fully decentralized FL** – The central authority which dictates when and how training of a particular model should be performed is missing. In such situations, certain edge nodes could communicate peer-to-peer with other edge nodes in its vicinity to exchange model updates [27]. Also, a blockchain approach may be applied to verify and keep track of updates to a certain global model [7,17].

Depending on the number of edge nodes (clients) participating in federated learning, we recognize the following cases [13]:

- **Cross-device FL** – In this case, the focus is on mobile and IoT devices and the number of participating edge nodes can be even millions. Having in mind such a large number of edge nodes, a centralized server must select a subset of edge devices to perform one round of federated updates. Edge nodes can be seen here as unreliable, since limited computing resources or network issues may cause significant latency or even a complete failure during the training process.
- **Cross-silo FL** – In this case, tens or hundreds of edge nodes are participating. In a federated environment, it is necessary to have larger data centers like banks or hospitals, which are generally more reliable than edge IoT devices. With a smaller number of edge nodes, it is not needed to select subsets of edge nodes to participate in the training process.

In both scenarios, the central server organizes the training process i.e., the order in which the edge nodes submit their model updates to the server. Several strategies are considered in literature [31]:

- **Concurrent FL** – In this case, all participating edge nodes carry out a single federated learning step (usually it is one epoch of training). The server waits for all edge nodes to submit their updates and after that it aggregates all updates using some algorithm for federated averaging [13,23]. In the cross-silo setting where clients are reliable, synchronization is rather straightforward. In cross-device FL, edge device failure and/or network instability must be considered. However, there are some solutions like: implementing a timeout to eliminate devices which take too long to respond to model updates, or some novel approaches which support asynchronous or semi-asynchronous updates to global models [3,5].
- **Incremental FL** – The server arranges N edge nodes in a queue, $E_1...E_n$. Following the specified order, clients update the global model by running local training on the global model using available local training datasets D_i. After successful local training, the updated model M_i is submitted to the server. The main drawback of this approach is possible loss of knowledge. In fact, when edge node E_{i+1} updates the global model, the performance of the newly updated model can significantly drop on the validation set of the previous edge node E_i.
- **Cyclic-incremental FL** – This approach is oriented towards tackling the problem of knowledge loss in the previous approach [31]. The idea is to eliminate waiting until each edge node E_i runs an entire round of training (sometimes it can include hundreds of epochs). So, the queue is transformed into a circular list where edge nodes $E_1...E_n$ update the model for one epoch each. After the last node finishes its update round, node E_1 again initializes the update process. In such a manner, each edge node at each step makes slight adjustments to the global model.

In spite of the fact that both mentioned approaches have their own unique problems, there are some common issues. Data distribution is an important issue which includes two problems: the number of data points at each edge node and the statistical distribution from which data points were drawn. Federated learning cannot make any assumptions about the statistical distribution of data points, which causes clients which have access to more data usually have a greater representation of the global dataset. Local models that are trained on small datasets are prone to overfitting and usually show low performance on new data instances. As a consequence, for smaller clients the incentive is clear – to gain access to better models. However, incentive seems to be lost for edge nodes which have bigger datasets. Again, some new methods have been developed to solve such problems, like personalized federated learning [6,33] and meta learning [12].

Furthermore, apart from considering data partitioning in federated environments, it is necessary to also consider feature sets [13,36]. Based on this criterion, we can distinguish two forms of FL. **Horizontal federated learning** assumes that all clients have access to the same feature set. In **Vertical federated learning** different clients can collect different features for the same instance. Finally, for FL could be considered different institutions which can have different feature sets, but also different sample spaces. In this case, we have a new FL paradigm called **federated transfer learning**.

Federated learning is mostly based on supervised learning and availability of labeled data. However, often [3] the realistic scenarios are that for different reasons data is partially labeled or not labeled. Different approaches such as semi-supervised learning could help to consider a variety of problems and domains which could be successfully solved by FL. In fact, using a small amount of labeled data, it is possible to create pseudo-labelled datasets which can be used to optimize these models. A typical scenario could be that a central server can have a small amount of labeled data, while the clients have unlabeled data. Some authors [3,5] proposed semi-supervised learning to FL, and thus expand its reach while achieving promising results.

3   Challenges that Federated Learning Brings

Federated learning is branching out in numerous directions and opens new and challenging issues in contemporary scientific research and industrial applications. Generally, interesting aspects are consideration of the number of participating clients, the data distribution, machine learning tasks, orchestration methods and strategies, etc. However, some challenges are specific to certain setups, while others are common across multiple federated scenarios. Some of the characteristic challenges will be briefly discussed in the rest of the section.

3.1   Privacy

Privacy preservation of sensitive data located at clients was originally a driving factor for conceptualizing this approach. FL naturally seems to protect the data since it does not require data to leave the edge. Initially, the two-way client-server communication which only exchanges information of updated model weights was considered safe. However, it has since been argued that these weight updates carry hidden information of the dataset from which they were created. This phenomenon is known as deep leakage or feature leakage from gradients [20,38]. An untrustworthy party may be able to reconstruct the initial dataset based on a certain edge node's weight updates [20]. This is an unintended security vulnerability which threatens the core assumptions of standard federated learning. Being aware of such security vulnerabilities, some solutions have been proposed. Different methods developed under the umbrella of **Differential privacy (DP)** can be reliable in solving the mentioned problems. DP encompasses methods for anonymizing datasets and altering them in such a way to make it harder for attackers to infer which individual or instance features from the dataset belong to. DP methods are particularly effective in FL as the original data cannot be reconstructed since the updates were a result of training on modified data. A negative aspect of this approach is the possibility of lowering the performance of the models being trained on real data [37]. When applying DP to FL tasks, it is often necessary to conduct prior tests to consider possible effects of varying amounts of augmentation on the performance of ML models [8,20].

Another contemporary approach for security and privacy preservation of sensitive data which helps in reducing the negative effects of feature leakages is **Homomorphic encryption (HE)**. Similarly, like the DP approach, HE is an umbrella term that incorporates different methods and techniques that allow users to perform operations and computations on encrypted data. When results are achieved and sent to the origin and decrypted, the results are the same as the results obtained from applying the same computations on unencrypted data. In [8] authors demonstrated the use of HE in fully decentralized federated learning. In this approach, edge nodes encrypt the model updates generated through local training. After that, they share the encrypted gradients with neighboring edge nodes. Other, less effective and less advantageous methods include sharing fewer gradients with the server or other collaborating clients or dimensionality reduction of the data [20].

Privacy also extends to trust issues in client-server settings and clients willing to collaborate and share knowledge must apply some form of defense mechanism. The differential privacy and homomorphic encryption techniques are often applied in practice [20,37]. In cases where clients cannot fully trust servers, a fully decentralized (i.e., serverless) approach offers an alternative. Decentralized approaches can rely on empowering technologies like blockchain [7,17] or they can be entirely peer-to-peer and have a more torrent-like approach [27].

On the other hand, what to do in situations when servers also cannot fully trust edge nodes. **Model poisoning** [5,30] is a form of attack on the global federated models where clients send damaging updates to the FL coordinator with the intention of disrupting the convergence of the global model. Model poisoning is a general term describing updates which disrupt the training process and slow down or even completely sabotage model convergence. This attack is quite hard to counter in federated environments since the server does not have access to original training data [5]. Furthermore, there is a question of identifying truly malicious training participants from those who simply do not have quality data [15]. Privacy can also be enhanced through split learning [10,13], which is an approach where learning starts at the edge and finishes in the cloud. Basically, the "head" of a deep neural network is located at the server while the other half, which handles input of data, is located at the client side. In this case, the training of a single model is done by both the client and the server.

3.2 Personalization

Federated learning supports creating a global model which can generalize well on the entirety of the global dataset, but it is affected by data distribution between clients. Generally, it is expected that in the typical FL setting based on the federated averaging algorithm, clients with less data available will contribute less to the quality and reliability of the overall model. Consequently, their datasets will be less represented in the global model and local models will be more accurate than the global federated model.

Some proposals to solve this problem are reported in different papers [5,12, 15,16] and we will present them briefly in the rest of the section.

A widely accepted solution to the mentioned problem is known as **Federated transfer learning** [15]. First activity is that edge nodes collaborate in training global models. After that step edge nodes download the global model and start with transfer learning locally i.e., fine-tuning of the global model is performed on their local data distribution.

The second possible solution is based on fair resource allocation in a federated learning environment [16]. After each iteration of federated updates, the resulting global model would be validated by all participating clients. The essence of this approach is: when some clients notice poorer performance of the model, the server could shift training in their favor, assigning higher significance to their weight updates of the global model. The possible negative aspect of such a solution is increasing the risk of being vulnerable to model poisoning attacks [5].

As a solution to achieve better performing models for certain edge nodes that have specific data distributions, personalized federated learning (PFL) has been proposed. Contrary to local ML where for each of the N edge nodes a different model exists in traditional FL a single global model which would ideally generalize well on all edge nodes is created. Personalized federated learning goes in a slightly different direction where multiple global models are created, each one best suited for a subset of edge nodes. To achieve better performance of models, a kind of prior clustering of edge nodes is welcomed [1,2,28,33,34]. It has been stated in [34] that it is expected that cluster specific models converge significantly faster [34] compared to models trained without clustering. An additional advantage is that numerous clients with small datasets which are not able to train their own useful models can use reliable global models [1].

3.3   Communication Latency

In the majority of cases in FL environments, almost all computationally intensive work is put on the edge. Since edge nodes can be IoT devices without enough computational power, local model optimization may take an unacceptable long time. It is especially problematic when clients with low computing power may have larger datasets and need longer time to train models. If these updates get disregarded by the coordinating server, computation power at the edge device is wasted. To solve the problem, different approaches to introduce asynchronous federated learning protocols are reported [4,35]. Real world settings also often have data arriving in streams, as it is collected. Online learning presented in [4] handles data arriving in streams and was coupled with asynchronous FL.

3.4   Other Challenges

Certain critical systems that include IoT settings which are massively distributed have very high accuracy requirements. In [32], short term electrical load forecasting of households is pointed out as a problem which could be tackled with FL, as it requires privacy protection. The prediction of electrical usage requires high accuracy, which is why personalized federated learning methods such as clustered aggregation must be implemented [34].

One among several bottlenecks for FL is communication efficiency [4,9,15,21] as the number of participating edge devices in each round can be quite high. It is very important to solve the communication overhead issue. Asynchronous FL [35] presents an acceptable communication cost. However, better approaches like extending local training done at the edge [5] have successfully decreased the number of transmitted messages between the client and server. The essence of this approach is that the server lets clients run multiple epochs before submitting their updates instead of having each edge node run only one epoch of training.

Another approach is presented in [37] where federated learning is considered from the perspective of the client. The authors considered the question of what incentive clients have to participate in FL. Clients which have big datasets may not benefit much from FL as it can happen that the global model has worse performance than their local model. On the contrary, clients which have small datasets can have more benefits from this approach. However, a classical drawback is that local models are prone to overfitting and lose the ability to generalize effectively [31,33].

4   Application of Federated Learning to Different Domains

Federated learning faces many challenges and open questions, attracting the research community. It has a lot of possibilities to be applied in different domains in academia and industry. Contemporary FL applications are predominantly in domains where the focus is on IoT and security and privacy preserving datasets like medicine, banking and similar domains.

The use of FL in medicine is a kind of guarantee of providing a high level of security and privacy [11,29]. The approach based on tensor factorization and federated models is presented in [14]. To protect the privacy of involved patients and under the assumption that a federated server can only be semi-trusted only summarized information is transferred to the cloud. Also, different federated orchestration strategies are evaluated [31] and it has been shown that FL can achieve results in medicine that are comparable with results obtained by centralized learning methods. Patients' privacy is achieved through application of different methods among which differential privacy is dominant. Unification of FL with some other contemporary technologies (like digital twins) is considered in [24] where it helps to reduce the spread of infectious diseases [24]. By modeling cities and simulating certain responses to the spread of disease, it could be possible to reduce its negative effect. Also, the cold start problem was pointed out once a disease first emerges in some environment.

The Internet of Things can also have great benefits from applying FL to some workflows. One among the biggest concerns in this area is communication overhead because of the numerous devices participating in the process. High accuracy is needed for tasks like electrical load forecasting [32] which need to be aided by personalization methods such as in [34] or methods which are proposed in [1,2]. Some advantages of implementations of fully decentralized FL based on blockchain and development of several advanced approaches are presented in [7]. In the presented solution, specific care is taken of problems like edge node authentication. However, additional work is necessary on compressing these models to reduce communication costs and on incentive mechanisms to encourage clients to join the FL process. Federated learning may soon find itself utilized in telecommunication. New 5G and 6G networks and telecommunication architectures [22] embed intelligence at the network level. The intelligent O-RAN architecture would see this intelligence optimize resource allocation and various other tasks at the edge [22,25]. This new architecture would be fully virtualized and would be able to run real-time, near real-time or non-real-time applications, which would more often than not involve utilization of machine learning models [25]. According to [21], decentralized ML offers support to reduce energy consumption and network bandwidth.

One very interesting and challenging area where applications of intelligent techniques are rapidly increasing is agriculture. The knowledge and experience gained in using intelligent techniques in industrial settings are excellent starting points for their application to food production. Factories have already experienced great benefits from IoT integrations which involve the use of digital twins to help facilitate their processes. This can be carried over to agriculture where the use of digital twins may help in modeling and simulating fields and the effect of various parameters on crop yield [26]. As symbiosis of FL and digital twins is already applied [24], it can be expected that soon similar implementations in agriculture will bring significant benefits.

Banking and finance also have various challenges which slow down the integration of ML systems. However, federated learning may provide better solutions and answers [18] to some of these blocking issues which could pave the way for future successful integration into such systems.

5   Conclusion and Future Challenges

The intention of this brief literature review was to focus on the latest research of FL in order to identify the latest research developments, future research directions, challenges, and open problems in this area. Federated learning as a new, powerful distributed intelligent paradigm can take on various forms in order to fit a diverse set of problems in numerous domains, economy and the industrial sector. Based on presented research results, numerous opportunities for future work can be identified. Some notable issues which have emerged are connected to communication costs and performance of federated models trained by different algorithms and strategies.

Communication costs have a significant impact on the real-world application of FL and it could be interesting to determine the relationship between model performance and communication cost. It is also viable to research other techniques which could reduce the overhead of communication, other than extending model training at the edge by some fixed number of epochs.

Although numerous experimental evaluations have been done to compare the performance of federated models trained by different algorithms, there is little research done on the influence of the federated orchestration strategy on the performance of models. For successful evaluation, it is necessary to work with variations in dataset sizes available at the edge and the sequence in which institutions make updates.

References

1. Armacki, A., Bajovic, D., Jakovetic, D., Kar, S.: One-shot federated learning for model clustering and learning in heterogeneous environments. arXiv preprint arXiv:2209.10866 (2022)
2. Armacki, A., Bajovic, D., Jakovetic, D., Kar, S.: Personalized federated learning via convex clustering. In: 2022 IEEE International Smart Cities Conference (ISC2), pp. 1–7. IEEE (2022)
3. Bian, J., Fu, Z., Xu, J.: FedSEAL: semi-supervised federated learning with self-ensemble learning and negative learning. arXiv preprint arXiv:2110.07829 (2021)
4. Chen, Y., Ning, Y., Slawski, M., Rangwala, H.: Asynchronous online federated learning for edge devices with non-IID data. In: 2020 IEEE International Conference on Big Data (Big Data), pp. 15–24. IEEE (2020)
5. Diao, E., Ding, J., Tarokh, V.: SemiFL: semi-supervised federated learning for unlabeled clients with alternate training. In: Advances in Neural Information Processing Systems, vol. 35, pp. 17871–17884 (2022)
6. Fallah, A., Mokhtari, A., Ozdaglar, A.: Personalized federated learning: a meta-learning approach. arXiv preprint arXiv:2002.07948 (2020)
7. Feng, C., Liu, B., Yu, K., Goudos, S.K., Wan, S.: Blockchain-empowered decentralized horizontal federated learning for 5G-enabled UAVs. IEEE Trans. Ind. Inf. **18**(5), 3582–3592 (2021)
8. Froelicher, D., et al.: Truly privacy-preserving federated analytics for precision medicine with multiparty homomorphic encryption. Nat. Commun. **12**(1), 5910 (2021)
9. Gadekallu, T.R., Pham, Q.V., Huynh-The, T., Bhattacharya, S., Maddikunta, P.K.R., Liyanage, M.: Federated learning for big data: a survey on opportunities, applications, and future directions. arXiv preprint arXiv:2110.04160 (2021)
10. Gao, Y., et al.: End-to-end evaluation of federated learning and split learning for internet of things. arXiv preprint arXiv:2003.13376 (2020)
11. Ivanovic, M., Autexier, S., Kokkonidis, M., Rust, J.: Quality medical data management within an open AI architecture - cancer patients case. Connect. Sci. **35**(1), 2194581 (2023). https://doi.org/10.1080/09540091.2023.2194581
12. Jiang, Y., Konečný, J., Rush, K., Kannan, S.: Improving federated learning personalization via model agnostic meta learning. arXiv preprint arXiv:1909.12488 (2019)
13. Kairouz, P., et al.: Advances and open problems in federated learning. Found. Trends® Mach. Learn. **14**(1–2), 1–210 (2021)

14. Kim, Y., Sun, J., Yu, H., Jiang, X.: Federated tensor factorization for computational phenotyping. In: Proceedings of the 23rd ACM SIGKDD International Conference on Knowledge Discovery and Data Mining, pp. 887–895 (2017)
15. Li, L., Fan, Y., Tse, M., Lin, K.Y.: A review of applications in federated learning. Comput. Ind. Eng. **149**, 106854 (2020)
16. Li, T., Sanjabi, M., Beirami, A., Smith, V.: Fair resource allocation in federated learning. arXiv preprint arXiv:1905.10497 (2019)
17. Li, Y., Chen, C., Liu, N., Huang, H., Zheng, Z., Yan, Q.: A blockchain-based decentralized federated learning framework with committee consensus. IEEE Netw. **35**(1), 234–241 (2020)
18. Long, G., Tan, Y., Jiang, J., Zhang, C.: Federated learning for open banking. In: Yang, Q., Fan, L., Yu, H. (eds.) Federated Learning. LNCS (LNAI), vol. 12500, pp. 240–254. Springer, Cham (2020). https://doi.org/10.1007/978-3-030-63076-8_17
19. McMahan, B., Moore, E., Ramage, D., Hampson, S., Arcas, B.A.: Communication-efficient learning of deep networks from decentralized data. In: Artificial Intelligence and Statistics, pp. 1273–1282. PMLR (2017)
20. Melis, L., Song, C., De Cristofaro, E., Shmatikov, V.: Exploiting unintended feature leakage in collaborative learning. In: 2019 IEEE Symposium on Security and Privacy (SP), pp. 691–706. IEEE (2019)
21. Niknam, S., Dhillon, H.S., Reed, J.H.: Federated learning for wireless communications: motivation, opportunities, and challenges. IEEE Commun. Mag. **58**(6), 46–51 (2020)
22. Niknam, S., et al.: Intelligent O-RAN for beyond 5G and 6G wireless networks. In: 2022 IEEE Globecom Workshops (GC Wkshps), pp. 215–220. IEEE (2022)
23. Nilsson, A., Smith, S., Ulm, G., Gustavsson, E., Jirstrand, M.: A performance evaluation of federated learning algorithms. In: Proceedings of the Second Workshop on Distributed Infrastructures for Deep Learning, pp. 1–8 (2018)
24. Pang, J., Huang, Y., Xie, Z., Li, J., Cai, Z.: Collaborative city digital twin for the Covid-19 pandemic: a federated learning solution. Tsinghua Sci. Technol. **26**(5), 759–771 (2021)
25. Polese, M., Bonati, L., D'Oro, S., Basagni, S., Melodia, T.: ColO-RAN: developing machine learning-based xApps for open RAN closed-loop control on programmable experimental platforms. IEEE Trans. Mob. Comput. (2022)
26. Pylianidis, C., Osinga, S., Athanasiadis, I.N.: Introducing digital twins to agriculture. Comput. Electron. Agric. **184**, 105942 (2021)
27. Roy, A.G., Siddiqui, S., Pölsterl, S., Navab, N., Wachinger, C.: BrainTorrent: a peer-to-peer environment for decentralized federated learning. arXiv preprint arXiv:1905.06731 (2019)
28. Sattler, F., Müller, K.R., Samek, W.: Clustered federated learning: model-agnostic distributed multitask optimization under privacy constraints. IEEE Trans. Neural Netw. Learn. Syst. **32**(8), 3710–3722 (2020)
29. Savić, M., et al.: The application of machine learning techniques in prediction of quality of life features for cancer patients. Comput. Sci. Inf. Syst. **20**(1), 381–404 (2023)
30. Shejwalkar, V., Houmansadr, A., Kairouz, P., Ramage, D.: Back to the drawing board: a critical evaluation of poisoning attacks on production federated learning. In: 2022 IEEE Symposium on Security and Privacy (SP), pp. 1354–1371. IEEE (2022)
31. Sheller, M.J., et al.: Federated learning in medicine: facilitating multi-institutional collaborations without sharing patient data. Sci. Rep. **10**(1), 1–12 (2020)

32. Taïk, A., Cherkaoui, S.: Electrical load forecasting using edge computing and federated learning. In: 2020 IEEE International Conference on Communications (ICC), ICC 2020, pp. 1–6. IEEE (2020)
33. Tan, A.Z., Yu, H., Cui, L., Yang, Q.: Towards personalized federated learning. IEEE Trans. Neural Netw. Learn. Syst. (2022)
34. Tun, Y.L., Thar, K., Thwal, C.M., Hong, C.S.: Federated learning based energy demand prediction with clustered aggregation. In: 2021 IEEE International Conference on Big Data and Smart Computing (BigComp), pp. 164–167. IEEE (2021)
35. Wu, W., He, L., Lin, W., Mao, R., Maple, C., Jarvis, S.: SAFA: a semi-asynchronous protocol for fast federated learning with low overhead. IEEE Trans. Comput. **70**(5), 655–668 (2020)
36. Yang, Q., Liu, Y., Chen, T., Tong, Y.: Federated machine learning: concept and applications. ACM Trans. Intell. Syst. Technol. (TIST) **10**(2), 1–19 (2019)
37. Yu, T., Bagdasaryan, E., Shmatikov, V.: Salvaging federated learning by local adaptation. arXiv preprint arXiv:2002.04758 (2020)
38. Zhu, L., Liu, Z., Han, S.: Deep leakage from gradients. In: Advances in Neural Information Processing Systems, vol. 32 (2019)

Cooperative Strategies for Decision Making and Optimization

A New Ant Population Based Improvement Heuristic for Solving Large Scale TSP

Samia Sammoud$^{(\boxtimes)}$ ⓘ, Ines Alaya ⓘ, and Moncef Tagina

Laboratory of Research in Artificial Intelligence (LARIA),
ENSI, University of Manouba, Manouba, Tunisia
{samia.sammoud,ines.alaya,moncef.tagina}@ensi-uma.tn

Abstract. Solving large-scale Traveling Salesman Problems (TSPs) has become a new challenge for the Ant Colony Optimization metaheuristic (ACO). Indeed, traditional ACO algorithms suffer from problems of stagnation and premature convergence and their computational cost increases remarkably as the problem size does. In this paper, we propose a new algorithm inspired by the ACO metaheuristic for symmetric large-scale TSPs. The basic idea of this new algorithm, called Ant-IH, is to change the classic role played by ants in order to accelerate the convergence speed. In fact, in our approach artificial ants are not anymore used to construct solutions but to improve the quality of a population of solutions using a guided local search strategy. To validate the performance of Ant-IH, we conduct the experiments on various TSPLIB instances. The experimental results show that our proposed algorithm is more efficient for solving symmetric large-scale TSPs than the compared algorithms.

Keywords: Ant colony optimization · Local search · Convergence speed

1 Introduction

Ant colony optimization (ACO) is a metaheuristic inspired by the behavior of real ant colonies [1]. In nature, ants communicate with each other by leaving pheromone trails to indicate the shortest paths to food sources. ACO is based on this communication mechanism and applies it to optimization problems.

ACO was originally developed to solve the Traveling Salesman Problem [2], but it has since been successfully applied to a variety of optimization problems including the quadratic assignment [3], vehicle routing [4–6], knapsack problems [7–9] and Scheduling problems [10–12], etc. It is widely used in various industries, such as transportation, logistics, and telecommunications.

However, ACO algorithms still suffer from problems of stagnation and premature convergence and the time needed by ants to build their solutions increases exponentially with the problem size. These disadvantages make ACO algorithms less competitive than the other metaheuristics and prevent them from solving large-scale instances.

© The Author(s), under exclusive license to Springer Nature Switzerland AG 2023
N. T. Nguyen et al. (Eds.): ICCCI 2023, CCIS 1864, pp. 495–507, 2023.
https://doi.org/10.1007/978-3-031-41774-0_39

To overcome these drawbacks, we propose a new ACO algorithm, called Ant-IH, for solving large-scale TSP problems. This new approach mainly differs from traditional ACO algorithms in the way how it uses ants. In fact, ants will not construct the solutions themselves but rather they will try to improve the quality of some initial solutions by using a pheromone guided 2-Opt function.

To summarize, our main contributions can be presented as follows:

1) We introduce, Ant-IH, a new variant that combines features from ACO and the iterated local search. This variant is a population based local search inspired by the ACO metaheuristic. It inherits its random criteria, pheromone update and evaporation mechanisms from the ACO but it uses them differently in order to guide the ant's search.
2) Ant-IH is based on an improvement procedure and not a construction procedure as in ACO metaheuristic, therefore it spends less time constructing solutions compared with traditional ACO algorithms.
3) Artificial ants perform a pheromone guided local search strategy to improve the quality of an initial population of solutions previously produced by the Nearest Neighbor Heuristic.
4) In our approach, new mechanisms for avoiding problems of stagnation and local optima are proposed. Indeed, Ant-IH accepts worsening movements with probability and this improves its ability to escape from local minima. It also replaces the non-scalable solutions by new ones randomly chosen from a so-called backup population.
5) The new variant shows a marked improvement in performance over traditional ACO algorithms and appears to be comparable to other evolutionary approaches.

The remainder of this paper is organized as follows. In the next section, we review related work. Section 3 is dedicated to explain the basic idea of our new approach. The results section (Sect. 4) is divided into two parts: first we start by comparing Ant-IH with ACO algorithms using large-scale TSP instances from the TSPLIB [13]. Then, another experimental study is performed to compare it with other recent evolutionary algorithms. The last section conclude this work.

2   Ant Colony Optimization

As shown in Algorithm 1, the basic steps of the ACO metaheuristic are as follows:

- Initialization: At the beginning of the algorithm, each ant is placed on some randomly chosen city.
- Solution construction: Each ant builds a solution by probabilistically selecting candidate cities based on the pheromone concentrations in the environment.
- Pheromone updating: After all ants have constructed their solutions, the pheromone levels are updated based on the quality of the solutions found.
- Termination: The algorithm terminates after a specified number of iterations or when a satisfactory solution is found.

ACO has many variants, including Ant System [14], Max-Min Ant System (MMAS) [15], and Ant Colony System (ACS) [16]. Each variant differs in the way pheromone trails are updated and how candidate cities are selected.

Algorithm 1. ACO meta-heuristic

Initialize parameters
repeat
  for each ant **do**
  construct_solution ()
  end for
  Evaporate_pheromone ()
  Deposite_pheromone ()
  Update best solution
until termination criteria is met
Return best solution

---

3 Proposed Approach

Algorithm 2. Algorithmic scheme of Ant-IH

Initialize the sizes of the initial population N_i and the backup population N_b
Generate N_i solutions: x_i $i \in 1, \ldots, N_i$ (**Using Algorithm 3**)
Initialize pheromone trails and the best-so-far solution X_{best}
for Max-iter **do**
  for each ant k **do**
    Produce a new solution $x_k^{'}$ **(Using Algorithm 4)**
    Replace x_k by $x_k^{'}$
    if $x_k^{'}$ is better than X_{best} **then**
     Replace X_{best} by $x_k^{'}$
     $Counter(X_{best}) = 0$
    else
     $Counter(X_{best}) = Counter(X_{best}) + 1$
    end if
  end for
  Update the trail level according to Eq. 2 and Eq. 3
  Update the backup population **(Algorithm 6)**
  if $Counter(X_{best}) >$ limit **then**
    for each solution x_i $i \in 1, \ldots, N_i$ **do**
    Replace x_i with a solution randomly chosen from the backup population
    end for
    $Counter(X_{best}) = 0$
  end if
end for
Output: Return best-solution X_{best}

As shown in Algorithm 2, Ant-IH starts by generating an initial population of solutions using the Nearest Neighbor Heuristic. Then, each ant takes a solution from the current population and performs a pheromone guided local search strategy to improve its quality.

At the end, all the obtained solutions are evaluated and only the best-iteration ant is allowed to update the pheromone trails.

Ant-IH proposes two mechanisms to avoid problems of stagnation and local optima. First, it uses a degradation acceptance criteria which allows ants to occasionally accept poorer quality solutions. In addition, when a problem of stagnation is met the population is automatically updated by new solutions. Indeed, a counter parameter is associated with the best overall solution, when its value becomes greater than a control parameter, called "limit", than all the solutions will be replaced by new ones randomly choosen from a backup population. This backup population contains a copy of the best found solutions during the program execution. The goal of using this second population is to speed up the local search process by replacing the abandoned solutions with others of similar quality.

3.1 The First Population Initialization

To generate an initial population of solutions, Ant-IH uses the Nearest Neighbour Heuristic (NNH). Thus, it spends less time constructing solutions compared with traditional ACO algorithms.

The main steps of the NNH are summarized in Algorithm 3. First, an arbitrarily chosen city is selected as a partial solution. Then, we iteratively choose the closet city to move ahead. The algorithm stops when all cities have been visited.

Algorithm 3. Nearest Neighbor Heuristic

Mark all the cities as unvisited
Select an arbitrary city and set it as the current city u
$S_{NNH} \leftarrow u$
Mark u as visited
Do
   Find out the shortest edge connecting city u and an unvisited city v
   Set v as the current city u
   $S_{NNH} \leftarrow u$
   Mark u as visited
until all the cities are visited
Output: return S_{NNH}

3.2 Pheromone Guided Local Search

In improvement heuristics, like 2-Opt [17] algorithm, best solutions are found by iteratively modifying a current solution using local movements. However, searching for all possible neighbors could be extremely expensive, especially when dealing with large-scale problems.

In Ant-IH, we recourse to pheromone to calculate for each edge a fitness value which reflects its priority to be preserved or rejected. Then according to the obtained results, we create a dynamic list (DL) containing a reduced set of 2-Opt movements. Each ant uses this list to look for an improving move or one that satisfies the degradation acceptance criteria. If such movement is found then the search is terminated, otherwise, the DL will be updated by new candidates and the search is then restarted. The process described above is outlined with more details in Algorithm 4.

Algorithm 4. Pheromone Guided Local Search

Choose an initial solution S_k
Generate the DL **(Algorithm 5)**
while (DL is not empty and no solution is accepted) **do**
  if(untested pairs remain in the DL) **then**
    Select an edge pair$((c_i, c_{i+1}), (c_j, c_{j+1}))$ from the DL
    Apply the 2-opt movement to obtain a new solution S_k'
    if $(S_k'$ is better than $S_k)$ **then**
      S_k' replaces S_k(an improvement is found)
    else
      Generate a random number r in [0,1]
      Calculate P=Fitness (c_i, c_j)+Fitness(c_{i+1}, c_{j+1}) (Eq. 1)
      if $(r<P)$
        S_k' replaces S_k(A degradation is accepted)
      else
        S_k is retained
      end if
    end if
  else
    Update the DL with new candidates
  end if
end while
Output: return S_k

– Dynamic List generation

To create the DL, the main steps described by Algorithm 5 are followed. At the beginning, we pick an initial solution, then we calculate the fitness values of its edges. After the fitness calculation, we create a static list by sorting edges in ascending order, based on the obtained results. The following formula is used to calculate these fitness values:

$$Fitness(i,j) = \frac{\tau_{ij}^{\alpha} \times \eta_{ij}^{\beta}}{\sum_{\forall ab \in N^k} \tau_{ab}^{\alpha} \times \eta_{ab}^{\beta}} \tag{1}$$

where N^k the set of edges of the current solution, τ_{ij} the pheromone value associated with the edge (i, j) and $\eta_{ij} = \frac{1}{d_{ij}}$ the heuristic information (d_{ij} is the distance between the two cities i and j).

Once the sorted list is generated, the edge with the lowest fitness value is selected and denoted as E_{lowest}. Now, we have just to associate E_{lowest} with each of its non-adjacent edges to formulate candidate pairs.

Algorithm 5. Dynamic List construction
___
Step1: Choose an initial solution S_k
    Create a list L containing the edges and sort them ascending according to their fitness values.
Step2: Select the edge with the lowest fitness value (E_{lowest}).
Step3:
    For each edge e in L **do**
      if (e is non-adjacent to E_{lowest}) **do**
        insert the pair(E_{lowest}, e) in the Dynamic List (DL)
      end if
    end for
return Candidate List

The DL is automatically updated when no improving movements are available. In this case, E_{lowest} will be replaced by its successor in the sorted list (generated in step 1) and the same principle described by Algorithm 5 will be followed to create new candidates.

– Degradation acceptance criteria

In Ant-IH, worsening movements are accepted only if they meet the degradation acceptance criteria. This depends on the new edges that will result after the 2-Opt movement. Indeed, the sum of the fitness values of these edges (denoted as P) is compared to a number r in [0, 1] generated randomly and the degradation is accepted whenever r < P.

3.3   Update Phase

In this part, we explain how the backup population and the pheromone trails are updated.

– Update strategy for the backup population

As presented in Algorithm 6, the backup population is iteratively updated by the best-iteration solution. Thus during the first cycles and if the backup population is not yet saturated, the best-iteration solution is automatically added. Then, it will eventually take the place of the worst solution in the backup population only if it has a better cost.

Algorithm 6. The backup population updating

---

input:

the best-iteration solution $Best - iter_{sol}$

the current_size (the current number of solutions in the backup population)

The N_b parameter (the maximum number of solutions that the backup population can contain)

if (current_size $< N_b$) **then**

insert $Best - iter_{sol}$ in the backup population.

else

select the worst solution $Worst_{sol}$ in the backup population

if ($Best - iter_{sol}$ is better than $Worst_{sol}$) **then**

$Best - iter_{sol}$ replaces $Worst_{sol}$.

end if

end if

– Pheromone update

During this stage, the pheromone trails are updated by the best-iteration ant. Basically, Ant-IH follows the MMAS [15] scheme and uses the same pheromone-updating rules given by following equations:

$$\tau_{ij} = \left[(1 - \rho) \times \tau_{ij}(t) + \Delta\tau_{ij}^{best} \right]_{\tau_{min}}^{\tau_{max}} \tag{2}$$

where τ_{max} and τ_{min} the upper and the lower limits of the pheromone trail, $\rho \in [0, 1[$ the evaporation rate and $\Delta\tau_{ij}^{best}$ the quantity of pheromone laid on the edge (i, j) by the best ant (iteration-best and best-so-far):

$$\Delta_{ij}^{best} = \begin{cases} \frac{Q}{L^{best}} & if\ ij \in best - tour \\ 0 & otherwise \end{cases} \tag{3}$$

where L_{best} is the length of the tour of the best ant and Q a positive constant.

3.4   Improvements over the Original Approach Ant-PLS

Ant-IH is proposed as a new variant of a new approach we published recently in [18]. This approach, called Ant-PLS (Ant-Population based Local Search), is based on the same main idea as Ant-IH: using ants to improve initial solutions instead of constructing them from zero. However, the experimental results have shown that its effectiveness degrades when the problem size increases. Thus, we decided to revisit this approach and propose few adjustments that may improve its effectiveness in solving large-scale problems.

The population update and the number of moves allowed per iteration are the main differences between the two approaches. Indeed, Ant-PLS [18] allows several moves per iteration, but the pheromone is updated only when all ants have finished their search. However, in the new variant, only one movement is allowed per iteration. This condition seemed necessary to guarantee the pheromone update after each movement. Thus, the pheromonal information will be effectively exploited to guide the ant's search. In addition, Ant-PLS [18] replaces the abandoned solutions by others generated by the same starting heuristic (NNH), while the new variant uses the backup population to make this update. In fact, we noticed that the NNH loses effectiveness when dealing with large-scale problems, and if it will be used to update the abandoned solutions then we will take a lot of time to go back to the same level previously reached by ants.

The way the counter parameter is used by the two approaches is another difference. Indeed, Ant-PLS [18] assigns a counter to each solution, while in Ant-IH this counter is associated with the best-so-far solution. This decision is required to reduce the complexity of the new variant and to improve its convergence speed.

4   Tests and Results

In this section, two separate comparisons are performed. The first compares Ant-IH to Ant-PLS [18], and to MMAS [15] and ACS [16] to determine whether it is a competitive alternative to traditional ACO algorithms. Then, a second comparison to other state-of-the-art algorithms is provided to better prove the competitiveness and efficiency of our new variant.

4.1   Comparison to Other ACO Algorithms

In this comparison, all algorithms are implemented in C++, and run on 2GHz Intel Core i3 with 4GB memory. Since the proposed method is compared to Ant-PLS [18] and other standard ACO algorithms, a summary of the parameters for each method can be found in Table 1, knowing that these parameters were empirically found.

Codes of MMAS [15] and ACS [16] were taken from the GitHub site and their parameter setting is the same as in [15] and [16] except the number of ants which will be set, as Ant-IH, to 10.

Table 1. Parameter setting for the compared algorithms. "N_i" means the number of ants (i.e. the size of the initial population) and "N_b" means the backup population size.

Algorithm	N_i	q_0	α	β	rho	limit	τ_{min}	τ_{max}	N_b
MMAS	10	–	1	2	0.98	–	Dynamically optimized		–
ACS	10	0.9	0.1	2	0.9	–	–	–	–
Ant-PLS	10	–	1	2	0.99	15	0.01	6	–
Ant-IH	10	–	3	1	0.99	250	0.01	6	100

Table 2. Average and best solution of each algorithm for all the used TSP instances (best result in bold).

TSP	Time (s)	Best solution				Average on 20 runs			
		ACS	MMAS	Ant-PLS	Ant-IH	ACS	MMAS	Ant-PLS	Ant-IH
rat783	800	10449	10405	10134	**9386**	10500,2	10496,6	10351	**9474,0**
u1060		261702	260367	260100	**253087**	270335,6	268953,0	272045,2	**254911,2**
pcb1173		69543	68732	70240	**64276**	69906,1	69509,7	70760,7	**64496,1**
fl1400	1000	24417	23796	24541	**22578**	24520,5	24216,0	24713,9	**22812,7**
fl1577		25723	25569	24664	**24212**	25880,6	25871,7	25422,9	**24672,0**
u1817	1800	66083	66327	66630	**62945**	67230,2	67031,2	68255,5	**63341,9**
u2152	2000	74636	74699	75161	**70815**	75256,1	75164,8	76157	**71258,8**

As we can see in Table 2, our new variant was first compared to Ant-PLS [18] to show the efficiency of provided improvements. Then, it was compared to MMAS [15] and ACS [16], since it presents a new idea different from traditional ACO algorithms.

According to the experimental results, we noticed that our algorithm is more efficient in terms of solution quality and convergence speed than all the compared algorithms. In fact, the best found solutions and the average lengths obtained by Ant-IH are significantly better than those found by the other methods in all the TSP instances considered in this comparison.

The results confirm, as shown in Table 2, that Ant-PLS [18] falls behind traditional ACO in solving large-scale TSP instances. Indeed, compared to MMAS [15], the best solutions found by Ant-PLS [18] are better only for rat783,u1060 and fl1577. Also, Ant-PLS [18] obtains a shorter distance on average only for two instances (rat783 and fl1577), while MMAS [15] obtains better average solutions for 5 instances. In addition, ACS [16] outperforms Ant-PLS [18] and obtains better average solutions for 5 instances. Also, the best solutions found by ACS [16] are better than those found by Ant-PLS [18] for 4 instances.

To summarize, the obvious advantages of our new variant, compared to the other approaches, are the convergence speed and efficiency in solving large-scale TSPs.

To see if there is a significant difference between our new method and the compared algorithms, the Wilcoxon signed ranks test [19] is used at a significance level of 5%. The goal of this test is to determine if the solutions found by our approach are different from those found by the other approaches in a statistically significant manner. The results of the Wilcoxon test are summarized in Table 3. The plus sign ($+$) means that the difference is significant (<0.05) and the minus sign ($-$) means that it is not. According to the statistical results, we conclude that Ant-IH has significantly better performance than the other algorithms for all the tested TSP instances.

Table 3. Wilcoxon test: Ant-IH vs Ant-PLS, MMAS and ACS

TSP	Wilcoxon test: Ant-IH vs		
	MMAS [15]	ACS [16]	Ant-PLS [18]
rat783	+	+	+
u1060	+	+	+
pcb1173	+	+	+
fl1400	+	+	+
fl1577	+	+	+
u1817	+	+	+
u2152	+	+	+

4.2   Comparison to Other State-of-the-art Algorithms

In this part, various TSP instances are used to evaluate Ant-IH and compare it against, first, two improved ACO algorithms named Partial-ACO [20] and P-ACO [20]. Then it is compared to other evolutionary algorithms GA [21] and DFWA [21].

In this experiment, Ant-IH was run with the same parameter settings of the mentioned methods. Indeed, we used the same number of ants used by the improved ACO algorithms. However, our approach was run only for 2000 cycles unlike Partial-ACO [20] and P-ACO [20] which were run for 100,000 cycles.

For the second comparison, our approach was run with the same termination condition (time in seconds) used by GA [20] and DFWA [21].

We can clearly notice from Table 4, that despite Ant-IH was executed only for 2000 cycles, it was able to find better solutions than both P-ACO [20] and Partial-ACO [20]. Indeed, our algorithm always obtains a shorter distance on average for all the TSP instances.

Table 4. Comparison of the average solutions found by Ant-IH and other recent ACO algorithms.

TSP Instance	P-ACO	Partial -ACO	Ant-IH
pcb442	52890.4	52159.2	**51989.2**
d657	55834.7	51029.8	**50770.2**
rat783	9165.3	9126.5	**9059.6**
pr1002	279457.8	269562.2	**268820.1**
pr2392	428952.9	413831.6	**409214.6**

According to Table 5, Ant-IH is more efficient than the GA [21] and returns better results on the average values for all the tested TSP instances. In addition,

Table 5. Comparison of the average solutions found by Ant-IH, GA and DFWA.

TSP Instance	GA	DFWA	Ant-IH
rat575	7099.3	7042.6	**7039.5**
gr666	3293.8	3295.0	**3288.7**
rat783	9487.5	9201.2	**9142.4**
dsj1000	20469872.6	19792718.5	**19780645.1**
pcb1173	63745.1	**60861.6**	60975.4
nrw1379	63603.1	**59268.2**	59673.3
fl1400	22652.5	21237.5	**21222.3**
u2319	266052.9	241753.1	**241634,4**

the results reveal that the average solutions found by Ant-IH are shorter than those found by DFWA [21] for 6 TSP instances. In fact, DFWA [21] obtains better solutions only for the nrw1379 and pcb1173 instances.

4.3   Global Analysis

In this section, we try to draw some general conclusions about all the analysis realized in this experimental study. We have compared our new variant to the original version Ant-PLS [18] and to traditional ACO algorithms to show that Ant-PLS's efficiency decreases when dealing with large size instances and prove that our new variant can be a better alternative to solve this kind of problems. Ant-PLS [18] is a newly proposed swarm intelligence algorithm. It has shown good performance against traditional ACO algorithms in solving the Traveling Salesman Problem. However, when applied to large-scale instances, this algorithm was unable to compete with MMAS [15] and ACS [16] algorithms, contrary to our new variant which achieved better results. Indeed, the experimental results show that our method was more efficient and obtains the best results in all the tested instances. Also, the statistical test showed that this difference is significant. Furthermore, the obtained results have shown the positive effect of the proposed adjustments on the performance of the original version.

The use of the backup population was very helpful to improve both the convergence speed and the solution quality. Indeed, replacing non-scalable solutions with others of the same quality is better than replacing them with others of poor quality and waste a lot of time to go back to the same level already reached.

Allowing only one movement per iteration was also beneficial because we will guarantee the pheromone update after each movement and therefore the pheromonal information will be used more effectively. Indeed, in Ant-PLS [10] this update phase is incorporated at the end of each iteration, so the pheromone is not modified when we pass from one movement to another. Also, when applying several movements we can go throw better intermediate solutions and at the end, if we accepted degradation, then we will end up with a poor quality solution.

In order to assess the competitiveness of our method, we have provided a comparison to other state-of-the-art algorithms. Furthermore, Ant-ILS has been compared to P-ACO [20] and Partial-ACO [20], new improved ACO algorithms. Then, it was compared to the Genetic Algorithm [21] and the DFWA [21] approach which simulates the fireworks explosion process. According to the results of this comparison, it was noticed that Ant-ILS was able to compete with other evolutionary algorithms.

5   Conclusions

In this paper, a new approach inspired by the ACO metaheuristic is introduced for solving the large-scale TSPs. The goal of this new approach is to rapid the convergence speed of the ACO algorithms by changing the classical role played by ants.

Indeed, our proposed algorithm is based on a guided local search procedure and not a construction procedure as in ACO metaheuristic. A comparison of Ant-IH to relevant state-of-the-art algorithms MMAS, ACS and Ant-PLS, proved that our method outdid these algorithms, on solving large-scale TSP instances. In fact, the obtained results reveal that Ant-IH was more performant in terms of solution quality and convergence speed than the compared algorithms.

At the end of this study, Ant-IH was compared with other recent evolutionary algorithms P-ACO, Partial-ACO, GA and DFWA. The results show that our approach outperforms these algorithms and obtains better solutions in average for almost all the TSP instances.

Further work will mainly concern the application of Ant-IH on other types of combinatorial problems to show its capability to solve different types of combinatorial problems.

References

1. Dorigo, M., Stutzle, S.: Ant colony optimization: overview and recent advances. In: Handbook of Metaheuristics, pp. 311–351 (2019)
2. Li, D., Sun, H.X.: An application research of TSP based on genetic algorithm. In: Science Technology of Heilongjiang Province, vol. 13, p. 27 (2009)
3. Gambardella, L.M., Taillard, D., Dorigo, M.: Ant colonies for the quadratic assignment problem. J. Oper. Res. Soc. 50(2), 167–176 (1999). https://doi.org/10.1057/palgrave.jors.2600676
4. Bullnheimer, B., Hartl, R.F., Strauss, C.: An improved ant system algorithm for the vehicle routing problem. Ann. Oper. Res. 89, 319–328 (1999). https://doi.org/10.1023/A:1018940026670
5. Balaprakash, P., Birattari, M., Sttzle, T., Marco, D.: Estimation-based metaheuristics for the single vehicle routing problem with stochastic demands and customers. Comput. Optim. Appl. 61(2), 463–487 (2015). https://doi.org/10.1007/s10589-014-9719-z
6. Bianchi, L., et al.: Hybrid metaheuristics for the vehicle routing problem with stochastic demands. J. Math. Model. Algorithms 5(1), 91–110 (2006). https://doi.org/10.1007/s10852-005-9033-y

7. Zouari, W., Alaya, I., Tagina, M.: A hybrid ant colony algorithm with a local search for the strongly correlated knapsack problem. In: IEEE/ACS 14th International Conference on Computer Systems and Applications (AICCSA), pp. 527–533 (2017). https://doi.org/10.1109/AICCSA.2017.61

8. Mansour, I.B., Alaya, I., Tagina, M.: A gradual weight-based ant colony approach for solving the multiobjective multidimensional knapsack problem. Evol. Intell. **12**, 253–272 (2019). https://doi.org/10.1007/s12065-019-00222-9

9. Alaya, I., Solnon, C., Ghedira, K.: Ant colony optimization for multi-objective optimization problems. In: IEEE 19th International Conference on Tools with Artificial Intelligence (ICTAI), pp. 450–457 (2007). https://doi.org/10.1109/ICTAI.2007.108

10. Blum, C., Sampels, M.: Ant colony optimization for FOP shop scheduling: a case study on different pheromone representations. In: Proceedings of the 2002 Congress on Evolutionary Computation, CEC 2002 (Cat. No.02TH8600), vol. 2, pp. 1558–1563 (2002). https://doi.org/10.1109/CEC.2002.1004474

11. Fernandez, S., Alvarez, S., Díaz, D., Iglesias, M., Ena, B.: Scheduling a galvanizing line by ant colony optimization. In: Dorigo, M., et al. (eds.) ANTS 2014. LNCS, vol. 8667, pp. 146–157. Springer, Cham (2014). https://doi.org/10.1007/978-3-319-09952-1_13

12. den Besten, M., Stützle, T., Dorigo, M.: Ant colony optimization for the total weighted tardiness problem. In: Schoenauer, M., et al. (eds.) PPSN 2000. LNCS, vol. 1917, pp. 611–620. Springer, Heidelberg (2000). https://doi.org/10.1007/3-540-45356-3_60

13. Reinelt, G.: Benchmark-TSPLIB: a traveling salesman problem library. ORSA J. Comput. (1991). http://comopt.ifi.uni-heidelberg.de/software/TSPLIB95/

14. Dorigo, M., Maniezzo, M., Colorni, V.: The ant system: optimization by a colony of cooperating agents. IEEE Trans. Syst. Man Cybern. B **26**(1), 1–13 (1996)

15. Sttzle, T., Hoos, H.H.: MAX-MIN ant system. Future Gener. Comput. Syst. **16**(8), 889–914 (2000). https://doi.org/10.1016/S0167-739X(00)00043-1

16. Dorigo, M., Gambardella, L.M.: Ant colony system: a cooperative learning approach to the traveling salesman problem. IEEE Trans. Evol. Comput. **1**(1), 53–66 (1997). https://doi.org/10.1109/4235.585892

17. Croes, G.A.: A method for solving traveling-salesman problems. Oper. Res. **6**(6), 791–812 (1958). https://doi.org/10.1287/opre.6.6.791

18. Sammoud, S., Alaya, I.: A new ant colony optimization metaheuristic based on pheromone guided local search instead of constructive approach. In: Genetic and Evolutionary Computation Conference (GECCO 2022), Boston, MA, USA, p. 9. ACM, New York (2022). https://doi.org/10.1145/3512290.3528733

19. Kafadar, K., Sheskin, D.J.: Handbook of Parametric and Nonparametric Statistical Procedures, 5th edn. Chapman and Hall/CRC (2007). https://doi.org/10.1201/9780429186196

20. Chitty, D.M.: Applying ACO to large scale TSP instances. In: Chao, F., Schockaert, S., Zhang, Q. (eds.) UKCI 2017. AISC, vol. 650, pp. 104–118. Springer, Cham (2018). https://doi.org/10.1007/978-3-319-66939-7_9

21. Xue, J.J., Wang, Y., Li, H., Xiao, J.Y.: Discrete fireworks algorithm for aircraft mission planning. In: Tan, Y., Shi, Y., Niu, B. (eds.) ICSI 2016. LNCS, vol. 9712, pp. 544–551. Springer, Cham (2016). https://doi.org/10.1007/978-3-319-41000-5_54

Comparison of Various Mutation Operators of the Bacterial Memetic Algorithm on the Traveling Salesman Problem

Ákos Holló-Szabó[ID] and János Botzheim[(✉)][ID]

Department of Artificial Intelligence, Faculty of Informatics,
Eötvös Loránd University, Pázmány P. Sétány 1/A, 1117 Budapest, Hungary
botzheim@inf.elte.hu

Abstract. Bacterial memetic algorithms (BMA) are a relatively new branch of evolutionary algorithms that are good alternatives to traditional genetic algorithms. They meant a significant breakthrough regarding order-based optimizations like the traveling salesman problem. In BMA the selection and mutation steps are replaced by bacterial mutation. During bacterial mutation each specimen of the population is improved separately by cloning them, mutating each clone, and then selecting one as a replacement for the original specimen. The bacterial mutation is one of the most innovative and critical steps of the BMA. Bacterial mutations have many variants, but documentation lacks detailed statistics and behavior models. In this publication, we compare different bacterial mutation operators. The gathered data and observations will support all future research targeting BMA.

Keywords: Traveling Salesman Problem · Bacterial Memetic Algorithm · Bacterial Mutation

1 Introduction

Evolutionary algorithms (EA) are meta-heuristics inspired by the evolutionary process of nature. EAs iterate on a pool of solutions (population) for the target problem improving on the solutions by mixing their properties (genes) and editing the individuals (mutation). This approach results in a global search applicable for most optimization problems. The most common type of Evolutionary Algorithms are the Genetic Algorithms [4] (GA). GAs are criticized for their slow convergence and high computational complexity. If population size, solution size, and iteration count are proportional to the input size of the problem, then the computational complexity is at least $O(s^3)$, where s is the size of the problem. However, in order to reduce the probability of the optimization running into local minima, more complexity might be required.

N. T. Nguyen et al. (Eds.): ICCCI 2023, CCIS 1864, pp. 508–520, 2023.
https://doi.org/10.1007/978-3-031-41774-0_40

Most modern genetic algorithms are hybridized by local search algorithms to speed up convergence, however the problem of computational complexity still remains.

Bacterial Memetic Algorithms (BMA) (see [1]) are a relatively new branch of evolutionary algorithms with a smaller computational complexity and higher convergence speed. It consists only of three steps: gene transfer, local search, and bacterial mutation. During gene transfer information is transferred from one solution to another resulting in a global convergence led by the best solutions. Local search is usually applied to some of the best solutions to speed up convergence. Bacterial mutation is a pseudo global search focusing on one solution at a time. In this step the solution is cloned, and each clone is mutated. A segment (set of properties) is selected from the solution and modified in each clone separately. The segment is limited in length, therefore each clone is still similar to the original solution. Mutation is mostly done by a random function ensuring probability for less expected improvements. The original solution is overridden by the selected clone (better clone, higher probability) at the end of the bacterial mutation.

During BMA each step drives the convergence in different ways. Gene transfer is a global search affecting the population as a whole. Local search is focusing on the best individual. Bacterial mutation reduces the chance of staying in a local minimum while still improving on the solutions. This is the main difference compared to GA where mutation slows down convergence by focusing on gene pool diversity instead of improvement rate. This results in the faster and more stable convergence of BMA. Also by bacterial mutation being a pseudo global search there is no need for a big population, reducing the computational complexity to at least $O(s^2)$ instead of at least $O(s^3)$.

During our research we restricted the scope to permutation based optimizations because of their unique characteristics and challenges. Most modern research focuses on optimization of continuous functions with many continuous parameters represented by a vector of a continuous space. Many techniques are using gradients to guide the search towards the global optimum. However in case of permutations we do not have a gradient, rendering most common techniques inapplicable. We are working on abstract methods to deal with permutation based problems in general, while presenting our recent results on the traveling salesman problem.

The traveling salesman problem (TSP) [2] could be mathematically formulated as searching for a minimal weight Hamiltonian cycle on a weighted complete graph. If the graph is directional, then the cycles could be binary matched by the order or permutation of other vertices starting from a selected vertex. The cycle is usually referred to as a trip of the salesman, the selected vertex is the center and the other vertices are the objectives or clients. Since the number of possible permutations increase factorially to the size of the problem finding an optimum takes $O(c!)$ time where c is the number of customers. In most algorithms we represent each solution with a permutation evaluated based on the distance graph. In case of EAs we can refer to each element of the permutation as a gene and as specimen to the permutation as a whole.

The goal of this paper is to compare methods introduced for the bacterial mutation step of BMA and draw conclusions that will support the future improvement of the step and therefore the entire algorithm.

2 Problem Statement

We introduced new operators for the BMA in preceding research (see [5]). Our results were promising and we continue improving on the architecture. Most descriptions introduced in the paper are based on best practices discovered during our research.

Table 1. Parameters of bacterial mutation

Mark	Meaning	Scaling
c	number of customers	
mc	mutation count	1 to 10
ccc	clone cycle count	proportional to $sqrt(c)$
cc	clone count	around 50
sl	segment length	4 to 16

The most crucial step of BMA is the bacterial mutation described as follows. Multiple specimen are selected. Bacterial mutation consists of ccc iterations (clone cycle), where a segment is selected in each iteration. In case of permutations specimen are integer arrays and the selected segment is an integer range of positions in the indices of the array. During one cloning cycle cc clones (copies) are created from the selected specimen (see Table 1). Each clone is mutated on the segment of the iteration by the mutation operator and then evaluated. This mutation must result in a valid permutation to be evaluated therefore the mutation can be interpreted as reordering the selected genes. If any clone is better than the original solution then it is overwritten by the properties of that clone. This process is then repeated multiple times within the same bacterial mutation.

The logic of bacterial mutation can be divided into three sub-steps with multiple strategy options for each:

– **Selection:** It is not required to run the mutation on all specimen exactly once. The performance of the algorithm can be improved by focusing on some of the best solutions and solutions with highest potential for improvement. This sub-step is the implementation of this selection for mutation logic. Since the population required for a BMA is very small, we did not find it necessary to implement more advanced strategies for this step. We either selected the best specimen for mutation (radical elitist) or the best specimen and a few at random (half elitist). Therefore, we did not find it necessary to include this sub-step in the experiments listed in Sect. 4.

- **Cloning:** During bacterial mutation after all cloning cycles are complete, all genes should be touched at least by one mutation. It is not required to use the same mutation operator on each clone. For example a limited number of eugenic clones might be generated to look for typical solutions related to the current one (see [6] and [3]). This step is the implementation of this segment and operator selection strategy. (How many clones should be created? Where to mutate which? How to mutate which?) Variants of this sub-step are described in Sect. 3.
- **Mutation:** As mentioned in Sect. 1 the specimen is a permutation in case of a TSP. During the mutation of an individual clone we are working on the selected segment of the specimen. The goal of the mutation operator is to find a better order of the elements of the segments than the current one. Not necessarily the optimal order! It is preferred to have small, but continuous improvements compared to having big but rare improvements. Always selecting the best order drives the optimization into local minima. The goal is quick improvements with some probability for all better orders than the current one. For any mutation operator, there will be an optimal segment size where this probability distribution is optimal. Therefore, the size of the segment is a constant with a value depending on the selected operator. Since the computational complexity of the operators depend only on the size of the segment, most mutation operators have an $O(1)$ runtime. Variants of this sub-step are described in Sect. 3.

For selection we use a pseudo elitist solution where the best solution is always mutated, while only a few other solutions are selected. We decided upon this technique to minimize budget consumption, where the budget is the number of solution evaluations. The focus of this paper is the other two sub-steps of the mutation instead. During cloning a mutation strategy is executed that not just selects the mutated segment, but assign the mutation operators to individual clones. The segment can be one continuous set of positions, a spread set of positions, or a spread set of edges of the Hamiltonian cycle. Since we work with permutations and the cost of a trip is determined by which customer is followed by which customer, we are working with continuous segments only. During experiments clone count was 40 and clone cycle count was 5 resulting in 200 mutation operator calls. The step can be improved by improving on the segment selection and operator assignment strategies. Most crucial is to improve on the bacterial mutation step. By implementing more precise operators, the size of the selected segment can be increased since the probability to find a better solution per operation increases. A bigger segment size means the operator moves from a local search to a global search making bigger improvement possible.

However, the number of possible clones increases proportional to $sl!$ (see Table 1). That is why we compare new and existing operators to each other while increasing the segment length. By finding the current optimal sl magnitude we can target the next magnitude. The long term goal is to find solutions with $O(sl^2)$ performance for better scaling with better performance speeding up convergence and increasing the distance values traveling towards their optimal position.

3   Operators and Cloning Strategies

Bacterial mutation operators take a solution and segment selection information then return a solution altered on that segment. Solutions can be eugenic (meaning for a given input always the same output is returned) or randomized.

In case of eugenic operators the goal is usually to check solutions as far from the current solution or each other as possible. However, the distance of two permutations is hard to define. The distance can be defined by the number of positions holding different values or the required number two positions have to be switched to get the other permutation. In case of TSP the most optimal technique is to count the number of edges present in the Hamiltonian cycle of the selected permutation but not present in the Hamiltonian cycle of the other. By this definition there are multiple permutations in maximal distance of a given permutation since the only restriction is that no value is followed by the same value as followed by in the original permutation.

Randomized solutions are building on the fact that, if all segment permutations have a non zero probability to be generated then by generating solutions all the best solution will emerge given enough time. The probability of generating the best segment permutation follows a Poisson distribution. Therefore, the probability of such segment permutation can be increased simply by increasing the cc parameter. However, instead of always generating the best segment permutation (it would be too rigid), the goal is simply to generate better permutations with higher probability. The current approach is to use simple probability based heuristics as mutation operators.

3.1   Opposition Operator

The goal of an opposition operator in case of vector based optimizations is to mirror a solution to the center of the solution space. It is most useful in cases, where the mirrored vector is expected to have a similar cost, while belonging to the environment of another local minimum. The similarity means it has a high potential to have a similar score or even an improvement, while the relatively big distance might help to avoid the current nearby local minima. In the case of permutations a similar effect can be achieved by reversing the order of the values of the segment. This is also a maximal distance solution since in our case the problem is asymmetrical therefore there are no common edges between the two Hamiltonian cycles, even if all edges are parallel with edges of the original segment.

3.2   Modulo Stepper Strategy

We originally applied modulo stepping to generate as many permutations as far from each other as possible during the initialization of the population. During modulo stepper initialization a base permutation is generated randomly. All other permutations are generated from this solution by walking the permutation with different step sizes. If we walk the permutation with the step size of one then we start from the first position and walking the entire array of the permutation in sequence. In the case of step size two we start at the second position then take the fourth and returning to some of the first positions when the end of the array is reached. During the walk a new permutation is generated by filling an array by the touched values. If a value is touched second time in the same walk then steps with size of one are made until the first value not present yet in the new permutation. Since in the case of a bacterial mutation we are reordering a segment the new order can be described by a segment sized permutation. Therefore a modulo stepper initialization can be used to generate clones with maximal distances from each other.

3.3 Cloning Strategies

After cloning we can choose to mutate one of the clones by the opposition operator. Or generate a few clones with any operator but also generate their opposition. Moreover, some of the clones can be generated by modulo stepper optimization. These kind of strategies can help in avoiding local minima in the long term but might also slow down the convergence. For example in real life cases road networks are not symmetrical, but almost symmetrical radically reducing the chance for big improvement by opposition operator.

3.4 Random Operator

During the full random bacterial mutation the positions of the segment are shuffled randomly. In case of sl segment size $1/sl!$ is the probability of the generation of the best possible clone on a given segment. This means in the case of cc clones $1 - (sl! - 1/sl!)^{cc}$ is the probability of the best possible clones. Therefore in the case of any sl and target probability there is a sufficient cc. In case of small segments the generation of the optimal clone is almost guaranteed even with 40 clones.

3.5 Sequential Heuristic

Instead of full random generation the probabilities of better solutions could be increased by heuristic approaches. The sequential heuristic is a reconstruction method starting with an empty array. A value is selected for the next free position in each iteration. The values not added yet have probabilities of selection proportional to the multiplicative inverse of the weight of edges from the vertex corresponding to the previous value to the vertex corresponding to the given value. For the weighted random selection a roulette wheel selection variant is applied. If the nearest neighbor were the next element instead of a randomly selected one, the options would be reduced so radically that the last values could not be selected optimally. By allowing the selection of less optimal candidates, there is still probability to select the optimal values at the end of the generation.

3.6   Edge Builder Heuristic

We can convert the problem of finding the optimal clone to a smaller TSP by building a new weighted complete graph. We take the edges between the elements of the segment, edges from the element before the segment, and edges to the vertex after the segment. By uniting the vertex before and after the segment we get a new complete graph with size of $sl + 1$. The edge builder heuristic works by selecting edges by weighted probability and then disabling edges that would result in cycles when selected. This selection probability weight should be proportional to the multiplicative inverse of the length of an edge. The roulette wheel selection can be also applied for the selection. It takes $O(1)$ time to check if an edge should be disabled given the correct support structures. Edges should be selected until a Hamiltonian path is built which is trivial to complete to a cycle.

3.7   Improved Edge Builder Heuristic

The edge builder heuristic can be improved by better calculation of the weights. Since by selection of an edge other edges are disabled, the weight of those edges should be included in the calculation of selection probabilities. The three groups of these trivial edges are the edges with same source, edges with same target, and the parallel edge. The weight of the first two groups are averaged and the three values of the three groups are added together before dividing the original weight of the edge.

3.8   Improved Edge Builder Heuristic with Recalculations

As edges are excluded from selection the weights of the edges could be recalculated. This increases the required run time by a magnitude, but might improve the performance of the operator.

3.9   Integrated TSP Solvers

In Sect. 3.6 we introduced how the task to find the optimal sequence can be converted to a small TSP. However since the goal of the long term research is to increase the segment size by magnitudes it is a false premise to build on its current value. The edge builder heuristic for example has an $O(c^3)$ run time, and the only reason it does not increase the calculation complexity of the whole algorithm, is that we view the segment size as a constant value. In the case of TSP we could implement many other algorithms that would solve the problem better than the edge builder heuristic. We could use genetic algorithms, a smaller instance of BMA into itself, or neural networks. However, all solutions have higher complexity than the required $O(c^2)$ and might be too aggressive. We are going to review the possibility of these algorithms in future research.

4 Statistics

4.1 Dataset

We generated random distance matrices with different sizes, 10 instances for each size. The smallest size was a graph with 4 vertices (3 customers) and this size was doubled, the biggest problem size being 64. Each value was randomly generated between 1 and 10000, then the graph is optimized by the Floyd algorithm. Floyd is well known algorithm used for calculating the length of all minimal distance routes between any two vertices of a graph without calculating the actual route. It is necessary in the case of TSP, where triangle inequality is expected. All distance matrices are available on Github: Link

Instead of running the entire BMA on the generated tasks, only the cloning strategy and mutation operator are ran with the entire permutations as selected segment. Also each run is made with a predefined solution as input instead of a random one. This way we could complete the runs in minimal time and compare the operator and strategy variants on the same segment. Problem sizes of 128 and above unfortunately would take too much time. We estimated that it would take years to collect sufficient amount and variety of data at the current stage of development.

4.2 Scenarios

We ran 25 scenarios for each Bacterial Mutation Operator, Cloning Strategy, size, instance combination. The tested operators were: Full Random, Opposition, Sequential Heuristic, Improved Edge Builder and Improved Edge Builder with Recalculation. The tested strategies were: Elitist, Elitist with opposition of original, and Elitist with modulo stepper group. In the case of the modulo stepper the base permutation is random and the maximal number of permutations are generated from it, while the rest of the clones are generated with the configured operator. In all cases the mutation is ran with $cc = 40$ and $ccc = 5$ meaning 200 clones are generated in one run and 5000 during the 25 runs of one scenario.

4.3 Comparison

On problem size 4 most configurations always found the optimal solution. The only exception is the runs with the opposition operator since this eugenic generation always returned the same solution instead of generating different clones (see Fig. 1). We still kept these runs for reference and display of the modulo stepper cloning strategy. In the cases where the original permutation and its opposition were not the optimal solution, but modulo stepper strategy was used, optimal solution was still found in at least 80% of the times (see Fig. 2).

In the case of problem size 8 the data is already more informative.

On the first instance the edge builder and sequential heuristics always find the optimum (see Fig. 3). The random operator under performs, only finding the

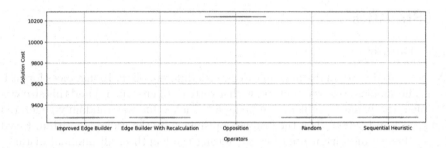

Fig. 1. Scenario with size 4, first version and elitist strategy

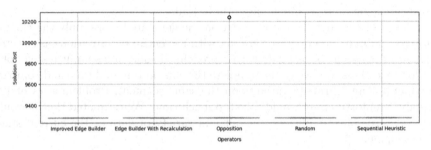

Fig. 2. Scenario with size 4, first version and modulo stepper strategy

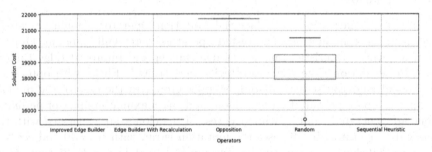

Fig. 3. Scenario with size 8, first version and elitist strategy

best solution once in 15 runs. The modulo stepper strategy founds no optimal solutions in the case of the opposition operator (see Fig. 4).

On the second instance the sequential heuristic almost always finds the optimal solution. The edge builder heuristics found the optimal solution only 45% of the time (see Fig. 5). The modulo stepper solution found optimum when opposition operator was used otherwise (see Fig. 6). The random operator found the optimum once out of 5 tries.

On the third instance the improved edge builder performed around 60% slightly better than the sequential heuristic with 55% (see Fig. 7). Unexpectedly the Edge builder heuristic with recalculation performed a lot worse around 50%. Random found the optimal solution only once and modulo stepper with opposition found it only once.

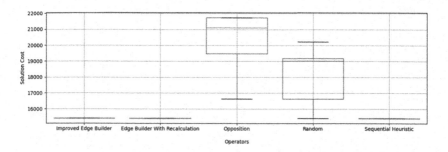

Fig. 4. Scenario with size 8, first version and modulo stepper strategy

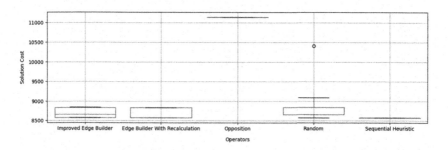

Fig. 5. Scenario with size 8, second version and elitist strategy

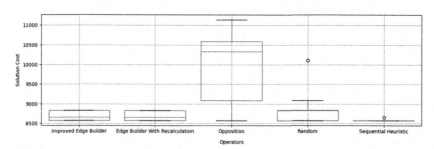

Fig. 6. Scenario with size 8, second version and modulo stepper strategy

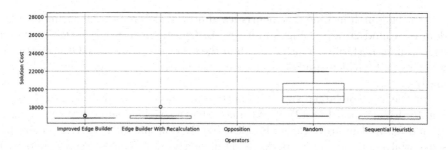

Fig. 7. Scenario with size 8, third version and elitist strategy

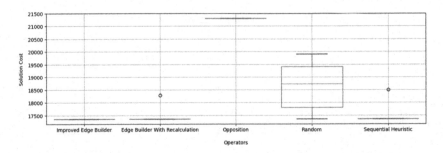

Fig. 8. Scenario with size 8, fourth version and elitist strategy

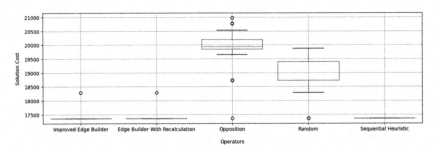

Fig. 9. Scenario with size 8, fourth version and modulo stepper strategy

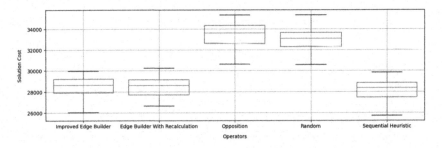

Fig. 10. Scenario with size 16, sixth version and modulo stepper strategy

On the fourth instance the heuristics almost always found the optimum, random is around 20% (see Fig. 8 and Fig. 9). On the fifth instance the improved edge builder performed a lot better than the other two heuristics. Other instance with size of 8 yielded similar results with either edge builder or sequential dominating.

In the case of larger sizes the optimum generation is not consistent (see Fig. 10, Fig. 11, and Fig. 12). The three heuristics yielded similar results on size 16 and 32, and improved edge builder slightly dominated. However, on size 64 sequential heuristics under perform significantly. It produces results almost as random generation compared to the two edge builder heuristics.

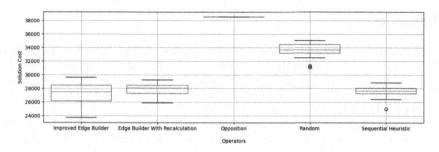

Fig. 11. Scenario with size 32, ninth version and elitist strategy

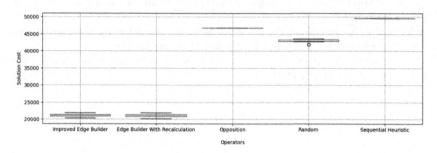

Fig. 12. Scenario with size 64, first version and elitist strategy

5   Conclusion

Modulo stepper takes up too many clones and opposition rarely yields a better clone than other operators. Problem size of 8 was the biggest problem size, where operators were still reliable. However, having a segment size of 16 may speed up convergence at the start of the algorithm. Improved Edge builder heuristic is better than sequential heuristic for the biggest segment sizes. However, recalculation yielded almost no improvement compared to the other edge builder heuristic.

We could improve on the operators by using multiple operators at the same time with statistical cloning strategy, but it would not perform much better on a segment size 32 task. The results of edge builder heuristics are promising compared to alternatives. A segment size of 64 looks probable for the near future meaning the optimal segment size could be quadrupled. Experiments on bigger data sizes are already in progress. We are going to develop and integrate new probability based heuristics in the future.

References

1. Botzheim, J., Cabrita, C., Kóczy, L.T., Ruano, A.E.: Fuzzy rule extraction by bacterial memetic algorithms. Int. J. Intell. Syst. **24**(3), 312–339 (2009). https://doi.org/10.1002/int.20338. https://onlinelibrary.wiley.com/doi/abs/10.1002/int.20338
2. Cormen, T.H., Leiserson, C.E., Rivest, R.L., Stein, C.: Introduction to Algorithms, 3rd edn. The MIT Press, Cambridge (2009)
3. Földesi, P., Botzheim, J.: Modeling of loss aversion in solving fuzzy road transport traveling salesman problem using eugenic bacterial memetic algorithm. Memetic Comput. **2**, 259–271 (2010)
4. Holland, J.H.: Adaptation in Natural and Artificial Systems: An Introductory Analysis with Applications to Biology, Control, and Artificial Intelligence. MIT Press, Cambridge (1992)
5. Holló-Szabó, Á., Botzheim, J.: Bacterial memetic algorithm for asymmetric capacitated vehicle routing problem. Electronics **11**(3758) (2022)
6. Ye, J., Tanaka, M., Tanino, T.: Eugenics-based genetic algorithm. IEICE Trans. Inform. Syst. **5**, 600–607 (1996)

Comparing Lamarckian and Baldwinian Approaches in Memetic Optimization

Mei Jiaojiao$^{(\boxtimes)}$, László Gulyás , and János Botzheim

Department of Artificial Intelligence, Faculty of Informatics, ELTE Eötvös Loránd
University, Pázmány Péter Sétány 1/A, Budapest 1117, Hungary
{v6fisc,lgulyas,botzheim}@inf.elte.hu

Abstract. Memetic optimization (MO) unifies local and global search
in non-monotonic, 'rugged' search spaces. As an enhancement of genetic
optimization, where global search is via crossover and local search
through random mutation, MO employs advanced techniques for local
search and its integration with the global counterpart. This paper compares two approaches to memetic optimization (MO) based on the Baldwinian and Lamarckian theories of evolution. These theories propose
that individuals' behaviors are enhanced not only through crossover and
mutation but also via lifetime learning. The Baldwinian approach suggests that learned behaviors impact genotype-phenotype mappings, leading to changes in individuals' fitness. In contrast, the Lamarckian approach posits that learned behaviors not only affect individual fitness but
also transfer to offspring. Our study demonstrates that genetic algorithms outperform memetic algorithms in general unimodal and multimodal functions, whereas memetic algorithms utilizing the Baldwinian
and Lamarckian approaches excel in fixed-dimension multimodal functions, uncovering more global minima and generating superior solutions.
These findings, derived from extensive experiments on the CEC-BC-2017
test functions, provide valuable insights for algorithm selection and optimization in various problem domains.

Keywords: Memetic Optimization · Baldwinian effect · Lamarckian
evolution · Local Search

1 Introduction

Genetic Algorithm (GA) is a powerful tool for solving large-scale optimization
problems in both research and industry [9]. It is based on the Darwinian theory of
evolution and consists of three operators: selection, crossover, and mutation [2].
The process starts with a population of randomly generated individuals, each
of which represents a solution to the optimization problem, then measures their
fitness (i.e., the quality of the solution), selects the most adapted individuals,
creates new offspring through crossover and mutation, and repeats the process
until better populations are found [4,9,10,17]. The selection operator chooses the

© The Author(s), under exclusive license to Springer Nature Switzerland AG 2023
N. T. Nguyen et al. (Eds.): ICCCI 2023, CCIS 1864, pp. 521–533, 2023.
https://doi.org/10.1007/978-3-031-41774-0_41

fittest individuals to produce offspring, ensuring that GA always maintains the best solution in each generation [4,9,10,17]. The crossover operator swaps genes between parents to create new solutions, while the mutation operator randomly alters genes to increase diversity [4,9,10,17].The fitness function evaluates how well an individual is adapted to its environment,which is the objective function of the optimization problem. A fitness landscape is a way to conceptualize the relative locations between individuals and a fitness function [8,20].

Memetic algorithm (MA) is an extension of the genetic algorithm (GA) that combines a mixed population-based approach with an individual's learning procedure to enable local fine-tuning [11,12]. By introducing local search heuristics into the framework of stochastic global search techniques, MA reduces the probability of GA's premature convergence [12,15,16]. The local search procedure (LSP) is a type of optimization method that explores a small space nearby the current solution and replaces it with a better one if it exists [3]. The crossover and mutation operators in GA allow individuals to jump across the fitness function landscape and explore the local environment, respectively. MA reinforces local search based on mutation, but it may not always lead to improvement, especially when the population has already reached a local optimum [12]. Despite this limitation, memetic algorithms have the potential to bridge local and global search and produce collaborative effects.

In GA and MA, genotype refers to an individual's genetic makeup, while phenotype refers to an individual's observable traits resulting from interactions between the genotype and the environment [19]. Both the Baldwinian and Lamarckian evolution suggest that an individual's learned behaviors can affect their offspring's evolution [5,19]. According to the Baldwinian approach, learned behaviors affect the mapping of genotypes to phenotypes, which ultimately results in changes to the fitness of individuals. The Lamarckian approach assumes that not only will the learned behaviors affect the fitness of individuals, but they will also be passed on to the offspring. The difference is that phenotype is not inherited to the offspring in Baldwinian approach, but it can be in Lamarckian approach [1,6,7,19,21]. These perspectives offer a valuable structure for constructing memetic optimization algorithms. Baldwinian approach can increase population diversity and exploration ability [7,13], while Lamarckian approach potentially accelerates finding global minima in dynamic environments [14]. These studies [1,6,7,13,14,19,21] have focused on the genotype-to-phenotype mapping and how individual learning affects the evolution of populations, Bereta et al. [1] compared the Baldwin effect and Lamarckian evolution, but only for the Euclidean Steiner tree problem. However, a comprehensive assessment of the two approaches is still lacking.

The paper presents two implementations of the memetic algorithm, which combine local search procedures with a genetic algorithm based on the Baldwinian effect and Lamarckian theory of evolution. The performance is evaluated on benchmark functions CEC-BC-2017 and compared to a baseline genetic algorithm [18]. As these functions span various categories and dimensions, they offer a thorough evaluation of the proposed algorithms. This study uniquely compares two memetic algorithms using diverse benchmark functions.

The paper is organized as follows: Sect. 1 provides the background and motivation for the study. Section 2 presents the implementation details of the proposed algorithm, including the description of selection, crossover, mutation, and local search operators, as well as the methodology for selecting optimal parameters. Section 3 provides a detailed analysis of the experimental results, drawing conclusions from our findings. Additionally, Sect. 4 discusses potential avenues for future research.

2   Methods

2.1   Baseline and Memetic Algorithms

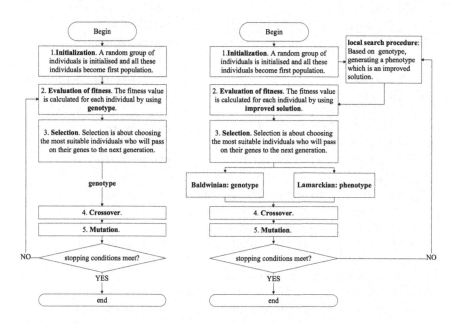

Fig. 1. Flowchart of Baseline(left) and Memetic algorithm(right).

The steady-state genetic algorithm [18], which serves as the baseline for the experiments in the paper, begins by randomly initializing a population of individuals. The algorithm then evaluates their fitness, selects individuals for reproduction, produces their offspring through crossover and mutation, and adds a fixed number of new individuals in each generation. However, to maintain a constant population size, the algorithm deletes an equal number of individuals that are deemed less fit or not well adapted to their environment. This process is repeated until a satisfactory solution is found. Figure 1(left) illustrates the flowchart of the baseline genetic algorithm, while Fig. 1(right) shows the flowchart of the memetic algorithm. The memetic algorithm builds upon the baseline by including a local search operator to enhance its performance. The difference between the Baldwinian and Lamarckian approaches lies in the way they incorporate the genotype and phenotype in the crossover operation. The Baldwinian approach involves using genotypes to perform crossover, while the Lamarckian approach uses phenotypes.

Table 1. CEC-BC-2017 benchmark functions

Function	D	Domain	Optimum
$F1 = \sum_{i=1}^{D} x_i^2$	100	$[-100, 100]$	0
$F2 = \sum_{i=1}^{D} |x_i| + \prod_{i=1}^{D} |x_i|$	100	$[-100, 100]$	0
$F3 = \sum_{i=1}^{D} \left(\sum_{i=1}^{D} = (x_i)^2 \right)$	100	$[-100, 100]$	0
$F4 = \max |x_i|$	100	$[-100, 100]$	0
$F5 = \sum_{i=1}^{D-1} \left(100 \left(x_{i+1} - x_i^2 \right)^2 + (x_i - 1)^2 \right)$	100	$[-30, 30]$	0
$F6 = \sum_{i=1}^{D-1} (x_i + 0.5)^2$	100	$[-100, 100]$	0
$F7 = \sum_{i=1}^{D} \left(i x_i^4 \right)$	100	$[-1.28, 1.28]$	0
$F8 = \sum_{i=1}^{D} \left(-x_i \sin \left(\sqrt{|x_i|} \right) \right)$	100	$[-500, 500]$	$-418.98 \cdot D$
$F9 = \sum_{i=1}^{D} \left(x_i^2 - 10 \cos (2\pi x_i) + 10 \right)$	100	$[-5.12, 5.12]$	0
$F10 = -20 \exp \left(-0.2 \sqrt{\frac{1}{D} \sum_{i=1}^{D} x_i^2} \right) -$ $\exp \left(\frac{1}{D} \sum_{i=1}^{D} \cos 2\pi x_i \right) + 20 + e$	100	$[-32, 32]$	0
$F11 = \frac{1}{4000} \sum_{i=1}^{D} x_i^2 - \prod_{i=1}^{D} \cos \frac{x_i}{\sqrt{i}} + 1$	100	$[-600, 600]$	0
$F12 = \frac{\pi}{D} (10 \sin^2 (\pi y_1) +$ $\sum_{i=1}^{D-1} (y_i - 1)^2 \cdot (1 + 10 \sin^2(\pi y_{i+1})) + (y_D - 1)^2) +$ $\sum_{i=1}^{D} U(x_i, 10, 100, 4)$	100	$[-50, 50]$	0
$F13 = 0.1(\sin^2(3\pi x_1) + \sum_{i=1}^{D-1} (x_i - 1)^2 (1$ $+ \sin^2 (3\pi x_i + 1)) + (x_D - 1)^2 \left(1 + \sin^2 (2\pi x_D) \right))$ $+ \sum_{i=1}^{D} U(x_i, 5, 100, 4)$	100	$[-50, 50]$	0
$a = [[-32, -16, 0, 16, 32, -32, -16, 0, 16, 32, -32,$ $-16, 0, 16, 32, -32, -16, 0, 16, 32, -32, -16, 0, 16, 32]$ $, [-32, -32, -32, -32, -32, -16, -16, -16, -16,$ $-16, 0, 0, 0, 0, 0, 16, 16, 16, 16, 16, 32, 32, 32, 32, 32]]$ $F14 = \left(\frac{1}{500} + \sum_{j=1}^{25} \frac{1}{j + \sum_{i=1}^{2} (x_i - a_{ij})^6} \right)^{-1}$	2	$[-65, 65]$	1
$a = [.1957, .1947, .1735, .16, .0844, .0627, .0456,$ $.0342, .0323, .0235, .0246]$ $b = [.25, .5, 1, 2, 4, 6, 8, 10, 12, 14, 16]; b = 1./b$ $F15 = \sum_{i=1}^{11} \left(a_i - \frac{x_1 (b_i^2 + b_i x_2)}{b_i^2 + b_i x_3 + x_4} \right)^2$	4	$[-5, 5]$	0.0003
$F16 = 4x_1^2 - 2.1x_1^4 + \frac{1}{3}x_1^6 + x_1 x_2 - 4x_2^2 + 4x_2^4$	2	$[-5, 5]$	-1.0316
$F17 = \left(x_2 - \frac{5.1}{4\pi^2} x_1^2 + \frac{5}{\pi} x_1 - 6 \right)^2 +$ $10 \left(1 - \frac{1}{8\pi} \right) \cos (x_1) + 10$	2	$[-5, 5]$	0.398

(*continued*)

Table 1. (*continued*)

Function	D	Domain	Optimum
$F18 = [1 + (x_1 + x_2 + 1)^2 (19 - 14x_1 + 3x_1^2$ $-14x_2 + 6x_1x_2 + 3x_2^2)] \cdot [30 + (2x_1 - 3x_2)^2 \cdot$ $(18 - 32x_1 + 12x_1^2 + 48x_2 - 36x_1x_2 + 27x_2^2)]$	2	$[-2, -2]$	3
$a = [[3, 10, 30], [.1, 10, 35], [3, 10, 30], [.1, 10, 35]]$ $c = [1, 1.2, 3, 3.2]$ $p = [[.3689, .117, .2673], [.4699, .4387, .747], [.1091,$ $.8732, .5547], [.03815, .5743, .8828]]$ $F19 = -\sum_{i=1}^{4} \left(c_i \exp \left(-\sum_{j=1}^{3} a_{ij} (x_j - p_{ij})^2 \right) \right)$	3	$[0, 1]$	-3.86
$a = [[10, 3, 17, 3.5, 1.7, 8], [.05, 10, 17, .1, 8, 14], [3,$ $3.5, 1.7, 10, 17, 8], [17, 8, .05, 10, .1, 14]]$ $c = [1, 1.2, 3, 3.2]$ $p = [[.1312, .1696, .5569, .0124, .8283, .5886], [.2329,$ $.4135, .8307, .3736, .1004, .9991], [.2348, .1415, .3522,$ $.2883, .3047, .6650], [.4047, .8828, .8732, .5743, .1091,$ $.0381]]$ $F20 = -\sum_{i=1}^{4} \left(c_i \exp \left(-\sum_{j=1}^{6} a_{ij} (x_j - p_{ij})^2 \right) \right)$	6	$[0, 1]$	-3.32
$a = [[4, 4, 4, 4], [1, 1, 1, 1], [8, 8, 8, 8], [6, 6, 6, 6], [$ $3, 7, 3, 7]]; c = [.1, .2, .2, .4, .4]$ $F21 = -\sum_{i=1}^{5} \left((X - a_i)(X - a_i)^T + c_i \right)^{-1}$	4	$[0, 10]$	-10.1532
$a = [[4, 4, 4, 4], [1, 1, 1, 1], [8, 8, 8, 8], [6, 6, 6, 6], [3,$ $7, 3, 7], [2, 9, 2, 9], [5, 5, 3, 3]].$ $c = [.1, .2, .2, .4, .4, .6, .3]$ $F22 = -\sum_{i=1}^{7} \left((X - a_i)(X - a_i)^T + c_i \right)^{-1}$	4	$[0, 10]$	-10.4028
$a = [[4, 4, 4, 4], [1, 1, 1, 1], [8, 8, 8, 8], [6, 6, 6, 6], [3,$ $7, 3, 7], [2, 9, 2, 9], [5, 5, 3, 3], [8, 1, 8, 1], [6, 2, 6, 2], [7,$ $3.6, 7, 3.6]].c = [.1, .2, .2, .4, .4, .6, .3, .7, .5, .5]$ $F23 = -\sum_{i=1}^{10} \left((X - a_i)(X - a_i)^T + c_i \right)^{-1}$	4	$[0, 10]$	-10.5363
Where $U(x, a, k, m) = k((x - a)^m)(x > a) + k((-x - a)^m)(x < (-a))$			

Table 1 provides detailed information on each of CEC-BC-2017 benchmark functions. The functions were divided into three groups: unimodal functions (F1 to F7), multimodal functions (F8 to F13), and multimodal functions with fixed dimensions (F14 to F23). Table 2 provides detailed information about the symbol, parameters, and tested values. Regarding Table 2, *iter*, and δ are parameters used as stopping criteria in the program. *iter* represents the maximum number of iterations allowed, δ represents the maximum number of evaluations of the test function. *gg* represents the probability of an individual being selected to participate in the production of offspring in the population. C_r, M_r, and LS_r represent the probability of each gene in an individual undergoing crossover, mutation, and local search operations, respectively. S, C_t, M_t, and LS_t represent the types of operators used for selection, crossover, mutation, and local search, respectively.

Table 2. This table lists the parameters and their corresponding values that were explored in the study.

Symbol	Parameters	Tested Values
$iter$	Number of Generations	1000000
M_r	Mutation Rate	0.03, 0.06, 0.1, 0.2, 0.5
β	Number of Individuals	100, 200, 400, 500
C_r	Crossover Rate	0.5, 0.6, 0.7, 0.9, 1.0
M_t	Mutation Type	normal, uniform
C_t	Crossover Type	probabilistic crossover, single point crossover, two point crossover, linear combination crossover
LS_r	Local Search Rate	0.01, 0.05, 0.01, 0.3, 0.5
LS_t	Local Search Type	uniform, normal
R	Search Radius	0.01, 0.03, 0.05, 0.1, 0.15
D	Dimension	10, 50, 100, 400 (irrelevant for functions with fixed dimensions)
gg	Generation Gap	0.01, 0.05, 0.2, 0.5, 0.8, 0.99
S	Selection Method	steady state genetic algorithm, sorted selection part, sorted selection all, roulette wheel selection
LLS	Length of Local Search	1, 4, 10
RLS_r	Redo Local Search Rate	0, 0.1, 0.2
γ	Number of Runs	10
δ	Number of Evaluations	$D \cdot 10000$
F	Test Functions	5, 8, 21
$Algo.$	Algorithm	Baseline, Baldwin, Lamarck

β represents the population size, D represents the dimension of the test function, γ represents the number of times a particular parameter combination is run, F represents the specific test function being used, and $Algo.$ represents the algorithm being applied. LLS refers to the number of solutions generated by the local search procedure each time it is applied. RLS_r represents the probability that individuals who are not removed from the population during the evolutionary process can improve their genes through a local search procedure. R is a parameter used to control the range of new genes generated through mutation and local search operations. Pseudocode in Algorithm 1 combines the Baseline, Baldwinian, and Lamarckian algorithms.

Table 3. Selection operators

S	Eligible Individuals	Partners	Non-eligible Individuals
(1)	Individual with the best fitness	All individuals except the non-eligible individual	Individual with the worst fitness
(2)	$gg \cdot \beta$ individuals with best fitness, rounded up	All individuals except the non-eligible individuals	$gg \cdot \beta$ individuals with worst fitness, rounded up
(3)	$gg \cdot \beta$ individuals with best fitness, rounded up	All individuals	$gg \cdot \beta$ individuals with worst fitness, rounded up
(4)	Select $gg \cdot \beta$ non-repeated individuals with $InvProb_i$	All individuals except for non-eligible individuals	Select $gg \cdot \beta$ non-repeated individuals with $Prob_i$

Algorithm 1. Baseline and Memetic algorithms

Input: $iter$, M_r, β, C_r, M_t, C_t, LS_r, LS_t, R, D, gg, S, LLS, RLS_r, δ, F, $Algo$.

1: $iter$ counter $\leftarrow 0$, δ counter $\leftarrow 0$
2: <u>**Funct**</u> Initialization (β, F, D, R, $Algo.$, LLS, $LS_r^{\bullet}$, LS_t)
3: **for** $i = 0$; $i < \beta$; $i++$ **do**
4:      randomly generate a genotype(F, D)
5:      **if** $Algo.$ is Baseline **then**
6:          fitness $\leftarrow F$(genotype)
7:          δ counter $+ = 1$
8:      **else**
9:          phenotype $= LSP(LLS, LS_r, LS_t, F, D, R$, genotype)
10:         fitness $\leftarrow F$(phenotype)
11:         δ counter $+ = (1+LLS)$
12:     **end if**
13: **end for**
14: **return** the population
15: sort the population based on fitness
16: save the best solution, $iter$ counter $+ = 1$
17: **while** $iter$ counter $< iter$ and δ counter $< \delta$ **do**
18:     <u>**Funct**</u> Selection(gg, S, β, the population)
19:     **return** eligible individuals, partners, non-eligible individuals
20:     **for all** eligible individuals **do**
21:         randomly choose a partner from partners
22:         **if** $Algo.$ is Baseline or Baldwin **then**
23:             crossover(parents, C_r, C_t, D, $Algo.$) using parents' genotypes
24:         **else if** $Algo.$ is Lamarck **then**
25:             crossover(parents, C_r, C_t, D, $Algo.$) using parents' phenotypes
26:         **end if**
27:         <u>**Funct**</u> Mutation(M_r, M_t, F, D, R, result of crossover)
28:         **return** genotype of a new individual
29:         **if** $Algo.$ is Baseline **then**
30:             fitness $\leftarrow F$(genotype), δ counter $+ = 1$
31:         **else**
32:             phenotype $= LSP(LLS, LS_r, LS_t, F, D, R$, genotype)
33:             fitness $\leftarrow F$(phenotype), δ counter $+ = (1+LLS)$
34:         **end if**
35:     **end for**
36:     delete non-eligible individuals in the population
37:     **for all** individuals in the rest of population **do**
38:         **if** a random probability $< RLS_r$ and $Algo.$ is Lamarck or Baldwin **then**
39:             phenotype $= LSP(LLS, LS_r, LS_t, F, D, R$, genotype)
40:             δ counter $+ = (LLS)$
41:         **end if**
42:     **end for**
43:     add the new individuals into the population
44:     sort the population based on fitness
45:     save the best solution, $iter$ counter $+ = 1$
46: **end while**

Output: Best solution of all generations

2.2   Operators

Selection Operators. Table 3 shows the details of four selection operators: (1) steady state genetic algorithm, (2) sorted selection part, (3) sorted selection all, and (4) roulette wheel selection. Each of these operators takes population, gg and β as inputs and returns three lists: eligible individuals, partners, and non-eligible individuals. In (4), the probability $Prob_i$ of selecting each individual i based on their fitness is: $Prob_i = \frac{|fitness_i|}{\sum_{j=1}^{\beta} |fitness_j|}$, and inverse probability is $InvProb_i = 1 - Prob_i$.

Crossover Operators. There are four types of crossover operators implemented in genetic algorithms: (1) single point crossover, (2) two point crossover, (3) probabilistic crossover, and (4) linear combination crossover. If there are two possible child solutions, the operator randomly selects one of them to return. Let P_1 and P_2 be the two parents' genotypes/phenotypes, $P_1[i]$ and $P_2[i]$ denote the i-th element of the parent solutions. Both genotypes and phenotypes are D-dimensional vectors. For single point crossover, let c be a random index between 1 and $D - 1$. The child solutions $Child_1$ and $Child_2$ are then:

$$Child_1 = [P_1[1:c], P_2[c+1:D]]$$
$$Child_2 = [P_2[1:c], P_1[c+1:D]] \tag{1}$$

In two point crossover, two random indices c_1 and c_2 are chosen between 1 and $D - 1$, where $c_1 < c_2$. The child solutions are formed accordingly.

$$Child_1 = [P_1[1:c_1], P_2[c_1+1:c_2], P_1[c_2+1:D]]$$
$$Child_2 = [P_2[1:c_1], P_1[c_1+1:c_2], P_2[c_2+1:D]] \tag{2}$$

In probabilistic crossover, each gene in the child solution $Child$ is determined by comparing a randomly generated float r (between 0 and 1) with C_r. Let $r[i]$ be a random float generated independently for i-th gene in the child solution.

$$Child_i = \begin{cases} P_1[i], & \text{if } r[i] \leq C_r \\ P_2[i], & \text{otherwise} \end{cases} \tag{3}$$

For linear combination crossover, the i-th gene of the child $Child_i$ is:

$$Child_i = C_r \cdot P_1[i] + (1 - C_r) \cdot P_2[i] \tag{4}$$

Mutation Operators. For uniform mutation, the mutation amount is sampled from a uniform distribution $U(-3 \cdot STD, 3 \cdot STD)$, where $STD = R \cdot Domain$. $Domain$ is the domain of the function being optimized. For normal mutation, the mutation amount is sampled from a normal distribution $N(0, STD^2)$. The mutation is applied to each gene in the child solution with probability M_r.

Uniform Mutation: $NewGene = OldGene + U(-3 \cdot STD, 3 \cdot STD)$

Normal Mutation: $NewGene = OldGene + N(0, STD^2)$ $\tag{5}$

$OldGene$ represents the gene value obtained after crossover, $NewGene$ represents the mutated gene value.

Local Search Operators. Local search operators are a more advanced alternative to mutation operators that iteratively improve upon solutions by generating multiple candidates and selecting the best option at each step, controlled by the LLS parameter. Algorithm 2 shows the procedure for local search used in this paper.

Algorithm 2. Local search procedure

Funct LSP(LLS, LS_r, LS_t, F, D, R, genotype)

1: **for** i=0; i< LLS; i++ **do**
2:     new solution = Mutation(LS_r, LS_t, F, D, R, genotype)
3:     **if** F(new solution) < F(genotype) **then**
4:         genotype ← new solution
5:     **end if**
6: **end for**
7: phenotype ← genotype
8: **return** phenotype

2.3   Top 5 Parameter Combinations

To identify the best parameter combinations, we evaluated the performance of the baseline algorithm for three functions in different groups. Let $F(x^*)$ be the fitness value at the global minimum x^* of a fitness function F. For a parameter combination θ, the score $Score_{F,\theta}$ of the fitness function F with θ is calculated as:

$$Score_{F,\theta} = \sum_{j=1}^{\gamma}(F(x_{\theta,j}) - F(x^*)) \tag{6}$$

γ represents the number of solutions generated for each θ, and $F(x_{\theta,j})$ is the fitness value of the j-th solution for F with θ. The scores are ranked in reverse order, with higher scores $Score_{F_i,\theta}$ receiving lower ranks $R_{F_i,\theta}$, as the objective is to minimize the fitness function. F_i represents the i-th fitness function under evaluation. The goal is to find the parameter combinations with the smallest aggregated ranking scores. Mathematically, this can be expressed as:

$$\arg\min \sum_{i\in 5,8,21} R_{F_i,\theta} \tag{7}$$

The top 5 parameter combinations for our algorithms are: (1) $\beta = 200$, $C_r = 0.7$, $LLS = 1$; (2) $\beta = 100$, $C_r = 0.7$, $LLS = 1$; (3) $\beta = 200$, $C_r = 0.6$, $LLS = 4$; (4) $\beta = 100$, $C_r = 0.6$, $LLS = 4$; (5)$\beta = 200$, $C_r = 0.7$, $LLS = 4$. The other parameters are the same: $iter$: 1000000, M_r: 0.03, M_t: normal, C_t: probabilistic crossover, LS_r: 0.5, LS_t: uniform, R: 0.05, D: 100 (Irrelevant for Functions with Fixed Dimensions), gg: 0.05, S: Sorted Selection Part, RLS_r: 0, δ: $D \cdot 10000$, and γ: 10.

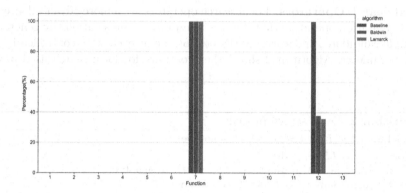

Fig. 2. Barplots representing the percentage of finding the optimal value for F1 to F13. Each group of three bars, from left to right, represents the Baseline, Baldwinian, and Lamarckian algorithms, respectively.

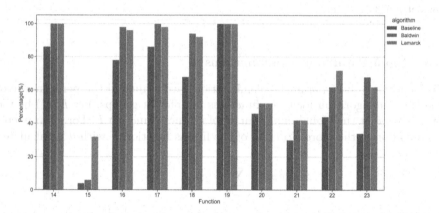

Fig. 3. Percentage of successfully finding the optimal value for F14 to F23.

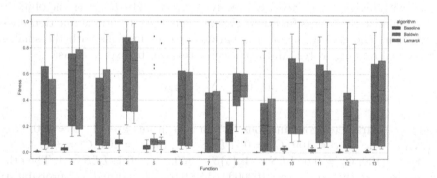

Fig. 4. Boxplots of the best solutions found by the Baseline, Baldwinian, and Lamarckian algorithms for F1 to F13. Each function has three colored boxes grouped together on the x-axis, and the y-axis represents the fitness value, normalized to the range of [0, 1] using the max-min normalization method.

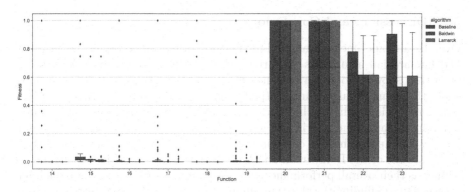

Fig. 5. Boxplots of the best solutions found by the Baseline, Baldwinian, and Lamarckian algorithms for F14 to F23, similar to Fig. 4, but with a different set of objective functions being optimized.

3   Results

3.1   Description of the Results

We present the results of our experiments, which aimed at the comparison of the performance for the Baseline, Baldwinian, and Lamarckian algorithms on various functions. We assessed the algorithms' success rates in finding the global optimal value and analyzed the distribution of solutions using boxplots.

First, our experiments evaluated the performance of the Baseline, Baldwinian, and Lamarckian algorithms on various unimodal and multimodal functions showed Table 1. Let s_{ij} be a binary variable that equals 1 if the j-th run for the i-th parameter combination was successful (i.e., met the criterion of $abs(solution - global\ minimum) \leq 0.0001$), and 0 otherwise. The percentage of successful runs for each algorithm was calculated as $\frac{\sum_{i=1}^{5} \sum_{j=1}^{\gamma} s_{ij}}{5 \cdot \gamma}$. Our results, as shown in Fig. 2, indicate that only in the case of 2 out of 13 objective functions were the algorithms successful in finding the minimum value using all three algorithms. All algorithms had a 100 percent success rate in finding the minimum value for F7, but the Baseline algorithm performed better than the memetic algorithms in minimizing F12. In contrast, our results show that the Baldwinian and Lamarckian algorithms outperformed the Baseline algorithm on multimodal functions with fixed dimensions, as shown in Fig. 3. The success rate of the memetic algorithms was consistently higher than that of the Baseline algorithm across all functions from F14 to F23.

Second, to further analyze the distribution of the best solutions found, boxplots of the minimum values found of each run are provided. According to Fig. 4, the boxplots for the Baseline algorithm are generally shorter and more tightly clustered compared to the memetic algorithms for unimodal and multimodal functions (F1 to F13). For multimodal functions with fixed dimensions (F14 to F23), the boxplots for memetic algorithms are more tightly packed and have fewer outliers, as seen in Fig. 5.

3.2 Discussions and Conclusions

Overall, our experiments evaluated the performance of the Baseline, Baldwinian, and Lamarckian algorithms on various objective functions. First, the Baseline algorithm showed good performance on unimodal and multimodal functions, while the memetic algorithms outperformed on fixed-dimensional multimodal functions. This highlights the effectiveness of incorporating local search procedures in optimization algorithms, supporting the value of the Baldwinian and Lamarckian approaches for constructing memetic optimization algorithms. Second, in terms of the Baldwinian and Lamarckian algorithms, there was no clear winner as their overall performance was comparable. They both achieved similar success rates in finding the global minimum and exhibited similar distributions of best solutions found. However, subtle differences in their performance on specific functions were observed. This suggests that the choice between these approaches may depend on the specific characteristics of the objective function being optimized.

4 Future Work

Future work can consider the following directions in the field of memetic optimization algorithms using the Lamarck and Baldwin frameworks. Firstly, there is a need to explore novel local search procedures to enhance the efficiency and effectiveness of these algorithms. Additionally, investigating algorithm parameter tuning, while considering the potential time-consuming nature of running one million evaluations, is crucial to optimizing the performance of memetic algorithms. Comparative studies with other metaheuristic algorithms would provide valuable insights into the strengths and weaknesses of memetic approaches. Furthermore, conducting real-world applications and case studies would validate the practical efficacy of memetic algorithms in solving complex optimization problems. By pursuing these research directions, the field can advance and further enhance the performance and applicability of memetic optimization algorithms.

References

1. Bereta, M.: Baldwin effect and Lamarckian evolution in a memetic algorithm for Euclidean Steiner tree problem. Memetic Comput. **11**(1), 35–52 (2019)
2. Dawkins, R.: The Selfish Gene. Oxford University Press, Oxford (1978)
3. García-Martínez, C., Lozano, M.: Local search based on genetic algorithms. In: Siarry, P., Michalewicz, Z. (eds.) Advances in Metaheuristics for Hard Optimization. NCS, pp. 199–221. Springer, Cham (2008). https://doi.org/10.1007/978-3-540-72960-0_10
4. Grefenstette, J.J., Baker, J.E.: How genetic algorithms work: a critical look at implicit parallelism. In: International Conference on Genetic Algorithms (1989)
5. Hinton, G.E., Nowlan, S.J.: How learning can guide evolution. Complex Syst. **1** (1996)

6. Houck, C., Joines, J., Kay, M.: Utilizing Lamarckian evolution and the Baldwin effect in hybrid genetic algorithms (1996)
7. Ishibuchi, H., Kaige, S., Narukawa, K.: Comparison between Lamarckian and Baldwinian repair on multiobjective 0/1 Knapsack problems. In: Coello Coello, C.A., Hernández Aguirre, A., Zitzler, E. (eds.) EMO 2005. LNCS, vol. 3410, pp. 370–385. Springer, Heidelberg (2005). https://doi.org/10.1007/978-3-540-31880-4_26
8. Kallel, L., Naudts, B., Reeves, C.R.: Properties of fitness functions and search landscapes. In: Kallel, L., Naudts, B., Rogers, A. (eds.) Theoretical Aspects of Evolutionary Computing. NCS, pp. 175–206. Springer, Heidelberg (2001). https://doi.org/10.1007/978-3-662-04448-3_8
9. Katoch, S., Chauhan, S.S., Kumar, V.: A review on genetic algorithm: past, present, and future. Multimed. Tools Appl. 80, 8091–8126 (2021)
10. Mitchell, M.: An Introduction to Genetic Algorithms. MIT Press, Cambridge (1998)
11. Moscato, P., et al.: On evolution, search, optimization, genetic algorithms and martial arts: towards memetic algorithms. Caltech Concurrent Computation Program, C3P Report 826(1989), 37 (1989)
12. Neri, F., Cotta, C., Moscato, P.: Handbook of Memetic Algorithms, vol. 379. Springer, Heidelberg (2011)
13. Paenke, I., Jin, Y., Branke, J.: Balancing population-and individual-level adaptation in changing environments. Adapt. Behav. 17(2), 153–174 (2009)
14. Paenke, I., Sendhoff, B., Rowe, J., Fernando, C.: On the adaptive disadvantage of Lamarckianism in rapidly changing environments. In: Almeida e Costa, F., Rocha, L.M., Costa, E., Harvey, I., Coutinho, A. (eds.) ECAL 2007. LNCS (LNAI), vol. 4648, pp. 355–364. Springer, Heidelberg (2007). https://doi.org/10.1007/978-3-540-74913-4_36
15. Pandey, H.M., Chaudhary, A., Mehrotra, D.: A comparative review of approaches to prevent premature convergence in GA. Appl. Soft Comput. 24, 1047–1077 (2014)
16. Radcliffe, N.J., Surry, P.D.: Formal memetic algorithms. In: Fogarty, T.C. (ed.) AISB EC 1994. LNCS, vol. 865, pp. 1–16. Springer, Heidelberg (1994). https://doi.org/10.1007/3-540-58483-8_1
17. Sastry, K., Goldberg, D., Kendall, G.: Genetic algorithms. In: Burke, E.K., Kendall, G. (eds.) Search Methodologies, pp. 97–125. Springer, Boston (2005). https://doi.org/10.1007/0-387-28356-0_4
18. Syswerda, G.: A study of reproduction in generational and steady-state genetic algorithms. In: Foundations of Genetic Algorithms, vol. 1, pp. 94–101. Elsevier (1991)
19. Turney, P.D.: Myths and legends of the Baldwin effect. CoRR cs.LG/0212036 (2002). http://arxiv.org/abs/cs/0212036
20. Van Cleve, J., Weissman, D.B.: Measuring ruggedness in fitness landscapes. Proc. Natl. Acad. Sci. 112(24), 7345–7346 (2015)
21. Whitley, D., Gordon, V.S., Mathias, K.: Lamarckian evolution, the Baldwin effect and function optimization. In: Davidor, Y., Schwefel, H.-P., Männer, R. (eds.) PPSN 1994. LNCS, vol. 866, pp. 5–15. Springer, Heidelberg (1994). https://doi.org/10.1007/3-540-58484-6_245

A Fitness Approximation Assisted Hyper-heuristic for the Permutation Flowshop Problem

Asma Cherrered[1][(✉)] , Imene Racha Mekki[1] , Karima Benatchba[2] ,
and Fatima Benbouzid-Si Tayeb[2]

[1] University Of Science And Technology Houari Boumediene (USTHB) of Algiers,
Algiers, Algeria
asmacherrered@gmail.com
[2] Laboratoire des Méthodes de Conception de Systèmes (LMCS), Ecole nationale
Supérieure d'Informatique (ESI), BP 68M-16270 Oued Smar, Algiers, Algeria

Abstract. Hyper-heuristics can be applied to solve complex optimization problems. Recently, an efficient hyper-heuristic (HHGA) was proposed for solving the permutation flowshop problem (PFSP), one of the most important scheduling type in modern industries. HHGA is a hyper genetic algorithm (GA) that evolves GAs to solve the PFSP. It designs, automatically, efficient GA per instance. However, HHGA evolves in a huge search space (more than 9 million GAs). Moreover, at each generation, HHGA needs to execute many GAs, which requires a very large number of fitness evaluations; thus, inducing huge computational overhead. To overcome this problem, this paper aims at integrating machine learning techniques into HHGA. The objective is to approximate, in an offline approach, the fitness function, reducing considerably the execution time of HHGA while maintaining its quality. The experimental results on Taillard's widely used benchmark problems show that the proposed fitness approximation-assisted HHGA is able to achieve competitive performance on a limited computational budget.

Keywords: Hyper-heuristics · Genetic algorithm · Permutation Flowshop problem · Machine learning · Fitness function

1 Introduction

Scheduling problems in the permutation flow shop environment (PFSP) are an important class of problems widely encountered in areas such as manufacturing and large-scale product fabrication with high social or economic impact [30]. The PFSP is a typical NP-hard combinatorial optimization problem [11] that aims to find the sequence of processing a set of n jobs in the same order on a set of m machines. Nonetheless, with the increase in the number of jobs and machines, the solutions' space and the difficulty of solving the problem will increase rapidly. As a result, it is very difficult to get a satisfactory solution in a short amount of

N. T. Nguyen et al. (Eds.): ICCCI 2023, CCIS 1864, pp. 534–545, 2023.
https://doi.org/10.1007/978-3-031-41774-0_42

time. Therefore, heuristics and metaheuristics (MHs) approaches have become the mainstream research on this topic. Recent research achievements solving the PFSP can be found in [1,2,8,10,15,18,24]. For comprehensive reviews of the problem under different constraints, we refer the interested reader to [9,21,29].

However, even though the fruitful research results on the PFSP, no method seems to perform well in all instances. This was effectively proven by the No Free Lunch Theorem [33]. As a result, in recent years, hyper-heuristics (HHs) have become more popular for optimization problems [6,23,27]. Instead of exploring the solutions' search space, they explore the heuristics' search space to generate heuristic sequences looking for better solutions for a problem or an instance of a problem [32]. However, it should be emphasized that, in the literature, the use of HHs for solving scheduling problems in general and PFSP in particular, are limited [3,4,22].

Nonetheless, in spite of the performance of HHs in solving real-world computational problems, the HH evolution process is often computationally expensive when compared with a methodology that operates directly on the solution space mainly due to the computationally expensive determination of the solution and fitness evaluation.

In the last decade, the integration of machine learning (ML) techniques into optimization methods has gained considerable interest which has yielded numerous research articles [5,14]. When integrating ML techniques into MHs, the main goal is to improve the efficiency of MHs either through speeding up the search process by performing approximations or injecting knowledge into the search process or through finding better solutions by replacing the expert knowledge and experience with better decisions obtained using ML techniques. In this regard, various studies have been done on the integration of ML techniques into MHs for different purposes, including parameter setting, fitness evaluation [16,31], solution initialization, and operator selection [13,26].

Recently, Ahmed Bacha *et al.* [3] proposed HHGA, a competitive HH that generates, an effective GA per instance for the PFSP. However, HHGA is computationally expensive as the evaluation of its solutions' fitness requires the execution of many GAs during the search process. Indeed, fitness evaluation is one of the key components of HHs, that consumes most of the execution time, to guide the search process toward the promising regions of the search space. In this regard, we propose an ML approach to approximate the fitness function, in order to reduce considerably the execution time of HHGA while maintaining its quality.

The rest of this paper is organized as follows: Sect. 2 introduces the PFSP. Section 3 provides first the HHGA and its drawback, then our proposed ML-assisted approach to solve the latter. The experimental results are given in Sect. 4. The conclusion is given in the final section.

2   Problem Domain Description

The formal PFSP consists in determining the processing order of a set $J = \{J_1, J_2, ..., J_n\}$ of n independent jobs through a set $M = \{M_1, M_2, ..., M_m\}$ of m

sequential machines. In this aspect, all n jobs are processed in the m machines in the same order. The processing of job J_j on machine m_i, takes an uninterrupted processing time p_{ij}.

The assumptions and constraints of the PFSP are summarized as follows:

- At time zero, all jobs are available and ready for processing and no preemption is allowed;
- Each job is processed on only one machine while each machine can handle only one job at a time;
- The number of jobs and their execution time on each machine is known ahead and independent;
- Execution times include setup time, processing time, and transportation time;
- Once a job starts to be processed on a machine, this process cannot be interrupted before its completion;
- Each machine processes the job in the same sequence.

In this paper, the goal is to find a sequence that minimizes the makespan C_{max} which is the total completion time of the schedule. When all jobs are scheduled, C_{max} is equal to c_{mn} the time at which machine M_m finishes processing the nth job. The resulting problem is the PFSP with makespan criterion, denoted $Fm|prmu|\ C_{max}$, where m is the number of machines, n the number of jobs, $prmu$ denotes that only permutation schedules are allowed, and C_{max} denotes the makespan minimization as the optimization criterion.

3   Proposed Offline Surrogate-Assisted Approach

HHGA [3] is a hyper-GA that evolves GAs to solve the PFSP. It designs, automatically, efficient GA per instance. The main purpose of HHGA is to generate the most appropriate GA configuration for the considered PFSP instance. HHGA's two layers are defined as follows (1) (Fig. 1):

- **The hyper-heuristic layer** is a high-level GA that evolves low-level GAs, allowing the generation of efficient GA per instance. The evaluation of HHGA on an instance is done by running the low-level GAs on this instance, thus computing C_{max}. To measure their qualities on an instance i, we use the relative percentage deviation (RPD) computed as follows:

$$RPD_i = \frac{C_{max} - UpperBound_i}{UpperBound_i} \times 100$$

Where C_{max} is the makespan of the best solution found by the low-level GA and $UpperBound_i$ is the makespan of the best-known solution for the instance i[1]

---

[1] HHGA uses the updates of the upper bound which are available in Taillard's site; http://mistic.heig-vd.ch/taillard/.

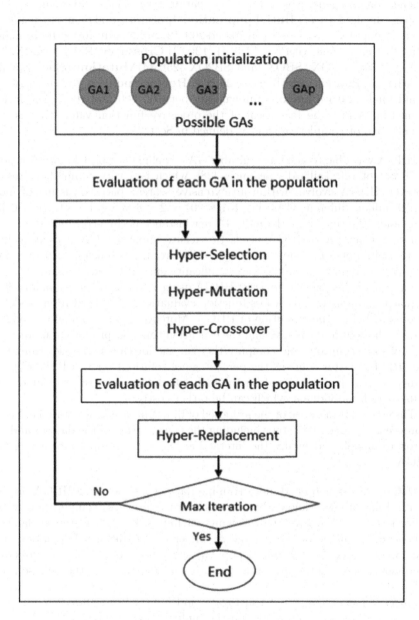

Fig. 1. HHGA architecture [3]

– **The problem layer** is mainly composed of low-level GAs. A GA is composed of components and encoded as a vector of hyper-genes. A component (hyper-gene) can be a genetic operator *op* or a parameter *p*. The standard and specific operators used are (1) **Initial population**: Stochastic and Semi-stochastic [3] with a population size between 50 and 200; (2) **Selection**: Roulette, Ranking, and K-tournament with $k \in \{2, 3, 4\}$ [12]; (3) **Crossover**: PMX, OX, IX, 2X, [19] SJOX, SJ2OX, SBOX, and SB2OX [25]; (4)**Mutation**: Shift, random exchange, Position, and Inverse [20]; (5) **Replacement**: $\alpha + \beta$ strategy; (6) and finally **Numbers of generations** between 800 and 1000. The fitness function is just the reciprocal of the objective function value, that is, the makespan or completion time as defined in Sect. 2.

HHGA was able to generate suitable GAs reaching the best-known solutions for 50 out of 120 Taillard's instances [28], which is a very competitive result. However, HHGA evolves within an extensive search space consisting of more than 9 million different GAs, i.e. $151 \times 201 \times 2 \times 8 \times 5 \times 1 = 9\ 712\ 320$ [3]. As a result, the search for the best GA per instance is time-consuming. Indeed, with each generation, HHGA needs to execute numerous GAs, resulting in a substantial number of fitness evaluations. As a result, significant computational resources are required, leading to a significant computational burden.

The aim of this paper is to assist HHGA using a surrogate model, in an offline approach, to approximate fitness function evaluations. A substitution model is, thus, built, before the execution of HHGA. Moreover, to reach a good trade-off between the solution's quality and the execution time, we propose to predict the C_{max} of some solutions and compute the real one for the others, according to a rate (R). The latter controls the percentage of solutions for which the C_{max} is predicted. This is done to reduce the high computational cost associated with evaluating all individuals, which can be rather costly.

The general framework of the proposed offline approach is illustrated in Fig. 2. It proceeds in three main steps including the construction of the dataset and the surrogate model, and finally the interaction between the surrogate model and HHGA.

– *Dataset Construction.* Build a training dataset by executing HHGA on several Taillard's well-known benchmarks with real fitness computation of the low-level GA. We save the following attributes for each instance: name of benchmark, name of the instance, number of generations, Population size, Strategies used for the initial population's generation, selection, crossover, crossover rate, mutation, mutation rate, and the C_{max} of the best solution found.
– *Model Construction.* Build a surrogate model of the fitness function, by training a machine learning model on the built dataset to predict the C_{max}. To assist HHGA two regression models were used: Random forest (RF), and Support vector regression (SVR).
– *Interaction.* In this step, we substitute the fitness function, i.e. the evaluation of each GA with the low-level GA, by the surrogate model. First with RF,

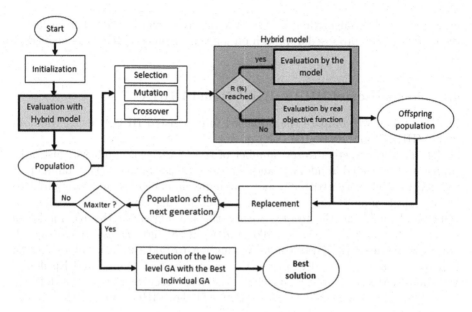

Fig. 2. HHGA with surrogate model.

then with SVR, resulting in 2 algorithms respectively HHRF and HHSVR. If the surrogate model evaluates all individuals, HHRF and HHSVR may converge to a local optimum. As a result, it should be used in conjunction with the true fitness function evaluation to avoid false convergence.

To do so, two strategies are proposed. The first uses a static value of R during the search process. The second strategy is a dynamic one where the number of solutions effectively computed decreases during the search process, according to the rate R.

4   Experimental Results and Analysis

In this section, we present the results of performed experiments to assess the proposed surrogate approach. We implemented our algorithms in C# and ran experiments on Intel Xeon CPU E5-2650 with 2.0 GHz (8 Cores) and 32 GB main memory on IBNBADIS CERIST computational cluster. In order to check the effectiveness of the models and compare their impact on the performance of our HHGA, we compared HHRF and HHSVR with a fully assisted HHGA where the fitness of all solutions are predicted (100%). Then, we performed a set of tests to find the rate R for which there is a good trade-off between the solutions' quality and execution time. All experiments have been carried out using the well-known flowshop benchmark of Taillard classified according to their number of tasks $n \in \{20, 50, 100, 200, 500\}$ and their number of machines $m \in \{5, 10, 20\}$ named $n \times m$. Each benchmark has 10 instances. The instances used for the experiments are those of benchmarks 20×5, 50×20, and 200×10. To assess the performance of our algorithm, we used the relative deviation (RPD) to measure the quality of the proposed approach on a given instance i (RPD) as defined in Sect. 3.

4.1   Comparison of HHRF, HHSVR and HHGA

In this section, we compare the proposed fully assisted HHGA, using Random Forest (HHRF) and SVR (HHSVR) models.

RF has 4 parameters to set: number of trees (n_trees), number of instances (n_instance) selected randomly, and for each Decision tree (DT), number of selected attributes (n_attribut), and minimum number of samples required to be at a leaf node (Min_samples_leaf). After testing several combinations of values and analyzing the results, we set the parameters of the RF model as follows: n_trees=30, $n\_instance$=200, $n\_attribut$=8, and $Min\_samples\_leaf$=2. For SVR, we used the GridSearchCV function to find the best values for the hyperparameters: kernel, Regularization parameter C, Gamma, and Epsilon ϵ. We conducted several tests and chose the most recurrent values as follows: $C = 100$, $\epsilon = 0.5$, $kernel = Gaussian(rbf)$. For HHGA we fix the Hyper-Number of individuals to 30.

Table 1 shows RPDs and significant CPU time reduction (Gain-CPU) for benchmarks 20×5, 50×20, and 200×10. Gain-CPU of assisted approach is computed as follows:

$$\text{Gain-CPU} = \frac{HHRF(SVR)_{CPU}}{HHGA_{CPU}} \times 100$$

For benchmark 20×5, both models are efficient compared to HHGA as they achieve a great reduction of time: 96.77% and 98.56% on average for HHRF and HHSVR respectively (see Table 1). Moreover, HHRF and HHSVR give, on average, very close values for RPDs, respectively 0.393 and 0.38, whereas HHGA gives 0,041. With HHRF, we have achieved a deviation rate equal to 0 for tai001, tai006, tai008, tai009, and tai010, and close to 0 for tai005. On the other hand, for HHSVR, a deviation rate of 0 was observed for tai001, tai005, tai006, and tai008. These results are very promising and show the efficiency of the proposed approaches. However, we notice a slightly bigger difference when comparing the average RPDs of HHRF and HHSVR for benchmark 50×20, respectively 3.41 and 2.43, whereas HHGA gives 1,146 (see Table 1). The gain in CPU time is as important as the one for benchmark 20×5: 97.34% for HHRF and 94.42% for HHSVR. One can notice that for the 10 instances of benchmark 200×10, the gain of CPU is significant: 93.6% and 86.75% for HHRF and HHSVR respectively. Moreover, the average RPDs of HHRF and HHSVR, respectively 0.66 and 0.59, are very interesting as the average RPD of HHGA is 0,11. We can conclude that both algorithms maintain the quality of solutions while reducing significantly CPU time.

Table 1. Comparison between HHSVR and HHRF

Benchmark	Instance	RPD HHGA	RPD HHRF	RPD HHSVR	Gain-CPU HHRF (%)	Gain-CPU HHSVR (%)
20 × 5	tai001	0	0	0	−96,76	**−98,77**
	tai002	0	0,44	**0,15**	−95,82	**−97,74**
	tai003	0	1,57	**0,65**	−98,03	**−99,26**
	tai004	0	**0,46**	0,70	−97,08	**−98,12**
	tai005	0	0,08	0	−96,42	**−99,81**
	tai006	0	0	0	−96,23	**−98,80**
	tai007	0,41	1,37	**0,41**	−97,18	**−97,96**
	tai008	0	0	0	−97,49	**−98,09**
	tai009	0	0	0,81	−97,18	**−98,21**
	tai010	0	0	1,08	−95,55	**−98,87**
	Average	0,041	0,393	**0,38**	−96,77	**−98,56**
50 × 20	tai051	1,16	3,06	**1,58**	**−99,73**	−97,98
	tai052	2,02	**3,67**	5,45	−98,83	**−99,78**
	tai053	1,12	3,84	**2,36**	**−94,75**	−92,60
	tai054	0,96	3,97	**2,61**	**−99,12**	−98,25
	tai055	0,8	3,37	**1,50**	−95,80	**−97,00**
	tai056	1,14	2,63	**2,61**	**−96,78**	−93,85
	tai057	0,94	4,13	**1,62**	**−99,71**	−94,99
	tai058	1,35	3,44	**2,44**	**−97,95**	−97,41
	tai059	0,85	3,47	**2,14**	**−99,09**	−97,95
	tai060	1,12	2,55	**1,97**	**−91,64**	−74,36
	Average	1,146	3,41	**2,43**	**−97,34**	−94,42
200 × 10	tai091	0,09	**0,34**	0,51	−99,51	**−99,94**
	tai092	0,27	0,99	**0,74**	**−95,17**	−93,01
	tai093	0,3	0,94	**0,87**	**−91,46**	−86,06
	tai094	0,03	0,78	**0,46**	−86,27	**−95,67**
	tai095	0,03	0,48	**0,41**	**−90,25**	−85,71
	tai096	0,04	1,36	**0,50**	**−99,38**	−81,85
	tai097	0,05	**0,25**	0,76	**−99,27**	−82,88
	tai098	0,1	0,72	**0,45**	**−92,48**	−88,41
	tai099	0,11	**0,31**	0,39	**−92,63**	−64,86
	tai100	0,093	**0,48**	0,78	**−91,57**	−89,13
	Average	0,11	0,66	**0,59**	**−93,6**	−86,75

4.2   Static vs Dynamic Assisted Hyper-heuristics

In this section, we will compare the static and dynamic surrogate strategies using the same initial population. At first, the value of R is static during the search process. We used respectively 0%, 20%, 50%, 80% and 100% resulting in five different algorithms named $HHRF_{R\%}$. One can note that $HHRF_{0\%}$ is HHGA and it is given for comparative purposes. In the dynamic strategy, R is initialized to 100%. Thus all solutions are effectively computed during the first generation. Then, it is decreased by 3% at each generation. This version of the algorithm is named $HHRF_{Dyn}$.

For the studied three benchmarks, Fig. 3 shows a considerable decrease in CPU time. As expected, as the value of R decreases, CPU time increases.

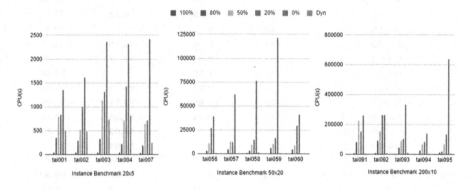

Fig. 3. Evaluation of CPU according to rate R for the three benchmarks

The results of benchmark 20×5 (Table 2) are remarkable for almost all algorithms. For example, for $R = 50\%$, $HHRF_{50\%}$ reaches an RPD of zero for seven instances out of ten. Overall, when comparing average RPDs, we note that $HHRF_{50\%}$ and $HHRF_{20\%}$ gave the best results followed by $HHRF_{Dyn}$. This pattern is noticed for benchmark 50×20 (Table 2). As for 200×10, an effective computation of 20% is sufficient to have competitive results. Moreover, the performances of $HHRF_{80\%}$ and $HHRF_{Dyn}$ are very close.

We can conclude from our tests that the rate R of effectively computed solutions' fitness function depends on the benchmarks. An interesting result, though, is that $HHRF_{Dyn}$ performance is always competitive with the best algorithm.

Table 2. Evaluation of HHRF according to rate R

Instance	$HHRF_{0\%}$	$HHRF_{20\%}$	$HHRF_{50\%}$	$HHRF_{80\%}$	$HHRF_{100\%}$	$HHRF_{Dyn}$
tai001	0	0	0	0	0,62	1,48
tai002	0	0,44	0	0,44	0,44	0,51
tai003	0	0	0	0	3,6	0
tai004	0	1,16	0,69	0,85	0,46	0,69
tai005	0	0	1,21	0	1,37	0,72
tai006	0	1.25	0	1,25	0	0
tai007	0,41	0,41	1,37	0,41	1,37	1,37
tai008	0	0,41	0	0	0,66	0
tai009	0	0	0	5,52	1,86	1,13
tai010	0	0	0	0	0,54	0
Average	0,041	0,36	0,33	0,84	1,09	0,59
tai051	1,53	2,96	3,84	5	4	4,2
tai052	1,62	3,1	3,94	3,1	6,4	7,19
tai053	2,33	4,75	1,53	5,6	4,6	1,53
tai054	1,63	5,23	2,2	2,4	3,3	2,17
tai055	1,46	1,38	1,7	1,2	3,4	2,21
tai056	1,62	2,41	3,9	3,2	17,1	3,45
tai057	1,32	3,34	5,6	3,9	4,6	2,69
tai058	2,08	3,68	5,3	4,3	5,3	4,65
tai059	1,28	2,83	2,6	3	3,6	3,63
tai060	1,81	4,5	3,1	3,8	4,2	3,16
Average	1,67	3,42	3,39	3,57	5,68	3,49
tai091	0,09	0,32	0,52	0,21	0,32	0,81
tai092	0,54	0,41	0,48	0,46	0,87	0,42
tai093	0,24	0,94	0,87	0,86	1,43	0,39
tai094	0	0,77	0,46	0,3	0,2	0,45
tai095	0,12	0,12	0,12	0,12	0,12	0,48
tai096	0,21	0,21	0,43	0,44	0,81	0,35
tai097	0,13	0,82	1,57	0,52	0,82	0,5
tai098	0,2	0,63	0,91	0,45	0,3	0,91
tai099	0,26	0,26	0	0,26	1,23	0,26
tai100	0,49	0,78	0,49	0,78	0,98	0,1
Average	0.23	0,53	0,58	0,44	0,712	0,45

5 Conclusion

We have proposed a Hyper-heuristic approach assisted by substitution in an Offline approach, HHS-Offline. We integrated into the hyper-heuristic a model that replaces the effective objective function computation during the search process, at a certain rate. Two models were used, $HHRF$ and $HHSVR$. In order to evaluate our approach, we carried out experiments on the well-known Taillard benchmarks. The tests and results have shown that the proposed approach with its different models gave significant results in terms of quality and execution time. Although the results obtained are promising, we intend to investigate the use of other surrogate models such as Neural Networks and an online approach.

References

1. Abu Doush, I., Al-Betar, M., Awadallah, M., Alyasseri, Z., Makhadmeh, S., El-Abd, M.: Island neighboring heuristics harmony search algorithm for flow shop scheduling with blocking. Swarm Evol. Comput. **74**, 101127 (2022)
2. Alawad, N., Abed-alguni, B.: Discrete Jaya with refraction learning and three mutation methods for the permutation flow shop scheduling problem. J. Supercomput **78**, 3517–3538 (2022)
3. Bacha, S.Z.A., Belahdji, M.W., Benatchba, K., Tayeb, F.B.S.: A new hyperheuristic to generate effective instance GA for the permutation flow shop problem, Procedia Comput. Sci. **159**, 1365–1374 (2019). http://dx.doi.org/10.1016/j.procs.2019.09.307. Knowledge-Based and Intelligent Information and Engineering Systems: Proceedings of the 23rd International Conference KES2019 (2019)
4. Bacha, S.Z.A., Benatchba, K., Tayeb, F.B.S.: Adaptive search space to generate a per-instance genetic algorithm for the permutation flow shop problem. Appl. Soft Comput. **124**, 109079 (2022)
5. Bengio, Y., Lodi, A., Prouvost, A.: Machine learning for combinatorial optimization: a methodological tour d'horizon. Eur. J. Oper. Res. **290**(2), 405–421 (2021)
6. Burke, E.K., Kendall, G., Mısır, M., zcan, E. O.: Monte Carlo hyper-heuristics for examination timetabling, Ann. Oper. Res. **196**(1) 73–90 (2012)
7. Chen, R., Yang, B., Li, S., Wang, S.: A self-learning genetic algorithm based on reinforcement learning for flexible job-shop scheduling problem. Comput. Ind. Eng. **149**, 106778 (2020)
8. Fernandez-Viagas, V., Prata, B., Framinan, J.: A critical-path based iterated local search for the green permutation flowshop problem. Comput. Ind. Eng. **169**, 108276 (2022)
9. Fernandez-Viagas, V., Ruiz, R., Framinan, J.M.: A new vision of approximate methods for the permutation flowshop to minimise makespan: state-of-the-art and computational evaluation. Eur. J. Oper. Res. **257**, 707–721 (2017)
10. Fernandez-Viagas, V., Talens, C., Framinan, J.: Assembly flowshop scheduling problem: speed-up procedure and computational evaluation. Eur. J. Oper. Res. **299**, 869–882 (2022)
11. Garey, M.R., Johnson, D.S., Sethi, R.: The complexity of flowshop and jobshop scheduling. Math. Oper. Res. **1**(2), 117–129 (1976)
12. Goldberg, D.E., Deb, K.: A comparative analysis of selection schemes used in genetic algorithms. In: Foundations of Genetic Algorithms, vol. 1, pp. 69–93. Elsevier (1991)
13. Karimi-Mamaghan, M., Mohammadi, M., Meyer, P., Karimi-Mamaghan, A.M., Talbi, E.G.: Machine learning at the service of meta-heuristics for solving combinatorial optimization problems: a state-of-the-art. Eur. J. Oper. Res. **296**(2), 393–422 (2022)
14. Karimi-Mamaghan, M., Pasdeloup, B., Mohammadi, M., Meyer, P.: A learning-based iterated local search algorithm for solving the traveling salesman problem. In: Dorronsoro, B., Amodeo, L., Pavone, M., Ruiz, P. (eds.) OLA 2021. CCIS, vol. 1443, pp. 45–61. Springer, Cham (2021). https://doi.org/10.1007/978-3-030-85672-4_4
15. Lee, J.H., Kim, H.J.: Reinforcement learning for robotic flow shop scheduling with processing time variations. Int. J. Prod. Res. **60**, 2346–2368 (2022)
16. Lim, D., Jin, Y., Ong, Y.-S., Sendhoff, B.: Generalizing surrogate-assisted evolutionary computation. IEEE Trans. Evol. Comput. **14**, 329–355 (2009)

17. Lin, Q., Gao, L., Li, X., Zhang, C.: A hybrid backtracking search algorithm for permutation flow-shop scheduling problem. Comput. Ind. Eng. **85**, 437–446 (2015)
18. Morais, M., Ribeiro, M., da Silva, R., Mariani, V., Coelho, L.: Discrete differential evolution metaheuristics for permutation flow shop scheduling problems. Comput. Ind. Eng. **166**, 107956 (2022)
19. Michalewicz, Z., Hartley, S.J.: Genetic algorithms+ data structures= evolution programs. Math. Intell. **18**(3), 71 (1996)
20. Nearchou, A.C.: The effect of various operators on the genetic search for large scheduling problems. Int. J. Prod. Econ. **88**(2), 191–203 (2004)
21. Neufeld, J., Gupta, J., Buscher, U.: A comprehensive review of flowshop group scheduling literature. Comput. Oper. Res. **70**, 56–74 (2016)
22. Nugraheni, C.E., Abednego, L.: A tabu-search based constructive hyper-heuristics for scheduling problems in textile industry. J. Ind. Intell. Inf. **5**(2) (2017)
23. Pandiri, V., Singh, A.: A hyper-heuristic based artificial bee colony algorithm for k-interconnected multi-depot multi-traveling salesman problem. Inf. Sci. **463**, 261–281 (2018)
24. Ruiz, R., Pan, Q.K., Naderi, B.: Iterated Greedy methods for the distributed permutation flowshop scheduling problem. Omega **83**, 213–222 (2019)
25. Ruiz, R., Maroto, C., Alcaraz, J.: Two new robust genetic algorithms for the flowshop scheduling problem. Omega **34**(5), 461–476 (2006)
26. Song, H., Triguero, I., Özcan, E.: A review on the self and dual interactions between machine learning and optimisation. Prog. Artif. Intell. **8**(2), 143–165 (2019). https://doi.org/10.1007/s13748-019-00185-z
27. Soria-Alcaraz, J.A., Ochoa, G., Swan, J., Carpio, M., Puga, H., Burke, E.K.: Effective learning hyper-heuristics for the course timetabling problem. Eur. J. Oper. Res. **238**(1), 77–86 (2014)
28. Taillard, E.: Benchmarks for basic scheduling problems. Eur. J. Oper. Res. **64**(2), 278–285 (1993). ISSN 0377–2217
29. Tanzila, A., Asif, A.S.: A comparative analysis of heuristic metaheuristic and exact approach to minimize make span of permutation flow shop scheduling. Am. J. Ind. Eng. **8**(1), 1–8 (2021)
30. Tasgetiren, F.M., Pan, Q.K., Suganthan, P.N., Buyukdagli, O.: A variable iterated greedy algorithm with differential evolution for the no-idle permutation flowshop scheduling problem. Comput. Oper. Res. **40**, 1729–1743 (2013)
31. Tong, H., Huang, C., Minku, L.L., Yao, X.: Surrogate models in evolutionary single-objective optimization: a new taxonomy and experimental study. Inf. Sci. **562** 414–437 (2021)
32. Wilson, J.: Search methodologies: introductory tutorials in optimization and decision support techniques (2007)
33. Wolpert, D.H., Macready, W.G.: No free lunch theorems for optimization. IEEE Trans. Evol. Comput. **1**(1), 67–82 (1997)

Generalized Objective Function to Ensure Robust Evaluation for Evolutionary Storage Location Assignment Algorithms

Polina Görbe[(✉)] [ID] and Tamás Bódis [ID]

Széchenyi University, Egyetem sqr. 1, 9026 Győr, Hungary
gorbe.polina@sze.hu

Abstract. The efficiency of warehouse operations can be measured by various indicators, but the main one is the lead time, which is heavily influenced by the order picking, as this is the most time- and labor-intensive process in the warehouse operation. In order to reduce lead times, many researchers are working on the topic of Storage Location Assignment Problem (SLAP) The optimized SLA is designed to improve picking efficiency, so that the picker does not have to travel long distances unnecessarily in a picker-to-parts system. During the optimization process, it is necessary to evaluate the SLA in an appropriate way, on the basis of which it is possible to measure whether the objectives are approximated by the results or not. It is also very important to evaluate regularly the SLA during the period after optimization to get an up-to-date information about the assignment of the storage items. The results of regular evaluations can be used to check whether the SLA is effective and lead times are good or whether optimization and reassignment is necessary. Based on studies and experience, SLAs are reassessed and optimized following significant inefficiencies, resulting in relocation tasks and additional work and costs for warehouses. The authors' research concept includes avoiding large-scale relocation tasks by continuously review the SLA. While other studies evaluate the optimized SLA by running picking lists, but it usually would be necessary to get information about the assignment of the entire warehouse. Furthermore, since assigning thousands of items to thousands of positions is a huge combinational problem, evolutionary algorithm would be necessary to apply. It is also requiring time-effective and generalized individual evolution method to make us possible tactical SLA optimization.

The aim of this paper is to describe a novel generalized SLA evaluation method where each of the located items is evaluated to obtain a more accurate optimization result. Furthermore, unlike other research, the aim is to ensure that the optimization concept and the evaluation method are not only specified for one warehouse but can be used in other warehouses as well.

Keywords: Storage-location-assignment · Objective function · Combinatorial optimization

---

N. T. Nguyen et al. (Eds.): ICCCI 2023, CCIS 1864, pp. 546–559, 2023.
https://doi.org/10.1007/978-3-031-41774-0_43

1 Introduction

It is well known that the order picking is the most time-consuming task in warehouse operations, and the general goal is to minimize the lead time to be able to perform more orders within the usual short time window with the given resources. The picking efficiency is influenced by the definition of the routing and the storage location assignment (SLA) in the warehouse. There are several SLA policies to assign the items into the warehouse. When warehouses experience inefficiencies, typically the storage location assignment is reviewed and optimized [1]. In the literature storage location assignment problem (SLAP) deals with this topic [2]. The topicality of the topic is reflected in the fact that the optimization of SLAs has been studied from several angles. Several authors published studies on solving SLA. In the state-of-the-art researches, it is clearly visible that the topic has been investigated from several points of view by combining different storage and order picking logics, and information is also available on the methods used to investigate the feasibility of solving the problem [2–4].

In the course of the research, as the presented relevant literature review shows, we observed that many authors deal with SLA optimization using different methods, heuristics and algorithms, in most cases they have specified the study for a specific case, however there is no mention of the possibilities to maintain efficiency after optimization. Based on this experience, it was thought that it would be worth exploring a possible method for maintaining an ideal SLA. An intelligent system concept presented by authors, which is the Adaptive Storage Location Assignment (ASLA). The purpose of ASLA is to optimize SLA based on the available data, and then use this data to recommend items for the depleted storage location that need to be moved to the front or back of the warehouse based on demand. It is important to emphasize that 100% optimal results cannot be achieved, since most likely the location requested by the optimal SLA will not be empty. But based on trade-offs, the empty storage location nearby may be ideal and will be offered for the replenishing task. In critical cases, a repositioning task is cannot be completely excluded, but the time spent on the repositioning task can be significantly reduced and it can be integrated into daily operations without requiring overtime. The goal of the conception to be applicable not only to a specific circumstance, but also to other warehouses with minimal modification and appropriate data. The authors have published this concept previously [5]. Since assigning thousands of items to thousands of positions is a huge combinational problem, evolutionary algorithm would be necessary to apply. It is also requiring time-effective and generalized individual evolution method to make us possible tactical SLA optimization. The review of the evolutional methods and objective function highlighted most of the research evaluates the assignment based on sample picking lists. It is proper solution if a given case would be analyzed, but our case requires more generalized and time-effective objective function for the evolutionary algorithm used on tactical level. In contrast to the methodology used in the investigated studies, a new method for evaluating the effectiveness of the optimization process and the SLA has been formulated that takes into account the state of the entire product placement. The aim of this article is to present a new evaluation method and the associated objective function based on the ASLA concept. We present the results of testing the objective function using various case studies.

2   Research Goals

The discussed research is focusing on how to maintain a near ideal SLA while minimizing the repositioning tasks. The concept of Adaptive Storage Location Assignment
(ASLA) has been formulated, the aim of which is to periodically optimize SLA based
on actual conditions adapting and applying the results to daily operations by adap-
tively replenishing the depleting picking locations based on the current ideal SLA. The
ASLA (Fig. 1) starts with the demand analysis, when based on the previously defined
time period the booked orders from the ERP (Enterprise Resource Planning) will be
investigated and classified. After the SLA optimized the necessary relocation tasks are
managed. The ideal SLA is entered into the WMS (Warehouse Management System) and
on this basis the replenishment tasks are managed. A near ideal SLA can be maintained
by periodically reviewing and re-running the process.

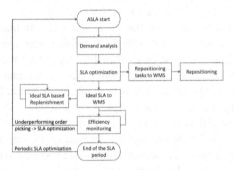

Fig. 1.   ASLA workflow [5]

The goal is to make ASLA not just a solution for one warehouse, but also applicable to
other warehouses with the right modifications. We have already examined the conditions
for storage location assignment, which can be implemented using ASLA. In the Fast-
Moving Consumer Goods (FMCG) sector, ASLA can be a solution for warehouses where
the storage structure is more complex, number of items is high, picking efficiency can
deteriorate rapidly and the travel distances increases over time during picking processes.
Such complex problems can be addressed by the concept [6].

Because of the complexity, the authors started to investigate what heuristics and algorithms have been used by other authors for optimize and what algorithm might be ideal
for the ASLA concept to work quickly and efficiently. The Storage location assignment
problem (SLAP) is strongly NP-hard combinatorial problem [7], because many items
need to be stored in a warehouse with a large storage capacity and therefore the number
of combinations is large. In the research we examined iterative heuristics and algorithm
[8, 17], Simulated Annealing algorithm [10], Neighborhood Search method [11], clustering algorithm [9, 13], apriori algorithm [12], Genetic Algorithm [15] and a combined
Iterated Local Search algorithm with Tabu Thresholding [16] were investigated, and in
a study, heuristics was compared with genetic algorithm [14].

The steps of the optimization process include the evaluation of the results. The
operation of ASLA is also based on a continuous evaluation, so it is necessary to fit

it with an appropriate objective function. After learning about the algorithms used to optimize product placement in the Picker-to-parts system, the evaluation methods of the researches studied were also investigated. As de Koster et al. determined in a previous study: The main factor is to minimize the length of the picking route and to reduce picking time [1]. This is still the aim and the objective of the evaluation methods examined. Kübler et al. perform relocation optimizations taking into account the frequency value of the products to achieve a shorter total travel distance during order picking tasks. Storage location assignment changed by relocation is checked against order picking lists to ensure that the correct result has been achieved [8]. Zhang used generated picking lists to evaluate the results of the algorithm they studied in their research [9]. In their subsequent research the authors performed the optimization by considering S-routing and during the evaluation they also ran picking lists on the route to check whether the total travel distance decreased [10]. Silva et al. were integrated the SLAP and Order picking problem (OPP) and solve them as a single problem that they name as storage location and order picking problem (SLOPP). To test the different routing policies, the same order picking task was performed by authors [11]. Öncan in his study of picking planning problems focused on the order batching aspect. The evaluation was carried out for three layouts with different lengths of generated picking tasks [16]. Li et al. at their objective function examined the allocated and unallocated items and the connection between the items. The items also classified by the order frequency to the A, B and C classes. After optimizing the SLA, a randomly selected order picking list is used to compute the travel distance of order picking [18]. In the later research the objective function of Li et al. is also to minimize the total expected travel distance. Optimization takes into account the order frequency of products and the relationship between products ordered together. Picking lists were run to check the results of the different scenarios and compared [12]. Dijkstra and Roodbergen examined the SLA optimization based on the class-based ordering of items and with the four routing method (return, S-shape, largest gap, midpoint). Generated picking tasks were used to investigate the routings and layout [19]. In another research the authors used randomly generated order picking lists for the evaluation of the results, and also investigated the weighting of the parameters and the clustering during the evaluation [13]. In Wang et al.'s research where the optimization is performed by swapping pairs of items, for evaluation picking lists of prioritized orders are used [17].

The evaluation methods of the studies examined in our research all show that the results of the optimization procedure are evaluated using picking lists. This evaluation method narrows down the possibilities and can be applied to specific tasks in the cases under consideration. Since our optimization method and concept differs from previous research, it was necessary to improve the evaluation method. The general applicability of the method we have studied and formulated is therefore a new approach to the subject. To implement of the evaluation method, it was necessary to investigate what variations exist for which ASLA should work. The detailed results of the complexity analysis are not presented in this article, but in general the cases identified are grouped as follows. We considered simpler and more complex cases and looked at the number of possible allocation variations. In the first group, we include storage where only one type of item is allowed in a given location. We looked at when the number of storage locations equals the number of products to be stored, and when there are more and less products than available storage location. In the second group, we looked at typical cases where there are multiple items in a location, with the number of items to be stored being less than, equal to or more than the number of picking locations available. The further we look, the more we see that the number of possible SLA is increasing. For the more complex, parameterizable cases, we have found that the more aspects to consider for each warehouse, such as zones or to handle the ordered together items, the more variations there are, which is difficult to handle. The concept described should be applicable to the cases under consideration.

In the next sections, the evaluation method was defined and tested for the cases when the number of item type and the storage locations are equal.

3 Evaluation Method

We started from the optimization problems to implement the evaluation. As detailed in the previous section, typically a picking task is run to evaluate the optimized SLA and the goal is to minimize the length of the picking route. This type of evaluation typically examines the results using generated order picking lists. The selection of order picking lists has a significant impact on the result and does not provide information on the whole product placement. In addition, running these lists and evaluating the results is slow. To overcome this and to maintain efficiency, a quick and general evaluation is needed. In our research, during the optimization we would like to minimize the distance between the frequented products and the depot point and evaluate the entire SLA and thus aim for an overall value that is kept to a minimum. The primary consideration was to define a variable value for each product that varies as a function of the distance data due to the product location and by aggregating this data we can quantify the current SLA status.

To evaluate the whole SLA, data such as the picking frequency, which is similar to the turnover speed, is needed for the products, like an indicator number. This can be used to categorize the products stored and handled in the warehouse in a similar way to the Pareto principle. If the operation of a particular warehouse requires it, we should take into account which products are stored together in groups. In addition, we believe that an important aspect to consider is which products are regularly ordered together, are stored close to each other and we aim to be able to evaluate this with the objective function. In addition, the distance of the picking locations from the manipulation area should also be taken into account. The necessary data can be obtained from historical ordering data and from the warehouse layout.

3.1 Notations, Fundamental Principles and Assumptions

Parameters:

t is the time-period under examination,

p is a given picking location,

i is the item which handled in the warehouse,

f_{pt} is the number of picking of the item on the p picking location at the t time-period,

l_p is the distance of the p picking location from the depot,

F_t is the summarized item order lines during the t time-period,

j_t is the number of pickings of the item is non-assigned on picking location at the t time-period,

g_n is a given group of items,

lg_n is the distance between items ($i_1, ..., i_n$) within a group,

Ig_n is the number of items within a group,

o_{i_1,i_2} is the order frequency of two ordered together items (i_1, i_2) during the t time-period,

l_{i_1,i_2} is the distance between of two items,

ω_n is the weight of the components.

Fundamental principles and assumptions:

1. The objective is to minimize the total value of the storage location assignment (Eq. 5.).
2. We consider a manual picker-to-parts system in a warehouse.
3. Since we consider a low-level system, vertical movements can be neglected.
4. Each item type is stored only in one location, and each location contains only a single type of item.
5. We assume that the item ordering frequency of the near future is known based on the actual and historical customer demand.
6. We assume that, if necessary, we know which items should be stored together.
7. We assume that, if necessary, we know which items are ordered together.

3.2 Formulas for the Objective Function

We constructed a complex objective function which has four components.

$$\sum_p \left(\frac{f_{pt}}{F_t} \cdot l_p\right) \tag{1}$$

Equation (1) gives a frequency value based on the order frequencies. It takes into account the ordering frequencies per item for a given period and how far they are from the Depot point. This illustrates that if the products that need to be picked frequently are close to the buffer points at the manipulation area, the SLA is ideal.

$$\frac{1}{\sum_i \frac{j_t}{F_t}} \tag{2}$$

The Eq. (2) is the Non-assigned component of our objective function. Sometimes not all products in the warehouse can be assigned a low-level picking location, so it takes into account how many products were not assigned to a picking location and with what frequency they had to be picked during the period under consideration. Ideally, products that need to be picked infrequently should not be given picking location, but the picking frequency of these products can change rapidly due to rapidly changing demands.

$$\sum_g \frac{\sum lg_n}{Ig_n} \tag{3}$$

The third component of objective function (3) evaluates the range of products stored together. Some warehouses require that identical products are either grouped together in an area or grouped according to some criteria and stored directly next to each other.

$$\sum_i \left(\frac{o_{i_1,i_2}}{\sum_i o_{i_1,i_2}} \cdot l_{i_1,i_2} \right) \tag{4}$$

The fourth component (4) evaluates the range of products ordered together. It can be used to check the distance between products that are regularly ordered together. For optimization purposes, it is advisable to store them close to each other in the warehouse, taking into account the picking frequencies. A certain compromise is necessary, as we have to give up the ideal SLA because of the frequency component of objective function in some direction.

$$\min \left(\frac{\omega_1 \cdot \sum_p (\frac{f_{pt}}{F_t} \cdot l_p)}{\omega_2 \cdot \frac{1}{\sum_i \frac{f_t}{F_t}}} + \omega_3 \cdot \sum_g \frac{\sum lg_n}{lg_n} + \omega_4 \cdot \sum_i \left(\frac{o_{i_1,i_2}}{\sum_i o_{i_1,i_2}} \cdot l_{i_1,i_2} \right) \right) \tag{5}$$

The described components operate on the basis of Eq. 5. We aim for the minimum; the lowest result will be the appropriate SLA when comparing the results of the optimization process evaluation. Each component of the objective function has a weight value (ω_n). As mentioned above, the aim of our research is not to apply the ASLA concept and the associated evaluation method to only one case, the weights are used to specify the objective function for different operational warehouses with minimal changes. In the operation of a given warehouse, whichever aspect is more relevant, the weight of that component is increased. If a criterion is not taken into account, the value of the weight can be minimized, or the component of the objective function can be omitted. The weights for Eqs. (1), (3) and (4) can be placed between 0-∞, but for the non-assigned (2) component of the objective function they must be placed between 1-∞. Weights are not used in the evaluation in this article, each weight is equal to 1, so that the focus is on the operation of the members of the objective function. The range of weights requires further investigation and will be published in a forthcoming article.

3.3 Steps for Calculating the Objective Function

To use the objective function first need to determine the frequency value of the items based on the frequency of picking and distance from the depot (Eq. 1.). Secondly need to determine the non-assigned component based on the quantity and frequency value of unallocated products (Eq. 2.). Determine the value of items stored together by group (Eq. 3.). At the fourth step it is need to determine the value of items ordered together based on their distance from each other. Calculate the objective function as specified.

4 Results and Discussions

The aim of this section is to evaluate the objective function with analytical examples to prove that it is a well-directed and a workable solution. The application of the objective function can be implemented in a more general framework. The study used a sample layout of 120 picking locations and typical arrangement of racks for testing.

The applicability of the objective function was tested for 3 cases:
-Random storage.
-Class-based arrangement.
-Arrangement that considered all aspects.

All of the above apply to cases of SLA. In all three cases, the range of items to be stored together and the location of the items ordered together are taken into account for the evaluation of the objective function. In line with real-life operations, we also look at items that have been denied picking location due to lack of storage space.

4.1 Data Relating of the Examination

Table 1. Groups of products stored together

Group	ItemID	Category
Group1	ITM_G_001	A
	ITM_G_002	B
	ITM_G_003	B
	ITM_G_004	C
	ITM_G_005	C
	ITM_G_006	B
	ITM_G_007	B
	ITM_G_008	A
	ITM_G_009	C
	ITM_G_010	C
Group2	ITM_G_011	C
	ITM_G_012	C
	ITM_G_013	C
	ITM_G_014	B
	ITM_G_015	B
	ITM_G_016	A
	ITM_G_017	C
	ITM_G_018	B

The same layout as for the initial objective function was considered for the test. The warehouse layout shows 120 picking locations. The items are defined by ABC ordering frequency category with a ratio of 10–20-70%. So, 12 of items is A, 24 of items is B and 64 of items is C are allocated to picking storage locations. Groupings have been made according to certain criteria. The items that need to be stored together has been divided into two groups. From the total item set, the two groups were randomly selected.

Table 2. Relationship between products ordered together (OT)

Main Item	Connected Item	Number of orders
ITM_019	ITM_020	2
	ITM_021	5
ITM_022	ITM_023	4
	ITM_G_013	7
	ITM_G_002	11
	ITM_024	3
ITM_G_007	ITM_025	4
ITM_027	ITM_026	1
	ITM_028	6

Table 3. Non-assigned items

ItemID	Category
ITM_029	B
ITM_030	B
ITM_031	B
ITM_032	C
ITM_033	C
ITM_034	C
ITM_035	C
ITM_036	C
ITM_037	C
ITM_038	C

The aim of ensuring that the two groups did not have the same number of items, so the Group1 contains 10 items and Group2 contains 8 items. The grouping is shown in the Table 1. For the co-ordering aspect, there are 4 main items that are considered, and the frequency and relationship of the items co-ordered with them is as follows. Table 2 shows the relationship between the products ordered together. In addition, there are another 10 items that have not been allocated to picking storage due to lack of storage location. There are the Non-assigned items, which is shown in Table 3 below. In both the 2 and 3 tables, the number of items has been defined so that they are different but manageable in the analysis.

The next chapters will highlight some possible industrial cases and the SLA will be evaluated based on formula. The goal is to validate each part of the formula with analytic examples.

4.2 The Examined Cases

Evaluation of Full Random Storage

In this case, the items are placed in the picking location areas without following any logic, the items are stored in the free locations. There are logics that suggest that it makes sense to follow this arrangement, either due to the characteristic of the products, but in our opinion, it may not be ideal for short lead times for efficient operations, especially for warehouses where multiple orders need to be picked and the picking frequency of items are also high. A favorable initial condition for testing optimization is the full random layout. In order to test the objective function, we therefore chose this case as the initial condition. Comparative table (Table 4.) shows the result of the evaluation, the value of each component of the objective function. It can be clearly seen that the value of the Frequency component is not so high for random assignment, but if we consider the range of items that need to be stored together and those that are ordered together, we can see from the values that they are very far apart and therefore the overall value of the objective function is high. On the Fig. 2. at the random storage part the layout clearly shows the scattering of the class-based items and the items tested under different aspects - stored together (Group1, Group2), ordered together (OT).

Class-Based Storage Evaluation

Items are sorted into ABC categories according to the frequency of picking based on order data. This is a well-established practice in SLA, as the items that need to be picked more frequently have a shorter distance to travel, are picked faster, and therefore picking efficiency is good. The focus of this case was on optimization by ABC category, with no changes to the range of items stored and ordered together. The comparison table (Table 4.) clearly shows that compared to Case 1, the value of Frequency has improved and due to the characteristics of the items, in some cases, our value has improved for the items stored together, but worsened for the items ordered together. It can still be said that the overall value of the Objective Function has improved significantly compared to the Case 1. The layout shows the class-based arrangement clearly on the Fig. 2., but the items of the other aspects are still scattered.

Evaluation All Aspects into Account

In the Case 3, we have taken into account the different aspects, i.e. we have tried to represent a layout where items that need to be stored together and items that are frequently ordered together are located close to each other in the warehouse, keeping in mind the ABC categories. The results of the test clearly show that the Frequency value has increased compared to Case 2 i.e., it is slightly worse, but the third and fourth terms of the objective function give much better results, so overall the objective function is the best. Compared to the initial starting point, which was 138.081, down to 40.8087, we achieved a verifiably better result in the evaluation. The layout shows on the Fig. 2. at all aspects considered storage part, that the items are arranged with all aspects taken into account.

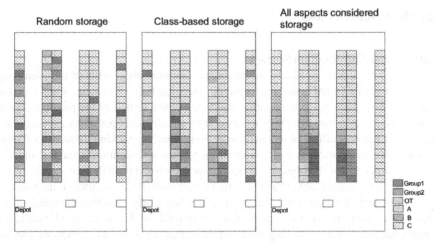

Fig. 2. Random; Class-based; All aspects considered storage from the cases described

Table 4. Comparison table of Objective Function results in several cases

	Case1	Case2	Case3
Frequency	9,3497	8,8376	9,1620
Non-assigned	18,5745	18,5745	18,5745
Stored together	105,1824	91,3115	25,2333
Ordered together	32,3948	41,0454	15,0822
Calculated OF	138,081	132,833	40,8087

4.3   Buffer Locations

To smoothly maintain near-ideal SLA with replenishment tasks, it is necessary to have a certain amount of buffer location that can be used to perform replenishment or, if necessary, repositioning tasks. The buffer does not appear in the objective function but is necessary for operation. We continued the examination with the best performing case (Case 3). We used 5% of the total storage space as buffer space in the first round and 10% in the second round. These empty locations are randomly distributed in the layout as shown in Fig. 3. It is important to point out that these are not dedicated locations in the picking area but change as a result of the fluidity of the flow. Importantly, we should set a limit on the intervals at which we need to free up location according to the buffer capacity. When comparing the two cases, it was necessary to determine that 6 picking location should be freed for 5% and 12 for 10% buffer capacity. Of the allocated products, the least frequented items were classified in the Non-assigned group. Based on this, we reallocated the items by category and criteria and recalculated the objective function for the buffer cases. The value of objective function was 41.1432 for a 5% buffer and 41.3721 for a 10% buffer. The detailed results are shown in Table 5. It can be seen that the value of the objective function is slightly increased compared to the favorable

Case 3, but it is significantly below the value of Case 1 and Case 2. To some extent, a trade-off is necessary in determining the number of buffer locations. The results have also been represented on layout and are shown in Fig. 3.

Table 5. Comparison table of Objective Function results in several cases of buffer

	Buffer 0%	Buffer 5%	Buffer 10%
Frequency	9,1620	8,6948	8,3103
Non-assigned	18,5745	10,504	7,8649
Stored together	25,2333	25,2333	25,2333
Ordered together	15,0822	15,0822	15,0822
Calculated OF	40,8087	41,1432	41,3721

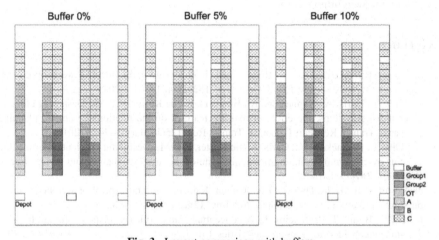

Fig. 3. Layout comparison with buffers

5 Conclusion

Of all warehouse operations, picking process is the most cost- and time-consuming. SLA in the warehouse has a big impact on picking efficiency. There are many studies on the subject from different approaches, but little is said about the maintenance of the state in the various optimization solutions. That is why the authors of this article started to research this issue and formulated a new concept, called ASLA, which aims to maintain a near-ideal SLA by performing replenish tasks. The concept is based on continuous evaluation. The aim of this article was to present a new method for evaluating SLA. Previous research has formulated an evaluative objective function for the optimization of SLA in a given warehouse and picking lists are used. Based on our ASLA concept, the objective function can be applied to different warehouses with minimal changes and the right data. In developing the objective function, an important aspect for us was that the larger the warehouse capacity and the more products we want to assign, the bigger the combinatorial problem. An evolutionary algorithm can provide the solution, but this requires an evolution method that is time-effective and generalizable to individual evolution. In this article, the objective function is described, and the results of tests carried out using analytical examples are also presented. Our results so far show that the objective function is well applicable, since the value of the objective function is significantly reduced by the optimized SLA compared to the baseline. In a larger warehouse, measured with more picking locations, a much greater contrast can be achieved between the two values. The objective function does not require any algorithm development, it can be implemented in MS Excel with the right data, but the algorithm is required to maintain the optimized SLA based on our concept, so it is part of the evaluations. Further research to improve the ASLA algorithm and evaluation. In addition, we aim to investigate the objective function at a deeper level by testing the results with a picking list, different routing, more complex SLA based on the complexity test and other layouts, as well as fine-tuning the weighting criteria.

References

1. de Koster, R.B.M., Le-Duc, T., Roodbergen, K.J.: Design and control of warehouse order picking: a literature review. Eur. J. Oper. Res. **182**(2), 481–501 (2007)
2. van Gils, T., Caris, A., Ramaekers, K., Braekers, K., de Koster, R.B.M.: Designing efficient order picking systems: the effect of real-life features on the relationship among planning problems. Transp. Res. Part E: Logist. Transp. Rev. **125**(January), 47–73 (2019)
3. van Gils, T., Ramaekers, K., Caris, A., de Koster, R.B.M.: Designing efficient order picking systems by combining planning problems: state-of-the-art classification and review. Eur. J. Oper. Res. **267**(1), 1–15 (2018)
4. de Koster, R.B.M., Le-Duc, T., Roodbergen, K.J.: Design and control of warehouse order picking: a literature review. Comput. Ind. Eng. **129**(2), 396–411 (2019)
5. Görbe, P., Bódis, T., Botzheim, J.: A conceptual framework for adaptive storage location assignment considering order characteristics. Eur. J. Sci. Technol. (April), 610–614 (2020)
6. Görbe, P., Bódis, T., Földesi, P.: Trade-offs in warehousing storage location reassignment. Int. J. Logist. Syst. Manag. (1742–7967 1742–7975): **1**(1), 1 (2023)
7. Frazelle, E.H.: Stock location assignment and order picking productivity. Doctoral Dissertation, Georgia Institute of Technology (1989)
8. Kübler, P., Glock, C.H., Bauernhansl, T.: A new iterative method for solving the joint dynamic storage location assignment, order batching and picker routing problem in manual picker-to-parts warehouses. Comput. Ind. Eng. **147**, 106645 (2020)
9. Zhang, Y.: Correlated storage assignment strategy to reduce travel distance in order picking. IFAC-PapersOnLine **49**(2), 30–35 (2016)
10. Zhang, R.Q., Wang, M., Pan, X.: New model of the storage location assignment problem considering demand correlation pattern. Comput. Ind. Eng. **129**, 210–219 (2019)
11. Silva, A., Coelho, L.C., Darvish, M., Renaud, J.: Integrating storage location and order picking problems in warehouse planning. Transp. Res. Part E: Logist. Transp. Rev. **140**(July), 102003 (2020)
12. Li, Y., Méndez-Mediavilla, F.A., Temponi, C., Kim, J., Jimenez, J.A.: A heuristic storage location assignment based on frequent itemset classes to improve order picking operations. Appl. Sci. (Switzerland) MDPI AG **11**(4), 1–15 (2021)

13. Trindade, M.A.M., Sousa, P.S.A., Moreira, M.R.A.: Improving order-picking operations with precedence constraints through efficient storage location assignment: evidence from a retail company, U Porto. J. Eng. **7**(3), 34–52 (2021)
14. Park, C., Seo, J.: Comparing heuristic algorithms of the planar storage location assignment problem. Transp. Res. Part E: Logist. Transp. Rev. **46**(1), 171–185 (2010)
15. Pan, J.C.H., Shih, P.H., Wu, M.H., Lin, J.H.: A storage assignment heuristic method based on genetic algorithm for a pick-and-pass warehousing system. Comput. Ind. Eng. **81**, 1–13 (2015)
16. Öncan, T.: MILP formulations and an iterated local search algorithm with Tabu thresholding for the order batching problem. Eur. J. Oper. Res. **243**(1), 142–155 (2015)
17. Wang, M., Zhang, R.Q., Fan, K.: Improving order-picking operation through efficient storage location assignment: a new approach. Comput. Ind. Eng. **139**(October 2019), 106186 (2020)
18. Li, J., Moghaddam, M., Nof, S.Y.: Dynamic storage assignment with product affinity and ABC classification—a case study. Int. J. Adv. Manufact. Technol. **84**(9–12), 2179–2194 (2016)
19. Dijkstra, A.S., Roodbergen, K.J.: Exact route-length formulas and a storage location assignment heuristic for picker-to-parts warehouses. Transp. Res. Part E: Logist. Transp. Rev. **102**, 38–59 (2017)

Bacterial Evolutionary Algorithm Based Autoencoder Architecture Search for Anomaly Detection

Hunor István Lukács[1,2](✉) ⓘ, Tamás Fischl[2] ⓘ, and János Botzheim[1] ⓘ

[1] Department of Artificial Intelligence, Faculty of Informatics, Eötvös Loránd University, Pázmány P. Sétány 1/A, 1117 Budapest, Hungary
{botzheim,cqd3yu}@inf.elte.hu
[2] Robert Bosch Kft, Budapest, Gyömrői út 104, 1103 Budapest, Hungary
tamas.fischl@hu.bosch.com

Abstract. This paper presents an architecture optimization approach, based on evolutionary algorithms, which helps in finding the optimal architecture depth, shortening the time that one has to invest in an uncertain number of test runs to find the right architecture. The provided algorithm is applied in the field of anomaly detection, which consists of searching for small amounts (ppm) of anomalies in large datasets using autoencoder models.

Nowadays, as a result of the continuous digitization efforts visible in the industry, the data of semi-finished and finished products and production processes are becoming available in increasing quantities. A lot of data can be connected through databases, which offer the possibility of recognizing connections that have been hidden to this day. Quality assurance in industry also requires that deviations within limit values and specifications are investigated (outlier detection). The analyzed data is extracted from the production of a MEMS (Micro Electro Mechanical System) based inertial sensor used in the automotive industry, thus the paper reflects on real problems arising in industry, while the results of the suggested method are validated by domain experts.

The presented method in this paper shows how the bacterial evolutionary algorithm combined with an abstraction, based on rational quadratic Bézier curves, can be used in the autoencoder architecture search, and thus be applied to anomaly detection challenges appearing in the industry.

Keywords: Architecture optimization · Bézier curve · Anomaly detection · MEMS Inertial Sensor

1 Introduction

With the spread of digitalization in industry, more and more data is becoming available in manufacturing, product development and services. Analyzing and

N. T. Nguyen et al. (Eds.): ICCCI 2023, CCIS 1864, pp. 560–572, 2023.
https://doi.org/10.1007/978-3-031-41774-0_44

evaluating this data is also a big task, and there are numerous methods for solving it. Today, the use of artificial intelligence to analyze industrial data is becoming important in the field of understanding the correlation in the data.

Numerous AI-based model architectures are available for identifying and inferring relationships in data. In many cases, however, the modeling process is iterative, in which finding the right architecture (providing the right accuracy for a given task) is the result of multiple iterations.

This article analyses data from the production of a MEMS (Micro Electro Mechanical System) based inertial sensor [5] used in the automotive industry. Within that, it deals with the topic of anomaly detection, which consists of searching for small amounts (ppm) of anomalies in the data using an autoencoder neural network architecture.

The nature of the effects in the data set (and in data sets in general) can also be diverse. They can be the result of random measurement error (not a real error), or the result of systematic behavior either from the product or the environment, or a combination of both. Overall, however, the identification of these deviations is of paramount importance for the manufacture of the product. If it is considered that an initial deviation that is within the measurement limits may lead to an out-of-specification deviation later in the product life cycle, then the detection and identification of these deviations is part of the quality assurance process.

Although in the present case the autoencoder architecture is given to solve the problem, it is nevertheless not possible to determine in advance the depth of the architecture that is best suited for the task, i.e. how many hidden layers will lead to the best solution. Just as in this case it is not known which data in the dataset can be called an anomaly.

Thus, this paper aims at the bacterial optimization of this chosen autoencoder architecture on the chosen MEMS based inertial production data set.

2   Problem Statement

Given a dataset and based on expert knowledge a few data points are labeled as anomalies, these are the *ground truth anomalies*. We would like to find an optimal autoencoder architecture, which can split the dataset into inliers and outliers (anomalies) such that all the ground truth anomalies are labeled as anomalies and also to find all the so far undiscovered, real anomalies.

Our dataset is originating from an automotive inertial sensor production. Data are measurement data of the product from the production process from component up to the final measurement. After the data cleaning and preprocessing procedures, our dataset consists of 430k data point, and 61 features, while the number of ground truth anomalies is 4. Figure 1b. shows how the 4 ground truth anomalies appear in the correlation of two features. These 4 data points can not be discovered by the Standard Scaler method, since it only investigates the data feature-by-feature, neglecting the correlations between features, thus finds only those outliers which have standard deviation greater than a given threshold with respect to a single feature. However, this anomaly detection problem [3] can be solved via autoencoders (Sect. 2.1), if the architecture is set appropriately.

This paper aims to find a solution for such architecture optimization problem based on evolutionary algorithm, thus automatizing the architecture adjustment.

2.1 Symmetric Autoencoder

Autoencoder [2] is a type of artificial neural network which is used in unsupervised learning tasks to learn an efficient coding of unlabeled data. The autoencoder model contains an encoder, a code, and a decoder (as shown in Fig. 1a). It consists of two main functions, the encoding and the decoding functions. The encoding function transforms the input data into an encoded representation, while the decoding function is used in the recreation of the original input data from the encoded representation. Using these functions, the autoencoder can perform a dimension reduction (typically) in order to learn an efficient representation.

In the case of symmetric autoencoders, the symmetricity refers to the architectural symmetry between the encoder and the decoder. The decoder's architecture is the mirrored encoder on the code.

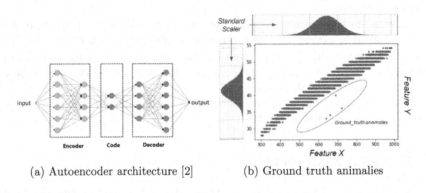

(a) Autoencoder architecture [2]   (b) Ground truth animalies

Fig. 1. Autoencoder architecture and the ground truth anomalies

3   Proposed Method

3.1   Bacterial Evolutionary Algorithm

The bacterial evolutionary algorithm (BEA) [6] is a general optimization method, where each bacterium represents a solution to the original problem. In our case, each bacterium represents a symmetric autoencoder architecture with fully-connected structure. The optimization process consists of three main steps, first is the random generation of the initial population, then the two main operators,

---

Algorithm 1. Bacterial Evolutionary Algorithm

1: initialize population randomly
2: **do**
3:      apply bacterial mutation operator (Section 3.4)
4:      apply gene transfer operator (Section 3.5)
5: **while** stopping criteria not reached

---

the bacterial mutation (Sect. 3.4) and the gene transfer (Sect. 3.5) are performed in each generation as illustrated in Algorithm 1. The number of generations is the stopping criteria, and it is indicated by the N_{gen} hyperparameter. At the end of the algorithm, the solution will be the bacterium with the lowest error value according to the evaluation criteria (Sect. 3.3).

3.2   Encoding Method

Each bacterium encodes a symmetric autoencoder in an abstract space, which is based on the quadratic Bézier curves. Bézier curves are used to represent the relationship between the number of neurons in the model's layers. Any desired architecture can be represented by a well-chosen Bézier curve with an appropriate degree of curvature, following the presented method and tailoring the constraints accordingly. In this paper, the quadratic Bézier curve is used.

Due to symmetricity (Sect. 2.1), it's enough to encode the encoder's architecture, whilst the decoder's architecture is simply just the mirrored encoder on the code. The architecture representation in the abstract space based on Bézier curves is presented in Fig. 2.

Bézier Curve. The quadratic Bézier curve is the path traced by the $B(t)$ function, given the control points P_0, P_1, and P_2. Rational Bézier curves add adjustable weights w_0, w_1, and w_2 to the control points P_0, P_1, and P_2 respectively:

$$B(t) = \frac{P_0 \cdot w_0 \cdot (1-t)^2 + P_1 \cdot w_1 \cdot 2 \cdot t \cdot (1-t) + P_2 \cdot w_2 \cdot t^2}{w_0 \cdot (1-t)^2 + w_1 \cdot 2 \cdot t \cdot (1-t) + w_2 \cdot t^2}, 0 \leq t \leq 1 \quad (1)$$

The modification of the curve, by changing the parameters of the $B(t)$ functions described by the Eq. (1), will lead to different architectures.

Constraints and DoF. The architecture encoding has the following constraints in the abstract representation:

1) P_0 is fixed at $[0,\ inp_{dim}]$
2) The x coordinate of the P_2 point is fixed at 1
3) The x coordinate of $P_1 \in [0,1]$
4) The y coordinate of $P_1 \in [code\_size, inp_{dim}]$

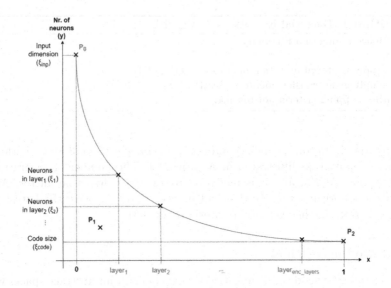

Fig. 2. Individual representation in the abstract space using Bézier curve

5) $w_0 = w_2 = 1$, while $w_1 = 5$

The inp_{dim} refers to the number of nodes in the input layer, while the *code_size* denotes the number of nodes in the code. The constraint regarding the y coordinate of the P_1 control point is important, since we are encoding a symmetric autoencoder architecture. If this value were greater than the input dimension, the autoencoder could learn the identity. In other, non-autoencoder architectures, this constraint won't be necessary.

The constraint regarding the weight values is important because we want to make sure that moving the P_1 control point will have effect on the curve. If the w_1 value were low, then all the curves generated by three control points would be just a line between P_0 and P_2.

The degrees of freedom (DoF) is 4 and these are as follows:

1) *code_size* (The y coordinate of the P_2 point)
2) N_{enc_layers}: Number of hidden layers in the encoder (same as in the decoder)
3) The x coordinate of the P_1 control point
4) The y coordinate of the P_1 control point

Since the DoF is four, each bacterial individual represents a symmetric autoencoder architecture with fully-connected structure using only four values.

From Abstract Representation to Architecture. We take N_{enc_layers} equidistant points in the [0, 1] interval on the horizontal axis, as illustrated in Fig. 2 by $layer_1$, $layer_2$, ..., $layer_{enc\_layers}$. By projecting these points onto the curve, we get the corresponding N_{enc_layers} intersection points. The rounded

y coordinate values of the intersection points show the number of neurons the corresponding layers will contain, these will be denoted by ξ_i.

In order to get the y coordinates of the intersection points, first we have to calculate the t timestamp corresponding to the x coordinate. For this we have to solve the quadratic equation w.r.t t. Let's denote with P_{i_x} and P_{i_y} the x and y coordinates of the P_i control point, respectively. Then we get the a, b, and c coefficients as follows:

$$a = P_{0_x} \cdot w_0 - 2 \cdot P_{1_x} \cdot w_1 + P_{2_x} \cdot w_2 - x \cdot w_0 + x \cdot 2 \cdot w_1 - x \cdot w_2$$
$$b = 2 \cdot P_{0_x} \cdot w_0 + 2 \cdot P_{1_x} \cdot w_1 + x \cdot 2 \cdot w_0 - x \cdot 2 \cdot w_1 \qquad (2)$$
$$c = P_{0_x} \cdot w_0 - x \cdot w_0.$$

From these coefficients t value can be computed as: $0 = a \cdot t^2 + b \cdot t + c$, where t has to be in the $[0, 1]$ interval.

Then, by substituting the derived t value in Eq. 1 we derive the intersection point's y coordinates on the Bézier curve corresponding to the t timestamp. The rounded y coordinates will be the ξ_i values. Then the associated autoencoder architecture has the following form:

$$Encoder : [\xi_{inp}, \xi_1] \rightarrow [\xi_1, \xi_2] \rightarrow \cdots \rightarrow [\xi_{enc\_layers}, \xi_{code}] \qquad (3)$$

$$Decoder : [\xi_{code}, \xi_{enc\_layers}] \rightarrow \cdots \rightarrow [\xi_2, \xi_1] \rightarrow [\xi_1, \xi_{inp}] \qquad (4)$$

where ξ_i is the number of neurons/nodes in the ith layer, ξ_{inp} is the number of nodes in the input layer, ξ_{code} is the number of nodes in the code, while ξ_{enc_layers} is the number of nodes in the N_{enc_layers}-th layer. $[\xi_{in}, \xi_{out}]$ represents a fully connected layer with ξ_{in} number of input nodes and ξ_{out} number of output nodes.

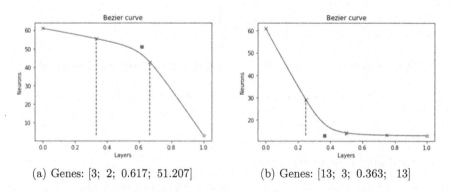

(a) Genes: [3; 2; 0.617; 51.207]   (b) Genes: [13; 3; 0.363;   13]

Fig. 3. Examples for abstract (Bézier curve) representations

Table 1. Examples: Bacteria and the corresponding architectures

Id	Bacterium Genes	Autoencoder architecture (fully connected layers)
1	[3; 2; 0.617; 51.207]	$[61, 55] \rightarrow [55, 43] \rightarrow [43, 3] \rightarrow [3, 43] \rightarrow [43, 55] \rightarrow$ $[55, 61]$
2	[13; 3; 0.363; 13]	$[61, 29] \rightarrow [29, 14] \rightarrow [14, 13] \rightarrow [13, 13] \rightarrow$ $[13, 13] \rightarrow [13, 14] \rightarrow [14, 29] \rightarrow [29, 61]$

Examples: Individuals, Abstract Representations, and the Associated Architectures

Figure 3 present 2 different bacteria, while Table 1 shows the corresponding architectures. The input dimension is 61.

In Table 1 each bacterium has the following form:

[*code size*; N_{enc_layers}; P_{1_x}; P_{1_y}], referring to the 4 DoF, while in the autoencoder architecture, $[IN, OUT]$ represents a fully connected layer with IN number of input nodes and OUT number of output nodes.

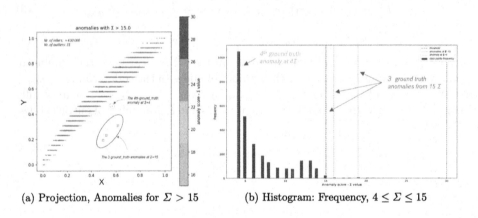

(a) Projection, Anomalies for $\Sigma > 15$ (b) Histogram: Frequency, $4 \leq \Sigma \leq 15$

Fig. 4. Anomalies, threshold value

3.3   Evaluation of Individuals

By the evaluation of the individual, we assign an error value to it, so it rewards accuracy and penalizes complexity.

The final error value of an individual has the following form:

$$error = loss + \lambda \cdot complexity \tag{5}$$

where λ is a hyperparameter of the algorithm, which represents the tradeoff between the accuracy and complexity.

In our case, determining the loss value for an individual consists of two steps. First, we train an autoencoder with the architecture encoded by the individual. At the beginning of the evolutionary algorithm we split our dataset into train set (70%), validation set (15%), and test set (15%). In order to prevent overfitting, early stopping is applied combined with a learning rate scheduler. In the second step, according to a threshold value on the standard deviation (Σ) of the reconstruction errors, the trained autoencoder splits the whole dataset into two parts, the inliers and the anomalies. The data points whose reconstruction error is less than the threshold value are the inliers, whilst the rest data points are the anomalies. A different threshold value is determined for each architecture, such that all the ground truth anomalies belong to the anomalies, and at the same time, we would like to find all real anomalies. Figure 4a illustrates, how on a trained model, a selected threshold value affects the appearing anomalies. Note, that in this figure a 61 dimensional dataset is projected onto a plane, stretched by 2 features. In this experiment, the autoencoder with manually set architecture has the following layers: 61 nodes in the *input layer*, 57 nodes in the *code*, and 61 nodes in the *output layer*. Figure 4b shows how would the quantity of anomalies change by choosing different Σ values, and also that the 3 of the ground truth anomalies are located outside 15 Σ, while the 4th one is located at $\Sigma = 4$.

Then the loss term is the ratio between the number of data points labeled as anomalies and the number of data points in the whole dataset.

$$loss_{anomaly} = \frac{N_{anomalies}}{N_{all\_data\_points}} \qquad (6)$$

The complexity term is the ratio between the trainable parameters of the model (N_{params_model}) and the maximum possible trainable parameters that a model can have (N_{params_max}). In our case, the trainable parameters are the weights and biases in the artificial neural network. The maximum possible trainable parameters an individual can have is determined by the N_{enc_layers} hyperparameter of the algorithm. This hyperparameter shows what the maximum number of layers is in the encoder's architecture between the input layer and the code (which will be mirrored in the decoder). In order to get the number of maximum possible trainable parameters, we assume that each layer contains the maximum amount of neurons, which in our case is the input layer's neuron number.

$$complexity = \frac{N_{params\_model}}{N_{params\_max}} = \frac{N_{params\_model}}{2 \cdot (N_{enc\_layers} + 1) \cdot (inp_{dim}^2 + inp_{dim})} \qquad (7)$$

3.4 Bacterial Mutation

The bacterial mutation operator is applied for each individual in the population [7]. It creates N_{clones} +1 number of clones for each individual. One group of genes is randomly selected and changed in N_{clones} clones, with one remaining unchanged.

The best clone from $N_{clones}+1$ clones is selected to transfer the mutated genes into the other N_{clones} clones.

The same process executes again with the yet-unselected group of genes, and repeats until all the genes in the bacterial chromosome are selected exactly once.

The best clone replaces the original individual in the population, discarding the other clones.

3.5   Gene Transfer

The gene transfer operator works on the population level. According to error definition, the bacterial population is divided into two halves, where the individuals with a low error value belong to the Superior Half, while individuals with a higher error value belong to the Inferior Half. A randomly chosen individual from the Superior Half of the population (*Donor*) transfers genes to another randomly chosen bacterium from the Inferior Half (*Acceptor*). The number of genes transferred is l_{gt}, which is a parameter of the algorithm.

After transferring the genes, the population is sorted again, and the procedure is repeated N_{inf} times.

4   Simulation Results

4.1   Model Training

In order to evaluate a bacterial individual, first we have to train the encoded autoencoder model. The model training procedures between bacteria are independent of each other. The goal of this training process is to train the autoencoder such that the reconstruction error on the validation set to be minimal. Different architectures yield different minimum validation errors. In the training procedure in our experiments, we used the techniques below.

Mini-Batch Training. For training the model, we used mini-batch training [1]. The mini-batch is a group of samples, fixed size subset of the original dataset, and in each iteration we train the model on a different subset until all the samples of the original dataset are used. The hyperparameter, which shows the size of a batch, is the N_{batch_size}.

Early Stopping. In order to avoid overfitting, we used early stopping [8], which is an optimization technique and a form of regularization. The early stopping is used for stopping the training process before the model starts to overfit. In order to decide if the model is overfitting in the early stopping technique, the validation loss is tracked. As soon as the validation loss is increasing or at least not decreasing for $N_{patience}$ iterations, the learning procedure stops. The $N_{patience}$ is a hyperparameter of the algorithm. The other stopping criteria is the $N_{max\_iteration}$ the maximum iteration number.

Adam Optimizer. For the training of the autoencoder, the Adam optimizer [4] is used, which is an extended version of stochastic gradient descent, it uses adaptive learning rates based on the second moments of the gradients, and calculates the exponential moving average of the gradients and the square gradients.

Learning Rate Schedule. The Adam optimizer uses adaptive learning rate, thus all the parameters will be updated with an individual learning rate. All the individual learning rates use the initial learning rate, which is a parameter of the algorithm, as an upper limit. By decreasing this learning rate during training, we can reduce the loss at the latest steps.

The learning rate is decreasing during training using the following schedule. First, we set the *learning_rates* $= [lr_1, lr_2, \ldots, lr_n]$ list, which is a hyperparameter and contains the learning rates $(lr_1, \ldots, lr_n)$ in decreasing order. At the beginning of training, the learning rate parameter of Adam is lr_1. Decreasing the learning rate happens as follows. The optimizer uses the learning rate lr_i and when the early stopper is triggered, we set the learning rate to the next (decreased) value lr_{i+1} and reset the early stopper's counter. If the early stopper is triggered when using the lr_n, then we stop the training.

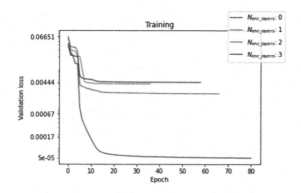

Fig. 5. Training models with different architectures

Experiments on Model Training. In our experiments[1] the following hyperparameters were used: $N_{batch\_size} = 256$, $N_{max\_iteration} = 100$, $N_{patience} = 3$, *learning_rates* $= [10^{-3}, 10^{-4}]$. In Fig. 5 we can follow, on four randomly chosen models with different architectures, how the validation loss decreases over the epochs. The N_{enc_layers} parameter shows how many layers the model has in the encoder (code excluded), and it refers to the N_{enc_layers} parameter (Fig. 2). Note, that if the N_{enc_layers} is 0, then the corresponding architecture consists of only an input layer, code, and output layer.

---

[1] System configuration: Intel(R) Xeon(R) Gold 6248R CPU @ 3.00GHz, 3 x NVIDIA Tesla T4 (16 GB) GPU, 256 GB RAM.

4.2   Results

In the first experiment, the λ value is set to 10^{-4}, while in the second experiment, its value is 10^{-1}.

All the other hyperparameters are the same in both experiments. The used hyperparameters for the bacterial evolutionary algorithm (Sect. 3.1) are as follows: $N_{gen} = 10, N_{ind} = 3, N_{clone} = 3, N_{inf} = 2$, while the maximum number of layers N_{enc_layers} is set to 3. Thus, the number of all gene mutations through the training is 95.

Fig. 6. Error through evolution, $\lambda = 10^{-4}$

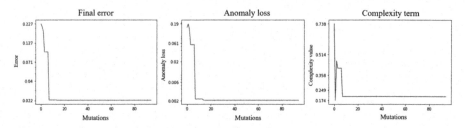

Fig. 7. Error through evolution, $\lambda = 10^{-1}$

Evolution. Figures 6 and 7 depict how the error (Eq. (5)) is decreasing through all the gene mutations, which includes all the mutations from the bacterial mutation (Sect. 3.4) and gene transfer operators (Sect. 3.5) through the iterations. On the blue curve the evolution of the error value is presented, which has two components, the $loss_{anomaly}$ and the *complexity*, as Eq. (5) shows. The green curve shows the corresponding anomaly loss, and the red is the complexity term.

Error Meshgrid. Figures 8a and 8b present the 3-dimensional meshgrid where we can follow how the error value is affected by the number of layers and the number of trainable parameters in the model. It is observable that the highest

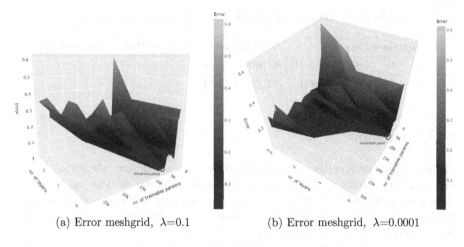

(a) Error meshgrid, λ=0.1   (b) Error meshgrid, λ=0.0001

Fig. 8. Error meshgrids

peak in error value occurs when the number of layers is the highest and the number of trainable parameters is low. These architectures have the highest anomaly loss. In both cases, the minimum error points are found where the number of layers is minimal and the number of trainable parameters is high.

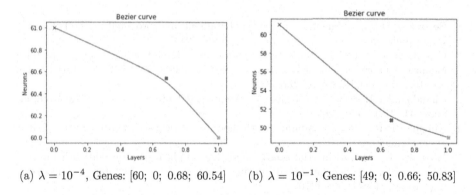

(a) $\lambda = 10^{-4}$, Genes: [60; 0; 0.68; 60.54]   (b) $\lambda = 10^{-1}$, Genes: [49; 0; 0.66; 50.83]

Fig. 9. Abstract representations (Bézier curves) of the solutions

Solutions. Figure 9 presents the two solutions (Figs. 9a and 9b) for the 2 different λ values, while Table 2 presents the corresponding architectures. The notations are the same as presented in Sect. 3.2.

Table 2. Solutions: Bacteria and the corresponding architectures

Id	Bacterium Genes	Autoencoder architecture (fully connected layers)
a	[60; 0; 0.681; 60.541]	[61, 60] → [60, 61]
b	[49; 0; 0.66; 50.834]	[61, 49] → [49, 61]

5   Conclusion

The results of the architecture, optimized by the evolutionary algorithm, match well with the results of the manually adjusted architecture. The most optimal autoencoder architecture yielded the optimum exactly at the expected location, demonstrating that bacterial optimization can be effective in finding the right architecture for model development.

Although the computational demand of bacterial optimization may be higher, it can help to find the optimal architecture depth for simple and even complex data sets, shortening the time that one has to invest in an uncertain number of test runs to find the right architecture. Due to the iteration of the bacterial algorithm is time-consuming, but it can be parallelized, and therefore the extra time for the training can be reduced further.

References

1. Bertsekas, D.P.: Incremental gradient, subgradient, and proximal methods for convex optimization: a survey. Optimization 2010 (2015)
2. Cao, Z., et al.: Scalable distribution systems state estimation using long short-term memory networks as surrogates. IEEE Access **8**, 23359–23368 (2020). https://doi.org/10.1109/ACCESS.2020.2967638
3. Chandola, V., Banerjee, A., Kumar, V.: Anomaly detection: a survey. ACM Comput. Surv. **41**, 15:1-15:58 (2009)
4. Kingma, D.P., Ba, J.: Adam: A Method for Stochastic Optimization. CoRR abs/1412.6980 (2014)
5. Maenaka, K.: MEMS inertial sensors and their applications. In: 2008 5th International Conference on Networked Sensing Systems, pp. 71–73 (2008). https://doi.org/10.1109/INSS.2008.4610859
6. Nawa, N.E., Furuhashi, T.: Fuzzy system parameters discovery by bacterial evolutionary algorithm. IEEE Trans. Fuzzy Syst. **7**(5), 608–616 (1999). https://doi.org/10.1109/91.797983
7. Phiri, C.C., et al.: Fuzzy rule-based model for outlier detection in a topical negative pressure wound therapy device. ISA Trans. **117**, 16–27 (2021). https://doi.org/10.1016/j.isatra.2021.01.046
8. Zhang, T., Yu, B.: Boosting with early stopping: convergence and consistency. Ann. Stat. **33**(4) (2005). https://doi.org/10.1214/009053605000000255

Digital Content Understanding and Application for Industry 4.0

Improved Object Detection by Utilizing the Image Stream

István Reményi[1]([⊠]) [ID], Bálint Domián[2], and Zoltán Kárász[3]

[1] Department of Artificial Intelligence, Faculty of Informatics, ELTE Eötvös Loránd University, Pázmány Péter sétány 1/A, Budapest 1117, Hungary
remenyi@inf.elte.hu
[2] Department of Data Sciences and Engineering, Faculty of Informatics, ELTE Eötvös Loránd University, Pázmány Péter sétány 1/C, Budapest 1117, Hungary
bu1t3@inf.elte.hu
[3] Robert Bosch Kft., Budapest, Hungary
zoltan.karasz@hu.bosch.com

Abstract. If we evaluate any deep learning-based object detection architecture on consecutive camera frames, one of the problems is that flickering can occur. Even the tiniest changes in the object placed on the image plane can destabilize the detection performance, not to mention the upcoming occlusions in the sensorial perspective of a dynamic scene. In an online methodology, namely in a driving assist (autonomous driving) scenario, utilizing the temporal information can be one of the tricks against the mentioned problems. The focus of this article is to demonstrate that the information from past images can be fed to an object detection model as integrated recurrent layers in an independent multiscale sense. We based our idea on the convolutional Gated Recurrent Unit (GRU) by Mitsubishi Research [1], where they applied it in the Single Shot Detector (SSD) architecture right before the detection layer. This proved to extract information from the consecutive frames and improve the network's precision. Currently, we are adapting the You Only Look Once V3 (YOLOv3) architecture [2] with an extension to capture multi-scale information flow. For the YOLOv3 model's training purposes, we used the driving-oriented KITTI object detection dataset. We have measured the change in precision and inference time to the base model's capabilities to evaluate the efficiency of the recurrent extension.

Keywords: Object Detection · Autonomous Driving · Temporal Investigation

1 Introduction

One of the main steps in developing deep learning-based object detectors was when the objects' position-, volume regression, and classification were organized into a common architecture. Among these one-shot detector candidates was the

N. T. Nguyen et al. (Eds.): ICCCI 2023, CCIS 1864, pp. 575–584, 2023.
https://doi.org/10.1007/978-3-031-41774-0_45

SSD model [8]. Although this was a huge leap while working on a highly redundant information source such as camera frames, the object detection models' inference speed could not really be caught up to real-time. At least up until the arrival of further optimizations in architecture design. This statement was the main reason for excluding deep learning from online applications such as driving assist systems, where being a (detection) module in a goal-designed pipeline requires strict timing limits. Keeping a low calculation profile for object detection - considered one of the most expensive modules - is the key to the applicability [4].

When working with neural networks an architectural challenge is to regress variable number of valid output for different inputs, as in object detection cases. Faster R-CNN introduced the anchor based concept, where a (lower resolution) grid is stretched over the input image and for each cell inside a fixed number of potential object detection candidates are presented. This concept became popular, one of the most promising extension is when SSD fed the bounding box regression with features sampled form their encoder at different resolutions (Fig. 1) [8]. Following these foot-steps YOLOv3 further extended the detection architecture with an adaptation of the feature pyramid network, namely it's output is based on three different output scale levels. On each scale there is the differently stretched grid packed with anchors (Fig. 2) [2]. Figure 3 highlights one object candidate, where output is based on the given anchor volume priors. Extent (b_w, b_h) is expressed as the multiplication of priors (p_x, p_y) and exponentially scaled regression output (t_w, t_h). Location prediction (b_x, b_y) is relative inside the selected cell, sigmoid function (σ) is called over (t_x, t_y) [2,11].

As a purpose-built and optimized convolution-based object detection architecture, YOLOv3 brought the potential of real-time inferencing, but some assumptions made this achievement possible. Redmond et. all provided some comparisons (see Fig. 4) between their selected model configuration and other potent architectures. From this, we can read that along with the architecture design, the limited input resolution was one of the enablers.

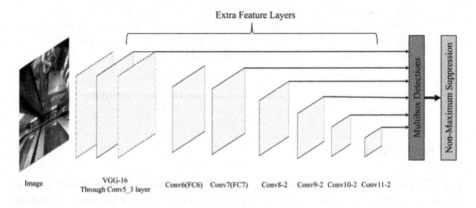

Fig. 1. SSD network architecture [3]

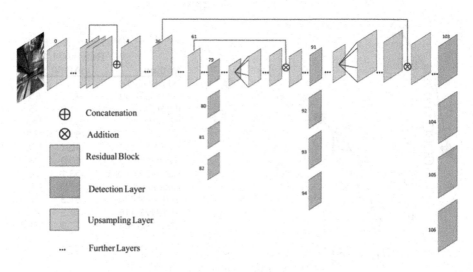

Fig. 2. YOLOv3 network architecture [3]

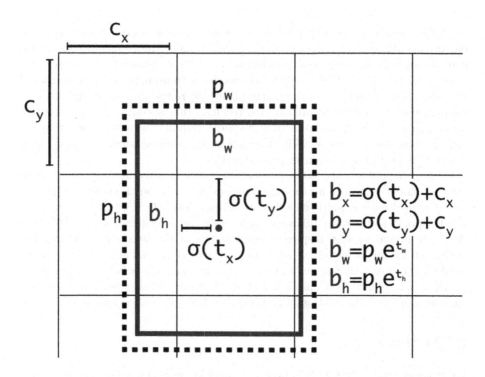

Fig. 3. Sample bounding box output with an achor prior [11]

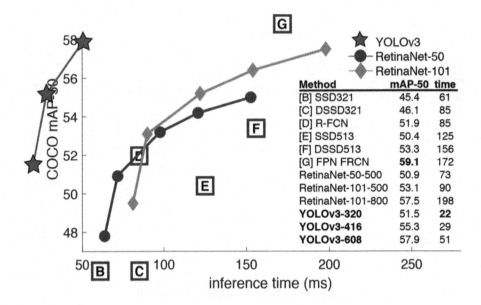

Fig. 4. Performance comparison from [2]

To aid some of the performance instability of the object detection models' in time domain, [1] introduced the application of the recurrent concept on convolutional neural networks, positioned before the non-maximum suppression-based detection head. This combination produces thousands of two-dimensional bounding box candidates on the image plane, where the candidate suggestion is supported by the recurrent information condensation of compressed consecutive image frames, while the non-maximum suppression acts as a filter based on the objects' volumes (see Fig. 5). With their effort, the original paper's authors could reach 2.7% performance gain in precision [1].

Our main goal was not to create an entirely new architecture but to extend an existing model's capabilities to store temporal information. Therefore, YOLOv3 was equipped with a multi-scale detection head, into which we wanted to inject the temporal features on different scale levels in a recurrent form. Although there are newer use-case-inspired improvements of the selected model, further optimizations might introduce some trade-off between speed and accuracy, so we would like to insist that in our tests, the original version is a better candidate in terms of precision [5–7]. Considering this, we can report that our patented [10] changes made a 7.1% mAP gain compared to the unmodified baseline.

2   Methods

We have selected the YOLOv3 and its Darknet53 implementation version for our investigation. It contains 53 convolution layers for feature encoding and another 54 for detection outputs. It can be summarized as convolutional (75), shortcut

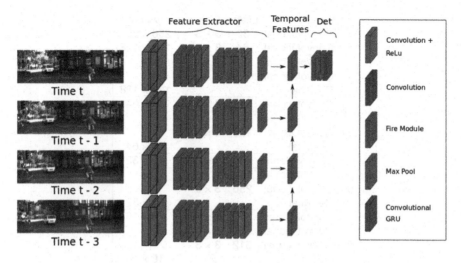

Fig. 5. The original extension of SSD with GRU [1]

(23), route (4), upsample (2), yolo (3), and Fig. 6 collects the basic organization of the layers.

The architecture's output structure is organized into three grid layouts at different resolutions to capture the object detection candidates at different stages. The 416×416 input resolution and the convolution layer details in [2], 13×13, 26×26, and 52×52 grid is stretched on the images, in which for each grid cell, three different anchors are assigned to represent the potential candidates. From this aspect, having a properly configured anchor set in the YOLOv3 architecture is a must. This way, a-prior information can be fed into the network, like the common bounding box shapes and sizes. Initially, nine base anchors were used, and the centroids were calculated via K nearest neighbor algorithm. We also did this pre-calculation on our selected dataset (train split), on which the finalized box sizes are: [12 10], [15 33], [25 16], [33 62], [43 23], [65 36], [89 54], [121 114], [125 61] in the shape of [width, height]. The network uses the first three anchors on the highest resolution, the next three on the middle resolution, and the remaining set on lower resolution - meaning that there is an explicit constraint on where the model should output its detections based on the actual sizes.

Following the recommendations of [1], for temporal memory, we selected GRU, mostly due to the simplified gated update mechanism. Its convolutional version combines sparse and structure-aware data processing (compared to fully connected layers) and recurrent memory for temporal information conservation. Inside the GRU cell, a state representation holds the temporal information at every timestamp. To modify its value, there is an update gate mechanism for direct information exchange, but the final output of the cell is defined by interpolation between the updated state and the candidate state representation calculated from the input itself. The following equations summarize the behavior of the cell:

	Type	Filters	Size	Output
	Convolutional	32	3 × 3	256 × 256
	Convolutional	64	3 × 3 / 2	128 × 128
1×	Convolutional	32	1 × 1	
	Convolutional	64	3 × 3	
	Residual			128 × 128
	Convolutional	128	3 × 3 / 2	64 × 64
2×	Convolutional	64	1 × 1	
	Convolutional	128	3 × 3	
	Residual			64 × 64
	Convolutional	256	3 × 3 / 2	32 × 32
8×	Convolutional	128	1 × 1	
	Convolutional	256	3 × 3	
	Residual			32 × 32
	Convolutional	512	3 × 3 / 2	16 × 16
8×	Convolutional	256	1 × 1	
	Convolutional	512	3 × 3	
	Residual			16 × 16
	Convolutional	1024	3 × 3 / 2	8 × 8
4×	Convolutional	512	1 × 1	
	Convolutional	1024	3 × 3	
	Residual			8 × 8
	Avgpool		Global	
	Connected		1000	
	Softmax			

Fig. 6. Layer structure of YOLOv3 feature encoding [2]

$$z_t = \sigma(W_z * x_t + U_z * h_{t-1})$$
$$r_t = \sigma(W_r * x_t + U_r * h_{t-1})$$
$$\hat{h}_t = tanh(W * x_t + U * (r_t \odot h_{t-1}))$$
$$h_t = (1 - z_t)h_{t-1} + z_t\hat{h}_t$$

(1)

where $*$ denotes the convolution and $\odot$ denotes the Hadamard product. The variable x_t, h_t are the input and output; z_t, r_t, $\hat{h}_t$ are the update gate, reset gate, and candidate activation; W_* and U_* are the learnable weights [1,12].

Based on the closeness of the multiple resolution output branches inside the YOLOv3, we nominated three layers for our investigations: the 37th, 62nd, and 80th convolutional layers inside the feature encoder. We replaced them with the previously described recurrent cell. Inside each GRU the kernel sizes are 3×3, and zero padding was applied without any modification at the given layers' original depth.

3   Dataset and Metrics

For evaluation, we have chosen the KITTI dataset. This collection contains sampled 7481 images from diverse location environments (city, highway, university, residential area) with around 40.000 bounding box labels. Their successor three frames are also stored for every labeled image, so it can serve as a basis for temporal investigations [9]. One way to keep the low computational profile, the images can be under-sampled; this technique was utilized for the original evaluation of both the SSD and YOLOv3 where the images contained 416×416 pixels [2,8]. This meant, in our case, that the 1242×375 resolution was down-sampled by 3×3, and we zero-padded by the second dimension to generate square-like inputs. This decision was driven by the fact that we wanted to compare the performance of pre-trained and trained from-scratch versions, and we needed to be aligned with the pretraining circumstances. We used scaling mirroring, rotating, contrast-, and color space modification to augment the dataset.

During testing, we also aligned ourselves to [9]. In addition, we have used the Intersection-Over-Union (IOU) based Average Precision (AP) metric, where the IOU association between the predicted ($pred_i$)- and ground truth (gt_j) objects are calculated as in Eq. (2) and Eq. (3).

$$IOU(pred_i, gt_j) = \frac{AREA(pred_i \cap gt_j)}{AREA(pred_i \cup gt_j)} < \epsilon \tag{2}$$

$$AP = \sum_{k=0}^{K} (R(k) - R(k+1)) \cdot P_{interp}(R(k)), \tag{3}$$

where AP is the Riemann integral of the K-point interpolated Precision X Recall (P x R) curve [13].

In our tests, we used the fixed value of $\epsilon = 0.5$. The IOU association, recall, and precision can calculate the full confusion matrix. To limit our scopes to driving assist systems, the reports will concentrate on TP, and FP values, and to cover the method's overall potential, a selection of class-wise interpolated AP and their mean (mAP). Also, the reports will highlight the well-represented classes, but of course, the mAP scores are calculated on every available data sample.

4   Results

First, we downloaded an already pre-trained set of weights from [14]. We wanted to measure the additional performance of the GRU cell extensions when the model - mostly its feature encoder part - is on top of its potential. Without any changes in the model, we achieved 80.94% mAP (Table 1.).

Then we replaced the 80th convolutional layer (positioned at the end of the feature encoder) with a GRU cell - to reproduce the statements about the added value of recurrent information originating from [1]. This needed some fine-tuning with the stacked consecutive four frames. We followed the configuration recommendations in [11], with slight modifications. We applied 10^{-3} for the initial learning rate with 0.25 exponential scheduling at every 120th epoch. We set the weight decay to be 10^{-6}. Each training duration was at least 360 epochs (this setup was applied for every training). After tuning, we measured a 7.45%

performance increase, as expected. To understand what happened, we also report the TP/FP measures where we can notice the slightly higher FP numbers. Except for the Car category, the best-represented class in the KITTI dataset, with a more bounding box than the remaining classes. We replaced all the nominated layers for the multiscale temporal encoded information preservation test. Here we can also spot the increasing FP numbers on the poorly-represented classes, but overall the fine-tuning resulted in 88.11% mAP.

Table 1. Comparison of **pretrained** YOLOv3, its 1 GRU-, and its 3 GRU extension performances
(TP = True Positive; FP = False Positive; AP = Average Precision).

Class	Unmodified			1 GRU ext.			3 GRU ext.		
	TP	FP	AP	TP	FP	AP	TP	FP	AP
Car	2529	238	86.2%	2595	171	91.8%	2616	171	92.1%
Truck	246	19	90.1%	258	49	95.6%	259	145	94.6%
Pedestrian	396	52	76.4%	394	139	78.7%	404	412	82.2%
Cyclist	166	109	80.0%	171	86	85.6%	172	163	86.9%
	mAP = 80.94%			mAP = 87.45%			mAP = 88.11%		

For our second test, we wanted to measure the performance gain without the effectiveness of the pre-trained weights. For this comparison, we trained the YOLOv3 architecture from scratch (random layer initialization is aligned with the PyTorch recommendations). The mAP score of the unmodified architecture was 75.95%. The lack of performance can be originated from the changes in the training configuration, but our intentions were not to optimize to the extreme but to have a fair baseline. After training the GRU extended version (also from scratch), we measured a 2% performance gain with increased FP numbers, also, for the Car category (Table 2.). Although recurrence can improve detection capabilities, this raises the question of training strategy: having a one-frame optimized and fine-tuned weight set is better than doing both in one pass.

As to our performance measures, the original YOLOv3 in inference mode can run at 29 FPS on 416 × 416 input resolution. The inference of 186 images with batch size 4 took 25.56 s on the KITTI validation set. For one additional GRU layer at layer 80, the runtime is 1 min 35 s. Here we have to mention that due to the random sampled nature of the dataset, our naive implementation does not have any pipeline optimization. Unlike an online application, every input frame has to be encoded for each sample, where consecutive frames are processed once and can be fed to the GRU in an encoded form. Keeping this in mind, every sample contains 4 images, but the validation set's processing time is less than 4 times higher. This is because the detection head runs once, and only the feature encoder is utilized 4 times. The same evaluation with three additional GRU cells lasted 1min. 50 s, with an additional 15 s overhead.

Table 2. Comparison of **trained from scratch** YOLOv3 and its 3 GRU extension performances
(TP = True Positive; FP = False Positive; AP = Average Precision).

Class	Unmodified			3 GRU ext.		
	TP	FP	AP	TP	FP	AP
Car	2452	251	85.9%	2518	488	86.9%
Truck	235	42	84.2%	241	73	87.0%
Pedestrian	328	156	59.3%	343	323	59.9%
Cyclist	144	60	71.0%	149	131	69.7%
	mAP = 75.95%			mAP = 77.95%		

5 Conclusions

In this article, we wanted to utilize the temporal information of the consecutive image frames for two-dimensional object detection. To reach our goals, we adopted the GRU extension of the SSD architecture in a multiscale fashion on a performance-wise more suitable YOLOv3 model to evaluate in an autonomous driving concept. When we replaced one layer in the pre-trained model with a convolutional GRU, we observed 6.5% mAP gain. By replacing two further recurrent layers, we measured a 7.1% mAP increase. This demonstrates that our original hypothesis on exploiting the multi-scale temporal information can stabilize its detection itself and scale with the applied number of recurrent cells. Performance-wise, we observed that the run time scaled just with the number of consecutive frames used. This means a low computation profile can be achieved with a properly optimized implementation where object detection is frame-wise modularized.

After covering the performance gain as a standalone object detector, we need to understand the modification's impact on the whole system into which it is integrated. Our future plan is to integrate the multiscale GRU extension into an autonomous driving pipeline, where we can investigate its effect on object tracking and trajectory planning algorithms.

Funding Information. SUPPORTED BY THE KDP-2021 PROGRAM OF THE MINISTRY OF INNOVATION AND TECHNOLOGY FROM THE SOURCE OF THE NATIONAL RESEARCH, DEVELOPMENT AND INNOVATION FUND.

References

1. Broad, A., Jones, M., Lee, T.Y.: Recurrent multi-frame single shot detector for video object detection. In BMVC, p. 94 (2018)
2. Redmon, J., Farhadi, A.: YOLOv3: an incremental improvement (Version 1) (2018). arXiv. https://doi.org/10.48550/ARXIV.1804.02767

3. Dai, Y., Liu, W., Li, H., Liu, L.: Efficient foreign object detection between PSDs and metro doors via deep neural networks. IEEE Access **8**, 46723–46734 (2020). https://doi.org/10.1109/ACCESS.2020.2978912

4. Yurtsever, E., Lambert, J., Carballo, A., Takeda, K.: A survey of autonomous driving: common practices and emerging technologies. IEEE Access, **8** (2020). https://doi.org/10.1109/access.2020.2983149

5. Deng, L., Li, H., Liu, H., Gu, J.: A lightweight YOLOv3 algorithm used for safety helmet detection. Sci. Rep. Nat. Portfolio **12**, 10981 (2022). https://doi.org/10.1038/s41598-022-15272-w

6. Khasawneh, N., Fraiwan, M., Fraiwan, L.: Detection of K-complexes in EEG signals using deep transfer learning and YOLOv3. Cluster Comput. (2022). https://doi.org/10.1007/s10586-022-03802-0

7. Chen, X., Lv, J., Fang, Y., Du, S.: Online detection of surface defects based on improved YOLOV3. Sensors **22**, 817 (2022). https://doi.org/10.3390/s22030817

8. Liu, W., et al.: SSD: single shot multibox detector. In: Leibe, B., Matas, J., Sebe, N., Welling, M. (eds.) ECCV 2016. LNCS, vol. 9905, pp. 21–37. Springer, Cham (2016). https://doi.org/10.1007/978-3-319-46448-0_2

9. Geiger, A., Lenz, P., Stiller, C., Urtasun, R.: Vision meets robotics: the KITTI dataset. Int. J. Rob. Res. **32**(11), 1231–1237 (2013). https://doi.org/10.1177/0278364913491297

10. Reményi, I., Domián, B., Kárász, Z.: Verbesserte Objekterkennung und -verfolgung aus einer Sequenz von Bildrahmen (DE102021206301A1). DPMA (2022). https://register.dpma.de/DPMAregister/pat/PatSchrifteneinsicht?docId=DE1020212063
01A1

11. Redmon, J., Farhadi, A.: YOLO9000: better, faster, stronger. In: Proceedings - 30th IEEE Conference on Computer Vision and Pattern Recognition, CVPR 2017, vol. 2017-January, pp. 6517–6525 (2017). https://doi.org/10.1109/CVPR.2017.690

12. Chung, J., Gulcehre, C., Cho, K., Bengio, Y.: Empirical evaluation of gated recurrent neural networks on sequence modeling (Version 1) (2014). arXiv. https://doi.org/10.48550/ARXIV.1412.3555

13. Padilla, R., Passos, W.L., Dias, T.L., Netto, S.L., Da Silva, E.A.: A comparative analysis of object detection metrics with a companion open-source toolkit. Electronics **10**(3), 279 (2021). https://doi.org/10.3390/electronics10030279

14. GitHub - packyan/PyTorch-YOLOv3-kitti: use yolov3 pytorch to train kitti. https://github.com/packyan/PyTorch-YOLOv3-kitti. Accessed 31 Feb 2023

Combination of DE-GAN with CNN-LSTM for Arabic OCR on Images with Colorful Backgrounds

Abdelkarim Mars[1]([✉]), Karim Dabbabi[2], Salah Zrigui[1,3], and Mounir Zrigui[1]

[1] Research Laboratory in Algebra, Numbers Theory and Intelligent Systems Faculty of Sciences of Monastir, Monastir, Tunisia
Abdelkarim.mars@gmail.com, Mounir.Zrigui@fsm.rnu.tn
[2] Research Unite of Analyze and Processing of Electrical and Energetic Systems, Faculty of Sciences of Tunis, Tunis, Tunisia
[3] DATAMOVE-Date Aware Large Scale Computing, LIG, Grenoble, France

Abstract. In this paper, a combination of the conditional generative adversarial network (DE-GAN) with the convolutional neural network (CNN) and long short time memory (LSTM) is proposed in order to improve the performance of optical character recognition (OCR) in the case of images with a colored background. For DE-GAN, it is introduced for the purpose of generating cleaned images. Then, these cleaned images are entered into the CNN model to extract their feature representations. These are next entered as sequences into the LSTM method to label them. Ultimately, Connectionist temporal component (CTC) model is applied to align the data. Experimental results showed that the combination of DE-GAN with CNN-LSTM has succeeded in achieving good results in terms of accuracy for OCR task.

Keywords: DE-GAN · CNN-LSTM · Arabic OCR · a colored background · generator · discriminator

1 Introduction

The need for efficient tools to recognize text from images has led the researchers to expand their research into optical character recognition (OCR) in recent years [1–3]. The task performed by optical character recognition (OCR) is to put the processed and digitized documents (e.g., scanned and handwritten documents, images, etc.) into appropriate forms and to make them understandable by human or computer vision systems for further automatic content-based search on recognized documents. Two types of documents can be considered for automatic transcription: printed texts and handwritten texts. For the former, it is reliable technology these days, while the latter is still a challenge. The main difficulty with written texts compared to the printed ones is not being segmented due to ill-defined boundaries. In this regard, connectionist temporal classification (CTC) was introduced to allow neural networks to be trained and thus to recognize sequences without exploring explicit segmentation [4].

N. T. Nguyen et al. (Eds.): ICCCI 2023, CCIS 1864, pp. 585–596, 2023.
https://doi.org/10.1007/978-3-031-41774-0_46

Additionally, all the advanced solutions [5, 6] were based on deep learning and CTC loss to deal with such a complex problem. However, large amounts of annotated data are required to train these neural networks in a supervised fashion. Additionally, the task of annotating images of text has the disadvantage of being expensive and time consuming. As we have explored handwritten texts associated with the corresponding transcriptions, we therefore reversed the annotation procedure by exploring an annotation system such as in [7].

In this work, we address the challenge of generating realistic data and then tackle the problem of training neural networks using such synthetic data with the aim of ameliorating the performance of handwritten text recognition. For the problem of image generation, it was previously approached using many techniques [7, 8] based on several models of a few characters, either handwritten or constructed using Bezier curves. This type of solutions based on the models of simply concatenated characters has the drawback that the distribution of real-word images cannot be faithfully reproduced [7]. As an alternative, an online method was explored by approximating handwriting as a trajectory recorded with a computer pen. The suggested model generated a given word by producing a sequence of pen positions. Long-short temporal memory (LSTM) combined with the recurrent neural network (RNN) is such a model that has been explored to predict such a sequence and thus handwriting is synthetized on the target chain depending on the condition of the neural network. However, this model was not well suitable to some useful features explored for offline recognition, such as line weight variations and background text. On the other hand, Generative Adversarial Networks (GAN) [9] can provide a powerful framework for the task of generative modeling. This architecture makes it possible to generate very realistic and diverse images. Moreover, it has been considered in the work of [9] to be an ideal solution for this task over auto-encoders in terms of variation, high quality and stability [10]. X^{2}.

Additionally, generative models have gained a lot of attention due to their ability to process multi-model outputs, capture high-dimensional probability distributions, and impute missing data [11]. Despite this good potential, they still only applied to handwritten profiling [12], to the translation of fonts [13], and to removal of staff lines from images in a musical score [14], where good results have been obtained. It was noted in [15] that conditional generative adversarial networks (cGANs) and a variant of GANs work well for image-to-image translation (edges to photo, labels to façade, day to night and B to color, etc.). As for GANs, they learn a generative data model, while those of conditional GANs (cGANs) they learn a conditional generative model, where they follow the conditions put on an input image and generate the corresponding output one [11]. The motivation behind our study is to preserve the text and to remove the conditioned images. Thus, cGANs can be a suitable solution because the document enhancement follows the same process as that of conditioned images.

Also, the main idea of our study is to obtain correct results on images with a colored background. This colored background remains a challenge compared to that of black and white with noise, which can be removed with certain image processing methods or an appropriate filter. In this paper, our application focus on Arabic OCR by recognizing text from a colored background using the combination of Document Enhancement Generative Adversarial Networks (DE-GAN) [11] with the Conventional neural network and LSTM

(CNN-LSTM). Much work has been done in the area of OCR for Arabic text such as that of [3] in which a full OCR pipeline was proposed for Arabic text supporting multiple fonts and presenting language independent.

Reading text from images with a colored background is a difficult task for OCR engines. Thus, none of them managed to achieve a high recognition rate for this special task. Nevertheless, many methods have been applied to overcome this weakness. In most cases, these approaches relied on image preprocessing, providing images more suitable for OCR [37].

In our study, CNN was introduced instead of fully connected neural networks in order to solve the problem of scaling larger images. Thus, a few neurons from the hidden layers were fully connected to all the neurons from the previous layers. Besides, LSTM model was combined with CNN to solve vanishing and explosion problems and facing the fixed size of input and output issue for CNN model. Moreover, it was employed to extract relevant information from feature sequences. Each time, the input images were generated by DE-GAN, their feature representations were then extracted using the CNN model and fed into the LSTM to label the sequences successively [37]. CTC was ultimately used to process the alignment of the data using primarily the loss function. This combination of DE-GAN with CNN-LSTM once again leverages the power of DE-GAN to extract text from conditioned images and enhance degraded document images. The overall performance of Arabic OCR system will therefore be improved. To the authors' knowledge, no work has been done on the Arabic OCR system using such a combination and in the case of a colored background.

The remaining sections of the document are given as follows: In Sect. 2, a description of the proposed Arabic OCR system is presented. The analysis and discussion of the different results are exhibited in Sect. 3. Conclusions and further research directions are provided in Sect. 4.

2 Method and Materials

2.1 The Proposed Model

The general architecture of the proposed approach, which is the combination of DE-GANN with CNN-LSTM, is given by the block diagram in Fig. 1. First, the input images are preprocessed to correct the problems caused by lightning and seizure. The preprocessed images are further cleaned and generated using the DE-GAN model, and then these cleaned images are entered into the CNN model to extract their feature representations. These are fed in the form of sequences in the LSTM model to label them consecutively. After that, the CTC model is applied to perform the data alignment and transcription by exploring the loss function. Thus, the recognized text will be provided.

Preprocessing Images. This step consists of three phases: smoothing, standardization of size and thinning.

Smoothing. The image of the character can be marred by noise due to the acquisition of artefacts and most often to the quality of the document, leading either to missing points (holes) or to impasto or growths and therefore to an overload of points. Thus, smoothing techniques can be solutions for these problems.

Standardization of Size. As the size of the characters differs from one way of writing to another, the parameters of the image will therefore be unstable. Thus, a nature pre-processing technique to create characters of the same size is required. In our work, we have used the normalization algorithm explored from the OpenCV1 python library.

　　Thinning. To facilitate the processing of the images, they should be reduced in size. For example, the size of an image can be reduced to one dimension and thus the character will be reduced to one pixel. This is called thickness.

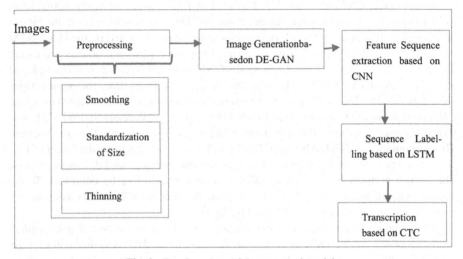

Fig. 1. The flowchart of the proposed model.

Image Generation Based on DE-GAN Model. The type of Generative Adversarial Network (GAN) used in our work is that of [11], known as conditional generative networks (cGAN). This model was called DE-GAN in [11] because the objective was to generate clean document images providing degraded images.

　　In general, GANs are composed of two neural networks: a discriminator D and a generator G that are characterized by the parameters φD and φG, respectively. For the generator, it is explored in order to learn an application of a random noise vector z to an image y, $G\varphi G{:}z \rightarrow y$. However, the discriminator was intended to discriminate the image generated by G from that of ground truth. Concerning a given y, D should give the probability value $D\varphi D$ to indicate if its state is fake or real, such as: y $\rightarrow$ P(real). Those two networks compete each other in a min-max game [11] so that if the first wins, the second loses. Each time, the generator tries to produce an image close to the ground truth, while the discriminator will improve its fake image prediction. This is called the adversarial learning. The same process is followed by cGANs with a simple difference that the latter incorporate the additional parameter x, which represents the conditioned image. At this level, the mapping is learnt by the generator from an image x and a random noise vector z to an image y, such that: $G\varphi G{:}\ \{x,\ z\} \rightarrow y$. From its part, the discriminator also tries to find the conditioned image so that its process becomes as: $D\varphi D{:}\ \{x,\ y\} \rightarrow$ P(real).

In this way, a clean image represented by IC will be generated by the generator every time a degraded image IW is inputted. The production of an image very close to the ground truth one known as IGT, represents the main objective of the generator. For this task, the training of cGANs is carried out by following the adversarial loss function such that:

$$L_{GAN}(\varphi_G, \varphi_D) = E_{I^W, I^{GT}} log\left[D_{\varphi D}(I^W, I^{GT})\right] + E_{I^W} log\left[1 - D_{\varphi D}(I^W, G_{\varphi G}(I^W))\right] (1)$$

The description of the generator and discriminator network architecture is given in the following subsections.

Generator. The generator was explored to perform the task of an image-to-image translation. Additionally, auto-encoder models were primarily devoted to accomplish this task. These models were composed of a sequence of convolutional layers called an encoder where its task was to perform down sampling to a particular layer. This process was then reversed in a sequence of convolutional layers and ascending sampling called a decoder. Nonetheless, the encoder-decoder model has two main drawbacks for the above-mentioned task: the first is that a lot of information is lost due to down-sampling and therefore the model has difficulty recovering it later whenever a prediction of the input image is made with the same size. However, the second is related to the flow of image information, including the bottleneck, which passes from one layer to another. For this, many unwanted redundant features can sometimes be exchanged.

Consequently, energy and time losses can be caused. Thus, the structure of U-net model was used because it follows the skip connections. Every two layers, these connections are added for the purpose of recovering images with less deterioration.

Moreover, these connections were explored in the case of training a very deep learning model in order to avoid the vanishing of the gradient and exploding problems.

Additionally, some batch normalization layers were added in order to speed up the training.

Discriminator. The discriminator was represented by a fully convolutional network (FCN), composed of six convolutional layers from which the probabilities that the generated image was real were outputted as a 2D matrix. Each time, two input images were entered into the discriminator, which were the clean image (cleaned by the generator or ground truth) and its degraded version. The two images were concatenated to give a tensor of shape $256 \times 256 \times 2$. The obtained volume then continued its propagation in the model until the last layer where it was found in a $16 \times 16 \times 1$ matrix. The probabilities of the discriminator were included in this matrix; if they were close to 1 then the ground truth image was represented by the cleaned one, otherwise when they were close to 0 then the clean image was generated by the generator. For the last layer, a sigmoid was used as an activation function for it. On other hand, the discriminator will not be used after completing the training and for a given degraded image, the generative network will only be explored to enhance it. However, this discriminator retains the function of forcing the generator during training to provide better results.

Extraction of Feature Sequence. In this study, the convolutional neural network (CNN) model was composed of convolutional layers and max-pooling ones. These layers were explored to extract a sequential representation of the characteristics of a given image. All the images were first scaled to the same height before being fed into the network. The feature maps produced by the convolutional layers were then explored to extract a sequence of feature vectors. This was the input for the LSTM model. The generation of each feature vector of each sequence was performed in particular on the feature maps by columns from left to right. In other words, the i-th columns of all maps were concatenated and represented by the i-th feature vector. For the width of each column, it was fixed to a single pixel.

Regarding the layers of convolution, max-pooling, and element-wise activation function, they were considered as transition invariants as they operated on local regions. Consequently, each rectangular region of the original image was represented by a column of the feature map. In the same order, these columns represented the rectangular regions from left to right on the feature maps.

Sequence Labeling. At the top of the convolutional layers, a deep bidirectional recurrent neural network has been built. For each frame xt in the sequence of features $x = x_1, \ldots, x_T$, the recurrent layers have the function of predicting the distribution of a label yt.

LSTM is considered to be directional by only exploring past contexts. In image-based sequences, however, the use of two-direction contexts is useful because they complement each other. Therefore, in this study we have combined two LSTMs into a bidirectional LSTM, where the first is forward, while the other is backward. Moreover, we have stacked multiple bidirectional LSTMs in order to obtain a deep bidirectional LSTM. The latter structure was used because it demonstrated a higher level of abstraction than a superficial level in addition to its ability to show significant improvements for the speech recognition task [16].

For recurrent layers, the propagation of error differentials was done in the opposite direction to the arrows. Furthermore, the sequence of propagated differentials was concatenated into maps at the bottom of the recurrent layers. Thus, the operation of converting feature maps into feature sequences was reversed and returned to the convolutional layers. Map-to-Sequence was created in practice, which was defined as a custom network layer that represented the bridge between recurrent and convolutional layers.

Transcription. The transcription process is defined as the conversion of per-frame predictions into a label sequence performed by RNN. It is devoted to the search for the sequence label with the highest probability conditioned by the predictions per frame.

In this study, the Connectionist Temporal Classification (CTC) layer was adapted as a conditional probability to predict the probability of label sequence [17]. Indeed, the probability for the sequence of labels I was conditioned on the predictions per-frame $y = y_1, \ldots, y_T$, and it did not take into account the location of each label in the sequence I.

Also, the construction of the BK tree for a lexicon was first performed offline. A quick online search is then performed using the tree, searching for sequences with an edit distance less than or equal to the query sequence.

2.2 Arabic OCR Database

We explored the database of [18] consisting of approximately 50,000 cropped images with embedded Arabic text. The generation of the different labels of this database was carried out from a corpus of Arabic words comprising 15,000 words.

2.3 The Training Process

DE-GAN. In the training process, the patches resulting from the degraded images of size 256×256 are entered into the generator. The discriminator then receives the produced images and the ground truth patches with the degraded ones. After that, the generator is forced by the discriminator to produce outputs which can be discriminated from the "real" images, but it maximizes its efforts to detect the "fakes" ones from the generator. An illustration of the training process is given in Fig. 2. Adam was used as an optimizer in this process with a learning rate of le-4.

CNN-BLSTM. For a give training dataset $X = \{I_i, I_i\}$, where I_i denotes the training image and I_i represents the ground truth label sequence. The minimization of the negative log-likelihood of the conditional probability of the ground truth is given such that:

$$\mathcal{O} = - \sum_{I_i, I_i \in X} \log p(l_i | y_i) \tag{2}$$

where y_i represents the sequence provided by the convolutional and recurrent layers from I_i.

The calculation of a cost value is performed directly by this objective function from an image and its sequence of ground truth labels. Manual labeling of all individual components in training images was removed and the network was trained only on image and sequence pairs. Additionally, network training is performed using a stochastic gradient descendant (SGD) where their gradients were calculated using a back propagation algorithm. For the back-propagation of error differentials in the transcription layer, it was performed using a forward-backward algorithm. However, these error differentials were calculated in the case of recurrent layers by the application of Back-Propagation Through Time (BPTT).

As for the optimization, it was carried out using ADADELTA [19] in order to automatically calculate the learning rates per dimension. This method has the advantage of not requiring any manual adjustment of a learning rate and the most important thing is that it can converge faster than the momentum approach [20].

3 Results and Discussions

3.1 Results

To clean up the images, the Noisy Office Database [21] containing different types of degradation was explored where 112 images were used for training, while the remaining 32 were explored for testing. A set of overlapped patches of size 256×256 pixels was

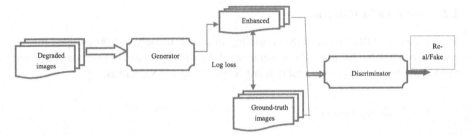

Fig. 2. Scheme of the proposed DE-GAN.

extracted from the 112 training images, resulting in 1356 generated pairs of patches which were entered into the DE-GAN model. This test was done in order to prove the adversarial training effect. Also, another model was trained which is the U-net. 15% of the training images were additionally explored as a validation set for this model.

For the network architecture, it is given in Table 1. As for the architecture of the convolutional layers, they were designed based on VGG-Very Deep architectures [22]. This was done in order to adapt them very well for the recognition of Arabic texts. Rectangular 1×2 size pooling windows were fitted instead of conventional square windows in the 3rd and 4th maximum pooling layers. This allows feature maps to be produced with greater width and therefore a longer feature sequence can be explored.

Typically, 10 characters are 100x32 in size from which the generation of a sequence of 25 frames is performed. This length is longer than most Arabic words. For rectangular pooling windows, they can provide rectangular receptive fields, conducive to the recognition of certain characters having narrow shapes. In order to speed up the training process for the deep convolutional layers and for the recurrent ones, two batch normalization layers [23] were introduced after the 5th and 6th convolutional layers.

On the other hand, the network has been implemented in the Torch7 framework for the transcription layer, BK-tree data structure and LSTM units. Furthermore, the experiments were performed on an Acer laptop with a 2.5 GHz processor and 64 GB RAM. For the training of the networks, it was done with ADADELTA by setting the parameter ρ to 0.9. All images were scaled to 100×32 during training in an effort to speed up the training process. As for the test images, they were scaled to height 32 and their widths in turn were scaled proportionally to this height.

Good results were obtained on the database with the proposed model using the DE-GAN approach in terms of evaluated performance (PNSR = 24.75, F-Measure = 92.25, Accuracy = 95.65%, and Average Run Time/words = 2.5 s) compared to those obtained with Cycle-GAN [24]. Moreover, these results exceeded those obtained by multidimensional RNNs (MDRNN) [25] on the same database (As shown in Table 1). Similarly, DE-GAN method contributed to achieve satisfactory performance on AcTiV-R [26] by reaching better results for the evaluated metrics (PNSR = 27.25, F-Measure = 97.75, Accuracy = 97.95%, and Average Run Time/words = 1.6s). Similarly, DE-GAN method contributed to achieve satisfactory performance on AcTiV-R [26] by reaching better results for the evaluated metrics, as indicated in Table 2 (PNSR = 27.25, F-Measure = 97.75, Accuracy = 97.95%, and Average Run Time/words = 1.6 s).

Table 1. Results of different methods obtained on database.

Model	PSNR	F-Measure	Accuracy (%)	Average Run Time/words (s)
DE-GAN	24.75	95.25	95.65	2.5
Cycle-GAN	18.45	92.15	92.35	3.7
Multi-Dimensional	19.95	93.75	93.95	
RNNs (MDRNNs)+CTC				3.0

Moreover, it should be noted that the obtained results were better improved when the proposed model designed based on DE-GAN was tested on images with black and white background corrupted by noise (as shown in Table 3).

Table 2. Results of different methods obtained on AcTiV-R database.

Model	PSNR	F-Measure	Accuracy (%)	Average Run Time/words (s)
DE-GAN	27.75	97.75	97.95	1.6
Cycle-GAN	24.45	95.15	95.45	2.8
Multi-Dimensional	25.25	96.65	96.85	
RNNs (MDRNNs)+CTC				2.1

3.2 Discussions

A lot of work has been done for Arabic OCR with various Arabic databases with different fonts and sizes. From Table 3, it can be clearly seen that the proposed model led to acceptable and competitive results compared to those obtained by state-of-the-art models [27, 29, 31, 33]. Overall, we can say that our method succeeded in obtaining these results despite the slight difference in the recorded results obtained in our tests with the different tested approaches compared to those achieved with these state-of-the-art models. This largely refers to the colored background of the various images included in the explored database, in addition to the noise added to these images. Also, exploring the CNN layer stack and adding the pooling layers can be useful to strengthen the feature extraction step by extracting the consistent features.

Table 3. Results of different methods obtained on different Arabic OCR databases.

Heading level	Database	Accuracy (%)
Font-in dependent word and character segmentation algorithm [27]	Watan-2004 [28]	99.89
Projection-Based Approach [29]	[30]	99.9
SVM with RBF kernel+HOG features [31]	Urdu printed textimages (UPTI) [32]	
Fuzzy K-Nearest Neighbor classifier (F-KNN) [33]	APTI Database and PATS-A01 [34]	97.3 and 87.13
MDLSTM [35]	EASTR-42 K [36]	97.52

4   Conclusion

An Arabic OCR model for recognizing Arabic text from scanned images with a colored background has been proposed. This model was built on the basis of DE-GAN and CNN-LSTM which helped to achieve good accuracy in the case of noisy conditions. This feat was mainly due to the large capacity of the DE-GAN combination which demonstrated good power in generating clean images.

As further work, we suggest testing the proposed model with the combination of CNN model and an attention transformer (CNN-attention-transformer) to improve the learning of contextual representations in the feature extraction step and learning long-term sequences, and thus improve the performance of the whole system. Moreover, we propose to evaluate the DE-GAN model in the context of environmental noise in order to ensure the overall performance of the system in real conditions.

References

1. Namysl, M., Konya, I.: Efficient, lexicon-free OCR using deep learning. In: 2019 International Conference on Document Analysis and Recognition (ICDAR), vol.15, pp. 295–301. IEEE (2019)
2. Dixit, S., Bharath, M., Amith, Y., Goutham, A.K., Harshitha, D.: Optical recognition of digital characters using machine learning. Int. J. Res. Stud. Comput. Sci. Eng. 5(1), 9–16 (2018)
3. Mansouri, S., Charhad, M., Zrigui, M.: Arabic text detection in news video based on line segment detector. Res. Comput. Sci. 132, 97–106 (2017)
4. Graves, A., Fernandez, S., Gomez, F., Schmidhuber, J.: Connectionist temporal classification: labelling unsegmented sequence data with recurrent neural nets. In: Proceedings of the 23rd International Conference on Machine Learning, pp. 369–376 (2006)
5. Bluche, T., Messina, R.: Gated convolutional recurrent neural networks for multilingual handwriting recognition. In: 2017 14th IAPR international conference on document analysis and recognition (ICDAR), vol.10, pp. 646–651. IEEE (2017)
6. Amari, R., Noubigh, Z., Zrigui, S., Berchech, D., Nicolas, H., Zrigui, M.: Deep convolutional neural network for Arabic speech recognition. ICCCI 2022, 120–134 (2022)
7. Alonso, E., Moysst, B., Messina, R.: Adversarial generation of handwritten text images conditioned on sequences. In: 2019 International Conference on Document Analysis and Recognition (ICDAR), vol. 7, pp. 481–486. IEEE (2019)

8. Elanwar, R.I.: The state of the art in handwriting synthesis. In: 2nd International Conference on New Paradigms in Electronics & information Technology (peit 2013), vol. 3, pp-157–165. Luxor, Egypt (2013)

9. Goodfellow, I., et al.: Generative adversarial nets. NIPS **27**(2), 105–112 (2014)

10. Karras, T., Aila, T., Laine, S., Lehtinen, J.: Progressive growing of GANs for improved quality, stability, and variation. arXiv preprint **17**(10), 10196 (2017)

11. Souibgui, M.A., Kessentini, Y.: DE-GAN: a conditional generative adversarial network for document enhancement. IEEE Trans. Pattern Anal. Mach. Intell. **19**(6), 319–326 (2020)

12. Ghosh, A., Bhattacharya, B., Chowdhury, S.B.R.: Handwriting profiling using generative adversarial networks. In: AAAI Conference on Artificial Intelligence, vol. 31, pp. 520–528 (2017)

13. Bhunia, A.K., et al.: Word level font-to-font image translation using convolutional recurrent generative adversarial networks. In: 2018 24th International Conference on Pattern Recognition (ICPR), vol.15, pp. 3645–3650. IEEE (2018)

14. Konwer, A., et al.: Staff line removal using generative adversarial networks. In: 2018 24th International Conference on Pattern Recognition (ICPR), vol. 25, pp. 1103–1108. IEEE (2018)

15. Isola, P., Zhu, J.-Y., Zhou, T., Efros, A.: Image-to-image translation with conditional adversarial networks. In: Proceedings of the IEEE conference on computer vision and pattern recognition., pp. 1125–1134 (2017)

16. Graves, A., Mohamed, A., Hinton, G.E.: Speech recognition with deep recurrent neural networks. In: ICASSP, vol.9, pp. 6645–6649. IEEE (2013)

17. Graves, A., Fernandez, S., Gomez, F.J., Schmidhuber, J.: Connectionist temporal classification: labelling unsegmented sequence data with recurrent neural networks. In: Proceedings of the 23rd international conference on Machine learning., pp. 369–376. (2006)

18. Mendeley Data. https://data.mendeley.com/datasets/gfc32vndz8

19. Zeiler, M.D.: ADADELTA: an adaptive learning rate method. arXiv preprint **12**(12), 5701 (2012)

20. Rumelhart, D.E., Hinton, G.E., Williams, R.J.: Neurocomputing: foundations of research. In: Learning Representations by Back-propagating Errors, MIT Press (1988)

21. Zamora-Martinez, F., España-Boquera, S., Castro-Bleda, M.J.: Behaviour-based clustering of neural networks applied to document enhancement. In: Sandoval, F., Prieto, A., Cabestany, J., Graña, M. (eds.) Computational and Ambient Intelligence. IWANN 2007. Lecture Notes in Computer Science, vol. 4507, pp. 144–151. Springer, Heidelberg (2007). https://doi.org/10.1007/978-3-540-73007-1_18

22. Simonyan, K., Zisserman, A.: Very deep convolutional networks for large-scale image recognition. arXiv preprint **14**(9), 1556 (2014)

23. Ioffe, S., Szegedy, C.: Batch normalization: Accelerating deep network training by reducing internal covariate shift. In: International conference on machine learning. PMLR, pp. 448–456. (2015)

24. Zhu, J.-Y., Park, T., Isola, P., Efros, A.: Unpaired imageto-image translation using cycle-consistent adversarial networks. arXiv preprint **12**(7), 722–730 (2017)

25. Graves, A.: Offline Arabic handwriting recognition with multidimensional recurrent neural networks. In: Märgner, V., El Abed, H. (eds.) Guide to OCR for Arabic Scripts. Springer, London (2012). https://doi.org/10.1007/978-1-4471-4072-6_12

26. Zayene, O., Masmoudi Touj, S., Hennebert, J., Ingold, R., Essoukri Ben Amara, N.: Open datasets and tools for Arabic text detection and recognition in news video frames. J. Imag. **4**(2), 32 (2018)

27. Osman, H., et al.: An efficient language-independent multi-font OCR for Arabic Script. arXiv preprint **10**(2), 09115 (2020)

28. Abbas, M.: Alwatan (2004). https://sites.google.com/site/mouradabbas9/corpora

29. Qaroush, A., Jaber, B., Mohammad, K., Washaha, M., Maali, E., Nayef, N.: An efficient, font independent word and character segmentation algorithm for printed Arabic text. J. King Saud Univ.-Comput. Inf. Sci. **34**(1), 1330–1344 (2022)

30. Slimane, F. Ingold, R., KanounS., Alimi, A.M., Hennebert, J.: A new Arabic printed text image database and evaluation protocols. In: 2009 10th International Conference on Document Analysis and Recognition, pp. 946–950 (2009)

31. Awais, M., Iqbal, S., Rasool, Q., Kousar, T.: Optical Character Recognition of Urdu Text using Histogram of Oriented Gradient Features (2022)

32. Sagheer, M.W., He, C.L., Nobile, N., Suen, C.Y.: Holistic Urdu handwritten word recognition using support vector machine. In: 2010 20th International Conference on Pattern Recognition, pp. 1900–1903. IEEE (2010)

33. Darwish, S.M., Elzoghaly, K.O.: An enhanced offline printed Arabic OCR model based on bio-inspired fuzzy classifier. IEEE Access **8**(1), 117770–117781 (2020)

34. Slimane, F., Ingold, R., Kanoun, S., Alimi, A.M., Hennebert, J.: A new Arabic printed text image database and evaluation protocols. In: 2009 10th International Conference on Document Analysis and Recognition, pp. 946–950. IEEE (2009)

35. Salah, A.l.: Arabic optical character recognition: a review. Comput. Model. Eng. Sci. **135**(3), 1825–1861(2023)

36. Ahmed, S. B., Naz, S., Razzak, M.I., Yusof, R.B.: A novel dataset for English-Arabic scene text recognition (EASTR)-42K and its evaluation using invariant feature extraction on detected extremal regions. IEEE Access **7**(10), 19801–19820 (2019)

37. Butt, H., Raza, M.R., Ramzan, M.J., Ali, M.J., Haris, M.: Attention-based CNN-RNN Arabic text recognition from natural scene images. Forecasting **3**, 520–540 (2021). https://doi.org/10.3390/forecast3030033

38. Fasha, M., Hammo, B., Obeid, N., Widian, J.:. A Hybrid Deep Learning Model for Arabic Text Recognition (2020)

A Solution for Building a V-Museum Based on Virtual Reality Application

Sinh Van Nguyen[1](✉)[iD], Duy Bao Dinh[1], Son Thanh Le[1], Sach Thanh Le[2],
Lam S.Q. Pham[1], Marcin Maleszka[3], and Lam V.D. Nguyen[1]

[1] International University of Ho Chi Minh City, VNU-HCM, Ho Chi Minh City,
Vietnam
nvsinh@hcmiu.edu.vn
[2] Ho Chi Minh City University of Technology, VNU-HCM, Ho Chi Minh City,
Vietnam
[3] Wroclaw University of Science and Technology, Wrocław, Poland
https://it.hcmiu.edu.vn, https://cse.hcmut.edu.vn,
https://kis.pwr.edu.pl/en/

Abstract. Digital transformation is a trend of technology studied and developed in every field recent years. Digitizing and moving real-world heritages into a dataset and visualizing them in a digital environment has been widely explored and improved by using a VR (Virtual Reality) technology. The application of VR and its implementation are being utilized in high-tech areas such as medical training, archaeology, digital heritage, digital museum, entertainment, etc. This paper conducts a depth research in 3D models processing and propose a solution for building a VR application of the real museum to preserve and exhibit the cultural heritage of Vietnam. Our proposed method includes the following steps: research on the different methods of converting the real world objects into the 3D world of VR; developing an immersive and interactive museum environment. This research establishes a framework and workflow to create a VR software, laying the foundation for further research and development for VR environment simulations in other fields.

Keywords: Digital transformation · VR & AR application · Digital heritage · V-Museum · 3D objects

1 Introduction

The development of high-tech devices can help to enhance our senses. They support us increasing abilities of thinking, imagining, interacting the activities in both virtual and real world. As mentioned in [1], VR has function to simulate, copy and transform characteristics of the real world into a virtual world such

This research is funded by Vietnam National University Ho Chi Minh City (VNU-HCM) under grant number DS2023-28-01.

that users can handle and interact as in the real life. AR (Augmented Reality) is considered as another version of real world that is enhanced by using sensors, sounds and pictures to make more reality. MR (Mixed Reality or called Hybrid Reality) is a combination of VR and AR, a mixed world between the real and the virtual, where the real and digital objects are existed and interacted together in the real time. While XR (eXtended Reality) refers to all VR, AR and MR, and covers to the ecosystem revolving around XR. Among these Metaverse, VR seems most popular and close to us. The several services and application of VR are rapidly developed in entertainment, virtual meetings and creative products. They are made easier using VR such as decorations, art pieces, sculpting, design and architecture, etc. An important part of the VR application at the moment is ability to give users a realistic experience in a place far from their homes. Besides, VR tourism and VR exhibition are effective solutions to apply this techniques in reconstruction and visualization of the 3D objects. In the field of digital heritages, VR is applied in simulation and visualization. One of the VR research is to reconstruct and simulate the 3D data objects through digital environments. A research for preserving and showcasing valuable heritages and artifacts is an interesting example for VR application as presented in [2]. In the previous work [3], we suggested a method for reconstructing the 3D objects to build a museum online. The research is based on knowledge of computer graphics, geometric modeling and image processing to reconstruct the 3D heritage objects and visualize them on the VR application. The artifacts of heritage models are restored approximately their initial shapes. However, the voice processing as a tour-guide is not supported in the application. This paper present a completed solution for reconstructing and visualizing 3D objects on VR application, and furthermore improving optimization and ability to interact. We first explore the pipeline of developing a VR museum environment based on the Oculus Quest 2. The next step is building a constructed model into a VR application with an effective and improved function. The final step is to conduct research and propose algorithms for interacting and applying them to showcase the 3D simulated objects in a VR museum. This research has high applicability and will become a good reference for future researchers to develop and create an effective application of virtual worlds. They are not only applied in V-Museums, but also in different environments and fields with an optimized design and high flexibility interactions. The remaining of the paper is structured following sections. The next section covers related work and applications in practice. Our proposed method is presented in Sect. 3. We implement the method and present obtained results in Sect. 4. The evaluation and comparison to the existing methods and application are discussed in Sect. 5. The conclusion of the paper is presented in last section (Sect. 6).

2   Related Work

This section presents the existing methods and their application of AR and VR in both scientific researches and practice. Janowska et.al. [1] presented a survey how to perform digital transformation of museums in Poland. As mentioned in the paper, the proliferation of information and communications technology (ICT) allows the digitization of museum collections and increases their availability to the public. How to preserve and advertise the cultural heritages by processing and transforming the real heritage objects into a virtual world. Besides, the research expressed an important part of the cultural policy, is a priority for the European Union, resulting in increased funding of digitization initiatives. Minh et. al. [4] suggested a method for building and visualizing 3D objects of statues on both VR and AR application. The application performed on the VR Headset (Oculus Quest) and the Android Mobile-App (smartphone). The application simulated a V-Museum with basic functions that allows users interact directly with the statues as in the real world. This research opened a variety of application in practice such as V-Museum, tourism, training and entertainment, etc. The next improved step of Sinh et.al. [3] was to propose an improved method for digitizing, reconstructing and visualizing heritage objects for the purpose of artifact preservation. The method is based on techniques and knowledge in computer graphics, geometric modeling, and computer vision. The novelty of method is focused on building and restoring the tangible heritages from 3D scanning data. The surface of artifacts is reconstructed by filling the triangular holes. Comparing to the several methods, this research obtained the shapes of 3D objects that approximate the initial of real objects. However, both of above researches and these application need to support sound and the real spaces of the real museum to enhance more reality. Roman [5] conducted a project based on photogrammetry and its application to construct and create 3D data objects. Using capabilities of modern devices and their utility tools like smartphone and computer with high resolution cameras that allow to measure distances, heights, inclinations of edges and facets, magnetic azimuths. After that, a geometrical model of the real object is built and calibrated to obtain a 3D object. The method is evaluated successful in proposing a cost-effective and feasible for individuals or organizers in data gathering and model quality creating. The obtained 3D objects approximates the geometric structure of real objects. The resulting accuracy and shape of the models correspond to the requirements of the object's historic structures. Renju et. al. [6] presented a method for 3D digitizing pipeline using 3D scans, applied in the field of cultural heritage preservation. By using the 3D techniques based on both geometry computation and texture mapping that can be recovered, enabling digital archiving, building a V-Museum of artifacts. The outputs are various visual representations of the archaeological artefacts, such as photographs, 3D models. In general, the above methods have been proved an effective solution of capturing and visualizing data from real world objects into 3D virtual models. That leads advantages in building a V-Museum and plays an important role in cultural heritage protection. Wei et.al. [7] suggested a method to develop a completed framework for creating 3D digital objects from the real archaeological artefacts and historical tangible heritages in Malaysia. The research is based on the terrestrial laser scanning (TLS) combined with taking photograph in close distance (or called close-range photogrammetry: CRP). With the support of high-tech devices, the outputs of the framework are very high resolution of photorealistic 3D models that can be used to build a V-Museum application. Beyond the scope of digitizing and obtaining the 3D object models, the development of VR application and it's applicability is also explored by Antonios et.al. [8] in their research on 3D reconstruction of historical cities for gaming purposes. This study details more on the gamification and application flow than the process of scanning and generating 3D mesh models. Showing how the 3D visualization technology has developed throughout the times. Many projects aims at reconstructing old heritage for preservation and education. A similar project by Salsabil et.al. [9] outlines the flow of building and implementing scanned objects into a 3D application and visualizing them on an online database. However their VR implementation is simple and quiet with only viewing function. The heritage and archeology are not only brings humanity historical and cultural values but also in scientific. That is reason why there are a lot of researches, not only in digital heritage, but also in medical and education. Creating a virtual environment where users can free act, interact and immerse in a realistic world with the support of only a VR headset is an advancement of science. Pottle et. al. [10] states VR offers benefits for learners and educators, delivering cost-effective, repeatable, standardized clinical training on demand. A large body of evidence supports VR simulation in all industries, including health-care. Another research is proved by Jaehong et. al. [11] shown that the teachers have positive attitudes towards AR and it is effected on the continuous using of them in the classroom along with several previous studies [12].

3   Proposed Method

In this paper, we present our completed method for obtaining, processing, reconstructing and building a VR application of a V-Museum. The method includes following steps (see Fig. 1). We first obtain data from the real objects of tangible cultural heritages at the history museum of Ho Chi Minh City, Vietnam [13]. The obtained dataset is then processed by removing noise data points and reconstructing the 3D objects. The next step is creating and building a virtual room for exhibition. The last step is deploying VR application on the VR Headset (Oculus Quest 2).

3.1   Obtaining Data

Ho Chi Minh City (HCMC) is one of the largest city and located in the south of Vietnam. The history museum of HCMC stores a lot of tangible heritages, where exhibits two main contents: nature and archeology with historical and cultural values of Vietnamese [13]. The heritages includes various images, artifacts, maps, and diagrams, the basic features of the geological structure, topography and mineral resources were introduced. There are also archaeological sites that prove this land was inhabited 3,500 years ago. We use a 3D scanner (the R-EVO7 S 2000 SCAN articulated measuring arm with laser scanner [14]) to scan and obtain data of the objects surface. For each statue, its surface is scanned following 8 different surround directions (see Fig. 2).

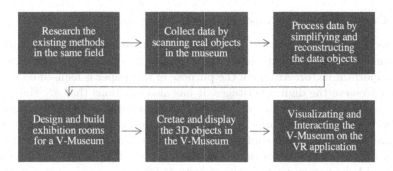

Fig. 1. Our completed proposed method for building a V-Museum.

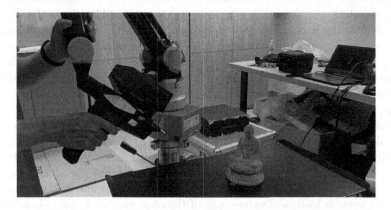

Fig. 2. The R-EVO7 S 2000 3D Scanner is used to scan data.

After obtaining data of the real objects, the output dataset is a 3D point cloud of each statue. The density of 3D points is dense or sparse depending on the scanning process. In the next step, we process to archive the best 3D model for each of them.

3.2   Processing Obtained Data

With the support of a very high quality 3D scanning R-EVO7, the obtained data is close to its original's shape of the real objects. However, the scanning process cannot approach exactly to regions in the object's surface like groove, crack or complex concave. In this section, we restore the object's surface based on characteristics of geometric modeling. In the previous work, we proposed a method to fill holes and reconstruct the 3D objects on both point clouds and mesh [15,16]. The first step is simplifying the obtained data based on computation of density points and local curvature of the object's surface [17]. The next step is filling the holes on the surface that are created during scanning step [16].

3.3   Computing and Constructing V-Museum

This section presents how to design and build a room for exhibition of a V-Museum. To ensure user experience of the application, the design of user interface is an important factor. Although the purpose of this paper is focused on research how to preserve the digital heritages, it has also functions that are similar to a video game, where users can traverse, explore and interact with the environment. We use the existing functions of Unity API to develop our V-Museum such as intuitive controls, layouts, components for user design. Our application consists of creating the mappings for input controls, movement options, user interaction and other behaviors of users to the objects as follows:

- Setup objects and space: Normally, the VR headset is designed for users who are standing and controlling objects in the room. Therefore, the object is located on the pedestal such that its height fits with the exhibition aesthetic as well as ensuring the user comfortable while viewing artifacts. An important step to decorate objects like texture mapping, color processing, shading and lighting, etc., will be implemented to enhance reality. Besides, a virtual user interface that contains components (like button, text-box, scroll-bar, checkbox, radio-button, etc.,) are necessary to control interactions of user. Three buttons are created on the pedestal to control position, rotate object and display historical information of the object. The functions of object manipulation by using VR controllers, means that the objects can be moved, rotated, scaled up and down dynamically. A function to restore the object comeback to its original status is convenient for visitors. Showing the information of the object such as historical values, age of the objects, etc., to provide additional knowledge to the visitors.
- Create interaction: Creating virtual interactions for the V-Museum is a new feature comparing to the traditional museums. Establishing a smooth and intuitive interaction system to improve the attraction of the application. Using controllers of the Oculus Quest 2 is as user hands that can handle and manipulate objects. The interactions allow users enable or disable the object's information text. The action to interact the objects is created based on two features: (i) Physical movement (the object move itself): like gravity, collide with other objects. (ii) User movement (the user interact to the objects) such as rotation and positional movement. These actions simulate a realistic interaction that is similar to the real world. We have also perform many algorithms to control objects such as multiplying transform matrices, matching the controller transform with the object transform, creating attachment points, verifying physics system and checking conditions. The function to scale objects allows users to expand or shrink the objects by pinching and moving the controllers. This action can make objects larger or smaller, whereas we cannot do the same manipulation in the traditional museum. This characteristic is an improved solution of our application.
- Create movement: The movement in the V-Museum is not only created for objects but also for users or visitors. We implement a function that simulates "walking" through the museum of users. The two functions of rotation and

location are controlled by two controller: the left thumb stick Y axis (forward and backward) handles the character movement in the virtual world. The right thumb stick X axis (left and right) controls the character rotation.

3.4 Creating Interactions for VR

In this section, we implement a list of algorithms based on the IDE of Unity 3D. Each algorithm is presented step by step to handle a task. Starting with a room to exhibit, the object's models are set up and displayed in the room. We handle the 3D objects and show their historical information for visualizing and visiting. The first algorithms (Algorithm 1) is importing the mesh's model onto the Unity. The next one (Algorithm 2) is to build a V-Museum. Algorithm 3 integrates Unity scenes to be used with a VR Headset. Algorithm 4 controls interaction of object's moving. Algorithm 5 handles movement of players. Algorithm 6 is expanding and shrinking objects. The last algorithm (Algorithm 7) is processing text-to-speech to read exhibit description.

Algorithm 1. Importing mesh's models of the objects to Unity

1: **Input**
2:     3D mesh and Textures of Object
3: **Process:**
4:     Load raw mesh into Unity scene
5:     Create objects using features (color, reflection, transparency, quality)
6:     Optimize textures and shaders
7:     Move and scale objects in scene
8:     Use source code (C#) to handle objects
9:     Save objects with Unity Prefabs and place into V-Museum
10: **Output:**
11:     Integrated 3D objects to Unity

Algorithm 2. Building space for a V-Museum

1: **Input**
2:     An exhibit room of Museum
3:     The objects (from output of Algorithm 1)
4: **Process:**
5:     Import Museum 3D model
6:     Create VR avatar
7:     Set up UI, design sound and lighting
8:     Locate object's models and note their information
9:     Use source code (C#) to process objects (adjust lighting, bake scene)
10:     Adjust settings and code for each object
11: **Output:**
12:     A V-Museum scene in Unity

Algorithm 3. Integrating Unity scenes to be used with VR Headset

1: **Input**
2:    A V-Museum (from output of Algorithm 2)
3: **Process:**
4:    Implement XR SDK for VR headset (e.g. Oculus Quest 2)
5:    Integrate user Avatar with XR-Rig
6:    Bind controls for movement, UI, interactions
7:    Sync camera movement to head movement
8:    Add C# scripts for expanded interaction features
9:    Adjust VR settings for optimize the display (FPS: frames per second)
10: **Output:**
11:    Playable V-Museum application with VR Headset

Algorithm 4. Controlling interaction of object's moving

1: **Input**
2:    Hand controllers and C# scripts for the objects
3: **Process:**
4:    Read controller inputs and position in 3D coordinates
5:    Move the held object to the position of the hand controllers
6:    Rotate the held object to the rotation of the hand controllers
7:    Detect and handle collisions/physics of the movement
8: **Output:**
9:    A V-Museum with interactions as in the reality

Algorithm 5. Handling movement of players

1: **Input**
2:    Hand controllers and C# scripts for player
3: **Process:**
4:    Read controller inputs and headset looking direction in 3D coordinates
5:    Calculate movement parameters (speed, look direction, thumbsticks direction)
6:    Apply movement to camera and avatar in 3D space
7:    Detect and handle collisions/physics of the movement
8: **Output:**
9:    A V-Museum with additional movement function

Algorithm 6. Expanding and shrinking objects

1: **Input**
2:    Hand controllers and C# scripts for objects
3: **Process:**
4:    Read controller inputs and position in 3D coordinates
5:    Calculate scale parameters (distance between controllers, object scale)
6:    Shrink or expand objects according to the ratio change of distance between controllers
7:    Detect and handle collisions/physics of the movement
8: **Output:**
9:    Added features to zoom-in/out the objects

Algorithm 7. Converting text to speech to read objects description

---

1: **Input**
2:    Text information of the objects
3: **Process:**
4:    Configure speaker voice (speed, pitch, gain)
5:    Read text description of objects
6:    Result audio file is generated and cached in headset's memory
7:    Audio file is opened to user using the headset speakers
8: **Output:**
9:    A V-Museum with audio function

---

4   Implementation and Results

We implement our proposed method in the Unity, using C# programming language to program, process and control all the 3D object's of the real models. As default, the Unity 3D toolkit [18] does not support developing and testing with VR out of the box. Some additional packages and modifications can be added to allow the usage of some development SDK created by Unity for building VR application. The Unity XR Tech, a framework that enables direct integration of multiple platforms. The tech stack consists of an API that exposes common functionality, across the platforms Unity supports and enables XR hardware and software providers to develop their own Unity plugins. The Unity has developed a new plugin framework (called XR SDK) that enables XR providers to integrate the Unity engine using its full features. This plugin-based approach improves Unity's ability to make quickly bug fixes, distribute SDK updates from platform partners, and to support new XR devices and runtimes without having to modify the core engine. The unity XR tech stack allows developing VR platforms. One benefit of the XR tech stack is that it abstracts the underlying architecture and add compatibility of many different headset SDKs. So the final application can be executed not only on the Oculus platform but also in other VR hardware (steamVR, HoloLens, PlaystationVR, ect.,). Upon this framework the application will be built, using C# code and another development toolkit called XR Interaction Toolkit to create and implement more advanced features.

Besides, the function to control the artifacts is supported by using hands with finger animations. The XR Interaction Toolkit API illustrate finger movements when the user presses buttons on the controllers. The hand models will move in the VR space in accordance with the controller movements in the real world. Therefore, user can see where their hands are controlling objects to improve interactive experience as in the reality. The powerful Unity3D engine enables accurate physics simulation such as collisions, gravity, momentum, by adding certain components to the objects in the scene and activating them dynamically by C# scripts. The objects while grabbed will follow the controller's position and rotation. With this control scheme, objects can be picked up and rotated using the controllers motion tracking. By moving and rotating the hand holding the controller, the virtual hands would also rotate and interact the artifacts. This process allows handling 360° with close-up of the models. Figure 3 is an exhibit room designed by adding, locating objects and their buttons to control on each object.

Fig. 3. The exhibit room of our V-Museum: see https://youtu.be/LJQ2LUYDrOU

5   Evaluation and Comparison

A vital part of a VR application is deployed on the native hardware of the Oculus Quest 2 instead of a PC that is limited resources on the mobile hardware. Furthermore, performance of the application is measured in FPS (frames per second). It is one of the most important metrics of user comfort and optimal quality. If the FPS is low or inconsistent that can cause disoriented, dizzy or even headaches to the users. For this reason, optimizing the graphics and algorithms is necessary to ensure application quality. The following performance factors [20] relate to the optimization techniques:

- Processing the Bake Lightmaps..
- Using high resolution of the object's surface with low cost computation
- Simulating the minimal interactions (only active the current objects)
- Performing the ambient occlusion.
- Reducing the image post processing.

We compare the features of our V-Museum application with the previous research [4] (an application of V-Museum based on VR & AR) and the Vietnam Museum [23] to show the improved features of our V-Museum (see Table 1). Our application can run fine on different VR headsets. The interactions of user to the objects are diverse (e.g. rotation, zoom in/out, movement with natural actions and sound) comparing to the research in [24]. The sound and voice are additional factors to make the application more realistic. These features are neccessary and important functions compared to the previous application [4] and close to the reality of visiting the HCMC Museum.

Table 1. Comparing the features of V-Museum applications

Features	Apps		
	Application in [4]	VN-Museum [23]	Our V-Museum
VR Platform	Oculus Quest 2	Web-based application	All kinds of VR headsets
Object's models	The 3D point cloud	Web 360 images	High quality of 3D mesh
Audio function	No	No	Yes
Interaction	Rotate objects	Viewing 360	Full interaction
Movement	Continuous	Teleport	Continuous
Lighting/shadow	Yes	No	Yes
Different views	Static view	Web 360	Dynamic and automatic view
Physical simulation	No	No	Yes
User setting	No	No	Yes
Dynamic description	Yes	Yes	Yes
UI and UX	No	No	Yes

6   Conclusion

In this research, we have studied and implemented a V-Museum with full functions as in the real world. This VR application is applied in the HCMC Museum of Vietnam. This is also one of the digital transformation step in cultural heritages. The research is performed based on the combination of geometric modeling, creating 3D graphical models and visualizing them in the virtual environment of the real heritages. Comparing to the previous application [4,23,24], our application has more functions and features with different interactions of the objects. The visitors are immersed in the exhibition of digital heritages and the application is used in practice as a tour at HCMC museum. We will develop and complete the whole project, such that the users and visitors will be experimented in the digital space as in practice of HCMC museum.

Acknowledgments. This research is funded by Vietnam National University Ho Chi Minh City (VNU-HCM) under grant number DS2023-28-01. We would like to thank for the fund.

References

1. Janowska, A.A., Malik, R.: Digitization in museums: between a fashionable trend and market awareness. Studia z Polityki Publicznej, **7**(3), 31–45 (2020). https://doi.org/10.33119/KSzPP/2020.3.2
2. Van Nguyen, S., Tran, H.M., Maleszka, M.: Geometric modeling: background for processing the 3D objects. Appl. Intell. **51**(8), 6182–6201 (2021). ISSN: 1573–7497, (SCI-E, Q2, IF: 5.08)
3. Van Nguyen, S., Le, S.T., Tran, M.K., Tran, H.M.: Reconstruction of 3D digital heritage objects for VR and AR applications. J. Inf. Telecommun. **6**(3), 254–269 (2022)
4. Tran, M.K., Nguyen, S.V., To, N.T., Maleszka, M.: Processing and visualizing the 3D models in digital heritage. In: Nguyen, N.T., Iliadis, L., Maglogiannis, I., Trawiński, B. (eds.) ICCCI 2021. LNCS (LNAI), vol. 12876, pp. 613–625. Springer, Cham (2021). https://doi.org/10.1007/978-3-030-88081-1_46
5. Shults, R.: New opportunities of low-cost photogrammetry for culture heritage preservation. Int. Arch. Photogramm. Remote Sens. Spatial Inf. Sci., **XLII-5/W1**, 481–486 (2017). https://doi.org/10.5194/isprs-archives-XLII-5-W1-481-2017
6. Li, R., Luo, T., Zha, H.: 3D digitization and its applications in cultural heritage. In: Ioannides, M., Fellner, D., Georgopoulos, A., Hadjimitsis, D.G. (eds.) EuroMed 2010. LNCS, vol. 6436, pp. 381–388. Springer, Heidelberg (2010). https://doi.org/10.1007/978-3-642-16873-4_29
7. Wei, O.C., et al.: Three dimensional recording and photorealistic model reconstruction for virtual museum application - an experience in Malaysia. ISPRS - Int. Arch. Photogrammetry, Remote Sens. Spat. Inf. Sci. **XLII-2/W9**, 763–771 (2019). https://doi.org/10.5194/isprs-archives-XLII-2-W9-763-2019
8. Kargas, A., Loumos, G., Varoutas, D.: Using different ways of 3D Reconstruction of historical cities for gaming purposes: the case study of Nafplio. Heritage. **2**(3), 1799–1811 (2019). https://doi.org/10.3390/heritage2030110
9. Ahmed, S., Islam, R., Himalay, S.S., Uddin, J.: Preserving heritage sites using 3D modeling and virtual reality technology. In: Proceedings of the 3rd International Conference on Cryptography, Security and Privacy (ICCSP 2019). Association for Computing Machinery, New York, NY, USA, pp. 267–272 (2019). https://doi.org/10.1145/3309074.3309116

10. Pottle, J.: Virtual reality and the transformation of medical education. Future Healthc. J. **6**(3), 181–185 (2019). https://doi.org/10.7861/fhj.2019-0036. PMID: 31660522; PMCID: PMC6798020
11. Jang, J., Ko, Y., Shin, W.S., Han, I.: Augmented reality and virtual reality for learning: an examination using an extended technology acceptance model. IEEE Access **9**, 6798–6809 (2021). https://doi.org/10.1109/ACCESS.2020.3048708
12. Abd Majid, F., Mohd Shamsudin, N.: Identifying factors affecting acceptance of virtual reality in classrooms based on technology acceptance model (TAM). Asian J. Univ. Educ. **15**(2), 1–10 (2019). ISSN 1823–7797
13. Museum of Ho Chi Minh City, Vietnam. https://hcmc-museum.edu.vn/en/trang-chu-english/. Accessed Jan 2023
14. Metrology, R-EVO S-SCAN Articulated measuring arm with laser scanner. https://www.rpsmetrology.com/en/product/r-evo-s-scan/. Accessed Jan 2023
15. Nguyen, V.S., Tran, K.M., Tran, M.H.: Filling hole on the surface of 3D point clouds based on reverse computation of Bezier curves. In: Bhateja, V., Nguyen, B.L., Nguyen, N.G., Satapathy, S.C., Le, D.-N. (eds.) Information Systems Design and Intelligent Applications. AISC, vol. 672, pp. 334–345. Springer, Singapore (2018). https://doi.org/10.1007/978-981-10-7512-4_34
16. Van Sinh, N., Ha, T.M., Thanh, N.T.: Filling holes on the surface of 3D point clouds based on tangent plane of hole boundary points. In: Proceedings of the Seventh International Symposium on Information and Communication Technology (SoICT), pp. 331–338. ACM (2016). ISBN: 978-1-4503-4815-7
17. Nguyen, V.S., Bac, A., Daniel, M.: Simplification of 3D point clouds sampled from elevation surfaces. In: 21st International Conference on Computer Graphics, Visualization and Computer Vision WSCG 2013, Plzen, Czech Republic, pp. 60–69 (2013). ISBN: 978-80-86943-75-6, Rank B
18. Unity Manual - XR Plugin Framework, Unity Documentation. https://docs.unity3d.com/Manual/XRPluginArchitecture.html. Accessed Jan 2023
19. IGIIID - Museum VR Complete Edition asset pack on Unity Asset store. https://assetstore.unity.com/packages/3d/environments/museum-vr-complete-edition-89652. Accessed Jan 2023
20. Unity Manual - Normal map (Bump mapping), Unity Documentation. https://docs.unity3d.com/Manual/StandardShaderMaterialParameterNormalMap.html. Accessed Jan 2023
21. Vietnamese National Historical Museum - E-Heritage Digital Museum. https://baovatquocgia.baotangso.com/. Accessed Jan 2023
22. VR360 - Museum Tourism. https://vr360.com.vn/khu-du-lich-bao-tang. Accessed Jan 2023
23. Vietnam national museum of history. https://baovatquocgia.baotangso.com. Accessed Feb 2023
24. Kadri, M., Khalloufi, H., Azough, A.: V-museum: a virtual museum based on augmented and virtual realities for cultural heritage mediation. In: International Conference on Intelligent Systems and Computer Vision (ISCV), Fez, Morocco, 2020, pp. 1–5. IEEE (2020). https://doi.org/10.1109/ISCV49265.2020.9204253

Synthetic Football Sprite Animations Learned Across the Pitch

Alexandru Ionascu[✉], Sebastian Stefaniga, and Mihail Gaianu

Department of Computer Science, Faculty of Mathematics and Computer Science,
West University of Timisoara, Timisoara, Romania
`alexandru.ionascu96@e-uvt.ro`

Abstract. In previous sporting scene synthesis and 3D reconstruction pipelines, gathering an extensive database of sprite animations has been problematic and often the cause of unrealistic renders. We present a video processing framework for collecting and rendering sprite animations - applied on the football pitch. The main idea is to maximize the available information in a football scene by transferring the motion from all the players across the pitch to an individual. All the players on a football pitch provide a wide variety of poses and animation key-frames. In our experiments, even if we successfully capture clean video samples of a target player for 10 s, we can render an order of magnitude more animation key-frames - worth of minutes. The framework is also extensible for other sports, but football is particularly relevant for this task, highlighting the team's impact on the pitch.

Keywords: Computer Vision · Video Processing · Segmentation · Depth Estimation · GAN · Animation Transfer

1 Introduction

Computer-generated scenes are now part of the football world. Video assistant referee is part of the game, and almost any 3D football scene reconstruction is quickly available for the viewers. However, these enhancements are possible with hardware outside the viewer's scope. Stereo cameras were the first natural advancement, a priori camera calibration; secondly, more static and dynamic cameras pivot around the pitch for 360° views. In addition, some experiments can benefit from specific depth sensors, and we even have tracking sensors inside the ball.

With the help of additional hardware, we can augment the live broadcast football experience, commentaries, and analysis. For example, we can analyze potentially different outcomes after the match, starting with in-game moments from build-up play or set pieces, via specific computer software.

The football field is highly dynamic, and it is sporadic to be able to track a player for a few seconds without encountering occlusions. On the other hand, we cannot deny that we have an incredible amount of football videos online, most

© The Author(s), under exclusive license to Springer Nature Switzerland AG 2023
N. T. Nguyen et al. (Eds.): ICCCI 2023, CCIS 1864, pp. 610–618, 2023.
https://doi.org/10.1007/978-3-031-41774-0_48

of which are from TV broadcasts. Hence, we aim to maximize the data we can extract and process from a football game in the monocular video.

For a regular football game, a 90-minute match (or 5400 s), we will have to deal with approximately a minimum of 162 K–324 K frames individually, depending if we have 30–60 frames per second. Intuitively, this task requires individual segmentation, tracking, discarding the errors, and key-frame animation grouping - tasks that are challenging to approach at this scale. Of course, some tasks can be computer-automated, but we will always risk inflicting some errors.

The core idea of this framework is to focus only on the most iconic, player-specific animations and fill the set of possible poses and animation key-frames with generic ones collected across the pitch. In other words, if we capture a clean video sample of 10 s of Lionel Messi, we try to synthesize Lionel Messi's animation frames - worth of minutes, based on the animation key-frames performed by the other players in the scene. Intuitively, this should be a 10–20× reduction in the size of our original problem. The scope of our experiments is to evaluate the feasibility and the trade-offs and to explore potential improvements.

This framework will start with instance segmentation and masking. At this point, we will have a set of sprites - from multiple people. Then, we use the on-screen coordinates tracking to form animation key sets with the sprites - in an intermediary version, but human intervention is often required. Now we need an intermediary representation of the human body. Since the football players in the broadcast camera scene are relatively small, we will estimate the depth maps for our instances and then apply image-to-image or video-to-video techniques. In this way, we generally represent a specific type of movement in depth sprites (Fig. 1).

Fig. 1. Broadcast TV football footage from our experiment. There are 16 players in this frame and 1 referee. In this example, there are 4 occlusions, and one cameraman is detected.

2   Related Work

In general, rendering 3D interactive environments reached a spectacular state-of-the-art realism. Simultaneously, human rendering progressed, although traditional 3D rendering approaches have triggered doubts about whether neural models can outperform them. The scope of our work follows the same idea by trying to work under a 3D controlled environment and a neural approach for human rendering.

Each framework component has been previously used in sports scene synthesis and 3D reconstructions, either neural or procedural. However, football has certain particularities. In computer vision, football is one of the most challenging scene types due to the high number of individuals on the pitch and nearby it, constant occlusions, and ever-changing camera parameters.

Sprite gathering leads us to consider two principal paths: supervised and unsupervised. In practical scenarios, we might use a hybrid solution to approach a more significant scale factor in video frame processing while introducing minimal errors. Human intervention is also occasionally present to correct errors. We also make a two-sided distinction in principles: correct the errors early to prevent error propagation or let the erroneous images pass through the pipeline and leverage the fact that errors are predictable and correctable by any machine-learning-based components in the pipeline.

Previous work [11] demonstrated the ability to decompose a scene in a sprite dictionary autonomously. However, our task for the following experiment will focus only on athletes under different poses, even though we will not add interactivity with the ball.

Human body parameters and pose representation can be implemented in several ways. We can use simple numerical representations, SMPL [8] is very popular for this task, and it generally represents a baseline for 3D reconstructions. On a similar note, we have the natural extension [9] for working with deformable models applied to human avatars, and also, more recently, [12]. Another similar implementation, but this time using a much larger space representation, would be [7].

This decision is closely related to the next step: **animation transfer**. If we consider an image-to-image approach (or video-to-video), it will make sense to represent our body and pose under the same dimensional space. In our case, we can estimate the depth maps for each detected player on the field. Alternatively, we can use another intermediate representation to represent our scene correspondence, such as the one described in [5] - considering the high redundancy we encounter in football scenes. Nevertheless, the approach is non-exclusive; we can use our approach as a preprocessing phase to synthesize the input video.

In comparison with other sport reconstruction pipelines [10,13] we notice a few differences, but primarily, our novelty counts on the impact of the collective animations across the scene. The biggest challenges, previously, were regarding the database size of collected sprites, and this problem is primarily visible during state transitions - we aim to enlarge the sprite gathering and processing steps to prevent this from happening. While there are parts of images that are compared

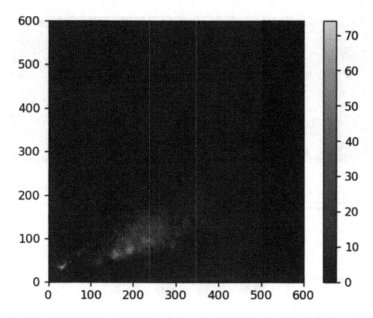

Fig. 2. Distribution of the sprites in size, extracted from video highlights of Lionel Messi playing in Real Madrid - Barcelona in 4K resolution.

to an existing database of sprites, and an image-to-image step is in use, we will only consider the images captured completely - we can have sprites containing partial human body but we have no end-goal for this application (Fig. 2).

3   Proposed Method

3.1   Overview

For the first step of sprite gathering, we use PointRend [4] as our image segmentation and masking processing method in a frame-by-frame manner. Secondly, we easily track the on-the-screen coordinates to group the sprites in animation key-frames. This process is prone to errors, while it can be automatized; for the scope of the experiment, the frames were manually regrouped when needed. This step is optional towards our end goal but requires highlighting the individual animation alongside the generic one (Fig. 3).

The next step for depth estimation for a single image is using GLPN [3]. Lastly, for the image-to-image part, we will use a conditional GAN [1] based on pix2pix [2], with an additional alpha channel. Also, before the training, we will apply additional color normalization - for both player sprites and depth maps, jittering and mirroring.

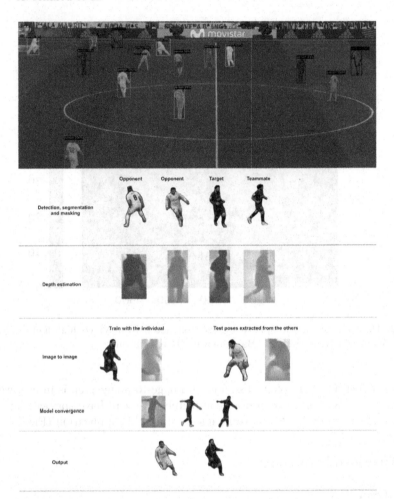

Fig. 3. The proposed framework step by step. From top-to-bottom, we start with player detection, segmentation, and masking. Next, we obtain a sprite dataset and keep our target player separately - in this case, Lionel Messi. Then, we proceed with depth estimation for all our extracted sprites. Lastly, we train an image-to-image generative model with our individual-target data and test it with the collective depths from poses across the pitch. Our result will be the sprites of Lionel Messi in novel target poses.

3.2 Implementation

For this experiment, our input video consists of 15 min highlights of Lionel Messi playing for Barcelona, facing Real Madrid. The video has 4K resolution and 50 FPS. We sampled 1150 frames for our start of the dataset - frames sampled linearly in a short frames-interval of a maximum of 2 s (100 frames), counting from a set of manually selected starting points. These will result in a database of

19,250 extracted sprites, many containing erroneous body patches. The average sprite size in our dataset is 263 in height and 140 in width.

We will choose Lionel Messi as our target individual player - consisting of a dataset of 538 images - manually cleaned. Those images must be paired with the corresponding estimated depths, mainly representing the training part, but we also use an 80%-10%-10% split for test and validation sets. Since the masking result comes in different shapes, we apply to resize and padding to convert images to 256 × 256 size with 4 channels - including the alpha layer.

We use the predicted depth maps to predict novel poses, except for the images where GLPN failed to provide contextual depth information. This results in a set of 17,898 depth predictions, which can be fed into the generator.

We run up to 80,000 steps for our pix2pix training, preserving the original implementation details from the original paper [2]. The image-to-image experiment used Tesla K80 GPU, Tensorflow, and Keras.

Fig. 4. Framework application demo with synthetic sprites. Lionel Messi is our target player in the middle. On the left, we have the next extracted sprite. On the right, we have our synthesized sprite with our framework - with a lower level of detail - yet realistic.

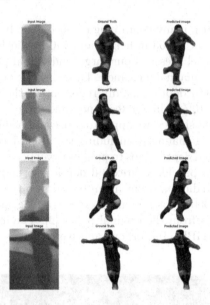

Fig. 5. Image to image step from the framework. GAN training after 40,000 steps. Poses can be reconstructed from depths.

4 Evaluation

We can see that the final output of the pipeline is well-shaped around the depth of the pose, but the prediction has fewer details, which appear blurry. However, the loss of details in the original size of 256×256 appears less significant when projected back to the original pitch. While most poses are reconstructed correctly, the uncommon poses are hallucinated - for example, if we use a goalkeeper-specific depth pose (Table 1).

Table 1. Average image similarities on test dataset.

Average MSE	Average RMSE	Average UQI
0.9888	0.9809	0.7343

4.1 Limitations and Future Work

Our experiments provided good generalizations on common poses. Nevertheless, the generative model could learn the training set well; some details may need to be more prominent on common poses, and the unusual poses are generally impractical. Moreover, even though we target a margin of factor increase in obtaining novel potential poses, some angles are more challenging to reconstruct from others.

For a complete experience, we currently need more physics of the game. Consequently, we do not reconstruct the ball interaction and interactions with the other players. The future directions for delivering the whole experience include integrating an existing physics-based simulator. For example, we have seen [6] - typically used for reinforcement learning. However, it is entirely plausible to consider compressing the sprites produced by our framework. Then we can use it in a real-time shader program, replacing our predicted depth with actual depth buffers.

5   Conclusions

We presented a video processing framework for generating new football animation frames. Individually, obtaining clean and non-hallucinating sprites from a broadcast TV scene is challenging. Our work relies on collecting human sprites across the pitch. We use a depth map estimator and an image-to-image generative model to combine specific player animation with generic animations performed by the other 20+ players on the field. In this way, a clean video sample worth seconds individually is worth minutes collectively.

References

1. Goodfellow, I., et al.: Generative adversarial networks, 1–9. arXiv preprint arXiv:1406.2661 (2014)
2. Isola, P., Zhu, J.Y., Zhou, T., Efros, A.A.: Image-to-image translation with conditional adversarial networks. In: Proceedings of the IEEE Conference on Computer Vision and Pattern Recognition, pp. 1125–1134 (2017)
3. Kim, D., Ga, W., Ahn, P., Joo, D., Chun, S., Kim, J.: Global-local path networks for monocular depth estimation with vertical cutdepth. arXiv preprint arXiv:2201.07436 (2022)
4. Kirillov, A., Wu, Y., He, K., Girshick, R.: PointRend: image segmentation as rendering. In: Proceedings of the IEEE/CVF Conference on Computer Vision and Pattern Recognition, pp. 9799–9808 (2020)
5. Klose, F., Wang, O., Bazin, J.C., Magnor, M., Sorkine-Hornung, A.: Sampling based scene-space video processing. ACM Trans. Graph. (TOG) **34**(4), 1–11 (2015)
6. Kurach, K., et al.: Google research football: a novel reinforcement learning environment. In: Proceedings of the AAAI Conference on Artificial Intelligence, vol. 34, pp. 4501–4510 (2020)
7. Lin, Z., Huang, A., Huang, Z., Hu, C., Zhou, S.: Collaborative neural rendering using anime character sheets. arXiv preprint arXiv:2207.05378 (2022)
8. Loper, M., Mahmood, N., Romero, J., Pons-Moll, G., Black, M.J.: SMPL: a skinned multi-person linear model. ACM Trans. Graph. (TOG) **34**(6), 1–16 (2015)
9. Prokudin, S., Black, M.J., Romero, J.: SMPLpix: neural avatars from 3D human models. In: Proceedings of the IEEE/CVF Winter Conference on Applications of Computer Vision, pp. 1810–1819 (2021)
10. Rematas, K., Kemelmacher-Shlizerman, I., Curless, B., Seitz, S.: Soccer on your tabletop. In: Proceedings of the IEEE Conference on Computer Vision and Pattern Recognition, pp. 4738–4747 (2018)

11. Smirnov, D., Gharbi, M., Fisher, M., Guizilini, V., Efros, A., Solomon, J.M.: MarioNette: self-supervised sprite learning. In: Advances in Neural Information Processing Systems, vol. 34, pp. 5494–5505 (2021)

12. Xiu, Y., Yang, J., Tzionas, D., Black, M.J.: ICON: implicit clothed humans obtained from normals. In: 2022 IEEE/CVF Conference on Computer Vision and Pattern Recognition (CVPR), pp. 13286–13296. IEEE (2022)

13. Zhang, H., Sciutto, C., Agrawala, M., Fatahalian, K.: Vid2player: controllable video sprites that behave and appear like professional tennis players. ACM Trans. Graph. (TOG) 40(3), 1–16 (2021)

Solving the Hydrophobic-Polar Model with Nested Monte Carlo Search

Milo Roucairol[✉][iD] and Tristan Cazenave[✉][iD]

LAMSADE, Université Paris Dauphine - PSL, CNRS, Paris, France
milo.roucairol@dauphine.eu, tristan.cazenave@lamsade.dauphine.fr

Abstract. In this paper we present a new Monte Carlo Search (MCS) algorithm for finding the ground state energy of proteins in the Hydrophobic-Polar-model (HP model). We also compare it to other MCS algorithms not usually used on the HP model as well as to other approaches and provide an overview of the state of the art algorithms used on the HP model.

Keywords: Protein folding · Monte Carlo Search · MCTS · HP model · optimization · pruning

1 Introduction

Monte Carlo search algorithms have proven to be powerful as game playing agents, with recent successes like AlphaGo [14]. These algorithms have the advantage of only needing an evaluation function for the final state of the space they explore.

Protein folding is crucial to our understanding of biology and designing drugs, however, trying our algorithms directly on accurate models could be counterproductive. In this paper, we use a new MCS algorithm to fold proteins in a simplified lattice based model called the HP model.

First, we will present the protein folding and the HP model, then the different algorithms we used to explore the problem space and finally the results of our experiments.

2 The Problem

2.1 Protein Folding

With recent developments in ARNm technology, it is now possible to incite cells to produce a specific protein [8], like the spike protein used in COVID-19 vaccines. Unfortunately, deducing the shape a protein will take given the amino acids sequence is not obvious nor trivial. That is a reason protein folding is a very important problem in molecular biology and medicine.

Proteins are chains of amino acids (primary structure), they can fold in many different ways, the secondary structure is the shape the protein will take at a

N. T. Nguyen et al. (Eds.): ICCCI 2023, CCIS 1864, pp. 619–631, 2023.
https://doi.org/10.1007/978-3-031-41774-0_49

local level (a coil for example), the tertiary structure is the global shape of the protein with less discernible patterns, finally, the quaternary structure is how a protein can assemble with another. Here we are interested in predicting the ground state energy folding (secondary and tertiary structure) from the primary structure. Many forces drive the folding, which prevents the creation of a very accurate simulator, the main driving force is the hydrophobic one.

One can not approach protein folding without mentioning DeepMind's AlphaFold [10]. Placing first at the Critical Assessment of Techniques for Protein Structure Prediction in 2018 and 2020, it is the best program for protein structure prediction yet. AlphaFold uses machine learning on a large protein database to train neural networks, in addition to physics based rules in order to predict the folding of a protein.

AlphaFold is the greatest achievement to protein folding prediction in decades, but the research is not over yet. AlphaFold accuracy can still be perfected, and by using neural networks the explainability is low and the model may not be able to predict the structure of proteins never seen before. Our objective here is to provide a better algorithm than the other MCS algorithms for Monte Carlo physics simulation, which may be more explainable than AlphaFold and other MCS algorithms, but should currently be way less accurate than Alphafold if it was applied on the same problem.

2.2 Hydrophobic-Polar Model

The HP model was introduced in 1985 by Ken Dill [4]. The main idea behind the creation of the HP model is that the Hydrophobic-Polar (HP) force is the main force driving the folding of a protein, thus it is the only one used here.

The HP model is a simplified lattice based model for protein folding, it exists in 2D and 3D versions.

In the HP model, proteins are represented as a chain of H and P residues (amino acids), the chain is then folded onto a grid, two residues can not share the same positions. The residue contacts determine the energy of a chain, usually, the reward for an H-H connection is -1, and 0 for H-P and P-P contacts in a context of minimization (since the ground energy state is the state with the least potential energy). Other rewards can be used to obtain different results or guide the search.

2.3 State of the Art on HP Model

The HP model has seen a number of algorithms trying to solve it. All of the best performing algorithms on the HP model are Monte Carlo based, policy learning using neural networks or reinforcement learning like NRPA [12] led to poor results. In these Monte Carlo algorithms, we can identify two types, the chain growth algorithms and the replica exchange ones.

The chain growth methods add the residues one after the other, next to the previous one, it is similar to a self avoiding walk and it is the method we used in our own algorithm.

The replica exchange methods use pull moves, pulling the chain at one point by rotating a residue around one of its neighbors, symmetrically rotating a part of the chain or pulling from one side of the chain. This means the entirety of the chain is present on the lattice at any given state of the search and is in a physically possible conformation, this method is used in simulated annealing like Monte Carlo algorithms. To see a representation of these moves see Chris Thchuk, Alena Shmygelska, and Holger H Hoos REMC article [16].

Here is a short review of the methods we encountered.

1) PERM: Initially used on Self Avoiding Walks (SAW), PERM is a chain growth algorithm and was used on the HP model by Peter Grassberger in 1997 [7]. It stands for Pruned Enriched Rosenbluth Method, the idea is to explore the possible chains uniformly with a bias on the immediate gain, cutting (pruning) branches leading to too few choices and poor performances, and cloning (enriching) branches that lead to great results. PERM has seen many new versions until 2011 [9], mainly proposed by its creator, Peter Grassberger. It still is one of the best algorithms available but has been outperformed by pull-moves based more recent algorithms. We reproduced PERM, but our results with this algorithm did not live up to the expectations, it matched UCT's (see part 4.3) performances.

2) REMC: Introduced in 2007 by Chris Thachuk, Alena Shmygelska and Holger H Hoos [16], the Replica Exchange Monte Carlo algorithm uses pull moves and simulated annealing. That algorithm keeps only a certain number of replicas (it was determined the best number of replicas for the 3D HP model was 2), each with a given temperature. At each step the algorithm mutates each replica with a Monte-Carlo Search using the pull moves, the probabilities of keeping a mutation are decided by the score gain (energy loss) of the mutated state and the temperature. Then, once each state is produced through mutation, the replicas are then again swapped probabilistically according to their score (energy) and temperatures.

3) Wang-Landau sampling: Introduced in 2012 on the HP model, the Wang-Landau sampling (WLS) [17] method seems to be the new best algorithm for solving the HP model. It is a replica-exchange (simulated annealing) algorithm that uses the same pull moves as the REMC, but also uses moves consisting in cutting and joining of the molecule (thus reallocating all the residues according to their position), together they are named the Monte-Carlo trial moves. With these moves, the WLS explores the conformation space to estimate a histogram of the energies of these conformations. With this histogram, the WLS can then direct the exchange of the replicas.

3   Algorithm

3.1   Biased Growth

In a similar way to the PERM algorithm [9], we try to favor the immediate reward when building/folding the molecule. To do this, we use biased playouts, the chances of selecting a move m from M the possible moves from state S follows a softmax distribution with b the bias factor:

$$\frac{exp(G_m * b)}{\sum_{i \in M_S} exp(G_i * b)} \tag{1}$$

$M_{c\text{-}state}$ denotes the legal moves available from the state *current-state*. $G_{M_{c\text{-}state}}$ denotes the immediate gains of each legal moves available from the state *current-state*.

Algorithm 1. The biased growth playout algorithm.

```
 1: function PLAYOUT(c-state, b)
 2:     ply ← 0
 3:     seq ← {}
 4:     while c-state is not terminal do
 5:         gains ← G_{M_{c-state}}
 6:         move ← softMaxChoice(M_{c-state}, gains * b)
 7:         current-state ← play(c-state, move)
 8:         seq[ply] ← move
 9:         ply+ = 1
10:     end while
11:     return score(current-state), seq
12: end function
```

3.2   Nested Monte Carlo Search

NMCS [1] is a Monte Carlo Search algorithm that recursively calls lower level NMCS on children states of the current state in order to decide which move to play next, the lowest level of NMCS being a random playout, selecting uniformly the move to execute among the possible moves. A heuristic can be added to the playout move choices, and it is the case here with the biased growth playouts.

Algorithm 2 gives the NMCS algorithm, l is the nesting level and b the playout bias.

Algorithm 2. The NMCS algorithm.

```
 1: function NMCS(c-state, l, b)
 2:     if l = 0 then return playout(c-state, b)
 3:     else
 4:         best-score ← −∞
 5:         best-sequence ← []
 6:         ply ← 0
 7:         while c-state is not terminal do
 8:             for each move in M_{c-state} do
 9:                 n-st ← play(c-state, move)
10:                 (score, seq) ← NMCS(n-st, l − 1, b)
11:                 if score ≥ best-score then
12:                     best-score ← score
13:                     best-sequence[ply..] ← move + seq
14:                 end if
15:             end for
16:             next-move ← best-sequence[ply]
17:             ply ← ply + 1
18:             c-state ← play(c-state, next-move)
19:         end while
20:         return (best-score, best-sequence)
21:     end if
22: end function
```

3.3 Lazy Nested Monte Carlo Search

The lazy NMCS inherits its main features from the NMCS, but solves an obstacle encountered on this problem. Solving the 3D HP model with the NMCS requires using a level of 4 at least, however, it requires computing many 3 level NMCS, already very costly, one for each possible move the level 4 NMCS can make. The main idea behind the lazy NMCS is that there are moves that lead to low potential states, to do so, we estimate the potential of a state by launching a number of biased growth playouts and calculating the mean of their scores, then we compare that score to a threshold (relative to the number of moves already done) calculated from the previous estimations to decide if we want to expand the search tree from this state, or prune it. To update the pruning threshold tr, it is possible to use a mean, a median, or a max from the previous estimations, here we use the max as it gave the best results on these problems.

In the following pseudocode in Algorithm 3, p is the number of playouts used to evaluate a state and r is the ratio to the threshold a state will be pruned on. l is the nesting level and b is the playout bias.

From line 9 to line 14, the state is evaluated with the mean of p playouts.

From line 15 to line 17, the threshold list is extended on the first entry of a new molecule length, this step is not needed if the list is initialized with the right size from the start for problems we know the maximum number of moves that will be played.

From lines 18 to 120, the threshold is updated with the evaluation.

Algorithm 3. The Lazy NMCS algorithm.

```
1: tr ← []
2: function LNMCS(c-st, l, b, p, r)
3:     if level = 0 then return PLAYOUT(c-st, b)
4:     else
5:         best-score ← −∞
6:         best-sq ← []
7:         ply ← 0
8:         while c-st is not terminal do
9:             for each move in M_{c-state} do
10:                n-st ← play(c-st, move)
11:                for i in 0..p do
12:                    (playoutSc, _) ← playout(n-st, b)
13:                    es ← es + playoutSc/p
14:                end for
15:                if tr.length() < c-st.nbplay + 1 then
16:                    tr.push(0.0)
17:                end if
18:                if tr[c-state.nbplay] < es then
19:                    tr[c-state.nbplay] ← es
20:                end if
21:                if es < ratio ∗ tr[c-st.nbplay] then
22:                    (sc, sq) ←LNMCS(c.1, 0, b, p, r)
23:                else
24:                    (sc, sq) ←LNMCS(c.1, l − 1, b, p, r)
25:                end if
26:                if sc ≥ best-score then
27:                    best-score ← sc
28:                    best-sq[ply..] ← move + sq
29:                end if
30:            end for
31:            next-move ← best-sq[ply]
32:            ply ← ply + 1
33:            c-st ← play(c-st, next-move)
34:        end while
35:        return (best-score, best-sq)
36:    end if
37: end function
```

From lines 21 to 25, it is decided with the evaluation, the pruning ratio, and the corresponding threshold if the search will be costly or not.

As you can see there is only one FOR loop iterating over the moves in this implementation of the LNMCS, which means the evaluation is incomplete when the algorithm decides whether to prune the first branches or not. This is a minor flaw in this version of the algorithm and it is easily fixed by ulterior versions (along with other shortcomings). Nonetheless, the experiments were made with this "prototype" version of the algorithm.

4 Results

4.1 Lazy Nested Monte Carlo Search

Experimental Setup. We conducted experiments on the 10 molecules with 48 mers from the benchmark we can find in Holger's [16] and Hsu's [9] work, here on Table 1. -E* denotes (the opposite of) the speculated energy of the lowest energy state.

Table 1. The benchmark's molecules and their speculated lowest energy state

ID	molecule	-E*
1	HPHHPPHHHHPHHHPPHHPPHPH HHPHPHHPPHHPPPHPPPPPPPPHH	32
2	HHHHPHHPHHHHHPPHPPHHPPH PPPPPHPPHPPPHPPHHPPHHHHPH	34
3	PHPHHPHHHHHHPPHPHPPHPHH PHPHPPPHPPHHPPHHPPHPHPPHP	34
4	PHPHHPPHPHHHPPHHPHHPPPH HHHHPPHPHHPHPHPPPPHPPHPHP	33
5	PPHPPPHPHHHHPPHHHHPHHPH HHPPHPHPHPPHPPPPPPHHPHHPH	32
6	HHHPPPHHPHPHHPHHPHHPHPP PPPPPHPHPPHPPPHPPHHHHHHPH	32
7	PHPPPPHPHHHPHPHHHHPHHPH HPPPHPHPPPHHHHPPHHPPHHPPPH	32
8	PHHPHHHPHHHHPPHHHPPPPP HPHHPPHHPHPPPHHPHPHPHHPPP	31
9	PHPHPPPPHPHPHPPHPHHHHHH PPHHHPHPPHPHHPPHPHHHPPPPH	34
10	PHHPPPPPPHHPPPHHHPHPPHP HHPPHPPHPPHHPPHHHHHHPPHH	33

To obtain our results, we used the lazy NMCS with a timeout of 150 s, if the algorithm has not found a conformation with the lowest known energy before the end of the timeout then we restart the algorithm until that happens. In our experiments, the playout biased growth gives an immediate gain of 1 to any legal H-H connection, but also a penalty of −0.2 to the HP connections, this was made in order to incite the biased growth to keep a maximum of H mers open to future connections, we did not experiment on that variable.

Molecule 4 used a lazy NMCS with a threshold based on the mean of the evaluation playouts with the following parameters:

level	4
#eval playouts	10
pruning ratio	0.97
playout bias	20

The other molecules used a lazy NMCS with a threshold based on the best average from a batch of evaluation playouts with the following parameters:

level	5
#eval playouts	20
pruning ratio	0.9
playout bias	20

Results. Different methods of evaluation and pruning can greatly change the performance of the algorithm, and some methods can be ineffective on a set of molecules while being capable on another set (Table 2).

Table 2. Mean time and interquartile (in minutes) of LNMCS on the benchmark molecules to reach a state with the lowest state energy

ID	mean time	interquartile
1	5.5	5
2	12.5	15.5
3	10	14
4	20	25
5	10	10
6	+− 180	−
7	+− 60	−
8	13.5	12
9	+− 120	−
10	7	9

These results are displayed in minutes and were obtained on a 3.50GHz Intel core i5-6600K CPU, the lowest state energy are the -E* featured in Table 1.

Our LNMCS performed very poorly on molecules 6 and 7, we were not able to gather enough data to compute the statistics. This was unexpected since only molecules 4 and 9 are difficult for PERM (the state of the art chain growth algorithm) to solve according to Grassberger and Hsu's latest paper [9], and molecule 4 posed fewer problems. However, the lazy NMCS could attain the second best energy level very reliably in less than 150 s in half of the launches with both molecules.

LNMCS was also able to easily reach the second best level of energy on molecule 9 but could only reach the optimal state every 2 h approximately, that result was expected since PERM encounters difficulties with that molecule too.

4.2 Comparing LNMCS to Deep Reinforcement Learning in AlphaZero Style

Experimental Setup. Recent results on the HP model were brought to our attention in Deng et al's work [3]. Experiments were realized on 8 other HP strings in Table 3 using a neural network based Monte Carlo Search method, in AlphaZero's manner. To the best of our knowledge, this is a first for the HP model.

Table 3. The second benchmark's molecules and their speculated lowest energy state

ID	molecule	-E*
S1	HPHPPHHPHPPHPHHPPHPH	11
S2	HHPPHPPHPPHPPHPPHPPHPPHH	13
S3	PPHPPHHPPPPHHPPPPHHPPPPHH	9
S4	PPPHHPPHHPPPPPHHHHHHHPPHH PPPPHHPPHPP	18
S5	PPHPPHHPPHHPPPPPHHHHHHHH HPPPPPPHHPPHHPPHPPHHHHHH	31
S6	HHPHPHPHPHHHHPHPPPHPPPHPP PPHPPPHPPPHPHHHHPHPHPHPHH	31
S7	PPHHHPHHHHHHHHPPPHHHHHHHH HHPHPPPHHHHHHHHHHHHPPPP HHHHHHPHHPHP	52
S8	HHHHHHHHHHHHHPHPHPPHHPPHHP PHPPHHPPHHPPHPPHHPPHHPPHPHP HHHHHHHHHHHH	56

We launched our LNMCS with a threshold based on the best average from a batch of evaluation playouts with the same parameters as with most previous results:

level	5
#eval playouts	20
pruning ratio	0.9
playout bias	20

Table 4. Best scores obtained by LNMCS on the second benchmark molecules

ID	our -E*	LNMCS time to previous -E*	previous -E*
S1	11	30 s	11
S2	13	25 s	13
S3	9	5 s	9
S4	18	0.73 s	18
S5	31	103 s	31
S6	31	143 s	31
S7	54	14 s	52
S8	58	135 s	56

Results. In Table 4 we show that LNMCS is able to outperform this recent method as well.

Due to a typo on S6 in [3], molecule S6 was retrieved from [13]. The times displayed in Table 4 show approximately how much time is necessary to reach the previous lowest energy state for each molecule.

As you can see in Table 4, our LNMCS was able to very quickly get to the lowest know state energy and was even able to find new optimums for molecules S7 and S8. However, despite the LNMCS performing better, our own UCT with biased playouts is inferior to their UCT with the priors approach. We think using priors on the LNMCS could lead to even better results than the ones presented in this paper.

4.3   Other MCS Algorithms

We tried to solve The HP model with a variety of different Monte Carlo algorithms. We only applied these algorithms to the first molecule from the benchmark, the results presented in this section are only to give an idea of these algorithms' performances and do not necessarily reflect their potential on the HP model.

Nested Monte Carlo Search. The good performances of the NMCS [1] compared to the other algorithms presented in this section is what made us decide to try to improve it for this problem into the LNMCS: the NMCS was able to find the optimal value on the molecule in less than 10mn.

In Fig. 2 and Fig. 1 we compare performances of the level 5 NMCS and the level 5 LNMCS with a ratio of 0.9 on molecule 1, with both a playout bias of 20 over 20 runs with a 150 s timeout.

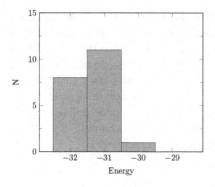

Fig. 1. Energy distribution with the Lazy NMCS

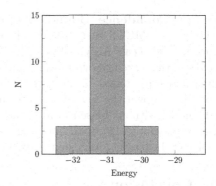

Fig. 2. Energy distribution with the NMCS

As you can see in Figs. 1 and 2, the LNMCS provides a substantial performance gain over the NMCS on this problem. Lowest energy conformations are way sparser than the second lowest energy conformations, being able to reach them 3 or 4 times as often is a great improvement.

Nested Rollout Policy Adaptation. The NRPA [12] is similar to the NMCS, the main difference is that the NRPA learns a policy to decide which move to play during playouts, that policy discovery is interesting for many problems which are too complex to implement a handmade policy (like we did here). On many problems the NRPA outperforms the NMCS, however, in this case it was not able to. The performance of the NRPA and GNRPA [2] are widely dependent on the move representations, here it is the number corresponding to the number of residues already placed and its direction and NRPA and GNRPA with a bias of 20 were not able to reach the optimal energies (-28 or -29 for the GNRPA when -32 is the best known). Other moves representations were tried, using the last few previous moves instead of the number of residues already placed for example, but none were able to provide better performances. Our inability to obtain good results with NRPA does not mean it is impossible to solve this problem with it.

Greedy Best First Search with Playouts. The Greedy BFS [5] is a simple search algorithm that uses a ranked list of the nodes to open according to their scores given by an evaluation function. Iteratively, the Greedy BFS opens the best node from the list and launches the evaluation function on every child of this node to insert them in the ranked list. Here we evaluate the children with their results with one or multiple playouts. This method converges rapidly to a "good enough" solution (a local minimum), -29 when the best known is -32 on molecule 1, but then improves very little, it is due to a large number of good scoring states that do not lead to an optimal solution, making the search too exhaustive. Pruning the search tree could improve the results of this method.

Upper Confidence Bounds Applied to Trees. UCT [11] is the most widely used MCTS method, namely in outstanding works like alphazero [15] and AstraZeneca's AiZynthFinder [6]. It iteratively starts from the initial state, go down the search tree following a formula, and launches layouts once it finds an unvisited state, based on the results of each playout, the value used to determine how to go down the search tree are updated. UCT does not work well on the HP model without biased growth (achieving about the same scores as a single biased playout, -18), with biased growth it achieves scores around $-28/-29$ on molecule 1, like the other non-NMCS algorithms discussed here.

5 Conclusion

In this paper, we proposed a new (prototype) Monte Carlo Search algorithm that has the advantage to be easier to implement than most usual HP model algorithms and is applicable to more problems. It is also shown to be an improvement on the NMCS algorithm for this specific problem and to outperform novel neural network based methods. We have applied LNMCS to other problems, and it has not been outperformed by any other algorithm on any of these problems yet, we also made slight changes to the algorithm towards a final version (hence the use of the term "prototype" here) in papers soon to be published.

In future works, we aim to apply LNMCS to more problems and find ways to improve its performance. We also aim to use a prior neural network to further improve LNMCS performance on the HP model problem.

You can find our codes for the HP model, the LNMCS, and the other algorithms here: https://github.com/RoucairolMilo/HPmodelICCCI

References

1. Cazenave, T.: Nested Monte-Carlo search. In: Boutilier, C. (ed.) IJCAI, pp. 456–461 (2009)
2. Cazenave, T.: Generalized nested rollout policy adaptation. In: Cazenave, T., Teytaud, O., Winands, M.H.M. (eds.) MCS 2020. CCIS, vol. 1379, pp. 71–83. Springer, Cham (2021). https://doi.org/10.1007/978-3-030-89453-5_6
3. Deng, H., Yuan, X., Tian, Y., Hu, J.: Neural-augmented two-stage Monte Carlo tree search with over-sampling for protein folding in HP model. IEEJ Trans. Electr. Electron. Eng. **17**(5), 685–694 (2022)
4. Dill, K.A.: Theory for the folding and stability of globular proteins. Biochemistry **24**(6), 1501–1509 (1985)
5. Doran, J.E., Michie, D.: Experiments with the graph traverser program. Proc. Royal Soc. London. Ser. A. Math. Phys. Sci. **294**(1437), 235–259 (1966)
6. Genheden, S., Thakkar, A., Chadimová, V., Reymond, J.L., Engkvist, O., Bjerrum, E.: AiZynthFinder: a fast, robust and flexible open-source software for retrosynthetic planning. J. Cheminformatics **12**(1), 70 (2020). https://doi.org/10.1186/s13321-020-00472-1. https://jcheminf.biomedcentral.com/articles/10.1186/s13321-020-00472-1
7. Grassberger, P.: Pruned-enriched Rosenbluth method: simulations of polymers of chain length up to 1 000 000. Phys. Rev. E **56**(3), 3682 (1997)

8. Gros, F., Gilbert, W., Hiatt, H.H., Attardi, G., Spahr, P.F., Watson, J.D.: Molecular and biological characterization of messenger RNA. In: Cold Spring Harbor Symposia on Quantitative Biology vol. 26, pp. 111–132. Cold Spring Harbor Laboratory Press (1961)
9. Hsu, H.P., Grassberger, P.: A review of Monte Carlo simulations of polymers with PERM. J. Stat. Phys. **144**(3), 597–637 (2011)
10. Jumper, J., et al.: Highly accurate protein structure prediction with AlphaFold. Nature **596**(7873), 583–589 (2021)
11. Kocsis, L., Szepesvári, C.: Bandit based Monte-Carlo planning. In: Fürnkranz, J., Scheffer, T., Spiliopoulou, M. (eds.) ECML 2006. LNCS (LNAI), vol. 4212, pp. 282–293. Springer, Heidelberg (2006). https://doi.org/10.1007/11871842_29
12. Rosin, C.D.: Nested rollout policy adaptation for Monte Carlo tree search. In: IJCAI 2011, Proceedings of the 22nd International Joint Conference on Artificial Intelligence, pp. 649–654 (2011)
13. Santana, R., Larrañaga, P., Lozano, J.A.: Protein folding in simplified models with estimation of distribution algorithms. IEEE Trans. Evol. Comput. **12**(4), 418–438 (2008)
14. Silver, D., et al.: Mastering the game of go with deep neural networks and tree search. Nature **529**, 484–489 (2016)
15. Silver, D., et al.: Mastering chess and shogi by self-play with a general reinforcement learning algorithm. arXiv:1712.01815 [cs] (2017), https://arxiv.org/abs/1712.01815, arXiv: 1712.01815
16. Thachuk, C., Shmygelska, A., Hoos, H.H.: A replica exchange Monte Carlo algorithm for protein folding in the HP model. BMC Bioinform. **8**(1), 342 (2007)
17. Wüst, T., Landau, D.P.: Optimized Wang-Landau sampling of lattice polymers: ground state search and folding thermodynamics of HP model proteins. J. Chem. Phys. **137**(6), 064903 (2012)

Ground Truth Data Generator in Automotive Infrared Sensor Vision Problems Using a Minimum Set of Operations

Sorin Valcan[1,2]([✉])[iD] and Mihail Gaianu[1,2][iD]

[1] West University of Timisoara, Timisoara, Romania
sorin.valcan96@e-uvt.ro
[2] UX Department, Continental Automotive Romania, Timisoara, Romania

Abstract. In image vision we call a ground truth data generator any kind of software tool or algorithm that contributes in a semi or fully automatic way to the extraction of ground truth labels from a data set. The main purpose of such automation is to reduce as much as possible the manual effort of labeling a big number of frames. Above all, such a generator must be precise and avoid false positives because its results shall be used as training data for neural networks. In this paper we present a minimum set of operations required for fully automatic generation of labels from existing grayscale images in automotive image vision problems such as eye detection or traffic sign recognition. Multiple configurations based on these operations have been created to fit various desired features. We shifted the focus from algorithms development for ground truth data generation to understanding the particularities of an object or sign in the grayscale spectrum and defining correct configurations to detect them. We will present these configurations and the results obtained in the ground truth data generation process.

Keywords: Object detection · Driver monitoring · Safety features · Ground truth data · Infrared sensors

1 Introduction

In our days neural networks models have become a popular solution in image vision problems due to their good capability of learning patterns and good processing performance in the inference phase. It has become much easier to train a network to learn a desired feature with all its small or big variations than writing a classic algorithm that should somehow incorporate all the possible ways and specific shapes in which that feature could appear in an image. Such a complicated algorithm not only has big chances to become computationally inefficient, but writing the algorithm itself can be costly and take a long period of time.

The general adoption of neural networks as a satisfying solution has shifted the focus from algorithms development to the new trend of data science where

© The Author(s), under exclusive license to Springer Nature Switzerland AG 2023
N. T. Nguyen et al. (Eds.): ICCCI 2023, CCIS 1864, pp. 632–644, 2023.
https://doi.org/10.1007/978-3-031-41774-0_50

most of the effort is allocated in data acquisition and preparation before the neural network training process. Data acquisition usually refers of obtaining the images either from some already existing sources or going out and recording as many images as needed with the desired object or sign.

Data preprocessing is a much more complicated area because it involves tasks like labeling which means marking each image with the location of the correct detection, cleanup which can involve some processes of removing outliers or irrelevant samples and data sets generation for training and testing where it is very important to test the model on data not used in the training phase.

From all these tasks involved in the new data science approach the most repetitive and stressful for one individual is the labeling process. Here a person or a team of persons need to focus on marking images for multiple hours in a very repetitive process which becomes tiring and results in human errors. Because of these natural problems, usually the solution is to double check the labeling work which is hoped to remove partially or totally the existing errors but which is in no way different to the initial process of labeling.

Our work is focused on removing the manual work of labeling data in image vision problems with experiments performed in the automotive area of driver monitoring systems. Because of the complicated nature of the automotive systems, we work with images from infrared sensors that guarantee visibility at night which results in processing on grayscale images.

1.1 Related Work

To approach the fully automation of the labeling process the solution will definitely be found in the area of algorithms that perform the detection considered as ground truth labels. Because of this, one could take multiple eye detection implementations ([1–6]) with proven results and use their outputs as training and testing data for neural networks.

There have been work done in the area of semi automation for the labeling process with interactive helping tools ([7–9]) developed in order to ease the manual work. This approach is usually the preferred way to go for various tasks but not necessarily in the automotive or medical industry where the resulted data sets are required to be manual labeled by experts and verified multiple times in order to make sure a future neural network will be trained with correct data.

Another approach to mention is the generation of synthetic ground truth data using either generative neural networks or other specific software [10]. Not many experiments have been performed in the automotive or medical area using synthetic generated data since it is hard to believe such images could truly contain the necessary details from the real world.

Deep learning techniques have had success across a multitude of domains, including human trajectory prediction in the context of autonomous vehicles ([11]). In trajectory prediction, human behavior is often modeled using discrete modes that can represent high-level maneuvers like accelerating, braking, and turning ([12]).

2   Problem Description

2.1   Current Proved Method

The main purpose of this work is a proof of concept in training neural networks for face feature detection using an existing data set with drivers from an automotive driver monitoring project without performing any kind of manual labeling. The data set contains more than 2 million frames with over 100 subjects from different ethnicity: Caucasian, African, Asian and Latino.

To avoid the manual labeling effort we implemented a very precise eye detection algorithm in [13] that was mainly focused on accuracy of detection. This resulted in a very big number of frames where eye labels were missing but the existing labels were correct in 99% of cases.

Using this generated ground truth data we trained neural networks for eye detection and showed a huge improvement [14]. By taking the very correct and very inconsistent automatically generated data, the resulted neural network managed to be very correct and much more consistent. The machine learning model managed to overcome the limits of the initial algorithm and detected frames and subjects that were not observed in the fully automatic labeling phase.

This process was then extended to detect other facial features like nostrils and mouth using an extension of the initial ground truth generator for eyes and the same drivers data set [15].

The main difference between the algorithm in [13] and other detection methods presented in the related work is that our approach was to focus very much on the accuracy of the generated ground truth data. We preferred to leave recordings with 80–100% of frames not marked but make sure the existing labels were correct. This reduces a lot the wrong data present in neural network training. In case of a full labeling on all frames many of them would be redundant anyway because the driver is looking forward and not moving for long sequences.

2.2   A General Ground Truth Data Generator Approach

The thing to do now is to generalize the proposed method from above and use it in other detections. If one would like to detect traffic signs using a neural network, a new ground truth data generation algorithm would need to be implemented. It is the same for any detection required in image vision.

In this paper we want to remove the necessity of algorithm development in the fully automatic ground truth data generation process by proposing a minimal set of operations performed directly on the grayscale images and combination of resulted maps to perform various detections.

Ones remaining job is to create a set of rules based on these operations to match the desired feature to be detected in the data set with enough strictness to avoid wrong labels.

Performing detections in the grayscale spectrum can be much harder compared to an RGB image. In RGB to detect eyes one can use the color of the skin, the white of the sclera surrounded by skin and the deep black of the pupil. To detect traffic signs, one can use the colours of the specific signs to directly point an algorithm in the interest area.

In grayscale everything is just a variation of intensities from black to white which can make an algorithm output the desired feature in places one could hardly believe because the color variations are the same even if for the human eye looking at the image it makes no sense.

It remains the job of the individual creating the set of rules to fully understand the characteristics of the desired feature in the grayscale image and constrain the detection as much as possible in order to create a data set of ground truth data that has good accuracy labels and without significant false positives.

3 Methods

In this section we will show the minimum set of operations we use in our ground truth data generation. These are the base operations one should use in a set of rules to define how the hues of gray in a grayscale image shape the object to be detected.

3.1 Average Comparisons Operation

The average comparisons is the operation used to define different shapes that characterize an object. The inputs of this operation are defined as:

$$G = (g_{ij})_{0 \leq i < h, 0 \leq j < w} \tag{1}$$

$$B = \{(x_0, y_0, w_0, h_0), (x_1, y_1, w_1, h_1)...(x_m, y_m, w_m, h_m)\} \tag{2}$$

$$C = \{(bb1_0, bb2_0, ct_0, f_0), (bb1_1, bb2_1, ct_1, f_1)...(bb1_n, bb2_n, ct_n, f_n)\}$$
$$0 \leq bb1 < m, 0 \leq bb2 < m, bb1 \neq bb2 \tag{3}$$

$$O = (x, y)_{0 \leq x < h, 0 \leq y < w} \tag{4}$$

Here G is a bidimensional matrix representing the grayscale input image where detection should be performed. B is a set of m bounding boxes that together will traverse the entire grayscale image. For each one, the average value of the pixels inside will be computed. The coordinates of the bounding boxes are relative to the pixel coordinate where the processing is happening at a specific moment.

Using the averages computed with the bounding boxes defined in B, C represents a set of n comparison tests. Here bb1 and bb2 indexes point to the desired bounding boxes from B, ct is the comparison type chosen from {ZONE1_GREATER, ZONE2_GREATER, ZONE12_EQUAL} and f is the factor used as minimum (for ct as greater) or maximum (for ct as equal) difference between the two averages to pass the comparison test.

The last input O represents the pixel coordinate in the output map where the valid passing of all comparisons tests in C will be marked with white.

The operation is performed as follows, for each pixel location in the image G:

- The relative coordinates of the bounding boxes in B are converted to absolute coordinates in G
- For each bounding box in B, the average pixel value inside it is computed
- For each comparison test in C, the test is performed
- In case all tests in C are valid, the coordinate O will be set to white in the output map or black otherwise

The output of this operation is a black and white map of the same dimension with the input grayscale image G which contains white for locations where all the comparisons succeeded and black otherwise.

One can use this operation to define the shape in the grayscale spectrum of the object that needs to be detected. Multiple average comparisons should be defined for one desired object in order to extract as many different characteristics as possible.

Each average comparison can output white pixels in both the location where the desired feature exist or doesn't exist. This is because a similar shape of gray colours can be found in different places on image. The following operations performed on the maps resulted from the average comparisons should help unify the detected shapes in a logical way so that only locations that truly contain the feature will remain on the map.

3.2 Map Existence Operation

The map existence operation is creating a relation between two average comparisons resulted maps. The following inputs are necessary for this operation:

$$A = (a_{ij})_{0 \leq i < h, 0 \leq j < w} \in \{0, 255\} \tag{5}$$

$$B = (b_{ij})_{0 \leq i < h, 0 \leq j < w} \in \{0, 255\} \tag{6}$$

$$S = (x, y, w, h) \tag{7}$$

Inputs A and B represent two black and white maps resulted from the average comparisons. The white pixels (value 255) will represent locations where a specific characteristic of an object has been detected. S represents a bounding box with relative coordinates to the current processed location.

The map existence operation performs the following steps:

- Each pixel in A with white value is taken into consideration
- The relative bounding box S is converted to absolute values based on each white pixel in A

– If B contains at least one white pixel inside the bounding box S, the respective white pixel in A will remain unchanged, otherwise it will become black

The output of this operation is the altered map A which should contain only the white points respecting the existence rule of characteristic B.

This operation has the purpose to create a logical correlation between two detected characteristics. Characteristic A may be detected in multiple locations on the grayscale image but it has greater chances to truly represent the desired object in the image if characteristic B is present around in bounding box S. This operation helps to remove the unwanted detections of A with help of other characteristics represented by B.

3.3   Map Non-existence Operation

The map non-existence operation is defined by the same inputs, outputs and rules as the existence operation defined in Sect. 3.2. The only difference here is that a white pixel in map A will remain unchanged if map B does not contain any white pixel inside bounding box S. This operation helps to ensure a specific characteristic B is not present anywhere inside bounding box S of map A.

3.4   Max White Shape Selection Operation

This operation is basically the capacity to iterate through a black and white map and keep only the white spot with a defined maximum number of points. This is usually the final operation performed on a map, to determine the final location of the desired object as the biggest white spot available. In case the specific map reached the end of operations and does not contain any white pixel, it means the object has not been detected in the image.

3.5   Set of Operations for Detection

To create a set of operations to perform a detection, one should first extract the main characteristic of the desired object using Sect. 3.1. As many bounding boxes and comparison rules must be added to constrain the algorithm detect the characteristic in as few locations as possible. In case of a too complicated or strict average comparison rule, the object may only be detected in idealistic scenarios which should be avoided.

Once the characteristics have been extracted using Sect. 3.1, the next step is to add as many Sects. 3.2 and 3.3 operations between the extracted maps to constrain the algorithm to keep only the white areas where the characteristics have big chances to truly represent the desired object.

Usually at the end, but not necessarily then, the Sect.3.4 operation should be performed to select the final position of the detection. If one considers necessary, this operation can be used at any time on any characteristic map computed between other operations.

4   Experiments

In this section we will present some experiments and sets of rules created to perform detections. Our main target is to generate ground truth data for face features compared to the previous algorithm described in [13]. Additional to this, we will present detections performed for other signs and objects to prove the utility of this algorithms in other areas.

Because of limited space available here we will only present the full definition for one average comparison operation to exemplify it's usage. The other rules will have a general explanation provided.

4.1   Eye Detection

In [13] we presented a ground truth data generator used for eye detection on recordings with drivers. In this paper we are performing a similar ground truth data generation but without using a complex and very specific algorithm. Here we created two sets of rules using operations from Sect. 3, one set for left eye and another for the right eye.

Table 1. Average comparison operation for left eye outer corner detection

Information	Details
Operation Type	Average comparisons
Bounding boxes	0:(30,6,5,5), 1:(35,9,5,5), 2:(40,12,5,5), 3:(45,15,5,5), 4:(20,16,5,5), 5:(25,19,5,5), 6:(30,22,5,5), 7:(35,25,5,5), 8:(20,0,5,5), 9:(25,0,5,5), 10:(15,25,5,5), 11:(20,25,5,5), 12:(25,25,5,5), 13:(30,25,5,5), 14:(0,36,10,10), 15:(10,36,10,10), 16:(20,36,10,10), 17:(30,36,10,10), 18:(0,46,10,10), 19:(10,46,10,10), 20:(20,46,10,10), 21:(30,46,10,10), 22:(45,21,5,5), 23:(45,26,5,5), 24:(45,31,5,5)
Comparison tests	(0,4,Z1G,3), (1,5,Z1G,3), (2,6,Z1G,3), (3,7,Z1G,3), (8,4,Z1G,3), (8,5,Z1G,3), (8,6,Z1G,3), (8,7,Z1G,3), (9,4,Z1G,3), (9,5,Z1G,3), (9,6,Z1G,3), (9,7,Z1G,3), (0,10,Z1G,3), (0,11,Z1G,3), (0,12,Z1G,3), (0,13,Z1G,3), (14,4,Z1G,3), (15,5,Z1G,3), (16,6,Z1G,3), (17,7,Z1G,3), (18,4,Z1G,3), (19,5,Z1G,3), (20,6,Z1G,3), (21,7,Z1G,3), (22,4,Z1G,3), (23,4,Z1G,3), (24,4,Z1G,3)
Output location	(40, 19)

In Table 1 are presented the bounding boxes and comparison tests used to mark the area of the left eye outer corner. These bounding boxes iterate on the entire input image and mark with white pixels only the locations where the shape described in the table is present. A visualisation of the resulted map is presented in Fig. 1.

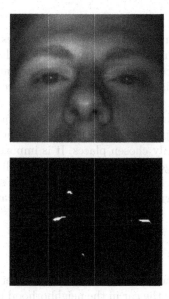

Fig. 1. Visualisation of map resulted with rules in Table 1

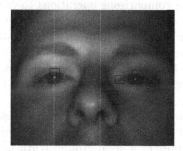

Fig. 2. Extracted characteristics for detection of left eye

It can be observed the inner corner of the right eye is detected with the same pattern of the left eye outer rules. There is also a marked area on the eyebrow and another one at the nostrils. The correct location of the left eye outer corner is kept using other characteristics presented in Fig. 2.

We also use the upper shape of the right eye in order to validate the marked area of the left eye. This is done with the map existence and non existence operations from 3.2 and 3.3. There are in total 6 average comparison, 7 map non-existence, 7 map existence and 1 max white shape selection operations used to detect the left eye. A similar mirror process is performed for the right eye.

With the ground truth data generator from [13] there have been 397.906 frames with both eyes labeled. The generator in the current paper is capable of detecting the eyes independent from one another resulting in frames where only one eye is marked. With this minimal set of operations we generated 313.953

labels for left eye and 361.065 labels for the right eye. It can also be noted that the problems with recordings where drivers wear glasses and a bright reflection is present does not exist anymore. Those problems were described in [13]. The rules added for eye detection constrain the algorithm so much to fit on the correct spots that glasses frame have no longer a bad influence like frequent jumping of the detection.

The generated labels have contained the eye in more than 96% of the cases. The wrong detections appear on the nose between the eyes, at a corner of the mouth or in other randomly chosen places. It is important to specify that most of the wrong labels are generated on a relative small number of drivers with some specific problematic facial characteristics for the set of rules. We were able to generate some sets of rules that work very well on most persons in the data set.

4.2   Give Way Traffic Sign Detection

To demonstrate other area of utility of this minimal set of operations, we took a grayscale sensor and drove the car in the neighborhood to create a few recordings containing the give way traffic sign.

We created 3 average comparisons operations to extract the characteristics highlighted in Fig. 3. Those were followed by 2 map existence operations to check the 3 characteristics are present around one another and kept the maximum white shape as a valid detection.

As presented in Fig. 4 we managed to generated ground truth data for this traffic with 99% accuracy. There were only a few wrong bounding boxes detected on a pedestrian crossing.

Those rules were not capable to detect the traffic sign on absolutely every frame. It only generated data on approximately 30% of the cases where it was present which should represent a good ground truth basis for the training of a neural network.

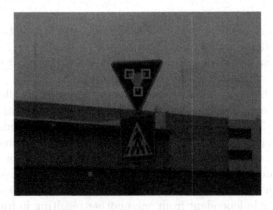

Fig. 3. Extracted characteristics of the give way traffic sign

Fig. 4. Examples of ground truth generated data for give way traffic sign

4.3   West University of Timisoara Logo Detection

To demonstrate another possible usage for the minimal set of operations presented in this paper, we created a minimal set of operations to detect the logo of the West University of Timisoara in various places in our office or even on a picture with the university building that is publicly available at a search on the internet.

To detect this logo, we create 4 average comparison and 3 map existence operations to check the grouping together of the 4 characteristics. Figure 5 present some outputs from our experiment.

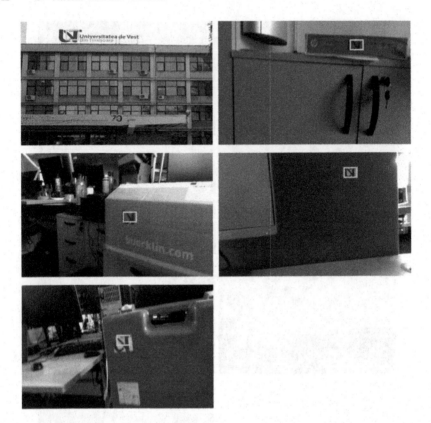

Fig. 5. Examples of ground truth generated data for the logo of the West University of Timisoara

The detection of the logo was correct in 99% of cases which represented around 20% of the frames where it was visible. A very few wrong labels were generated on a keyboard in the office.

5   Discussion

The process of generating ground truth data through manual work implies a tiring and repetitive process that leads to a lot of subjectivity and errors from the individuals involved in it. To train a neural network a relative small part of the entire data truly require labels, with the machine learning algorithms capable to learn the desired feature in a very general way.

The automation of the labeling process can start from existing algorithms. The necessity of writing a different algorithm for each new feature can be replaced by a very good understanding of the patterns involved in the problem.

Work done in [14] and [15] support the opinion that automatically generated ground truth data can train very good neural networks.

In this paper we presented detections based on the same minimal set of operations. Are this operations enough? New operations may be necessary for more complicated patterns. However, a basis for a solid automation that removes manual work and algorithm development in the labeling process may take shape with such experiments.

6 Conclusion

This paper presented a minimal set of operations that anyone can use to generate ground truth data in an grayscale image vision problem. Multiple use cases were presented with applications in automotive industry but not only.

We wanted to present a proof of concept where no manual work is required in image vision problems. Previously available experiments together with the automation presented in this paper should help simplify the work of data scientists.

References

1. Swirski, L., Bulling, A., Anddodgson, N.: Ro-bust real-time pupil tracking in highly off-axis images. In: Proceedings of the ETRA (2012)
2. Fuhl, W., Eivazi, S., Hosp, B., Eivazi, A., Rosenstiel, W., Kasneci, E.: BORE: boosted-oriented edge optimization for robust, real time remote pupil center detection. In: Eye Tracking Research and Applications, ETRA, p. 12. (2018)
3. Fuhl, W., Kübler, T.C., Hospach, D., Bringmann, O., Rosenstiel, W., Kasneci, E.: Ways of improving the precision of eye tracking data: controlling the influence of dirt and dust on pupil detection. J. Eye Mov. Res. **10**, 3 (2017)
4. Fuhl, W., Santini, T., Kübler, T.C., Kasneci, E.: ElSe: ellipse selection for robust pupil detection in real-world environments. In: Proceedings of the Ninth Biennial ACM Symposium on Eye Tracking Research & Applications (ETRA), pp. 123–130 (2016)
5. Gu, H., Su, G., Du, C.: Feature points extraction from faces. In: Image and Vision Computing New Zealand. https://citeseerx.ist.psu.edu/viewdoc/download? doi=10.1.1.110.519&rep=rep1&type=pdf
6. Paul, S.K., Uddin, M.S., Bouakaz, S.: Face recognition using eyes, nostrils and mouth features. In: 16th International Conference Computer and Information Technology, pp. 117–120 (2014). https://doi.org/10.1109/ICCITechn.2014.6997378
7. Demirkus, M., Clark, J.J., Arbel, T.: Robust semi-automatic head pose labeling for real-world face video sequences. Multimed. Tools Appl. **70**, 495–523 (2014). https://doi.org/10.1007/s11042-012-1352-1
8. Tian, Y., Liu, W., Xiao, R., Wen, F., Tang, X.: A Face Annotation Framework with Partial Clustering and Interactive Labeling. In: IEEE Conference on Computer Vision and Pattern Recognition, pp. 1–8 (2007). https://doi.org/10.1109/CVPR. 2007.383282
9. Le, V., Brandt, J., Lin, Z., Bourdev, L., Huang, T.S.: Interactive facial feature localization. In: Fitzgibbon, A., Lazebnik, S., Perona, P., Sato, Y., Schmid, C. (eds.) ECCV 2012. LNCS, vol. 7574, pp. 679–692. Springer, Heidelberg (2012). https://doi.org/10.1007/978-3-642-33712-3_49

10. Świrski , L., Dodgson, N.: Rendering synthetic ground truth images for eye tracker evaluation. In: Proceedings of the Symposium on Eye Tracking Research and Applications (2014). https://doi.org/10.1145/2578153.2578188
11. Leon, F., Gavrilescu, M., A review of tracking and trajectory prediction methods for autonomous driving. Mathematics **9**(6), 37 (2021). Article number 660. https://doi.org/10.3390/math9060660
12. Salzmann, T., Ivanovic, B., Chakravarty, P., Pavone, M.: Trajectron++: dynamically-feasible trajectory forecasting with heterogeneous data. In: Vedaldi, A., Bischof, H., Brox, T., Frahm, J.-M. (eds.) ECCV 2020. LNCS, vol. 12363, pp. 683–700. Springer, Cham (2020). https://doi.org/10.1007/978-3-030-58523-5_40
13. Valcan, S., Gaianu, M.: Ground truth data generator for eye location on infrared driver recordings. J. Imaging **7**, 162 (2021). https://doi.org/10.3390/jimaging7090162
14. Valcan, S., Gaianu, M.: Eye detection for drivers using convolutional neural networks with automatically generated ground truth data. In: 2022 24th International Symposium on Symbolic and Numeric Algorithms for Scientific Computing (SYNASC) (2022)
15. Valcan, S., Gaianu, M.: Nostrils and mouth detection for drivers using convolutional neural networks with automatically generated ground truth data. In: 9th Annual Conference on Computational Science & Computational Intelligence (CSCI 2022) (2022)

Theoretical and Empirical Testing of the Randomness of a Quantum Random Number Generator with Quantum Entanglement

Piotr Paweł Jóźwiak[✉] [iD]

Wrocław University of Science and Technology, Wrocław, Poland
piotr.jozwiak@pwr.edu.pl

Abstract. The quality of random numbers is directly related to the quality of cryptographic systems. Algorithmic methods of obtaining random numbers are slowly becoming insufficiently secure given the advent of soon commercially available quantum computers. The incremental power that quantum computers will offer will make it possible to break currently used cryptographic systems. The answer to this is the need to develop random number generators that are free of any kind of transitive phenomena. Much hope is placed in quantum random number sources due to their probabilistic nature. This paper discusses two complementary methods of testing a quantum random number source - empirical and theoretical testing. The presented concept of random number generation based on quantum entanglement makes it possible to perform not only empirical testing, but, fundamentally more importantly, also theoretical testing based on the Bell-CHSH inequality breaking test. This paper presents a proposal for a QRNG quality measure using photon entanglement levels. Empirical methods for randomness testing based on statistical hypothesis testing and their interpretation are also discussed.

Keywords: random numbers · test · quantum random number generator · quantum entanglement

1 Introduction

For more than decades, the issue of random number generation has been an important subject of scientific research. Today, the need for high-performance random number generators is even more urgent than it was a dozen years ago. This is a direct result of the increasingly advanced research into developing a quantum computer. In 2019, Google announced that it had successfully developed a quantum computer that realizes the goal of quantum supremacy [2–4] over classical silicon processors. As evidence, computational results were presented in which a computational task estimated to require 10000 computing years was solved in 200 s on a quantum processor [1]. As can be seen from the above example, the scale of problems that can be easily solved using quantum computers incomparably exceeds the capabilities of classical computers.

N. T. Nguyen et al. (Eds.): ICCCI 2023, CCIS 1864, pp. 645–657, 2023.
https://doi.org/10.1007/978-3-031-41774-0_51

While in the initial phases access to novel quantum computers will be limited for financial reasons, in the near future quantum solutions will begin to displace classical supercomputing centers. It will become possible to perform research requiring significant computing power, as well as to break various types of IT security systems including cryptography.

In view of the above, the need to obtain truly random number sequences to maintain the security of cryptographic systems becomes obvious. Only such numbers can ensure that any fast quantum computer will not be able to break a cipher using strings derived from truly random number generators. Undoubtedly, for such a situation to occur, one-time pad key-based cryptography must be used [18].

In the context of random number generation, the term 'random' is also used as a synonym for independent, unpredictable and unique distribution. The question of whether a probabilistic model can give an accurate description of reality is a philosophical question, directly related to the question of whether the universe is deterministic or not. In this context, it does not seem possible to give an answer that would satisfy everyone. On the other hand, there are chaotic processes in nature, such as radioactive decay or thermal noise in a transistor, which allow the development of random generators whose behavior is consistent with the expectations placed on true randomness [7]. Particularly good sources of random numbers are generators using quantum mechanics phenomena, which fundamentally provide unpredictability and randomness according to the Copenhagen interpretation [11]. The experimentally confirmed projection of the wave function, which is a linear combination of basis vectors representing classical states onto these basis vectors (otherwise known as the wave function collapse constituting the quantum information-destroying measurement), named after one of the co-authors of quantum mechanics, the von Neumann projection allows one to conclude that quantum measurement is intrinsically absolutely random [12]. It is in this phenomenon that the possibility of obtaining high-quality random number generators is seen.

2   Theoretical Versus Empirical Testing of Randomness

Generating good quality strings is not an easy issue, thus demonstrating the level of randomness of a given generator also poses many problems.

The best approach to testing random number generators is to analyze the design of the generator operation. In this case, it does not matter whether it is an algorithmic or physical generator. Theoretical testing involves examining the generator and demonstrating its weaknesses based on its design or operating principle. Knuth calls these **theoretical tests** [5]. Of course, they do not exhaust the need for further research on the generator in question, but this approach gives a better understanding of the method being generated, and thus may show weaknesses that need to be further tested on, e.g. statistically. Unfortunately, this method is often very difficult to carry out, as there can be problems in selecting mathematical tools to carry out tests and proving formalisms. Sometimes the difficulty encountered may also be insurmountable, as a result of using a physical process that does not lend itself easily to mathematical description or research approaches. Researchers around the world use various quantum mechanics phenomena to generate random numbers because of its probabilistic nature. It is the probabilistic description of the phenomena of quantum mechanics, in this case, that provides the foundation for the theoretical testing necessary for randomness. In the case of theoretical testing of the randomness of mathematical algorithms used to generate random numbers, e.g. the Linear Congruential Generator (LCG) [5], a mathematical proof is sought to demonstrate, for example, the cyclicity of the generated sequences. Thus, it is difficult to speak of unpredictability or uniqueness in such a situation. This is possible due to the fact that any mathematical algorithm determines successive states in a deterministic manner. We find a similar observation in the case of descriptions of phenomena of classical physics. These are fundamentally deterministic, although they have an additional advantage over mathematical algorithms, in the form of the difficulty of writing down a formal record of the phenomenon in question or of measuring all the variables affecting the dynamics of the phenomenon in question. Quantum mechanics simplifies this problem, so to speak, because it itself has a probabilistic description and the fundamental uniqueness of the processes taking place. There is no way within quantum mechanics to reproduce the state of a system that has been measured at a given point in time. Thus, the theoretical testing of quantum random number generators can be reduced to the problem of demonstrating the occurrence of a quantum phenomenon in a given generator. However, not every mechanism of quantum mechanics as of today can be easily confirmed.

Because there are many difficulties in theoretical testing, the most common approach used to test generators is **empirical testing** [5], which uses statistical methods to assess randomness. Each such test examines the quality of the randomness of the data from a specific point of view by testing certain statistical characteristics, such as the frequency of singularities or m-bit blocks in the number sequence under test. Most empirical randomness tests are based on statistical hypothesis testing. Individual tests compare certain characteristics of the data with an expected test statistic that is pre-computed for random infinite sequences. In this context, randomness is a probabilistic property and can be characterized and described in terms of probability [6]. This is due to the fact that even a good random number generator produces sequences with characteristics that differ significantly from the expected values in the tests. With this approach, it is not possible to distinguish whether a given 'bad' sequence was obtained from a faulty generator or whether this sequence came from a good generator by chance. In an empirical study of randomness, randomness is expressed as the probability that a perfect random number generator would have produced a sequence with the same or lower quality of randomness than those exhibited by the sequence under analysis.

Unfortunately, with an empirical approach, it is not possible to develop a single statistical test that would confidently examine all relevant characteristics of a sequence in terms of assessing its randomness. Each test focuses on a specific single characteristic. Therefore, in order to be able to assess the quality of a generator with greater certainty, it has to be sampled by a whole set of statistical tests that are chosen to examine different properties of randomness, unpredictability, chaos, etc. Such groups of tests are encapsulated in so-called test batteries. There are many solutions available on the market in the form of libraries of randomness tests. The most popular of these are: NIST Statistical Test [8] - 15 statistical tests; Diehard/Dieharder [9] developed by Georg Marsaglia and refined by Robert Brown, and consisting of about 30 tests; TestU01 [10] implemented at the University of Montreal and consisting of 9 testing modules, where each module has several to a dozen tests.

While theoretical tests are much more certain to prove the randomness of a given source, simultaneous statistical testing should not be abandoned. In order to obtain the highest possible confidence in the quality of the generator, both classes of tests should be performed simultaneously. This is particularly important in the case of quantum random number sources, where the quantum source itself is indisputably random, however, implementation errors when measuring the eigenstates of observables easily introduce a deterministic component, called bias, into the resulting number sequence. This is where statistical testing makes it possible to detect such faults.

3 Statistical Testing of Randomness

Empirical randomness testing uses various types of statistical tests to examine randomness based on hypothesis testing. Generally, in this type of testing, we are formulating null hypothesis H_0, which generally reads: *the sequence under test is random*. Directly related to the definition of the null hypothesis is the alternative hypothesis H_1, which takes the opposite claim to H_0, namely that: *the sequence under test is not random*. Initially, the position is taken that the null hypothesis is true and, on the basis of a given statistical test, an attempt is made to show that it is not. If the test is confirmatory then the null hypothesis is rejected and the alternative hypothesis is accepted as valid for the given random sequence under test. Otherwise, there is no basis for rejecting the null hypothesis H_0.

Directly related to hypothesis testing is the determination of the significance level α for a given test. For the accepted level of agreement α, the critical area R_α is found. If the value of the statistic K does not belong to the critical area R_α, we have no grounds to reject the hypothesis of randomness of the sample. Otherwise, we reject the null hypothesis and accept the alternative hypothesis that the sample is not random. A significance level of $\alpha = 0.01$ is usually adopted.

To allow easier analysis of the results, each statistical test provides a result in the form of a number called P_{value}. Each P_{value} is the probability that an ideal random number generator would generate a sequence of numbers less random than the sequence being tested. Note that if P_{value} for the test equals 0, then the sequence of numbers appears to be completely non-random. In order to accurately test a sequence of numbers against the null hypothesis of randomness, we need to perform multiple statistical tests. Each statistical test examining different characteristics provides a nonnormal value for the statistic. Only the calculation of P_{value} introduces a standardized measure for the entire set of statistical tests.

A positive pass of a given statistical test is taken to mean that the inequality $P_{value} > \alpha$ must be satisfied. In addition, in order to be considered that a given sequence does not show grounds for rejecting the hypothesis of its randomness, the sequence must obtain positive results for all tests in the battery [8].

4   Theoretically Testable True Random Number Generator Using Quantum Entanglement

As mentioned earlier, the preferred way to prove the randomness of a generator is by theoretical testing over empirical testing. However, not every generator easily lends itself to theoretical testing. This paper presents an example of a quantum generator that offers the possibility of theoretical as well as empirical testing. The random number generator presented is an adaptation of an optical system used to test quantum entanglement. In general, random number generators using quantum optics operate on the basis of spatial non-determinism, using photons that will travel along different optical paths. Not being able to predict, but only knowing the probability of taking one of the two paths is a practical use of optical phenomenon to generate random numbers. Semi-permeable mirrors are used for this purpose. In the simplest terms, individual photons travelling through such a mirror have a 50% chance of reflecting off or passing through the mirror at an angle of 45. Using appropriate photon detectors, for both possible optical paths we obtain the simplest binary number generator, depending on which detector a given photon is spotted we generate the corresponding bit value at the output. The quality of such a generator is strongly related to the quality of the optics, on which the uniform distribution of the probability of defeat or reflection from the mirror depends. The detectors themselves are also not insignificant and must have identical characteristics. As can be seen in the simplified description of such a generator, the indicated realizations are not an easy task, as they require tuning of the optics and high quality components. In such a system, it is difficult to assess whether the system is free of errors that may manifest themselves in classical system operation.

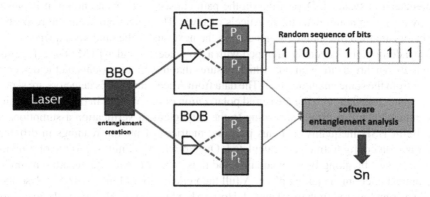

Fig. 1. Diagram of a quantum random number generator with verification of photon entanglement.

A certain solution to this problem may be the use of an optical system used to study quantum entanglement of photons. The assumptions are based on an arrangement developed by a team of researchers working to prove the absence of hidden variables in entangled systems, defined as the EPR paradox (Einstei, Podolski, Rosen) [13]. A team led by Alain Aspect [14] experimentally demonstrated the absence of hidden variables in such a system, proving the Bell/CHSH inequality to be broken. The system used to prove the existence of quantum entanglement is ideally suited to develop this scheme towards the generation of random numbers, together with verification of the quality of the generator, based on the demonstration of the level of quantum entanglement. It is also worth mentioning here that Alain Aspect was awarded the Nobel Prize in 2022 for confirming the existence of quantum entanglement as the foundation of quantum mechanics [20]. This type of approach increases confidence that the generator does in fact use quantum mechanics. A schematic of such a quantum generator is shown in Fig. 1.

The system consists of two modules Alice and Bob. Both systems are equipped with photon detectors set to different polarizations. The entangled photons are obtained by pumping a BBO (Beta Barium Borate) crystal with a laser beam, where the phenomenon of spontaneous parametric down-conversion (SPDC) occurs. A pumping photon of higher energy passing through the BBO crystal undergoes down-conversion into two photons of lower energies. According to the conservation of energy and momentum principle, the two photons in total have the same energy as the photon entering the crystal. The photons at the intersection of the two light cones have no specific polarization and are mutually entangled.

As a result of pumping a BBO crystal with a laser beam, two cones of oppositely polarized photons are obtained at the exit of the crystal. Photons that fly on a trajectory at the intersection of these two cones undergo a type II spontaneous parametric down-conversion process, in which the resulting two photons are mutually entangled in an anti-correlated state.

The basis for the randomness of the system is based on a fundamental problem of quantum mechanics of optical path selection called the "*which path problem*" [15]. The separated entangled photons follow two separate paths (optical fibres) to the Alice and Bob detection systems. Depending on the path chosen by a given photon, it is picked up by a single-photon detector in Alice's receiver. The detections from the respective detectors are then the source for generating the next bits of the random sequence.

In addition, the system is equipped with a Bob receiver and a TTM (Time-Tagging-Module) synchronization circuit, which ensures that the photon counts on the detectors come from the same entangled pair. The data from Alice's and Bob's detectors are sent to a computer together with the measured polarization of the photons in order to determine the entanglement measures according to the entanglement verification assumptions of the Bell/CHSH inequality. For this purpose, matrices of photon readings in different polarization configurations are calculated. Overcoming the limit of a value of 2 by the counts means breaking Bell's inequality and thus demonstrating the quantum nature of the optical phenomena taking place. A full theoretical proof of this issue was described in a paper by four researchers Clauser J, Horne M., Shimony A., Holt R. on the exclusion of the existence of hidden local variables in quantum mechanics [16], the theory posited in the EPR paradox [17]. The CHSH inequality was named after the first letters of the researchers' names, which proves that obtaining a value of the counting matrix larger than 2 and reaching a maximum of $2\sqrt{2}$ proves the truth of the probabilistic description of the behaviour of elementary particles in quantum mechanics. As mentioned earlier, the experimental proof was carried out by Alain Aspect in his paper [14]. Therefore, we obtain a proof of the absence of a deterministic basis for physical phenomena, since in quantum mechanics phenomena have a fully probabilistic description. This follows directly from the von Neuman axiom of measurement [19], in which we are unable to determine the polarization of a photon until the moment of measurement. It is only at the moment of this measurement that a photon in a superposition state (both polarizations simultaneously) selects one of the polarization and its collapse occurs. The two photons in the entangled state realize a common wave function describing their eigenvalues, so they remain in a correlated state, i.e. if one photon has a vertical polarization at the moment of measurement, the other photon in the entangled state will have a horizontal polarization.

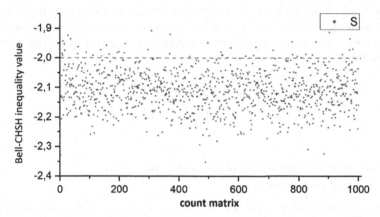

Fig. 2. Diagram of the Bell-CHSH inequality values before tuning of the optics system.

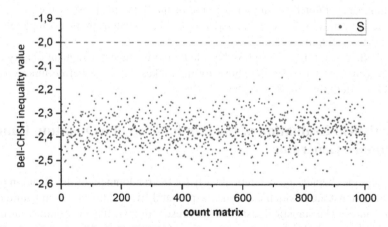

Fig. 3. Diagram of the Bell-CHSH inequality values after tuning of the optics system.

The values of the Bell/CHSH inequality that were measured on the random number generator are shown in Figs. 2 and 3. Figure 2 shows the count values of the Bell/CHSH inequality for the count matrix before the final tuning of the optics. The accompanying graph shows that there is a breakage of the Bell/CHSH inequality for the majority of the count matrices. However, a small fraction remained within the limits of the classical measurements, not overcoming the absolute value $|2|$. After alignment of the system, all count matrices showed a breaking of the Bell-CHSH inequality, as shown in the graph of Fig. 3 by the position of the individual count matrix values between $-2\sqrt{2}$ and -2.

Although most of the series showed a breaking of the Bell/CHSH inequality, however, they did not reach the limits of $-2\sqrt{2}$, which means that we have not reached a pure Bell state, but only the entangled photons are in a mixed state. This is due to the decoherence that the photons undergo during their path in the optical fibers where they interact with their surroundings. The aim of this research is to test whether such a mixed state is sufficient to generate good quality random numbers.

A measure of the quality of a quantum random number generator using quantum entanglement as a source of randomness is proposed in the form of the formula Z normalizing the mean value of the entanglement to the interval [0,1]. This formula is given the form:

$$Z = \frac{\left|\frac{1}{n}\sum_{i=1}^{n}s_i\right| - 2}{\left(2\sqrt{2} - 2\right)} \tag{1}$$

where:

- s_i – the degree of entanglement of the i – th counting matrix
- n – number of counting matrices

If the measure takes negative or zero values, we reject such a generator as non-quantum. For values in the interval $0 < Z \leq 1$, we assume that the generator is quantum with the entanglement quality determined by the value of Z. The above method of evaluating a generator is an implementation of the theoretical test of the randomness of a generator, by showing that the underlying source of entropy is a completely non-deterministic quantum source.

For both cases in Figs. 2 and 3, the calculation of the entanglement quality of the quantum generator based on the above formula takes the value before tuning to $Z \approx 0.1338$ and after tuning to $Z \approx 0.4544$.

5   Statistical Evaluation of the Randomness of a Quantum Random Number Generator

In the previous chapter, the theoretical basis for the randomness of the quantum generator was demonstrated, which confirms the probabilistic and thus random nature of the random source. The statistical tests that we present in this chapter should confirm that the source does not exhibit statistical deviations from theoretically random sources. We perform these tests because of the possibility of implementation errors in the generator's measurement equipment. At the same time, these tests provide an additional safeguard and final confirmation of the randomness of a given generator.

A sequence of 819,200,000 bits was generated from the generator described in Chapter 4. This sequence was statistically tested with the NIST (National Institute of

Standards and Technology) test battery described in paper [8]. This battery is the reference standard for randomness testing in the USA. It was created to test new encryption algorithms after the Data Encryption Standard (DES) algorithm was broken. The NIST battery allowed the successor to the DES algorithm to emerge, which was the AES (Advanced Encryption Standard) algorithm [6].

```
-------------------------------------------------------------------------
RESULTS FOR THE UNIFORMITY OF P-VALUES AND THE PROPORTION OF PASSING SEQUENCES
-------------------------------------------------------------------------
 C1  C2  C3  C4  C5  C6  C7  C8  C9 C10  P-VALUE  PROPORTION  STATISTICAL TEST
-------------------------------------------------------------------------
 93  91 104 107 115 100  98 102  98  92 0.837781  0.9920   Frequency
 99  84  93 105 103  96 105 100 105 110 0.829047  0.9910   BlockFrequency
102  81  90 103 111 101 102 114  98  98 0.530120  0.9860   CumulativeSums
 94  95  96 100 106  88 105 112  98 106 0.862883  0.9900   CumulativeSums
 97  99 124  95  93  85  91 107 102 107 0.298282  0.9930   Runs
 74 101 110  97 115  99 117  90 100  97 0.118812  0.9910   LongestRun
104 111  95 114  80  88 106 115  98  89 0.168112  0.9880   Rank
112  97  88  96  93  95 105 102  93 119 0.508172  0.9850   FFT
 92 101  93 101 107 100  98 102 102 104 0.992670  0.9910   NonOverlappingTemplate (1)
106  91  84  99  99  95 101 109  99 117 0.562591  0.9890   NonOverlappingTemplate (2)
    ...
 97 113  94 106  99  98 100  91  96 106 0.919131  0.9960   NonOverlappingTemplate (148)
 95  99 104 106  91 105 100  99  99 102 0.992952  0.9890   OverlappingTemplate
107 122 104  85 103 101  87 100 102  89 0.291091  0.9850   Universal
 87 113 112  93 102  88  92 101 114  98 0.397688  0.9960   ApproximateEntropy
 70  60  71  50  60  61  52  63  44  44 0.094864  0.9791   RandomExcursions
 52  53  67  69  42  56  63  65  51  57 0.252423  0.9896   RandomExcursions
 59  61  61  65  51  64  51  42  56  65 0.440519  0.9896   RandomExcursions
 65  65  63  64  53  54  53  63  53  42 0.408649  0.9861   RandomExcursions
 68  60  52  63  62  49  58  47  62  54 0.607920  0.9913   RandomExcursions
 53  72  73  58  62  60  49  48  46  54 0.116818  0.9913   RandomExcursions
 63  65  52  53  53  64  50  64  52  59 0.755611  0.9913   RandomExcursions
 58  56  61  57  59  52  63  59  60  50 0.979681  0.9948   RandomExcursions
 54  58  59  57  59  61  62  57  57  51 0.995711  0.9930   RandomExcursionsVariant
 54  57  52  53  73  68  50  59  52  57 0.450330  0.9930   RandomExcursionsVariant
 57  53  56  56  69  60  57  60  48  59 0.863760  0.9896   RandomExcursionsVariant
 57  51  66  66  66  64  48  51  60  46 0.343431  0.9930   RandomExcursionsVariant
 57  61  56  58  69  63  50  49  64  48 0.560868  0.9930   RandomExcursionsVariant
 55  69  51  63  53  55  57  64  55  53 0.796169  0.9861   RandomExcursionsVariant
 69  61  53  67  43  55  50  53  62  62 0.321491  0.9826   RandomExcursionsVariant
 70  68  48  57  43  52  58  61  67  51 0.159457  0.9843   RandomExcursionsVariant
 64  68  51  58  66  57  45  60  62  44 0.266211  0.9826   RandomExcursionsVariant
 67  62  56  64  57  59  53  52  57  48 0.809184  0.9878   RandomExcursionsVariant
 75  52  57  52  68  67  47  48  59  50 0.104252  0.9896   RandomExcursionsVariant
 64  65  56  52  67  59  43  61  51  57 0.473637  0.9948   RandomExcursionsVariant
 69  67  45  62  55  56  48  64  61  48 0.254683  0.9990   RandomExcursionsVariant
 61  65  69  58  51  46  57  60  59  59 0.528851  0.9983   RandomExcursionsVariant
 60  70  64  58  53  60  54  51  60  45 0.543010  0.9948   RandomExcursionsVariant
 59  65  68  50  76  54  49  48  58  48 0.101036  0.9878   RandomExcursionsVariant
 60  60  70  66  55  56  49  52  61  46 0.460249  0.9878   RandomExcursionsVariant
 62  64  61  56  50  66  63  51  47  55 0.640773  0.9896   RandomExcursionsVariant
 98  97  92  99  92  93 107 107  94 121 0.568739  0.9850   Serial
 99  85 100 109  90 103 104  96  99 115 0.664168  0.9870   Serial
103  95  99  93  99 106 113  95  88 109 0.798139  0.9880   LinearComplexity
```

Fig. 4. Final results of the NIST statistical tests.

The NIST battery consists of 15 statistical tests (*Frequency, Block Frequency, Cumulative Sums, Runs, Longest Run, Rank, FFT, Non Overlapping Template, Overlapping Template, Universal, Approximate Entropy, Random Excursions, Random Excursions*

Variant, Serial, Linear Complexity). Each of the statistical tests performed provides multiple P_{value} relative to the random sequence under test. This is because the input sequence is divided into smaller samples, called streams, and the test is performed separately for each stream. In order to be able to evaluate the sequence holistically, an appropriate interpretation of the provided sets of P_{value} sub-sequences needs to be made. NIST has proposed two methods for interpreting these results [8]:

- Uniformity of P_{value} distribution - the resulting P_{value} are expected to uniformly cover the interval [0,1). The χ^2 statistic is used for this purpose.
- Proportion of positive P_{value} to number of streams - the number of successful tests is expected to lie within a predetermined range.

In order to adjudicate that the tested sequence is random, it is assumed that both tests must be positive for all 15 statistical tests.

In addition, the *Random Excursions, Random Excursions Variant* and *Serial* tests are performed several times for different test parameters. Thus, they provide multiple final P_{value} values. The same is true for the *Non Overlapping Template* test, whose number of final results is directly related to the length of the templates. For a default template length value of $m = 9$, 148 possible aperiodic patterns are obtained, thus yielding 148 P_{value} values, where each assesses randomness against a single pattern. A detailed description of the tests can be found in [8].

The final results of the statistical tests of the tested quantum random sequence are shown in Fig. 4. Due to the very large number of 148 P_{value} values for the *Non Overlapping Template* test, most of the results have not been included in the figure, but this does not preclude them from actually being carried out. All 148 tests were successful.

Each test provided two outcome values: the P_{value} indicating the evenness of the distribution of sub-sequence scores for each test, and the *Proportion*, which indicates the ratio of positive tests to all tests performed on the sub-sequences tested.

The uniformity of the distribution of P_{value} values is the first way to interpret the statistical results. The detailed numbers of individual P_{value} values for the sub-sequences are shown in Fig. 4 in columns C1 from C10. These values represent the frequency of occurrence of P_{value} values for sub-sequences in ten equal intervals. The final result is calculated from the χ^2 statistic. The quality of the fit is determined from the formula [8]:

$$\chi^2 = \sum_{i=1}^{10} \frac{\left(F_i - \frac{s}{10}\right)^2}{\frac{s}{10}} \tag{2}$$

where:

- F_i – is the number of P_{value} counts in i -th interval
- s – number of sequences/streams tested with a given statistical test

The final evaluation of the tested sequence is obtained by determining the P_{value} according to the formula [8]:

$$P_{value} = \text{igamc}\left(\frac{9}{2}, \frac{\chi^2}{2}\right) \tag{3}$$

where:

– igamc – is an incomplete Gamma Function

The test is considered positive, i.e. providing no grounds for rejecting the hypothesis of randomness of the tested sequence when the P_{value} is greater than the preset level of significance, which in this case is $\alpha = 0.01$. As can be seen in the final results, all P_{value} values of the uniform distribution are greater than the significance level α. Thus, according to the first interpretation, all tests were successful.

Let us now analyze the second way of interpreting the results. The probability that a random sequence passes a given test is equal to the complement of the significance level $1 - \alpha$. In the case of multiple random sequences, the proportion of sequences that pass a given test is usually different, but close to the value $(1 - \alpha)$. Thus, a random sequence is expected to have a number of positive test results of all sub-sequences around the value $(1 - \alpha)$. This interval is determined from the formula [6]:

$$(1 - \alpha) \pm 3\sqrt{\frac{\alpha(1 - \alpha)}{s}} \tag{4}$$

where:

– α – significance level
– s – number of sequences/streams tested with a given statistical test

Thus, for the default significance level of $\alpha = 0.01$ adopted by the NIST battery, a positive statistical test can be said to pass when, out of $s = 1000$ sequences tested with a given test, the proportion of positive tests is in the range [0.9805608; 0.999439]. This means that for every 1000 sequences tested with a given test, there must be at least 981 to a maximum of 999 positive tests. The results of the calculation of the proportion are shown in Fig. 4 in the *PROPORTION* column. As can be seen, all results fall within the indicated range. Thus, there are no grounds to reject the hypothesis of randomness of the tested sequence also due to the second way of interpreting the results.

Finally, all statistical tests were successful. This means that we have no grounds for rejecting the hypothesis of randomness of the tested sequence.

6 Summary

This paper presents two approaches, theoretical and empirical, for testing random number generators. The two approaches are complementary; the use of one does not preclude the need to use the other approach. In the case of quantum random number generators, theoretical randomness testing can be reduced to demonstrating that the generator uses a quantum, and therefore completely probabilistic, phenomenon to generate randomness. This paper presents an example of a quantum generator that yields to this type of testing. A measure of the quality of the generator is also proposed, allowing the degree of quantum entanglement to be determined, resulting in the ability to quantify the level of quantum phenomenon in the generator.

The paper discusses the problems that arise with both approaches to randomness testing. In particular, in the case of theoretical testing, the problem of feasibility of this type of testing is pointed out, which is strongly related to the type of randomness source. Different methods are used for algorithmic generators, others for generators based on classical or quantum physics phenomena. For statistical tests, it is important to note that the fundamental problem with this approach is trying to determine which tests to perform and how long to test. There is no single statistical test that can comprehensively assess the randomness of a given sequence of numbers. Thus, there is a need to build entire test batteries, consisting of multiple statistical tests. There is no clear answer as to how many tests are sufficient to be confident about the randomness of a generator. This is due to the very nature of statistical hypothesis testing, which only provides evidence to reject the random hypothesis, but if the tests do not provide it, we are still not certain that the generator is random. We simply have no basis for claiming that it is not. Statistical testing has the character of a negative criterion. A separate problem is that by increasing the number of statistical tests, we also increase the probability that a number of tests will be false negatives. Finding the golden mean is very difficult. Even more difficult is selecting the right tests for a particular source and parameterizing them. Current batteries of tests such as NIST [8], Dieharder [9] or TestU01 [10] were developed for testing algorithmic sources of randomness. Thus, it is uncertain whether they fully address the problems that may arise in quantum sources of randomness. This issue requires separate research that will test the test suites themselves for completeness and fit with this new class of random number generators.

Additionally, in this paper we also discusses how to interpret a number of statistical test results. The results of a statistical test of the randomness of a quantum random number source using quantum entanglement, for which a theoretical approach had previously been evaluated, are presented. Both approaches, theoretical and empirical, showed that the generator provides good quality random numbers. Thus, in the generator concept discussed here, we have much more confidence in the true randomness of the numbers than for sources that have only undergone statistical testing.

A separate problem that is not discussed in the paper is the performance itself and the possibility of building a commercial solution on the basis of the presented prototype. The prototype discussed delivers numbers at a rate of a few megabytes per second, which is not a satisfactory result. Algorithmic sources can deliver a much higher volume of numbers in the same time. The issue of miniaturization and stability of the discussed generator concept also provides a number of problems to be solved.

References

1. Arute, F., et. al.: Quantum supremacy using a programmable superconducting processor. Nature **574**, 505–510 (2019)
2. Boixo, S., et al.: Characterizing quantum supremacy in near-term devices. Nat. Phys. **14**, 595 (2018)
3. Bremner, M.J., Montanaro, A., Shepherd, D.J.: Average-case complexity versus approximate simulation of commuting quantum computations. Phys. Rev. Lett. **117**, 080501 (2016)
4. Neill, C., et al.: A blueprint for demonstrating quantum supremacy with superconducting qubits. Science **360**, 195–199 (2018)
5. Knuth, D.E.: The Art of Computer Programming, Vol 2: Seminumerical Algorithms. Addison-Wesley USA (1997)

6. Sys, M., Riha, Z., Matyas, V., Marton, K., Suciu, A.: On the interpretation of results from the NIST statistical test suite. Roman. J. Inf. Sci. Tech. **18**(1), 18–32 (2015)
7. Maurer, U.M.: A universal statistical test for random bit generators. J. Cryptol. **5**(2), 89–105 (1992)
8. Rukhin, J., et al.: A statistical test suite for random and pseudorandom number generators for cryptographic applications. National Institute of Standards and Technology (2010)
9. Brown, R.G.: Dieharder, Robert G. Brown's General Tools Page. https://webhome.phy.duke.edu/~rgb/General/dieharder.php. Accessed 20 2021
10. L'Ecuyer, P., Simard, R.: TestU01: a C library for empirical testing of random number generators. ACM Trans. Math. Softw. **33**(4), 1–40 (2007)
11. Landau, L., Lifszyc, J.: Mechanika kwantowa, teoria nierelatywistyczna. PWN, Warszawa (2012)
12. von Neumann, J.: Mathematical Foundations of Quantum Mechanics. Princeton University Press, Princeton (1955)
13. Bell, J.S.: On the Einstein Podolsky Rosen Paradox. Physics **1**(3), 195–200 (1964)
14. Aspect, A., Grangier, P., Roger, G.: Experimental realization of Einstein-Podolsky-Rosen-Bohm Gedankenexperiment: A New Violation of Bell's Inequalities. Phys. Rev. Lett. **49**(2), 91 (1982)
15. Vo Van, T., Vu Duc, V.: Which-way identification by an asymmetrical double-slit experiment with monochromatic photons. Scientific Reports **12**(3709) (2022)
16. Clauser, J.F., Horne, M.A., Shimony, A., Holt, R.A.: Proposed experiment to test local hidden-variable theories. Phys. Rev. Lett. **23**, 880–884 (1969)
17. Einstein, A., Podolsky, B., Rosen, N.: Can quantum mechanical description of physical reality be considered complete. Phys. Rev. **47** (1935)
18. Shannon, C.: Communication Theory of Secrecy Systems (PDF). Bell Syst. Tech. J. **28**(4), 656–715 (1949). https://doi.org/10.1002/j.1538-7305.1949.tb00928.x
19. Mello, P.A.: The von Neumann Model of Measurement in Quantum Mechanics. Instituto de Física, Universidad Nacional Autónoma de México, (2013) https://doi.org/10.48550/arXiv.1311.7649
20. Alain Aspect – Facts at Nobel Prize. https://www.nobelprize.org/prizes/physics/2022/aspect/facts/. Accessed 20 Jan 2023

Computational Intelligence in Medical Applications

Robust Brain Age Estimation via Regression Models and MRI-Derived Features

Mansoor Ahmed[1] , Usama Sardar[1] , Sarwan Ali[2] , Shafiq Alam[3] ,

Murray Patterson[2(✉)] , and Imdad Ullah Khan[1(✉)]

[1] Lahore University of Management Sciences, Lahore, Pakistan
{mansoor.ahmed,usama.sardar,imdad.khan}@lums.edu.pk
[2] Georgia State University, Atlanta, GA, USA
[3] Massey University, Auckland, New Zealand

Abstract. The determination of biological brain age is a crucial biomarker in the assessment of neurological disorders and understanding of the morphological changes that occur during aging. Various machine learning models have been proposed for estimating brain age through Magnetic Resonance Imaging (MRI) of healthy controls. However, developing a robust brain age estimation (BAE) framework has been challenging due to the selection of appropriate MRI-derived features and the high cost of MRI acquisition. In this study, we present a novel BAE framework using the Open Big Healthy Brain (OpenBHB) dataset, which is a new multi-site and publicly available benchmark dataset that includes region-wise feature metrics derived from T1-weighted (T1-w) brain MRI scans of 3965 healthy controls aged between 6 to 86 years. Our approach integrates three different MRI-derived region-wise features and different regression models, resulting in a highly accurate brain age estimation with a Mean Absolute Error (MAE) of 3.25 years, demonstrating the framework's robustness. We also analyze our model's regression-based performance on gender-wise (male and female) healthy test groups. The proposed BAE framework provides a new approach for estimating brain age, which has important implications for the understanding of neurological disorders and age-related brain changes.

Keywords: Neuroimaging · T1-weighted MRI · Brain Age · Machine Learning · Artificial Intelligence · Destrieux atlas

1 Introduction

The biological brain age, or simply brain age, is the estimated brain age (in years) that quantifies how old a person's brain is. In contrast, the chronological age is the person's actual age relative to the calendar birth date. We call the difference between the brain age and the chronological age as Brain Estimated Age Difference (Brain-EAD). The brain age of people with various neurological disorders is known to be different from its chronological brain age and is also an important biomarker for neurodegenerative disorders [7, 17]. For instance, Brain-EAD of Alzheimer's Disease (AD) patients is greater than Parkinson's Disease (PD) patients [5].

M. Patterson and I. U. Khan—Equal contribution.

© The Author(s), under exclusive license to Springer Nature Switzerland AG 2023
N. T. Nguyen et al. (Eds.): ICCCI 2023, CCIS 1864, pp. 661–674, 2023.
https://doi.org/10.1007/978-3-031-41774-0_52

Brain-EAD is a data-driven biomarker that exploits brain features derived from neuroimaging modalities such as brain MRIs by leveraging machine learning algorithms for brain age prediction [13]. A major challenge in developing efficient BAE frameworks is the selection of appropriate features that fully capture healthy aging and, ultimately, the machine learning model [10]. Existing BAE approaches have widely used region-wise features such as the global brain volumes [6,11] or cortical measurements [1–4,23] such as cortical thickness, volume, surface area, and curvatures yielding lesser accuracy. Some other approaches have used very high-dimensional voxel-wise features requiring computationally expensive resources for dimensionality reduction, such as Principal Component Analysis [2]. To address these limitations, we propose the fusion of the region-wise features, i.e., global Gray Matter (GM), White Matter (WM), and Cerebrospinal Fluid (CSF) volumes and cortical measurements of parcellated regions of interest (ROI), for building a BAE framework. Therefore, we hypothesize that integrating the region-wise features may carry potentially complementary information about brain age, resulting in an improved BAE model.

In this paper, we build a BAE framework using three different sets of region-wise features derived from the T1-weighted MRI of healthy individuals by training a Generalized Linear regression Model (GLM). We evaluated the model performance on the three separate feature sets and compared them with the integrated feature set. Additionally, we compare the model performance on gender-wise (male and female) healthy test groups. Our experiments demonstrate that our model outperforms previous methods of efficiently estimating brain age from T1-weighted MRI scans.

The significant contributions of this paper are the following:

1. We propose the first brain age estimation model that integrates the distinct region-wise features, i.e., global GM and CSF volumes and cortical measurements of Desikan [8] and Destrieux [12] ROI.
2. We compare the performance of BAE frameworks developed using individual region-wise metrics derived from T1-w MRI and on the gender-wise (male/female) hold-out test sets.
3. Our model achieves improved BAE accuracy compared to the previously known BAE models using region-wise features derived from T1-w brain MRIs.

The rest of the paper is organized as follows: Sect. 2 provides a review of the BAE framework. Section 3 provides the details of our proposed models. Section 4 details the experimental design, and Sect. 5 analyzes and discusses the experimental results and comparisons of different models. Finally, Sect. 6 concludes the paper.

2   Related Work

In this section, we introduce the brain age estimation (BAE) problem, a comparison of features derived from MRI for BAE, multi-site MRI studies, and evaluation metrics used for assessing the performance of BAE models.

2.1 BAE Framework

Biological brain age is determined by training a supervised machine learning model on MRIs of cognitively healthy subjects. This model takes input features (extracted from MRIs) as independent variables and outputs the brain age (in years) as the dependent variable. Since all the subjects are "healthy", their Brain-EAD is assumed to be zero. Thus, the BAE model attempts to fit a function (of features) for age. A subject's brain age difference, Brain-EAD, or brain age gap, is the difference between the estimated biological and chronological ages. If the observed Brain-EAD is (significantly) higher than 0, then the subject may have a certain underlying neurological disorder (aging their brain faster) [5]. In contrast, it has been observed that the Brain-EAD of long-term meditation practitioners is (significantly) less than 0 (slower rate of brain aging) [24].

Analysis of T1-weighted MRIs is commonly employed as they provide high-resolution images of the GM and WM [26] while providing information about atrophy in the brain's anatomical structures [19]. Some studies also used multi-modal MRIs by integrating structural and functional MRI (fMRI) to estimate brain age [3,33]. To build BAE models, different machine learning algorithms such as Support Vector Regression (SVR) [3,4], Gaussian Process Regression (GPR) [1,2], Relevance Vector Regression (RVR) [14], and Generalized Linear Models (GLM) [28] have been applied to the features extracted from T1-w MRI [22]. Similarly, researchers have applied deep learning algorithms, such as 3D convolutional neural networks (CNNs), to predict brain age using voxel-wise features extracted from GM and WM segmented T1-weighted images [7,20].

2.2 Features Selection

MRIs contain valuable structural and functional information about alterations in the human brain, such as the reduction in global volumes with age. It has been observed that GM volume monotonically decreases from the 20 s to the 70 s, WM volume shows minor changes, while CSF volumes, conversely, increase from the 20 s to the 70 s [32]. Capturing the morphological similarities and alterations in the individual brain with age is necessary for building accurate BAE models and varies greatly with the structural measures being used [10]. Currently, different local and global brain features are derived from the T1-weighted MRI for brain age estimation. These features are broadly categorized into region-wise [21,23], voxel-wise [14,29], and surface-based metrics [30].

The model's accuracy was degraded when individual features derived from T1-w MRI were used. Franke et al. predicted brain age using the voxel-wise features from T1-w MRI with an MAE of 4.98 years [14]. Similarly, Cole et al. used GM and WM volumes and demonstrated the MAE to be 4.65 years [6]. Liu et al. built a BAE framework using region-wise cortical measurements and attained a Mean Absolute Error (MAE) of 3.73 years [23]. On the contrary, promising results were obtained when these features were integrated [2,7]. Authors in [4] and [2] integrated gray matter voxel-wise maps and region-wise metrics and achieved MAE of 4.63 and 3.7 years respectively. The authors of [20] combined surface-based and voxel-wise features and showed that prediction accuracy decreases compared to individual features. Still, there is no clear understanding of the selection of appropriate features, and it can be assessed that integrating the different region-wise features derived from the T1-w brain MRIs results in improved BAE models.

3   Proposed Model

In this section, we first analyze and describe the different MRI-derived region-wise features and classify participants into different age groups or clusters. Then, we build our BAE model by integrating the three region-wise features and evaluate the performance on an independent healthy test set.

3.1   Participants and Exclusion Criteria

The OpenBHB dataset[1] contains the MRI-derived features of a total of 3983 HCs collected from 10 different sources with 60 individual MRI acquisition sites. These data sources are Autism Brain Imaging Data Exchange (ABIDE-1 and ABIDE-2)[2], brain Genomics Superstruct Project (GSP)[3], consortium for Reliability and Reproducibility (CoRR)[4], information eXtraction from Images (IXI)[5], brainomics/Localizer[6], MPI-Leipzig[7], narratives (NAR)[8], neuroimaging Predictors of Creativity in Healthy Adults (NPC)[9], and the reading Brain Project L1 Adults (RBP)[10]. We excluded 18 samples from our analysis because of duplicate IDs with conflicting ages and used the remaining dataset ($m = 3965$). The dataset has an overall uniform gender distribution with an equal distribution in each of the 10 age bins (male = 2079, female = 1886) (see Fig. 1).

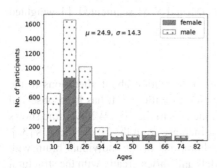

Fig. 1. Age and gender distribution of the participants.

Table 1. Demographic characteristics of the training and test set subjects.

	Training set	Test set
No. of HC	3172	793
Age ± std (years)	25.2 ± 14.6	23.8 ± 12.8
Sex (M/F)	1661/1548	434/359

---

[1] The dataset was provided (in part) by Neurospin, CEA, France.
[2] http://fcon_1000.projects.nitrc.org/indi/abide/.
[3] https://www.nitrc.org/projects/gspdata.
[4] http://fcon_1000.projects.nitrc.org/indi/CoRR/html/.
[5] http://brain-development.org/ixi-dataset/.
[6] https://osf.io/vhtf6/wiki/Localizer/.
[7] https://openneuro.org/datasets/ds000221/.
[8] https://openneuro.org/datasets/ds002345/.
[9] https://openneuro.org/datasets/ds002330/.
[10] https://openneuro.org/datasets/ds003974/.

3.2 Sampling Method

An $80 - 20\%$ random split was followed to divide the data into training and testing sets with uniform gender distribution in both sets. The test set was further divided into male and female hold-out sets, as shown in Table 1.

3.3 MRI Processing

The MRIs of all HC are uniformly pre-processed using FreeSurfer and CAT12, while a semi-automatic quality control was also performed on the images before extracting different features [9]. Later, the volumetric measurements of different brain atlases or regions of interest (ROI) were computed.

CAT12 ROI. The CAT12 Voxel-Based Morphometry (VBM) pipeline, as explained in [16], was followed, which includes non-linear registration to $1.5 \ mm^3$ MNI template, Gray Matter (GM), White Matter (WM), and Cerebrospinal Fluid (CSF) tissue segmentation, bias correction of intensity non-uniformities, and segmentation modulation by scaling with the number of volume changes due to spatial registration [9]. We used GM and CSF volumes averaged on the Neuromorphometrics atlas comprising the volumes of 142 cortical and sub-cortical regions of both hemispheres (see Fig. 2).

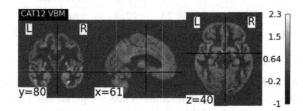

Fig. 2. An illustration of GM maps generated by CAT12.

Desikan ROI. Using FreeSurfer, the MRIs are pre-processed by intensity normalization, skull stripping, segmentation of GM and WM, hemispheric-based tessellations, topology corrections, inflation, and registration to the "fsaverage" template [9]. Then, the measurements for the widely-used cortical parcellations Desikan-Killiany atlas [8] (automated labeling of the human cerebral cortex into the gyral-based region of interest) containing the surface area (mm^2), GM volume (mm^3), cortical thickness (mm), thickness std dev (mm), integrated rectified mean curvature (mm^{-1}), integrated rectified Gaussian curvature (mm^{-2}), and the intrinsic curvature index of each brain region are obtained. The two principal curvatures of each regional surface are computed and represented as k_1 and k_2. Hence,

$$\text{Mean curvature} = 1/2(k_1 + k_2) \qquad \text{Gaussian curvature} = k_1 \times k_2$$

These measurements for Desikan parcellation $(2 \times 7 \times 34)$ were used to train the BAE model. We call these features set "Desikan-ROI".

Destrieux ROI. The MRI preprocessing pipeline is the same as Desikan ROI, with varying brain regions in both brain parcellations. The features constitute the seven cortical measurements (as explained in Desikan ROI) of the Destrieux atlas [12] comprising 74 global regions of interest for each hemisphere.

We call the concatenation of Desikan ROI, Destrieux ROI, and CAT12 ROI "all region-wise" metrics.

3.4 Feature Engineering and Model Selection

Let $X^{m \times n} \in \mathbf{R}^{m \times n}$ be the data matrix of HCs with m being the number of subjects and n being the MRI-derived features while $Y^{m \times 1}$ be their chronological ages.

We visualized the feature separation for the three age groups (adults, adolescents, and elders) computed through k-means clustering using t-distributed Stochastic Neighbor Embedding (t-SNE) [25] plots. The summary of k-means clustering of ages is presented in Table 2.

Table 2. Summary of 3-means clustering of the participants' ages (in years).

Cluster ID	Min	Max	Mean	Frequency	Group
0	6	17	11.6	620	Adolescents
2	17	42	23	2223	Adults
1	42	86	61.1	366	Elders

We represent the region-wise features of 3 age groups using t-SNE, as shown in Fig. 3. We can observe that the "Adolescents" class (in green color) shows a separate group and is far away from the "Elders" class (in blue color). We also computed the correlation of features to test the statistical dependence with age (target variable). The features were min-max normalized to bring the values between 0 and 1 before training the regression model, $x_{scaled} = {}^{x - x_{min}}/_{x_{max} - x_{min}}$.

We trained different regression models such as Support Vector Regression (SVR), Relevance Vector Regression (RVR), Linear Regression (LR), and Generalised Linear Model (GLM) to predict the brain age of the healthy test subjects. More formally, $Y_m^{pred} = \beta_1 x_{m1} + \beta_2 x_{m2} + ... + \beta_n x_{mn} + c$, where β_1, β_2, and β_n are the unknown parameters while x_{m1}, x_{m1}, and x_{mn} are the selected brain MRI features.

3.5 Working Algorithm

Algorithm 1 describes our brain age estimation model. In line 1, we take data as input with their corresponding age vector. We train regression models on the input data of the m training samples in lines 3 to 5 of the algorithm. Lastly, we validate the accuracy of our model using 10-fold cross-validation in line 6 and predict the brain ages of an unseen healthy test set in line 7 of the algorithm.

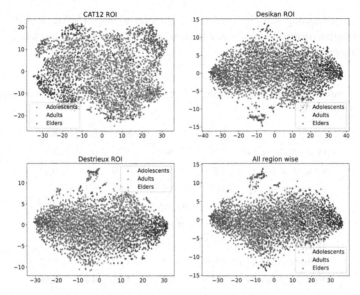

Fig. 3. t-SNE representation for different region-wise features of the three age groups.

Algorithm 1. Brain age estimation model.

1: **Data:** $X^{m \times n} \leftarrow$ Data matrix of m subjects, $Y^{m \times 1} \leftarrow$ chronological ages of m subjects.
2: **Result:** Let Y^{pred} be the estimated ages of m subjects.
3: **for** m subjects **do**   ▷ Model training
4:     Train a regression model using the $X^{m \times n}$ with age labels $Y^{m \times 1}$
5: **end for**
6: Validate the prediction accuracy of the regression model   ▷ Testing the regression model
7: Estimate the brain age Y^{pred} of HC test set

---

4   Experimental Evaluation

In this section, we first present the existing baseline brain age estimation models. Then, we analyze the regression models used for developing BAE frameworks and choosing the best-performing algorithm using the evaluation metrics of MAE, RMSE, and R^2.

4.1   Baseline Models

We report comparison results of the proposed BAE model with the state-of-the-art BAE frameworks using T1-weighted MRI in Table 3. The evaluation metrics for these brain age estimation models vary. For instance, some studies [4,23] have used MAE, RMSE, and R^2 to assess the performance of their models while others [6,15,20] have used only MAE and R^2 to evaluate their BAE frameworks. The individual cohorts or subsets of healthy brain MRIs in the present study have previously been used in other BAE studies. For instance, [4,6,23] used the healthy brain MRI samples from IXI or ABIDE for brain age estimation that were also included in this study. Based on the age range, the number of training samples, and the evaluation metrics (MAE, RMSE, and R^2), our model outperforms the previously known brain age estimation models using T1-w MRIs as shown in Table 3.

Table 3. A comparison of the studies conducted for brain age estimation using T1-weighted MRI and our proposed model.

Study	# HC	Age-range	MAE	RMSE	R^2
Beheshti et al. [4]	788	18–94	4.7	6.13	0.89
Cole et al. [6]	2001	18–90	4.16	–	0.95
Aycheh et al. [1]	2119	45–91	4.05	5.16	–
Jonsson et al. [20]	1264	20–86	3.85	–	0.87
Liu et al. [23]	2501	20–94	3.73	4.81	0.95
Baecker et al. [2]	10824	47–73	3.7	4.65	–
Fujimoto et al. [15]	1099	20–75	3.59	–	0.95
Proposed model	**3965**	**6–86**	**3.25**	**4.72**	**0.90**

4.2   Regression Algorithms

We compare the performance of each regression model (LR, SVR, RVR, and GLM) using different region-wise features in Table 4. Our analysis showed that GLM outperformed the other models, achieving lower mean absolute error (MAE) with the FreeSurfer Desikan and Destrieux ROI features. In contrast, RVR achieved better performance with the CAT12 ROI features. However, GLM produced the lowest MAE for all features combined, i.e., all region-wise (MAE = 3.25 years).

5   Results and Discussion

In this section, we present the results of our proposed model and compare them to existing baselines. We begin by showing the regression results using different evaluation metrics and methods in Table 4. Specifically, we trained the regression algorithms (LR, SVR, RVR, and GLM) on each feature set and computed the performance evaluation metrics after tuning the hyperparameters. We then selected the best-performing model based on lower mean absolute error (MAE), root mean squared error (RMSE), and higher R^2 score.

We present scatter plots to show the difference between the chronological age and the estimated brain age using region-wise MRI-derived features in Fig. 4. This relationship is shown for both the male (number of samples = 434) and female (number of samples = 359) test participants. Box plots in Fig. 5 show the brain-EAD using different region-wise features for both genders. We test our BAE model on the MRI-derived features of healthy individuals, as shown in the right sub-table in Table 5.

Integrating all region-wise feature metrics from T1-w MRI improved the BAE framework, resulting in lower MAE and RMSE than using individual feature metrics. The highest performance with individual feature metrics was achieved using the

Table 4. Regression results for different MRI-derived region-wise features (LR: Linear Regression, SVR: Support Vector Regression, RVR: Relevance Vector Regression, GLM: Generalized Linear Model).

Features	Algo.	MAE ↓	RMSE ↓	R^2 ↑
CAT12 ROI	LR	4.24	5.73	0.85
	SVR	4.26	5.85	0.85
	RVR	**3.94**	**5.32**	**0.86**
	GLM	4.02	5.88	0.84
Desikan ROI	LR	5.37	7.11	0.78
	SVR	5.28	7.14	0.77
	RVR	5.87	10.76	0.46
	GLM	**4.23**	**6.4**	**0.81**
Destrieux ROI	LR	5.31	7.03	0.79
	SVR	5.12	6.99	0.80
	RVR	5.50	11.31	0.41
	GLM	**3.9**	**5.81**	**0.84**
CAT12 ROI + Desikan ROI	LR	4.21	5.54	0.86
	SVR	4.12	5.51	0.86
	RVR	3.56	4.92	0.89
	GLM	**3.4**	**5.02**	**0.88**
CAT12 ROI + Destrieux ROI	LR	4.61	5.97	0.85
	SVR	4.42	5.65	0.87
	RVR	3.74	5.00	0.88
	GLM	**3.33**	**4.87**	**0.89**
Desikan ROI + Destrieux ROI	LR	5.74	7.58	0.74
	SVR	5.17	6.82	0.80
	RVR	5.54	11.08	0.43
	GLM	**3.77**	**5.58**	**0.86**
All region wise	LR	5.31	6.62	0.79
	SVR	4.49	5.73	0.85
	RVR	3.37	4.91	0.89
	GLM	**3.25**	**4.73**	**0.90**

Destrieux-ROI features because we utilized seven cortical measurements or explanatory variables for 148 brain regions, unlike previous studies that used fewer variables [4,23]. Conversely, the individual global volumetric measurements, CAT12 ROI, of the segmented GM and CSF achieved lower performance (higher MAE). The improved performance of our BAE model is also because of an overall greater sample size ($m = 3965$) compared to the previously known models [6,20,23] and wider age range compared to the state-of-the-art BAE models [1,2,4].

Table 5. Performance comparison of the brain age estimation framework for different MRI-derived region features of the male and female healthy test set (left sub table) and complete (containing male and female combined) healthy test set (right sub table).

MRI features	Male			Female			Complete Data		
	MAE ↓	RMSE ↓	R^2 ↑	MAE ↓	RMSE ↓	R^2 ↑	MAE ↓	RMSE ↓	R^2 ↑
CAT12 ROI	3.9	5.68	0.86	4.17	6.11	0.81	3.94	5.32	0.87
Desikan ROI	4.39	6.93	0.79	4.03	5.69	0.83	4.23	6.4	0.81
Destrieux ROI	3.98	6.05	0.84	3.81	5.51	0.84	3.9	5.81	0.84
CAT12 ROI + Desikan ROI	3.29	4.94	0.89	3.54	5.11	0.87	3.4	5.02	0.88
CAT12 ROI + Destrieux ROI	3.24	4.78	0.90	3.44	4.97	0.87	3.33	4.87	0.89
Desikan ROI + Destrieux ROI	3.89	5.92	0.85	3.63	5.14	0.87	3.77	5.58	0.86
All region	**3.19**	**4.67**	**0.91**	**3.32**	**4.79**	**0.88**	**3.25**	**4.73**	**0.90**

We also observed that the choice of machine learning model greatly affects the performance of BAE using different region-wise MRI-derived features. Table 4 shows that Generalized Linear Model (GLM) performed better on Desikan ROI and Destrieux ROI region-wise features compared to Linear Regression (LR), linear Support Vector Regression (SVR), and Relevance Vector Regression (RVR). On the contrary, RVR improved accuracy on the CAT12 ROI features compared to LR, SVR, and GLM. These results are consistent with the BAE models in [22, 27].

The brain-EAD of the healthy test set is evident from Fig. 5 using different region-wise features. It shows that integrating the three region-wise structural measurements decreases brain-EAD ($\mu \approx 0$). While, individually, CAT12 ROI and Desikan ROI showed similar results with the highest brain-EAD. Similarly, the scatter plots between the chronological age and brain age in Fig. 4 show that the proposed model generalizes well for adolescents and adults (lesser Brain-EAD), while outliers exist among older healthy subjects because of the non-uniform age distribution across the different age groups. Another important observation is that the BAE model overestimates for younger subjects while underestimates for older subjects [6, 33] as shown in Fig. 4.

We tested the proposed model separately on male and female subjects and found that the model performed slightly better for male participants (MAE = 3.19 years) compared to the female subjects (MAE = 3.32 years). This difference in performance is also observed in [13] because of both genders' local and global brain anatomy and the normal aging trajectory [11, 31]. Finally, in the case of CAT12 ROI, the GM volume shows a strong -ve correlation with age ($r \approx -0.5$), while CSF volume shows a strong +ve correlation with age ($r \approx 0.5$). These observations are consistent with previous studies indicating that GM volume decreases with age, while CSF volume increases gradually with age [11, 18].

The present study has three limitations. First, besides using an extensive collection of healthy brain MRIs aged 6–86 years, the participants' age distribution is right-skewed compared to [3, 23]. A future research direction can include more adult and elder healthy training samples to explore the impact on the accuracy of the BAE model. Second, we only used the global volumetric features on the Neuromorphometrics atlas

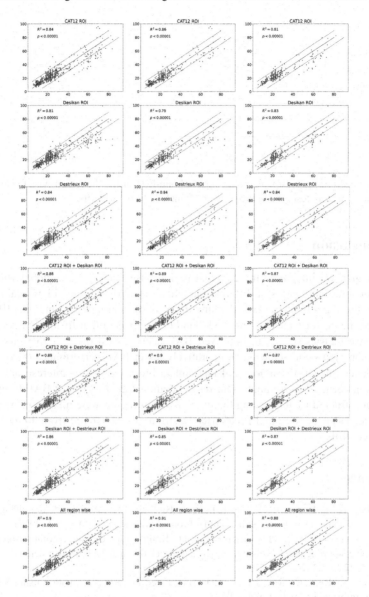

Fig. 4. (from left to right) Scatter plots showing the chronological age (years) vs. estimated brain age (years) of all healthy test subjects, the male healthy test subjects, and the female healthy test subjects using different MRI-derived region-wise features.

and did not explore other voxel-based atlases like Suit and Cobra. Third, the current approach only uses T1-w brain MRIs for brain age estimation and does not consider multimodal data such as fMRI used recently in [3, 33].

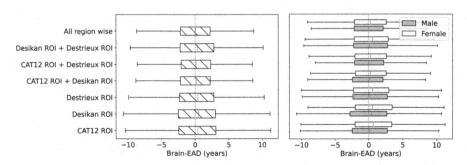

Fig. 5. (from left to right) Box plots showing the brain-EAD using the region-wise features of the independent, healthy test set and the male and female hold-out test sets.

6   Conclusion

In this paper, we integrated the different region-wise features, i.e., global volumetric and cortical measurements of different parcellations, derived using T1-w healthy brain MRIs to develop a BAE framework using the novel benchmark dataset, OpenBHB. We evaluated the performance of our model and demonstrated that fusion of the different region-wise metrics results in improved BAE accuracy (MAE = 3.25 years). These features, on their own, achieved comparatively lesser BAE performance (MAE = 4.23 years) depending on the number of anatomical brain regions of interest and the different volumetric measurements. Our results demonstrate that robust BAE frameworks can be constructed by integrating the three different region-wise metrics (CAT12 ROI, FreeSurfer Desikan ROI, and FreeSurfer Destrieux ROI) derived from T1-w MRIs of healthy controls.

References

1. Aycheh, H.M., Seong, J.K., Shin, J.H., et al.: Biological brain age prediction using cortical thickness data: a large scale cohort study. Front. Aging Neurosci. **10**, 252 (2018)
2. Baecker, L., Dafflon, J., Da Costa, P.F., et al.: Brain age prediction: a comparison between machine learning models using region and voxel based morphometric data. Hum. Brain Mapp. **42**(8), 2332–2346 (2021)
3. Basodi, S., Raja, R., Ray, B., et al.: Decentralized brain age estimation using MRI data. Neuroinformatics **20**, 981–990 (2022)
4. Beheshti, I., Maikusa, N., Matsuda, H.: The accuracy of T1-weighted voxel-wise and region-wise metrics for brain age estimation. Comput. Meth. Program. Biomed. **214**, 106585 (2022)
5. Beheshti, I., Mishra, S., Sone, D., et al.: T1-weighted MRI-driven brain age estimation in Alzheimer's disease and Parkinson's disease. Aging Dis. **11**(3), 618 (2020)
6. Cole, J.H., Poudel, R.P., Tsagkrasoulis, D., et al.: Predicting brain age with deep learning from raw imaging data results in a reliable and heritable biomarker. Neuroimage **163**, 115–124 (2017)
7. Cole, J.H., Ritchie, S.J., Bastin, M.E., et al.: Brain age predicts mortality. Mol. Psychiatry **23**(5), 1385–1392 (2017)

8. Desikan, R.S., Ségonne, F., Fischl, B., et al.: An automated labeling system for subdividing the human cerebral cortex on MRI scans into gyral-based regions of interest. Neuroimage **31**(3), 968–980 (2006)
9. Dufumier, B., Grigis, A., Victor, J., et al.: OpenBHB: a large-scale multi-site brain MRI data-set for age prediction and debiasing. Neuroimage **263**, 119637 (2022)
10. Ediri Arachchi, W., Peng, Y., Zhang, X., et al.: A systematic characterization of structural brain changes in schizophrenia. Neurosci. Bull. **36**(10), 1107–1122 (2020)
11. Farokhian, F., Yang, C., Beheshti, I., et al.: Age-related gray and white matter changes in normal adult brains. Aging Dis. **8**(6), 899–909 (2017)
12. Fischl, B., Van Der Kouwe, A., Destrieux, C., et al.: Automatically parcellating the human cerebral cortex. Cereb. Cortex **14**(1), 11–22 (2004)
13. Franke, K., Gaser, C.: Ten years of BrainAGE as a neuroimaging biomarker of brain aging: what insights have we gained? Front. Neurol. **10**, 789 (2019)
14. Franke, K., Ziegler, G., Klöppel, S., et al.: Estimating the age of healthy subjects from T1-weighted MRI scans using kernel methods: exploring the influence of various parameters. Neuroimage **50**(3), 883–892 (2010)
15. Fujimoto, R., Ito, K., Wu, K., et al.: Brain age estimation from T1-weighted images using effective local features. In: Proceedings of the Annual International Conference of the IEEE Engineering in Medicine and Biology Society, EMBS, pp. 3028–3031 (2017)
16. Gaser, C., Dahnke, R.: CAT - A Computational Anatomy Toolbox for the Analysis of Structural MRI Data. bioRxiv (2022)
17. Gaser, C., Franke, K., Klöppel, S., et al.: BrainAGE in mild cognitive impaired patients: predicting the conversion to Alzheimer's Disease. PLoS ONE **8**(6), e67346 (2013)
18. Hafkemeijer, A., Altmann-Schneider, I., de Craen, A.J., et al.: Associations between age and gray matter volume in anatomical brain networks in middle-aged to older adults. Aging Cell **13**(6), 1068–1074 (2014)
19. Jiang, H., Lu, N., Chen, K., et al.: Predicting brain age of healthy adults based on structural MRI parcellation using convolutional neural networks. Front. Neurol. **10**, 1346 (2020)
20. Jónsson, B.A., Bjornsdottir, G., Thorgeirsson, T., et al.: Brain age prediction using deep learning uncovers associated sequence variants. Nat. Commun. **10**(1), 5409 (2019)
21. Lee, P.L., Kuo, C.Y., Wang, P.N., et al.: Regional rather than global brain age mediates cognitive function in cerebral small vessel disease. Brain Commun. **4**(5) (2022)
22. Lee, W.H., Antoniades, M., Schnack, H.G., et al.: Brain age prediction in schizophrenia: does the choice of machine learning algorithm matter? Psychiatry Res. Neuroimaging **310**, 111270 (2021)
23. Liu, X., Beheshti, I., Zheng, W., et al.: Brain age estimation using multi-feature-based networks. Comput. Biol. Med. **143**, 105285 (2022)
24. Luders, E., Cherbuin, N., Gaser, C.: Estimating brain age using high-resolution pattern recognition: younger brains in long term meditation practitioners. Neuroimage **134**, 508–513 (2016)
25. Van der Maaten, L., Hinton, G.: Visualizing data using t-SNE. J. Mach. Learn. Res. **9**(11), 2579–2604 (2008)
26. Mikheev, A., Nevsky, G., Govindan, S., et al.: Fully automatic segmentation of the brain from T1-weighted MRI using bridge burner algorithm. J. Magn. Reson. Imaging?: JMRI **27**(6), 1235–1241 (2008)
27. Mishra, S., Beheshti, I., Khanna, P.: A review of neuroimaging-driven brain age estimation for identification of brain disorders and health conditions. IEEE Rev. Biomed. Eng. **16**, 371–385 (2021)
28. Modabbernia, A., Whalley, H.C., Glahn, D.C., et al.: Systematic evaluation of ML algorithms for neuroanatomically-based age prediction in youth. Hum. Brain Mapp. **43**(17), 5126–5140 (2022)

29. Nenadić, I., Dietzek, M., Langbein, K., et al.: BrainAGE Score Indicates Accelerated Brain Aging in Schizophrenia, but Not Bipolar Disorder. Psychiatry Research: Neuroimaging **266**, 86–89 (2017)
30. Sajedi, H., Pardakhti, N.: Age Prediction Based on Brain MRI Image: A Survey. J. Med. Syst. **43**(8), 279 (2019)
31. Sanford, N., Ge, R., Antoniades, M., et al.: Sex differences in predictors and regional patterns of brain age gap estimates. Hum. Brain Mapp. **43**(15), 4689–4698 (2022)
32. Taki, Y., Thyreau, B., Kinomura, S., et al.: Correlations among brain gray matter volumes, age, gender, and hemisphere in healthy individuals. PLoS ONE **6**(7), e22734 (2011)
33. Taylor, A., Zhang, F., Niu, X., et al.: Investigating the temporal pattern of neuroimaging-based brain age estimation as a biomarker for Alzheimer's disease related neurodegeneration. Neuroimage **263**, 119621 (2022)

Efficient Analysis of Patient Length of Stay in Hospitals Using Classification and Clustering Approaches

Sheikh Sharfuddin Mim[1]([envelope])[ID], Doina Logofatu[1][ID], and Florin Leon[2][ID]

[1] Frankfurt University of Applied Sciences, Frankfurt am Main, Germany
bit.mim@gmail.com, logofatu@fb2.fra-uas.de
[2] Technical University of Iasi, Iasi, Romania
florin.leon@academic.tuiasi.ro

Abstract. To maintain resource efficiency and high-quality care, hospitals must estimate a patient's length of stay (LOS). Machine learning-based prediction algorithms can help. The healthcare industry has become a massive data hub due to its increasing adoption of information technology, but most of this data is kept within the medical institution and not shared with others due to privacy concerns, making it difficult to build effective predictive analytics that need a lot of training data. Using MIMIC database data extraction, we will create two models and offer exploratory and predictive insights. The first model predicts the likelihood of a category event like a patient's stay. Based on their characteristics and admission circumstances, we will classify patients as short, medium, or long-term stays. The second model groups patients according to the variety of patient-caretaker interactions, such as procedures, drugs prescribed, and inputs taken, which can be used to approximate a patient's physical or human resource requirements during their stay. We want to blend two models to assess attributes connected to a patient's background, illness, and therapy. We intend to improve healthcare systems, proactive resource allocation, and patient care by applying predictive analytics and grouping patients by hospital resource utilization. Multinomial Logistic Regression (MLR), Random Forest (RF), and Gradient Boosting Machine (GBM) were developed for the classification problem. Grouping is accomplished using K-Means.

Keywords: Patient Length of Stay (LOS) · Machine Learning · Multinomial Logistic Regression (MLR) · Random Forest (RF) · Gradient Boosting Machine (GBM) · K-Means · Classification and Clustering Analysis

1 Introduction

Chronic diseases are now one of the leading causes of death and disability in the US [1]. Changes in lifestyle and diet are linked to four of the most common

© The Author(s), under exclusive license to Springer Nature Switzerland AG 2023
N. T. Nguyen et al. (Eds.): ICCCI 2023, CCIS 1864, pp. 675–688, 2023.
https://doi.org/10.1007/978-3-031-41774-0_53

chronic diseases: obstructive pulmonary disease, type 2 diabetes, cancer, and cardiovascular disease. Complex and chronic illnesses have driven an increase in long-term hospital stays in recent years [2], and managing patient admissions and hospital stays costs the US over $377.5 billion per year [3]. Longer hospital stays increase the likelihood of hospital-acquired conditions and overburden hospitals with limited resources and capacity [4]. Predicting a patient's hospital stay and understanding how they use hospital resources has significant financial and social value. Being able to do so may help hospitals allocate resources to accommodate patients faster, which can improve patient care, reduce unnecessary stays, and save money that can be invested in health infrastructure. Machine learning and data mining are increasingly used to gain insights from healthcare data, which can help public health agencies and hospitals manage human and financial resources. Past descriptive, predictive, and hypothesis-driven studies have examined the prevalence of intensive care admissions, diagnoses, and complications and shown a growing potential to impact clinical practice [5]. The Medical Information Mart for Intensive Care (MIMIC) database provides a comprehensive stream of patient hospitalization records [6]. Our investigation uses MIMIC database data to develop two models (classification and clustering) and provide predictive and exploratory insights. For the classification task, *Multinomial Logistic Regression (MLR)*, *Random Forest (RF)*, and *Gradient Boosting Machine (GBM)* were built. *K-Means* is used for clustering purpose. R Studio was used for data preparation, visualization, and model construction. [7]

2   Related Work

LOS is commonly estimated based on the patient's hospital stay. Bisection and periodic tests examine prediction algorithms in decision tree methods like Adaboost, Bagging, and Random Forest (Ma et al.; 2020 [8]). One of Xiamen's main hospitals provided 11,206 respiratory disease admission records for the study. Studies rarely used hospital data to predict duration of stay, although some used insurance claims. Also good. Bagging had 0.723 accuracy, 0.296 RMSE, and 0.831 R2 in the bisection test. Insurance data tactics yielded greater results. Bagging and Adaboost predicted LOS better than bisection and periodic testing, respectively.

Using the cutting-edge R package tidy models for machine learning, several researchers successfully implemented multiple algorithms for respiratory problem patients using the MIMIC-III dataset (Williams Batista and Sanchez-Arias; 2020 [9]). This shows that new LOS forecasting methods are not always algorithmic. The C5.0 classification model, Support Vector Machine, and Random Forest fared better in ICU LOS prediction, depending on the dataset. Classifying LOS as A (less than 3 days), B (3–5 days), and C (5+ days) helped classify. In another study, researchers employed Lasso, Elastic Net, Linear, and Ridge regression techniques to anticipate LOS using the MIMIC-II dataset of ICU inpatients. Lasso, Elastic Net, and Ridge outperformed the linear regressor since the medical dataset characteristics are not linearly linked. The average of the three regressors predicted LOS since they all performed well. Patients who undergo more tests remain longer; however, the rationale is unclear.

Medical datasets include non-linear feature correlations; therefore, linear relationship machine learning methods fail. One study used an artificial neural network-based non-linear feature selection technique (Kabir and Farrokhvar; 2019 [10]. Before applying the model, LOS was binary, characterized as short-term or long-term. SVM, LR, and ANN fitted LOS classification subsets. The ANN outperformed the SVM and LR, demonstrating the non-linear relationship between the LOS and its predictor, which can be better identified using non-linear classifiers like the ANN.

3   Data Description and Preparation

The Massachusetts Institute of Technology Computational Physiology lab created the open-access MIMIC III database. The Harvard University teaching hospital Beth Israel Deaconess Medical Center in Boston, Massachusetts, has 60,000 intensive care unit admissions in its database. Over 50,000 adult patients and 8,000 newborns stay. Patients were recorded June 2001-October 2012. We analyzed a subset of Dr. Alexander Scarlat's MIMIC III database on Kaggle [11]. This dataset includes patient demographics, admission details, and conditions, as well as the average daily number of patient-caretaker interactions like drug prescriptions and clinical notes. The data also includes patient stay length and death during admission. Figure 1 outlines all variables.

3.1   Variable Cleaning and Transformation

Three categorical variables had null values upon data exploration. Most categorical variables had "unknown" or "unspecified" categories, so null values and categories with no information were grouped together. Misspelled words and variations of the same category (i.e., "GI" vs. "Gastrointestinal") were encoded into the same group in several categorical classes. "White - European" and "White - Russian" for patient ethnicity were intuitively reclassified as "White" due to high cardinality. Over 15,000 patient diagnosis categories existed. Thus, to simplify feature selection, we chose a few of the most common admission diagnoses and a few of interest and renamed the rest "Other". Since patient IDs were unique and the admission procedure variable was text, both were removed from the analysis.

3.2   Target Variable Creation - Length of Stay (LOS)

From 0 to 294 days, LOS was a continuous variable. LOS was divided into three classes with equal numbers of observations to create a categorical target for the classification task: **Short stays**: 0–5 days, **Medium stays**: 6–10 days, and **Long stays**: greater than 10 days.

MIMIC III Data Description		
Variable Name	**Type**	**Description**
LOS days	Continuous	Length of stay in days across all units
LOSgroupNum	Categorical	Categorized length of stay
Categorical predictors		
Gender	Binary	Gender of the patients (Male or Female)
Admit type	Categorical	Type of admission (i.e. Emergency, elective)
Admit Diagnosis	Categorical	Diagnosis upon admission
Insurance	Categorical	Insurance type of the patients
Religion	Categorical	Religious belief of the patients
Marital status	Categorical	Marital status
Ethnicity	Categorical	Ethnicity
Admit procedure	Categorical	Procedure upon admission
Expired hospital	Binary	Flag indicating if a patient has died during stay
Continuous predictors		
Age	Continuous	Age of the patients (in years)
Num callouts	Continuous	Avg. daily number of callouts for consultation
Num procedures	Continuous	Avg. daily number of procedures performed
Num diagnoses	Continuous	Avg. daily number of diagnosis made during stay
Num drugs prescribed	Continuous	Avg. daily number of drugs prescribed
Num CPT events	Continuous	Avg. daily number of events recorded in current procedural terminology code
Num inputs	Continuous	Avg. daily number of events related to fluid inputs for patients (i.e. IV)
Num labs	Continuous	Avg. daily number of events relating to laboratory tests
Num micro labs	Continuous	Avg. daily number of microbiology tests
Num notes	Continuous	Avg. daily number of notes associated with hospital stay (nursing, MD notes, radiology etc)
Num outputs	Continuous	Avg. daily number number of outputs and measurements (i.e. HR, IV line change)
Num transfers	Continuous	Avg. daily number of transfers of patients to different locations within the hospital
Num chart events	Continuous	Avg. daily number of events occurring on a patient chart
Total num interactions	Continuous	Total aggregated number of interactions of any type during the stay (summary of above)

Fig. 1. Predictors descriptions [7].

3.3 Variable Exploration and Relationships

We used histograms and box-plots to visualize variable categories by reducing high-cardinality categorical variables to fewer classes. These tools analyzed categorical frequencies for variables like patient admission type, insurance type, religion, marital status, and ethnicity. By visualizing categorical predictors, we were able to infer that older patients had longer hospital stays, while younger patients had the shortest (Fig. 2). Emergency admissions dominated hospital admissions, but mortality rates were low. Most patients were neonates or middle-older aged and covered by Medicare or private insurance. Compared to other ethnic groups, white patients were older (Fig. 3).

3.4 Outlier Detection and Collinearity

Clustering models are distance-based and sensitive to outliers. Thus, we used the *outlierTest()* function on numerical variables describing patient-caretaker interactions to find anomalies. Although the latter observations can provide useful information about unusual patient cases or exceptions, we decided to remove

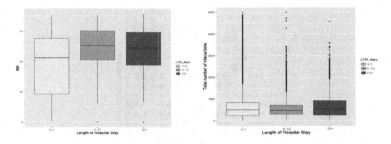

Fig. 2. Length of patient stay by age & total number of patient-caretaker interactions.

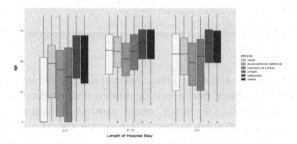

Fig. 3. Length of patient stay by age and ethnicity.

them because they can significantly influence cluster centroids and cluster formation. The correlation matrix results from the correlation test *cor()* and the Variance Inflation Factors (VIF) test were used to assess collinearity for continuous predictors. In order to avoid multicollinearity, some patient-caretaker interaction variables were excluded from the clustering model due to high collinearity. The correlation matrix (Fig. 4) shows highly correlated variables with coefficients above 0.75.

4   Model Selection and Methodology

We built classification and clustering models due to the data's richness. Patients are classified into short, medium, and long-term stays by the classification model. Based on patient-caretaker interactions during a stay, the clustering model seeks to identify patterns and similarities.

4.1   Classification Model

Feature Selection. Only predictors recorded upon hospital admission were included in the classification model to predict rather than simply observe the patient's length of stay. The continuous predictors described patient treatment

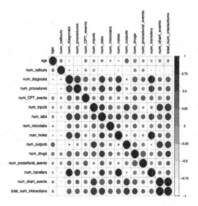

Fig. 4. Correlation matrix for continuous predictors.

and care events, except for age. Thus, continuous predictors describing measures, tests, and procedures performed or observed throughout a patient's hospital stay were excluded. The latter would produce a high-performing model but would misrepresent feature validity. Except for age, the remaining classification variables were categorical after feature engineering. We used the Python Scipy package to perform Chi-Squared tests of independence at 0.05 for feature selection. Since the target variable and predictors are categorical, Chi-Squared, a hypothesis test, was chosen as the best feature selection method. We used contingency tables to test whether length of stay (LOS) and each candidate predictor were significantly related. We used Bonferroni-adjusted post-hoc tests to perform pair-wise comparisons and identify LOS-related categories for candidate predictors. Since self-paid insurance was unavoidable, it was removed. Our categorical predictors dropped from 50 to 38, dummified before model building. Only age, which increased with the length of stay, was considered for modeling. Table 1 shows the list of all classification model predictors. [7]

Model Selection. Identifying the pros and cons of popular models for the classification task was the first step in building the classification model. Linear probability models, multinominal logistic regression models, linear discriminant analysis, quadratic discriminant analysis, and tree-based models like classification trees, random forests, and gradient boosted trees were considered. Due to its lack of probability boundaries and linearity assumptions, the linear probability model was excluded from model testing. Linear and quadratic discriminant analysis models were also abandoned because the predictors were mostly categorical. We tested a *multinomial logistic regression (MLR)* model instead of a simple logistic regression model because our classification task was multiclass in nature. Finally, instead of simple classification trees, which have a high classification variance, *Random Forest (RF)* and *Gradient Boosting Machine (GBM)* tree-based models were chosen. Overall, MLR, RF, and GBM models were built.

Table 1. Selected features for Classification model.

Variable Name	Classes
Age	(continuous predictor)
Gender Male	(binary predictor)
Admit type	Elective, Emergency, Newborn, Urgent
Admit location	Clinical referral, Emergency room, HMO referral, Physician referral, Transfer from hospital
Admit diagnosis	Congestive heart failure, Coronary artery disease, Diabetic Ketoacidosis, Fever, Gastrointestinal bleed, Intracranial hemorrhage, Liver failure, Newborn, Overdose, Pneumonia, Sepsis, Other
Religion	Catholic, Unspecified
Marital Status	Married, Divorced, Widowed, Unknown
Ethnicity	African American, Asian, Hispanic or Latino, White, Unknown

Model Training. For the selected models, 70% and 30% of observations were randomly split into training and test validation sets. The models assigned length of stay labels to each test observation based on the highest probability of the predicted value after training on the training dataset. We calculated each prediction's test accuracy, error rate, and 95% confidence interval by comparing the predicted classifications to the test dataset's observed classifications. Accuracy and recall were used to assess the model's ability to predict short, medium, and long-term stays. Confusion matrices compared the predicted length of stay to the observed length of stay. Recall (Eq. 1) assesses the classifiers' completeness and the prediction model's ability to accurately identify patients' length of stay (true positives), while precision (Eq. 2) is the ratio of correctly classified observations to the total number of positive observations (true and false positives). The accuracy (Eq. 3) indicates the proportion of correct predictions, whereas the error rate (Eq. 4) indicates the proportion of incorrect predictions [12–14].

$$recall = \frac{TP}{TP + FN} \tag{1}$$

$$precision = \frac{TP}{TP + FP} \tag{2}$$

$$accuracy = \frac{TP + TN}{Total(TP + TN + FP + FN)} \tag{3}$$

$$error\,rate = 1 - accuracy \tag{4}$$

RF and GBM were trained on 200 trees to compare. After comparing the base models, GBM had the highest test accuracy; therefore, we further optimized this model by performing hyper-parameter tuning. We specified different numbers of boosting iterations to build, maximum tree depths, and shrinkage parameters based on recommended ranges for datasets of similar size, and performed a five-fold cross validation for each combination of hyper-parameters to determine their optimal levels. [7]

4.2   Clustering Model

Feature Selection. We explored unsupervised methods for clustering patients by the average daily number of patient-caretaker interactions as a metric of the quantity of human or physical resources consumed by patients during their stay to supplement the classification task findings. The clustering exercise aimed to identify hidden similarities between patients by putting them into homogeneous groups to determine which were more expensive. We targeted a priority patient group of 1349 patients by selecting only "emergency" admissions with one of the hospital's five most common conditions: gastrointestinal hemorrhage, coronary artery disease, pneumonia, sepsis, or congestive heart failure. We then clustered patients by eight quantitative variables: number of diagnoses, number of procedures, number of inputs and outputs, number of labs and microbiology labs, number of drugs prescribed, and number of procedural events. Variables were scaled using min-max normalization before clustering due to their various ranges.

Cluster Formation Using K-Means. K-Means was used to cluster patients into specified groups. Three methods were used to estimate the optimal number of clusters: the elbow method, the silhouette method, and the NbClust package in R, which analyzes 30 indices to obtain the best cluster number. These measures strive to maximize variation between clusters while limiting variation within each cluster. Using these strategies, we found three clusters to be best. After allocating each patient to a cluster, Principal Component Analysis (PCA) was applied to the dataset to perform dimension reduction to depict the clusters by the top two principal components, and the characteristics of patients assigned to each cluster were plotted.

5   Results and Discussion

5.1   Patients Classification by Length of Hospital Stay

Accuracy and Error Rate. Table 2 shows model prediction performance. The GBM model has 45.7% accuracy with a 95% confidence interval (CI) of 0.4523–0.462, outperforming the other two models. The GBM successively develops trees using the ensemble approach, employing past tree knowledge to increase aggregate performance. We expected the boosting algorithm to outperform the other examined models. Classification models perform poorly overall.

Table 2. Accuracy and error rate of classification models.

Performance	Model		
	MLR	RF	GBM
Accuracy (%)	43.8	43.6	45.7
Error Rate (%)	56.2	56.4	54.3
95% CI	(0.4293, 0.4389)	(0.4315, 0.441)	(0.4523, 0.462)

Precision and Recall of Classification Models. The confusion matrices
(Table 3) show that all models fared well at detecting short stays. However,
the models were far less likely to detect medium and long-term stays when
they occurred, suggesting that they overwhelmingly predicted short stays. After
examining recall, the GBM model predicted 64% of short stays, 27.4% of medium
stays, and 40.9% of long stays. Class precision was similar. 48.6% of predictions
for short stays were short, 44.2% for medium stays and 41.7% for long stays
were accurate. The GBM model's better recall and poorer precision for short
stays verify our observation that the model performs best at identifying patients
with short stays but still performs poorly due to its frequent misclassification of
patients with medium and long stays.

Table 3. Confusion matrices of classification models.

Predicted	Actual								
	MLR			RF			GBM		
	Short	Medium	Long	Short	Medium	Long	Short	Medium	Long
Short	9752	4936	5469	12904	8162	8783	10263	5516	5345
Medium	2618	3678	2309	1841	2907	1571	2298	3472	2077
Long	3947	4067	4776	1302	1612	2200	3486	3693	5132

Feature Importance. The MLR, RF, and GBM models each have their own
unique importance, so we employed three separate methods to identify which
predictors were most important in determining patient stays. The MLR model's
VarImp() function calculated the sum of the absolute values of the variables'
coefficients. The RF model's *VarImpPlot()* dotchart was interpreted graphically.
GBM's *summary()* function graphs predictor influence. Table 4 shows the top
four predictors of the three models and suggests that age, admission location,
and admission diagnosis were the most relevant in predicting the length of stay.

5.2 Clustering of Patients by Patient-Caretaker Interactions

Figure 5, three clusters explained 64.5% of the patients' variance, evaluated as
the variation between clusters compared to the total variation. Cluster 3 rep-

Table 4. Top four most important predictors for classification models.

Rank	MLR	RF	GBM
1	Admit diagnosis: Liver failure	Age	Age
2	Admit location: Transfer	Admit location: Physician Referral	Admit location: Unknown
3	Admit location: Unknown	Admit location: Clinic Referral	Ethnicity: Unknown
4	Admit diagnosis: Overdose	Admit diagnosis: Coronary Heart Disease	Insurance Government

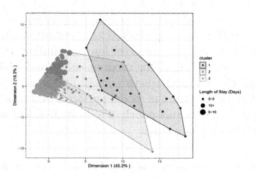

Fig. 5. Results of K-Means clustering of patients by patient-caretaker interactions.

resents the majority of patients, who had fewer average daily patient-caretaker interactions and less variation. Cluster 1 has the most patient-caretaker interactions, while cluster 2 has more variation. According to a relative frequency analysis (Fig. 6) of patient characteristics within each cluster, Cluster 1 is exclusively made up of patients with short stays, most of whom died during their stay. The highest relative proportion of admissions to the emergency room occurred in this cluster, and sepsis was the most common diagnosis upon admission. Cluster 3 patients stay longer, have lower mortality, and have the lowest relative frequency of emergency admissions. Cluster 2 is "intermediate" between clusters 1 and 3, with characteristics from both. We also looked at patients' insurance status, ethnicity, and age across these clusters. Overall, patient-caretaker interaction cluster development is poor. We found 19 patients in cluster 1, 129 in cluster 2, and 1201 in cluster 3. Patients in these clusters have many traits despite their differences.

5.3 Discussion and Managerial Implications

Our classification studies show that patient characteristics, diagnosis, and admission conditions alone cannot predict hospital stay length. Given that several external factors, such as physician availability, specialized equipment, and case

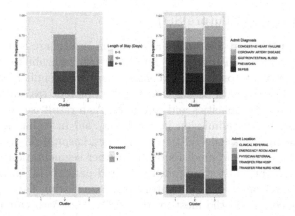

Fig. 6. Relative frequency of patient traits clustered by patient-caretaker interactions.

management effectiveness, can affect a patient's hospital stay, this is unsurprising. Patients may be used in medical research and training in teaching hospitals like Beth Israel Deaconness Medical Center. Thus, patient stays may be extended if extra lab tests are needed or if treating one problem uncovers other conditions. Our categorization analysis showed that the models were best at predicting short stays but overstated their likelihood, making medium and long-term stays difficult to predict. Hospitals will likely underestimate patient stays using our existing model, which could result in inadequate beds, staff, and resources to meet capacity needs. Given the substantial danger of misinformation in healthcare resource allocation and patient care, we do not advise hospitals to base choices simply on patient demographics and admission status. Our K-Means clustering model provided some crucial findings. For patients admitted under one of the top five most common emergency diagnoses, cluster 1 had the highest and most variable patient-caretaker interactions and the highest potential daily "cost" to the hospital. These patients had the shortest stays, the most sepsis diagnoses, and the highest mortality rates. Sepsis is a medical emergency that rapidly progresses to septic shock, causing tissue destruction and organ failure [15]. The high-fatality conditions in this cluster of patients may explain the huge range in patient-caretaker interactions. Patients either died before treatment or died during therapy. In clusters 2 and 3, the majority of patients had fewer and less variable patient-caretaker interactions and longer stays. Interactions may be significant immediately after admission but plateau once the patient is stabilized. These groups had fewer deaths and more gastrointestinal bleed, coronary artery disease, and congestive heart failure. These conditions range in severity but are not life-threatening. We found a few significant traits associated with patient-caretaker interactions, mostly related to a patient's condition rather than demographics. The distribution of clusters implies that some patients may use more resources every day, but most use the same amount. We hypothesize that due to cluster overlap, patient-caretaker interactions may differ depending on patient history and condition severity.

5.4   Limitations and Future Steps

Model Interpretation. Predictive analytics in healthcare is difficult because mathematical models must account for model generalizability and the large variation in treatment costs and outcomes even across similar patient groups. Patients have various health issues that require different treatments. They also enter units of varying capacities and resources. As a result, segmenting patients based on diagnosis and admission location may aid in estimating stay length costs. Since the data was collected across 11 years, hospital programs, units, and divisions may have restructured, requiring further segmentation into comparable time periods. Our cluster approach clustered patients by diagnosis, number of procedures, and number of laboratory exams, allowing us to predict which patient groups consumed the most average daily resources. Our results cannot quantify the dollar cost of each patient category to hospitals because obtaining patient vitals is far cheaper than surgery. The exploratory cluster model did not produce perfectly heterogeneous clusters; therefore, only a few features may be interpreted. [7]

Sample Bias. The Beth Israel Deaconess Medical Center, a Harvard University teaching hospital and one of the nation's top hospitals, provided the data for the analysis. The median age of all patients was 59, and most were white and covered by private insurance or Medicare (federal health coverage for people 65 and older). Compared to the US average of 1.48–0.77 deaths per 1,000 emergency room admissions, 70% of patients were emergency room admissions, and over 10% of admitted patients died [16]. The patient profile in the dataset shows that this sample of patients is not representative of the demographic composition of patients across the US, hence our findings should not be extrapolated to the US population. [7]

Feature Validity. The classification model lacks comprehensive measures. We had six categorical predictors (admit type, admit location, admit diagnosis, religion, marital status, and ethnicity), one binary predictor (gender male), and one continuous predictor (age). The MIMIC III database provides more extensive information on the patient-caretaker interactions we investigated, but we used only the average quantity of these measures rather than the results of tests, operations, and patient notes. The categorization model's prediction value can be improved by including critical admission metrics such as body mass index (BMI), heart rate, temperature, and nervous reflexes, as well as general indicators like pain levels and pre-existing medical conditions. [7]

6   Conclusion

This effort sought to develop models that explain hospitalization patterns. We developed classification and clustering models using retrospective data from the MIMIC III dataset to identify factors that may affect patient stay length. We were able to examine the performance of three predictive classification models and found that the dataset's restrictions prevent the models from predicting patient length of stay. However, we were able to describe three groups of patients based on hospital resource utilization, characteristics, diagnoses, and potential causes of mortality during their stay, making the current data more suitable for exploratory purposes. This work helped us understand the intricacy of health care analytics tools and the practical ramifications of these models. Predictive modeling can improve human resources management, prognostic and diagnostic analysis, and early disease and disability identification. Data collection, algorithm tuning, and model interpretation must be done in a way that benefits the people, communities, and populations they serve to operationalize predictive models for such activities. When human lives are at stake, such models can have big benefits.

References

1. World Health Organization (WHO): Integrated chronic disease prevention and control (2020)
2. Friedman, B., Jiang, H.J., Elixhauser, A., Segal, A.: Hospital inpatient costs for adults with multiple chronic conditions. Med. Care Res. Rev. **63**(3), 327–346 (2006)
3. Health Catalyst: Patient-centered LOS reduction initiative improves outcomes, saves costs (2016)
4. Hassan, M., David, K.: Hospital length of stay and probability of acquiring infection. Int. J. Pharm. Healthc. Mark. **4**(4), 324–338 (2010)
5. Panch, T., Szolovits, P., Atun, R.: Artificial intelligence, machine learning and health systems. J. Glob. Health **8**(2), 020303 (2018)
6. Alistair, E.W., et al.: MIMIC III, a freely accessible critical care database. Sci. Data **3**, 1–9 (2016)
7. Courtemanche-Martel, S., Wang, D.: A classification and clustering analysis of patient hospital stays. Final Project Report, Master of Management in Analytics, Desautels Faculty of Management, McGill University (2020)
8. Ma, F., Yu, L., Ye, L., Yao, D.D., Zhuang, W.: Length-of-stay prediction for pediatric patients with respiratory diseases using decision tree methods. IEEE J. Biomed. Health Inform. **24**(9), 2651–2662 (2020)
9. Williams Batista, R., Sanchez-Arias, R.: A methodology for estimating hospital intensive care unit length of stay using novel machine learning tools. In: 19th IEEE International Conference on Machine Learning and Applications (ICMLA), pp. 827–832 (2020)
10. Kabir, S., Farrokhvar, L.: Non-linear feature selection for prediction of hospital length of stay. In: 18th IEEE International Conference on Machine Learning and Applications (ICMLA), pp. 945–950 (2019)
11. Scarlat, A.: MIMIC-III Dataset - MIMIC3d aggregated data: ICU aggregated data as number of interactions between patient and hospital (2019)
12. Prajwal, C.N.: Confusion matrix in R—A Complete Guide (2022). https://www.digitalocean.com/community/tutorials/confusion-matrix-in-r
13. Wisdom, B.D.: Understanding the Confusion Matrix (II) (2019). https://dev.to/overridedeveloper/understanding-the-confusion-matrix-264i

14. Shmueli, B.: Multi-class metrics made simple, Part I: precision and recall (2019). https://towardsdatascience.com/multi-class-metrics-made-simple-part-i-precision-and-recall-9250280bddc2
15. Centers for Disease Control and Prevention (CDC): What is sepsis? (2022)
16. Shmerling, R.H.: Where people die (2018)

Electrocardiogram-Based Heart Disease Classification with Machine Learning Techniques

Hai Thanh Nguyen$^{(\boxtimes)}$ ⓘ, An Hoang Cao ⓘ, and Phuong Ha Dang Bui$^{(\boxtimes)}$ ⓘ

Can Tho University, Can Tho, Vietnam
{nthai.cit,bdhphuong}@ctu.edu.vn

Abstract. Automatic extraction of relevant and reliable information from electrocardiogram (ECG) signals is essential for heart disease diagnosis and treatment. This study proposes deep learning model based on improved one-dimensional convolutional neural network (1D-CNN) architecture for classifying heart disease using ECG data. First, we collect ECG recordings from patients with and without heart disease. Then, the relevant features are extracted from the ECG data, which is a critical step as the features' quality directly impacts the predictive models' performance. Next, we apply the predictive models, encompassing 1D-CNN, Support Vector Machine (SVM), and Logistic Regression, combined with fine-tuned hyperparameters and StandardScaler, to improve heart disease prediction performance. The experimental results show that the proposed deep learning model using 1D-CNN combined with fine-tuning hyperparameters and StandardScaler can achieve better classification results on ECG-based heart disease classification tasks than previous studies.

Keywords: Electrocardiogram · Heart Disease · 1D-Convolutional Neural Network · Fine-tuned Hyperparameters

1 Introduction

Cardiovascular disease is one of the most common causes of death worldwide annually. Early detection of abnormal heart conditions can avoid sudden cardiac death and other dangerous illnesses caused by heart disease. In addition, the early heart disease diagnosis helps doctors know the patient' s condition and offer reasonable and early treatment plans. ECG, a non-invasive diagnostic tool that records the heart's electrical activity through electrodes placed on the chest, arms, and legs, is widely used in diagnosing heart disease [1]. The ECG signals are the recordings of the cardiac system's bioelectrical activities, which can be used to identify abnormal heart rhythms, heart damage, and other conditions that may indicate an increased risk of heart disease.

Many researchers have recently applied deep learning architectures to analyze ECG data for predicting the likelihood of heart disease and identifying specific risk factors and characteristics associated with heart disease as well. This

© The Author(s), under exclusive license to Springer Nature Switzerland AG 2023
N. T. Nguyen et al. (Eds.): ICCCI 2023, CCIS 1864, pp. 689–701, 2023.
https://doi.org/10.1007/978-3-031-41774-0_54

research proposes ECG-based heart disease prediction model using an improved 1D-CNN algorithm. First, the ECG recordings are obtained from many patients with and without heart disease. The data are preprocessed to remove noise and ensure signal quality. Then, the relevant features are extracted from the ECG data. Next, the predictive models based on deep learning frameworks, comprising 1D-CNN, SVM, and Logistic Regression, combined with fine-tuned hyperparameters and StandardScaler, are applied to classify heart disease. Finally, the performance of these predictive models is evaluated using various metrics, e.g., accuracy, precision, recall, and F1-score. We can see from the experimental results that the proposed deep learning model based on 1D-CNN combined with fine-tuned hyperparameters and StandardScaler can improve the performance in classifying ECG-based heart disease.

In the rest of this paper, the related work applied machine learning and statistical models for heart disease prediction are briefly presented in Sect. 2. Section 3 proposes deep learning model based on the improved 1D-CNN framework for classifying heart disease using ECG data. Section 4 evaluates the performance of the proposed improved 1D-CNN model and compares it to those of some state-of-the-art studies to evaluate the proposed approach's effectiveness. Finally, the conclusion is discussed in Sect. 5.

2   Related Work

Recently there have been numerous studies in predicting heart disease based on ECG data, using various machine learning and statistical methods. Notably, Wang et al. [2] presented an improved CNN-based method to classify arrhythmia's heartbeat automatically. In a study [3], Xu and Liu developed a Holter data CNN heartbeat classifier based on coupled-convolution layer structure and adopted the dropout mechanism to classify ECG heartbeat. Another work [4] was introduced by Sahker et al. proposed an ECG classification model applying generative adversarial networks for restoring the balance of the dataset, then using two deep learning approaches-an end-to-end approach and a two-stage hierarchical approach-based on deep CNNs for eliminating hand-engineering features by combining feature extraction, feature reduction, and classification. In the study [5], the authors presented a prediction method based on six types of machine learning techniques, including linear discriminant analysis, linear and quadratic SVMs, decision tree, k-nearest neighbor, and artificial neural networks to identify the most significant parameters extracted from ECG signals for cardiovascular disease prediction. Wang et al. [6] proposed an ECG classification method using Continuous Wavelet Transform (CWT) and CNN. In the method, CWT was used for decomposing ECG signals to obtain different time-frequency components, and CNN was used for feature extraction from the 2D scalogram composed of the above time-frequency components. Hassan et al. [7] presented a cardiac arrhythmia classification model, which combined CNN and Bidirectional Long Short-Term Memory (BLSTM) using MIT-BIH and St-Petersburg datasets. In another work [8], the authors developed an ECG heartbeat classification model based on a CNN-BLSTM-based classifier to classify ECG heartbeats of MIT-BIH imbalanced dataset. Cui et al. [9] presented a deep learning-based multidimensional feature fusion method that combines traditional approaches and 1D-CNN to find the optimal feature set for ECG arrhythmia classification. In a study [10], Rafi and Akthar proposed an ECG classification method based on a hybrid deep-learning approach that incorporates both a revolution and a recurrent deep neural network for reliably identifying the cardiac beats. In work [11], Farag developed a tiny CNN classifier combined with the matched filter theory for inter-patient ECG classification and arrhythmia detection. Exciting work in [12] applied a cardiac disease detection model which used discrete wavelet transform for preprocessing to remove unwanted noise or artifacts and a non-linear vector decomposed neural network to enhance heart disease prediction performance.

Numerous studies have explored the robustness of machine learning applied to medical data. However, the applications of such approaches are limited to ECG data on heart disease. In addition, heart disease is dangerous and must be detected early to deploy treatments as soon as possible. Therefore, our study aims to predict heart disease based on ECG data by leveraging the powers of machine learning algorithms.

3   Methods

In this section, the main steps are applied to solve the problem of predicting heart disease based on ECG data, as shown in Fig. 1. These steps will be described in detail in the following sections.

3.1   ECG Data Collection

This study proposes the improved 1D-CNN model to classify heart rate types on the ECG dataset. The data used in this work are two collections of heartbeat signals derived from two famous datasets in heartbeat classification, MIT-BIH Arrhythmia dataset [13] and PTB Diagnostic ECG dataset [14]. Both datasets provide enough samples to support deep neural network training. Furthermore, the normal and different arrhythmias cases and myocardial infarctions on the ECG can correlate to the signals. These signals have been preprocessed and segmented, and each segment corresponds to a pulse.

3.2   Data Prepropcessing

Although ECG data obtained from the MIT-BIH database is expected not to contain as much disruptive noise as ECG data obtained directly from a patient, it still contains some noise that requires attention to improve the subsequent steps of the system. Therefore, the signal preprocessing step is focused on removing noise from ECG recordings. Below is an illustration (Fig. 2) of the samples of the MIT-BIH Arrhythmia dataset.

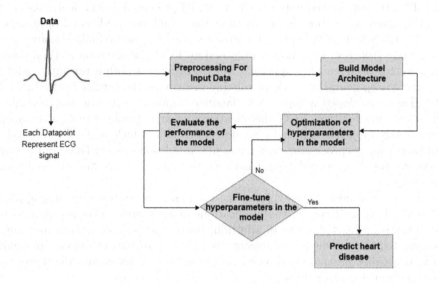

Fig. 1. Heart disease prediction based on ECG data

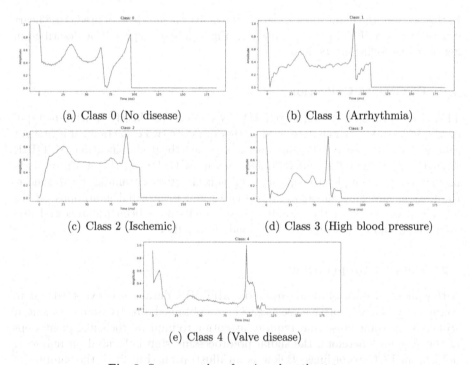

(a) Class 0 (No disease)　　　　　(b) Class 1 (Arrhythmia)

(c) Class 2 (Ischemic)　　　　　(d) Class 3 (High blood pressure)

(e) Class 4 (Valve disease)

Fig. 2. Some samples of various heartbeat types

As a first step, mean removal is applied to remove the noise in the ECG signals. Next, the unwanted component is removed by subtracting the mean of the ECG recording from every sample point, and the signal baseline amplitude is pulled back to level zero. However, nearly all ECG recordings also have high and low-frequency noise present, which is brought on by various causes, including muscular contraction, breathing movements, inadequate electrode contact, and the presence of other external equipment. Therefore, the next step is to eliminate the low-frequency noise components once the high-frequency noise has been removed. This low-frequency noise manifests as baseline wandering, mainly brought on by the patient's breathing. Finally, all ECG recordings are subjected to a derivative-based (high pass) filter to eliminate this low-frequency noise, which passes high frequencies but attenuates low frequencies.

3.3   Convolutional Neural Network on 1D Data (1D-CNN)

CNN has become one of the most popular artificial intelligence techniques because of its excellent ability to recognize traits automatically. Moreover, 1D-CNN can be ideal for real-time applications because of its low processing demands on 1D data. The proposed CNN model consists of two 1D convolution layers and two fully connected layers enabled by the ReLU activation function-feature map for the related input [15].

Firstly, we divided the dataset into training and testing sets and performed preliminary steps such as segmenting each ECG signal into small segments and normalizing signal values. Subsequently, we construct a simple CNN model with two 1D convolution layers and two fully connected layers [7]. The model is trained on the training dataset for 100 epochs with a learning rate of 0.001. The results obtained indicate that the model is capable of accurately classifying different types of heart rhythms from ECG signals with high accuracy. We also utilize data augmentation techniques such as rotation and flipping to increase the diversity of the training dataset and reduce model overfitting. Finally, based on the outcomes of experiments, we predict cardiac diseases, precisely five types represented in the ECG data.

4   Experimental Results

In this section, we evaluate the performance of the proposed improved 1D-CNN model. These results are compared to the results of some state-of-the-art studies to evaluate the effectiveness of the proposed approach.

4.1   Dataset Description

In this study, we use the MIT-BIH dataset, which contains 48 half-hour segments of two-channel ambulatory ECG recordings from 47 subjects participating in BIH Arrhythmia Laboratory research between 1975 and 1979. Then, 23 recordings were randomly selected from a pool of 4000 24-hour ambulatory ECG record-ings taken by a mixed group of inpatients (approximately 60%) and outpatients (about 40%) at Boston's Beth Israel Hospital. To include less common but clini-cally relevant arrhythmias that would not be well represented in a small random sample, the remaining 25 recordings from the same set were chosen [16].

Table 1 briefly reviews all classes referred to in the dataset, where N stands for normal and no arrhythmia, S stands for Supra-ventricular premature, V stands for Ventricular escape, and F stands for Fusion of ventricular and normal, and Q stands for Fusion of paced and normal unclassifiable. In the study, they are trained on a set of 109446 samples shown in Fig. 3 and a test set of 21892 samples, where N is 72471 samples, S is 2223 samples, V is 5788 samples, F is 641 samples, and finally Q is 6431 samples.

Table 1. Summary for each category in dataset

Category	Label	Annotations	Type of disease
N	0	Normal	No disease
S	1	Supraventricular ectopic	Arrhythmia
V	2	Ventricular ectopic	Ischemic
F	3	Fusion	High blood pressure
Q	4	Unknown	Valve disease

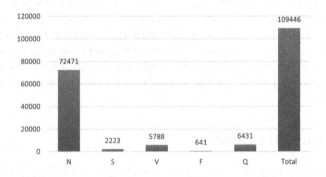

Fig. 3. The number of samples of each class

4.2   Environmental Settings

All the above processes are coded and applied on the Jupyter Notebook envi-ronment. These notebooks provide users an interactive environment to analyze data and train machine learning models. It is run on a PC with Intel(R) i5-6500

CPU 3.20 GHz and 8 GB RAM. The trained model was created with 100 epochs and a batch size 256.

To evaluate the performance of the proposed model, this study uses several evaluation matrices such as accuracy, recall, precision, and F1-score.

4.3 Experimental Results

Scenario 1: Comparison Between Using Default Hyperparameters and Fine-Tuned Hyperparameters. This section compares three popular machine learning algorithms, including 1D-CNN, SVM, and Logistic Regression, with default values of hyperparameters and fine-tuned hyperparameters (Table 2).

Table 2. Classification report between using default hyperparameters and fine-tuned hyperparameters

	Default hyperparameters			Fine-tuned hyperparameters		
	1D-CNN	SVM	LR	1D-CNN	SVM	LR
N	0.99	0.98	0.95	0.99	0.96	0.95
S	0.84	0.71	0.46	0.83	0.61	0.51
V	0.96	0.91	0.45	0.95	0.42	0.44
F	0.79	0.59	0.38	0.81	0.45	0.40
Q	0.99	0.95	0.91	0.99	0.92	0.91
Accuracy	0.98	0.97	0.91	0.98	0.92	0.91
Macro avg	0.91	0.83	0.63	0.92	0.67	0.64
Weighted avg	0.98	0.97	0.90	0.98	0.91	0.90

This study has leveraged the RandomizedSearchCV method [17] to seek optimal hyperparameters. RandomizedSearchCV selects random values for hyperparameters with 3-fold cross-validation on the training set. For the comparison, we use the default value of hyperparameters for the considered algorithms.

The selected values of hyperparameters in Table 2 include Logistic Regression algorithms (penalty = 'l2', C = 1.0, solver = 'lbfgs', max-iter = 100), SVM (kernel = 'linear', C = 1.0) and 1D-CNN (epochs = 100, batch-size = 64). For the Logistic Regression algorithm, the accuracy shows that with fine-tuned hyperparameters, a value of 0.91 is obtained, and with default hyperparameters, it is also 0.91. For the SVM algorithm, the accuracy is not improved, with the fine-tuned hyperparameters achieving a value of 0.92 compared to 0.97 of the default hyperparameters. For the 1D-CNN algorithm, the accuracy shows no improvement, with the fine-tuned hyperparameters achieving value of 0.98 compared with 0.98 of the default hyperparameters.

Scenario 2: Comparison Between Using a Scaler and Without Scaler.
While training a machine learning model, a scaling method such as Standard-Scaler can help improve the model's performance by bringing the data values to the same range. This makes it easier for the model to learn relationships and avoid problems like a boom or vanishing gradients and can improve the performance as shown in [18]. This study compares the performance of three machine learning algorithms, comprising 1D-CNN, SVM, and Logistic Regression when combining with StandardScaler and without StandardScaler.

As can be seen from Table 3, for the Logistic Regression algorithm, when we run the experiment with default hyperparameters, the accuracy, Macro-average accuracy (Macro avg), and Weighted average accuracy (Weighted avg) without using the scaler are 0.91, 0.58, and 0.89, respectively, and those of using the scaler are 0.91, 0.64, 0.90, respectively, which shows that the results are not much difference. For SVM, the accuracy, Macro avg, and Weighted avg without the scaler are 0.92, 0.67, and 0.91, respectively, while the performance with the scaler are 0.97, 0.84, 0.97, which shows an improvement when using the scaler. For the 1D-CNN, using the scaler, we can reach the accuracy performance, Macro avg, and Weighted avg are 0.98, 0.90, and 0.98, respectively, whereas those of without using the scaler are 0.98, 0.91, and 0.98, respectively, which shows that there are not much difference between two approaches.

The experimental results show that all three machine learning architectures can be improved effectively by using StandardScaler. However, there are some factors which we need to pay attention, e.g., the amount of data, network structure, selected hyperparameters, etc., to ensure that the training takes place effectively and precisely.

Table 3. Classification report with default hyperparameters for using the scaler and without using the scaler

| | Without StandardScaler | | | Using StandardScaler | | |
	1D-CNN	SVM	LR	1D-CNN	SVM	LR
N	0.99	0.96	0.95	0.99	0.98	0.95
S	0.83	0.61	0.33	0.81	0.71	0.53
V	0.96	0.42	0.43	0.95	0.91	0.43
F	0.80	0.45	0.25	0.77	0.62	0.39
Q	0.99	0.92	0.92	0.99	0.95	0.92
Accuracy	0.98	0.92	0.91	0.98	0.97	0.91
Macro avg	0.91	0.67	0.58	0.90	0.84	0.64
Weighted avg	0.98	0.91	0.89	0.98	0.97	0.90

Scenario 3: The Performance of Using a Scaler Combined with Fine-Tuned Hyperparameters. We can see from Table 4, for the Logistic Regression algorithm, when we run the experiment using the scaler combined with fine-tuned hyperparameters, the accuracy, Macro avg, and Weighted avg are 0.91, 0.65, 0.90, while without using the scaler and running with default hyperparameters, those values obtain 0.91, 0.63 and 0.90 (Table 2), which shows that the results are not much difference. For the SVM algorithm, with fine-tuned hyperparameters and using the scaler, the accuracy, Macro avg, and Weighted avg are 0.98, 0.87, and 0.98, respectively, whereas those of without using the scaler and running with default hyperparameters are 0.97, 0.83, and 0.97, respectively, which shows an improvement when using the scaler and running with fine-tuned hyperparameters. Similar to the 1D-CNN algorithm, using the scaler combined with fine-tuned hyperparameters, the accuracy, Macro avg, and Weighted avg are 0.99, 0.94, and 0.99, respectively. When not using the scaler combined with default hyperparameters, those values are 0.98, 0.91, and 0.98, which shows a significant improvement when using the scaler and running with fine-tuned hyperparameters. In summary, using the scaler combined with fine-tuned hyperparameters can improve the models' performance on heart disease classification.

Table 4 also shows that the 1D-CNN algorithm gives better results than other algorithms, followed by SVM, which is slightly better than the Logistic Regression algorithm. Moreover, from Fig. 4a, the 1D-CNN algorithm shows high accuracy in all classes. The results are much higher than the other algorithms. Therefore, we choose the 1D-CNN algorithm for our proposed model.

The classification accuracy results for the MIT-BIH data set were approximately 95.70% with a relatively flat curve after 100 training epochs. Whereas the validation datasets had an accuracy of between 96.70% and 99.30%, the curve was stable as revealed in Fig. 5a. Therefore, the loss curve of the training set from 0.26 to 0.16 is pretty flat. Meanwhile, the validation loss is reduced to 0.11 to 0.03 across epochs (Fig. 5b). The results show that the loss is significantly reduced, and the accuracy is relatively high. All are presented in Fig. 5.

Table 4. Classification results of the improved algorithms by using StandardScaler combined with fine-tuned hyperparameters with RandomizedSearchCV

	1D-CNN	SVM	LogisticRegression
N	0.99	0.99	0.95
S	0.88	0.75	0.55
V	0.97	0.94	0.44
F	0.84	0.68	0.40
Q	1.00	0.98	0.92
Accuracy	0.99	0.98	0.91
Macro avg	0.94	0.87	0.65
Weighted avg	0.99	0.98	0.90

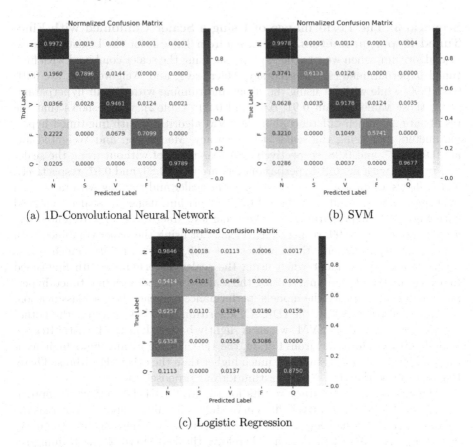

(a) 1D-Convolutional Neural Network   (b) SVM

(c) Logistic Regression

Fig. 4. Confusion matrices of various algorithms

4.4   Comparison with Previous Studies and Discussion

Table 5 shows that the proposed method outperforms the others. Furthermore, the best hyperparameter retrieved by the method was picked and was among the hyperparameters' learning rates. Therefore, it can be said that the suggested model has been improved using the 1D-CNN combined with the scaler and fine-tuned hyperparameters, which worked in the manner mentioned above.

The proposed improved 1D-CNN model using the scaler combined with fine-tuned hyperparameters plays an important role in improving the model's accuracy. Therefore, the model can scrutinize these layers more effectively than in the learning process. Table 5 compares the results of different approaches. Nazrul Anuar [5] achieved a 90.0% accuracy in identifying four arrhythmia classes by applying ANN. At the same time, MM Farag [11] designed a CNN model capable of automatically classifying five distinct types of heartbeats in ECG readings achieving an accuracy of 97.13%. Amin Shoughi [8] reported 98.71% accuracy for categorizing five classes by using the CNN with the Bi-LSTM model. SK

Table 5. Classification performance of the proposed improved 1D-CNN model compared to some state-of-the-art studies

Studies	Architecture	Accuracy (%)	Precision (%)	Recall (%)	F1-score (%)
Proposed Model	**CNN on 1D data**	**99.30**	**95.30**	**93.30**	**94.40**
Nayan Nazrul Anuar [5]	ANN	90.0	–	–	–
Tao Wang [6]	CNN with CWT	98.74	–	–	68.76
M. Mohamed Suhail [12]	CNN with DWT	90.67	–	–	–
Abdelrahman M. Shaker [4]	CNN with GAN	98.30	90.0	97.70	–
Mohammad Rafi [10]	CNN and RNN	98.0	90.80	84.40	97.40
Amin Shoughi [8]	CNN with BI-LSTM	98.71	92.50	94.40	–
MM Farag [11]	CNN	97.13	–	91.00	88.30

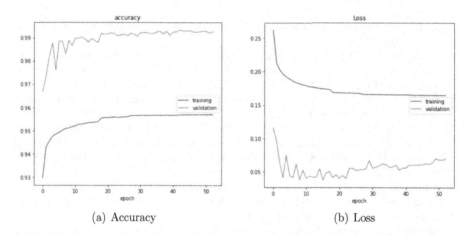

(a) Accuracy   (b) Loss

Fig. 5. An illustration of training and testing performance of 1D-CNN during epochs.

Mohammad Rafi [10] designed a CNN model with RNN capable of automatically classifying five types of heartbeat in ECG datasets, which achieves an accuracy of 98.0%, while Abdelrahman M. Shaker [4] with CNN and GAN models achieves an accuracy of 98.30%. We achieve promising results which overcome the state-of-the-art studies by improving the 1D-CNN model using the scaler combined with fine-tuned hyperparameters. Our refined model yielded an impressive accuracy of 99.30%, which we consider a highly favorable outcome.

5   Conclusion

Machine learning has emerged as a critical tool in medicine and automatic diagnosis owing to its ability to achieve high accuracy in medical data analysis. This study proposes a novel approach to improve machine learning's performance in electrocardiogram-based heart disease prediction by using the scaler combined with fine-tuned hyperparameters. As shown from the experiments, the results of the proposed approach, which improved the 1D-CNN model by using the scaler combined with fine-tuned hyperparameters, can get better results than previous studies, with 99.30%, 95.30%, 93.30%, and 94.40% in accuracy, precision, recall, and F1-score, respectively. However, independently fine-tuned hyperparameters did not significantly improve the performance. In addition, classic machine learning algorithms such as SVM and Logistic Regression can benefit from scaler rather than fine-tuned hyperparameters.

Further studies can explore 2D convolutional networks to leverage deep learning advancements on images. Moreover, patterns of abnormalities in electrocardiograms should be further analyzed to detect heart diseases early.

References

1. Sattar, Y., Chhabra, L.: Electrocardiogram. In: StatPearls [Internet]. StatPearls Publishing (2022)
2. Wang, H., Shi, H., Chen, X., Zhao, L., Huang, Y., Liu, C.: An improved convolutional neural network based approach for automated heartbeat classification. J. Med. Syst. **44**(2), 1–9 (2019). https://doi.org/10.1007/s10916-019-1511-2
3. Xu, X., Liu, H.: ECG heartbeat classification using convolutional neural networks. IEEE Access **8**, 8614–8619 (2020). https://doi.org/10.1109/access.2020.2964749
4. Shaker, A.M., Tantawi, M., Shedeed, H.A., Tolba, M.F.: Generalization of convolutional neural networks for ECG classification using generative adversarial networks. IEEE Access **8**, 35592–35605 (2020). https://doi.org/10.1109/ACCESS.2020.2974712
5. Anuar, N.N., et al.: Cardiovascular disease prediction from electrocardiogram by using machine learning. Int. J. Online Biomed. Eng. (iJOE) **16**(07), 34 (2020). https://doi.org/10.3991/ijoe.v16i07.13569
6. Wang, T., Lu, C., Sun, Y., Yang, M., Liu, C., Ou, C.: Automatic ECG classification using continuous wavelet transform and convolutional neural network. Entropy **23**(1), 119 (2021). https://doi.org/10.3390/e23010119
7. Hassan, S.U., Zahid, M.S.M., Abdullah, T.A., Husain, K.: Classification of cardiac arrhythmia using a convolutional neural network and bi-directional long short-term memory. Digit. Health **8**, 205520762211027 (2022). https://doi.org/10.1177/20552076221102766
8. Shoughi, A., Dowlatshahi, M.B.: A practical system based on CNN-BLSTM network for accurate classification of ECG heartbeats of MIT-BIH imbalanced dataset. In: 2021 26th International Computer Conference, Computer Society of Iran (CSICC), pp. 1–6 (2021). https://doi.org/10.1109/CSICC52343.2021.9420620
9. Cui, J., Wang, L., He, X., Albuquerque, V.H.C.D., AlQahtani, S.A., Hassan, M.M.: Deep learning-based multidimensional feature fusion for classification of ECG arrhythmia. Neural Comput. Appl. (2021). https://doi.org/10.1007/s00521-021-06487-5
10. Rafi, S.M., Akthar, S.: ECG classification using a hybrid deeplearning approach. In: 2021 International Conference on Artificial Intelligence and Smart Systems (ICAIS), pp. 302–305 (2021). https://doi.org/10.1109/ICAIS50930.2021.9395897

11. Farag, M.M.: A tiny matched filter-based CNN for inter-patient ECG classification and arrhythmia detection at the edge. Sensors **23**(3), 1365 (2023). https://doi.org/10.3390/s23031365

12. Suhail, M.M., Razak, T.A.: Cardiac disease detection from ECG signal using discrete wavelet transform with machine learning method. Diabetes Res. Clin. Pract. **187**, 109852 (2022). https://doi.org/10.1016/j.diabres.2022.109852

13. Moody, G.B., Mark, R.G.: MIT-BIH arrhythmia database (1992). https://physionet.org/content/mitdb/

14. Bousseljot, R.D., Kreiseler, D., Schnabel, A.: The PTB diagnostic ECG database (2004). https://physionet.org/content/ptbdb/

15. Schmidhuber, J.: Deep learning in neural networks: an overview. Neural Netw. **61**, 85–117 (2015). https://doi.org/10.1016/j.neunet.2014.09.003

16. Kachuee, M., Fazeli, S., Sarrafzadeh, M.: ECG heartbeat classification: a deep transferable representation. In: 2018 IEEE International Conference on Healthcare Informatics (ICHI), pp. 443–444 (2018)

17. Liu, Y., Wang, P., Li, Y., Wen, L., Deng, X.: Air quality prediction models based on meteorological factors and real-time data of industrial waste gas. Sci. Rep. **12**(1), 9253 (2022). https://doi.org/10.1038/s41598-022-13579-2

18. Raju, V.N.G., Lakshmi, K.P., Jain, V.M., Kalidindi, A., Padma, V.: Study the influence of normalization/transformation process on the accuracy of supervised classification. In: 2020 Third International Conference on Smart Systems and Inventive Technology (ICSSIT), pp. 729–735 (2020)

SS-FL: Self-Supervised Federated Learning for COVID-19 Detection from Chest X-Ray Images

Ines Feki[1,2]([envelope]), Sourour Ammar[1,2][ORCID], and Yousri Kessentini[1,2][ORCID]

[1] Digital Research Center of Sfax, B.P. 275, Sakiet Ezzit, 3021 Sfax, Tunisia
`ines.feki.doc@enetcom.usf.tn,`
`{sourour.ammar,yousri.kessentini}@crns.rnrt.tn`
[2] SM@RTS: Laboratory of Signals, systeMs, aRtificial Intelligence and neTworkS,
Sfax, Tunisia

Abstract. Recently Federated Learning has gained considerable popularity and becomes an attractive learning paradigm due to the privacy and the computational advantages that it offers. However, it is facing a major challenge: the lack of labeled data on certain federated settings. This is known as label deficiency challenge and it remains less studied. To address this challenge and related problems, we propose in this work a simple Self-Supervised Federated Learning based framework for COVID-19 detection from chest X-ray images, named (SS-FL). Due to the scarcity of radiological images of COVID-19 and the confidentiality considerations, the aim of this framework is to benefit from the large amount of available unlabeled chest X-ray images to learn useful visual representations that will help in distinguishing COVID-19 from other pathologies. We propose to train a deep neural network in a self-supervised way on large unlabeled dataset at server-side and then to fine-tune it, in a federated fashion, on a small amount of labeled data at clients-sides. Our simulation results show that the use of the self-supervised pre-training step at server level allows to improve the accuracy compared with the classic supervised FL: an improvement of 3.1% on COVID-19 dataset. We also highlight the ability of pre-training a global model with unlabeled data to speed up the overall federated training process.

Keywords: Self-supervised learning · Federated Learning · Chest X-ray images · COVID-19 detection

1 Introduction

In machine learning, training deep models need to have access to very large datasets to achieve good performance. However, collecting data is a big challenge especially in sensitive domains, such as the healthcare domain, due to the privacy and data-ownership challenges of medical data. With the advantage of

N. T. Nguyen et al. (Eds.): ICCCI 2023, CCIS 1864, pp. 702–714, 2023.
https://doi.org/10.1007/978-3-031-41774-0_55

privacy-preserving data, Federated Learning (FL) is currently the most attractive distributed machine learning framework. Indeed, FL enables decentralized clients to collaborate and train a shared model while preserving data privacy [26]. In general, the standard training process of FL begins from the server which distributes an initial global model to a random subset of participating clients. Then, each client optimizes its local model by training on its own local data in parallel. Those trained local models are transferred to the server which aggregates received parameters and updates the global model to construct a new one. The success of existing FL algorithms in computer vision is heavily dependent on the quality and the information content of the visual representations learned from the input images [24,28]. In this context, there are many works in the field of FL that assume that fully labeled samples are available at the clients [2,7,11].

As a decentralized approach, FL has successfully resolved the problem of privacy of medical imaging data, but assuming that data is available in fully labeled format is in itself problematic. Indeed, one of the commonly encountered problems in the medical domain (and in most other fields) is label deficiency. In fact, data generated at edge devices is typically unlabeled. However, collection and annotation of large datasets are costly and time-consuming. Some recent works [17,23,25] tried to address the label deficiency problem in FL assuming that only a fraction of labeled data is available and using semi-supervised learning techniques to build a global model. More recently, the authors in [30] proposed a federated self-supervised pre-training method as a solution for heterogeneous data distributions problems and label deficiency in FL. Another problem that may occur when few labeled data is available on the client-side is the difficulty of convergence of local models. This problem can highly affect the resulting global model generated by aggregating those local models (sent by each client at each round). In addition, the random initialization of the global model at the beginning of the FL process - which will serve as the initial weights for all local models - can also affect the convergence of the models. To address these challenges, we must find solutions to fully leverage the available data without annotations on the one hand and to improve the performance of the distributed model on the other hand.

Given the rapid or exponential increase in the amount of data and the high cost of manual annotation, recent progress in Self-supervised learning (referred as SSL) have shown tremendous improvement in reducing the amount of labeled data required to achieve state-of-the-art performance. Moreover, unlike supervised learning which relies heavily on the label information, self-supervised pre-training uses only the unlabeled dataset to learn features from different visual representations for a later fine-tuning using only a small fraction of labeled data.

In view of the self-supervised learning advantages, we have exploited this technique in order to improve the performance of the traditional FL strategy. In this work, we propose to combine the self-supervised learning with the FL in a new framework called *SS-FL: Self-supervised Federated Learning framework*. In fact, we propose to use self-supervised learning at the server-side to build an initial model that has benefited from a large amount of unlabeled data to learn useful image representations. This model will be used as a starting model for the FL process. The proposed framework is then consisting of two phases: 1) a pre-training stage at server level (centralized way) to build a starting model on unlabeled data, and 2) a fine-tuning stage (supervised learning) in a federated (decentralized) fashion. In this work we deal with the detection of COVID-19 disease from chest X-ray images. To investigate the effectiveness of the proposed framework, we carried out simulations on a Chest X-ray images dataset (COVID-19 dataset containing images belonging to three classes) and we compared the performance of the obtained model with and without using the self-supervised pre-training stage. We experimentally show that our framework surpasses the classic FL in terms of accuracy on the COVID-19 dataset and converges faster.

The remaining paper is organized as follows: Sect. 2 cites the related works. Section 3 describes an overview of our proposed framework. Section 4 is dedicated to the experimental study and the obtained results. Finally, we conclude this study in Sect. 5.

2   Related Work

We review in this section related works about the FL and the SSL approaches.

2.1   Federated Learning (FL)

Federated Learning is a popularized deep learning approach that enable distributed clients to train, collaboratively, deep models on their own data with privacy preserving. Since the appearance of the influential paper [26], FL has become an active research area to address the problems of centralized learning and data privacy. In view of the FL advantages, many works such as [1, 15, 27, 31] have been introduced in the computer vision field and healthcare domain, where data is submitted to privacy rules. Other works exploited this technique to detect the COVID-19 disease based on Chest X-ray images. For example, in our previous paper [7], we presented a collaborative federated learning framework allowing multiple medical institutions to screen COVID-19 disease from Chest X-ray images using deep learning without sharing patient data. Also, the work in [19] used blockchain technology based federated learning to detect COVID-19 using CT images. In [36], the authors proposed a novel dynamic fusion-based federated learning approach for medical diagnostic image analysis to detect COVID-19 infections. However, despite the advantages of the FL, it could not overcome the challenge of lack of annotations of training data that researchers are facing. Indeed, existing supervised federated learning algorithms such as FedAvg [26], FedProx [21], and FedNova [34] assume that all client's data is labeled and the server is the responsible to push the federated process with random parameters which usually leads to non-guaranteed convergence issues.

2.2   Self-Supervised Learning (SSL)

To address the label deficiency issue in FL, recent works [16,17,22,23,25,37] use semi-supervised methods (such as pseudo labeling [20]) by assuming that the server or client has a fraction of labeled data to train a global model. However, the main challenging setting is the fully unsupervised training without using any labels in server or client parts.

Self-supervised learning is a popular method which aims to exploit unlabeled data to learn meaningful representations of samples without human supervision [35]. Recently, much research work has focused on the development of self-supervised methods in computer vision across different applications [8,32]. In addition, we mention as an example our recent work [6] where we demonstrated that the use of self-supervised learning on unlabeled data is able to learn useful visual representations from Chest X-ray images, and only few labeled data samples are sufficient to reach the same accuracy of a supervised model learnt on the whole annotated dataset. More specifically, Self-supervised contrastive learning is one of several related approaches that used SSL by forcing the visual representations to stay close to each other for similar pairs and far apart for dissimilar pairs in the latent space [4,13]. It has recently shown promising results in computer vision. As an example, we cite the work in [4] that proposed to use contrastive SSL following 3 steps: first, some data augmentation operations are performed on input images, secondly, visual representation are learned on these inputs, and finally a few-shot classification is made. The authors in [33] also used contrastive SSL on multiple views to understand the importance of view selection. In the same direction, the authors in [10] have explored contrastive SSL to classify agricultural images. Since these existing works have shown a great improvement in reducing the amount of labeled data required to achieve good performance, we have focused our attention to exploit this recent progress in SSL in order to improve the FL performances and address the label deficiency issue in such conditions. But it remains still unclear how these SSL methods can be incorporated into FL to perform federated results. In the literature, there are very few works such as [12] which have examined recent progress in SSL community (such as SimCLR [4], SimSiam [5], BYOL [9] and SwAV [3]) in a federated setting.

In the present work, we have concentrated our efforts to incorporate the SSL into the FL framework and we demonstrate how well performance would be significantly improved compared to classic supervised FL.

3   Proposed Framework

We describe in this section the main components of our proposed *SS-FL* framework for COVID-19 detection from Chest X-ray images. The idea of this proposition is to combine the self-supervised learning principle with the FL to deal with limited labeled data scenarios. Indeed, this framework consists of the following steps: 1) First, we perform a self-supervised pre-training of a base encoder on a large amount of unlabeled Chest X-ray images using contrastive learning.

This step allows us to learn useful visual representations from X-ray images. The obtained model is then used to initialize the parameters of the server that will enable federated learning. 2) Secondly, we perform supervised fine-tuning on a small labeled chest X-ray dataset, belonging to a medical institution, in a federated way. Figure 1 shows the summary of our proposed method. Our aim is to improve the federated learning process by initializing the server model by a better model that benefits from the useful representations learned during the pre-training step.

3.1 Self-Supervised Pre-training Step at Server Level

For the pre-training step, we adopt the SimCLR [4] algorithm which consists of four components as described in the blue box on the right of Fig. 1: $\mathcal{T}(.)$ as a stochastic data augmentation module, $f(.)$ is a Resnet-50 as a neural network base encoder, $g(.)$ is 2-layer MLP as projection head, and a contrastive loss function $\mathcal{L}_c(.)$ (described in Eq. 1).

For Each input image x from the unlabeled dataset, we apply $\mathcal{T}(x)$ twice to obtain two copies $\tilde{x}_i$ and $\tilde{x}_j$ of the image. Both copies are given as input for the ResNet-50 encoder $(f(.))$ to get a normalized embedding vector. The obtained vector is then propagated through the projection head $(g(.))$ to obtain a 224-dimensional features vector. After that, we compute the supervised contrastive loss on the output of the projection head by using Eq. 1.

$$\mathcal{L}_c = -\log \frac{exp(sim(z_i, z_j)/\tau)}{\sum_{k=1}^{2N} \mathbb{1}_{[k \neq i]} exp(sim(z_i, z_k)/\tau)} \tag{1}$$

where z_i, and z_j denote the output of the projection head for $\tilde{x}_i$ and $\tilde{x}_j$, respectively, $\mathbb{1}_{[k \neq i]}$ is an indicator function (equal to 1 if $k \neq i$), N is the size of the batch of images, τ is a temperature parameter, and $sim(.)$ is a similarity measure.

As SimCLR, our framework learns representations to distinguish between similar and dissimilar images by encouraging the two generated views $\tilde{x}_i$ and $\tilde{x}_j$ from the same image x to be similar, and two views $\tilde{x}_i$ and $\tilde{x}_k$ $(k \neq i)$ from different images to be dissimilar.

This step is made only once before the starting of the federated process. After the pre-training is finished, we totally discard the projection head $g(.)$ from the network and we conserve only the base encoder $f(.)$ with its weights learnt from the unlabeled data. The output of this step will then be the weights of the base encoder referred as w^{0*}. These weights will be used to initialize the weights of the global model at the starting point of the federated process, at server level.

3.2 Supervised Federated Fine-Tuning Step

At this step, the knowledge is transferred from the previous step (self-supervised pre-training) to the target task to fine-tune the created model in a federated fashion on the clients-sides.

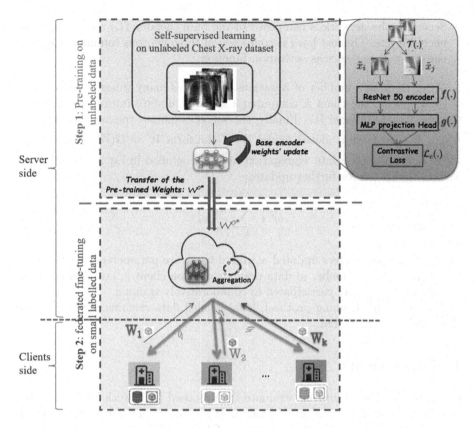

Fig. 1. Overview of self-supervised federated learning framework SS-FL that consists of two steps: 1) Before the federated process starts and before the server starts sending parameters to the clients, a pre-training step is performed at server level. 2) At the beginning of the second step (fine-tuning step), the server produces a global encoder with weights w^0* and broadcasts the global model to each collaborating client. Each client fine-tunes its local model with the labeled local data and uploads the updates of its model w_k to the central server. The server produces a global model with new weights via model weights averaging.

Indeed, a federated learning setting consists of a set of K clients, with each client k having local data instances X_k of size n_k drawn from the local data distribution D_k. At round t_1, the server sends an initial model with its weights w^0 to a set of contributing clients. The sent model will be used to initialize each local model at client side. In classic federated frameworks, this global model is generally initialized with random weights at server level. In our framework, the global model is built as follows:

– First, the base encoder $f(.)$ with its weights w^{0*}, adjusted during the pre-training phase, is transferred from the first step (self-supervised pre-training) and used to initialize the weights w^0 of the global model, so that $w^0 \leftarrow w^{0*}$.

– Secondly, the network is composed of the base encoder $f(.)$ and 2 fully connected layers. The last layer is composed of three neurons (number of output classes) with softmax as activation function.

After running a number of iterations of SGD as many times as the number of local epochs, the client k computes a gradient update in order to generate the new updated model W_k. Finally, the server combines the local models W_1, $W_2,...,$ W_N to learn a global model $\widehat{W}$ of the form $\widehat{W} = G(W_1, W_2, ..., W_N)$, where G is an appropriate aggregation function detailed in Eq. 2, and sends $\widehat{W}$ back to the clients for further updates.

$$w^t \leftarrow \sum_{k=1}^{K} \frac{n_k}{n} w_k^t \tag{2}$$

where w^t are parameters updated at round t, w_k^t are parameters sent by client k at round t, n_k is number of data points stored on client k, and n is the total number of data points participated in collaboratively training.

Following this training protocol, local labeled data remains private to each client and is never shared.

4   Experiments

In this section, we empirically evaluate the proposed framework SS-FL and discuss the potential of using a self-supervised learning as a pre-training phase in improving the federated learning results for COVID-19 detection. First, we introduce the dataset used in our simulations. Then, we present the implementation details. Finally, we present and discuss the experimental results.

4.1   Data Preparation

To maintain the idea of data privacy in FL, we perform server-side pretraining and client-side fine-tuning on two different input datasets. For the pretraining phase, we use the CheXpert Dataset [18], a large dataset of labeled CXR images released in 2019 by Stanford University to promote research into chest disease using XRays. The CheXpert dataset contains to date 224,316 chest radiographs of 65,240 patients collected by the studies of Stanford Hospital in both inpatient and outpatient centers and performed between October 2002 and July 2017. The CheXpert dataset consists of 14 labeled observations, meaning that each image is labeled with 14 different diseases. More than one view is available for a particular patient (frontal and lateral views). The choice of this database is justified by the fact that the class COVID-19 does not exist in this database since it is collected before the appearance of Corona disease. This makes the situation more challenging. During the pre-training phase, we consider the whole

CheXpert dataset discarding the labels where images are merged to consider them as unlabeled dataset. As a result, we obtain $223,414$ unlabeled chest X-ray images for the pre-training phase.

For the fine-tuning phase and the evaluation step, we use the COVID-19 Radiography Database [29], a large open source database of chest X-ray images for "COVID-19" positive cases along with "Normal" and "Viral Pneumonia" images. This dataset is collected from different publicly accessible datasets, online sources and published papers.

Because the number of images in this database is expected to increase over time with more available data, our taken dataset consists of a set of 15,153 chest X-ray images belonging to three classes: Normal (healthy), COVID-19, and Viral Pneumonia. It contains 10,192 chest X-ray images diagnosed as Normal (not affected patients), 3,616 chest X-ray images diagnosed as COVID-19, and 1,345 chest X-ray images for Viral Pneumonia. We randomly split the dataset into 12,121 training images (80% of the images and referred by D_{train}) and 3,032 test images (20% of the images and referred by the D_{test}).

We construct a FL-COVID dataset using the dataset D_{train} and D_{test} split both into K subsets. All our simulations are done using $K = 4$ clients. All clients have the same amount of data (25%) according to the same distribution. To mimic the real-world federated scenarios, each client only contains the data from one real-world site (i.e.,hospital) without overlapping, and all images from the same patient only appear in either training or testing set of the same client. Thus, we assign 3,788 images (904 COVID-19 cases, 336 Viral Pneumonia cases and 2548 Normal cases) for each client. The FL-COVID dataset is used during the fine-tuning phase.

4.2   Implementation Details

In this work, we adopt the SimCLR algorithm for self-supervised pre-training. For the model architecture, we use ResNet-50 [14] as the backbone of the Sim-CLR framework. For the pre-training protocol, we do not know how many categories the images belong to. In our approach, the images are ordered in a batch of 128 samples and we train SimCLR for 500 epochs with learning rate= 0.1.

On the output of the ResNet-50 base encoder, we use a 2-layer MLP projection head to obtain a vector of 224-dimensional embedding. This feature vector is used for contrastive learning using the contrastive loss (NT-Xent) with temperature equal to 0.1. For the FL fine-tuning step, we fine-tune the network using the standard SGD optimizer for minimizing the classification loss function and then updating the network parameters. The learning rate is set to 0.001, and the batch size to 2.

Regarding the number of rounds, we fine-tune our models up to 200 communication rounds and present the accuracy for after each round, in order to investigate its behavior during the federated learning process.

For data Augmentation: During pre-training and as those used by SimCLR, we randomly crop patches of size $224 \times 224 \times 3$ from original images for all the dataset, followed by Gaussian blur and color distortion (strength =0). During fine-tuning, we randomly resize and crop the images to $224 \times 224 \times 3$. In addition, we perform horizontal and vertical flips.

4.3   Experimental Results

In this section, we provide our experimental results on the Chest X-ray dataset, and we investigate the potential of including the pre-training step in order to improve the FL performances when dealing with the label deficiency problem. For that, we evaluate the proposed framework SS-FL and we compare its achievement regarding the classical supervised FL framework. The performance in terms of accuracy of both methods is drawn in Fig. 2. We also present a performance analysis on the confusion matrix of the proposed SS-FL and the classical supervised FL framework (given in Fig. 3 and Fig. 4).

We plot in Fig. 2 the accuracy scores on the test dataset D_{test} against the number of communication rounds for both methods (SS-FL and Supervised FL).

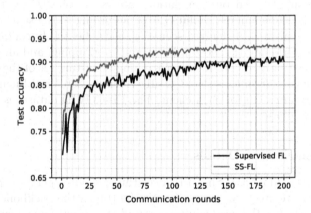

Fig. 2. Comparison of SS-FL to supervised FL in terms of accuracy on test dataset. (Color figure online)

For the SS-FL method, the accuracy curve (red curve in Fig. 2) shows that the performance of the model is indeed progressing and able to converge over 200 communication rounds. Moreover, SS-FL method outperforms the supervised FL baseline (black curve) even at the beginning of the first rounds. After 200 rounds, the SS-FL method achieves an accuracy of 93.23% on the test set, against only 90.13% for the supervised FL method, with an improvement of 3.1%.

However, the accuracy of the supervised FL method is fluctuating and the convergence to close values begin only after several rounds. This behavior is due to the convergence difficulties that the global model is facing when the server aggregates the updates sent by each contributing client. We recall that the starting model at round zero is initialized with random weights. In fact, as the training data is small at each client, the learned local models can be more personalized for this local data. On the other hand, the SS-FL accuracy presents smoother fluctuations. This result highlights the ability of the pre-training step to provide a better initial model for the FL process leading to an easiest convergence.

In addition, it can be seen from Fig. 2 that the SS-FL method requires less rounds than the supervised FL method to converge to the same accuracy rate. In fact, SS-FL requires only 40 rounds to achieve an accuracy rate of 90%, whereas the supervised FL method requires more than 120 rounds to achieve the same accuracy. Thus, we find that our method has lower communication costs than supervised FL.

In conclusion, the obtained results show that classic supervised FL on small labeled datasets at clients sides is indeed challenging, and using a self-supervised learning as pre-training step (in SS-FL) allows to learn useful visual representations and then helps the FL process to converge quickly into a better model.

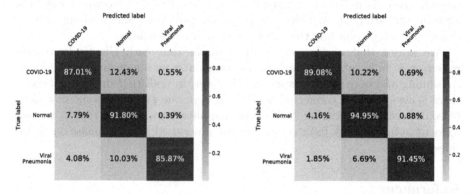

Fig. 3. Confusion matrix of the supervised FL based model

Fig. 4. Confusion Matrix of the self-supervised FL based model

To support this investigation, we provide in Fig. 3 and Fig. 4 two confusion matrices for the SS-FL and the supervised FL methods, respectively. Since the diagonal elements are the correctly predicted samples, for the SS-FL, the model correctly predicts a total of 2827 samples from a total of 3032 samples in D_{test} leading to an overall accuracy of 93.23%. However, for the supervised federated learning method, the model correctly predicted only 2733 on the same test set D_{test} leading to an accuracy of 90.13%. The confusion matrix presented by Fig. 4 reveals that the SS-FL model outperforms the supervised FL model on all three classes: an improvement of 2.07% for "COVID-19" class, 3.15% for the class "Normal" and 5.58% for the "Viral Pneumonia" class.

We recall that the dataset used during the pre-training step is collected before the corona virus outbreak. Thus, it is sure that this disease's characteristics are not shown during the first step of SS-FL. Although this, we find that the SS-FL method provides better results on the "COVID-19" class (an improvement of

2.07%) than the supervised FL method. This result highlights the ability of the pre-training step to learn useful representations even on never seen classes.

5   Conclusion and Future Work

Classical federated learning algorithms require that each client trains a random initialized model received from the server and consider supervised learning tasks where labels are naturally available on each client which is severely limiting and may have drastic detrimental effects on the performance. In this paper, we deal with the label deficiency problem and we present a self-supervised federated learning framework (SS-FL) for COVID-19 detection from chest X-ray images. This framework consists of two steps. First, we perform a self-supervised learning on a large amount of unlabeled chest X-ray dataset in order to learn useful visual representations. This step is performed at server level, and the pre-trained model will be used as a starting point to the federated process. Secondly, the pre-trained model is fine-tuned on small labeled datasets in a federated way. The experimental study showed that the proposed framework allows to improve the overall accuracy regarding the supervised federated scenario.

We notice that our present work assumes that each client's local data resources is fully labeled, which is not pragmatic as annotating data is time consuming and may require expertise. However, in realistic federated networks, there is always a new connected device and each one generates some new unlabeled data resulting from interactions with applications. For that reason, we plan to focus in future work to integrate the self-supervised learning phase on clients sides.

References

1. Baheti, P., Sikka, M., Arya, K.V., Rajesh, R.: Federated learning on distributed medical records for detection of lung nodules. In: Proceedings of the 15th International Joint Conference on Computer Vision, Imaging and Computer Graphics Theory and Applications, pp. 445–451 (2020). https://doi.org/10.5220/0009144704450451
2. Caldas, S., et al.: LEAF: a benchmark for federated settings. CoRR abs/1812.01097 (2018). http://arxiv.org/abs/1812.01097
3. Caron, M., Misra, I., Mairal, J., Goyal, P., Bojanowski, P., Joulin, A.: Unsupervised learning of visual features by contrasting cluster assignments. In: Proceedings of the 34th International Conference on Neural Information Processing Systems (NIPS 2020), pp. 9912–9924 (2020)
4. Chen, T., Kornblith, S., Norouzi, M., Hinton, G.: A simple framework for contrastive learning of visual representations. In: International Conference on Machine Learning (ICML 2020) (2020)
5. Chen, X., He, K.: Exploring simple Siamese representation learning. CoRR abs/2011.10566 (2020)

6. Feki, I., Ammar, S., Kessentini, Y.: Self-supervised learning for COVID-19 detection from chest x-ray images. In: Bennour, A., Ensari, T., Kessentini, Y., Eom, S. (eds.) Intelligent Systems and Pattern Recognition, ISPR 2022. Communications in Computer and Information Science, vol. 1589, pp. 78–89. Springer, Cham (2022). https://doi.org/10.1007/978-3-031-08277-1_7

7. Feki, I., Ammar, S., Kessentini, Y., Muhammad, K.: Federated learning for COVID-19 screening from chest x-ray images. Appl. Soft Comput. **106**, 107330 (2021). https://doi.org/10.1016/j.asoc.2021.107330

8. Feng, Z., Xu, C., Tao, D.: Self-supervised representation learning by rotation feature decoupling. In: 2019 IEEE/CVF Conference on Computer Vision and Pattern Recognition (CVPR), pp. 10356–10366 (2019). https://doi.org/10.1109/CVPR.2019.01061

9. Grill, J.B., et al.: Bootstrap your own latent a new approach to self-supervised learning. In: Proceedings of the 34th International Conference on Neural Information Processing Systems (NIPS 2020), pp. 21271–21284 (2020)

10. Güldenring, R., Nalpantidis, L.: Self-supervised contrastive learning on agricultural images. Comput. Electron. Agric. **191**, 106510 (2021). https://doi.org/10.1016/j.compag.2021.106510

11. Hao, M., Li, H., Xu, G., Liu, S., Yang, H.: Towards efficient and privacy-preserving federated deep learning. In: ICC 2019–2019 IEEE International Conference on Communications (ICC), pp. 1–6 (2019). https://doi.org/10.1109/ICC.2019.8761267

12. He, C., Yang, Z., Mushtaq, E., Lee, S., Soltanolkotabi, M., Avestimehr, S.: SSFL: tackling label deficiency in federated learning via personalized self-supervision. ICLR (2022)

13. He, K., Fan, H., Wu, Y., Xie, S., Girshick, R.: Momentum contrast for unsupervised visual representation learning. In: Proceedings of the IEEE/CVF Conference on Computer Vision and Pattern Recognition (CVPR), pp. 9729–9738 (2020)

14. He, K., Zhang, X., Ren, S., Sun, J.: Deep residual learning for image recognition. In: Proceedings of the IEEE Conference on Computer Vision and Pattern Recognition, pp. 770–778 (2016). https://doi.org/10.1109/CVPR.2016.90

15. Huang, L., Shea, A.L., Qian, H., Masurkar, A., Deng, H., Liu, D.: Patient clustering improves efficiency of federated machine learning to predict mortality and hospital stay time using distributed electronic medical records. J. Biomed. Inform. **99**, 103291 (2019). https://doi.org/10.1016/j.jbi.2019.103291

16. Itahara, S., Nishio, T., Koda, Y., Morikura, M., Yamamoto, K.: Distillation-based semi-supervised federated learning for communication-efficient collaborative training with non-IID private data. IEEE Trans. Mob. Comput. **22**(01), 191–205 (2023). https://doi.org/10.1109/TMC.2021.3070013

17. Jeong, W., Yoon, J., Yang, E., Hwang, S.J.: Federated semi-supervised learning with inter-client consistency. ArXiv abs/2006.12097 (2020)

18. Jeremy, I., et al.: CheXpert: a large chest radiograph dataset with uncertainty labels and expert comparison. CoRR, vol. abs/1901.0703 (2019)

19. Kumar, R., et al.: Blockchain-federated-learning and deep learning models for COVID-19 detection using CT imaging. In: Electrical Engineering and Systems Science(EESS) (2020). https://doi.org/10.48550/arXiv.2007.06537

20. Lee, D.H.: Pseudo-label: the simple and efficient semi-supervised learning method for deep neural networks. In: ICML 2013 Workshop: Challenges in Representation Learning (WREPL) (2013)

21. Li, T., Sahu, A.K., Zaheer, M., Sanjabi, M., Talwalkar, A., Smith, V.: Federated optimization in heterogeneous networks. arXiv preprint arXiv:1812.06127 (2020)

22. Liang, X., Liu, Y., Luo, J., He, Y., Chen, T., Yang, Q.: Self-supervised cross-silo federated neural architecture search. CoRR abs/2101.11896 (2021)

23. Liu, Y., Yuan, X., Zhao, R., Zheng, Y., Zheng, Y.: RC-SSFL: towards robust and communication-efficient semi-supervised federated learning system. arXiv preprint arXiv:2012.04432 (2020)

24. Liu, Y., Zhang, L., Ge, N., Li, G.: A systematic literature review on federated learning: from a model quality perspective. CoRR abs/2012.01973 (2020). https://arxiv.org/abs/2012.01973

25. Long, Z., et al.: FedSemi: an adaptive federated semi-supervised learning framework. arXiv preprint arXiv:2012.03292 (2020)

26. McMahan, H.B., Moore, E., Ramage, D., Hampson, S., Arcas, B.A.: Communication-efficient learning of deep networks from decentralized data. In: Artificial Intelligence and Statistics (AISTATS), pp. 1273–1282 (2017)

27. Nguyen, D.C., Ding, M., Pathirana, P.N., Seneviratne, A., Zomaya, A.Y.: Federated learning for COVID-19 detection with generative adversarial networks in edge cloud computing. IEEE Internet Things J. **9**(12), 10257–10271 (2022). https://doi.org/10.1109/JIOT.2021.3120998

28. Pejó, B.: The good, the bad, and the ugly: quality inference in federated learning. CoRR abs/2007.06236 (2020). https://arxiv.org/abs/2007.06236

29. Rahman, T.: COVID-19 radiography database (2021). https://www.kaggle.com/tawsifurrahman/covid19-radiography-database

30. Rui, Y., et al.: Label-efficient self-supervised federated learning for tackling data heterogeneity in medical imaging. IEEE Trans. Med. Imaging **42**, 1932–1943 (2023). https://doi.org/10.1109/tmi.2022.3233574

31. Sheller, M.J., et al.: Federated learning in medicine: facilitating multi-institutional collaborations without sharing patient data. Sci. Rep. **10**, 12598 (2020). https://doi.org/10.1038/s41598-020-69250-1

32. Souibgui, M.A., et al.: Text-DIAE: a self-supervised degradation invariant autoencoders for text recognition and document enhancement. arXiv preprint arXiv:2203.04814 (2022)

33. Tian, Y., Sun, C., Poole, B., Krishnan, D., Schmid, C., Isola, P.: What makes for good views for contrastive learning. In: International Conference on Neural Information Processing Systems (NIPS 2020) (2020)

34. Wang, J., Liu, Q., Liang, H., Joshi, G., Poor, H.V.: Tackling the objective inconsistency problem in heterogeneous federated optimization. In: Proceedings of the 34th International Conference on Neural Information Processing Systems (NIPS 2020), pp. 7611–7623 (2020)

35. Wang, Y., Zhang, J., Kan, M., Shan, S., Chen, X.: Self-supervised equivariant attention mechanism for weakly supervised semantic segmentation. In: Proceedings of the IEEE Conference on Computer Vision and Pattern Recognition (CVPR) (2020)

36. Zhang, W., et al.: Dynamic-fusion-based federated learning for COVID-19 detection. IEEE Internet Things J. **8**(21), 15884–15891 (2021). https://doi.org/10.1109/JIOT.2021.3056185

37. Zhao, Y., Liu, H., Li, H., Barnaghi, P.M., Haddadi, H.: Semi-supervised federated learning for activity recognition. CoRR abs/2011.00851 (2020)

A New Approach for the Diagnosis of Children Personality Disorders Based on Semantic Analysis

Aiman Chakroun[✉], Mariem Mefteh, and Nadia Bouassida

Mir@cl Laboratory, Sfax University, Sfax, Tunisia
Aimanchakroun@gmail.com

Abstract. Psychology is the scientific study of behavior and experience, of how humans and animals feel, think, learn and adapt to their environment. When psychology meets modern technology in computer science, it creates Psycho-informatics. In this paper, we propose an approach and its tool, for the benefits of children having psychological issues. This approach extracts the different traits from raw documentations of personality disorders based on semantic analysis. These traits are then used to build, automatically, a personalized test depending on the disorder(s) estimated by the psychiatrist. The responses of the child's parent on this test are then analyzed to generate a report for the psychiatrist, which would be useful in the precise diagnosis of the child.

Keywords: Personality disorders · Children psychology · Semantics

1 Introduction

Computer science profoundly changes our practices and knowledge: bioinformatics makes possible the manipulation of genes, chemical computing makes it possible to walk among molecules in an adapted visual universe, etc. Likewise, the boundary between computer science and psychology becomes permeable [8].

Psychology is the scientific study of behaviour and mental processes that uses scientific methods to study how, when, where and why we feel, think and act the way we do, and uses psychological interventions to influence people [1]. Personality traits have been studied in psychology for a long time [15]; they are enduring patterns of perceiving, relating to, and thinking about the environment and oneself that are exhibited in a wide range of social and personal contexts [6]. More specifically, personality disorders are inflexible and maladaptive patterns of behavior reflecting extreme variants of normal personality traits that have become rigid and dysfunctional [19]. Ten prototypical personality disorders were listed in the *Diagnostic and Statistical Manual of Mental Disorders* (DSM-5) [6], including the *antisocial, avoidant, borderline, dependent, histrionic, narcissistic, obsessive-compulsive, paranoid, schizoid,* and *schizotypal* personality disorders.

When psychology is combined with modern technology, it creates *psycho-informatics* [24]. Psycho-informatics is an emerging interdisciplinary field that

© The Author(s), under exclusive license to Springer Nature Switzerland AG 2023
N. T. Nguyen et al. (Eds.): ICCCI 2023, CCIS 1864, pp. 715–727, 2023.
https://doi.org/10.1007/978-3-031-41774-0_56

uses principles from computer science for the acquisition, organization, and synthesis of data collected from psychology to reveal information about psychological traits such as personality and mood [29]. It took place when psychologists and biologists, in 1960, used artificial intelligence to understand how animals and humans plan their actions and act [1]. Diving into further study, it is noticed that further advancements can be introduced to the traditional methods of treating psychological problems; with the help of these advancements, psychologists will be able to treat their patients in a better and more efficient way [29]. In today's generation, children are constantly facing psychological problems, which they cannot express to anyone but which can be remarkable to their parents throughout strange behavior. Consequently, the number of patients in this age group visiting psychiatrists is increasing, with the need of their parents to find solutions for their problems. The majority of psychiatrists start by collecting the personality traits of the patient as a first step for the therapy. In most cases, they rely on widely used tests, such as Minnesota test [16], Rorschach test [26], etc. Nobody can deny the importance of these tests in the diagnosis phase. However, each test is used to identify specific disorders and diseases.

In this paper, we propose a novel approach, which is dedicated to psychiatrists and parents, both, for the diagnosis step. This approach takes as inputs textual descriptions of personality disorders written *freely* in English, i.e. with no need for preprocessing. They can be in the form of items or even quite complex paragraphs. These descriptions are then analyzed semantically through a natural language processing technique called the semantic model (SM) [21] as a means to extract semantic information from raw sentences. In addition, our approach relies on the Term Frequency/Inverse Document Frequency (TF/IDF) numerical statistic method [17] and the Density-Based Spatial Clustering of Applications with Noise (DBSCAN) algorithm [7], in order to identify the list of personality disorders' traits. The generated traits are used to build automatically personalized psychological tests, according to the disorder(s) estimated by the psychiatrist. This test is then fulfilled by the child's parent, at home, instead of making it in stressful conditions in the psychiatrist's clinic. The result constitutes a support to the psychiatrist to validate the estimated disorder(s) of the patient. Moreover, our approach generates a report which contains the percentages of each estimated disorder, as well as its approved traits. This report would help the psychiatrist to diagnose, efficiently, the child state, which would reflect a good quality of the proposed therapeutic plan, in an optimal time. Our approach is implemented with a tool, which automates all its steps. More specifically, this tool distributes these latter between a server side and a client side. Indeed, a C# code is created and executed on an IIS web server to analyze, semantically, textual descriptions and generate a traits' list. Besides, a mobile application is developed, which is dedicated for the psychiatrists and the parents to build personalized tests and generate psychological reports.

As a proof of concept, this paper also presents an experimental evaluation of our approach. The experimental evaluation measured the quality of the personality traits' list extracted by our approach through the *precision, recall, and*

F-measure rates, in comparison with those identified by an expert, by starting from the same inputs.

The remainder of this paper is organized as follows. In Sect. 2, we describe briefly the concept of the semantic model. In Sect. 3, we overview currently proposed works on psycho-informatics. In Sect. 4, we present our approach and its implementing tool. In Sect. 5, we discuss the experimental evaluation results. Finally, in Sect. 6, we summarize the paper and highlight our future works.

2   Background

The semantic model (SM) [21] represents formally raw ideas, following the way in which we think, independently of the used natural language and without resorting to operational details (like creating variables, defining their types, methods signatures, etc.). It is based on a set of patterns, called *mapping rules* as a means to represent formally these ideas. The semantic model treats several features of the natural language (called *entities*), like *concepts* (any "thing" from the real world, being abstract or concrete), *properties* (describe concepts), *statements* (declarative clauses that may be true or false), *sentences* (made up of clauses, possibly connected by links), etc.

For instance, the SM supports many types of statements, like the *predicate statement*. In fact, a *predicate* refers to a verb that requires a number of arguments, depending on its type (intransitive, transitive or ditransitive). An argument refers to any constituent that is strictly (semantically) required by the verb. Each argument corresponds to a specific semantic role. A semantic role is the underlying relation that a constituent has with the main verb in a clause, like *Manner* (i.e. a way of doing something, using the conjunction *by* for example), *Agent* (i.e. the entity that performs the action), *Object* (i.e. the entity that undergoes the action), *Possessed* (i.e. something that is owned or in the disposal of someone/something), etc.

Due to space limitation, we refer the reader to our reference [21] for more details on the semantic model features and mapping rules.

3   Related Work

Currently, the work that falls within the domain of psycho-informatics is quite scattered; indeed, it is published in two rather separate scientific communities (psychology and computer science) [23]. In this section, we will present some existing works on the fusion of the psychology and the computer science domain, i.e. psycho-informatics.

Some existing works were focused on big data monitoring in the context of psycho-informatics. In this sight, Markowetz et al. [18] suggested a method that collects, stores, and analyzes massive amounts of indicative data at little cost and without risks or stress for patients or participants, by tracking user behavior with smartphones. Likewise, Montag et al. [23] proposed an approach which handles large data sets derived from heavily used devices, such as smartphones or online social network sites, in order to shed light on a large number of psychological traits, including personality and mood. Similarly, Muizz et al. [24] proposed a method that aims to dissect human conduct in detail with the help of large information by estimating the seriousness of an individual's downturn and web fixation. The needed information are recorded with the help of cell phones or computers in an electronic structure and are stored in big data storage. Besides, Gerlach et al. [9] developed an approach to the identification of personality types, applied to four large data sets comprising more than 1.5 million participants; their approach identified four distinct personality types and showed that these types appear as a small subset of a much more numerous set of spurious solutions in typical clustering approaches. In addition, Kosinski et al. [15] investigated over 58,000 Facebook users and demonstrated that it is possible to predict sexuality, ethnicity, or political attitudes, as well as personality from Facebook "Likes".

In another context, Madhaffar et al. [20] presented a deep learning approach for depressive episode detection on mobile devices, called DL4DED; it is based on a convolutional neural network and a long short-term memory network to identify the status of a patient's voice extracted from spontaneous phone calls. Moreover, based on image processing techniques, Qin and Gao [25], Hu et al. [13] and Jin et al. [28] predicted personality characteristics from the person's entire facial image features.

On the other hand, some works were interested in predicting psychological variables from online social networks, such as Facebook and Twitter by using the Five Factor Model [10]. For instance, Gosling et al. [12] revealed several connections between personality and self-reported Facebook features, such as the positive relationship between Extroversion and frequency of Facebook usage and engagement in the site. Similarly, Correa et al. [4] and Zhong et al. [30] focused on the amount of time spent using social media and social networking sites and showed that certain personality traits are correlated with total internet usage and with the propensity of individuals to use these tools. In addition, Chittaranjan et al. [3] investigated the relationship between automatically extracted behavioral characteristics derived from rich smartphone data and self-reported Big-Five personality traits based on a machine learning method to detect the personality trait of a user based on smartphone usage.

No one can deny the importance of the aforementioned works and the several challenges they exhibit. In particular, most of them aim to collect indicative data from mobile and web applications in order to estimate the personality kinds and behaviors of a large number of participants. However, in this paper, we propose a novel approach dedicated to the children having psychological problems. This approach treats several personality disorders; indeed, it recognizes the maximum number of personality disorders' traits from reliable resources, such as DSM-5 [6]. The generated traits' list is used to (i) build personalized psychological tests, and to (ii) generate reports for the psychiatrists for the diagnosis phase and for the assignment of adequate therapeutic plans to patients in an optimal time.

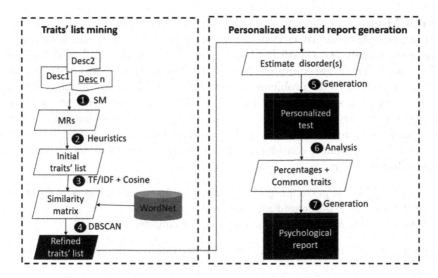

Fig. 1. Functional structure of our approach

4   Our Approach for the Diagnosis of Children Personality Disorders

In order to extract the maximum amount of information for each personality disorder, our approach operates in two phases: *traits' list mining*, followed by *personalized test and report generation* (see Fig. 1). Our approach is implemented through a tool, which is composed of two main parts:

- The first part focuses on the generation of the traits' list by exploiting the semantics of the input personality disorders descriptions; the involved process is implemented as C# classes on an IIS server.
- The second part implements the personalized test construction and the report generation phase of our approach through a mobile application, called Psy-Home (**Psy**chology at **Home**), dedicated to the psychiatrists and the parents of children having psychological problems. This part relies on the generated traits' list throughout a web API.

In fact, the repartition of the involved tasks, between a server and a client side, aims to generate the traits' list only for one time, instead of generating the same list from the same inputs each time the mobile application is installed and launched on a new device. In the remainder of this section, we detail each phase of our approach.

4.1   Traits List Mining

The goal of this phase is to first extract the traits' list corresponding to personality disorder descriptions.

Traits Mining. In this phase, our approach accepts the textual descriptions of the personality disorders (txt files), which are taken from different reliable resources, namely the DSM5 [6], Bockian et al. [2], Kerber [14], and Goldberg [11]. It parses these descriptions to identify the traits of each personality disorder. In fact, it overcomes the problems inherent to natural language ambiguities, and different levels of specification details. To handle these concerns, our approach applies the SM on the input documents and applies a set of heuristics on the generated mapping rules to mine the involved pertinent information (step 1 in Fig. 1). For instance, considering the following descriptions for the narcissic personality disorder:

1. *"The narcissistic personality is characterized by exaggerating self-importance in the form of self-aggrandizing behavior"*
2. *"Overestimate himself and has limitless self-confidence"*

Applying the SM on these descriptions, we get the following mapping rules:

```
[MR1]
    (statement, (action, exaggerate),
      (agent, (personality,narcissistic )),
      (object, self-importance),(manner, (behavior,
        (property statement, (object, greatness),
        (destination, self))))))))
[MR2]
    (copulative,
      (statement, (action, overestimate),(object, self)),
      (statement, possession concept relation,(possessed,
      (self-confidence, limitless))))
```

Where *"statement"* stands for the type of the clause; *"action"* is the predicate class; *"agent"*, *"object"*, *"destination"*, *"possessed"* and *"manner"* represent the semantic roles of the corresponding predicate arguments; *"copulative"* is the type of the involved compression; *"possession concept relation"* and *"property statement"* are two types of statements.

Afterwards, the generated mapping rules will be used to extract the pertinent information for each trait. The application of the MRs is guided by a set of heuristics to produce a list of traits (step 2 in Fig. 1). Due to space limitation, we will present the two following heuristics:

Heuristic. *Find the action predicate statements. Neglect the "agent" argument. Get the predicate if it does not correspond to an abstract verb (e.g. "enable", "provide", "offer", "permit"...). Get the other eventual arguments within the obtained mapping rule.*

For example, following the guidelines of this heuristic, we eliminate the expression *"(agent, (personality, narcissistic))"* from MR1 in the generated examples.

Heuristic. If the mapping rule corresponds to a possession concept relation statement, then neglect the "possessor", keep the "possessed" concept and the other eventual arguments.

For example, only the part *(possessed, (self-confidence, limitless))* is kept from MR2 in our running example.

After applying the guidelines of all the proposed heuristics, our approach extracts the initial traits' list from the resulting MRs. For example, it generates the following traits from MR1 and MR2:

1. exaggerate self-importance by greatness to self behaviour
2. limitless self-confidence

The next step refines the traits' list by using an unsupervised classification method.

Traits List Refinement. This step ensures that the traits have a unified vocabulary without redundancies. Towards this end, our approach proceeds with the classification of the list of traits, using an unsupervised classification method (steps 3 and 4 in Fig. 1). For this purpose, we relied on the widely used TF/IDF method, which calculates the *cosine similarity*, combined with the *DBSCAN* algorithm, in order to refine the initial traits' list. Indeed, DBSCAN accepts input points as values instead of terms. In our case, the traits are composed of terms instead of numbers. Thus, we relied on the TF/IDF method and the similarity matrix, in order to build the traits list and to refine it by removing the eventual noises in the resulting traits' classes.

TF/IDF involves the construction of documents and queries. In our case, a query is composed of the grammatical units (i.e. terms) of one trait; a document contains the same units of a query, added to their synonyms extracted from the WordNet ontology [22]. More specifically, our approach starts with assigning a weight to a term i in a document j as follows:

$$w_{ij} = tf_{i,j} \times idf_{i,j} = tf_{i,j} \times \log(\frac{m}{D(i)}) \tag{1}$$

where: w_{ij} is the weight of the term i in the document j; $tf_{i,j}$ is the frequency of the term i in the document j; m is the total number of documents in the collection; and $D(i)$ is the number of documents where the term i occurs. As a second step, our approach calculates the cosine between documents and queries, as follows:

$$\cos(\overrightarrow{d_i}, \overrightarrow{q}) = \frac{\sum_{t_j \in T} w_{ij} \times w_{qj}}{\sqrt{\sum_{t_j \in T} w_{qj}^2 \times \sum_{t_j \in T} w_{ij}^2}} \in [0, 1] \tag{2}$$

where d_i is the document i; q is the query; $(\overrightarrow{d_i}, \overrightarrow{q})$ is the angle between the vectors $\overrightarrow{d_i}$ and $\overrightarrow{q}$; w_{ij} is the weight of the term t_j in d_i; w_{qj} is the weight of the term t_j in q; T is the set of terms contained in the documents.

After performing TF/IDF and computing the cosine similarity matrix, our approach applies the DBSCAN algorithm on the generated matrix, in order to group documents into semantic classes. For example, our approach generates a class which contains the following traits: "*envy*", "*envious of others*" and "*feeling envious of others*". Based on this classification, the first name in each list is automatically attributed as the name of the class to reflect its content (because all the names in a class have the same meaning).

After applying this step on the traits' list, we get a reduced and refined list of traits, which contains not redundant traits. In practice, our tool generates a JSON file, untitled "*Traits.json*", which contains the resulting traits' list and which is accessible via a web API. Figure 2 shows an extract from the generated JSON file.

```
{
    "Paranoid":[
        "Hypersensitivity",
        "Pervasive distrust",
        "Bear persistently grudges",
        "Read hidden demeaning or threatening meaning in benign remarks or events",
        "Perceive attack on his or her character or reputation",
        "Recurrent suspicions to fidelity of spouse or sexual partner",
        "Jealousy",
        "Rivalries",
        "Risk of committing homicidal act",
        "Overestimation of oneself or hypertrophy of the ego"
    ],
```

Fig. 2. Extract from the generated JSON file of the traits' list

4.2   Personalized Test and Report Generation

The goal of this phase is to build personalized tests and to generate the corresponding reports for the psychiatrists. As we mentioned before, in practice, this phase is implemented by our tool as a mobile application, entitled PsyHome. This application relies on the traits list built in the *Traits.json* file. It accesses to this file through a web API, developed in .NET, which returns the traits' list when the application is installed and launched in the client devices, (i.e. the psychiatrists and the parents devices). Figure 3 shows some interfaces from this application.

Before estimating the child disorder, the psychiatrist can look for specific personality traits in PsyHome, as a refresh of his information about a specific disorder. For example, Fig. 3a shows the displayed interface of the Antisocial personality disorder. Similarly, at the end of the medical consultation, the psychiatrist estimates the possible personality disorder(s) of the patient (i.e. the child). A list of disorders are displayed (see Fig. 3b), from which he selects one or more disorders. Then, PsyHome generates a personalized test, which is composed of questions about the traits of the selected disorder(s), combined with those of other eventual ones, whose names are included in the traits of the estimated disorders (step 5 in Fig. 1). For instance, the Borderline disorder contains the trait "*paranoid ideation or severe dissociative symptoms*". Our tool detects

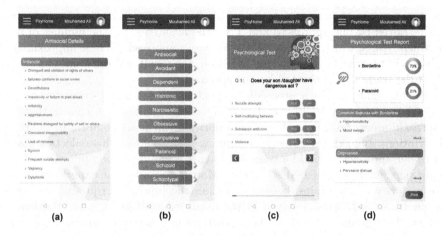

Fig. 3. Some interfaces from PsyHome mobile application

the word "*paranoid*" and includes the traits of the Paranoid disorder in the test which focuses on the Borderline disorder. The traits are put in the form of YES/NO questions, starting with the clause "*Does your son/daughter have*", in the generated test (see Fig. 3c). In case where the trait starts with a verb instead of a noun group, the question starts with the clause "*Does your son/daughter*". The parent of the patient is then asked to fulfil the test, at home, without being in stressful conditions in the psychiatrist clinic. When accomplished, PsyHome builds a report for the psychiatrist (steps 6 and 7 in Fig. 1), which contains the percentages of the estimated personality disorder(s), as well as the traits approved by the parent (see Fig. 3d). This report is useful for the psychiatrist in many ways: *(i)* the test is done by the parent in quiet stable conditions without stress (in fact stress could affect the results); *(ii)* the time taken to treat the child is reduced by avoiding the eventual appointments delays, which could take weeks if the psychiatrist's clinic is always full; *(iii)* providing a guide for the precise diagnosis of the patient in an optimal time, and *(iv)* offering a useful support assigning the most accurate therapeutic plan to the child.

5   Evaluation

The overall objective of this section is to show the ability of our approach in generating traits' list of high quality. To this end, we propose to evaluate the conformity degree between the generated traits' list and the traits retrieved by an expert. More specifically, we gave to an expert (a voluntary psychologist) the same input documents to our approach, i.e. the personality disorders' descriptions. We asked him to focus on the semantics of the descriptions, in order to approximate the values of TP (true positives, i.e. the number of true traits retrieved by our approach), FP (false positives, i.e. the number of traits generated by our approach but absent in the expert's list), FN (false negatives, i.e. the number of pertinent traits within the input descriptions, which were not retrieved by our approach) and TN (true negatives, i.e. the number of non-pertinent traits, which were not retrieved by our approach). These approximated values will be used to measure the precision, the recall and the F-measure rates [5] of the traits' list generated by our approach.

In this sight, we got a precision (respectively recall and F-measure) rate of 81.33% (respectively 94,13% and 87.26%). This result shows clearly that our approach mines the traits, where the majority of them are conform to the input descriptions. Indeed, the F-measure value is close to 90%. This reflects the ability of our approach to build a traits list having a significant compliance with the input personality disorders descriptions. More specifically, the expert noted that the majority of the traits, he deduced from the input descriptions, are found in our traits' list. This is shown in the recall value of 94,13%. In addition, he judged that the majority of the false positives may serve to enrich significantly the traits list, and consequently the quality of the generated tests and reports. Indeed, many parents do not have a well knowledge on psychology, and thus, building quite detailed questions would help them to understand correctly their aims. Similarly, concerning the precision rate, we got a precision value of 81,33%. This implies the presence of some false positives, like "*interpret motives as malevolent*" for the Paranoid disorder, which, when examined closely, are considered as enrichment to the traits' list, especially to the question "*Does your child have suspiciousness of others?*". This helps to get more precise report for the psychiatrist. On the other hand, the expert found that some traits reflect indirectly other traits, which are considered as false positives. For example, he considered that the trait "*attention seeking*" has the same sense as the trait "*concern to please physically*", and thus, he puts only the first trait in his list (i.e. the second trait is a false positive). However, there was no information in the input descriptions that the one reflects the other. This concern is caused by the full automation of our approach.

Note that a key issue when performing experiments in the validity of the results: are the statistical tests used correctly? are the issues under investigation really investigated in the study? to which domain are the results possible to generalize? [27] Despite our challenging results, at the evaluation stage, when labelling datasets and especially health related datasets, we need more than one expert. In fact, it is very important that cross-labelling techniques are used at this stage because of the delicacy of these applications. The second concern of our approach is the use of TF/IDF and DBSCAN methods, instead of new classification methods, namely the modern machine learning methods, like genetic algorithms, neural networks, which increases the scalability of our approach.

6   Conclusion

In this paper, we presented a novel approach, and its implementing tool, which aim to improve the wellbeing of children having psychological problems. This approach is dedicated to the psychiatrists and the children's parents. It helps the psychiatrists to diagnose, more precisely and in a reduced time, the eventual personality disorders of children and teenagers, and thus, to propose the adequate therapeutic plans in an optimal time. More specifically, our approach extracts a trait list for the most famous personality disorders which are present in the DSM-5 manual. It accepts as inputs the descriptions for these disorders from reliable resources. These descriptions can be in the form of simple items or even paragraphs composed of complex sentences. To handle this challenge, our approach relies on several techniques like the TF/IDF method, the DBSCAN algorithm and the semantic model, in order to provide a solution for building personalized psychological tests and analyzing their results. We evaluated our approach based on an expert's feedback. The correct and complete traits' list generated by our approach is challenging; it allows saving the time for the psychologists and the parents to the children's treatment in an optimal time.

Evidently, even though our empirical evaluation produced encouraging results, our approach must be extended with additional traits of other psychological diseases, such as the *depression*, the *bi-polar*, etc. This extension would provide a solid ground for the performance of our approach. As a solution, we plan to treat automatically the evolution of the generated traits' list based on new *language-independent* descriptions. Indeed, many reliable resources on personality disorders and psychological diseases are available in languages, different from English. Such an extension would enhance considerably the quality of the reports built by our approach, and thus the more adequate therapeutic plans proposed by the psychiatrists. For example, the Borderline personality disorder traits are very close to those of the bipolar disease. Besides, the bipolar involves the manic and the depressive poles. If the psychiatrist diagnoses the psychological state of the patient as a Borderline personality disorder instead of bipolar, and that the low humor of the patient is caused by the depressive trait of this disorder, this psychiatrist may prescribe an antidepressant, instead of a mood stabilizer; this medication would aggravate the situation of the patient by promoting the reappearance of the manic pole, which is considerably dangerous. Thus, including other psychological diseases in our traits' list is highly recommended in this case. In addition, we plan to conduct an evaluation on large set of real cases and to evaluate the generated reports based on several psychiatrists feedback as experts, instead of one expert. Moreover, we plan to rely on modern machine learning methods in order to automate the process of the personalized test building depending on the patient state.

References

1. Ayandele, O.: Basic Psychology. Hope Publications Ltd., Ibadan (2016)
2. Bockian, N.R., Smith, J.C., Berghuis, D.J.: The Personality Disorders Treatment Planner: Includes DSM-5 Updates. Wiley, New York (2016)
3. Chittaranjan, Gokul, B.J., Gatica-Perez, D.: Mining large-scale smartphone data for personality studies. Pers. Ubiquit. Comput. **17**, 433–450 (2013). https://doi.org/10.1007/s00779-011-0490-1

4. Correa, T., Hinsley, A.W., de Zuniga, H.G.: Who interacts on the web? The intersection of users personality and social media use. Comput. Hum. Behav. **26**(2), 247–253 (2010)

5. Dalianis, H.: Evaluation metrics and evaluation. In: Dalianis, H. (ed.) Clinical Text Mining, pp. 45–53. Springer, Cham (2018). https://doi.org/10.1007/978-3-319-78503-5_6

6. Kupfer, D.J., et al.: 5th edn. American Psychiatric Publishing. A Division of American Psychiatric Association, Washington, DC (2013)

7. Ester, M., Peter Kriegel, H., Sander, J., Xu, X.: A density-based algorithm for discovering clusters in large spatial databases with noise. In: Proceedings of the International Conference on Knowledge Discovery and Data Mining, pp. 226–231. AAAI Press (1996)

8. Finkel, A.: L'analyse cognitive, la psychologie numérique et la formation des enseignants à l' université. Pratiques Psychologiques **23**(3), 303–323 (2017). https://doi.org/10.1016/j.prps.2017.05.006

9. Gerlach, M., Farb, B., Revelle, W., Amaral, L.A.N.: A robust data-driven approach identifies four personality types across four large data sets. Nat. Hum. Behav. **2**, 735–742 (2018). https://doi.org/10.1038/s41562-018-0419-z

10. Goldberg, L.: Language and individual differences: the search for universal in personality lexicons. Rev. Pers. Soc. Psychol. **2**, 141–165 (1981)

11. Goldberg, L.R.: The structure of phenotypic personality traits. Am. Psychol. **48**(1), 26 (1993)

12. Gosling, S.D., Augustine, A., Vazire, S., Holtzman, N., Gaddis, S.: Manifestations of personality in online social networks: self-reported Facebook-related behaviors and observable profile information. Cyberpsychol. Behav. Soc. Netw. **14**(9) (2011). https://doi.org/10.1089/cyber.2010.0087

13. Hu, S., et al.: Signatures of personality on dense 3D facial images. Sci. Rep. **7**(1), 73 (2017)

14. Kerber, A., Roth, M., Herzberg, P.Y.: Personality types revisited-a literature-informed and data-driven approach to an integration of prototypical and dimensional constructs of personality description. PLOS ONE **16**(1), 1–27 (2021)

15. Kosinski, M., Bachrach, Y., Kohli, P., Stillwell, D., Graepel, T.: Manifestations of user personality in website choice and behaviour on online social networks. Mach. Learn. **95**(3), 357–380 (2013). https://doi.org/10.1007/s10994-013-5415-y

16. Lee, T.T.C.: Minnesota multiphasic personality inventory (MMPI). In: Zeigler-Hill, V., Shackelford, T.K. (eds.) Encyclopedia of Personality and Individual Differences, pp. 2915–2918. Springer, Cham (2020). https://doi.org/10.1007/978-3-319-24612-3_914

17. Manning, C.D., Raghavan, P., Schütze, H.: Introduction to Information Retrieval. Cambridge University Press, New York (2008)

18. Markowetz, A., Blaszkiewicz, K., Montag, C., Switala, C., Schlaepfer, T.: Psychoinformatics: big data shaping modern psychometrics. Med. Hypotheses **82** (2014). https://doi.org/10.1016/j.mehy.2013.11.030

19. Marty, M., Segal, D.: DSM-5: Diagnostic and Statistical Manual of Mental Disorders, pp. 965–970 (2015)

20. Mdhaffar, A., et al.: DL4DED: deep learning for depressive episode detection on mobile devices. In: Pagán, J., Mokhtari, M., Aloulou, H., Abdulrazak, B., Cabrera, M.F. (eds.) ICOST 2019. LNCS, vol. 11862, pp. 109–121. Springer, Cham (2019). https://doi.org/10.1007/978-3-030-32785-9_10

21. Mefteh, M., Bouassida, N., Ben-Abdallah, H.: Towards naturalistic programming: mapping language-independent requirements to constrained language specifications. Sci. Comput. Program. **166**, 89–119 (2018). https://doi.org/10.1016/j.scico. 2018.05.006

22. Miller, G.A.: WordNet: a lexical database for English. Commun. ACM **38**(11), 39–41 (1995). https://doi.org/10.1145/219717.219748

23. Montag, C., Duke, E., Markowetz, A.: Toward psychoinformatics: computer science meets psychology. Comput. Math. Methods Med. **2016** (2016). https://doi.org/10. 1155/2016/2983685

24. Muizz, R.A., Uddin, M.S., Sakib, M.M.N., Islam, S., Ahmed, N.: BigPsy: a big data framework to support psycho-informatics. Master's thesis, Brac University (6 2021)

25. Qin, R., Gao, W., Xu, H., Hu, Z.: Modern physiognomy: an investigation o predicting personality traits and intelligence from the human face. Sci. China Inf. Sci. **61** (2018). https://doi.org/10.1007/s00779-011-0490-1

26. Rorschach, H., Oberholzer, E., Lemkau, P.V., Morgenthaler, W.: Psychodiagnostics: a diagnostic test based on perception: including Rorschach's paper the application of the form interpretation test (published posthumously by Dr. Emil Oberholzer). Verlag Hans Huber, Berne, Switzerland (1942)

27. Thelin, T., Runeson, P., Wohlin, C., Olsson, T., Andersson, C.: Evaluation of usage-based reading-conclusions after three experiments. Empirical Softw. Eng. **9**(1–2), 77–110 (2004)

28. Xu, J., Tian, W., Lv, G., Liu, S., Fan, Y.: 2.5D facial personality prediction based on deep learning. J. Adv. Transp. **2021** (2021)

29. Yarkoni, T.: Psychoinformatics new horizons at the interface of the psychological and computing sciences. Curr. Dir. Psychol. Sci. **21**, 391–397 (2012). https://doi. org/10.1177/0963721412457362

30. Zhong, B., Hardin, M., Sun, T.: Less effortful thinking leads to more social networking? The associations between the use of social network sites and personality traits. Comput. Hum. Behav. **27**(3), 1265–1271 (2011). https://doi.org/10.1016/j. chb.2011.01.008

Comparative Analysis of Human Action Recognition Classification for Ambient Assisted Living

Ainur Zhumasheva[1]([✉]) [iD], Madina Mansurova[1] [iD], Gulshat Amirkhanova[1] [iD], and Rollan Alimgazy[2] [iD]

[1] Al-Farabi Kazakh National University, Almaty, Kazakhstan
ainur93ardak@gmail.com
[2] International Information Technology University, Almaty, Kazakhstan

Abstract. Technologies of Ambient Intelligence - an environment filled with computing systems and devices that react and have a certain impact on the presence of a person in this environment. Namely, by making life easier and better for the elderly by designing and developing new functions, services and information and communication technology systems. This study is aimed at reviewing and presenting a new approach to the issue of detecting anomalies and potentially dangerous situations for human health and life - a system for calculating a person's posture by constructing a vector skeleton. The advantage of this method is rather moderate system requirements for computing software and the possibility of its rapid implementation from the planning stage to the final implementation. Extracting the main features from a sequence of images to evaluate parameters such as posture, position and activity of a person and their subsequent categorization and ordering using neural network algorithms. This procedure is necessary to determine the frames for the content of scenarios with a potential threat to an elderly person, for example, a fall. In particular, the most recent and advanced body of libraries has been created in the last five years to make skeleton-based algorithms more accessible for research and subsequent application. Since these libraries will be included for practical applications in video surveillance, medical care. This report presents a comparative classification of various libraries of the human pose calculation system by constructing a vector skeleton based on prepared images and videos. In all tests performed, the parameter for evaluating the performance of these libraries for algorithms such as PoseNet, MoveNet and BlazePose is the percentage of correctly calculated joint vectors. According to the results of the study and the tests carried out, the most effective method for identifying various positions of a person in videos is MoveNet.

Keywords: MoveNet · PoseNet · BlazePose · HAR · AAL

1 Introduction

Based on population-based environmental studies conducted over the past few years, it can be concluded that the most common injuries in the elderly (65 years and older) and two-thirds of all serious facial injuries are caused by various types of falls [1, 2,

© The Author(s), under exclusive license to Springer Nature Switzerland AG 2023
N. T. Nguyen et al. (Eds.): ICCCI 2023, CCIS 1864, pp. 728–739, 2023.
https://doi.org/10.1007/978-3-031-41774-0_57

35]. In addition, the World Health Organization (WHO) in its report also defines falls in the elderly, indicating 29–36% for people over 65 and 33–45% for people over 60 [3]. Unfortunately, demographic aging is also a national problem in Kazakhstan, without significant differences [4, 5]. An ecological study of the population of the city of Semey, East Kazakhstan, is presented in [4]. An analysis of the most common injuries showed that most injuries were caused by falls (82.2%), followed by inanimate objects (7.7%) and mechanical impacts (4.6%) [5]. This analysis shows that older people need care and protection, especially if they have health problems. We believe that an accurate and efficient automated system that can help health authorities can have a significant social impact in improving the overall quality of life of people, particularly the elderly and people who have disabilities. The relevance of this method over the past 20 years is confirmed by the constantly updated and increasing number of libraries created as a result of increased attention to the problems of using neural network algorithms in ambient intelligence systems.

An innovative HAR system is presented in [7], which combines the capabilities of video devices and the potential of deep learning technology to recognize the most common daily movements and postures of people in the house.

This can be observed during the Covid-19 pandemic when the elderly and the disabled need remote monitoring [36]. Posture assessment can aid in remote fall detection and real-time alerts by using posture assessment to constantly monitor high-risk areas in the home where falls may occur and to immediately alert caregivers and family members when someone falls or falls. Has abnormal movements.

Human pose recognition uses photographs or video footage to identify parts of the human body; HPR is now a common task in computer vision. Pose recognition is often used in medicine [8, 9], sports performance evaluation [10–13], and video inspection [14–16]. In this application, human base points are used to validate the pose and classify the pose. Human key points collected from various parts of the human body can be used to detect situations of child abduction or child abuse through intelligent video surveillance. In healthcare, key points from identified body parts can be used to confirm correct posture for exercise therapy, monitoring, and rehabilitation at home. Key points from different parts of the body can also be compared with standard ground-truth poses to evaluate the efficiency and accuracy of the athlete's movements.

As the demand for human pose recognition grows, several skeletal-based human posture recognition methods have been developed and compiled into a library for the convenience of researchers. The functionality of HPR data is important to the reliability of many of the practical applications in which it is included. For example, to ensure the reliability of the program, the HPR library must be able to recognize the correct posture of patients performing unlimited rehabilitation postures in various home settings. The situation becomes more complicated when common difficulties such as incorrect camera orientation or self-coverage [18, 19] prevent the detection of critical points of the skeleton. Recently, four leading pose recognition libraries, PoseNet [20], MoveNet [21], and BlazePose [22], have been increasingly used in various applications. Problems commonly encountered when evaluating poses from the three HPE libraries include "improper camera placement" and "self-photo effect". Each library has its own strategy to overcome these issues, but the strengths and weaknesses of the three HPE libraries have not yet been determined. Therefore, it is important to compare the results of these libraries to determine how reliable they are in detecting different human attitudes. Therefore, these three HPR models were compared using images and videos. To the authors' knowledge, this is the first time that the performance of BlazePose, MoveNet, and PoseNet has been evaluated and investigated using image and video datasets. The Table 1 shows a list of the application in medicine in last 4 year.

Table 1. Applications of PoseNet, MoveNet, OpenPose, and MediaPipe Pose in Medicine

HPR library	Year	Purpose of application
PoseNet [20]	2020	Application for Physiotherapy Exercises. [8]
	2021	Yoga Pose Detection for healthcare.[10]
MoveNet [21]	2022	A healthcare system for physical therapy medical rehabilitation [14]
BlazePose [22]	2022	A posture corrector system.[13]

2 Pose Recognition Models

In this research, tests were carried out in which the process of launching the detector on the first frame of the video recording was carried out to localize a person in the image space, followed by the creation of a bounding box. Next, this tracker takes control and predicts landmarks based on the data received within the previously created ROI bounding box. The tracker continues this process on all subsequent frames. In video recording, using the ROI of the previous frame and then calling the detection model again only if it cannot track the person with a high degree of confidence.

For pose estimation, various pose estimation methods based on deep learning can be used. These calculation algorithms and approaches are generally classified into top-down and bottom-up algorithms and posture estimation approaches. The top-down approach to analyzing human posture is a rather naive and traditional method. When capturing a still or moving image of a person, it uses object detection to first determine exactly where the object is before drawing a bounding box around it. Once the bounding box is received, it is passed to the pose estimation function, which then extracts the important points of the body from that bounding box. Although this method is quite simple, it has a number of disadvantages, one of the most significant of which are the specific application of this method, as well as high computational costs and an execution environment that is directly proportional to the number of people in the image being processed.

The bottom-up approach is the exact opposite of the top-down approach and is more appropriate in some situations. This approach is to combine systems into more complex systems. This method first draws key points on an image and then tries to match it with different people in that image. Starting with small individual elements, this method then uses and connects them together to create a complete picture, in the case of HPR models, a skeleton.

Table 2. Characteristics of HPR models

HPR Libraries	Year of realization	Maximum number of keypoints	Position of keypoints in the body parts	Type of Pose	Method	Under Lying Network
PoseNet [20]	2017	17	Head, upper body, lower body	Single- and multi-person	Top-down	ResNet and MobileNet
MoveNet [21]	2021	17	Head, upper body, lower body	Single- and multi-person	Bottom-up	MobileNet V2
BlazePose [22]	2020	33	Head, upper body, lower body	Single- and multi-person	Top-down	CNN

This section presents an analysis of the three main HPR models, namely: PoseNet, MoveNet and BlazePose. Table 2 provides a brief technical specification for each method. Two HPR models have 17 of the most encountered key points when building a pose. These points are the eyes, ears and nose are as parts of the head, with a total of 5 key points. Next comes the upper body, which consists of the 6 most common key points on the arms, namely the shoulders, elbows, and wrists. And the last is the lower body, which consists of 6 key points located on the legs, namely the hips, knees and ankles. One model detecting the posture and position of the human body locates 33 major key landmarks on the human body. These points are elbows, knees, ankles, hands and so on. Keypoint detection, in turn, is a major branch of the subject matter of computer vision, also called image recognition. The other classes in this branch are Classification, Discovery, and Segmentation.

PoseNet, which was introduced in 2017 [20], utilizes two different iterations of the algorithm, one strategy is used to estimate a single pose and the other is used to estimate multiple poses from an input video or image. Both methods can detect 17 key points from a single person. The computation time for the multi-face method is slightly longer than for the single face pose estimation algorithm. However, this does not depend on the number of detected faces. If there are many people in the provided video or photo, then when using the single face method, key points may be mixed. Estimating a person's pose is easy and fast, but the person must be present in the image/video, otherwise several key points may be evaluated as part of the same object. PoseNet has two standard architectures: the MobileNet v1 architecture and the ResNet50 architecture. The models in the MobileNet v1 architecture are smaller and faster, but less accurate; the ResNet50 variant [24] is larger and slower, but more accurate; both MobileNet v1 and ResNet50 support one-to-many target evaluation.

MoveNet is a fast and relatively accurate model that captures the 17 main points of the body. The model is available in two flavors called Lightning and Thunder in TF Hub - Lightning for applications where latency is critical, and Thunder for applications where high accuracy is required. Both models run faster than real time (over 30 frames per second) on most modern desktops, laptops and mobile phones. In 2021, an open position model called MoveNet was introduced [21]. Heat maps use MoveNet to display human access points. Feature extraction tools and some extraordinary architecture predictionsTo maintain sequential order, Table 2b has been changed to Table 3. Please check and correct if necessary..

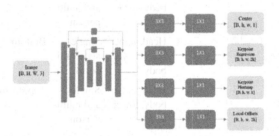

Fig. 1. MoveNet architecture

MoveNet [21] calculates four processes at the same time, as shown in (Fig. 1) To determine the location of each atom, a heat map of its center is built, and then the location with the highest estimate is selected. The cue points resulting from the regression are then used to organize a set of cue points for the individual. If the set of key points obtained because of the regression matches an individual, then he is identified. In addition, each pixel is multiplied by a weight that is inversely proportional to its distance from the regression key point. Thus, important information from background subjects can be excluded from the calculation. The final set of key points is determined by the maximum heatmap value of each key point channel.

BlazePose is a lightweight CNN architecture developed by Google for human body pose estimation, capable of calculating the (x, y, z) coordinates of 33 major body points. BlazePose consists of two machine learning models, a detector, and an estimator. Position estimation is performed in an ML pipeline with a two-stage tracking detector. The detector is used to locate the region of interest. The detector then predicts 33 critical points. The topology we use is shown in (Fig. 2).

For video, the detector is activated only in the first frame [25]. In addition, six keypoints for the head, six for the upper body, and four for the lower body are provided by Pose. Top-down and bottom-up methods can be used to define keypoints in the HPR library. The top-down method first determines the number of people based on the input data, and then assigns a separate bounding area to each person [26]. Keypoints in each boundary region are then evaluated. In the "bottom-up" method, the base points are determined at the first stage, in contrast to the "top-down" method [27].

Keypoints are then identified according to the specific person. There are three libraries for estimating human pose: PoseNet, MediaPipe Stance, and MoveNet, with PoseNet and Blaze Pose using the top-down method, and MoveNet using the bottom-up method. Blaze Pose uses Convolutional Neural Network (CNN) while PoseNet uses ResNet.

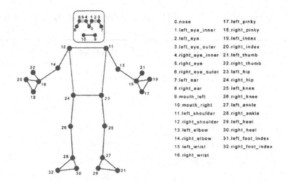

Fig. 2. BlazePose keypoint topology

3 Discussion

3.1 Video Dataset

The video source datasets used in this experiment were the Penn Action [28] datasets, respectively. The data share 6 upper body keypoints and 6 lower body keypoints. Penn Action only provides keypoint at the head position.

Penn Action [28] is a video dataset that consists of 2326 video sequences with 15 actions. It is commonly used in HPE experiments [29–31]. Each video sequence contains RGB image frames and annotations. Annotations include various human actions, 2D bounding boxes to determine the position of the person, and skeletal key points in body parts. Each human instance is labeled with 13 key points.

3.2 Metrics Experiment Results

To organize an experiment to evaluate the effectiveness of libraries, we must assess the poses at the important locations of the human body's matrix. Evaluation metrics are critical in determining the quality of libraries. If the distance between the expected and genuine connections is within a specific proportion of the diagonal of the bounding box, the discovered link is considered accurate. The use of a metric requires that all joints' correctness is evaluated using the same error threshold. The proportion of identified joints was employed as an assessment parameter in this study to quantify the performance of the libraries used [32–34].

The detection accuracy of method libraries is measured using the Euclidean distance between the ground truth and anticipated key points in pixels. The accuracy score increases as the metric value increases. The first experiment for the video dataset compared the performance of each pose recognition library for each video frame, whereas the second experiment looked at how well each library performed for each body component of each motion. Each activity's *Percentage of Detected Joints* was computed.

MoveNet had 9-actions, followed by PoseNet-8, and BlazePose-6. MoveNet had the best overall outcome, with over 50% *Percentage of Detected Joints* across all activities. BlazePose had the worst performance, with a 9-action PDJ of less than 50%.

Table 3. Overall Percentage *of Detected Joints* (%) average in each action.

Actions	Blaze Pose	PoseNet	MoveNet
1	66.62	68.47	67.70
2	92.57	91.61	61.68
3	74.21	77.55	80.58
4	48.92	41.20	61.05
5	49.34	82.36	75.67
6	47.00	77.47	81.42
7	41.10	69.72	69.31
8	62.43	55.78	92.18
9	78.03	76.23	71.85
Average PDJ (%)	62.25	71.18	73.49

The Table 3 indicates the highest and lowest *Percentage of Detected Joints* values for each library for each action to test and apply the performance of the libraries for each activity. The libraries performed best in Action 8 out of the nine activities (skiing). Blaze Pose performed the worst of all action in motion 7 (zooming away from the camera). BlazePose and PoseNet, coincidentally, performed the poorest in motion 4. (Half squat). The last row of the table highlights the overall average values for all activities. MoveNet, BlazePose, and PoseNet ranked top to lowest in terms of performance. MoveNct, BlazePose, and PoseNet scores all declined between 65% and 70%. Blaze Pose recognized 8 actions (see table), achieving 75% to 100%, which was greater than MoveNet, but its total performance was 3.14% lower (Fig. 3).

3.3 Tested Active Recognition

This section summarizes the key findings of this investigation. In contrast to other active recognition libraries, MoveNet earned the greatest Percentage of Detected Joints values in terms of minimum, first quartile, and third quartile values. The PoseNet method has the most accurate calculation of the human skeleton and has the ability to track a person in space Table 3, compared to the other two models.

One of the disadvantages PoseNet was due to the fact that it can connect vectors by keypoint if there is more than one person on the frame. It can be clearly seen in the Fig. 4. While the BlazeNet cannot detect keypoints 25–31(Fig. 4) on the body because the object is close to the camera. In the picture, you can see confirmation of the percentage indicators of the metric. All keypoints are clearly distributed in the model MoveNet.

A lower percentage of accuracy was shown by the PoseNet method. It has a number of drawbacks, due to which the accuracy of this method is not constant under conditions of movement and a changing distance from a person to a camera lens, mainly the top-down approach. This method has very low accuracy on close distance, as well as troubles in detecting moving objects, as seen on the applied pictures.

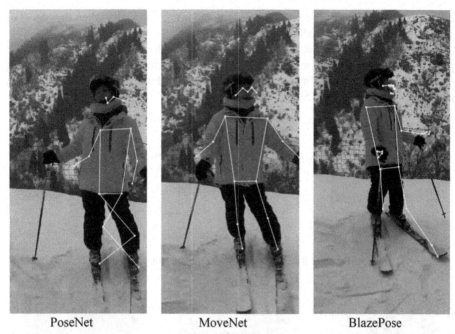

PoseNet   MoveNet   BlazePose

Fig. 3. Human Skeleton Recognition Results in Comparison of Three Methods

Pose Net   **Move Net**   **Blasé Pose**

Fig. 4. The difference between the three models when there is more than one person on the frame.

The MoveNet method showed the highest accuracy when building a vector skeleton model. By applying a newer and more efficient bottom-up method, the recognized pose is the most accurate final result. The method determined the object both at close and far distances (Fig. 4), did not lose focus when the object moved. The most common problem with other methods of rendering is the impossibility of algorithms to correctly calculate the positions of the joints of the legs and arms, especially when the object of study moves away or approaches the camera.

On Figs. 5, 6 and 7 Comparison of three models in the frame. Although relatively good, however, the PoseNet method showed worse performance compared to MoveNet. Its main problem is the inability to correctly determine and build a human figure, resulting in an inaccurate result (Fig. 5).

Fig. 5. **PoseNet** Sample video frame and detection result of Action

Fig. 6. **MoveNet** Sample video frame and detection result of Action

Fig. 7. **BlazePose** Sample video frame and detection result of Action

Also, when an object approaches the camera, the top-down algorithm showed the lowest performance. The BlazePose method showed (Fig. 7) the lowest accuracy in this study. The algorithm is only able to detect objects at a certain distance and camera position. At a distance closer than 2 m (Fig. 7), the method showed relatively good results, however, it quickly loses its effectiveness at a distance from the camera further than 4 m. Also, this method loses its accuracy as the number of people in the frame increases. The main problem in this case is the inability of this method to adequately calculate all the joints and correctly determine them. On (Figs. 5, 6 and 7) can immediately notice the unfinished cons of each model.

4 Conclusion

In conclusion, body part detection performance will suffer when confronted with challenges such as camera misalignment or self-occlusion. These concerns are well handled by MoveNet, BlasePose, and PoseNet. BlazePose has the lowest reliability in video detection because it loses track when self-occlusion with body components occurred. The tests in this work were limited to assessing the performance of three libraries for human posture identification using value range. Based on all the above material, we can conclude that the most accurate method is MoveNet. This method has the most accurate calculation of the human skeleton and has the ability to track a person in space, in comparison with the other two models. MoveNet is based on a bottom-up method of assessing human posture and skeleton, while the alternatives to this model BlasePose and PoseNet use a top-down approach.

A comparative analysis of the human skeletal score in the article was carried out to obtain a system in future studies designed to classify each data frame and provide the classification result for a further decision algorithm. Which can trigger an alarm to help the fallen person based on the classified position. Using all the results obtained on the MoveNet model, in the future, human posture recognition will be carried out based on machine learning for Ambient Assisted Living.

References

1. Kannus, P., Sievänen, H., Palvanen, M., Järvinen, T., Parkkari, J.: Prevention of falls and consequent injuries in elderly people. Lancet **366**(9500), 1885–1893 (2005)
2. Seifert, J.: Incidence and economic burden of injuries in the United States, 926 (2007)
3. Park, S.-H.: Tools for assessing fall risk in the elderly: a systematic review and meta-analysis. Aging Clin. Exp. Res. **30**(1), 1–16 (2017). https://doi.org/10.1007/s40520-017-0749-0
4. Tlemissov, A., et al.: Does the number of injuries among elderly people in Kazakhstan increase during Ramadan? Public Health **142**, 70 (2017)
5. Abdirova, T.M., et al.: The culture of active aging. J. Pharm. Sci. Res. **10**(4), 805–807 (2018)
6. Bianchi, V., Bassoli, M., Lombardo, G., Fornacciari, P., Mordonini, M., De Munari, I.: IoT wearable sensor and deep learning: an integrated approach for personalized human activity recognition in a smart home environment. IEEE Internet Things J. **6**(5), 8553–8562 (2019)
7. Park, J.H., Song, K., Kim, Y.-S.: A kidnapping detection using human pose estimation in intelligent video surveillance systems. J. Korea Soc. Comput. Inf. **23**, 9–16 (2018)
8. Thyagarajmurthy, A., Ninad, M.G., Rakesh, B.G., Niranjan, S., Manvi, B.: Anomaly detection in surveillance video using pose estimation. In: Sridhar, V., Padma, M., Rao, K. (eds.) Emerging Research in Electronics, Computer Science and Technology. Lecture Notes in Electrical Engineering, vol. 545, pp. 753–766. Springer, Singapore (2019). https://link.springer.com/chapter/10.1007/978-981-13-5802-9_66. Accessed 27 Oct 2022
9. Lamas, A., et al.: Human pose estimation for mitigating false negatives in weapon detection in video-surveillance. Neurocomputing **489**, 488–503 (2022)
10. Shah, D., Rautela, V., Sharma, C., Florence, A.: Yoga pose detection using Posenet and k-NN. In: 2021 International Conference on Computing, Communication and Green Engineering (CCGE), pp. 1–4, Pune, India (2021). https://doi.org/10.1109/CCGE50943.2021.9776451
11. Zou, J., et al.: Intelligent fitness trainer system based on human pose estimation. In: Sun, S., Fu, M., Xu, L. (eds.) Signal and Information Processing, Networking and Computers. ICSINC 2018. Lecture Notes in Electrical Engineering, vol. 550, pp. 593–599. Springer, Singapore (2018). https://doi.org/10.1007/978-981-13-7123-3_69

12. Suda, S., Makino, Y., Shinoda, H.: Prediction of volleyball trajectory using skeletal motions of setter player. In: Proceedings of the 10th Augmented Human International Conference, Reims, France, 11–12 March 2019; pp. 1–8 (2019)

13. Wang, J., Qiu, K., Peng, H., Fu, J., Zhu, J.: AI coach: deep human pose estimation and analysis for personalized athletic training assistance. In: Proceedings of the 27th ACM International Conference on Multimedia, Nice, France, 21–25 October 2019, pp. 374–382 (2019)

14. Bejinariu, S., Luca, R., Costin, H., Rotaru, F., Onu, I.: Medical rehabilitation assessment using gait analysis in video sequences. In: 2022 E-Health and Bioengineering Conference (EHB), Iasi, Romania, pp. 01-04 (2022). https://doi.org/10.1109/EHB55594.2022.9991604

15. Shapoval, S., García Zapirain, B., Mendez Zorrilla, A., Mugueta-Aguinaga, I.: Biofeedback applied to interactive serious games to monitor frailty in an elderly population. Appl. Sci. **11**, 3502 (2021)

16. Chua, J., Ong, L.Y., Leow, M.C.: Telehealth using PoseNet-based system for in-home rehabilitation. Future Internet **13**, 173 (2021)

17. Jeon, H., Yoon, Y., Kim, D.: Lightweight 2D human pose estimation for fitness coaching system. In: Proceedings of the 2021 36th International Technical Conference on Circuits/Systems, Computers and Communications (ITC-CSCC), Jeju, Republic of Korea, 27–30 June 2021, pp. 1–4 (2021)

18. Park, H.J., Baek, J.W., Kim, J.H.: Imagery based parametric classification of correct and incorrect motion for push-up counter using OpenPose. In: Proceedings of the 2020 IEEE 16th International Conference on Automation Science and Engineering (CASE), Hong Kong, China, 20–21 August 2020, pp. 1389–1394 (2020)

19. Nguyen, H.T.P., Woo, Y., Huynh, N.N., Jeong, H.: Scoring of human body-balance ability on wobble board based on the geometric solution. Appl. Sci. **12**, 5967 (2022)

20. Kendall, A., Grimes, M., Cipolla, R.: PoseNet: a convolutional network for real-time 6-DOF Camera relocalization. In: 2015 IEEE International Conference on Computer Vision (ICCV), Santiago, Chile, pp. 2938–2946 (2015). https://doi.org/10.1109/ICCV.2015.336

21. Bajpai, R., Joshi, D.: MoveNet: a deep neural network for joint profile prediction across variable walking speeds and slopes. IEEE Trans. Instrum. Meas. **70**, 1–11, 2021, Article no. 2508511. https://doi.org/10.1109/TIM.2021.3073720

22. Alsawadi, M.S., Rio, M.: Human action recognition using BlazePose skeleton on spatial temporal graph convolutional neural networks. In: 2022 9th International Conference on Information Technology, Computer, and Electrical Engineering (ICITACEE), Semarang, Indonesia, pp. 206–211 (2022). https://doi.org/10.1109/ICITACEE55701.2022.9924010

23. Jawale, C.D., Joshi, K.A., Gogate, S.K., Badgujar, C.: Elcare: elderly care with fall detection. J. Phys. Conf. Ser. **2273**, 012019 (2022)

24. Pishchulin, L., et al.: DeepCut: joint subset partition and labeling for multi person pose estimation. In: Proceedings of the IEEE Conference on Computer Vision and Pattern Recognition, Las Vegas, NV, USA, 30 June 2016, pp. 4929–4937 (2016)

25. Min, Z.: Human body pose intelligent estimation based on BlazePose. In: 2022 IEEE International Conference on Electrical Engineering, Big Data and Algorithms (EEBDA), Changchun, China, pp. 150–153 (2022). https://doi.org/10.1109/EEBDA53927.2022.9745022

26. Joseph, R., Ayyappan, M., Shetty, T., Gaonkar, G., Nagpal, A.: BeFit—a real-time workout analyzer. In: Proceedings of the Sentimental Analysis and Deep Learning; Springer: Singapore, 2022; pp. 303–318 (2022). https://link.springer.com/chapter/10.1007/978-981-16-5157-1_24. Accessed 27 Oct 2022

27. Trejo, E.W., Yuan, P.: Recognition of Yoga poses through an interactive system with kinect device. In: 2018 2nd International Conference on Robotics and Automation Sciences (ICRAS), Wuhan, China, pp. 1–5 (2018). https://doi.org/10.1109/ICRAS.2018.8443267

28. Agarwal, S., et al.: FitMe: a fitness application for accurate pose estimation using deep learning. In: 2021 2nd International Conference on Secure Cyber Computing and Communications (ICSCCC), Jalandhar, India, pp. 232–237 (2021). https://doi.org/10.1109/ICSCCC 51823.2021.9478168

29. Nakai, M., Tsunoda, Y., Hayashi, H., Murakoshi, H.: Prediction of Basketball free throw shooting by openpose. In: Kojima, K., Sakamoto, M., Mineshima, K., Satoh, K. (eds.) New Frontiers in Artificial Intelligence. JSAI-isAI 2018. Lecture Notes in Computer Science, vol. 11717, pp. 435–446. Springer, Cham (2018). https://doi.org/10.1007/978-3-030-31605-1_31.

30. Zheng, C., et al.: Deep learning-based human pose estimation: a survey. arXiv (2020). arXiv: 2012.13392

31. Papandreou, G., et al.: Towards accurate multi-person pose estimation in the wild. In: Proceedings of the IEEE Conference on Computer Vision and Pattern Recognition, Honolulu, HI, USA, 21–26 July 2017, pp. 4903–4911 (2017)

32. Andriluka, M., Pishchulin, L., Gehler, P., Schiele, B.: 2D human pose estimation: New benchmark and state of the art analysis. In: Proceedings of the IEEE Conference on Computer Vision and Pattern Recognition, Columbus, OH, USA, 28 June 2014, pp. 3686–3693 (2014)

33. Liu,J., Shi, M., Chen, Q., Fu, H., Tai, C.L.: Normalized human pose features for human action video alignment. In: Proceedings of the IEEE/CVF International Conference on Computer Vision, Montreal, BC, Canada, 11–17 October 2021, pp. 11521–11531 (2021)

34. Ahmedt-Aristizabal, D., Nguyen, K., Denman, S., Sridharan, S., Dionisio, S., Fookes, C.: Deep motion analysis for epileptic seizure classification. In: Proceedings of the 2018 40th Annual International Conference of the IEEE Engineering in Medicine and Biology Society (EMBC), Honolulu, HI, USA, 18–21 July 2018, pp. 3578–3581 (2018)

35. Kistaubayev, Y., Mutanov, G., Mansurova, M., Saxenbayeva, Z., Shakan, Y.: Ethereum-based information system for digital higher education registry and verification of student achievement documents. Future Internet 15, 3 (2023). https://doi.org/10.3390/fi15010003

36. Yelure, B.S., Deokule, N.S., Mane, S.S., Bhosale, M.V., Chavan, A.B., Satpute, V.C.: Remote monitoring of Covid-19 patients using IoT and AI. In: 2022 Second International Conference on Artificial Intelligence and Smart Energy (ICAIS), Coimbatore, India, pp. 73–80 (2022). https://doi.org/10.1109/ICAIS53314.2022.9742750

Overview of Time Series Classification Based on Symbolic Discretization for ECG Applications

Mariem Taktak[1]([envelope]) [ORCID] and Slim Triki[2]

[1] Higher Institute of Applied Sciences and Technologies of Sousse, Sousse, Tunisia
Mariem.Taktak@issatso.u-sousse.tn
[2] National Engineering School of Sfax, Sfax, Tunisia
slim.triki@enis.tn

Abstract. This paper presents a comprehensive review of the Time Series (TS) data classification based on symbolic representation. In particular, we will focus on the classification of the Electro-Cardio Graphic (ECG) signal whatever the application it is used for. That is, we review the TS symbolic discretization in order to guide practitioners to make appropriate choice which meet their requirements in the ECG classification problem. We believe that scalability challenge in a real-time monitoring of cardiovascular patients, for example, require adapted representation that enhance dimensionality reduction before conducting classification process. Furthermore, an overview of the recent classification methods based on ordered symbolic attributes is detailed.

Keywords: Time Series · Symbolic Discretization · Classification · ECG

1 Introduction

Monitoring and analysis of cardiovascular patients using data driven techniques such as artificial intelligence, data mining or knowledge discovery are arising with the advanced technologies environments such as IoT, smart city and E-health. In this context, ECG classification system based on machine learning is still an active research area. In addition, collecting ECG data from sensors which reflect the electrical activity of the heart has been shown to represent important recognition capabilities due to the personal aspects that influence the generation of these signals. Whatever the ECG is used for, an efficient compression algorithm is typically required to deal with the large amount of the collected data. Moreover, these data have typical structures of Time Series (TS) data since ECG sensors record their values over time. It is well known that a key feature that distinguishes TS to other kinds of data is its shape. For example, looking at the following real-valued TS = [25.3, 25.3, 25.4, 25.4, 25.3, 25.2, 25.2, 25.1, . . . , 24.6, 24.6] cannot lead to any recognized signal. But this change after plotting the TS (see Fig. 1) where we can easily recognize the heartbeat shape of an electro-cardio graphic signal. In order to deal with the large amount of ECG data, TS representation and discretization are mainly applied for dimension reduction. An effective discretization algorithm not only reduces memory usage but also improve interpretability of the extracted knowledge from the ECG signal.

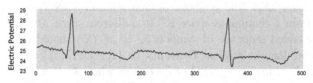

Fig. 1. Plot of an ECG signal.

Additionally, many ECG classification algorithms can benefit from the discrete representation. In this work, we aim to explore symbolic discretization methods over the recent state-of-the art TS classification for ECG applications.

2 Mapping TS into Sequence of Symbols

A lot of TS mapping techniques have been proposed in the two last decades. However, our first review is limited to the techniques proposed to treat the typical TS datamining problem such as: query by content, clustering, classification, motif detection, and rule discovery. Subsequently, we will focus on the mapping methods proposed for the TS classification problem. In contrast to other TS datamining problem, the TS classification involves building predictive models for a discrete target variable representing a class label. That is, this work focuses on reviewing predictive models built from ordered symbolic attributes. As depicted in the diagram of Fig. 2, we first divide the mapping techniques depending on the TS data dimension being as univariate or multivariate.

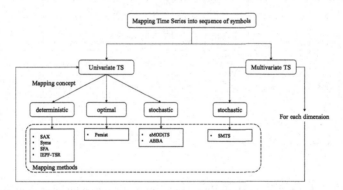

Fig. 2. Overview of our survey about mapping TS into sequence of symbols.

In the next level, the existing concept for mapping a TS into sequence of symbols can be classified into three main types namely: deterministic, optimal and stochastic. In fact, we rely the mapping process to the type of the discretization methods used to transform the original real-valued raw data into a sequence of symbols. Broadly speaking, discretization is the process of transforming continuous space valued into a discrete valued. More formally, let $\mathbf{T} = (\mathbf{X}, \mathbf{y})$ a list of m pair $\{X_i, y_i\}_{i \in [1,\ldots,m]}$ where $X_i = (x_1^i, x_2^i, \ldots, x_N^i) \in \mathbb{R}^N$ is a continuous time series with N observation and y_i is its discrete class label. The symbolic discretization of a TS X_i can be defined as a mapping $\mathcal{M}$ from a continuous space $\mathbb{R}^N$ to a discrete space $\mathbb{A}^n$ such that $n \ll N$. That is, the obtained sequence of symbols $S_i = \mathcal{M}(X_i)$ should be of considerably lower dimension than the original TS with $S_i = \{s_1^i, s_2^i, \ldots, s_n^i\}$ and s_j^i is an element of an alphabet $\mathbb{A} = \{a_1, a_2, \ldots, a_k\}$ of k symbols where $k \ll n$. Ideally, such a map should preserve important information of the TS like its shape. This is achieved by controlling an error of approximate reconstruction of the original TS. In the context of the TS datamining, additional properties are also required when a specific application are needed. For example, in the mining task based on the similarity matching, the lower bound property for the mapping process is mandatory in order to avoid false dismissal. In the TS literature review, we found that the most discretization methods were developed for the univariate case as we can see from the diagram in Fig. 2. In table 1 we give a summary of literature studies by highlighting their features and other useful information.

Table 1. Summary of reviewed symbolic mapping approaches.

Authors	Method	Parameters	Feature	Feature Complexity	Technique	Dimension	Algorithm	Supervised	data mining application
Lin et al. [1]	SAX	win,n,alphabet	mean	O(N)	PAA + equal-probability (normal distribution) binning	univariate	deterministic	no	
Morchen & Ultsch [6]	Persist	bin_boundaries	self-transition probability	O(N*N)	equal-frenquency binning + Symmetric Kullback-Leibler divergence	univariate	optimal	no	
Zalewski et al. [2]	Symb	n,k	mean's first order difference	O(N+1)	PAA + k-means	univariate	deterministic	no	Query by Content,
Marquez-Grajales et al. [5]	eMODITS	W={w1,w2,...,wi},alpha bet,n,Population_size, total_generation	mean	O(N)	PAA + evolutionary multi-objective (to find multi-breakpoints)	univariate	stochastic	yes	Clustering, Classification, Motif Detection, Rule Discovery.
Schafer & Hogqvist [7]	SFA	win,n	Discrete Fourier coefficients	O(N*log(N))	Multiple Coefficient Binning + equal-depth binning for each coefficient	univariate	deterministic	no	
Chen et al. [3]	IEPF-TSR	approximation_tol	[start_time, mean, trend]	O(N*L)	PLA + Iterative end point fitting	univariate	deterministic	no	
Baydogan & Runger [8]	SMTS	n_tree	[Time, raw time series, first differences]	O(1)	random forest	multivariate	stochastic	yes	Classification
Elsworth & Guttel [4]	ABBA	approximation_tol	[length, increment]	O(N*L)	PLA + clustering	univariate	stochastic	no	Motif Detection, Rule Discovery.

win: sliding window size
alphabet: alphabet size
n: word size
N: length of the TS
L: number of PLA segment

Among the deterministic algorithm, the Symbolic Aggregate approXimation (SAX) was the first to guarantee the lower bound property which make it the most popular in the TS datamining application [1]. The proposed map by SAX begins with the approximation of the original TS through Piecewise Aggregation Approximation (PAA) to extract a reduced feature vector of a mean value. Subsequently, SAX quantize each mean value in Q bins $Q = \{q_1, q_2, \ldots, q_Q\}$ such that the area under a Normal $\mathcal{N}(\mu, \sigma)$ curve follows

$P(q_{i+1}) - P(q_i) = \frac{1}{Q}$. In practice, the original TS is z-normalized before applying SAX so that the quantization Normal curve have $\mu = 0$ and $\sigma = 1$. Figure (3.a) gives an illustrative example of mapping process by SAX.

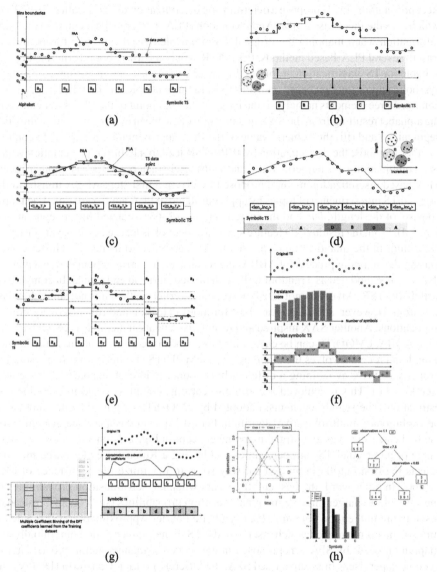

Fig. 3. Illustrative example of mapping process by (a) SAX, (b) symb, (c) IEPF-TSR, (d) ABBA, (e) eMODiT, (f) Persist, (g) SFA and (h) SMTS.

Although its efficiency, SAX ignore the important information related to the local tendency of the TS data. In order to preserve slope information, another deterministic method was proposed and so-called *Symb* [2]. The mapping methods by *Symb* exploit the first order difference of the SAX feature vector to learn, in an unsupervised way, a codebook from the training set. The resulting codebook is used later in the discretization of a new TS data. That is, the feature vector is quantized into k-cluster by assigning each entry to the closest cluster centroid. An illustrative example is shown in Fig. (3.b). Recently, authors in [3] propose a deterministic discretization method, called IEPF-TSR, which uses the Piecewise Linear Approximation (PLA) to merge the mean with the slope information when mapping the original TS into triplet-based symbolic forms. In contrast to several PLA-based methods, IEPF-TSR satisfy the lower bound criteria, then it is suitable for TS classification problems. Figure (3.c) demonstrates an example of a triplet symbolic approximation based on IEPF-TSR. In this example, the first triplet $\langle 1, a_3, T_1 \rangle$ combine three elements namely, (i) the index of the start point of the PLA segment, 1, (ii) the alphabet resulting from the SAX quantization of the mean of all data points within this segment, a_3 and (iii) the numeric value of the PLA approximation trend, T_1. In contrast to other methods, the discretization by IEPF-TSR lead to a hybrid representation which is a combination of a numeric value and a string characters. ABBA is another recent PLA-based discretization method proposed by [4]. In a first step, ABBA transform the original TS into sequence of tuples by applying adaptive PLA approximation. Each tuple consists of the length, *len*, and the increment, *inc*, of its associated linear segment (see Fig. 3.d). From the resulted 2D feature space, a codebook is learned by k-mean clustering algorithm. In the quantization step, each tuple is assigned to its nearest cluster center. During the mapping process by ABBA, the reconstruction error is bounded in a manner that it can be modeled as a random walk with pinned start and end points. In comparison with IEPF-TSR, ABBA do not satisfy lower bound criterion then it is not suited for classification. However, ABBA appears best for motif detection and rule discovery mining applications. Another SAX inspired and recent discretization methods is eMODiTS [5]. Like ABBA, eMODiTS can be categorized as a stochastic discretization method, since a random process involves the mapping steps. eMODiTS attempt to improve resolution property of SAX by defining a different bins boundary in each adapted PAA segment (see Fig. 3.e). This is achieved according to entropy, complexity and information loss estimation. The search mechanism adopted by eMODiTs is quite complex and based on evolutionary multi-objective algorithm. Persist [6] is an unsupervised discretization method categorized as an optimal mapping concept in Fig. 2. Persist divides the values range of an original TS into percentiles and having a Kulback-Leibler based measure selects the best cutoffs in an optimal way so as to maximize the persistence of each symbol. In other word, the best cutoffs occurs when the self-transition probabilities of the symbols are larger than the marginal transition probabilities (see Fig. 3.f). Instead of discretizing in the time domain, SFA (Symbolic Fourier Approximation) [7] is a deterministic mapping method which discretize the TS in the frequency domain. Initially, the mapping process by SFA was proposed in unsupervised manner and improved later to become supervised. In unsupervised SFA, the Discrete Fourier Transform (DFT) of the original TS is computed and only subset of first coefficients is kept. Let X_i a TS of length N then $DFT(X_i) = \left(real_1^i, img_1^i, \ldots, real_{\frac{n}{2}}^i, img_{\frac{n}{2}}^i \right)$ is its approximation by discrete Fourier where n is the number of Fourier coefficient used to map X_i into sequence of n symbols. In supervised SFA the Fourier coefficients are first ranked based on ANOVA statistical test and a subset of first ranked coefficient is kept. Retained Fourier coefficients represent the novel feature vector of the TS data. By applying the DFT on all the TS in the training database, we obtain a matrix whose row are TS and columns are SFA features (i.e., Fourier coefficients). Subsequently, each column of this matrix is quantized uniformly based on the quantiles of the Fourier coefficients. Then, the unsupervised SFA maps the TS into symbols as illustrated in the Fig. (3.g). In the supervised SFA, the bin boundaries in the quantized step are defined based on impurity criterion. In the multivariate case, the SMTS was propose in [8] as a stochastic mapping method where symbols are learned in a supervised way. In a first step of the SMTS, the univariate TS of the training dataset are concatenated and augmented by their time indexes and first different values to form a novel feature matrix denoted as $M = \left[I, X_1, diff\,(X_1), \ldots, X_N, diff\,(X_N) \right]$ where $I = [1, \ldots, N]^T$ and $diff\,(X_i) = \left[\left(x_2^i - x_1^i \right), \ldots, \left(x_N^i - x_{N-1}^i \right) \right]^T$.. In a second step, a random forest tree learner is applied on this matrix. Through this latter step, interaction between attributes values over time index are detected and the feature space is divided in order in accordance to each instance class. That is, each instance is assigned to a terminal node of the tree and then a symbol is associated to each terminal node as illustrate the Fig. (3.h).

3 TS Classification Based on Symbolic Representation

3.1 SAX Shape-Based Classification

Without loss of generality, SAX shape-based classification algorithm leverages the similarity measure between symbolic representation of the TS to find a predefined number of training sample nearest in distance to the testing sample. Typically, the number of nearest neighbors is fixed to one which lead to the simple 1NN classifier. Let $\tilde{X} = \{s_1, \ldots, s_n\}$ and $\tilde{Y} = \{q_1, \ldots, q_n\}$ two sequences of symbols resulting from a mapping by SAX of two TS; $X = [x_1, \ldots, x_N]$ and $Y = [y_1, \ldots, y_N]$ respectively. The SAX dissimilarity measure between $\tilde{X}$ and $\tilde{Y}$ is defined as follow:

$$MINDIST\left(\tilde{X}, \tilde{Y} \right) = \sqrt{\frac{N}{n}} \sqrt{\sum_{k=1}^{n} dist(s_k, q_k)} \tag{1}$$

where $dist(\cdot, \cdot)$ is a precomputed distance table.

Since the first publication of SAX dissimilarity measure, several extensions were proposed and a summary of the reviewed methods can be found in Table 2 and their dimensionality reduction ratios are listed in Table 3. That is, ESAX extend the single SAX-feature (i.e., the mean) by the extraction of the minimum and the maximum points values in each PAA segment [9]. This is of great importance for us to deal with ECG signal because the peak values are important pattern. However, ESAX require triple storage size compared to SAX but still use the Eq. (1) to measure similarity between two ESAX symbolic sequence. Overlap-SAX is another SAX shape-based classifier where author in [10] propose to incorporate trend information by swapping the end points of each subsequence with the end points of the neighboring subsequence. Therefore, Overlap-SAX preserve the similarity matching with Eq. (1) while keeping the SAX storage size.

Table 2. List of reviewed SAX shape-based TS classification.

Authors	Method		Classifier	Technique
Lin et al. [1]	SAX shape-based	SAX	1NN (dissimilarity measure)	MINDIST()
Lkhagva et al. [9]		ESAX		
Muhammad Fuad [10]		OverlapSAX		
Sun et al. [11]		SAX-TD		TD-DIST()
Zan & Yamana [12]		SAX-SD		SD-DIST()
He et al. [13]		SAX-BD		BD-DIST()
Chen et al. [3]		IEPF-TSR		TSR_DIST()

Table 3. Compression ratio of reviewed SAX-based with 1NN classifier.

Methods	SAX	ESAX	OverlapSAX	1d-SAX	SAX-TD	SAX-SD	SAX-BD	IEPF-TSR
Dimensionality Reduction	s/N	3*s/N	s/N	2*s/N	(2*s+1)/N	2*s/N	3*s/N	3*s/N

Unlike Overlap-SAX, authors in [11] proposed a novel SAX extension called SAX-TD. Additional SAX-features in SAX-TD method are the range between the first value (res. Last value) and the mean value of each PAA subsequence. This result in a hybrid (numeric and symbolic) representation where each SAX symbol is augmented by the trend variation at the start and the end of each PAA segment. In the extension called SAX-SD, authors [12] adopt the standard deviation value as the only one additional statistical feature which integrate the amount of variability between the actual and mean value. Recently, authors in [13] proposes the SAX-BD method with a novel feature, called Boundary Distance (BD), to estimate the trend information within each PAA segment. The idea behind BD is simple and consist to adapt SAX-TD features with the ESAX features. In other word, the start and the end points used in the SAX-TD are replaced by the minimum and the maximum points used in the ESAX representation. In order to see the advantage of the above-mentioned SAX shape-based classifier we conduct a hierarchical clustering with average linking applied on first 6 instances from the ECG200 database [14]. As we can see on Fig. 4, all SAX-based dissimilarity measure correctly clusters ECG signal with minor difference related to instance's order in a group. That is, SAX-based classifier successfully isolates the second instance which show a discriminative pattern shape at its end (rapid decrease followed by a positive peak). This is achieved with a compression ratio 4 and an alphabet size 6.

3.2 Symbolic Features for Classification

Ordered symbolic attributes resulting from TS discretization are used in several research work to extract higher level structural information through a dictionary-based classification. At the core of any dictionary classifier is the statistic used in natural language processing. Table 4 gives a summary of reviewed SAX feature classification methods while Table 5 gives a summary of reviewed SFA-based classification methods. Based on the SAX discretization, Bag-Of-Pattern (BOP) was first proposed in [15]. BOP results

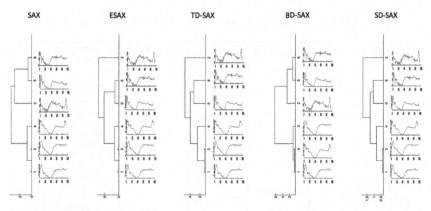

Fig. 4. Dendrogram clustering of the first 6 instances from the ECG200 database.

from the transformation of each TS subsequence, within a sliding window, into SAX symbols. Therefore, by scanning the symbols, a histogram-based representation of unique words is obtained. In practice, BOP with 1NN represent a simple but efficient classifier which addresses the scalability in classification of a very long TS data. In order to improve the BOP performance, several extensions were proposed such as BOPF [16], HBOP [17] and TBOPE [18]. To provide an interpretable TS data classification, authors in [19] propose SAX-VSM as an alternative to the BOP-based classifier. SAX-VSM also takes the advantage of the SAX and extract a set of words by sliding a window through TS. During the training phase, SAX-VSM determine, for each class, the term frequency-inverse document frequency (TF-IDF) of each unique word in the dictionary. Finally, cosine similarity between frequency words and learned TF-IDF words is used to do the classification. Another structure-based TS data classification using SAX is Representative Pattern Mining (RPM) [20]. RPM focus on finding the most representative subsequence (i.e., shapelets) for the classification task. After SAX discretion of a TS data, RPM takes advantage of grammatical inference techniques to automatically find recurrent and correlated patterns of variables lengths. This pool of patterns is further refined so that the most representative pattern that capture the properties of a specific class are selected.

Another recent shapelet-based classification called BSPCOVER was proposed in [21]. BSPCOVER begin by generating a pool of SAX's candidate words by sliding a window over TS, then filter out identical and highly similar candidates via Bloom filters and similarity matching, respectively. After that, a p-Cover algorithm is applied in order to select shapelet candidates that maximally represent each class in the TS database. MiSTiCl [22] is another recent shapelet-based classifier where frequent patterns are extracted using a string mining algorithm. In contrast to RPM, MiSTCl extract pattern with varying SAX discretization parameters. Extracted frequent patterns are used to create a novel feature matrix. Finally, classification model can be trained by any off-the-shelf algorithms. Other grammatical-based classifier was proposed in [23] and called Domain Series Corpus (DSCo). As its name suggest, DSCo apply the SAX with sliding window technique on training TS data to build a corpus and subsequently each class is

Table 4. List of reviewed SAX-feature methods for structural TS classification.

Authors	Method		Classifier	Technique
Lin et al. [15]	SAX-feature	BOP	Dictionary-based classifier	Histogram of Bag-of-Pattern + Euclidean distance
Li & Lin [16]		BOPF		Centroid of BoP for each class + cosine similarity measure
Liang et al. [17]		HBOP		Histogram of Hybrid BoP + similarity matching
Bai et al. [18]		TBOPE		Ensemble of BOP with Trend + cosine similarity measure
Senin et al. [19]		SAX-VSM		BoW (TF-iDF weights) for each class + cosine similarity measure
Daoyan Li [23]		DSCo-NG	n-gram models	model-based classifier
Wang et al. [20]		RPM	shapelet transformation-based classifier	SAX + Sequiture + SVM
Li et al. [21]		BSPCOVER		SAX + Bloom filter + similarity matching + p-Cover algorithm
Raza & Kramer [22]		MiSTiCl	subsequence (or pattern)-based classifier	off-the-shelf classifier algorithms
Marquez-Grajales et al. [5]		eMODITs	J48 classifier (decision tree)	each symbol is an attribute used as a classification feature

Table 5. List of reviewed structural-based classifiers based on SFA.

Authors	Method		Classifier	Technique
Patrick Schafer [24]	SFA-feature	BOSS	Ensemble	Histogram of Bag-of-SFA words
		BOSS-VS	Ensemble	TF-iDF weighted Bag-discrminative BOP
Schafer & Leser [25]		WEASEL	Ensemble	from supervised SFA representation

summarized with an n-gram Language Model (LM). The classification is performed by checking which LM is the best fit for the tested TS. Based on the SFA discretization, a Bag-Of-SFA-Symbol (BOSS) was proposed and extended later to BOSS in Vector Space (BOSSVS) [24]. BOSS and BOSSVS are similar in principle with BOP and SAX-VSM respectively. However, instead of extracting subsequences of one fixed window size, WEASEL [25] slides repeatedly through the TS with varying window size. Therefore, the SFA discretization is concatenated with the window size and word frequency is counted with every iteration. Then, relevant bag-of-words are retained based on a statistical test measure.

3.3 Hybrid SAX and SFA Features for Classification

Stimulated by how flies look at the world, authors in [26] proposed the "compound eye" to classify TS through thousands of lenses. Abbreviated by Co-eye, this method combines SAX and SFA with different lenses (i.e., with different discretization parameters) to have a multi-resolution representation of the TS data. The latter property is important in some kind of ECG signal. For example, in the case of the NonInvasiveFelatECGThorax1signal [14] which record the ECG from the left and the right thorax, a low resolution allows to have a global view of classes but a high resolution in some intervals is required to detect the fine change between classes (see highlighted zone in Fig. 5). After multi-resolution symbolic representation, Co-eye build a random forest where low confident forests are pruned and classification with soft dynamic vote is performed by the remained forest.

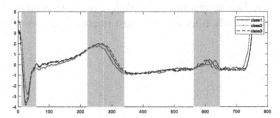

Fig. 5. Plot display of 1 sample from 3 classes in the NonInvasiveFetalECGThorax1 database.

Another hybrid classifier was proposed in [27] and called mtSS_SEQL + LR. This classifier is an ensemble of multiple sequence learner algorithm which uses a multiple symbolic representation that combine SAX with SFA to find a set of discriminative subsequences by employing a brunch-and-bound feature search strategy. Table 6 give a summary of these methods.

Table 6. List of reviewed classifiers based on SAX and SFA.

Authors	Method		Classifier	Technique
Abdallah & Gaber [26]	SAX & SFA feature	Co-eye	Random Forest	Histogram of SAX and SFA bag-of-words
Le Nguyen el al. [27]		mtSS-SEQL+LR	ensemble of sequence learner	Multiple representation (SFA + SAX) from multiple domains (Temporal + Frequential)

3.4 ECG Classification Results

We conduct experiments on ECG signals available from the public UCR archive benchmark [6]. In particular, we select the TS databases namely; ECG200, ECG5000, ECGFiveDays, NonInvasiveFetalECGthorax1, NonInvasiveFetalECGThorax2 and TwoLeadECG to evaluate reviewed classification methods based on ordered symbolic attributes of the TS data. The evaluation metric for each single ECG database would be the accuracy ratio on the test set. Among SAX shape-based classifier we can see from Fig. (6.a) that SAX-SD and SAX-TD show the better performance on all ECG databases with an average classification accuracy of 85%. Figure (6.b) show the classification accuracy of the remained reviewed classifier. Among them, BSPCOVER, mtSS-SEQL+LR, MiSTiCl and WEASEL provide the better average classification accuracy of 94% over the six ECG databases. Two of them uses SAX symbols and only one uses SAF symbols while the remainder uses the combination of SAX and SFA symbols. Surprisingly, Co-eye classifier which combine SAX and SFA is not as performant as those using single form of symbolic feature. In comparison with Co-eye, mtSS-SEQL+LR uses greedy feature selection strategy to effectively filter out irrelevant symbolic representation before conducting classification while Co-eye uses all symbolic features to learn random forest and only filter out the most unconfident forest before conducting classification.

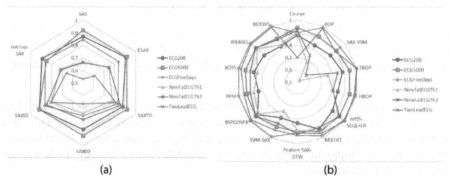

(a)   (b)

Fig. 6. Classification accuracy of reviewed (a) SAX shape-based classifier, (b) symbolic feature-based classifiers.

In addition, shapelet-based classification like RPM and BSPCOVER has the advantage to visualize discriminative part in the ECG signal which help practitioner to distinguish between classes in monitoring application or discovering anomaly pattern in heart disease inspection. Therefore, these classification algorithms are usually accompanied by a visual toolkit[1,2]. This Graphical User Interface make the classification a shallow process with more interpretation capability. This is of great interest in ECG application. Typically, shapelet-based classifier requires expensive time to learn a model. However, it is possible to overcome this issue by discretization technique which reduce the TS dimension and consequently the computation time cost. Figure 7 show a comparison of running time in training and testing between three shapelet classifier and the BOSS classifier on ECGFiveDays and TwoLeadECG databases.

---

[1] https://github.com/GrammarViz2/grammarviz2_src.

[2] https://www.comp.hkbu.edu.hk/~csgzli/tsc/visualet.jar.

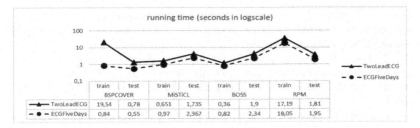

Fig. 7. Comparison of running time (in seconds) between four classifiers.

4 Conclusion

In this paper, we have presented a review on symbolic discretization of the TS and have focused on recent literatures that uses ordered symbolics attributes in TS classification. We give a comprehensive overview for practitioners who attempt to use ECG in classification application. Based on experimental results, we suggest the use of the symbolic attribute in structural-based classifier rather that shape-based. Furthermore, we recommend the use of a shapelet-based classifier which provide useful feedback information and make the classification of the ECG more interpretable for a human being.

References

1. Lin, J., Keogh, E., Lee, W., Lonardi, S.: Experiencing SAX: a novel symbolic representation of time series. Data Min. Knowl. Disc. **15**(2), 107–144 (2007)
2. Zalewski, W., Silva, F., Wu, C.F., Lee, H.D., Maletzke, A.G.: A symbolic representation method to preserve the characteristic slope of time series. SBIA **2012**, 132–141 (2012)
3. Chen, H., Du, J., Zhang, W., Li, B.: An iterative end point fitting-based trend segmentation representation of time series and its distance measure. Multimedia Tools Appl. **79**, 13481–13499 (2020)
4. Elsworth, S., Guttel, S.: ABBA: adaptive Brownian bridge-based symbolic aggregation of time series. Data Min. Knowl. Disc. **34**, 1175–1200 (2020)
5. Marquez-Grajales, A., Acosta-Mesa, H.G., Mezura-Montes, E., Graff, M.: A multibreakpoints approach for symbolic discretization of time series. Knowl. Inf. Syst. **62**, 2795–2834 (2020)
6. Morchen F., Ultsch, A.: Optimizing time series discretization for knowledge discovery. In: KDD 2005, August 21–24, Chicago, USA (2005)
7. Schafer, P., Hogqvist, M.: SFA: a symbolic fourier approximation and index for similarity search in high dimensional datasets. In: EDBT 2012, ACM Press, Germany, p. 516 (2012)
8. Baydogan, S., Runger, G.: Learning a symbolic representation for multivariate time series classification. Data Min. Knowl. Disc. **29**(2), 400–422 (2015)
9. Lkhagva, B., Suzuki, Y., Kawagoe, K.: New time series data representation ESAX for financial applications. In: IEEE International Conference on Data Engineering, pp. 17–22 (2006)
10. Muhammad Fuad, M.M.: Modifying the symbolic aggregate approximation method to capture segment trend information. In: Torra, V., Narukawa, Y., Nin, J., Agell, N. (eds.) Modeling Decisions for Artificial Intelligence. MDAI 2020. Lecture Notes in Computer Science, vol. 12256, pp. 230–239. Springer, Cham (2020). https://doi.org/10.1007/978-3-030-57524-3_19
11. Sun, Y., Li, J., Liu, J., Sun, B., Chow, C.: An improvement of symbolic aggregate approximation distance measure for time series. Neurocomputing **138**, 189–198 (2014)

12. Zan, C.T., Yamama, H.: An improved symbolic aggregate approximation distance measure based on its statistical features. In: Proceeding of the 18th International Conference on IIWAS, Singapore, November 28–30 (2016)

13. He, Z., Long, S., Ma, X., Zhao, H.: A boundary distance-based symbolic aggregate approximation method for time series data. Algorithms **13**, 284–304 (2020)

14. Dau, H.A., et al.: 'The UCR time series archive. IEEE/CAA J. Autom. Sin. **6**, 1293–1305 (2019)

15. Lin, J., Khade, R., Li, Y.: Rotation-invariant similarity in time series using bag-of-patterns representation. J. Intell. Inf. Syst. **39**, 287–315 (2012)

16. Li, X., Lin, J.: Linear time complexity time series classification with bag-of-pattern-features. ICDM **2017**, 277–286 (2017)

17. Liang, S., Zhang, Y., Ma, J.:. Enhancing Linear Time Complexity Time Series Classification with Hybrid Bag-Of-Patterns. In: Nah, Y., Cui, B., Lee, SW., Yu, J.X., Moon, YS., Whang, S.E. (eds.) Database Systems for Advanced Applications. DASFAA 2020. Lecture Notes in Computer Science, vol. 12112, pp. 717-735. Springer, Cham (2020). https://doi.org/10.1007/978-3-030-59410-7_50

18. Bai B., Li G., Wang S., Wu Z., Wen Y.: Time series classification based on multi-feature dictionary representation and ensemble learning. Expert Syst. Appl. **169**, 114162 (2021)

19. Senin P., Malinchik, S.: SAX-VSM: interpretable time series classification using SAX and vector space model. In: IEEE International Conference on Data Mining, pp. 1175–1180 (2013)

20. Wang X., et al.: Rpm: Representative pattern mining for efficient time series classification. In: 19th International Conference on Extending Database Technology (2016)

21. Li, G., Choi, B., Xu, J., Bhowmick, S.S., Chun, K., Wong, G.L.: Efficient shaplete discovery for time series classification. IEEE Trans. Knowl. Data Eng. **34**(3), 1149–1163 (2020)

22. Raza, A., Kramer, S.: Accelerating pattern-based time series classification: a linear time and space string mining approach. Knowl. Inf. Syst. **62**, 1113–1141 (2020)

23. Daoyuan, L., Tegawendé, F.B., Jacques, K., Yves, L.T.: DSCo-NG: a practical language modeling approach for time series classification. In: 15th International Symposium, IDA 2016, Stockholm, 13–15 Octobre (2016)

24. Schafer, P.: The BOSS is concerned with time series classification in the presence of noise. Data Min. Knowl. Disc. **29**(6), 1505–1530 (2015)

25. Schafer, P., Leser, U.: Fast and accurate time series classification with WEASEL. In: Proceedings of the 2017 ACM on Conference on Information and Knowledge Management - CIKM 2017 pp 637–646 (2017)

26. Abdallah, Z., Gaber, M.: Co-eye: a multi-resolution ensemble classifier for symbolic approximation time series. Mach. Learn. **109**, 2029–2061 (2020)

27. Le Nguyen, T., Gsponner, S., Ilie, I., O'Reilly, M., Ifrim, G.: Interpretable time series classification using linear models and multi-resolution multi-domain symbolic representations. Data Min. Knowl. Discov. **33**(4), 1183–1222 (2019)

Res_1D_CNN and BiLSTM
with Attention Mechanism Integration
for Arrhythmia Diagnosis

Wissal Midani[1,3](✉)(iD), Wael Ouarda[2](iD), and Mounir Ben Ayed[1,4](iD)

[1] REGIM-Lab: REsearch Groups in Intelligent Machines, National Engineering
School of Sfax (ENIS), University of Sfax, BP 1173, 3038 Sfax, Tunisia
`wissal.midani15@gmail.com`, `wissalelmidani@fsegs.u-sfax.tn`,
`mounir.benayed@fss.usf.tn`
[2] Digital Research Centre of Sfax, Sfax, Tunisia
`wael.ouarda@crns.rnrt.tn`
[3] Faculty of Economics and Management of Sfax, University of Sfax, Road Airport
Km 4, 3018 Sfax, Tunisia
[4] Faculty of Sciences of Sfax, University of Sfax, Road Sokra Km 4, 3000 Sfax,
Tunisia

Abstract. An electrocardiogram (ECG) is the most common test used
to diagnose an arrhythmia, which arrhythmia is related to abnormal electrical activities of the heart that can be reflected by the ECG which plays
the main role in heart disease analysis. However, it is still a challenge to
detect arrhythmia based on ECG basic characteristics because of the non-
stationary nature of ECG signal even cardiologists faced challenges in
arrhythmia diagnosis. Therefore, automatic arrhythmia detection-based
ECG signals with height accuracy is a serious and indispensable task.
Hence In this paper, we propose a new deep learning-based approach
which is a combination of Res 1D CNN for spatial feature extraction
and BiLSTM to learn temporal features in two directions with an attention layer to focus only on informative information. A comprehensive
experimental study has been made in this research, which shows that
the proposed approach offers the most efficient tool for accurate classification and ranks top of the list of recently published algorithms on
the MIT-BIH arrhythmia dataset based on the AMII standard. A 5-fold
cross-validation is carried out. The proposed model achieved an accuracy,
recall, precision, and F1-score of 97.17%, 83.48%, 92.25%, and 87.08%,
respectively. The proposed model provides a robust tool for the early
detection of arrhythmias.

Keywords: Res 1D CNN · BiLSTM · Attention mechanism ·
Arrhythmia classification · AMII standard · Spatial-Temporal features

1   Introduction

Cardiovascular Disease (CVD) is an essential cause of silent death in the world.
In 2019, the American Heart Association showed by statistics that more than

N. T. Nguyen et al. (Eds.): ICCCI 2023, CCIS 1864, pp. 753–764, 2023.
https://doi.org/10.1007/978-3-031-41774-0_59

17.6 million deaths were closely related to heart failure and it is predestined that these statistics will reach 23.6 million in 2030 [1]. Cardiac arrhythmia is one of the most important CVD that also leads to sudden cardiac death, which is almost 80% of deaths caused [2]. An arrhythmia appears when the blood cannot be pumped to the body fast enough by the heart, so an arrhythmia is abnormal electrical activities in the electrocardiography (ECG).

The most common solution for detecting arrhythmias is to record an electrocardiogram (ECG) because it provides a massive volume of heart information [3], which displays the heart's electrical activity over time from electrodes placed on the skin. However, the ECG signal is a nonstationary time series, so there are no specific morphology features, The properties of the ECG signal change from person to person and within the same person, which makes it hard and difficult for cardiologists to efficiently detect arrhythmia diseases via visual assessment [4,5].

To process the issue of ECG signal visual assessment, various computer-aided studies have been proposed. In addition, these methods are composed of three steps, first preprocessing step, then feature extraction and feature reduction step, and finally classification step. After the ECG preprocesses various types of signal noise are removed, then hand-crafted features are extracted from the processed signal, and these features are essential information related to the heart. Generally, in literature, the techniques used to feature extraction include hidden Markov model (HMM) [6], spectral analysis [7,8], higher-order statistics (HOS) [9], time-frequency analysis [10], etc. Then, feature reduction methods such as principal component analysis (PCA) [10,11], independent component analysis (ICA) [9,10,12], etc., are applied after feature extraction to minimize feature dimensions. Finally, for arrhythmia classification, these features are trained with a classifier such as support vector machine (SVM) [8], neural networks (NN) [13], cluster analysis [14], random forest [15], etc. Handcrafted methods have notably increased classification performance; unfortunately, this performance is insufficient because the healthcare domain is sensitive, and it is quite hard for these methods to boost classification performance, which is because, in the feature extraction step the ECG features are variable in morphology and timing in inter- and intra-patient paradigms spatially in the clinical practice where the signal is noisy with the baseline wanders, power line interference, muscle contraction, ect.

In recent years, deep neural networks DNN have obtained high success in wide healthcare problems thanks to their power of automatic feature extraction ability in biomedical signal [16,17] and medical images [18]. Hannun et al. [19], propose an end-to-end deep feature extraction without any handcraft features by developing a DNN for 12 rhythm classification and shows the efficiency of DNN where the accuracy of classification of the proposed DNN is higher than the accuracy of cardiologists. Also, Liu et al. [20] propose Attention-Based Convolutional Neural Networks (ABCNN), it is composed by CNN for feature extraction and multi-head attention for ECG informative dependencies, they demonstrate the power of ABCNN informative features extraction by features visualization. To increase the performance Hong et al. [21] propose an ECG interpreter, where they propose DNN model for ECG signal delineation to extract features waves such as P, complex QRS, and p waves then a sliding window is applied to learn

Table 1. Summary of AMII standards for MITBIH heartbeats dataset.

AAMI class	MIT-BIH class	MIT-BIH heartbeat name	Number
Normal beats (N)	N	Normal beat	90 589
	L	Left bundle branch block beat	
	R	Right bundle branch block beat	
	e	Atrial escape beat	
	j	Nodal escape	
Supraventricular ectopic beats (SVEB)	A	Atrial premature beat	7 236
	a	Aberrated atrial premature beat	
	J	Nodal (junctional) premature beat	
	S	Supraventricular premature beat	
Ventricular ectopic beat (VEB)	V	Premature ventricular contraction	2 779
	E	Ventricular escape beat	
Fusion beats (F)	F	Fusion of ventricular and normal beat	803
Unknown beats (Q)	/	Paced beat	8 039
	f	Fusion of paced and normal beat	
	Q	Unclassified beat	

the features waves with 3 RR interval length. Sen et al. [22] applicate their method to an inter-patient paradigm, where they test the model on an unseen dataset and validate the model with 5 cross-validations, then fed RR interval into the model which is composed of a convolutional layer for feature extraction. In addition, Lui et al. [4] combinate two-dimensional convolutional neural network TD-CNN with BiLSTM to extract the spatial-temporal features, the use TD-CNN for local spatial features, and BiLSTM to learn temporal dependencies in two directions. Sassi et al. [23] proposes a freezing-based convolutional neural network learning using a morphological transformation of CT images to classify COVID-19 cohorts to help in prognostication pneumonia disease monitoring.

2 Materials and Methods

2.1 Dataset

In this work, a public database is considered. MIT-BIH Arrhythmia Database (MITDB) [24] is available on Physionet [25]. MITDB 47 individual subjects, each record containing two leads (lead II and lead V5) sampled at 360 Hz with 11-bit resolution. Each record in this database is separately annotated by more than two cardiologists. MITBIH is based on the Association for the Advancement of Medical Instrumentation (AAMI) standard [24], MITBIH includes five classes of arrhythmias N, S, V, F, and Q, and each class contains many subclasses illustrated in Table 1.

2.2   Algorithm Overview

The proposed method is shown in Fig. 1. Each ECG lead is first preprocessed, normalized, and segmented to RR interval. The proposed end-to-end model is trained and tested for arrhythmia classification.

Preprocessing. In the preprocessing step, for each patient, the two ECG leads are processed separately. To segment the ECG signal into RR intervals, the R position of beats is detected with annotation. Then, those RR sequences were first scaled in the range of [0,1], and then standardized. Subsequently, all RR beats are resampled from 360 Hz to 125 Hz.

Model Architecture. The proposed contribution is illustrated in Fig. 2, The model is designed to solve the variability features in morphology and timing by extracting spatial-temporal features. The model adopted in this study is constructed with three different deep network structures integrated into a 1D conventional neural network, BiLSTM layer, and Attention layer. The final output is the classification result based on the feature vector analysis.

We proposed Res-1D convolutional DNN to detect arrhythmias were is inspired by Resnet [26], which takes as input the RR interval. The input is fed directly into the 1D convolutional layer to obtain the feature map representations with a kernel size K= 7. The proposed architecture is composed of 17 layers; to force the optimization of the tractable network, shortcut connections are employed like the residual network architecture [19]. The proposed Res-1D convolutional consists of 3 residual blocks with two 1D convolutional layers per block. The convolutional layers have a filter width of 64*2k where k is a hyperparameter that starts at 0 and is incremented by 1 for each residual block with a constant kernel size K= 7. Between each residual block, another 1D convolutional is applied with the same hyper-parameter as the next residual block. After

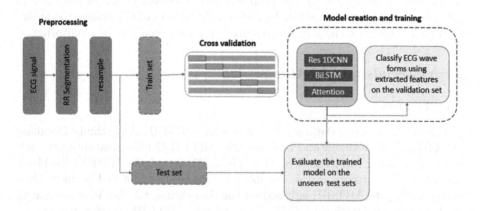

Fig. 1. Structure of the proposed method contains the preprocessing steps with model training and validation process on MIT-BIH dataset with a test phase.

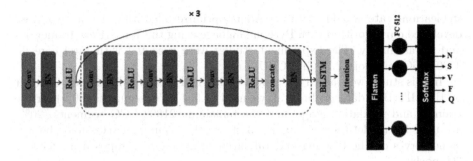

Fig. 2. The proposed architecture.

each 1D convolutional layer, we applied batch normalization and a ReLU activation function. After each concatenation, a max-pooling layer with a stride of 5 is applied to reduce the feature maps dimension and minimize the parameter's model which will decrease the problem of overfitting.

After end-to-end spatial feature extraction with the proposed Res 1D convolutional, the output is fed into one single BiLSTM layer to learn from the spatial feature vector and extract features in two temporal directions. To focus on the informative and essential information of the ECG signal and increase the arrhythmia detection performance, an Attention layer is applied that helps to give attention to the location of the abnormal wave to make Res 1D convolutional more investigative and interpretative.

At the end of our proposed model, a flatten layer is used to regulate Attention output information and to make it suitable for the next following fully connected (FC) layers. A set of dense layers with a dropout layer of 0.5 drop probability was added between the FC layers to boost the generalization ability of the model, a 512/2K in K starts at 0 and is incremented by 1 for each dense layer, exception of the last dense layer with five-unit and softmax activation was placed at the end of the network, to recognize and classified automatically the ECG beat classes.

2.3 Performance Evaluation

Our proposed architecture was evaluated with five-fold cross-validation. First, the MIT-BIH dataset is randomly spilled into five equal portions, where data distribution in each fold have approximately the same size and the same data condition combination. Then, we used four portions for the training model and one portion for model validation. This cross-validation will repeat five times. Finally, we calculate the average score of all five-folds to evaluate the model performance.

3 Results

The hyperparameters of the proposed Res 1D CNN BiLSTM with attention mechanism are stable during the training stage such as the batch size of 32 and the learning rate of 0.001 with the Adam optimizer algorithm. In this work, we developed our algorithm with Python language using the TensorFlow framework and Keras library. The experiment studies were executed with Intel core i5-4200U, 6Go memory 2.30 GHz CPU.

In this study, we trained our model with 5-fold cross-validation and tested it on the MIT-BID dataset. In total, we used 87,554 ECG segments (80%) for the training and validation stage, and the remaining 21892 ECG segments (20%) are used for model testing. Figure 3 shows the accuracy curves and the loss value curves on the training and validation stage for the proposed model over 30 epochs.

To assess Res 1D CNN performance for ECG classification four evaluation metrics are employed which are accuracy (ACC), F1-score (F1), precision, and recall. All metrics are calculated from the confusion matrix using the equations below:

$$Accuracy = \frac{TP + TN}{TP + TN + FP + FN} \tag{1}$$

$$Recall = \frac{TP}{TP + FN} \tag{2}$$

$$Precision = \frac{TP}{TP + FP} \tag{3}$$

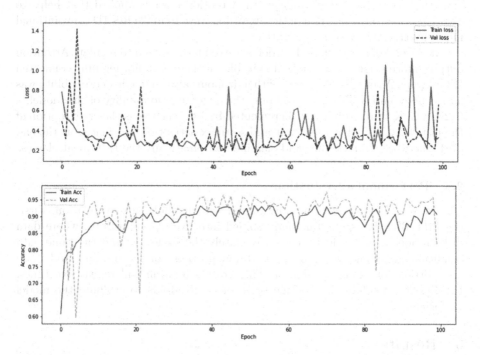

Fig. 3. Performance graphs of our proposed architecture on MIT-BIH dataset during the training stage.

$$F1 - score = \frac{2 * Precision * Recall}{Precision + Recall} \tag{4}$$

An observation from Table 2 is that the highest performance results were obtained with Res 1D CNN, and the lowest architecture is 1 D CNN, which attained 93.64% and 97.14% accuracy respectively.

Table 2. Five cross-validation averages with different CNN model architectures

Architectures	Acc(%±SD)	Recall(%±SD)	Precision(%±SD)	F1(%±SD)
1D CNN	91.75±0.06	92.33±0.32	68.56±0.3	75.64±0.24
Res 1D CNN	94.76±0.02	93.08±0.41	76.38±0.25	82.72±0.18
Res 1D CNN+BiLSTM	95.89±0.04	94.14 ±0.48	78.84±0.28	84.23±0.19
Res 1D CNN+BiLSTM+Att	**97.68± 0.06**	**95.46±0.23**	**82.02±0.21**	**87,64±0.22**

The result is self-evident, the shortcut connections are employed in many researches to force the model optimization. The first part is for the spatial features and is composed of 1D convolutional, also to increase the performance of our model a BiLSTM was added to learn the temporal features in two directions because the input is a time series signal, in the end, temporal feature extracted from BiLSTM is fed into attention layer to give greater weight to the important information. For those reasons, our proposed architecture is more performance than the other models as illustrated in Tabel 2 with an accuracy of 97.68%, recall of 95.46%, precision of 82.02%, and F1_score of 87,64%.

Table 3. Performance values of arrhythmia classes on test data.

Classes	Acc(%)	Recall(%)	Precision(%)	F1_score(%)
Non-ectopic (N)	**99.87**	98.80	**99.31**	**98.46**
Ventricular ectopic (V)	98.46	94.41	92.68	93.11
Supraventricular ectopic (S)	95.01	82.03	71.35	76.89
Fusion (F)	92.72	86.62	57.84	68.78
Unknown (Q)	99.81	**99.42**	96.23	98.2
Overall	**97.17**	**92,25**	**83.48**	**87,08**

Tabel 3 details the proposed classification performance on test data MIT BIH dataset based on the evaluation metrics criteria. The overall performance results showed that an accuracy of 97.17%, recall of 83.48%, precision of 92,25 %, and F1-score of 87,08% was achieved. The highest accuracy of 99.87%, recall of 99.31%, and F1-score of 98.46% were obtained for the non-ectopic (N) class with a high precision value of 98.80% obtained for the unknown (Q) class. Unfortunately, the lowest accuracy of 92.77%, recall of 57.84%, and F1-score

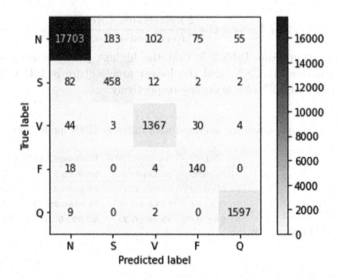

Fig. 4. Confusion matrix of the proposed model.

of 78.68% were obtained for Fusion (F) class and the lowest precision of 82.03% was obtained for the Supraventricular ectopic (S) class. Figure 4 shows the proposed model confusion matrix based on the test data. The confusion matrix was used to illustrate the dissentients between the different classes. The proposed model classified 21 265 out of 21892 ECG segments correctly during the test stage, yielding an overall F1-score of 87.08% and overall accuracy of 97.17%. It is referred from this confusion matrix that the model predicts the most classification mistakes between the Supraventricular ectopic (S) heartbeat records and the Non-ectopic (N) records. The Proposed Res 1D CNN misclassified 82 Supraventricular ectopic heartbeats into the Non-ectopic class. Similarly, 183 Non-ectopic heartbeats were incorrectly classified in the Supraventricular ectopic class. A representation of some actual Supraventricular ectopic (S) signals which had been misclassified as an Non-ectopic (N) signals is illustrated in Fig. 5.

In Fig. 5 the QRS complex features of Supraventricular ectopic (S) heartbeat are identical to LBBB or RBBB morphology, where they are a subclass of Non-ectopic (N). Generally, as the (N) beats, (S) is considered as an early atrial heartbeat that is in charge of the atrioventricular node and the subsequent ventricular electrical state that represents the ECG morphological features or the QRS representation wave. From here we can conclude the reason for our proposed model confusion, is that the (N) beats and the (S) beat have the exact QRS morphology representation.

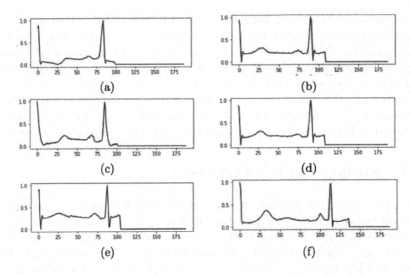

Fig. 5. Supraventricular ectopic (S) heartbeats which were predicted as Non-ectopic (N) heartbeats.

4 Discussion

In this study, an automatic classification approach for ECG arrhythmia detection is composed of three steps, spatial feature extraction using Res 1D CNN, temporal feature extraction in two directions using BiLSTM, and attention layer to focus on the informative and essential information of the ECG signal. Our model was trained and validated with 5-fold cross-validations on the same dataset MIT-BIH database. Table 4 provides some studies in the literature that have been identified ECG arrhythmia on MIT-BIH database and a comparison between them and the classification performance of the proposed model.The proposed methods of wang et al. [29], Shi et al. [28], Wang et al. [30], and Liu et al. [27] have a lower accuracy lower than our method. However, all those algorithms

Table 4. Performance comparison between the proposed model and other ECG state-of-the-art studies on MIT-BIH database.

Study	Input segment	Method	Result
Liu et al. [27],2019	RR interval	CNNLRSVM	Acc:95.54%
Shi et al. [28],2019	single heartbeat	XGBoost Hierarchical Classification Method	Acc:92.1%
Wang et al. [29],2020	single heartbeat	Dually Fully CNN	Acc:93.4%
Wang et al. [30],2022	Three heartbeats	1D CNN with THML	Acc:94.4%
Proposed method	**RR interval**	**Res 1D CNN with BiLSTM and Attention layer**	**Acc:97.17%**

use the end-to-end approach without requiring to feature extraction step. Those researches demonstrate that the CNN approach can extract features from the ECG signal. The CNN extracts only spatial features without giving attention to temporal features. More then Res 1D CNN for spatial features We add a BiL-STM layer at the end d 1D CNN to learn and extract temporal features from the output of 1D CNN in two directions, for this reason, our proposed model is efficient, it fuses the spatial feature and temporal with and makes a focus on this fusion to extract and learn the essential information of the ECG signal.

5   Conclusion and Perspectives

In this research, a novel hybrid model was designed for automatic arrhythmia detection based on AMII standard from ECG signals. This model is an end-to-end features extraction approach where the features are extracted in two steps: spatial feature based on Res 1D CNN and temporal features based on the Bidirectional LSTM layer, after the two steps an attention layer was added to give attention to informative features extracted from CNN and BiLSTM. The contextual model can distinguish the different arrhythmia types from the ECG signal automatically. Our architecture was verified using the five-fold cross-validation on the MIT-BIH database based on AMII standards while attending the higher classification performance compared with the state-of-the art studies. The main point of this research is that the combination of the 1D-CNN, the Bidirectional LSTM and Attention mechanism not only reinforce the model to extract the crucial characteristics automatically from the original signal but also helps to improve the achievement of heartbeats analyses without any handcraft interference. Moreover, the proposed model can detect automatically five different classes efficiently and also addresses the diagnostic error that faces most cardiologists without any ECG signal preprocessing and features extraction approach. In future works, we will include data augmentation to increase classification performance.

References

1. Benjamin, E.J., et al.: Heart disease and stroke statistics-2019 update: a report from the American heart association. Circulation **139**(10), e56–e528 (2019)
2. Brenyo, A., Aktas, M.K.: Review of complementary and alternative medical treatment of arrhythmias. Am. J. Cardiol. **113**(5), 897–903 (2014)
3. Midani, W., Fki, Z., BenAyed, M.: Online anomaly detection in ECG signal using hierarchical temporal memory. In: 2019 Fifth International Conference on Advances in Biomedical Engineering (ICABME), pp. 1–4 IEEE (2019)
4. Liu, F., Zhou, X., Cao, J., Wang, Z., Wang, H., Zhang, Y.: Arrhythmias classification by integrating stacked bidirectional LSTM and two-dimensional CNN. In: Yang, Q., Zhou, Z.-H., Gong, Z., Zhang, M.-L., Huang, S.-J. (eds.) PAKDD 2019. LNCS (LNAI), Part II, vol. 11440, pp. 136–149. Springer, Cham (2019). https://doi.org/10.1007/978-3-030-16145-3_11

5. Gtif, I., et al.: Oxidative stress markers-driven prognostic model to predict post-discharge mortality in heart failure with reduced ejection fraction. Front. Cardiovasc. Med. **9**, 1017673 (2022)

6. Chang, P.-C., Lin, J.-J., Hsieh, J.-C., Weng, J.: Myocardial infarction classification with multi-lead ECG using hidden Markov models and gaussian mixture models. Appl. Soft Comput. **12**(10), 3165–3175 (2012)

7. Javadi, M., Arani, S.A.A.A., Sajedin, A., Ebrahimpour, R.: Classification of ECG arrhythmia by a modular neural network based on mixture of experts and negatively correlated learning. Biomed. Signal Process. Control **8**(3), 289–296 (2013)

8. Khalaf, A.F., Owis, M.I., Yassine, I.A.: A novel technique for cardiac arrhythmia classification using spectral correlation and support vector machines. Expert Syst. Appl. **42**(21), 8361–8368 (2015)

9. Kutlu, Y., Kuntalp, D.: Feature extraction for ECG heartbeats using higher order statistics of WPD coefficients. Comput. Meth. Programs Biomed. **105**(3), 257–267 (2012)

10. Elhaj, F.A., Salim, N., Harris, A.R., Swee, T.T., Ahmed, T.: Arrhythmia recognition and classification using combined linear and nonlinear features of ECG signals. Comput. Meth. Programs Biomed. **127**, 52–63 (2016)

11. Martis, R.J., Acharya, U.R., Min, L.C.: ECG beat classification using PCA, LDA, ICA and discrete wavelet transform. Biomed. Signal Process. Control **8**(5), 437–448 (2013)

12. Wang, Z., Zhou, X., Zhao, W., Liu, F., Ni, H., Yu, Z.: Assessing the severity of sleep apnea syndrome based on ballistocardiogram. PLoS ONE **12**(4), e0175351 (2017)

13. Liu, F., Zhou, X., Wang, Z., Ni, H., Wang, T.: OSA-weigher: an automated computational framework for identifying obstructive sleep apnea based on event phase segmentation, Journal of Ambient Intelligence and Humanized. Computing **10**, 1937–1954 (2019)

14. Yeh, Y.-C., Chiou, C.W., Lin, H.-J.: Analyzing ECG for cardiac arrhythmia using cluster analysis. Expert Syst. Appl. **39**(1), 1000–1010 (2012)

15. Liu, F., Zhou, X., Wang, Z., Wang, T., Ni, H., Yang, J.: Identifying obstructive sleep apnea by exploiting fine-grained BCG features based on event phase segmentation. In: 2016 IEEE 16th International Conference on Bioinformatics and Bioengineering (BIBE), pp. 293–300. IEEE (2016)

16. Midani, W., Ouarda, W., Ayed, M.B.: DeepArr: an investigative tool for arrhythmia detection using a contextual deep neural network from electrocardiograms (ECG) signals. Biomed. Signal Process. Control **85**, 104954 (2023)

17. Tmamna, J., Ayed, E.B., Ayed, M.B.: Deep learning for internet of things in fog computing: survey and open issues. In: 2020 5th International Conference on Advanced Technologies for Signal and Image Processing (ATSIP), pp. 1–6. IEEE (2020)

18. Ben Ahmed, I., Ouarda, W., Ben Amar, C.: Hybrid UNET model segmentation for an early breast cancer detection using ultrasound images. In: Nguyen, N.T., Manolopoulos, Y., Chbeir, R., Kozierkiewicz, A., Trawiński, B. (eds.) ICCCI 2022. Lecture Notes in Computer Science, vol. 13501, pp. 464–476. Springer, Cham (2022). https://doi.org/10.1007/978-3-031-16014-1_37

19. Hannun, A.Y., et al.: Cardiologist-level arrhythmia detection and classification in ambulatory electrocardiograms using a deep neural network. Nat. Med. **25**(1), 65–69 (2019)

20. Liu, Z., Zhang, X.: ECG-based heart arrhythmia diagnosis through attentional convolutional neural networks. In: 2021 IEEE International Conference on Internet of Things and Intelligence Systems (IoTaIS), pp. 156–162. IEEE (2021)

21. Hong, J., Li, H.-J., Yang, C.-C., Han, C.-L., Hsieh, J.-C.: A clinical study on atrial fibrillation, premature ventricular contraction, and premature atrial contraction screening based on an ECG deep learning model. Appl. Soft Comput. **126**, 109213 (2022)

22. Liu, S., Wang, A., Deng, X., Yang, C.: MGNN: a multiscale grouped convolutional neural network for efficient atrial fibrillation detection. Comput. Biol. Med. **148**, 105863 (2022)

23. Sassi, A., Ouarda, W., Amar, C.B.: Deep content information retrieval for COVID-19 detection from chromatic CT scans. Arab. J. Sci. Eng. **48**(2), 1935–1945 (2023)

24. Moody, G.B., Mark, R.G.: The impact of the MIT-BIH arrhythmia database. IEEE Eng. Med. Biol. Mag. **20**(3), 45–50 (2001)

25. Goldberger, A.L., et al.: PhysioBank, PhysioToolkit, and PhysioNet: components of a new research resource for complex physiologic signals. Circulation **101**(23), e215–e220 (2000)

26. Leibe, B., Matas, J., Sebe, N., Welling, M. (eds.) Computer Vision-ECCV 2016: 14th European Conference, Amsterdam, The Netherlands, 11–14 October 2016, Proceedings, Part IV, vol. 9908, Springer, Cham (2016)

27. Liu, J., Song, S., Sun, G., Fu, Yu.: Classification of ECG arrhythmia using CNN, SVM and LDA. In: Sun, X., Pan, Z., Bertino, E. (eds.) ICAIS 2019. LNCS, vol. 11633, pp. 191–201. Springer, Cham (2019). https://doi.org/10.1007/978-3-030-24265-7_17

28. Shi, H., Wang, H., Huang, Y., Zhao, L., Qin, C., Liu, C.: A hierarchical method based on weighted extreme gradient boosting in ECG heartbeat classification. Comput. Meth. Programs Biomed. **171**, 1–10 (2019)

29. Wang, H., et al.: A high-precision arrhythmia classification method based on dual fully connected neural network. Biomed. Signal Process. Control **58**, 101874 (2020)

30. Wang, L.-H., et al.: Three-heartbeat multilead ECG recognition method for arrhythmia classification. IEEE Access **10**, 44046–44061 (2022)

Author Index

N. T. Nguyen et al. (Eds.): ICCCI 2023, CCIS 1864, pp. 765–767, 2023.
https://doi.org/10.1007/978-3-031-41774-0

Printed in the United States
by Baker & Taylor Publisher Services

Printed in the United States
by Baker & Taylor Publisher Services